Warman's
ANTIQUES
AND THEIR PRICES
26th Edition

*The Standard Price Reference for antiques
and collectibles, for collectors, dealers
and professionals in the trade.*

Edited by
Harry L. Rinker

**Completely illustrated
and authenticated**

**Wallace-Homestead Book Company
Radnor, Pennsylvania**

ISBN 0-87069-623-8
ISSN 0196-2272
Library of Congress Catalog Card No. 82-643542
Manufactured in the United States of America

1 2 3 4 5 6 7 8 9 0   1 0 9 8 7 6 5 4 3 2

EDITORIAL STAFF, 26TH EDITION

Lissa L. Bryan-Smith
and Richard M. Smith
Holiday Antiques
Box 208, R. D. 1
Danville, PA 17821
(717) 275-7796
Christmas Items

Craig Dinner
P. O. Box 455
Valley Stream, NY
11582
(516) 825-0145
Doorstops

Regis and Mary Ferson
122 Arden Rd.
Pittsburgh, PA 15216
(412) 563-1964
Milk Glass

Doug Flynn and Al
Bolton
Holloway House
P. O. Box 547
Mesilla, NM 88046-0547
(505) 527-4555
*British Royalty
Commemoratives*

Ron Fox
Fox-Terry Steins, Inc.
416 Throop St.
N. Babylon, NY 11704
(516) 669-7232
Mettlach, Steins

Roselyn Gerson
12 Alnwick Rd.
Malverne, NY 11565
Compacts

Walter Glenn
Geode Ltd.
3393 Peachtree Rd.
Atlanta, GA 30326
(404) 261-9346
Frankart

Dan Golden
5375-C Avendia Encinas
Carlsbad, CA 92008-
4362
(619) 438-8383
Telephones

Ted Hake
Hake's Americana &
Collectibles
P. O. Box 1444
York, PA 17405
(717) 848-1333
*Disneyana, Political
Items*

John High
415 E. 52nd St.
New York, NY 10022
(212) 758-1692
Stevengraphs

Joan Hull
1376 Nevada
Huron, SD 57350
(605) 352-1685
Hull Pottery

David and Sue Irons
Irons Antiques
R. D. #4, Box 101
Northampton, PA 18067
(215) 262-9335
Irons

William J. Jenks
Golden Webb Antiques,
Inc.
P. O. Box 1274
Wilkes-Barre, PA 18703
(717) 288-3039
Pattern Glass

Lon Knickerbocker
20 William St.
Dansville, NY 14437
(716) 335-6506
Whimsies, Glass

Judy Knauer
1224 Spring Valley Lane
West Chester, PA 19380
(215) 431-3477
Toothpicks

Edward W. Leach
381 Trenton Ave.
Paterson, NJ 07503
(201) 684-5398
Shaving Mugs

Ron Lieberman
The Family Album
R. D. #1, Box 42
Glen Rock, PA 17327
(717) 235-2134
Books, Americana

Elaine J. Luartes
Athena Antiques
100 Beta Dr.
Franklin, TN 37064
(615) 377-3442
Jewelry

Clarence and Betty
Maier
The Burmese Cruet
P. O. Box 432
Montgomeryville, PA
18936
(215) 855-5388
*Burmese Glass, Crown
Milano, Royal Flemish*

James S. Maxwell, Jr.
P. O. Box 367
Lampeter, PA 17537
(717) 464-5573
Banks, Mechanical

Joan Collett Oates
5912 Kingsfield Dr.
W. Bloomfield, MI
48322
(313) 661-2335
Phoenix Bird Pattern

INTRODUCTION

Warman's provides the keys needed by auctioneers, collectors, and dealers to open the doors to understanding and dealing with the complexities of the antiques market. A price list is only one of the many tools needed today.

Warman's 26th Edition contains histories, reference books, periodicals, collectors' clubs, and museums. Useful buying and collecting hints also are provided.

Warman's is designed to be your introduction to the exciting world of antiques. As you advance beyond this book into specialized collecting areas, **Warman's** hopes you will remember with fondness where you received your start. When you encounter items outside your area of specialty, remember **Warman's** remains your key to unlocking the information you need, just as it has for over forty–four years.

ORGANIZATION

Listings: Objects are listed alphabetically by category, beginning with ABC Plates and ending with Zsolnay Pottery. If you have trouble identifying the category in which your object belongs, use the extensive index at the back of the book. It is designed to guide you to the proper category.

We have attempted to make the listings descriptive enough so that specific objects can be identified. We also have placed emphasis on those items which are actively being sold in the marketplace. Nevertheless, some harder–to–find objects are included in order to demonstrate the market spread.

Each year as the market changes, we carefully consider which categories to include, which to drop, and which to add. **Warman's** is a direct response to the developing trends in the marketplace. To further help collectors and dealers, Wallace–Homestead Book Company also publishes the *Warman's Encyclopedia of Antiques and Collectibles*. These volumes in the Warman format concentrate on a specific collecting group, e.g., Americana, Country, English & Continental Pottery & Porcelain, and Oriental Antiques.

History: Every collector should know something about the history of his object. We have presented a capsule background for each category. In many cases the background contains collecting hints or tips to help you spot reproductions.

References: Special references are listed for each category to help collectors learn more about their objects. Included are author, title, publisher [if published by a small firm or individual, we have indicated "published by author"], and date of publication or most recent edition.

Finding these books may present a problem. The antiques and collectibles field is blessed with a dedicated core of book dealers who stock these specialized publications. You will find them at flea markets, antiques shows, and advertised in leading publications in the field. Many dealers publish annual or semi–annual catalogs. Ask to be put on their mailing lists. Books go out–of–print quickly, yet many books printed over twenty–five years ago remain the standard work in a category. Used book dealers often can turn up many of these valuable reference sources.

Periodicals: Generally, the newsletter or bulletin of a collectors' club focuses on the specific publication needs within a category. However, there are other publications, not associated with collectors' clubs, of which the collector and dealer should be aware. These are covered under specific categories.

In addition, there are general interest newspapers and magazines which deserve to be brought to our user's attention. These are:

Antique Review, P. O. Box 538, Worthington, OH 43085
Antique Trader Weekly, P. O. Box 1050, Dubuque, IA 52001
Antique Week, P. O. Box 90, Knightstown, IN 46148
Antiques (The Magazine Antiques), 551 Fifth Avenue, New York, NY 10017
Antique & The Arts Weekly, Bee Publishing Company, 5 Church Hill Road, Newton, CT 06470
Antiques & Collecting Hobbies, 1006 South Michigan Avenue, Chicago, IL 60605
Collector News & Antique Reporter, Box 156, Grundy Center, IA 50638
Collectors Journal, P. O. Box 601, Vinton, IA 52349
Collectors' Showcase, P. O. Box 837, Tulsa, OK 74101
Maine Antique Digest, P. O. Box 358, Waldoboro, ME 04572
MidAtlantic Monthly Antiques Magazine, P. O. Box 908, Henderson, NC 27536
New England Antiques Journal, 4 Church Street, Ware, MA 01082
New York–Pennsylvania Collector, Drawer C, Fishers, NY 14453
Southern Antiques, P. O. Box 1107, Decatur, GA 30031
West Coast Peddler, P. O. Box 5134, Whittier, CA 90607
Yesteryear, P. O. Box 2, Princeton, WI 54968

It is impossible to list all the national and regional publications in the antiques and collectibles field. The above is merely a sampling. A check with your local library will bring many other publications to your attention.

Collectors' Clubs: The large number of collectors' clubs adds vitality to the antiques and collectibles fields. Their publications and conventions produce knowledge which often cannot be found anywhere else. Many of these clubs are short–lived; others are so strong that they have regional and local chapters.

Museums: The best way to study a specific field is to see as many documented examples as possible. For this reason, we have listed museums where significant collections in that category are on display. Special attention must be directed to the complex of museums which make up the Smithsonian Institution in Washington, D.C.

Reproductions: Reproductions are a major concern to all collectors and dealers. Most reproductions are unmarked; the newness of their appearance is often the best clue to uncovering them. Specific objects known to be reproduced are marked within the listings with an asterisk (*).

Index: A great deal of effort has been expended to make our index useful. Always try to find the most specific reference. For example, if you have a piece of china, look first for the maker's name and second for the type. The key is to ask the right questions of yourself.

Photographs: You may encounter a piece you cannot identify well enough to use the index. Consult the photographs and marks. If you own the last several editions of **Warman's**, you have assembled a valuable photographic reference to the antiques and collectibles field.

PRICE NOTES

In assigning prices we assume the object is in very good condition. If otherwise, we note this in our description. It would be ideal to suggest that mint, or unused, examples of all objects do exist. The reality is that objects from the past were used, whether they be glass, china, dolls, or toys. Because of this, some normal wear must be expected. In fact, if an object such as furniture does not show wear, its origins may be more suspect than if it does show wear.

Whenever possible, we have tried to provide a broad listing of prices within a category so you have a "feel" for the market. We emphasize the middle range of prices within a category, while also listing some objects of high and low value to show the market spread.

We do not use ranges because they tend to confuse rather than help the collector and dealer. How do you determine if your object is at the high or low end of the range? There is a high degree of flexibility in pricing in the antiques field. If you want to set ranges, add or subtract 10% from our prices.

One of the hardest variants with which to deal is the regional fluctuation of prices. Victorian furniture brings widely differing prices in New York, Chicago, New Orleans, or San Francisco. We have tried to strike a balance. Know your region and subject before investing heavily. If the best prices for cameo glass are in Montreal or Toronto, then be prepared to go there if you want to save money or add choice pieces to your collection. Research and patience are key factors to building a collection of merit.

Another factor that affects prices is a sale by a leading dealer or private collector. We have tempered both dealer and auction house figures.

PRICE RESEARCH

Everyone asks—where do we get our prices? They come from many sources.

First, we rely on auctions. Auction houses and auctioneers do not always command the highest prices. If they did, why would so many dealers buy from them? The key to understanding auction prices is to know when a price is in the high or low range. We think we do this and do it well.

Second, we work closely with dealers. We screen our contacts to make certain they have a full knowledge of the market. Dealers make their living from selling antiques; they cannot afford to have a price guide which is not in touch with the market.

Over forty antiques and collectibles magazines, newspapers, and journals come into our office regularly. They are excellent barometers of what is moving and what is not. We don't hesitate to call an advertiser and ask if their listed merchandise sold.

When the editorial staff is doing field work, we identify ourselves. Our conversations with dealers and collectors around the country have enhanced this book. Teams from **Warman's** are in the field at antiques shows, flea markets, and auctions recording prices and taking photographs.

Collectors work closely with us. They are specialists whose devotion to research and accurate information is inspiring. Generally, they are not dealers. Whenever we have asked them for help, they have responded willingly and admirably.

BOARD OF ADVISORS

Our Board of Advisors are specialists, both dealers and collectors, who feel a commitment to accurate information. You'll find their names listed in the front of the book. Several have authored a major reference work on their subject.

Members of the Board of Advisors file lists of prices in their categories for which they are responsible. They help select and often supply the photographs used. If you wish to buy or sell an object in their field of expertise, drop them a note along with an SASE. If time or interest permits, they will respond.

BUYER'S GUIDE, NOT SELLER'S GUIDE

Warman's is designed to be a buyer's guide to what you would have to pay to purchase an object on the open market from a dealer or collector. **It is not a seller's guide to prices.** People frequently make this mistake. In doing so, they deceive themselves. If you have an object listed in this book and wish to sell it to a dealer, you should expect to receive approximately fifty percent (50%) of the listed value. If the object is not anticipated to be resold quickly, expect to receive even less.

A private collector may pay more, perhaps 70% to 80% of our list price. Your object will have to be something needed for his or her collection. If you have an extremely rare object or an object of exceptionally high value, these guidelines do not apply.

Examine your piece as objectively as possible. As an antiques and collectibles appraiser, I spend a great deal of time telling people their treasures are not ''gold'' at all, but items readily available in the marketplace.

In respect to buying and selling, a simple philosophy is that a good purchase occurs when both the buyer and seller are happy with the price. Don't look back. Hindsight has little value in the antiques field. Given time, things tend to balance out.

COMMENTS INVITED

Warman's Antiques and Their Prices continues to be the leader in the antiques and collectibles price guide field because we listen to our readers. Readers are encouraged to send their comments and suggestions to Harry L. Rinker, Consulting Editor, Wallace–Homestead, c/o Rinker Enterprises, Inc., P. O. Box 248, Zionsville, PA 18092.

ACKNOWLEDGMENTS

This has been a year of transition for Rinker Enterprises, Inc. After preparing *Warman's* in a cabin in the woods for ten years, Rinker Enterprises, Inc., moved to the former Vera Cruz Elementary School on February 1, 1991. Available space increased ten fold. Dreams became reality. A new era, reflected by the changes that you see in this twenty–sixth edition, began.

The move would not have been possible without the total support of my staff. Ellen Schroy, Senior Editor, now carries the added burden of having talked me into buying the building. She is reminded of this each time there is a major maintenance problem!

As a staff, we shared Terese Oswald's loss of her husband, Dean. Ellen, Dana, Diane, and the other Rinkettes covered until Terese was able to rejoin us. We are all delighted that she could continue.

You will find the Rinkettes pictured once again in the back of the book. As you can see, the group has grown. Among the new faces are Nancy Butt, Beverly Marriner, and Diane Stoneback. Never assume that I edit this book alone. It is not a one-person job.

When the picture of the "Rinkettes" first appeared in the twenty–fifth edition of this book, some suggested that the concept was sexist. Nothing could be further from the truth. Chris Allen coined the term "Rinkettes" at an Antiques and Collectibles Information Service summer seminar several years ago. It was adopted by my staff, female and male alike. We see ourselves akin to a music group from the Rock 'n' Roll era. What is important is the music we make together, not whether one wears pants or skirts. And, at Rinker Enterprises, Inc., we prefer to write our own music.

There were two key elements that made the move to Vera Cruz possible—the staff at Rinker Enterprises and Chilton Books. It is wonderful to work for a client that asks "how can I help" more often than "what are you prepared to do for me." Thanks to Christopher Kuppig, Elsie Comninos, Edna Jones, Troy Vozzella, and Tim Scott.

Of course, any client is willing to help when they know the product they are supporting is going to do well. The Rinkettes and I only edit this book. Neil Levin and his marketing staff sell it. Kudos for a job that exceeded everyone's expectations.

A desire to never stand still is one of the plus factors of working with Chilton Books. When we proposed introducing an annual *Warman's Antiques and Collectibles Pocket Reference* to this book, Chilton's response was an immediate "let's do it." We did.

Finally, thanks to two groups without whom this book would not exist—those who provided information for the listings and those who buy and use it. We appreciate your support and promise to continue to produce a product that warrants your continued support year after year.

Rinker Enterprises, Inc.   Harry L. Rinker
P. O. Box 248   Editor
Zionsville, PA 18092
January 1992

STATE OF THE MARKET

The antiques and collectibles market is feeling the full effects of the recession. The news is bad on all fronts. Antiques and collectibles show gates are down. Collectors are being more and more selective in what they buy and are watching prices as never before. Many dealers are having their worst year in a decade. There are exceptions, as there always will be exceptions. However, when viewed as a whole, these are not the "best of times." The good news is that the antiques and collectibles field is not in a depression.

Unpredictable and *spotty* best describe the current state of the antiques and collectibles field. No one is certain exactly what will happen next. A dealer can have a great show one week and sell nothing the next. An auction can achieve record prices for some pieces while also experiencing two to three times its normal buy–in rate. A show gate that matches or even exceeds last year's is no guarantee that there will be active buying on the floor.

The bright spot in this otherwise gloomy picture is that few individuals have given up. Appraisers, auctioneers, collectors, dealers, and others have tightened their belts. They are coping. The survival instinct in the antiques and collectibles field is very high. The few that fall by the wayside are quickly replaced.

However, survival means adjustments. Look for profound changes in the antiques and collectibles market in the mid-1990s, changes ranging from what is being sold to how it is being sold. Attitudes that have been governing collecting and dealing for almost a century are going to be radically altered. There already are signs of change.

The hottest portion of the current market is post–World War II material, from 1950s designer furniture to Captain America action figures. The post–war market is fueled by availability, affordability, and trendiness. It also has attracted the attention of the "big boys." Christie's and Sotheby's competed openly for the right to auction the American toy holdings of bankrupt Mint & Boxed. In December 1991 Sotheby's auctioned a major comic book collection.

There are more twentieth-century categories and listings in this edition of *Warman's Antiques and Their Prices* than ever before. As the nation's leading general antiques and collectibles guide, *Warman's* keeps pace, unlike some of its competitors who continue to focus only on traditional categories. Look for more twentieth-century material in subsequent editions of *Warman's*. This is where the action is.

One of the primary factors behind the popularity of post–World War II collectibles is the attempt on the part of many collectors to recapture their childhood. For the vast majority of the American population, their childhood dates from the 1950s or later. Most individuals born during the first quarter of the decade are selling, rather than collecting. While the number of collectors for Eddie Cantor material decreases each year, the number of Kiss collectors increases.

There is a negative side to the post–war material—speculation fever. In the late 1970s speculators were major players in the eighteenth and early nineteenth century American antiques sector. Their sell–off in the early 1980s created a temporary pause in an otherwise boom market. The 1990s speculator focuses heavily on post–World War II collectibles and concentrates on material less than ten years old. I bought a Dick Tracy Playmates "The Tramp" figure on sale for $3.14. Within the past month, sellers have advertised it in *Toy Shop* for $8.00 and $15.00. This price diversity is clear proof of the speculative nature of recently discontinued material. It takes time to develop a secondary resale market that has a set of prices upon which collectors and dealers can rely—ask any dealer who has bought an item that is priced so high that no dealer or collector is willing to buy it.

In the early 1980s I put forth Rinker's Thirty Year Rule: "For the first thirty years of anything's life, all its value is speculative." Individuals have argued with me to change the number of years to twenty–five or twenty to reflect current market practices. I think not. I remain convinced that thirty is the right number.

In most dealers' minds, the clear winner in 1991 was the auctioneer. A common dealer complaint is "I cannot buy at auction anymore." Normally a dealer expects to acquire fifty percent or more of his merchandise through auction. For many dealers the answer to their frustration is to become auctioneers themselves. The catalog and trade paper advertisement mail/telephone auction continued to grow in 1991. Most operators of these auctions are unlicensed. Few comply with state auction laws. The potential for abuse is enormous. Beware.

Antiques malls are either a blessing or a curse depending on who you talk to. 1991 saw the first chinks in the antiques malls' armor. Many malls exhausted their dealer waiting list. They look full only because existing dealers spread out to fill in the gaps. A large number of smaller malls, those consisting of five to twenty dealers, went out of business. Tenants floated in and out depending on season, rather than remaining on a long term basis. The field is over-malled. Enough is enough.

In discussing the current market with dealers and show promoters who are surviving, it became apparent that there are four keys to survival— customer service, responsibility for goods sold, taking a long term position, and offering quality pieces at reasonable prices. These trends should become even more wide-spread in 1992.

During much of the 1980s, the antiques and collectibles market was not customer service oriented. There were plenty of customers. Why cultivate them? The recession changed this. The buyer is regaining his rightful place in the buyer/ seller equation. The antiques and collectibles market is at its best when there is a perfect balance between buyer and seller.

The traditional adherence to *caveat emptor*, "let the buyer beware," is changing. More and more sellers are backing their merchandise with a "no questions asked, money back guarantee." One show promoter has offered to pay dealers "for reproduction, fake or new pieces that a dealer may have inadvertently purchased." *Antique Week* has declared "War" on reproductions. Finally, sellers understand that they must take full responsibility for what they sell.

Learning to adopt a long, not short term position, is going to require a major readjustment in thinking. Many individuals turned to the antiques and collectibles field because it required so little commitment. The 1990s recession is going to last several years. There will be no quick in and out of the antiques and collectibles market in 1992.

Further, little is gained, with the exception of enjoyment, by paying a price for an object that one never will be able to realize through resale in one's lifetime. Many 1980s owners of record setting fine art and toys have been unable to recover their purchase price when offering their material for resale in the 1990s market. Antiques and collectibles are risky financial investments at best.

The final survival key for the 1990s is to offer quality pieces at reasonable prices. Since collector–dealers constitute a large majority of the sellers in the trade, they acquire needed capital by offering choice pieces from their private collections. The infusion of this material keeps buyers active. However, one of the most constant dealer complaints is the inability to replace quality pieces sold at a price that allows for a viable profit.

In 1991 the antiques and collectibles press finally admitted there is a recession in the trade. This is a major concession in a media that is largely "good news" oriented. Despite the fact that bad news reporting is carefully controlled and tempered, many dealers complain openly that the trade papers and their writers are responsible for the problems created by the recession. Talk about a cart and horse scenario.

All signs point to a 1992 market in which "buying right" will dominate over "selling right." Middle market dealers will have to check their desire for a "score" on every piece in favor of more modest returns. Sellers stressing volume sales and quick turnover appear to be in a better financial position than those relying solely on high ticket, high profit merchandise.

The importance of the foreign buyer in the American antiques and collectibles market decreased in 1991. The recession is causing caution worldwide. European dealers have turned their attention from American markets to raiding the former communist countries. Do not read too much into this trend. When the world economy recovers, European and Japanese buyers will come back to the American market with a vengeance. Enjoy the lull while you can.

1991 was a year when everyone blamed someone else rather than themselves for the problems in the market. All too often we forgot to look in the mirror. As 1991 ended there was a growing acceptance that the only way to end the recession was to roll up one's sleeves and do what needs to be done. This is a very positive sign. It means that the market is on the right track.

The 1992 market promises to be a great place to buy. Sellers have lowered prices, especially in the middle and low sectors of the market. There are bargains, plenty of them. There is a wide selection of merchandise. Many pieces from private collections entered the market in 1991.

Those who hold back based on the premise that the market will decline even further may be making a major mistake. Many categories already have established a bottom. After all, the best market for both buyer and seller is a stable market. After the wild ride of the 1980s, it is time for a little comfort and relief.

AUCTION HOUSES

The following auction houses cooperate with Rinker Enterprises, Inc., by providing catalogs of their auctions and price lists. This information is used to prepare *Warman's Antiques and Their Prices*, volumes in the Warman's Encyclopedia of Antiques and Collectibles, and Wallace–Homestead Book Company publications. This support is most appreciated.

Sanford Alderfer Auction Company
501 Fairgrounds Rd.
Hatfield, PA 19440
(215) 368-5477

Al Anderson
P. O. Box 644
Troy, OH 45373
(513) 339-0850

W. Graham Arader III
1000 Boxwood Court
King of Prussia, PA 19406
(215) 825-6570

Ark Antiques
Box 3133
New Haven, CT 06515
(203) 387-3754

Arthur Auctioneering
R. D. 2
Hughesville, PA 17737
(717) 584-3697

Noel Barrett Antiques and Auctions Ltd.
P. O. Box 1001
Carversville, PA 18913
(215) 297-5109

Robert F. Batchelder
1 West Butler Ave.
Ambler, PA 19002
(215) 643-1430

Biders Antiques, Inc.
241 South Union St.
Lawrence, MA 01843
(508) 688-4347

Richard A. Bourne Co., Inc.
Corporation St.
P. O. Box 141
Hyannis Port, MA 02647
(508) 775-0797

Butterfield's
220 San Bruno Ave.
San Francisco, CA 94103
(415) 861-7500

Christie's
502 Park Ave.
New York, NY 10022
(212) 546-1000

Christie's East
219 E. 67th St.
New York, NY 10021
(212) 606-0400

Christmas Morning
1850 Crown Rd., Suite 1111
Dallas, TX 75234
(817) 236-1155

Marvin Cohen Auctions
Box 425, Routes 20 & 22
New Lebanon, NY 12125
(518) 794-9333

Collector's Auction Services
P. O. Box 13732
Seneca, PA 16346
(814) 677-6070

Marlin G. Denlinger
RR 3, Box 3775
Morrisville, VT 05661
(802) 888-2774

William Doyle Galleries, Inc.
175 E. 87th St.
New York, NY 10128
(212) 427-2730

Early Auction Co.
123 Main St.
Milford, OH 45150
(513) 831-4833

Fine Arts Co. of Philadelphia, Inc.
1808 Chestnut St.
Philadelphia, PA 19103
(215) 563-9275

William A. Fox Auctions, Inc.
676 Morris Ave.
Springfield, NJ 07081
(201) 467-2366

Ron Fox
F. T. S. Inc.
416 Throop St.
N. Babylon, NY 11704
(516) 669-7232

Garth's Auction, Inc.
2690 Stratford Rd.
P. O. Box 369
Delaware, OH 43015
(614) 362-4771 or 369-5085

Glass-Works Auctions
P. O. Box 187-102
Jefferson St.
East Greenville, PA
18041
(215) 679-5849

Grandma's Trunk
The Millards
P. O. Box 404
Northport, IN 49670
(616) 386-5351

Guerney's
136 East 73rd St.
New York, NY 10021
(212) 794-2280

Ken Farmer Realty &
Auction Co.
1122 Norwood St.
Radford, VA 24141
(703) 639-0939

Hake's Americana and
Collectibles
P. O. Box 1444
York, PA 17405
(717) 848-1333

Harmer Rooke
Numismatists, Inc.
3 East 57th St.
New York, NY 10022
(212) 751-4122

Hart Galleries
2311 Westheimer
Houston, TX 77098
(713) 524-2979 or
523-7389

Norman C. Heckler &
Company
Bradford Corner RD.
Woodstock Valley, CT
06282
(203) 974-1634

Leslie Hindman, Inc.
215 West Ohio St.
Chicago, IL 60610
(312) 670-0010

Michael Ivankovich
Antiques
P. O. Box 2458
Doylestown, PA 18901
(215) 345-6094

James D. Julia, Inc.
P. O. Box 830
Fairfield, ME 04937
(207) 453-7904

Charles E. Kirtley
P. O. Box 2273
Elizabeth City, NC
27906
(919) 335-1262

Howard Lowery
3818 W. Magnolia Blvd.
Burbank, CA 91505
(818) 972-9080

Les Paul's
2615 Magnolia St.,
Suite A
Oakland, CA 94607
(415) 832-2615

Alex G. Malloy, Inc.
P. O. Box 38
South Salem, NY 10590
(203) 438-0396

Martin Auctioneers, Inc.
Larry L. Martin
P. O. Box 477
Intercourse, PA 17534
(717) 768-8108

Robert Merry Auction
Company
5501 Milburn Rd.
St. Louis, MO 63129
(314) 487-3992

Mid-Hudson Auction
Galleries
One Idlewild Ave.
Cornwall-On-Hudson,
NY 12520
(214) 534-7828

Milwaukee Auction
Galleries
318 N. Water
Milwaukee, WI 53202
(414) 271-1105

Neal Alford Company
4139 Magazine St.
New Orleans, LA 70115
(504) 899-5329

New England Auction
Gallery
Box 2273
W. Peabody, MA 01960
(508) 535-3140

New Hampshire Book
Auctions
Woodbury Rd.
Weare, NH 03281
(603) 529-1700

Nostalgia Publications,
Inc.
21 South Lake Dr.
Hackensack, NJ 07601
(201) 488-4536

Richard Opfer
Auctioneering, Inc.
1919 Greenspring Dr.
Timonium, MD 21093
(410) 252-5035

Pettigrew Auction
Company
1645 South Tejon St.
Colorado Springs, CO
80906
(719) 633-7963

Postcards International
P. O. Box 2930
New Haven, CT 06515-
0030
(203) 865-0814

David Rago Arts &
Crafts
P. O. Box 3592
Station E
Trenton, NJ 08629
(609) 585-2546

Lloyd Ralston Toys
173 Post Rd.
Fairfield, CT 06432
(203) 255-1233 or
366-3399

Renzel's Auction Service
P. O. Box 222
Emigsville, PA 17318
(717) 764-6412

R. Niel & Elaine
Reynolds
Box 133
Waterford, VA 22190
(703) 882-3574

Roan Bros. Auction
Gallery
R.D. 3, Box 118
Cogan Station, PA 17728
(717) 494-0170

Stanton's Auctioneers &
Realtors
144 South Main St.
Vermontville, MI 49096
(517) 726-0181

Robert W. Skinner Inc.
Bolton Gallery
357 Main St.
Bolton, MA 01740
(508) 779-6241

Smith House Toy Sales
26 Adlington Rd.
Eliot, ME 03903
(207) 439-4614

Sotheby's
1334 York Ave.
New York, NY 10021
(212) 606-7000

Swann Galleries, Inc.
104 E. 25th St.
New York, NY 10010
(212) 254-4710

Theriault's
P. O. Box 151
Annapolis, MD 21401
(301) 224-3655

Western Glass Auctions
1288 W. 11th St.,
Suite #230
Tracy, CA 95376
(209) 832-4527

Winter Associates
21 Cooke St., Box 823
Plainville, CT 06062
(203) 793-0288

Wolf's Auction Gallery
13015 Larchmere Blvd.
Shaker Heights, OH
44120
(216) 231-3888

Woody Auction
Douglass, KS 67039
(316) 746-2694

ABBREVIATIONS

The following are standard abbreviations which we have used throughout this edition of **Warman's**.

ah = applied handle
C = century
c = circa
circ = circular
cov = cover
d = diameter or depth
dec = decorated
DQ = Diamond Quilted
emb = embossed
ext. = exterior
FE = first edition
ftd = footed
ground = background
h = height
hp = hand painted
hs = high standard
imp = impressed
int. = interior
irid = iridescent
IVT = inverted thumbprint
j = jewels
K = karat
l = length

litho = lithograph
ls = low standard
MIB = mint in box
mkd = marked
MOP = mother of pearl
NE = New England
No. = number
opal = opalescent
orig = original
os = orig stopper
pat = patent
pcs = pieces
pr = pair
rect = rectangular
sgd = signed
sngl = single
SP = silver plated
SS = Sterling silver
sq = square
w = width
yg = yellow gold
# = numbered

ABC PLATES

History: The majority of early ABC plates were manufactured in England, imported into the United States, and achieved their greatest popularity from 1780 to 1860. Since a formal education was limited in the early 19th century, the ABC plate was a method of educating the poor for a few pennies.

ABC plates are found in glass, pewter, porcelain, pottery, and tin. Porcelain plates range in diameter from 4⅜ to slightly over 9½ inches. The rim usually contains the alphabet and/or numbers; the center features animals, great men, maxims, or nursery rhymes.

References: Susan and Al Bagdade, *Warman's English & Continental Pottery & Porcelain, 2nd Edition*, Wallace–Homestead, 1991; Mildred L. and Joseph P. Chalala, *A Collector's Guide to ABC Plates, Mugs and Things*, Pridemark Press, 1980.

Plate, raised alphabet border, maxim "Constant Dropping Wears Away Stones And Little Strokes Fall Great Oaks," multicolored transfer of boy chopping tree, 7″ d, $75.00.

GLASS

Christmas Eve, 6″ d, Santa on chimney, clear	65.00
Clock, 7″ d, blue	35.00
Ducks, 6″ d, amber	45.00
Emma, girl's head center, beaded rim, Higbee	85.00
Floral Bouquet with bow, clear	50.00
Hen and Chicks, 6″ d, clear	40.00
Rabbit in Cabbage Patch, frosted center, stippled edge	40.00
Sancho Panza and Dabble, frosted center, clear border	52.50
Star Medallion, 6″ d, clear	40.00

PORCELAIN OR POTTERY

Baby Bunting and Little Dog Bunch	55.00
Boy, 6″ d, fishing, Staffordshire	35.00
Campbell Kid	50.00
Deaf and Dumb, 6½″ d, sign language, pink transfer, hands making signs of alphabet on inner rim, two dressed cats in center, H Aynsley & Co, London, England, c1904	150.00
Elephant, two girls, pink transfer, Staffordshire	85.00
Franklin Maxim, Like Rest Consumes Faster Than Labor While the Used Key is Always Bright	80.00
Goat Herd Boy, 5″ d, horn, dog and goat center, emb border	75.00
Harvest Home, 5½″ d, hay wagon, emb border, J G Meakin, c1870	75.00
Men Fighting on Donkeys, 7″ d	65.00
Niagara From The Edge Of The American Falls, 7¼″ d, Staffordshire	125.00
Organ Grinder, 8¼″ d, Staffordshire	40.00
Punch and Judy, 7″ d, ironstone, blue transfer, marked "Allertons, England"	75.00
Robinson Crusoe, 6³⁄₁₆″ d, pink transfer scene, Brownhills Pottery Co, England, 1887–88	110.00
Rule of Three, 8″ d, three black men raising glasses, Staffordshire	200.00
Shepherd Boy, 5¼″ d, horn, dog, and goat	75.00
Stag's Head, 6″ d	30.00
The Baker, 7″ d, worker putting loaves of bread into brick oven, Staffordshire	135.00
The Leopard, 7½″ d, sq brown and green transfer scene, Brownhills Pottery Co, 1882	110.00
Titmouse, 7¼″ d, polychrome enamel trim, Staffordshire, c1884	90.00
Washington, 7¼″ d, Staffordshire	90.00
Zebra, 6⅛″ d, transfer printed, polychrome trim, emb border, Powell & Bishop, 1876–78	85.00

TIN

Cat with yarn, 4″ d	35.00
Children, 2″ d	65.00
Girl on swing, 3½″ d	40.00
Hey Diddle Diddle, 8″ d	55.00
Mary had a Little Lamb, 8″ d	90.00
Sea Horse, 8″ d, hp, bear and children border	25.00
Tom Thumb, 3″ d	40.00
Victoria and Albert, 6″ d, names and busts	150.00

ADAMS ROSE

History: Adams Rose, made c1820–40 by Adams and Son in the Staffordshire district of England, is decorated with brilliant red roses and green leaves on a white ground.

G. Jones and Son, England, made a variant known as "Late Adams Rose." The colors are not as brilliant and the ground is a "dirty" white. It commands less than the price of the early pattern.

Reference: Susan and Al Bagdade, *Warman's English & Continental Pottery & Porcelain, 2nd Edition,* Wallace–Homestead, 1991.

Plate, early, 7¼″ d, $145.00.

Bowl, 8¾″ d, early	600.00
Creamer, early	340.00
Cup and Saucer, handleless, late	65.00
Cup Plate, 4¼″ d	48.00
Milk Pitcher	
4⅞″ h, c1840	75.00
6¾″ h, bulbous, emb	130.00
Plate	
7¼″ d, early	145.00
7½″ d, late	35.00
8½″ d, late	45.00
8¾″ d, late	50.00
9¼″ d, early	175.00
9½″ d, late	65.00
10½″ d, early	225.00
Platter, 15″ l, oval, early, c1820	300.00
Soup, flange rim, late	75.00
Sugar, cov, late	150.00
Teapot, late	210.00
Vegetable Dish, cov, 12⅝″ l, c1850	500.00
Wash Bowl and Pitcher, early	1,000.00

ADVERTISING

History: Before the days of mass media, advertisers relied on colorful product labels and advertising giveaways to promote their products. Containers were made to appeal to the buyer by the use of stylish lithographs and bright colors.

Many of the illustrations used the product in the advertisement so that even an illiterate buyer could identify a product.

Advertisements were put on almost every household object imaginable and were constant reminders to use the product or visit a certain establishment.

References: Al Bergevin, *Drugstore Tins and Their Prices,* Wallace–Homestead Book Company, 1990; Al Bergevin, *Food and Drink Containers and Their Prices,* Wallace–Homestead Book Company, 1988; Ray Klug, *Antique Advertising Encyclopedia,* Vol. 1 (1978) and Vol. 2 (1985), L–W Promotions; Ralph and Terry Kovel, *Kovels' Advertising Collectibles Price List,* Crown Publishers Inc., 1986; L–W Promotions (ed.), *Antique Advertising Handbook and Price Guide,* L–W Book Sales, 1988; Douglas Congdon–Martin, *Antique Advertising: America for Sale,* Schiffer Publishing, 1991; James H. Stahl, *Collectors Guide To Key–Wind Coffee Tins With Price Guide,* L–W Book Sales, 1991; Robert W. and Harriet Swedberg, *Tins 'N' Bins,* Wallace–Homestead Book Company, 1985.

Collectors' Clubs: The Ephemera Society of America, P.O. Box 37, Schoharie, NY 12157; Tin Container Collectors Association, P.O. Box 440101, Aurora, CA 80014.

Periodical: *National Association of Paper and Advertising Collectibles,* P.O. Box 500, Mount Joy, PA 17552.

Additional Listings: See *Warman's Americana & Collectibles* for more examples.

Ashtray	
Firestone Tire	22.00
Fisk Tires, 6½″ d, rubber, clear glass insert	20.00
Marguerite Cigars, 7¼″ d, glass, clear, woman and adv graphics, 1920–30	300.00
Peacemaker, figural gun	45.00

Box, Waltke's Baby Doll Soap, Proctor & Gamble, 2½ x 4 x 1½″, $5.00.

Badge, Dupont Gopher Ordinance
Works, MN 20.00
Bag, Red Goose Shoes, paper 15.00
Bank
  Red Circle Coffee, tin 15.00
  Snow Crest Beverages, Salem, MA,
    bottle type, figural standing bear,
    clear glass 20.00
Banner, Union Leader Tobacco 175.00
Bin, Tiger Chewing Tobacco, 1915–25 70.00
Blotter, Morton's Salt, 4 x 9", unused,
  c1930 .... 15.00
Booklet, Grand American Handicap
  Union Metallic Cartridge Co, celluloid
  cov, 1905 .... 55.00
Box
  Armour's Sliced Bacon, cardboard . 13.00
  Ayer's Cherry Pectoral/Dr J C Ayer &
    C, Lowell, MA, wood, black print,
    stenciled 80.00
  Buxton's Rheumatic Cure, wood,
    black print, stenciled 50.00
  Cascade Ginger Ale, pictures water-
    fall, holds six bottles 35.00
  Coldwell Lawnmower, wood 30.00
  Dalton's Sarsaparilla and Nerve
    Tonic, wood, black print, stenciled 65.00
  Dr Kilmer's Ocean Weed Heart Rem-
    edy, wood, multicolored print, sten-
    ciled 220.00
  Ocean Spray Cranberries, wood ... 18.00
  Warner's Safe Cure, wood, black
    print, stenciled 75.00

**Brochure, Wrigley's Mother Goose,
1915, 4 x 5⅞", $20.00.**

Calendar
  Atlantic Steel Co, 1943, wartime pic-
    tures 20.00
  Browns Iron Bitters, revolving, 1888 70.00
  Consumers Brewing Co, 17 x 12",
    factory scene, 1913 .... 350.00
  DeLaval, 24 x 12", litho, 1925 ..... 25.00

Ebling Brewing Co, 25 x 17", factory
  scene, framed, 1903 .... 225.00
Firestone Tire & Rubber Co, 34 x 17",
  paper, litho, c1911 .... 1,600.00
John Hancock Mutual Life Insurance,
  litho on paper, 10 x 8" 60.00
Mobil, 1969 .... 15.00
Nehi, 19¼ x 8½", 1927, framed under
  glass 50.00
Peters Cartridge Company, 30 x
  13½", pictures grouse in field, in-
  complete, 1926 .... 40.00
Change Mat, Camel Cigarettes, 9",
  round, rubber, marked "Have A Real
  Cigarette" 45.00
Change Receiver, Clark's Teaberry
  Gum, double sided, green vaseline
  glass, red and yellow decals, 1920s 90.00
Change Tray
  Arthur M Butts Wagons, Autos, Sport-
    ing Tools, 3¼ x 5" 30.00
  Baker's Breakfast Cocoa, 6", 1920s . 140.00
  Best Automatic Electric Iron, iron in
    center, city landscape background,
    c1920 .... 45.00
  Columbus Brewing Co, Christopher
    Columbus in center, c1898 ..... 20.00
  Continental Life Insurance, company
    building, 4" d, c1920 .... 35.00
  Eversweet, 5½ x 3", draped female
    with flowers, c1910 .... 60.00
  Frank Jones Homestead Ale, 5" d .. 30.00
  Henry Elias Brewing Co, emb tin, 4"
    d, c1900 .... 45.00
  J Chr Hupfel Brewing Corp, emb tin,
    4" d, c1910 .... 35.00
  J W Sheets Choice Groceries, wood-
    land scene border, 3¼ x 5" 30.00
  Muehlebach Pilsner Beer, "Purest
    and Best", 5" d 30.00
  Pepsi Cola, litho, 1890s 675.00
  Rigby's La Toco Havana Cigar, clas-
    sical girl in center with cherubs,
    c1920 .... 15.00
Charger, 24" d, Miller High Life Beer, tin,
  litho, girl sitting on crescent moon
  holding product, c1907 .... 950.00
Clock
  Budweiser, team and wagon scene . 125.00
  Lucky Strike, 23" h, orig finish and
    label on back, New Haven Clock
    Co, 1900–20 .... 275.00
  Merricks Spool Cotton, New Haven
    Clock Co, 24" h, 1900–20 ...... 500.00
  Royal Crown Cola, lights up 185.00
Display Rack, Golden Burst Popcorn,
  counter type 45.00
Door Push
  Chesterfield King, tin, 9 x 4⅛", c1950 60.00
  Crescent Flour, tin, emb, pictures
    sack of flour, 9½ x 3¾", c1930 .. 110.00
  Kramer's Beverages, tin 30.00

Salada Tea, porcelain	65.00
Sweetie, tin, emb bottle, 11½ x 4", c1930	25.00

Fan

Emerson's Drugs Ginger, soda fountain giveaway, girl playing tennis .	50.00
Marshall Field & Co, paper	35.00
Figure, Red Goose, chalk, 12" h	125.00
Game, Champion Spark Plugs, Champion Road Race, 18 x 12" playing board, cut–out spinner, six cut–out race cars, instructions	45.00
Grater, Fels Naptha	8.00
Jar, Planter Peanut, 10½" h, paper label, 1920s	250.00
Jug, Barbwells Root Beer, 11½" h, stoneware, emb elk on one side, raised lettering on other	45.00
Kettle, 4¾" h, SSS For The Blood, bronze, 1900–20	320.00

Measuring Cup, Hellick's Rain Flakes, Geo. F. Hellick Coffee Co., Easton, PA, blue and white litho tin, $35.00.

Menu Board, Dybala Orange Drink ...	65.00
Milk Bottle, Farm Fresh Tools, stoneware, pictures rooster	20.00

Mirror

Dr Van Dykes Holland Bitters, black and red, white ground	110.00
Edna Jetticks, You'll Stride with Pride	55.00
Mountain States Telephone & Telegraph Co, 3½" d	45.00
Old Reliable Coffee	50.00
Yucatan Gum, pocket	48.00

Mug

Ambassador Scotch, ceramic	20.00
Buckeye Root Beer, ceramic	55.00
Schering Pharmaceutical	15.00
Paperweight, National Lead Company, 3¼", cast lead, pictures early Dutch Boy painter, Phoenix Metal	30.00
Print, Hire's Root Beer, 12½ x 9½", framed	40.00
Recipe Booklet, Kraft Cheese, 3 x 7", 1936	12.00
Roulette Wheel, ReaLemon Soda, wood	30.00

Mirror, Ballard's Obelisk, Louisville, Parisian Nov. Co., Chicago, 1¾" d, $35.00.

Sign

American Bicycle Safety Club, tin, small, orig envelope	75.00
Arbuckles Ariosa Coffee, 30 x 21", paper, litho, c1889	450.00
Brookfield Rye, 33" h, tin, lady standing wearing see–through gown holding product, artist sgd, framed, c1902	2,000.00
Budweiser Anheuser Busch, 11½ x 32¼", tin, 1910–20	200.00
Clark's Mile End Spool Cotton, paper, litho, 18 x 12", c1920	40.00
Colgan's Chips, 26 x 20", paper, litho, "The Gum That's Round!," c1910	3,000.00
Columbian Bottled Beer, 13 x 9½", tin, emb, c1905	150.00
Cyclone Twister, 12 x 10", cardboard, litho	25.00
Dairy Made Ice Cream, 28 x 19", baby at beach with cone, 1920–30	150.00
Dandy Shandy, 12 x 9", cardboard, "Down goes the Thermometer, Down goes Dandy Shandy," 1930s	120.00
Deering Ideal Reaper, 19 x 30", paper, litho, matted and framed, c1905–15	130.00
DeLaval, 31½ x 19½", tin, litho, orig frame, 1915–25	500.00
Derby Pipe Tobacco, 14½ x 10½", cardboard, orig frame	225.00
Fehr's Malt–Tonic, 28½ x 23", tin, semi–nude and flying cherubs, framed, c1903	1,250.00
Fencing Club Pure Rye, 36 x 23", tin, lady sitting holding sword, c1901 .	2,700.00
Finck's Detroit–Special Overalls, 12 x 9", tin, litho, "Wears Like a Pig's Nose" and "Try a Pair–The Man Who Thinks Invests in Fincks," c1930s	40.00
Fraser's Axle Grease, 25 x 38", tin, framed	750.00

Pinback Button, Winchester, Junior Rifle Corps, celluloid, ⅞″ d, $35.00.

George Lawrence Dog Chains and Leads, 7″, sq, litho on tin, c1915 . | 30.00
Gossard Corsets, 25 x 50″, paper, litho, 1920s . . . . | 15.00
Grand Union Tea Co, 9 x 6½″, diecut, winter scene encircled by holly, seashell on top, c1910 . . . . | 25.00
Greyhound, porcelain, orig bracket . | 395.00
Harvard Brewing Co, 32 x 23″, paper, litho, Harvard and Yale rowing teams competing, factory on bottom, c1901 . . . . | 1,050.00
Jell-O 10¢, 42 x 20″, paper, litho, c1900 . . . . | 950.00
Just Foods, paper, litho, framed, 1930s . . . . | 70.00
Lord Salisbury Cigarettes, 19 x 10″, tin, framed . . . . | 75.00
Lycoming Rubber Boots and Shoes, 24 x 17″, paper, litho, man standing in stream helps lady walk across stones, c1905 . . . . | 1,500.00
Marathon Ohio Oil Co, runner . . . . . | 175.00
Mavis Chocolate Drink, tin, flanged . | 125.00
Nation–Wide Grocers, 20 x 121″, emb enamel . . . . | 40.00
Nehi Beverages, 54 x 18″, tin, pictures bottle, red, green, and orange | 40.00
Orange Crush, tin, emb bottle cap . . | 55.00
Pedigree Whiskey, 19 x 27″, tin, emb, c1895 . . . . | 600.00
Quaker Maid Rye, 40 x 27″, tin, litho, c1905 . . . . | 200.00
Remington Game Loads, 29 x 19″, paper, litho, 1910–20 . . . . | 225.00
Rice's Seeds, 15½ x 44″, paper, litho, 1930s . . . . | 50.00
Royal Crown Cola, 60″, diecut bottle | 350.00
Salvet Worm Destroyer, 9 x 13″, counter top type, tin, emb, 1905–15 . . | 120.00
Snow King Baking Powder, 20 x 36″, diecut, figural, cardboard, litho, c1900 . . . . | 375.00
Texaco Fire Chief, porcelain . . . . . . | 49.00
The Devilish Good 5¢ Cigar, 9¾ x

13½″, product box in center, flaming letters, emb, 1890s . . . . | 70.00
Union Leader Cut Plug, 12 x 8½″, tin, pictures product, c1920 . . . . | 130.00
White Mountain Ice Cream Freezer, 21½ x 15½″, paper, litho, c1905 . | 1,200.00

Sugar Sack
National Golden Brown Sugar . . . . . | 10.00
Quaker Soft Cane Sugar, 14 x 22″, burlap, 25 lb, Keystone logo and maiden, red and blue lettering . . . | 15.00

Thermometer
Bireley's, yellow, bottle . . . . | 85.00
Cobbs Creek Whiskey, 38″, steel, red, white, and blue, dated 1936 . . . . | 125.00
Dr Pepper, round . . . . | 75.00
Hires, bottle shape . . . . | 75.00
Mission Orange, 16″, bottle . . . . | 75.00
Nature Remedy, porcelain . . . . | 95.00
Standard Heating Oils, orig box . . . | 30.00
Tums . . . . | 37.50
Vicks . . . . | 30.00
Winston, round . . . . | 25.00

Tin, Tiger Chewing Tobacco, rect, 6 x 3¾ x 2¼″, $60.00.

Tin
Big Ben Tobacco, pocket . . . . | 20.00
Bonomo's Hard Candy . . . . | 25.00
Boyers Railroad Salve, 4 x 6″, litho . | 230.00
Campfire Marshmallow . . . . | 28.00
Choice Family Tea, 8½ x 4¼″ . . . . . | 20.00
Colgates Baby Talc, 6¼″, c1920 . . . | 35.00
Comfort Powder, pictures baby, 4″ h, 2½″ d . . . . | 100.00
Curtiss and Harvey Gun Powder, 1 lb | 40.00
Drako Brand Coffee, drake on sides, c1920 . . . . | 140.00
Dream Girl Talcum . . . . | 43.00
Golden Pheasant Condoms . . . . . . | 75.00
Governor Coffee, pictures Edward Tipten first Ohio Governor, c1915 . | 50.00
Granger Tobacco . . . . | 32.50
Hi-Plane Tobacco, pocket . . . . | 20.00
Humpty Dumpty Borated Talc, 7¼″ h, Humpty Dumpty scene, c1908 . . . | 50.00

Laxamints	10.00
Maxwell House Tea, 4½" h, 3½" sq,	
blue, orange lettering	60.00
Monarch Cocoa, 5"	25.00
Moore Bros Antiparasitic, 4" h, "Worm	
& Tonic Powders for Horses &	
Dogs"	100.00
Mrs Tucker's Shortening	25.00
Nestles Egyptian Henna	18.00
Orcico Cigar, Indian in center, c1919	60.00
Penslar Baby Powder, silhouette of	
children playing	58.00
Punch Cigar, 5½" h, round, Punch	
medallion on front and back	80.00
Ramses Condoms	90.00
Regina Moth Proofing Liquid, pint . .	10.00
Schotts Butter Pretzels, 1940s	25.00
Snowdrift Coconut, 1920	25.00
Stein's Burnt Cork, Blackface makeup	25.00
Tiger Tobacco, round, 1 lb, c1910 . .	200.00
Tiny Tot Talcum, pictures baby	75.00
Unguentine, sq, 1 lb	25.00
US Marine Flake Cut, pocket, c1910	130.00
Velvet Night Talcum	38.00
Victoria Brand Tea, 5 lb	20.00
Welsh Rabbit Biscuit, 10 x 4½ x 2",	
family at tea time, 1910–20	60.00
Yankee Boy Plug Cut, c1915	360.00
Tray	
A Hupfel's Sons Brewery, tin, 13" d,	
"Remember the Maine," c1898 . .	350.00
Arctic Ice Cream, 13" d, polar bear on	
ice cap, c1920	240.00
Brookfield Rye Whiskey, 12 x 17", tin,	
litho, c1905	300.00
Christian Feigenspan Brewing Co,	
13" d, sgd by artist A Asti	25.00
Clysmic, King of Table Waters, 16 x	
12½", lady sitting with foot in water	
holding large bottle, elk drinking	
from water, c1910	450.00
Drink Orange Julip, 10½ x 13", 1920s	120.00
Elmira Ice Cream, 12½" d, tin, litho,	
1920s	225.00
Excelsior Brewing Co, tin, oval, 16 x	
13", c1902	425.00
F & M Schaefer Brewing Co, 16½ x	
13½", oval, beer barrel in center,	
c1902	200.00
Hampden Brewing Co, 13" d, 1930s	120.00
Hyan Dry Ginger Ale, 10½ x 13", baby	
on bottle airplane, 1920s	60.00
Miller High Life, 13" d, girl sitting on	
crescent moon, 1907	150.00
Milwaukee Brewing of San Francisco	
Golden State Beer, 13 x 10", c1910	275.00
Nafruco, 10½ x 13", 1911 copyright .	330.00
Orange Crush, 10½ x 13", black fig-	
ure crushing orange, c1929	400.00
Pabst Blue Ribbon, 13 x 10½", gen-	
tleman with product, c1933	30.00
Supreme Bread, tin, pictures Uncle	

Pete dining with squirrel, travel	
game on reverse	45.00
The West End Brewing Co, 13" d,	
1905–15	500.00
White Rock Beer, 13¼", round	250.00
Wielands Extra Pale Lager Beer, 13"	
d, Indian maiden, c1902	850.00
Yuengling's Ice Cream, 13" d, lady	
holding tray with dish of ice cream,	
1920	80.00
Umbrella, Bliss Herbs For The Blood,	
orange, black lettering, 1900	410.00
Watch Fob	
Savage Rifles, silver	120.00
Willy's Knight	35.00
Whistle, Sun Bright Cleanser, can	
shape	25.00

ADVERTISING TRADE CARDS

History: Advertising trade cards are small, thin cardboard cards made to advertise the merits of a product and usually bear the name and address of a merchant.

With the invention of lithography, colorful trade cards became a popular advertising media in the late 19th and early 20th centuries. They were made especially to appeal to children. Young and old alike collected and treasured them in albums and scrapbooks. Very few are dated; 1880 to 1893 were the prime years for trade cards; 1810 to 1850 cards can be found, but rarely. By 1900 trade cards were rapidly losing their popularity. By 1910 they had all but vanished.

References: Kit Barry, *The Advertising Trade Card,* Book 1, Iris Publishing Co., 1981; Robert Jay, *The Trade Card In Nineteenth–Century America,* University of Missouri Press, 1987; Jim and Cathy McQuary, *Collectors Guide To Advertising Cards,* L–W Promotions, 1975; Murray Card (International) Ltd., *Cigarette Card Values: Murray's 1991 Guide To Cigarette & Other Trade Cards,* published by author, 1991.

Additional Listings: See *Warman's Americana & Collectibles* for more examples.

CLOTHING

Celluloid Waterproof Collars, Cuffs &	
Shirt Bosoms	2.50
Climax Hats, lady wearing hat	4.00
F Mayer Boot & Shoe Co, Milwaukee,	
three boys playing hopscotch	4.00
Hodges Hat & Bonnet Bleachery	2.00
Koch Bros, Allentown's Leading Cloth-	
ing Makers, Maud Humphrey, 1902 .	12.00
Paris Kid Gloves, diecut	3.00
Solar Tip Shoes, children, 1878	10.00
Warner's Corset, black and white	2.50

COFFEE

Great Atlantic & Pacific Tea Company, 8 x 9″, 1884	35.00
Lion Coffee, diecut, male frog	10.00

FARM MACHINERY

Eclipse Halter, multicolored, black and white cow in stall, 3 x 5″, 1884	5.00
Kemp & Burpee Manure Spreader	3.00
Milwaukee Harvester, pretty woman	8.00
Moline Wagon Co, Moline, IL, couple in wagon	4.00
Stoddard Tiger, King of Rakes	5.00
Wm Deering & Company, two girls and dog, 4 x 6½″, c1890	20.00

FOOD

Baker's Chocolate, early 1900s	100.00
Borden's Milk, baby drumming milk can, 1886	20.00
Cudahy Meats, diecut, pig, folder type	10.00
Daniels & Smith, groceries	2.50
Dunham's Coconut	1.00
Falstaff Lemp Beer, colorful	55.00
Fleischmann Co, black couple	10.00
Heinz Pickle, pickle shape, girl holding product	3.00
Hires Root Beer, boy and dog, 1892	20.00
Horlick's Malted Milk, diecut	3.00
Maiden Blush Vinegar, children playing	4.00
Renown Table Salt	1.50
Royal Baking Powder, mechanical, 1920s	40.00
Sanford's Ginger, black girl rocking baby	75.00
Snyder's Catsup, mechanical	10.00
Warner's Safe Yeast, girl smelling flowers	2.50

MEDICINE

Ayer's Cherry Pectoral, girl holding basket	6.00
Burdock's Bitters	5.00
Chesebrough Manufacturing Co, Vaseline, girl playing with cat and two puppies	3.00
Dr Seth Arnold's Cough Killer, girl holding puppy	5.00
Humphrey's Witch Hazel Oil, lady picking flowers	4.00
Kendall's Spavin Cure, black jockey and race horse, 4 x 6″, c1890	10.00
Morse's Pills, girl feeding two kittens, 1890	4.00
Parker's Ginger Tonic, girl sitting in chair	5.00
Scott's Emulsion of Cod Liver Oil, fisherman carrying fish, 1884	15.00

Medicine, Hires Cough Cure, Charles E. Hires Co., adv on back, 3 x 5″, $10.00.

MISCELLANEOUS

Cudahy Packing Co, mechanical, 19th C	85.00
Fairbank's Scales, elephant	2.00
Forepaugh Wild West Show, multicolored, 4 x 5″, c1890	20.00
Hotchkiss & Co, revolving cannon	5.00
Hoyt's Cologne, Germany	6.00
National Cash Register, mechanical	45.00
Page Fence, woman and charging bull	4.00
Pratts Astral Oil, Statue of Liberty, 1883	25.00
Ryders Excursion, paddle wheel, 1881	20.00
State Line, anchored ship	10.00

PIANOS AND ORGANS

Estey Organ, bear scene	5.00
Weaver Organ & Piano Co, Victorian girl waving to ship, 1898	5.00

SOAP AND CLEANERS

Dixon's Stove Polish, child	2.00
Enoch Morgan & Sons, Sapolio, boy wearing fancy clothes	3.00
Fairbank's White Star Soap, man riding bicycle	2.00
Pear's Soap, lovely lady	15.00
Pyle's Pearline, Pearline Soap Co, court jester	3.00
White Swan Soap	1.50

STOVES AND RANGES

Gold Coin and Gold Medal Stoves & Ranges	2.00
Peninsular Stoves, diecut, stand–up	6.00

Thread, Kerr & Co., NY, 3¼ x 4¾", $5.00.

THREAD AND SEWING

Clark's Thread, Queen Margaret	**15.00**
Domestic Sewing Machine, farm scene	**6.00**
Golden Eagle Knitting Wools, Willey & Pearson, Ltd, woman wearing green dress	**3.00**
J & P Coats Thread, four kittens sewing	**15.00**
New Home Sewing Machine Co, diecut, multicolored, 7 x 9", c1890	**20.00**
Willimantic Thread, children riding horse	**20.00**

TOBACCO

Mail Pouch Tobacco, boy wearing diaper	**20.00**
Neudecker's Tobacco, roses in high heel shoe, late 1800s	**15.00**
Player's Cigarettes, set of 50, poultry series, 1930s	**1.25**
Sweet Caporal Cigarettes, actress, 1890s	**2.50**

AGATA GLASS

History: Agata glass was invented in 1887 by Joseph Locke of the New England Glass Company, Cambridge, Massachusetts.

Agata glass was produced by using a piece of peachblow glass, coating it with metallic stain, spattering the surface with alcohol, and firing. The result was a high gloss, mottled appearance of oil droplets floating on a watery surface. Shading usually ranged from opaque pink to dark rose. Pieces are known in a pastel opaque green. A few pieces have been found in a satin finish.

Bowl	
5" d, tricornered	**1,400.00**
5⅜" d, crimped rim	**600.00**
6½" d, ruffled top	**1,800.00**
Celery, 7" h, sq, fluted top	**580.00**
Creamer	**1,200.00**
Finger Bowl, 5¼" d, 2⅝" h, crushed raspberry shading to creamy pink, all	

over gold mottling with bits of blue mottling	**975.00**
Juice Glass, 3¾" h	**825.00**
Pitcher, 6⅜" h, crimped rim	**1,650.00**
Spooner, 4½" h, green opaque, gold band and mottling	**650.00**
Toothpick, 2¾" h, cylindrical	**550.00**
Tumbler, 3¾" h, wild rose color fading to cream at base, profuse mottling .	**545.00**

Bowl, tricorn, 5" d, $1,400.00.

Vase	
4½" h, sq, pinched sides, ruffled 4 scalloped rim	**550.00**
9" h, lily shape	**1,200.00**

AMBERINA GLASS

History: Joseph Locke developed Amberina glass in 1883 for the New England Glass Works. "Amberina," a trade name, describes a transparent glass which shades from deep ruby to amber color. It was made by adding powdered gold to the ingredients for an amber glass batch. A portion of the glass was reheated later to produce the shading effect. Usually it was the bottom which was reheated to form the deep red; however, reverse examples have been found.

Most early Amberina is of flint quality glass, blown or pattern molded. Patterns include Diamond Quilted, Daisy and Button, Venetian Diamond, Diamond and Star, and Thumbprint.

In addition to the New England Glass Works, the Mt. Washington Glass Company of New Bedford, Massachusetts, copied the glass in the 1880s and sold it at first under the Amberina trade name and later as "Rose Amber." It is difficult to distinguish pieces from these two New England factories. Boston and Sandwich Glass Works never produced the glass.

Amberina glass also was made in the 1890s by several Midwest factories, among which was Hobbs, Brockunier & Co. Trade names included "Ruby Amber Ware" and "Watermelon." The Midwest glass shaded from cranberry to amber and resulted from a thin flashing of cranberry applied to the reheated portion. This created a sharp demarkation between the two colors. This less expensive version caused the death knell for the New England variety.

In 1884 Edward D. Libbey was assigned the trade name "Amberina" by the New England Glass Works. Production occurred in 1900, but ceased shortly thereafter. In the 1920s Edward Libbey renewed production at his Toledo, Ohio, plant for a short period. The glass was of high quality. Amberina from this era is marked "Libbey" in script on the pontil.

Reproduction Alert: Reproductions abound.

Bowl, coin spot variant pattern, flared hexagonal ruffled rim, 9″ d, 4½″ h, $600.00.

Berry Bowl, 5″ sq, Daisy & Button, set
of four 330.00
Bowl
  5″ d, fuchsia
    Rect rim 250.00
    Tricorn 250.00
  7½″ d, DQ, roll over scalloped edge 180.00
Butter Pat, 2¾″ d, sq, notched corners,
  Daisy & Button, pr 190.00
Butter Tub, cov, 5″ d, Daisy & Button,
  amber faceted cut knob, minor roughness 550.00
Canoe, 4½″ l, Daisy & Button 330.00
Carafe, 7⅛″ h, IVT, reversed color,
  swirled neck 150.00
Celery
  5¾″ h, scalloped sq top, pinched
    paneled sides 120.00
  7″ h, scalloped top, DQ 375.00
Center Bowl, 12″ l, 7″ h, oval, crimped
  top, enameled bird on flowering berry
  branch, Moser 2,310.00
Compote, 6½″ d, 4″ h, slightly scalloped
  rim, fuchsia ribbed bowl, baluster
  stem, marked "Libbey Amberina" . . 715.00
Cordial, 4½″ h, trumpet shape 225.00
Creamer and Sugar, 4½″ h, DQ, crimp
  top, amber reeded handles, pr 610.00
Cruet, 6¾″ h, 3″ d, amber cut faceted
  orig stopper, amber applied handle . 225.00
Curtain Tiebacks, pr, orig shanks 150.00
Finger Bowl
  4½″ d, DQ, fuchsia 250.00

4¾″ d, Coin Spot and DQ, etched
  "World's Fair, 1893," scalloped rim 385.00
  5½″ d, scalloped rim 140.00
Hair Receiver, 4″ d, 2″ h, ribbed, fuchsia,
  marked "Libbey" 660.00
Ice Cream Dish, 5¾″ d, sq, Daisy &
  Button, scalloped corners 100.00
Lamp, hand, 10¾″ h overall, 5″ base,
  Baby Hobnail, 6 applied shell feet, 5
  amber leaf–like extensions rising to
  middle of lamp, applied amber branch
  handle 475.00
Mint Bowl, 5″ d, 1¾″ h, fuchsia, honey-
  comb, ftd 935.00
Pickle Castor, 6¾″ h, pewter cov, IVT,
  enameled floral dec, Mt Washington 225.00
Pitcher
  5″ h, tankard, Daisy & Button 330.00
  6½″ h, Coin Spot Opalescent 220.00
  6¾″ h, Hobnail, Hobbs, Brockunier &
    Co 165.00
  7¼″ h, Optic, bulbous, reeded applied
    handle 265.00
  8½″ h, triangular top, IVT, amber
    reeded applied handle, Mt Wash-
    ington 225.00
Plate, 7″ d, Daisy & Button 315.00
Punch Cup, 4″ h, ribbed, amber reeded
  handle 250.00
Ramekin, underplate, 2¼″ h, 4¼″ d,
  slightly ribbed, New England Glass
  Works 200.00
Rose Bowl
  4″ h, Inverted Coin Spot, rigaree col-
    lar 420.00
  6″ h, tricorn rim, int. and ext. DQ,
    three applied amber reeded feet . 550.00
Spooner, 4½″ h, Inverted Coin Spot,
  fold–in crimped rim 330.00
Syrup, 5½″ h, bulbous, Inverted Coin
  Spot, silver collared spout, handle,
  and hinged lid 1,375.00
Tea Cup and Saucer, 2½″ h, 4½″ d sau-
  cer, etched "World's Fair, 1893" . . . 420.00
Toothpick
  2¼″ h
    DQ, fuchsia, crimp rim 360.00
    Venetian DQ, tricorn 305.00
  3″ h, Daisy & Button, trifoot 235.00
Tumbler
  DQ 100.00
  Inverted DQ, fuchsia 137.50
Tumble–Up, IVT, water carafe and
  matching tumbler 325.00
Vase
  3″ h, 5″ d, squatty, ribbed, flared scal-
    loped rim 200.00
  6″ h, lily, deep amber base 250.00
  8″ h, oviform, waisted neck, ribbed,
    wafer and ball stem, marked "Lib-
    bey" 715.00

9" h, bud, elongated, ribbed, marked
"Libbey" 625.00
12" h, lily, ribbed 325.00
Whiskey Glass, 2½" h, DQ 120.00
Wine, 4½" h, optic ribbed 200.00

AMBERINA GLASS—PLATED

History: The New England Glass Company,
Cambridge, Massachusetts, first made Plated Amberina in 1886; Edward Libbey patented the process for the company in 1889.

Plated Amberina was made by taking a gather
of chartreuse or cream opalescent glass, dipping
it in Amberina and working the two, often utilizing
a mold. The finished product had a deep amber to
deep ruby red shading, a fiery opalescent lining,
and often vertical ribbing for enhancement. Designs ranged from simple forms to complex pieces
with collars, feet, gilding, and etching.

A cased Wheeling glass of similar appearance
had an opaque white lining, but is not opalescent
and the body is not ribbed.

Vase, bulbous base, ribbed, $2,500.00.

Bowl, 8" d, 3¼" h, ruffled 1,600.00
Celery Vase 2,600.00
Cruet, 6¾" h, faceted amber stopper . 3,200.00
Lamp Shade, 14" d, hanging, swirled,
ribbed 4,750.00
Parfait, applied amber handle, c1886 . 1,250.00
Pitcher, milk, applied amber handle, orig
"Aurora" label 7,000.00
Punch Cup, vertical ribs, applied handle 1,500.00
Salt Shaker, orig top 1,000.00
Spooner, 4" h, paneled, ground pontil . 2,000.00
Syrup Pitcher, orig top, applied handle 5,500.00
Tumbler, 3¾" h, vertical ribs 2,250.00
Vase, lily shape
7¼" h 2,500.00
9¾" h 5,500.00

AMPHORA

History: The Amphora Porcelain Works was
one of several pottery companies located in the
Teplitz-Turn region of Bohemia in the late 19th
and early 20th centuries. It is best known for art
pottery, especially Art Nouveau and Art Deco
pieces.

Several markings were used, including the
name and location of the pottery and the Imperial
mark which included a crown. Prior to WWI, Bohemia was part of the Austro-Hungarian Empire, so
the word "Austria" may appear as part of the mark.
After WWI the word "Czechoslovakia" may be part
of the mark.

Reference: Susan and Al Bagdade, *Warman's
English & Continental Pottery & Porcelain,* 2nd
Edition, Wallace–Homestead, 1991.

Additional Listings: Teplitz.

Bowl, 12 x 15", reticulated, applied
leaves and chestnuts, two double
twisted gold handles, ftd, sgd 625.00
Center Bowl, 17" d, oval, undulating rim,
applied scrolled handles, green
glaze, grapevines and bunches dec,
four scrolled feet, imp "Amphora
8192/56," c1900 . . . . 325.00
Centerpiece, 18½ x 18½", matte
glazed, figure, baby Dionysius wearing wreath of grapes on head, holding
two thyrsos, sitting on ram with two
empty basket molded containers, rect
base, painted amber and green, gilt
highlights, cream ground, imp "Amphora" and crown mark 420.00

**Vase, pink roses, green shaded
ground, imp crown and Amphora
marks, minor chips on roses, 11" h,
$300.00.**

Ewer
  9½″ h, handles, spout, oval reserve
    of gladiator **125.00**
  13″ h, children in forest dec **100.00**
Figure
  8″ h, girl, selling roses, marked "Am-
    phora–Teplitz" **150.00**
  10″ h, lion stalking over rocky cliff for-
    mation **275.00**
Vase
  7″ h, beige, purple and red gooseber-
    ries, sgd **150.00**
  9″ h, bottle form, gilt rim and high-
    lights, green thistles, royal blue
    ground, base imp "Amphora/Aus-
    tria/Turn/Pans 1900 RSTK," pr ... **425.00**

ANIMAL COLLECTIBLES

History: The representation of animals as a theme in fine arts, decorative arts, and utilitarian products dates back to antiquity. Some religions endowed certain animals with mystical properties. Authors throughout written history embodied them with human characteristics.

Collecting by animal theme has been practiced for centuries. Until the early 1970s most collectors were of the closet variety. However, the formation of collector's clubs and marketing crazes, e.g., flamingo, pig, and penguin, brought most collectors out into the open.

The animal collector differs from other collectors in that they care little about the date when an object was made or even its aesthetic quality. The key is that the object is in the image of their favorite animal.

References: Peter Johnson, *Cats & Dogs: Phillips Collectors Guides*, Dunestyle Publishing Ltd., 1988; Alice Muncaster and Ellen Yanow, *The Cat Made Me Buy It*, Crown, 1984; Alice Muncaster and Ellen Yanow Sawyer, *The Cat Sold It!*, Crown, 1986; Herbert N. Schiffer, *Collectible Rabbits*, Schiffer Publishing, Ltd., 1990; Mike Schneider, *Animal Figures*, Schiffer Publishing, Ltd., 1990.

Periodicals: *The Canine Collector's Companion*, P.O. Box 2948, Portland, OR 97208; *The Owl's Nest*, Howards Alphanumeric, P.O. Box 5491, Fresno, CA 93755.

Collector's Clubs: Cat Collectors, 31311 Blair Drive, Warren, MI 48092; Equine Collectors Club, Box 4764 New River Stage II, Phoenix, AZ 85027; The Frog Pond, P.O. Box 193, Beech Grove, IN 46107; The National Elephant Collector's Society, 89 Massachusetts Avenue, Box 7, Boston, MA 02115; Russell's Owl Collector Club, P.O. Box 1292, Bandon, OR 97411.

Additional Listings: See specific animal collectible categories in *Warman's Americana & Collectibles*.

BIRDS

Bonbon Dish, 4″ h, 9″ l, peacocks, sterling silver, stamped, chased, dish formed by spreading tail feathers, Durgin for Gorham, Concord, NY, pr **1,320.00**
Bottle Opener, figural, cast iron
  3¼″ h, cockatoo, orange, and yellow chest, red and orange comb, green base, black ground, John Wright Co **100.00**
  3⅜″ h, pelican, red and black, yellow beak, orange feet, green base, Wilton Products **50.00**
Carving, 8¼″ h, 11¼″ l, bluejay, wood, relief carved, orig yellow and alligatored paint, burl base, early to mid 20th C **450.00**
Dish, 6″ h, 8½″ l, swan, sterling silver, glass molded body, silver chased wings, neck, and head, pr **2,475.00**
Figure, 6″ h, chalk, old worn polychrome paint, old chips, minor head damage **205.00**
Iron, 2¾″ l, swan, miniature, cast iron, orig trivet, worn red paint **65.00**
Limited Edition Collector Plate, 10½″ d, Lenox, Edward Marshall Boehm artist, cardinal, 1976 .... **60.00**
Paperweight, 3″ h, swan, cast lead, pr **70.00**
Poster, 63 x 47″, peacock, Cognac Jacquet, Bouchet, Vercasson, Paris, multicolored peacock, green and yellow ground, red letters **550.00**
Shaker, 5½″ h, 11″ l, pheasants, sterling silver, chased, male and female, long folded pointed tails, removable necks, perforated breasts, monogram on male, retailed by Marshall Field & Co, Chicago, set of four **3,020.00**

BOVINE

Carousel Animal, 19″ h, 39″ l, bull, carved and painted wood, full body, horns, sweeping tail, running position, black and white, minor repairs **1,760.00**
Folk Art, 21″ h, 15″ w, carved wood, stylized head of steer, brown paint, light brown stripe, white markings, leather ears, real steer horns, 19th C **880.00**
Painting, 26 x 37″, G Brasseur, Pasture with Cows, oil on canvas, modern frame **850.00**
Weathervane, 29″ l, cow, molded copper, cast tail and horns, applied ears, verdigris surface **3,000.00**

CATS

Bank, 9½″ h, chalk, full body, seated, worn polychrome paint **200.00**
Children's Book, *Kittens and Cats,* Eu-

lalie Osgood Grover, Houghton Mifflin
   CO, 1911 .... **25.00**
Doorstop, 9½" h, cast iron, flat silhouette, painted black **235.00**
Figure
   4" h, pottery, Whieldon type, brown
     tortoise shell glaze, old repair, small
     chips **650.00**
   9½" h, chalk, seated, worn orig poly-
     chrome paint, chipped nose **1,250.00**
   15¾" h, ceramic, marked "Royal
     Dux" **125.00**
Folk Art, 4½" h, 5" l, carved wood, cross
   hatched coat, orig white, black, and
   brown paint, red trim, Schimmel type **350.00**
Painting, 15 x 22", Daniel Merlin, The
   Captivating Toy, sgd, four kittens and
   ball of yarn, c1900 .... **10,500.00**
Pip–Squeak
   4⅜" h, papier mache, orig black paint,
     polychrome trim, wear, damage to
     ears, replaced leather **45.00**
   7¾" h, composition, seated cat, white,
     orange and black markings, bel-
     lows base **1,200.00**
Toy, 5" l, pull, wood, orig polychrome
   paint, platform with wheels **75.00**

**Dog, pitcher, copper luster, multico-
lored enameled greyhound and bull,
c1820–30, 7½" h, $450.00.**

DOGS

Boot Scraper, 9¼" h, cast steel, Scottie,
   low relief, edge tooling, old black
   paint **95.00**
Figure
   7¼" h, china, Whippets holding rab-
     bits, standing, Staffordshire, 19th
     C, pr **625.00**
   8¾" h, china, seated, green and
     white, polychrome enamel and lus-
     ter, Staffordshire, pr **400.00**

9" h, Galena pottery, freestanding
   front legs, red clay, rich brown mottled glaze, minor edge chips, large
   chip on tail **650.00**
10" h, 8¾" l, chalk, pug, full body,
   worn red and black paint **300.00**
12¾" h, china, seated, white, polychrome enamel, worn gilt, Staffordshire, pr **250.00**
Folk Art, 3⅞" h, primitive carved wood,
   good patina, late **105.00**
Inkwell, 10" l, bronze, hound lapping at
   dish, French, 19th C **1,670.00**
Painting
   10¾ x 8½", John Singer Sargent,
     Pointy, oil on panel, artist initials
     lower right, titled upper left, full sig-
     nature and inscription on reverse,
     c1881 .... **34,100.00**
   16 x 20", Arthur Wardle, Rabbiting,
     three terriers hunting rabbits **24,000.00**
   17 x 21", George Horlor, What Will He
     Do With It, dated 1882 .... **34,000.00**
Sculpture
   12" h, white marble, King Charles
     spaniel, sgd "Rebaldi," Italian, 19th
     C **6,735.00**
   16" h, bronze, retriever with pheasant
     in mouth, Jules Moigniez, c1870 . **5,280.00**
Textile, 19¾ x 18¾", needlepoint panel,
   dog on cushion, shaded brown, blue,
   white, and olive, sgd and dated "H
   1885," old worn gilt frame **475.00**
Weathervane, 16" h, 31" l, molded copper, setter, good verdigris surface,
   bullet hole, EG Washburne & Co,
   Danvers, MA, late 19th or early 20th
   C **5,250.00**

EAGLES

Figure
   15" h, bisque, soft coloring, marked
     "Bald Eagle by Andrea, Japan" .. **85.00**
   17½" h, 23½" wing span, cast iron,
     good details, old gold paint, mod-
     ern wood base **135.00**
Folk Art
   13½" h, carved pine, old natural fin-
     ish, traces of gilt, minor damage to
     spread wings **275.00**
   13¾" h, carved and painted pine,
     glass eyes, naturalistic colors,
     green painted base **1,300.00**

ELEPHANTS

Bottle Opener, 3¹⁄₁₆" h, figural, sitting,
   trunk in circle, gray, pink, nostrils,
   white details **35.00**
Figure
   2⅝" l, pink quartz, wood base **45.00**

20" l, bronze, walking, Oriental, wood
base, one ivory tusk glued **375.00**
Screen, 96" w, 84" h, three panel, elephant family moving through jungle,
brightly colored parrot in tree, sgd
"Ernest Brierly" **2,750.00**

FOWL

Bottle Opener, 3⅞" h, figural, metal,
black body, red comb, orange–yellow
beak and feet, green base, John
Wright Co **50.00**
Box, cov, 10½" l, porcelain, two ducks,
bright enamels, Oriental **550.00**
Carousel Animal, 32" h, 35" l, rooster,
laminated wood, relief carving, layers
of old worn polychrome paint, glass
eyes, age cracks, old repairs, re-
placed base **1,500.00**
Folk Art
5⅞" h, rooster, carved pine, old patina, red comb, Mountz type, dam-
aged comb **65.00**
6⅛" h, chicken, pine, old patina, glass
eyes, Mountz type, damaged beak **25.00**
6¼" h, chicken, wood and papier
mache, orig polychrome paint, minor edge flaking, damage to beak
and legs **145.00**
12¼" h, rooster, carved wood, an-
tiqued polychrome paint, minor
wear **275.00**
15" h, rooster, sheet metal, ham-
mered three dimensional body,
edge tooling, wrought iron legs . . **2,300.00**
Game Plates, turkey, 21" l platter, eight
10" d plates, brown transfer, polychrome, marked "Ralph Wood, Bur-
slem, England" **150.00**
Painting, 5 x 6¾", Adrien Joseph Ver-
hoeven–Ball, Farmyard Fowl and
Roosters, Chickens and a Peacock in
a Landscape, oil on panel, sgd and
dated 1870, pr **2,000.00**
Weathervane, rooster
20½" h, 21¾" l, copper and cast zinc,
strutting, perched on arrow, gilt loss **1,300.00**
25" h, cast iron and tin, hollow zinc
body, traces of old paint, name
"James" as balance **350.00**
33" h, 32" w, molded copper, swell
body, cut copper comb, crop, and
tail, painted green, yellow, brown,
and white, repairs **5,225.00**

FOXES

Painting, 40¼ x 32½", Carl Fredrik
Kioeboe, The Escape/Winter Scene
with Fox and Rabbit, oil on canvas,
sgd lower right, framed **2,500.00**

**Fox, stirrup cup, orange–brown, black
muzzle, eyes, and rim, cracked, 5" l,
$250.00.**

Poster, 40½ x 30", La Fleche, Backer,
Dresden, brown fox, green and brown
ground **330.00**
Weathervane, 13¾" h, 31" l, copper,
verdigris surface, traces of bolle, 19th
C **1,700.00**

**Horse, figure, Scottish Highland, tan,
brown mane and tail, marked "Highland, Beswick, England," 7" h, $48.00.**

HORSES

Carousel Animal, 28½" h, 38" l, laminated wood, good relief carving, old
worn polychrome repaint, glass eyes,
worn velvet seat, old repairs, modern
stand **1,800.00**
Diorama
9" h, 60" l, Amish farm scene, full
bodied carved wood animals and
figures, five horse–drawn wagons,
painted background, early 20th C **700.00**
14¾" h, 60" l, livery stall, nine full bodied cast iron horses, individual illuminated stalls, painted details,
early 20th C **1,500.00**

Figure, 9¾" h, 12" l, bronze, rearing, raised forelegs, pricked ears, flared nostrils, long curly mane falling over right side of neck, partly bound tail flying, rear legs resting on later brass plaque, attributed to workshop of Francesco Fanelli, mid 17th C **19,800.00**

Painting
10 x 12½", watercolor, primitive brown and black horse, pink cloth belt, blue grass, sgd on back "Henry Lapp 1873," rosewood veneer frame **1,150.00**
16 x 19", Suzanne Wamsley, Paris Prince, pastel on paper, sgd and dated lower right, 1983 .... **1,045.00**
23 x 28", Catherine Bloomfield, Premier Ministre, gouache on paper, sgd and dated lower left, 1982 ... **1,210.00**

Poster
33 x 23", James Montgomery Flagg, "Help Him To Help U.S.!," The American Red Star Animal Relief, National Headquarters, Albany, NY, Uncle Sam with horse **440.00**
49½ x 35", Horse Super Cigarettes, red horse, deep blue ground **250.00**

Weathervane
18" h, painted, J Howard & Co, Bridgewater, MA, third quarter 19th C **4,000.00**
19" h, 43½" l, molded copper, full body, Dexter, fine verdigris surface, Cushing and White, Waltham, MA, second half 19th C, hole at underside **4,250.00**
19½" h, 35½" l, molded zinc, full body, flowing mane and tail, painted black, repairs to tail **1,210.00**
22" w, copper, Stallion, sgd "Westervelt" on bar, AB and WT Westervelt, Church, NY, 1883 ... **5,500.00**
28" l, copper, running, Black Hawk, hollow body, molded detail, green patina, soldered repairs, modern wood base **1,750.00**

OWLS

Andirons, 14" h, cast iron, copper wash, perched on branch, yellow glass eyes, c1920, pr **150.00**
Barometer, 11" h, carved walnut, English **65.00**
Calendar, 8½" w, 18¾" h, twelve color lithographs, different bird on each month, muted tones surround, Theo van Hoytema, Holland, 1908 ...... **1,100.00**
Calendar Plate, owl on open book, 1912, Berlin, NE **30.00**
Candy Container, 4⅜" h, stylized feathers, gold tin screw cap **85.00**
Fairy Lamp, 4" h, bisque, glass eyes . **250.00**

Folk Art
3¾" h, primitive carving, hardwood, old brown finish, round base **45.00**
12½" h, carved wood, relief carving, orig paint, glass eyes **125.00**
Inkwell, 8 x 4", brass, glass inset, hinged lid, pen tray, 2" owl figure **85.00**
Mask, papier mache, c1915 .... **90.00**
Stein, half liter, Bibite on shield held between claws, Mettlach #2036 ..... **950.00**
Vase, 12½" h, ruffled rim, two handles, marked "Royal Nishiki Nippon Hand Painted" **365.00**

PARROTS

Figure
13" h, porcelain, bright polychrome, marked "Germany," minor edge damage, painted repair **125.00**
24" h, porcelain, pink, blue, green, yellow, and rust, trunk form base, applied and molded trailing fruiting vines, scattered flowers, dome scrolled base, underglaze blue crossed arrows mark, French, early 20th C, pr **3,575.00**
Folk Art, 17¼" h, carved wood, orig polychrome paint, glass eyes, seated on perch, 20th C **350.00**
Urn, cov, 17¾" h, baluster, domed cov, waisted circular stepped base, applied overall flowering vines and scattered insects, three perched parrots, lid with parrot finial, Potschappel, overglaze blue factory mark, minor repairs, pr **2,100.00**

SHEEP

Magazine Cover, orig art, Harper's, May, 1895, Edward Penfield illus, woman with ship, green, red, and blue **250.00**
Painting
22 x 28", British School, Sheep and Poultry in a Landscape, oil on cradled panel, 19th C **2,100.00**
22¼ x 31", AF Tait, Sheep in a Pasture, oil on canvas, sgd "AF Tait, NA NY '95," modern gilt frame ... **4,750.00**
Stamp, 4¼" h, carved stone ram, dark patina, Oriental characters **145.00**

WILD ANIMALS

Architectural Element, 29½" h, 38" w, lions, cast stone, painted white, curly manes, open jaws, one forepaw resting on sphere, molded rect base, pr **990.00**
Carving, 6½" l, leopard, wood, painted spots, one tooth chipped **45.00**

Doorstop, 13" h, lion, cast brass, rampant lion, dark patina, wood base . . **85.00**
Figure, 8½" h, 29½" l, panther, bronze, left forepaw outstretched, curling tail resting on ground, laidback ears, snarling jaws, base inscribed "Andre Basseire, Cire Perdu Leblanc Barbedienna A Paris 18/25," later granite oblong base, French **1,650.00**

ARCHITECTURAL ELEMENTS

History: Architectural elements are those items which have been removed or salvaged from buildings, ships, or gardens. Many are hand crafted. Frequently they are carved in stone or exotic woods. Part of their desirability is due to the fact that it would be extremely costly to duplicate the items today.

The current trend of preservation and recycling architectural elements has led to the establishment and growth of organized salvage operations that specialize in removal and resale of elements. Special auctions are now held to sell architectural elements from churches, mansions, office buildings, etc. Today's decorators often design an entire room around one architectural element, such as a Victorian marble bar or mural, or use several as key accent pieces.

References: Ronald S. Barlow (Comp.), *Victorian Houseware: Hardware and Kitchenware*, Windmill Publishing Co., 1991; J. L. Mott Iron Works, *Mott's Illustrated Catalog of Victorian Plumbing Fixtures for Bathrooms and Kitchens*, Dover Publications, 1987; Alan Robertson, *Architectural Antiques*, Chronicle Books, 1987; J. P. White's Pyghtle Works, Bedford, England, *Garden Furniture and Ornament*, Apollo Books, 1987.

Additional Listings: Stained Glass.

Aquarium, 42" h, 40" l, 17½" d, cast iron, pierced scroll base, circular waffle–iron pattern removable plant stands, Victorian, sgd "Fullis Bros, St. Louis" **715.00**
Aviary, 60 x 144", iron and wirework, faceted onion dome top, rect vertical cage, arched sides, radiating spandrels, painted white, French **4,500.00**
Baluster, 18½" h, walnut and inlaid ivory, late Georgian, early 19th C **120.00**
Bench Ends, pr
27½" h, cast stone, modeled as winged crouching sphinxes, reverse and stiles molded with ribbon tied pendant fruiting vines **770.00**
36" h, pottery, modeled as crouching sphinxes, mottled cream colored glaze, stamped "Doulton Lambeth, London," c1890 . . . . **1,980.00**
Bird Bath
32" h, 24" d, carved stone, circular,

Garden Furniture, cast iron, A. Bach, Philadelphia, c1860, 3 pc set, $500.00.

steeply tapering sides, separate sq section pyramidal stand, 19th C . . **360.00**
33½" h, carved marble, Nanna Matthews Bryant, c1920 . . . . **4,400.00**
Ceiling, pressed copper, 31 x 5', elaborate floral dec **1,200.00**
Cistern
12½" h, 31½" l, granite, sq **275.00**
15½" h, 34½" l, red sandstone, rect **715.00**
Doorway, 126" h, ext., pine, pitched projected cornice, fan light with incised dec, reeded pilasters, painted, Federal, Trenton, NJ, c1800, 1928 measured drawing **6,500.00**
Entry Figures, pr, bronze
47" h, lion, seated on haunches, dark green mottled patina **6,050.00**
48" l, reclining dogs, stippled integral rect base, variegated golden–brown patina **3,575.00**
Figure
15½" h, Abyssinian Cat, seated, bronze, green patina **250.00**
26" h, dwarf, cast stone, bearded, potbelly, clutching moneyback, weathered patina **300.00**
31½" h, little girl and rabbit, short dress, clutching pet against hip, standing on rockwork base, cast lead, painted gray, c1930 . . . . . . **825.00**
34½" h, 27" l, deer, bronze, standing, head raised, weathered patina . . . **1,760.00**
33" l, recumbent doe and fawn, bronze, patina **412.00**
67" h, gray painted lead putto, seated on draped plinth, gazing at dove, cylindrical sandstone pedestal . . . **2,475.00**
86" h and 71" h, standing cranes, bronze, one with craned neck, other with neck bent backwards gazing, mottled brown patina, pr . **3,300.00**
Fountain, 54" h, terra cotta, shallow cir-

cular basin, deeply everted lip, molded relief laurel and flowers, putto on one side, naked winged mermaid with crossed arms as baluster, coved circular base, acanthus cast scrolled feet, weathered patina, minor losses, repaired basin **4,125.00**

Fountain Head, 33″ h, lead, figural, standing naked infant strangling a cockerel, integral circular base, weathered patina **1,870.00**

Furniture
Cast Stone, table, hexagonal top, molded leaf and bead border, triform festooned standard, conforming base, mossy weathered patina, Baroque style **1,210.00**

Wirework, Victorian style, pr 40″ l settees, circular plant stand, armchair, painted white **1,540.00**

Gate Pediment, 32″ h, 89″ l, arched form, scrolls and foliate dec, two dragon heads, wrought iron, painted black, parcel gilt, Continental **715.00**

Jardiniere
8½″ h, 13″ d, Neoclassical, lead, beaded upper and lower border, relief cast sides, foliate arabesques and cartouches, English, late 19th C **550.00**

29½″ h, Victorian, rustic, terra cotta, pierced tree trunk form base, mid 19th C **825.00**

Mailbox, 44″ h, painted metal, pagoda form, front and sides molded in relief of equestrian postmen, foliage cast baluster pedestal, rect base, painted dark green, Victorian **675.00**

Mortar, 12¼″ d, marble, 19th C **200.00**

Pedestal
44″ h, circular top, ring turned cylindrical pedestal, Greek key carved median band, lobed melon base, octagonal foot, Sienna marble, late 19th C **550.00**

52″ h, 12″ d, columnar, circular top, fluted shaft, molded plinth base, painted white, pr **525.00**

Pediment Ornament, 38″ w, eagle, carved wood, full feathers, gold paint, 19th C **500.00**

Planter, 35½″ h, 35½″ d, circular basket, rusticated sq pedestal base, cast stone, 19th C **1,980.00**

Radiator Grill, 45½″ h, 39″ w, Art Deco, French, c1930, later oak top with canted corners, molded edge, pierced wrought iron grill, rounded rect grate, center rect bosses **900.00**

Sundial, 41″ h, carrara marble, acanthus carved baluster, fluted and volute carved capital, chamfered gray mar-

ble sq top, cast bronze dial, Greek Key border, quadruple paw footed base, concave sided plinth, Neoclassical, Continental, 19th C **2,200.00**

Transom Window, 9 x 30¾″, leaded glass, finely plated, dusty pink and deep purple wisteria blossoms, green leaves, mottled lavender branches, twilight ground, marked "Tiffany Studios," oak frame **2,500.00**

Urn
19½″ h, bronze, campagna, ovolo and beaded everted rim, flaring body, lobed lower section, applied fluted loop handles, grotesque mask terminals, coved circular socle, stepped sq foot, weathered green–brown patina, Neoclassical, early 19th C **1,650.00**

24″ h, cast iron, painted black, everted lobed rim, acanthus cast lower section, modeled satyr mask handles, coved socle, sq foot, Continental, late 19th C, pr **1,210.00**

24½″ h, cast iron, painted black, ribbon bound reeded lip, basketwork frieze, cast garland medallion with emperor, lion mask side handles with winged putto, coved circular socle, sq foot, Continental, late 19th C, pr **2,750.00**

34½″ h, cast iron, painted black, fluted flaring form, circular fluted socle, sq base, separate flared shallow plinth, pr **2,200.00**

45″ h, cast stone, bountiful filled fruit basket, molded C–scroll border, acanthus cast volute handles, lobed hemispherical stand, fluted spreading socle, sq foot, pr **5,225.00**

46″ h, 30″ w, lobed form, foliate swags, swan neck handles, plinth base, gray, neoclassical style, pr . **4,400.00**

Wall Bracket, carved alabaster, crouching heraldic lion, egg and dart carved serpentine fronted platform, holding vacant escutcheon between paw and knees, Continental, mid 19th C, pr . **1,540.00**

Wall Fountain, 67″ h, glazed terra cotta, swelling cartouche form, grotesque snarling mask emptying to shell shaped basin, flanked by C–scrolls, standing putto emptying to ewer, cracked cream glaze, pastel pale green and blue accents, Italian Rococo style **1,870.00**

ART DECO

History: The Art Deco period was named for an exhibition, "l'Exposition Internationale des Arts

Décorative et Industriels Modernes,'' held in Paris in 1927. It is a later period than Art Nouveau, but sometimes the two styles overlap since they were closely related in time.

Art Deco designs are angular with simple lines. This was the period of skyscrapers, movie idols, and the cubist works of Picasso and Legras. Art Deco motifs were used for every conceivable object being produced in the 1920s and 1930s (ceramics, furniture, glass, and metals) not only in Europe but in America as well.

References: Victor Arwas, *Glass: Art Nouveau To Art Deco*, Rizzoli, 1977; Lillian Baker, *Art Nouveau & Art Deco Jewelry: An Identification & Value Guide*, Collector Books, 1981; Bryan Catley, *Art Deco And Other Figures*, Antique Collectors' Club; Tony Fusco, *The Official Identification And Price Guide To Art Deco*, House of Collectibles, 1988; Mary Gaston, *Collector's Guide To Art Deco*, Collector Books, 1989; Robert Heide and John Gilman, *Popular Art Deco: Depression Era Style And Design*, Abbeville Press, 1991; Katherine Morrison McClinton, *Art Deco: A Guide For Collectors*, reprint, Clarkson N. Potter, 1986; Wolf Uecker, *Art Nouveau and Art Deco Lamps and Candlesticks*, Abbeville Press, 1986.

Collectors' Club: Art Deco Societies of America, 3447 Sheridan Avenue, Miami Beach, FL 33140.

Museums: Art Institute of Chicago, Chicago, IL; Corning Museum of Glass, Corning, NY; Jones Museum of Glass and Ceramics, Sebago, ME.

Additional Listings: Furniture and Jewelry. Also check glass, pottery, and metal categories.

Bookends, Spalter, bronze wash, celluloid faces, marble base, 5″ h, 5″ l base, pr, $325.00.

Ashtray
  4″ d, three rearing malachite green horses, heavy glass dish, Czechoslovakia **150.00**
  10″ h, figural nude holding tray overhead, copper colored metal, marked "Rembrandt" **185.00**
  32″ h, Jeeves, wooden, figural, butler **125.00**

Bookends, pr, figural
  Nudes, 5 x 7″, cast iron, full figure nude woman kneeling, leg extended forward, body arched back, bronze finish **70.00**
  Race Horse and Jockey, white metal, bronze finish **75.00**
Bottle, 10½″ h, figural, Napoleon, wearing gray uniform, black cocked hat stopper, marked "Robj Paris France" **335.00**
Bowl, rect, rust and pink, hp flowers, gold handle, marked "Royal Winton" **45.00**
Box, cov, 2¼″ l, sterling silver, rounded ends, linear blue and white enamel dec, monogram, cabochon saphires, vermeil wash int. **110.00**
Candelabra
  9¾″ h, sterling silver, three light, chamfered flaring central shafts, circular base, engraved cipher monogram, Elgin Silversmith Inc, c1945, pr **175.00**
  12½″ h, silverplated, five rose form candle sockets, nude girl on base **250.00**
Centerpiece, 24¼″ h, triangular wrought iron base, delicately fashioned blossoms and leaves, blue porcelain Sevres bowl, French, c1925 ...... **600.00**
Cigar Dispenser, iron, black and red, marked "Cigarola" **35.00**
Cigarette Box, cov, 8½ ″ l, 5¼″ d, 2¾″ h, burlwood, rect hinged lid, rounded ends, light and dark veneers, fitted int., c1920 .... **135.00**
Cigarette Case, 3 x 3½″, hinged rect case, silver, horizontal reeded bands with 14K red and green gold bands, medallion with engraved monogram, Elgin, c1915–30 .... **300.00**
Clock
  6½″ h, alarm, blue mirrored glass and chromed metal circular case, rect chromium base, designed by Gilbert Rohde for Herman Miller Clock Co, Zeeland, MI, c1932 .... **600.00**
  8″ h, lamp, two figural bronze washed white metal ladies hold 6″ d center clock, glass lamp shade **150.00**
  15¼″ h, mantel, arched marble case, black marble banding, gilt bronze floral dec, four circular gilt bronze feet, French, c1925 .... **800.00**
Cocktail Shaker, chrome, alternating hammered and smooth horizontal panels, dec black wood handle, marked "Farber Bros" **20.00**
Cologne Bottle, acid treated glass, enameled cobalt blue and yellow stylized flowers, large mushroom stopper **175.00**
Doorstop, 7 x 9″, bronze, woman standing, holding out skirt of clinging gown **165.00**
Dresser Set, Coquille d'Oeuf, sq tray,

brush, mirror, cov box, make up tray, black ground, eggshell linear dec, box sgd "Jean Dunand," 6 pcs **3,250.00**

Figure

8¼" h, male dancer, purple costume, female dancer in pale yellow and coral costume, sgd "C Werner, Hutschenreuther" **345.00**

14⅛" h, bronze, young woman, standing on toes, arms extending high at sides, enameled jewel band dec on forehead, brown enameled hair, gray and red marble plinth base, inscribed "Grundmann," Germany **575.00**

18⅛" h, man playing tennis, wood, chrome, and rubber, bald, wearing T shirt and baggy pants, flattened circular base, imp "SK" within a triangle, c1930 .... **1,100.00**

Fish Bowl, 4½ x 8¼ x 9", pale amber glass, molded figural chalkware base, orig label **65.00**

Furniture

Buffet, 66" l, burl walnut, American, c1925 .... **1,000.00**

Chest of Drawers, 44½ x 35", parchment covered, rect top, three tapering drawers, pyramidal mirrored stiles, bracket feet, back branded "Quigley," French, c1925 .... **2,750.00**

Game Table, 48" l, 30" h, oak, hinged leaf, felt lined inner compartment, American **600.00**

Magazine Stand, 15" h, bronze, two centaurs **225.00**

Vanity, 43 x 23¾", rect top, two drawers, cupboard doors flanking recessed door, mirrored glass panels **425.00**

Lamp, table

16½" h, conical frosted glass shade,

fluted chrome standard, circular blue mirrored base, c1920 ...... **330.00**

23" h, gilt metal hinged extension fixture, white silk shade, black onyx angular quatraform base **200.00**

23" h, 18" d shade, angular octagonal glass shade, monochromatic stylized foliage, spherical base, conforming quatraform platform **990.00**

Perfume Bottle, 3¼ x 6½", cased cranberry glass, deep cut opposing triangles, high matching stopper **125.00**

Powder Box, 5½" w, black glass base, silverplated cov, wolf hound finial .. **65.00**

Torcheres, mantel, 10½" h, orange glass cylinders, black hp silhouette scenes of dancing women and children, pr **385.00**

Vanity Set, lady's, traveling, 14 karat gold, engine turned striated design, center oval medallion on each pc engraved with cipher, 11¾" hand mirror, fitted blue leather carrying case, McChesney Co, Newark, NJ, retailed by Cartier, c1920–31, 18 pcs **6,500.00**

Vase, Boch Freres, blue, turquoise, and yellow bands, ivory crackle glaze, numbered, 8¼" h, $350.00.

Vase

6" h, lacquer, spherical, black ground, gold, gray, and red fanciful animals, lacquered "Jean Dunand" **2,400.00**

6¼" h, sterling silver, oval, flared sides, applied bands of parcel gilt scalloping, detachable silverplate liner, Jeans E Puiforcat, Paris, c1940 .... **7,100.00**

6½" h, lacquer, spherical, black, red, and silver, vertical stripes and lightning bolts, silver gilt highlights, lacquered "Jean Dunand" **5,000.00**

9¼" h, silver, tapering, squat stems pierced with scrolling blossoms and cast fruit, circular spreading feet, La Paglia for International, c1935, pr **1,200.00**

Purse, celluloid, plastic clasp, metal hinges, mfg by Llewellyn, Inc., trademark "Llewsid Jewel," 8¼" w, $55.00.

ART NOUVEAU

History: Art Nouveau is the French term for the "new art" which had its beginning in the early 1890s and continued for the next 40 years. The flowing and sensuous female forms used in this period were popular in Europe and America. Among the most recognized artists of this period were Gallé, Lalique, and Tiffany.

Art Nouveau can be identified by its flowing, sensuous lines, floral forms, insects, and the feminine form. These designs were incorporated on almost everything produced at that time, from art glass to furniture, silver, and personal objects.

References: Victor Arwas, *Glass: Art Nouveau To Art Deco*, Rizzoli, 1977; Lillian Baker, *Art Nouveau & Art Deco Jewelry: An Identification & Value Guide*, Collector Books, 1981; Giovanni Fanelli and Ezio Godoli, *Art Nouveau Postcards*, Rizzoli International Publication, Inc., 1987; Albert Christian Revi, *American Art Nouveau Glass*, reprint, Schiffer Publishing, 1981; Wolf Uecker, *Art Nouveau and Art Deco Lamps and Candlesticks*, Abbeville Press, 1986.

Additional Listings: Furniture and Jewelry. Also check glass, pottery, and metal categories.

Candy Dish, sterling silver, water lily motif, 7⅝ x 6⅝ x 1½", $250.00.

Basket, 9½" l, sterling silver, monogram, marked "Frank W Smith Silver Co Inc for Bailey, Banks, and Biddle Co" .. **350.00**
Billiards Table, 121 x 66 x 32", walnut, leather playing surface, six leather pockets with rosewood borders, six flared sq form legs, geometric patterns of ebony and MOP, Brunswick, c1916 .... **8,500.00**
Bust, porcelain, 28¼" h, Daphne, finely featured, garland in hair, self base, molded name **1,700.00**
Candelabra, 19" h, bronze, trumpet shape, floral candlecups, entwined stems, cut–out base, naturalistic designs, sgd "J Preston, Chicago" ... **2,750.00**

Calling Card Tray, 4½ x 7", pewter, relief molded woman with flowing hair ... **75.00**
Centerpiece, 20½" h, 22" w, resilvered metal standard of female, three ruffled overshot rubena bowls **1,500.00**
Clock, 7¼", gilt bronze, enameled dial, tapering tall case, trailing fruiting vines repousse, marked "Susse Freres, Paris," c1900 .... **575.00**
Creamer and Sugar, silverplated, marked "Meriden" **100.00**
Figure
  9½" h, nymph skipping rope, gilt bronze, rouge marble circular base, inscribed "A Marionnet," French, c1910 .... **385.00**
  14½" h, girl, gilt bronze, long skirt, low girdle and breastplates over mesh bodice, draped beaded necklace, ivory head, arms, and feet, coved circular gray–green and black marble base, incised "A Gori" **3,200.00**
Fireplace Tools, 40" h, poker, shovel, and broom on stand, silver alloy, looped handles terminating in wavy tendrils, marked "S Hart" **2,750.00**
Furniture
  Bed, 54" w, 57½" h, marquetry, inlaid floral designs, carved tendrils and brass overlay on headboard and footboard, stamped "BL 106 6B," French **1,430.00**
  Dining Suite, walnut, 96" h buffet, 55" h credenza, 28¾" h table, and four side chairs, walnut, buffet with arched crest over rounded rect beveled glass mirror, flanked by leaf and pod sprigs, two glazed cabinet doors, lower section with molded edges, two drawers with berried gilt bronze pulls, two cupboard doors with arched panels and central leaf carved supports, stiles continuing to form slightly splayed feet, 7 pcs, c1900 ...... **2,475.00**
  Fireplace Screen, 29" l, 42" h, Majorelle, carved walnut, shaped rect, arching open crest, central V form of intersecting wood bands of carved clematis vines, two orig ivory and white silk upholstered panels, molded downswept supports, c1900 .... **2,200.00**
  Parlor Suite, Majorelle style, escargot pattern, carved mahogany, 55" l settee, two armchairs, two side chairs, molded and dipped crestrails, carved and pierced stiles, rect upholstered seats, cabriole legs, 5 pcs **4,125.00**
  Stand, corner, 15" w, 15" d, 42" h, marquetry, floral and foliate inlay,

green marble top, brass hardware, French **2,200.00**
Table
Occasional, French
21" w, 24" h, oak and marquetry, Galle, two tiers, shaped rect top, conforming undertier, inlaid thistles, splayed fluted supports **1,200.00**
24¼" d, 22" h, walnut and marquetry, shaped circular top, reeded stepped edge enclosing scene of magpie perching among oak leaves and acorns, four waisted reeded clustered tapering supports **800.00**
Side, 22½" l, 27½" h, nest of four, rect top, marquetry, pierced organic trestle supports, shaped stretcher, marquetry includes landscape, seascape, three cats, and flowers **2,250.00**
Garniture, sterling silver, Iris pattern, Shreve & Co, San Francisco, c1909, 15½" cov vase, two flanking vases, inverted pyriform bodies, domed circular feet, applied chased bearded iris dec, bell mark, 3 pcs **2,475.00**
Hors D'oevres Tray, 10" l, figural, applied peacock in center, pearlized china, artist sgd, marked "ES Germany–Prov Saxe" **245.00**

Inkwell, cast metal, bronze, 4¾ x 9¾", $45.00.

Jardiniere, 12" d, bronze, circular, cast lily pads and buds, dark green patina, c1900 .... **550.00**
Lamp, table
25" h, 15½" d gold textured squatty dome shade, three repeat green, opalescent, and ruby floral glass inserts, graceful tri–prong arms and stem, inset amber jeweled moons and cut–out stars, three raised female masks, leaf pods, and lilies

on base, artist initials "BL," marked "Eichberg" **5,000.00**
29" h, patinated metal, figural, slender girl with butterfly wings, holding arching branch with applied enameled green leaves, two stems ending in leaf form light sockets, hanging frosted green grape cluster shades, green and brown patina, marble base, inscribed "J Causse," applied metal tag imp "Papillon/par J Causse (Statuaire)" **1,210.00**
Letter Opener, brass, dagger shape ... **15.00**
Magnifying Glass, 2⅛" d glass, 6¼" l, sterling silver hollow handle, scrolled leaves dec, marked "Blackinton, 1904" **110.00**
Match Holder, 5" h, painted bronze, figural, imp marks, Franz Bergman, c1910 .... **475.00**

Mug, majolica, yellow, brown, and green, German, 3¾" d base, 3¾" h, $95.00.

Pitcher, 14½" h, glass, silverplated mountings, cylindrical body, bulbous base, hinged lid, scrolled handle, green leaves, fuchsia blossoms, and band of iris, four scroll feet **330.00**
Postal Scale, 4¼" h, desk type, sterling silver, cased, monogram, marked "Shreve & Co," c1900 .... **250.00**
Shoe Horn, sterling handle **50.00**
Textile, throw pillow, 16½" sq, dark blue velour, grape appliques, scrolled plum stitched pattern, self welt, pr **250.00**
Tray, 16¼ x 26½", bowed rect, raised gallery, marquetry, inlaid scene of silhouetted castle, fruiting grapevine cascading in foreground, spread winged crane form handles, signed "Galle" in marquetry **500.00**
Vase
6" h, bronze, cast cherub faces in swirling sea, brown patina, gilded

faces, artist sgd "Jules Meliedon
1896, Louchet" **315.00**
9⅛" h, glass, gold luster, threaded,
applied dec, feather design, bogus
Tiffany signature **1,200.00**
14¼" h, pottery, cylindrical, flared bulbous base, low circular foot, relief
molded hollyhocks and leaves,
white matte glaze, translucent
green glazed int., inscribed monogram, marked "L. C. Tiffany Stu-
dios," c1900–28 . . . . **3,575.00**
Wall Shelf, 21" l, demilune, fruitwood,
pale gray glass overlaid in shades of
purple, meandering river and forest
scene, shaped demilune shelf and
bracket, signed "Jacques Gruber" in
cameo, c1900 . . . . **2,250.00**
Wine Glass, gold and copper floral dec,
cut swirl stems, gold leaves on base,
set of eight **700.00**

ART PEWTER

History: Pewter objects produced during the Art
Nouveau, Arts and Crafts, and Art Deco periods
are gaining in popularity. These mostly utilitarian
objects, e.g., tea sets, trays, and bowls, were elaborately decorated and produced in the Jugendstil
manner by German firms, such as Kayserzinn, and
Austrian companies, such as Orivit. In England,
Liberty and Company marketed Tudric Pewter,
which often had a hammered surface and was
embellished with enameling or semi-precious
stones. Most pieces of art pewter contain the maker's mark.

FIEN ZINN

Bowl, 9½", large open rim handles,
marked "S Rothhan, Fien Zinn" . . . **50.00**
Pitcher, 12", marked "Wien, Fien Zinn" **85.00**

JUGENDSTIL

Tray, 9" l, 8½" w, shaped triangular harp
form, relief dec, standing figure of
woman with one bare arm resting on
top of harp, diaphanous flowing gown
swirling at feet, two slender branches
form handles, leaves spreading
across dished surface, imp "B" and
"OX" **335.00**

KAYSERZINN

Candy Dish, leaf shape, marked #4065 **100.00**
Chamberstick, Art Nouveau floral dec . **75.00**
Vase, 7¾" h, wheat and butterflies dec,
marked #4310 . . . . **125.00**

**Kayserzinn, covered bowl, bulbous
sides, ftd, sunflowers motif, 7½" d,
numbered, $125.00.**

LIBERTY

Biscuit Box, 4¾" d, 4½" h, hammered
texture, raised geometric motifs, dark
patina, designed by Archibald Knox,
1904, marked "JB 2765" **425.00**

ORVIT

Pitcher, claret type, green glass insert,
Art Nouveau vines and floral dec . . **90.00**
Wine Cooler, 8 x 10½", floral dec **275.00**

TUDRIC

Centerpiece, 9¾" d, two handles, circular dish, raised base, sinuous blossoms and stems, inscribed, stamped
"Tudric," c1900 . . . . **500.00**
Clock, 5½" h, desk, rect, repoussé wind-
ing vines and berries dec, Arabic numerals enameled in red, green, and
blue, stamped "Tudric" **350.00**
Vase, 6" h, floriform, double tendril handles, small bulbous bowl, slender tapering stem, spreading circular foot,
imp "English Pewter/029/2," de-
signed for Liberty, c1903 . . . . **825.00**

URANIA

Candelabra, 13¼" h, flattened oval
pierced standard, low relief casting,
linear motifs, flanking branches at
right angles, conical cup, tapering cylindrical nozzle, imp "Urania/Hutton,
Sheffield/1376," pr **550.00**

ART POTTERY (GENERAL)

History: The period of art pottery reached its
zenith in the late 19th and early 20th century. Over
a hundred companies produced individually designed and often decorated wares which served a
utilitarian as well as an aesthetic purpose. Artists

moved about from company to company, some forming their own firms.

Quality of design, beauty in glazes, and condition are the keys in buying art pottery. This category covers companies not found elsewhere in the guide.

References: Paul Evans, *Art Pottery of the United States, Second Edition,* Feingold & Lewis Publishing Co., 1987; Lucile Henzke, *Art Pottery of America,* Schiffer Publishing, Ltd., 1982; Ralph and Terry Kovel, *The Kovels' Collector's Guide to American Art Pottery,* Crown Publishers, Inc., 1974.

Periodical: *Arts & Crafts Quarterly,* Station E, P.O. Box 3592, Trenton, NJ 08629.

Collectors' Club: American Art Pottery Association, 9825 Upton Circle, Bloomington, MN 55431.

Additional Listings: See Cambridge, Clewell, Clifton, Cowan, Dedham, Fulper, Grueby, Jugtown, Marblehead, Moorcroft, Newcomb, North Dakota School of Mines, Ohr, Owens, Paul Revere, Peters and Reed, Rookwood, Roseville, Van Briggle, Weller, and Zanesville.

Walrath, figure, nude, face supported by hands, mustard glaze over green base, imp "Walrath/1912," 14¾" l, $485.00.

Arequipa Pottery (1911–1918), Marin County, CA
Bowl
  1½ x 4¾", octagonal, gray matte, die mark **125.00**
  9 x 4¾", flower and leaf mold, black and white **150.00**
Vase
  7½" h, dark matte blue, 1912 . . . . **350.00**
  11½" h, 5½" d, reticulated, bunches of blue wisteria, rose high-glazes, mottled matte ochre ground, matte green leaves, dec by Frederick H Rhead **4,400.00**
Batchelder, Los Angeles, CA, center bowl, 18½" d, wide everted rim, int. glazed in pale green, purple ext., in-scribed "5 EA Batchelder/Kinneloa/Kiln" **625.00**
E Bennett Pottery Co (1845–1936), Baltimore, MD, vase, 8½ x 8", pillow, Arabian man on horseback, brown, green, and cream scene, green ground, base incised "Albion," "E Bennett Pottery Co, 1896," and "KB" **1,100.00**
California Faience (1916–1930), Berkley, CA
Bookends, pr, eagle, blue matte . . . **675.00**
Bowl, 10½", black matte, turquoise int., frog, pedestal base **150.00**
Box, 1½ x 4½ x 3½", raspberry tile top, cloisonne dec **100.00**
Potpourri Jar, 4½" h, Oriental shape, yellow matte, incised mark **225.00**
Vase
  6½", red glossy glaze, large styl-ized carved leaves **180.00**
  10", baluster, salmon ground, tan drip dec **200.00**
Kenton Hills (1939–1942), Erlanger, KY
Ashtray, 7 x 6½", stylized horse head shape, turquoise glossy glaze, marked **45.00**
Bowl, 3½", olive glossy glaze **100.00**
Vase, 7 x 6", brown irid glaze **120.00**
McLaughlin, M Louise (1876–1906), Cincinnati, OH, vase, 4½ x 4", bulbous, Impressionist style brown flowers and green leaves, marbled beige ground, sgd in script "L McL Cincinnati 1878" and "81" **800.00**
Merrimac Pottery, (1897–1908), Newburyport, MA, vase, 12" h, 9½" d, bulbous, smooth feathered matte blue-green glaze, imp mark, small glaze base chips **550.00**
Middle Lane Pottery (1894–1946), East Hampton and West Hampton, NY, vase
  4¾ x 4", bulbous, upright neck, irid orange and brown flame glaze, sgd in script "Brouwer," "M" with flame **1,000.00**
  6 x 5½", smooth, dark purple irid glaze, incised flame mark **1,100.00**
Mullany, American, 20th C, vase, 9" d, 6" h, wide flat rim, black glaze, bulbous red clay body, mat white glaze dec, sgd on base **110.00**
Natzler, American studio potter, 20th C, bowl
  2 x 3½", chartreuse high glaze, ink mark **385.00**
  4½ x 8", wide, flaring, fine metallic silvery–black porous flambe, black block mark, slight rim chip **945.00**
  4½ x 8¾", ovoid, smooth matte bright yellow glaze, ink mark **1,210.00**
Pewabic Pottery (1903–1961), Detroit, MI

Box, cov, 5" w, 3¾" d, 1¾" h, rect, cut corner top, imp stylized peacock dec, irid blue green glaze, imp "Pewabic, Detroit," early 20th C **275.00**

Plate, 9", hp, cottage scene border . **150.00**

Tile, 2¾", floral nosegay dec, blue luster, matte white ground **65.00**

Vase

5 x 3¾", cylindrical, closed rim, thick, uneven brown matte finish, early maple leaf mark **245.00**

6½ x 4½", gourd shape, cut back design, stylized jonquils, long stems, smooth matte green glaze, die stamped mark **1,760.00**

Pisgah Forest (1913–present), Mt Pisgah, NC

Creamer, blue, pink int. **15.00**

Cup and Saucer, yellow and pink . . **25.00**

Pitcher, 6¼" h, Cameo ware, band of Indians on horses around rim, mottled turquoise high glaze, emb mark **325.00**

Urn, 4¼", white crackle, pink int., 1936 . . . . **35.00**

Vase

7", turquoise, 1949 . . . . **85.00**

10", bulbous, green mottled glaze, 1928 . . . . **128.00**

University City (1910–1915), University City, MO, vase

3½ x 3½", U–shaped, sheets of white snowflake crystals, white porcelain ground, imp "U–C" and "1912" . . **945.00**

4¼ x 4", bulbous, heavy, brown to tan flambé glaze, incised "UC" **295.00**

Walley Pottery, Sterling, MA, early 20th C, bowl, cov, 4½ x 8", applied large leaves, drippy organic matte green glaze, imp mark **1,210.00**

Walrath Pottery (1900–1920), Rochester, NY

Bowl, 4¾", green florals, brown ground **225.00**

Figure, 6", lion, seated, one paw lifted, 1913 . . . . **250.00**

Flower Bowl, 9½ x 9½", brown and green lily pads on ext., center seated nude figure, tall weed flower frogs, incised "Walrath 1412 Pottery" **880.00**

Mug, 6", brown florals, green matte ground, sgd "RB," incised mark . . **250.00**

Pitcher, 10", two colored stylized floral band, brown matte **250.00**

Vase, 4¾", cylindrical, hp buds and leaves, green ground **750.00**

Wheatley, Cincinnati, OH, c1900

Bowl, 7½" d, 3¼" h, relief dec, open petal flowers and leaves, matte green glaze, raised mark and number, retail label **880.00**

Oil Lamp, 7¼" h, 9½" d, four sq buttressed feet, organic curdled matte green glaze **880.00**

Tile, 7¾" sq, emb lion, organic matte brown glaze **250.00**

Vase

8" h, yellow, daisies dec, 1880 . . . **385.00**

12 x 7¾ x 3", oval, French Limoges style painting by Martin Rettig on one side, schooners on ocean, deep blue high glaze, artist sgd, incised "No 50, TJW & Co, 1880," some restoration to glaze chips **1,760.00**

ARTS AND CRAFTS MOVEMENT

History: The Arts and Crafts Movement in American decorative arts took place between 1895 and 1920. Leading proponents of the movement were Elbert Hubbard and his Roycrofters, the brothers Stickley, Frank Lloyd Wright, Charles and Henry Greene, George Niedecken, and Lucia and Arthur Mathews.

The movement was marked by individualistic design (although the movement was national in scope) and re-emphasis on handcraftsmanship and appearance. A reform of industrial society was part of the long range goal. Most pieces of furniture favored a rectilinear approach and were made of oak.

References: Steven Adams, *The Arts & Crafts Movement,* Chartwell Books, Inc., 1987; David M. Cathers, *Furniture of the American Arts and Crafts Movement,* New American Library, 1981; Paul Evans, *Art Pottery Of The United States, 2nd Edition,* Feingold & Lewis Publishing, 1987; Malcolm Haslam, *Collector's Style Guides: Arts and Crafts,* Ballantine Books, 1988; Bruce Johnson, *The Official Identification And Price Guide To Arts And Crafts,* House of Collectibles, 1988; Wendy Kaplan, *The Art That Is Life: The Arts And Crafts Movement In America 1875–1920,* Boston Museum of Fine Arts, 1987; Coy L. Ludwig. *The Arts and Crafts Movement In New York State, 1890s–1920s,* Gallery Association of New York State, 1983.

Periodical: *Arts and Crafts Quarterly,* Station E, P.O. Box 3592, Trenton, NJ 08629.

Museum: Museum of Modern Art, New York, NY.

Additional Listings: Roycroft Items, Stickleys, and art pottery categories.

Box, cov, 2 x 4½ x 4", copper, cedar lined, enameled lid scene of white Spanish ship, black details, blue sea, polished **250.00**

Clock, 75½" h, tall case, overhanging top, brass numerals, dial over leaded glass cabinet door, arched side

Footstool, leather cov, branded mark, Roycroft, 10 x 15", $250.00.

panels, tapering foot, weights and pendulums, c1910 .... 935.00

Furniture

Desk, 32" w, 43½" h, Lifetime, No. 8548, gallery top, drop front int., fitted compartments, two long drawers, arched apron, round copper pulls, escutcheon plate missing, decal on lower side stretcher, c1910 .... 550.00

Dining Room Set, Limbert, oak, 59¼" l sideboard, 35¾" l server, No. 409 54" pedestal base table with four boxed leaves, seven No. 891 dining chairs, branded mark, c1910 . 5,500.00

Magazine Stand, 48" h, toby style, oak, rect top, four shelves, canted plant sides, arched cut–out base . 360.00

Rocker

34½" h, rounded flat open arms, raised front posts, four concave horizontal rails 110.00

36" h, Harden and Co, shaped crest trail, wide vertical slat flanked by two narrow slats, spring cushion seat, paper label 200.00

Room Divider, 27 x 46" frame, leaded glass, stained glass grape pattern on trellis, contemporary oak frame, wrought iron hardware 1,400.00

Wall Shelf, 26⅛" w, 6⅛" d, 36" h reticulated plank ends, D shaped handles, four shelves, exposed keyed tenons 110.00

Lamp

Floor, 72" h, wicker, pyramid shape shade, sq column, rect open work design, sq base, green stain 1,200.00

Table, 22" h, 18" d geometric white and polychrome leaded glass shade, plain gunmetal brass base 825.00

Wall, 8" h, 15" w, reticulated backplate, center hinged demilune shape shade in leaded grid pattern, green irid glass back 360.00

Lantern

13" h, Stickley No. 324 style, patin-

ated metal framework, stenciled, textured yellow glass shade 360.00

20" l, Handel, hexagonal verdigris framework, crackled glass panels at top, tapered body, pink floral motif, pink slag and green glass, c1910, set of 3 .... 4,275.00

Linen, 15 x 15½", embroidered pair of peacocks drinking at fountain, blues and greens, framed 110.00

Mailbox, 12" l, hammered copper, wall mounted 110.00

Mirror

11¼" w, 15" h, rect, wide patinated metal framework, low relief roses and vines, Glasgow, Scotland, c1915 .... 375.00

11¼" w, 18½" h, carved and gilded frame, ink mark "GIB 1910," Boston Society of Arts and Crafts paper label, Boston 550.00

Mug, 6 x 5", bisque fired, sq handle, motto around rim "The Joys That Are To Come," white and green painted and incised narcissus, incised Jervis mark and "O, B" 475.00

Print

Hall, Norma Bassett, "Mt Hood, Oregon," tall evergreens against snow capped Mount Hood, woodcut, sgd and numbered, 10 x 8" 770.00

Lindenmuth, Todd, "The Seiner's," polychrome on paper, fishing boats on water, woodblock, sgd, framed, 15 x 15½" 1,045.00

Norton, Elizabeth, "Goldfish No. 1," four goldfish swimming in seaweed, band of snails at base, gold, green, and black, orig Marshall Fields frame, woodblock, sgd and dated 1924, 9 x 6" 550.00

Rug

3' x 5', drugget, yellow and aubergine flowers, caramel border, tan ground, pr 3,520.00

11' 10" x 11' 2", designed by George Niedeken for Horicon, WI residence, 1923–26, wool, stylized beige scrolls accented by navy blue flowers, ... 2,500.00

Teapot, 5½" h, brass, detachable lid, squat body, pivoted rect cane cov handle, imp stamp "Jan Eisenloffel," 1903 .... 220.00

Textile, tapestry, 11½ x 13½", landscape, green and brown trees, framed 420.00

Tray, 10¾" l, sterling silver, Kalo, oval, scalloped rim, monogram base, stamped "Sterling Hand Wrought at The Kalo Shop," 14 troy ozs 425.00

Wall Sconces, 10½" h, wrought metal,

copper colored patina, hammered repousse overlapping leaf pattern, mica shades, fitted for electricity, c1910, pr — **660.00**

AUSTRIAN WARE

History: Over a hundred potteries were located in the Austro-Hungarian Empire in the late 19th and early 20th centuries. Although Carlsbad was the center of the industry, the factories spread as far as modern day Czechoslovakia.

Many of the factories were either owned or supported by Americans; hence, their wares were produced mainly for export to the United States. Responding to the 1891 law that imported products must be marked as to country of origin, many wares do not have a factory mark, but only the word "Austrian."

Reference: Susan and Al Bagdade, *Warman's English & Continental Pottery & Porcelain, 2nd Edition,* Wallace–Homestead, 1991.

Additional Listings: Amphora, Carlsbad, Royal Dux, and Royal Vienna.

Book Cover, brass, reserved and delicately tooled, sinuous blossoms, stems, and pendant flowers — **800.00**
Bouillon, underplate, pink floral dec, white ground, set of six — **90.00**
Bowl, 10½" d, glazed pottery, gnarled branch section, grape bunch at one end, incised mark, c1900 — **315.00**
Celery Tray, 12" l, scalloped border, pink roses, green leaves, gold trim — **65.00**
Ewer, 5 x 7", squatty, gold handle and spout, tan, blue, and cream ground, multicolored mum dec, green leaves, crown Vienna, Austria mark — **100.00**
Figure, 7" l, boy fishing, hat, feather plume, shirt, vest, breeches, and clogs, crouching on banks of river, rect plinth, copper–brown patina, inscribed "Berndorf," c1900 — **385.00**

Sherbet, ftd, blue florals, gold trim, irid int., marked "Royal Austria," 3" h, $15.00.

Inkwell, Wiener Werkstatte pottery, double well and pen tray, glossy blue glaze, green accents, reticulated back, imp monogram, 9¼ x 8 x 4½", early 20th C — **200.00**
Loving Cup, three handles, hp, raspberries, marked "Vienna, Austria" — **125.00**
Plate, 9½" d, pink and yellow roses, green leaves in center and border, gold scalloped rim, marked "MZ Austria," set of six — **85.00**
Portrait Ware, 11½" h, vase, girl, tan and blue dress, gold chain and earrings with blue stones, blue flowers in hair, green shading to yellow and tan, crown Austria mark — **150.00**
Powder Box, 3 x 4", yellow flowers, green leaves, white ground, marked "O & EG" — **35.00**
Stamp Box, cov, 4¼ x 3⅛", ftd, two compartments, hp, roses, gold trim — **45.00**
Vase
7⅛" h, molded pillar, irid green, pink int. — **80.00**
17" h, Royal Wedding, cream to tan ground, two gold floral handles, floral dec, gold trim, floral base relief, sgd "Robert Hanke" — **225.00**
Wine Glass, pale amber, set of six — **35.00**

AUTOGRAPHS

History: Autographs occur in a wide variety of formats—letters, documents, photographs, books, cards, etc. Most collectors focus on a particular person, country, or category, e.g. signers of the Declaration of Independence.

The condition and content of letters and documents bears significantly on value. Collectors should know their source since forgeries abound and copy machines compound the problem. Further, some signatures of recent presidents and movie stars are done by machine rather than by the persons themselves. A good dealer or advanced collector can help one spot the differences.

The leading auction sources for autographs are Swann Galleries, Sotheby's, and Christie's, all located in New York City.

References: Mary A. Benjamin, *Autographs: A Key To Collecting,* reprint, Dover, 1986; Charles Hamilton, *American Autographs,* University of Oklahoma Press, 1983; Robert W. Pelton, *Collecting Autographs For Fun And Profit,* Betterway Publications, 1987; George Sanders, Helen Sanders, Ralph Roberts, *Collector's Guide To Autographs,* Wallace–Homestead, 1990; George Sanders, Helen Sanders, Ralph Roberts, *The Price Guide To Autographs, 2nd Edition,* Wallace–Homestead, 1991.

Periodical: *The Autograph Collector's Magazine,* P.O. Box 55328, Stockton, CA 95205.

Collectors' Clubs: Manuscript Society, 350 Niagara Street, Burbank, CA 95105; Universal Autograph Collectors Club, P.O. Box 6181, Washington, DC 20044.

Additional Listings: See *Warman's Americana & Collectibles* for more examples.

The following abbreviations denote type of autograph material and their sizes.

ADS	Autograph Document Signed
ALS	Autograph Letter Signed
AQS	Autograph Quotation Signed
CS	Card Signed
DS	Document Signed
LS	Letter Signed
PS	Photograph Signed
TLS	Typed Letter Signed

Sizes (approximate):

Folio	12 x 16 inches
4to	8 x 10 inches
8vo	5 x 7 inches
12mo	3 x 5 inches

COLONIAL AMERICA

Greene, General Nathaneal, ALS, 2 pgs, integral address leaf, 4to, Camp Springfield, June 1779, to Col James Abale, orders supplies to be sent, mentions General Washington, sgd "Nath Greene Qmr," framed **1,600.00**

Gridley, Richard, Revolutionary War General, order to James Fitter, Pay Office, Horse Guards, for payment of 42 sterling to Jonathan and John Amory, sgd Boston, June 25, 1771 . **450.00**

Hamilton, Alexander, ALS, 1 pg, 4to, Philadelphia, August 1794, requesting tents and camp equipage to be sent to New Jersey Militia **850.00**

Hancock, John, PDS, 1 pg, oblong 4to, Watertown, November 1775, sgd by Hancock and Charles Thomson, Secretary, appointing Edward Wigglesworth colonel in Continental Army, worn along folds, repaired on verso . **3,000.00**

Morris, Robert, Signer of Declaration of Independence, ALS, Phila, Oct 23, 1794, re payments of drafts for delivering flour to France, integral address leaf bears circular "22/OC" postmark **975.00**

Otis, James, orator and patriot, DS, appointing James Warren as sheriff of Plymouth County, over 100 words .. **325.00**

Washington, George, ALS, 1 page, folio, Headquarters, Middle Brook, 19 March 1779, to Colonel Wigglesworth, re resignation, strengthened along folds, copy of 1 page 8vo resolution, sgd by Chas Thompson (sic) **9,000.00**

EUROPEAN

Charles X, King of France, DS, folio, sgd as Comte d'Artois, conferring decoration, Paris, September, 1816, creased, foxed along folds **100.00**

Francisco, Franco, PS, 14 x 10", bust length, military dress, inscribed on mat **325.00**

Hitler, Adolf, PS, 8vo, black and white, matte finish, bust pose, suit and tie, serious expression, 2 x 1" black ink signature **2,950.00**

Lafayette, Gilbert Marquis De, ALS, 1 page, 4to, Paris, January, 1820, sgd "Lafayette," discusses news from Spain, framed with engraved portrait **550.00**

Lehmann, Ernest A., German aeronautical engineer, commander of *Graf Zeppelin* and *Hindenburg,* PS, 4 x 6", sepia, bust pose in uniform, smoking pipe **675.00**

Mussolini, Benito, PS, 12 x 8", bust length, military uniform, sgd on mat "Benito Mussolini Roma 23 Mayo 1928–VI" **1,700.00**

Pasteur, Louis, French bacteriologist, ALS, 1882, 5 x 8" plain paper, in French, reply to letter **1,600.00**

Rommel, Erwin, DS, 8 x 6", typed, Feb 1942, promotion for Karl Ditmer, huge blue pencil signature **2,250.00**

GENERAL

Barnum, P. T., check, payable to S. H. Hurd for $500, October 17, 1865 ... **390.00**

Bell, Alexander Graham, 3½" sq magazine picture, sgd lower white margin **275.00**

Edison, Thomas, check, to Walter N. Archer, January 16, 1929 .... **425.00**

Hopkinson, Joseph, ANS, to the Mayor of Philadelphia John Scott, introducing J. W. Audubon, September 30, 1833 .... **390.00**

Kelly, Emmett, orig art, blue ink self sketch of character Weary Willie, detailed bust pose, sgd Best Wishes to Jack from Emmett Kelly, 1967, 12mo sketch on 6 x 9" menu from Showcase Restaurant, New York City ... **1,200.00**

Lewis, Meriweather, promissory note, "No. 6," 8vo, Gov of Louisiana Territory, drawn by hand payable to Thomas Prather, Louisville, February 15, 1808 .... **1,100.00**

MacArthur, Douglas, WWII commander, book, MacArthur, His Rendezvous With History, Major General Courtney Whitney, Knopf, 1956, first edition, titled page inscribed to General Richard K Sutherland with admiration of his great service to the Nation in the Pacific War, sgd by both Whitney and MacArthur, orig dust jacket **500.00**

Penn, William, DS, 12¼ x 15", vellum, August 12, 1705, wax seal in orig case, land grant in Philadelphia to Francis and Elizabeth Fox **810.00**

Pope Pius X, PS, silver print photograph showing him seated, also sgd by Archbishop of Balisa and the Bishop of Sao Paulo, 1906 . . . .   **1,275.00**

LITERATURE

Doyle, Arthur Conan, ALS, Haslemere, May 5, 1904, to Mackenzie Bell about Charles Martineau, framed with envelope **175.00**

Fitzgerald, F. Scott, CS, to Paul Clute about his poems **250.00**

Grey, Zane, State of Oregon hunting license, dated September 2, 1925, signed in three places **890.00**

Lewis, Sinclair, book, *Arrowsmith*, Harcourt, Brace, 1925, second printing, ANS on 1st blank end paper, poor book condition, signature good **195.00**

Longfellow, Henry Wadsworth, ALS, to Cary & Hart, Philadelphia, concerning the details of publication of various of his works, dated December 3, 1844   **475.00**

O'Neill, Eugene, book *Dynamo*, 1929, limited edition of 775, No. 331, bound in blue–green vellum, gilt lettering, purple board box **175.00**

Torrence, Ridgley, ALS, 8vo, 1922, mentions "fortunate experience" in Miami, etc **35.00**

Twain, Mark, CS, framed with photograph **200.00**

MUSIC

Carmichael, Hoagy, AMQS, 8vo, 1 pg, no date, three bars from "Stardust" .   **150.00**

Copland, Aaron, ADS, 5 x 8" program for Westchester Conservatory of Music 80th Birthday Salute to Aaron Copland, signature on cov **195.00**

Gershwin, George, 4to sheet music, Rhapsody in Blue for Jazz Band and Piano, orig color wrappers, inscribed on title page, NY, 1925 . . . .   **4,600.00**

Perlman, Itzhak, PS, 4to, black and white glossy, young pose, 1966 . . . .   **45.00**

Pavarotti, Luciano, 14 x 11" poster of movie "Yes Giorgio" **35.00**

Presley, Elvis, DS, 9 x 11" contract, Oct 18, 1957, 3 pages, employment agreement between Hal B. Wallis, Joseph H. Hazen, and Elvis, each sgd in full **3,000.00**

Salieri, Antonio, orig autograph musical manuscript, oblong folio, 2 pgs, titled "Il maestro e la scolaro" **950.00**

Strauss, Richard, AQS, signature and 2 bars of music on approx 6 x 5" blank side of Excelsior Hotel–Italie Florence   **1,000.00**

PRESIDENTIAL, AMERICAN

Buchanan, James, four language ship's paper, for Francis E. Strawburg, master of the ship "Congress" bound for the Pacific Ocean, sgd August 2, 1858 . . . .   **1,275.00**

Cleveland, Grover, CS, and wife Frances F. Cleveland, ink signatures on matching Executive Mansion, Washington cards, pr **500.00**

Grant, Ulysses S, DS, 1 pg, 4to, Washington, September 1871, order to affix seal on pardon for John Wiggins, framed with engraved portrait **400.00**

Harding, Warren G, and Herbert Hoover, DS, 4to, 1 leaf from register of Ritz–Carlton Hotel, Atlantic City, 1921, sgd by Harding, who also signs for Mrs. Harding, Hoover, and George B Christian, Jr., framed with newspaper clippings **225.00**

Hoover, Herbert, TLS, 4to, White House stationery, 1932, to Colonel L. W. Oliver re new Veterans Administration hospital in western NY area, large black ink full signature **695.00**

Jefferson, Thomas, ALS, written to Mrs. Eleanor Worthington acknowledging the receipt of the seeds of the Serpentine Cucumber and the debts of an old friendship, April 22, 1826 . . .   **2,950.00**

Lincoln, Abraham, ADS, 1 page, folio, vellum, paper seal, Washington, March 1863, appointing Winslow L. Kidder Assistant Adjutant General of Volunteers, countersigned by Edwin M. Stanton, small tears on edges, laid down, framed with engraved portrait   **3,200.00**

Madison, James, check, Office of Pay and Deposit of the Bank of Columbia, Washington, filled in and sgd, March 27, 1816 . . . .   **1,585.00**

Pierce, Franklin, appointment of Edwin C. Bailey as Deputy Postmaster at Boston, September 23, 1853, seal attached **650.00**

Roosevelt, Eleanor, PS, full length, evening gown, by Harris & Ewing, 6 x 9", signed on image **250.00**

Roosevelt, Franklin D, TLS, 1 page, 4to, White House, Washington, December 1944, framed with photograph **325.00**

Taft, William H., ALS, appointing Rear Admiral Charles F. Stokes a member

and vice–chairman of the War Relief
Board of the American National Red
Cross, dated December 11, 1912 .. **450.00**

Wilson, Woodrow, TLS, 1 page, 8vo,
White House, 29 December 1917 .. **175.00**

SHOW BUSINESS

Crawford, Joan, TLS, 8vo, 1½ pgs, September 8, 1959, to Walter Smally, objects to statement saying she was noisy during a performance of someone else **75.00**

Fields, W. C., PS, 14 x 11″, standing in costume worn in *Poppy,* sgd "Bill Fields," inscribed to Arthur Samuels, author of *Poppy,* Oct 1928 .... **1,700.00**

Garbo, Greta, check, Chase Manhattan Bank, filled in and signed, envelope **2,500.00**

Hart, William S., PS, sepia, 7 x 8″, full pose, large sentiment and full signature in lower right corner **200.00**

Kelly, Grace and Cary Grant, matted lobby photo, 15 x 13″, romantic pose, formal attire, plain page sgd Best Wishes Grace Kelly/Cary Grant **850.00**

Kern, Jerome, PS, 11 x 14″, seated at piano, sgd and inscribed **1,700.00**

Monroe, Marilyn, and Joe DiMaggio, menu, cut to 4 x 3″, matted, 9 x 7″ black and white glossy photo, sgd "Warmest Regards/Marilyn Monroe &," his signed full name underneath, dated Saturday, May 16, 1953 .... **2,000.00**

Novarro, Ramon, PS, 10 x 13″, silent film star, close–up bust portrait **250.00**

Baseball, Hank Aaron, $25.00.

SPORTS

Agassi, Andre, PS, 4to, color, action close–up **75.00**

Clemente, Roberto, 5 x 8″ magazine cov, Pirates uniform, sgd in blue ballpoint **295.00**

Cobb, Ty, check, oblong 8vo, 1945,

drawn on First National Bank of Nevada, filled in and sgd by Cobb as "Tyrus R. Cobb," cancellation markings **100.00**

Dempsey, Jack, PS, sepia, 4to, full length pose in boxing stance, sgd "Best regards/Jack Dempsey/Nov. 22, '27" **75.00**

Robinson, Sugar Ray, PS, Boxing magazine cov, color action, bold signature **125.00**

Ruth, Babe, 1939 Commemorative U. S. Postage Stamp, The Centennial of Baseball **375.00**

Williams, Ted, sgd baseball, signature on sweetspot, holder **75.00**

STATESMAN, AMERICAN

Acheson, Dean, TLS, 4to, 1 page, Jan 23, 1954, to Ellis of Four Freedoms Foundation thanking him for photographs **25.00**

Clinton, De Witt, DS, appointment of Elisha Waters as an Ensign in the 24th Regiment of Infantry, March 27, 1819 .... **95.00**

Colfax, Schuyler, envelope, addressed in another hand, franked by Colfax at upper right, Washington postmark at left, Vice Pres under Grant **75.00**

Davis, Jefferson, ALS, endorsement on a letter concerning the Allegheny Valley R. R. Co., April 28, 1853 ...... **485.00**

Hall, A. Oakley, Mayor of NYC, ALS, 8vo, 4pp, Executive Depart., City Hall, response to inquiry re: "the new charter," envelope included **300.00**

Holmes, Oliver Wendell, calling card, February 13, 1913 .... **490.00**

Jay, John, DS, appointing Henry Saltsman Pay Master of the Regiment of Militia in the county of Montgomery, April 18, 1800 .... **790.00**

King, Preston, ALS, 4to, 8 pgs, Washington, Feb 6, 1851, to Gideon Welles, Lincoln's Sec. of Navy, political letter concerning the presidential election to be held the following year **275.00**

Sumner, Charles, ALS, 12mo, 1 page, "Senate Chamber, Aug. 25," stating he has not received letters from Webster on specific subject **25.00**

AUTOMOBILES

History: Automobiles can be classified into several categories. In 1947 the Antique Automobile Club of America devised a system whereby any motor vehicle (car, bus, motorcycle, etc.) made prior to 1930 is an "antique" car. The Classic Car

Club of America expanded the list focusing on luxury models from 1925 to 1948. The Milestone Car Society developed a list for cars in the 1948 to 1964 period.

Some states, such as Pennsylvania, have devised a dual registration system for older cars—antique and classic. Models from the 1960s and 1970s, especially convertibles and limited production models, fall into the "classic" designation depending how they are used.

References: Quentin Craft, *Classic Old Car Value Guide, 23rd Edition,* published by author, 1989; James M. Flammang, *Standard Catalog of American Cars, 1976–1986, 2nd Edition,* Krause Publications, 1989; John A. Gunnel, *Standard Catalog of American Cars, 1946–1975, Second Edition,* Krause Publications, 1987; Beverly Kimes and Henry Austin Clark, Jr., *Standard Catalog of American Cars, 1805–1942, Second Edition,* Krause Publications, 1989; Jim Lenzke and Ken Buttolph, *Standard Guide to Cars & Prices, 1991 Edition,* Krause Publications, 1991.

Periodicals: *Hemmings Motor News,* Box 100, Bennington, VT 05201; *Old Cars Price Guide,* 700 E. State Street, Iola, WI 54990; *Old Cars Weekly,* 700 E. State Street, Iola, WI 54990.

Collectors' Clubs: Antique Automobile Club of America, 501 W. Governor Road, Hershey, PA 17033; Classic Car Club of America, P.O. Box 443, Madison, NJ 07940; Milestone Car Society, P.O. Box 50850, Indianapolis, IN 46250.

Note: The prices below are based upon a car in running condition, with a high percentage of original parts, and somewhere between 60% and 80% restored. *Prices can vary by as much as 30% in either direction.*

Many older cars, especially if restored, now exceed $15,000.00. Their limited availability makes them difficult to price. Auctions, more than any other source, are the true determinant of value at this level. Especially helpful are the catalogs and sale bills of Kruse Auctioneers, Inc., Auburn, IN 46706.

Auburn
  1915, Model 4–36, Touring, 4 cyl. . . **17,000.00**
  1935, Model 653, Sedan, 6 cyl. **8,500.00**
Bentley
  1953, Park Ward, Convertible, 4.6
    Litre engine **28,000.00**
  1963, S3, Sedan, four door, right
    hand drive, taupe leather int., re-
    painted **16,500.00**
Bricklin, 1975, Model SV–1, Gullwing
  Coupe **8,000.00**
Buick
  1908, Model 10, Touring, 4 cyl. **12,000.00**
  1941, Roadmaster, Sedan, 8 cyl. . . . **15,000.00**
Cadillac
  1931, Model 370, Cabriolet, V–12 . . **42,000.00**
  1956, Sedan, blue body, cream top . **11,500.00**

  1963, Convertible, red, white top . . . **7,500.00**
Chandler, 1927, Big Six, Sedan, 6 cyl. **4,800.00**
Chevrolet
  1933, Eagle, Coupe, rumble seat, 6
    cyl. **6,000.00**
  1953, Sedan, four door **10,000.00**
  1958, Corvette, Roadster, V–8 . . . . **15,000.00**
  1965, Corvair, Convertible, 6 cyl. . . . **4,000.00**
  1968, Impala Coupe, V–8 engine . . **1,200.00**

Chevrolet, 1931, Model AE, two door sedan, 6 cylinder, $10,000.00.

Chrysler
  1932, Imperial, Sedan, 6 cyl. **9,000.00**
  1939, Imperial **9,000.00**
  1956, New Yorker, Hemming engine **9,000.00**
  1959, Saratoga, Sedan, V–8 . . . . . . **3,000.00**
Columbia, 1925, Six, Sedan, 6 cyl. . . **8,000.00**
Cunningham, 1929, Model V9, Roads-
  ter, 6 cyl. **20,000.00**
Daniels, 1920, Submarine, Speedster,
  V–8 . . . . **24,500.00**
Dayton, 1913, Tandem, Cycle, 2 cyl. . **3,000.00**
Delahaye, 1935, Superflux, Roadster, 6
  cyl. **12,000.00**
DeSoto
  1931, Model 31, Coupe, rumble seat,
    6 cyl. **4,200.00**
  1952, Firedome, Convertible Coupe,
    V–8 . . . . **6,000.00**
Dodge
  1921, Model 21, Touring, 4 cyl. **3,500.00**
  1949, Wayfarer, Roadster, 6 cyl. . . . **4,000.00**
  1966, Charger, Coupe, V–8 . . . . . . **2,200.00**
Dort, 1924, Model 27, Touring, 6 cyl. . **4,000.00**
Dragon, 1906, Model 25, Touring, 4 cyl. **5,500.00**
Drexel, 1916, Model 7–60, seven pas-
  senger touring, 4 cyl. **5,000.00**
Duesenberg, 1931, LeBaron–J, Con-
  vertible Berline, 8 cyl. **125,000.00**
Durant, 1928, Model M, Sedan, 4 cyl. . **4,800.00**
Edsel, 1959, Ranger, V–8 engine **2,850.00**
Excalibur SS, 1973, Model SSK,
  Roadster, V–8 . . . . **11,500.00**
Falcon, 1922, Touring, 4 cyl. **5,000.00**
Ferrair, 1956, Tipo 375, Touring, V–12 **27,000.00**
Ford
  1903, Model A, Runabout, 2 cyl. . . . **11,500.00**

1927, Model T, Coupe, green **6,500.00**
1929, Model A, Coupe, rumble seat,
  orig title **9,000.00**
1930, Model A, Sedan **9,000.00**
1940, Deluxe, Sedan Delivery, V–8 . **6,800.00**
1960, Galaxie, Victoria, V–8 . . . . . . **3,000.00**
1963, Falcon, Convertible **3,500.00**
Franklin
1930, Model 14, Convertible Sedan,
  6 cyl. **20,000.00**
1933, Olympic, Cabriolet, 6 cyl. **7,000.00**
Fritchle, 1916, Touring, 4 cyl. **5,000.00**
Gardner, 1929, Model 130, Roadster, 8
  cyl. **12,000.00**
Graham–Paige, 1941, Hollywood, Con-
  vertible Coupe, 6 cyl. **10,000.00**
Grant, 1921, Model HZ, Sedan, 6 cyl. . **4,500.00**
Hillman, 1967, Huskey, Station Wagon,
  1.7 litre **1,250.00**
Hudson, 1935, Terraplane Fordor, Se-
  dan, black, brown int. **6,900.00**
Jaguar
1951, Mark VII, Sedan, 6 cyl. **3,600.00**
1966, XKE, Sport Racing, 4.2 litre . . **6,500.00**
Julian, 1922, Model 60, Coupe, 8 cyl. . **10,000.00**
Lambert, 1909, Roadster, 6 cyl. **8,000.00**
LaSalle
1939, hearse **14,500.00**
1940, Model 52, Club Coupe, V–8 . **5,000.00**
Lincoln, 1935, Dietrich, Convertible
  Coupe, V–12 . . . . **28,000.00**
Lotus, 1966, Mark 46 Europa, Coupe,
  1.5 litre **2,100.00**
Mercedes–Benz
1935, Model 170–V, Limousine **15,000.00**
1956, Model 190SL, Convertible, 4
  cyl. **9,000.00**
Mercury
1940, Series 09A, Convertible, 8 cyl. **10,000.00**
1955, Monterey, Sedan **1,500.00**
1963, Comet S–22, Convertible, 8 cyl. **2,400.00**
Nash
1954, Ambassador, two door hardtop,
  8 cyl. **1,250.00**
1962, Metropolitan, Convertible, 4 cyl. **4,000.00**
Oldsmobile
1942, Model 66, Station Wagon, 6 cyl. **4,000.00**
1966, Toronado, Coupe, V–8 . . . . . **3,100.00**
Opel, 1938, Admiral, Drophead Coupe,
  3.6 litre **1,700.00**
Packard
1928, Model 426, roadster, 6 cyl. . . **14,000.00**
1940, Darrin, Convertible Victoria, 8
  cyl. **25,000.00**
Peugeot, 1939, Darl mat, Coupe, 2.1
  litre **1,200.00**
Pittsburgh, 1911, Touring, seven pas-
  senger, 6 cyl. **6,500.00**
Plymouth
1928, Model Q, Sport Roadster, 4 cyl. **8,500.00**
1942, Model P145, Sedan, 6 cyl. . . . **2,500.00**

1957, Fury, Convertible, V–8 cyl. . . . **4,000.00**
Pontiac
1955, Star Chief, four door **7,500.00**
1958, Bonneville, two door hardtop,
  V–8 . . . . **2,800.00**
1966, GTO, Convertible, V–8 . . . . . **5,200.00**
Porsche, 1969, Model 911 T, Coupe, 4
  cyl. **6,800.00**
Renault, 1955, Fregate, Convertible, 2
  litre **2,000.00**
Rolls Royce
1929, Pall Mall, Touring, 6 cyl. **60,000.00**
1952, Silver Dawn, Touring Limou-
  sine, 6 cyl. **18,000.00**
1971, Corniche Coupe **25,850.00**
Studebaker
1933, President, Convertible, 8 cyl. . **10,000.00**
1949, Champion, Convertible, 6 cyl. **4,800.00**
1963, Avanti, Coupe, V–8 . . . . **5,000.00**
Stutz
1914, Bearcat, Roadster, 6 cyl. **45,000.00**
1927, Black Hawk, Speedster, 8 cyl. **8,000.00**
Sunbeam, 1958, Alpine, Sport, 4 cyl. . **2,800.00**

MISCELLANEOUS

Fire Engine
Diamond T, 1947, pumper **2,500.00**
Dodge, 1945, pumper, American
  LaFrance, 6 cyl. **2,500.00**
Ford
1929, Model AA **4,800.00**
1940, pumper, flat V–8 . . . . **6,500.00**
Mack, 1936, pumper, Hale pump . . . **4,000.00**
Motorcycle
BSA, 1943, Military **3,800.00**
Harley–Davidson, 1952, Model K . . **1,800.00**
Indian
1930, Scout, Model 101 . . . . **5,500.00**
1948, Chief **7,500.00**
Triumph, 1921, Baby **1,500.00**
Truck
Chevrolet
1932, Huckster **6,000.00**
1937, Sedan delivery, 6 cyl. **5,500.00**
1957, Pickup, ½ ton, Short Bed,
  V–6 . . . . **2,300.00**
Dodge
1937, Pickup, ¾ ton, Slant 6 . . . . . **2,000.00**
1957, Sweptside, ½ ton, V–8 . . . . **850.00**
Ford
1941, F–1 Stake, V–8 . . . . **2,500.00**
1956, F–100, Custom Cab, V–8 . . **2,500.00**
1962, Falcon, Ranchero, 6 cyl. . . **2,500.00**
Plymouth, 1938, Pickup, High Side,
  Slant 6 . . . . **2,400.00**
Stewart, Pickup, 1 ton, 4 cyl. **3,200.00**
VW, Pickup, short bed, 1600 cc . . . **1,400.00**
Willys
1928, Model 70, Sedan, 6 cyl. . . . **1,800.00**
1941, Americar, Sedan, 4 cyl. . . . **1,800.00**

AUTOMOBILIA

History: The amount of items related to the automobile is endless. Collectors seem to fit into three groups—those collecting parts to restore a car, those collecting information about a company or certain model for research purposes, and those trying to use automobile items for decorative purposes. Most material changes hands at the hundreds of swap meets and auto shows around the country.

References: Scott Anderson, *Check The Oil: Gas Station Collectibles With Prices,* Wallace–Homestead, 1986; Gordon Gardiner and Alistair Morris, *The Price Guide and Identification of Automobilia,* Antique Collectors' Club; Brian Jewell, *Motor Badges & Figureheads,* Midas Books, 1978; Dan Smith, *Accessory Mascots, The Automotive Accents Of Yesteryear, 1910–1940,* Published by author, 1989.

Periodical: *Hemmings Motor News,* Box 100, Bennington, VT 05201.

Pinback Button, International United Automobile Workers of America, red border, lavender gear, 1" d, $8.50.

Advertising	
Ashtray, Buick, Convertible, 1947 ..	15.00
Paperweight, Yellow Taxicab Service, round, 3"	30.00
Sign	
Cadillac Sales & Service, porcelain, double sided, 42"	1,350.00
Champion Spark Plugs, porcelain, 13 x 30", pictures early plug ...	950.00
Chevy Bel Air, tin, red convertible, 1957	95.00
Economy Auto, porcelain, double sided, Scotsman sitting on 1940s car holding sign, 18 x 36"	1,600.00
Ford Batteries Sales & Service, porcelain, 15 x 24"	575.00
Marathon Ohio Oil Co, with runner	175.00
Plymouth Service, porcelain, double sided, 16 x 20"	1,150.00

Rambler Parts/Service, double sided, porcelain, 42"	550.00
Air Pump, Cadillac, 4 cyl., 1913–14 ..	75.00
Bottle, Marquette Oil, emb, tin spout ..	25.00
Brochure	
Buick Wildcat Sportster, 1955	15.00
DeSoto, dealers, 1951	20.00
Hudson, 1950	25.00
Rambler, dealers, 1962	15.00
Catalog, Ford, Model T, 10 pgs, 1923, 7 x 11"	65.00
Chauffeur's Badge	
Arkansas, 1925	18.00
Kentucky, 1928	18.00
New York, 1921	12.00
Emblem, Old Trails Auto Association, metal, 1920s	20.00
Encyclopedia, *Dyke's Automobile Encyclopedia,* 940 pgs, 1919	30.00
Floor Mat, Buick, red rubber, 1963 ...	55.00
Folder, Buick, 1952	20.00
Gas Cap, Ford, metal	8.00
Gearshift Knob, glass, green and white swirls	18.00
Headlights, pr	
Ford Model A, chrome, orig lens ...	200.00
Franklin, 1928	230.00
Hood, Ford, 1936	35.00
Hood Ornament	
Art Deco, metal, lady with flowing hair	45.00
Hudson, 1949	85.00
Mack, bulldog, chrome	30.00
Horn	
Spartonet, push down handle	60.00
Trojan United, electric	50.00
Yoders Super Goose, chrome, bulb type	35.00
Hubcap	
Chevrolet, 1957	15.00
Durant, 6½"	60.00
Edsel, spinner type	35.00
Jack	
Hudson, 1930	25.00
Jaguar	30.00
License Plate	
1913, New Jersey, graniteware	75.00
1931, New York	25.00
1938, Alabama	40.00
Lubrication Chart, Quaker State, 22 x 35", 1938	30.00
Magazine	
Motor Age, January 14, 1904	18.50
Willy–Overland, 48 pgs, 1912	55.00
Manual	
Chevrolet, Model D, 1920s	12.00
Chilton's Motor Age Flat Rate & Service Manual, 1952	25.00
Ford, owner's, 1950	20.00
Stoddard–Dayton, c1908	65.00
Radiator Cap	
Chevrolet, Viking, 1929	150.00
Lincoln, figural, greyhound, 1930s ..	125.00

BACCARAT GLASS

History: The Sainte-Anne glassworks at Baccarat in the Voges, France, was founded in 1764 and produced utilitarian soda glass. In 1816 Aime-Gabriel d'Artiques purchased the glassworks, and a Royal Warrant was issued in 1817 for the opening of Verrerie de Vonche á Baccarat. The firm concentrated on lead crystal glass products. In 1824 a limited company was created.

From 1823 to 1857 Baccarat and Saint-Louis glassworks had a commercial agreement and used the same outlets. No merger occurred. Baccarat began the production of paperweights in 1846. In the late 19th century the firm achieved an international reputation for cut glass table services, chandeliers, display vases and centerpieces, and sculptures. Products eventually included all forms of glassware. The firm still is active today.

Additional Listing: Paperweights.

Fairy Lamp, Rose Tiente, 3⅞" h, sgd, $275.00.

Biscuit Jar, vaseline, shaded frosted to clear, swirling flowers, sgd 200.00
Bowl
  8" d, Rose Tiente, scalloped, ftd, sgd   100.00
  14" d, 3½" h, wide flattened rim, narrow knopped annual foot, etched "Baccarat, France" 500.00
Candlesticks, pr, 10¾" h, Eiffel Tower pattern, Rose Tiente 225.00
Champagne Bucket, 9¼" h, tapering cylindrical, rect stop fluted molded sides, stamped "Baccarat, France" .   400.00
Cigar Lighter, Rose Tiente, SP top . . .   125.00
Cologne Bottle
  5½" h, Rose Tiente, Diamond Point Swirl, orig stopper 95.00
  7" h, crystal, frosted rosette ground, gold floral swags and bows, cut faceted stopper, pr 330.00
Crystal Ball, 6" d, clear, acid stamped "Baccarat," 3¼" h clear glass cylindrical dished stand, low circular foot, retailed by Tiffany and Co, pr 1,430.00
Decanter, 9¾" h, Rose Tiente, orig stopper 115.00
Dresser Jar, 5⅜" d, round, double cut overlay, pink cut to clear over opaque white, cut vertical panels, gold dec .   125.00
Epergne, 15" h, scalloped edges, Rose Tiente, 3 pcs 450.00
Fairy Lamp, 3⅞" h, shaded white to clear 275.00
Finger Bowl, 4¾" d bowl, 6¼" d underplate, ruby, medallions and flowers gold dec 325.00
Goblet
  Perfection pattern 36.00
  Vintage pattern, cone shaped amber bowl, etched grape design, cut stem and base, set of 6 . . . .   100.00
Jar, cov, 7" d, cameo cut, gilt metal mounts, imp "Baccarat" 350.00
Jewelry Box, 4" d, 2¾" h, hinged lid, Button and Bow pattern, sapphire blue, brass fittings 125.00
Lamp, table, crystal and gilt metal, pr
  Column form 3,200.00
  Urn form 3,000.00
Pitcher, 9¼" h, Rose Tiente, Helical Twist pattern 275.00
Rose Bowl, 3" h, cranberry, lacy enamel dec 150.00
Sweetmeat Jar, cranberry colored strawberries, blossoms, and leaves, cut back to clear ground of ferns, SP cov and handle, sgd 350.00
Toothpick Holder, 2½" h, scalloped, Rose Tiente 100.00
Tumbler, Rose Tiente, Swirl pattern . .   60.00
Tumble–Up, Rose Tiente, Swirl pattern, carafe and tumbler 200.00
Vase, 8¼" h, bamboo stalk form, relief molded leaf sprig at side, coiled snake around base, enameled and gilt insects, early 20th C, sgd 500.00

BANKS, MECHANICAL

History: Banks which display some form of action while utilizing a coin are considered mechanical banks. Although mechanical banks are known which date back to ancient Greece and Rome, the majority of collectors center their interests in those made between 1867 and 1928 in Germany, England, and the United States. Recently there has been an upsurge of interest in later types, some of which date into the 1970s.

Initial research suggested that approximately

250 to 300 different or variant designs of banks were made in the early period. Today that number has been revised to 2,000–3,000 types and varieties. The field remains ripe for discovery and research.

Over 80% of all cast iron mechanical banks produced between 1869 and 1928 were made by J.E. Stevens Co., Cromwell, Connecticut. Tin banks tend to be German in origin.

While rarity is a factor in value, appeal of design, action, quality of manufacture, country of origin, and history of collector interest also are important. Radical price fluctuations may occur with an imbalance of these factors. Rare banks may sell for a few hundred dollars while one of more common design with greater appeal will sell in the thousands.

The prices on our list represent fairly what a bank sells for in the specialized collectors' market. Some banks are hard to find and establishing a price outside auction is difficult.

The prices listed are for original old mechanical banks with minor repairs, in sound operating condition, and with a majority of the original paint intact.

References: Al Davidson, *Penny Lane, A History Of Antique Mechanical Toy Banks,* Long's Americana, 1987; Bill Norman, *The Bank Book: The Encyclopedia of Mechanical Bank Collecting,* Collectors' Showcase, 1984.

Collectors' Club: Mechanical Bank Collectors of America, P.O. Box 128, Allegan, MI 49010.

Reproduction Alert: Reproductions, fakes, and forgeries exist for many banks. Forgeries of some mechanical banks were made as early as 1937, so age alone is not a guarantee of authenticity. In our listing two asterisks indicate banks for which serious forgeries exist and one asterisk indicates banks for which casual reproductions have been made.

Advisor: James S. Maxwell, Jr.

Acrobat, J. & E. Stevens Co., Cromwell, CT, designed by Edward L. Morris, patent date April 3, 1883, $1,800.00.

Alligator, grabs coin in mouth, tin	1,150.00
**American Sewing Machine, iron	2,000.00
Australian William Tell, brass, wood, and tin	1,200.00
Automatic Coin Savings, tin, strong man in leopard skin holding man by hair	2,000.00
Bank of Education & Economy	550.00
Barking Dog, wood and steel	1,400.00
**Bear, standing, iron	350.00
**Billy Goat, iron	1,000.00
**Bismark, iron	2,350.00
Bowing Man in Cupola, iron	3,000.00
**Boy & Bull Dog, iron	550.00
**Boy on Trapeze, iron	875.00
*Boy Scout Camp, iron	2,000.00
**Boys Stealing Watermelons, iron	850.00
British Lion, tin	850.00
**Bull & Bear, iron	12,000.00
*Bull Dog, iron, coin on nose	650.00
Bull Dog Savings, iron, key wind	2,000.00
Bull Tosses Boy in Well, brass	2,200.00
Bureau	
Tin, Ideal	475.00
Wood	
Serrill Pat. Appld. For	400.00
Stenciling on front	350.00
**Butting Buffalo, iron	950.00
Butting Ram, man thumbs nose	1,700.00
**Calamity, iron	4,500.00
**Called Out, orig unpainted iron	10,000.00
Called Out, lead master pattern	12,000.00
Calumet with Calumet Kid, tin can	150.00
Calumet with Soldier, tin can	1,000.00
Calumet with Sailor, tin can	1,2000.00
**Cannon, U.S. & Spain	1,850.00
Cat & Mouse, iron and brass, cat standing upright	12,000.00
Cat Chasing Mouse in Building, tin	2,400.00
Chandlers, iron	250.00
Child's Bank, Clark Thread	350.00
**Chimpanzee, iron and tin	1,150.00
Chinaman, iron, reclining	1,650.00
**Circus Ticket Collector, man at barrel	800.00
Clown & Dog, tin	850.00
Clown, tin, black face	250.00
**Clown, Harlequin, Columbine, iron	14,500.00
**Clown on Globe, iron	775.00
Coin Registering, iron, domed building	300.00
Confectionery, iron	2,800.00
Crescent Cash Register, iron	125.00
Crowing Rooster, tin	275.00
Dapper Dan, tin	450.00
Darky Bust, tin	450.00
**Dentist, iron	2,200.00
Dog Goes Into House, lead and brass	3,800.00
**Dog With Tray, iron, oval base	1,000.00
Ducks, lead, two	650.00
Electric Safe, steel	150.00
Elephant Baby, lead, with clown at table	3,700.00
**Elephant With Howdah, iron, man pops out	375.00

**Elephant With Locked Howdah, iron, oval base	600.00
**Elephant, iron, "Light of Asia" on wheels	675.00
Elephant, tin, Royal Trick	850.00
**Elephant On Wheels, iron, trunk moves Face, wood	700.00 875.00
**Feed the Kitty, iron	400.00
**Ferris Wheel, iron and tin, marked "Bowen's Pat."	1,400.00
Fire Alarm, tin	1,250.00
Flip The Frog, tin	950.00
Football, iron, black man and watermelon	14,000.00
Fortune Teller Safe, iron	450.00
Freedman (man at desk)	38,500.00
**Forty–Niner, iron	400.00
Frog On Arched Track, tin	2,000.00
Frog On Rock, iron	350.00
Fun Producing Savings, tin	275.00
Germania Exchange, iron, tin and lead	2,800.00
**Giant Standing, iron	6,800.00
**Girl in Victorian Chair, iron	2,350.00
Give Me A Penny, wood	700.00
**Glutton, brass, lifts turkey	425.00
Golden Gate Key, aluminum	125.00
Grasshopper, tin, wind–up	5,000.00
Guessing, lead and iron, man's figure	2,000.00
Hall's Excelsior, iron and wood, policeman figure	1,400.00
Hall's Lilliput, Type II	250.00
Hall's Yankee Notion, brass	850.00
Harold Lloyd, tin	950.00
Hillman Coin Bank, wood, iron, and glass	3,200.00
**Hold The Fort, iron, five holes	1,400.00
Home, iron	375.00
Home With Dormer Windows, iron	475.00
**Horse Race, iron, tin horses, flanged base	2,000.00
**Humpty Dumpty, iron	425.00
I Always Did 'Spize a Mule, black, sitting on bench	575.00
Huntley And Palmers Readings	250.00
*Indian And Bear, iron, white bear	750.00
**Initiating First Degree, iron	2,800.00
Jack on Roof, tin	300.00
Joe Socko, tin	275.00
John R. Jennings Money Box, wood	2,800.00
Jolly Joe Clown, tin	400.00
**Jolly Nigger	
Aluminum, string tie	100.00
Iron	150.00
Jonah And Whale, iron, ftd base	12,500.00
Key, iron, World's Fair	300.00
Kick Inn, paper on wood	275.00
**Leap Frog, iron	1,250.00
**Lighthouse, iron	600.00
Lion Hunter, iron	1,650.00
Little High Hat, iron	500.00
Little Jocko Musical, tin	900.00
Little Moe, iron, tip hat	450.00

Long May It Wave, iron and wood	400.00
Lucky Wheel Money Box, tin	150.00
**Magic Safe, iron	175.00
**Magician, iron	1,650.00
**Mama Katzenjammer, iron, 1930s	550.00
Mama Katzenjammer, iron, 1905–08, low cut dress with white fringe	3,700.00
Man on Chimney	550.00
**Mason, iron	1,450.00
Merry–Go–Round, mechanical	4,500.00
Metropolitan, iron	150.00
Mikado, iron	7,500.00
Minstrel, tin	450.00
Model Railroad Stamp Dispenser, tin	650.00
Model Railroad Sweet Dispenser	650.00
Model Savings, tin	500.00
*Monkey & Coconut, iron	750.00
Monkey & Parrot, tin	200.00
Monkey With Tray, tin	350.00
Moonface, iron	20,000.00
Mosque, iron	450.00
*Mule Entering Barn, iron	650.00
Musical Church, wood, rotating tower	2,500.00
Musical Savings, wood house	1,200.00
New, iron, lever in center	450.00
New Creedmoor Bank, iron	450.00
**Novelty, iron	400.00
Old Woman In The Shoe	180,000.00

Organ Grinder, cat and dog, Kyser & Rex Co., Frankford, PA, patent June 13, 1882, $650.00.

**Organ Grinder With Performing Bear, iron	1,600.00
Owl, iron, slot in head	250.00
Owl, turns head, iron	225.00
*Paddy & Pig, iron	875.00
Pascal Savings, tin	250.00
**Peg Leg Begger, iron	600.00
**Pelican With Rabbit, iron	700.00
**Piano, iron, old conversion to musical	2,200.00
Pig In High Chair, iron	450.00
Pistol, stamped metal	325.00
Postman, tin, English	250.00

Presto, iron, penny changes to quarter	3,700.00
Pump & Bucket, iron	425.00
*Punch & Judy, iron	750.00
Punch & Judy, tin	1,500.00
Queen Victoria Bust, iron	5,000.00
**Rabbit, iron, large	275.00
Rabbit In Cabbage	250.00
**Red Riding Hood, iron	5,500.00
Rival, iron	5,000.00
Roller–skating, iron	4,000.00
Safety Locomotive, iron	250.00
Saluting Sailor, tin	500.00
Sam Segal's Aim to Save Target, iron	4,500.00
Savo, tin, round, children	125.00
Scotchman, tin	375.00
Sentry, tin, raises rifle	550.00
Shoot The Hat, brass	2,500.00
Signal Cabin, tin	150.00
Snake & Frog In Pond, tin	1,200.00
*Speaking Dog, iron	750.00
Sportsman, iron, fowler	4,500.00
**Squirrel & Tree Stump, iron	800.00
Stollwerk, tin, Victoria	250.00
Sweet Thrift, tin	150.00
*Tammany, iron	275.00
*Tank & Cannon, aluminum	200.00
Target, iron, fort and cannon	2,750.00
Ten Cent Adding Bank, iron	400.00
Thrifty Tom's Jigger, tin	400.00
Tiger, tin	950.00
Time Lock Savings, iron	1,100.00
Toboggan, SP Britannia metal	850.00
Treasure Chest Music, pot metal	375.00
**Trick Dog, iron, solid base	450.00
*Trick Pony, iron	675.00
Trick Savings, wood, front drawer	125.00
Try Your Weight Scale, tin	250.00
**Uncle Remus, iron	1,650.00
**Uncle Sam Bust, iron	475.00
Uncle Tom, iron, star base	250.00
United States Bank, iron, picture pops up	875.00
Viennese soldier, lead	1,800.00
Volunteer, iron	450.00
Watch Dog Safe, iron	250.00
Weeden's Plantation, tin, wind–up	650.00
Wimbledon, iron	1,600.00
Wishbone, brass	6,000.00
Woodpecker, tin, 1920s	850.00

BANKS, STILL

History: Banks with no mechanical action are known as still banks. The first still banks were made of wood, pottery, or from gourds. Redware and stoneware banks, made by America's early potters, are prized possessions of today's collectors.

Still banks reached a "golden age" with the arrival of the cast iron bank. Leading manufacturing companies include Arcade Mfg. Co., J. Chein & Co., Hubley, J. & E. Stevens and A. C. Williams. The banks often were ornately painted to enhance their appeal. During the cast iron era, banks and other businesses used the still bank as a form of advertising for attracting customers.

The tin lithograph bank, again frequently with advertising, did not reach its zenith until the 1930 to 1955 period. The tin bank was an important premium, whether it be a Pabst Blue Ribbon beer can bank or a Gerber's Orange Juice bank. Most tin advertising banks resembled the packaging shape of the product.

Almost every substance has been used to make a still bank–diecast white metal, aluminum, brass, plastic, glass, etc. Many of the early glass candy containers also converted to a bank when the candy was eaten. Thousands of varieties of still banks were made, and hundreds of new varieties appear on the market each year.

References: Earnest Ida and Jane Pitman, *Dictionary of Still Banks*, Long's Americana, 1980; Andy and Susan Moore, *Penny Bank Book, Collecting Still Banks*, Schiffer Publishing, Ltd., 1984; Hubert B. Whiting, *Old Iron Still Banks*, Forward's Color Productions, Inc. 1968, out of print.

Collectors' Club: Still Bank Collectors Club of America, 62 South Hazelwood, Newark, OH 43055.

Museum: Margaret Woodbury Strong Museum, Rochester, NY.

GLASS

Barrel, emb	12.00
Dog, 3¼" barrel	75.00
Fruit Jar, Atlas Mason Jar	15.00
House	
3¼", Save With Pittsburgh Paints, clear, pressed	25.00
4", brick, orig brown paint, milk glass, orig mustard label on bottom	40.00
Kewpie, 3⅛" h, pressed glass with polychrome	75.00
Liberty Bell, dated 1919	20.00
*Log Cabin, 4", milk glass	20.00
Milk Bottle, 4½", Elsie The Borden Cow	25.00
Monkey, 5"	35.00
Owl, 7", carnival glass, marigold	25.00
Schoolhouse, milk glass	50.00

METAL, Cast Iron unless otherwise stated.

Animal

Boston Bull, 4⅜" h, seated, polychrome	85.00
Camel, 7¼" l, gold, red and orange	215.00
Cat with ball, 5⅝" l, gray, gold ball	150.00
*Deer, 9½", antlers	55.00
*Donkey, 6¾"	100.00
*Elephant, 4", gold trim	115.00

Cast iron, standing lion, painted, 5" h, $45.00.

Goose, 3¾", "Red Goose School Shoes" adv 100.00
Hippopotamus, 5" l, black 200.00
Newfoundland, 3⅝" h, black 40.00
Pig, 2½", "Decker's Iowana," gold . . 65.00
Possum, 2½", gold or silver 165.00
*Scottie, 3⁵⁄₁₆", black 70.00
Seal, 3⅜" h, gold 240.00
*Sheep, 5¼", gold 65.00
Turkey 70.00
Other
Baseball Player, 5¾", gold or blue . . 75.00
Battleship, "Maine", 4½", japan finish 125.00
Beehive 60.00
Bicentennial, 1776–1976, 6 x 6" . . . 40.00
Boy Scout, 5¾", gold 65.00
Building, 7", "Columbia," nickel finish 80.00
Bungalow, 3¾" h, polychrome, porch 175.00
Captain Kidd, 5⅝", c1901 . . . . 225.00
Castle, 3" h, brown japanning, gold trim 250.00
Clock, "Time Is Money," 3³⁄₁₆", black 55.00
Colonial House, 3" h, gold and green 95.00
Devil, 4¼", two faced, red 285.00
Dutch Girl, 5¼", flowers 35.00
Fireman 100.00
Frowning Face, 5¾" h, unpainted . . 485.00
Garage, 2½" h, aluminum, two car, red 135.00
Gingerbread House, 2½", tin, German 35.00
Gothic Bank, 4⅜", early tin, American 40.00
Globe, 5¾", on stand, eagle finial, red 90.00
Goodyear Zeppelin Hanger, 2⁵⁄₁₆", aluminum 130.00
Helmet, German, 4⅞" l, lead, olive drab, key trap 175.00
High Rise, 5½" h, silver, gold trim . . 65.00
Hot Water Heater, Rex, 7¾" h, green litho finish 20.00
Independence Hall, Tower Bank, bell 220.00
*Junior Cash Register, 5¼", nickel finish 75.00
Mary, 4⅜", lamb 190.00
Mutt and Jeff, 5⅛" h, gold 85.00

Pass Around The Hat, 2⅜", black . . 60.00
Plymouth Rock, 3⅞", dated "1620," white metal 20.00
Porky Pig, 4⁷⁄₁₆", tree trunk, white metal 60.00
Radio, 4½", "Majestic," steel back . . 45.00
Rose Window, 2¼" h, brown japanning 145.00
Safe, 4", "Mascot," tin 25.00
Statue of Liberty, 6⅜", silver 75.00
Stop Sign, 4½", painted 140.00
Stove, 5⅜", "Gas Stove Bank," black 80.00
Taxi, 4", "Yellow Cab," Arcade 240.00
Teddy Roosevelt, 5" h, gold, red and silver trim 145.00
U.S. Mailbox, 4¾", silver 30.00
"White City Puzzle Pail," 3⅛", nickel finish 48.00
Windmill, 3⅜", brass, silvered 65.00

POTTERY

Apple, 2½", redware 90.00
Bear, 12", ceramic, black and white, Hamm's 30.00
Cat
4", head, amber glaze, brown and tan sponging, emb features 110.00
5½", sitting in basket, blue and green 35.00
Donkey, white, Staffordshire 40.00
Duck, 2¾", blue and white spongeware 65.00
Elephant 25.00
Frog, 4" 40.00
Incense Burner 25.00
Kewpie, chalkware, black 50.00
Mail Box, 3¾", U.S. Mail, red, white, and blue 40.00
Owl, 6¾", brown glaze, yellow eyes . . 70.00
Peach, 2⅝", pale yellow and peach . . 50.00
Peacock, 5", multicolored glaze 75.00
Pig
6" l, blue and brown sponge spatter 100.00
10", sewer pipe, tooled eyelashes . . 400.00
Shoe, 5", high button, tan 80.00

BARBER BOTTLES

History: Barber bottles, colorful glass bottles found on shelves and counters in barber shops, held the liquids barbers used daily. A specific liquid was kept in a specific bottle which the barber knew by color, design, or lettering.

The bulk liquids were kept in utilitarian containers under the counter or in a storage room.

Barber bottles are found in many types of glass: art glass with varied decoration, pattern glass, and commercially prepared and labeled bottles.

References: Richard Holiner, *Collecting Barber Bottles*, Collector Books, 1986; Ralph & Terry Kovel, *The Kovels' Bottle Price List, Eighth Edition,*

Crown Publishers, Inc. 1987; Philip L. Krumholz, *Value Guide For Barberiana & Shaving Collectibles*, Ad Libs Publishing Co., 1988.

Note: Prices are for bottles without original stoppers unless otherwise noted.

Amethyst
 6½" h, ribbed, white and red enamel dec, pontil, sheared lip **60.00**
 7½" h, ribbed, green, pink, white, and gold enamel dec, pontil, rolled lip . **130.00**
Art Nouveau, 8" h, cobalt blue, yellow enamel dec, open pontil, rolled lip . . **265.00**
Clear Glass, 7⅛" h, etched dec, village scene, fluted neck, smooth base, rolled lip **120.00**
Cobalt Blue
 6⅝" h, ribbed body, white and gold enamel dec, open pontil, sheared and tooled lip **100.00**
 7⅞" h, ribbed pattern, white enamel and gold gilt dec, open pontil, sheared lip **90.00**
Cranberry, 7⅛" h, hobnail pattern, polished pontil **120.00**
Frosted, 8" h, raised floral design, pontil ground, pr **75.00**
Lavender, 7" h, ribbed body, orange, blue, and white enamel dec, open pontil, rolled lip **110.00**
Mary Gregory
 7⅝" h, yellow green, white enamel dec and "Vegederma," open pontil, rolled lip **630.00**
 8⅛" h, cobalt blue, white enamel dec, open pontils, rolled lips **550.00**
Milk Glass, 8¾" h, hp dec, ferns and "Lac De France," base stamped "R H Hegener Barber Supplies, Minneapolis, Minn" **165.00**
Opalescent, Coin Dot, pink **90.00**

Opalescent, blue ground, 7" h, $115.00.

Opalized
 6⅞" h
  Stars and Stripes pattern, robins egg blue, polished pontil, rolled lip **250.00**
  Swirl Ribbed pattern, turquoise blue, polished pontil, rolled lip . **275.00**
 7" h
  Spanish Lace pattern, white, polished pontil, rolled lip **120.00**
  Stars and Stripes pattern, cranberry and white polished pontil, rolled lip **300.00**
 7⅛" h, cranberry, white Daisy and Fern pattern, melon sides, smooth base, rolled lip **75.00**
 7⅜" h, lemon yellow, melon rib sides, smooth base, rolled lip **60.00**
Spatter Glass, 8¼" h, red and white . . **150.00**
Turquoise Blue, 9" h, ribbed body, green, orange, white, and pink enamel dec, open pontil, rolled lip . . **355.00**

BAROMETERS

History: A barometer is an instrument which measures atmospheric pressure which, in turn, aids weather forecasting. Low pressure indicates the coming of rain, snow, or storm; high pressure signifies fair weather.

Most barometers use an evacuated and graduated glass tube which contains a column of mercury and are classified by the shape of the case. An aneroid barometer has no liquid and works by a needle connected to the top of a metal box in which a partial vacuum is maintained. The movement of the top moves the needle.

Banjo
 38½", mahogany case, hygrometer, thermometer, barometer with balancing level, A & V Cattania **400.00**
 39¼", Regency, mahogany, sgd "A Intross & Co, Chalham," early 19th C **500.00**
 40", Louis XVI, carved giltwood, pierced foliate scrolls and swagged drapery, two lovebirds under laurel arbor cresting, dial inscribed "Robert Op, Passage St Pierre 4 A Versailles," late 18th C **1,210.00**
 45½", mahogany case, broken arch pediment, marked "Lione & Co, 81 Holborn St, London," early 19th C **1,870.00**
Desk, figural, tin, Weather House, chalk man and woman, painted dec, sgd "Alvan Lovejoy, Boston" **170.00**
Stick
 34¼" h, carved giltwood and molded gesso, hexagonal frame, paper dial, France, c1800 . . . . **770.00**

37" h, engraved silvered brass scale, ebonized backboard, Central Scientific Co, Chicago, IL, 1940 .... **130.00**

37¼" h, gimbal, acanthus carved, Rodgerson of Liverpool, 19th C .. **5,175.00**

38" h, mahogany case, carved dec, engraved ivory color dials and silvered brass scale, W Weichert, Cardiff, 1890 .... **440.00**

38½" h
  B Wood, mahogany veneered case, four engraved silvered brass dials, scrolled crest with turned finial, Liverpool, England, c1850 .... **410.00**

  S Lilly, mahogany veneered case, satinwood banding, four engraved silvered brass dials, scrolled crest with brass finial, Edinburgh, 1850 .... **1,150.00**

English, mahogany, inlaid dec, fahrenheit and centigrade scales, marked "Short & Mason, London," 33½" l, 12½" w, $1,400.00.

Wheel
  37⅝" h, rosewood grain painted case, inscribed dial, c1860 .... **550.00**
  39" h, inlaid mahogany case, scrolled pediment crest, shaped base, late 18th C **935.00**
  42" h, mahogany, shaped case, L Solomons, Bath Warantes, Regency period, early 19th C **825.00**

BASKETS

History: Baskets were invented when man first required containers to gather, store, and transport goods. Today's collector, influenced by the country look, focuses on baskets made of splint, rye straw, or willow. Emphasis is placed on handmade examples. Nails or staples, wide splints which are thin and evenly cut, or a wire bail handle denote factory construction which can date back to the mid-19th century. Painted or woven decorated baskets rarely are handmade, unless they are American Indian in origin.

Baskets are collected by (a) type–berry, egg, or field, (b) region–Nantucket or Shaker, and (c) composition–splint, rye, or willow. Stick to examples in very good condition; damaged baskets are a poor investment even at a low price.

References: Frances Johnson, *Wallace-Homestead Price Guide To Baskets, Second Edition*, Wallace-Homestead, 1989; Martha Wetherbee and Nathan Taylor, *Legend of the Bushwhacker Basket*, published by author, 1986; Christoph Will, *International Basketry For Weavers and Collectors*, Schiffer Publishing, Ltd., 1985.

Reproduction Alert: Modern reproductions abound, made by diverse groups ranging from craft revivalists to foreign manufacturers.

Urn shape, natural color, coiled handles, pr, 6½" h, $65.00.

Berry
  8 x 9½ x 5", splint, melon rib, old red paint **200.00**
  10¾ x 11½ x 5½", woven splint, buttocks type, wood handle **125.00**
Cheese, 24" d, woven splint, gray scrubbed finish, blue paint trace ... **475.00**
Egg
  11 x 11 x 6", finely woven splint, bentwood handle **140.00**

13 x 14 x 7½", splint, radiating rib
design, bentwood handle **100.00**
15 x 17", woven splint, bentwood handle, weathered gray scrubbed finial **55.00**
Gathering
13 x 10½ x 7¼", rect, handle on each
end, 19th C **75.00**
17 x 23 x 7¾", woven splint, oblong,
built up rim handles **75.00**
18 x 9 x 13", woven splint, bentwood
handles, faded red and blue design **75.00**
Herb Drying, 20½ x 21¼", loosely
woven, natural splint **355.00**
Laundry
19" d, 11¾" h, round, woven splint,
wrapped rim with hand holds, cop-
per wire woven in bottom **100.00**
19½ x 27", rect, woven splint, wood
bottom, bentwood rim handles,
worn finish **55.00**
20" d, 11½" h, woven splint, wrapped
rim, rect rim handholds, copper
wire laced bottom **125.00**
Market
7" d, 4¼" h, flat woven splint, wrapped
rim, bentwood handle **30.00**
7 x 11", woven splint, wrapped rim,
bentwood handle **100.00**
10" d, 5¼" h, woven splint, wrapped
rim, bentwood swivel handle **225.00**
12" d, 7¾" h, woven splint, wrapped
rim, bentwood handle, brown **335.00**
12½ x 17½", woven splint, wrapped
rim, bentwood handle, open lattice
bottom **100.00**
16 x 14½ x 12", buttocks type, 19th
C **150.00**
18 x 15 x 11", buttocks type, 19th C **150.00**
Nantucket
8" d, circular, swing handle, label
"Made on South Shoals Light Ship
1860 Bought in Nantucket April
1860 T L Allen" on bottom **700.00**
10½" d, round, swing handle **525.00**
13¼" l, oval, swing handle, handwrit-
ten label on bottom **1,400.00**
Picnic, 7¾ x 15 x 6", splint, double
hinged lid, green and natural pattern
int., bentwood handle **110.00**
Sewing, cov, 11½" d, woven splint,
painted pale blue, late 19th C **175.00**
Storage
6¼" d, 3½" h, woven splint, wrapped
rim, small bentwood rim handles . **350.00**
12½ x 19", natural woven splint, overlapping lid, banded design painted
red and blue **75.00**
Utility
6½ x 8¼", wrapped rim, bentwood
handles, green and white painted
floral dec **300.00**
8¾" d, 4¼" h, natural woven splint,

painted blue, yellow, and green
banded design, sgd "Mary Sylves-
ter" **110.00**
9½" d, 7" h, woven splint, bentwood
handle, worn green paint **200.00**
Wall, 11" w, 10½" h, woven splint,
carved loops for hanging, central di-
vider, 19th C **220.00**
Work, 17 x 24", woven splint, bentwood
end handles **50.00**

BATTERSEA ENAMELS

History: Battersea enamel is a generic term for
English enamel-on-copper objects of the 18th century.

In 1753 Stephen Theodore Janssen established
a factory to produce "Trinkets and Curiosities En-
amelled on Copper" at York House, Battersea,
London. Here the new invention of transfer printing developed a high degree of excellence, and the
resulting trifles delighted fashionable Georgian society.

Recent research has shown that enamels actually were being produced in London and the
Midlands several years before York House was
established. However, most enamel trinkets still
are referred to as "Battersea Enamels," even
though they were probably made in other work-
shops in London, Birmingham, Bilston, Wednes-
bury, or Liverpool.

All manner of charming items were made, including snuff and patch boxes bearing mottos and
memory gems. (By adding a mirror inside the lid,
a snuff box became patch box). Many figural whimsies, called "toys," were created to amuse a gay
and fashionable world. Many other elaborate articles, e.g., candlesticks, salts, tea caddies, and
bonbonnières, were made for the tables of the
newly rich middle classes.

Reference: Susan Benjamin, *English Enamel
Boxes*, Merrimack Publishers Circle, 1978.

Advisors: Barbara and Melvin Alpren.

**Box, floral dec, blue ground, gold trim,
2¼ x 3¼", $265.00.**

Bonbonniere, reclining cow, natural colors, grassy mound, floral lid, Bilston, c1770 .... **3,500.00**

Candlesticks, 6" h, pink ground, all–over nosegays, pastels, Bilston, 1770 ... **3,300.00**

Etui, white tapered column, pastoral scenes within reserves, gilt scrolling and diaper work, int. fitted with perfume bottle, writing slide, pencil, and bodkin, Bilston, c1770 .... **2,950.00**

Patch Box

   1¼" round, "A Small Token of Friendship," pink, South Staffordshire, c1780 .... **450.00**

   1½" oval

      Pastoral riverside scene, full color, pale green top and bottom, Bilston, c1780 .... **495.00**

      "Peace and Plenty," cobalt and white doves, Wednesbury, c1780 **695.00**

   1½" rect, "Let us in Love Unite," yellow, white top, Bilston, c1780 .... **495.00**

   1¾" oval, "Virtue is the greatest ornament of the fair," pink base, white and pastel top, South Staffordshire, c1780 .... **595.00**

Potpourri Box, 3½ x 2", reticulated top, floral cut–outs, South Staffordshire, c1770 .... **1,400.00**

Topsy–Turvy Box, 2¼" oval, white, "Before and After Marriage," humorous drawing of couple whose smiles turn into frowns when box is turned upside down, Bilston, c1780 .... **1,200.00**

Traveling Writing Casket, 3 x 1¼ x 1¼", white, blue, and gold enamel all–over geometric pattern, writing implements, polished brass rope mounts, Bilston, c1770 .... **3,900.00**

BAVARIAN CHINA

History: Bavaria, Germany, was an important porcelain production center, similar to the Staffordshire district in England. The name Bavarian China refers to companies operating in Bavaria, among which were Hutschenreuther, Thomas, and Zeh, Scherzer & Co. (Z. S. & Co.). Very little of the production from this area was imported into the United States prior to 1870.

Reference: Susan and Al Bagdade, *Warman's English & Continental Pottery & Porcelain, 2nd Edition,* Wallace–Homestead, 1991.

Bowl, 9½" d, large orange poppies, green leaves dec **65.00**

Celery Tray, 11" l, basket of fruit in center, luster edge, c1900 .... **35.00**

Charger, scalloped rim, game bird in woodland scene, bunches of pink and yellow roses, connecting garlands .. **75.00**

Chocolate Set, chocolate pot, cov, 6 cups and saucers, shaded blue to white, large white leaves, pink, red, and white roses, crown mark **235.00**

Cup and Saucer, roses and foliage, gold handle **20.00**

Dinner Service, 108 pcs, service for 12, serving pcs, Baronet–Belclaire, black and platinum rose, platinum rim, c1950 .... **500.00**

Creamer and Sugar, purple and white pansy dec, marked "Meschendorf, Bavaria," $45.00.

Figurine, 10½" h, dark blue and pale orange marabou standing beside tan and navy cactus, marked "Hutschenreuther Selb– Bavaria, K. Tutter" .. **250.00**

Fish Set, thirteen plates, matching sauceboat, artist sgd **400.00**

Hair Receiver, 3½ x 2½", apple blossom dec, marked "T. S. & Co" **50.00**

Pitcher, 9" h, bulbous, blackberry dec, shaded ground, burnished gold lizard handle, sgd "D. Churchill" **110.00**

Plate

   6" d, salad, gold and white **10.00**

   8½" d, hp, poinsettia dec **45.00**

   9½" d, red berries, green leaves, white ground, scalloped border .. **25.00**

Platter, 16" l, Dresden flowers **90.00**

Portrait Plate, 9" d, side view of lady, sgd "L. B. Chaffee, R. C. Bavaria" . **70.00**

Punch Bowl, hp roses int. and ext., gold pedestal base, marked "H & C" ... **250.00**

Ramekin, underplate, ruffled, small red roses with green foliage, gold rim .. **40.00**

Salt and Pepper Shakers, pink apple blossom sprays, white ground, reticulated gold tops, pr **25.00**

Shaving Mug, pink carnations, marked "Royal Bavarian" **50.00**

Sugar, cov, white, green grapes dec .. **30.00**

Sugar Shaker, hp, pastel pansies **50.00**

Toothpick Holder, barrel shape, pink roses **30.00**

Vase, 4¾" h, hp, florals, sgd **20.00**

BELLEEK

History: Belleek, a thin, ivory colored, almost iridescent–type porcelain, was first made in 1857 in county Fermanagh, Ireland. Production continued until World War I, was discontinued for a period of time, and then resumed. The Shamrock pattern is most familiar, but many patterns were made, including Limpet, Tridacna, and Grasses.

Irish Belleek has several identifying marks, e.g., the Harp and Hound (1865–80) and Harp, Hound, and Castle (1863–91). After 1891 the word "Ireland" or "Erie" was added. Some pieces are marked "Belleek Co., Fermanagh."

There is an Irish saying: If a newly married couple receives a gift of Belleek, their marriage will be blessed with lasting happiness.

Several American firms made a Belleek–type porcelain. The first was Ott and Brewer Co. of Trenton, New Jersey, in 1884, followed by Willets. Other firms included The Ceramic Art Co. (1889), American Art China Works (1892), Columbian Art Co. (1893), and Lenox, Inc. (1904).

Reference: Mary Frank Gaston, *American Belleek,* Collector Books, 1984.

Collectors' Club: The Belleek Collectors' Society, 144 W. Britannia Street, Taunton, MA 02780.

Additional Listings: Lenox.

Abbreviations: 1BM = 1st Black Mark; 2BM = 2nd Black Mark; 3BM = 3rd Black Mark; 4GM = 4th Green Mark; 5GM = 5th Green Mark.

Irish, vase, Princess, second black mark, 9¼" h, $425.00.

AMERICAN

Bowl, 9" d, green, heavy gold trim, white curled handle, Lenox green wreath mark	90.00
Cup and Saucer, 6" h, square pedestal base, undecorated, Willets brown mark	35.00
Demitasse Cup, liner, gold band border, SS holder with saucer, Lenox green wreath mark	55.00
Dresser Set, cov powder box, pin tray, buffer and container, nail brush, pin cushion, hp violets, artist sgd "M.R.", Willets brown mark, 6 pcs	550.00
Dresser Tray, roses	115.00

Figure

4" h

Elephant, white, Lenox green wreath mark	315.00
Swan, green, Lenox green wreath mark	65.00
Loving Cup, three handles, wine keeper in wine cellar, artist sgd, SS repoussé collar, CAC mark	185.00
Mask, 7½" h, lady's face, black, Lenox green wreath mark	175.00
Mug, hp, gooseberries, artist sgd	125.00
Perfume, figural, rabbit, white, Lenox green wreath mark, pr	525.00
Pitcher, 5½" h, body indentation, tree branch shaped handle, gold paste floral dec, Willets brown mark	375.00
Powder Box, 4 x 6", pink, gold wheat on lid, Lenox green wreath mark	40.00

Salt

1" d, gold rim, Willets brown mark	15.00
2" d, gold ftd, green ground, pink rose ext., single pink rose int., gold rim, CAC mark	25.00
Salt and Pepper Shakers, pr, 1" d salt, 2" h egg shape pepper, pink roses, Lenox green palette mark	35.00

Vase

8½" h, bulbous shape, pine cone and branches decor, Lenox green wreath mark	55.00
12" h, 8½" d, applied handles, floral ground, artist sgd, CAC mark	475.00

IRISH

Ashtray, 4½" d, shamrock horseshoe, 4GM	45.00

Basket

8" d, Melvin, sq, decorative border, twig handles, turquoise–blue, four applied violet floral sprays, green leaves	550.00
8½" d, Sydenham, three strands, circular, twig handles, four applied flo-	

ral sprays, pearl luster glaze, imp
mark **990.00**
Box, cov, 3" h, Forget–Me–Not, ftd,
globular, applied flowerheads, conical
knop, pearl luster glaze, 3BM **385.00**
Cup and Saucer, 6" d, 2" h, Shamrock
pattern, 2BM **200.00**
Cake Plate
   Limpet pattern, 2BM **175.00**
   Shamrock pattern, 3BM **125.00**
Creamer, Lotus pattern, green handle,
2BM **75.00**
Creamer and Sugar
   Lily pattern, 5GM **45.00**
   Lotus pattern, 5GM **45.00**
   Tridacna, green rim, 3BM **115.00**
Dish, 6½" w, heart shape, 3BM **95.00**
Figure
   3½" h, Terrier, 4GM **35.00**
   4½" h, Swan, 3BM **65.00**
   14⅝" h
      Affection, multicolored, 1BM **2,500.00**
      Meditation, multicolored, 1BM . . . **2,500.00**
Flower Holder, 3½" h, Seahorse, one
with white head, other with brown,
1BM, pr **1,200.00**
Sandwich Tray, Mask pattern, 2BM . . . **275.00**
Sugar
   Cleary pattern, 3BM **60.00**
   Shamrock pattern, cov, 3BM **65.00**
Tea and Dessert Service, Eugene
Sheran, partially decorated, c1887,
32 pcs **7,900.00**
Tea Set, Grass Ware, 3⅜" h teapot,
creamer, cov sugar, waste bowl, two
teacups and saucers, pink highlights,
purple luster, brown and gilt trim, 1BM **880.00**
Tub, 3¼" d, Shamrock pattern, 3BM . . **55.00**
Vase, Shamrock pattern
   6¼" h, tree trunk, 2BM **145.00**
   6½" h, harp, 5GM **40.00**
   7⅞" h, panel, yellow gilt, 6GM **65.00**

BELLS

History: Bells have been used for centuries for
many different purposes. They have been traced
as far back as 2697 B.C., though at that time they
did not have any true tone. One of the oldest bells
is the "crotal," a tiny sphere with small holes and
a ball or stone or metal inside. This type now
appears as sleigh bells.

True bell making began when bronze, the mixing
of tin and copper, was discovered. There are now
many types of materials of which bells are made—
almost as many materials as there are uses for
them.

Bells of the late 19th century show a high degree
of workmanship and artistic style. Glass bells from
this period are examples of the glass blower's talent and the glass manufacturer's product.

Collectors' Club: American Bell Association,
Rt. 1, Box 286, Natronia Heights, PA 15065.

Additional Listings: See *Warman's Americana
& Collectibles* for more examples.

**Porcelain, figural, peasant woman,
multicolored, unglazed clapper,
marked "Bayeux," French Faience, 8¼"
h, $85.00.**

Bicycle, eagle, cast brass, nickel plated **85.00**
Church Steeple, cast iron, Hollsboro,
OH, 1886 . . . . **220.00**
Desk
   Bronze, white marble base, side tap,
   c1875 . . . . **45.00**
   Silverplate, windup, open filigree
   skirt, top knob **85.00**
Dinner
   3¾" h, SS, spot hammered, applied
   leaves and pods, baluster form
   handle with inlaid polychrome
   enamel design, Tiffany & Co, New
   York, 1879–85 . . . . **5,500.00**
   4¼" h, chased foliage design, applied
   cast copper and brass ornament,
   tapered cylindrical handle, silver
   clapper, marked "Dominick & Haff,"
   1880 . . . . **1,100.00**
Glass
   Amethyst, flint, metal lace trim,
   painted crowing rooster on top of
   handle **350.00**
   Burmese, 6¼" h, shaded deep pink
   to ivory, satin finish **70.00**
   Custard, "Alamo–Built 1718, San An-
   tonio, TX," gilt band **90.00**
   Heisey, frosted, Victorian Belle **125.00**
   Vaseline, flint, ornate metal lace trim,
   elephant with green eyes and red
   mouth on top of handle **325.00**
Hand, figural, brass
   Bust, 3⅝" h, lady, quilted pattern bell **35.00**

Monk, 5″ h, carrying umbrella and basket	**75.00**
Turtle, bell bracket and striker on shell	**30.00**
Locomotive, 17 x 17″, brass, cradle and yoke	**800.00**
Marriage, 12″ h, brown, clear fancy handle	**125.00**
School	
6″ h, brass, handled	**25.00**
6½″ h, hand, brass, turned maple handle, marked "No 6"	**65.00**
Ship, brass	**30.00**
Sleigh	
Four bells, 12″ l, nickel plated shaft, arched strap	**45.00**
Thirty bells, leather strap	**125.00**
Table, 4⅝″ h, SS, cupid blowing horn, figural handle, frosted finish, foliate strap work border, Gorham Mfg Co, c1870	**725.00**

J. NORTON
BENNINGTON
VT.

BENNINGTON AND BENNINGTON-TYPE POTTERY

History: In 1845 Christopher Webber Fenton joined Julius Norton, his brother-in-law, in the manufacturing of stoneware pottery in Bennington, Vermont. Fenton sought to expand the company's products and glazes; Norton wanted to concentrate solely on stoneware. In 1847 Fenton broke away and established his own factory.

Fenton introduced the famous Rockingham glaze, developed in England and named after the Marquis of Rockingham, to America. In 1849 he patented a flint enamel glaze, "Fenton's Enamel," which added flecks, spots, or streaks of color (usually blues, greens, yellows, and oranges) to the brown Rockingham glaze. Forms included candlesticks, coachman bottles, cow creamers, poodles, sugar bowls, and toby pitchers.

Fenton produced the little known scroddled ware, commonly called lava or agate ware. Scroddled ware is composed of different colored clays, mixed with cream colored clay, molded, turned on a potter's wheel, coated with feldspar and flint, and fired. It was not produced in quantity, as there was little demand for it.

Fenton also introduced Parian ware to America. Parian was developed in England in 1842 and known as "Statuary ware." Parian is a translucent porcelain which has no glaze and resembles marble. Bennington made the blue and white variety in the form of vases, cologne bottles, and trinkets.

Five different marks were used, with many variations. Only about twenty percent of the pieces carried any mark; some forms were almost always marked, others never. Marks: (a) 1849 mark (4 variations) for flint enamel and Rockingham; (b) E. Fenton's Works, 1845–47, on Parian and occasionally on scroddled ware; (c) U. S. Pottery Co., ribbon mark, 1852–58, on Parian and blue and white porcelain; (d) U. S. Pottery Co., lozenge mark, 1852–58, on Parian; and (e) U. S. Pottery, oval mark, 1853–58, mainly on scroddled ware.

The hound handled pitcher is probably the best known Bennington piece. Hound handled pitchers also were made by some 30 potteries in over 55 different variations. Rockingham glaze was used by over 150 potteries in 11 states, mainly the Mid-West, between 1830 and 1900.

References: Richard Carter Barret, *How To Identify Bennington Pottery*, Stephen Greene Press, 1964; Laura Woodside Watkins, *Early New England Potters And Their Wares*, Harvard University Press, 1950.

Museums: Bennington Museum, Bennington, VT; East Liverpool Museum of Ceramics, East Liverpool, OH.

Additional Listings: Stoneware.

Bennington, Snuff Jar, figural, toby, 1850 mark, $395.00.

BENNINGTON POTTERY

Bank, 7″ h, globular, mottled flint enamel glaze, short stem, circular foot, spiral finial, imp owner's name	**165.00**
Book Flask, flint enamel	
Bennington Battle, letter "J" marked on bottom	**475.00**
Bennington Companion, 10¾″, dark brown, amber, blue and green glaze, repaired	**700.00**
Departed Spirits, 5¾″, mottled brown glaze	**350.00**
Untitled, "470" marked on spine . . .	**225.00**

Bottle, figural, coachman
  10⅜" h, Rockingham glaze, dated
    1849 . . . . 250.00
  10¾" h, wearing tricorn hat, mottled
    brown Rockingham glaze, green
    specks, dated 1849 . . . . 700.00
Candlestick, 6¾" h, columnar, yellow–
  brown, flint enamel, blue glaze 400.00
Creamer, 5½" h, figural, cow, Rockingham glaze, imp "N" 300.00
Cuspidor, diamond pattern
  8" d, scroddled ware, squatty waisted
    form 550.00
  8½" d, cylindrical body, waisted sides,
    mottled flint enamel glaze 275.00
Dish, 9¼", flint enamel, marked "Fenton
  Co," 1849 . . . . 400.00
Foot Bath, 19½" l, flint enamel, brown
  and cream mottled glaze, blue and
  amber highlights, Scalloped Rib pattern, crack beside handle 700.00
Frame, flint, scalloped edge, holds 3 x
  3¼" picture 425.00
Goblet, 4½" h, Rockingham glaze 275.00
Pitcher
  7⅜", baluster, Tulip & Heart pattern,
    mottled flint enamel glaze, angled
    handle 850.00
  7¾" h, Parian, Sunflower pattern, rib-
    bon mark 190.00
  8", Parian, white, tulip and sunflower
    pattern, c1852 . . . . 225.00
  8¼", Parian, Pond Lily pattern, ribbon
    mark 165.00
  9" h, seated hunter and hounds
    scene, glazed 175.00
  9½", Rockingham glaze 1,000.00
  10" h, parian, Cascade pattern, imp
    "United States Pottery Co, Ben-
    nington, VT" 150.00
Pitcher and Washbowl Set, 10½"
  pitcher, 13 x 4⅜" bowl, Diamond pattern, flint enamel glaze, orange, yellow, and green, 1849 mark 950.00
Snuff Jar, 4", toby hat, Rockingham
  glaze, Fenton, 1849 mark 400.00
Soap Dish, 5¼", flint enamel, olive
  brown and cream, glazed, green
  flecks, dated 1849 . . . . 125.00
Teapot, 7⅜" h, flint enamel, Alternate
  Rib pattern, marked 500.00
Vase
  8" h, parian, youth and maid, oversize
    sheaf 35.00
  8⅞" h, Belleek type, eagle form, tow
    small chips 200.00
  9½" h, waisted cylindrical, Paul & Vir-
    ginia pattern, relief molded figures
    and landscape scene, blue ground,
    ftd 350.00
  9¾" h, tulip, scroddled, variegated
    brown clays 1,500.00

BENNINGTON–TYPE

Figure, 3" h, monkey, glazed 125.00
Food Mold, 6⅝", turk's head, Rock-
  ingham glaze 90.00
Mixing Bowl, 14¼ x 5¼", Rockingham
  glaze 190.00

Bennington Type, pitcher, seated cupid, scalloped top, medium brown, shaped handle, 7" h, $145.00.

Pitcher, 10½", paneled, Rockingham
  glaze, c1850 . . . . 225.00
Soap Dish, 4 x 2½", round, Rockingham
  glaze 100.00

BISCUIT JARS

History: The biscuit or cracker jar was the fore-runner of the cookie jar. They were made of various materials by leading glassworks and potteries of the late 19th and early 20th centuries.

Note: All items listed have silver plated mountings unless otherwise noted.

Bristol
  6½" h, allover enameled pink, blue,
    white, and yellow floral dec, green
    leaves, silver plated top, rim, and
    handle 110.00
  7½" h, tan enameled trees and her-
    ons, silver plated rim, lid, and han-
    dle, strawberry finial 200.00
Cased Glass, 6¼" h, blue, enameled,
  pink roses and green leaves, silver
  plated top, rim, and handle 135.00
Cranberry, 9 x 6¼", clear feet, flower
  prunt underneath, and ribbed finial
  knob, two clear ring applied handles 170.00
Emerald Green, 7¾" h, white and pink

Jasperware, white classical cameos, black ground, silverplated handle, rim, and lid, imp "Wedgwood," 6" h, $425.00.

enameled daisies and gold leaves dec, brass top, rim, and handle	**200.00**
Loetz Type, 6½" h, translucent white mother–of–pearl irid, green raindrop spatter, melon swirls, plated lid, rim, and handle	**200.00**
Nippon, 4½ x 7¼", sq, white, multicolored floral bands, gold outlines and trim, marked "E E"	**85.00**
Pairpoint, 9½" h, burnt orange, floral dec, blown–out floral base, sgd	**325.00**
Royal Bayreuth	
Poppy, red, blue mark	**650.00**
Tomato	**265.00**
Satin Glass, 7¼" h, pink, shell pattern base, enameled floral dec, SP lid and handle	**300.00**
Stevens and Williams, 5½ x 7¾", amber and green applied leaves, cream opaque ext., deep pink int., SP rim, lid, and handle	**275.00**
Vaseline, 7" h, threaded, silver plated rim, lid, and handle	**145.00**
Wave Crest, 5½ x 9", yellow roses, molded multicolored swirl ground, incised floral and leaf dec on lid, marked "Quadruple Plate"	**390.00**
Wedgwood, 5¼ x 7¾", jasperware, white floral dec, lavender ground, acorn finial, artist sgd "Barnard" . . .	**710.00**

BISQUE

History: Bisque or biscuit china is the name given to wares that have been fired once and are not glazed.

Bisque figurines and busts were popular during the Victorian era, being used on fireplace mantels, dining room buffets, and end tables. Manufacturing was centered in the United States and Europe. By the mid–20th century the Japanese were the principal source of bisque items, especially character related items.

Reference: Susan and Al Bagdade, *Warman's English & Continental Pottery & Porcelain, 2nd Edition,* Wallace–Homestead, 1991; Elyse Karlin, *Children Figurines of Bisque and Chinawares, 1850–1950,* Schiffer Publishing, Ltd., 1990.

Box, egg shape, relief windmill scene, ftd	**45.00**
Dish, cov, 9 x 6½ x 5½", dog, brown and white, green blanket, white and gilt basketweave base	**500.00**

Figures, boy and girl, classical period dress, pale blue and white, unmarked, French, pr, $1,900.00.

Figure	
Babies, 3 pcs, crying, sitting, crawling, marked "Japan"	**25.00**
Bonnie Prince Charlie, 8", French . .	**30.00**
Man offering lady a rose, Victorian costumes, polychrome, 20¾" h, German, 19th C, pr	**300.00**
Mother dog teaching two puppies how to read, one puppy on red pillow, tan book base, 3¼" h	**65.00**
Flower Pot, figural, carriage, four wheels, pale blue and pink, white ground, gold dots, royal markings dec	**140.00**
Match Holder, figural	
Dog, dressed in man's clothing and top hat, Germany	**70.00**
Dutch girl, copper and gold trim . . .	**35.00**
Nodder	
2½ x 3½", jester, seated holding pipe, pastel peach and white, gold trim .	**75.00**

3½" h, hobo, holding walking stick, green coat, tan pants, bottle in pocket	**210.00**
4¼" h, lady seated, white and turquoise Oriental style robe, gold trim, holding fan	**150.00**

Piano Baby

Crawling crying, marked "Made in Japan"	**15.00**
Lying on stomach, wearing bib, dog and cat, 6¾" l, Germany	**100.00**
Planter, girl with water jug, sitting by well, coral and green	**50.00**
Salt, 3" d, figural, walnut, cream, branch base, matching spoon	**70.00**
Tobacco Jar, figural, boy, hair forms cov, marked "Heubach"	**150.00**
Wall Plaque, pr, 10¼" d, light green, scrolled and pierced scallop, white relief figures in center, man playing mandolin, lady wearing hat, c1900	**250.00**

BITTERS BOTTLES

History: Bitters, a "remedy" made from natural herbs and other mixtures with an alcohol base, often was viewed as the universal cure-all. The names given to various bitter mixtures were imaginative, though the bitters seldom cured what their makers claimed.

The manufacturers of bitters needed a way to sell and advertise their products. They designed bottles in many shapes, sizes, and colors to attract the buyer. Many forms of advertising, including trade cards, billboards, signs, almanacs, and novelties proclaimed the virtues of a specific bitter.

During the Civil War a tax was levied on alcoholic beverages. Since bitters were identified as medicines, they were exempt from this tax. The alcohol content was never mentioned. In 1907 when the Pure Foods Regulations went into effect, "an honest statement of content on every label" put most of the manufacturers out of business.

References: Carlyn Ring, *For Bitters Only*, 1980; J. H. Thompson, *Bitters Bottles*, Century House, 1947; Richard Watson, *Bitters Bottles*, Thomas Nelson and Sons, 1965.

Periodical: *Antique Bottle and Glass Collector*, P.O. Box 187, East Greenville, PA 18041.

A S Hopkins Union Stomach Bitters, 9¾" h, greenish–yellow, applied tapered collar lip, smooth base	**255.00**
Alpine Herb Bitters, 9⅝" h, amber, sq, smooth base, tooled lip	**165.00**
Baker's Orange Grove Bitters, 9½" h, yellowish amber, smooth base, applied mouth	**175.00**
Bell's Cocktail Bitters Jas M Bell & Co, New York, 10½" h, amber, applied ring, smooth base	**440.00**

Augauer Bitters, green, paper label front and back, $85.00.

Berkshire Bitters Amann & Co, Cincinnati, OH, 4" h, pig shape, emb, golden amber, sheared lip, smooth base	**660.00**
Big Bill Best Bitters, 12" h, amber, smooth base, tooled lip, emb lead neck seal, orig contents	**120.00**
Browns Celebrated Indian Herb Bitters/ Patented Feb 11, 1868, 12¼" h, figural, emb, golden amber, ground lip, smooth base	**330.00**
Bourbon Whiskey Bitters, 9¾" h, barrel shape, cherry puce, applied sq collar, smooth base	**500.00**
Buhrers Gentian Bitters, 9⅛" h, amber, smooth base, applied mouth	**75.00**
Caldwell's Herb Bitters/The Great Tonic, triangular, beveled and lattice work panels, yellow–amber, applied tapered lip, iron pontil	**385.00**
Clarke's Vegetable Sherry Wine Bitters, 14" h, aqua, smooth base, applied mouth	**550.00**
Dr A S Hopkins Union Stomach Bitters, Hartford, CT, 9⅝" h, yellow, olive tint, sq, smooth base, applied mouth	**120.00**
Dr Loew's Celebrated Stomach Bitters & Nerve Tonic, 9¼" h, green, smooth base, tooled lip	**125.00**
Dr Petzold's Genuine German Bitters, Incpt 1862, The Great Elixir of Life, 6¾" h, amber, smooth base, tooled lip	**210.00**
Drake's Plantation Bitters, 9¾" h, puce, tapered lip, smooth base, Arabesque design	**265.00**
Godfrey's Celebrated Cordial Bitters, NY, 10" h, aqua, pontil, applied mouth	**1,210.00**
Greeley's Bourbon Bitters, barrel shape, 9¼" h, smokey grayish– brown, sq collared lip, smooth base	**190.00**
H P Herb's Wild Cherry Bitters, Reading, PA, 9¾" h, cabin shape, amber, smooth base	**265.00**

Hall's Bitters, 9¼" h, barrel shape, yellow, sq collar, smooth base **265.00**

Hibernia Bitters, 9¾" h, amber, sq, smooth base, tooled lip **80.00**

Holtzermans Patent Stomach Bitters, 9¾" h, cabin shape, amber, sloping collar, smooth base **140.00**

Hops & Malt Bitters, 9⅜" h, golden amber, tapered collar lip, smooth base . **220.00**

Hygeia Bitters, Fox & Co, 8⅜" h, amber, smooth base, applied mouth **120.00**

Kelly's Old Cabin Bitters, 9" h, cabin shape, amber, sloping collar lip, smooth base **710.00**

Keystone Bitters, 9¾" h, barrel shape, golden amber, applied tapered collar, sq lip, smooth base **140.00**

McKeever's Army Bitters, 10⅝" h, amber, sloping collared lip, smooth base **1,590.00**

Mist of the Morning Sole Agents Barnett & Lumley, 9¾" h, golden amber, sloping collar lip, smooth base **220.00**

Morning Bitters, Incep Tum 5869, 12⅞" h, triangular shape, amber, applied tapered collar lip, iron pontil **200.00**

National Bitters, 12⅝" h, corn cob shape, puce amber, applied ring lip, smooth base **330.00**

Old Sachem Bitters and Wigwam Tonic, 9½" h, barrel shape, deep wine to amethyst, smooth base, applied mouth **470.00**

Red Jacket Bitters, Monheimer & Co, 9½" h, sq, amber, smooth base, tooled lip **90.00**

Rex Kidney and Liver Bitters, The Best laxative and Blood Purifier, 9⅝" h, amber, smooth base, ABM lip, orig contents **70.00**

Schroeder's Bitters, Louisville, KY, 11¾" h, amber, smooth base, tooled lip . . **360.00**

Simon's Centennial Bitters, 9⅞" h, George Washington bust shape, aqua, smooth base, applied mouth . **600.00**

Sol Frank's Panacea Bitters, Frank Hayman & Rhine/Sole Proprietors, New York, 10¼" h, lighthouse shape, amber, sloping collar, ring lip, smooth base **500.00**

S O Richardson's Bitters, South Reading, MA, 7" h, deep aqua to teal, open pontil, applied mouth **220.00**

Suffolk Bitters, Philbrook & Tucker, Boston, 10⅛" l, pig shape, amber, smooth base, applied mouth **500.00**

Sunny Castle Stomach Bitters, Jos Dudenhoefer, Milwaukee, 9" h, sq, amber, smooth base, tooled lip **90.00**

The Fish Bitters/W H Ware Patented 1866, 11¾" h, amber, olive tint, flattened sq collar lip, smooth base . . . **190.00**

Warner's Safe Bitters, 7⅜" h, amber, smooth base, applied mouth **250.00**

Yoghim Bros Celebrated Stomach Bitters, 8¾" h, golden amber, tapered collar lip, smooth base **220.00**

Zingari Bitters, 11⅞" h, amber, smooth base, applied mouth **120.00**

BLACK MEMORABILIA

History: The term "Black memorabilia" refers to a broad range of collectibles that often overlap other collecting fields, e.g., toys, post cards, etc. It also encompasses African artifacts, items created by slaves or related to the slavery era, modern Black cultural contributions to literature, art, etc., and material associated with the Civil Rights Movement and the Black experience throughout history.

The earliest known examples of Black memorabilia include primitive African designs and tribal artifacts. Black Americana dates back to the arrival of African natives upon American shores.

The advent of the 1900s saw an incredible amount and variety of material depicting Blacks, most often in a derogatory and dehumanizing manner that clearly reflected the stereotypical attitude held toward the Black race during this period. The popularity of Black portrayals in this unflattering fashion flourished as the century wore on.

As the growth of the Civil Rights Movement escalated and aroused public awareness to the Black plight, attitudes changed. Public outrage and pressure eventually put a halt to these offensive stereotypes during the early 1950s.

Black representations are still being produced in many forms, but no longer in the demoralizing designs of the past. These modern objects, while not as historically significant as earlier examples, will become the Black memorabilia of tomorrow.

References: Patiki Gibbs, *Black Collectibles Sold In America*, Collector Books, 1987; Patiki Gibbs and Tyson Gibbs, *The Collector's Encyclopedia of Black Dolls*, Collector Books, 1987; Douglas Congdon Martin, *Images in Black: 150 years of Black Collectibles*, Schiffer Publishing, Ltd., 1990; Dawn Reno, *Collecting Black Americana*, Crown Publishing Co., 1986; Darrell A. Smith, *Black Americana: A Personal Collection*, Black Relics, Inc., 1988; Jackie Young, *Black Collectibles: Mammy and Her Friends*, Schiffer Publishing, Ltd., 1988.

Periodical: *Black Ethnic Collectibles*, 1401 Asbury Court, Hyattsville, MD 20782.

Reproduction Alert. Reproductions are becoming an increasing problem, from advertising signs (Bull Durham tobacco) to mechanical banks (Jolly Nigger). If the object looks new to you, chances are that it is new.

Advertising
Box, 11½″ w, Masons Challenge
Blacking, wood, paper label **75.00**
Fan, Coon Chicken Inn **25.00**
Poster, 14½ x 22½″, O'Baby Choco-
late Dairy Drink, cardboard, multi-
colored **140.00**

**Advertising Trade Card, Howe Scales,
black trapped in cotton bale being
weighed, multicolored scene, printed
by Donaldson Brothers, NY, adv on
back for Howe Scales, Bordon Shelleck
& Co, Chicago, St. Louis, $10.00.**

Sign
Old Time Gingerbread Molasses,
26 x 20″, paper, litho, pictures
Mammy, c1900 . . . .   **4,750.00**
Runnymede Club Whiskey, 6¼ x
20″, black and white photo of
nine black babies, c1897 . . . . .   **650.00**
Tin, 11″ h, C D Kenney, Mammy's
Favorite Brand Coffee **125.00**
Tray
Harvard Brewing Co, 12″ d, couple
being served by black waiter,
1920 . . . .   **130.00**
Straight Whiskey, 12″ d, black man
standing by horse, 1905–15 . . .   **325.00**
Ashtray, 4″ h figure, tray between legs,
boy eating watermelon, ceramic and
glass, black, yellow, red, and green .   **45.00**
Bank
3″ h, two–faced boy, cast iron, painted   **55.00**
5¼″ h, mammy with hands on hips,
cast iron, painted, red, white, blue,
and brown **45.00**
5½″ h, sharecropper, cast iron,
painted, gold, black, and red **110.00**
5¾″ h, mammy with spoon, cast iron,
painted, gold **18.00**
6″ h, Jolly N, mechanical, aluminum   **385.00**

Bell, 4″ h, Mammy, silvered metal,
painted wood and cloth **25.00**
Bottle, Mammy **150.00**
Cigar Cutter, 6½″ h, cast iron figure,
wood base, painted, depressing right
arm activates mouth cutter, Rohlfing
& Co **575.00**
Clock, 8½″ h, painted composition male
face, pendulum tin tie, eyes move,
Lux **385.00**
Cookie Jar
Chef **245.00**
Mammy
Mosaic Tile, yellow dress **575.00**
National Silver **300.00**
Pearl China **900.00**
Creamer and Sugar, F & F **90.00**
Dexterity Puzzle, 2½″ d, woman, emb
litho tin, mirror on reverse, Germany   **25.00**
Doll
8″ h, composition head, wood arms
and legs, multicolored cloth dress,
painted **250.00**
18″ h, Cream of Wheat, cloth, apron
and hat, red, white, and blue **80.00**
Doorstop, 13½″ h, Mammy, cast iron,
painted, Littco label **250.00**
Figure
African Woman, 5¼″ h, cast iron, removable head basket, yellow and
green **220.00**
Boy with cigar, 3¾″ h, lead, painted,
red, yellow, and green **12.50**
Sprinklin' Sambo, wood, orig label . .   **195.00**
Woman, 5″ h, seated, wearing yellow
and green ball gown, head moves,
composition, painted **12.00**

**Gum, Goudey's Pick–A–Ninny Chew-
img Gum, Goudey Gum Co, Boston,
MA, blue letters, orange ground, $5.00.**

Game
Amos & Andy Acrobat Figures, MIB,
1940s **65.00**
Chocolate Splash, target game, Willis
G Young Mfg, Chicago, 1916 copy-
right **100.00**
Little Black Sambo Target Game,
litho metal, stand, 23″ h **80.00**

Mammy Ring Toss Game, 12″ h, paper wood and metal figure with cloth covering, wood base, four wood rings 90.00

Grocery List, Mammy, "We Needs," wood, orig pegs 65.00

Hitching Post, 25″ h, jockey shape, repainted, 19th C 250.00

Lunch Box, Dixie Kid Tobacco, tin, black child 150.00

Match Holder, 5¾″ h, ceramic, woman, scalloped collar and sleeves 30.00

Menu, Coon Chicken Inn 35.00

Mug, 5″ h, ceramic, black butler with food tray, titled "Junior Feed 1915" . 75.00

Nodder, 7″ h, ceramic, baby, seated holding fruit, wearing straw hat and earrings 40.00

Pencil Holder, 5½″ l, celluloid, alligator with black's head in mouth, c1930 .. 15.00

Perfume Bottle, miniature, black boy, pr 16.00

Pie Bird, Chef 30.00

Planter, boy with watermelon, black and gold 20.00

Post Card, Pickaninnies photo, 1912 . 15.00

Ring Holder, wall type, negro 30.00

Salt and Pepper Shaker, pr, boys seated on green peas 35.00

Sheet Music
  Aunt Jemima's Picnic Day, 1914 ... 20.00
  My Sugar Coated Chocolate Boy, 1919 .... 10.00
  When The Coons Are On The Move, 1901, matted and framed 55.00

Spice Set, Negro, four containers, wood rack 40.00

String Holder, plaster, boy, bending beside watermelon 30.00

Teapot, Mammy, Weller 985.00

Toaster Cover, Mammy, marked "Souvenir of New Orleans" 30.00

Toy
  Bojangle Dances Again, 8½″ h, mechanical, stenciled wood figure, litho tin base, arms and hat, orig box, Clown Toy Mfg 170.00
  Boy on horse, 5¼″ h, tin boy, wood horse, wheeled platform, painted . 25.00
  Dancers, 8″ h, wind–up, litho tin, cut–out figures 235.00
  Jazzbo–Jim, 9″ h, wind–up, litho tin, Unique Art 250.00
  Sweeping Maid, 8″ h, wind–up, litho tin, red, yellow, green, and white, Lindstrom Corp 170.00

Wall Plaque, 5 x 8″, youngster with pigtails, red parasol, gray dress, yellow accents, c1950 .... 20.00

Water Sprinkler, Mammy 150.00

Wall Hanging, 6″ h, ceramic, bust of girl with watermelon, painted 45.00

Wall Memo, Mammy, plastic 60.00

BLOWN THREE MOLD

History: The Jamestown colony in Virginia introduced glass making into America. The artisans used a "free blown" method.

Blowing molten glass into molds was not introduced into America until the early 1800s. Blown three mold glass used a pre–designed mold that consisted of two, three, or more hinged parts. The glass maker placed a quantity of molten glass on the tip of a rod or tube, inserted it into the mold, blew air into the tube, waited until the glass cooled, and removed the finished product. The three part mold is the most common and lends its name to this entire category.

The impressed decorations on blown mold glass usually are reversed, i.e., what is raised or convex on the outside will be concave on the inside. This is useful in identifying the blown form.

By 1850 American made glassware was in relatively common usage. The increased demand led to large factories and the creation of a technology which eliminated the smaller companies.

Reference: George S. and Helen McKearin, *American Glass,* reprint, Crown Publishers, 1941, 1948.

Collectors' Club: National Early American Glass Club, 7417 Allison Street, Hyattsville, MD 20784.

Bottle, olive amber, Keene, McKearin GIII–16 .... 185.00

Bowl, 5⅝″ d, clear, folded rim, pontil, twelve diamond base, McKearin GII–6 .... 90.00

Celery Vase, Pittsburgh, GV–21 ..... 650.00

Cordial, 2⅞″ h, clear, ringed base, pontil, heavy circular foot, formed free hand, McKearin GII–16 .... 450.00

Decanter, olive amber, Keene, NH, McKearin G–III–16, $475.00.

Creamer, 3½" h, applied handle **90.00**
Cruet, 7¾" h, cobalt blue, scroll scale pattern, ribbed base, pontil, applied handle, French **250.00**
Decanter
  McKearin GI–18, 7" h, clear, pt **110.00**
  McKearin GII–43, clear, mushroom stopper, 1½ pt **990.00**
  McKearin GIII–2, clear pt **140.00**
  McKearin GIII–19, amethyst, missing stopper **100.00**
  McKearin GV–12, clear, qt **110.00**
  McKearin GV–14, pr, clear, baroque, matching stopper, qt **385.00**
  McKearin GV–17, clear, Horn of Plenty pattern, qt **770.00**
Dish, clear
  5¼" d, McKearin GII–16 . . . . **55.00**
  5½" d, McKearin GII–18 . . . . **40.00**
  6¼" d, McKearin GII–16 . . . . **165.00**
Flask
  5¼" h, clear, arch and diamond pattern, sheared mouth, pontil, Continental **300.00**
  7¼" h, deep yellow–green, chemical deposit on one rib, plain base, McKearin GI–22, ex–William Elsholz and George S McKearin collections **1,250.00**
Flip Glass, clear
  5½" h, McKearin GII–18 . . . . **140.00**
  5⅞" h, McKearin GIII–22 . . . . **220.00**
  6" h, McKearin GII–18 . . . . **100.00**
Inkwell
  Amber, McKearin GIII–29 . . . . **80.00**
  Deep olive amber, McKearin GIII–29 **90.00**
Miniature
  Decanter, 2⅝" h, clear, McKearin GIII–12 . . . . **140.00**
  Tumbler, 1¾" h, clear, McKearin GII–16 . . . . **35.00**
Mustard, 4¼" h, clear, pontil, cork stopper, orig paper label, McKearin GI–15 **45.00**
Pitcher
  7" h, clear, base of handle reglued, McKearin GIII–5 . . . . **120.00**
  8⅛", clear, Horn of Plenty pattern, applied hollow blown handle, McKearin GV–17, ex–William Elsholz and George S. McKearin collections **2,400.00**
Salt, basket shape, clear **110.00**
Sauce Dish, 4⁹⁄₁₆", deep purple–blue, McKearin GIII–23, ex–William Elsholz and Crawford Wettlaufer collections . **3,250.00**
Toilet Bottle, 5⅞", light yellow–green, orig stopper, McKearin GI–3, Type 2, ex–William Elsholz collection **700.00**
Vase, 9" h, clear, engraved flowers, leaves, and berries, Mckearin GV–21 **7,260.00**
Vinegar Bottle, cobalt blue
  Ribbed, stopper, McKearin GI–7 . . . **275.00**

Swirled, stopper, McKearin GI–13 . . **385.00**
Whiskey Glass, 2⅜" h, clear, applied handle, McKearin GII–18 . . . . **275.00**

BOEHM PORCELAINS

History: Edward Marshall Boehm was born on August 21, 1913. Boehm's childhood was spent at the McConogh School, a rural Baltimore County, Maryland, school dedicated to caring for homeless boys. He studied animal husbandry at the University of Maryland, serving as manager of Longacre Farms on the Eastern Shore of Maryland upon graduation. During World War II, Boehm joined the Air Force and was assigned as a therapist to a convalescent center in Pawling, New York. After the war, he moved to Great Neck, Long Island, and worked as an assistant veterinarian.

In 1949 Boehm quit his job to open a potter studio in Trenton, New Jersey. His initial sculptures consisted of Herefords, Percherons, and dogs done in hard-paste porcelain. The first five to six years were a struggle, with several partnerships beginning and ending during the period. In the early 1950s Boehm's art porcelain sculptures began appearing in major department stores. When Eisenhower presented a Boehm sculpture to Queen Elizabeth and Prince Philip during their visit to the United States in 1957, Boehm's career accelerated.

Boehm had a reputation for being opinionated, prejudiced, and unforgiving. His contributions were the image concepts and techniques used to produce the sculptures. Thousands of prototype sculptures were made, with over 400 put into actual production. The actual work was done by skilled artisans. Boehm died on January 29, 1969.

In the early 1970s a second production studio was opened in Malvern, England, as Boehm Studios. The tradition begun by Boehm continues today.

Reference: Reese Palley, *The Porcelain Art of Edward Marshall Boehm*, Harrison House, division of Crown Publishers, 1988.

BIRDS

American Avocet, #40134 . . . . **1,250.00**
American Eagle, #498 . . . . **950.00**
Blue Heron, #200–19 . . . . **275.00**
Blue Jays, #466 . . . . **4,900.00**
Bobwhite Quail, #407 . . . . **1,200.00**
California Quail, #433, pr **1,750.00**
Canadian Geese, #408, pr **575.00**
Capped Chickadee, #438, 9" **450.00**
Cardinal, female, #415, 15" h **600.00**
Crested Flycatcher, baby, #458C **170.00**
Downy Woodpeckers, #427 . . . . **1,000.00**
English Nuthatch, #1001 . . . . **650.00**
Fledgling Eastern Bluebird, #442 . . . . **135.00**
Goldfinch, thistle, #457 . . . . **1,000.00**

Hummingbird, cactus base, #440, 8½" h	900.00
Kingfisher, #449, 6" h	135.00
Lark Sparrow, #400–35	2,750.00
Lesser, Prairie Chicken, #464	2,750.00
Oven Bird, 10" h	725.00
Pelican, #40161, 21"	1,000.00
Prothonotary Warbler, #445	575.00
Ring Neck Pheasants, #409	800.00
Robin, baby, #4375, 3½" h	135.00
Ruby Crowned Kinglets, #434	875.00
Song Sparrow, #400–59	475.00
Tumbler Pigeons, #416	750.00

FLOWERS

Blue Nile Rose, #300–80	1,450.00
Daisies, #3002	750.00
Grace de Monaco Rose, #300–71	1,900.00
Magnolia Grandiflora, #300–12	1,500.00
Pascali Rose, #30093	1,500.00
Pussy Willows, #200–28, pr	175.00
Queen Elizabeth Rose, #30091	1,200.00
Roy Hartley Begonia, #300–41	1,500.00

BOHEMIAN GLASS

History: The once independent country of Bohemia, now a part of Czechoslovakia, produced a variety of fine glassware: etched, cut, overlay, and colored. Their glassware was first imported into America in the early 1820s and continues today.

Bohemia is known for its "flashed" glass that was produced in the familiar ruby color, as well as amber, green, blue, and black. Common patterns include "Deer and Castle," "Deer and Pine Tree," and "Vintage."

Most of the Bohemian glass encountered in today's market is of the 1875–1900 period. Bohemian–type glass also was made in England, Switzerland, and Germany.

Reproduction Alert.

Beaker, 5½" h, amber flashed, engraved, animals and building, C scroll panels, flared foot, c1860	95.00
Bowl, 12½" d, double cut overlay, cobalt blue cut to clear	250.00
Box, domed lid, ruby flashed, Vintage, engraved clear and frosted grape clusters and vines, gilt brass fittings	125.00
Candy Dish, cov, ruby flashed, Deer and Castle, clear and frosted	90.00
Celery Dish, ruby flashed, Deer and Castle, clear and frosted	80.00
Cologne Bottle, 5" h, cobalt blue, tiered body dec, white and gold flowers and scrolls	150.00
Compote	
7" d, amber flashed, cut leaf and floral	

dec, green band at top, pedestal base	100.00
9½ x 6½", amber flashed, Deer and Castle, engraved clear and frosted animals, castle, and trees	150.00
Decanter, 14¾" h, crystal, octagonal, greenish tint, engraved forest and deer scene, orig stopper	80.00
Flip Glass, 6 x 6", clear, cut, engraved forest scene with fox and birds	100.00
Goblet	
6¾" h, white and cranberry overlay, thistle form bowl, six teardrop panels alternately enameled with floral bouquets and cut with blocks of diamonds, faceted knop and spreading scalloped foot, gilt trim	600.00
7½" h, cranberry, gold and enamel dec, artist sgd	125.00
Jar	
7" h, cov, barrel shape, bands of clear engraving, red satin discs, barrel finial	125.00
9½" h, cov, ruby flashed	145.00
Mantel Lusters, 6½" d, 12¼" h, cranberry cut overlay, cut scalloped tops, white overlay panels, multicolored flowers, allover gold flowers and scrolls, clear cut prisms, pr	1,000.00
Mug, 6" h, ruby flashed, engraved castle and trees, applied clear handle, sgd "Volmer, 1893"	80.00
Perfume Bottle, 7" h, ruby flashed, Deer and Castle, clear and frosted, gold dec	90.00
Pickle Jar, cov, 6" h, ruby flashed, Deer and Castle, clear and frosted	50.00
Powder Box, 4¼" d, round, straight sides, flat top, ruby flashed, etched cov with leaping stag, forest setting, landscape and birds on sides, clear base	100.00

Vases, blue cut to clear, center medallion of peasant in tree, vertical panels with castle, deer, partridge, and swan, matched pr, 9" h, $265.00.

Rose Bowl, 8½" d, ruby flashed, Deer
and Castle, clear and frosted **225.00**
Spa Glass, 5" h, waisted cylindrical,
white and cranberry overlay, six vertical cut panels, named engraved and
gilt architectural views, white enamel
and gilt scrolls **360.00**
Stein, 3 x 6½", ruby flashed, engraved
cathedral panel, leaves, and scrolls,
pewter mounts, ruby flashed inset lid **300.00**
Sugar Shaker, ruby flashed, Bird and
Castle, clear and frosted **70.00**
Teapot, 11" w, cranberry cut to clear,
panels of flowers, gilt spout and handle **185.00**
Tumbler
4" h, ruby flashed, cut design, gold
dec, set of 4 .... **125.00**
4¼" h, engraved scene, early 19th C **150.00**
Vase, 10" h, 6" d, cranberry cut to clear,
buzz star, shooting star panels, German **350.00**
Whiskey Glass, pr, 3¼" h, engraved,
clear, early 19th C **225.00**

BOOKS—THE AMERICAN WEST

History: The settlement of the American frontier has been a major theme in American literature since the eighteenth century. During the nineteenth century, a highly romanticized image of the American West of the Great Plains became a viable part of American literature. Identified by historians as the "frontier myth," this image was continued by movies and television through the 1960s. This West is one of cowboy heroes–both mythical and real.

In sharp contrast to the romanticized West are the personal accounts of exploration, settlement, and life written by those who experienced it first hand. These books are especially prized by collectors.

Western collectors also focus on books about the American Indians. Eagerly sought are nineteenth century books with colored plates.

Because of the specialized nature of book on the American West, titles tend to go out–of–print very rapidly. Many are privately published by the authors or small firms.

Many books were published in several printings and editions. Place your emphasis on first editions. Popular editions were often issued. These generally were printed on lesser quality paper and have poorer bindings. Avoid them whenever possible.

Many of these books had dust jackets. The book should not be considered complete if the jacket has been lost. Also check to make certain that all illustrations are present.

There are a number of dealers who specialize in out–of–print books about the American West.

Your local librarian can help you—do not hesitate to ask. It may take from a few months to several years to find a particular book, but eventually your patience will be rewarded.

References: Allen Ahearn, *Book Collecting: A Comprehensive Guide*, G. P. Putnam's Sons, 1989; Allen and Patricia Ahearn, *Collected Books, The Guide To Values,* G. P. Putnam's Sons, 1991; *American Book Prices Current, Volume 97, 1991*, Bancroft/Parkman, Inc., 1992; John Carter (revised by Nicolas Barker), *ABC For Book Collectors, Sixth Edition*, Granada Publishing, 1980; Editors of Collector Books, *Huxford's Old Book Value Guide, Third Edition*, Collector Books, 1991; Jean Peters, ed., *Book Collecting: A Modern Guide*, R. R. Bowker Company, 1977; Jean Peters, ed., *Collectible Books: Some New Paths*, R. R. Bowker Company, 1979.

See: *Warman's Americana & Collectibles* for additional listings in the Big Little Books, Books: Limited Editions Club, Cookbooks, Paperback Books, and Pulp Magazines categories.

Advisor: Ron Lieberman.

Adams, Andy
Cattle Brands, Boston, 1906 ...... **75.00**
Wells Brothers, Boston & NY, 1911,
1st ed, 1st printing **45.00**
Adams, Ramon F., A Fitting Death For
Billy The Kid, Norman, 1960 ...... **45.00**
Allen, Jules Verne, Cowboy Lore, San
Antonio, 1933, 1st ed, sgd limited ed
of 200 copies **50.00**
Appler, A. C., The Younger Brothers,
NY, 1955, 1st ed **20.00**
Austin, Mary, The Land Of Little Rain,
Boston, 1903 .... **75.00**
Barrett, S. M., editor, Geronimo's Story
Of His Life, NY, 1906, 1st ed **75.00**
Bartholomew, Ed, Wild Bill Longley–A
Texas Hard Case, Houston, 1953 .. **40.00**
Beadle, J. H., Life In Utah: Or The Mys-
teries And Crime of Mormonism, Phil-
adelphia, 1870 .... **75.00**
Belle, Frances P., Joaquin Murrieta,
Chicago, 1925, 1st ed, limited to 975
copies **60.00**
Breckenridge, William M., Helldorado,
Boston, 1928, 1st ed **75.00**
Bryant, Edwin, Rocky Mountain Adven-
tures, NY, 1889, 1st ed **40.00**
Buel, J. W., Heroes Of The Plains Or
Lives & Wonderful Adventures, St
Louis, 1881, 1st ed **125.00**
Burch, J. P., A True Store Of Chas. W.
Quantrell And His Guerrilla Band,
Vega, Texas, 1923 .... **40.00**
Burr, F. A. and Hinton, R. J., The Life Of
General Philip H. Sheridan, Provi-
dence, 1888, 1st ed **60.00**
Burt, Struthers, The Diary Of A Dude
Wrangler, NY, 1924, 1st ed **25.00**

Canton, Frank M., *Frontier Trails*, Boston, 1930, 1st ed **70.00**
Chapel, Charles Edward, *Guns Of The Old West*, NY, 1961, 1st ed **50.00**
Chisholm, Alexander, *The Old Chisholm Trail*, Salt Lake City, 1964, 1st ed . . **50.00**
Cody, W. F., *Life And Adventures Of Buffalo Bill*, Chicago, 1917, 1st ed . **35.00**
Cody, Wm. F., *The Story Of The Wild West & Campfire Chats*, Chicago, 1888, 1st ed **70.00**
Davis, Richard Harding, *The West From A Car Window*, NY, 1892, 1st ed . . . **40.00**
De Quille, Dan, *A History Of The Comstock Silver Lode And Mines*, Virginia City, Nevada, 1889, 1st ed **150.00**
Dodge, Col. Richard Irving, *Our Wild Indians; Thirty–Three Years Personal Experience*, Hartford, 1882, 1st ed . **75.00**
Drago, Harry Sinclair
Outlaws On Horseback, NY, 1964, 1st ed **30.00**
Wild, Wooly, And Wicked, NY, 1960, 1st ed **35.00**
Emory, Col. W. H., *Notes Of A Military Reconnoissance From Fort Leavenworth In Missouri–To San Diego, Calif, 1848*, Washington, 1848 . . . . **300.00**
Forsee, Aylesa, *William Henry Jackson Pioneer Photographer Of The West*, NY, 1964, 1st ed **25.00**
Furlong, Charles Wellington, *Let'er Buck–A Story Of The Passing Of The Old West*, NY, 1921 . . . . **30.00**
Gandy, Lew Cass, *The Tabors–A Footnote Of Western History*, NY, 1934, 1st ed **35.00**
Greer, James Kimmins, *Colonel Jack Hays*, NY, 1952, 1st ed **90.00**
Grigsby, Melvin, *The Smoked Yank*, Sioux Falls, 1888, 1st ed **90.00**
Hagedorn, Herman, *Roosevelt In The Bad Lands*, Boston, 1921, 1st ed . . **30.00**
Hamner, Laura V., *Short Grass & Longhorns*, Norman, 1943, 1st ed **45.00**
Hinton, R. J., *The Resources And Natural Wealth Of Arizona*, San Francisco, 1878, 1st ed **150.00**
Holbrook, Stewart H., *Little Annie Oakley And Other Rugged People*, NY, 1948, 1st ed **25.00**
Hope, Ascott R., *The Men Of The Backwoods*, NY, 1880, 1st ed **30.00**
Houghton, Eliza P. Donner, *The Expedition Of The Donner Party And Its Tragic Fate*, Chicago, 1911, 1st ed . **100.00**
Howard, Maj. Gen. O. O., *Famous Indian Chiefs I Have Known*, NY, 1908 **125.00**
Howe, Henry, *Historical Collections Of The Great West*, Cincinnati, 1852 . . **70.00**
Inman, Col., Henry, *The Great Salt Lake Trail*, NY, 1898, 1st ed **100.00**

Jackson, Clarence S., *Picture Maker Of The West–William H Jackson*, NY, 1947, 1st ed, dj **85.00**
Jackson, Joseph Henry, *Tintypes In Gold, Four Studies In Robbery*, NY, 1939, 1st ed, 1st printing **25.00**
James, Will
Cow Country, NY, 1927, 1st ed **75.00**
Cowboys North And South, NY, 1926 **50.00**
Lone Cowboy–My Life Story, NY, 1930, 1st ed **35.00**
Smoky, NY, 1926, 1st ed **45.00**
Johnson, Fletcher, *Life Of Sitting Bull And History Of The Indian Wars 1890–91*, Edgewood, 1891, 1st ed . **50.00**
Kelly, Luther S., edited by M. M. Quaife, *Yellowstone Kelly*, New Haven, 1926 **80.00**
King, Capt. Charles, *Campaigning With Crook*, NY, 1890 . . . . **70.00**
Klette, Ernest, *The Crimson Trail of Jauquin Murieta*, Los Angeles, 1926, 1st ed **45.00**
Laut, Agnes, *The Overlaid Trail*, NY, 1929, 1st ed **25.00**
Meeker, Ezra, *The Ox Team; Or The Oregon Trail 1851–1906*, Omaha, 1906, 1st ed **50.00**
Monaghan, Jay, *Last Of The Badmen*, Indianapolis, 1946, 1st ed **35.00**
Myers, John Myers, *The Last Chance–Tombstone's Early Years*, NY, 1950, 1st ed **35.00**
Nix, Ed, *Oklahombres*, 1929, 1st ed . . **75.00**
Otero, Miguel Antonio, *My Life On The Frontier*, NY, 1935, 1st ed **75.00**
Poe, John W., *The Death Of Billy The Kid*, Boston & NY, 1933, 1st ed **50.00**
Post, C. C., *Ten Years A Cowboy*, Chicago, 1888 . . . . **25.00**
Price, George F., (Capt. 5th Cav.), *Across The Continent With The Fifth Cavalry*, NY, 1883, 1st ed **200.00**
Rascoe, Burton, *Belle Starr, The Bandit Queen*, NY, 1941, 1st ed **40.00**
Remington, Frederic, *Done In The Open*, NY, 1902, 1st ed **175.00**
Rosa, Joseph G., *They Called Him Wild Bill–The Life And Adventures Of James Butler Hickok*, Norman, 1964, 1st ed **40.00**
Shields, G. O., *The Battle Of The Big Hole*, Chicago, 1889, 1st ed **175.00**
Shirley, Glen, *Heck Thomas–Frontier Marshal*, Philadelphia & NY, 1962, 1st ed **30.00**
Summerhays, Martha, *Vanished Arizona Recollections Of My Army Life*, 1908, 1st ed **70.00**
Sutley, Zack T., *The Last Frontier*, NY, 1930 . . . . **45.00**
Thayer, William M., *Marvels Of The New West*, Norwich, 1888 . . . . **45.00**

Thompson, Col. William, *Reminiscences Of A Pioneer*, San Francisco, 1912, 1st ed **80.00**
Van Tramp, John C., *Prairie And Rocky Mountain Adventures; Or Life In The West*, Columbus, 1866, 1st ed **50.00**
Vestal, Stanley, *Kit Carson, The Happy Warrior Of The Old West*, Boston, 1928, 1st ed **60.00**
Walsh, Richard J., *The Making Of Buffalo Bill*, Indianapolis, 1928, 1st ed .   **30.00**
Waters, Frank, *The Earp Brothers Of Tombstone–The Story Of Mrs. Virgil Earp*, NY, 1960, 1st ed **45.00**
Webb, Walter Prescott, *The Texas Rangers–A Century Of Frontier Defense*, Boston, 1935, 1st ed **65.00**
Wheeler, Col. Homer, *Buffalo Days*, Indianapolis, 1925, 1st ed **75.00**
Wilstach, Frank J., *Wild Bill Hickok*, NY, 1926, 1st ed **30.00**

BOOTJACKS

History: Bootjacks are metal or wooden devices that facilitate the removal of boots. Bootjacks are used by placing the heel of the boot in the "U" shaped opening, putting a foot on the back of the bootjack, and pulling the front boot off the foot.

Cast iron, beetle type, $60.00.

Brass, 10", beetle **90.00**
Cast Iron
    9¾" l, Naughty Nelly, old worn polychrome repaint **45.00**
    10¾" l, lyre shaped **50.00**
    11½" l, intertwined scrolls form letter M **25.00**
    11¾" l, cricket, emb lacy design . . .   **25.00**
    12" l
        Tree center, footed **30.00**
        Vine design **35.00**
Wood
    10" l, tiger stripe maple **20.00**
    13" l, maple, hand hewn **15.00**
    15" l, Folk Art, monkey, painted suit, c1900 . . . .   **30.00**
    22" l, walnut, heart and diamond openwork **40.00**

24" l, pine, rose head nails, pierced for hanging **40.00**
25" l, pine, oval ends, sq nails **28.00**

BOTTLES, GENERAL

History: Cosmetic bottles held special creams, oils, and cosmetics designed to enhance the beauty of the user. Some also claimed, especially on their colorful labels, to cure or provide relief from common ailments.

A number of household items, e.g., cleaning fluids and polishes, required glass storage containers. Many are collected for their fine lithograph labels.

Mineral water bottles contained water from a natural spring. Spring water was favored by health conscious people between the 1850s and 1900s.

Nursing bottles, used to feed the young and sickly, were a great help to the housewife because of graduated measures, replaceable nipples, ease of cleaning, sterilizing, and reuse.

References: Ralph & Terry Kovel, *The Kovels' Bottle Price List, Eighth Edition*, Crown Publishers, Inc., 1987; Jim Megura, *The Official Identification and Price Guide To Bottles, Eleventh Edition*, House of Collectibles, 1991; Carlo & Dorothy Sellari, *The Standard Old Bottle Price Guide*, Collector Books, 1989.

Periodicals: *Antique Bottle And Glass Collector*, P.O. Box 187, East Greenville, PA 18041; *Bottles and Extras*, Box 154, Happy Camp, CA 96039.

Collectors' Club: Federation of Historical Bottle Collectors, 14521 Atlantic, Riverdale, IL 60627.

Museum: Naitonal Bottle Museum, Ballston Spa, NY.

Additional Listings: Barber Bottles, Bitter Bottles, Figural Bottles, Food Bottles, Ink Bottles, Medicine Bottles, Poison Bottles, Sarsaparilla Bottles and Snuff Bottles. Also see the bottle categories in *Warman's Americana & Collectibles* for more examples.

COSMETICS

De Vry's Dandero–Off Hair Tonic, 6½", clear, label **10.00**
Hagans Magnolia Balm, 5", milk glass, beveled corners, ring top **12.00**
Hyacinthia Toilet Hair Dressing, 6", rect, aqua, applied lip, open pontil **25.00**
Kranks Cold Cream, 2¾" h, milk glass   **5.00**
Pompeian Massage Cream, 2¾" h, amethyst **5.00**
Violet Dulce Vanishing Cream, 2½", eight panels **5.00**

HOUSEHOLD

Bull Dog Brand Liquid Glue, 3½", aqua, ring collar **4.00**

Everett & Barron Co, Shoe Polish, 4¾", oval, clear	2.00
E Z Stove Polish, 6", aqua	6.00
Hubbard's Vegetable Germicide, Disinfectant and Deodorizer, 4¾", clear	6.00
Imperial Polish Co, 7¼", aqua, label	4.00
Jennings Bluing, 7", aqua, blob top	5.00
Larkin Soap Co, 3½", clear	4.00
Spalding's Glue, 4", aqua	2.00
Sperm Sewing Machine Oil, 5½", clear	4.00

MINERAL OR SPRING WATER

Adirondack Spring, Westport, NY, emerald green, double collar lip, smooth base	250.00
Artesian Spring Co, olive–green, applied double collar lip, smooth base, 1860–70	60.00
Campbell Mineral Spring Co, Burlington, VT, aqua, double collar lip, smooth base	740.00
Congress & Empire Spring Co, Hotchkiss Sons, yellow–olive, applied double collar lip, smooth base	165.00
Deep Rock Spring, aqua, applied double collar lip, smooth base	110.00
Excelsior Spring, Saratoga, NY, emerald green, applied double collar lip, smooth base	90.00
Gettysburg Katalysine Water, forest green, double collar lip, smooth base	70.00
Gulford Mineral Spring Water, yellow–olive, tapered double collar lip, smooth base	80.00
Kissingen Water, Hanbury Smith, olive–green, tapered collar lip, smooth base	55.00
Middletown Mineral Spring Co, emerald green, double collar lip, smooth base	55.00
Richfield Springs NY Sulphur Water, emerald green, applied double collar lip, smooth base	410.00
Saratoga Vichy Water, amber, tapered double collar lip, smooth base	220.00
St Regis Water Massena Springs, medium blue–green, tapered double collar lip, smooth base	145.00
Vermont Spring, Saxe & Co, Sheldon, VT, yellow–amber, tapered double collar lip, smooth base	410.00
Whelan, DJ, Troy, NY, aqua, blob top lip, smooth base	90.00

NURSING

Acme, clear, lay–down type, emb	60.00
Cala Nurser, 7⅛" h, oval, clear, emb, ring on neck	5.00
Empire Nursing Bottle, 6½", bent neck, emb	50.00
Graduated, 6½" h, clear	10.00
Grip Tite, Teat & Valve, clear, emb	25.00

Nursing, clear, emb "The Empire Nursing Bottle," 5½" h, $50.00.

Miller Sanitate, clear, emb	35.00
Mother's Comfort, clear, turtle type	20.00
Nonpareil Nurser, 5½", aqua	15.00

BRASS

History: Brass is a durable, malleable, and ductile metal alloy consisting mainly of copper and zinc. It achieved its greatest popularity for utilitarian and decorative art items in the eighteenth and nineteenth centuries.

References: Mary Frank Gaston, *Antique Brass: Identification and Values,* Collector Books, 1985; Peter, Nancy, and Herbert Schiffer, *The Brass Book,* Schiffer Publishing, Ltd, 1978.

Additional Listings: Bells, Candlesticks, Fireplace Equipment, and Scientific Instruments.

Reproduction Alert: Many modern reproductions are being made of earlier brass forms, especially in the areas of buckets, fireplace equipment, and kettles.

Andirons, pr	
17" h, double lemon top	200.00
23" h, ball feet, spurred legs, steeple tops with matching log stops, early 19th C	700.00
27" h, ball feet, double log stops, early 19th C	900.00
Ashtray, 4½ x 5", figural, bull's head, relief, protruding curled horns	50.00
Basinette, 43" l, 35" h crosier, Edwardian, crosier suspending a knotted rope basket, oval brass basin, decorative stand, scrolled legs	1,150.00
Book Stand, 9" h, folding, pierced and scrolled, rect base, English	160.00
Box, 6¾" l, hanging, emb floral dec	25.00
Bucket, 22½" d, tapered cylinder, rolled rim, iron bail handle, 19th C	350.00

Candlesticks, pr, beehive, push–ups, 9″ h, $165.00.

Call Bell, 6¼″ h, red granite base	25.00
Candle Box, 12″ l, hanging, scalloped back, minor dents	150.00
Candelabra, pr, 21″ h, ornate	100.00
Candleholder, pr, 27″ l, bracket type, faceted candle arm fitted with nine candle sockets, mid 18th C	1,100.00
Candlestick, pr	
8½″ h, sq ftd base	50.00
9″ h, Continental, baluster stem, c1680	200.00
10″ h, fluted, English, 18th C	225.00
Candy Scoop, 8″ l	30.00
Chamber Stick	
4⅞″ h, gadroon molding, ejector, rect base, English, late 18th C, early 19th C	50.00
16″ h, pushup	60.00
Cigar Cutter, pocket type	40.00
Coal Hod, 9½″ h, hammered, 20th C .	75.00
Dish, 15½″ d, ftd, Dutch, late 19th C . .	50.00
Door Knob Set, pear shape, England, 19th C	45.00
Door Knocker, 4″, bear	75.00
Doorstop, 13″ h, pineapple, cast	115.00
Fireplace Fender	
49″ l, paw feet	350.00
56″ l	125.00
Fireplace Fan, 38″ w, 25″ h, folding, griffin detail	65.00
Girandoles, pr, 10″ h, clear cut prisms, eagle bases	125.00
Incense Burner, 4⅜″ h, foo dog	75.00
Inkwell	
5½″ l, triple, three monkeys, hear no evil, see no evil, and speak no evil pose, hinged heads, Victorian, late 19th C	80.00
11″ l, pierced scrolled back plate, two ink pots, pen tray, Victorian style .	110.00
Jam Kettle, 13″ d, handwrought iron rim, bail handle, early 19th C	50.00
Jardiniere, 6½ x 9½″, engraved dragon dec, China	55.00
Kettle	
11″ d, iron bail handle, label "H W Hayden, Waterbury, Conn"	75.00
13¾″ d, cylindrical, molded rim, iron bail handle	70.00
Kettle Shelf	
9″ l, reticulated top, English	70.00
13¾″ l, oval, reticulated top	85.00
Lamp	
Bracket, chimney and reflector, electrified	440.00
Desk, opaque white shade	60.00
Pan, 16½″ h, bird mounted on top, Eastern	225.00
Skater's	
6¾″ h, clear globe	65.00
7⅛″ h, cobalt blue globe	95.00
Table, pr, fox head, hunter horn holds shade, c1900	595.00
Whale oil, 5⅛″ l, 3″ h, pear shape, pickwick and orig double drop burner	45.00
Milk Pail	300.00
Miniature Table, 6¾″ h, tilt–top	50.00
Mortar and Pestle, 4½″ h	70.00
Pie Crimper, 4½″ l, wheel on each end	35.00
Pitcher, 7″ h, Continental, late 19th C .	50.00
Plant Stand, 23″ h, paw feet	75.00
Salt, cov, 3″ d, 4¾″ h, paw feet	85.00
Sconces, pr, 14″ h, French Empire style, mounted swan supporting wreath in mouth holding three candle arms . .	550.00
Scuttle, 7″ h, repousse floral dec, scoop, Victorian	100.00
Sewing Bird, 5″ h, cast iron clamp . . .	90.00
Shelf, 20 x 14 x 8″, hanging, reticulated unicorn and vine pediment, glazed oval sides, drawer, late 19th C	70.00
Stencil, 13⅝″ sq, cut–out rooster figure and "H A & Co, 56 Boston"	210.00
Sundial, 7⅞″ d, octagonal, engraved face, dated 1689	750.00
Taper Jack, 5½″ h, scissor form, floral dec, adjustable shaft, pierced base, marked "H R," mid 18th C	410.00
Tea Kettle, 11″ d, 15¼″ h, unusual spout, copper rivets, 19th C	175.00
Teapot, 8¼″ h, dragons and trees dec, Oriental	40.00
Vase, 10½″ h, cloisonne bands, Oriental	60.00
Wafer Iron, 4″ d, 17″ l, geometric floral design, wrought iron handles	65.00
Warming Pan, orig turned handle	150.00
Wash Bowl, 15″ d, Georgian, circular handle, 19th C	90.00

Watch Holder, 8½" h, Rococo style,
scroll, leaf, and floral dec **80.00**

BREAD PLATES

History: Beginning in the mid-1880s, special
trays or platters were made for serving bread and
rolls. Designated by collectors as "bread plates,"
these small trays or platters can be found in porcelain, glass (especially pattern glass), and metals.

Bread plates often were part of a china or glass
set. However, many glass companies made special plates which honored national heroes, com-
memorated historical or special events, offered a
moral maxim, or supported a religious attitude. The
theme on the plate could be either in a horizontal
or vertical format. The favorite shape for these
plates is oval, with a common length being ten
inches.

Reference: Anna Maude Stuart, *Bread Plates
And Platters*, published by author, 1965.

Additional Listings: Pattern Glass.

Garfield Memorial, 10″ d, clear, $48.00.

China
  Nippon, gaudy, green and gold, pink
    asters **225.00**
  Noritake, 10″, gold handled, hp scene
    in center, wide border, hp stylized
    flowers, maroon wreath **65.00**
Milk Glass
  Liberty Bell, John Hancock signature,
    handles **260.00**
  William J Bryan **40.00**
  Wheat & Barley **60.00**
Pattern Glass
  Aurora, 10″ round, large star in center,
    ruby stained **35.00**
  Be Industrious, 12 x 8¼″, oval, clear,
    handled **50.00**

Beaded Grape, sq **30.00**
Butterfly & Fan, clear **40.00**
Canadian, 10″, clear **45.00**
Continental Hall, 12¾″ l, hand holds   **75.00**
Cupid and Venus, amber **75.00**
Daisy and Button, 13″, apple green .   **60.00**
Deer and Pine Tree, blue **100.00**
Egyptian, Cleopatra in center, 13″ l .   **50.00**
Fern **30.00**
Give Us This Day, round, rosette cen-
  ter and border **65.00**
Good Luck **45.00**
Horseshoe, 14 x 10″, double hor-
  seshoe handles **65.00**
Iowa, motto **80.00**
Lattice, Waste Not Want Not, 11½″ l   **32.00**
Lion, 12″, frosted, including lion han-
  dles, GUTDODB **125.00**
Maple Leaf, oval, vaseline, 13 x 9½″   **45.00**
Moon and Star, rect, clear **45.00**
Nellie Bly, clear, 11″ l **170.00**
Old State House, sapphire blue . . .   **175.00**
Palmette, 9″, handled **30.00**
Queen Anne **50.00**
Rock of Ages, 12⅞″ l, clear and opa-
  lescent, colored and clear combi-
  nations, c1870 . . . .   **175.00**
Scroll and Flowers, 12″ d **35.00**
Shell and Tassel, round **55.00**
Tennessee, colored jewels **75.00**
Three Presidents, frosted center . . .   **85.00**
US Coin, frosted coins **300.00**
Wildflower, sq **28.00**
Tin, 12¾″ l, painted fruit and leaf motif
  border, brown ground, 19th C **3,025.00**

BRIDE'S BASKETS

History: A ruffled edge, glass bowl in a metal
holder was a popular wedding gift in the 1880–
1910 era, hence, the name of "bride's basket."
The glass bowls can be found in most glass types
of the period. The metal holder was generally silver
plated with a bail handle, thus enhancing the basket image.

Over the years, bowls and bases became separated and married pieces resulted. When the
base has been lost, the bowl is sold separately.

Reference: John Mebane, *Collecting Bride's
Baskets And other Glass Fancies*, Wallace–
Homestead, 1976.

Reproduction Alert: The glass bowls have
been reproduced.

Note: Items listed have silver plated holder unless otherwise noted.

Cased
  8¼″ w, sq, deep rose and white ext.,
    white int., dragon, floral, and leaf
    dec, ruffled edge, Mt Washington .   **650.00**

9⅜" d, shaded pink int. with gold floral dec, clear ruffled rim, white ext. . . **100.00**

10 x 14¼", white int., cobalt blue ext., enameled gold flowers and leaves, ruffled rim, SP frame, emb leaves **400.00**

Cranberry, Victorian, ornate ruffled insert **85.00**

Custard

10" w, sq, melon ribbed, enameled daisies, applied rubena crystal rim, twisted and beaded handle, ftd, emb SP frame, marked "Wilcox" . **425.00**

12" d, three lobed form, cased pink, amber rim, enameled flower dec, SP stand **450.00**

Hobnail, 10½" d, pink, enameled flowers, ruffled rim, reticulated SP frame **225.00**

Loetz, irid blue, silver threading, coin spots, brass holder **375.00**

Opaque, 10⅛" d, white, apricot satin finished int., white butterflies and flowers, silver plated holder **250.00**

Pairpoint, peppermint stick rim shaded to frosted bowl, silverplated frame with six medallions of busts of Roman warriors, ftd, 8¾" d bowl, $150.00.

Pairpoint, pink and white, ornate ruffled edge **325.00**

Peachblow

9¼" d, yellow flowers dec, orig SP holder **45.00**

11½" d, dec, sterling silver stand . . . **200.00**

Satin Glass

14" d, rose pink, scalloped, rippled, ribbed, and swirled, lacy allover enamel and gold flower pattern, figural silverplate base with hummingbird, sgd "Eagle & Co" **1,100.00**

11 x 15½", deep rose, enamel swan and floral dec, heavy bronze holder with birds perched on top **400.00**

Schlegelmilch, floral center, ornate, ftd **50.00**

Spangled Glass, 10⅜" d, multicolored,

ruby, cranberry, and green, ivory–yellow ground, silver flecks **100.00**

Spatter, yellow, brown, and purple, ruffled and crimped, SP holder **240.00**

BRISTOL GLASS

History: Bristol glass is a designation given to a semi–opaque glass, usually decorated with enamel and cased with another color.

Initially, the term referred only to glass made in Bristol, England, in the 17th and 18th centuries. By the Victorian era firms on the Continent and in America were copying the glass and its forms.

Biscuit Jar, 6½" h, white, brown leaves and white flowers **150.00**

Bowl, light blue, cupid playing mandolin, gold trim **35.00**

Cake Stand, celadon green, enameled herons in flight, gold trim **125.00**

Candlestick, 7" h, soft green, gold band, pr **60.00**

Cruet, 2¼ x 4¾", blue, white flowers, gold leaves, applied blue handle, matching ball stopper **90.00**

Decanter, 8", blue, matching stopper . . **75.00**

Dresser Set, two cologne bottles, cov powder jar, white, gilt butterflies dec, clear stoppers **50.00**

Ewer, 17", white, enameled cupid scene **80.00**

Hatpin Holder, 6⅛", ftd, blue, enameled jewels, gold dec **100.00**

Marmalade Jar, white, floral dec, plated handled frame **85.00**

Mug, 5" h, white, eagle and "Liberty" . . **375.00**

Perfume Bottle, 3¼", squat, blue, gold band, white enameled flowers and leaves, matching stopper **100.00**

Pickle Castor, pink, flower dec **300.00**

Perfume Bottles, blue neck, teardrop stopper, gilt, hp bluebird in center medallion, pr, $215.00.

Puff Box, cov, round, blue, gold dec . .	**30.00**
Rose Bowl, 3½", shaded blue, crimped edge	**60.00**
Scent Bottle, 6½" h, blue, multicolored florals, stopper	**100.00**
Sugar Shaker, 4¾", white, hp flowers .	**60.00**
Sweetmeat Jar	
3 x 5½", deep pink, enameled flying duck, leaves, blue flower dec, white lining, SP rim, lid, and bail handle	**100.00**
5¾ x 4½", green, enameled garlands of pink, white, yellow, blue, and green flowers, four butterflies, SP rim, lid, and bail handle	**120.00**
Vase	
8½" h, pr, cobalt blue dec	**110.00**
11", tan, coralene florals and butterflies, gold trim, pr	**300.00**
18" h, urn form, pink, boy and girl with lamb on gold	**550.00**

BRITISH ROYALTY COMMEMORATIVES

History: British commemorative china, souvenirs to commemorate coronations and other royal events, dates from the 1600s, with the early pieces being rather crude in design and form. The development of transfer printing, c1780, led to a much closer likeness of the reigning monarch on the ware.

Few commemorative pieces predating Queen Victoria's reign are found today at popular prices. Items associated with Queen Elizabeth II and her children, e. g., the wedding of HRH Prince Andrew and Miss Sarah Ferguson and the subsequent birth of their daughter HRH Princess Beatrice, are very common.

Some British Royalty commemoratives are easily recognized by their portraits of past or present monarchs. Some may be in silhouette profile. Other royal symbols include crowns, dragons, royal coats of arms, national flowers, swords, scepters, dates, messages, and initials.

References: Malcolm Davey and Doug Mannion, *50 Years of Royal Commemorative China 1887–1937,* Dayman Publications, 1988; Peter Johnson, *Royal Memorabilia: A Phillips Collectors Guide,* Dunestyle Publishing Ltd., 1988; John May, *Victoria Remembered, A Royal History 1817–1861,* London, 1983; John and Jennifer May, *Commemorative Pottery 1780–1900, A Guide for Collectors,* Charles Scribner's Sons, 1972; Josephine Jackson, *Fired For Royalty,* Heaton Moor, 1977; David Rogers, *Coronation Souvenirs and Commemoratives,* Latimer New Dimensions, Ltd., 1975; Sussex Commemorative Ware Centre, *200 Commemoratives,* Metra Print Enterprises, 1979; Geoffrey Warren, *Royal Souvenirs,* Orbis, 1977; Audrey B. Zeder, *British Royal Commemoratives,* Wallace-Homestead, 1986.

Additional Listings: See *Warman's Americana & Collectibles* for more examples.

Advisors: Douglas Flynn and Alan Bolton.

Beaker	
Edward VIII, Investiture as Prince of Wales, 1911, 3½" h, color portrait, Royal Wintonia	**140.00**
George V/Mary, Coronation, 4⅜" h, color portraits along with Prince of Wales, unmarked	**80.00**
Bowl	
China, George VI/Elizabeth, 1937 Coronation, sepia Marcus Adams portrait, color dec, 6" sq, J & G Meakin	**40.00**
Pressed Glass	
Elizabeth II, Coronation, 8" d, 4¼" w at bottom, crown shape	**40.00**
Edward VIII, 1937 Coronation, profile in well, 10" d	**65.00**
Victoria, 1897 Jubilee, 19¼" d, amber	**65.00**
Box	
Elizabeth II, 25th Anniversary of Coronation, 4¼" d, Coalport	**40.00**
Elizabeth, The Queen Mother, 80th Birthday, color portrait, 4" d, Crown Staffordshire	**65.00**
Cup and Saucer	
Charles/Diana, 1981 Wedding, Royal Albert	**25.00**
Charles, 1969 Investiture as Prince of Wales	**50.00**
George V/Mary, 1911 Coronation, color portraits, no mark	**55.00**
Edward VII/Alexandra, 1902 Coronation, Foley	**45.00**
Jug	
Edward VII, In Memoriam, brown and green, relief portrait, 6¼" h	**65.00**
Elizabeth II, 1953 Coronation, color portrait, 3¾" h, Royal Stafford . . .	**60.00**
Lithophane	
Alexandra, 1902, cup, crown, and cypher, 2¾" h	**175.00**
Edward VII, 1902, mug, crown, and cypher, 2¾" h	**90.00**
George V, 1911, mug, crown, and cypher, 2¾" h	**140.00**
Mary, 1911, cup, crown, and cypher, 2¾" h	**250.00**
Loving Cup	
Charles/Diana, 1981 Wedding, brown on white portraits, Royal Doulton, limited edition 5,000	**85.00**
Elizabeth II, 1972 Silver Wedding Anniversary, 3" h, Paragon	**150.00**
Elizabeth, The Queen Mother, 80th Birthday, gold profile, 3" h, Royal Crown Derby, limited edition 500 .	**225.00**

Mug, Edward VIII, Coronation, multi-colored decal, dated May 1939, marked "Minton," $30.00.

Victoria, 1897 Jubilee, brown portrait,
4″ h **175.00**
William, 1982 Birth, 3″ h, Paragon .. **110.00**
Mug
Andrew/Sarah, 1986 Wedding, color
portraits, 3¾″ h, Calclough **27.50**
Duke/Duchess of Windsor, In Memoriam, black and white portraits;
birth, marriage, accession, abdica-
tion, death dates, 3⅜″ h, Dorincourt **50.00**

Edward VII/Alexandra, 1902 Coronation, 3″ h, Johnson Brothers **55.00**
Edward VIII, 1937 Coronation, sepia
portrait, 3½″ h, Empire **40.00**

Elizabeth II, 60th Birthday, color portrait, 3½″ h, Coronet **20.00**
Henry, 1984 Birth, blue design, silver
trim, 4¼″ h, R Guyatt design,
Wedgwood, limited edition 1,000 . **65.00**
Victoria, 1887 Jubilee, black and
white portrait, 3″ h, CTM **100.00**

Victoria, 150th Anniversary of Coronation, 3⅝″ h, Caverswall **40.00**
William 3rd Birthday, Henry 1st Birthday, black and white portraits, 2⅝″
h, Dorincourt, limited edition 150 . **50.00**
Paperweight
Edward VIII, 1937 Coronation, black
and white portrait, 4¼ x 1⅛″ **25.00**

George VI/Elizabeth, 1937 Coronation, black and white Marcus Adams portrait, 2½″ d **35.00**
Victoria/Albert, black and white portraits, color and glitter, 2⅞″ **30.00**

Pin Tray
Edward VII/Alexandra, 1902 Coronation, sepia portraits, 4″ d **40.00**
Edward VIII, 1937 Coronation, 4⅞ x
3¾″, Hammersley **48.00**

Elizabeth II, 1959 Canada visit, sepia
photograph, 4¼″ sq **28.00**
Victoria, 1897 Jubilee, sepia portrait,
5″ d **40.00**
Pitcher
Elizabeth II, 1953 Coronation, brown
portrait, 6¼″ h, Royal Doulton ... **175.00**
Victoria, 1887 Jubilee, black and
white portrait, 5″ h **120.00**

Plate, Edward VII, portraits of Edward VII and Alexandra, cobalt border with gilt tracery, pierced for hanging, 9″ d, $55.00.

Plate
Andrew/Sarah, 1986 Wedding, silhouette portraits, 8½″ d, Caverswall, limited edition 1,500 ...... **45.00**
Charles, 1969 Investiture as Prince of
Wales, sepia portrait, 8″ d, Coronet **65.00**
Edward VII/Alexandra, 1902 Corona-
tion, blue and white portraits, 10¼″
d **170.00**
Edward VII/Alexandra, 1902 Corona-
tion, 7″ d, Royal Copenhagen ... **190.00**
Elizabeth II, 60th Birthday, large color
portrait, 10½″ d, Coalport, limited
edition 20,000 .... **80.00**
George VI/Elizabeth, 1937 Coronation, sepia portraits, 9½ x 8¼″,
Shelley **75.00**
Victoria, 1887 Jubilee, orange and
white portrait, 10½″ d, Royal
Worcester **125.00**
Victoria, 1897 Jubilee, color portrait,
servicemen, ships, 8″ d **165.00**
Victoria, 150th Anniversary of Coronation, gold portrait, 10½″ d, Caverswall, limited edition 150 ..... **135.00**

Playing Cards
 Edward VIII, 1919 Canada visit, color portrait, single deck, C Goodall & Co 75.00
 Elizabeth II, 1977 Jubilee, sepia portrait, single deck, Waddingtons ... 25.00
 George V/Mary, 1911 Coronation, color portraits, double deck 75.00
 George VI/Elizabeth, 1937 Coronation, color portrait, double deck, Canadian Playing Card Co 65.00
Shaving Mug
 Edward VII/Alexandra, 1902 Coronation, color portraits, 3¾" h 100.00
 Edward VIII, 1937 Coronation, sepia portrait, 4" h, no mark 90.00
 Elizabeth II, 1953 Coronation, color portrait, 4" h 65.00
 George VI/Elizabeth, 1937 Coronation, sepia portraits, 4½" h, Shelley 100.00

Spoon, Queen Victoria, Diamond Jubilee, sterling silver, gold wash, coronation scene in bowl, elaborate dec on both sides of handle, 6¼" l, $150.00.

Teapot
 Charlotte, In Memoriam, black and white dec, 6" h 250.00
 Edward VII/Alexandra, 1902 Coronation, color portraits, 4¾" h 70.00
 Elizabeth II, 1953 Coronation, relief portraits, white on royal blue jasperware, 5" h, Wedgwood 225.00
 George V/Mary, 1911 Coronation, color portraits (also Prince of Wales), 6" h, bone china, no mark 250.00
 Victoria, 1897 Jubilee, color coat of arms, 6" h, Aynsley 220.00
Tea Set, Elizabeth II, 1953 Coronation, teapot, creamer, and sugar, relief portraits, light blue on white Queensware, Wedgwood 275.00
Tin
 Edward VII/Alexandra, 1902 Coronation, color portraits, hinged, 4¼ x 5½" 65.00
 Edward VII/Alexandra, 1907 Cardiff visit, color portraits, 6 x 3½", J S Fry & Sons 48.00
 Edward VIII, 1937 Coronation, color portrait, hinged lid, 5¾ x 3¾", Riley's Toffee 45.00

Elizabeth II, 1953 Coronation, color portrait, 10 x 7", E Sharp 30.00
George V/Mary, 1935 Jubilee, color portrait, 6¾ x 4½" 45.00
Victoria, 1897 Jubilee, color portraits (young, mature), hinged lid, 3¼ x 3" 100.00
Vase, Edward VII, Memorial, 3¼", includes birth, accession, and death dates, Goss 125.00

BRONZE

History: Bronze is an alloy of copper, tin, and traces of other metals. It has been used since Biblical times not only for art objects, but also for utilitarian purposes. After a slump in the Middle Ages, bronze was revived in the 17th century and continued in popularity until the early 20th century.

Reference: Lynne and Fritz Weber, *Jacobsen's Eleventh Painting and Bronze Price Guide, January 1988 to January 1990,* Jacobsen's Publications, 1990.

Notes: Do not confuse a "bronzed" object with a true bronze. A bronzed object usually is made of white metal and then coated with a reddish–brown material to give it a bronze appearance. A magnet will stick to it.

A signed bronze commands a higher market price than an unsigned one. There also are "signed" reproductions on the market. It is very important to know the history of the mold and the background of the foundry.

Ashtray, 7½" d, circular leaf form, applied salamander, c1910 .... 100.00
Bookends, pr
 6¾" h, cupid, swathed in swirl of fabric, tip–toeing with bow in hand, other young girl with flowing hair and bouquet in hand, inscribed "Cast By Griffoul, Newark, NJ," early 20th C 400.00
 9" h, daffodil silhouette, imp mark of G Thew, 1928 .... 210.00
Bowl, 5" d, four lion head medallions, linear border, sgd "Tiffany & Co" ... 190.00
Box, 5¾" h, cricket cage with mouse, Oriental 350.00
Bust, 6½" h, Lincoln, cast relief 10.00
Cake Basket, 9½" d, 7⅝" h, circular bowl, molded pedestal, flat arch handle with enameled mottled red, pink, and amber, imp "Favrile, Louis C Tiffany Furnaces, IN, 511" and monogram, 1918–28 .... 1,210.00
Candelabra, 21" h, pr, three acanthus and scrolled arms, reeded urn form

candle sockets, turned and floral
banding, French Empire **1,700.00**
Cemetery Flag Holder, 12¼" h, cast ea-
gle with banner **15.00**
Desk Set, 6 pcs, ink stand, letter holder,
perpetual calendar, pr blotter holders,
and pen tray, Tiffany **1,375.00**
Dish, 4¼ x 6¼", oval, girl picking ap-
ples, naughty view on reverse **40.00**
Dresser Box, 3½" l, woman portrait on
lid, sgd "Perin" **135.00**

**French Army Officer, Franco–Prussian
War, holding paper inscribed "Alsace–
Lorraine," inscription on base "Nous
L'Aurons," sgd "L. Gregoire," mid
1870s, 13⅜" h, $1,300.00.**

Figure
5" h, robin, cold painted, Vienna . . . **350.00**
5¼" h, little girl, close fitted cap, long
billowing dress, sailor collar, large
sweeping broom, irregular shaped
plinth, black patina, inscribed "E Si-
mone, Fond: Art–Lagana Napoli,"
c1900 . . . . **250.00**
6¼" l, greyhound, reclining, scratch-
ing flank with one hind leg, green–
brown patina, rect Sienna marble
plinth, c1900 . . . . **440.00**
7" l, bull dog, marble base, collar
marked "EKH 1920" **375.00**
9¼" h, Marly horse, rearing, loin cloth
on groom, naturalistic plant cast
plinth, black patina, after Guillaume
Coustou, c1900 . . . . **300.00**
11" h, classical lady wearing Grecian
attire, standing by flowering vine
draped pedestal, smelling flower,
sgd "Huzel", c1860 . . . . **850.00**

15" l, Heron, stalking, sgd "Cain" . . **165.00**
Jar
9½" h, lotus shape, Oriental **60.00**
12" h, colored metal inlay, Oriental . **725.00**
14⅝" h, foo dog, Chinese **165.00**
Lamp, pr, 18" h, 24¼" d, bracket, worn
gold paint **670.00**
Matchsafe, Zodiac pattern, matching
ashtray, sgd "Tiffany Studios, New
York," numbered **160.00**
Pencil Sharpener, sewing machine
shape **15.00**
Pitcher, 6" h, baluster shape, tapering
spout, applied scrolled handle, low relief dec, Continental, 16th C **550.00**
Planter
8" h, squat form, cut–out coin dec, on
rim, cut–out handles, cylindrical
feet, Japan, late 19th C **520.00**
10½" d, high relief marsh marigolds
with green patina, stamped "Tiffany
Studios New York 3617" **9,900.00**
Plaque
9⅜ x 10", seated braves, one with
arms outstretched offering corn, relief sgd "Raymond Averill Porter
1911–50" **375.00**
10¾" w, 13¼" h, oval, Indian head,
greenish patina **150.00**
Sculpture
Dachshunds, pr, 6⅝" l, 5½" w, 5¼" h,
Emmanuel Fremiet, French, 19th C **1,000.00**
Hunting Dog, 8¼" l, pointing,
mounted on red marble base, Carl
Kauba, 19th C **220.00**
Three Cranes, 20" h, chrome plated,
black marble base, sgd "Rochard" **325.00**
Winston Churchill, 5¾" h, marble
base, dated 1949, R A Pickering . **80.00**
Statue
20" h, Mercury, messenger god, sgd
"M Amodie, Napoli" **700.00**
69¼" h, Roman soldier, labeled
"Honor Patria," sgd "E Picault" . . **1,400.00**
Tieback, 14½" l, set of 6, scrolled plate,
reeded scroll arm with leaf and fruit
detail, early 20th C **250.00**
Tray, 8" d, Greek Key pattern, dore fin-
ish, pedestal base, sgd "Tiffany Studios, New York," numbered **170.00**
Vase
7⅛" h, ovoid, tapered, elongated lip
dec on collar, rope design band at
top, scrolls and medallions on upright band on each side, stamped
"Gurschner" and "Made in Aus-
tria," c1900 . . . . **1,650.00**
11" h, gilt flowers in relief, Japanese,
c1920 . . . . **125.00**
12¼" h, baluster, three band relief
dec, dark brown patina, imp char-
acter signature, Japan, late 19th C **1,980.00**

BUFFALO POTTERY
1907

DELDARE WARE,
UNDERGLAZE

BUFFALO POTTERY

History: Buffalo Pottery Co., Buffalo, New York, was chartered in 1901. The first kiln was fired in October 1903. Larkin Soap Company established Buffalo Pottery to produce premiums for its extensive mail order business. Wares also were sold to the public by better department and jewelry stores. Elbert Hubbard and Frank L. Wright, who designed the Larkin Administration Building in Buffalo in 1904, were two prominent names associated with the Larkin Company.

Early production consisted mainly of dinner sets of semi–vitreous china. Buffalo was the first pottery in the United States to produce successfully the Blue Willow pattern, marked "First Old Willow Ware Mfg. in America." Buffalo also made a line of hand decorated, multicolored willow ware, called Gaudy Willow. Other early items include a series of game, fowl, and fish sets, pitchers, jugs, and a line of commemorative, historical, and advertising plates and mugs.

In 1908–09 and 1921–23, Buffalo Pottery produced the line for which it is most famous, Deldare Ware. The earliest of this olive green, semi–vitreous china depicts hand decorated scenes from English artist Cecil Aldin's *Fallowfield Hunt*. Hunt scenes were only done in 1908–09. English village scenes also were characteristic and found throughout the series. Most are artist signed.

In 1911 Buffalo Pottery produced Emerald Deldare, which used scenes from Goldsmith's *The Three Tours of Dr. Syntax* and an Art Nouveau type border. Completely decorated Art Nouveau pieces also were made.

In 1912 Abino was born. Abino was done on Deldare bodies and showed sailing, windmill, and seascape scenes. The main color was rust. All pieces are artist signed and numbered.

In 1915 the pottery was modernized, giving it the ability to produce vitrified china. Consequently, hotel and institutional ware became their main production, with hand decorated ware de–emphasized. Buffalo china became a leader in producing and designing the most famous railroad, hotel, and restaurant patterns. These wares, especially railroad items, are eagerly sought by collectors.

In the early 1920s, fine china was made for home use, e.g., the Bluebird pattern. In 1950 Buffalo made their first Christmas plate. They were given away to customers and employees from 1950–60. Hample Equipment Co. ordered some in 1962. The Christmas plates are very scarce.

The Buffalo China Company made "Buffalo Pottery" and "Buffalo China," the difference being that one is semi–vitreous ware and the other vitrified. In 1956 the company was reorganized, and Buffalo China became the corporate name. Today Buffalo China is owned by Oneida Silver Company. The Larkin family no longer is involved.

Reference: Seymour and Violet Altman, *The Book Of Buffalo Pottery*, reprinted by Schiffer Publishing, 1987.

Note: Numbers in parenthesis refer to plates in the Altman's book.

Advisor: Seymour & Violet Altman.

Mug, Calumet Club, Buffalo, NY souvenir, green, 1915, 4⅜″ h, $90.00.

ABINO WARE

Candlestick, 9″, sailing ships, 1913 (251)	**475.00**
Pitcher 7″, Portland Head Light (256)	**700.00**
Plaque	
12¼″, sailing ships (241)	**1,000.00**
13½″, pasture scene (244)	**2,500.00**
Tankard, 10½″, sailing scene (255)	**900.00**

BLUE AND WHITE WILLOW

Blue Willow	
Creamer, double lip (30)	**15.00**
Plate, 9¼″ (75)	**25.00**
Relish (27)	**45.00**
Gaudy Willow	
Pitcher, 8″ (C*)	**350.00**
Plate, 10½″, (28)	**125.00**

CHRISTMAS PLATES

1950 (260)	**50.00**
1956 (266)	**50.00**
1962 (271)	**225.00**

COMMERCIAL SERVICES

Cake Plate, Roycroft Inn, 10" (288) .. **150.00**
Plate
   B & O Railroad, Harpers Ferry, 9½"
    (282) **300.00**
   Mont Clair Hotel, 10½" (293) **100.00**
Platter, George Washington Service,
   (275) **600.00**

DELDARE

Bowl, Ye Village Street, 8", fern, insert
   (153) **450.00**
Cake Plate, 10", Ye Village Gossips,
   1908 (142) **325.00**
Calendar Plate, 1910 .... **1,800.00**
Calling Card Tray, Ye Lion Inn (173) .. **300.00**
Chocolate Pot, 9" (163) **1,500.00**
Dresser Tray, 9 x 12", Dancing Ye Min-
   uet, 1909 (144) **550.00**
Humidor, 7", octagonal, Ye Lion Inn
   (174) **675.00**
Mug, 3½", Fallowfield Hunt, 1909 (122) **235.00**
Nut Bowl, 8" Ye Lion Inn (175) **475.00**
Pitcher, 9", With A Cane Superior Air
   (167) **525.00**
Plate
   6½", Fallowfield Hunt, 1909 (132) .. **120.00**
   9½", Ye Olden Times, 1908(145) .. **160.00**
Powder Jar, cov, Ye Village Street (143) **300.00**
Relish Dish, Fallowfield Hunt, The Dash
   (135) **350.00**
Sugar, cov, village scenes, 1925 (138) **200.00**
Tankard, 12 x 7", The Fallowfield Hunt,
   The Hunt Supper scene, six men, two
   dogs celebrating, painted by L Streis-
   sel, ink mark, 1909 .... **725.00**
Tea Tile, 6", Traveling In Ye Olden Days
   (140) **300.00**
Teapot, 3¼", Scenes of Village Life,
   1909 (138) **250.00**
Vase, 8", fashionable men and women
   (162) **675.00**
   5¼", Scenes of Village Life in Ye
   Olden Days **375.00**

DELDARE SPECIALS

Humidor, 8", There Was An Old Sailor
   (227) **750.00**
Mug, 4½", Indian scene (231) **500.00**
Salt and Pepper Shakers, pr, Art Nouveau **500.00**

EMERALD DELDARE

Cup and Saucer, Dr Syntax At Liverpool
   (181) **275.00**
Fruit Bowl, octagonal, Art Nouveau dec,
   matching underplate (183) **3,550.00**

Humidor, 7" Dr Syntax Returned Home **850.00**
Inkwell, Art Nouveau dec (196) **5,000.00**
Plaque, 13½", Penn's Treaty With The
   Indians, 1911 (217) **1,500.00**
Tea Tray, 10¼ x 13¾", Dr Syntax Mis-
   takes A Gentleman's House For An
   Inn (180) **875.00**

Saucer, advertising, "The Wanamaker
Store, Philadelphia, Largest In The
World, 1861–Jubilee Year–1911," green
and white, 4⅜" d, $60.00.

GAME SETS

Plate
   9", fish, striped bass (60) **70.00**
   9½", Champion–Bromley Crib Dog
   (73) **500.00**
Platter, oval, Buffalo Hunt, 1907 (62) . **175.00**

HISTORICAL, COMMEMORATIVE, AND ADVERTISING WARE

Mug, 4½"
   Calumet Club (111) **75.00**
   Fraternity Hall (109) **75.00**
Pitcher, Holland **250.00**
Plate
   7½", Gate Circle, Buffalo, NY (97) .. **90.00**
   9", Women's Christian Temperance
   Union, 1908 (86B) **150.00**

MISCELLANEOUS

Canister Set, cov, 1906, each (353) .. **40.00**
Dinner Set, 100 pcs, Kenmore (315) .. **500.00**
Jug, Landing of Roger Williams (36) .. **550.00**
Plate, 10¼", eleven Roosevelt Bear
   scenes, 1906 .... **700.00**
Punch Set, Tom and Jerry (352) **150.00**
Rose Bowl, 3¾", Geranium, 1907 (358) **95.00**
Teapot, Argyle, matching teaball (336) **200.00**

BURMESE GLASS

History: Burmese glass is a translucent art glass originated by Frederick Shirley and manufactured by the Mt. Washington Glass Co., New Bedford, Massachusetts, from 1885 to c1891.

Burmese glass shades from a soft lemon to a salmon pink. Uranium was used to attain the yellow color and gold was added to the batch so that on reheating one end turned pink. Upon reheating again, the edges would revert to the yellow coloring. The blending of the colors was so gradual that it was difficult to determine where one color ended and the other began.

Although some of the glass has a surface that is glossy, most of it is acid finished. The majority of the items were free blown, but some were blown molded in a ribbed, hobnail, or diamond quilted design.

American–made Burmese is quite thin, fragile, and brittle. The only factory licensed to make Burmese was Thos. Webb & Sons in England. Out of deference to Queen Victoria, they called their wares "Queen's Burmese."

Reproduction Alert: Reproductions abound in almost every form. Since uranium can no longer be used, some of the reproductions are easy to spot. In the 1950s, Gunderson produced many pieces in imitation of Burmese.

MW = Mount Washington
Wb = Webb
a.f. = acid finish
s.f. = shiny finish
Advisors: Clarence and Betty Maier.

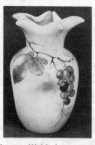

Vase, Thomas Webb, hp, grapes, vines, and leaves, rolled star rim, relief mark on base, registration mark, 4⅝" h, $695.00.

Biscuit Jar, 6" h, autumn leaves dec,
   acid 1,072.00
Bon Bon, 2¾" w, 5" l, 2¾" h, MW, s.f.,
   rect, gently rounded corners 585.00
Bowl, 5" d, MW, a.f., ball shape, four

fold–down edges on top, berry pontil,
   four applied feet 475.00
Castor Set, MW, a.f., pr cruets with lapidary stoppers, pr of ribbed salt and
   pepper shakers, orig Pairpoint silverplated frame 2,250.00
Champagne Glass, 5½" h, shaded raspberry to yellow, circular base, two
   handles 265.00
Cruet, 6½" h, MW, a.f., melon ribbed
   body, orig mushroom stopper 1,285.00
Epergne, 9½" h, Wb, a.f., two undecorated fairy lamps, sgd Clarke bases,
   twin bud vases, centered metal standard holding upright vase, SP stand 1,500.00
Ewer, 10" h, 8½" d base, MW, a.f., applied handle, heat check at upper
   junction 335.00
Fairy Lamp, 5½" h, 7½" d, Wb, a.f., Criklite, undecorated, pleated base, imp
   sgd "Thos Webb & Sons Queen's
   Burmeseware Patented," clear glass
   candle cup sgd "Clarke's Criklite
   Trade Mark," fairy logo, three pcs .. 1,075.00
Hall Lamp, 9½" l, ACB, cylindrical
   shade, four hummingbirds perched
   on floral branches, gold wash metal
   cut–out frame 1,210.00
Hat, 1¼" h, Pairpoint, s.f., c1930 .... 500.00
Jack In The Pulpit, 12" h, MW, a.f., pie
   crust crimped edge, heavy enamel
   floral dec 1,200.00
Lamp Shade, 5" d, MW, s.f., gas fixture 315.00
Pitcher, 9" h, MW, a.f., tankard, rural
   scene and florals, Longfellow verse . 3,250.00
Rose Bowl
   3" d, 2⅞" h, Wb, a.f., eight crimp top,
     lavender five petal flowers, green
     and brown leaves 400.00
   3½" h, floral dec, hexagon top 360.00
Salt, master, 5" d, 6¾" h, Wb, s.f., ruffled, silverplated holder 465.00
Sweetmeat, 7" h, Wb, a.f., cylindrical,
   bittersweet and gold foliage, SP collar, lid, and bail handle, sgd 485.00
Toothpick Holder, 2¾" h, MW, a.f., cylindrical, crimped top, Optic DQ pattern,
   orig paper label 500.00
Tumbler, prunus blossom dec, thin walls 875.00
Vase
   5" h, s.f., flared, bulbous base 250.00
   7" h, 4" w, MW, a.f., double gourd
     shape, green, beige, and pale
     brown maiden hair fern dec, deep
     salmon shaded to brilliant yellow
     base 900.00
   8" h, MW, a.f., lily 585.00
   12½" h, MW, a.f., slender neck, bul-
     bous base, two small handles,
     wafer base, dainty daisy blossoms,
     shadow foliage, gold branches ... 1,950.00
   25" h, s.f., trumpet 750.00

BUSTS

History: The portrait bust has its origins in pagan and Christian tradition. Greek and Roman heroes, and later images of Christian saints, dominate the early examples. Busts of the "ordinary man" first appeared in the Renaissance.

Busts of the nobility, poets, and other notable persons dominated the 18th and 19th centuries, especially those designed for use in a home library. Because of the large number of these library busts, excellent examples can be found at reasonable prices, depending on artist, subject, and material.

Reference: Lynne and Fritz Weber, *Jacobsen's Eleventh Painting and Bronze Price Guide, January 1988 to January 1990,* Jacobsen's Publications, 1990.

Additional Listings: Ivory, Parian Ware, Soapstone, and Wedgwood.

George Washington, Staffordshire, 8¼" h, $100.00.

Alabaster, woman
6⅞" h, white, oval base	**65.00**
16" h, Renaissance style, marble base	**400.00**

Bisque, 18" h, classical lady, smiling, wearing silver and gold trimmed helmet with gilt eagle mounted on top, gold socle, France, 19th C **600.00**

Bronze
6¾" h, child, gilt, green onyx base, marked "S Klaber & Co Founder, NY"	**10.00**
10" h, Marechal Joseph Jacques Joffre, reddish–brown patina, inscribed	**2,250.00**
22" h, girl, inscribed signature	**1,050.00**

Lead, 28" h, Goddess, Hera, diadem in parted hair, loose tunic tied at shoulders, 18th C **1,150.00**

Majolica, 29½" h, Charles V, Order of the Golden Fleece around neck intaglio dec, scrolling foliage, mustard, rust, and green edge epaulets, 16th C **2,500.00**

Marble
15½" h, Greek slave, inscribed "H Powers Sculp"	**15,400.00**
21" h, child, fluted and ivy entwined pedestal, sgd, "C B Ives, Fecit Romae"	**1,850.00**
37" h, Emperor Augustus, short curly hair, white socle, 18th C	**9,000.00**

Oak, 15", Benjamin Franklin, old brown alligatored finish, black carved "Harris" **725.00**

Parian, May Queen, Ceramic and Crystal Palace Art Union, pub April 1, 1868...Copeland, 13" h **110.00**

Plaster, 35" h, George Washington, cast, orig bronze finish **110.00**

Terra Cotta, 30", court lady, Louis XVI style, sgd "Coustou" **500.00**

BUTTER PRINTS

History: Butter prints divide into two categories: butter molds and butter stamps. Butter molds are generally of three piece construction—the design, the screw-in handle, and the case. Molds both shape and stamp the butter at the same time. Butter stamps are of one-piece construction, sometimes two pieces if the handle is from a separate piece of wood. Stamps decorate the top of butter after it is molded.

The earliest prints were one piece and hand carved, often thick and deeply carved. Later prints were factory made with the design forced into the wood by a metal die.

Some of the most common designs are sheaves of wheat, leaves, flowers, and pineapples. Animal designs and Germanic tulips are difficult to find. Rare prints include unusual shapes, such as half-rounded and lollipop, and those with designs on both sides.

Reference: Paul E. Kindig, *Butter Prints And Molds,* Schiffer Publishing, Ltd., 1986.

Reproduction Alert: Reproductions of butter prints date as early as the 1940s.

MOLD

Anchor, 2¾" d, carved wood	**175.00**
Pineapple, 4⅜" d, carved wood	**325.00**
Roses, 5 x 8", carved maple, serrated edges	**145.00**
Sheaf of Wheat, 4½ x 8¼", carved, rect, gray scrubbed finish	**55.00**
Sunflower, 3½" d, carved wood	**50.00**
Thistle, 3⅝" d, carved wood	**100.00**

**Stamp, scallop design, reeded border,
3½" d, 2⅝" h, $90.00.**

STAMP

Cow, 4¼" d, turned handle 150.00
Eagle, shield, and stars, 4½" d, handle
missing 200.00
Floral Design
  4½" d, stylized, turned handle 55.00
  5¼" l, wheel type 100.00
Foliage and Flowers, 4¾" d, 5½" l, wal-
nut, elaborate carving 60.00
Lamb and Cross, 4⅛" d, carved, zig–
zag band around center design,
raised rim, scrubbed finish 125.00
Leaf, 3¼" d, turned inserted handle, refinished 45.00
Leaf and Branch, 3⅝" d, 2¼" l, fruit-
wood, carved 55.00
Pineapple
  4⅝" d, carved, stylized, band of
  dashes on rim, turned handle,
  scrubbed finish 65.00
  4⅞" h, carved 30.00
Pinwheel, 3¾" d, four teardrop and triangular arms form design, old dark
finish 110.00
Rectangular Shape, 4" l, 2½" w, 1⅝" d,
carved heart, tulip, and domed stars 75.00
Rosette, 5⅞" l, lollipop type, carved,
hardwood 100.00
Scallop, 3½" d, reeded border 90.00
Sheaf of Wheat, 6¾" l, stylized design,
notched rim band 200.00
Star, 7" l, lollipop type, zig–zag band
rim, flared end handle, old patina . . 300.00
Strawberry
  2⅞" d, 4½" l, fruitwood, carved 40.00
  4¾" d, carved, rope twist rim band,
  inserted handle, scrubbed finish . . 100.00
Sunflower, 4¼" d, carved, feather
leaves, turned inserted handle, old
dark finish 430.00
Thistle, 2½" d, turned handle 45.00

Tulip
  4½" d, carved, sawtooth border, 19th
  C 220.00
  4⅜" d, carved stylized blossom with
  leaf sprigs, turned handle,
  scrubbed finish 110.00

CALENDAR PLATES

History: Calendar plates were first made in England in the late 1880s. They became popular in
the United States after 1900, the peak years being
1909 to 1915. The majority of the advertising
plates were made of porcelain or pottery with a
calendar, the name of a store or business, and
either a scene, portrait, animal, or flowers. Some
also were made of glass or tin.

Additional Listings: See *Warman's Americana
& Collectibles* for more examples.

**1912, Compliments of J. F. Lauck, Pal-
myra, PA, light gray border, multicolored transfer, marked "Sterling
China," 8⅜" d, $65.00.**

1907, Christmas scene and holly center 75.00
1908, hunting dog, Pittston, PA 35.00
1908, 9½", two monks drinking wine . . 65.00
1908, roses center 55.00
1909, 8¼", flowers 18.00
1909, 9", woman and man in patio gar-
den 25.00
1910, Betsy Ross, Dresden 30.00
1910, boxer portrait center 45.00
1910, ships and windmills 20.00
1910, swimming hole scene 30.00
1911, 7½", compliments of Hilding Nelson, New Britain, CT 30.00
1911, 8", hunt scene, Markell Drug Co,
Chelsea 25.00
1911, Cash Grocery Store, W C Van-
derberg, Hoopston, IL adv, cherub
center 45.00

1911, deer in meadow, scenic panels between months	**35.00**
1912, 9¼", Martha Washington	**35.00**
1913, Quebec country scene	**30.00**
1913, roses and holly	**25.00**
1914, 6¾", Point Arena, CA	**25.00**
1915, 9", black boy eating watermelon	**35.00**
1916, 7½", man in canoe, IA	**25.00**
1916, 8¼", eagle with shield and American flag	**32.00**
1917, cat center	**25.00**
1919, ship scene	**25.00**
1920, The Great War, MO	**25.00**
1921, 9", bluebirds and fruit	**25.00**
1922, dog watching rabbit	**30.00**
1923, Hudsonville, MI	**35.00**
1929, 6¼", flowers, Valentine, NE	**25.00**

CALLING CARD CASES AND RECEIVERS

History: Calling cards, usually carried in specially designed cases, played an important social role in the United States from the period of the Civil War until the end of World War I. When making a formal visit, a caller left his card in a receiver (card dish) in the front hall. Strict rules of etiquette developed. For example, the lady in a family was expected to make calls of congratulations, visits to the ill, and condolence.

The cards themselves were small, embossed or engraved with the caller's name, and often carried a floral design. Many hand done examples, especially in Spencerian script, can be found. The cards themselves are considered collectible and range in price from a few cents to several dollars.

Note: Don't confuse a calling card case with a match safe.

CALLING CARD CASES

Abalone, 3¾", rect, pearl inlay, diamond pattern, 19th C	**75.00**
Ivory, 4" l, rect, wood inlay, block rows center framed with diamond design rim band,	**155.00**
Mother–of–Pearl, 3¾" l, rect, oval ivory reserve with carved floral relief, 19th C	**125.00**
Pearl, carved classical profile of woman, floral engraving	**35.00**
Sterling Silver, 3⅜" l, chased scrolled borders, chain holder, Nathanial Mills, Birmingham, England, 1849–50	**190.00**
Tortoise Shell, 3¾" l, ivory inlay, nacre and colored metal	**85.00**

CALLING CARD RECEIVERS

Art Deco, figural, lady, cast metal, painted green	**85.00**

Calling Card Receiver, Art Nouveau, bronze, 10½" w, 7¼" l, 1½" h at handles, $485.00.

Crystal, blown out flowers, pedestal base	**35.00**
Hand Painted China, 10", roses, gold handles	**30.00**
Nippon, 7½", white and pink flowers, green leave, rolled edges, cobalt ground, blue mark	**150.00**
Sterling Silver, marked "S Kirk & Sons," 1880	**125.00**

CAMBRIDGE GLASS

History: Cambridge Glass Company, Cambridge, Ohio, was incorporated in 1901. Initially, the company made clear tableware, later expanding into colored, etched, and engraved glass. Over 40 different hues were produced in blown and pressed glass.

Five different marks were employed during the production years, but not every piece was marked.

The plant closed in 1954. Some of the molds were later sold to the Imperial Glass Company, Bellaire, Ohio.

References: National Cambridge Collectors, Inc., *The Cambridge Glass Co., Cambridge, Ohio* (reprint of 1930 catalog and supplements through 1934), Collector Books, 1976; National Cambridge Collectors, Inc., *The Cambridge Glass Co., Cambridge, Ohio, 1949 Thru 1953* (catalog reprint), Collector Books, 1976; National Cambridge Collectors, Inc., *Colors In Cambridge Glass,* Collector Books, 1984; Mark Nye, *Cambridge Stemware,* published by author, 1985.

Collectors' Club: National Cambridge Collectors, Inc., P.O. Box 416, Cambridge, OH 43725.

Ashtray	
Caprice, blue, triangular, 3" d	**10.00**
Nude Stem #3011, Carmen	**250.00**
Basket, Crown Tuscan, 10" h	**475.00**

Bowl
  Cleo, green, 14½" d, flared 60.00
  Flying Nude, crystal 450.00
  Mt Vernon, amber, 12" d 40.00
Butter, cov, Diane, crystal 135.00
Cake Plate
  Crown Tuscan, 12" d, ftd 125.00
  Wildflowers, 11½" d, two handles . .   65.00
Candlesticks, pr
  Etch #739, pink 25.00
  Mocha, amber, dolphins 300.00
Candy, cov
  Arcadia, crystal, ftd 45.00
  Elaine, dark emerald 275.00
  Mocha, amber 40.00
Celery, Mocha, amber, 11½" l 20.00
Champagne, Nude Stem #3011, dec,
  frosted stem, Rockwell sgd 650.00
Cheese, Apple Blossom, yellow 35.00

**Cigarette Box, cov, pink, dolphin feet,
4¾ x 4", $35.00.**

Claret, Nude Stem #3011, dec, frosted
  stem, Rockwell sgd 695.00
Cocktail
  Mt Vernon, amber 20.00
  Nude Stem #3011
    Amethyst bowl, Crown Tuscan
      stem and foot 795.00
    Yellow, frosted stem and foot 125.00
Compote
  Caprice Alpine, crystal, 5" d 45.00
  Nude Stem #3011, crystal 475.00
Console Set, Apple Blossom, amber,
  center bowl, three lite keyhole candle-
  sticks, 3 pcs 125.00
Cordial
  Apple Blossom, yellow 95.00
  Mocha, amber 22.00
Cornucopia, Crown Tuscan 35.00
Creamer, Caprice Alpine, crystal 9.50
Cup and Saucer
  Caprice, blue 40.00
  Cleo, amber 15.00

Etch #739, pink 25.00
Decanter, Mt Vernon, amber 40.00
Flower Frog
  Draped nude, 8½" h
    Amber 195.00
    Crystal 65.00
  Geisha, dark amber 450.00
  Roselady, amber 250.00
Goblet
  Candlelight, crystal 27.50
  Cleo, pink 35.00
  Mt Vernon, amber 17.50
  Nude Stem #3011, dec, frosted stem,
    Rockwell sgd 695.00
Ice Bucket, Etch #957, pink 55.00
Ice Tea
  Apple Blossom, light emerald 35.00
  Caprice, crystal 18.00
Ivy Bowl, Caprice, blue, 5" d 275.00
Juice, Caprice, blue 35.00
Lemon Plate, Caprice, blue 20.00
Mayonnaise, 3 pcs
  Arcadia, crystal 35.00
  Cleo, pink 110.00
  Etch #725, green 60.00
Mustard, cov, Etch #701, pink 75.00
Oyster Cocktail, Cleo, pink 27.50
Plate
  Caprice, blue, 9½" d, dinner 125.00
  Cleo, green, 8" d 9.50
Rosepoint, crystal, 8" d 23.00
Puff Box, pink, fighting cocks, round . .   60.00
Relish, Arcadia, crystal, 8" d, three part   35.00
Salt and Pepper Shakers, pr, Nautilus,
  Crown Tuscan 375.00
Salt, open, Caprice, frosted 17.50
Server, Apple Blossom, light emerald,
  center handle 75.00
Sherbet, Arcadia, crystal 10.00
Sugar
  Caprice, blue 27.50
  Everglade, blue, ftd 75.00
Sweetmeat, Cleo, pink 25.00
Tumbler
  Apple Blossom, amber 24.00
  Caprice, crystal 16.00
  Hunt Scene, green, gold trim, 4½" h   45.00
Urn, cov, Martha Washington, heather-
  bloom 110.00
Vanity Set, #680, flashed light blue,
  gold dec 45.00
Vase
  Crown Tuscan, bud, 10" h 45.00
  Lorna, yellow, 7" h, shape #3025 . . .   24.00
  Nude Stem #3011, amber, bud 750.00
Water Set, Gyro Optic, pistachio, pitcher
  and 5 tumblers 175.00
Whiskey, Etch #739, pink 45.00
Wine
  Apple Blossom, yellow 38.00
  Caprice, crystal 30.00
  Nude Stem #3011, topaz 575.00

CAMBRIDGE

CAMBRIDGE POTTERY

History: The Cambridge Art Pottery was incorporated in Ohio in 1900. Between 1901 and 1909 the firm produced the usual line of jardinieres, tankards, and vases with underglazed slip decorations and glazes similar to other Ohio potteries. Line names included Terrhea, Oakwood, Otoe, and others.

In 1904 the company introduced Guernsey kitchenware. It was so well received that it became the plant's primary product. In 1909 the company's name was changed to Guernsey Earthenware Company.

All wares were marked.

Vase, green, acorn mark, 6½″ h, $120.00.

Bank, 3¼″ h, 6″ l, pig shape, dark glaze	125.00
Bowl, 8½″ d, 5¾″ h, matte green glaze, ftd, four imp acorn marks	115.00
Custard Cup, Guernsey mark	40.00
Ewer, 5″ h, Oakwood, marbleized green, brown, and yellow	85.00
Pitcher, 16½″ h, tankard, mold #263, two ears of corn, incised signature	650.00
Tile, 6″ sq, majolica type glaze, high relief florals	85.00
Vase	
5½″ h, ovoid, grapes and leaves, artist sgd	125.00

6½″ h, tapering sides, inward flaring collar, raised sq motif with raised circles, green matte finish, acorn mark	120.00
8″ h, Oakwood, mold #235, saucer base, extended body, applied shaped handles, high glaze, tones of yellow, green, and brown	150.00

CAMEO GLASS

History: Cameo glass is a form of cased glass. A shell of glass was prepared; then one or more layers of glass of a different color(s) was faced to the first. A design was then cut through the outer layer(s) leaving the inner layer(s) exposed.

This type of art glass originated in Alexandria, Egypt, 100–200 A.D. The oldest and most famous example of cameo glass is the Barberini or Portland vase which was found near Rome in 1582. It contained the ashes of Emperor Alexander Serverus who was assassinated in 235 A.D.

Emile Gallé is probably one of the best known artists of cameo glass. He established a factory at Nancy, France, in 1884. Although much of the glass bears his signature, he was primarily the designer. On many pieces, assistants did the actual work, even signing his name. Glass made after his death in 1904 has a star before the name Gallé. Other makers of French cameo glass include D'Argental, Daum Nancy, LeGras, and Delatte.

English cameo does not have as many layers of glass (colors) and cuttings as do French pieces. The outer layer is usually white, and cuttings are very fine and delicate. Most pieces are not signed. The best known makers are Thomas Webb & Sons and Stevens and Williams.

References: Victor Arwas, *Glass Art Nouveau to Art Deco*, Rizzoli International Publications, Inc., 1977; Ray and Lee Grover, *English Cameo Glass*, Crown Publishers, Inc., 1980; Tim Newark, *Emile Galle*, The Apple Press, 1989; Albert C. Revi, *Nineteenth Century Glass*, reprint, Schiffer Publishing, Ltd., 1981; John A. Shuman, III, *The Collector's Encyclopedia of American Art Glass*, Collector Books, 1988.

AMERICAN

Honesdale, vase, 14¼″ h, flaring, deep green over crystal, Art Nouveau iris dec, gold trim, base sgd in gold	875.00
Mt Washington, bowl, 10″ d, ruffled, pink, griffin and floral band, acid stamp sgd	990.00
New England Glass Co, lamp, fluid, 10¾″ h, 8″ d, pink birds and flowers, white ground, iron base, brass font	325.00
Tiffany, vase, 8½″ h, ovoid, white calla lilies, lime green leaves and insect,	

Vase, Daum Nancy, enameled thistle pattern, bronze base, 5¾″ h, $500.00.

pearly irid body, inscribed "L.C.T. X1175," c1892–1928 . . . . **5,500.00**
Weis
   Vase, 5½″ h, cylindrical shape, lavender flowers, pale lavender and white ground **385.00**

ENGLISH

Stevens and Williams
   Lamp, 8″ h, red fuchsias and leaves, yellow ground, sgd **2,650.00**
   Vase, 5⅝″ h, baluster, translucent lime green ground, etched pendant dogwood blossoms, flowering rose bushes, lower section with reserved arched frieze of alternating blossoms and squares, waisted neck with conforming frieze **2,500.00**
Unknown Maker
   Biscuit Jar, 5½″ d, 6½″ h, frosted vaseline ground, opaque white carved berries and leaves, SP top, rim, and handle **2,225.00**
   Marmalade Jar, 4″ d, 3¾″ h, white roses and leaves, red ground, hallmarked sterling silver lid and bail . **1,980.00**
   Perfume, 4½″ h, pear shape, red, white star flowers and leaves, hallmarked sterling hinged lid, glass stopper **1,045.00**
   Rose Bowl, 3″ h, white morning glories, brown ground **350.00**
   Vase, 4½″ h, white anemone, leafy stems, and butterfly, red ground, floral rim band **1,100.00**

Webb, Thomas & Sons
   Compote, 10″ d, 4″ h, pink and white flowers, blue ground, sgd **2,000.00**
   Fairy Lamp, 5″ d, 2″ h, blue, fold-down rim, white cameo forget–me–nots and insect on base, sgd "Thomas Webb & Sons" **615.00**
   Inkwell, 3½ x 4″, bluish–white flowers, frosted amber ground, SS hinged top, sgd **950.00**
   Perfume, 3″ h, bulbous, ivory, serpent weaving through textured design, hinged, hallmarked silver swirl top **770.00**
   Vase
      5½″ d, squatty, blue, gingo ferns, marked **1,100.00**
      6¼″ h, red butterfly, trumpet flower, and leaves, bright yellow ground, sgd "Thomas Webb & Sons" . . **1,320.00**

Vase, Le Gras, sunset, rust to orange to gray to green, black scene, 5″ h, 3½″ d, 4¾″ w, $525.00.

FRENCH

Arsall, vase
   5½″ h, pink daffodils, frosted ground, sgd **440.00**
   10″ h, light brown mums shading to dark brown, pink ground, small bubble on inside top rim, sgd **690.00**
   12″ h, autumn colored leaves and pods, frosted ground, sgd **660.00**
Chouvenin, vase, 8″ h, scenic, windmills and trees, shades of brown, frosted brown to yellow ground, sgd **475.00**
Daum Nancy
   Bowl, 4¾″ d, deep blue grape pods, autumn color leaves and vines, mottled yellow, pink, and amethyst ground, quad fold rim, cameo sgd **825.00**
   Box, cov, 4¾ x 2¾″, green grapes and leaves, tan ground **500.00**

Cologne, 4" h, deeply carved red poppies and green leaves, pink ground, vertical lines, gold rim and stopper with dragonflies, sgd and cross mark **5,000.00**

Creamer, 4½" h, colorful enameled tulips, mottled green and peach ground, cameo cut handle **365.00**

Jar, 3¼" h, red flower buds, green leaves, lavender and opalescent ground **250.00**

Lamp, table
  17" h, double dome shade, brown foliated trees and grasses, lake shore, frosted amber sky, 8½" d baluster form base, shade sgd "Daum Nancy, France," base initials "DN" with cross **16,500.00**
  24" h, enamel dec, branched red apple blossoms, frosted amber ground, 9" h urn shaped stem, gold ftd acanthus leaf base, sgd "Daum Nancy, France" **935.00**

Perfume, 3" h, gold outlined blue poppies and stars, frosted blue ground, matching inset stopper, sgd and cross mark **600.00**

Pitcher, 10¼" h, red bleeding hearts, mottled red and green leafy stems, mottled frosty and pink ground, pulled handle, sgd **9,900.00**

Salt, 2", blackbirds in snow **275.00**

Vase
  3" h, 4" l, miniature pillow, sgd "Daum Nancy" on base
    Fall, mottled orange and yellow sky, enameled snow **2,530.00**
    Summer, chartreuse and green forest scene **2,530.00**
  11½" h, mold blown woodland scene, dark green foliage trees, peering village, mottled orange and yellow sky, sgd on bottom . **10,175.00**
  11¾" h, ftd, red flowers, green leaves, frosted red and gold mottled ground, cameo sgd **3,410.00**

De Latte, vase, 4½" h, deep burgundy gooseberries and leaves, sgd in cameo **440.00**

De Vez
  Rose Bowl, 3½" d, cobalt blue foliated trees and mountains, pink to yellow sky and water, scalloped rim, sgd **500.00**
  Vase
    6" h, island in lake scene with mountains, purple, brown, and peach on white, white background **440.00**
    8" h, tubular, three color scenic brown castle and trees, blue mountains, frosted ground, sgd **1,320.00**

Galle
  Atomizer, 9" h, tapered, red wisteria, frosted citron ground, orig bulb, sgd **1,100.00**
  Bowl
    4¾" d, deep blue grape pods, autumn color leaves and vines, mottled yellow, pink, and amethyst ground, quad fold rim, sgd **825.00**
    5" d, 3¾" h, deep brown pine cones, pale blue ground, sgd .. **700.00**
    10½" l, 3½" h, boat shape, pale lavender hydrangeas, frosted ground, sgd with star **1,600.00**
  Perfume, 5½" h, tri–ribbed, carved pink orchid, leaves, and buds, clear emerald green ground, silver foot, collar, and emb floral dome cov, sgd "Cristallerie E Galle" **6,600.00**
  Toothpick, 2½" h, chartreuse and medium green seed pods and leafy branches, frosted and orange ground, sgd **420.00**
  Urn, 7⅞" h, ftd, burgundy leaves and pods, pale gold ground, deep cut dark burgundy leaves, sgd **1,540.00**
  Vase
    2½" h, orange leaves and berries, sgd **440.00**
    3¾" h, stick, green thistles, peach shaded to green ground, cameo sgd **440.00**
    4½" h, bud, cylinder, frosted, layered amber, cut blossoms, pods, and leaves, sgd on side **525.00**
    5½" h, tapered, shiny brown eucalyptus, bluish–gray ground, sgd **500.00**
    6" h, barrel shape, clusters of red hawthorn berries, leafy branches, frosty and orange ground, sgd **935.00**
    7" h, flat sided stick, shiny brown hydrangeas, frosted gold ground, horizontal cameo sgd **550.00**
    10¼" h
      Scenic, deep purple trees, blue mountains, frosted yellow ground, cameo sgd **5,000.00**
      Tri–shape, lavender hydrangeas, wide green leaves, frosted mottled orange ground, cameo sgd **2,000.00**
    11½" h, molded pink fuchsia, brown leaves, mottled frost and yellow ground, cameo sgd **17,050.00**
    12" h, molded red hyacinth, shaded burgundy leaves, frosted amber ground, cameo sgd, base stamped "Made in France" ... **16,500.00**
    14" h, chartreuse and medium green branched seed pods and leaves, frosty orange ground, sgd **1,375.00**

17" h, stick, chartreuse wisteria, frosted and pink ground **2,255.00**
Gautier, vase, 4¼" h, blue scenic trees, birds in flight, frosted to pale green ground, gold color metal base and rim, sgd **470.00**
Le Gras, vase
    5⅞" h, plum leaves, frosty white ground **110.00**
    8" h, bulbous, maroon floral vines, frosted textured ground **525.00**
    8½" h, stick, enamel red leaf and vine, sgd **500.00**
    8¾" h scalloped oval shape, landscape scene, green, brown, peach, and frosty white **630.00**
    11" h, landscape scene, brown, peach, green, and frosty white . . . **710.00**
    15½" h, heavy mottled brown, white, and clear, etched Art Deco bird motif **770.00**
Le Verre Francais
    Bowl, 9" d, 4½" h, shiny brown and gold stylized floral clusters, frosted gold ground **440.00**
    Ewer, 12" h, orange geometric design, white ground, blue handle and rim **500.00**
    Vase
        8¼" h, stylized shiny brown leaves, frosted orange mottled ground, sgd **425.00**
        10¾" h, apricot amber, etched Art Deco florals, base edge etched "Le Verre Francaise Charder" . **1,045.00**
        12⅞" h, mottled orange and peach, leaves and seed pattern **575.00**
Richard
    Vase
        5" h, brown foliage, blue ground . **275.00**
        6¼" h, pine boughs with pine cones and mountains, yellow ground . **110.00**
        7¾" h, reddish–brown leaves, frosty yellow–green ground . . . **220.00**
    Wine, 7¾" h, cobalt blue scenic water and sailboats on frosted ground, notched stem **330.00**
Unknown Maker, pitcher, 11" h, fall color Woodbine vine and berries, mottled frost, maroon, and blue ground, applied branch handle entwines ribbed body **3,850.00**
Velez, vase, 8½" h, ftd, tapered, deep cranberry shaded sky silhouettes autumn green foliage trees and woodland grasses, pale green hills and trees along river bank, sgd "Velez" . **1,045.00**
Verreri D'Art, vase
    8" h, yellow azaleas and leafy branches, hammered textured purple to cream tapered body, applied silver double handles, silver cut–

out raspberry and leaves on rim, shoulder, and ftd base, sgd in gold "Verreri D'Art, De Lorraine, S & C, Depose" **11,500.00**
9" h, ftd, tapered amber body, lady and armored warrior, band of assorted animals and birds in medallions, gold ground, enamel leaves, sgd in gold "Verreri D'Art, De Lorraine, S & C, Depose" . . . **8,250.00**

CAMERAS

History: The collecting of cameras, except in isolated instances, started about 1970. Although photography generally is considered to have had its beginning in 1839, it is very unusual to find a camera made before 1880. These cameras and others made before 1925 are considered to be antique cameras. Most cameras made after 1925 that are no longer in production are considered to be classic cameras. American, German, and Japanese cameras are found most often.

Value of cameras is affected by both exterior and mechanical conditions. Particular attention must be given to the condition of the bellows if cameras have them.

References: Jim and Joan McKeown, *Price Guide To Antique And Classic Still Cameras, 1989–90, Seventh Edition,* published by authors, 1990; *Jason Schneider On Camera Collecting, Book Three,* Wallace–Homestead, 1985; Douglas St. Denny, *The Jessop International Blue Book, 1990–1991, Second Gold Edition,* Jessop Specialist Publishing, 1990; John Wade, *The Camera, From the 11th Century to the Present Day,* Jessop Specialist Publishing, 1990.

Periodical: *Camera Shopper,* One Magnolia Hill, West Hartford, CT 06117.

Collectors' Clubs: National Stereoscopic Association, P.O. Box 14801, Columbus, OH 43214; Photographic Historical Society, P.O. Box 9563, Rochester, NY 14604.

Museum: George Eastman Museum, Rochester, NY; Smithsonian Institution, Washington, DC.

Additional Listings: See *Warman's Americana & Collectibles* for more examples.

Argus, Model A, 35 mm, f4.5/50mm fixed focus anastigmat lens, c1936–1941, (Ann Arbor, MI) **20.00**
Baldinette, folding 35mm, f2.9/50, Schneider Radionar, Balda–Werke, 1950, (Dresden, Germany) **48.00**
Bell & Howell, Filmo Turret Movie Camera, 8 mm, triple lens holder, variable speeds, 16–64 frames, c1938, (Chicago, IL) **15.00**
Busch, Verascope F–40, f3.5/40 Berthiot lens, guillotine shutter to 250, RF, 1950s, (Chicago, IL) **375.00**

Century, Grand, 5 x 7″, $195.00.

Ciro, Ciroflex B, c1948, (Delaware, OH)	15.00
Coronet, midget, bakelite, black, 15 mm roll film, c1935, (Birmingham, England)	35.00
Devry, 16 mm movie camera, c1932, (Chicago, IL)	25.00
Dossert Detective Camera, box, 4 x 5″ plate, reflex viewing, leather cover designed to look like satchel, c1885, Dossert Detective Camera Co (New York, NY)	675.00
Dubroni, Le Photographe de Poche, wooden box, porcelain int. for in–camera processing, cl860, (Maison Dubroni, Paris)	3,000.00
Eastman Kodak (Rochester, NY)	
Automatic Kodak Junior, No. 2C, c1916–27	15.00
Boy Scout Camera, 1⅝ x 2½″, 127 roll film, green vest pocket, emblem on bed, 1930–34	40.00
Medalist II, 2¼ x 3¼″, 620 film, f3.5/100mm Ektar, flash supermatic shutter, 1946–52	150.00
No. 2, Folding Pocket, 101 roll film, 3½ x 3½″, 1899–1903	15.00
No. 4 Bullet, box, c1896	50.00
Weno Hawk–Eye Box, #7	25.00
Foth, Derby 11, folding, (Berlin, Germany)	40.00
Genie, brass magazine–box, string–set shutter, push–pull action changes plates and actuates exposure counter, c1892, (Philadelphia, PA)	450.00
Ingento, 3A Folding, Burke & James, (Chicago, IL)	35.00
Kalimar A, 35 mm, non–RF, f3.5/45mm Terionar lens, c1950, (Japan)	25.00
Leitz (Wetzier, Germany)	
Leica E (Standard), black, c1932–46	275.00
Leica M2, black, c1950	400.00
Nikon, Nikon F Photomatic, 35 mm, c1965, (Tokyo, Japan)	150.00

Revere, Ranger Model 81, 8 mm movie camera, c1947, (Chicago, IL)	10.00
Seneca, Busy Bee, box, c1903, (Rochester, NY)	70.00
Tom Thumb Camera Radio, Automatic Radio Mfg Co, 1948, (Boston, MA)	110.00
Tynar, 10 x 14mm exposures on specially loaded 16mm cassettes, single speed guillotine shutter, c1950, (Los Angeles, CA)	40.00
Universal Camera Corp (New York, NY)	
Roamer 63, 100 mm f6.3 lens, 120 roll film	10.00
Univex AF, compact, collapsing for Number 00 roll film, cast metal body, 1930s	15.00
Vitar 35 mm, Flash Chronomatic shutter	15.00
Vidmar, Vidax, folding, 120 roll film, c1951, (USA)	250.00

CAMPHOR GLASS

History: Camphor glass derives its name from its color. Most pieces have a cloudy white appearance, similar to gum camphor; the remainder has a pale colored tint. Camphor glass is made by treating the glass with hydrofluoric acid vapors.

Powder Jar, cov, pink salmon, emb flowers, lovebirds finial, 4½″ h, 5″ d, $48.00.

Bowl, 10″ d, fluted rim, polished pontil	125.00
Box, 5″ d, hinged, holly spray	75.00
Candlestick, pr, 7″ h, roses, hp	70.00
Creamer, 3¾″ h	35.00
Cruet, hp, enameled roses, orig stopper	40.00
Miniature Lamp, 4½″ h, hp, violets	75.00
Perfume Bottle, orig stopper	
6½″ h	40.00
8½″ h, pinch type, mushroom stopper	45.00
Place Card Holder, 3¾″ d, ftd	35.00

Plate
6½″ d, Easter Greetings	**35.00**
7¼″ d, owl dec	**40.00**

Powder Jar, cov, 4½″ d, pink–salmon, emb flowers on lid, figural love birds finial ... **48.00**
Rose Bowl, hp violets, green leaves .. **45.00**
Salt and Pepper Shakers, pr, blue, Swirl pattern, orig tops ... **40.00**
Sugar Shaker, 3½″ h, yellow, pressed leaf dec, SP top ... **50.00**
Toothpick Holder
Bucket	**30.00**
Swirled, ruffled top	**35.00**

Vase
8″ h, fan shape, clear leaf design and trim ... **80.00**
10½″ h, Grecian shape, double handles, clear base ... **100.00**

CANDLESTICKS

History: The domestic use of candlesticks is traced to the 14th century. The earliest was a picket type, named for the sharp point used to hold the candle. The socket type was established by the mid-1660s.

From 1700 to the present, candlestick design mirrored furniture design. By the late 17th century, a baluster stem was introduced, replacing the earlier Doric or clustered column stem. After 1730 candlesticks reflected rococo ornateness. Neoclassic styles followed in the 1760s. Each new era produced a new grouping of candlesticks.

However, some styles became universal and remained in production for centuries. For this reason, it is important to examine the manufacturing techniques of the piece when attempting to date a candlestick.

References: Margaret and Douglas Archer, *The Collector's Encyclopedia Of Glass Candlesticks*, Collector Books, 1983; Tom Felt and Bob O'Grady, *Heisey Candlesticks, Candelabra, and Lamps*, Heisey Collectors of America, 1984; Ronald F. Michaelis, *Old Domestic Base–Metal Candlesticks*, Antique Collectors' Club; Wolf Uecker, *Art Nouveau and Art Deco Lamps and Candlesticks*, Abbeville Press, 1986.

Brass
5″ h, octagonal base	**75.00**
7¼″ h, Queen Anne style, octagonal feet, turned shafts, 19th C, pr	**225.00**
7⅝″ h, pr, pushups, diamond quilted and beehive detail	**375.00**
7¾″ h, pr, side pushups	**250.00**
9″ h, pr	**110.00**
9⅜″ h, pr, mid drip pans	**300.00**
10″ h, fluted, English, 18th C, pr	**250.00**
13″ h, open spiral stems, pr	**300.00**

Bronze, 18″ h, tall slender form, glass

blown into socket, sgd "Tiffany Studios, 21100″ ... **1,400.00**
Copper, 11″ h, pear shape, partly hammered, applied silver beads and reeded bands, monogrammed, detachable nozzles, Tiffany & Co, New York, 1891–1902, pr ... **4,125.00**
Glass
Cambridge, Rose Point, ram's head	**200.00**
Camphor, 7″, hp, roses, pr	**75.00**
Cut, 9½″ h, hobstars, teardrop stem	**230.00**
Early American, 7″ h, canary yellow, dolphin, Pittsburgh, pr	**850.00**
Imperial, 7½″, pressed, crystal, orig stickers	**30.00**
Opalescent, 6½″ h, yellow, dolphin, Bakewell, Pears & Co, Pittsburgh, pr	**150.00**
Sandwich, flint, clear dolphin, petal sockets, pr	**450.00**

Ivory, 9″ h, pr, Egyptian caryatid stems **160.00**
Paperweight, 6¾″ h, clear stem, concentric rings of pastel canes base, Whitefriars ... **200.00**
Pewter
6½″ h, weighted base, snuffer provision, c1700	**225.00**
7½″ h, Jack–O–Diamonds, pr, English, 19th C	**90.00**
8″ h, pr, American	**400.00**
8¾″ h, pushup ejectors, English, 1800–25	**375.00**

Steel, 7¼″ h, wrought, spiral pushup, wood base ... **200.00**
Sterling Silver
9″, baluster shaft, surmounted urns, beaded base, drip pan, Goodnow & Jenks ... **220.00**

Porcelain, Samson, pastel colors, gold anchor marks, 8¼″ h, pr, $500.00.

11⅛″, engraved and initialed fluted tapered stem, fluted vase shape socket, detachable drip pan with reeded border, octagonal base with reeded border and engraved dec, Bigelow, Kennard & Co, Boston, 1920, pr **350.00**

Tin, 4 x 5½″, saucer base with lift, ring handle, c1840 . . . . **60.00**

Wood, 7½″, turned base with four turned columns, tin collar and socket, adjustable thumb screw **160.00**

Tank, Victory Glass Co., Jeanette, PA, $40.00.

CANDY CONTAINERS

History: In 1876 Croft, Wilbur and Co. filled a small glass Liberty Bell with candy and sold it at the Centennial Exposition in Philadelphia. From that date until the 1960s, glass candy containers remained popular and served to outline American history, particularly transportation.

Jeannette, Pennsylvania, a center for the packaging of candy in containers, was home to J. C. Crosetti, J. H. Millstein, T. H. Stough, and Victory Glass. Other early manufacturers included: George Borgfeldt, New York, New York; Cambridge Glass, Cambridge, Ohio; Eagle Glass, Wheeling, West Virginia; L. E. Smith, Mt. Pleasant, Pennsylvania; and West Brothers, Grapeville, Pennsylvania.

Candy containers with original paint, candy, and closures command a high premium, but be aware of reproduced parts and repainting. The closure is a critical part of each container; its loss detracts significantly from the value.

Small figural perfumes and other miniatures often are sold as candy containers.

References: George Eikelberner and Serge Agadjanian, *The Complete American Glass Candy Containers Handbook*, revised and published by Adele L. Bowden, 1986; Jennie Long, *An Album Of Candy Containers*, published by author, Volume I: 1978, Volume II: 1983.

Collectors' Club: Candy Container Collectors of America, P.O. Box 1088, Washington, PA 15301.

Museums: Cambridge Glass Museum, Cambridge, OH; L. E. Smith Glass, Mt. Pleasant, PA.

Additional Listings: See *Warman's Americana & Collectibles* for more examples.

Automobile, coupe, 5¼″ l, 3″ h, clear, pressed, long hood, snap on tin closure **75.00**

Bath Tub, 4¾″ l, 1⅞″ h, clear, pressed, open top, traces of white paint, sides marked "Dolly's Bath Tub," Victory Glass Co, Jeannette, PA, USA **2,200.00**

Battleship, 5½″ l, clear **25.00**

Bird, 5″ h, perched on stump, wood,

composition, and chalk, polychrome dec **25.00**

Black Cat For Luck, 4¼″ h, glass, painted, black **1,540.00**

Building, tin, 1914 . . . . **30.00**

Bus, Victory Lines Special, gray paint, cardboard closure **50.00**

Cannon, 4¾″ l, pressed glass, metal frame and wheels **290.00**

Cash Register, 3 x 1½ x 2⅝″, clear, pressed, gold paint, tin slide closure, Dugan Glass Co, Indiana, PA **325.00**

Chest of Drawers, clear, pressed, inserted mirror, painted gold and black trim, tin slide closure **125.00**

Chick, composition
3″ h, painted, orange, yellow, and white, lead legs **60.00**
5″ h, cardboard base, Germany . . . **12.00**

Chicken, 3⅞″ h, composition, red shirt, white pants, head pulls off **100.00**

Clarinet, musical, tin whistle, cardboard tube **30.00**

Clock, 3¼ x 2½ x 1¾″, opaque, white, pressed, painted gilt scrolls, pink rose and green leaf spray, tin slide closure **150.00**

Dog, 3½″ h, begging, clear, pressed, round open base **150.00**

Elf on rocking horse, 3½″ h, pressed glass, painted, no closure **155.00**

Fire Truck, with ladders **25.00**

Football, tin, Germany **18.00**

Ghost Head, 3½″, papier mache, flannel shroud **135.00**

Girl, celluloid, crepe paper dress **20.00**

Gun, 3⅝″ l, 2″ h, clear, molded, cream enamel screw cap, waffle type pattern grip **12.00**

Hat, clear, opaque white and stained colors, screw tin brim **60.00**

Horse and Wagon, glass **35.00**

House, 3″ h, tin, litho, multicolored, glass insert with wire trap **110.00**

Indian, 5″ l, riding motorcycle with sidecar, pressed glass, no closure . . . **330.00**

Kettle, 2″ h, 2¼″ d, clear, pressed, three

feet, cardboard closure, T H Stough
Co 45.00
Kewpie, 3″ h, glass, painted, no closure 110.00
Lantern, barn type, glass, tin bottom,
friction closure 50.00
Limousine, 4⅛ x 1¹⁵⁄₁₆ x 2½″, clear,
pressed, black painted tin wheels,
open top, 1912–14 . . . . 70.00
Mailbox, 3¼″ 50.00
Motorcycle, man on top with side car,
clear, pressed, painted, red tin snap
closure, Victory Glass Co, Jeannette,
PA 350.00
Nursing Bottle, clear, pressed, natural
wood nipple closure, T H Stough Co,
1940–50 . . . . 15.00
Owl, 4⅜″ h, clear, pressed, stylized
feather design, gold tin screw cap . . 80.00
Piccolo, musical, tin whistle, cardboard
tube 45.00
Political Elephant, 2¾″, GOP 110.00
Pumper, 5″ l, pressed glass, tin wheels
and bottom 100.00
Pumpkin Head, 8¾″ h, composition,
painted, multicolored, paper hat . . . 165.00
Puppy, 2½″ h, papier mache, painted
white, black muzzle, glass eyes . . . 30.00
Purse, 4⅛ x 2½ x 3⅝″, clear, pressed,
light emerald, alligator leather design,
gilded metal parts, gold souvenir
panel, aluminum closure 275.00
Rabbit
Eating carrot 35.00
Riding motorcycle, composition,
painted, orange, blue, green, and
red, spring neck 110.00
Seated
5½″ h, composition and wood, simulated fur, glass eyes 45.00
9½″ l, composition, brown, pink,
and white, glass eyes 45.00
Standing, 7½″ l, composition, painted,
brown, glass eyes 170.00
With cart, 7¾″ l, papier mache rabbit,
wood cart 110.00
Record Player, with horn 200.00
Refrigerator, clear, pressed, painted
white, gilded hinges, handles, and
latches, four legs, USA–VG Co–
Jeannette, PA 1,000.00
Rooster, composition, painted
7½″ h, lead legs 200.00
9¼″ h, policeman, wood jointed neck,
blue, yellow, orange, and green . . 25.00
Santa
5¼″ h, pressed glass, painted, red,
gold, and white 310.00
6½″ h, cardboard, painted face, upper
body lifts off, Germany 145.00
Soldier, 5⅛″ h, holding sword, molded,
painted, stepped plinth type base, tin
slide closure 800.00

Ship, 6½″, SS Colorado 325.00
Squirrel, 5″ h, sitting on stump holding
nut, clear, pressed, emb leaves, twig,
and acorn design, tree bark ground,
metal screw top 1,200.00
Statue of Liberty, 5¾″ h, clear, lead top 1,100.00
Suitcase, 3⅝″, emb straps, tin closure,
wire handle 35.00
Telephone, desk type, French, Crosetti 20.00
Topsy–Turvy, 3¼″ h, composition, card-
board base 110.00
Traffic Sign, 4½″, marked "Don't Park
Here" 60.00
Turkey, papier mache 20.00
Wolf, 4⅝″, holding book 50.00
World's Fair Exposition, 1892, pressed
glass, no closure 290.00

CANES

History: Canes and walking sticks were important accessories in a gentleman's wardrobe in the
18th and 19th centuries. They often served both
a decorative and utilitarian function. Collectors frequently view carved canes in wood and ivory as
folk art and pay higher prices for them. Glass
canes and walking sticks were glass makers'
whimsies, ornamental rather than practical.

References: Joyce E. Blake, *Glasshouse
Whimsies,* published by author, 1984; Catherine
Dike, *Cane Curiosa,* published by author, 1983;
Catherine Dike, *La Canne: Objet d'Art,* published
by author, 1987.

Periodical: Linda Beeman, *Cane Collector's
Chronicle,* 15 Second Street NE, Washington, DC
20002.

CANES

Glass
30″, aqua, twisted handle and tip . . 110.00

Ivory handle, ebony shaft, 35″ l, $50.00.

33", honey amber, ribbed handle, corkscrew bottom **200.00**

36", latticino, pink and white swirls . **235.00**

58", burgundy swirl stripes **225.00**

Ivory, 34¾", tapered shaft, carved fist clenching coiled snake handle, late 19th C **1,650.00**

Scrimshaw

29¾", wood shaft, L shape whale ivory handle, mid 19th C **55.00**

33", five sections, ebonized wood, wood and whalebone separators, whale ivory top with L shape handle, mid 19th C **250.00**

35", shark vertebrae, mounted on iron rod, whale's tooth handle, mid 19th C **110.00**

35¾", whalebone, C shape handle, 19th C **330.00**

Wood

30¾", rosewood, whale's tooth handle **65.00**

33½", ebonized, SS knop and reeded head, horn tip, late 19th C **250.00**

35½", ebonized, gold knop, foliate design and engraved name and date on shaft, imp marks **330.00**

38", tapered, carved and incised Masonic designs, 19th C **110.00**

WALKING STICKS

Ebony, 32½", amethyst head with pierced gold filled laurel borders, 19th C **275.00**

Folk Art, 36", pine, carved clenched fist, cuff and cuff link, and snake, old varnish finish **110.00**

Glass, 54½", clear, gold int. **70.00**

Tortoiseshell, 34", handle with repousse and chased foliage, Continental, 19th C **1,100.00**

Wood

34¼", relief carved inscriptions of Thomas Jefferson's life **225.00**

35", tapered, carved insects, snakes, and reptiles, hand molded grip, inscribed "made by F T Smith for B Chambe," 19th C **440.00**

35¾", tapered octagonal shaft **55.00**

CANTON CHINA

History: Canton china is a type of oriental porcelain made in the Canton region of China from the late 18th century and early 19th century to the present and produced largely for export. Canton china is hand decorated in light to dark blue underglaze on white. Design motifs include houses, mountains, trees, boats, and a bridge. A design similar to "willow china" is the most common.

Borders on early Canton feature a rain and cloud motif (a thick band of diagonal lines with a scalloped bottom). Later pieces usually have a straight line border. The markings "Made in China" and "China" indicate wares which date after 1891.

Early, c1790–1840, plates are very heavy and often have an unfinished bottom, while serving pieces have an overall "orange peel" bottom. Early covered pieces, such as tureens, vegetable dishes, sugars, etc., have strawberry finials and twisted handles. Later ones have round finials and straight, single handles.

Reference: Sandra Andacht, *Oriental Antiques & Art: An Identification And Value Guide,* Wallace-Homestead, 1987.

Reproduction Alert: Several museum gift shops and private manufacturers are issuing reproductions of Canton china.

Advisor: Mark Saville.

Bowl, 10" d

Round, scalloped, c1830 . . . . **775.00**

Square, cut corners, c1830 . . . . **1,200.00**

Butter Dish, 3 pcs, c1840 . . . . **700.00**

Butter Pat, early **80.00**

Candlesticks, pr, 7" h, trumpet shape . **2,850.00**

Charger, 14" d, early, c1835 . . . . **800.00**

Coffeepot, 10" h, domed lid, c1850 . . . **900.00**

Creamer, 4" h, pear shape, c1840 . . . **235.00**

Egg Cup, 2½" h, early, c1840 . . . . **125.00**

Fruit Basket, 9¾" l, reticulated, matching undertray, c1840 . . . . **1,100.00**

Ginger Jar, cov, 6" h, c1840 . . . . **275.00**

Hot Water Dish, 8½" d, c1845 . . . . . . **400.00**

Kettle Stand, 7" h, c1830 . . . . **225.00**

Pie Dish, early, c1840

7" d **300.00**

9" d **425.00**

Pitcher, 10" h, c1830 . . . . **1,300.00**

Plate, early, c1820–30

6" d, butter **60.00**

7½" d, salad **75.00**

Plate, water edge scene, c1800–20, 10" d, $65.00.

8″ d, dessert	**90.00**
9″ d, lunch	**110.00**
10″ d, dinner	**150.00**
Platter, early, c1830–40	
13″ l, rect	**375.00**
16″ l, rect	**650.00**
17″ l, well–in–tree	**750.00**
Salt, master, c1830	**500.00**
Saucer	
Straight line border, late, c1875	**75.00**
Twig shape handle, c1850	**105.00**
Serving Dish, early, c1840	
10″ d, open	**300.00**
12″ l, rect, open	**450.00**
Spoon, firemarks, early, c1835	**50.00**
Sugar, Cov, twisted handles	**360.00**
Teapot	
6″ h, drum shape, c1830	**500.00**
7″ h, lighthouse shape, c1825	**650.00**
Tile, sq, early, c1820	**325.00**
Tureen	
8″ d, undertray	**750.00**
13″ l, undertray, c1820	**2,400.00**
Vegetable Dish, cov, 8½ x 9½″, sq, c1840	**475.00**

CAPO-DI-MONTE

History: In 1743 King Charles of Naples established a soft paste porcelain factory near Naples which made figures and dinnerware. In 1760 many of the workmen and most of the molds were taken to Buen Retiro, near Madrid, Spain. A new factory opened in Naples in 1771 and added hard paste porcelains. In 1834 the Doccia factory in Florence purchased the molds and continued their production in Italy.

Capo-di-Monte was copied heavily by factories in Hungary, Germany, France, and Italy.

Reference: Susan and Al Bagdade, *Warman's English & Continental Pottery & Porcelain,* 2nd *Edition,* Wallace–Homestead, 1991.

Reproduction Alert: Many of the pieces in today's market are of recent vintage. Do not be fooled by the crown over the "N" mark; it also was copied.

Box, gilt metal mounting	
6⅛″ l, hinged, rect, relief molded, three maidens and young, sides molded with baby Bacchantes tending to grapevines, overglaze blue crowned "N" mark	**1,100.00**
11½″ l, oval, Greek gods molded on lid, ribbon tied floral garland, gilt ground, side frieze of mask flanked by two sphinxes between scrolling	

Glove Box, pastels, low relief molded putti, 10½″ l, 5½″ h, $500.00.

acanthus above gilt guilloche band enclosing flowerheads, underglaze blue crowned "N" mark	**1,320.00**
Candleholder, 3″ h, raised flowers and nude figures	**100.00**
Compote, cov, 9″ h, oval, relief molded cherubs on sides, cherub finial and handles	**225.00**
Cup and Saucer, molded cup ext. with sea nymphs swimming in the ocean, gilt int. with painted floral sprigs, molded putti on saucers, underglaze blue crowned "N" mark, set of twelve	**2,475.00**
Demitasse Set, 17 pcs, covered pot, creamer, sugar, six ftd cups and saucers, large round ftd tray, artist sgd .	**250.00**
Ferner, 11″ l, oval, relief molded and enameled allegorial figures, full relief female mask at each end	**100.00**
Figure	
8½ x 9½″, Young Photographer, boy kneeling with camera, girl on brick wall, crown/N/initials	**170.00**
14″ h, African Crowned Crane, one foot in water, other with water plants on base, sgd "G Armani" .	**180.00**
Jewel Box, 9¾″ l, oval, relief molded and brightly painted frieze of drunken cherub being carried away by baby satyrs, domed cov with Venus, entwined rose garland and feather borders, 19th C	**350.00**
Plaque, 22½ x 16½″, harvest scene, high relief, velvet covered molded frame	**290.00**
Plate, semi–nudes bathing beside brook relief, floral festoon border . . .	**100.00**
Snuff Box, 3¼″ d, hinged lid, cartouche shape, molded basketweave and flowerhead ext., painted int. with court lady and page examining portrait of gentleman, gold mountings, c1740, minor restoration	**1,650.00**
Stein, garden scene, adults and children, lion on cov, sgd	**120.00**
Tea Set, 9″ h cov teapot, creamer, cov sugar, four cake plates, cups, and saucers, relief molded scenes of classical figures, landscape settings, mul-	

ticolored enamels, crowned "N" mark, c1900, 15 pcs **275.00**

Urn, 21⅛" h, cov, ovoid, central molded frieze of Nereids and putti, molded floral garlands, gadroon upper section, acanthus molded lower section, socle foot with putti, sq plinth base, applied ram's head handles, domed cov, acorn finial, underglaze crowned "N" mark, minor chips and losses, pr **1,650.00**

Vase, 13" h, cylindrical, pedestal base, ring and domed foot, relief molded scantily clad classical figures, polychrome dec, relief molded putti around base, late, pr **250.00**

CARLSBAD CHINA

History: Because of changing European boundaries during the last 100 years, German–speaking Carlsbad has found itself located first in the Austro-Hungarian Empire, then in Germany, and currently in Czechoslovakia. Carlsbad was one of the leading pottery manufacturing centers in Bohemia.

Wares from the numerous Carlsbad potteries are lumped together under the term "Carlsbad China." Most pieces on the market are post-1891, although several potteries date to the early 19th century.

Reference: Susan and Al Bagdade, *Warman's English & Continental Pottery & Porcelain, 2nd Edition,* Wallace–Homestead, 1991.

Ashtray, 5¼" d, multicolored Dutch men and women strolling waterfront **15.00**

Bowl
8¾", shallow, gold center with death of King Lear, green border, artist sgd **70.00**
10", portrait, green border, gold tracings, sgd "Boucher, Victoria Carlsbad, Austria" **60.00**

Butter Dish, 7½" d, cov, pink flowers, green leaves, wavy gold lines, white ground **55.00**

Chocolate Pot, 10", blue, scenic portrait, marked "Carlsbad Victoria" **110.00**

Creamer and Sugar, Bluebird pattern, marked "Victoria Carlsbad" **55.00**

Cup and Saucer, set of 6, rosebuds, vines, and leaves, c1875 . . . . **125.00**

Ewer
6", cream, pastel pink, gold, floral dec **75.00**
14", handles, light green, floral dec, gold trim, marked "Carlsbad, Victoria" **80.00**

Hair Receiver, 4" d, cobalt blue flowers, emb basketweave at top, gold trim, white ground **30.00**

Oyster Plates, 8¾", set of 10, lavender flowers, gold outlining, white ground **100.00**

Pin Tray, 8½", irregular scalloped shape, roses, green leaves, white ground, marked "Victoria, Carlsbad, Austria" **30.00**

Pitcher
7" h, two cherubs at fountain, pink and white ground, gold handle . . . **25.00**
8" h, cream, gold floral dec, ornate handle **60.00**

Plate, floral center, lilac reticulated border, gilt edge, marked, 6½" d, $15.00.

Plate
7½" d, multicolored portrait of young girl, pierced for hanging **30.00**
9", cherries, hp, sgd **25.00**

Powder Box, cov, 5" d, Bluebird pattern, Victoria, Carlsbad **45.00**

Soup Tureen, cov, white, deep pink and yellow roses, green leaves, gold trim buckle handles and finial, imp mark . **65.00**

Sugar Shaker, 5½", egg shape, floral dec **60.00**

Urn, 14½" h, rose bouquet, shaded ivory ground, marked "Carlsbad, Austria" **145.00**

Vase
8" h, double gourd shape, multicolored florals **30.00**
9½" h, center medallion of four Grecian figures, dark blue–green ground, ornate cream handles . . . **48.00**

CARNIVAL GLASS

History: Carnival glass, an American invention, is colored pressed glass with a fired on iridescent finish. It was first manufactured about 1905 and was immensely popular both in America and abroad. Over 1,000 different patterns have been identified. Production of old carnival glass patterns ended in 1930.

Most of the popular patterns of carnival glass were produced by five companies—Dugan, Fenton, Imperial, Millersburg, and Northwood. Northwood patterns frequently are found with the "N" trademark. Dugan used a diamond trademark on several patterns.

In carnival glass, color is the most important factor in pricing. The color of a piece is determined by holding the piece to the light and looking through it.

References: Bill Edwards, *The Standard Encyclopedia of Carnival Glass, Revised Third Edition*, Collector Books, 1991; Marion T. Hartung, *First Book of Carnival Glass to Tenth Book of Carnival Glass* [series of 10 books], published by author, 1968 to 1982; Thomas E. Sprain, *Carnival Glass Tumblers, New and Reproduced,* published by author, 1984.

Collectors' Clubs: American Carnival Glass Association, 4579 Clover Hill Circle, Walnutport, PA 18088; Collectible Carnival Glass Association, 2360 N. Old S.R.9, Columbus, IN 47203; Heart of America Carnival Glass Association, 3048 Tamarak Drive, Manhattan, KS 66502; International Carnival Glass Association, Inc., R.D. #1, Box 14, Mentone, IN 46539; New England Carnival Glass Club, 12 Sherwood Road, West Hartford, CT 06117.

Cherry Circle, bonbon, marigold, 7⅜" d, $40.00.

Marigold	70.00
Blueberry, Fenton	
Pitcher, blue	500.00
Tumbler	
Blue	75.00
Marigold	35.00
White	185.00
Brooklyn Bridge, Dugan, 8¾" d, 2⅞" h, marigold, shiny finish, fluted scalloped edge	275.00
Carolina Dogwood, Westmoreland	
Bowl, 8½" d	
Aqua opalescent	375.00
Peach opalescent	150.00
Bride's Bowl, peach opalescent	325.00
Plate, 8½" d, peach opalescent	475.00
Cherry, Fenton	
Bonbon, aqua, two handles	275.00
Bowl, green	150.00
Calling Card Tray, aqua	125.00
Plate, 6" d, marigold	40.00
Cherry Circle, Fenton, bowl, 10" d, ruffled, Orange Tree ext., white	100.00
Coin Dot, Northwood	
Bowl	
6" d, green	20.00
8" d, aqua, stippled	45.00
9" d, vaseline, ruffled	55.00
Pitcher, marigold	150.00
Plate, purple	60.00
Rose Bowl, marigold	45.00
Tumbler, marigold	50.00
Corinth, Dugan	
Banana Boat, marigold	30.00
Rose bowl, ice blue	110.00
Country Kitchen, Millersburg	
Bowl, 5" d, marigold, ruffled	80.00
Butter Dish, cov, purple	350.00
Spooner, marigold	100.00
Daisy, Fenton	
Bonbon, marigold	85.00
Nut bowl, blue	220.00
Daisy and Plume, Northwood	
Candy Dish, green	65.00
Compote, aqua	60.00
Rose Bowl, marigold	80.00

Acorn, Fenton
Bowl	
5" d, blue, ribbon candy rim	60.00
7" d, amber, ruffled	110.00
9" d, purple, ribbon candy rim	50.00
Apple Blossom Twigs, Dugan	
Banana Boat, peach opalescent, ruffled	175.00
Bowl	
8" d, marigold	50.00
10" d, purple	250.00
Plate, 9" d, blue	110.00
Vase, amethyst	50.00
Autumn Acorns, Fenton	
Bowl, 9" d	
Blue	75.00
Green	40.00
Marigold	50.00
Beaded Shell, Dugan	
Berry set, master and three ftd sauces, purple	185.00
Creamer, marigold	60.00
Mug, purple	65.00
Rose Bowl, green	40.00
Spooner, marigold	40.00
Table Set, marigold, 4 pcs	250.00
Tumbler	
Blue	45.00
Lavender	95.00

Dragon and Lotus, Fenton
Bowl, blue	75.00
Plate, 9½" d, marigold	650.00

Drapery, Northwood
Bowl, 8" d, pastel	50.00
Candy Dish, marigold	150.00
Rose Bowl, green	85.00
Vase, ice green	55.00

Embossed Mums, Northwood
Bonbon, pastel	100.00
Bowl, 9" d, marigold	45.00
Plate, irid	1,750.00

Feather Stitch, Fenton, bowl, blue ... 290.00

Flute, Imperial and Millersburg
Breakfast Set, individual size, green	115.00
Goblet, marigold	15.00
Sauce, green	60.00
Sherbet	25.00
Toothpick, amethyst	55.00

Good Luck, Northwood
Bowl
7" d, green, ruffled	200.00
8" d, purple, piecrust	235.00
Plate, 9" d	
Green	500.00
Marigold	225.00

Grape, Northwood, nut bowl, 8" d, scroll feet, amethyst ... 65.00

Grape and Cable, Fenton and Northwood
Banana Boat, blue	335.00
Berry Set, master and six sauces, green	200.00
Bowl, aqua opalescent, stippled	2,600.00
Butter Dish, cov, amethyst	95.00
Creamer and Sugar, amethyst	85.00
Cup and Saucer, marigold	250.00
Ice Cream Bowl, white	130.00
Plate, green	85.00
Sweetmeat, cov, Northwood, amethyst, sgd	250.00

Heavy Grape, Imperial, chop plate, amethyst ... 400.00

Hobnail, Millersburg
Butter Dish, cov, marigold	350.00
Cuspidor, purple	475.00
Rose Bowl	
Amethyst	475.00
Marigold	50.00

Hobstar and Feather, Millersburg
Punch Bowl, two pcs, marigold, vaseline base, chip on inside rim	525.00
Punch Cup, green	30.00
Rose Bowl, green	1,500.00

Horse Heads, Fenton
Bowl, blue	100.00
Jack In The Pulpit Vase, vaseline	135.00
Nut Bowl, vaseline	210.00
Plate, 8" d, marigold	145.00
Rose Bowl, marigold	110.00

Inverted Strawberry, Imperial, tumbler, amethyst, marked "Nearcut" ... 300.00

Jeweled Heart, Dugan
Bowl, white	165.00
Calling Card Tray, peach opalescent, turned up sides	45.00
Pitcher, marigold	650.00
Sauce, purple	40.00
Tumbler, amber	115.00

Leaf and Flower, Millersburg, compote, green ... 190.00

Lion, Fenton
Bowl
5" d, marigold, low	95.00
7" d, blue	300.00
Plate, 7" d, marigold	500.00

Little Fishes, Fenton
Bowl
6" d, ftd	65.00
10" d, blue, ftd	250.00
Sauce Dish, 5" d, marigold	55.00

Little Flowers, Fenton
Berry Set, master bowl and six sauces, green	240.00

Heavy Grape, bonbon, purple, $60.00.

Millersburg Diamond, tumbler, marigold, $45.00.

Bowl
5" d, marigold	30.00
8" d, blue	100.00
10" d, lavender, ruffled	115.00
Nut Bowl, marigold	65.00
Plate, 6" d, marigold	185.00

Lotus and Grape, Fenton
Bonbon, green, two handles	50.00

Bowl
5" d, blue, ftd	40.00
7" d, marigold, ftd	45.00
Ice Cream Bowl, 8½" d, Persian blue	400.00
Plate, 9" d, green	1,500.00

Louisa, Westmoreland
Bowl, 8" d, green, ftd	45.00
Nut Bowl, marigold, ftd	30.00
Plate, 9½" d, teal blue, ftd	100.00
Rose Bowl, lavender, ftd	70.00
Salt and Pepper Shakers, pr, marigold	20.00

Many Stars, Millersburg
Bowl, 8" d, marigold	130.00
Ice Cream Bowl, 10" d, green	375.00

Nautilus, Dugan
Bowl, ftd, amethyst	130.00
Creamer, purple	170.00
Sugar Bowl, peach opalescent	250.00

Palm Beach, United States Glass Co
Banana Boat, purple	115.00
Bowl, 5" d, marigold, turned in sides	90.00
Butter Dish, cov, white	200.00
Creamer, marigold	70.00
Pitcher, marigold	400.00
Rose Bowl, amber	125.00
Sauce, white	40.00
Spooner, white	85.00
Tumbler, marigold	200.00

Peacock and Urn, Fenton and Millersburg
Bowl
Blue	300.00
Marigold, with bee	350.00
Compote, 5" d, aqua	325.00
Ice Cream Bowl, 10" d, purple	250.00
Plate, 6½" d, marigold	165.00
Sauce, green	75.00

Peacock at the Fountain, Northwood
Berry Set, master and six sauces, marigold	200.00
Butter Dish, cov, purple	225.00
Compote, marigold	400.00
Creamer, purple	90.00
Punch Bowl and Base, marigold	350.00
Punch Cup, blue	50.00
Sauce, ice blue	75.00
Sugar Bowl, white	180.00
Water Set, pitcher, six tumblers, cobalt blue	600.00

Peacock on Fence, Northwood
Bowl
8" d, blue, piecrust rim	375.00
9" d, marigold, ruffled rim	200.00

Peacock, bowl, purple, 8¾" d, $125.00.

Plate, 9" d	
Ice green	2,100.00
Purple	600.00
White	400.00

Plaid, Fenton
Bowl, blue	90.00
Plate, 9" d, marigold	125.00

Rose Show, Northwood
Bowl, 8¾" d, marigold	125.00
Plate, aqua opalescent	2,000.00

Singing Birds
Creamer, marigold	40.00
Sugar, marigold	45.00

Stag and Holly, Fenton
Bowl, amethyst	160.00
Rose Bowl, marigold	375.00

Stippled Rays, Fenton, plate, 7" d, marigold	35.00

Strawberry, Northwood, plate, 9" d, basketweave ext., green, irid, sgd	425.00

Three Fruits, Northwood
Bonbon, green	80.00
Bowl, aqua opalescent	400.00
Compote, marigold	50.00
Plate, marigold	160.00

Three In One, Imperial, bowl, 8¾" d, smoky	20.00

Wide Panels, United States Glass Co
Plate, red	90.00
Salt, marigold	40.00

Wishbone, Northwood
Bowl, ftd, amethyst	130.00
Epergne, aqua	275.00

CAROUSEL FIGURES

History: By the late 17th century, carousels were found in most capital cities of Europe. In 1867 Gustav Dentzel carved America's first carousel. Other leading American manufacturers include Charles I. D. Looff, Allan Herschell, Charles Parker, and William F. Mangels.

Original paint is not critical, since figures were

repainted annually. Park paint indicates layers of accumulated paint; stripped means paint removed to show carving; restored involves stripping and repainting in the original colors.

References: Charlotte Dinger, *Art Of The Carousel,* Carousel Art, Inc., 1983; Tobin Fraley, *The Carousel Animal,* Tobin Fraley Studios, 1983; Frederick Fried, *The Pictorial History Of The Carrousel,* Vestal Press, 1964; William Manns, Peggy Shank, and Marianne Stevens, *Painted Ponies: American Carousel Art,* Zon International Publishing, 1986.

Periodicals: *Carrousel Art,* P.O. Box 992, Garden Grove, CA 92642; *The Carousel News & Trader,* 87 Park Avenue West, Suite 206, Mansfield, OH 44902.

Collectors' Clubs: The American Carousel Society, 60 East 8th Street, #12K, New York, NY 10003; National Amusement Park Historical Association, P.O. Box 83, Mount Prospect, IL 60056; National Carousel Association, P.O. Box 8115, Zanesville, OH 43702.

Cat, racing, carved and painted, fish in
 mouth, tail up, 54″ l, Gustav Dentzel,
 c1903 . . . . **27,500.00**
Donkey, rearing, carved bells, expres-
 sive face, bell on neck strap, orig handle, 60″ l, Bayol, France, c1895 . . . **16,500.00**
Dragon, leaping, scaly body, carved
 double saddle, fierce expression,
 etched mirrored and jeweled eye,
 hinged neck, 69″ l, Anderson, En-
 gland, c1900 . . . . **11,000.00**
Elephant, walking, painted scalloped
 blanket, carved saddle, 52″ l, Ameri-
 can, c1880 . . . . **11,550.00**
Giraffe, standing, criss–cross blanket,
 48″ l, Charles Looff, c1895 . . . . **13,200.00**
Horse
 Jumper
  Armored, latticework blanket, jew-

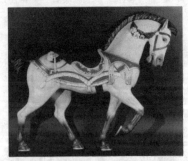

**Horse, outside row, stander, PTC,
Muller Period, c1906, $49,500.00.**

eled trappings, breastplate medallion, 50″ l, C W Parker Amuse-
  ment Co, c1905 . . . . **6,600.00**
 Tapered head, reverse swept
  mane, spirited expression, 52″ l,
  M C Illions, c1910 . . . . **5,500.00**
Prancer, inner row, flowing mane,
 parted forelock, scalloped straps,
 draped blanket, 54″ l, Gustav Den-
 tzel, c1900 . . . . **16,500.00**
Standing, outside row
 Flowing mane, draped forelock,
  jeweled trappings, sword and
  scabbard, fishscale armor, 64″ l,
  Charles Carmel, c1915 . . . . . . **29,700.00**
 Protruding peek–a–boo mane, or-
  nately carved, jeweled trappings
  and blanket, 62″ l, MC Illions &
  Sons, c1921 . . . . **45,100.00**
Mule, jumping, animated pose, folded
 blanket, scrolled saddle, 52″ l, Herschell–Spillman, c1914 . . . . **6,600.00**
Pig, running, protruding tongue, painted
 collar and blanket, 42″ l, Chanvin,
 France, c1895 . . . . **3,520.00**
Rabbit, running, white body, tassel dec
 on layered trappings, fur detail, 46″ l,
 Hubner, Germany, c1890 . . . . **4,950.00**
Rooster, running, 38″ h, 32″ l, Pennsyl-
 vania, 19th C **1,750.00**
Sea Dragon, horse front legs, scaly fish
 tail, fierce expression, jeweled straps
 and blanket, repainted, 66″ l, Charles
 Looff, c1900 . . . . **20,900.00**
Stag, attributed to Looff, New York,
 leaping, carved and painted, scrolled
 saddle pommel, real antlers, glass
 eyes, 61″ l, c1895 . . . . **13,200.00**
Zebra, standing, outside row, painted,
 layered blanket, fringed straps, 56″ l,
 E Joy Morris, Philadelphia Toboggan
 Co, c1903 . . . . **22,000.00**

CASTLEFORD

History: Castleford is a soft paste porcelain made in Yorkshire, England, in the 1800s for the American trade. The ware has a warm, white ground, scalloped rims (resembling castle tops), and is trimmed in deep blue. Occasionally pieces are decorated further with a coat of arms, eagles, or Lady Liberty.

Creamer, 4¼″ h, white, parian, deep
 blue striping, emb classical scenes of
 cherubs **100.00**
Milk Jug, 4¾″ h, oval, relief of American
 Eagle on one side, Liberty and cap
 on reverse, acanthus leaf border . . . **150.00**
Sugar, cov, relief of classical figure leaning on urn, acanthus leaf panel, blue

Milk Jug, oval, American eagle on one side, Liberty and Cap on reverse, acanthus leaf dec, 4¾" h, $150.00.

enamel border, scalloped edge, three enamel bands on cov 245.00
Teapot and Stand, 9¼" h, blue enamel trim, relief molded classical scenes within panels, leafy borders, floral finial, slide cov, imp mark, minor chips, finial reglued 440.00
Tea Set, cov teapot, milk jug, cov sugar bowl, relief panels of mythological figures, animals, and shell, bead border, fluted base, dolphin knob, blue enamel line border, glazed int. 400.00

CASTOR SETS

History: A castor set consists of matched condiment bottles within a frame or holder. The bottles are for condiments such as salt, pepper, oil, vinegar, and mustard. The most commonly found castor set consists of three to five glass bottles in a silver-plated frame.

Although castor sets were known as early as the 1700s, most of the sets encountered today date from the 1870 to 1915 period when they enjoyed great popularity.

3 bottles, clear, Daisy and Button, toothpick holder center, matching glass holder 110.00
3 bottles, clear, Ribbed Palm pattern, pewter tops and frame 175.00
3 bottles, cranberry glass, silverplated crescent moon shape frame, orig spoon 175.00
4 bottles, clear, mold blown, pewter lids and frame, domed base, loop handle, 8" h, marked "I Trask," early 19th C 300.00
4 bottles, ruby stained, Ruby Thumbprint pattern, glass frame 355.00
4 bottles, cranberry glass, IVT pattern, enameled floral dec, silverplated frame, marked "Meriden" 100.00
4 bottles, Gothic Arch pattern, pewter frame 115.00

4 bottles, green cut to clear, sq bottles and silverplated frame 335.00
4 bottles, King's Crown, SP frame . . . 150.00
4 bottles, mismatched cut bottles and two salt dishes, silverplated frame, 9⅜" h 110.00
4 bottles, Venecia pattern, rubena, glass frame 145.00
5 bottles, Baccarat glass, Rose Tiente pattern, silverplated frame 175.00
5 bottles, Bellflower pattern, pressed stopper, pewter frame with pedestal, 11" 275.00
5 bottles, china, Willowware pattern, matching frame 120.00
5 bottles, clear, 13½" h holder, Meriden 225.00
5 bottles, clear, allover lunar and geometric design, SS mounts and frame, shell shape foot, 8½" h, English hallmarks, c1750 . . . . 600.00
5 bottles, cut, ornate Rogers & Brothers frame 150.00
5 bottles, cut, SS frame, three ball and claw feet, open cartouche circular handle, English hallmarks, c1861 . . 375.00
5 bottles, etched, amberina, cut stoppers, gilt frame 2,000.00
5 bottles, etched, wreath and polka dots pattern, rib trimmed frame 150.00
5 bottles, Gothic Arches pattern, pewter frame 100.00
5 bottles, Honeycomb pattern, ornate Wilcox frame 250.00
5 bottles, ruby cut to clear, silverplated frame 190.00

Two bottles, Quimper, blue sponge trim, 5⅜" h, 8" w, $150.00.

6 bottles, clear cut diamond point panels, rotating sterling silver frame, allover flowers, paw feet, loop handle, 11½" h, Gorham Mfg Co, c1880 . . . 2,200.00
6 bottles, clear, fluted glass, SS stand, circular, vertical fluted border, central ring of cast antheminon and ivy leaf

dec, 11" h, sgd "Tiffany & Co, NY," c1865	**1,250.00**
6 bottle, cut, silverplated pewter frame with mechanical door housing, Gleason	**1,500.00**
6 bottles, etched, wreath design, Reed & Barton frame with cupid	**350.00**
6 bottles, pressed, silverplated Simpson, Hall, and Miller frame	**125.00**

CATALOGS

History: The first American mail order catalog was issued by Benjamin Franklin in 1744. This popular advertising tool helped to spread inventions, innovations, fashions, and other necessities of life to rural America. Catalogs were profusely illustrated and are studied today to date an object, identify its manufacturer, study its distribution, and determine its historical importance.

References: Don Fredgant, *American Trade Catalogs: Identification and Value Guide*, Collector Books, 1984; Lawrence B. Romaine, *A Guide To American Trade Catalogs 1744–1900*, R. R. Bowker, 1960.

Additional Listings: See *Warman's Americana & Collectibles* for more examples.

Starrett Precision Tools, The L. S. Starrett Company, Athol, MA, Catalog 26, 1938 copyright, 4⅞ x 7", $20.00.

Ario's Cowboy Catalog, 66 pgs, 1942	15.00
Bannermann Military Goods, 1931	140.00
Billiard, 1909	75.00
Brown & Sharpe Small Tools, 1938	20.00
Chandler and Barber Metal Working Tools, 1907	15.00
Chicago Engineer Supply Co, hard cov, 528 pgs, 1915	25.00
Crane Co, Valves, Fittings, 743 pgs, 1923	15.00

Derby Desk Co, mission style furniture, 1920s	30.00
DeVilbiss Automotive, 60 pgs	20.00
E I Horsman, Manufacturer of Games, Toys, Home Amusements & Novelties, 1880–81	500.00
Elgin National Watch Co, materials	20.00
Fenestra Windows, c1920	15.00
Fischer, C, 120 pgs, 1902, 9½ x 12½"	100.00
Ford, Model T, 10 pgs, 1923, 7 x 11"	65.00
Greer and Laing, hardware, 1900s	125.00
Heywood Wakefield Furniture, c1927	55.00
International Harvester, 1940, dealer's	15.00
International Trucks, Model SL, 8 pgs, 9 x 12"	20.00
Iver Johnson Fishing Tackle, 1917, 195 pgs	25.00
Iver Johnson Sporting Goods, 1916, 196 pgs	26.00
John Plain Co, jewelry and watches, 97 pgs, 1925	25.00
Johnson Smith, 1935	65.00
Joys Modern Boat Equipment, 1937	50.00
Lincraft Rustic Furniture, Fences, c1920	15.00
Mershow Co Firearm Accessories and Police Equipment, 1940	20.00
Mitchell Motion Picture Cameras, 44 pgs, 1937, 9 x 11½"	35.00
Modern Shoemaking International, April, 1916	100.00
Montgomery Ward, 1925	30.00
National, 1925–26, 20 pgs, ladies hats	75.00
Oldsmobile, 1946, 24 pgs	20.00
Oliver Chilled Plows	20.00
Olson Rugs, 1931	12.00
Parry Buggies	200.00
Phillip Bernard Co Farm Equipment #7	15.00
Plymouth, 1937	20.00
Restuarant Supplies, 1923	25.00
Rookwood, 1904	350.00
Rubber Swim Caps, c1920	18.00
Scranton Lace Curtains, 1918	12.00
Sears, 1958	30.00
Stromber, Carburetors, 1939	50.00
Thomas Register of American Manufacturers, 5,200 pgs, 1937	150.00
Victor Red Seal Records, 1924	20.00
Western Auto, Ford Supply Co, 1929	25.00
White Frost Sanitary Refrigerator	55.00
Winton Six, 54 pgs, 1913, hard cov, 5¼ x 8"	50.00

CELADON

History: The term celadon, meaning a pale grayish green color, is derived from the theatrical character Celadon, who wore costumes of varying shades of grayish green, in Honore d'Urfe's 17th century pastoral romance, "L'Astree." French Jesuits living in China applied it to a specific type of Chinese porcelain.

Celadon divides into two types. Northern celadon, made during the Sung Dynasty up to the 1120s, has a gray to brownish body, relief decoration, and monochrome olive green glaze.

Southern (Lung-ch'uan) celadon, made during the Sung Dynasty and much later, is paint decorated with floral and other scenic designs and found in forms which would appeal to the European and American export market. Many of the Southern pieces date from 1825 to 1885. A blue square with Chinese or pseudo-Chinese characters appears on pieces after 1850. Later pieces also have a larger and sparser decorative patterning.

Reproduction Alert.

Bowl, shallow, ftd, celadon ground, peacock center, pink floral dec, c1810, 7″ d, $250.00.

Bowl

5½″ d, barrel shape, two monster masks, stylized floral motifs, band of applied floral bosses, crackled glaze shading from gray–green to brown–green, imperfections, Chinese, Ming Dynasty **1,200.00**

7⅛″ d, conical, int. imp floral roundel, wide band of leafy blossoms, pooled muted green glaze, fine crackle pattern, Korean, Koryo Dynasty **400.00**

14¾″ d, deep rounded sides, waisted rim, everted lip, ext. with interwoven bands of flowering magnolias, three cylindrical applied monster head feet, pale gray–green glaze, unglazed base, Chinese .. **935.00**

Censor, tripod, Chinese

10¾″ d, compressed globular form, three monster head supports, ext. carved with Eight Trigrams, thick gray–green crackle glaze, int. central portion and base unglazed, kiln flaws, Longquan, Ming Dynasty .. **660.00**

11⅝″ d, shallow rounded form, three paw feet, stylized monster mask heads, ext. bagua motifs, overhanging lip, pale olive green crackle glaze, unglazed int. well and raised circular base, rim chips and cracks, 19th C **660.00**

Dish, 6¾″ d, steep sides, everted rim, small ring foot, muted green glaze, wide crackle pattern, Korean, Koryo Dynasty **275.00**

Fish Bowl, 8⁷⁄₁₆″ d, flattened rim, carved petals, int. with two small swimming fish, luminous glaze **350.00**

Ginger Jar, 6″ h, bulbous, multicolored relief floral dec, dark green leaves, gold trim **175.00**

Jardiniere, 12″ h, circular, pale green glaze, molded alternating shaped medallions with stags and owls, bird and floral border, pr **500.00**

Libation Cup, 3¾″ h, steep taper sides, foliate rim, dragon and clouds, blue–green glaze, 19th C **200.00**

Olive Jar, ovoid, tapering to waisted neck, dished mouth, iron–oxide scrolls beneath translucent olive–green glaze, Korean, Yi Dynasty ... **375.00**

Planter, 7½″ d, cylindrical, molded, bundle of bamboo stalks tied together with blue and white ribbon, stylized calligraphy, glazed deep celadon ... **225.00**

Vase, 7¾″ h, Hu form, low relief, handles **1,750.00**

CELLULOID ITEMS

History: In 1869 brothers J. W. Hyatt and I. S. Hyatt developed celluloid, the world's first synthetic plastic, as an ivory substitute because elephant herds were being slaughtered for their ivory tusks.

Known as "Ivorine" or "French Ivory," celluloid was made of nitrocellulose and camphor. Early pieces have a creamy color with stripes and grooves to imitate the texture of ivory or bone. The 1897 Sears catalog featured celluloid items. Celluloid was used widely until synthetics replaced it in the early 1950s. Celluloid often is used as a generic term for all early plastics.

Advertising

Calendar, pocket type, pictures graniteware **20.00**

Pencil Box, Red Goose Shoes **75.00**

Album, photograph, floral cov **75.00**

Animal

Peacock on pedestal, 5½″ h **25.00**

Swan **10.00**

Box
Glove, hp floral dec on cov, pink lin-
ing, dated 1869 . . . .   35.00
Necktie, 2½ x 3 x 4″, creamy ivory,
gold and floral dec on cov 42.00
Candlestick, 5″, creamy ivory 10.00
Cane Handle, carved dog's head, glass
eyes 30.00
Collar Box, white chrysanthemums and
green leaves on cov, velvet lined . . .   45.00
Comb, lady's, creamy ivory 18.00
Doll, 10″, French, elaborate costume,
marked "270" 50.00
Door Knob, creamy ivory 35.00
Dresser Set, 11 pcs, green, gold dec,
leather case 100.00
Frame, 4 x 3″, creamy ivory, reticulated
border, easel back 25.00
Hair Receiver, rect, yellow, dark green
floral design 8.00
Nail File, folding, emb floral dec 12.00
Napkin Ring, creamy ivory 10.00

**Perfume bottle holder, orig bottle and
stopper, $18.50.**

Powder Box
Round, scalloped ivory top, amber
base, marked "Pearltone, Pyralin,
DuBarry" 8.00
World War II military hat shape, blue
and white 12.00
Rattle, blue and white, c1930 . . . .   12.00
Roly Poly, chicken 10.00
Scissors, manicure, 4″, creamy ivory
handle 12.00
Stick Pin, color portrait of woman, yel-
low and green ribbons, "Welcome to
Eugene, Oregon" 25.00
Toy, wind–up
Clown, 7½″, marked "Occupied Ja-
pan" 60.00
Penguin, 3″, marked "Made In Japan"   30.00
Reindeer, pulls sleigh, ringing bell . .   135.00
Tatting Shuttle 8.00
Travel Kit, tube contains brush, razor,
and two blades, cap ends, orig in-
structions 50.00

CHALKWARE

History: William Hutchinson, an Englishman, invented chalkware in 1848. It was a substance used
by sculptors to imitate marble. It also was used to
harden plaster of Paris, creating confusion between the two products.

Chalkware often copied many of the popular
Staffordshire items of the 1820 to 1870 period. It
was cheap, gayly decorated, and sold by vendors.
The Pennsylvania German "folk art" pieces are
from this period.

Carnivals, circuses, fairs, and amusement parks
used chalkware pieces as prizes during the late
19th and 20th centuries. They often were poorly
made and gaudy. Don't confuse them with the
earlier pieces. Prices for these chalkware items
range from ten to fifty dollars.

References: Thomas G. Morris, *Carnival Chalk
Prize,* Prize Publishers, 1985; Ted Soufe, *Midway
Mania: A Collectors Guide To Carnival Plaster
Figurines, Prizes, and Equipment 1900–1950,* L-
W, Inc., 1985.

Additional Listings: See Carnival Chalkware
in *Warman's Americana & Collectibles.*

Bank, dove
9½″ 325.00
11″ h, worn orig polychrome paint . .   350.00
Bookends, pr, 8″, Arabian Knights, male
and female, red, gold, and brown . .   75.00
Bust, 20″, Hiawatha, 1890s 120.00

**Dachsund, black–brown, 4¾″ h, 5½″ l,
$35.00.**

Figure
Angel, 3¾″ h, kneeling, orig poly-
chrome paint 225.00
Cat, 10″, seated with mouse, octag-
onal base 450.00
Dog, 7″, spaniel, standing, red and
black 225.00
Dove, 12″, perched on stump, cher-
ries and leaves, pr 525.00

Love Birds, 3⅛" h, pr on base facing each other, orig polychrome paint	250.00
Squirrel, 6¾", orig paint	525.00
Stag, 16", painted details, rect base	400.00
Woman, 9½" h, holding parasol, orig polychrome paint	225.00
Garniture, 11", leafy pomegranate, pedestal, multicolored	800.00
Match Holder, 6", figural, man with long nose and beard, Northwestern National Insurance Co adv, c1890	100.00
Nodder, 6", cat, orig red and black dec	325.00
Plaque, 9" h, horse head, orig polychrome paint	100.00
Wall Pocket, basket shape	15.00

CHARACTER ITEMS

History: In many cases, toys and other products using the image of fictional comic, movie, and radio characters occur simultaneously with the origin of the character. The first Dick Tracy toy was manufactured within less than a year after the strip first appeared.

The "golden age" of character material is the TV era of the mid-1950s through the late 1960s. Some radio premium collectors might argue this point. Today, television and movie producers often have their product licensing arranged well in advance of the initial release.

Do not overlook the characters created by advertising agencies, e.g., Tony the Tiger. They represent a major collecting subcategory.

This category includes only objects related to fictional characters. Sometimes the line can become very blurred. Bill Boyd's portrayal of Hopalong Cassidy turned Clarence Mulford's fictional hero into a real-life entity in the minds of many.

References: William Crouch, Jr. and Lawrence Doucet, *The Authorized Guide to Dick Tracy Collectibles,* Wallace–Homestead, 1990; Fred Grandinetti, *Popeye: The Collectible,* Krause Publications, 1990; David Longest, *Character Toys and Collectibles,* Collector Books, 1984; David Longest, *Character Toys And Collectibles, Second Series,* Collector Books, 1987; Richard O'Brien, *Collecting Toys, A Collector's Identification & Value Guide, No. 5,* Books Americana, 1990.

Additional Listings: See *Warman's Americana & Collectibles* for expanded listings in Cartoon Characters, Cowboy Collectibles, Movie Personalities and Memorabilia, Shirley Temple, and Space Adventurers.

Amos and Andy	
Ashtray and Matchholder, plaster	25.00
Diecut, 3 x 5", cardboard, Amos, Andy, and Kingfish, 1931	20.00
Poster, 13 x 29", multicolored, Campbell's Soup ad, radio show listings, framed	125.00

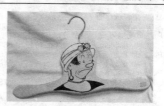

Maggie, hanger, wood, pink ground, 15 x 8¾" h, $25.00.

Sheet Music, 6 pgs, "Three Little Words," from movie "Check and Double Check," 1930 copyright	25.00
Betty Boop	
Decal Sheet, c1920, set of twelve	10.00
Match Safe, 1¼" w, sq, celluloid, c1930	150.00
Perfume Bottle, 3½" h, figural, glass, c1930	30.00
Pin, gold colored metal with attached link chain to Scotty dog, Fleisher Studios copyright, 1930s, attached to orig sample retail card	150.00
Wall Pocket, Betty and Bimbo, luster glaze, Fleisher Studios copyright	100.00
Blondie and Dagwood	
Coloring Book, Blondie, 1959, unused	10.00
Game, Blondie Goes To Leisureland, orig 8 x 11" envelope, Westinghouse premium, 1940 copyright	25.00
Marionette, 14" h, Dagwood, wood and plastic, Hazell, 1950s, MIB	45.00
Napkin Holder, ceramic	40.00
Pencil, Dagwood, 1949, unused	12.50
Pinback Button,¹³⁄₁₆" d, litho, Dagwood, Kellogg's Pep	10.00
Stationery Set, Blondie, 1950s, unused	10.00
Brownies, Palmer Cox	
Book, *The Brownie Primer,* A Flanagan Co, Chicago, 1905, hard cover, 6 x 8", 96 pages	30.00
Plate, 7" d, octagonal, china, full color illus of three Brownies, dressed as Uncle Sam, Scotsman, and golfer, soft blue ground, gold trim, sgd "La Francaise Porcelain"	75.00
Stickpin, black, white, and green enamel, c1896	20.00
Buster Brown	
Bank, iron, horseshoe shape, Buster Brown, Tige, and horse	125.00
Clicker, 1¾" l, litho metal, "Brown Shoe Co." inscription, c1930	15.00
Drawing Book, 8 pgs, thin film tracing sheets between illus page, six neatly traced sheets, issued by Emerson Piano Co	45.00

Mask, diecut, stiff paper, Froggy the Gremlin, 1946 . . . . 40.00
Paddle Board, 5 x 10", cardboard, rubber ball attached by string, 1946 . . . . 60.00
Pinback Button, ⅞" d, multicolored, Buster Brown Hose Supporter . . . 18.00
Pitcher, 4" h, white, china, full color illus, early 1900s 75.00
Toy, 5" h, squeaker, rubber, Froggy, Rempel, 1948 . . . . 100.00

Campbell Kids, adv sign, metal, 23¼" l, 14½" h, $65.00.

Campbell Kids
Child's knife, fork, and spoon, SP . . 50.00
Reverse Painting on Glass, 7½ x 9½", kids loading baskets in a vegetable patch, "C" on shirt, 11 x 12½" gray wood frame, c1970 . . . 60.00
Salt and Pepper Shakers, pr, 4½" h, plastic, 1950 . . . . 20.00
Thermometer, tin, figural, adv 35.00
Toy, squeeze, doll 75.00
Captain Marvel
Game, Shazam, paper, 1944 . . . . . 30.00
Magic Flute, orig card, 1946 . . . . . 65.00
Pennant, felt, dark blue, maroon picture 20.00
Wristwatch, red strap, orig box, copyright 1948, Fawcett Publications . 125.00
Captain Video
Figure, spaceman, Kellogg's premium 10.00
Gun, Rite-O-Lite 40.00
Key Chain, rocket, puzzle, 1950s . . 15.00
Pen, rocketship, 1950s 20.00
Tab, Purity Bread 30.00
Toy, Secret Ray Gun 95.00
Charlie The Tuna
Bathroom Scale, 13" w, "Sorry Charlie" 40.00
Clock 35.00
Lamp, 9" h, plaster figure 50.00
Wrist Watch, "Sorry Charlie," orig case, 1971 . . . . 75.00
Ella Cinders, book, ice cream premium 18.00

Dennis The Menace
Coloring Book, 1960, unused 12.50
Doll, orig box 125.00
Game, baseball, MIB 95.00
Mug, 4" h, plastic, picturing Dennis, 1950s 15.00
Paper Dolls, Back-Yard Picnic Set, punch-out dolls and picnic items, Whitman, 1960 . . . . 25.00
Puzzle, Whitman, TV photo 12.00
Spoon, 6" l, SP, emb figure at top of handle, name vertically on handle, 1950s 25.00
Elsie The Cow
Bank, 6½" h, marked "Master Caster," 1950 . . . . 75.00
Charm, ½" h, full dimensional Elsie, white hard plastic, c1940 . . . . . . 18.50
Creamer and Sugar, Elsie and Elmer, orig labels 75.00
Doll, 15" h, vinyl head, plush, c1950 50.00
Mechanical Pencil 75.00
Pin, ½ x ¾" diecut, enameled metal, Second 100 Years, 1957, white Elsie, yellow daisy, blue ground, Borden copyright on back 25.00
Pinback Button
1¾" d, cello, red and white, "Drink Rosenberger's Milk, Smile," white illus of Elsie in center . . . 15.00
2¼" d, emb brass, raised head, c1940 . . . . 25.00
Ring, plastic, green, color inset picture, Borden Company copyright, c1950 . . . . 50.00
Felix The Cat
Doll, 8½" l, wood, jointed, decals, leather ears, Schoenhut, c1920 . . 200.00
Figure, 13" h, composition, jointed arms 350.00
Pin, 1" l, black letter, bright yellow litho, "30 Comics/Herald and Examiner," c1930 . . . . 50.00
Place Card Holder, celluloid 1¾" Felix figure, ½" h arched back black cat, base, glossy black holder, Japanese, 1930s 80.00
Post Card, 3¼ x 5", German, ham radio operator, Stutgart radio call letters, 1949 postmark 50.00
Puzzle, 13 x 10½", Built-Rite, 1949 . 15.00
Valentine, diecut, jointed cardboard, full color, valentine pictured on his tail, "Purr Around If You Want To Be My Valentine" inscription, Pat Sullivan copyright, c1920 . . . . . . 15.00
Yarn Holder, 6½" l, diecut wood, black images, inscription "Felix Keeps On Knitting," "Pathe Presents" symbol in center, c1920–30 35.00
Flintstones, The, Hanna Barbera Studios

Activity Book, Hanna Barbera, 1974, unused **10.00**
Bank, 13" h, plastic, Fred, 1971 ... **20.00**
Colorforms Set, 1972, unused ... **18.50**
Gerber Baby, pinback button, 1½" d, orange and black litho, Gerber Foods trademark, issued for annual picnic, 1954 .... **20.00**
Barney Google
Candy Container, Spark Plug, glass **75.00**
Coloring Book, 1968 .... **10.00**
Green Hornet
Color Magic Rub–Off, 1966, MIB ... **55.00**
Ring, flicker, plastic, silver color **7.50**
Viewmaster, three reels, 16 page booklet, 1966 .... **48.00**
Happy Hooligan
Figure, 8¼" h, bisque, worried expression, tin can hat, orange, black, blue, and yellow **75.00**
Post Card, 3½ x 5½", full color illus, inked inscription, Nov 1905 postmark **17.50**
Stick Pin, 2¼" h, brass **35.00**
Toy, nesting **45.00**
Henry, coloring book, #1, 1935 ..... **35.00**
Hopalong Cassidy
Badge, metal, silver, star shape, raised portrait at center, c1950 ... **20.00**
Coloring Book, 1950, large size ... **28.00**
Ring, adjustable, silvered brass, portrait on top with initials and the Bar 20 symbol, c1950 .... **30.00**
Rug, chenille **100.00**
Shirt, button, red trim slit pocket and collar, six different images, red inscription, "Little Champ Of Hollywood" label, size 12, early 1950s **150.00**
Tablet, 8 x 10", color photo cov, facsimile signature, unused, early 1950s **20.00**
Howdy Doody
Bank, 6½ x 5", ceramic, riding pig .. **45.00**
Belt, suede, emb face **30.00**
Cake Decorating Set **35.00**
Game, Flub–A–Dub–Flip–A–Ring .. **24.00**
Handkerchief, 8 x 8¼", cotton **15.00**
Marionette, 16" h, wood and stuffed cloth, composition hands, movable lower mouth, plastic jiggle eyes, fully strung, hand control board, printed instructions **200.00**
Pencil Case, vinyl, red **20.00**
Record Spindle Spinner, 4" h plastic figure, movable mouth, figure mounted on 3" d plastic base, center hole for placement over record player spindle, inscription "Hi Ya Kids/Watch Me Go Round On Your Record" on base, Kagran copyright, 1951–56 .... **50.00**
Wall Light Shade, parchment like heavy paper, plastic edge lacing, soft blue, red, and yellow illus, off white background, Kagran copyright c1951–56, orig wall mount .. **75.00**
Jiggs and Maggie
Paperweight, glass **35.00**
Pin, 1" l, Jiggs, black letter, bright yellow litho, "30 Comics/Herald and Examiner," c1930 .... **50.00**
Pinback Button, 13/16" d, litho, Maggie, Kellogg's Pep **18.00**
Salt and Pepper Shakers, pr, ceramic **45.00**
Li'l Abner
Bottle, 7½" h, Shmoo, blue glass, marked "Baldwin Lab, 1950" **30.00**
Coloring Book, Saalfield, #2370, 144 pages, 1941, some pages neatly colored **25.00**
Pinback Button
2⅛" d, white Shmoo, dark green ground **45.00**
3" d, bright red, black, and white, "Ah Likes Elvis But Ah Loves The Hit Musical Li'l Abner/St James Theater," yellow ground . **30.00**
Salt and Pepper Shakers, pr, 4" h, Shmoo, black face details, "Made In Japan" foil sticker, late 1940s . **85.00**
Little Orphan Annie
Clicker, red, white, and black, Mysto members, 1941 .... **35.00**
Doll, ABC Toys, 1940 .... **25.00**
Gravy Boat, lusterware, white, orange, yellow, and black **175.00**
Mug, Ovaltine **60.00**
Nodder, 3½" h, painted bisque, stamped on back "Orphan Annie," 1930s **150.00**
Pastry Set, miniature baking utensils, two aluminum mixing spoons, wood pestle shape rolling pin, flour cup, and 6 x 8" rolling board, boxed, Transogram "Gold Medal" Toy, 1930s **75.00**
Whistle, tin, signal, three tones **30.00**
Lone Ranger
Badge, 1" d, Safety Scout **15.00**
Guitar, 30" l, Jefferson, orig box ... **80.00**
Hartland Figure, orig box **225.00**
Holster, 9" l stiff cardboard, colored to resemble tan leather, steer design, brand initials "GA", inscription in rope script, khaki web army style belt, includes a 7" l aluminum single shot cap pistol with white plastic grips, boxed, 1942 copyright **75.00**
Pencil Case, 1 x 4 x 8¼", textured stiff cardboard, gold cov design is lightly emb, dark blue background, American Lead Pencil Co, Lone Ranger copyright, 1930s **40.00**
Print Set, 1940s, unused, orig box . **40.00**

Rifle, 24" l, plastic, simulated metal
and wood parts, gold script inscription, emb Indian head and bear in
woods on sides of stock, clicking
sound, sighting scope, c1960 ... 25.00
Toy, litho tin windup, Range Rider,
Marx, MIB 500.00

Charlie McCarthy
Bubble Gum Wrapper 12.00
Handkerchief, 9 x 9½", linen like fab-
ric, corner inscribed "Charlie Mc-
Carthy In At The Races," white
ground, bright red, blue, yellow, and
black race horse center, late 1930s 30.00
Pinback Button, ¾" d, celluloid, black
and white portrait of Charlie, c1930 65.00
Notepad, 5½ x 9", black, white, and
green, lined paper, 1938 .... 20.00
Ring, plastic, green, black and white
photo, c1940 .... 30.00
Valentine, diecut cardboard 17.50

Mr. Peanut
Bank, 8½" h, molded tan plastic, coin
slot in top of hat, inscription on hat
brim, c1950 .... 40.00
Night Light, 8¼" h, plastic, electric,
glows in the dark, Atlantic City souvenir sticker 72.00
Pencil, mechanical, 5¼" l, red and
white plastic, cylinder at top contains miniature tan figure, inscription on side, c1940–50 .... 15.00

Moon Mullins
Baking Set, Pillsbury Comicookie,
1937, MIB 35.00
Nodder, bisque, marked "Germany" 75.00
Pinback Button, 1½" d, black and
white, Moon Mullins Knothole
Gang, c1930 .... 45.00

Annie Oakley
Coloring Book, 11 x 14", Whitman,
soft color, 1955, unused 18.00
Costume, child's, c1950 .... 70.00
Game, Milton Bradley, c1950 ..... 35.00
Hartland Figure, orig horse, hat, and
gun 140.00
Magic Erasable Picture, Transogram,
1959 .... 40.00
Paper Dolls, 10½ x 13", Whitman,
1954, neatly cut 60.00
Suspenders, 4½ x 12", card, multi-
colored, elastic, Annie Oakley on
one, Tagg on other, c1960 ..... 15.00

Our Gang, pencil box, 1930s 60.00

Popeye
Charm, celluloid 5.00
Children's Book, Popeye Borrows A
Baby Nurse, Whitman #712 .... 40.00
Dot–To–Dot Book, Golden, 1978 ... 8.00
Figure, 14" h, chalkware 125.00
Lamp, figural, 16" h, dark maroon with
gold accent striped shade, gray

Popeye, Big Little Book, *Popeye Ghost Ship To Treasure Island,* Paul S. Newman, Whitman, #2008, $7.50.

metal base with 8" h figure, arms
around brown lamp pole 150.00
Mug, 4" h, Olive Oyl, figural 15.00
Phonograph, Emerson 40.00
Salt and Pepper Shakers, pr, 3" h,
Vandor 30.00
Sticker Book, Lowe #2631 .... 35.00
Watch, 1¼" d, silver colored metal
case, dial pictures Popeye holding
spinach can, gray leather bands,
c1960 .... 50.00

Red Ryder
Book, Red Ryder and Circus Luck,
Whitman Better Little Book #1466,
1949 .... 25.00
Glove Case, black enameled metal
and cardboard, illus on lid, leather
carrying handle, elastic straps for
holding supplies, silvered metal
spring clip fasteners, 1951 salesman program, Wells–Lamont Glove
Company 150.00
Paint Book, 1941, unused 35.00
Target Game, litho cardboard, Whitman, 1939 .... 55.00

Reddy Kilowatt
Cookie Cutter 40.00
Cuff Links 80.00
Earrings, 1" h, figural, brass, 2¾ x 3"
yellow, blue, and red presentation
folder with verse, 1955 copyright . 20.00
Magic Gripper, 5" d textured rubber
disk, yellow, red illus, orig 5¼" sq
envelope 30.00
Pen and Pencil Set 40.00

Rocky Jones, Space Ranger
Coloring Book, Whitman, cockpit cov,
1951 .... 30.00
Pinback Button, membership 42.00
Wings, pin 40.00

Wrist Watch **120.00**
Rootie Kazootie
  Game, card, Rootie Kazootie Word
    Game, Ed–U–Cards, 1953 . . . . .   **20.00**
  Handkerchief, 9" sq, Gala Poochie
    Pup **15.00**
  Puppet, 11" h, vinyl head, cloth base-
    ball uniform body **30.00**
Skippy
  Pinback Button, 1⅛" d, red, white,
    and blue, litho, "Skippy Ice Cream,"
    c1930 . . . .   **15.00**
  Sign, 24 x 36", diecut cardboard,
    "Fro–joy" ice cream container,
    color, 1930s **200.00**
Smitty, coloring book, McLoughlin Bros,
  1932, 24 pages **45.00**
Straight Shooter (Tom Mix)
  Coloring Book, 8½ x 11", health and
    hygiene, Ralston premium, unused   **75.00**
  Ring, brass, checkerboard logo on
    top with steer head and gun design
    on sides, 1935 . . . .   **50.00**
Dick Tracy
  Book
    Family Fun Book, Tip Top Bread,
      1940 . . . .   **65.00**
    *Secret Service Patrol Secret Code
      Book,* 12 pages, Quaker pre-
      mium, 1938 . . . .   **60.00**
  Camera, 3 x 5", plastic, black, Sey-
    more Products, Chicago **45.00**
  Candy Wrapper, Johnson Caramels   **20.00**
  Game, Dick Tracy Electronic Target
    Game, battery operated, silent ray
    gun, shoots a beam of light at a
    revolving cardboard drum, elec-
    tronic photocell bull's eye, auto-
    matic scorekeeper, 11" black plas-
    tic pistol, instruction sheet,
    American Doll & Toy Corp, 1961
    copyright, unused **100.00**
  Greeting Card, Christmas, orig en-
    velope, c1950 . . . .   **45.00**
  Newspaper, Sunday comic page,
    1940, Chester Gould **40.00**
  Salt and Pepper Shaker, pr, plaster,
    Dick and Junior **35.00**
  Toy, 18" l, tin, squad car, friction, Marx   **300.00**
  Trading Card, Big Little Book, 1939 .   **35.00**
  Water Pistol, plastic, 1955 . . . .   **35.00**
Woody Woodpecker
  Coloring Book, Learn To Draw, 1958,
    neatly colored **12.00**
  Figure, 5½" h, plastic, red, orig tag .   **20.00**
  Ring, plastic, white, metallic blue and
    white disk, c1960 . . . .   **20.00**
Yellow Kid
  Cigar Box, 3½ x 4¼ x 9", wood, illus
    and name inscription in bright gold,
    brass hinges, label inside "Smoke
    Yellow Kid Cigars/Manuf'd By B. R.

    Fleming, Curwesville, Pa." tax label
    strips on back, c1896 . . . .   **200.00**
  Figure, 7¼" h, paper, full dimensional,
    hollowed thin papier mache, solid
    dark red painted back, Pulver
    Chewing Gum, Old King Cole Pa-
    pier Machine Co, Canton, OH . . .   **225.00**
  Pinback Button, No 14, Kid dressed
    to go to a ball **20.00**
  Post Card, 3¾ x 6", full color illus for
    month of October, issued as re-
    minder from Ohio hardware com-
    pany, 1911 post mark **40.00**

CHELSEA

History: Chelsea is a fine English porcelain designed to compete with Meissen. The factory began operating in the Chelsea area of London, England, in the 1740s. Chelsea products are divided
into four periods: (1) Early period, 1740s, with incised triangle and raised anchor mark; (2) The
1750s, with red raised anchor mark; (3) The
1760s, the gold anchor period; and (4) The Derby
period from 1770–1783. In 1924 a large number
of the molds and models of figurines were found
at the Spode-Copeland Works, and many items
were brought back into circulation.

Reference: Susan and Al Bagdade, *Warman's
English & Continental Pottery & Porcelain,* 2nd
Edition, Wallace–Homestead, 1991.

Bowl
  6½" d, molded leaves on ext., floral
    spray in center, red anchor **1,000.00**
  8¾" d, swirled ribs, scalloped, floral
    and foliage dec **575.00**
Candlestick, pr, 7½", figural, draped
  putti, sitting on tree stump holding
  flower, scroll molded base encircled
  in puce, gilt, wax pan **825.00**

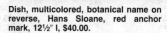

**Dish, multicolored, botanical name on
reverse, Hans Sloane, red anchor
mark, 12½" l, $40.00.**

Cup and Saucer, multicolored exotic
  birds, white ground gold anchor mark,
  c1765 .... **750.00**
Dish
  6³⁄₁₆", pr, flower sprays and leaves,
    silver form molded edge, red an-
    chor mark, c1755 .... **350.00**
  6½", Flying Dog, Kakiemon style, ten
    sided, red anchor mark, c1755 .. **1,250.00**
Figure, pr, 14" h, fruit and flower sellers
  with animals, multicolored clothing,
  shaped socles, gold anchor mark,
  late 18th C **600.00**
Plate
  8½" d, multicolored floral design,
    scalloped rim, gold anchor mark . **450.00**
  9" d, botanical, Hans Sloane type, red
    anchor period, c1756, set of six . **4,675.00**
Platter, 16" l, stag head crest **500.00**
Scent Bottle, 3" h, cupid at altar, applied
  florals, 1760s **2,400.00**
Soup Plate, 9⅜", octagonal, center
  painted with iron–red and gold phoenix in flight, yellow breasted blue and
  iron–red pheasant, turquoise rock,
  iron–red, blue, turquoise, and gold
  flowering tree, ridged rim, iron–red
  floral border, red anchor, c1753 .... **2,000.00**
Teapot, 6¼" h, multicolored floral dec,
  D and anchor mark **750.00**

"CHELSEA" GRANDMOTHER'S WARE

History: "Chelsea" Grandmother's ware identifies a group of tableware with raised reliefs of
either grapes, sprigs of flowers, or thistles on a
white ground. Some examples are lustered.

The ware was made in the first half of the 19th
century in England's Staffordshire district by a
large number of manufacturers. The "Chelsea" label is a misnomer, but commonly accepted in the
antiques field.

Bowl, 8", Grape **30.00**
Butter Pat, 4" d, Sprig **12.00**
Cake Plate
  9", Sprig **35.00**
  10", Grape **40.00**
Creamer
  Grape **30.00**
  Sprig **50.00**
Cup, Grape **22.50**
Cup and Saucer, Thistle **25.00**
Egg Cup, Grape **25.00**
Milk Pitcher, Sprig **50.00**
Plate
  7", Sprig **18.00**
  8", Grape **20.00**
  9", Sprig **30.00**

**Egg Cup, Grape pattern, marked
"Royal Adderley/Blue Chelsea/Ridg-
way Potters Ltd," $25.00.**

Ramekin, blue, underplate, Sprig **12.00**
Sauce Dish, Sprig **5.00**
Sugar, cov, 7½", Sprig **110.00**
Teapot, 10", octagonal, Grape luster .. **125.00**

CHILDREN'S BOOKS

History: Because there is a bit of the child in
all of us, collectors always have been attracted to
children's books. In the 19th century, books were
popular gifts for children, with most of the children's classics written and published during this
time. These books were treasured and often kept
throughout a lifetime.

Developments in printing made it possible to
include more attractive black and white illustrations
and color plates. The work of artists and illustrators
has added value beyond the text itself.

References: Barbara Bader, *American Picture
Books From Noah's Ark To The Beast Within*,
Macmillan, 1976; E. Lee Baumgarten, *Price List
for Children's and Illustrated Books For the Years
1880–1940, Sorted by Artist*, published by author,
1990; Margery Fisher, *Who's Who In Children's
Books: A Treasury of the Familiar Characters of
Childhood*, Holt, Rinehart and Winston, 1975; Virginia Haviland, *Children's Literature, A Guide To
Reference Sources*, Library of Congress, 1966,
first supplement 1972, second supplement 1977,
third supplement 1982; Bettina Hurlimann, *Three
Centuries Of Children's Books In Europe*, tr. and
ed. by Brian W. Alderson, World, 1968; Cornelia
L. Meigs, ed., *A Critical History of Children's Literature*, 2nd ed., Macmillan, 1969.

Periodicals: *Book Source Monthly*, P. O. Box
567, Cazenova, NY 13035; *Martha's KidLit Newsletter*, P. O. Box 1488, Ames, IA 50010.

Libraries: Free Library of Philadelphia, PA; Library of Congress, Washington, D.C.; Pierpont

Morgan Library, New York, NY; Toronto Public Library, Toronto, Ontario, Canada.

Advisor: Joyce Magee.

Additional Listings: See *Warman's Americana & Collectibles* for more examples and an extensive listing of collectors' clubs.

Note: dj = dust jacket; wraps = paper covers; pgs = pages; unp = unpaged; n.d. = no date; teg = top edges gilt.

Thornton W. Burgess, *The Adventures of Paddy The Beaver*, Bedtime Story Books, Boston, Little, Brown & Co., 1917, 4¾ x 7″, $12.00.

Allingham, William, *In Fairy Land,* Richard Doyle, illus, Longmans, Green, 1870, 31 pgs, 1st ed **550.00**

Barrows, Marjorie, *Muggins Mouse,* Deith Ward, illus, Reilly & Lee, 1932, 60 pgs **50.00**

Buck, Pearl S., *Johnny Jack and His Beginnings,* Werth, illus, John Day, 1954, 47 pgs, 1st ed, dj **30.00**

Burnett, Frances, Hodgson, *Sara Crewe or What Happened at Miss Minchin's,* Reginald Birch, illus Scribner's, 1888, 83 pgs, 1st ed **75.00**

Chapin, Anna, *True Story of Humpty Dumpty,* Ethel Betts, illus, Dodd, 1905, 206 pgs, 1st ed **95.00**

Clyne, Geraldine, *The Jolly Jump-ups And Their New House,* McLoughlin, 1939, unp, 6 pop-ups **35.00**

Disney, Walt, *Dance of the Hours from Fantasia,,* Harper, 1940, unp, 1st ed **40.00**

Dr. Seuss, *Bartholomew and the Oobleck,* Random House, 1949, unp, 1st ed, sgd **75.00**

Field, Rachel, *Hitty: Her First Hundred Years,* Dorothy Lathrop, illus, Macmillan, 1929, 207 pgs, 1st ed, sgd by Lathrop **70.00**

Garer, Elvira, *Ezekiel,* Holt, 1937, unp, 1st ed, dj **35.00**

Greenaway, Kate, *Almanac for 1889,* Routledge, n.d. adv. a.e.g. **100.00**

Harris, Joel Chandler, *The Tar Baby and other Rhymes of Uncle Remus,* A. B. Frost & E. W. Kemple, illus, D. Appleton, 1904 190 pgs, 1st ed . . . **70.00**

Hoffmann, Heinrich, *Slovenly Peter,* Fritz Dredel, illus, German to English by Mark Twain, limited edition club, 1935, 34 pgs, numbered ed in box . **135.00**

Kipling, Rudyard, *Just So Stories,* Macmillan, 1902, 249 pgs, 1st ed **125.00**

Lenski, Lois, *The Easter Rabbit's Parade,* Oxford, 1936, 32 pgs, 1st ed . **45.00**

McCready, T.L., *Biggity Bantam,* Tasha Tudork, illus, Ariel/Farrar Straus, Young, 1954, unp, 1st ed, dj **55.00**

Moore, Clement, *The Night Before Christmas,* Elizabeth MacKinstry, illus, Dutton, 1928, unp, 1st ed **65.00**

Newberry, Clare, *Babette,* Harper, 1937, 30 pgs, 1st ed, dj **43.00**

Nura, *Nura's Garden of Betty & Booth,* Morrow, 1935, 41 pgs, 1st ed **50.00**

Owen, Dora, *The Book of Fairy Poetry,* Warwide Goble, illus, Longmans, 1920, 129 pgs, 1st ed **95.00**

Phillpotts, Eden, *The Girl and the Fawn,* Frank Branquyn, illus, London, 1916, 78 pgs, dj **125.00**

Pyle, Howard, *The Garden Behind the Moon,* Scribner's, 1895, 192 pgs, 1st ed **115.00**

Sarg, Tony, *Where is Tommy?* Greenberg, 1932, unp, 1st ed **55.00**

Southwold, Stephen, *The Book of Animal Tales,* Honor/C. Appleton, illus, Crowell, n.d. c1930, 286 pgs **50.00**

Tarcov, Edith, *Rumpelstiltskin,* Edward Gorey, illus, Four Winds, 1974, 46 pgs, 1st ed, dj **45.00**

Tate, Sally Jane, *Sally's ABC Sewed in a Sampler in 1795,* Dugald Stewart Walker, illus, Harcourt, Brace, 1929, unp, 1st ed **65.00**

Thompson, Kay, *Eloise,* Hilary Knight, illus, Simon and Schuster, 1955, 65 pgs, 1st ed, dj **50.00**

Upton, Bertha, *The Golliwogg's Desert Island,* Florence K. Upton, illus, Longmans and Green, 1906, unp, 1st ed **100.00**

Wilder, Laura Ingalls, *On The Banks Of Plum Creek,* Helen Sewell & Mildred Boyle, illus, Harper & Row, 1937, 239 pgs, 1st ed **65.00**

Zaffo, George, *Peter On The Paddleboat,* Saalfield, 1946, unp, spiral, dj, animated **25.00**

CHILDREN'S FEEDING DISHES

History: Unlike toy dishes meant for play, children's feeding dishes are the items actually used in the feeding of a child. Their colorful designs of animals, nursery rhymes, and children's activities are meant to appeal to the child and make meal times fun. Many plates have a unit to hold hot water, thus keeping the food warm.

Although glass and porcelain examples from the late 19th and early 20th centuries are most popular, collectors are beginning to seek some of the plastic examples from the 1920s to 1940s, especially those with Disney designs on them.

References: Doris Lechler, *Children's Glass Dishes, China and Furniture,* Collector Books, 1983; Doris Lechler, *Children's Glass Dishes, China, Furniture, Volume II,* Collector Books, 1986; Lorraine May Punchard, *Child's Play,* published by author, 1982; Margaret & Kenn Whitmyer, *Children's Dishes,* Collector Books, 1984.

Cup, brown transfer train scene, yellow handle, marked "Portland Pottery," 2½" h, $35.00.

Baby Dish, 8" d, warming type, red circus decals, white ground, divided, marked "Hazel Atlas"	18.00
Bowl	
6¾" d, Beach Baby, marked "P. K. Unity, Germany"	42.00
9" d, Sing A Song of Sixpence	40.00
Breakfast Set, plate, bowl, and creamer, white, blue design of children playing	75.00
Christening Mug, sterling silver, hallmarked, "R. Redgrave, R. A.," London, c1865	500.00
Creamer	
Bunnykins, marked "Royal Doulton"	40.00
Buster Brown	50.00
Cup and Saucer	
Boy, girl, and bunny, red mark, Germany	12.00
Century of Progress, nursery rhyme dec, marked "Shenango," 1933	48.00
Old Mother Hubbard, marked "Royal Doulton"	50.00
Sand Baby, marked "Royal Bayreuth"	75.00
Egg Cup, Bunnykins, marked "Royal Doulton"	10.00
Mug, Snow Babies, sledding, Royal Bayreuth, blue mark	80.00
Plate	
4½" d, children playing, Kate Greenaway illus	75.00
6½" d, Sunbonnet Babies, Royal Bayreuth, blue mark	
Babies sewing	165.00
Babies washing	130.00
7½" d, hexagon, emb floral border, green transfer of child and cat, marked "Davenport"	85.00
8½" d, Uncle Wiggily	50.00
Sugar, Bunnykins, marked "Royal Doulton"	20.00

CHILDREN'S NURSERY ITEMS

History: The nursery is a place where children live in a miniature world. Things come in two sizes. Child scale designates items actually used for the care, housing, and feeding of the child. Toy or doll scale denotes items used by the child in play and for creating a fantasy environment which copies that of an adult or his own.

Cheap labor and building costs during the Victorian era enabled the nursery to reach a high level of popularity. Most collectors focus on items from the 1880 to 1930 period.

References: Doris Lechler, *Children's Glass Dishes, China, and Furniture,* Collector Books, 1983; Doris Lechler, *Children's Glass Dishes, China, Furniture, Volume II,* Collector Books, 1986; Doris Lechler, *English Toy China,* Antique Publications, 1989; Doris Lechler, *French and German Dolls, Dishes and Accessories,* Antique Publications, 1991; Doris Lechler, *Toy Glass,* Antique Publications, 1989; Anthony and Peter Miall, *The Victorian Nursery Book,* Pantheon Books, 1980; Lorraine May Punchard, *Child's Play,* published by author, 1982.

Additional Listings: Children's Books, Children's Feeding Dishes, Children's Toy Dishes, Dolls, Games, Miniatures, and Toys.

Blocks, set of 36, 1¾", alphabet, animals, and stripes, polychrome	110.00
Bonnet	
Crocheted, white, Popcorn Stitch pattern	18.00
Organdy, white, blue ribbons and trim, orig store tag	20.00
Booties, blue leather, Victorian	30.00
Carriage, Victorian, ornate, orig upholstery and blue and cream paint, fringe around top, 1860	330.00
Chamber Set, 8 pcs, wash bowl, pitcher, chamber pot, cov, soap, toothbrush	

Chamber Pot, blue and white Oriental scene, 8" d, 4¾" h, $165.00.

and comb holder, and slop bucket, hp floral dec	**175.00**
Christening Dress, white, 19th C	**65.00**
Furniture	
Bed, 29 x 48 x 30½", turned posts and legs, four rails with lattice slats, solid board bottom, old green paint over red	**75.00**
Chair, 30", Hepplewhite, Martha Washington style, arm, upholstered back and seat	**650.00**
Cradle, 37" l, walnut, dovetailed, cut out rockers, shaped sides, hand holds	**225.00**
Highchair, Victorian, oak, pressed back, cane seat, converts to stroller	**400.00**
Rocker, 26" h, ladder back, three slats, turned arms and finials, old dark finish	**150.00**
Mug	
Copper Luster, 2½", putty colored band, marked "Eliza"	**50.00**
Glass, raised alphabet and girl looking at Christmas tree and boy at desk scene	**125.00**
Nurser Bottle, glass, blue	**20.00**
Quilt, 40 x 58", nursery rhyme characters, embroidered names	**100.00**
Rattle, celluloid	
Bell shape	**15.00**
Cat shape, pink	**15.00**
Puffin Bird, 3½" h	**10.00**
Rocking Horse, 40" h, 34" l, wood head, red burlap cov, straw filled, wood legs, red paint, red felt and leather saddle, hair mane, marked "Cebasco, Made in Germany"	**975.00**
Sled, 27½", Victorian maple and steamed oak, red center board with stenciled flowers and transfer portrait of Indian, marked "No 52, Paris Mfg Co, So Paris Maine"	**1,000.00**
Spoon, Gerber	**8.00**
Tea Set, ironstone, three 5¾" d plates, 5⅜" teapot, 3¾" d waste bowl, sugar, four cups and saucers, red transfer of Punch and Judy	**170.00**
Teething Ring, celluloid, silver bells . .	**18.00**

Tricycle, wood frame and wheels, black striping, orig red paint **500.00**

CHILDREN'S TOY DISHES

History: Dishes made for children often served a dual purpose—playthings and a means of learning social graces. Dish sets came in two sizes. The first was for actual use by the child when entertaining friends. The second, a smaller size than the first, was for use with dolls.

Children's dish sets often were made as a side line to a major manufacturing line either as a complement to the family service or as a way to use up the last of the day's batch of materials. The artwork of famous illustrators, such as Palmer Cox, Kate Greenaway, and Rose O'Neill, can be found on porcelain sets.

References: Doris Lechler, *Children's Glass Dishes, China and Furniture,* Collector Books, 1983, 1991 value update; Doris Lechler, *Children's Glass Dishes, China, Furniture, Volume II* Collector Books, 1986; Doris Lechler, *English Toy China,* Antique Publications, 1989; Doris Lechler, *French and German Dolls, Dishes, and Accessories,* Antique Publications, 1991; Doris Lechler, *Toy Glass,* Antique Publications, 1989; Lorraine May Punchard, *Child's Play,* published by author, 1982; Margaret & Kenn Whitmyer, *Children's Dishes,* Collector Books, 1984.

Tea Set, akro agate glass, The Little American Maid Tea Set, No. 335, opaque, octagonal dishes in three colors, orig box, $125.00.

Akro Agate
Dinner Service, Interior Panel, small, green Transoptic, four cups and saucers, four plates, creamer, cov teapot	**80.00**

Water Service, Stippled Band, amber,
pitcher and six tumblers **65.00**
Bohemian Glass, decanter and glasses,
ruby flashed, Vintage dec, 5 pcs . . . **125.00**
China
Cheese Dish, cov, hunting scene,
Royal Bayreuth **58.00**
Chocolate Pot, Model T car with pas-
sengers **85.00**
Creamer, Phoenix Bird **18.00**
Cup
Phoenix Bird **12.00**
Willow Ware, blue, marked "Occu-
pied Japan" **6.50**
Dinner Set
23 pcs, Moss Rose **85.00**
25 pcs, Blue Willow **145.00**
Sugar, cov, Phoenix Bird **25.00**
Tea Set
English, Allerton, Staffordshire
Stag, brown transfer, 20 pcs . . . **280.00**
Japanese, gray dragon dec, 21 pcs **75.00**
Tureen, attached tray, marked "Por-
celaine Empire" **8.50**
Milk Glass
Creamer, Wild Rose **65.00**
Cup, Nursery Rhyme **20.00**
Ice Cream Platter, White Rose **60.00**
Punch Cup, Wild Rose **15.00**
Punch Set, White Rose, lemon stain,
punch bowl, six cups **200.00**
Spooner, Wild Rose **45.00**
Pattern Glass
Berry Set, Wheat Sheaf, 7 pcs **80.00**
Butter, cov
Hobnail with Thumbprint base, blue **95.00**
Pennsylvania, green, gold dec . . . **145.00**
Cake Stand
Fine Cup and Fan **35.00**
Palm Leaf Fan **30.00**
Condiment Set, Hickman, open salt,
pepper shaker, cruet, and leaf
shaped tray **60.00**
Creamer
Buzz Saw **10.00**
Drum **70.00**
Lamb **70.00**
Twin Snowshoes **15.00**
Whirligig **15.00**
Cup and Saucer, Lion **45.00**
Mug, Grapevine **20.00**
Pitcher
Colonial, clear **10.00**
Oval Star, clear **15.00**
Portland, gold **35.00**
Punch Set, Wheat Sheaf, 7 pcs . . . **70.00**
Rose Bowl, Star **25.00**
Saucer, Puss in Boots **7.00**
Spooner
Diamond and Panels **15.00**
Tulip and Honeycomb **10.00**
Whirligig **15.00**

Sugar
Beaded Swirl **35.00**
Drum **60.00**
Menagerie, bear, blue **225.00**
Tulip and Honeycomb **25.00**
Table Set
Fernland, olive, 4 pcs **115.00**
Nursery Rhyme, 4 pcs **210.00**
Water Set, Nursery Rhyme, pitcher,
six tumblers **225.00**
Tin
Dinner Set, 16 pcs, four dinner plates,
dessert plates, cups, and saucers,
strawberry dec, white ground,
marked "J. Chein" **30.00**
Ice Cream Freezer, 5½" h, hand
crank, Baby Jeannette Freezer,
Jeannette Toy & Novelty Co, Jean-
nette, PA, includes instructions . . **80.00**

CHRISTMAS ITEMS

History: The celebration of Christmas dates
back to Roman times. Several customs associated
with modern Christmas celebrations are traced
back to early pagan rituals.

Father Christmas, believed to have evolved in
Europe in the 7th Century, was a combination of
the pagan god Thor, who judged and punished the
good and bad, and St. Nicholas, the generous
Bishop of Myra. Kris Kringle originated in Germany
and was brought to America by the Germans and
Swiss who settled in Pennsylvania in the late 18th
century.

In 1822 Clement C. Moore wrote "A Visit From
St. Nicholas" and developed the character of
Santa Claus into what we know today. Thomas
Nast did a series of drawings for *Harper's Weekly*
from 1863 until 1886 and further solidified the
character and appearance of Santa Claus.

References: Robert Brenner, *Christmas Past*,
Schiffer Publishing, Ltd., 1986; George Johnson,
Christmas Ornaments, Lights & Decorations, Col-
lector Books, 1987, 1990 value update; Nancy
Schiffer, *Christmas Ornaments: A Festive Study*,
Schiffer Publishing, Ltd., 1984; Margaret & Kenn
Whitmyer, *Christmas Collectibles*, Collector
Books, 1987, 1990 value update.

Periodicals: *Golden Glow of Christmas Past*,
P.O. Box 14808, Chicago, IL 60614; *Hearts of
Holly, The Holiday Collectors Newsletter*, P.O. Box
105, Amherst, NH 03031; *Ornament Collector*, R.
R. #1, Canton, IL 61520.

Additional Listings: See *Warman's Americana
& Collectibles* for more examples.

Advisor: Lissa L. Bryan-Smith and Richard M.
Smith.

Banner, 19", diecut, star, Merry Xmas in
tail, German, 1920s **45.00**

Book
- *Night Before Christmas,* diecut, house shape, Graham 65.00
- *Visit from Santa Claus,* McLoughlin, 1899 .... 90.00

Candle Holder, 5½", blue clay ball, counter–balance style 25.00

Candy Container, 2½ x 3", drum, vertical gold stripes, silver star, Dresden 100.00

Christmas Fence
- Feather, 65", evergreen hedge, Germany 525.00
- Wooden
  - Folding, red and green 40.00
  - Lighted, red, 6 sections and gate . 65.00

Children's Book, *The Night Before Christmas,* Thomas Nash, Frances Brundage, illustrator, Saalfield Pub. Co., Akron, Ohio, $35.00.

Church, musical, wind–up, plays "Silent Night," mica covered, wood 28.00

Costume, Santa, hooded mask, 1930s 120.00

Deer
- 5" h, metal, brown, marked "Germany" 35.00
- 6" h, glass, silvered, blown glass base, German 40.00

Light Bulb
- Angel, clear, molded wings, orange hair, Japan 35.00
- Candy Cane, 3", milk glass, red and white 35.00
- Father Christmas, 9", orig box, Japan 100.00
- Lantern, molded swirls, multicolored, Germany 45.00
- Santa, with tree 20.00
- Star 8.00

Light Set, bubble, one string, orig box . 20.00

Ornament
- Blown
  - Frog, 4", yellow, black, and red .. 100.00

Santa, 4½", red, gold molded legs and tree 55.00

Sparrow, white, spun glass tail, 1920s 15.00

Chromolithograph
- Child, sleeping, surrounded by toys, tinsel 28.00
- Father Christmas, red coat, standing, toys attached to belt 35.00
- Young Couple, arms linked, tinsel 20.00

Celluloid, Santa, 5", made in USA, Irwin 12.00

Cotton Batting
- Dog, standing on back legs 20.00
- Girl, composition face, skis with poles, 5½" h, Japan 110.00
- Santa, composition face, faded red coat, black legs 100.00

Dresden
- Fish, silver, two sided 150.00
- Guitar, 4" 145.00
- Purse, 1½", red 100.00
- Star, 2" h, gold 15.00

Ornament, glass, Punch, yellow hat and base, white face, blue eyes, red lips, 5¾" h, $75.00.

Glass
- Angel, head 75.00
- Bell, red, white, and blue 25.00
- Cat in Shoe 95.00
- Crown, gold 16.00
- Deer, silvered, glass hook 40.00
- Devil, head and neck 130.00
- Los Angeles Zeppelin 275.00
- Santa, red suit, green tree 35.00
- Stork, clip 42.00
- Sugar Bowl 22.00
- Teapot 23.00

Kugels
  2" h, oval, ribbed 22.00
  4" d, round, blue 60.00
  Wax, early, angel, small 40.00
Putz Material
  Animal
    Camel, 7" h, composition body,
      hide covering, wood legs 50.00
    Cow, 6" h, composition body, cloth
      cov, wood legs 40.00
    Ram, 4" h, celluloid 10.00
    Sheep
      2" h, composition on stuffed
        body, cotton covering, wood
        legs 25.00
      8" h, composition on stuffed
        body, cotton covering, wood
        legs 85.00
    House, 4", cardboard and mica, Jap-
      anese 6.00
    Village, cigar box, four houses and
      church 100.00
  Santa
    6½", celluloid face, papier mache
      boots, Japan 135.00
    7¼", blue, Belsnickle, Germany 695.00
    10", papier mache face and boots,
      Japan 100.00
    Sheet Music, "Silver Bells," E T Paul . 25.00
    Spoon, 4¼" l, child's, SP, Santa, sleigh,
      and deer in bowl 65.00
    Star, 8½ x 3", tin, gold and red paint,
      patented 1926 .... 50.00
  Stocking
    Felt, 10¾", stamped Santa face ... 65.00
    Silk, 6", gold, hp cherries, dated 1882 85.00
  Toy, Santa
    Pop–up, litho cov cardboard, chim-
      ney, top opens, cloth cov Santa,
      composition face, c1910, German 110.00
    Wilson Walkie, Santa, red, orig box . 40.00
  Tree
    12" h, brush, green, snow, Japanese 10.00
    24" h, feather, white, sq red base,
      West Germany 90.00
    32", feather, turned wood base, Ger-
      many 255.00
  Tree Stand
    5 x 11", cast iron, painted, Santa's
      head in relief 265.00
    15 x 18 x 18", cast iron, inverted cone,
      tripod foot, 1920s 65.00

CIGAR CUTTERS

History: Counter and pocket cigar cutters were used at the end of the 19th and the beginning of the 20th centuries. They were a popular form of advertising. Pocket-type cigar cutters often were a fine piece of jewelry that was attached to a watch chain.

COUNTERTOP

Advertising
  East Rock Cigars, glass top with
    mountain scene 80.00
  Gentlemen's Preference, El Santo,
    glass base 115.00
  Great Ohio 5¢ Cigar, cast iron, pig
    shape 425.00
  Plug Tobacco, iron, star, dated 1885 65.00
  Strauss & Hamburger, Chicago, oak,
    match holder, lighter, cigar cutter,
    and container, 7½ x 11" 100.00
Figural
  Bulldog, cast iron, desk type 40.00
  Donkey, cast iron, tail plunger cutter 200.00
  Horse's head, bridle, flowing mane,
    SP, 5¾" 100.00

Pocket, scissors type, sterling silver, 2⅛" l, $40.00.

POCKET

Advertising
  New Bachelor, brass 20.00
  Swift & Co, watch chain 45.00
Figural
  Bakelite, log, wood grain design ... 15.00
  Silver metal, dog's head, 5¾" l 65.00
Knife Type
  Brass
    Girl on potty 90.00
    Revolver, black onyx handle, 3½" 150.00
  Ivory, boar tusk, sterling silver mount 200.00
Scissors Type, sterling silver, floral ... 25.00

CIGAR STORE FIGURES

History: Cigar store figures were familiar sights in front of cigar stores and tobacco shops from about 1840. Figural themes included Sir Walter Raleigh, sailors, Punch figures, and ladies, with Indians being the most popular.

Most figures were carved in wood, although figures also were made in metal and papier-mâché for a short time. Most carvings were life size or slightly smaller and brightly painted. A coating of tar acted as a preservative against the weather. Of the few surviving figures, only a small number have their original bases. Most replacements are due to years of wear and usage by dogs.

Use of figures declined when local ordinances were passed requiring shop keepers to move the figures inside at night. This soon became too much trouble, and other forms of advertising developed.

Reference: A.W. Pendergast and W. Porter Ware, *Cigar Store Figures*, The Lightner Publishing Corp., 1953.

American, warrior, polychrome, 108″ h, $11,100.00.

Indian
Chief, 70¼″ h, pine, carved and painted, wearing red, white, and blue feathered headdress, gold and red gown, holds dagger in right hand, tobacco and cigars in left, black painted pedestal base, 19th C **2,640.00**
Maiden, 28″ h, pine, carved and painted, wearing three feathered headdress, standing on circular base, missing one arm, c1870 . . . **3,575.00**
Princess, 79″ h, pine, carved and painted, feathered headdress and sash, red and green costume, carved and yellow painted fringe, blue leggings and moccasins, one foot raised on tobacco block, holds tobacco leaves and pink rose in right hand, platform base, c1875 . **10,450.00**
Warrior, 108″ h, holding staff in left hand, hatchet in right, polychrome dec **11,100.00**

Punch, 50″ h, pine, carved and painted, holds bunch of cigars in one hand, other hand raised, circular base, early 20th C **2,750.00**
Racetrack Tout, 78″ h, holds can in left hand offers jacket sheets in right, four cigars in jacket pocket, black top hat, repainted, stood in front of Opera House Restaurant, Nantucket, 19th C **42,500.00**
Virginian, 80″ h, pine, carved and painted, black man wearing crown of red, green, orange, and gold tobacco leaves, tobacco leaves kilt and armbands, mounted on composition base in black painted wood frame, c1870 **13,200.00**

CINNABAR

History: Cinnabar is a ware made of numerous layers of a heavy mercuric sulfide and often referred to as vermillion, the red hue in which it is most commonly found. It was carved into boxes, buttons, snuff bottles, and vases. The best examples were made in China.

Reference: Sandra Andacht, *Oriental Antiques & Art: An Identification And Value Guide,* Wallace-Homestead, 1987.

Snuff Bottle, lapis lazuli top, late 19th C, 2¾″ h, $300.00.

Box, cov, 12″ d, 6½″ h, compressed globular, deeply carved scene of gentlemen in garden, pavilion, rocky outcroppings and trees, base with roundel scenes of children in landscapes, peonies and foliate meander ground, raised foot with keyfret pattern below band of stylized lotus lappets, 19th C **880.00**
Cigarette Case, 6⅛″ l, rect hinged top, cinnabar lacquer and ivory, carved courtly scene, key fret band border . **350.00**
Dish, 14½″, carved, three maidens in palace courtyard scene, lotus scrolls on sides, barbed and lobed rim **225.00**

Ginger Jar, 9", ivory, marked "China," pr	650.00
Plate, 7", carved village scene	185.00
Snuff Bottle, 3½", carved scene, figures in garden, carved matching stopper, c1825	250.00
Sweetmeat, 4½ x 9 x 9", carved, open-work cov, eight Buddhist Emblems, latticework platform galleried base, diaper ground	1,320.00
Table Screen, 22¼", figural scene with monk rowing boat, reverse with 3 dragons above rock, flower scroll border, stand	300.00
Tray, 8 x 12", carved garden scene	225.00
Vase	
10", landscape, eight people in garden	250.00
12¼", six lobed per shape, carved with flowering plants, flower scrolls at neck, 19th C	200.00

CLAMBROTH GLASS

History: Clambroth glass is a semi-opaque, grayish-white glass which resembles the color of the broth from clams. Pieces are found in both a smooth finish and a rough sandy finish. The Sandwich Glass Co. and other manufacturers made clambroth glass.

Barber Bottle, Bay Rum, porcelain stopper, 7⅝" h, $35.00.

Barber Bottle	65.00
Candlesticks, pr	
7¼" h, hexagonal petal top, Sandwich	225.00
8¾" h, reeded, scalloped base	100.00
Ewer, 10⅞" h, green applied handle and band, pewter fittings	55.00
Ladle, 9½" l	40.00
Lamp Shade, pr, sgd "Northwood"	45.00

Mug, Lacy Medallion, souvenir	35.00
Pomade Jar, 3¾" h, bear, made for F B Strouse, NY	375.00
Salt, master, Sawtooth, Sandwich, c1850	50.00
Soap Dish, cov, orig insert, Robin and Wheat pattern	100.00
Talcum Shaker	25.00
Toothpick Holder, souvenir	35.00

CLARICE CLIFF

History: Clarice Cliff, born on January 20, 1899, in Tunstall, Staffordshire, England, was one of the major pottery designers of the twentieth century. At the age of thirteen, she left school and went to Lingard, Webster & Company where she learned free-hand painting. In 1916 Cliff was employed at A. J. Wilkinson's Royal Staffordshire Pottery, Burslem. She supplemented her in-house training by attending a local school of art in the evening.

In 1927 her employer sent her to study sculpture for a few months at the Royal College of Art in London. Upon returning, she was placed in charge of a small team of paintresses at the Newport Pottery, taken over by Wilkinson in 1920. Cliff designed a series of decorative motifs which were marketed as "Bizarre Ware" at the 1928 British Industries Fair.

Throughout the 1930s Cliff added new shapes and designs to the line. Her inspiration came from art magazines, books on gardening, and plants and flowers. Cliff and her Bizarre Girls gave painting demonstrations in stores of leading English retailers. The popularity of the line increased.

World War II halted production. When the war ended, the hand painting of china was not renewed. In 1964 Midwinter bought the Wilkinson and Newport firms.

The original pattern names for some patterns have not survived. It is safe to rely on the handwritten or transfer printed name on the base. The Newport Pattern books in the Wilkinson's archives at the Hanley Library also are helpful.

Bizarre and Fantasque are not patterns. Rather they are range names, Bizarre being used from 1928 to 1937 and Fantasque used from 1929 to 1934.

References: Leonard R. Griffin and Louis Meisel, *Clarice Cliff & The Bizarre Affair*, Thames and Hudson, 1988; Howard Watson, *Collecting Clarice Cliff*, Kevin Francis Publishing Ltd., 1988.

Collector's Club: Clarice Cliff Collectors Club, Fantasque House, Tennis Drive, The Park, Nottingham, NG7 1AE, England.

Reproduction Alert: In 1986 fake *Lotus* vases appeared in London and quickly spread worldwide. Very poor painting and patchy, uneven toffee-colored Honeyglaze are the clues to spotting them. Collectors also must be alert to patterns being added to plain items bearing the "Clarice Cliff" backstamp.

In the summer of 1985, Midwinters produced a series of limited edition reproductions to honor Clarice Cliff. They are clearly dated 1985 and contain a special amalgamated backstamp.

Ashtray, Tonquin pattern, Royal Staffordshire Pottery, Wilkinson, Ltd . . .	35.00
Biscuit Jar, 8" h, Honolulu	1,700.00
Bowl, 10" d, Umbrellas pattern	900.00
Condiment Set, 3 pcs, Cabbage Flower pattern, conical shape	300.00
Cracker Jar, 9¼" h, Bizarre ware, My Garden pattern, rattan handle	355.00
Creamer and Sugar, Bizarre ware, ovoid, hp landscape scene	250.00
Cup and Saucer, Crows pattern	75.00
Dinner Set	
Service for six, Coral Fir pattern, includes candleholders	1,850.00
Service for twelve, black, red, orange, and yellow dec bands on ivory . . .	3,400.00
Flower Frog, Autumn Crocus pattern .	340.00
Honey Pot, Beehive, stripes	300.00
Jam Pot, Melon cylindrical	400.00
Marmalade Jar, cov, Capri pattern, orange dec	300.00
Plate	
6" d, Bizarre ware, stylized branches and foliage center design, black concentric rings	100.00
10" d, Citrus Delicia	300.00
Sugar Sifter, Crocus, conical	300.00

Teapot, Bizarre Ware, multicolored, 5" h, $200.00.

Teapot, cov, Tonquin pattern, reddish brown	100.00
Vase	
7" h, Geometric, cylinder	1,000.00
8" h, Oranges, triangle	1,200.00
12¼" h, Lovebirds, yellow ground, Newport Pottery mark	225.00
Vegetable Bowl, Tonquin pattern, reddish brown	35.00
Wall Plaque, 13" d, Bizarre, orange, yellow, and lavender flowers	595.00

CLEWELL POTTERY

History: Charles Walter Clewell was first a metal worker and second a potter. In the early 1900s he opened a small shop in Canton, Ohio, to produce metal overlay pottery.

Metal on pottery was not a new idea, but Clewell was perhaps the first to completely mask the ceramic body with copper, brass, "silvered" and "bronzed" metals. One result was a product whose patina added to the character of the piece over time.

Most of the wares are marked with a simple incised "CLEWELL" along with a code number. Because Clewell used pottery blanks from other firms, the names "Owens" or "Weller" are sometimes found.

Since Clewell operated on a small scale with little outside assistance, only a limited quantity of his artwork exists. He retired at the age of 79 in 1955, choosing not to reveal his technique to anyone else.

References: Paul Evans, *Art Pottery of the United States, 2nd Edition,* Feingold & Lewis Publishing Corp., 1987; Ralph and Terry Kovel, *The Kovels' Collector's Guide To American Art Pottery,* Crown Publishers, Inc., 1974.

Vase, bronze tones, Vance Avon blank, 2 pcs, 12½" h, 5⅝" w, $350.00.

Ashtray, 3¾", copper clad, label "Compliments Canton Bridge Co"	50.00
Bowl, 8", blue–green patina	125.00
Jardiniere, 14" h, ovoid, matte finish . .	75.00
Mug, 4½" h, metal clad, riveted design, applied monogram, relief signature .	30.00
Pitcher, 5¾", copper clad, green patina	150.00
Vase	
4" h, ovoid, glossy green and brown patina	325.00
5½" h, ovoid, green patina, sgd	250.00

6" h, seed form, green and brown patina, sgd **230.00**
7" h, ovoid, streaked blue green patina **275.00**
7½" h, streaked green patina **500.00**
8" h, ovoid, brown to green foot, sgd "Clewell 45936" **375.00**
8½" h, baluster, brown patina on top, green foot **500.00**
9" h, baluster, green two brown areas, cushion foot **90.00**
9½" h, cylinder, pinched rim, veined copper foot **100.00**
15" h, ovoid, brown, deep blue green streaked, cushion foot, inscribed ... **900.00**

CLIFTON

CLIFTON POTTERY

History: The Clifton Art Pottery, Newark, New Jersey, was established by William A. Long, once associated with Londhuna Pottery, and Fred Tschirner, a chemist.

Production consisted of two major lines: Crystal Patina, which resembled true porcelain with a subdued crystal-like glaze, and Indian Ware or Western Influence, an adaptation of the American Indians' unglazed and decorated pottery with a high glazed black interior. Other lines included Robin's Egg Blue and Tirrube. Robin's Egg Blue is a variation of the crystal patina line but in blue-green instead of straw colored hues and with a less prominent "crushed crystal" effect in the glaze. Tirrube is on a terra-cotta ground; features brightly colored, slip decorated flowers; and is often artist signed.

Marks are incised or impressed. Early pieces may be dated and shape numbers impressed. Indian wares are identified by tribes.

References: Paul Evans, *Art Pottery Of The United States, 2nd Edition,* Feingold & Lewis Publishing Corp., 1987; Ralph and Terry Kovel, *The Kovels' Collector's Guide To American Art Pottery,* Crown Publishers, Inc., 1974.

Bowl, 8" d, 5" h, Indian Ware, small neck and rim, squatty bulbous body, dark brown bands, redware ground, Four Mile Ruin, AZ, inspired design, stamped **150.00**
Oil Lamp, 12 x 11", bulbous, brass fixture, earth tones, geometric pattern, sgd in script, numbered, initials **770.00**

Teapot, matte finish, yellow and green glaze, stamp mark, imp numbers, 5½" h, $150.00.

Vase
2½ x 3½", Indian Ware, squatty, bulbous shoulder, matte red, tan, and black S–curve dec, base inscribed "Mississippi," and numbered **50.00**
5 x 7½", bulbous, earth tones, bisque clay, banded geometric dec, die stamped, numbered, marked "Little Colorado, Ariz" **250.00**
8 x 10", Indian Ware, wide short neck, squatty bulbous body, geometric Indian motifs, brown and beige glazes, Homolobi tribe, sgd "Clifton 233," c1910 .... **360.00**

CLOCKS

History: The sundial was the first man-made device for measuring time. Its basic disadvantage is well expressed in the saying: "Do like the sundial, count only the sunny days."

With need for greater dependability, man developed the water clock, oil clock, and the sand clock respectively. All these clocks worked on the same principle—time was measured by the amount of material passing from one container to another.

The wheel clock was the next major step. These clocks can be traced back to the 13th century. Many improvements on the basic wheel clock were made and continue to be made. In 1934 the quartz crystal movement was introduced.

Recently an atomic clock has been invented that measures time by the frequency of radiation and only varies one second in a thousand years.

Identifying the proper model name for a clock is critical in establishing price. Condition of works also is a critical factor. Examine the works to see how many original parts remain. If repairs are needed, try to include this in your estimate of purchase price. Few clocks are purchased purely for decorative value.

References: *Collectors Guide To Clocks Price Guide,* L–W Promotions, 1973 (revised 1986 price list); Roy Ehrhardt, *Clock Identification And Price Guide: Book I,* rev. ed., Heart of America Press, 1979; Roy Ehrhardt, *Clock Identification And Price Guide: Book II,* Heart of America Press, 1979; Roy Ehrhardt, ed., *The Official Price Guide To Antique Clocks,* House of Collectibles, Third Edition, 1985; Rick Ortenburger, *Vienna Regulators And Factory Clocks,* Schiffer Publishing, 1990; Robert W. & Harriett Swedberg, *American Clocks and Clock-makers,* Wallace–Homestead, 1989.

Collectors' Club: National Association of Watch and Clock Collectors, Inc., P.O. Box 33, Columbia, PA 17512.

Museums: American Clock & Watch Museum, Bristol, CT; Museum of National Association of Watch and Clock Collectors, Columbia, PA.

Advertising, Baird Clock Co., Chicago, IL, 15 day Seth Thomas movement, blue, cream dial, c1890, 19¾″ d dial, 30½″ h, $1,600.00.

MISCELLANEOUS

Advertising
Gem Damaskeene Razor, oak, illus center, 8 day time movement with pendulum inscribed "Pure Drugs," paper label on reverse, 27½″ h .. **2,200.00**
Halls Ice Cream, Waterbury Clock Co, Waterbury, CT, 1890, pressed oak case, black and gold tablet, 8 day time movement with pendulum, paper on tin dial, 38″ h **220.00**
Alarm
Ansonia Clock Co, Ansonia, CT, patented Apr 23, 1878, nickel plated case, beveled glass, bell on top, 30 hour time and alarm movement

Alarm, Warren Telechron Co., Ashland, MA, octagonal pumpkin Bakelite case, $40.00.

with winding mechanism, sgd dial and case, 4″ h **75.00**
Gilbert Clock Co, Winsted, CT, 1890, nickel plated case, top mounted with rolling bell swings back and forth causing hammer to strike, paper dial, 30 hour time and alarm lever movement, 10¾″ h **75.00**
Parker Clock Co, Meriden, CT, 1900, Model #60, brass case mounted on brass bell, beveled glass, painted dial, inscribed, 5″ h **140.00**
Seth Thomas Clock Co, Thomaston, CT, 1885, student lever model, nickel plated and gilded case, paper on zinc dial, 30 hour time and alarm lever movement, 7″ h **75.00**
Terry Clock Co, Terryville, CT, 1875, ebonized cast iron case, paper on zinc dial, 30 hour time and alarm movement, fixed pendulum, paper label, 6″ h **30.00**
Unmarked, Germany, c1920, animated, carved chapel, Friar ringing bell, 30 hour lever movement, simulated porcelain dial with gilt center, 13¼″ h **500.00**
Westclox, American, c1925, Art Deco white metal case, silvered dial, 30 hour time and alarm movement, 3″ h **30.00**
Automated, Thomas Armstrong & Bros, Manchester, England, 1880, ship's hull cross section shape revealing engine room, crankshaft powered by spring movement, deck mounted with timepiece with inscribed silvered dial, aneroid barometer, thermometer, compass and cannons, brass and nickel plated brass case, 8 day time lever movement, carved stone base, 17¼″ h **8,800.00**
Blinking Eye, figural
Dog, Bradley & Hubbard cast iron

case, orig paint, paper on zinc dial, 20 hour movement, fixed pendulum, 8½" h **1,430.00**

John Bull, Chauncey Jerome, Bristol, CT, 1870, 30 hour time and movement, paper on zinc dial, 16" h ... **880.00**

Lion, Bradley & Hubbard cast iron case, orig paint, 30 hour time movement, fixed pendulum, 8" h . **1,950.00**

Monkey, German, 1900, multicolored white metal, animated mouth, 9¾" h **440.00**

Organ Grinder, Waterbury Clock Co, Waterbury, CT, 1870, painted cast iron case, eyes move up and down, paper on zinc dial, 30 hour lever movement, 17¼" h **1,700.00**

Owl, German, c1900, nickel plated front, green eyes, paper dial, 30 hour lever movement, 6½" h **465.00**

Sambo, balance wheel, 30 hour time movement, 16" h **630.00**

Topsy, Waterbury Clock Co, Waterbury, CT, 1870, balance wheel, 30 hour time movement, 17" h **600.00**

Figural, Gilbert Clock Co, Preacher & Drunk, cast and painted white metal, 30 hour time lever movement, paper dial, 9" h **230.00**

Car, Waltham, 8 day time movement, 3¼" d **90.00**

Gravity

Europe

19¾" h, engraved silvered brass dial, pierced brass hands, 30 hour movement with crown wheel escapement **4,620.00**

37" h, 1875, ebonized case, pitched head and bracket, 30 hour movement with crown wheel escapement, white porcelain dial with Arabic numerals surrounded with gilded shelled shape dial, inlaid oak board behind sawtooth track **3,740.00**

Germany, carved base, 30 hour time movement, sawtooth bar driven, porcelain dial inscribed "Anno 1750," 26½" h **360.00**

Unmarked, brass case, painted glass dial, 10¼" **135.00**

Night Light

American, 1890, milk glass dial, brass mounts, 30 hour lever movement, 6" h **65.00**

Arfandaux, Paris, France, c1850, cast iron base, gilt brass mounts, lacy style clear glass, frosted glass dial, 30 hour fusee verge escapement movement, pierced and engraved balance cock, 14" h **770.00**

France, 1890, metal, figural, woman

supports 30 hour movement with crown wheel escapement and short pendulum, cast and painted, revolving white glass shade, 20" h . **330.00**

Standard Novelty Co, New York, c1885, nickel plated case, revolving milk glass shade, 30 hour time lever movement, 6½" h **250.00**

Unknown Maker, 1880, gas, milk glass dial, cast brass rim and dec, 30 hour time movement, unsigned, 6" h **80.00**

Novelty

Birdcage, metal cage, gold painted, two plastic birds, one moves with balance wheel, other with alarm mechanism, 30 hour lever movement, 7" h **55.00**

Dog, cast metal case, revolving eyes indicate hour and minute, 5¼" h . **550.00**

Doll, Ansonia Clock Co, Ansonia, CT, c1900, swinging boy, gilded and cast white metal case, paper dial, 30 hour time movement, 11¾" h . **825.00**

Commemorative, Admiral Dewey, gilded iron case, 30 hour lever movement, 10" h **165.00**

Train, Ansonia Clock Co, New York, pat 1878, white metal train front case, includes engineers and amber reflector, 30 hour balance wheel movement with paper dial, gilt highlights, 8" h **600.00**

Woman, Junghans Clock Co, Germany, c1920, mounted on turned base, cast figure supports brass case, 30 hour lever movement, inscribed white porcelain dial, 15½" h **600.00**

Paperweight, E N Welch Mfg Co

Amber glass case, octagon, porcelain dial, 30 hour lever movement, 4" h **155.00**

Blue glass case, porcelain dial, 30 hour lever movement, 4" h **110.00**

Ship

Ashcroft Mfg Co, New York, c1920, cast brass case mounted on walnut base, engraved brass dial, seconds indicator, 8 day double wind time lever movement, chipped bezel glass, 12½" h **355.00**

Seth Thomas, Thomaston, CT, 1900, brass case, silvered dial inscribed, "Kelvin White & Co Nautical Instruments Boston–New York, Seth Thomas," 30 hour lever movement, bell strike, later mahogany base, 10¼" h **330.00**

Waterbury Clock Co, Waterbury, CT, 1940, cast brass case, ship's wheel bezel, silvered dial, 8 day jeweled lever movement, bell strike, 8" d . **250.00**

Stick, Japan, 19th C
  Ebonized rosewood case, brass numerals, small drawer holds winding key, engraved plates, crown wheel escapement with hairspring and balance, lead weight, removable hood, 15½" h 935.00
  Rosewood, brass numerals, small drawer holds winding key, pierced and engraved plates, crown wheel escapement with hairspring and balance, strike mechanism with weight powers time train movement, 19" h 3,300.00
Stove, cast iron, 30 hour time and alarm hair spring movement, 9¾" h, c1900   100.00

SHELF

Acorn
  Brown, J C, and Forestville Mfg Co, laminated rosewood veneered case, painted tablet with floral dec and geometric designs, painted zinc dial, 8 day time and strike double fusee movement with pendulum, 19" h 5,000.00
  Forestville Mfg Co, Bristol, CT, 1847, laminated wood, 8 day time and strike lyre movement, detached fusees mounted on case bottom, painted dial and glass tablet, pendulum, 24½" h 4,400.00
Animated
  France, 1880, The Steam Hammer, cast brass case, marble base, hammer attached to escapement, 8 day time and strike movement, black metal dial with applied brass numerals, 18" h 2,750.00
  Germany, c1900, carved case, Cathedral shape, door opens to Friar ringing the bell in steeple, 30 hour movement with pendulum striking two hammers on single bell, 31" h   1,100.00
Beehive
  Ansonia, rosewood case, 30 hour time and strike movement, 18¾" .   80.00
  Beals, J J, Boston, MA, 1860, overpasted label, mahogany veneered case, enameled zinc dial, J C Brown 8 day time, strike, and alarm movement, 18¾" h 200.00
  Brewster, E C, Bristol, CT, c1845, Kirk's patent iron back plate, lyre mounted gong, 8 day time and strike repeating movement, pendulum, paper label, 19" h 550.00
  Brewster & Ingraham, Bristol, CT, 1850, mahogany veneered case, cut glass tablet, painted zinc dial, 8 day time and strike movement with

orig brass springs and pendulum, 19" h 440.00
  Brown, J C and Forestville Mfg Co, Bristol, CT, 1850, rosewood veneered case, ripple molding, cut glass tablet, painted zinc dial, 8 day time and strike movement with pendulum, 19" h 880.00
  Ingraham, E & A, Bristol, CT, 1850, mahogany veneered case, etched glass tablet, enameled zinc dial, 8 day time and strike movement with pendulum, 19" h 220.00
  Unknown Maker, England, c1906, electric, mahogany case, satinwood banding, engraved silvered dial, balance wheel mounted with coil, dated and numbered 2769, 10¾" h 850.00
  Welch, E N, Forestville, CT
    Mahogany veneered case, rippled door, cut glass tablet, painted zinc dial, 8 day time and strike movement with pendulum, 19" h   500.00
    Rosewood veneered case, cut glass tablet, paper label, enameled zinc dial, 8 day time and strike movement, pendulum, 19" h, 1865 . . . .   385.00
Box or Cottage
  Atkins Clock Co, Bristol, CT, 1870, rosewood veneered case, black and gold tablet, enameled zinc dial, paper label, 30 hour time movement, pendulum, 10" h 250.00
  Chauncey Jerome, Bristol, CT, 1860, ebonized wood case, mother–of–pearl inlay, gold dec, inscribed enameled zinc dial, 30 hour time and strike fusee movement, 13" h   330.00
  Favnor, German, c1940, oak case, stained glass insert on door, silvered dial, 8 day three–train movement with Westminster chimes and pendulum, 28" h 55.00
  Gilbert Mfg Co, Winsted, CT, 1875, rosewood veneered case, gilded moldings, dec tablet, enameled zinc dial, paper label, 8 day time and strike movement, pendulum, 13½" h 80.00
  Jerome, Chauncey, New Haven, CT, 1850, rosewood veneer case, painted zinc dial, 8 day time and strike fusee movement, 13½" h . .   250.00
  New England Clock Co, Bristol, CT, 1850, painted tablet, painted zinc dial, 30 hour time and alarm movement with pendulum, 11" h 425.00
  Terry, S B, Terryville, CT, 1860, applied dec paper on case surface, frosted glass tablet, enameled zinc

dial, 30 hour ladder movement with pendulum, 10½" h **825.00**

Unknown Maker

Connecticut, 1875, rosewood veneered case, two black and gold tablets, painted zinc dial, 30 hour time and strike movement with pendulum, 13½" h **75.00**

German, 1930, oak case, rippled dec, silvered dial, 8 day three–train movement, five chime rods, silvered pendulum, 30" h **190.00**

Bracket

Kienzle Clock Co, New York and Germany, c1930, mahogany case, engraved silvered brass dial, 8 day time and strike three–train movement, Westminster chimes, pendulum, brass plaque on back, 15¾" h **200.00**

Quosig, S, Germany, c1850, walnut case, brass carrying handle, glazed doors and case sides, pewter and brass engraved dial, pierced brass hands, 8 day movement with crown wheel escapement, 19¾" h **2,200.00**

Unknown Maker

China, 19th C, rosewood, revolving base, cabriole legs, glazed door with inlaid mother–of–pearl, porcelain dial with engraved brass, 8 day time and strike fusee movement, crown wheel escapement, sweep seconds, and pendulum, 18½" h **1,000.00**

Japan, 1850, rosewood case, 30 hour time and strike pillar movement with engraved front and back plates, time train fusee, vertical crown wheel escapement, revolving hour dial, two zodiac sign apertures, 10" h **5,500.00**

Calendar

Ansonia Brass & Copper Co, Ansonia, CT, 1870, rosewood veneered case, drop finials, painted tablet, enameled zinc dial, 8 day time and strike movement with iron weights and pendulum, 32¾" h . .   **660.00**

Burwell Mfg Co, Bristol, CT, c1860, rosewood veneered case, laminated and turned bezels, black and gold tablet, upper paper on zinc dial, lower enameled zinc dial, 8 day time and strike movement with rolling pinions, two iron weights and pendulum, 36" h **660.00**

Davis Clock Co, Texarkana, AK, 1890, pressed and carved oak case, two black and gold tablets, paper on zinc dial, 8 day time and strike movement, simple calendar

Calendar, shelf, Ithaca, #3½ Parlor, walnut case, ebony trim, black double dials, crystal pendulum, 3,000.00.

mechanism, pressed brass pendulum, 27½" h **600.00**

William L Gilbert, Winsted, CT, c1870, rosewood veneered case, black and gold tablet, painted zinc dial, 8 day time and strike movement with pendulum, 17½" h **1,155.00**

Ingraham, E Clock Co, Bristol, CT, rosewood veneered case, laminated bezels, painted tablet, enameled zinc dial, 8 day time and strike movement with pendulum, Josiah K Seem calendar dial, 22" h **925.00**

Ithaca Calendar Clock Co, Ithaca, NY, c1870

No 3½ Parlor, walnut, ebonized wood trim, two dials, black paper with silver numerals upper, lower with silver numerals and maker's name, 8 day time and strike movement, cut glass pendulum, 20½" h **3,000.00**

No 10 Farmers model, carved walnut case, paper on zinc dial, inscribed lower dial, 8 day time and strike movement, nickel plated pendulum, 26" h **880.00**

No 11 Octagon model, walnut case, inscribed paper on zinc dial, 8 day time and strike movement by E N Welch, pendulum, 21" h **550.00**

Jerome & Co, New Haven, CT, 1900, nickel plated case, paper dial with date indicator, 30 hour lever movement, pierced crest, 7½" h **75.00**

Seth Thomas Clock Co, Thomaston, CT, c1875

Fashion #1, rosewood veneered case, paper on zinc dial, 8 day time and strike movement with pendulum, orig instructions on inside door, 28½" h **990.00**

Fashion #2, walnut case, three turned finials, paper on zinc dials, 8 day time and strike movement with pendulum, 31½" h **880.00**

Fashion #5, walnut case, three turned finials, painted zinc dials, 8 day time and strike movement, cathedral gong, damascene dec nickel plated pendulum, gold inscribed tablet, 31½" h **1,590.00**

Waterbury Clock Co, C W Feishtinger Patent Calendar, Waterbury, CT, 1895, walnut case, registers date and month, day of week on bottom case, 8 day time, strike, and alarm movement with pendulum, painted zinc dials, gold dec glass, 22" h . . **660.00**

Welch, E N Mfg Co, Forestville, CT, c1880, Arditi model, date, day, and month indicators, 8 day time and strike movement, paper on zinc dials, pendulum, 27" h **600.00**

Carriage

H & H, France, 1890, beveled glass panels, porcelain dial, gold five minute markers, 8 day lever time movement, leather covered carrying case, 4" h **340.00**

Unknown Maker, French, repeater movement, made for Shreve, Crump & Low, 7¾" h **2,100.00**

Commemorative

E Ingraham & Co, Bristol, CT

Admiral George Dewey, flags, cannonballs, stars, and anchors, oak case, orig gold tablet, gilded lead pendulum, 8 day time and strike movement with steel plates, 23" h, 1899 . . . . **300.00**

President McKinley, flags, cannonballs, stars, and anchors, oak case, orig gold tablet with ship and flags, gilded lead pendulum, 8 day time and strike movement with steel plates, 23" h, 1900 . . **300.00**

E N Welch, Forestville, CT, 1900, President Theodore Roosevelt, pressed oak case, crest portrait, soldiers on side brackets, patriotic glass, paper on zinc dial, 8 day time and strike movement, pendulum, 24¼" h **250.00**

Unknown Maker, French, 19th C, 8

day movement, hour repeater, 5½" h **425.00**

Cuckoo

A Frankfield & Co, New York, c1890, carved oak case, grapes and grape leaves, 8 day time and strike movement, paper label on case int., pendulum, 17½" h **465.00**

Unknown Maker, Germany, c1900, carved oak case, 30 hour time and strike movement, pendulum, 16½" h **275.00**

French, Mantel

Brass, gilded, enameled dec panels, 8 day time and strike movement, 12" h **600.00**

Bronze, gold, figural, Diana the Huntress, playing flute, 21¾" h **2,310.00**

Marble case, black, incised gold dec, inset green stone panels, Brocot escapement time dial, aneroid barometer dial, and perpetual calendar dial with moon phase, 8 day time and strike movement with pendulum, 18½" h **2,300.00**

Slate cased tambour, 8 day time and strike outside escapement movement, replaced base, 19½" l, c1880 **110.00**

Garniture, French, 3 pcs

Marble, black, cast brass mounts surmounted by urn, dial engraved and gilded with Roman numerals, 8 day time and strike movement with pendulum, two conforming dec vases, 19" h clock, dial inscribed "Shreve, Crump & Low," c1880 . . . . **550.00**

Gingerbread (Kitchen)

Ansonia Clock Co, Ansonia, CT, 1890, carved and pressed walnut case, paper on zinc dial, silver dec glass, 8 day time and strike movement with pendulum, 22" h **100.00**

Ingraham, E, Bristol, CT, c1900, oak case

Admiral Dewey bust pressed on crest, carved nautical motifs, gold dec tablet with warship, paper on brass dial, 8 day time and strike movement with pendulum cast of lead with shields and eagle, refinished, 23" h **330.00**

Capitol dome pressed on crest, gold dec tablet, paper on zinc dial, 8 day time and strike movement with calendar mechanism and pendulum, paper label on reverse of case, 22" h **275.00**

Welch, E N, Forestville, CT, c1900, Admiral Sampson bust pressed on crest with nautical motifs, gold dec tablet with warship, paper on brass dial, 8 day time and strike movement with pendulum cast of lead with eagle and shield, 24½" h ... **275.00**

Lantern

Forman, Francis, St Paules, England, 17th C, engraved brass dial, single hand, pierced engraved fret, 30 hour time and strike movement, orig balance escapement, 14" h .. **3,850.00**

Hitchman, Henry, Pickadilley, London, 1775, engraved dial and nameplate surrounded with spandrels, 30 hour pull–up time and alarm movement, crown wheel escapement, short pendulum and single hand, brass weight, 9" h **2,970.00**

Mantel, Louis Majorelle, rosewood, iron metal work, bronze patina, 8" h, $1,500.00.

Mantel

Ansonia Clock Co, Ansonia, NY, c1900, ebonized cast iron case, applied and incised gilt dec, porcelain dial with outside escapement, 8 day time and strike movement with pendulum, 12" h **330.00**

Bulle, France, 1920, engraved silver and gilt dial, battery movement with pendulum oscillating over curved magnet, ebonized base, round glass dome, 10½" h **170.00**

Eureka Clock Co, London, c1906, electric, mahogany case, quarter column inlaid with brass banding, porcelain dial, bi–metallic balance wheel mounted with coil, dated and numbered 7945, 15½" h **1,100.00**

Jungans Clock Co, Germany, c1930,

mahogany case, three–train movement, silvered dial with attached brass numerals, pendulum, 10½" h **45.00**

McInnes, J, Bunbarton, England, c1790, gothic, mahogany veneered case, ebony banding, pierced brass inserts, engraved brass dial, 8 day time and strike movement, 18" h **880.00**

Poole Mfg Co, New York City, 1940, battery operated brass movement with round movement support column, engraved silvered dial with seconds indicator, turned wood base, glass dome, 10¾" h **200.00**

Sozet, Mereville, France, 1890, black marble case, incised gold dec, figure mounted on top, black and gold dial, 8 day time and strike movement with pendulum, discolored, 19¼" h **30.00**

Waterbury Clock Co, Waterbury, CT, c1930, tambour, mahogany case, three–train movement striking Westminster chimes, silvered dial with attached brass numerals, 9¾" h **55.00**

Massachusetts Shelf

Hubbard, Daniel, Medfield, MA, c1820, Federal, mahogany and eglomise, shaped crest, urn and foliate form finial, rect eglomise door dec with lyres and foliate motifs, gold painted dished dial, hinged eglomise door with mill and waterfall scene, molded base, gilt wood ball feet, 36" **42,000.00**

Willard, Aaron, Boston, c1820, Federal, mahogany and eglomise, shaped crest, brass eagle finial, door dec with polychrome foliate and lyre motifs, white painted dished dial above eglomise panel painted with corner lyre motifs, oval mirror, brass ball feet, 34½" **9,500.00**

Metal

Iron

Terry, S B, Terryville, CT, 1852, ebonized, mother–of–pearl inlay, painted gold dec, enameled zinc dial, 30 hour time movement, torsion balance, marked "Oct 5th 1852," 8½" h **1,000.00**

Terry Clock Co, Waterbury, CT, 1870, ebonized, striped dec, paper on zinc dial, 8 day time movement, fixed pendulum, broken bezel glass, 8¾" h **80.00**

Ogee

Ansonia Brass & Copper Co, Ansonia, CT, 1845, rosewood veneered case, painted table, enameled zinc dial, 30 hour time and strike movement with iron weights and pendulum, 25¾″ h **250.00**

Ansonia Clock Co, Ansonia, CT, 1850, mahogany veneered case, black and silver dec tablet, enameled zinc dial, 30 hour time and strike movement with iron weights and pendulum, 25½″ h **90.00**

Atkins & Porter, Bristol, CT, c1845, mahogany veneered case, glass tablet, painted zinc dial, 30 hour time and strike movement with cast iron weights, missing pendulum and key, 26″ h **470.00**

Beals, J J, Boston, MA, 1840, mahogany veneered case, frosted glass tablet, enameled wood dial, 30 hour time and strike wood movement with iron weights and pendulum, 26″ h **75.00**

Birge & Fuller, Bristol, CT, 1840, mahogany case, frosted tablet, painted wood dial, 8 day time and strike strap brass movement with pendulum and iron weights, 29¾″ h **220.00**

Brewster & Ingraham, Bristol, CT, 1850, mahogany veneered case, cut glass tablet, painted zinc dial, 30 hour time and strike movement with orig brass springs and pendulum, 17½″ h **250.00**

Brewster, E C & Co, Bristol CT, 1850, veneered, mirror tablet, Charles Kirk cast iron backplate 8 day time and strike spring driven movement, rack and snail strike, orig finish, 28″ h **275.00**

Brown, J C, Bristol, CT, c1850, mahogany and rosewood veneered case, painted wood dial, 8 day time and strike movement with iron weights and pendulum, 29″ h **330.00**

Forestville Mfg Co, Bristol, CT, mahogany veneered case
Enameled wood dial, 8 day time and strike movement with pendulum and iron weights, orig finish, 31″ h, 1840 .... **170.00**
Boston Harbor view on glass tablet, inscribed 8 day time and strike movement with two iron weights and pendulum, enameled wood dial, 28½″ h, 1850 .... **275.00**
Fulton side wheeler steamship dec tablet, inscribed enameled wood dial, 8 day time and strike lyre movement with iron weights and pendulum, 29″ h, 1850 .... **385.00**

Gilbert, Jerome & Grant, Bristol, CT, 1840, mahogany veneered case,

two painted tablets, brass dial, 30 hour time and strike movement with pendulum and iron weights, 25″ h **330.00**

William Gilbert, Winsted, CT, c1860, veneered case with matching figured mahogany veneered panels, frosted tablet, 30 hour time and strike fusee movement with pendulum, 17″ h **220.00**

Ives, Joseph, Plainville, CT, c1840, mahogany, veneered case, glazed door, painted tablet, paper label, 8 day time and strike movement, iron weights, roller pinions and pendulum, carved and gilded crest, 31″ h **940.00**

Jerome, Chauncey, New Haven, CT
26″ h, mahogany veneered case, Merchants Exchange, Philadelphia pictured on tablet, inscribed enameled wood dial, 30 hour time and strike movement, iron weights and pendulum **140.00**
30″ h, mahogany veneered case, painted tablet, enameled wood dial, 8 day time and strike movement with iron weights and pendulum, 1850 .... **500.00**

Johnson, William S, New York, 1850, mahogany veneered case, painted tablet, Chauncey Boardman 8 day time and strike fusee movement with pendulum, 19¼″ h **385.00**

Jones, Jacob, Concord, NH, 1820, mahogany veneered case, one painted tablet, one mirror tablet, enameled iron dial, 8 day time and strike movement with lead weights and pendulum, 31¾″ h **2,310.00**

Smith & Goodrich, Bristol, CT, 1850, rosewood veneered case, floral tablet, painted zinc dial, 30 hour time and strike fusee movement with pendulum, 15½″ h **385.00**

Smith, Philip L, Marcellus, NY, c1830, mahogany veneered case, mounted print behind lower glass, enameled wood dial, 8 day time and strike movement with strap brass plates, iron pendulum and stamped brass pendulum bob, two iron weights, 36″ h **500.00**

Terry, Eli Jr & Co, Terryville, CT, 1845, mahogany veneered case, mirror tablet, enameled wood dial, 8 day time and strike movement with iron weights and pendulum, 33½″ h **300.00**

Terry, Silas B, Plymouth, CT, 1840, rosewood and mahogany veneered case, wood dial with brass seconds disc, 8 day time and strike movement, 34½″ h **440.00**

Seth Thomas, Thomaston, CT, 1863, mahogany veneered case, colorful floral tablet, enameled zinc dial inscribed "Patented May 19, 1863," paper label, 30 hour time and strike lyre movement with pendulum, 16½" h **250.00**

Union Manufacturing Co, Bristol, CT, 1845, mahogany veneered case, painted tablet, wood dial with winged cherubs and floral dec, 30 hour time and strike movement, 26" h **165.00**

Waterbury Clock Co, Waterbury, CT, 1850, rosewood veneered case, dec glass tablet, enameled zinc dial, 30 hour time and strike movement with iron weights and pendulum, 25¾" h **90.00**

Welch, E N, Forestville, CT, 1850
Mahogany veneered case, Hotel Saratoga on glass tablet, enameled zinc dial, 8 day time and strike movement with iron weights and pendulum, 29" h . . **165.00**
Rosewood veneered case, Baltimore Cemetery scene on tablet, painted zinc dial, paper label, 8 day time and strike movement with iron weights and pendulum, 29" h **140.00**

Welton, Hiram, Terryville, CT, c1845, mahogany veneered case, enameled wood dial, 30 hour time and strike movement with attached alarm mechanism with lead weights, 19¼" h **525.00**

Pillar and Scroll
Atkins & Downs, 1830–40, 30 hour weight driven wood time and strike movement, orig pendulum, 31¼" h **120.00**
Neal, Elisha, New Hartford, CT, 1830, mahogany, scrolled crest, turned columns, painted tablet, painted wood dial, 30 hour time and strike wood movement, iron weights and pendulum, three brass finials, 29¼" h **1,100.00**
Stow, Solomon, mahogany veneered case, inlaid maple plinths, painted tablet, enameled wood dial, 30 hour time and strike wood movement, iron weights and pendulum, three brass finials, 29" h **710.00**
Seth Thomas, mahogany case, inlaid satinwood panels, brass finials, turned columns, painted tablet, enameled wood dial, 30 hour time and strike strap wood movement with center pendulum, 30" h **2,100.00**
Unknown Maker, American, c1950, mahogany case, Seth Thomas 8

day time and strike movement, nautical painted tablet, 22½" h . . . **75.00**
Porcelain or China Case, Royal Bonn case, porcelain dial, 8 day time and strike movement with pendulum, France, 13¾" h **500.00**
Shelf
Atkins Clock Manufacturing Co, Bristol, CT, 1840, rosewood veneered case, painted tablet and mirror tablet, enameled zinc dial, 30 day time double wind movement, lever spring, 17¾" h **1,320.00**
Bartholomew, E & G W, 1830–40, carved columns, Eagle splat, 30 hour wood time and strike movement, orig label, 34½" h **275.00**
Birge & Ives, Bristol, CT, 1832, triple decker, carved mahogany eagle splat, columns, and feet, gilded columns painted tablet, mirror tablet, enameled wood dial, strap brass time and strike movement with iron weights and pendulum, 36½" h . . **935.00**
Birge & Mallory, Bristol, CT, column and cornice, mahogany, painted tablet, mirror tablet, painted wood dial, 8 day time and strike strap brass movement with iron weights and pendulum, 36" h **500.00**
Birge, John & Co, Bristol, CT, c1848, mahogany, gilded plaster crest, painted dec columns, painted tablet, enameled wood dial, 8 day time and strike brass movement with iron weights and pendulum, 35" h **440.00**
Blakeslee, E Jr, New York, c1845, mahogany veneered case, painted tablet, enameled wood dial, Davies Patent lever strike mechanism marked on 30 hour movement with iron weights and pendulum, refinished case, 26" h **250.00**
Boardman & Wells, Bristol, CT, 1840, split column, stenciled splat, painted tablet, enameled wood dial, 30 hour time and strike wood movement, iron weights and pendulum, 31½" h **220.00**
Brewster, E C, Bristol, CT, 1840, mahogany veneered case, painted tablet, painted zinc dial, 20 hour time and strike movement with pendulum, Kirk's Patent iron backplate, 20¼" h **385.00**
Brewster, N L, Bristol, CT, c1860, rosewood veneered case with turned columns, painted tablet with coat of arms, painted zinc dial, pendulum, Joseph Ives tin plate 30 hour movement, squirrel cage roll-

ing pinion escapement, tin plates, and roller pinions, 17½" h **1,870.00**

Brown, J C and Forestville Mfg Co, Bristol, CT, 1850, rosewood veneered case, painted tablet, painted zinc dial, 8 day time and strike movement, orig finish, 15" h **500.00**

Conant, William S, New York, 1860, mahogany and rosewood veneered case, molded crest and base, four turned columns, enameled wood door, 30 hour time and strike weight driven movement, 25¾" h **500.00**

Connecticut Clock Co, 1850, rosewood veneered case, glass tablet, painted zinc dial, Miles Morse 8 day time and strike movement with pendulum, 15" h **440.00**

Crane, A D, rosewood and mahogany veneered case, orig cut and frosted glass door, glass and paper dial, overpasted paper label, 8 day time and strike movement with torsion suspension and three ball pendulum, iron weights, 20½" h **3,300.00**

Dutton, David, Mount Vernon, NH, c1830, strawberry dec on dial, 30 hour wood time and strike movement, 33¾" h **140.00**

Goodrich, Chauncey, Bristol, CT, 1860, Empire style, mahogany veneered case, two painted tablets, enameled zinc dial, 8 day time and strike movement with pendulum, refinished case, 20½" h **710.00**

Goodwin, E O, Bristol, CT, 1852, mahogany veneered case, three painted tablets, painted zinc dial, Brewster & Ingraham 8 day time and strike movement, refinished, 20½" h **710.00**

Hart, Orrin, Bristol, CT, 1835, stenciled columns and splat, enameled wood dial, 30 hour time and strike Groaner wood movement, pendulum and iron weights, 34¼" h **220.00**

Hotchkiss & Benedict, Auburn, NY, 1830, mahogany veneered case, carved crest and capitals, painted tablet, black painted dial with gold dec, 8 day time and strike movement with flying eagle pendulum, iron weights, refinished, 37½" h .. **880.00**

Hotchkiss, Spencer & Co, Salem Bridge, CT, 1830, mahogany veneered case, stenciled half round columns, molded cornice, gold leaf dec dial, 8 day Salem Bridge time movement with pendulum and lead weight, turned feet, 28" h **1,485.00**

Ingraham, E & Co, Bristol, CT, 1875, rosewood veneered case, gold dec

tablet, paper on zinc dial, 8 day time and strike movement with pendulum, 16½" h **120.00**

Ives, C & L C, Bristol, CT, 1835, triple decker, mahogany and veneer case, enameled wood dial, ebonized ball feet and columns, eagle dec crest, 8 day time and strike strap brass movement with pendulum, refinished case, 36½" h .. **2,640.00**

Jerome & Co, New Haven, CT, 1875, rosewood veneered case, gutta percha panels behind glass, 8 day time and strike movement with pendulum, 16" h **165.00**

Jerome & Darrow, c1830, stenciled half columns and splat, carved pineapple finial and paw feet, 30" h **770.00**

Kroeber, F, New York, 1875, carved poplar case, porcelain dial, 8 day time and strike movement with glass pendulum, refinished case, 20" h **200.00**

Manross, Elisha, Bristol, CT, 1850, rosewood veneered case, line inlay, painted zinc dial, 30 hour time and strike movement with pendulum, 14" h **355.00**

Marsh, George, Bristol, CT, 1835, split stenciled column, glazed door with mirror, painted tablet, enameled wood dial, 8 day time and strike movement, ivory bushings, iron weights, pendulum, 35½" h .. **660.00**

Morse, Miles, Plymouth, CT, 1825, mahogany veneered case with inlaid satinwood panels, turned columns, enameled dial, painted tablet with mustard background, 8 day Salem Bridge movement with iron weights, 26½" h **7,700.00**

New Haven Clock Co, New Haven, CT, 1860, Empire style, mahogany veneered case, painted dec columns, enameled zinc dial, two tablets, 8 day time, strike, and alarm movement with pendulum, 20½" h **440.00**

Pratt, Daniel, Jr, Reading, MA, 1843, mahogany veneered case, mirror tablet, enameled wood dial, 30 hour time and strike movement with weights and pendulum, 28" h **330.00**

Seymour, Willimas & Porter, Unionville, CT, c1835, mahogany case, carved basket of fruit crest, columns, and paw feet, enameled wood dial, 8 day time and strike wood movement, with weights and pendulum, 37¼" h **600.00**

Smith & Goodrich, Bristol, CT, 1850, mahogany veneer, painted tablet with eagle, shield, and arrows, 30 hour time and strike fusee movement with pendulum, 14¾" h **355.00**

Sperry & Shaw, New York, 1845, mahogany veneered case, painted floral dec tablet, enameled wood dial, 30 hour time and strike movement with lead weights and pendulum, 19¾" h **135.00**

Spring, S C & Co, Bristol, CT, c1865, rosewood veneered case, ebonized columns, black and gold tablet, painted zinc dial, 8 day time and strike strap movement with iron weights and pendulum, 30½" h . . **440.00**

Terry, Samuel, 1830–40, half column and splat, 30 hour time and strike movement, 34¾" h **120.00**

Terry, Silas B, Terryville, CT, 1840, mahogany veneered case, molded door, painted tablet, 30 hour weight driven brass time and strike movement with orig iron weights and pendulum, 24" h **2,530.00**

The Year Clock Co, New York, 1888, ebonized case with brass mounts, cut glass tablet, green paper label, glass dial with paper back, Aaron Crane patent torsion suspension with six ball pendulum and one year fusee time and strike movement, 21½" h **6,000.00**

Seth Thomas, Thomaston, CT, 1875 Mahogany and veneered case, Empire style, gilded basket of fruit on crest, stenciled columns, paw feet, 30 hour time and strike wood movement with orig weights, 37" h **1,100.00**

Rosewood veneered case, two dec tablets, painted zinc dial, 8 day time and strike movement with pendulum and iron weights, 32½" h **330.00**

Walnut case, gold band dec, enameled zinc dial, 8 day time and strike movement with cathedral gong, silver dec tablet, nickel plated pendulum with damascene dec, 19" h **175.00**

Unknown Maker, walnut case with pitched top, glazed door, enameled dial, Joseph Ives 30 day double wind movement and cast iron frame with lever spring attached, pendulum, 26" h **880.00**

Votti, G, Philadelphia, PA, c1885, elaborate case, raised gilded and silvered gesso dec, 8 day movement with escapement and pendulum, silvered brass dial with applied numerals and damascene dec, 29½" h **1,430.00**

Shelf, E. N. Welch, teardrop, walnut, 8 day movement, 22½" h, $300.00.

Welch, E N, Forestville, CT, 1880, carved walnut case with three turned finials, paper on zinc dial, 8 day time and strike movement with emb pendulum, 26" h **330.00**

Welch Spring & Co, Forestville, CT, 1870, Venetian model, rosewood veneered case, gilded columns, black and gold tablet, 8 day time and strike movement with pendulum, 17" h **165.00**

Williams, Orton, Prestons & Co, Farmington, CT, 1835, mahogany case, stenciled columns and splat, painted tablet, 30 hour time and strike wood movement with iron weights and pendulum, 32" h **110.00**

Skeleton

Bolt, Thomas & Co, Liverpool, England, 1870, silvered and engraved pierced brass dial, 8 day time and strike fusee movement with recoil escapement, ebonized wood base, glass dome, pendulum, 15" h . . . **1,870.00**

Ithaca Calendar Clock Co, Ithaca, NY, 1890, nickel plated cast frames and dials, black and silver paper day and month indicators, 8 day time and strike movement, walnut base, ball feet, glass dome, pendulum, 14½" h **2,975.00**

Lamport, W H, Plymouth, England, 1860, glass dome, rosewood veneered base, engraved silvered dial, 8 day time fusee movement, 14" h **1,430.00**

Terry Clock Co, Waterbury, CT, 1875,

glass dome, porcelain dial, pressed brass dial, 8 day double wind time movement, painted dec on base, 11½" h **990.00**

Terryville Clock Co, Waterbury, CT, 1875, glass dome, porcelain dial, pressed brass ornamentation, day double wind time movement, painted dec base, 9" h **710.00**

Unknown Maker, England, c1870, Cathedral model, silvered brass dial, 8 day time fusee movement, marble and ebonized wood oval base, glass dome, pendulum, 16½" h **600.00**

Steeple

Ansonia Brass & Copper Co, Ansonia, CT, 1875, mahogany veneered case, dec tablet, 8 day time and strike movement with pendulum, 20" h **250.00**

Birge, John, Bristol, CT, 1850, steeple on steeple, mahogany veneered case, painted zinc dial, 8 day time and strike fusee movement with pendulum, 26½" h **1,050.00**

Birge & Fuller, Bristol, CT, 1845, mahogany veneered case, four turned candles, painted tablet, painted zinc dial, 8 day time and strike movement with lever spring, pendulum, 26" h **1,760.00**

Boardman, Chauncey, Bristol, CT, 1845

20" h, mahogany veneered case, frosted glass tablet, painted zinc dial, 30 hour time, strike, and alarm triple fusee movement with pendulum **440.00**

21¾" h, mahogany veneered case, painted zinc dial, 30 hour time and strike movement, Joseph Ives patent lever spring, pendulum **4,125.00**

Brewster & Ingraham, Bristol, CT, 1865, mahogany veneered case, turned columns, cut glass tablet, paper label, enameled zinc dial, 8 day time and strike movement, pendulum, 20" h **550.00**

Brown, J C, Forestville, CT, c1850, rosewood veneered case

Cut glass tablet, painted zinc dial, 30 hour time, strike, and alarm movement with pendulum, 16" h **355.00**

Etched glass tablet, painted zinc dial, 8 day time and strike fusee movement with pendulum, 20" h **825.00**

Forestville Hardware & Clock Co, Forestville, CT, 1853–55, mahogany veneered case, frosted glass tablet, turned finials, painted zinc

dial, 30 hour time movement with pendulum and key, 12¼" h **440.00**

Ingraham, E & A, Bristol, CT, c1855, mahogany veneered case, cut glass tablet, painted zinc dial, 30 hour time, strike, and alarm movement with pendulum, 20" h **500.00**

Jerome, Chauncey, New Haven, CT Mahogany veneered case

Dec tablet, enameled zinc dial, blue paper label, 30 hour time and strike fusee movement, pendulum, 20" h, 1850 . . . . . **250.00**

Frosted glass tablet, enameled zinc dial, 8 day time and strike fusee movement with pendulum, 19¾" h, 1840 . . . . **440.00**

Rosewood veneered case, glass tablet, enameled zinc dial, 30 hour time and strike movement with pendulum, 20" h **220.00**

Johnson, William S, New York, c1850, steeple on steeple, mahogany veneered case, turned finials, orig painted tablets, painted zinc dial, 8 day brass spring driven time and strike movement with pendulum, 23½" h **440.00**

Manross, Elisha, Bristol, CT, 1845

Mahogany veneered case, two geometric tablets, painted zinc dial, 8 day time and strike fusee strap brass movement with pendulum, 23½" h **660.00**

Rosewood veneered vertically, painted zinc dial, 8 day time and strike movement strap brass fusee movement with pendulum, 24" h **1,980.00**

Platt, A S & Co, Bristol, CT, 1850, mahogany veneered case, mirror tablet, enameled zinc dial, 30 hour time and strike fusee movement, 20" h **220.00**

Smith & Goodrich, Bristol, CT, 1845, mahogany veneered case, tablet with balloon and American flags, painted zinc dial, 30 hour time and strike fusee movement with pendulum, 20" h **500.00**

Terry & Andrews, Bristol, CT, 1850, mahogany veneered case, painted tablet, painted zinc dial, 8 day time and strike lyre movement with pendulum, 19½" h **575.00**

Terry, Silas B, Terryville, CT

Mahogany and rosewood case, painted wood dial, 30 hour time and strike with two wood fusee cones, wood winding drums, 25" h **6,600.00**

Mahogany veneered case, four finials, frosted glass tablet, enameled zinc dial, 30 hour time and strike movement with pendulum, 19¾″ h **275.00**

Terry & Andrews, Ansonia, CT, c1850, rosewood veneered vertically, painted zinc dial, 8 day time, strike, and alarm lyre movement, orig brass springs and pendulum, 20″ h **355.00**

Terryville Manufacturing Co, Terryville, CT, 1860, rosewood veneered case, nautical dec tablet, 30 hour time and strike movement with pendulum, 20″ h **410.00**

Unknown Maker, rosewood veneered case, applied rippled molding, etched glass tablet, painted zinc dial, converted Waterbury 8 day time and strike movement with pendulum, 20″ h **1,265.00**

Welch, E N, Forestville, CT
20″ h, rosewood veneered case, Iodine Springs on tablet, painted zinc dial, 8 day time, strike, and alarm movement, pendulum, c1865 . . . . **360.00**

23½″ h, rosewood veneered case, enameled zinc dial, 8 day time, strike, and alarm movement with pendulum, 1860 . . . . **940.00**

TALL CASE CLOCKS

Balch, Daniel, Newbury, MA, c1760, walnut, molded stepped pediment hood with three ball and eagle brass finials, engraved brass dial mounted with foliate spandrels, waisted case with arched hinged door, molded base with shaped pendant, bracket feet, stylized gilt highlights, 93½″ h, 20″ w, 10½″ d **5,500.00**

Bevan, Thomas, Marlborough, England, c1780, oak case, cross banded mahogany veneers, flat top, glazed door with turned columns, shaped waist door with quarter columns, straight bracket feet with central drop, inscribed engraved dial, 8 day time and strike movement plays musical tone on nest of bells on quarter hour, pendulum and three weights, 81½″ h . . **4,075.00**

Fouche, Bastide, St Savin, France, 1860, Morbier, pine grain painted case, 8 day time and strike movement with alarm, porcelain dial with brass dec, gridiron pendulum, two iron weights and one brass alarm weight, 94″ h **500.00**

Hallett, James, NY, c1790, Chippendale, mahogany, shaped crest hood,

three brass ball and steeple finials, arched glazed door, white painted dial, waisted case with arched hinged door, bracket feet, 96½″ h, 19″ w, 9½″ d **6,655.00**

Keim, John, Reading, PA, 1790, walnut case, molded flat top, glazed door, inscribed enameled dial, rect waist door with incurvate upper corners, inset base panel, turned feet, 30 hour time and strike pull–up movement with one iron weight and pendulum, 91¼″ h **880.00**

Lock, William, Taunton, England, 1780, carved oak case, arched hood, glazed doors with turned columns with gilded capitals, rect waist door, cut–out feet, 8 day time and strike movement, lead weights and pendulum, engraved silver and gilt dial with calendar aperture and month indicator, 80½″ h **1,200.00**

Mulliken, Samuel, Bradford, MA, 1750, cherry, hood with broken arch crest, applied dentil moldings, turned hood columns, engraved brass dial, tombstone waist door, flat fluted columns, straight bracket feet, 30 hour time and strike pull–up posted movement, iron weight and pendulum, 89½″ h **2,500.00**

Pyke, Joseph, London, England, 1840, Victorian, mahogany, engraved silvered dial, 8 day time movement with dead beat escapement, brass tubular pendulum and weight, case with sloping pediment, glazed door, applied bracket, 78½″ h **1,700.00**

Rittenhouse, David, Philadelphia, PA, c1765, walnut case, flat molded top, glazed hood door with turned columns, tombstone waist door, high bracket feet, 30 hour pull–up time and strike movement, iron weight and pendulum, engraved brass dial with pewter spandrels and inscribed nameplate, 90″ h **12,100.00**

Unknown Maker
European, 1830, pine case, pierced fret and three finials on hood, glazed door, turned columns, enameled dial, tombstone waist door, 8 day time and strike movement with weights and pendulum, 88¾″ h **1,100.00**

Federal, c1810, inlaid walnut, molded swan's neck crest, arched glazed door, white painted dial with moon phases, waisted case with cross banded hinged door, line inlaid quarter columns, fan inlaid base, shaped skirt, bracket feet, 103″ h, 20″ w, 10″ d **4,540.00**

Morbier, France, 1870, pine grain painted case, 8 day time, strike, and alarm movement, porcelain dial, pressed brass farm workers in field scene, brass pendulum and two iron weights, 91" h **770.00**

New England, c1810, Federal, cherrywood, pierced crest, two ball finials, white painted dial with calendar date and minute register, columns with brass caps, waisted case with oval inlaid door with quarter columns with brass caps, oval inlaid base, splayed bracket feet, 90¾" h, 18" w, 9" d **5,500.00**

Urletig, Valentin, Reading, PA, c1770, walnut case, broken arch hood, three carved finials, turned hood columns, tombstone waist door with inlaid initials, inlaid waist with turned and fluted quarter columns, flaring French feet, inscribed engraved brass dial with moon phase, 8 day time and strike movement, brass weights and pendulum, 96½" h **4,675.00**

Vandelle, C, Paris, France, 1880, Morbier, walnut case with inset panels, round pendulum opening, three–train 30 hour movement, three bells, porcelain dial, three iron weights, 96½" h **1,760.00**

Wilder, Joshua, Hingham, MA, c1810, Federal, inlaid mahogany, hood with two brass ball and steeple finials, white painted dial, turned columns, waisted case with hinged door, cross banded base above shaped skirt, bracket feet, 41½" h, 10½" w, 5½" d **25,850.00**

Williams, Dan, Neath, England, c1760, japanned case, arched hook, tombstone waist door, bracket feet, gilded and painted dec case, brass dial with calendar indicator and engraved boss, 8 day time and strike movement with weights and pendulum, 91¾" h **1,430.00**

WALL

Acorn, J C Brown and Forestville Mfg Co, Bristol, CT, 1850, laminated case with figured mahogany veneered front, painted glass tablet, enameled zinc dial, 8 day time movement with pendulum, 28½" h **1,000.00**

Banjo

Brewster & Ingraham, Bristol, CT, mahogany, painted zinc dial, black and gold glasses, 8 day time movement with pendulum, 31½" h **600.00**

Howard, E & Co, Boston, MA, 1870 28½" h, grain painted poplar case, paper on zinc dial, two red, black,

Wall, Howard E. Davis, Boston, $2,100.00.

and gold glass inserts, 8 day time movement, iron weight **1,760.00**

29¼" h, cherry grained case, two black and gold glasses, paper on zinc dial, 8 day time movement with damascene dec on front plate, orig iron weight and pendulum **5,000.00**

Howard & Davis, Boston, MA, 1850, cherry grained case, black and gold glasses, paper on zinc dial, 8 day time movement with damascene dec front plate, iron weight and pendulum, 32" h **1,980.00**

New Haven Clock Co, 1920s, mahogany case, 8 day spring–driven movement, triple wind time, 41½" h **410.00**

Stennes, Elmer O, presentation, 8 day weight driven time movement, case marked "10/74," 41¾" h . . . **2,200.00**

Taber, E, Boston, MA, 1820, mahogany, two painted tablets, brass finial, enameled iron dial, 8 day time movement with lead weight and pendulum, 34½" h **2,035.00**

Tift, Horace, Attleboro, MA, 1840, mahogany, finial on top, figured panels, enameled iron dial, 8 day time movement, iron weight and pendulum, 33¼" h **550.00**

Tower, Reuben, Hingham, MA, 1820, 8 day time and alarm movement, inscribed enameled iron dial, replaced bell on top, lead weight, 29½" h **3,500.00**

Unknown Maker, MA, 1820, gilded frame, eagle finial, brass side arms and bezel, two painted tablets, enameled iron dial, 8 day time movement with lead weight and pendulum, 33" h **525.00**

Waterbury Clock Co, 1920–30, miniature, 8 day jeweled time movement, 15" h **240.00**

Willard, Aaron, Boston, MA, c1825, mahogany and eglomise, gilt lemon form finial, white painted dial, inscribed "A Willard, Jr Boston," painted American eagle and shield on throat panel, brass side arms, hinged door with painted naval scene, 33 x 10" **5,500.00**

Calendar

Atkins Clock Co, Bristol, CT 1875, rosewood veneered and grain painted case, B B Lewis perpetual calendar indicates day, date, month, and time, painted zinc dial, 8 day time movement with pendulum, black and gold tablet, 24½" h **825.00**

William L Gilbert, Winsted, CT, 1875, carved and pressed oak case, dec glass panel with day, month, and date apertures, paper on zinc dial, 8 day time and strike movement, Thomas McCabe patent calendar mechanism with three revolving sheet metal discs, lever connected to strike train activates day and date discs, month disc moved manually, pendulum, 35½" h **1,875.00**

Maranville, Galusha, rosewood veneered case, carved side arms, black and gold tablet, painted zinc dial, William L Gilbert 8 day time weight driven movement with dead beat escapement, pendulum and iron weight, 34" h **1,925.00**

Seth Thomas, Thomaston, CT, c1870, rosewood veneered case, two painted zinc dials, lower inscribed "Made in USA, Seth Thomas Clock Co, Plymouth Hollow, CT, patented," 8 day time movement with pendulum, 27½" h **600.00**

Welch Spring & Co, Forestville, CT, c1885, Gale Drop Calendar, astronomical calendar with time, date, moon phase, sunrise, and sunset, and day of week, rosewood veneered and grain painted case, black and gold tablet, black paper label, 8 day time and strike movement marked "E N Welch" with pendulum, 30" h **3,850.00**

Cuckoo

Black Forest

23" h, bird crest, 8 day time and strike movement, 1870–80 . . . . **110.00**

26½" h, eagle crest, 8 day time and strike movement, c1880 . . . . . . **410.00**

Germany

19" h, carved case, bird with glass eyes on top, 30 hour three–train movement, single cuckoo bird and two doors open to dancing figures, 1940 . . . . **110.00**

22½" h, carved deer, trumpet, powder flask, and guns, 30 hour time and strike movement, paper instruction label, two weights and carved pendulum, c1890 . . . . . **275.00**

24½" h, carved case, bird with glass eyes on top, 30 hour three–train movement, double striking cuckoo birds, three weights and pendulum, 1940 . . . . **385.00**

Gallery

Ansonia, Ansonia, CT, 1890, laminated and turned case, paper on zinc dial, 8 day time movement with pendulum, 16" d **110.00**

Ansonia Brass & Copper Co, Ansonia, CT, 1880, rolled brass case, paper label, painted zinc dial, 30 hour lever movement, 8½" d **80.00**

Brewster & Ingraham, Bristol, CT, 1850, laminated and turned mahogany bezel, convex enameled wood dial, 8 day horizontal movement with upside–down pendulum suspension, 19¼" d **1,430.00**

Clark, J, Manchester, England, 1930, mahogany case, enameled dial, 8 day time and strike movement, tow chime rods, 15½" d **120.00**

Jerome, S B, New Haven, CT, 1865, ebonized canvas covered wood case, brass trim, enameled zinc dial, paper label, 30 hour lever movement, 9" d **165.00**

Marine Clock Mfg Co, New Haven, CT, c1850, rosewood veneered case, enameled zinc dial, 20 hour time and strike movement, Charles Kirk Patent double wheel escapement, 11" h **3,660.00**

New Haven Clock Co, New Haven, CT, 1875, octagon, rosewood veneered case, painted zinc dial, 30 hour time lever movement, 6¼" h **70.00**

Pomeroy, N, Bristol, CT, 1850, rippled octagon, rosewood veneered case, applied rippled moldings, painted zinc dial with balance wheel aperture, 8 day time lever movement, 10½" h **500.00**

Self Winding Clock Co, New York, 1940, enameled case and dial, dead–beat movement, battery wind mainspring, pendulum, 20" d **25.00**

Terryville Mfg Co, Terryville, CT, 1855, rosewood veneered case, enameled zinc dial, torsion pendulum, 8 day time movement, refinished **600.00**

Unknown Maker
Connecticut, 1875, rosewood veneered case, painted zinc dial, 30 hour lever movement, 8½" h . . **90.00**
French, brass spring driven 8 day time and strike movement, 12½" d **140.00**

Waterbury Clock Co, New York, 1880, laminated and turned walnut case, paper label, painted zinc dial with seconds indicator, 8 day time, double wind lever movement, 12" d . . **220.00**

Welch, E N Mfg Co, Forestville, CT, 1870, rosewood veneered octagon case, enameled zinc dial, 30 hour lever movement, 8¾" h **120.00**

Miscellaneous
Dutch, oak case, removable arched hood with ball finials, applied split columns and gilded capitals, applied brass dec on lower case, enameled iron dial, 30 hour time, strike, and alarm pull–up movement with pendulum and brass weights, 50" h **880.00**
Marine Lever, E N Welch, 1860, octagon, rosewood veneered case, 8 day brass time movement, second bit, 8¾" d **110.00**
Metal, Gilbert, c1875, iron, filigree, 8 day brass spring driven time and strike movement, 28" h **660.00**
Mission Oak, National Clock & Mfg Co, Chicago, IL, 1920, brass plated numerals and hands, 8 day time and strike movement with pendulum, 26" h **55.00**
Morbier, France
53" h, Stolz, 1880, 8 day time, strike, and alarm movement, three weights and brass pendulum, gridiron and lyre dec, porcelain dial **410.00**
57" h, 1850, porcelain dial surrounded by pressed brass, 30 hour time and strike movement, thermometer tube in pendulum, two brass weights **440.00**
58½" h, 1860, 8 day time and strike movement, calendar mechanism fitted with strike mechanism, iron weights, repousse pendulum, white porcelain dial inscribed "Barennes fils de l'aine'a Clairac" **690.00**
Oriental, Japan, 1800, engraved brass case and dial, 30 hour time, strike, and alarm movement with foliate escapement, cast iron

weight and four lead counterweights, 9" h **2,475.00**

Lyre
Sawin, John, Boston, MA, 1830, carved mahogany case, brass bezel, painted iron dial inscribed "Sawin," eagle finial, painted tablet, 8 day weight driven time movement, replaced finial and plinth, refinished and reglued, some replacements, 36½" **1,100.00**
Willard, Aaron, Roxbury, MA, 1820, carved mahogany case, painted tablet, wood panel, enameled iron dial inscribed "Aaron Willard, Patent, Roxbury," 8 day time movement with iron weight and pendulum, 38" h **1,480.00**

Ogee, George Hills, Plainville, CT, 1850, mahogany veneered case, mirror tablet, enameled zinc dial, 20 hour time and strike movement, 36½" h . **600.00**

Regulator
Atkins Clock co, Bristol, CT, 1860, rosewood veneered case, black and gold glass, enameled zinc dial, 8 day double wind time only weight driven movement with two brass weights and pendulum, 36½" h . . **660.00**
Becker, Gustave, Germany
45½" h, 1900, burl walnut veneered case, turned finials, bracket, and carved crest, porcelain dial, 8 day time and strike movement with pendulum and brass weights **1,100.00**
59" h, 1890, walnut veneered case with ebonized carved dec, turned finials, 30 day time and strike movement, porcelain dial, two brass weights, pendulum **3,300.00**
Brewster & Ingraham, Bristol, CT, 1860, rosewood veneered case, applied rippled molding, enameled zinc dial, 8 day time and strike movement with pendulum, 22" h . **275.00**
Ingraham, E & Co, Bristol, CT, 1880
Poplar case, grain painted dec, paper on zinc dial, 8 day time movement with calendar mechanism and pendulum, 24" h . . . **220.00**
Pressed oak case, paper on zinc dial, 8 day time movement, gilded lead pendulum, 25" h . . . **275.00**
Jerome, Chauncey, 1850, octagon, 8 day time and strike movement, 24" h **330.00**
Juguns, c1900, walnut case, eagle pediment, 8 day time and strike spring driven movement, 38" h . . **275.00**
Kroeber, F & Co, New York, 1880, Vienna Regulator #51, glazed

sides, porcelain dial with seconds indicator, 8 day time movement with brass weight and pendulum, 44" h **500.00**

National Clock & Mfg Co, Chicago, IL, 1900, mahogany case, black and gold tablets, paper on tin dial, 8 day time movement with calendar mechanism, brass pendulum, 39½" h **600.00**

Sessions
   Clinton model, 1920, oak case, 8 day time movement, 28" h **220.00**
   Model #2, 1910, oak case, 8 day time spring driven movement, 38½" h **300.00**

Sexty, Grantham, 1875, mahogany rosewood veneered case, carved twisted rope columns and bezel, enamel iron dial, 30 day time movement with brass weight and pendulum, 68½" h **1,100.00**

Sperry, Henry & Co, New York, c1850, mahogany veneered case, cross banding, carved brackets, painted tablet, enameled zinc dial, 8 day time movement with pendulum, 24½" h **330.00**

Terry, Silas B, Terryville, CT, 1840, rosewood veneered case, black and gold tablet, enameled zinc dial, 8 day time movement with dead beat escapement, gilded pendulum rod, lead weight, 37½" h **550.00**

Seth Thomas, Thomaston, CT
   Model #30, mahogany case, 8 day time only movement, second bit, 50" h, 1900 .... **1,540.00**
   Mahogany, enameled zinc dial with seconds indicator, 8 day time movement with brass weight and pendulum, 36½" h, 1890 ..... **770.00**
   Oak case, black and gold tablet, painted zinc dial, paper label, 8 day time movement, pendulum, 24" h, 1900 .... **355.00**

Unknown Maker
   French, 1900, walnut case, 8 day weight driven time and strike movement with second bit, 52½" h **500.00**
   Germany, c1900, various, carved and dec case, paper on dial, 8 day time and strike spring driven movement with pendulum, 40" h **150.00**

Waltham, 1900–10, oak case, 8 day time movement, 34" h **500.00**

Waterbury, Waterbury, CT, 1900, mahoganized poplar case, regular tablet, paper on zinc dial, seconds indicator, paper label on reverse, 30

day time movement, pendulum, 31" h **550.00**

Welch, E N, c1870, octagon, mahogany veneered case, 8 day time and strike movement, 24½" h **275.00**

School House
   New Haven, New Haven, CT, 1880, pressed oak case, gold dec tablet, paper on tin dial, 8 day time movement, calendar mechanism, 27½" h **360.00**
   Sessions Clock Co, Forestville, CT, c1900, oak case, paper on tin dial, 8 day time movement with pendulum, 19¼" h **500.00**

Wag on Wall
   Dutch, 18th C, 27" h
      Enameled dial with painted cherubs and floral dec, 30 hour time and alarm movement, turned pillars, verge escapement and outside count wheel, cast lead crest and side brackets on case, backboard and bracket painted with floral dec, canopy with cast lead dec, pendulum **1,000.00**
      Enameled dial with painted nautical motifs, gilded cast lead crest and side brackets, backboard and bracket painted with mermaids, canopy with gilded cast lead dec, 30 hour time and alarm movement with turned pillars, verge escapement and outside count wheel, pendulum **770.00**
   Germany, 1890, enameled wood dial, 30 hour time and strike three train Black Forest type movement activates animated Friar bows when strikes, pendulum and three tin weights, 16½" h **2,750.00**

CLOISONNÉ

History: Cloisonné is the art of enameling on metal. The design is drawn on the metal body. Wires, which follow the design, are glued or soldered on the body. The cells thus created are packed with enamel and fired; this step is repeated several times until the level of enamel is higher than the wires. A buffing and polishing process brings the level of enamels flush to the surface of the wires.

This art form has been practiced in various countries since 1300 B.C. and in the Orient since the early 15th century. Most cloisonné found today is from the late Victorian era, 1870–1900, and was made in China and Japan.

Beaker, 19½" h, spheroid, long flaring neck, galleried rim, stepped foot, bro-

Powder Jar, cov, yellow ground, multi-colored dec, 3¾" d, $72.00.

cade dec, green ground, Japanese, mid 19th C, pr 650.00
Bowl, 12" d, 3½" h, turned in rim, marine blue, variety of large lotus blossoms, clusters of small circle cloisonnes, cobalt border with silk–worm cloisonnes, overlapping pomegranates on bottom, Chinese 500.00
Box, cov
    4" l, 4" h, oval, reclining hoofed animal, pr 220.00
    6½" d, 3½" h, pink and brown dec, Chinese 335.00
    12" d, steep sloping sides, high splayed foot, int. polychrome enameled medallion of Buddha flanked by two arhats, lotus pond, two kinnara flying through cloud scrolls, turquoise ground, ext. with sinuous dragons winding through flowering lotus plants and Chinese characters of longevity and happiness, two character base mark of "Daimin," Chinese, Meiji period . . 600.00
Brush Pot, 5" h, asters and butterfly dec, light blue ground, sgd "Takeuchi," Japanese, c1875 . . . . 200.00
Charger
    17⅞" d, int. dec of large writhing dragon, blue ground, geometric patterned band, eight petal shaped reserves of ho–o alternating with suspended jewels, black ground, floral patterned rim band, warped, drilled, Meiji period 440.00
    23½" d, birds and butterfly hovering over peonies, chrysanthemums, morning glories, wisteria, and hydrangea, sky blue ground, brocade floral rim border, Meiji/Taisho period, pr 4,400.00
Cigarette Case, green, three dragons, multicolored, Chinese 150.00
Dish, 25⅜" d, shallow, circular, raised

ring foot, int. dec of blue, green, pink, purple, orange, yellow, brown, and gilt enameled peacocks perched on reticulated rocks, two songbirds perched on flowering magnolia branches, flowering roses and magnolias, underside enameled pale blue and gilt florets, two ruyi–lappet bands 660.00
Figure, animal, Chinese, teakwood base
    3" h, 3" l, singing frogs, pr 165.00
    3" h, 6" l, running boars, ridged back, pr 275.00
    3" h, 7½" l, fantailed goldfish, removable eyes, pr 330.00
    4" h, 5" l, lounging horses, pr 220.00
    5" h, 8" l, lounging, gold horned and bearded beasts, Oriental sgd, pr . . 412.50
Libation Cup, 5½" l, figural ram's head, blue, multicolored swirl and dragon design 250.00
Plate, 9¾" d, marine blue, two white cranes, scenic terrain, peonies, foliage, etc., Japanese 300.00
Potpourri Jar, cov, 4¼" h, 4⅛" d, multicolored flowers and butterflies, black, gold, and blue flowers, Japanese . . 275.00
Ruyi–Scepter, 22" l, carved wood and enamel, two long sinuous qilong with applied enamel ruyi–lappet heads, central cloisonne medallion, lotus flowers, pomegranates, antique objects, and interwoven floral scrolls, reverse carved with geometric diaper pattern, pr 770.00
Vase
    18" h, slender ovoid, tall waisted neck, slightly flaring rim, coral–red oval shaped reserves of birds and flowers, long undulating dragon and phoenix among stylized blossoms, green ground 715.00
    19¾" h, quadrangular, two sinuous dragons chasing flaming jewel, band of taotie masks, archaistic motifs, waisted neck with stylized archaistic ruyi–lappet band, gilt rims, four character Xuande mark, minor restorations, pr 770.00
    26" h, baluster, ext. with blue, green, pink, brown, black, and gilt enamels, orange–yellow ground, large interwoven lotus flowers, bats, auspicious emblems, shou medallions surrounding four large bronze reticulated medallions, two sinuous dragons chasing flaring jewel, ruyi–lappet border, two bronze qilong handles, band of interspersed bats, flaming jewels, and leafy tendril scrolls, turquoise enameled int., minor restoration and wear, pr 1,980.00

CLOTHING

History: While museums and a few private individuals have collected clothing for decades, it is only recently that collecting clothing has achieved a widespread popularity. Clothing reflects the social attitudes of a historical period.

Christening and wedding gowns abound and, hence, are not in large demand. Among the hardest items to find are men's clothing from the 19th and early 20th centuries. The most sought after clothing is by designers, such as Fortuny, Poirret, and Vionnet.

Note: Condition, size, age, and completeness are critical factors in purchasing clothing. Collectors divide into two groups: those collecting for aesthetic and historic value and those desiring to wear the garment. Prices are higher on the West coast; major auction houses focus on designer clothes and high fashion items.

References: C. Willett Cunnington, *English Women's Clothing in the Nineteenth Century*, Dover Publications, 1990 (reprint of 1937 book); Maryanne Dolan, *Vintage Clothing 1880–1960*, Second Edition, Books Americana, 1987; Cynthia Giles, *The Official Identification And Price Guide To Vintage Clothing*, House of Collectibles, 1989; Tina Irick–Nauer, *The First Price Guide to Antique and Vintage Clothes*, E.P. Dutton, 1983; Sheila Malouff, *Clothing With Prices*, Wallace–Homestead, 1983; Terry McCormick, *The Consumer's Guide To Vintage Clothing*, Dembner Books, 1987; Diane McGee, *A Passion For Fashion: Antique, Collectible, and Retro Clothes*, Simmons–Boardman Books, 1987.

Periodicals: *Vintage Clothing Newsletter*, P.O. Box 1422, Corvallis, OR 97339; *Vintage Fashions*, Hobby House Press, 900 Frederick Street, Cumberland, MD 21502.

Collectors' Club: The Costume Society of America, P.O. Box 761, Englishtown, NJ 07726.

Museums: Los Angeles County Museum (Costume and Textile Dept.), Los Angeles, CA; Metropolitan Museum of Art, New York, NY; Museum of Costume, Bath, England; Philadelphia Museum of Art, Philadelphia, PA; Smithsonian Institution (Inaugural Gown Collection), Washington, D.C.

Additional Listings: See *Warman's Americana & Collectibles* for more examples.

Baby Christening Outfit, cotton batiste, white, lace tiers	**35.00**
Bathing Tunic, sateen, 1915	**35.00**
Blouse	
Lace, black, long sleeves, 1920s	**25.00**
Nylon, white, satin trim, long sleeves, 1930s	**15.00**
Silk, taffeta, pale green, handmade bobbin lace trim, 1900	**400.00**
Bodice, satin, beige, fully lined, nine satin–lace covered buttons, pleated tail–back, 22″ fitted waist line, 9½″ ruf-	

fled cuff trim, semi–high neckline, lace overlay	**25.00**
Bolero, 18″ l, fur, leopard	**225.00**
Cape	
Gauze, black, stenciled foliate scrolls, tied at shoulders, hem threaded with striped Venetian glass beads, Fortuny, 36″ l	**400.00**
Satin, evening, semi–circular, hip length, ivory, brocade poppies, pink satin lining, ruffled pink and ivory silk organdy trim, ivory ostrich feather neck dec	**200.00**
Velvet, black, white fur collar and sleeves, 1930s	**75.00**
Chemise, silk, cream, Valenciennes lace trim, garlands of flowers embroidered in French knots, V neck, pale yellow ribbon	**275.00**
Coat, lady's	
Crepe, black, dots, fox trim, fringed neck, 1920s	**225.00**
Gabardine, lavender–gray, flaring form, panels of blue and gray silk, floral embroidery, gray rabbit fur collar	**120.00**
Leather, wrap style, lavender, long, tie belt, cuffed dolman sleeves, slash pockets, irid taffeta lining	**125.00**
Wool twill, blue, single breasted, wide lapels, slightly fitted waist, two clear plastic buttons, two false pockets, 15″ w at shoulders, 40″ l, designed by Galanos	**25.00**
Collar, velvet, black, rhinestones, beads and pearls, 1930s	**30.00**
Dress	
Day	
Cotton, turquoise, high neck, lace inserts, ruffled sleeves, 1895	**200.00**
Rayon, pink, blue piping, padded shoulders, 1935–45	**35.00**
Silk, irid green, lace trim, handmade, 1890–1900	**225.00**
Evening	
Gabardine, royal blue, net and silk	

Bed Jacket, satin crepe, peach, three pearl buttons, c1940, $25.00.

satin, self–colored piping, white
lace, black velvet trim, 1890–
1900 . . . . **225.00**
Lace, silk, 2 piece, nile green, long
waisted, snug fitting bodice, lay-
ered rows of ruffled skirt, hip
length jacket, 1928 . . . . **50.00**
Satin, red, ruffled edge, 1920s . . . **65.00**
Taffeta, black, sequin flowers, label
"Jeanne Lanvin, Paris Hiver,"
1938–39 . . . . **325.00**
Housecoat, mandarin style, blue silk
brocade, brown silk lining, black vel-
vet trim **45.00**
Jacket
Fur
Fox, brown, label "Henry Marshall,
Brooklyn," 1940–50 . . . . **250.00**
Seal, brown, white collar and cuffs,
Arnold Constable, 5th Ave label **100.00**
Silk, irid blue moire, full–length
sleeves and cording, c1855 . . . . . **70.00**
Taffeta and velvet, black, fitted waist,
c1900 . . . . **65.00**
Wool, pinstripe, black and white, silk
lined, 1910–20 . . . . **55.00**
Nightgown, silk, lace edge neckline,
embroidered, 1930s **85.00**
Pantaloon, cotton, white, eyelet em-
broidery trim and tucking, hand sewn **25.00**
Robe
Gauze, black, gilt foliate scrolls and
medallions, Fortuny, 44" l **1,000.00**
Silk, blue ground, eight couched gold
dragons chasing flaming pearls,
stylized clouds and bats, boashan
haishui band at hem, Chinese, mid
19th C **1,700.00**
Romper, child's, cotton, white, hand
tucking and embroidery **18.00**
Skirt
Felt, gray, velvet embroidered border,
c1880 . . . . **40.00**
Satin, red, peasant–type, black velvet
stripes, braiding, lace apron, 1906 **100.00**
Smoking Jacket, velvet, brown, silk
quilted collar, cuffs, and pockets, silk
lined, 1900–10 . . . . **75.00**
Suit, lady's
Linen, 3 pcs, size 12, c1910 . . . . . . **400.00**
Rayon, white and black print, padded
shoulders, peplum, 1935 . . . . **65.00**
Wool Gabardine, double breasted
jacket, straight skirt, Adrian, 1940s **150.00**
Sweater
Knit, cream, pastel floral embroidery
and beads, 1960–65 . . . . **45.00**
Wool, bolero style, lilac and gray . . . **12.50**
Teddy, French lace yoke, rose print on
white background **35.00**
Tuxedo, wool, black, cutaway coat,
pants button in front, 1900–10 . . . . **100.00**

CLOTHING ACCESSORIES

References: Rod Dyer & Ron Spark, *Fit To Be
Tied: Vintage Ties Of The Forties And Early Fifties,*
Abbeville, 1987; Roseann Ettinger, *Handbags,*
Schiffer Publishing, Ltd., 1991; Evelyn Haetig, *An-
tique Combs & Purses,* Gallery Graphics Press,
1983; Richard and Teresa Holiner, *Antique
Purses,* Second Edition, Collector Books, 1987;
Mary Trasko, *Heavenly Soles: Extraordinary
Twentieth–Century Shoes,* Abbeville Press, 1989.

Periodical: *Vintage Fashion,* Hobby House
Press, 900 Frederick Street, Cumberland, MD
21502.

Additional Listings: See *Warman's Americana
& Collectibles* for more examples.

Apron, cotton, hand sewn
Green and white check **40.00**
Patchwork design, waist length, ties **25.00**
Bonnet, baby
Crochet, ribbon insert, newborn . . . **15.00**
Organdy, white, blue ribbon and trim **18.00**
Camisole, crochet **25.00**
Fan
14" w, deep purple–blue feathers,
spreading floral spray with small robin painted pink, red, and white,
green leaves, pierced ivory sticks
and guards **35.00**
16" w, green silk and white net
shaped ground, green silk leaf bordered with gilt sequin flowerheads,
gilt dec edges, gilt pique faux ivory
guards and sticks, minor damages
and discoloration, Continental . . . **35.00**
Gloves, pr, 4¾" l, infants, leather, white
kidskin, silvered metal button snap,
imp "Dent's" **25.00**
Handbag, evening
Art Deco, brocade, engraved gold
filled frame **75.00**
Faille, black, marcasite set mount,
green onyx monogram, c1930 . . . **60.00**

**Hat, man's, straw, navy and red stripe,
orig. tag reads "Size 7, Cosmopolitan,"
1911, $35.00.**

Hat

Felt, skull cap, black, elaborate ostrich trim, French, label "Lorelei Designs" 25.00

Milan Braid, garden, black, ecru appliques, black feather edged ribbon trim 25.00

Silk, black, ruched crown with bow trim, large brim, ribbons, flowers and chartreuse feather trim 65.00

Velvet, black, 1939, MIB 28.00

Motorcycle Cap, boy's, embroidered blue wheel with silver wings 15.00

Night Cap, lady's

Satin, pink crochet work 10.00

Silk, purple, lace trim 20.00

Parasol

Child's, silk, black 85.00

Girl's, lace, black, Victorian 40.00

Lady's, white, embroidered, 1910 .. 60.00

Shawl

Chantilly type lace, black 25.00

Kashmir, paisley, rose 225.00

Lace, black, 12 x 66", 1925 ...... 45.00

Wool, black, black satin embroidery, silk fringe 75.00

Shoe

High Button

Leather, black 55.00

Satin, white 75.00

Pumps, sling back, lavender and blue floral, matching rosette on toe, Schiaparelli, 1940s 30.00

Stockings, white, stamped "Imperial Lisle" 10.00

COALPORT

History: In the mid-1750s Ambrose Gallimore established a pottery at Caughley in the Severn Gorge, Shropshire, England. Several other potteries, e.g., Jackfield, developed in the area.

About 1795 John Rose and Edward Blakeway built a pottery at Coalport, a new town founded along the right-of-way of the Shropshire Canal. Other potteries located adjacent to the canal were those of Walter Bradley and Anstice, Horton, and Rose. In 1799 Rose and Blakeway bought the "Royal Salopian China Manufactory" at Caughley. In 1814 this operation was moved to Coalport.

A bankruptcy in 1803 led to refinancing and a new name, John Rose and Company. In 1814 Anstice, Horton, and Rose was acquired. The South Wales potteries at Swansea and Nantgarw

were added. The expanded firm made fine quality, highly decorated ware. The plant enjoyed a renaissance in the 1888 to 1900 period.

World War I, decline in trade, and shift of the pottery industry away from the Severn Gorge brought hard times to Coalport. In 1926 the firm, now owned by Cauldon Potteries, moved from Coalport to Shelton. Later owners included Crescent Potteries, Brain & Co., Ltd., and finally, in 1967, Wedgwood.

References: Susan and Al Bagdade, *Warman's English & Continental Pottery & Porcelain*, 2nd Edition, Wallace–Homestead, 1991; Michael Messenger, *Coalport 1795–1926*, Antique Collectors' Club, 1990.

Additional Listings: Indian Tree Pattern.

Plate, Cigar pattern, multicolored, blue seashell dec on back, 8½" d, $185.00.

Bough Pot, 11½" h, hp landscape scene with two British soldiers, gilt floral dec, yellow ground, c1809 .... 350.00

Compote, 12" d, round, pedestal on sq foot, gilt scroll molded rim, flower sprays within, gilt and foliage surrounds, red ground, c1830 .... 450.00

Cup and Saucer, Harebell pattern 25.00

Dish, leaf shape, apple green, garden flower bouquet, gilt foliage, c1820 .. 90.00

Figure, Lady of Fashion

Allison 50.00

Girl with flower basket 20.00

Ginger Jar, cov, Blue Willow pattern .. 70.00

Plate, 9", pink roses, green garlands, heavy gold, artist sgd, made for Davis Collamore, NY 90.00

Soup Plate, 10" d, flowering branch centering oval reserve, gilt scalloped rim, burgundy band 20.00

Spill Vase, 5", set of 3, pink, garden flowers and gilt scroll bands, bird's head handles with gilt rings, flared rim, sq base, c1830 .... 875.00

Tureen, 12½", cov, iron red, yellow and gilt scattered flower sprays, gilt handles, flowerhead finial, c1850 . . . . . **400.00**

Vase, 7", waisted, pierced lip dec with leaf sprays and applied flowerheads, body with gilt highlighted leaf scrolls which form pierced handles, painted butterflies and floral sprays, magenta glazed lower section, scroll molded foot, quatrefoil base, underglaze blue mark **165.00**

COCA–COLA ITEMS

History: The originator of Coca–Cola was John Pemberton, a pharmacist from Atlanta, Georgia. In 1886 Dr. Pemberton introduced a patent medicine to relieve headaches, stomach disorders, and other minor maladies. Unfortunately, his failing health and meager finances forced him to sell his interest.

In 1888 Asa G. Candler became the sole owner of Coca–Cola. Candler improved the formula, increased the advertising budget, and widened the distribution. Accidentally, a "patient" was given a dose of the syrup mixed with carbonated water instead of still water. The result was a tastier, more refreshing drink.

As sales increased in the 1890s, Candler recognized that the product was more suitable for the soft drink market and began advertising it as such. From these beginnings a myriad of advertising items have been issued to invite all to "Drink Coca–Cola."

Dates of interest: "Coke" was first used in advertising in 1941. The distinctive shaped bottle was registered as a trademark on April 12, 1960.

References: Deborah Goldstein Hill, *Price Guide to Coca–Cola Collectibles,* Wallace–Homestead, 1991; Allan Petretti, *Petretti's Coca–Cola Collectibles Price Guide, 8th Edition,* Wallace–Homestead, 1991; Schroeder Publishing Co., *Goldstein's Coca–Cola Collectibles,* Collector Books, 1991; Al Wilson, *Collectors Guide To Coca–Cola Items, Volume I,* (revised: 1987) and *Volume II,* (1987), L–W Book Sales.

Collectors' Club: The Coca–Cola Collectors Club International, P.O. Box 546, Holmdel, NJ 07733.

Museum: Schmidt's Coca–Cola Museum, Elizabethtown, KY.

Additional Listings: See *Warman's Americana & Collectibles* for more examples.

Ashtray
   Aluminum, emb, 1950s **5.00**
   Glass, 1940s **10.00**
Banner, 69 x 16½", Drink Coca–Cola From The Bottle Through A Straw, canvas **1,150.00**

Baseball Scorekeeper, perpetual counter **400.00**
Bell, 2¼" h, enameled printing, c1920 . **200.00**
Blotter
   1929, man and woman toasting with Coke bottles **75.00**
   1936, 50th Anniversary 1886–1936 . **40.00**
Bookends, bottle shape, bronze, 1963 **130.00**
Bookmark, pretty lady **300.00**
Bottle Carrier, wood, holds six bottles, 1939 . . . . **45.00**
Bottle Opener
   Bone handle, 1930–40 . . . . **20.00**
   Nashville 50th Anniversary, gold plated, 1952 . . . . **40.00**
   Wall mount, toothed, c1930 . . . . . . **75.00**
Calendar, 1922, lady wearing hat holding glass, active baseball field background, 12 x 30" **1,210.00**
Catalog, 1936–41 Replacement Parts, The Reconditioning of Coolers for Coca–Cola **12.00**
Chair, child's, folding **25.00**
Change Purse, triangle shape, snap closure, c1908 . . . . **90.00**
Change Tray
   1909, 5½ x 3", oval **750.00**
   1910, oval, red borders, artist Hamilton **100.00**
   1914, Betty, 6 x 4¼" **70.00**
   1916, Elaine **135.00**
   1917, Elaine **90.00**
Cigar Band, bottle in center, 1930s . . . **75.00**
Clicker, metal, 1930s **60.00**
Clothing
   Necktie **20.00**
   Trousers **25.00**
   Windbreaker **25.00**
Coaster
   Cardboard, round, 1950s **4.00**
   Rubber, set of 4, orig envelope, 1940s **15.00**
Convention Badge, 1959 . . . . **35.00**
Cooler, unusual shape and size **300.00**
Dispenser, porcelain, German **400.00**
Door Push, 4 x 6", 1960s **30.00**
Envelope, unused, 1908 . . . . **10.00**
Festoon, Autumn Leaves, 1922 . . . . . **600.00**
Flag, German **65.00**
Fly Swatter, net with wood handle, Coca–Cola, Helena, Ark **10.00**
Game
   Cribbage Board, 1940s **45.00**
   Paddle Ball, c1950 . . . . **35.00**
   Punching Ball Game, mask and ball, orig box, 1930 . . . . **400.00**
Ice Pick, opener on one end **30.00**
Ice Tongs, wood handle with Coca–Cola adv, 1920s **150.00**
Knife, opens on each end **220.00**
Letterhead, used, handwritten and sgd, 1912 . . . . **100.00**
License Plate, red **20.00**

Menu Board, tin	40.00
Mirror, pocket, woman with flowing hair	130.00
Notebook, 2¾ x 4½", Compliments The Coca–Cola Co, 1905	150.00
Pencil Box, includes contents, 1930s	30.00
Pencil Holder, ceramic, 1960s	150.00
Playing Cards, double deck, 100th Anniversary, sealed	18.00
Poster, 50th Anniversary 1886–1936, two ladies sitting, each holding bottle	170.00
Radio, cooler shape, 7 x 12 x 9½", 1950	450.00
Ruler, wood, 1950s	5.00

Sign

3¼ x 11½", emb, tin, pictures product, framed, 1907	120.00
24 x 67", 1950s	25.00
20 x 11", cardboard, Welcome Friend, Have A Coke	60.00
31½ x 14", February 1946, American Art Works	225.00
54 x 18", tin, framed, 1951	50.00

Syrup Container

Can, paper label, 1950s	75.00
Jug, ceramic, paper label, early 1900s	100.00

Thermometer

17", 1950s	35.00
Gold, 1958	20.00
Thimble, 1920s	28.00

Toy, Buddy L

Racer	25.00
Truck	60.00

Tray, 1934, 13 x 10", $325.00.

Tray

1904, lovely girl, 13"	1,320.00
1914, Betty, 15 x 12¼"	90.00
1917, Elaine, 19 x 8½"	80.00
1938	85.00
1941	85.00
1942, 13 x 10½"	50.00
1950	20.00
Uniform Button, ¾", c1910	45.00
Vienna Art Plate, Topless Lady, Western Bottling Co, 1905	450.00

Watch Fob, "Drink Coca–Cola in Bottle–5¢," brass, emb, girl with product, 1905	250.00

Whistle

Plastic, c1950	12.00
Wood, 1920s	50.00
Window, 31 x 41", Coca–Cola adv and magazines across top	60.00

COFFEE MILLS

History: Coffee mills or grinders are utilitarian objects designed to grind fresh coffee beans. Before the advent of stay-fresh packaging, coffee mills were a necessity.

The first home size coffee grinders were introduced about 1890. The large commercial grinders designed for use in stores, restaurants, and hotels often bear an earlier patent date.

Reference: Terry Friend, *Coffee Mills,* Collector Books, 1982.

Delft design, blue and white, Germany, wall mounted, 14½" h, $85.00.

COUNTERTOP (COMMERCIAL)

Advertising, Elgin National Coffee, cast iron, Woodruff and Edwards Co, 24" h	325.00
Coles Mfg, No 7, cast iron, patented 1887, 27"	475.00
Elgin National, No 40, cast iron, two wheels	325.00
Enterprise, No 12, two wheels, eagle, patented 1898	625.00
Parker, No 5000, cast iron, patented 1897	275.00
S & H, cast iron, drawer, 12"	425.00

FLOOR MODEL (COMMERCIAL)

Enterprise, eagle on top, patented 1873, 72″	3,500.00
Fairbanks Morse, cast iron, brass hopper, 72″	1,300.00
Starr, cast iron, 72″	975.00

LAP (DOMESTIC)

A Kendrick & Sons, No 1, cast iron, brass hopper	100.00
Arcade	
Favorite, cast iron top and hopper	100.00
Imperial, wood and cast iron, 11″	75.00
Common, wood, box joints, cast iron hopper	75.00
Delmew, Simons Hardware, St Louis	75.00
J Fisher, Warranted, walnut, dovetailed, brass hopper	150.00
Landers, Frary & Clark, cast iron, corset shape, round sculpted cup and hopper, curved crank handle with wood knob	220.00
New Model, cast iron, drawer, 5½ x 4½ x 5½″	75.00
Unmarked, cherry, dovetailed, brass hopper, 4″	155.00
W W Weaver, walnut, dovetailed, pewter hopper	155.00

TABLE (DOMESTIC)

Arcade Imperial, wood and cast iron, 13″	75.00
Challenge Fast Grinder, wood base, cast iron hopper, crank, and handle, wood knob	80.00
Enterprise, cast iron, brass hopper, patented 1873	400.00
Grand Union Tea, cast iron, sq base, round hopper	100.00
New Home, cast iron top, enclosed hopper with wood box	75.00
Sun Mfg, wood, 13″	200.00

WALL (DOMESTIC)

Lunbrack, Czechoslovakia	70.00
National Specialty Co, Philadelphia, cast iron, orig red scroll, gilt dec	85.00
Unmarked, funnel hopper, made by blacksmith, c1790	180.00

COIN OPERATED ITEMS

History: Coin operated items include amusement games, pinball, jukeboxes, slot machines, vending machines, cash registers and other items operated by coins.

The first jukebox was developed about 1934 and played 78 RPM records. Jukeboxes were important parts of teenage life before the advent of portable radios and television.

The first pinball machine was introduced in 1931 by Gottlieb. Pinball machines continued to be popular until the advent of solid state games in 1977 and advanced electronic video games.

The first three-reel slot machine, the Liberty Bell, was invented in 1905 by Charles Fey in San Francisco. In 1910, Mills Novelty Company copyrighted the classic fruit symbols. Improvements and advancements have lead to the sophisticated machines of today.

Vending machines for candy, gum, and peanuts were popular from 1910 until 1940 and can be found in a wide range of sizes and shapes.

Because of the heavy usage these coin operated items received, many are restored and at the very least have been repainted by either the operator or manufacturer. Using reproduced mechanisms to restore pieces is acceptable in many cases, especially when the restored piece will be able to perform as originally intended.

References: Jerry Ayliffe, *American Premium Guide To Jukeboxes And Slot Machines, Gumballs, Trade Stimulators, Arcade*, Books Americana, 1985; Richard Bueschel, *Pinball I: Illustrated Historical Guide To Pinball Machines, Volume I*, Hoflin Publishing Ltd., 1988; Richard Bueschel, *Slots 1: Illustrated Guide to 100 Collectible Slot Machines, Volume 1*, Hoflin Publishing Ltd., 1989; Nic Costa, *Automatic Pleasures: The History Of The Coin Machine*, Kevin Francis Publishing Ltd., 1988; Bill Enes, *Silent Salesmen: An Encyclopedia Of Collectible Gum, Candy & Nut Machines*, published by author, 1987; Stephen K. Loots, *The Official Victory Glass Price Guide To Antique Jukeboxes, 1988 (Third) Edition, Jukebox Collector Newsletter*, 1988; Vincent Lynch, *American Jukebox The Classic Years*, Chronicle Books, 1990.

Periodicals: *Coin Machine Trader*, P.O. Box 602, Huron, SD 57350; *Coin–Op Newsletter*, 909 26th Street, N.W., Washington, DC 20037; *Jukebox Collector Newsletter*, 2545 SE 60th Street, Des Moines, IA 50317.

Additional Listings: See *Warman's Americana & Collectibles* for separate categories for Jukeboxes, Pinball Machines, Slot Machines, and Vending Machines.

GAME

Bally Fireball, pinball	1,700.00
Challenger, target practice, 10 shots for 1¢, ABT Mfg Corp, Chicago, USA, orange, black, and gold, key	275.00
Foxhunt, pinball, 5¢, 65 x 21 x 51″, Pat 1936, orig instruction card, 1940	175.00
Mutascope 2¢ Hockey, orig marquee	1,200.00
Over the Top 1¢ Skill Game, penny push–up, 8 x 20″	400.00

Play Football, arcade, Chester Pollard
   Amusement Co, c1924 . . . . **800.00**
Select–Em, dice game, Exhibit Supply
   Co, Chicago **275.00**

JUKEBOX

AMI, Model C **800.00**
Mills Throne of Music **750.00**
Rockola, #1422, 1946 . . . . **1,700.00**
Seeburg
   Model P148, light up side columns,
     top changes colors with revolving
     lights, blue glass mirrored tile front,
     5 plays for a quarter, 1948 . . . . . **1,450.00**
Wurlitzer, Model 1015, bubble tubes
   framing glazed front, veneered wood
   case, 50″ h, c1947 . . . . **2,700.00**

**Slot Machine, The Little Duke, early
1930s, $2,400.00.**

SLOT MACHINE

Berkley, 10¢, 3 reel, metal case, chrome
   dec, green **500.00**
Caille Commander Streamline, yellow
   case, 1930s **675.00**
Figural, Indian, holding Bursting Cherry
   slot machine, 3 reel, carved wood
   with headdress, restored **2,500.00**
Jennings
   Silver Moon, 5, countertop, 1941, re-
     stored **1,200.00**
   Standard Chief, 10¢, 3 reel, wood and
     chrome case **1,795.00**
Liberty Bell, 5¢, 3 reel, orig red, white,
   and blue, decal **160.00**
Mills, The Owl, 5¢, one wheel upright,
   oak cabinet carved with owl and foli-

age below color wheel, 5 way cast
   metal coin head, 64″, c1905, restored **7,000.00**
Pace, Comet Deluxe, 3 reel, twin jack-
   pots, restored, c1939 . . . . **1,500.00**
Wattling
   Blue Seal, 5¢, 3 reel, double jackpots,
     24″, c1932, restored **1,500.00**
   Rol–A–Top, 5¢, coin front **3,000.00**

VENDING

Acorn, 5¢, all purpose, Oak Mfg, 1940 **65.00**
Advance, 1¢, peanuts, football style
   globe, c1923 . . . . **140.00**
Bozo, balloons, includes pump to blow
   balloons, 60″, 1960 . . . . **125.00**
Columbus, 1¢, Gumball Machine, 15″ h,
   8″ d, cast iron, porcelain paint, light
   and dark green, orig key **300.00**
Dean, 1¢, gum, metal case, glass
   panels, 13 x 7 x 8″ **60.00**
Eat 'Em Hot Nuts, orig glass cup dis-
   penser, 1934 . . . . **275.00**
Jacob's, 5¢, cigars, 36″ w, patent 1907 **1,400.00**
Mansfield, 5¢, gum, 12″ h, 10½″ sq,
   etched glass front, glass sides **400.00**
Master, 1¢, peanuts, 16″ h, 8″ sq, cast
   metal, red and black paint, complete
   with orig keys, c1930s **120.00**
Pulver Yellow Kid, 1¢, gum, clockwork
   movement of Yellow Kid with insertion
   of penny **550.00**
Zeno, collar buttons **750.00**

MISCELLANEOUS

Cash Register, National, Model 542,
   brass, keys up to $99.99, receipt ma-
   chine at side, running totals at other
   side, crank operated, brass cash
   drawer, 24″ h **600.00**
Fare Box, Jonson, hand crank, patent
   1914, restored **225.00**
Piano, Seeburg style A, mandolin at-
   tachment, oak case, art glass panel **6,750.00**
Radio, hotel, "25 for 2 hours," gray
   metal case, 14 x 8 x 7½″, Corado,
   c1940 . . . . **65.00**
Telephone, Western Electric, wall type,
   oak, uses dimes, nickels, and quar-
   ters, c1920 . . . . **475.00**

COMIC BOOKS

History: Shortly after comics first appeared in
and newspapers of the 1890s, they were reprinted
in book format and often used as promotional giveaways by manufacturers, movie theaters, candy
stores, and stationery stores. The first modern format comic was issued in 1933.

The magic date is June 1938 when DC issued Action Comics No. 1, marking the first appearance of Superman. Thus began comics' "Golden Age," which lasted until the mid–1950s and witnessed the birth of the major comic book publishers, titles, and characters.

In 1954 Fredric Wertham authored *Seduction of the Innocent*, a book which pointed a guilt–laden finger at the comic industry for corrupting youth, causing juvenile delinquency and undermining American values. Many publishers were forced out of business, while others established a "comics code" to assure parents that their comics were compliant with morality and decency censures upheld by the code authority.

Comics "Silver Age," mid–1950s through the end of the 1960s, witnessed the revival of many of the characters from the Golden Age in new comic formats. The era began with *Showcase No. 4* in October 1956, which marked the origin and first appearance of the Silver-Age Flash.

While comics survived in the 1970s, it was a low point for the genre. In the early 1980s a revival occurred. In 1983 comic book publishers, aside from Marvel and DC, issued more titles than existed in the past forty years. The mid and late 1980s were a boom time, a trend which appears to be continuing into the 1990s.

References: Mike Benton, *The Comic Book In America, An Illustrated History*, Taylor Publishing Co., 1989; Ernst and Mary Gerber (compilers), *Photo–Journal Guide To Comics, Volume One (A–J)* and *Volume 2 (K–Z)*, Gerber Publishing Company, 1990; John Hegenberger, *Collector's Guide To Comic Books*, Wallace–Homestead, 1990; D. W. Howard, *Investing in Comics*, The World of Yesterday, 1988; Robert Overstreet, *The Official Overstreet Comic Book Price Guide, No. 21*, House of Collectibles, 1991.

Periodicals: *The Comics Buyer's Guide*, 700 State Street, Iola, WI 54990; *The Comics Buyer's Guide Price Guide*, 700 East State Street, Iola, WI 54990; *Comic Values Monthly*, Attic Books, P.O. Box 38, South Salem, NY 10590.

Museum: Museum of Cartoon Art, Rye, NY.

Reproduction Alert: Publishers frequently reprint popular stories, even complete books, so the buyer must pay strict attention to the title, not just the portion printed in outsized letters on the front cover. If there is any doubt, look inside at the fine print on the bottom of the inside cover or first page. The correct title will be printed there in capital letters.

Also pay attention to the size of the comic. Reprints often differ in size from the original.

Note: The comics listed below are in fine condition, meaning they may have a cover that has almost no wear; is still relatively flat, clean, and shiny; has no subscription crease, writing, yellowing at margins, or tape repairs. Minor color flaking is permitted at the spine, staples, or corners. Inside, a hint of yellowing is acceptable.

Walt Disney's Comics and Stories, Dell, August, #191, $3.50.

PRE/GOLDEN AGE

Detective Comics, No. 30, Dr. Death appears, National Periodical Publications/DC Comics	850.00
Fighting Yank, No. 1, Mystico, the Wonder Man appears	200.00
Plastic Man, No. 9, Quality Comics	85.00
Red Ryder Comics, No. 7, Dell Publishing	65.00
Shadow Comics, No. 2, The Avenger begins, Street & Smith Publications	200.00

GOLDEN AGE

Abbott and Costello, No. 8, St. John Publishing Co.	40.00
Adventures of Mighty Mouse, No. 4, St. John Publishing Co.	15.00
Archie's Pal, Jughead, No. 23, Archie Publications	15.00
Batman, No. 44, Joker story, National Periodical Publications/DC Comics	200.00
Billy the Kid, No. 24, Charlton Publications	10.00
Classic Comics, Gilberton Publications	
No. 1, Three Musketeers, sixth edition, 1946	20.00
No. 18, The Hunchback of Notre Dame, first Gilberton edition, March 1944	1,500.00
No. 98, The Red Badge of Courage, eight edition, June 1964	2.00
Davy Crockett, No. 632, Dell Publishing	12.50
Donald and Mickey Merry Christmas, No. 8, Donald in Toyland, 1948, Firestone Tire giveaway	100.00
Do You Believe in Nightmares?, No. 2, St. John Publishing	20.00
Ella Cinders, No. 4, United Features Syndicate	8.00

Fawcett Movie Comic
No. 12, "Rustlers on Horseback,"
Rocky Lane **50.00**
No. 20, "Ivanhoe," Liz Taylor **35.00**
First Romance Magazine, No. 8, Home
Comics (Harvey Publications) **4.00**
Frankenstein Comics, No. 19, Prize
Publications **20.00**
Gabby Hayes Western, No. 16, Fawcett **15.00**
Girls in Love, No. 1, May 1950, Fawcett **15.00**
Hopalong Cassidy, No. 40, Fawcett . . **12.50**
Intimate Confessions, No. 3, Realistic
Comics **25.00**
Jungle Jim, Four Color, No. 565, Dell
Publishing **6.00**
Little Audrey, No. 6, St. John Publishing **10.00**
Looney Tunes and Merrie Melodies
Comics, No. 73, Dell Publishing . . . **8.00**
Love Tales, No. 45, ZPC **5.00**
MAD, No. 34, Berg starts as a regular,
E. C. Comics **20.00**
March of Comics, Western Publishing
No. 58, Henry **17.50**
No. 171, Oswald the Rabbit **4.00**
No. 240, Tarzan **15.00**
No. 334, Lassie (TV) **3.00**
No. 421, Tweety & Sylvester **1.00**
Mister Mystery, No. 14, SPM Publishing **25.00**
Navy Combat, No. 13, Atlas Comics . . **4.00**
Pat Boone, No. 2, National Periodical
Publications **35.00**
Phantom Lady, No. 18, Fox Features
Syndicate **165.00**
Richie Rich, No. 23, Harvey Publica-
tions **9.00**
Rin Tin Tin, Four Color, No. 434, Dell
Publishing **17.50**
Rootie Kazootie, Four Color, No. 415,
Dell Publishing **15.00**
Roy Rogers, No. 46, Dell Publishing . . **15.00**
Sad Sack Laugh Special, No. 8, Harvey
Publications **2.00**
Secret Hearts, No. 4, National Periodi-
cal Publications **30.00**
Sergeant Preston of the Yukon, No. 13,
origin of Sergeant Preston, Dell Pub-
lishing **9.00**
Six Gun Heroes, No. 1, Rocky Lane,
Hopalong Cassidy, and Smiley Bur-
nette, Fawcett **80.00**
Smitty, No. 2, Dell Publishing **10.00**
Star Spangled Comics, No. 43, National
Periodical Publications **50.00**
Strange Tales, No. 57, Atlas **15.00**
Tell It To The Marines, No. 2, Madame
Cobra appears, Toby Press Publica-
tions **12.50**
Texas Rangers In Action, No. 16, Charl-
ton Comics **3.50**
Uncanny Tales, No. 6, Wolvertonish, At-
las Comics **30.00**

U. S. Marines In Action, No. 3, Avon
Periodicals **6.00**
War Comics, No. 46, Atlas Comics . . . **8.00**
Wild Boy Of The Congo, No. 10, Ziff–
Davis **12.50**
Wyatt Earp, No. 24, Marvel **5.00**
Zago, Jungle Prince, No. 3, Fox Fea-
tures Syndicate **40.00**

SILVER AGE

Adam/12, No. 4, Gold Key **2.50**
The Amazing Spiderman, No. 94, origin
retold, Marvel **12.50**
Astonshing Tales, No. 12, Man Thing,
Marvel **2.00**
The Beatles, No. 1, Dell Publishing . . **100.00**
Bomba, The Jungle Boy, No. 5, National
Periodical Publications **2.50**
Casper, The Friendly Ghost, No. 43,
Harvey Publications **8.00**
Conan, the Barbarian, No. 1, Marvel . . **50.00**
Cynthia Doyle, Nurse In Love, No. 52,
Charlton Publications **2.00**
Daredevil, No. 19, Marvel **14.00**
Dark Shadows, No. 6, Gold Key **15.00**
Dennis the Menace Giant, No. 8, In
Mexico, first printing **10.00**
Doctor Strange, No. 14, Marvel **1.50**
Fantastic Four, Marvel
No. 6, Sub/Mariner and Dr. Doom
team up **175.00**
No. 91 . . . . **3.00**
No. 217, Dazzler **1.25**
No. 340 . . . . **1.00**
The Flash, No. 112, origin and first ap-
pearance of Elongated Man **45.00**
Girl from U.N.C.L.E., No. 3, Gold Key . **7.50**
Hawkman, No. 20, National Periodical
Publications **5.00**
Heuy, Dewey And Louie Junior Wood-
chucks, No. 40, Gold Key . . . . **.75**
Iron Man, No. 64, Marvel **3.00**
Justice League Of America, No. 83,
Death of Spectre **2.00**
Korak, Son Of Tarzan, No. 9, Gold Key **6.00**
The Lucy Show, No. 3, Gold Key **10.00**
Magnus, Robot Fighter, No. 22, origin,
Gold Key **5.00**
Metal Men, No. 52, DC Comics **2.00**
Movie Comics, The Love Bug, Gold Key **4.00**
Nick Fury, Agent Of SHIELD, No. 7,
Marvel **4.00**
Planet Of The Apes, No. 10, Marvel . . **.60**
Powerman, No. 19, Marvel **2.00**
Ripley's Believe It Or Not, No. 27, Gold
Key **4.00**
The Scarecrow Of Romney Marsh, No.
10112/404, Gold Key **8.00**
Space Ghost, No. 1, 1967, Gold Key . **40.00**
The Sub/Marriner, No. 53, Marvel . . . **1.50**
Tower Of Shadows, No. 7, Marvel . . . **1.50**

The Twilight Zone, No. 6, Gold Key ..	5.00
The Unexpected, No. 123, DC Comics	2.00
X/Men, No. 112, Marvel	5.00

POST/SILVER AGE

Adentures Of The Fly, No. 21, Fly Girl, Archie Comics	18.00
Alien Nation: The Spartans, No. 2, Adventure Comics	2.50
Aztec Ace, No. 6, Elite	3.00
Battletech, No. 4, Blackthorne	1.75
Blood Sword Dynasty, No. 1, J. C. Productions	2.00
Bloody Bohes & Black Eyed Peas, No. 1, Galaxy	2.00
Captain Victory, No. 7, Pacific	1.00
Cerebus, No. 36, Aardvark Vanaheim .	7.50
Deadworld, No. 13, graphic cover, Arrow	3.00
DNAAgents, No. 10, Eclipse	2.00
Duck Tales, No. 14, Planet Blues, Walt Disney	1.50
E/Man, No. 20, First	1.25
FemForce, No. 6, AC Comics	2.00
Flaming Carrot, No. 12, Renegade ...	4.00
Howard Chaykin's American Flagg, No. 8, First	1.75
Love And Rockets, No. 16, Fantagraphics	3.00
Mister X, No. 5, Vortex	3.00
Roachmill, No. 10, Dark Horse	2.00
Rouge Trooper, No. 30, Quality	1.50
Slaine The Berserker, No. 10, Quality .	1.25
The Spirit, No. 7	3.00
Teenage Mutant Ninja Turles, Mirage No. 1, fourth printing	22.50
No. 9	15.00
No. 30	3.00
Three Rocketeers, No. 2, Eclipse	2.00
Transformers, No. 3	2.00
Ultra Klutz, No. 11, Onward Comics ..	1.50
Viet Nam Journal, No. 3, Apple	3.00
Zot, No. 7, Eclipse	2.00

COMPACTS

History: In the first quarter of the 20th century attitudes regarding cosmetics changed drastically. The use of make-up during the day was no longer looked upon with disdain. As women became "liberated" and as more and more of them entered the business world, the use of cosmetics became a routine and necessary part of a woman's grooming. Portable containers for cosmetics became a necessity.

Compacts were made in a myriad of shapes, styles, combinations and motifs, all reflecting the mood of the times. Every conceivable natural or man-made medium was used in the manufacture of compacts. Commemorative, premium, souvenir, patriotic, figural, combination compacts, Art Deco, and enamel compacts are a few examples of the compacts that were made in the United States and abroad. Compacts combined with cigarette cases, music boxes, watches, hatpins, canes, lighters, etc., also were very popular.

Compacts were made and used until the late 1950s when women opted for the "Au Naturel" look. The term "vintage" is used to distinguish compacts from the first half of the twentieth century from contemporary examples.

References: Roseann Ettinger, *Compacts and Smoking Accessories*, Schiffer Publishing, Ltd., 1991; Roselyn Gerson, *Ladies' Compacts of the 19th and 20th Centuries*, Wallace-Homestead Book Company, 1989.

Collector's Club: The Compact Collectors Club, P.O. Box Letter S, Lynbrook, NY 11563.

Advisor: Roselyn Gerson.

Additional Listings: See *Warman's Americana & Collectibles* for more examples.

Weltzunder blue marbleized enamel Kamra-Pak style vanity case and matching cigarette lighter, silvered metal cut out of map of US Zone, orig presentation box, Germany, $175.00.

American Maid, heart shape, goldtone, brocade lid, c1930	40.00
Amita, damascene with inlaid gold and silver Mt Fuji scene, black matte finish lid, Japan, c1920	125.00
Coro, enamel, black, horseshoe shape, case and watch, snap closure, powder and rouge compartments, c1920	150.00
Coty	
Flying Colors, gilt metal, spread eagle shape, red, white, and blue lipstick tube center, orig presentation box, c1940	200.00
Octagonal, polished nickel finish ...	75.00

Croco, sq, leather, white, zippered, multicolored cord in lid, Israel 50.00
D F Briggs Co, vanity case, gold filled, engine turned, enamel disk on lid, carrying chain 90.00
Delettrez, Wildflower, pale blue paper, floral spray on lid, 1940s 50.00
Dorette, snakeskin, zipper compartments, lipstick in lid 225.00
Dunhill vanity, silvered, cigarette lighter shape, sliding lipstick, c1920 . . . . . . 125.00
E A Bliss Co, compact/bracelet, vermeil nickel silver, etched floral dec on lid, applied cutout leaf shape metal band 150.00
Eastern Star, enameled, jeweled 45.00
Elizabeth Arden, harlequin shape, light blue, c1940 . . . . 75.00
Evans, bronzed metal, compact and cigarette, engine turned design, white cloisonne disk on lid, c1930 . . . . . . 75.00
Girey, Kamra–Pak, confetti plastic case, camera shape, compartments and slide–out lipstick, 1930–40 . . . . 65.00
Fuller, plastic, comb sleeve mounted on lid 40.00
Harmony, Boston, box shape, tan, snap closure, 1920s 50.00
Harriet Hubbard Ayer, engine turned, goldtone, center compartments 60.00
Illinois Watch Co, compact and watch, goldtone, engraved design on lid, 1930–40 . . . . 125.00
K & K, mother–of–pearl, gray, faux sapphires and rhinestones, 1930–40 . . 50.00
LaMode, heart shape, silverplated . . . 55.00
Marathon, goldtone, heart on lid, lid reveals locket 60.00
Mary Dunhill, satin goldtone, hinged, rhinestones and green stones set in thumbpiece 75.00
Mireve, enamel, black, sliding lipstick, perfume bottle, France 75.00
Rex, mesh, vanity pouch, white plastic beads, c1930 . . . . 50.00
Richard Hudnut, vanity clutch, fabric, white and gold, Tree of Life motif with green stones, 1940s 75.00
Timepact, enamel, black, elongated horseshoe shape, case and watch, powder and rouge compartments . . 175.00
Unknown Maker
Alligator, pull–out mirror 80.00
Girl Scout, satin goldtone, insignia on top 60.00
Hand Mirror shape
Goldtone, dec and engraved lid . . 90.00
Plastic, ivory color, Germany, 1920s 60.00
Horseshoe shape, gilt metal, tolled leather inserts on lid and back . . . 100.00
Wadsworth, Compakit, plastic, black, camera shape, compartment on front,

lipstick and cigarette lighter on top, cigarette compartment on bottom, c1940 . . . . 175.00
Whiting & Davis, vanity bag, silvered mesh, etched and engraved lid, braided carrying chain, 1920s 400.00
Zell Fifth Avenue, goldtone, poodle motif with red cabochon stones, lipstick fitted black grosgrain case, 1940–50 110.00

CONSOLIDATED GLASS COMPANY

History: The Consolidated Lamp and Glass Company resulted from the 1893 merger of the Wallace and McAfee Company, glass and lamp jobbers of Pittsburgh, and the Fostoria Shade & Lamp Company of Fostoria, Ohio. When the Fostoria, Ohio, plant burned down in 1895, Corapolis, Pennsylvania, donated a seven–acre tract of land near the center of town for a new factory. In 1911 the company was the largest lamp, globe, and shade works in the United States, employing over 400 workers.

In 1925 Reuben Haley, owner of an independent design firm, convinced John Lewis, president of Consolidated, to enter the giftware field utilizing a series of designs inspired by the 1925 Paris Exposition Internationale des Arts Decoratifs et Industriels Modernes and the work of Rene Lalique. Initially, the glass was marketed by Howard Selden through his showroom at 225 Fifth Avenue, New York, New York. The first two lines were Catalonian and Martele.

Additional patterns were added in the late 1920s: Florentine (January 1927), Chintz (January 1927), Ruba Rombic (January 1928), and Line 700 (January 1929). On April 2, 1932, Consolidated closed it doors. Kenneth Harley moved thirty–five to forty moulds to Phoenix. In March 1936 Consolidated reopened under new management. The "Harley" moulds were returned. During this period the famous Dancing Nymph line, based on an 8" salad plate in the 1926 Martele series, was introduced.

In August 1962 Consolidated was sold to Dietz Brothers. A major fire damaged the plant during a 1963 labor dispute. In 1964 the company closed its doors for good.

References: Ann Gilbert McDonald, *Evolution of the Night Lamp*, Wallace–Homestead Book Co., 1979; Jack D. Wilson, *Phoenix & Consolidated Art Glass, 1926–1980*, Antique Publications, 1989.

Bowl, Olive pattern, Martele line, green 60.00
Butter Dish, cov, Guttate, white, gold trim 45.00
Candlestick
Five Fruits pattern, Martele line, green 25.00

Hummingbird pattern, Martele line,
  green frosted **95.00**
Celery Tray, Florette, pink **35.00**
Compote, Fish
  Amber stain **60.00**
  Green **90.00**
Cruet
  Cone, 5¼″ h, pink, applied clear
    frosted handle, facet cup stopper . **300.00**
  Florette, pink, orig stopper **70.00**
Cup and Saucer, Dance of the Nudes,
  clear, frosted nudes **60.00**
Jug, Five Fruits, French Crystal, ftd .. **225.00**
Mayonnaise, Iris, amethyst **60.00**
Pickle Castor, Cone, pink, SP frame
  marked "Tufts," resilvered **200.00**
Pitcher
  Five Fruits, clear and frosted **350.00**
  Guttate, 9½″ h, pink satin, applied
    clear handle **175.00**
Plate
  Bird of Paradise, 8″ d, amber stain . **30.00**
  Dance of the Nudes, 10″ d **75.00**
Puff Box, Lovebirds, blue **95.00**
Salt Shaker, orig top
  Cone, blue **25.00**
  Guttate, green **30.00**
Snack Set, Five Fruits, amber stain .. **60.00**
Sugar Bowl, cov, Florette, pink **40.00**
Sugar Shaker, Cone
  Green, glossy finish, orig top **85.00**
  Yellow, satin **250.00**
Tumbler
  Cone, pink **45.00**
  Dance of the Nudes, 3½″ h **45.00**
  Five Fruits, green stain **20.00**

Vase, 700 Line, light blue, 7″ w, 6¾″ h, $135.00.

Vase
  Bird of Paradise, rect, blue **250.00**
  Bittersweet, amber stain **75.00**
  Blackberry, French Crystal **500.00**

Dance of the Nudes, 12″ h, white
  nudes, custard ground **350.00**
Dogwood, 11½″ h, ruby stain, ormolu
  mounts **375.00**
Dragonfly pattern, 6″ h, Martele line,
  clear and satin **50.00**
Fish, Martele line, cased, amethyst
  stain **300.00**
Katydid, blue, frosted **300.00**
Line 700
  7″ h, ruby stained **95.00**
  10″ h, blue, frosted int. **400.00**
Love Bird pattern, 10¾″ h, Martele
  line, green stain **275.00**
Pan, ruby stain **500.00**

CONTINENTAL CHINA AND PORCELAIN (GENERAL)

History: By 1700, porcelain factories existed in large numbers throughout Europe. In the mid-18th century the German factories at Meissen and Nymphenburg were dominant. As the century ended, French potteries assumed the leadership role. The "golden age" of Continental china and porcelains was from the 1740s to the 1840s.

Americans living in the last half of the 19th century eagerly sought the masterpieces of the European porcelain factories. In the early 20th century this style of china and porcelain was a "blue chip" among the antiques collectors.

References: Susan and Al Bagdade, *Warman's English & Continental Pottery & Porcelain, 2nd Edition,* Wallace–Homestead, 1991; Rachael Feild, *Macdonald Guide To Buying Antique Pottery & Porcelain,* Wallace-Homestead, 1987.

Additional Listings: France—Haviland, Limoges, Old Paris, Sarreguemines, and Sevres; Germany—Austrian Ware, Bavarian China, Carlsbad China, Dresden/Meissen, Rosenthal, Royal Bayreuth, Royal Bonn, Royal Rudolstadt, Royal Vienna, Schlegelmilch, and Villeroy and Boch; Italy—Capo-di-Monte.

FRENCH

Faience
  Figure, 21″, bisque, nymph, standing,
    polychrome, curled pale brown hair,
    wreath of fruiting sprigs, blue sash,
    floral print drape, tree trunk, mound
    base, imp factory mark, c1900 ... **1,000.00**
  Jardiniere, 22½″ d, yellow, green, and
    blue, painted chrysanthemums,
    scalloped rim **475.00**
Jacob Petit
  Clock Case, 15¾', portrait of French
    courtesan, sgd, c1840, chips **1,000.00**
  Vase, pr, 7″ h, cornucopia shape, multicolored floral garland, green
    ground, molded foliate scrollwork,

French Faience, plate, blue, red, and green florals, insect in center, marked "Rouen," 9¾" d, $175.00.

shaped rect base with scroll molding and emb floral sprigs and gilt highlighting, underglaze blue "J. P." mark **400.00**
Mennency
Figure, 9", lady, seated, polychrome and gilt dec, c1755, minor damage **3,300.00**
Gravy Boat, 9", marked "DVA", 18th C **950.00**
Orlik, breakfast set, small 5¾" h coffeepot, creamer, cov sugar, cup and saucer, bowl, two plates, gilt floral sprays, pink ground, overglaze red mark "Orlik/Made In France/Hand–painted" .. **200.00**
St. Cloud
Bonbonniere, cov, cat form, SS mountings, late 19th C **225.00**
Chamber Pot, cov, 4½", SS mountings, c1740 .... **1,200.00**
Cup and Saucer, pr, trembleuse, c1750 .... **600.00**
Samson
Jar, cov, pr, 12¼" h, armorial porcelain, fitted as lamps, Chinese Export **1,000.00**
Jardiniere, pr, bisque, tapering cylindrical body, relief molded continuous frieze of dancing putti holding floral garland, white foliate scroll border, blue ground, gilt ram's heads, pseudo interlaced L's enclosing AA mark, late 19th C **6,000.00**
Plate, 9", set of 8, octagonal, porcelain, armorial center, floral dec cavetto, gilded rim, Chinese Export, late 19th C **1,700.00**
Sauce Tureen, cov, 8½", armorial porcelain, Chinese Export **1,600.00**
Vieux Paris
Clock, 13" h, vase form, yellow ground, minor chips, c1820 ..... **950.00**

Tray, 13½", sq, mythological dec, iron red factory mark, Duc d'Angouleme factory, c1800 .... **450.00**
Vase, pr, 14¾", floral medallion, lavender ground, handles, sq marble plinth base, mounted as lamp, c1815 .... **3,125.00**

Sitzendorf, figure, young girl holding dead bird, pink trim, 8½" h, $200.00.

GERMAN

Berlin
Plaque, 10½ x 14¼", domestic int. scene, painted in the manner of Felix Schlesinger, c1870 .... **3,750.00**
Frankenthal
Figure, 8" h, lyre player, 18th C **475.00**
Tea Service, teapot, milk jug, four cups and saucers, polychrome dec of two lovers, rococo garden ornament, floral sprays, underglaze blue crowned monogram, modeler's, gilder's, and artist's marks, c1762–95 .... **3,200.00**
Furtsenberg
Cup and Saucer, purple dec, underglaze blue "F" mark, c1765 ..... **500.00**
Plate, pr, 9½" d, underglaze blue script "F" mark, painted by C G Albert, c1770 .... **1,200.00**
Platter, 14" d, circular, laurel leaves edge band, polychrome bird in tree center, late 18th C **650.00**
Hochst
Figure, 11", group of lovers, rococo arbor entwined with grapes, under-

glaze wheel mark, incised triangle, c1765, minor restoration **9,250.00**

Platter, 17½" l, oval, scrolling handles, pierced border, polychrome floral spray, underglaze blue wheel mark **1,700.00**

Sugar Bowl, 6¼" d, Meissen type dec, polychrome village scene, randomly scattered sprigs and sprays, underglaze blue crowned wheel mark **600.00**

Hutschenreuther

Plaque, 4" h, rect, profile portrait of beauty, long flowing hair, blue drapery, white diaphanous, sgd "Wagner" in lower left corner, imp factory monogram in circle, ornately carved gilt wood frame, c1900 . . . **1,000.00**

Portrait Plate, 9⅝" d, Princess de Lamballe, yellow roses and pink ribbons in hair, white ruffled dress, gray ground, imp factory mark, blue "lamb Dresden 135.K," artist sgd "Vorberger" **800.00**

Service Plate, 10⅞" d, central dec, summer flowers within heavily gilt cavetto, rim worked with scrolling acanthus, textured ground, underglaze green factory marks, minor rubbing, set of twelve **1,320.00**

Ludwigsburg

Figure, 5", peasant, modeled by Pierre Francois Lejeune, painted by D Chr Sausenhofer, underglaze blue crowned interlaced C's, c1765 **1,100.00**

Teapot, cov, 3½", painted, green, brown, blue, and iron–red, underglaze blue crowned interlaced C's, c1765 . . . . **1,100.00**

Nymphenburg

Cup and Saucer, painted large bouquet and scattered sprays, brown rims, imp shield mark, c1765 . . . . **200.00**

Potschcappel

Urn, 28" h, ovoid, figures in garden listening to musician, white ground, scattered floral sprays and sprigs, scrolled handles with partially draped female figure and applied flowerheads and leaves, gadrooned, floral encrusted cov, cartouche shaped shield flanked by two cupids, circular stand painted with four figural vignettes, shell and scroll molded borders, four spreading scroll feet with applied flowerheads, underglaze blue crossed lines mark with T, minor losses to flowers, firing cracks, pr **8,250.00**

Vase, 21" h, tall cylindrical neck, flaring globular body, Japanese taste dec, flowering cherry tree rising

from rockwork base with pheasants and animals, slightly crackled ground, underglaze blue cross mark surmounted by T, dec attributed by Carl Thieme, c1870, pr . . **1,650.00**

Saxony

Butter Pat, 2⅞" h, shaped rect, central painted spray of bright colored flowers, one corner surmounted by brightly painted figure of 18th C lady or gentleman, underglaze blue or gilt monogram over "Dresden, Saxony," set of thirteen **1,210.00**

Vase, cov, pr, 21½", polychrome floral dec, applied flowers and putti, gilt dec, massive floral finial, blue mark, 19th C, slight damage **1,250.00**

Unknown Manufacturer

Plaque, 4 x 5¼", oval, cupid portrait, tousled brown hair, blue eyes, pale blue clouds, gilt foliate frame, imp "12," c1900 . . . . **275.00**

Urn, 32½" h, cov, baluster, polychrome enamels, floral sprays and sprigs, applied flowerhead garlands, flanking putti, two birds perched on twigs, blue borders, gilt edges, domical cov with putto and floral festoons, socle base, minor losses, underglaze blue crossed E's mark with triangle of three dots, attributed to Ernst Teichert, late 19th C, pr **8,250.00**

Volkstedt

Teapot, swelled circular, faint ridging, dome cov, applied purple berry finial, purple floral sprigs, applied scroll handle, underglaze blue crossed pitchforks mark, handle restored, mid 18th C **250.00**

ITALIAN

Doccia

Charger, 15¾", Imari style, cobalt blue, iron–red, and gold, branches of flowering prunus and peonies, trellis, diaper, and floral panel borders, c1755 . . . . **300.00**

Cup, U form body, painted scene, Turk kneeling beside river, gilt edge cartouche, purple panels, c1750 . **200.00**

Tea Bowl, 3¼", chinoiserie figures, c1770 . . . . **450.00**

Naples

Ewer, 20", relief dec, bacchic scene in orchard, female rising from leaf ornaments handle, late 19th C . . . **350.00**

Vase, pr, 13½", Francis I of Bourbon and his consort portraits, rubbed gilding, sgd "Raffaele Giovine, 1823" **6,000.00**

COOKIE JARS

History: Cookie jars, colorful and often whimsical, are now an established collecting category in their own right. Do not be misled by the high prices released at the 1988 Andy Warhol auction. Many of the same cookie jars that sold for over one thousand dollars each can be found in the field for less than one hundred dollars.

Many cookie jar forms were manufactured by more than one company and, as a result, can be found with different marks. This resulted from mergers or splits by manufacturers, e.g., Brush-McCoy which is now Nelson McCoy. Moulds also were traded and sold among companies.

Cookie jars often were redesigned to reflect newer tastes. Hence, the same jar may be found in several different style variations.

References: Harold Nichols, *McCoy Cookie Jars: From The First To The Latest,* Nichols Publishing, 1987; Fred and Joyce Roerig, *Collector's Encyclopedia of Cookie Jars,* Collector Books, 1991; Ermagene Westfall, *An Illustrated Value Guide To Cookie Jars,* Collector Books, 1983.

Hull Pottery, Little Red Riding Hood, 13″ h, $100.00.

Abingdon, Humpty Dumpty	**200.00**
American Bisque	
Blackboard Girl	**80.00**
French Poodle	**40.00**
Grandma, gold trim	**90.00**
Picnic Basket	**75.00**
Puppy in Blue Pot	**50.00**
Seal on Igloo	**70.00**
Yarn Doll	**50.00**
Brush	
Donkey with Cart	**200.00**
Humpty Dumpty	**60.00**
Lantern	**85.00**
Pig	**175.00**
Cardinal, French chef	**65.00**
Fredericksburg Art Pottery Co	
Bear	**35.00**
Windmill	**25.00**
Gonder Art Potter, Sheriff, marked "Gonder Original, 950″	**225.00**
Hoan	
Donald Duck	**45.00**
Mickey Mouse	**50.00**
Maddux of California	
Humpty Dumpty	**85.00**
Queen of Tarts	**500.00**
Hull, Red Riding Hood, closed basket	**100.00**
McCoy Pottery	
Asparagus	**45.00**
Caboose	**90.00**
Chipmunk	**65.00**
Elephant	**100.00**
Jack–O–Lantern	**100.00**
Keebler Treehouse	**75.00**
Little Miss Muffet	**75.00**
Locomotive	**75.00**
Lollipops	**45.00**
Penguin	**75.00**
R2D2	**150.00**
Snoopy on Doghouse, white	**75.00**
Timmie Tortoise	**35.00**
Winnie the Pooh	**125.00**
Metlox	
Apple	**35.00**
Mammy, yellow	**250.00**
Puddles	**45.00**
Mosiac Tile, Mammy	**525.00**
Red Wing	
Baker, mottled blue	**90.00**
Dutch Girl	**60.00**
King of Tarts	**150.00**
Pineapple	**40.00**
Regal China	
Cat, gold	**400.00**
Oatmeal	**125.00**
Quaker Oats	**150.00**
Robinson Ransbottom	
Dutch Boy	**55.00**
Jocko the Monkey	**60.00**
Oscar	**40.00**
Peter, Peter, Pumpkin Eater	**60.00**
Tigers	**40.00**
Shawnee	
Cardinal French Chef	**115.00**
Dutch Boy	**150.00**
Puss N' Boots	**125.00**
Smiley Shamrocks	**175.00**
Sierra Vista	
Circus Wagon	**55.00**
Rooster	**40.00**
Stagecoach	**80.00**
Treasure Craft, farmer pig	**40.00**
Twin Winton	
Ark	**40.00**
Baby Bear	**35.00**
Dobbin	**35.00**
Jack in Box, marked "Twin Winton Calif USA"	**65.00**

Nestle Tollhouse 100.00
Ranger Bear 40.00

COPELAND

Vegetable Bowl, cov, Landscape pattern, blue–gray transfer, c1891, marked, $125.00.

COPELAND AND SPODE

History: In 1749 Josiah Spode was apprenticed to Thomas Whieldon and in 1754 worked for William Banks in Stoke-on-Trent. In the early 1760s Spode started his own pottery, making cream colored earthenware and blue printed whiteware. In 1770 he returned to Banks' factory as master, purchasing it in 1776.

Spode pioneered the use of steam powered pottery making machinery and mastered the art of transfer printing from copper plates. Spode opened a London shop in 1778 and sent William Copeland there circa 1784. A number of larger London locations followed. At the turn of the century Spode introduced bone china. In 1805 Josiah Spode II and William Copeland entered into a partnership for the London business. A series of partnerships between Josiah Spode II, Josiah Spode III, and William Taylor Copeland resulted.

In 1833 Copeland acquired Spode's London operations and the Stoke plants seven years later. William Taylor Copeland managed the business until his death in 1868. The business remained in the hands of Copeland heirs. In 1923 the plant was electrified; other modernizations followed.

In 1976 Spode merged with Worcester Royal Porcelain to become Royal Worcester Spode, Ltd.

References: Susan and Al Bagdade, *Warman's English & Continental Pottery & Porcelain, 2nd Edition,* Wallace–Homestead, 1991; D. Drakard & P. Holdway, *Spode Printed Wares,* Longmans, 1983; L. Whiter, *Spode: A History Of The Family, Factory, And Wares, 1733–1833,* Barrie & Jenkins, 1970.

Butter Dish, cov, Spode's Tower, blue,
  Copeland Spode 60.00
Creamer, 4″ h, Spode's Tower, blue
  transfer 48.00
Cup and Saucer, Rosalie 8.00
Dinner Set
  Felspar, 95 pcs, royal blue border outlined with gilt, puce printed Spode Felspar marks, iron–red Pat #3951, c1810 .... 1,600.00

Indian Tree, service for eight, 51 pcs, cov butter dish, vegetable bowl, 12″ d pedestal cake plate, Spode ... 375.00
Dish, 11½″ w, two handles, mushroom ground, gilt foliage, gilt scroll molded handles, puce Spode Felspar mark, c1800 .... 125.00
Figure
  17″ l, 17½″ h, bisque, seated young woman, bending over to mend fishing net draped over her lap, oval base inscribed "Mending The Net, Edward W. Lion, Sculptor, 1873, Art Union of London Copyright Reserved, Copeland L74″ 1,750.00
  21½″ h, parian ware, barefoot boy wearing breeches and jacket, scarf tied at throat, sickle lying on ground, pointing to letter concealed in tree stump, titled "The Trysting Tree," incised "C Halse, Sc/Pubd 1874," imp "Copeland/Copyright Reserved" 600.00
Jar, cov, 10″ h, globular, handled, Oriental style, apple green, birds on flowering peony branches, iron–red, pink, and gilt, gilt knob finial, Spode mark, Pat #3086, c1820 .... 700.00
Jardiniere, pr, 14 x 10¼″, rect gilt bronze frame inset with four porcelain panels, rose ground, transfer printed and enameled reserves of two ladies in 17th C costume, cartouche shaped border, gilt foliate C scrolls with polychrome floral festoons, four gilt bronze bun feet, brass liner, circular factory mark imprinted on each panel "Copeland & Garrett/Late Spode," c1833–47 .... 4,400.00
Jug, 6 /12″ d, 8¼″ h, bright blue ground, raised ivory figures on front and back, raised leaf trim around top, Copeland, made for Columbian Expo, 1893 ... 200.00
Pitcher, 7½″ h, deep blue glaze, raised white figures, tavern scenes and berries 210.00

Plaque, 5″ w, turquoise, printed multi-colored sporting trophy, gilt scroll and foliage surround, green Copeland mark, late 19th C **30.00**

Plate

8¾″ d, creamware, pink shell motif, gilt flowering foliage, brown net pattern ground, gilt rim, imp Spode mark, c1820 .... **80.00**

9½″ d, bird perched on snowy branch, holly leaves and berries **100.00**

10¼″ d

Rosalie **13.00**

Rose Briar **12.00**

Platter

9½″ l, oval, birds on gnarled tree trunk issuing oriental flowers, peonies, chrysanthemums, and foliage border, imp Copeland Spode oval mark, pat #4639, 19th C **100.00**

10½″ l, oval, creamware, pierced rim, Spode, marked, c1820 .... **75.00**

Potpourri Jar, 10″ h, pierced cov, flared rim and foot, Imari style, flowering plants, gilt knop finial, Spode mark, Pat #967, c1810 .... **600.00**

Soup Plate, black transfer printed, multicolored insert and flowering plants, scrolling floral foliage borders, Spode mark, pattern #2148, c1810, set of 12 .... **450.00**

Soup Tureen, cov, matching stand, 13″ h, compressed baluster, loop handles and finials, three peonies and fowl, rocky landscape, marked "Spode Stone China," mid 19th C **350.00**

Spill Vase, pr, 4¾″ h, flared rims, pale lilac, gilt octagonal panels with portrait of bearded man, band of pearls on rims and bases, Spode, c1820 .. **400.00**

Tray, 11½″ w, sq, rose spray center, floral bouquet in corners, blue ground with gilt scale pattern, Pat #1163, iron–red Spode, c1800 .... **350.00**

COPPER

History: Copper objects, such as kettles, tea kettles, warming pans, measures, etc., played an important part in the 19th century household. Outdoors, the apple butter kettle and still were the two principal copper items. Copper culinary objects were lined with a thin protective coating of tin to prevent poisoning. They were relined as needed.

Great emphasis is placed by collectors on signed pieces, especially those by American craftsmen. Since copper objects were made abroad as well, it is hard to identify unsigned examples.

References: Mary Frank Gaston, *Antique Copper*, Collector Books, 1985; Henry J. Kauffman,

Early American Copper, Tin, and Brass, Medill McBride Co., 1950.

Additional Listings: Arts and Crafts Movement and Roycroft.

Reproduction Alert: Many modern reproductions also exist.

Pub Measure, quart, Georgian, marked "1826 N–P" on spout, 6⅛″ h, $225.00.

Baking Pan, 11″ d, turk's head, swirled design, dovetailed construction, worn tin lining **60.00**

Bed Warmer, 38½″ l, engraved lid, wood handle, wrought iron ferule, European **75.00**

Bowl, 6½″ d, globular form, hand hammered, scalloped rim, brown patina, stamped "Harry Dixon San Francisco," c1920 .... **330.00**

Box, cov, 7 x 4 x 3″, rect, red enamel floral dec, stylized green and black enamel motifs, hinged lid, scroll feet, dark patina, Buffalo, NY, c1910 .... **440.00**

Coal Bucket, 12″ h, 10″ d, swing and side handles, German, late 19th C . **70.00**

Colander, 10¾″ d, punched star design **65.00**

Creamer, 3¾″ h, luster, polychrome floral band **65.00**

Desk Set, 7½″ l, blue opaline sander with matching inkwell **135.00**

Desk Tray, 12 x 4″, raised fish, seahorse, and foliage, hammered ground, stamped "Mawson, Keswick" **60.00**

Fish Poacher, 20½″ l, cov, oval, rolled rim, iron swing bail handle, C form handle on lid, 19th C **330.00**

Fruit Cooler, 15″ h, hammered, applied spherical handle, shallow cone shaped lid, bulbous body, geometric detail, four cut–out and stepped feet, c1905 .... **325.00**

Jug, 14½″ h, iron hoop base, Continental, late 19th C **500.00**

Haystack Measure, 18½″ h, dovetailed

construction, conical body, flared rim, tubular scroll handle, loop handle on front, marked "Anderson Brothers Makers, Glasgow, 4 gallons," Scotland, 19th C 140.00

Horn, coachman's, 48½" l 75.00

Kettle
  9½" d, cov, cylindrical, dovetailed construction, iron loop handles, domed cov with button finial, marked "Range Co, Cini, O" 90.00
  35½" d, 18" h, handmade, dovetailed, riveted construction, iron rim band, rounded bottom 375.00

Lantern, 15" h, hexagonal beveled glass panels, circular handle, 19th C 250.00

Milk Pail, 12" h, swing handle, stamped "1870," Dutch 500.00

Mug, 1 qt, tapered, 19th C 100.00

Planter, 15" l, oval, two ring handles, ftd, Victorian, late 19th C 150.00

Samovar, 15½" h 25.00

Sauce Pan, 7" d, dovetailed construction, cast iron handle 45.00

Skillet
  10½" d, wrought steel handle, stamped "Colony R I" 85.00
  12¼" d, cov, flared, riveted iron handle, marked "NN" 75.00

Tea Kettle
  6½" h, dovetailed construction, gooseneck spout, domed cov on raised rim, brass knob finial 60.00
  7" h, dovetailed construction, marked "W Heiss No 213 North St, Phila" 410.00
  8½" h, dovetailed, gooseneck spout, wood handle and finial 50.00
  11" h, gooseneck spout, brass band 65.00
  11" h, acorn finial, discolored 40.00
  13" h, dovetailed construction, gooseneck spout, domed cov with acorn finial, England, late 18th C 220.00
  Large, dovetailed construction, gooseneck spout, brass finial, marked "VII" on handle, Pennsylvania, early 19th C 450.00

Umbrella Stand, 25" h, hand hammered, flared rim, cylindrical body, two strap work loop handles, repousse medallion, riveted flared foot, c1910 .... 660.00

Vase, 11¾" h, hand hammered, baluster form, waisted neck, flared mouth, brown patina, imp "Jauchens, Old Copper, Shop, 36," 1915–16 ...... 390.00

Warming Pan
  Engraved lid, orig black painted turned wood handle 150.00
  Pierced lid, wrought iron and wood handle 150.00

Weathervane, 24" l, fish, iron mount, 20th C 500.00

CORALENE

History: Coralene is a glass or china object which has the design painted on the surface of the piece and tiny glass colorless beads applied with a fixative. The piece is placed in a muffle which fixes the enamel and sets the beads.

Several American and English companies made glass coralene in the 1880s. Seaweed or coral was the most common design. Other motifs were "Wheat Sheaf" and "Fleur-de-Lis." Most of the base glass was satin finished.

China and pottery coralene, made from the late 1890s to the post-WWII era, is referred to as Japanese coralene. The beading is opaque and inserted into the soft clay. Hence, it is only half to three-quarters visible.

Reproduction Alert: Reproductions are on the market, some using an old glass base. The beaded decoration on new coralene has been glued and can be scraped off.

Lamp Base, yellow satin raindrop ground, blue seaweed coralene, script sgd "Webb," 7¼" h, $265.00.

CHINA

Condiment Set, open salt, cov mustard, pepper shaker, white opaque ground, floral coralene dec, SP stand 245.00

Pitcher, 4½" h, 1909 pattern, red and brown ground, beaded yellow daffodil dec 950.00

Vase
  4¾" h, tan, morning glories, cobalt blue trim 130.00
  8" h, 6¾" w, melon ribbed, sq top, yellow drape coralene, rose shaded to pink ground, white int. . 830.00

GLASS

Bowl, 5½" d, blue MOP satin herringbone pattern, pink seaweed coralene, deeply crimped top, applied rim ... **615.00**

Cruet, pink satin, yellow coralene, orig stopper **400.00**

Pickle Castor, 10½" h, cranberry, IVT, butterflies and flowers coralene dec, ornate SP marked "Meriden" frame . **450.00**

Pitcher, 6¼" h, shaded yellow, white int., seaweed coralene **350.00**

Sweetmeat Jar, 3½" d, 4¾" h, cov, white Bristol body, orange seaweed coralene **325.00**

Tumbler, 3¾" h, satin glass, medium to light pink, white int., gold seaweed coralene, gold rim **225.00**

Vase

4½" h, flared rim, peachblow opal body, yellow seaweed coralene .. **175.00**

5½" h, ovoid, short wide cylindrical neck, clear shaded to cobalt blue body, yellow seaweed coralene .. **375.00**

11" h, slightly tapering cylindrical, cushion foot, short neck, cupped rim, glossy white shaded to blue Bristol glass, enameled pink morning glories and green leaves covered with coralene, orig French store label on base, pr **325.00**

CORKSCREWS

History: The corkscrew is composed of three parts: (1) handle, (2) shaft, and (3) worm or screw. The earliest known reference to "a Steele Worme used for drawing corks out of bottles" is 1681. Samuel Henshall, an Englishman, was granted the first patent in 1795.

Elaborate mechanisms were invented and patented from the early 1800s onward, especially in England. However, three basic types emerged: "T" handle (the most basic, simple form), lever, and mechanism. Variations on these three types run into the hundreds. Miniature corkscrews, employed for drawing corks from perfume and medicine bottles between 1750 and 1920, are among the most eagerly sought by collectors.

Nationalistic preferences were found in corkscrews. The English favored the helix worm and tended to coppertone their steel products. By the mid-18th century English and Irish silversmiths were making handles noted for their clean lines and practicality. Most English silver handles were hallmarked.

The Germans preferred the center worm and nickel plate. The Italians used chrome plate or massive solid brass. In the early 1800s the Dutch and French developed elaborately artistic silver handles.

Americans did not begin to manufacture quality corkscrews until the late 19th century. They favored the center worm and specialized in silver mounted tusks and carved staghorn for handles.

Table mounted, Yankee #7, 7¼" h, $275.00.

LEVER

Chrome plated steel, Italian (Vogliotti–Torino), double, wire helix, marked "Japan" and "Christian–Brothers–San Francisco 1908" **125.00**

Nickel plated steel

Helical worm, stamped "Patent, Weir's Patent 1280425 Sept, 1884/J. Helley & Son Maker" **75.00**

Hinged, retractable, scalloped casing, marked "The Handy" and "Patented Feb 24, 1891," round shaft with center worm **35.00**

MECHANISM

Bone handle, polished, English rack and pinion corkscrew brush and hanging ring, four plain post open barrel, narrow rack, long wire helix, side handle, sgd "Verinder," c1800 . **400.00**

Brass, four triangular posts, open cage, uncyphered solid cutworm, probably Italian, c1890 .... **220.00**

Bronze, rosewood handle with brush, marked "G. Twigg's Patent," c1868 . **400.00**

Nickel plated steel, open cage, swivel over collar on handle to raise shaft, hanging ring, cyphered center worm, German Pat 1892 .... **40.00**

Steel, cylindrical sheath, wood barrel handle with metal caps, metal rim stamped "Magic Cork Extractor Pat March 4–79, May 10–92," Mumford . **300.00**

MINIATURE

Chrome, two finger pull, wire helix, enamel City of Clacton **25.00**

Figural, 2″ l, elephant, brass, tail corkscrew, marked "Perage England,"
c1930 . . . .   30.00
Meissen, head of Johann Von Schiller,
poet and philosopher, uncyphered
center worm, head marked with
crossed swords under glaze, c1870   385.00
Steel, cut, nickel plated, 3″ peg and
worm, fluted wire helix, mid 18th C .   80.00

NOVELTY

Boar's head, silver, carved, scroll
mount, monogrammed, Archimedean
screw, nickel plated bell cap 265.00
Old Snifter, Senator Volstead standing,
brass corkscrew and bottle opener,
helical worm, fixed hat 200.00
Lady, figural, celluloid, white, folding
type, helical worm, stamped "Ges.
Gech," Germany 525.00

T–HANDLE

Figural, 5½″, horse head, carved, flowing mane, spirited glass eyes, tapered shaft, staghorn handle, center
worm with point, c1880 . . . .   250.00
Steel, scrolled handle, Archimedean
screw 55.00
Thomason type, brass, bone handle
with brush, helical worm 150.00

COSMOS GLASS

History: Cosmos glass is a milk glass pattern
made by the Consolidated Lamp and Glass Company, c1900.

Cosmos glass is identified by its distinctive pattern. The ground is a molded cross-cut design.
Relief molded flowers are painted in pink, blue,
and yellow. Cosmos glass comes in an extended
tableware line which includes several sizes and
shapes of lamps.

Butter Dish, cov
Opaque white 110.00
Pink band 200.00
Creamer 150.00
Lamp, 13½″ h, opaque white, dec,
shade and chimney, electrified 330.00
Pickle Castor, pink band, ftd silverplated
frame 400.00
Pitcher, 5″ 170.00
Salt and Pepper Shaker, pr 40.00
Scent Bottle, pink and blue floral, orig
stopper 135.00
Spooner 120.00

**Pitcher, pale pink band, blue, pink, and
yellow flowers, 9″ h, $225.00.**

Syrup 200.00
Tumbler, pink band 65.00

COWAN POTTERY

History: R. Guy Cowan founded the Cowan
Pottery in 1913 in Cleveland, Ohio. The establishment remained in almost continuous operation until 1931 when financial difficulties forced closure.

Early production was redware pottery. Later a
porcelain-like finish was perfected with special emphasis placed on glazes. Lustreware is one of the
most common types. Commercial wares marked
"Lakeware" were produced from 1927 to 1931.

Early marks include an incised "Cowan Pottery"
on the redware (1913–17), an impressed
"Cowan," and an impressed "Lakewood." The imprinted stylized semicircle, with or without the initials R. G., was later.

References: Paul Evans, *Art Pottery of the
United States, 2nd Edition,* Feingold & Lewis Pub-
lishing Corp., 1987; Ralph and Terry Kovel, *The
Kovels' Collector's Guide to American Art Pottery,*
Crown Publishers, Inc., 1974.

Museums: Cowan Pottery Museum, Rocky
River Public Library, Rocky River, OH; Everson
Museum of Art, Syracuse, NY.

Bowl, 8″ d, 5″ h, ftd, cream and yellow
glaze 40.00

Candleholders, pr, 5¾" h, figural, gazelle, glossy tan glaze **150.00**
Centerpiece Bowl, 6½" h, figural nude flower frog **165.00**
Cigarette Holder, figural, seahorse, ivory **45.00**
Cup and Saucer, melon dec, tan glaze   **30.00**
Flower Frog, figural
  Flamingo, 11¼" h, 6" d, perforated base, white glaze, die stamped twice **295.00**
  Nude, scarf dancer **200.00**
Plate, 11⅜" d, starfish and coral center, fish rim, turquoise ground, set of ten   **330.00**
Punch Bowl, 8" h, Jazz pattern, incised Cubist–inspired urban scenes, blue and black glaze, sgd "Viktor Schreckengost," imp "Cowan," c1931 . . . . . **15,400.00**
Soap Dish, 4" d, seahorse, blue **45.00**
Trivet, 6½" d, scalloped rim, bust of young girl framed by flower, sgd . . .   **265.00**

Vase, flat semi–circle, green tones, semi–crystaline glaze, 5¼" h, 8¼" w, $80.00.

Vase
  6" h, blue and green glaze, hp mushrooms **365.00**
  9" h, hp, dragonfly and cattails dec .   **125.00**

CRANBERRY GLASS

History: Cranberry glass is transparent and named for its color, achieved by adding powdered gold to a molten batch of amber glass which then is reheated at a low temperature to develop the cranberry or ruby color. The glass color first appeared in the last half of the 17th century, but was not made in American glass factories until the last half of the 19th century.

Cranberry glass was blown, mold blown, or pressed. Examples often are decorated with gold or enamel. Less expensive cranberry glass was made by substituting copper for gold and can be identified by its bluish-purple tint.

Reference: William Heacock and William Gamble, *Encyclopedia Of Victorian Colored Pattern Glass: Book 9, Cranberry Opalescent from A to Z,* Antique Publications, 1987.

Additional Listings: See specific categories, such as Bride's Baskets, Cruets, Jack-in-the-Pulpit Vases, etc.

Reproduction Alert: Reproductions abound. These pieces are heavier, off-color, and lack the quality of older examples.

Vase, gold enameled fern–like design, cup neck, ormolu stand, 4¼" h, $60.00.

Basket, clear applied art work, feet, and handle **70.00**
Bowl
  5½" d, 5½" h, applied amber lotus flowers and buds, gold highlights, enamel floral dec, three amber ftd   **770.00**
  7 ¾", paneled, flower dec, brass standard, mirrored base **100.00**
Butter Dish, cov, round, Hobnail pattern   **100.00**
Cologne Bottle, 7" h, dainty blue, white, and yellow flowers, green leaves, gold outlines and trim, orig clear ball stopper **180.00**
Creamer, 4¼" h, opalescent hobnail . .   **90.00**
Cruet, 9½", engraved flowers and leaves, applied clear handle, clear wafer foot, clear cut stopper **160.00**
Cup and Saucer, gold bands, enameled purple and white violets, gold handle   **125.00**
Decanter, 16¾", double cut overlay, cranberry cut to clear, orig matching stopper, applied clear handle, clear ftd base **110.00**
Dresser Bottle, gold dec **65.00**
Finger Bowl, scalloped, matching underplate **125.00**
Jam Dish, 4½" d, applied clear rim, SP holder **100.00**
Lamp
  Bracket, orig umbrella shade **165.00**
  Miniature, 8¼" h, bulbous, swirled, hobnail dec **300.00**
Perfume Bottle, 5½" h, pr, enameled,

beveled glass house shape casket, gilt brass fittings 335.00

Pickle Castor, 11" h, baby thumbprint, floral enameling, ornate ftd frame, saucer type base 425.00

Pitcher

6" h, Diamond Quilted pattern, clear applied handle, ground pontil 125.00

7" h, 5¼" w, water, bulbous, enameled purple–blue pansies and leaves, floral dec, applied clear glass loop handle 475.00

7⅛" h, opaque white mottling, clear applied handle 85.00

7½" h, IVT, clear applied handle, ruffled rim 80.00

7⅝" h, tankard shape, clear applied handle 70.00

9⅝" h, clear applied handle, ruffled rim 80.00

11½" h, tankard shape, clear applied handle, orig label, Dorflinger Glass Co 385.00

Rose Bowl, 4¾" h, egg shape, applied clear swags, scroll feet, berry pontil . 250.00

Salt, master

Clear pedestal base 125.00

Footed, enamel dec 200.00

Two vaseline rigaree rows, ftd handled metal frame 165.00

Sugar Shaker, 6¼", Venetian Diamond pattern 100.00

Toothpick, 3¾" h, applied vaseline rigaree 115.00

Tumble–Up Set, IVT 85.00

Tumbler, IVT 35.00

Urn, 12½", cov, allover cutting, raised diamonds, bands of bull's eyes, cut clear glass stem, sq pedestal base, cut dome cov, clear acorn finial 275.00

Vase

2⅞" h, white enameled scrolls and dot dec, gold trim 40.00

3½" h, gold enamel leaves, silver flowers and berries, pr 550.00

3⅞" h, hobnail, squatty bulbous . . . 85.00

4¾" h, ovoid, gold leaves, white enamel trees 375.00

5¼" h, boat shape, amber rigaree rim and feet, strawberry pontil 195.00

5¾" h, pr, sanded white enameled dec, Roman Key design, gold trim, ormolu feet 275.00

6¾" h, sanded gold leaf dec outlined with white enamel, pedestal foot . 85.00

7" h, pr, crackle 55.00

7½" h, emb ribs, applied clear feet, three swirled applied clear leaves around base 100.00

8⅞" h, bulbous, white enameled lilies of valley dec, cylinder neck 100.00

10" h, drapery pattern, clear applied scallops on top, clear foot on base   55.00

CROWN MILANO

History: Crown Milano is an American art glass produced by the Mt. Washington Glass Works, New Bedford, Massachusetts. The original patent was issued in 1886 to Frederick Shirley and Albert Steffin.

Normally it is an opaque white satin glass finished with light beige or ivory color ground embellished with fancy florals, decorations, and elaborate heavy raised gold. When marked, pieces carry an entwined CM with crown in purple enamel on the base. Sometimes paper labels were used. The silver plated mounts often have "MW" impressed or a Pairpoint mark as both Mount Washington and Pairpoint supplied mountings.

Advisors: Clarence and Betty Maier.

Biscuit Jar, melon shape, coral ground on bottom, brown ground on upper quarter, raised gold blossoms, leaves, and foliage, silver plated top, relief crab dec, sgd "CM/crown/521," lid sgd "MW," 6¼" d, 5½" h, $975.00.

Biscuit Jar, cov

7" d, raised gold spider mums, tinted green leaves, cream ground, gold wash rim, bail and lid marked "MW #4419" 1,210.00

7" d, 5¾" h, heavy gold flowers and leaves, peach color shadow leaves, emb fluted rim, partial orig paper label, marked "MW" 935.00

Bowl, 9" w, 5¾" h, cov, four enameled lush pink roses, purple tulips, spring flowers, white ground, pigtail handles, small lid, red mark and number "1013" 1,250.00

Box, 5" d base, cov, melon ribbed, white, shiny, emb, rose dec, hinged cov 300.00

Candle Vase, 9" h, raised gold flowers and beading, yellow–brown scrolls and red flowers, applied leaf double handles 935.00

Creamer and Sugar, sq, jeweled flowers, gold and green leaves outlined in raised gold, gold ribbed handles, pr . 750.00

Demitasse Cup and Saucer, 2" h, 5¼" d, pastel roses, tulips, and spring blossoms, brushed gold edges, gold dec handle 750.00

Jar
    4" h, gold enamel leaves, orange raised seaweed design, floral emb hinged metal lid and handle 660.00
    5¾" d, 4" h, squat, orange painted flowers and jeweled dec, yellow ground, plated silver cov 330.00
    7" d, 6" h, mottled aqua, pink, and white, raised jeweled seaweed and marine creatures dec, SP cov ... 550.00

Pickle Castor, forget–me–not dec, simulated Mt Washington peachblow ground, SP Pairpoint holder, orig tongs and lid 985.00

Sweetmeat Jar
    4" d, 5" h, heavy gold leaves, jeweled dec, DQ gold ground, twig finial, lid marked "MW" 660.00
    4" d, 6½" h, Burmese, heavy gold outlined autumn leaves and acorns, metal lid, Palmer Cox Brownie finial 935.00

Syrup Pitcher, melon ribbed body, oak branch, acorns, and leaves, raised gold outlines, SP lid 985.00

Tumbler, 3⅞" h, shiny finish, gold swag and ribbon dec, sgd 465.00

Vase
    5½" h, bulbous, petal top, gold outlined autumn leaves, raised gold berries, soft brown to tan ground . 1,430.00
    9" h, gray Kate Greenaway type boy and girl, floral bouquets, gray cut rim, raised gold twig dec, pr 1,300.00
    9¼" h, oak leaves and acorn dec, sgd 440.00
    12" h, flared, shiny, Albertine, gilt enamel scrolling, nine applied berry prunts, red mark 330.00

CRUETS

History: Cruets are small glass bottles, used to hold oil, vinegar, wine, etc., for the table. The high point of cruet use was during the Victorian era when a myriad of glass manufacturers made cruets in a wide assortment of patterns, colors, and sizes. All cruets had stoppers; most had handles.

References: Dean L Murray, *More Cruets Only*, Killgore Graphics, Inc., 1973; William Heacock, *Encyclopedia of Victorian Colored Pattern Glass: Book 6, Oil Cruets From A To Z*, Antique Publications, 1981.

Additional Listings: Pattern Glass and specific glass categories such as Amberina, Cranberry, and Satin.

Amethyst, blown, applied clear handle, clear ground stopper, 9¼" h, $65.00.

Amberina, 7", IVT, three petal top, amber applied handle and cut faceted stopper 175.00

Art Glass, red, gold trim, "God Bless America," capitol 75.00

Burmese, 6¼" h, ribbed, orig stopper, Mt Washington 710.00

Cranberry
    Diamond Quilted, 6" h, 4" w, blown molded, clear applied handle, cut stopper 125.00
    Hobnail 85.00
    Opal swirl, Fenton 100.00

Custard Glass
    Jackson, stopper missing 40.00
    Wild Bouquet pattern, 6½" h, fired–on dec 525.00

Cut Glass, sgd "Sinclair" 100.00

Opalescent
    Cactus, blue opal, Fenton 100.00
    Coin Dot 70.00
    Intaglio, blue and white 125.00

Pattern Glass
    Cape Cod 40.00
    Paneled Sprig, white opal lattice, stopper missing 70.00

Paneled Thistle **65.00**

Peachblow

Acid finish, 8″ h, applied reeded handle

Gundersen **750.00**

Wheeling, faceted amber stopper . **1,350.00**

Amber applied handle and stopper,

Wheeling **690.00**

Deep coloring, 6½″ h, petticoat shape, orig cut amber stopper-Wheeling **1,750.00**

Reverse Swirl, blue, heat checked handle, bruised stopper **100.00**

Rose Amber, 6″ h, 4½″ w, expanded IVT, orig amber stopper, Mt Washington **750.00**

Rubina Verde, 6¾″ h, 4″ w, IVT, petticoat shape, orig cut vaseline stopper, Wheeling **385.00**

Satin, 8¼″ h, DQ, MOP, white shaded to gold, clear frosted handle, orig frosted clear knobby stopper **585.00**

Slag, 6¾″ h, pressed, Hobstars pattern, matching stopper **35.00**

X–Ray, green, gold trim **155.00**

CUP PLATES

History: Many early cups and saucers were handleless, with deep saucers. The hot liquid was poured into the saucer and sipped from it. This necessitated another plate for the cup, the "cup plate."

The first cup plates made of pottery were of the Staffordshire variety. In the mid–1830s to 1840s, glass cup plates were favored. The Boston and Sandwich Glass Company was one of the main contributors to the lacy glass type.

It is extremely difficult to find glass cup plates in outstanding (mint) condition. Collectors expect some marks of usage, such as slight rim roughness, minor chipping (best if under rim), and in rarer patterns a portion of a scallop missing.

Reference: Ruth Webb Lee and James H. Rose, *American Glass Cup Plates*, published by author, 1948, reprinted by Charles E. Tuttle Co., Inc., in 1985.

Notes: The numbers used are from the Lee–Rose book in which all plates are illustrated.

Prices are based on plates in "average" condition.

GLASS

LR 11, 2¹³⁄₁₆″ d, clear, New England origin, small shallow rim chips and roughage **75.00**

LR 22–B, 3⁷⁄₁₆″ d, clear, pontil, New England origin, slight roughage **90.00**

LR 26, 3⁹⁄₁₆″ d, clear, attributed to Sandwich or New England Glass Co **150.00**

LR 37, 3¼″ d, opalescent, attributed to Sandwich or New England Glass Co, two heat checks in rim, light roughage **150.00**

LR 45, 3⁹⁄₁₆″ d, pale opalescent, attributed to Sandwich or New England Glass Co, mold overfill, slag deposit near center **100.00**

LR 51, 3¾″ d, clear, pontil, eastern origin, moderate rim roughage, few shallow flakes **175.00**

LR 58, 3⅜″ d, clambroth, unlisted, eastern origin **275.00**

LR 61, 3⅜″ d, opalescent, attributed to New England Glass Co **250.00**

LR 75–A, 3¹³⁄₁₆″ d, clear, attributed to New England Glass Co, one tiny rim flake **70.00**

LR 80, 3¾″ d, opalescent, New England origin **250.00**

LR 81, 3¾″ d, fiery red opalescent, New England origin **350.00**

LR 88, 3¹¹⁄₁₆″ d, deep opalescent opaque, attributed to Sandwich or New England Glass Co, two minute under rim flakes **175.00**

LR 95, 3⅝″ d, opalescent opaque, attributed to New England, tiny under rim nick **150.00**

LR 100, 3¼″ d, clear, attributed to Philadelphia area, normal mold roughness **95.00**

LR 121, 3¹⁄₁₆″ d, clear, lacy, midwestern, slight rim roughage, two minor nicks, mold overfill **100.00**

LR 242–A, 3½″ d, black amethyst, lacy, eastern origin, mold underfill and overfill **650.00**

LR 247, 3⁷⁄₁₆″ d, emerald green, lacy, attributed to Sandwich or New England Glass Co, small chip on one scallop **750.00**

LR 253, 3⁹⁄₁₆″ d, blue–green, Roman Rosette, midwestern origin, two very small rim nicks **300.00**

LR 259, 3⁷⁄₁₆″ d, clear, eastern origin, small chip on one point and one scallop, normal mold roughness **85.00**

LR 276, 3⁷⁄₁₆″ d, blue, lacy, Boston and Sandwich Glass Co, slight opalescence bloom **325.00**

LR 279, 2⅞″ d, light green, lacy, eastern origin, two chipped scallops **250.00**

LR 319, 3⁵⁄₁₆″ d, clear, one scallop missing, five have small flakes, normal mold roughness **100.00**

LR 399, 3⁵⁄₁₆″ d, clear, eastern origin, normal mold roughness **60.00**

LR 433, 4⅛″ d, clear, two chips, mold roughness **75.00**

LR 445, 3⁷⁄₁₆″ d, cloudy, midwestern origin, four bull's eyes missing, five chips, mold roughness **265.00**

LR 459M, jade opaque, twelve hearts,
near mint **450.00**
LR 516, 3¼" d, amethyst, attributed to
Sandwich, rim chip on underside, sur-
face spalls, and rim roughage **425.00**

**Historical, dark blue, Woodlands near
Philadelphia, Stubbs, 3⅛" d, $325.00.**

GLASS, HISTORICAL

LR 568, 3⁷⁄₁₆" d, clear, attributed to
Sandwich, one scallop tipped, mold
roughness **50.00**
LR 586–B, clear, Ringgold, Palo Alto,
stippled ground, small letters, Philadelphia area, 1847–48, trace of mold
roughness **650.00**
LR 595, 3¼" d, amber, attributed to
Sandwich, three small mold spalls,
one scallop missing, six scallops
tipped, one spall on underside, aver-
age mold roughness **265.00**
LR 615–A, 3⅜" d, clear, unknown origin,
Constitution **650.00**
LR 695, 3" d, clear, midwestern origin
two scallops tipped, normal mold
roughness **125.00**

PORCELAIN OR POTTERY

Gaudy Dutch, Butterfly pattern **750.00**
Leeds, 3¾" d, softpaste, gaudy blue and
white floral dec, very minor pinpoint
edge flakes **240.00**
Staffordshire, Historical
Franklin Tomb, 3½" d, dark blue,
Wood, faint hairline **600.00**
Landing of Lafayette, 4⅜" d, dark
blue, full border, Clews **425.00**
The Tyrants Foe...Lovejoy, 4" d, light
blue, unknown maker, minute pin-
point on foot rim **275.00**

Unidentified View of Country Estate,
4⅝" d, grapevine border series,
dark blue, Wood **60.00**
Staffordshire, Romantic
Balantyre, twelve sided, J Alcock . .   **50.00**
Garden Scenery, twelve sided, pink,
Mayer **30.00**
Wood & Sons, 4⅝" d, dark blue transfer
printed scene, two sailboats and row-
boat, shell border, imp mark **165.00**

CUSTARD GLASS

History: Custard glass was developed in England in the early 1880s. Harry Northwood made
the first American custard glass at his Indiana,
Pennsylvania, factory in 1898.

From 1898 until 1915, many manufacturers pro-
duced custard glass patterns, e.g., Dugan Glass,
Fenton, A. H. Heisey Glass Co., Jefferson Glass,
Northwood, Tarentum Glass, and U.S. Glass.
Cambridge and McKee continued the production
of custard glass into the Depression.

The ivory or creamy yellow custard color is
achieved by adding uranium salts to the molten
hot glass. The chemical content makes the glass
glow when held under a black light. The higher the
amount of uranium, the more luminous the color.
Northwood's custard glass has the smallest
amount of uranium, creating an ivory color; Heisey
used more, creating a deep yellow color.

Custard glass was made in patterned tableware
pieces. It also was made as souvenir items and
novelty pieces. Souvenir pieces are marked with
place names or hand-painted decorations, e.g.,
flowers. Patterns of custard glass often were highlighted in gold, enamel colors, and stains.

References: William Heacock, *Encyclopedia Of
Victorian Colored Pattern Glass, Book IV: Custard
Glass From A to Z*, Peacock Publications, 1980;
William Heacock, James Measell and Berry Wig-
gins, *Harry Northwood: The Early Years 1881–
1900*, Antique Publications, 1990.

Reproduction Alert: L. G. Wright Glass Co. has
reproduced pieces in the Argonaut Shell and
Grape and Cable patterns. It also introduced new
patterns, such as Floral and Grape and Vintage
Band. Moser reproduced toothpicks in Argonaut
Shell, Chrysanthemum Sprig, and Inverted Fan &
Feather.

Additional Listings: Pattern Glass.

Banana Boat, Geneva, 11" l, oval **125.00**
Berry Bowl
Individual
Fan **40.00**
Louis XV, gold trim **40.00**
Ring Band, gold and rose dec, Heisey   **40.00**
Master
Diamond with Peg **225.00**
Louis XV, gold trim **135.00**

Creamer, Argonaut Shell, 4¾″ h, $85.00.

Berry Set, Chrysanthemum Sprig, 11″ oval unsigned master, six individuals sgd "Northwood" script	675.00
Bowl, Grape and Cable, 7½″ d, basket-weave ext., nutmeg stain, Northwood	50.00
Butter, cov	
Chrysanthemum Sprig, 6″ h	275.00
Everglades	370.00
Georgia Gem, enamel dec	135.00
Intaglio	175.00
Louis XV	120.00
Victoria	280.00
Celery	
Georgia Gem	175.00
Ring Band	300.00
Victoria, gold trim, Tarentum	250.00
Cologne Bottle, Grape, nutmeg stain, orig stopper, marked "N"	400.00
Compote, jelly	
Argonaut Shell	160.00
Intaglio, green trim	100.00
Condiment Set, Creased Bale, 4 pcs .	180.00
Creamer	
Chrysanthemum Sprig, blue, gold dec	385.00
Fluted Scrolls	65.00
Geneva	75.00
Georgia Gem, dec	35.00
Heart with Thumbprint	80.00
Cruet	
Argonaut Shell, orig stopper	425.00
Chrysanthemum Sprig, clear stopper, goofus dec	60.00
Custard Cup, Winged Scroll	50.00
Dresser Tray, Winged Scroll, hp dec . .	165.00
Goblet, Grape and Gothic Arches, nut-meg stain	65.00
Hair Receiver	
Georgia Gem, souvenir	45.00
Winged Scroll	125.00
Hat, Grape and Gothic Arches	60.00
Humidor, Winged Scroll	175.00
Ice Cream Bowl, Peacock & Urn, individual size, Northwood	35.00
Ice Cream Set, Fan, master bowl, six serving dishes, 7 pcs	500.00
Napkin Ring, Diamond with Peg	145.00
Nappy	
Northwood Grape	50.00

Prayer Rug, 6″ d	50.00
Pin Tray, Chrysanthemum Sprig	50.00
Pitcher, water	
Argonaut Shell	300.00
Diamond with Peg, tankard	250.00
Fan	290.00
Plate, 7½″ d	
Prayer Rug	20.00
Three Fruits	22.00
Punch Cup	
Diamond with Peg	60.00
Inverted Fan and Feather	250.00
Northwood Grape	48.00
Rose Bowl, Grape and Gothic Arches .	75.00
Salt and Pepper Shakers, pr	
Chrysanthemum Sprig	150.00
Punty Band	85.00
Vine with Flowers	50.00
Sauce	
Cane Insert	30.00
Intaglio	35.00
Klondyke	42.50
Jefferson Optic, dec	15.00
Spooner	
Chrysanthemum Sprig, blue, gold trim	220.00
Geneva	50.00
Grape and Cable, nutmeg stain . . .	95.00
Grape and Gothic Arches	65.00
Sugar, cov	
Chrysanthemum Sprig, blue, gold dec	325.00
Everglades	150.00
Fluted Scrolls	150.00
Heart and Thumbprint, individual . . .	75.00
Victoria	175.00
Syrup	
Ring Band	300.00
Winged Scroll	350.00
Table Set, cov butter, creamer, cov sugar, spooner	
Argonaut Shell	400.00
Intaglio	500.00
Toothpick	
Chrysanthemum Sprig, blue	300.00
Diamond with Peg	55.00
Georgia Gem, souvenir	35.00
Maple Leaf	550.00
Ribbed Drape	150.00
Tumbler	
Cherry Scale	40.00
Chrysanthemum Sprig, set of 6	300.00
Geneva, red and green enamel dec	50.00
Grape and Gothic Arches, gold trim	60.00
Inverted Fan and Feather	100.00
Louis XV, gold trim	55.00
Ring Band	65.00
Wild Bouquet	25.00
Water Set, water pitcher and tumblers	
Fan, 5 pcs	500.00
Fluted Scrolls, gold trim, 5 pcs	350.00
Grape and Gothic Arches, 7 pcs . . .	600.00

CUT GLASS, AMERICAN

History: Glass is cut by the process of grinding decoration into the glass by means of abrasive-carrying metal wheels or stone wheels. A very ancient craft, it was revived in 1600 by Bohemians and spread through Europe, to Great Britain, and to America.

American cut glass came of age at the Centennial Exposition in 1876 and the World Columbian Exposition in 1893. The American public recognized American cut glass to be exceptional in quality and workmanship. America's most significant output of this high quality glass occurred from 1880 to 1917, a period now known as the "Brilliant Period."

About the 1890s some companies began adding an acid-etched "signature" to their glass. This signature may be the actual company name, its logo, or chosen symbol. Today, signed pieces can command a premium over unsigned pieces since the signature clearly establishes the origin.

However, caution should be exercised in regard to signature identification. Objects with forged signatures have been in existence for some time. To check for authenticity, run your finger tip or finger nail lightly over the area with the signature. As a general rule, a genuine signature cannot be felt; a forged signature exhibits a raised surface.

Many companies never used the acid-etched signature on the glass and may or may not have affixed paper labels to the items originally. Dorflinger Glass and the Meriden Glass Co. made cut glass of the highest quality, yet never acid-etched a signature on the glass. Furthermore, cut glass made before the 1890s was not signed. Many of these wood polished items, cut on blown blanks, were of excellent quality and often won awards at exhibitions.

Consequently, if collectors restrict themselves to signed pieces only, many beautiful pieces of the highest quality glass and workmanship will be missed.

References: E. S. Farrar & J. S. Spillman, *The Complete Cut & Engraved Glass Of Corning,* Crown Publishers [Corning Museum of Glass monograph], 1979; John Feller, *Dorflinger: America's Finest Glass, 1852–1921,* Antique Publications, 1988; J. Michael Pearson, *Encyclopedia Of American Cut & Engraved Glass,* Volumes I to III, published by author, 1975; Albert C. Revi, *American Cut & Engraved Glass,* Thomas Nelson, Inc., 1965; Martha Louise Swan, *American and Engraved Glass*, Wallace-Homestead, 1986; H. Weiner & F. Lipkowitz, *Rarities In American Cut Glass,* Collectors House of Books, 1975.

Collectors' Club: American Cut Glass Association, 1603 SE 19th, Suite 112, Edmond Professional Bldg., Edmond, OK 73013.

Museums: The Corning Museum of Glass, Corning, NY; High Museum of Art, Atlanta, GA; Huntington Galleries, Huntington, WV; Lightner Museum, St. Augustine, FL; Toledo Museum Of Art, Toledo, OH.

Ambrosia Bowl, 12″ d, 10¼″ h, panel and cut fruit	140.00
Banana Bowl, 11″ d, 6½″ h, Harvard, hobstar bottom	210.00
Basket, 8 x 11″, Harvard, hobstars, and prism cut	475.00
Bell	
5¾″ h, dinner size, hobstars, fans, strawberry diamond	255.00
6¾″ h, strawberry diamond and fan sharply cut, pattern cut on knob at end of stem as well	550.00
Berry Set, Regis pattern, sgd "Libbey" with saber, set of twelve	550.00
Bishop's Hat Bowl, 12″ d, 5″ h, intaglio diamond point cut, sgd "Tuthill"	275.00
Bonbon, 8″ d, 2″ h, Broadway pattern, Huntly, minor flakes	125.00
Bone Dish, 7 x 5″, Russian pattern, crescent shape, set of 4	355.00
Bowl	
7″ d, sq, Russian pattern, rayed center	605.00
8″ d, hobstars and cut arches	235.00
8¼″ d, border of hobstars with floral panels	110.00
9″ d	
Band of hobstars, starred hobs, triple sq rim, minute rim chips	250.00
Geometrical pattern, hobstars, flared fans, strawberry diamonds and deep miters, sgd "Roden Bros"	275.00
Hobstars, crosshatching, notched prism, sgd "Libbey" with saber	220.00
9″ d, 4½″ h, Alhambra pattern	770.00
10″ d, Primrose, intaglio, sgd "Hawkes"	200.00
10 x 6½ x 3″, rect, Snowflake and Holly pattern, rim chips, sgd "Sinclaire"	275.00
11½ x 18″, rect, intaglio rose cutting, hobstar bottom, sgd "Sinclaire"	165.00

Box, hinged cov, Feathered Star pattern, Heinz Brothers, 1900, $225.00.

12" d, 4" h, fold–over rim, floral cut, Pairpoint 200.00

Bread Tray

11 x 5", hobstars, sgd "Clark" 275.00

13" l, Holly and Snowflake pattern, Sinclaire 605.00

13¾ x 6¼", hobstars and cane, rim flake 250.00

Butter, cov, 5" h

7" d plate, Russian and floral 385.00

8" d plate

    Hobstar chain cut on figured blank 325.00

    Hobstars and fans, sgd "Libbey" . 425.00

Butter Pat, Cypress, Lauren 35.00

Candlesticks, pr

8" h

    Hollow teardrop stems, rayed bases, hobstars, hobnail, and diamonds 975.00

    Teardrop stems, floral and Harvard 325.00

11" h, teardrop stem, notched prisms, 24 pt hobstar base 600.00

11½" h, large air trap base, floral cut 470.00

12" h, Adelaide, amber, Pairpoint .. 365.00

14" h, teardrop stems, cut and engraved, sgd "Sinclaire," pr 325.00

Candy Basket, 3¾" h, engraved florals, Hawkes, sterling silver rim and handle 185.00

Canoe

11" l, Harvard 240.00

13½ x 4½", floral and leaves 75.00

Carafe

Clear button Russian 325.00

Harvard 160.00

Hobstars and notched prisms 110.00

Wedgemere, 9" h, Libbey 1,000.00

Casserole, cov, 8½ x 7" h, Palm, sgd "Taylor Bros" 1,300.00

Celery Tray

11 x 4½", hobstars, flashed fans, strawberry diamond, Unger Bros . 145.00

11 x 5", floral and Harvard pattern, double X–vesicas 110.00

12", hobstars, flashed double vesicas, sgd "Alford" 250.00

12 x 4", intaglio cut, Libbey pattern . 165.00

Creamer and Sugar, Heart pattern, hobstar base, notched handles, $195.00.

Champagne Bucket, 7 x 7", sgd "Hoare" 350.00

Champagne Goblet, Russian pattern, knobbed stem, rayed star base, set of 12 .... 660.00

Champagne Pitcher, 14½" h, hobstars and canes 430.00

Cheese and Cracker Dish, Double Lozenge 275.00

Cheese Dish, 6" h dome, 9" d plate, cobalt cut to clear, bull's eye and panel, large mitresplits on bottom of plate 200.00

Cigar Jar

7½", Middlesex, hollow stopper, lid to hold sponge, Dorflinger 475.00

9"

    Monarch, pattern cut lid hollow for sponge, hobstar base, Hoare .. 625.00

    Pattern cut lid hollow for sponge, hobstars, beaded split vesicas, hobstar base 550.00

Cigarette Holder, 4" l,¾" w, nailhead diamond, strawberry diamond, fans, and honeycomb 630.00

Claret Jug, 12" h, lapidary ring neck, hobstars and fan, faceted stopper .. 165.00

Cocktail Shaker, strawberry diamond and fan, SS top, sgd "Hawkes" 275.00

Cologne Bottle

5½" h, Russian cut, chip on top ... 715.00

6" h, Hob and Lace, green cased to clear, pattern cut stopper, Dorflinger 600.00

7½ x 2¾", Parisian, sq shape, Dorflinger, pr 620.00

Compote

9" d, 9" h, basketweave, air trap stem 715.00

Cordial Set, Flute, green cased to clear, 9" h handled decanter with ringed neck and matching colored stopper, set of 8 cordials, Dorflinger 875.00

Cracker Jar

6½" h, hobstars, fans, double "X" cut vesicas, strawberry diamond, curved–in sides, matching pattern cut glass lid rests into SS rim ... 800.00

7" d, floral cut, silverplate lid and bail handle, Pairpoint 275.00

Creamer and Sugar, 4" h, hobstars, nailhead, and fan, triple cut handles, pr 250.00

Cream Pitcher, 5¼" h, bulbous, notched fluted rim, Persian, clear hobstar center, triple notched handles 150.00

Cruet

6" h, Chrysanthemum, tri–pour spout, cut handle and stopper, Hawkes . 350.00

9½" h, Alhambra, honeycomb handle, tall pyramidal shape 675.00

Decanter

7" h, Lotus, ship's, pattern cut stopper, Egginton 380.00

11" h
  Argand, SS flip–top lid and handle,
    Hoare **700.00**
  Stopper cut in matching geometric
    pattern, sgd "Hawkes" **525.00**
12" h, Russian and Pillar, pattern cut
  stopper **1,100.00**
13" h, Russian pattern, ftd, triple
  notched handle, scalloped base,
  faceted stopper **715.00**
13½" h, Brazilian, heavy blank, bul-
  bous, wood polished, Hawkes . . . **650.00**
Dresser Tray, 12 x 8", hobstar and diamond with fan border **322.50**
Egg Nog Bowl, 12" d, 9½" h, pinwheel
  cut, two pcs **310.00**
Finger Bowl, underplate, Russian pat-
  tern, set of six **330.00**
Fernery, Expanding Star, three ftd . . . **325.00**
Flower Center
  5" h, 6" d, flat–bottomed, hobstars,
    flashed fans, hobstar chain and
    base **300.00**
  7½" h, 10" d, hobstars in diamond
    shape fields, fans, strawberry dia-
    mond, honeycomb neck **775.00**
  9" h, step–cut and scalloped rim, 48
    point hobstar base **750.00**
Flower Pot, 6 x 6", hobstars and fans,
  pyramidal starred fields **775.00**
Goblet, Russian pattern, knobbed stem,
  rayed star base, set of 15 . . . . **1,240.00**

**Knife Rest, master size, pinwheel cut
ball ends, 5" l, $90.00.**

Ice Bucket, 7" d, 8" d underplate, hobstars and notched prisms, double
  handles **935.00**
Ice Cream Tray
  10" l, oval, scalloped rim, rings of hob-
    stars surrounded by clear band,
    sgd "Taylor & TB" **577.50**
  14¼ x 7¼", Rose Combination pat-
    tern, Irving, clear blank **475.00**
Jar, cov, 5" d, emerald green cut to clear,
  hobstar, cross–cut diamond and fan,
  green star cut knob **145.00**
Mustard, cov, 3½" h, underplate, panel
  and notched prism, sgd "Maple City
  Glass" **220.00**

Nappy, handle
  5½" d, floral and cane **45.00**
  6" d, Russian pattern **90.00**
Orange Bowl, 10" d, pinwheel, notched
  prism and hobstar in vesicas **165.00**
Pastry Tray, 9" d, 7" h, floral, handle . . **90.00**
Pitcher, milk, 6" h, floral, hobstars, and
  cane **255.00**
Pitcher, water
  10" h
    Copper wheel cut leaves and but-
      terfly, sgd "Libbey" in circle . . . **150.00**
    Hobstars, miters, and crosshatches **150.00**
  11½" h, tankard, cane and hobstar
    cut, 24 point hobstar base **275.00**
  12" h, tankard, snowflake pattern, sgd
    "Libbey" in circle **1,072.00**
Plate
  6" d, Gothic pattern, Baker **65.00**
  7" d, Gloria pattern, Libbey **165.00**
  10" d, vintage intaglio, sgd "Tuthill" . **660.00**
Powder Box, cov, 4½" d, silver thread,
  vintage and floral, cross–cut dia-
  mond, sgd "Sinclaire" **330.00**
Punch Bowl
  12" d, 8" h, strawberry diamond and
    hearts, 2 pcs **550.00**
  12" d, 9" h, Dorflinger Colonial pat-
    tern, 2 pcs **550.00**
  12" d, 13" h, Arcadia pattern, pedestal **1,100.00**
Punch Cup, 2½" h, cranberry cut to
  clear, cross–cut diamond, clear han-
  dle **80.00**
Relish, 13" l, leaf shape, Russian pat-
  tern, clear buttons **315.00**
Rose Bowl
  5" d, allover geometric engraving,
    American, blown blank **180.00**
  5" h, brilliant period, free form, trian-
    gular, allover floral engraving, en-
    graved rim band, sgd "Libbey" . . **300.00**
  6" h, ftd, Hawkes Brunswick pattern **220.00**
Salad Bowl, 10 x 7", strawberry diamonds, underplate, minute nicks . . . **300.00**
Salad Server, strawberry diamonds, silverplate, Gorham **250.00**
Spittoon, lady's, 7½" h, 4½" d, fold–over
  rim, floral cut, Pairpoint **330.00**
Spooner, 4 x 8", flat, Lotus pattern, Eg-
  gington **80.00**
Sugar Shaker, 5" h, emerald green cut
  to clear, can and fan, marked "Ster-
  ling" floral repousse top **415.00**
Syrup, Russian pattern, hinged silver-
  plate top, cut handle **770.00**
Tray
  9½ x 6", rect, Persian cut **220.00**
  15" l, hobstars, cane, and central
    feather, sgd "Libbey" with saber . **605.00**
  16 x 11", cut in bows and feather de-
    sign, sgd "Sinclaire" **210.00**
Tumbler, Russian button cut, set of nine **315.00**

Vase
    5" h, Brazilian pattern, trumpet,
    Hawkes **155.00**
    8" h, trumpet, intaglio cut poppy, Tuth-
    ill **165.00**
    11" h, urn, Vintage cutting, two han-
    dles, brilliant period, Tuthill **475.00**
    12" h, 5" d, trumpet, notched vertical
    prism and sq cutting, starred but-
    tons, 24 point rayed base, sgd "J
    Hoare & Co" **275.00**
Water Carafe
    7½" h, Arcadia pattern, cut ring neck **165.00**
    8" h, Russian pattern panels sepa-
    rated by notched prism stripes, pr **660.00**
    14" h, trumpet, deep burgundy cut to
    clear, deep cut strawberry diamond
    and fans, cross–cutting, clear star
    cut base **415.00**
Water Set
    10½" pitcher, six 4⅛" tumblers, bril-
    liant period, Fortuna type pattern,
    fans at top **650.00**
    10¾" pitcher, six 4" tumblers, brilliant
    period
    Buzz stars separated by horizontal
    bands, diamond center and fans **500.00**
    Floral and butterfly, attributed to Ni-
    land **470.00**
Whiskey Decanter, pr
    11" h, panel cut, orig stopper **250.00**
    13" h, handle, panel cut, lapidary
    knob, sgd "Clair" **770.00**
Wine
    5" h
    Brazilian pattern, teardrop stem,
    fully cut foot, Hawkes **330.00**
    Burgess pattern, teardrop knob
    through stem **385.00**
    Cranberry cut to clear, fields of
    cross diamonds and fans, Dor-
    flinger, set of four **400.00**
    7" h, green cut to clear, engraved
    roses and vines, Hawkes, set of
    four **310.00**
    8½" h, green cut to clear, hobstars,
    fan, and cane, quintruple flute cut
    stem, double teardrop, hobstar
    base **175.00**

CUT VELVET

History: Several glass manufacturers made cut
velvet during the late Victorian era, c1870–1900.
An outer layer of pastel color was applied over a
white casing. The piece then was molded or cut
in a ribbed or diamond shape in high relief, ex-
posing portions of the casing. The finish had a
satin velvety feel, hence the name "cut velvet."

Biscuit Jar, pink, SP mountings and lid **265.00**
Celery Vase, 6½" h, box pleated top,
    DQ, deep blue over white, Mt Wash-
    ington **725.00**
Creamer, 3½" h, DQ, cranberry, applied
    multicolored enamel dec **365.00**
Ewer, 4¾" h, DQ, deep blue, applied
    frosted handle **165.00**
Finger Bowl, 4½" d, DQ, blue **135.00**
Pitcher, 10¾" h, DQ, blue **220.00**
Toothpick, 3⅝" h, DQ, yellow, sq mouth **190.00**

**Vase, light aqua shading to deep ro-
bin's egg blue, basket weave pattern,
acid sgd "Stevens & Williams," 10" h,
$985.00.**

Vase
    6" h, 9" d, DQ, deep orange, deeply
    ruffled top, Mt Washington **675.00**
    9" h, DQ, pale lavender, ruffled top . **330.00**
    13½" h, 6" d base, double gourd,
    pumpkin stem neck, DQ, pale gold,
    Mt Washington **650.00**

CZECHOSLOVAKIAN ITEMS

History: Objects marked "Made in Czechoslovakia" were produced after 1918 when the country
claimed its independence from the Austro–Hungarian Empire. The people became more cosmopolitan, liberated, and expanded their scope of life.
Their porcelains, pottery, and glassware reflect
many influences.

A specific manufacturer's mark may be identified
as being much earlier than 1918, but this only
indicates the factory existed in the Bohemian or
Austro–Hungarian Empire period.

References: Dale and Diane Barta and Helen
M. Rose, *Czechoslovakian Glass & Collectibles,*
Collector Books, 1991; Ruth A. Forsythe, *Made in*

Czechoslovakia, Richardson Printing Corp., 1982; Jacquelyne Y. Jones–North, *Czechoslovakian Perfume Bottles and Boudoir Accessories,* Antique Publications, 1990.

GLASS

Atomizer, 7½" h, brilliant period cut glass	95.00
Bowl, cased, yellow int., black ext., polished pontil	45.00
Lamp Shade, beaded, Forsythe "659"	35.00
Mantel Lusters, 12½" h, pr, ruby and white overlay, cup form waisted top, scalloped rim, cylindrical stem, faceted knop, domed spreading foot, polychrome floral sprays, gilt trim	360.00
Perfume Bottle	
5½" h, brilliant period cut glass	125.00
6¾" h, amber, large intaglio floral stopper	150.00
Plate, Bartered Bride, hp, pr	50.00
Powder Box, cov, round, yellow, black knob top	55.00
Vase	
6¾" h, gold iridescent, Oil Spot, flared, ruffled top, sgd	185.00
8¼", hp bubbly green glass, fox hunt scene, ftd	145.00

Teapot, multicolored classical scene, caramel luster ground, gold handle, white spout, $48.00.

POTTERY AND PORCELAIN

Cologne Bottle, 4", glossy blue, bow front	12.00
Pitcher, 4", red black handle	15.00
Plate	
10", Art Deco, maiden, black and yellow, 1920s	50.00
10¾" d, set of 8, encrusted gold with white center, marked "Czechoslovakia"	120.00
Teapot, cov, Chelsea style, delicate florals, matching underplate, marked "Emphila Czechoslovakia"	45.00

DAVENPORT
LONGPORT
STAFFORDSHIRE

DAVENPORT

History: John Davenport opened a pottery in Longport, Staffordshire, England in 1793. His ware was of high quality, light weight, and cream colored with a beautiful velvety texture.

The firm made soft-paste (Old Blue), luster trimmed ware, and pink luster with black transfer. There have been pieces of Gaudy Dutch and Spatterware found with the Davenport mark. Later Davenport became a leading maker of ironstone and early flow blue. His famous "Cyprus" pattern in mulberry became very popular. His heirs continued the business until the factory closed in 1886.

Reference: Susan and Al Bagdade, *Warman's English & Continental Pottery & Porcelain, 2nd Edition,* Wallace–Homestead, 1991.

Pitcher, ironstone, blue and orange Oriental design, gilt trim, green handle, marked "W Davenport & Co, Longport, Staff. Potteries," c1805, 6" h, $170.00.

Charger, 17½" l, oval, Venetian harbor scene, light blue transfer	70.00
Compote, 2½" h, 8½" d, turquoise and gold band, tiny raised flowers, hp scene with man fishing, cows at edge of lake, c1860, pr	195.00
Creamer, tan, jasperware, basketweave, incised anchor mark	50.00
Cup and Saucer, Amoy pattern, flow blue, 3¾" h cup, 6" d saucer, incised anchor mark	70.00
Cup Plate, Teaberry pattern, pink luster	30.00

Dish, ftd, tricorn, Belvoir Castle dec . .	85.00
Ewer, 9″ h, floral dec, multicolored, c1830	185.00
Mustard Pot, 3½″ h, hinged SP cov, turquoise, gilt foliage and florals, 1870–86	85.00
Pitcher, 8″ h, black transfer print of cathedral, pink luster trim	200.00
Plate	
8″ d, octagonal, floral dec, gold rim .	40.00
9⅛″ d, Legend of Montrose, transfer, 1850–70	50.00
Platter	
17¼″ l, Tyrol Hunter, brown transfer	100.00
18″ l, white, blue border, anchor mark, c1820	200.00
20″ l, rect, blue and white, transfer printed exotic bird and flower pattern, c1840	300.00
Punch Bowl, 14″ d, int. painted iron–red, blue, and gilt, chrysanthemum and rockwork, iron–red trellis border, rim with flowering foliage on blue ground, ext. with band of seaweed pattern in gilt on pale blue ground between bands of dark blue foliage, puce mark "Davenport, Manufacturers To Their Majesties, Long Port, Staffordshire," c1830	2,200.00
Sauce Dish, cov, ladle, creamware, molded leaves, lime green veining, early	425.00
Tazza, 9½″ d, octagonal, ftd, Imari pattern, c1860	110.00
Tea Set, teapot, creamer, and ftd sugar, blue and white, marked "Davenport," c1880	100.00
Tureen, 12″ l, Blue Willow pattern	150.00
Vegetable Dish, Berry pattern, imp sgd, anchor mark	50.00

DECOYS

History: Carved wooden decoys, used to lure ducks and geese to the hunter, have become widely recognized as an indigenous American folk art form in the past several years.

Many decoys are from the 1880–1930 period when commercial gunners commonly hunted using rigs of several hundred decoys. Many fine carvers also worked through the 1930s and 1940s.

The value of a decoy is based on several factors: (1) fame of the carver, (2) quality of the carving, (3) species of wild fowl–the most desirable are herons, swans, mergansers, and shorebirds, and (4) condition of the original paint (o.p.).

The inexperienced collector should be aware of several facts. The age of a decoy, per se, is usually of no importance in determining value. Since very few decoys were ever signed, it will be quite diffi-

cult to attribute most decoys to known carvers. Anyone who has not examined a known carver's work will be hard pressed to determine if the paint on one of his decoys is indeed original.

Repainting severely decreases a decoy's value. In addition, there are many fakes and reproductions on the market and even experienced collectors are occasionally fooled.

Decoys listed below are of average wear unless otherwise noted.

References: Joe Engers (general editor), *The Great Book of Wildfowl Decoys,* Thunder Bay Press, 1990; Henry A. Fleckenstein, Jr., *American Factory Decoys,* Schiffer Publishing, Ltd.; Ronald J. Fritz, *Michigan's Master Carver Oscar W. Peterson, 1887–1951,* Aardvark Publications, 1988; Gene and Linda Kangas, *Decoys: A North American Survey,* Hillcrest Publications, 1983; Gene and Linda Kangas, *Decoys,* Collector Books, 1992; Art, Brad and Scott Kimball, *The Fish Decoy,* Aardvark Publications, Inc., 1986; Carl F. Luckey, *Collecting Antique Bird Decoys: An Identification & Value Guide,* Books Americana, 1983.

Periodicals: *Decoy Hunter Magazine,* 901 North 9th, Clinton, IN 47842; *Decoy Magazine,* P.O. Box 1900, Montego Bay Station, Ocean City, MD 21842; *The Wild Fowl Art Journal,* Ward Foundation, 655 South Salisbury Blvd, Salisbury, MD 21801.

Black Breasted Plover, Harry V Shourds, orig paint	2,600.00
Black Duck	
Charles Thomas, Massachusetts, glass eyes, orig paint	350.00
Ira Hudson, preening, raised wings, outstretched neck, scratch feather paint	8,500.00
Mason Factory, challenge grade, snakey head, orig grade stamp on bottom	1,600.00
Unknown Maker, carved balsa body, wood head, glass eyes, orig paint, 15½″ l	145.00
Wildfowler, Connecticut, inlet head, glass eyes, worn orig paint, green overpaint on bottom and sides, 13″ l, c1900	195.00
Zeke McDonald, McDonald Island, St Clair Flats, Michigan, hollow body, glass eyes, worn orig paint, 17¼″ l, c1910	425.00
Black–Breasted Plover	
A E Crowell, oval brand on bottom .	2,750.00
Unknown maker, Long Island, orig paint	1,200.00
Bluebill, matted pair, Mason Factory, standard grade, glass eyes	1,325.00
Bluebill Drake	
Ira Hudson, professional replaced bill	700.00
Jim Kelson, Mt Clemens, Michigan, carved wing detail, feather stamp-	

ing, glass eyes, orig paint, orig keel
and weight, 13½" l, c1930 . . . . . . **275.00**

Sandusky, well shaped head, tack
eyes, orig paint traces, 19th C . . . **335.00**

Ward Brothers, pinch breast style,
sgd "Lem and Steve" under tail,
stamped on bottom, c1930 . . . . . **850.00**

Bluebill Hen

Irving Miller, Monroe, Michigan,
carved, wood, glass eyes, orig
paint, 11½" l **150.00**

Jim Kelson, Mt Clemens, Michigan,
tucked sleeper, balsa body, inset
tail, glass eyes, orig paint and keel,
12" l, c1948 . . . . **175.00**

Thomas Chambers, Canada Club,
hollow body, glass eyes, old re-
paint, 15¾" l, c1900 . . . . **525.00**

Blue–Wing Teal, matted pair, unknown
maker, carved, raised wing tips, un-
usual rocking head, orig paint **340.00**

Blue–Wing Teal Drake, Mason Factory,
premier grade, replaced eyes **825.00**

Brant

Unknown Maker, carved, wood, hollow body, glass eyes, orig paint,
branded "WRG," 22¼" l **160.00**

Ward Brothers, Maryland, carved,
hollow body, head turned left, sgd
"Lem and Steve," dated 1917 . . . **1,500.00**

Bufflehead Drake

Bob Kerr, carved detail, glass eyes,
orig paint, 10½" l, scratch carved
signature, c1980 . . . . **250.00**

Harry M Shourds, carved, hollow
body, painted eyes **1,800.00**

**Canadian Goose, St. Lawrence River,
c1940, $425.00.**

Canada Goose

A E Crowell, oval brand on bottom . **1,950.00**

Bill Eminght, Toledo, Ohio, cork body,
wood head and keel, orig paint,
shot scars, sgd and dated 1968,
24½" l **500.00**

Doug Jester, Virginia, old paint **450.00**

Hurley Conklin, carved, hollow body,
swimming position, branded "H
Conklin" on bottom **600.00**

Canvasback Matted Pair, Ward Broth-

ers, Crisfield, Maryland, carved,
wood, 1936 . . . . **35,200.00**

Canvasback Drake

Jim Kelson, Mt Clemens, Michigan,
hollow aluminum head, wood body,
feather stamping, relief carved
wings, orig paint and keel, 15½" l,
c1956 . . . . **200.00**

Miles Smith, Marine City, Michigan,
high head, balsa body, glass eyes,
orig paint, 19" l, c1933 . . . . **150.00**

Tom Chambers, Canada Club, Ontario, Canada, hollow body, glass
eyes, worn orig paint, 14⅝" l,
branded "HMJ" and "WLM," c1890 **600.00**

Canvasback Hen

Charles Bean, carved, wood, glass
eyes, orig paint, 14¾" l **225.00**

Frank Schmidt, orig paint, glass eyes,
relief carved wing tips, 16¼" l . . . **150.00**

Curlew

A E Crowell, hollow carved, orig paint **850.00**

Harry V Shourds, orig paint **2,000.00**

William Gibian, carved wings and
feathers, head turned back, carved
neck muscle, sgd on bottom **500.00**

Eider Drake, unknown maker, Maine,
carved bill, inlet neck, chip carved
body, turned–up tail, orig paint **700.00**

Goldeneye Drake

L E Bernard, Hale, Michigan, carved,
wood, glass eyes, old worn paint,
15½" l **45.00**

Stevens Factory, repainted, branded
on bottom **355.00**

Green Wing Teal, matted pair, Robert
Weeks **275.00**

Green Wing Teal Hen, Lem Ward,
carved, hollow body, raised feathers
and wing tips, head turned left, sgd
and dated 1959 . . . . **2,000.00**

Heron, unknown maker, carved wing
and tail, wrought iron legs **900.00**

Herring Gull, Charles Wilber, Highland
Heights, New Jersey, Barnegat Bay
Style, hollow body, carved split wing
tip, glass eyes, orig paint, 19" l **325.00**

Mallard, matted pair

Evans Factory, mammoth size, orig
paint **610.00**

Mason Factory, standard grade, tack
eyes, orig paint **660.00**

Mallard Drake

Ben Schmidt, Detroit, relief carved,
feather stamping, glass eyes, orig
paint, orig keel, 15¼" l, marked
"Mallard drake Benj Schmidt, De-
troit 1960" **450.00**

Bert Graves, carved, hollow body,
orig weighted bottom, branded "E l
Rogers" and "Cleary" **900.00**

Mason Factory, standard grade,

carved, wood, glass eyes, orig paint, 15¾" l 225.00

Mallard Hen
Ralph Johnston, Detroit, Michigan, high head, glass eyes, orig paint, 17½" l, marked "R D Johnston original keel 1948" in pencil 200.00
Robert Elliston, carved, hollow body, orig paint 1,700.00

Merganser Drake
A E Crowell, hooded, rect brand, sgd on bottom 1,210.00
Mason Factory, challenge grade, orig paint 675.00

Merganser Hen
George Boyd, head turned slightly, feathered paint 7,000.00
Hurley Conklin, hollow body, carved wing tips, branded "H Conklin" on bottom 350.00

Pintail Drake
Mason Factory, premier grade, sloping breast, orig paint 750.00
Zeke McDonald, Michigan, high head, hollow body, glass eyes, orig paint, c1910 . . . . 500.00

Pintail Hen, Mason Factory, premier grade, sloping breast, orig paint, marked "Big Point Co, Pathcourt, Ont, John S Meredith, member 1900–1920" 2,300.00

Plover, Joe Lincoln, winter plumage feather painting, orig paint 750.00

Red Breasted Merganser Drake
Amos Wallace, Maine, inlet neck, carved crest, detailed feathered paint 2,000.00
George Boyd, New Hampshire, carved, orig paint 8,000.00
George Huey, carved wing tips and eyes, inlet neck, head turned to left, inset leather comb, sgd "G R Huey" 800.00

Red Breasted Merganser, matted pair
Norman Hudson, Virginia, carved crests, bills, and tails, c1949 . . . . 900.00
Oscar Bibber, carved, hollow body, turned head, orig horsehair combs, orig paint 4,000.00
Willie Ross, Maine, graceful body, inlet neck, ostrich feather crests, orig paint 3,700.00

Redhead Drake
Charles Perdew, Illinois, carved, wood 43,450.00
R Madison Mitchell, carved, wood, orig paint, unused, 13" l 300.00
Frank Schmidt, Detroit, Michigan, orig paint, glass eyes, relief carved wing tips, 15½" l 200.00

Robin Snipe, Obediah Verity, carved wings and eyes, orig paint 4,250.00

Ruddy Duck Drake, Len Carneghi, Mt Clemens, Michigan, hollow body, glass eyes, orig paint, 10¾" l, sgd and dated "1972" 225.00

Ruddy Turnstone, unknown maker, orig paint 600.00

Sanderling, A E Crowell, rect brand, sgd on bottom 1,100.00

Sandpiper, A E Crowell, white rumped, rect brand, sgd on bottom 2,500.00

Sickle Bill Curlew, carved, wood, glass eyes, pitchfork tine beak, orig paint, 22" l 125.00

Surf Scoter, unknown maker, inlet neck, old paint 950.00

Swan, unknown maker, Chesapeake Bay, Maryland, carved, wood, braced neck, white paint, 30" l 880.00

Widgeon, matted pair, Charlie Joiner, Maryland, sgd on bottom 775.00

Widgeon Hen, Gilbert St Ours, Rhode Island, orig paint 125.00

Yellowlegs
Ira Hudson, Virginia, carved, wood . 23,650.00
Joe Lincoln, carved wings, split tail, stippled paint, branded "S" on bottom 1,700.00
William Gibian, carved wings and tips, sgd on bottom 525.00

DEDHAM POTTERY

History: Alexander W. Robertson established the Chelsea Pottery in Chelsea, Massachusetts, in 1860. In 1872 it was known as the Chelsea Keramic Art Works.

In 1895 the pottery moved to Dedham, and the name was changed to Dedham Pottery. Their principal product was gray crackleware dinnerware with a blue decoration, the rabbit pattern being the most popular. The factory closed in 1943.

The following marks help determine the approximate age of items: (1) Chelsea Keramic Art Works, "Robertson" impressed, 1876–1889; (2) C.P.U.S. impressed in a cloverleaf, 1891–1895; (3) Foreshortened rabbit, 1895–1896; (4) Conventional rabbit with "Dedham Pottery" stamped in blue, 1897; (5) Rabbit mark with "Registered", 1929–1943.

Reference: Lloyd E. Hawes, *The Dedham Pottery And The Earlier Robertson's Chelsea Potteries*, Dedham Historical Society, 1968.

Reproduction Alert: Several rabbit pattern pieces have been reproduced.

Plate, Azalea pattern, 6″ d, $70.00.

Bowl
2⅞″ h, cov, rabbit border, blue rabbit
mark on bottom 75.00
5¼″ d, rabbit border, blue rabbit
stamp on bottom and Davenport
mark 55.00
5¾″ d, cov, rabbit border, blue rabbit
stamp on bottom 165.00
5⅞″, rabbit border, blue stamp on bot-
tom 90.00
6⅞″ d, rabbit border, blue registered
mark on bottom 140.00
7½″ d, flared rim, rabbit border, blue
rabbit stamp on bottom 140.00
8″ sq, rabbit border 300.00
10⅝″ d, flared rim, rabbit border, blue
registered mark on bottom 110.00
Candlestick, pr
1⅜″ h, rabbit border, blue rabbit registered mark on bottom 330.00
1½″ h 220.00
Celery Tray, 10″ l, rabbit border 300.00
Coffeepot, 8″ h, rabbit border, blue rabbit stamp on bottom 165.00
Creamer
2¼″ h, rabbit border 55.00
4⅝″ h, rabbit border, blue registered
mark on bottom 140.00
Cup and Saucer, Azalea border, blue
rabbit stamp 50.00
Cup Plate, 4⅜″ d, rabbit border, blue
rabbit stamp on bottom 140.00
Egg Cup, 2½″ h, set of 6, blue rabbit
stamp on bottom 360.00
Flower Arranger, 4⅝″ d, blue rabbit
stamp on bottom 30.00
Mug, 6″ h, Rabbit, incised and stamped 330.00
Plate
6″ d, slightly raised Snow Tree border,
blue rabbit stamp on bottom 70.00
6⅛″ d, swan border, blue rabbit stamp
and two incised rabbits mark . . . 250.00
6¼″ d, rabbit border, blue stamp on
bottom 50.00

6½″ d, iris border, blue rabbit stamp 45.00
7½″ d
Horse Chestnut, stamped, imp
twice, base chip 125.00
Swan border, blue rabbit stamp and
two incised rabbits 255.00
7⅝″ d, rabbit border, blue rabbit
stamp 75.00
8¼″ d, horse chestnut border, blue
rabbit stamp 50.00
8⅜″ d
Magnolia border, blue rabbit stamp
and one incised rabbit mark . . . 25.00
Poppy, blue rabbit stamp, incised
rabbit and underlined X mark . . 45.00
8½″ d
Poppy pod border, crackleware
blue and white, painted poppies
in center, incised and painted
mark 660.00
Raised rabbit border, incised mark 45.00
Raised swimming duck border,
crackleware blue and white, in-
cised mark 165.00
Turkey, stamped and imp, minor
imperfections 135.00
8⅝″ d, raised rabbit border, incised
rabbit mark 55.00
8¾″ d, butterfly pattern, crackleware,
blue ink mark, imp bunny 415.00
8⅞″ d, Magnolia border, blue rabbit
stamp and two impressed mark . . 70.00
9¾″ d
Azalea border, blue rabbit mark on
bottom 40.00
Rabbit border, blue rabbit stamp on
bottom 40.00
9⅞″ d
Rabbit border, blue mark and two
incised rabbits on bottom 80.00
Turkey border, blue rabbit mark . . 35.00
10″ d
Blue grape cluster band, crackleware, rabbit ink mark 275.00
Moth border, blue rabbit mark on
bottom 40.00
Turkey, stamped 245.00
Sugar Bowl, cov, 4¼″ h, blue rabbit
mark on bottom 55.00
Tea Stand, 6″ d, Rabbit, stamped, early
20th C 165.00
Tile, 5½″ d, Rabbit 250.00
Tumbler, 3⅜″ h, rabbit border, blue
stamp on bottom 30.00
Vase
8″ h, Crackleware, short neck, swollen cylindrical form, blue jay resting
on branch, dated, stamped regis-
tered mark, 1931 . . . . 1,100.00
9 x 8½″, bulbous shoulder, multicolored volcanic glaze, incised
"HCR," ink mark "DP37C" 1,320.00

10½" h, experimental, short neck, swollen cylindrical body, semigloss tan glaze, incised "BW, Dedham Pottery HCR," late 19th C **275.00**

12½" h, pillow, rect neck, flattened ovoid body, two lion faces, rect foot, blue–green glossy glaze, stamped "Chelsea Keramic Works Robertson & Sons" **450.00**

13¼" h, pillow shape ovoid, flaring rect foot, blue glaze, small loop handles, imp "Chelsea Keramic Art Works Robertson & Sons," wear to glaze at handles **165.00**

DELFTWARE

History: Delftware is pottery of a soft red clay body with tin enamel glaze. The white, dense, opaque color came from adding tin ash to lead glaze. The first examples had blue designs on a white ground. Polychrome examples followed.

The name originally applied to pottery made in the region around Delft, Holland, beginning in the 16th century and ending in the late 18th century. Tin came from the Cornish mines in England. By the 17th and 18th centuries, English potters in London, Bristol, and Liverpool were copying the glaze and designs. Some designs unique to English potters also developed.

In Germany and France the ware is known as Faience, and in Italy as Majolica.

Reference: Susan and Al Bagdade, *Warman's English & Continental Pottery & Porcelain*, 2nd Edition, Wallace–Homestead, 1991.

Reproduction Alert: Much souvenir Delft-type material has been produced in the late 19th and 20th centuries to appeal to the foreign traveler. Don't confuse these modern pieces with the older examples.

Apothecary Jar, 4½" h, coat of arms, label, pr **750.00**

Bottle, 10", globular, flared garlic neck, blue and white, stylized baskets of flowers and trailing branches, Liverpool, c1770 .... **500.00**

Bowl, 12", blue and white, bird on flowering foliage and insert, int. with flower spray, yellow rim, band of stylized flowerheads, Liverpool, c1740 . **275.00**

Charger

13⅝", broad cavetto with flowers and geometric dec, bird and flowers in center, late 17th C, one faint age crack **600.00**

21", broad cavetto, plain center, scenes of Chinese at tea, shades of blue, mid 18th C **850.00**

Dish, 13½" d, deep, yellow and lavender flowers, green leaves, Lambeth **700.00**

Ewer, 8½", floral dec, zigzag band, blue, purple, and yellow ochre **250.00**

Figure, 4½" h, cows, polychrome, glazed, Dutch, pr **400.00**

Flower Brick, 5" l, rect, blue and white scene, buildings in landscape on long side, figure in boat on short sides, pierced top with blue dot pattern, four ogee feet, English, c1750 .... **375.00**

Ink Well

4 x 4 x 2", polychrome flowers, white ground **250.00**

4¼", handle, stylized floral dec, multicolored, Lambeth, English, c1700 **350.00**

Dish, blue Oriental design, white ground, English, c1760, 9" d, $285.00.

Jar, cov

9¾" h, birds and flowers dec, marked **650.00**

15¾" h, octagonal baluster, four peacocks on densely dec floral ground, border and cov with lappet band, blue fu dog finial, blue inscribed claw mark, Dutch **400.00**

17¼" h, ribbed octagonal baluster, blue and white, four cartouches with seashore landscapes, two panels with amorous couples, upper border of flowerheads and scrollwork, densely painted ground, lion form knob, inscribed "AL" ... **550.00**

Plate

9"

Blue and white, floral design, late 18th C **185.00**

Oriental motif, yellow rim **250.00**

10¾", floral design, chipped rim ... **350.00**

11¾" d, bust center, polychrome ... **155.00**

Shoe, 6¾", blue and white, high heel, pointed toe, molded buckle, band of trellis pattern ribbon, Bristol, c1760 . **600.00**

Soup Plate, 8¾", blue and white, fisherman on pier, boat, buildings, and trees in background, pine cones and foliage border, Bristol, c1760, pr . . . **375.00**

Stein

7½", blue and white florals, sponged purple dec, pewter lid and base, marked "BP" **450.00**

8½" h, Oriental motif, pewter base and lid, 1719 . . . . **1,500.00**

Tile, Dutch

15 x 10", William II on horseback . . **90.00**

17 x 12", river, boat, and horse scene, manganese **400.00**

Vase, 8" h, floral design, sgd "BP" . . . **275.00**

Wall Plaque, 16½", portrait of lady, flow blue, urn and letters mark, pierced for hanging **400.00**

DEPRESSION GLASS

History: Depression glass is a glassware made during the period of 1920–40. It was an inexpensive machine-made glass, produced by several companies in various patterns and colors. The number of pieces within a pattern also varied.

Depression glass was sold through variety stores, given as premiums, or packaged with certain products. Movie houses gave it away from 1935 until well into the 1940s.

Like pattern glass, knowing the proper name of a pattern is the key to collecting. Collectors should be prepared to do research.

References: Gene Florence, *Collectible Glassware from the 40's, 50's, 60's, An Illustrated Value Guide,* Collector Books, 1992; Gene Florence, *The Collector's Encyclopedia of Depression Glass, Revised Tenth Edition,* Collector Books, 1992; Gene Florence, *Elegant Glassware of the Depression Era, Fourth Edition,* Collector Books, 1990; Gene Florence, *Very Rare Glassware Of The Depression Years,* Collector Books, 1987; Gene Florence, *Very Rare Glassware of the Depression Years, Second Series,* Collector Books, 1991; Carl F. Luckey and Mary Burris, *An Identification & Value Guide to Depression Era Glassware, Second Edition,* Books Americana, 1986; Mark Schliesmann, *Price Survey, Second Edition,* Park Avenue Publications, Ltd, 1984; Hazel Marie Weatherman, *1984 Supplement & Price Trends for Colored Glassware Of The Depression Era, Book 1,* published by author, 1984.

Periodical: *The Daze,* Box 57, Otisville, MI 48463.

Collectors' Club: National Depression Glass Association, Inc., P.O. Box 11123, Springfield, OH 65808.

Reproduction Alert: Send a self addressed stamped business envelope to *The Daze* and request a copy of their glass reproduction list. It is one of the best bargains in the antiques business.

Additional Listings: See *Warman's Americana & Collectibles* for more examples.

AMERICAN PIONEER, Liberty Works, 1931–34. Made in crystal, green, and pink; limited production in amber.

	Crystal	Green	Pink
Bowl			
5½", handled.	9.50	12.00	9.50
8¾, cov.	75.00	100.00	75.00
9", handled	15.00	18.00	17.50
9¼", cov	75.00	100.00	75.00
10¾", console	30.00	40.00	32.50
Candlesticks, 6½", pr.	50.00	70.00	50.00
Candy Dish, cov, 1 lb.	65.00	80.00	65.00
Cheese & Comport	35.00	50.00	35.00
Coaster, 3½".	13.00	15.00	12.50
Creamer, 3½"	15.00	18.00	17.50
Cup & Saucer.	8.50	15.00	12.00
Goblet			
4", 3 oz, wine.	15.00	25.00	18.00
6", ftd, 8 oz, water	15.00	25.00	18.00
Ice Bucket, 6".	32.50	40.00	30.00
Lamp, 8½" h.	55.00	70.00	65.00
Pitcher			
5", cov, urn	110.00	160.00	110.00
7", cov	135.00	175.00	135.00
Plates			
8", luncheon	7.50	12.00	10.00

	Crystal	Green	Pink
11″, handled	12.00	15.00	12.00
Rose Bowl, ftd, flared	—	60.00	—
Sherbert			
3½″.	10.00	15.00	10.00
4¾″.	18.00	24.00	19.00
Sugar, 3½″.	12.00	18.00	15.00
Tumbler			
5 oz, juice	18.00	24.00	18.00
8 oz, 4″.	20.00	25.00	22.00
12 oz, 5″.	28.00	40.00	30.00
Vase			
7″.	55.00	65.00	60.00
8¼″.	60.00	65.00	68.00

CADENA, Tiffin Glass Company, early 1930s. Made in crystal, yellow, and some pink.

	Crystal	Yellow		Crystal	Yellow
Bowl, 6″ d, handle.	10.00	15.00	Oyster Cocktail	15.00	20.00
Candlesticks, pr	25.00	40.00	Pickle, 10″ d	12.50	20.00
Champagne, 6½″ h	17.50	30.00	Pitcher, ftd, cov	185.00	275.00
Cocktail, 5¼″ h	17.50	25.00	Plate		
Console Bowl, 12″ d	20.00	35.00	6″ d.	5.00	8.00
Cordial, 5¼″ h.	30.00	50.00	7 ¾″ d.	7.00	12.00
Cream Soup	15.00	22.00	9¼″ d	27.50	35.00
Creamer.	15.00	25.00	Saucer.	4.00	6.50
Cup	15.00	25.00	Sherbet, 4¾″ h	15.00	22.00
Decanter	—	225.00	Sugar.	15.00	24.00
Finger Bowl, ftd.	12.00	17.50	Tumbler, ftd		
Goblet, 7½″ h	20.00	28.00	4¼″ h	15.00	25.00
Grapefruit Bowl, ftd	17.50	30.00	5¼″ h	17.00	27.50
Mayonnaise, ftd, liner	25.00	36.00	Vase, 9″ h.	25.00	45.00

CORONATION, "Banded Rib," "Saxon," Hocking Glass Company, 1936–48. Made in green, pink, and royal ruby.

	Green	Pink	Royal Ruby
Bowl			
4¼″, berry	—	3.00	4.50
6½″, nappy	—	5.00	7.50

Dogwood, plate, grill, pink, $14.00.

Trojan, sandwich server, yellow, $32.50.

	Green	Pink	Royal Ruby
8″, berry, handled................	—	8.00	10.50
8″, no handles	20.00	—	—
Cup	—	3.50	4.50
Pitcher, 7¾″, 68 oz	—	150.00	—
Plate			
6″, sherbet.....................	—	1.50	—
8½″, luncheon	18.00	3.50	5.00
Saucer.........................	—	1.50	—
Sherbet	35.00	3.50	—
Tumbler, 5″, 10 oz, ftd	40.00	15.00	—

DANCING GIRL, Morgantown Glass Works, late 1920s, early 1930s. Made in blue, crystal, green, and pink.

	All Colors		All Colors
Champagne	25.00	Sherbet	25.00
Cocktail, 6⅛″ h	25.00	Sugar................	40.00
Creamer...............	45.00	Tumbler	
Goblet	25.00	4¼″ h	30.00
Oyster Cocktail, 2½″ h.....	20.00	4¾″ h	30.00
Pitcher	225.00	5½″ h	32.50
Plate		Vase, 10″ h, bud	40.00
5⅞″ d	10.00	Wine, 7¾″ h	40.00
7½″ d	17.50		

DOGWOOD, "Apple Blossom, Wild Rose," Macbeth-Evans Glass Co., 1929–1932. Made in cremax, crystal, green, monax, pink, yellow. Limited production in crystal, monax, yellow.

	Cremax	Green	Pink
Ashtray..........................	—	—	12.00
Bowl			
5½″, cereal	16.00	20.00	20.00
8½″, berry	42.50	60.00	35.00
10¼″, fruit.....................	65.00	120.00	200.00
Cake Plate, ftd, 13″................	145.00	75.00	75.00
Creamer..........................	—	40.00	15.00
Cup and Saucer	18.75	24.00	15.50
Pitcher, 8″, decorated	—	—	125.00
Plate			
6″, bread & butter................	20.00	6.00	6.00
8″, luncheon	—	6.00	5.00
9¼″, dinner	—	—	23.00
10½″, grill, all over pattern	—	12.00	14.00
Saucer...........................	18.00	6.50	4.00
Sherbet, low, ftd	—	40.00	19.00
Sugar, 2½″........................	—	25.75	15.00
Tumbler			
4″, 10 oz, decor.................	—	65.00	20.00
4¾″, 10 oz, decor	—	75.00	30.00
5″, 12 oz decor	—	80.00	35.00

FLANDERS, Tiffin Glass Company, mid 1910s–mid 1930s. Made in crystal, pink, and yellow.

	Crystal	Pink	Yellow
Bonbon, two handles	15.00	20.00	20.00
Console Bowl, 12" d	25.00	35.00	65.00
Candlesticks, pr	50.00	80.00	90.00
Candy Jar, cov	90.00	150.00	165.00
Celery, 11" l	25.00	30.00	35.00
Champagne	15.00	20.00	20.00
Compote, 6" d	65.00	75.00	80.00
Cordial	55.00	75.00	65.00
Creamer, ftd	45.00	65.00	75.00
Cup	25.00	35.00	38.00
Decanter	185.00	200.00	200.00
Finger Bowl, liner	20.00	24.00	24.00
Goblet	17.50	35.00	29.00
Mayonnaise, liner	25.00	45.00	50.00
Oyster Cocktail	35.00	40.00	40.00
Pickle, 7½" l	22.50	27.50	27.50
Pitcher, cov	175.00	200.00	210.00
Plate			
6" d	10.00	12.50	10.00
8" d	12.00	17.50	14.00
9½" d	30.00	40.00	40.00
Saucer	10.00	12.00	12.00
Sugar, ftd	45.00	65.00	70.00
Sundae	14.00	20.00	20.00
Tumbler, 9 oz, ftd	18.00	20.00	24.00
Whiskey, ftd	35.00	65.00	60.00

FLORENTINE NO. 1, "Old Florentine, Poppy No. 1," Hazel Atlas Co., 1932–1935. Made in cobalt blue, crystal, green, pink, yellow. Limited production in cobalt blue.

	Crystal	Green	Pink	Yellow
Ashtray, 5½"	20.00	20.00	25.00	35.00
Bowl				
5", berry	7.50	9.00	10.00	8.50
6", cereal	8.00	8.00	12.00	10.00
8½", master berry	14.00	15.50	22.00	18.00
9½", oval, veg. cov	28.00	27.75	36.00	35.00
Butter, cov	100.00	125.00	130.00	150.00
Coaster, 3¾"	13.00	12.50	21.00	14.00
Creamer				
Plain edge	7.50	12.50	10.00	12.00
Ruffled edge	18.00	17.50	35.00	23.00
Cup	6.00	7.00	7.50	8.00
Egg Cup, 3¼", 4 oz	10.00	19.50	—	—
Pitcher, 6½", 36 oz, ftd	40.00	38.00	55.00	40.00
Plate				
6", sherbet	5.25	7.50	6.50	5.50
8½", salad	5.50	9.00	8.25	12.00
10", dinner	9.00	14.00	17.00	17.00
10", grill	8.25	8.00	9.25	12.00
Platter, 10½", oval	15.00	22.00	16.00	18.00
Saucer	2.00	2.00	3.50	3.00
Salt and Pepper Shakers, pr	27.50	28.00	42.50	55.00
Sherbet	4.50	8.50	9.00	7.50

	Crystal	Green	Pink	Yellow
Sugar				
Plain edge............	6.00	8.50	10.00	11.00
Ruffled edge	13.50	14.00	18.00	21.00
Sugar Ltd	12.00	12.00	15.00	15.00
Tumbler				
3¼", 5 oz, ftd	20.00	20.00	—	—
3¾", 5 oz, juice	8.00	12.00	15.00	14.50
4¾", 10 oz, ftd, water....	12.00	12.00	18.00	18.00
5¼", 12 oz, ftd, iced tea ..	14.00	14.00	22.00	20.00

HEX OPTIC, "Honeycomb," Jeannette Glass Company, 1928–32. Made in green and pink.

	Green	Pink		Green	Pink
Bowl			8", luncheon	4.50	4.50
4¼", berry, small	4.00	4.50	Platter, 11"	8.50	8.50
7¼", mixing	10.00	10.00	Refrigerator Dish, 4 × 4"...	8.00	8.00
7½", berry, master	5.00	5.00	Refrigerator Stack Set, 3		
8¼", mixing	14.00	14.00	pcs	30.00	32.00
9", mixing	15.00	15.00	Salt and Pepper	18.00	18.00
10", mixing	18.00	18.00	Saucer................	2.50	3.00
Butter Dish	50.00	55.00	Sherbet	4.00	4.00
Creamer..............	4.00	4.25	Sugar................	4.00	5.00
Cup	2.50	2.50	Sugar Shaker	75.00	75.00
Ice Bucket, metal handle ...	20.00	24.00	Tumbler		
Pitcher			3¾", 9 oz, flat	4.00	4.00
5", 32 oz	17.00	17.00	5", 10 oz	6.00	6.50
9", 48 oz, ftd	30.00	30.00	7", ftd	5.50	5.50
Plate			Whiskey, 2", 1 oz	5.00	5.00
6", sherbet............	1.75	1.75			

MISS AMERICA, "Diamond Pattern," Hocking Glass Co., 1935–37. Made in crystal and pink, limited production in green, ice blue, and red.

	Crystal	Green	Pink	Red
Bowl				
4½", berry............	—	10.00	14.00	—
6¼", cereal	6.00	13.00	15.00	—
8", vegetable	30.00	—	45.00	300.00
8¾", fruit	25.00	—	40.00	—
10", vegetable, oval	14.00	—	14.50	—
Butter Dish, cov	175.00	—	375.00	—
Cake Plate, ftd, 12"	28.00	—	32.00	—
Candy Dish, cov, 11½"	50.00	—	115.00	—
Celery, 10½".............	10.00	—	20.00	—
Coaster	14.00	—	20.00	—
Comport, 5"	15.00	—	23.00	—
Creamer, ftd	12.00	—	14.00	135.00
Cup	6.50	11.00	17.00	—
Goblet				
3¾", 3 oz, wine	12.00	—	50.00	150.00
4¾", 5 oz, juice	21.50	—	50.00	—
5½", 10 oz, water.......	19.00	—	40.00	150.00
Pitcher				
8", 65 oz	50.00	—	85.00	—
8½", 65 oz, ice lip	55.00	—	90.00	—

Miss America, candy dish, cov, pink, $115.00.

Queen Mary, tumbler, 5″ h, pink, $30.00.

	Crystal	Green	Pink	Red
Plate				
5¾″, sherbert.	4.00	5.00	6.50	—
6¾″, bread & butter	—	6.00	9.50	—
8½″, luncheon	5.00	8.00	13.00	60.00
10″, dinner.	11.00	—	17.00	—
10¼″, grill	15.00	—	19.00	—
Platter, 12½″.	14.00	—	21.00	—
Relish				
8¾″, 4 part	8.00	—	16.50	—
11¾″, round.	20.00	—	125.00	—
Salt and Pepper	20.00	175.00	40.00	—
Saucer	3.00	—	5.00	—
Sherbet	5.00	—	15.00	—
Sugar.	6.50	—	12.00	125.00
Tumbler				
4″, 5 oz, juice.	16.00	—	32.00	—
4½″, 10 oz, water.	18.00	17.00	26.00	—
6¾″, 14 oz, iced tea.	27.00	—	62.50	—

OYSTER & PEARL, Anchor Hocking Corp., 1938–1940. Made in crystal, pink, ruby red, white fired on pink or green interior.

	Crystal	Pink	Red	White with Green	White with Pink
Bowl					
5¼″					
Handled	5.00	5.00	6.00	5.50	5.50
Heart shaped	5.00	5.00	—	6.00	6.00
Round	5.00	5.00	8.70	6.00	6.00
6½″, deep, handled	8.00	8.00	12.00	—	—
10½″, deep, fruit.	14.00	14.00	30.00	10.00	10.00
Candleholder, 3½″, pr	15.00	15.00	30.00	12.00	12.00
Plate, 13½″, sandwich	15.00	15.00	25.00	—	—
Relish, 10¼″, oblong	6.50	6.50	—	7.00	7.50

QUEEN MARY, "Vertical Ribbed," Hocking Glass Company, 1936–40. Made in crystal and pink.

	Crystal	Pink		Crystal	Pink
Ashtray			Plate		
2 × 3¾", oval	2.00	3.00	6", sherbet	2.00	5.00
3½", round	2.75	—	6⅝", bread and butter	3.00	5.50
Bowl			8½" salad	6.00	8.00
4", nappy	5.00	5.00	9¾", dinner	18.00	39.00
5", berry	7.50	5.00	12", sandwich	18.00	18.00
5½", two handles	8.00	22.00	14", serving	18.00	20.00
6", cereal	8.00	20.00	Punch Bowl, ftd, 12 cups	—	95.00
7"	7.00	13.00	Relish		
8¾", berry	6.00	8.00	12", 3 pt	6.00	24.50
Butter Dish, cov	20.00	25.00	14", 4 pt	7.50	26.00
Candlesticks, pr	20.00	—	Salt and Pepper	20.00	85.00
Candy Dish	12.00	15.00	Saucer	1.50	2.00
Celery	5.00	6.00	Sherbet	4.00	6.50
Cigarette Jar	4.00	5.00	Sugar	4.00	6.00
Coaster			Tumbler		
3½"	2.00	2.50	3½", 5 oz, juice	3.75	9.00
4¼", sq	4.50	4.50	4", 9 oz, water	5.00	10.00
Compote, 5¾"	4.50	5.00	5", 10 oz, ftd	12.00	30.00
Creamer	4.25	5.00			
Cup					
Large	3.25	3.75			
Small	3.00	4.00			

TROJAN, Fostoria Glass Company, 1929–44. Made in Rose pink, Topaz Yellow, limited production in green.

	Rose	Topaz		Rose	Topaz
Ashtray	25.00	25.00	Oil, ftd	250.00	275.00
Baker, 9" l	45.00	45.00	Oyster Cocktail, ftd	20.00	20.00
Bonbon	25.00	29.50	Parfait	35.00	35.00
Bouillon, ftd	16.00	16.00	Pitcher	250.00	250.00
Bowl			Plate		
5" d, fruit	15.00	17.50	6" d	6.00	6.00
6" d, cereal	20.00	20.00	7½" d	7.50	8.00
10" d	30.00	30.00	8¾" d	10.00	10.00
Candy, cov	150.00	150.00	9½" d	16.00	16.00
Celery, 11½" l	24.00	24.00	10 1/4" d, grill	35.00	35.00
Centerpiece, 12" d	25.00	25.00	Platter, 12" l	40.00	40.00
Champagne	17.50	17.50	Relish, 8½" d	35.00	35.00
Cheese and Cracker Set	45.00	45.00	Salt & Pepper Shakers, pr	70.00	72.00
Claret, 6" h	40.00	40.00	Sauce Boat	60.00	60.00
Compote, 5"	35.00	25.00	Saucer	5.00	5.00
Cordial, 4" h	65.00	65.00	Sherbet, 6" h	20.00	20.00
Cream Soup, ftd	24.00	20.00	Sugar, ftd	27.50	20.00
Creamer, ftd	27.50	25.00	Sweetmeat	25.00	25.00
Cup	27.50	27.50	Tray, 11" d, center handle	32.50	32.50
Finger Bowl, liner	22.00	22.00	Tumbler, 5¼" h, ftd	16.00	16.00
Goblet, 8¼" h	27.50	27.50	Vase, 8" h	175.00	125.00
Ice Dish	30.00	28.00	Vegetable Bowl, 9" l, oval	75.00	75.00
Lemon Bowl	16.00	16.00	Whipped Cream Pail	100.00	100.00
Mayonnaise, liner	125.00	95.00	Whiskey	49.50	49.50
Mint Bowl, ftd	17.50	17.50	Wine, 5½"	40.00	38.00

DISNEYANA

History: Walt Disney and the creations of the famous Disney Studios hold a place of fondness and enchantment in the hearts of people throughout the world. The release of "Steamboat Willie" featuring Mickey Mouse in 1928 heralded an entertainment empire.

Walt and his brother, Roy, showed shrewd business acumen. From the beginning they licensed the reproduction of Disney characters in products ranging from wristwatches to clothing. In 1984 Donald Duck celebrated his 50th birthday, and collectors took a renewed interest in material related to him.

The market in Disneyana has been established by a few determined dealers and auction houses. Hake's Americana and Collectibles of York, PA, offers several hundred Disneyana items in each of their bimonthly mail and phone bid auctions. Sotheby's collector carousel auctions often include Disney cels, and Lloyd Ralston Toys auctions include Disney toys.

References: Robert Heide & John Gilman, *Cartoon Collectibles,* 1984 (only covers Disney material); Richard Schickel, *The Disney Version: The Life, Times, Art and Commerce of Walt Disney,* Avon Books, 1968; Michael Stern, *Stern's Guide to Disney Collectibles, First Series,* (1989), *Second Series,* (1990), Collector Books; Tom Tumbusch, *Tomart's Illustrated Disneyana Catalog and Price Guide,* Vols. 1, 2, 3, and 4, Tomart Publications, 1985; Tom Tumbusch, *Tomart's Illustrated Disneyana Catalog and Price Guide, Condensed Edition,* Wallace-Homestead, 1989.

Archives: Walt Disney Archives, 500 South Buena Vista Street, Burbank, CA 91521.

Collectors' Club: Mouse Club, 2056 Cirone Way, San Jose, CA 95124.

Additional Listings: See *Warman's Americana & Collectibles* for more examples.

Advisor: Ted Hake.

Alice in Wonderland
  Fan Card, full color, caption "Walt Disney's All Cartoon Feature–Alice in Wonderland," 8 x 10" **40.00**
  Marionette, composition, blue dress, white apron, yellow hair, black felt hair bow, 14", by Peter Puppet Playthings, 1950s **75.00**
Bambi
  Alarm Clock, animated, Flower and Thumper on dial, second hand is butterfly on Bambi's tail, light blue metal case, 2½ x 4½ x 5", orig box, Bayard of France, 1972 . . . . **125.00**
  Bowl, cereal, 5" d, Bambi on bottom, butterfly on tail, flowers, Walt Disney Productions, c1940 . . . . **20.00**
  Figure, glazed ceramic, turned head looking at butterfly on tail, copyright

marked "Walt Disney Productions/ Japan, 2½ x 7 x 6½", c1960 . . . . **30.00**
Picture, framed, "Bambi and Mother," c1940, Courvoisier Galleries sticker, c1940 . . . . **250.00**
Davy Crockett, toy, "Walt Disney's Official Davy Crockett Western Prairie Wagon," red litho tin, full color scene, Mouseketeer symbol on side, orig brown carton with red illus, Adco–Liberty Mfg Co, c1950 . . . . **125.00**
Donald Duck
  Celluloid, Donald Duck as musketeer on the defense, 9¼ x 6¼" **150.00**
  Comic Book Art, orig 8 panel strip, pen and ink by Al Taliaferro, Walt Disney Comics #55, page 29, 19 x 13" **600.00**
  Doll, 16", leatherette, angry Donald, by Richard G. Krueger, c1935 . . . **400.00**
  Planter, figural, sitting on top of ABC blocks, 5½", Leeds, c1940 . . . . . **35.00**
  Toy, wooden, Donald playing xylophone, paper labels, Fisher Price #177, 6 x 11 x 13", c1940 . . . . . . **125.00**
Dumbo
  Figure, 5½" h, Baby Weems, seated, baby bonnet, incised No 41, Vernon Kilns, c1940 . . . . **400.00**
  Sketchpad, 24 ink drawings in sequence, stamped Disney Studios, c1940, 13 x 17" **300.00**
Fantasia
  Celluloid, satyrs and unicorns dancing in pasture, applied to airbrushed ground, Courvoisier Galleries label, sgd "Walt Disney" in pencil on mat, 1940, 11½ x 8" . . . **1,450.00**
  Planter, ceramic, dancing mushrooms, turquoise, high relief on

Mickey Mouse, watch, Ingersoll, orig band with silver dec, 1¼" d, $235.00.

both sides, 12″ l x 7″ w x 2″ d,
Vernon Kilns, c1940 .... **100.00**
Toy, carousel, unicorns, 25″, 1940 .. **225.00**

Goofy
Plate, china, Goofy seated on a crate,
brick wall and flowers in back, cameos of Bambi, Thumper, Flower,
two butterflies, and bluebird around
edge, marked "Beswick, England,
7″ **35.00**
Wristwatch, "Backwards," 17 jewels,
leather band, MIB **350.00**

Mickey Mouse
Bank, treasure chest, red leatherette,
brass trim, emb Mickey and Minnie
on top, marked "Zell Products" .. **175.00**
Button, 1¼″ celluloid, red, black,
white, Good Teeth, Mickey brushing Big Bad Wolf's teeth **65.00**
Game, Mickey Mouse Coming Home
Game, Marks Brothers, 2 x 9 x 20″
cardboard box, 16 x 16″ board,
multicolored **75.00**
Guitar, plastic, 6½ x 21″, yellow front,
large paper label, six plastic
strings, Walt Disney copyright,
c1970 .... **15.00**
Handkerchief, 7½″ sq, small black figure of Mickey in one corner, 1930s **20.00**
Hot Pad, fabric, beige, 6 x 6″, 3″ center stripe depicts Mickey images in
black, white, and red, c1930 .... **25.00**
Painting, Mickey and Minnie on country lane, Mickey pointing to moon,
tempera on card, sgd "Walt Dis-
ney," c1935, 15½ x 10½″ **2,500.00**
Umbrella, two silk screen poses of
Mickey, Minnie on satin–like cloth,
20″ l, Walt Disney Enterprises,
c1930 .... **150.00**

Minnie Mouse
Book, *Minnie Mouse And The Antique Chair,* Whitman, No 845,
hardcover, 5 x 5½″, 1948 ...... **20.00**
Figure
3½″ bisque, playing accordion, orig
label, c1930 .... **65.00**
3½″ bisque, carrying first aid kit,
c1930 .... **50.00**
Mug, Minnie brushing hair, marked
"Salem China" **45.00**

Pinocchio
Celluloid, Jiminy Crickett standing behind the eight ball with fists raised,
titled "I'll Teach You," applied to airbrushed ground, 1939, 10½ x 8″ . **1,400.00**
Plaque, wood, Jiminy Crickett and
Pinocchio seated on Gepetto's sideboard, Blue Fairy holding wand,
brown finish, blue dress, yellow
hair, white wings, and yellow hat, 4
x 5″, c1940 .... **75.00**

Pluto
Celluloid, Sheep Dog, Pluto walking
across desert with bone in mouth,
1949, 9 x 27″ **250.00**
Mug, glazed china, Pluto on one side,
seated Mickey Mouse on other, 3″,
c1930 .... **45.00**
Planter, glazed china, multicolored, 4
x 8 x 6½″, c1940 .... **30.00**
Salt Shaker, glazed china, Disney
copyright on base, 4″ h, c1960 .. **10.00**

**Snow White, dime register bank,
$85.00.**

Snow White
Drinking Glasses, 4½″ h, full figures,
poems on each, set of eight, Libbey, c1930 .... **150.00**
Handkerchief, small image of Snow
White, deer, rabbits, and birds, red,
white, blue, and brown, 8½″ sq,
c1938 .... **15.00**
Pin, molded celluloid, multicolored,
Snow White surrounded by dwarfs
with musical instruments, orig 3½ x
4″ white, blue, and yellow card, pin
1¾ x 2″ **25.00**
Pitcher, glazed china, raised figures,
multicolored, large handle with two
bluebirds and squirrel, music box
base plays "Whistle While You
Work," Wade Heath, England, 7½″
h, 6″ d, c1938 .... **250.00**

Three Little Pigs
Bisque Set, litho box, 2 x 3½ x 5″, top
shows wolf puffing at brick house,
3½″ figures, c1930 .... **175.00**
Plate, glazed white china, color center scene, Patriot China (Syracuse
China Co), 7″ **35.00**
Toothbrush Holder, bisque, pigs
shown with fife, fiddle, and orange
bricks, 2 x 3½ x 4″ **75.00**

Zorro
Dominoes, Zorro on horseback on
back, Halsman, 1950s **35.00**

Lunch Box, litho tin, raised figures,
thermos, c1950 . . . . **75.00**

DOLL HOUSES

History: Doll houses date from the 18th century
to modern times. Early doll houses often were
handmade, sometimes with only one room. The
most common type was made for a young girl to
fill with replicas of furniture scaled especially to fit
into a doll house. Specially sized dolls also were
made for doll houses. All types of accessories and
styles allowed a doll house to portray any historical
period.

References: Caroline Hamilton, *Decorative
Dollhouses*, Clarkson Potter, 1990; Flora Bill Jacobs, *Dolls' Houses in America: Historic Preservation in Miniature*, Charles Scribner's Sons, 1974;
Donald and Helene Mitchell, *Dollhouses, Past and
Present*, Collector Books, 1980; Eva Stille, *Doll
Kitchens 1800–1980,* Schiffer Publishing, Ltd.,
1988; Blair Whitton (ed.), *Bliss Toys And Dollhouses,* Dover, 1979.

Museums: Margaret Woodbury Strong Museum, Rochester, NY; Washington Dolls' House
and Toy Museum, Washington, D.C.

**R. Bliss, lithograph on board, hinged,
two int. rooms, rural 20th C style, 7½ x
11½ x 16¼", $700.00.**

Bliss, Victorian, two rooms, two story,
litho on wood, high steeple roof, dormer windows, spindled porch railing,
second floor balcony, 27 x 18 x 11" . **900.00**
Converse
Cottage, red and green litho on redwood, printed bay window, stone
base, roof dormer, 15 x 17" **400.00**
Red Robin Farm, double barn doors,
six stalls, nine orig animals, cupola
on roof, 1912, 19½ x 17" **425.00**
German
English Tudor, three rooms, cream,
brown trim, yellow recessed section, olive green door, red roof, orig

wallpaper, front opens in two sec-
tions, c1880, 21 x 12 x 17" **650.00**
Victorian style, one room, cardboard,
litho, three sided, hinged, wood furniture, marked "Made in Germany,"
c1880 . . . . **250.00**
Nita Gearhart, house, seven rooms,
wallpaper covered walls, handmade
wood furniture, ten handmade bisque
dolls, 10 x 25", c1976 . . . . **500.00**
McLoughlin, house, folding, two rooms,
dec int., orig box, America, 12 x 17 x
16" **770.00**
Schoenhut
Bungalow, one story, attic, yellow and
green, red roof, orig decal, 12¾ x
11 x 9" **350.00**
Mansion, two story, eight rooms, attic,
tan brick design, red roof, large dormer, 20 glass windows, orig decal,
1923, 29 x 26 x 30" **1,500.00**
Unknown Maker
One Story, four rooms, wood, tiled
green roof, eight pierced glazed
windows, hinged front door, white,
green trim, electrified, America,
c1930, 22 x 53 x 24" **550.00**
Three floors, four rooms, lithographed
paper on wood, pitched roof, fourteen glazed arched windows,
hinged front door, portico, America,
c1900, 18 x 27 x 43" h **880.00**
Two story, ornate, wood, litho brick,
hinged side and attic, two car garage, porch with railings and
benches, windows with shutters
and flower boxes, removable steps,
c1920 . . . . **100.00**

DOLLS

History: Dolls have been children's play toys for
centuries. Dolls also have served other functions.
During the 14th through 18th centuries doll making
was centered in Europe, mainly in Germany and
France. The French dolls produced in this era represented adults and were dressed in the latest
couturier designs. They were not children's toys.

During the mid–19th century, child and baby
dolls, made in wax, cloth, bisque, and porcelain,
were introduced. Facial features were hand
painted; wigs were made of mohair and human
hair. They were dressed in baby or children's fashions.

Marks from the various manufacturers are found
on the back of the head, neck, or back area. These
marks are very important in identifying the doll and
date of manufacture.

Doll making in the United States began to flourish in the 1900s with names like Effanbee, Madame Alexander, Ideal, and others.

References: Johana Gast Anderton, *More Twentieth Century Dolls From Bisque to Vinyl, Volumes A–H, Volumes I–Z, Revised Edition,* Wallace–Homestead, 1974; John Axe, *The Encyclopedia of Celebrity Dolls,* Hobby House Press Inc., 1983; Julie Collier, *The Official Identification And Price Guide To Antique & Modern Dolls, Fourth Edition,* House of Collectibles, 1989; Jan Foulke, *10th Blue Book Dolls and Values,* Hobby House Press Inc. 1991; R. Lane Herron, *Herron's Price Guide To Dolls,* Wallace–Homestead, 1990; Polly Judd, *Cloth Dolls, Identification and Price Guide,* Hobby House Press, 1990; Wendy Lavitt, *American Folk Dolls,* Alfred Knopf, Inc., 1982; Wendy Lavitt, *Dolls,* Alfred A. Knopf, 1983; Lydia and Joachim F. Richter, *Bru Dolls,* Hobby House Press, 1989; Patricia R. Smith, *Antique Collector's Dolls, First Series,* Collector Books, 1975, Updated Values, 1991; Patricia R. Smith, *Antique Collector's Dolls, Second Series,* Collector Books, 1991; Patricia R. Smith, *Modern Collector's Dolls, Editions 1, 2, 3, 4, 5,* Collector Books, 1973, 1975, 1976, 1979, 1984; Patricia Smith, *Shirley Temple Dolls and Collectibles,* Collector Books, 1977, 1992 value update; Patricia Smith, *Shirley Temple Dolls and Collectibles, Second Series,* Collector Books, 1979, 1992 value update; Patricia R. Smith *Patricia Smith's Doll Values Antique to Modern, Seventh Series,* Collector Books, 1991; Patricia R. Smith, *The Collector's Encyclopedia of Madame Alexander Dolls 1965–1990,* Collector Books, 1991; Patricia R. Smith, *The World of Alexander–kins,* Collector Books, 1985; Marjorie Victoria Sturges Uhl, *Madame Alexander, Ladies of Fashion,* Collector Books, 1982; Florence Theriault, *Theriault's Doll Registry Price Guide, Volume III,* published by author, 1988.

Periodicals: *Contemporary Doll Magazine,* Scott Publications, 30595 W. 8 Mile Road, Livonia, MI 48152; *Doll Reader,* Hobby House Press, Inc., 900 Frederick Street, Cumberland, MD 21502; *Dolls The Collector's Magazine,* P.O. Box 1972, Marion, OH 43305; *Doll Collector's Price Guide,* P.O. Box 11302, Des Moines, IA 503401; *Doll World,* International Doll World, P.O. Box 11307, Des Moines, IA 50340.

Collector's Clubs: Madame Alexander Fan Club, P.O. Box 146, New Lenox, IL 60451; United Federation of Doll Clubs, P.O. Box 14146, Parkville, MO 64152.

Museums: Margaret Woodbury Strong Museum, Rochester, NY; Yesteryears Museum, Sandwich, MA.

Additional Listings: See *Warman's Americana & Collectibles* for more examples.

Alabama Doll Co., 22½″ h, rag face, neck, and bust fabric stuffed, neck and bust sewn to torso, ears sewn to head, body, arms, legs, and hands also stuffed, flesh colored waterproof paint, features painted over, painted black shoes and white socks, orig clothes, c1900, marks: "Mrs S. S. Smith Manufacturer and Dealer to The Alabama Indestructible Doll, Roanoke, Ala, Patented Sept 26, 1905" **2,500.00**

Alt Beck Gottscalk
22″ h, solid domed bisque turned shoulderhead, kid body with gusseted joints, bisque forearms, blond human or mohair wig, blue glass inset eyes, closed mouth, well dressed, c1885, marks: 639 Made In Germany **1,150.00**

26″ h, Sweet Nell, bisque socket head, composition wood ball jointed body, brunette human hair wig, gray glass sleep eyes, real lashes, painted features, open mouth, four porcelain teeth, old clothes, c1910, marks: 1362 Made In Germany **875.00**

Arranbee Doll Co.
12″ h, My Dream Baby, bisque solid dome head, painted hair, glass sleep eyes, open mouth, dressed in nice old baby clothes, c1924, marks: A.M. 341 or 351 or ARRANBEE **400.00**

13″ h, Bottletot, all composition, baby body with bent arms and legs, molded painted hair, blue sleep eyes, open mouth, celluloid hands, orig clothes, right holds bottle marked Arranbee/Pat Aug. 10, 26, doll is unmarked **195.00**

16″ h, Nancy, all composition, body jointed at neck, shoulders and hips, molded or mohair wigged hair, painted or sleep eyes, closed mouth, marks: "Arranbee" or "Nancy" **250.00**

20″ h, Debu Teen, all composition swivel head, shoulderplate, composition or cloth body jointed at neck, shoulders and hips, human or mohair wig, sleep eyes with lashes, closed mouth, orig clothes, c1938, marks: "R & B" **250.00**

Averill
10″ h, Topsy & Eva, double–ender cloth doll, hp faces, one black with yarn hair, other white with painted hair, orig polka–dot cotton flip dress, red/white to blue/white, c1930, marked: paper tag, Georgene Novelties **135.00**

13″ h, Rag Dolls, all stuffed cloth heads, bodies, arms, and legs, yarn hair, painted mask faces, orig costumes, c1930, marks: A/GENUINE/(script)GEORGENE/DOLL/A

PRODUCT OF GEORGENE NOV-ELTIES INC. NEW YORK/ MADE IN U.S.A. **135.00**

16½" h, Bonnie Babe, celluloid head, cloth body arms and legs all stuffed but movable, molded painted hair, brown set glass eyes, smiling open closed mouth, two teeth, fine old clothing, c1926, marks: BONNIE BABE/Reg. U.S. PAT OFF/Copyright by Georgene Averill/Germany 34 (turtle mark) **650.00**

19" h, Baby Hendren, composition swivel head, stuffed cotton body, cry box, composition arms and legs, molded painted hair, blue tin decal sleep eyes, painted upper and lower lashes, open mouth, two teeth, nicely dressed, c1930, marks: BABY HENDREN on head **245.00**

23" h, Baby Georgene, composition head, arms and legs, cloth body, curly blond mohair wig, blue sleep eyes, closed mouth, undressed, orig shoes and socks, c1935 .... **3,500.00**

Bahr & Proschild

12" h, Character Baby, bisque socket head, composition baby bent limb body, solid dome, blue glass sleep eyes, open mouth, two upper teeth, well dressed, c1910, marks: BP 585 Germany **525.00**

22" h, Character Baby, bisque socket head, composition baby bent limb body, brunette human hair wig, brown glass sleep eyes, open mouth, two upper teeth, nicely dressed, c1915, marks: BP 585 Germany **775.00**

Belton Type, 14" h, child, bisque socket head, solid flat top with two or three holes for stringing, composition and wood ball jointed body, straight wrists, blue paperweight eyes, closed mouth, pierced ears, nicely dressed, c1875 French style clothing, incised 137 .... **2,700.00**

Bergmann, C. M., 15" h, bisque socket head, composition bent limb baby body, brunette mohair wig, almond shaped small gray glass sleep eyes, open mouth, two porcelain upper teeth, nicely dressed, marks: Simon & Halbig, C. M. Bergmann 612 Germany **1,400.00**

Borgfeldt, George

12½" h, Hug Me Kiddie, round all composition mask face, pink felt body, fleecy brunette hair, inset large round glass googlie type eyes (side glancing), closed watermelon type mouth, pug nose, orig clothes, c1911, marks: paper label **850.00**

24" h, Character Baby, bisque socket head, blond mohair wig, brown glass sleep eyes, open smiling mouth, two upper porcelain teeth, tongue, nicely dressed, c1913, marks: G 327B Germany A. M. .. **800.00**

Bru

13" h, Bru Jne Black Child, dark brown bisque socket head on shoulder plate, dark bisque lower arms, brown kid jointed body, wooden lower legs, brown paperweight eyes, closed mouth, black lambswool wig, nicely dressed in old fabric clothing, "modern" Bru marks: "BRU JNE" **1,478.00**

15" h, Bebe, bisque socket head, composition and wooden body with straight wrists, brown paperweight eyes, painted lashes, black eyeliner, brush stroked and feathered brows, closed mouth, modeled white space between shaded and accented lips, pierced ears, blond mohair wig over cork pate, orig clothing, marks: Bru Jne 5 on both head and body **10,500.00**

16" h

Bebe, bisque swivel head on shoulder plate with molded bosom, orig gusset–jointed kid body, bisque forearms, old french lambskin wig, brown paperweight eyes, painted lashes, black eyeliner, rose–blushed eyelids, softly feathered brows, closed mouth, shaded and accented lips, pierced ears, antique clothes, marks: incised with circle and dot **8,000.00**

French Fashion, very pale bisque swivel neck, wood jointed body, articulated arms, paperweight set eyes, human hair wig, early pierced ears **6,750.00**

Lady Type, bisque shoulderhead, kid body and limbs, closed mouth, pale blue paperweight eyes, pierced ears, blond mohair wig, wooden dome trunk, ten outfits with accessories, hat and stamped shoes marks: BRU JNE et CIE on one shoulder, DE-POSE P on other shoulder, "P" incised on head **4,000.00**

Smiling Fashion, bisque swivel neck, gusseted–kid body, rare bisque BRU hands, mohair wig, blue–green paperweight eyes, closed smiling mouth, orig fashion dress and hat **3,500.00**

17½" h, Bebe, bisque swivel head on bisque shoulderplate with modeled bosom, orig gusset–jointed kid body, bisque forearms, human hair wig, brown paperweight eyes, painted lashes, black eyeliner, rose–blushed eyelids, softly feathered brows, closed mouth, shaded and accented lips, modeled teeth, pierced ears, French styled old fabric costume, marks: circle dot, (early model) **2,625.00**

18" h, French Fashion, bisque swivel neck, sturdy kid body, bisque arms, mohair wig, blue paperweight eyes, closed mouth, early pierced in ears, couture made dress and hat **6,950.00**

19" h, Bru Jne Bebe #6, bisque shoulder head, bisque lower arms, gusseted kid body, wooden lower legs, blond lambswool wig, cork pate, closed mouth, blue paperweight eyes, painted upper and lower lashes, feathered eyebrows, pierced ears, 1880's nicely dressed fine old dress and bonnet **20,000.00**

20" h, Smiling Fashion #G, bisque swivel head shoulderplate, kid body, articulated wood arms, mohair wig, smiling closed mouth, blue set paperweight eyes, pierced ears, orig fashion dress, hat, and marked leather boots **5,300.00**

23½"h
Jne R #10, "mint" Bru Jne body, orig blond human hair wig, big brown eyes, open mouth, gorgeous clothes, old marked Bru shoes **7,500.00**

Cameo Doll Company
10" h, Margie, composition head, wooden segmented spool like body, arms and legs, molded

Cameo Doll Co., Giggle Doll, No. 9613, 12" h, $450.00.

painted hair, painted eyes, nose and mouth, undressed, c1929, marks: red triangular decal label on chest reads "MARGIE Des. & Copyright by Jos. Kallus" **250.00**

12" h, Betty Boop, composition swivel head, wooden segmented spool type arms and legs, molded painted black hair, side glancing eyes, tiny closed mouth, composition torso with molded and painted swim suit, wearing old cotton print dress, c1932, marks: heart shaped label on chest "BETTY BOOP Des. & Copyright by Fleischer Studios" **600.00**

13" h, Black Scooties, all composition, toddler body, jointed at neck, shoulders and hips, molded painted hair, painted eyes, closed smiling mouth, wrist tags **725.00**

15" h, Scooties, all composition, toddler body, jointed at neck, shoulders, and hips, molded painted hair, painted side glancing eyes, smiling closed mouth, undressed, c1925, wrist tags **600.00**

Chase, Martha, 16" h, boy, stockinet and cloth, cloth body jointed at shoulders, hips, elbows, and knees, molded and painted bobbed hair, oil painted facial features, nicely dressed, c1893–1930, marks: Chase Stockinet Doll stamped on left leg, Martha Chase, Pawtucket, Rhode Island **1,000.00**

Daniel et Cie, 26" h, Paris Bebe, bisque socket head, French composition body and wood jointed body, blond human hair wig, amber/brown paperweight inset eyes, closed mouth, pierced ears, costumed, c1885, marks: Paris Bebe Depose 11 Eiffel Tower symbol on body **4,700.00**

Dressel, Cuno & Otto, 7", toddler, bisque socket head, five piece composition toddler body, hair wig, almond shaped blue glass sleep eyes, open mouth, painted shoes and socks, nicely dressed, c1910–22, marks: Jutta 1914 8 .... **550.00**

Effanbee
2½" h, Wee Patsy, all composition, one piece body and head, composition arms and legs, jointed at hips and shoulders, molded and painted bobbed hair style, painted eyes, closed mouth, molded Mary Jane style shoes and socks, orig clothes, pin, and box, c1930, marks: Effanbee Wee Patsy on back **325.00**

14" h
First Patsy, all composition, well de-

fined molded hair, unusual painted eyes glance to side, open closed smiling type mouth, nicely dressed, old fabric clothes, c1926, marks: Effanbee/Patsy . **650.00**

Patsy, composition head and shoulderplate, cloth body with cry box, composition slightly bent arms and legs, rosy knees, molded hair, glued reddish–brown mohair wig, blue–gray tin sleep eyes, open mouth with four teeth, painted rosy cheeks, molded dimples, orig blue and white gingham dress, matching panties, shaded blue silk socks with diamond design, red imitation leather shoes, celluloid Effanbee button, red with gold heart and red silk bow, c1926, marks: Effanbee/Patsy **750.00**

20″ h, Charlie McCarthy, composition head, hands, and feet, cloth body and limbs, painted hair and eyes, open and closed ventriloquist mouth, strings at back of head, orig clothes, top hat, and book, c1937, marks: Edgar Bergan's Charlie McCarthy, An Effanbee Product . . **780.00**

24″ h, Dy–Dee Baby, hard plastic head, soft rubber jointed body, molded painted hair, open drinker mouth, soft rubber inset ears, orig coat and hat outfit, marks: Effanbee/Dy–Dee Baby/U. S. Pat. 1–857–485/England 880–00/France 723–980/Germany 5–85–647/Other Pat. Pending **350.00**

Fulper, 16″ h, toddler, bisque socket head, five piece composition toddler body, short bobbed brown curly tousled hair wig, set eyes, open mouth, nicely dressed, c1918–21, marks: CMU (in triangle) Fulper, (vertically) Made in USA **550.00**

Gaultier, 11″ h, bisque swivel head, kid lined bisque shoulderplate, kid fashion body with gusset jointing at hips, orig hair, blue paperweight inset eyes, closed mouth, pierced ears, well costumed, fancy straw bonnet, c1880, marked: F. G. on side of shoulder . . **1,750.00**

Gaultier and Gesland, 30″ h, bisque socket head, composition shoulderplate, stockinet body with composition lower arms and legs, blond human hair wig over cork pate, brown paperweight inset eyes, closed mouth, dimpled chin, pierced ears, nicely dressed, c1875, marks: F14G, body stamped E. Gesland on shoulder . . **6,250.00**

Greiner, Ludwig, 25″ h, papier mache

shoulderhead, muslin body, brown leather arms, stitched fingers, painted hair, painted blue upper glancing eyes, closed mouth, partially exposed ears, well dressed, c1860, marks: Greiner Improved Patent Heads, Pat. March 30th '58 . . . . **750.00**

Handwerck, Heinrich

20″ h, bisque socket head, composition and wood ball jointed body, brunette human hair wig, brown glass sleep eyes, open mouth, four porcelain teeth, pierced ears, well dressed, c1900, marks: Handwerck 109–11 Germany **725.00**

22″ h, bisque socket head, fully jointed composition body, brown glass sleep flirty eyes, blond wig, open mouth, four teeth, pierced ears, nice old red dress, lace trim overcoat, c1855, marks: Germany, Heinrich Handwerck, Simon & Halbig **550.00**

Hertel, Schwab & Co., 12″ h, bisque socket heat, composition bent limb baby body, blond mohair wig, blue glass side glancing googlie eyes, closed mouth, watermelon smile, well dressed, c1910, marks: 165 . . . . . . **3,000.00**

Heubach, Ernst

14″ h, Character Baby, bisque socket head, composition bent limb baby body, blond human hair wig, blue glass sleep eyes, open mouth, two upper teeth, wobbly tongue, nicely dressed, c1910, marks: Heubach Koppelsdorf 300.14/0 Germany . . **475.00**

23″ h, Child, bisque socket head, fully jointed composition body, brown wig, brown glass sleep eyes, open mouth, four teeth, well dressed, c1888, marks: Heubach Koppelsdorf 250 Germany **525.00**

Heubach, Gebruder, 10″ h, baby, bisque shoulderhead, muslin baby body, composition lower arms and legs, blond forehead curls, blue intaglio eyes, closed mouth, two white beaded teeth, nicely dressed, c1915 **450.00**

Horsman, E. I. and Co., 12″ h, Tynie Baby, solid dome infant head, flanged neck, muslin body, composition hands, blue glass sleep eyes, brown painted hair, pouty type mouth, nicely dressed, marks: copyright 1924 E. I. Horsman Inc., Made In Germany . . **650.00**

Ideal Novelty Co., 13″ h, Shirley Temple, all composition, socket head, composition body jointed at shoulders and hips, blond curly mohair wig, green tin sleep eyes, hair lashes, open smiling mouth, six upper teeth, orig clothing labeled "Genuine Shirley Temple Doll, Reg US Patent Off, Ideal Novelty & Toy Co., Made In USA," orig celluloid fan club pin, c1934, marks: Shirley Temple 13, Ideal on head and body **650.00**

Right: Emile Jumeau, marked "Jumeau 5," $5,700.00; left: Emile Jumeau, marked "Depose E57," $4,800.00.

Jumeau, Emile
  14" h, Tete Jumeau Bebe, bisque socket head, French composition and wood jointed body, brunette human hair over cork pate, blue paperweight inset eyes, closed mouth, pierced ears, orig clothes, c1879, marks: Depose tete Jumeau BTE SGDG4 . . . . **3,600.00**
  18" h, Standard Face, bisque swivel head on shoulderplate, wood body, bisque arms and legs, old wig, paperweight eyes, closed mouth, pierced ears, fashionably dressed, old fabric clothing, c1870, marks: Jumeau Medaille d'Or Paris **5,000.00**
Kammer & Reinhardt
  12" h
    Character Child, bisque socket head, composition ball jointed body, molded painted blond hair, blue painted eyes, closed mouth, blushed cheeks, sailor type suit, c1909 . . . . **32,000.00**
    Character Toddler, bisque socket head, composition bent limb toddler body, voice box, brunette mohair wig, brown glass sleep eyes, open mouth, two porcelain teeth, spring tongue, nicely dressed, c1915, marks: K * R Simon and Halbig 122 28 . . . . . . **1,200.00**
  15" h, Peter, bisque socket head, composition wood ball jointed body, blond mohair wig, painted features,

narrow blue eyes, closed mouth, pouty type, nicely dressed, c1915, marks: K * R 101 34 . . . . **3,700.00**
Kestner
  11" h, Hilda, solid dome bisque socket head, narrow almond shaped gray glass sleep eyes, painted features, open mouth, two porcelain teeth, old white baby dress with lace, c1915, marks: Hilda JDK 237, Made In Germany **2,950.00**
  21" h, Child, bisque socket head, composition and wood ball jointed body, plaster dome, hair wig, blue glass sleep eyes, open mouth, four porcelain teeth, pierced ears, nicely dressed, c1910, marks: Made In Germany 10 1/2 167 . . . . **850.00**
Kley and Hahn, 16" h, Walkure, bisque socket head, jointed composition body, straight wrists, glass sleep eyes, open mouth, nicely dressed, c1925, marks: K + H, Walkure Made In Germany **550.00**
Kruse, Kathy, 15" h, celluloid socket head, celluloid jointed body, blond human hair wig, blue inset eyes, closed mouth, orig clothes, c1958, marks: turtle mark, Modell Kathy Kruse T40 **425.00**
Lanternier & Cie, 18" h, Lady, bisque socket head with adult look, French composition and wood jointed lady body, brunette human hair wig, almond shaped brown glass inset eyes, open/closed mouth, row of molded teeth, pierced ears, nicely dressed, c1915, marks: Fabrication Francasie IL E Cie Limoges **950.00**
Lenci, 20" h, Child, all felt, swivel head, cloth body jointed at shoulders and hips, painted features, side glancing eyes, orig felt and organdy clothes, c1920, marks: Lenci, Made in Italy on cloth and paper tags, also stamped Lenci on bottom of foot **1,800.00**
Madam Alexander
  14" h, Snow White, all hard plastic, five piece body jointed at shoulders and hips, socket head, black saran wig, green plastic sleep eyes, real lashes, painted features, closed mouth, orig tagged ivory satin gown, gold leaf patterned brocade vest, c1952, marks: Walt Disney Snow White Madam Alexander U.S.A. **500.00**
  16" h
    David Copperfield, all cloth, one piece body and head, cloth arms and legs, mitted type hands, molded felt face mask, blond human hair wig, painted facial fea-

Madam Alexander, Dionne Quintuplets, orig costumes, wicker basket, 8″ h dolls, $1,200.00.

tures, brown side glancing eyes, closed mouth, orig blue flannel trousers, black felt jacket and top hat, white shirt and bow tie, orig labels sewn in seams marked "Madam Alexander" and "David Copperfield," early 1930s, marks: Alexander **650.00**

Snow White, all composition, socket head, five piece body jointed at shoulders and hips, black mohair or human hair wig, brown sleep eyes, real lashes, closed mouth, all orig clothes tagged "Snow White, Madam Alexander," c1937, marks: Princess Elizabeth Alexander Doll Co. **500.00**

Marseille, Armand, 20″ h, bisque socket head, composition and wood ball jointed body, blond mohair wig, brown glass sleep eyes, open mouth, nicely dressed in old fabric clothing, c1890, marks: 390 ASM, Made In Germany **375.00**

Mason and Taylor, 12″ h, all wooden, sculpted and painted, dowel body jointed at shoulders, elbows, hips, and knees, spoon shaped hands, all facial features painted, short blond hair, blue eyes, c1880 .... **850.00**

Ohlhover, Gebruder, 20″ h, Baby Type, bisque socket head, composition bent limb baby body, auburn human hair baby style wig, blue glass sleep eyes, real hair lashes, open mouth, two upper molded teeth, nicely dressed in old fabric christening dress, petticoat, and bonnet, c1915, marks: Revalo Germany 22–12 .... **750.00**

Putnam, Grace, 12″ h, Bye–Lo Baby, composition head, stamped muslin frog style body, celluloid hands, flanged neck, painted light brown hair, blue glass sleep eyes, closed mouth, orig tagged Bye-Lo clothing, celluloid

button, c1925, marks: Copr by Grace S Putnam, Cameo Doll Co., New York, N. Y., U.S.A., body stamped Bye Lo Baby, Pat. Pending by Grace S. Putnam **475.00**

Raggedy Ann and Andy

15½″ h, all cloth, movable arms and legs, brown yarn hair, button eyes, painted features, striped fabric stockings and black for socks, orig clothes, marks: Patented Sept. 7, 1915, pr **850.00**

18″ h, all cloth, red yarn hair, painted features, striped fabric and black cloth shoes, all orig clothing, c1938–63, marks: cloth label sewn in side seam of bodies, pr **375.00**

Revalo, 12″ h, Character, bisque socket head, composition body, molded short brown curly hair, molded blue ribbon with rosette trim, gray painted eyes and other features, open/closed mouth, nicely dressed, c1915 ..... **725.00**

Schoenau and Hoffmeister, 21″ h, Child, bisque socket head, composition ball jointed body, brunette human hair wig, brown glass sleep eyes, real hair lashes, open mouth, four porcelain teeth, old fabric clothing, c1901, marks: S (star with PB) H 1909 Germany **550.00**

Schoenhut, 19″ h, Pouty Character Girl, all wooden, spring jointed body, carved facial features, mohair wig, brown painted intaglio eyes, open/closed mouth, painted teeth, metal stand for foot, all orig clothing, celluloid pin, c1911–30, marks: Schoenhut Doll, Pat. Jan 17 '11, U.S.A. incised and paper label **2,050.00**

S.F.B.J.

19″ h, Character Toddler, bisque socket head, French composition toddler body, side hip jointing, socket wrists, blond human hair wig, blue glass sleep eyes, closed pouty type mouth, nicely dressed, c1910, marks: S. F. B. J. 252 Paris 8 .... **7,000.00**

27″ h, Character Toddler, bisque socket head, composition and wood hip jointed toddler body, human hair wig, half moon shaped brown glass sleep eyes, open mouth, beaded upper teeth, wobbler tongue, orig clothes, orig paper label on body, c1915, marks: 21 S.F.B.J. 251 Paris 12 .... **2,800.00**

Simon & Halbig, 38″ h, Child, bisque socket head, ball jointed composition body, human hair wig, open mouth, painted upper and lower lashes, brown paperweight eyes, feathered eyebrows, pierced ears, fancy clothes and bonnet, c1889, marks: Simon & Halbig 1249 Santa DEP Germany 17 **3,100.00**

Steiner, E. U., 16″ h, Child, bisque socket head, kid body with bisque lower arms and legs, blond mohair wig, brown glass inset eyes, open mouth, four teeth, nicely dressed, c1900, marks: E. U. Steiner (in diamond), Made In Germany **275.00**

German, bisque head, dated 1899, head marked "Heinrich Handwerck–Simon & Halbig," 29″ h, $850.00.

Steiner, Jules Nicholas, 15″ h, Le Petit Parisien Bebe, bisque socket head, French composition and wood jointed body, straight wrists, blond human hair wig, cardboard pate, blue paperweight eyes, closed mouth, pierced ears, fine couture costume, c1890, marks: Steiner Paris France A7 on head, body stamped Le Petit Parisien Bebe Steiner Medaille d'Or Paris 1889 . . . . **4,700.00**

DOOR KNOCKERS

History: Before the advent of the mechanical bell or electrical buzzer and chime, a door knocker was considered an essential door ornament to announce the arrival of visitors. Metal was used to cast or forge the various forms; many cast-iron examples were painted. Collectors like to find knockers with English registry marks.

BRASS

Atlantis, head, dolphin, and seashells .	75.00
Bust of William Shakespeare, 4″	75.00
Devil, head, serpent striker ring	40.00
Lady's hand and face, beaded cuff and ringed finger, 6¼″ l	125.00
Oval, ring knocker, monogrammed . . .	25.00
Pheasants	45.00
Sea Horse and seashell	80.00

BRONZE

Grecian head, 4½″	80.00
Hand, ruffled sleeve, 5″	75.00
Maenad's head, fruit vines in hair, 7″ h, Continental, 19th C	385.00

Sam Weller, 3½″ h, $35.00.

CAST IRON

Amish Boy, head	50.00
Betty Boop, figural	40.00
Fox, head, knocking ring in mouth, 5½″	75.00
Parrot, Hubley	125.00
Spider, hanging from web with bee, 3½″ l	100.00
Woodpecker, Hubley	145.00

DOORSTOPS

History: Doorstops became popular in the late 19th century. They can be found flat or three dimensional and were made in cast-iron, bronze, wood, and other material. Hubley, a leading toy manufacturer, made many examples.

References: Jeanne Bertoia, *Doorstops: Identification And Values*, Collector Books, 1985; Marilyn Hamburger and Beverly Lloyd, *Collecting Fi-*

gural Doorstops, A.S. Barnes and Company, 1978.

Reproduction Alert: Reproductions are proliferating as prices on genuine doorstops continue to rise. There is usually a slight reduction in size in a reproduced piece unless an original mold is used at which time size remains the same. Reproductions have less detail, lack of smoothness to the overall casting, and lack of detail in the paint. If there is any bright orange rusting, this is strongly indicative of a new piece. Beware. If it looks too good to be true, it usually is.

Notes: Pieces described below contain at least 80% or more of the original paint and are in very good condition. Repainting drastically reduces price and desirability. Poor original paint is preferred over repaint.

All listings are cast-iron and flatback castings unless otherwise noted.

Doorstops marked with an asterisk are currently being reproduced.

B + H = Bradley and Hubbard.
Advisor: Craig Dinner.

Basket, 11″ h, rose, ivory wicker basket, natural flowers, handle with bow, sgd "Hubley 121″ 135.00
Bear, 15″ h, holding and looking at honey pot, brown fur, black highlights 600.00
Bellhop, black, 7½″ h, carrying satchel, facing sideways, orange–red uniform and cap 375.00
Bowl, 7 x 7″, green–blue, natural colored fruit, sgd "Hubley, 456″ 100.00
Boy
9⅜″, "The Tiger," hands at side, riding outfit, cartoon like eyes, "FISH" on front, sgd "Hubley 269″ 685.00
10⅝″ h, wearing diapers directing traffic, police hat, red scarf, brown dog at side 450.00
11″ h, full figure, Dutch, hands in pocket, blue jump suit and hat, red belt and collar, brown shoes, blonde hair 395.00
12¾″ h, native wearing turban and leopard skin, one hand extended . 500.00
*Caddie, 8″ h, carrying brown and tan bag, white, brown knickers, red jacket 375.00
Cat
*7″, male and female holding each others waist, dressed 195.00
*8″, black, red ribbon and bow around neck, on pillow 125.00
9½″ h, 7″ w, full figure, Persian, sitting, gray, light markings, sgd "Hubley" inside casting 145.00
10½″ l, fireside, full figure, gray, light markings, sgd "Hubley" inside casting 145.00

Child, 17″ h, reaching, naked, flesh color, short curly brown hair 625.00
Clown, 10″ h, full figure, 2 sided, red suit, white collar, blue hat, black shoes 565.00
Cottage
6⅜″ h, three dimensional garden, tan roof, 3 red chimneys, flowers, 2 pc casting, Ann Hathaway 275.00
8⅝″ l, 5¾″ h, Cape type, blue roof, flowers, fenced garden, path, sgd "Eastern Speciality Mfg Co 14″ . . 135.00
Dancer
8⅞″ h, Art Deco couple doing Charleston, pink dress, black tux, red and black base, "FISH" on front, sgd "Hubley 270″ 485.00
11⅛″ h, black woman doing Rhumba, red, yellow, and blue dress, red kerchief 325.00
Dog
Boston Bull
9″ h, full figure, facing left, black, tan markings 100.00
10½″ h, facing right, black, white markings 55.00
Boxer, 8½ x 9″, full figure, facing forward, brown, tan markings 185.00
Japanese Spaniel, 9″ h, black and white, long curly hair, sgd "1267″ . 185.00
Pekingese, 14½″ l, 9″ h, full figure, life–like size and color, brown, sgd "Hubley" 525.00
*Puppies, 7″, three puppies in basket, natural colors, sgd "Copyright 1932 M Rosenstein, Lancaster, PA, USA" 265.00
Wire Haired Fox Terrier, 9 x 8″, full figure, facing sideways, tan, brown markings 90.00
Drum Major, 12⅝″ h, full figure, ivory pants, red hat with feather, yellow baton in right hand, left hand on waist, sq base 265.00
Duck, 7½″, white, green bush and grass 225.00
Elephant, 14″, pulling coconut out of palm tree, natural color 145.00
Fisherman, 6¼″ h, standing at wheel, hand blocking sun over eyes, rain gear 145.00
Fish, 9¾″ h, three, fantail, orig paint, sgd "Hubley 464″ 125.00
Flower
Goldenrods, 7⅛″ h, natural color, sgd "Hubley 268″ 185.00
Jonquil, 7″ yellow flowers, red and orange cups, sgd "Hubley 453″ . . . 150.00
Frog, 3″, full figure, sitting, yellow and green 40.00
Giraffe, 20¼″ h, tan, brown spots, squared off lines to casting 585.00

Girl

8¾" h, dark blue outfit and beanie, high white collar, black shoes, red hair, incised "663" **385.00**

9", French, holding skirt out at sides, hat, sgd "Hubley 23" **125.00**

Sunbonnet, blue hat, pink dress . . **225.00**

10⅞", bathing, yellow and red swimsuits, green and yellow bathing caps under umbrella, "FISH" on front, sgd "Hubley 250" **375.00**

*13¾" h, 9¾" l, white hat, flowing cape, holding orange jack–o–lantern with red cutout eyes, nose, and mouth **850.00**

Petunias and Asters, Hubley, pink, blue, and yellow flowers, green leaves, orange and cream basketweave base, 6½ x 9½", $125.00.

*Golfer, 10" h, overhead swing, hat and ball on ground, Hubley **325.00**

Grandpa Rabbit, 8⅝" h, crouched down, sitting with hands on knees, brown skin, red jacket, white shirt, cream colored pants and collar, watch hanging out of vest **510.00**

Guitar Player, 11⅞" h, flatback, yellow hat and pants, red jacket with green trim and waist band, brown guitar . . **295.00**

Horse, 7⅞" h, jumping fence, jockey, sgd "Eastern Spec Co #790" **175.00**

House

5½" h, 8¼" l, 2 story, attic, path to door, shutters, sgd "Sophia Smith House" **225.00**

6" h, woman walking up front stairs, grapevines, sgd "Eastern Spec Co" **165.00**

Indian Chief, 9¾" h, flatback, orange and tan headdress, yellow pants with blue stripes and red patches at ankles, green grass, sgd "A A Richardson," copyright 1927 . . . . **285.00**

*Kitten, 7" h, 3 kittens in wicker basket, sgd "M Rosenstein, c1932, Lancaster, PA" **335.00**

Lighthouse, 14" h, flatback, green rocks, black path, white lighthouse, red window and door trim **195.00**

*Mammy

8½" h, full figure, red dress, white apron, blue kerchief with white spots, sgd inside "Hubley 327" . . **125.00**

10" h, white scarf and apron, very dark blue dress, red kerchief on head, full figure, one pc casting . . **325.00**

12", full figure, blue dress, white apron, red kerchief with white spots, sgd "copyright Hubley" inside **315.00**

Messenger Boy, 10" h, bouquet in hand, cap, rosy checks, front sgd "FISH" . **335.00**

Monkey, 14⅜" h, hand reaching up, brown, tan, and white **500.00**

Musician, 6⅞" h

Black man playing saxophone, white pants, red jacket **425.00**

Black man playing drums, black paint **385.00**

Old Mill, 6¼" h, brown log mill, tan roof, white path, green bushes **225.00**

Owl, 9½" h, sits on books, sgd "Eastern Spec Co" **235.00**

Pan, 7" h, with flute, sitting on mushroom, green outfit, red hat and sleeves, green grass base **125.00**

Parrot, 13¾" h, in ring, two sided, heavy gold base, sgd "B & H" **215.00**

Penguin, 10" h, full figure, facing sideways, black, white chest, top hat and bow tie, yellow feet and beak, unsgd Hubley **275.00**

*Pheasant, 8½", brown, bright markings, green grass, sgd "Fred Everett" front, sgd "Hubley" back **235.00**

Policeman, 9½" h, leaning on red fire hydrant, blue uniform and tilted hat, comic character face, tan base, "Safety First" on front **625.00**

Popeye, 9" h, full figure, pipe in mouth, white hat, blue pants, black and red shirt, sgd "Hubley, 1929 King Features Syn, Made in USA" **700.00**

*Quail, 7¼" h, 2 brown, tan, and yellow birds, green, white, and yellow grass, Fred Everett on front, sgd "Hubley 459," **245.00**

Rabbit

8⅛" h, eating carrot, red sweater, brown pants **300.00**

15¼" h, sits on hind paws, tan, green grass, detailed casting, sgd "B & H 7800" **445.00**

Ringmaster, 10½" h, full figure, hands
clasped behind back, red jacket,
green pants, top hat 675.00
Rooster
 7", standing, black, colorful detail . .   135.00
 12", full figure, black, red comb, yellow claws and beak 295.00
 13" h, red comb, black and brown tail
  and chest, yellow stomach 325.00
Ship
 5¼" h, clipper, full sails, American flag
  on top mast, wave base, two rubber
  stoppers, sgd "CJO" 50.00
 11¼", three masts, full sail 25.00
Skier, 12½" h, full figure, woman, red
 scarf, gloves, and belt, blue ski suit
 and beret, wood skis at side 385.00
Squirrel, 9", sitting on stump eating nut,
 brown and tan 185.00
Stork, 13¾", white, yellow beak, orange
 feet, black markings, flowers and
 grass 275.00

Storybook
 Huckleberry Finn, 12½" h, floppy hat,
  pail, stick, Littco Products label . .   375.00
 Humpty Dumpty, 4½", full figure, sgd
  "661" inside 285.00
 Little Miss Muffet, 7¾" h, sitting on
  mushroom, blue dress, blonde hair   140.00
 Little Red Riding Hood
  7½" h, 9½" w, sgd "NUYDEA" . . .   410.00
  9½", basket at side, red cape, tan
   dress with blue pattern, blonde
   hair, sgd "Hubley" 385.00
 Mary Quite Contrary, 11⅜" h, blue
  hat, yellow dress and socks, green
  watering can, "Littco Products" la-
  bel 545.00
 Puss in Boots, flat back, head sticking
  out of boot, sgd "Creations Co
  1930" 325.00
Tiger, 8½" h, tan, black stripes, baseball
 bat on shoulder, black base 400.00
Whistler, 20¼" h, flatback, boy, hands in
 tan knickers, yellow striped baggy
 shirt, lips rounded as if to whistle, two
 rubber stoppers, sgd "B & H" 900.00
Windmill, 6¾" h, 6⅞" w, ivory, red roof,
 house at side, green base 95.00
Woman
 8" h, Colonial, sgd "Hubley" 115.00
 8½" h, minuet, one hand on hip . . .   175.00
 8¾" h, peasant, blue dress, black
  hair, fruit basket on head 125.00
 *11" h, flowers and shawl 145.00
 12" h, carrying parasol and hat box in
  left hand, satchel with "Phoebe" in
  right hand, flowered hat 285.00
Zinnias, 11⅝" h, multicolored flowers,
 blue and black vase, detailed casting,
 two rubber stoppers, sgd "B & H" . .   175.00

1727

Dresden
1883-93

Dresden
MODERN MARK

DRESDEN/MEISSEN

History: Augustus II, Elector of Saxony and
King of Poland, founded the Royal Saxon Porcelain Manufactory in the Albrechtsburg, Meissen, in
1710. Johann Frederick Boettger, an alchemist,
and Tschirnhaus, a nobleman, experimented with
kaolin clay from the Dresden area to produce porcelain. By 1720 the factory produced a whiter hard
paste porcelain than that from the Far East. The
factory experienced its golden age in the 1730–
50s period under the leadership of Samuel Stolzel,
kiln master, and Johann Gregor Herold, enameler.

Many marks were used by the Meissen factory.
The first was a pseudo-oriental mark in a square.
The famous crossed swords mark was adopted in
1724. A small dot between the hilts was used from
1763–74 and a star between the hilts from 1774
to 1814. Two modern marks are swords with a
hammer and sickle and swords with a crown.

The Meissen factory was destroyed and looted
by forces of Frederick the Great during the Seven
Years' War (1756–1763). It was reopened, but
never achieved its former greatness.

In the 19th century, the factory reissued some
of its earlier forms. These later wares are called
"Dresden" to differentiate them from the earlier
examples. Further, there were several other porcelain factories in the Dresden region and their
products also are grouped under the "Dresden"
designation of collectors.

Reference: Susan and Al Bagdade, *Warman's
English & Continental Pottery & Porcelain, 2nd
Edition,* Wallace–Homestead, 1991.

DRESDEN

Compote, 4½" h, ftd, gilt beaded banding, floral garlands, gilt scrolls, white
 ground, set of eighteen 475.00
Cup, 3½" d, white, relief prunus dec, two

Spill Vase, multicolored Scottish figure, tree trunk with game as spill holder, blue crossed swords mark, 12¼" h, $1,600.00.

handles, attributed to Boettger, unmarked, 1715 . . . . 250.00
Demitasse Cup and Saucer, floral reserves, blue ground 250.00
Dessert Plate, 9" d, central female portrait, heavily gilt, green ground, marked, c1910, set of 12 . . . . 1,000.00
Ewer, 5½" d, 12" h, flattened oval, maroon bands top and bottom, heavy gold trim, center scene of two ladies and cupid in garden, obverse with four children playing blind man's bluff, ornate gold handle, Wissmann mark, c1890 . . . . 800.00
Figure
7" h, Ballerina, young girl, white and pink lace dress, pink shoes, red hair, applied flowers on dress . . . 225.00
8 x 10½", Gypsy Lady with Goat, seated, sandals, red kerchief, young goat, crown mark 450.00
Jardiniere, 14½" d, painted and transfer print, central cartouche, courting couple in landscape, pale yellow borders, relief floral garlands, gilt highlights, scrolled feet late 19th C 385.00
Loving Cup, 6½" h, three handles, woodland scene with nymph, gold trim 450.00
Tea Caddy, 5¼" h, 3½" w, sq, lacy gold flowers on two panels, scene of courting boy and girl, crossed swords mark, "H" and "Dresden" 175.00
Urn, 12" h, cov, two panels of lovers, garden setting, red ground, floral dec, c1860–1920 . . . . 400.00
Vase
8½" h, portrait scene, cobalt blue ground, raised gold dec, artist sgd 375.00

13½" h, three panels, each with full figure portrait of young lady, marked "Dresden" 525.00

MEISSEN

Bowl, 10" d, gold and pink, raised leaf dec, c1920 . . . . 165.00
Candelabra, five light, shaped sq base, waisted plinth, applied cartouches with arms of Saxony and Poland, putti, seated maiden, floral dec tunic, purple drape, foliate stem spreading as light branch, foliate molded drip pan and nozzle, pink, turquoise, and gilt highlights, underglaze blue crossed swords mark, late 19th C, minor restoration, pr 4,675.00
Coffee Service, cov 10½" h coffeepot, creamer, cov sugar, twelve 6½" d cups and saucers, white ground, foliage gilt highlights, orig fitted case, underglaze blue crossed swords mark, early 20th C 2,750.00
Figure
7½" h, Pluto with pink drape and gilt crown, carrying struggling Proserpine, oval base with molded and applied gilt scrolls, underglaze blue crossed swords, incised and imp numbers, after model by J J Kaendler, c1900 . . . . 600.00
7¾" h, kissing couple, lady in white dress with scattered polychrome floral sprays, white cap, gentleman in gilted purple overcoat, black breeches, shaped oval base with applied flowerheads and leaves, underglaze blue crossed swords mark, iron–red inscribed numerals, imp numerals, after model by J J Kaendler, c1900 . . . . 775.00
8¼" h, cavalier and lady, standing side by side, lady in black dress dec with iron–red, purple, and blue floral sprays, white ruffled neckline and cap, holding fan, gentleman in orange and pale blue coat, dark puce breeches, oval base with applied flowerheads, underglaze blue crossed swords, incised and imp numbers, after model by J J Kaendler, c1900 . . . . 900.00
12" h, Diana, seated on sq socle, quiver at side, white, clear glaze, blue underglaze mark 875.00
Garniture, 12" h centerpiece, Baroque style basket, three applied cherubs with rose blossoms, matching pair of four light candelabra formed as seated women holding infants, similar rose dec, blue underglaze mark . . . 700.00

Plate, 9¾″ d, molded scrolls and flowers, white ground, blue enameled floral sprigs, underglaze blue factory mark	100.00
Soup Plate, floral dec, canceled underglaze factory mark, set of 12	650.00
Sugar Box, cov, 4½ x 3¼ x 3″, oval, yellow tiger, brown rim, rabbit finial, crossed swords mark, c1730	185.00
Teacup and Saucer, Kakiemon style birds and flowers, brown ground on cup, white ground saucer, underglaze blue crossed swords mark, pr	275.00
Wine Bottle Stand, 9″ h, 6¾″ d, flattened ovoid form, scalloped rim, pierced flowerhead and C scroll frieze, molded and painted pink grisalle body, storks and swans, raised shell molded foot, oval base, underglaze blue crossed swords mark, pr	2,750.00

DUNCAN AND MILLER

History: George Duncan, Harry B. and James B., his sons, and Augustus Heisey, his son-in-law, formed George Duncan & Sons in Pittsburgh, Pennsylvania, in 1865. The factory was located just two blocks from the Monongahela River, providing easy and cheap access by barge for materials needed to produce glass. The men, from Pittsburgh's southside, were descendants of generations of skilled glass makers.

The plant burned to the ground in 1892. James E. Duncan, Sr., selected a site for a new factory in Washington, Pennsylvania, where operations began on February 9, 1893. The plant prospered, producing fine glassware and table services for many years.

John E. Miller, one of the stockholders, was responsible for designing many fine patterns, the most famous being "Three Face." The firm incorporated, using the name The Duncan and Miller Glass Company until its plant closed in 1955. The company's slogan was "The Loveliest Glassware in America." The U.S. Glass Co. purchased the molds, equipment, and machinery in 1956.

References: Gail Krause, *The Encyclopedia Of Duncan Glass,* published by author, 1984; Gail Krause, *A Pictorial History Of Duncan & Miller Glass,* published by author, 1976; Gail Krause, *The Years Of Duncan,* published by author, 1980.

Collectors' Club: National Duncan Glass Society, P.O. Box 965, Washington, PA 15301.

Additional Listings: Pattern Glass.

Ashtray	
Patio, chartreuse	12.00
Teardrop, crystal, 3″ d	4.00
Terrace, crystal, 3½″ d	10.00
Basket, Hobnail, pink opal, 5″ h	95.00
Bouillon, Spiral Flutes, amber	14.50

Sanibel, relish dish, divided, pink, 8¾″ d, $25.00.

Bowl	
Canterbury, pink opal, 10″ d, flared	50.00
Caribbean, blue, 9½″ d, deep	95.00
Patio, crystal, 3½″ d, ftd	12.50
Candlestick, Canterbury, blue opal, 3½″ h	30.00
Candy, cov	
Canterbury, blue opal, three parts	75.00
Hobnail, blue opal	125.00
Patio, crystal	35.00
Champagne	
Caribbean, crystal	15.00
Dover, yellow, frosted	8.00
First Love, crystal	14.50
Hobnail, pink opal	22.50
Teardrop, crystal, 5″ h	7.00
Cheese Dish, cov, Sandwich, crystal	100.00
Cigarette Box, cov	
Patio, crystal	25.00
Spiral Flutes, green, silverplated cov	35.00
Coaster, Hobnail, crystal	4.00
Cocktail Goblet	
Caribbean, crystal	24.00
Dover, green	8.00
Hobnail, pink opal	30.00
Cocktail Shaker, Caribbean, blue	175.00
Compote	
Festive, blue, 7¾″ d	75.00
Spiral Flutes, crystal	25.00
Cordial, First Love, crystal	70.00
Creamer and Sugar, Festive, honey	45.00
Cruet, Hobnail, crystal, orig stopper	35.00
Cup and Saucer, Hobnail, crystal	12.50
Goblet, water	
Hobnail, pink opal	35.00
Sandwich, crystal	9.50
Waterford, amber	9.00
Grapefruit	
Puritan, crystal	3.00
Sandwich, crystal, 7″ d	16.00
Spiral Flutes, amber	17.50
Hat, Astaire, crystal	
3″ h	35.00

3¾″ h **45.00**
Iced Tea
  Hobnail, blue opal **30.00**
  Indian Tree, crystal **22.50**
  Sandwich, crystal **15.00**
Jelly, individual, Sandwich, crystal, 3¼″ d **12.00**
Juice
  Astaire, crystal **9.50**
  Hobnail, pink opal **22.50**
  Waterford, amber **7.00**
Martini Pitcher
  Canterbury, crystal **95.00**
  First Love, crystal **145.00**
Mayonnaise and Underplate, Canterbury, crystal **20.00**
Pitcher
  Hobnail, pink opal **275.00**
  Radiance, ½ gallon, sapphire blue, blown **85.00**
  Teardrop, 8½″ h, crystal **75.00**
Plate
  Canterbury, crystal, 7¾″ d **7.00**
  Caribbean, blue, 13½″ d **55.00**
  First Love, crystal, 6″ d **10.00**
  Hobnail, blue opal, 13¼″ d **65.00**
  Puritan, green, 9½″ d **14.50**
  Sandwich, crystal, 7″ d **8.00**
Relish
  Caribbean, blue, 12½″ d, five parts . . **95.00**
  Festive, blue, divided **54.00**
  Indian Tree, crystal, 9″ d, three parts **27.50**
  Terrace, crystal, 10¾″ d, five parts . **27.50**
Salt Shaker, First Love, crystal **25.00**
Seafood Cocktail, Spiral Flutes, green **15.00**
Sherbet
  Caribbean, crystal, low **15.00**
  Georgian, green **9.00**
  Spiral Flutes, green **8.00**
  Waterford, amber **7.00**
Sugar Shaker, Sandwich, crystal **95.00**
Swan
  3″ h, crystal, solid **20.00**
  10½″ h
  Biscayne Green **50.00**
    Chartreuse **50.00**
    Crystal, cutting **225.00**
  12″ h, ruby **50.00**
Sweetmeat, Spiral Flutes, crystal, 4½″ d **10.00**
Syrup, Sandwich, crystal **95.00**
Table Set, creamer, cov sugar, and spooner, Block and Swag, ruby stained **135.00**
Tray
  Canterbury, crystal, clover **15.00**
  Caribbean, crystal, center handle, 8″ d **50.00**
  Hobnail, crystal, 8″ d **10.00**
Tumbler, 10 oz
  Astaire, ruby **15.00**
  Hobnail, pink opal **30.00**
Urn
  Grecian Urn, crystal, 7″ h, handles . **25.00**
  Language of Flowers, 5½″ h **45.00**
Vase
  Canterbury, crystal, 2½″ h, flared . . **8.00**
  Caribbean, blue, 10½″ h, oval **75.00**
  Grecian Urn, crystal, 3¾″ h **12.50**
  Spiral Flutes, crystal, 10½″ h **30.00**
  Three Feathers, pink opal **85.00**
Violet Bowl, Indian Tree, crystal, 4½″ d, crimped top **55.00**
Whiskey, Spiral Flutes, crystal **4.00**
Wine
  Caribbean, blue **55.00**
  Spiral Flutes, green **14.50**

DURAND

History: Victor Durand (1870–1931), born in Baccarat, France, apprenticed at the Baccarat glass works where several generations of his family worked. In 1884 Victor came to America to join his father at the Whitall-Tatum & Co. in New Jersey. In 1897 father and son leased the Vineland Glass Manufacturing Company in Vineland, New Jersey. Products included inexpensive bottles, jars, and glass for scientific and medical purposes. By 1920 four separate companies existed.

When Quezal Art Glass and Decorating Company failed, Victor Durand recruited Martin Bach, Jr., Emil J. Larsen, William Wiedebine, and other Quezal men and opened an art glass shop at Vineland in December, 1924. Quezal style iridescent pieces were made. New innovations included cameo and intaglio designs, geometric Art Deco shapes, Venetian Lace, and oriental style pieces. In 1928 crackled glass, called Moorish Crackle and Egyptian Crackle, was made.

Much of Durand glass is not marked. Some bears a sticker labeled "Durand Art Glass," some have the name "Durand" scratched on the pontil, or "Durand inside a large "V". Etched numbers may be part of the marking.

Durand died in 1931. The Vineland Flint Glass Works was merged with Kimble Glass Company a year later, and the art glass line discontinued.

Bowl
  5″ h, luster glass, opal and blue floral, sgd and numbered **3,250.00**
  9¾″ d, butterscotch, partial silver sgd **315.00**
  11″ d, green swirl swag dec, clear ground, unsgd **150.00**
Candlesticks, 2¾″ h, mushroom, red, opal pulled florals, pale yellow base, pr **660.00**
Compote
  4½″ h, 6¼″ d, blue opal feather dec, yellow–green stem and foot **385.00**

5½″ h, ribbed amethyst, sgd and
numbered **200.00**
Decanter, 12″ h, blue cut to clear, mushroom stopper, unsgd **550.00**
Jar, 8½″ h, gold ground, blue swirl vine
dec **1,100.00**
Lamp Base, 12″ h vase, blue, green,
orange King Tut dec, opal ground,
drilled **360.00**
Lamp, table, 22″ h, ruby red, ribbed .. **550.00**
Mint Bowl, 6″ d, shallow, gold scalloped
rim, sgd "V Durand" **165.00**

**Plate, green, white floral center, 8″ d,
$185.00.**

Rose Bowl, 4″ h, clear, air traps, sgd
and numbered **330.00**
Vase
4¼″ h, blue irid, white leaves and
veining, sgd **660.00**
6″ h
Baluster, Aurene, irid blue, gold
threading, sgd and numbered .. **700.00**
Bulbous, flared top, gold swags on
green ground, gold int., sgd and
numbered **500.00**
6¾″ h
Bulbous, flared top, irid blue, King
Tut design **990.00**
Classical, irid blue, sgd and numbered, rough pontil **500.00**
7″ h, irid amber, intaglio florals, unsgd **150.00**
7½″ h, ovoid, opal cut to ice blue, sgd
and numbered **1,760.00**
8½″ h
Flared rim, butterscotch **315.00**
Fold over white rim, light green,
shiny, sgd and numbered **500.00**
9″ h, flared, bulbous, blue irid, sgd
and numbered **1,540.00**
10″ h
Blue–purple irid design, opal
ground, sgd "Durand" **550.00**
Butterscotch, two amber handles,
blue hearts and vines, sgd **2,100.00**

10″ h, 9½″ d, crackle, ovoid, blue and
white dec, gold ground **1,600.00**
11″ h, sq, gold and green, lily pad dec **550.00**
12″ h, gold irid, green leaves and
veining, sgd **930.00**
13″ h
Clear, green, white pulled feather
dec, sgd and numbered **1,210.00**
Gold mottled ground, clear amber
pedestal base **525.00**
14″ h, crackle glass, alternating blue
irid and frosted panels **550.00**
16″ h, stick, bulbous, irid blue, opal
lily pads and vines, sgd and numbered **2,310.00**

ENGLISH CHINA AND PORCELAIN (GENERAL)

History: The manufacture of china and porcelain was scattered throughout England, with the
majority of the factories located in the Staffordshire
district. The number of potteries was over one
thousand.

By the 19th century English china and porcelain
had achieved a world wide reputation for excellence. American stores imported large amounts for
their customers. The special production English
pieces of the 18th and early 19th centuries held a
position of great importance among early American antiques collectors.

References: Susan and Al Bagdade, *Warman's
English & Continental Pottery & Porcelain, 2nd
Edition,* Wallace–Homestead, 1991; David Battie
and Michael Turner, *The Price Guide to 19th and
20th Century British Porcelain, Antique Collectors'
Club;* Peter Bradshaw, *18th Century English Por-
celain Figures, 1745–1795,* Antiques Collectors'
Club; Geoffrey A. Godden, *Godden's Guide To
Mason's China And The Ironstone Wares,* Antique
Collectors' Club; Geoffrey A. Godden, *Lowestoft
Porcelain,* Antique Collectors' Club; R. K. Henry-
wood, *Relief Molded Jugs, 1820–1900,* Antique
Collectors' Club; Rachael Feild, *Macdonald Guide
To Buying Antique Pottery & Porcelain,* Wallace-
Homestead Book Company, 1987; Llewellyn Jew-
itt, *The Ceramic Art of Great Britain,* Sterling Pub-
lishing, 1985 (reprint of 1883 classic); Griselda
Lewis, *A Collector's History Of English Pottery,*
Antique Collectors' Club; Donald C. Peirce, *En-
glish Ceramics: The Frances and Emory Cocke
Collection,* High Museum of Art, 1988; Simon
Spero, *The Price Guide To 18th Century English
Porcelain,* Antique Collectors' Club.

Additional Listings: Castleford, Chelsea, Coal-
port, Copeland and Spode, Liverpool, Royal
Crown Derby, Royal Doulton, Royal Worcester,
Historical Staffordshire, Romantic Staffordshire,
Wedgwood, and Whieldon.

BARGEWARE

Teapot, 7½" h, allover brown glaze, enamel floral relief dec, imp motto "Mr A. Aldridge, Foleshill 1886," minor nicks **220.00**

Bow, bowl, blue paneled florals, white ground, c1753, 8" d, $3,500.00.

BOW

Bowl, 4½" d, blue trailing vine, white ground, c1770 .... **170.00**
Candlesticks, pr, two birds on flowering branches, dog and sheep on grassy base, wood stand, c1755 .... **1,200.00**
Cup and Saucer, three molded prunus branches, c1735 .... **175.00**
Egg Cup, 2½" h, two half flower panels, powder blue ground, pseudo Oriental mark, c1760 .... **850.00**
Figure
  5½" h, sportsman, seated, gun on arm, tricorn hat, white sq mound base, c1752 .... **310.00**
  9½" h, gardener, puce jacket, underglaze blue hat, turquoise breeches, black shoes, blue, puce, and gilt base, c1765 .... **750.00**
Pickle Dish, 4" l, leaf shape, painted flowers and grapes, molded veins, serrated edge, c1760 .... **140.00**
Plate
  7⅛" d, octagonal, center reserve Oriental island scene panel, circular and fan shape panels of landscapes and flowers border, pseudo Oriental mark, c1765 .... **440.00**
  9" d, Turk's Cap Lily, dragonfly and moths, c1755 .... **850.00**

COALBROOKDALE

Cologne Bottle, pr, 7½" h, raised floral dec, c1820 .... **750.00**
Inkstand, 10" l, floral encrusted, molded asters, leafy ground, scrolling handle, early 19th C **200.00**
Vase, cov, 15" h, pear shape, raised floral dec, gilt rim and cov, flower spray finial, c1840, pr **800.00**

CAUGHLEY

Creamer, 5¼" h, milkmaid and cow scene, marked "Salopian" **180.00**
Custard Cup, cov, 3⅛" d, Oriental river scene, blue printed buildings **25.00**
Jug, 7¼" h, cabbage leaf mold, gilt entwined "JPM" in oval gilt and blue cartouche, gilt and blue flowers from pink ribbon swags, mask spout, c1795 .... **290.00**
Tea Caddy, 5¼" h, blue printed bouquets and butterflies, c1770 ...... **70.00**

DERBY

Butter Dish, cov, 7" d, blue, iron–red, and gilt, flowering scrolling foliage bands, matching stand, c1800, pr .. **250.00**
Figure, 8" h and 8½" h, pastoral, boy resting against tree stump playing bagpipe, black hat, bleu–du–roi jacket, gilt trim, butter yellow breeches, girl with green hat, bleu–du–roi bodice, pink skirt, white apron with iron–red flowerheads, gilt centers, leaves, scroll molded mound base, crown and incised iron–red D mark, pr **2,000.00**
Jar, cov, 22" h, octagonal, iron red, bottle green, and leaf green, alternating cobalt blue and white grounds, gilding, grotesque sea serpent handles, now fitted as lamp with carved base, 19th C, pr **10,000.00**
Plaque, cluster of fruit, carved giltwood frame, c1830, pr **2,000.00**

FLIGHT, BARR, & BARR

Crocus Pot, 9" w, 4" d, 6¼" h, D form, molded columns and architrave, peach ground panels, ruined abbey landscape reserve, gilding **2,200.00**
Pastille Burner, 3½" h, cottage, four open chimneys, marked, c1815 .... **400.00**
Plate, 8" d, armorial, iron–red, gold, blue, and black arms and crest, Abbot quartering Bryan impaling Harris quartering another, iron–red and gray mantling, pink banderole, motto "Toujours Prest," gilt edged rim and salmon ground border, incised letter mark, crowned and plumed brown "Barr Flight & Barr Royal Porcelain Works, Worcester" oval mark, c1804–09 .... **975.00**

HICKS, MEIGH & JOHNSON

Sugar, cov, 8¼" d, printed and painted transfer, famille rose type dec, gilted, molded rim, handles, and finial, stand, c1860, pr **425.00**

Tureen, 11" l, octagonal, flaring rim, applied acanthus tip handle, underglaze blue and white, gilt, iron–red, dark red, and underglaze blue flower-heads, scrolling foliage, and vases, c1813–30 . . . . **350.00**

JACKFIELD

Creamer, 4¼" h, bulbous, emb grapes design, leaves, and tendrils, gilt high-lights, three paw feet, ear shape handle **150.00**

Sugar, cov, 4½" h, 3¾" d, scalloped SS rims, SS mounted cov and ornate pierced finial **225.00**

Teabowl and Saucer, plain **100.00**

LOWESTOFT

Coffeepot, cov, 9" h, dark blue, under-glaze river scene, Chinese man fish-ing, trellis diaper border, c1770–75 . **910.00**

Demitasse Cup and Saucer, blue un-derglaze **120.00**

Milk Jug, 3¼" h, dark blue underglaze, Chinese river scene, diaper border, brown rim, c1775 . . . . **200.00**

MASONS

Creamer, 4" h, Oriental style shape, marked "Mason's Patent Ironstone" **75.00**

Dessert Dish, Oriental floral dec, c1830 **50.00**

Ice Cooler, 14½" h, straight sides, two applied molded twig form handles, liner with dished gilt rimmed border, fluted high domed cov, inverted pear shaped knob, underglaze blue and enamel iron–red and gold florals, fo-liage, and vase shapes, imp "Ma-son's Patent Ironstone China," pr . . **2,750.00**

Jug, 8" h, octagonal, Hydra pattern, wa-isted straight neck, green enameled handle, lion head terminal, under-glaze blue and iron–red flowers and vase, two imp marks and printed rounded crown mark, c1813–30 . . . **300.00**

Platter, 13½ x 10¾", Double Landscape pattern, Oriental motif, deep green and brick red, c1883 . . . . **250.00**

Potpourri Vase, cov, pr, 25¼", hexago-nal body, cobalt blue, large gold styl-ized peony blossom, chrysanthe-mums, prunus, and butterflies, gold

and blue dragon handles and knobs, trellis diaper rim border, c1820–25 . . **1,650.00**

Punch Bowl, 14⅛" h, ironstone, famille rose type dec, c1825 . . . . **825.00**

NEW HALL

Creamer, Chinese figure on terrace, c1790 . . . . **170.00**

Dessert Set, two oval dishes, eight plates, bat printed and colored named views, lavender–blue borders, light blue ground, c1815 . . . . **425.00**

Dish, deep blue underglaze, orange flowers and leaves dec, gilt, c1825 . **120.00**

Sugar, cov, multicolored bands of flow-ering foliage, puce rims, two handles, c1790 . . . . **125.00**

Tea Set, 44 pcs, interwoven ribbon and leaf trails, blue and gilt oval medal-lions border, minor repairs, c1790 . . **1,450.00**

PLYMOUTH

Cream Jug, 3½" h, painted bouquets and sprays, iron–red loop and line rim, c1768 . . . . **265.00**

Creamboat, 4⅛" h, scroll edged puce outlined side panels, painted cockerel and peacock landscapes, molded ro-coco shape, spur handle **295.00**

Figure, 7½" h, two putti and goat, seated by flowering tree stump, yel-low, iron–red, and blue flowers, scroll molded base, c1770 . . . . **250.00**

Mug, 6½" w, blue painted Oriental land-scape, formal rim border, bell shape, c1769 . . . . **450.00**

WOODS

Bust, 15⅜" h, Sir Issac Newton, gray hair, brown drape, waisted rect mar-bled green and pink socle, c1800 . . **475.00**

Coffeepot, 9⅝" h, cauliflower form, overlapping leaves, green glaze, foli-age molded spout and handle, c1770 **375.00**

Dish, 8" l, 6" w, dark blue transfer of castle, imp "Wood" **150.00**

Figure, 7¼" h, squirrel, seated on haunches, eating nut, splashed man-ganese and yellow, grass mound base, c1760 . . . . **2,550.00**

Jug, 5¾" h, ovoid, cameos of Queen
  Caroline, pink luster ground, beaded
  edge, molded and painted floral bor-
  der, c1820 . . . . **395.00**
Plate, 10" d, blue feather edge, marked
  "E Wood & Sons" **55.00**
Stirrup Cup, 5½" l, modeled hound's
  head, translucent shades of brown,
  c1760 . . . . **1,900.00**
Whistle, 3⅞" h, modeled as seated
  sphinx, blue accents, oval green
  base, c1770 . . . . **500.00**

ENGLISH SOFTPASTE

History: Between 1820 and 1860 a large number of potteries in England's Staffordshire district
produced decorative wares with a soft earthenware (creamware) base and a plain white or yellow
glazed ground.

Design or "stick" spatterware was created by a
cut–sponge (stamp), hand painting, or transfer.
Blue was the dominant color. The earliest patterns
were carefully arranged geometrics and generally
covered the entire piece. Later pieces had a decorative border with a center motif, usually a tulip.
In the 1850s Elsmore and Foster developed the
Holly Leaf pattern.

King's Rose features a large, cabbage–type
rose in red, pale red, or pink. The pink rose often
is called "Queen's Rose." Secondary colors are
pastels of yellow, pink, and occasionally green.
The borders vary: a solid band, vined, lined, or
sectional. The King's Rose exists in an oyster motif.

Strawberry China ware comes in three types:
strawberries and strawberry leaves (often called
strawberry luster), green feather–like leaves with
pink flowers (often called cut–strawberry, primrose, or old strawberry), and a third type with the
decoration in relief. The first two types are characterized by rust red moldings. Most pieces have
a creamware ground. Davenport was one of the
many potteries who made this ware.

Yellow–glazed earthenware (canary luster) has
a canary yellow ground, transfer design which is
usually in black, and occasional luster decoration.
The earliest pieces date from the 1780s and have
a fine creamware base. A few hand painted pieces
are known. Not every piece has luster decoration.

Marked pieces are uncommon. Because the
ground is softpaste, the ware is subject to cracking
and chipping. Enamel colors and other types of
decoration do not hold well. It is not unusual to
see a piece with the decoration worn off.

Reference: Susan and Al Bagdade, *Warman's
English & Continental Pottery & Porcelain*, 2nd
Edition, Wallace–Homestead, 1991.

Additional Listings: Adams Rose, Gaudy
Dutch, Salopian Ware, Staffordshire Items.

DESIGN SPATTERWARE

Bowl, 7½" d, 4" h, polychrome stripes . **75.00**
Creamer, 4⅜" h, Gaudy Floral pattern,
  red, green, blue, and black, marked
  "Baker & Co, England" **65.00**
Cup and Saucer
  Floral pattern, red, blue, green, and
    black **45.00**
  Peony, red and green **175.00**
Jug
  5½" h, Holly Leaf, red and green . . . **150.00**
  7" h, barrel shape, blue, rosettes and
    fern prongs **180.00**
Pitcher, 10¾" h, red, green, and purple
  floral wreaths, red borders **160.00**
Plate, 8½" d, red and blue flower center,
  green leaves, black stick spatter bor-
  der **175.00**
Platter, 15⅝" l, Rosebud and Thistle
  pattern, red stripe and columbine,
  green spatter **235.00**
Sugar, cov, 5" h, white, blue, and red
  flowers, green leaves, closed ring and
  shell handles **100.00**
Teapot, cov, rose dec, pink and blue . **200.00**

**King's Rose, plate, pink border, 6½" d,
$45.00.**

KING'S ROSE

Coffeepot, pink, green, yellow, and red
  dec **800.00**
Creamer, helmet shape, brick red rose **225.00**
Cup and Saucer, handleless
  Applied yellow, red, pink, and green
    enamel dec **100.00**
  Line border, minor enamel wear . . . **130.00**
Plate
  6½" d, yellow puff balls, vine border **140.00**
  8⅜" d, emb feather edge border, red,
    green, brick–red, and yellow center
    flower dec, imp "Rogers" **75.00**

8⅞" d, brown and purple stick spatter, green stripes 65.00
Soup Plate, 9¼" d, broken band border, puff balls 145.00
Sugar, scalloped rim, ribbed, vine border, pink rose 165.00
Teapot Caddy, 8¼" h, enameled red, green, blue, and purple flowers, rust line border 50.00
Teapot, Queen Anne shape, minor chips on cov 450.00

STRAWBERRY CHINA

Bowl, 4" d 150.00
Cup and Saucer, pink border, scalloped edge 220.00
Plate
  5¾" d, strawberry center, strawberry and vine border, chipped 60.00
  8¼" d, Cut Strawberry 190.00
Relish Dish, 8¾" d, shell shape 120.00
Sugar, cov, raised strawberries, strawberry knob 130.00
Teabowl and Saucer, vine border 225.00
Vegetable Dish, cov, octagonal 375.00

Yellow–Glazed Earthenware, pitcher, iron–red and silver luster florals, canary ground, silver luster rim and handle, Staffordshire, c1810, 4¾" h, $475.00.

YELLOW GLAZED EARTHENWARE

Creamer, 4½" h, canary band, white reserves, rust transfers of woman and child playing badminton and writing, green and blue enamels, copper luster body 65.00
Jug
  4½" h, silver luster, round medallion of Peace as young girl 360.00
  5½" h, black transfer, canary ground,

silver luster banding and roundels with Hope and Charity, c1810 . . . 250.00
Mug, 2½" h, red transfer, children and beehive, purple luster band, canary ground 120.00
Pitcher
  5½" h, black transfer, Sir Francis Burdett, silver luster roundel, canary ground, c1835 . . . . 950.00
  6¾" h, russet transfer of mother and child in garden, "Token on Love," border molded with animals, early 19th C 300.00
Plate, 8½" d, red center transfer scene, molded acanthus border, imp "Wood" 275.00
Waste Bowl, 5⅜" d, 2⅞" h, red and green floral dec, emb floral rim 250.00

FAIRINGS, MATCH–STRIKERS, AND TRINKET BOXES

History: Fairings are small, charming china objects which were purchased or given away as prizes at English fairs in the 19th century. Although fairings are generally identified with England, they actually were manufactured in Germany by Conte and Boehme of Possneck.

Fairings depicted an amusing scene either of courtship and marriage, politics, war, children, and animals behaving as children. Over four hundred varieties have been identified. Most fairings bore a caption. Early examples, 1860–70, were of better quality than later ones. After 1890 the colors became more garish, and gilding was introduced.

The manufacturers of fairings also made match–strikers and trinket boxes. Some were captioned. The figures on the lids were identical to those of the fairings. The market for the match–strikers and trinket boxes was identical to that for the fairings.

Reference: Susan and Al Bagdade, *Warman's English & Continental Pottery & Porcelain, 2nd Edition,* Wallace–Homestead, 1991.

Advisors: Barbara and Melvin Alpren.

FAIRINGS

After the Race, cats in a basket 200.00
Five O'Clock Tea, group of cats 200.00
God Save The Queen, children singing around piano 350.00
Opportunity Creates Thieves, child and pig 150.00
Peep Through A Telescope, sailor and child 150.00
You Dirty Boy, mother scrubbing boy's ears 200.00

MATCH–STRIKERS

Button Hole Sir?, young lady flower seller 300.00

Dresser Box, "Paddling His Own Canoe," white, gold trim, green, 2¾" w, 2" d, 4⅛" h, $250.00.

Penny Please, Sir?, young lad match seller	275.00
Safe Messenger, dog carrying basket	275.00
Two children and teacher	200.00

TRINKET BOXES

Clock and anchor on dresser	175.00
Paddling His Own Canoe, child on dresser in canoe	250.00
Pins Madame?, dog in a cape	250.00
Swansea to Bristol, train engine	250.00
Windsor Castle	200.00

FAIRY LAMPS

History: Fairy lamps, originating in England in the 1840s, are candle burning night lamps. They were used in nurseries, hallways, and dim corners of the home.

Two leading candle manufacturers, the Price Candle Company and the Samuel Clarke Company, promoted fairy lamps as a means to sell candles. Both contracted with other manufacturers of glass, porcelain, and metal to produce the needed shades and cups. For example, Clarke used Worcester Royal Porcelain Company, Stuart & Sons, and Red House Glass Works in England, plus firms in France and Germany. Clarke's trademark was a small fairy with a wand surrounded by the words "Clarke Fairy Pyramid, Trade Mark."

Fittings were produced in a wide variety of styles. Shades ranged from pressed to cut glass, from Burmese to Nailsea. Cups are found in glass, porcelain, brass, nickel, and silver plate.

American firms selling fairy lamps included Diamond Candle Company of Brooklyn, Blue Cross Safety Candle Co., and Hobbs-Brockunier of Wheeling, West Virginia.

Fairy lamps are found in two pieces (cup and shade) and three pieces (cup with matching shade and saucer). Married pieces are common.

References: John F. Solverson, *Those Fascinating Little Lamps*, Antique Publications, 1988; John F. Solverson (comp.), *Those Fascinating Little Lamps, Miniature Lamps Value Guide*, Antique Publications, 1988.

Reproduction Alert: Reproductions abound.

Spatter, orange, red, yellow, and white, Clarke sgd clear base, 4½" h, $135.00.

Bisque, 4" h, figural, owl, cat, and dog, glass eyes, clear candle cup marked "Clarke"	250.00
Burmese, 7" h, salmon pink shaded to yellow, acid finish, matching ruffled base marked "Clarke's Patent Fairy Lamps," clear candle cup marked "Clarke," brass frame with two scrolling arms	750.00
Cranberry	
4½" h, crown shape overshot shade, clear base marked "Clarke," made for Queen Victoria's 50th Jubilee in 1887	200.00
5½" h, frosted cranberry verre moire dome shade, matching ruffled base, clear candle cup marked "Clarke"	500.00
Nailsea	
4" h, red verre moire dome shade, red base, clear glass candle cup marked "S Clarke's Pyramid Trade Mark" and "C W S Night Light"	485.00
5¼" h, cranberry frosted verre moire with white loopings, clear glass base marked "Clarke"	200.00
6½" h	
Blue verre moire, white loopings, dome shape shade, triangular	

shape base with three pinched folds, clear glass candle cup marked "S Clarke Patent Trade Mark Fairy" **845.00**

Red verre moire, white loopings, dome shape shade, six pinched pleated bowl shape base, clear glass candle cup marked "Clarke Fairy Patent Trade Mark" **850.00**

Overshot, 3½" h, yellow swirl, cased, clear glass base marked "Clarke" .. **115.00**

Peachblow, Thomas Webb & Sons

3¾" h, green leaf dec, clear glass base marked "Clarke" **400.00**

3⅞" h, cream lining, acid finished rose shaded pink, black lacy flower and leaf dec, clear base marked "Clarke," gold–washed metal stand **325.00**

Rose Mother–Of–Pearl, 3¾" h, clear glass base marked "S Clarke Fairy Pyramid" **385.00**

Sapphire Blue, 4⅝" h, DQ, melon ribbed, clear base marked "Clarke" . **170.00**

Satin

3⅝" h, apple green opaque shade, emb Swirl pattern, clear base marked "Clarke" **135.00**

5½" h, raspberry pink shade cased with white, matching base with turned down ruffled edge, clear glass candle cup insert **375.00**

6" d, lavender ruffled dome top, three gold inset jeweled medallions, ruffled base **330.00**

7½" h, shaded cased pink satin shade and base, house shaped shade with molded roof, bricks, and windows, up turned ruffled base, crystal holder, small candle cup **955.00**

Spatter, 5½" h, white spatter, chartreuse cased in crystal ground, swirled rib mold, heavy applied crystal feet and base trim, crystal candle cup **580.00**

FAMILLE ROSE

History: Famille Rose is Chinese export enameled porcelain in which the pink color predominates. It was made primarily in the 18th and 19th centuries. Other porcelains in the same group are Famille Jaune (yellow), Famille Noire (black), and Famille Verte (green).

Decorations include courtyard and home scenes, birds, and insects. Secondary colors are yellow, green, blue, aubergine, and black.

Mid to late 19th century Chinese export wares similar to Famille Rose are identified as Rose Canton, Rose Mandarin, and Rose Medallion.

Reference: Sandra Andacht, *Oriental Antiques & Art: An Identification And Value Guide,* Wallace-Homestead, 1987.

Jar, cov, botan, kika design, imitating cloisonne ground, surrounding fan shaped reserves of rooster and flowers, 5½" h, $185.00.

Bowl

8" d

Center floral reserve, figural dec ext. **100.00**

Scalloped, floral dec, yellow ground **220.00**

10" d, floral and scrolled border int., figural cartouche on gilt ground ext., 19th C **600.00**

11½" d, bouquet of flowers int., floral chain, elaborate rim borders, floral trellis ext. band and border, late 18th C **1,000.00**

Box, cov, pr, 4½" d, figural and floral dec **100.00**

Brush Washer, 7½" l, lotus pad shape, ducks, lotus blossoms, and pads int., 19th C **625.00**

Charger, 12" d, central figural dec, brocade border **250.00**

Creamer, cov, pear shape, ladies and child at play with landscape scene, Qianlong **410.00**

Dish, 8½" l, oval, central figural garden scene, foliated piercework basketry rim, multicolored flowers **700.00**

Garden Seat, 18¾" h, hexagonal, animals and cranes beneath ruyi borders with bats and fruit, pierced top and sides **1,800.00**

Ginger Jar, cov, 8½" h, cockerel and floral dec **110.00**

Jar, cov, pr

12" h, pseudo tobacco leaf dec, mounted as lamps **550.00**

18½" h, ovoid, scattered peony sprays and flowers, peacocks and exotic birds on rockwork, cloud collar band, domed lid, c1900 ..... **2,475.00**

Jardiniere, 21½" h, ovoid, continuous scene of maidens on pavilion terrace with landscape scene, lappet band at neck, stiff leaf lappets around base,

flattened rim with scrolling lotus tendril dec **330.00**
Mug, 5" h, Mandarin Palette, Quianlong, 1790 .... **425.00**
Plate, 10" d, pr, floral dec, ribbed body, Tongzhi mark **275.00**
Sauce Boat, 7" l, Meissen style harbor scene, c1750 .... **600.00**
Tea Caddy, 5½" h, Mandarin Palette, arched rect form, painted front, figures and pavilion reverse, c1780 ... **550.00**
Tea Service, 37 pcs, Millefleur pattern, teapot, cov sugar, creamer, six dessert plates, coffee cups, and saucers, eight tea cups and saucers **1,000.00**
Teapot, 4½" h, cov, drum form, floral dec, sepia garland with flowers on shoulder and cov, strawberry finial, c1790 .... **770.00**
Tray, 8" l, pr, oval, multicolored center armorial arms, underglaze blue diaper and trefoil borders, reticulated rim, late 18th C **1,000.00**
Tureen, 15" l, pr, goose form, relief feathers, detailed feet, neck, and iron red beak **1,500.00**
Umbrella Stand, medallions with hunting scenes surrounded by gilt scrolling foliate dec, black ground **275.00**
Vase
6½" h
Bird perched on flowering prunus tree dec **115.00**
Bottle form, figural dec **100.00**
10" h, bird in flowering tree dec, Rouleau **200.00**
16⅝" h, baluster form, trumpet neck, eight flowering chrysanthemum branches, pale yellow, blue, violet, and iron–red blooming flowers, six–character Guangxu mark **1,210.00**
17½" h, sq sectioned bottle, each face dec with seasonal flowers, brilliant enamels, shiny black ground, 19th C **1,300.00**

FENTON GLASS

History: The Fenton Art Glass Company began as a cutting shop in Martins Ferry, Ohio, in 1905. In 1906 Frank L. Fenton started to build a plant in Williamstown, West Virginia, and produced the first piece of glass in 1907. Early production included carnival, chocolate, custard, and pressed plus mold blown opalescent glass. In the 1920s stretch glass, Fenton dolphins, jade green, ruby, and art glass were added.

In the 1930s boudoir lamps, "Dancing Ladies," and various slags were produced. The 1940s saw crests of different colors being added to each piece by hand. Hobnail, opalescent, and two–color overlay pieces were popular items. Handles were added to different shapes, making the baskets they created as popular today as then.

Through the years Fenton has added beauty to their glass by decorating it with hand painting, acid etching, color staining, and copper wheel cutting. Several different paper labels have been used. In 1970 an oval raised trademark also was adopted.

References: Shirley Griffith, *A Pictorial Review Of Fenton White Hobnail Milk Glass,* published by author, 1984; William Heacock, *Fenton Glass: The First Twenty–Five Years,* O–Val Advertising Corp, 1978; William Heacock, *Fenton Glass: The Second Twenty–Five Years,* O–Val Advertising Corp, 1980; William Heacock, *Fenton Glass: The Third Twenty–Five Years,* O–Val Advertising Corp., 1989.

Collectors' Club: Fenton Art Glass Collectors Of America, Inc, P. O. Box 384, Williamstown, WV 26187.

Additional Listings: Carnival Glass.

Ashtray
Hobnail, French opalescent, fan ... **35.00**
Jade, ftd **10.00**
Basket
Hobnail
Blue opalescent, 7" h **50.00**
Cranberry opalescent, 4" h **85.00**
Jade **110.00**
Peach Crest, white milk glass handle, 7 x 5" **60.00**
Silver Crest, 7" h **40.00**
Bonbon
Hobnail, yellow opalescent **25.00**
Swan, green **20.00**
Bone Dish, Hobnail, yellow opalescent, crescent **35.00**
Boot, high, blue **15.00**
Bowl
Flame, rolled brim, 10" d **95.00**
Ming Green, 9" octagonal bowl, 15" d liner, c1935 .... **350.00**
Silver Crest, turquoise, crimped ... **9.00**
Cake Plate, ftd, 13" d
Hobnail, yellow opalescent **135.00**
Silver Crest **35.00**
Candlesticks, pr
Alpine, blue, two lite **175.00**
Flame, 8" h **125.00**
Ivory Crest, cornucopia style **40.00**
Venetian, Chinese red, 8¾" h **150.00**
Candy Dish, cov
Commemorative, crystal, 1976 .... **45.00**
Lambs tongue, green pastel **70.00**
Cologne stopper, Silver Crest, Charleston dec, 7" h, pr **75.00**
Compote, ftd
Silver Crest, turquoise, #7228 .... **24.00**
Silver Crest, Violet in Snow, 7" d ... **30.00**
Console Set, Ming Rose, cornucopia candlesticks, 12" oval bowl **115.00**

Creamer and Sugar, Hobnail, blue opalescent	45.00
Cruet Set, oil and vinegar	
Crystal, #3400/96	55.00
Hobnail, blue opalescent, 4" h	32.00
Dresser Set, Silver Crest, melon shaped cologne and powder jar	50.00
Epergne	
Hobnail, French opalescent	110.00
Silver Crest, large	145.00
Fruit Bowl, Hobnail, yellow opalescent, ftd, 11¾" d	110.00
Hat, top	
Hobnail, yellow, 3" h	40.00
Rib optic, French opalescent, 10" d	225.00
Ruby overlay, 4" h	45.00
Ivy Ball, ftd	
Cranberry overlay	135.00
Ruby overlay	55.00
Jug, handle	
Hobnail, French opalescent, 4½" h	45.00
Peach Crest, 9" h	48.00
Lamp	
Dresser, Hobnail, blue opalescent, cologne bottle base	35.00
Hurricane, Hobnail, French opalescent	225.00
Marmalade Set, 4 pcs, Hobnail, blue opalescent	75.00
Mayonnaise	
Chinese red, ftd	65.00
Hobnail, blue opalescent	65.00
Flame, 4" d	47.00
Mustard, 3 pcs, Hobnail, blue opalescent	30.00
Nut Compote, Silver Crest	21.00
Paperweight, Patriot Eagle, red	25.00
Pitcher, Hobnail	
Blue opalescent, 5½" h	50.00
Milk glass, white, water	40.00
Plate	
Dot Optic, opalescent, 9" d	125.00
French opalescent, leaf, 9" d	30.00
Silver Crest, 12" d	32.00
Rose Bowl, ftd	
Cranberry opalescent, polka dot	95.00
Jade	40.00
Periwinkle Blue	60.00
Salt and Pepper Shakers, pr, Hobnail, blue opalescent	40.00
Sherbet, Plymouth, cobalt blue	17.00
Slipper	
Cat, amber	12.00
Hobnail, blue opalescent	24.00
Sugar Shaker	
Cranberry opalescent, dot optic	125.00
Ruby overlay	95.00
Tidbit, Silver Crest, Violet in Snow, two tiers	25.00
Tumbler	
Sheffield, amethyst, 4" h	18.00
Stars and Stripes, cranberry opalescent, 3¾" h	90.00
Vase	
Cranberry Opalescent, dot optic	
4½" h	35.00
7" h	75.00
9" h	110.00
Florentine, green, fan	30.00
Hobnail, yellow opalescent, fan, 3½" h	45.00
Lime Opalescent, dot optic	130.00
Periwinkle Blue, fan, 5½" h	60.00
Ruby Overlay, diamond optic, 7½" h	45.00
Snow Crest, amber spiral optic, 11" h	75.00

FIESTA

History: The Homer Laughlin China Company introduced Fiesta dinnerware in January, 1936, at the Pottery and Glass Show in Pittsburgh, Pennsylvania. Fredrick Rhead designed the pattern; Arthur Kraft and Bill Bensford molded it. Dr. A. V. Bleininger and H. W. Thiemecke developed the glazes.

The original five colors were red, dark blue, light green (with a trace of blue), brilliant yellow, and ivory. A vigorous marketing campaign took place between 1939 and 1943. In 1938 turquoise was added; red was removed in 1943 because of the war effort and did not reappear until 1959. In 1951

Rose Bowl, Swirl, green opalescent, crimped top, 5½" d, 4½" h, $85.00.

light green, dark blue, and ivory were retired and forest green, rose, chartreuse, and gray were added to the line. Other color changes took place in the late 1950s, including the addition of a medium green.

Fiesta ware was redesigned in 1969 and discontinued in 1972–73. In 1986 Fiesta was reintroduced by Homer Laughlin China Company. The new china body shrinks more than the old semi–vitreous and ironstone pieces, thus making the new pieces slightly smaller than the earlier pieces. The modern colors are also different in tone or hue. The cobalt blue is darker than the old blue. Other modern colors are black, white, apricot, and rose.

References: Linda D. Farmer, *The Farmer's Wife Fiesta Inventory and Price Guide,* published by author, 1984; Sharon and Bob Huxford, *The Collector's Encyclopedia of Fiesta, Revised Seventh Edition,* Collector Books, 1992.

Reproduction Alert.

Additional Listings: See *Warman's Americana & Collectibles* for more examples.

Pitcher, disc, yellow, $65.00.

Ashtray
Chartreuse	55.00
Dark Green	65.00
Gray	80.00
Rose	70.00

Bowl
4¾" d
Chartreuse	18.00
Red	20.00
Rose	20.00

5½" d, fruit
Dark Green	35.00
Medium Green	58.00
Red	20.00
Rose	24.00

6" d, dessert
Chartreuse	30.00
Rose	40.00

Candleholder, bulb
Red	35.00
Yellow	28.00

Carafe
Cobalt Blue	150.00
Red	175.00
Turquoise	175.00

Casserole, cov
Chartreuse	175.00
Cobalt Blue	140.00
Dark Green	165.00
Gray	335.00
Turquoise	125.00

Chop Plate, 15" d
Chartreuse	125.00
Gray	125.00
Rose	47.00

Coffeepot, dark green | 165.00

Creamer
Chartreuse	15.00
Medium Green	55.00
Turquoise, stick handle	30.00

Creamer and Sugar Set, figure 8 tray, red creamer, yellow sugar, cobalt blue tray | 225.00

Cream Soup, rose | 65.00

Cup and Saucer
Dark Green	25.00
Gray	35.00
Rose	30.00
Yellow	20.00

Deep Plate
Medium Green	85.00
Rose	35.00
Yellow	20.00

Demitasse Coffeepot, light green | 225.00

Demitasse Cup and Saucer
Chartreuse	195.00
Ivory	50.00

Egg Cup
Dark green	85.00
Gray	150.00
Red	40.00
Rose	140.00

Jar, cov, large
Cobalt blue	250.00
Light green	225.00

Juice Tumbler, gray | 150.00

Marmalade, cov
Red	225.00
Turquoise	145.00

Mixing Bowl, nested, red, #1 | 95.00

Mug, light green | 50.00

Mustard, cov
Ivory	125.00
Turquoise	125.00

Nappy, medium green, 8½" d | 95.00

Onion Soup, cov, light green | 395.00

Pitcher, disc
Dark Green	170.00
Gray	180.00
Ivory	75.00
Turquoise	65.00
Yellow	65.00

Plate
6" d, medium green	15.00

10" d
Medium Green	80.00
Red, marked	25.00
Yellow, marked	18.00

Platter
Ivory	20.00
Medium Green	75.00
Salad, ftd, ivory	175.00

Sauce Boat
Cobalt Blue	45.00
Dark Green	40.00
Gray	55.00

Syrup
Green	225.00
Turquoise	225.00
Teapot, medium, dark green	200.00
Tray, figure 8, turquoise	295.00

Vase
8" h
Red	410.00
Yellow	295.00
10" h, cobalt blue	425.00
12" h, green	565.00

FIGURAL BOTTLES

History: Figural bottles, made of porcelain either in glaze or bisque form, achieved popularity in the late 1800s and remained popular to the 1930s. The majority of figural bottles were made in Germany, with Austria and Japan accounting for the balance. They averaged in size from three to eight inches.

Figural bottles were shipped to the United States empty and filled upon arrival. They were then given away to customers by brothels, dance halls, hotels, liquor stores, and taverns. Some were lettered with the names and addresses of the establishment; others had paper labels. Many were used for holidays, e.g., Christmas and New Year.

Figural bottles also were made in glass and other materials. The glass bottles held perfumes, foods, or beverages.

References: Ralph & Terry Kovel, *The Kovels' Bottle Price List, 8th Edition,*, Crown Publishers, 1987; Otha D. Wearin, *Statues That Pour*, Wallace-Homestead, 1965.

Periodical: *Antique Bottle And Glass Collector,* P.O. Box 187, East Greenville, PA 18041.

Additional Listings: See *Warman's Americana & Collectibles* for more examples.

BISQUE

Man, 4½" h, toasting "Your Health," flask style, tree bark back	75.00
Sailor, 6½", cartoon type, white pants, blue blouse, hat, high gloss front, marked "Made In Germany"	110.00
Turkey Trot, 6⅜" h, tree trunk back, made in Germany	140.00

Clock, clear glass, paper dial under glass, metal cap, marked "US" in relief on back, 4½" d, 5" h, $85.00.

GLASS

Book, 5" h, Coming Thro/The Rye, blue glaze	110.00
Dutchman, 10", milk glass, c1870	90.00
Ear of Corn, 10¾" h, clear, smooth base, tooled lip	40.00
Eiffel Tower, 14¾" h, clear, pontil, scared base, tooled lip	50.00
Elk's Tooth, 3⅞" h, milk glass, emb clock above elk head, smooth base, ground lip	60.00
Girl with Muff, 6¼" h, clear, smooth base, tooled lip	35.00
George Washington, 9¾" h, golden amber, double collared mouth, smooth base, Simon's Centennial Bitters	800.00
Grover Cleveland, 9½" h, bust, clear and frosted, tooled mouth, ground pontil scar	75.00
Indian Warrior, 12¼" h, yellow amber, tooled mouth, H Pharazyn	500.00
Kummel Bear, 11" h, black amethyst, smooth base, tooled lip	50.00
Pig, 3½" h, 7½" l, clear, smooth base, sheared and tooled lip, orig contents and seal	60.00
Skull, 4¼" h, cobalt blue, tooled mouth, emb "Poison"	2,900.00
Teddy Roosevelt, 6⅜" h, amethyst, smooth base, tooled lip	120.00
Woman wearing undergarments, 6¾" h, clear, smooth base, ground lip	40.00

POTTERY AND PORCELAIN

Book, 10½" h, Bennington Battle, brown, tan, cream, and green flint enamel	1,000.00

Canteen, painted bust of Lincoln, Gar-
field, and McKinley, half pint **380.00**
Coachman, 10½" h, tan and brown mot-
tled glaze, Bennington mark **275.00**
Cucumber, 11¾" l, stoneware, green
and cream mottled glaze **90.00**

FINDLAY ONYX GLASS

History: Findlay onyx glass, produced by Dalzell, Gilmore & Leighton Company, Findlay, Ohio,
was patented in 1889 for the firm by George W.
Leighton. Due to high production costs resulting
from a complex manufacturing process, the glass
was made only for a short time.

Layers of glass were plated to a bulb of opalescent glass through repeated dippings into a glass
pot. Each layer was cooled and reheated to develop opalescent qualities. A pattern mold then
was used to produce raised decorations of flowers
and leaves. A second mold gave the glass bulb its
full shape and form.

A platinum luster paint, producing pieces identified as silver or platinum onyx, was applied to the
raised decorations. The color was fixed in a muffle
kiln. Other colors such as cinnamon, cranberry,
cream, raspberry, and rose were achieved by using an outer glass plating which reacted strongly
to reheating. For example, a purple or orchid color
came from the addition of manganese and cobalt
to the glass mixture.

Reference: James Measell and Don E. Smith,
*Findlay Glass: The Glass Tableware Manufactur-
ers, 1886-1902,* Antique Publications, 1986.

**Tumbler, cinnamon, barrel shape, po-
lished rim, 3⅜" h, $850.00.**

Bowl, 7½" d, rose **425.00**
Celery, 6" h, cream **265.00**
Creamer, 4½" h, raspberry **275.00**
Dresser Box, cov, 5" d, cream, round . **650.00**
Mustard, cov, raspberry **550.00**
Pitcher, 8" h, amber florals and handle,
minor bubbles in inner liner **660.00**

Spooner, cream, platinum blossoms . . **265.00**
Sugar Shaker, 5½" h, raspberry **350.00**
Syrup, cov, cream, hinged metal thumb
lift lid, applied opalescent handle . . . **450.00**
Toothpick, 2½" h, cinnamon **400.00**

FINE ARTS

Notes: There is no way a listing of a hundred
paintings or less can accurately represent the
breadth and depth of the examples sold over the
last year. To attempt to make such a list would be
ludicrous.

In any calendar year, tens, if not hundreds of
thousands of paintings are sold. Prices range from
a few dollars to millions. Since each painting is
essentially a unique creation, it is difficult to establish comparables.

Since an essential purpose of *Warman's Antiques And Their Prices* is to assist its users in
finding information about a category, this "Fine
Arts" introduction has been written primarily to
identify the reference books that you will need to
find out more about a painting in your possession.

Artist Dictionaries: Emmanuel Benezit, *Dic-
tionnaire Critique et Documentaire des Peintres,
Sculpteurs, Dessinateurs et Graveurs,* 10 volumes, third edition, Grund, 1976; Mantle Fielding,
*Dictionary of American Painters, Sculptors and
Engravers,* Apollo Books, 1983; J. Johnson and A.
Greutzner, *Dictionary of British Artists, 1880–
1940: An Antique Collector's Club Research Project Listing 41,000 Artists,* Antique Collector's
Club, 1976; Les Krantz, *American Artists,* Facts
on File, 1985.

Introduction: Alan Bamberger, *Buy Art Smart,*
Wallace–Homestead Book Company, 1990.

Price Guide References, Basic: *Art At Auction
in America, 1991 edition,* Krexpress, 1990; William
T. Currier (compiler), *Currier's Price Guide To
American Artists 1645–1945 at Auction, 1989–
1990 Edition* , Currier Publications, 1989; William
T. Currier (compiler), *Currier's Price Guide To Eu-
ropean Artists 1545–1945 at Auction, 1989–1990
Edition, Currier Publications, 1989; Huxford's Fine
Art Value Guide, Volume III,* Collector Books, 1992;
Susan Theran, *The Official Price Guide To Fine
Art,* House of Collectibles, 1987.

Price Guide References, Advanced: Richard
Hislop (editor), *The Annual Art Sales Index,* Wey-
bridge, Surrey, England, Art Sales Index, Ltd.,
since 1969; Enrique Mayer, *International Auction
Record: Engravings, Drawings, Watercolors,
Paintings, Sculpture,* Paris, Editions Enrique
Mayer, since 1967; Susan Theran (editor), *Leon-
ard's Price Index of Art Auctions,* Auction Index,
Inc., since 1980.

Museum Directories: *American Art Directory,*
R. R. Bowker Co.; American Association of Mu-
seum, *The Official Museum Directory: United
States and Canada,* updated periodically.

FIREARM ACCESSORIES

History: Muzzle loading weapons of the 18th and early 19th centuries varied in caliber and required the owner to carry a variety of equipment with him, including a powder horn or flask, patches, flints or percussion caps, bullets, and bullet molds. In addition, military personnel were responsible for bayonets, slings, and miscellaneous cleaning equipment and spare parts.

In the mid-19th century, cartridge weapons replaced their black powder ancestors. Collectors seek anything associated with early ammunition from the cartridges themselves to advertising material. Handling old ammunition can be extremely dangerous due to decomposition of compounds. Seek advice from an experienced collector before becoming involved in this area.

Military related firearm accessories generally are worth more than their civilian counterparts. See "Militaria" for additional listings.

Reproduction Alert: The amount of reproduction and fake powder horns is large. Be very cautious!

Advertising Sign, Remington UMC, lithograph print, old hunter in log cabin in front of fireplace with hunting dog, advertising Remington game loads, 12 gauge quail load and 12 gauge heavy duck load, Watson artist, 16" x 21", old frame	625.00
Ammunition, Winchester 50–110–300 for Winchester Model 1886 rifles, good cond, very good labels, twenty cartridges	165.00
Bayonet	
Civil War Rifled Musket, blade of bayonet stamped "US," socket stamped "A," complete in orig black leather scabbard with brass tip, brown leather frog for attachment to belt stamped in 2 ovals "N. LUTZ/U.S./ORD. DEPT/SUB INSPECTOR"	200.00
U.S. Model 1816 Musket, blade deeply stamped "US/RJ," socket stamped with letter "S"	75.00
Book	
Sutherland, Robert Q., and R. L. Wilson, *The Book Of Colt Firearms,* dust jacket	750.00
Wilson, R. L.	
The Book Of Colt Engraving, first edition, dust jacket	250.00
The Book Of Winchester Engraving, first edition, dust jacket . . .	500.00
Bullet Mould	
American, brass, 12⅝" overall, 4½" turned wooden handles, casts 9 balls, bottom of mould engraved "A. Gladding," the left side engraved "Shot Mould 1 of 16 to a Pound,/6 of 18 and 2 of 20 to ditto," with intertwined initials "AG," the left side engraved "Providence December 18th, 1798" with slightly crude spread winged Federal eagle, handles with minor stress or grain cracks, brass mould with many nicks and little dents	3,250.00
Colt Navy Gang, steel, walnut handles, brass ferrules, casting 6 conical bullets, cavities fine, outer surfaces moderately pitted overall . .	250.00
Calendar, 1906 Peters, pictures hunters guide carrying a moose head on back and chopping off branch of tree, hunter in background, print entitled "Coming Out Ahead," 12¾" x 26", month of December only, framed . . .	1050.00
Cannon, firecracker, 4½" barrel, breech loading, 3⅜" cast iron wheels, 10" overall length, black lacquer finish, retaining most of orig finish, orig box withe legible label	500.00
Cartridge Board, Remington U.M.C., 46" x 33", board has large U.M.C. in center of picture of deer and elk in mountain scene, cartridges include everything from 22 BB Cap to (1") Gatling gun, cartridges identified through printing underneath them, retains all orig cartridges, ground touched up, non–orig frame	4,000.00
Catalog, Merwin, Hulbert & Co., Catalog No. 30, issued August 1, 1886, 6½ x 11", faded green paper cover with black printing, 32 pgs listing various pistols and ammunition offered by the company, text in Spanish and English, spine strengthened with Scotch tape	350.00
Grips, pair	
Colt Root, solid ivory, raised carved in extremely high relief on the left side with the American eagle standing on the shield clutching arrows and olive branches, the branches running in relief down the front side of the grip, the shield over a "LIBERTY" scroll, missing a tiny chip at the rear toe on each side .	650.00
Colt Root, one piece antique checkered ivory	425.00
Merwin Hulbert Army, ivory, raised carved on right side with the Mexican eagle and snake	325.00
Holster	
Colt Model 1851 KM, made for the Austrian Kreigs Marine Colt Navies, designed for the pistol with a pouch for the spare cylinder to the side and another pouch in front for	

the capper, brown leather, leather a bit dry, both closure straps broken but there **200.00**
Remington, Civil War, fits Remington new model Army revolver, retaining most of black lacquer finish, complete with flap strap **325.00**
Western style, brown, 10½" overall, tooled decoration around the pistol shape only, c1900, orig lined with red wood flannel, most of which is missing **250.00**

Powder Flask, tin, Indian Rifle Gun Powder, made by Hazard Powder Co., Hazardville, CT, 6½" l, 4" w, $45.00.

Flasks, Powder
Brass
8" overall, emb on both sides in an Art Nouveau style fluted pattern **50.00**
11½", body emb on both sides with a fluted pattern, lacquered finish, nickel plated top dispensing loader, adjustable to 6 "Drams," collar marked "PATENT APPLIED FOR" **150.00**
Brass and Horn, 8½" overall, pressed horn body, brass mounts, early 18th C, bottle design body **150.00**
Copper
8½" overall, emb on both sides with oak leaves and acorns, stag's head at top and face of fox at bottom, brass top stamped "G. & J. W. HAWKSLEY/SHEFFIELD" **100.00**
Batty Peace Flask, top marked "BATTY," dated "1848" and inspected "JAG," complete and orig throughout **250.00**
Horn, flattened, 11¼" overall, turned nozzle and hand carved rect wood plug, base cov with horn, fitted with 2 flattened iron carrying rings, old leather strap **75.00**

Rubber, pistol, 4⅝" overall, brass top, hard rubber body marked "GOOD–YEARS PATENT May.6.1851," exceptionally clear markings **100.00**
Flask, Shot, Leather
8¼", emb on both sides with large panel depicting a setter in the woods, one side marked 4 lbs. brass, top marked "AM. FLASK & CAP CO," near mint condition ... **60.00**
8½", emb on both sides with Highland scene showing a Scottish hunter alongside a fallen stag with 2 hounds, brass top **45.00**
Horn, Powder
9", relief carved ivory, body with scene of man with a boar spear surrounded by dogs which are attacking massive wild boar, spout with open mouth highly stylized monster's head which somewhat resembles a wild boar, base low grade silver with scalloped edges, bottom engraved "1746/Prael Colod," minor age cracks **750.00**
14", Daniel Hunt, 1771, pictures rooster, winged serpent, horse, several trees, and bard, trimmed at plug end, minor chipping **1,700.00**
13", PA, early 19th C, engraved with a figure of a spread–winged eagle American eagle with shield on its breast, grasping olive leaves and arrows in its talons, banner in beak inscribed "E Pluribus Unum," fully rigged sailing ship, interlacing hearts, figure of mermaid inscribed "Neptune," soldier on back of seahorse, compasses, horse tied up at stake, large fort–like building with mounted guns, faceted spout, raised ring **1,750.00**
17", military, wooden base with screw out filling plug, fitted with heavy brass rings at nozzle and base with brass sling swivel fittings for the orig 1⅜" wide dark brown leather carrying strap with iron buckle, typical of horns used by US and militia troops in early 19th C, strap broken **300.00**
Loading Tool
Ideal
44 S&W caliber, with mold **90.00**
44–40 caliber, Number Three, orig box **65.00**
Marlin, Model 1881, 38–55 caliber, decapping pin missing, otherwise complete, retaining 75% orig blue **150.00**
Winchester
32 Colt n.p. caliber, with mold ... **72.50**
45 Govt. caliber, 45–125 express hollow point mold **300.00**

45 Govt.–500 caliber, with mold, all
orig **140.00**
Padlock, W. F. Ames & Co., solid brass,
3⅛" overall, stamped "W.F.&CO." on
one side of hasp, other side stamped
"AMES SWORD Co. CHICOPEE
MASS. U.S.A./PAT. SEPT. 19, 1882,"
orig key **425.00**
Signal Cannon, Winchester, Deluxe, se-
rial number D113, deluxe chrome finish overall, 10 gauge, orig pine ship-
ping crate **325.00**
Surgeon's Kit, presentation, brass
bound walnut case, 18¾ x 9¾ x 3½",
fancy name plate with scalloped
edges on lid, engraved "Mr. Kirkland,"
lined with purple velvet, lid with orig
silver plate reading "Presented to Mr.
Kirkland/by/Sir George Beaumount/
as a mark on his part of the very/great
attention he received from him/while
suffering from the effects of a/severe
accident," int. with two trays of various medical tools, large saw not orig,
approximately 35% of tools missing . **750.00**
Tool, combination, military, 3 fittings for
attachment to the ramrod, screwdriver, nipple pick, and mainspring
vise **80.00**

FIREARMS

History: The 15th century arquebus was the
forerunner of the modern firearm. The Germans
refined the wheelock firing mechanism during the
16th and 17th centuries. English settlers arrived in
America with the smoothbore musket; German
settlers had rifled arms. Both used the new flintlock
firing mechanism.

A major advance was achieved when Whitney
introduced interchangeable parts into the manufacturing of rifles. The warfare of the 19th century
brought continued refinements in firearms. The
percussion ignition system was developed by the
1840s. Minie, a French military officer, produced a
viable projectile. By the end of the 19th century
cartridge weapons dominated the field.

Two factors control pricing firearms–condition
and rarity. The value of any particular antique firearm covers a very wide range. For instance, a Colt
1849 pocket model revolver with a 5" barrel can
be priced from $100.00 to $700.00 depending on
whether or not all the component parts are original,
whether some are missing, how much of the original finish (bluing) remains on the barrel and frame,
how much silver plating remains on the brass trigger guard and back strap, and the condition and
finish of the walnut grips. Be careful to note any
weapon's negative qualities. A Colt Paterson belt
revolver in fair condition will command a much
higher price than the Colt pocket model in very

fine condition. Know the production run of a firearm
before buying it.

References: Ralf Coykendall, Jr., *Coykendall's
Sporting Collectilbes Price Guide,* Lyons & Bur-
ford, 1991; Norman Flayderman, *Flayderman's
Guide To Antique American Firearms And Their
Values,* 5th ed., DBI Books, 1990; Joseph Kindig,
Jr., *Thoughts On The Kentucky Rifle In Its Golden
Age,* 1960, available in reprint; Russell and Steve
Quetermous, *Modern Guns: Identification & Val-
ues, Revised 8th Edition,* Collector Books, 1991.

Periodical: *Gun List,* 700 East State Street,
Iola, WI 54990.

FLINTLOCK PISTOLS — SINGLE SHOT

Belgium, pair, 60 caliber rifled bores,
6⅞" part octagonal and round barrels,
12½" overall, checkered grip, octagonal butts, brass hardware, no name
but Liege proofed at breech of each
piece, 4½" flat lockplates, goose neck
hammers, very good cond, all original
except for small repair on one piece **800.00**
English, Tower, 60 caliber, 12" round
barrel, full length military stock, brass
trigger guard, butt cap and sidelined,
lockplate mkd Tower behind hammer
and Crown over "GR" forward of
hammer, proofed on left side of barrel
at breech, crown on tang behind tang
screw, good cond, re–browned and
cleaned, replaced front sight, working
order **600.00**
European, blunderbuss, 70 caliber, 16"
brass barrel, brass trigger guard and
buttplate, full stock, lock plate marked
with a crown over "R" under pan,
good cond, mellow brass patina,
working order, all original **725.00**
European, military, 70 caliber, 9" round
barrel, full length stock, brass nose
cap, brass trigger guard and butt cap
with iron lanyard loop, no markings or
name, good cond, working order,
hammer welded and repaired, other-
wise original **200.00**
Kentucky, T. P. Cherington, 12½" octag-
onal smoothbore barrel, stamped "T.
P. CHERINGTON" on barrel and lockplate, 45 caliber, brightly polished iron
parts, walnut stock **2,500.00**
Kentucky, Daniel Sweltzer & Co, Lan-
caster, 1807–08, 10½" round barrel,
smoothbore, 54 caliber, walnut stock,
only lock may be by Sweitzer with
barrel from Guest **6,500.00**
U. S. Model 1805 (Harper's Ferry), 10"
round iron barrel with iron rib underneath holding ramrod pipe, lockplate
marked with spread eagle and shield

over "US" and vertically at rear "HARPER'S/FERRY" over "1808," 54 caliber, walnut half stock with brass buttplate and trigger guard (Flayderman 6A–008) **3,000.00**
U.S. Model 1836, Asa Waters, Millbury, MA, 54 caliber, smoothbore, 8½" round barrel, brass blade front sight, oval shaped rear sight on barrel tang, overall length 14", swivel type ramrod with button shaped head, all mounting of iron, lockplate marked "A. H. WATERS & Co/MILLBURY, MASS/1844" **1,250.00**

Percussion Pistol, single shot, French, Naval, smooth base, lock marked "Mre Rle de Chattellerault," metal ramrod on pivot, belt hook, 11¾" l, $175.00.

PERCUSSION PISTOLS — SINGLE SHOT

Note: Conversion of flintlock pistols to percussion was common practice. Most English and U.S. military flintlock listed above can be found in percussion. Values for these percussion converted pistols are 40% to 60% of the flintlock values given.

Dueling, pair, cased, J. E. Evans, 10" octagonal barrel, smoothbore barrel, patent breeches stamped "J. E. EVANS/PHILADE," scroll and border engraved patent breeches, trigger guards, and trigger plates, set triggers, 50 caliber, French style brass bound mahogany casing lined in purple velvet containing a powder flash, a can of Eley percussion caps, a screwdriver, a nipple wrench with a screw top containing a nipple–prick, cleaning rod, rammer, mallet head and handle, quantity of bullets, brass plaque on lid inscribed "Mr. Charlos Cambos Jr Philadelphia, Pa" **7,000.00**
English, belt, 14½" overall, 9" round brass barrel sgd "LONDON" and stamped with Birmingham proofs and

a maker's mark, fitted with a round drum for the percussion nipple, "LONDON WARRANTED" lock originally flintlock and converted to percussion with light engraving at rear of the plate and fitted with a plain flat hammer, both tangs of trigger guard shortened, 2 brass ramrod caps but no buttcap, left side fitted with 3" steel belt hook **400.00**
European, possibly Italian, 70 caliber, 7¾" part round/octagonal barrel swamped at muzzle, heavily burled full stock, deluxe wood, raised carving at tang, trigger guard, etc., heavy relief engraved silver trigger guard, side plate, escutcheon at tang, ram rod pipes and buttplate, even grey/brown patina **700.00**
Stocking & Co., 36 caliber, 4" part octagonal/round barrel, smooth walnut bag type grips, lightly mkd on top of barrel "Stocking, Worcester," mkd on left side of bar hammer 1848, retaining traces of original finish, mostly metal gray patina overall **175.00**
Tyron, Merrick & Co (partnership between George Tyron and Samuel Merrick, Phila. from 1832–38), 12¾" overall, 8" octagonal barrel, smoothbore, 64 caliber, top flat inlaid in gold letters "TYRON, MERRICK & Co," bottom flat stamped with English proofs, walnut half stock with checkered wrist, German silver patch box in butt, barrel keys, and forend tip, steel tailpipe and engraved trigger guard, unsgd back action lock, missing ramrod, break in stock at wrist repaired **450.00**
U.S. Model 1842 Navy, 54 caliber, smoothbore, 11⅝" overall length, swivel type ramrod with button shaped head, trigger guard and trigger plate are integral:
"N. P. AMES/SPRINGIELD/MASS." marked centrally on lock, "USN/1845" stamped vertically at rear of lock (Flayderman 6A–046) **800.00**
"US/DERINGER/PHILADELA" marked centrally on lock, "USN/1847" also on lock, barrel stamped "DERINGER/PHILADELPA" and "RC" (Flayderman 6A–049) **1,500.00**

PERCUSSION PISTOLS — MULTI–SHOT

Colt
1860 Army Model, 8" round barrel, marked "ADDRESS COL. SAML COLT, NEW YORK U.S. AMERICA," 44 caliber, 6 shot, cylinder en-

Percussion Pistol, revolver, Sharps Pepperbox No. 1, cal. 22, rimfire, four shot, 2.5″ round barrels, marked "C. Sharps/Patent 1859," and "C Sharps & Co, Philada, Pa," spur trigger, $150.00.

graved with naval battle scene, walnut grips (Flayderman 5B–092) ... **850.00**

Dragoon, Baby Model, 1848, 5″ barrel, marked "ADDRESS SAML COLT, NEW–YORK CITY," 31 caliber, 5 shot, octagonal barrel, stagecoach holdup cylinder, oval stop slots, varnished walnut one piece grips (Flayderman 5B–039) **1,750.00**

Dragoon, First Model, c1849, 7½″ part round, part octagonal barrel, marked "ADDRESS SAML COLT, NEW–YORK CITY –, COLT'S/PATENT," 44 caliber, 6 shot, cylinder engraved with Indian fight scene, square backed trigger guard, walnut grips (Flayderman 5B–023) .. **4,500.00**

Navy, 1851 Model, 7½″ octagonal barrel, marked "ADDRESS SAML COLT NEW YORK U.S. AMERICAN," 36 caliber, 6 shot, cylinder engraved with naval battle scene, round trigger guard, walnut grips (Flayderman 5B–124) **750.00**

Paterson Revolver, No. 5, Holster Model, c1838–40, 9″ octagonal barrel, marked "Patent Arms M'g Co., Paterson N:J–Colt's Pt.," 36 caliber, 5 shot, cylinder roll scene of stagecoach holdup, hidden trigger, varnished polished walnut grip (Flayderman 5B–007) **10,000.00**

Sidehammer (Root) Model 1855, 3½″ octagonal barrel marked "ADDRESS SMAL COLT, HARTFORD, CT," 18 caliber, cylinder engraved with Indian fight scene, hammer mounted on right side of frame, walnut grips (Flayderman 5B–065) **800.00**

Remington

Army Model, 1861, 8″ octagonal barrel, marked "PATENTED DEC. 17, 1861– MANUFACTURED BY REMINGTON'S ILION, NY," 44 caliber, 6 shot, walnut grips (Flayderman 5E–011) **650.00**

New Model Police Revolver, 1863–73, 5½″ octagonal barrel, marked "PATENTED SEPT. 14, 1858, MARCH 17, 1863/E. REMINGTON & SONS, ILION, NEW YORK, U.S.A./NEW MODEL," 36 caliber, 5 shot, walnut grips (Flayderman 5E–028) **550.00**

Remington–Beals, 1st Model, 3″ octagonal barrel marked "F. BEAL'S PATENT" and date, frame marked "REMINGTONS, ILION, NY," 31 caliber, 5 shot, gutta percha grips, round trigger guard (Flayderman 5E–001) **450.00**

Other

Deringer and Deringer Type

F. H. Clark & Co., Memphis, TN, c1850s–60s, 41 caliber, 3½″ barrel, marked "F. H. CLARK & CO./ MEMPHIS," German silver cap on forend, plaint unengraved silver mounts, oval shaped barrel wedge escutcheons, wooden ramrod (Flayderman 7D–012) .. **800.00**

Slotter & Co., Philadelphia, c1860–1869, 41 caliber, 3″ barrel, engraved German silver mountings, varnished walnut stock, checkered handle (Flayderman 7D–026) **600.00**

Pepperbox

Thomas K Bacon, Norwich, CT, c1852–58, single action, underhammer, 31 caliber, 6 shot, 4″ ribbed barrel, large curved finger spur for cocking, engraved nipple shield, walnut grips (Flayderman 7B–00a) **400.00**

Sharps & Hankins, Philadelphia, PA, c1859–74, Model 3A, Serial No. 1759, 32 caliber short rimfire, 4 shot, marked "ADDRESS SHARPS & HANKINS, PHILADELPHIA, PENN." on top of barrel and "SHARPS PATENT/ JAN.25, 1859" on right side of frame, circular sideplate and button barrel release on left side of frame, gutta percha grips, complete and orig throughout, barrels with 20–30% blue mixed with age brown, frame with dulled aged silver color (Flayderman 5F–083) **275.00**

Swedish, "Darling," 30 caliber, 4 shot, 7¾″ overall, 3½″ barrel, bottom of butt carved with initials "JM," nipple protection shield loose and marred all the way around with deep scuff marks, otherwise complete and orig **250.00**

REVOLVERS (CARTRIDGE)

Bayard–Bergmann Model 1910/21 Semi Auto, 9MM caliber, 4″ barrel, serive front and rear sights, detachable magazine, smooth walnut grips, Serial No. 2516, left side of slide mkd "Anciens Etablissements Pieper, Herstal–Liege, Bergmann's Patent, M. 19 10/21. Brevete, S.G.D.G.," 90 to 95% blue **1,150.00**

Browning, Medalist Target, 22 long rifle caliber, 6¾″ barrel with vent, rib, and target sights, checkered wood grips, Serial No. 32836U3S, retaining 99.9% bright blue, case with red felt lining, barrel weights, etc. **550.00**

Charter Arms, Pathfinder 22, Serial No. 119194, 22 caliber, 3″ barrel, orig carton and papers **950.00**

Colt

New Service Target, 44 Russian caliber, 7½″ barrel with target front sight, fleur-de-lis checkered wood grips, Serial No. 13281, retaining 50 to 70% blue overall, wear on grips **675.00**

1878, double action, 32/20 caliber, 4¾″ barrel, black hard rubber bird head grips, Serial No. 50311, good cond, retaining 40 to 50% original nickel overall, working order **550.00**

1911–A1 U. S. Army, 45ACP caliber, 5″ barrel, brown plastic checkered grips, Serial No. 1012836, retaining 90% parkerized finish, original U. S. leather shoulder holster **475.00**

Erfurt 1908 Luger, military, 9MM caliber, 3⅞″ barrel, checkered wood grips, Serial No. 8907n and dated 1918, nickel plated with 98 to 99% of remaining, no magazine **275.00**

German 1908 Navy Luger, 9MM caliber, 6″ barrel, DWM on top of toggle, dated 1917 over chamber, checkered wooden grips, wooden bottom magazine with number 3892/a, Serial No. 1031/a, mkd on left side of barrel extension, crown over "M" in two places and smaller crown at the forward end next to barrel and small crown over barrel, small 1917 on forward left side of frame, 95 to 98% military blue . . . **2,250.00**

German WW–I Luger, Erfurt, dated 1918, 9MM caliber, 4″ barrel, checkered wood grips, all matching numbers 5388 including magazine, 95% military blue **700.00**

High Standard, Model G, Semi–Auto, 380 ACP caliber, 5″ barrel, checkered black plastic grips, Serial No. 7399, retaining 98 to 99% bright blue **310.00**

Japanese Papa Nambu, 8MM caliber, 4¾″ barrel, fixed front and adjustable rear military sights, checkered wood grips, Serial No. 5842, Magazine No. 5952, retaining 90% military blue . . **875.00**

Mauser, Model HSC Double Action Pocket, 7.65 MM, 32 ACP caliber, checkered wood grips, Srial No. 915603, retaining 98 to 99% bright blue **425.00**

Remington, Model 51, Serial No. PA30819, 380 caliber, 97–98% orig blue **380.00**

Ruger, New Model Blackhawk, 41 magnum caliber, 6½″ barrel, fixed front and adjustable rear sights, smooth wood grips with Ruger logo, Serial No. 41-008979, retaining 98 to 99% bright blue **275.00**

Smith & Wesson

Mark II, hand ejector, second model, originally 455 caliber but cylinder altered to hand 45 Colt caliber, 6½″ barrel, service sights, lanyard loop on butt, non-original staghorn trips, Serial No. 12945 on butt and barrel and 63733 on cylinder, non-factory engraved in an oak leaf pattern, retaining 95 to 98% bright blue **275.00**

Model 3, Russian, third model, 44 S & W Russian caliber, 6½″ barrel with pinned front sight blade, spur on trigger guard, smooth walnut grips, backstrap and butt are cut for shoulder stock, lanyard loop on butt removed, slot on cutt cut for stock was milled through serial number, Serial No. 46823, number on cylinder and barrel top strap is 7740, retaining 95 to 98% nickel finish . **1,900.00**

Model 27, target revolver, early five screw model, 6″ barrel with target front and rear sights, target hammer and trigger, smooth wood grips with S & W monogram, Serial No. S107589, cased in mahogany S & W case, retianing 99.9% bright blue **375.00**

Star, Model PD, presentation, Serial No. 1363196, 45 caliber, plain wood grips with special Toledo work gold damascened medallions, the right the American eagle and shield, the left "John Amber/FROM/YOUR FRIENDS AND STAR" **950.00**

Stevens, Offhand Target No. 35, 22″ long caliber, 6″ part octagonal/round barrel, bead front and sporting rear sights, smooth walnut grip, Serial No.

49171, retaining 50% blue on barrel, 90 to 95% nickel on frame and grip . **175.00**

Steyr, 1915 Semi Auto, 38 auto caliber, 5⅛″ barrel, checkered wood grips, Serial No. 2388K, fair to good cond, completely parkerized over a lightly pitted surface **150.00**

Walther, PP22, Serial No. 302362P, 22 caliber, extended checkered wood grips and magazine extension, Nazi proofs, 95% orig dull blue War time finish **625.00**

Dan Wesson, Model 15, Serial No. 10245, 357 Magnum caliber, 5¾″ barrel, orig carton with spare 5¾″ barrel and a pair of finger groove grips . . . **200.00**

FLINTLOCK LONG ARMS

Charleville, Model 1777, musket, 69 caliber, 44¾″ barrel, mkd on left side of barrel at breech 1814 and proofed, marked on tang Model 1777, lockplate mkd under pan in two lines, "Manuf., By de Charleville," full length military musket stock and proofed in circle on right butt "MR" and dated 1814, very good cond, metal gray patina finish overall, original flint, working order **1,500.00**

Kentucky, John Armstrong, 50 caliber, smooth bore, 41¼″ octagonal barrel slightly swamped at muzzle, brass base front sight with silver blade, open sporting rear sight, signed on top of barrel "John Armstrong," recovered to flint using the correct old parts, 4¾″ lockplate with "JA" engraved forward of goose neck hammer, full length tiger maple raised carved stock, brass hardware, round silver nameplate at tang, and engraved silverplate with eagle at cheekpiece, ramrod old replacement **13,500.00**

Kentucky, Peter White, 45 caliber rifled bore, 43⅝″ slim octagonal barrel, slightly swamped at muzzle, brass base with silver blade front sight and open sporting rear sight, full length tiger maple Kentucky rifle stock, raised carving at either end of left cheek piece, raised carving around top tang, sideplate, and lockplate, brass hardware, three brass barrels keys with silver escutcheons and large eagle engraved on oval silver inlay in cheek piece, barrel is lightly signed "Peter White" and lockplate engraved "P W," one silver inlay on either side of stock in tear drop to rear of sideplate and lockplate, two silver

inlays on either side of dobule set trigger, professionally reconverted to flint, restoration throughout **8,500.00**

U.S. Model 1816 Musket, Type II, made at Springfield Armory, 69 caliber, single shot, muzzleloader, 42″ round barrel, walnut stock, lockplate marked "SPRING/FIELD/1829," complete with orig issue bayonet in black leather scabbard, throat mount marked "R DINGEE/N–YORK" (Flayderman 9A–197) **4,000.00**

PERCUSSION LONG ARMS

Note: Conversion of flintlock long arms to percussion was common practice. Most English, French, and U.S. military flintlock model long arms listed in the previous section can be found in percussion. Values for these percussion converted long arms are 40% to 60% of the flintlock values previously noted.

English Infantry Rifle, 577 caliber, 48½″ overall, 33″ round barrel, stud for a saber bayonet, 900 yard folding sight, lock stamped with a large crown and engraved "John O. Evans 1860," all iron furniture, two clamping barrel ends, lock still retains orig nipple protector and chain **950.00**

Kentucky, 52¼″ overall, 36¾″ heavy octagonal barrel, top flat engraved with a rope pattern and "L. Biddle" in script (Levi Biddle, Shanesville, OH, c1834–45), lightly engraved percussion lock with indistinct maker's mark, tiger stripped bull stock with brass forend cap, 3 ramrod pipes, trigger guard and butt plate, fancy engraved German silver openwork patch box, long toe plate and stripe along comb, fitted with 15 German silver inlays, missing one inlay, stock with old refinish **2,500.00**

Kentucky, 56″ overall, 40½″ octagonal barrel, 38 caliber, signed on top flat "FRANCOIS GOME" (No record maker, possibly owner), lightly engraved "JOSH GOLCHER" lock secured with a large pin with hammered head rather than usual screw, tiger stripped full stock with all German silver mounts including open work patch box with light engraving and 15 inlays including the large oval on the check rest which is engraved with a classic primitive American eagle, old partial break in stock at rear of barrel, otherwise complete and orig **1,750.00**

Kentucky, 56¼″ overall, 41″ octagonal barrel, 41 caliber, simple scroll engraving on 3 upper flats at the breech, top flat stamped "N. SHENNENFELT" (Nicholas Shennenfelt, working in PA between about 1823 and 1871), engraved percussion lock stamped "J. STEATHAM," elaborate brass furniture including trigger guard and butt plate, engraved open work patchbox, engraved toe plate and rib along the comb, openwork sideplate and forend wear plate, 3 ramrod pipes and forend cap, stock with 46 engraved German silver inlays of varied shapes and designs, bad break in stock in front of lock, repair on barrel tang, could use professional restoration .. **3,500.00**

Remington Model 1863 (Zouave Rifle), Contract Rifle, c1862–65, 58 caliber, single shot, muzzleloader, 33″ round barrel, walnut stock, brass patchbox on right side of butt which still retains orig spare nipple and worm, screw fitting for ramrod, 7 groove rifle, lockplate marked ahead of hammer, American eagle over small "U.S.," two lines under bolster "REMINGTON'S/ILION, N.Y.," horizontally dated at rear "1863" (Flayderman 5E–076) **2,500.00**

U. S. Model 1855, Rifled Musket, made at Harper's Ferry Armory, c1857–61, 58 caliber, single shot, muzzleloader, 33″ round barrel, two barrel bands, walnut stock, patchbox on right side of butt, lockplate marked "U.S./HARPERS FERRY," dated "1858," barrel with same date, complete with orig "U.S." marked bayonet in black leather brass mounted scabbard (Flayderman 9A–308) **3,000.00**

REPRODUCTION LONG ARMS

Kentucky, flintlock, 32 caliber rifled bore, 43″ octagon barrel, B.R.J. engraved on top of barrel, brass blade front and sporting rear sights, full length stock with brass hardware, retaining 90% blue on barrel **350.00**

Kentucky, flintlock, 45 caliber rifled bore, 40″ round and octagonal barrel, full length tiger maple stock, raised carving, brass hardware and patch box, soft light blue patina finish on barrel **975.00**

Kentucky, percussion, full stock, 40 caliber rifled bore, 40″ octagonal barrel, hooded front sight with insert, tang peep sight, double set triggers, bird's-eye maple wood, somewhat crudely made **135.00**

RIFLES

Colt, Model 722, bolt action, sporting, 222 Remington caliber, 26″ round barrel, ramp front sight with bead, slot blank rear and Lyman Wolvertine All–Weather scope and Buehler top mount, re–stocked by Brownell master stock makers with pistol grip, fleur-de-lis checkering, cheek piece Brownell thin brown rubber recoil pad measuring 14″ over pad, schnable forearm tip, Serial No. 369980, retainings 99% original blue on barrel **675.00**

Griffin & Howe, custom magnum, 416 Rigby caliber, 26″ round barrel with hooded ramp front sight, three leaf express rear sight, Griffin & Howe custom stock with factory checkering, cheek piece, ebony forearm cap and Griffin & Howe engraved and checkered steel buttplate with trap, sling, and swing swivels, Griffin & Howe Serial No. 1029, retaining 95 to 98% original blue overall **7,125.00**

Japanese World War II, bolt action, military paratrooper's take–down rifle, 7.7MM caliber, 26″ barrel with military front and rear sights, pistol grip stock with original sling swivels and cleaning rod, Serial No. 14047, with matching number on bolt handle, 95% plus original military blue finish **610.00**

Marlin

Model 1892, 32 rimfire caliber, 24″ round barrel, bead front and sporting rear sights, full magazine, straight grip stock with smooth buttplate, Serial No. 436841, retaining 75% original blue **225.00**

Model 1894, lever action, 38/40 caliber, 24″ round barrel, blade front and sporting rear sights, full magazine, straight grip stock with smooth steel buttplate, Serial No. 1827, retaining 98 to 99% original blue on barrel **700.00**

Remington

Model 121, 22 long rifle caliber, 24¾″ round barrel, bead front and sporting rear sight, pistol grip stock with Remington checkered buttplate, Serial No. 95123, retaining 98% original blue **360.00**

Model 513-T, target, 22 long rifle caliber, 27″ round target barrel, front sight missing, Redfield target rear sight, heavy target type pistol grip stock with checkered steel buttplate, sling, and swivels, 95% original blue **150.00**

Ruger, Model 77, 25/250 caliber, 24″

varmit weight barrel made without sights, Redfield 20X telescope with Ruger mounts, pistol grip stock with factory checkering, pistol grip cap and Ruger red rubber recoil pads, Serial No. 70-56331, retaining 98 to 99% original bright blue overall **425.00**

Savage, Model 99, 308 Winchester caliber, 24″ round barrel, bead front sight and Mabel's sporting rear sight, pistol grip stock with factory checkering, swing swivels and Savage aluminum buttplate, Serial No 1010685, retaining 95% of original blue on barrel . . **275.00**

Springfield, Model 1868, trapdoor, 45/70 caliber, 32⅝″ military round barrel with military front and military adjustable rear sights, breech black marked 1869 over crossed arrows and small eagle head, full length military stock with musket buttplate and sling swivels, Serial number on side of frame 7988, "V" proofed inspected on left side of barrel at breech, 90 to 95% original blue **385.00**

Standard Arms Company, Model G, automatic and slide action, 30 REM caliber, 22″ barrel, ivory bead front and sporting rear sights, straight grip deluxe stock with brass buttplate and pump operating handle, Serial No. 5634, retaining 75% original blue . . **275.00**

Stevens Favorite Single Shot Boys Rifle, 22 long rifle caliber, 22½″ part round and part octagon barrel, blade front and sporting rear sights, straight grip stock with Stevens hard rubber buttplate, retaining 95% original blue on barrel **140.00**

Underwood World War II M–1 Carbine, 30 M–1 caliber, 18″ barrel, military front and rear sights, carbine stock with sling, Serial No. 5098832, rebuilt, 95% plus parkerized finish **275.00**

Weatherby, Deluxe, bolt action, sporting, 257 Weatherby magnum caliber, 26″ light weight round barrel, early Weatherby with a Mauser action with the South Gate, CA, address, hooded ramp front sight, no provision for rear sight, mounted with a Lyman Alaskan All Weather scope in a Paul Jaeger detachable side mount, all factory installed, Deluxe bird's–eye maple stock with fleur–de–lis checkering, pistol grip, cheek piece, black line recoil pad, five inlays of different color wood in stock, Serial No. 1914, new and unfired, retaining 99.9% original bright blue overall **1400.00**

Winchester
Model 1894, saddle ring carbine, 30–30 caliber, 20″ carbine barrel with carbine front and rear sights, full magazine, carbine butt stock with carbine buttplate, Serial No. 846048, retaining 95% original blue on barrel and magazine **360.00**

Model 9422M, take–down, 22 magnum caliber, 22″ round barrel, hooded ramp front and sporting rear sights, full magazine, pistol grip stock with pistol grip cap and crescent buttplate, Serial No. F550820, formerly property of G. L. Alcock, President of U. S. Repeating Arms Co., new **255.00**

SHOTGUNS

Baikal, Model TOZ-34E, Souvenir, 20 gauge, 28″ over and under barrel, modified and full choke, ventilated rib, engraved receiver, walnut, hand checkered and pistol grip stock and forearm, imported from the Soviet Union **450.00**

Belgium Browning
A-5, semi-auto, 20 gauge, 26″ ventilated rib barrel, pistol grip stock with round knob, factory checkering and Browing hard rubber buttplate, Serial No. 8Z12624, retaining 99.9% original bright blue overall . **630.00**

Diana Grade Over/Under, 12 gauge, 28″ barrels with ventilated rib, full and modified choke, single selective trigger, auto–ejectors, deluxe pistol grip stock with round knob, Browning hard rubber buttplate, factory checkering, engraved frame and signed "V. Doyen," Serial No. 35045, retaining 99% original blue on barrels **3,300.00**

A. H. Fox Gun Company, Sterling Worth Grade Double Barrel, 12 gauge, 28″ barrels, full and modified choke, pistol grip stock with factory checkering and hard rubber pistol grip cap and buttplate, double triggers with extractor, Serial No. 82848, retaining 90% original blue, but thin **350.00**

Harrington & Richardson, Model 400, 16 gauge, 28″ barrel, slide action, hammerless, repeating, full choke, 5–shot tubular, semi–pistol grip stock & grooved slide handle, recoil pad . . . **110.00**

Ithaca, Model 66, Supersingle, 20 gauge, 30″ barrel, full choke, lever action, exposed hammar, single shot, checkered straight stock and forearm **65.00**

Ivor Johnson, double barrel, 16 gauge,

30" barrels, full and modified choke, box lock action with Miller single trigger and auto ejectors, pistol grip stock with factory checkering, hard rubber pistol grip, sling swivels, and period Jostam red rubber recoil pad, Serial No. 4850E, retaining 75 to 90% original blue **400.00**

Parker, Double Barrel, early lifter action, 12 gauge, 30" Damascus barrel, improved cylinder and modified choke, number "2" frame, "F" grade engraved full sidelock action with hammers, pistol grip stock with factory checkering and smooth steel buttplate, Serial No. 17584, retaining 50 to 60% original Damascus finish ... **275.00**

Remington, Model 870, 12 gauge, 28" barrel, ventilated rib, modified choke, slide action, hammerless, side ejection, 4-shot tubular, fluted comb, pistol grip stock **175.00**

L. C. Smith
  Double Barrel, field grade, 12 gauge, 28" barrels, full and modified choke, double triggers with extractors, pistol grip stock with factory checkering, pistol grip cap and hard rubber buttplate measuring 14½" over plate, Serial No. FW131892, retaining 90% original blue **615.00**
  Double Barrel, premier skeet, 12 gauge, 26" barrels, skeet chokes, beaver tail forearm, single selective trigger with auto ejectors, engraved sidelocks with a clay pigeon and scroll onright side and a flying quail plus scrolls on left side, straight grip stock with factory checkering and checkered butt, Serial No. FWE54862, retaining 95% original blue **910.00**

Winchester
  Model 12, pump action, skeet gun, 20 gauge, 26" solid rib barrel, WS-1 Skeet choke, pistol grip stock with factory checkering, pistol grip cap and non-original black rubber recoil pad measuring 14⅝" over pad, beaver tail forearm with factory checkering, Serial No. 746092, retains 90 to 95% original bright blue overall **725.00**
  Model 12, 12 gauge, 28" barrel, modified coke, pistol grip stock with poorly installed Red head recoil pad, 13¼" pull over pad, Serial No. 895716, retaining 50 to 70% original blue overall **165.00**
  Model 42, field grade, 410 gauge, 26" plain barrel, full coke, pistol grip stock with Winchester hard rubber

buttplate, Serial No. 56793, retaining 97 to 99% original bright blue . **750.00**

COMMEMORATIVE PIECES AND REPLICAS

Note: The resale of modern commemorative weapons is in its infancy. It will take another ten years to establish a viable secondary market. However, these weapons are sold regularly at firearm auctions, often with strong results.

Pistol
Colt, Maine Sesquicentennial 1820–1970 Revolver, 22 long rifle caliber, 4¾" barrel, plastic pearl grips, Serial No. 1294MES, original pine case, new, unfired, cyclinder has never been turned **275.00**
Colt, NRA Centennial, single action, 357 magnum caliber, 5½" barrel, smooth wood grips with NRA logo, Serial No. NRA3969, cased in original NRA presentation case, new, unfired, cylinder never turned **550.00**
Rifle
  Winchester Model 94, Oliver Winchester Commemorative, 38/55 caliber, 24" octagonal barrel, blade front and sporting rear sights, full magazine, straight grip stock with fleur-de-lis checkering, crescent buttplate, Serial No. OFW12335, new, unfired, original box with jacket **440.00**
  Winchester, Model 1966 Commemorative, 30/30 caliber, 26" octagon barrel, blade front and sporting rear sights, straight grip stock with crescent butt, Serial No. 30657, original brown carton, new, unfired, and retaining 100% original gold finish .. **250.00**
  Winchester Model 9422, Boy Scout of American Commemortive, 22 caliber, S. L. or long rifle, 20½" barrel, straight grip stock with crescent butt, hooded front and sporting rear sights, factory engraved frame, Serial No. BSA 1910, original box with all papers, purchased by G. L. Alcock, President U. S. Repeating Arms Co., new, unfired, 1985 ... **425.00**

FIREHOUSE COLLECTIBLES

History: The volunteer fire company has played a vital role in the protection and social growth of many towns and rural areas. Paid professional firemen usually are found only in large metropolitan areas. Each fire company prided itself on equipment and uniforms. Conventions and parades gave the fire companies a chance to show off their equipment. These events produced a wealth of firehouse related memorabilia.

References: Chuck Deluca, *Firehouse Memorabilia: A Collectors Reference,* Maritime Antique Auctions, 1989; Mary Jane and James Piatti, *Firehouse Collectibles,* The Engine House, 1979.

Periodical: *The Fire Mark Circle of the Americas,* 2859 Marlin Dr., Chamblee, GA 30341.

Museums: Insurance Company of North America (INA) Museum, Philadelphia, PA; Oklahoma State Fireman's Association Museum, Oklahoma City, OK; San Francisco Fire Dept. Memorial Museum, San Francisco, CA.

Additional Listings: See *Warman's Americana & Collectibles* for more examples.

Alarm Box, marked "Gamewell" and "Telegraph Station," 1880s	75.00
Badge, 1½ x 2¼", Tri–County Firemen's Convention, brass, diecut pendant with fire symbols, hanger bar with lantern and "July 2–3, 1897"	25.00
Bell, 11", brass, iron back	100.00
Belt, red, black, and white	
41½" l, marked "1, 1st Assistant"	100.00
43" l, marked "Hampden"	65.00
52" l, marked "Director"	125.00
Book, *The Fire Chief's Handbook,* Shepperd, 1932, illus	20.00
Bucket, leather	
10½" h, orig black paint, white letters, "J Tubbs, No 2"	525.00
12" h, polychrome dec, inscribed "Harnden & Co," 19th C	275.00
13" h, ceremonial parade type, hand painted, town consumed in flames with fire fighters scene, inscribed "Asa C Dix" and Enterprise Fire Club," dated 1810, mustard yellow ground, dark green saddle stitched rim, leather cased rope handle	3,025.00
Catalog, American La France No 10, photos	110.00
Fire Extinguisher	
Babcock, American La France Fire Engine Co, Elmira, NY, grenade, amber glass	550.00
Fireen Safety First Fire Ext Co, canister	25.00
Hayward's Hand Fire Grenade, yellow, ground mouth, smooth base, 6¼" h, c1870	75.00
Red Comet, red, metal canister, red glass bulb	40.00
Sinclair, grenade, glass, cobalt blue	425.00
Fire Mark, cast iron, oval	
8 x 11½", relief molded design, pumper framed by "Fire Department Insurance," polychrome paint	410.00
8 x 12", black, gold eagle and banner dec, marked "Eagle Ins Co Cin O"	930.00

Hat, parade type, top hat style	
Composition, painted bust portrait of Thomas Jefferson, gilt bordered banners inscribed "Independent Hose Co" and "JH" in script on back, shield with initials "JH," 7¼" h	8,250.00
Pressed Felt, painted black, red banners inscribed "Franklin–Fire Co" and crossed American flags with shield inscribed "4," reverse with gilt number "4" entwined with red banner inscribed "Haste to the Rescue," red painted underbrim, 19th C, 5" h	4,400.00

Helmet, leather, black, gold eagle, red and white letters, made by Cairns & Brothers, NY, size 7¼", $165.00.

Helmet	
Leather, four comb type, painted red, black brim, gilt inscribed shield "No 3–EBD," orig padded straw liner, early 19th C	1,760.00
Oilcloth, blue, tin shield inscribed "Niagara 3 Brunswick," red underbrim, early 19th C	1,100.00
Hose Nozzle	
Brass, 16" l, removable, double handle, marked "Akron Brass Mfg Co, Inc"	140.00
Bronze, emb roses and "Santa Rosa"	30.00
Lantern	
Alf Roamite, steel and copper	250.00
Dietz, King Fire Dept, copper bottom	135.00
Photograph, sepia, fire engine drawn by three horses, 10th, New York City, c1900	80.00
Presentation Trumpet	
Coin Silver, 16¼" h, derby style bell, inscribed "Presented by the City of Lowell to Mazeppa Engine Company No 10 for the Third Best Horizontal Playing July 4, 1856"	1,430.00
Silverplated, 17¾" h, chased floral design, steamer, helmet, crossed trumpets, and ladder dec, inscribed	

"Presented to Captain Joseph Frye by the members of the Bradlee Hose Co No 10, March 11, 1870" **1,650.00**

Sign, 10 x 14", tin, painted, eagle on shield, black edge background, red and yellow foliate designs, ribbon banner with "Rainbow Fire Company" **800.00**

Watch Fob, West Penna Volunteer Firemen, aluminum, strap, 1926 ...... **25.00**

FIREPLACE EQUIPMENT

History: The fireplace was a gathering point in the colonial home for heat, meals, and social interaction. It maintained its dominant position until the introduction of central heating in the mid-19th century.

Because of the continued popularity of the fireplace, accessories still are manufactured, usually in an early American motif.

Reproduction Alert: Modern blacksmiths are reproducing many old iron implements.

Additional Listings: Brass and Iron.

Fender, brass and iron, 20" l, 6½" h, $100.00.

Andirons, pr
18" h, cast iron, cat form, glass eyes **400.00**
19" h, brass, sgd "Whittingham, New York" **750.00**
20¼" h, wrought iron, knife blade, spade feet, goose neck finials ... **675.00**
24¾" h, Federal, metal, urn finial, tapered standards, sq plinth cabriole legs, claw and ball feet, includes shovel and tongs **1,430.00**
31" h, brass, urn top, columnar, spur supports, claw and ball feet **250.00**

Bellows
19½" l, stenciled leaf and fruit design, red ground, 19th C **275.00**
29½" l, carved comic face, English . **85.00**
Bench, fireside, 54 x 48 x 24", pine, red graining, high back **200.00**
Chestnut Roaster, 23" l, brass, reticulated detail, England **150.00**
Clock, mantel
10" h, ceramic case, blue and white Delft type dec, marked "Made in France" **125.00**
14¾" h, 25" l, black onyx, relief floral carving, red onyx inlay, gilded brass face trim, Roman numerals, marked "Tiffany & Comp" **650.00**
Coal Hod, 25" h, brass, hammered, emb tavern scenes **45.00**
Fender
18½" h, brass, two uprights, removable rail, Continental **475.00**
28½" l, brass and iron **75.00**
39" w, D form, iron wire screen, brass top and bottom moldings, brass ball feet, English **355.00**
46" l, brass, Federal style **200.00**
70 x 12½ x 6¼", wrought iron, simple detail **125.00**
Fire Back, 22½ x 27", cast, high relief design, anchors and fleur–de–lis, arched crest, marked "IFC," dated 1788 .... **950.00**
Fire Dog, pr, 5¾" h, 20" l, wrought iron, snake like head, twisted and tooled detail **175.00**
Fireplace Screen
30¾" h, cast brass, ornate scrolling design **750.00**
31 x 22½", Louis XV style, ormolu and mesh, cartouche form **1,300.00**
Fireplace Crane
17½" w, 14½" h, wrought iron **65.00**
24" l, 16" h, wrought iron, scroll work and three hooks **50.00**
Firetool Stand, 62" h, bronze, double eagle finial, turned standard, tripod base, claw feet **130.00**
Flue Cover
7½" d, lady, multicolored, gilt trim .. **30.00**
8½" d, hp winter scene **25.00**
9¼" d, lithograph cherub and angel, pink and white, reverse painted border **55.00**
Grate, 9 x 17½", cast iron, mid 19th C **75.00**
Heat Reflector, 8 x 6½", tin, semi–circular form, pierced heart, diamonds, dots, and stars design, loop handle . **500.00**
Log Box, 15 x 35 x 13", walnut, dovetailed case, hinged top **125.00**
Mantel, 69¼ x 56½", Federal style, poplar, applied moldings, stop and dec fluting, pine repairs **600.00**

Mantel Mirror
  66 x 50″, Revival, baroque, walnut,
    gold painted trim **350.00**
  68 x 61″, Louis XV style, giltwood,
    carved acorn, leaf, and acanthus .   **650.00**
Pole Screen
  19½ x 25¼ x 58″, mahogany, Queen
    Anne, two figures and landscape
    scene, 18th C **770.00**
  34½″ h, cherry, adjustable pleated
    green silk screen, tripod base with
    spider legs, turned base and pole,
    urn finial, folding shelf with "Polly
    Pomeroy Starr" and "1781" **11,000.00**
  35½ x 29¼″, fruitwood, shell and
    scroll design, scrolled legs, floral
    needlepoint panel **300.00**
  51″ h, mahogany, circular frame with
    young boy in needlework, tripod
    base, New England, 19th C **3,300.00**
Toaster, hearth
  Iron and Wire, inlaid brass initials "I
    H," heart hanger on handle end . .   **350.00**
  Wrought Iron, hand wrought **300.00**
Tools
  Set, 30″ h stand, three tools, brass,
    19th C **75.00**
  Shovel and Tong, brass, American,
    c1800 . . . .   **425.00**
  Trivet, wrought iron, adjustable spit . .   **700.00**

FISCHER J.
BUDAPEST.

FISCHER CHINA

History: In 1893 Moritz Fischer founded his factory in Herend, Hungary, a center of porcelain production from the 1790s.

Confusion exists about Fischer china because of its resemblance to the wares of Meissen, Sevres, and Oriental export. It often was bought and sold as the product of these firms. Forged marks of other potteries are found on Herend pieces. The mark "MF," often joined, is the mark of Moritz Fischer's pottery.

Fischer's Herend is hard paste ware with luminosity and exquisite decoration. Pieces are designated by pattern names, the best known being Chantilly Fruit, Rothschild Bird, Chinese Bouquet, Victoria Butterfly, and Parsley.

Fischer also made figural birds and animal groups, Magyar figures (individually and in groups), and Herend eagles poised for flight.

Reference: Susan and Al Bagdade, *Warman's English & Continental Pottery & Porcelain, 2nd Edition,* Wallace–Homestead, 1991.

Potpourri Jar, hexagonal, reticulated, multicolored floral and vine design, domed top, rose finial, 7″ h, $300.00.

Cache Pot, 5″, Rothchild Bird pattern,
  handled **160.00**
Charger, 13″, multicolored enamel floral
  dec, gold trim **325.00**
Ewer
  7½″, enameled floral dec **200.00**
  16½″, reticulated body, rose, blue,
    green, and gold enamel floral dec   **275.00**
Jar, cov, 7¼″ h, multicolored floral motif,
  raised relief medallions with reticulated
    fleur–de–lis, white ground,
    matching oval reticulated finial **250.00**
Nappy, 4½″, triangular shape, Victoria
  Butterfly pattern, gold trim **125.00**
Pitcher, 12″, reticulated, multicolored
  floral dec **285.00**
Plate, 7½″, luncheon, Chantilly Fruit
  pattern **90.00**
Sauce Boat, underplate, matching china
  ladle
    Parsley pattern **225.00**
    Victoria Butterfly pattern **250.00**
Tureen, cov, 8½″, Chantilly Fruit pattern,
  natural molded fruit finial, handled . .   **300.00**
Urn, 12″, reticulated, blue floral dec,
  shield mark **325.00**
Vase, reticulated
  8″, blue flowers and green leaves,
    gold handles, shield mark **230.00**
  10½″, floral dec, pink, blue, green,
    and white **200.00**

FITZHUGH

History: Fitzhugh, one of the most recognized Chinese Export porcelain patterns, was named for the Fitzhugh family for whom the first dinner service was made. The peak period of production was from 1780 to 1850.

Fitzhugh features an oval center medallion or monogram surrounded by four groups of flowers or emblems. The border is similar to that on Nanking china. Occasional border variations are found. Butterfly and honeycomb are among the rarest.

Blue is the common color. Color is a key factor in pricing with rarity in ascending order of orange, green, sepia, mulberry, yellow, black, and gold. Combinations of colors are scarce.

Reference: Sandra Andacht, *Oriental Antiques & Art: An Identification And Value Guide,* Wallace-Homestead, 1987.

Reproduction Alert: Spode Porcelain Company, England, and Vista Alegre, Portugal, currently are producing copies of the Fitzhugh pattern. Oriental copies also are available.

Plate, orange, 9⅝" d, $300.00.

Basket, oval, reticulated, blue	
10⅞" l	450.00
11" l, matching undertray, handles	1,500.00
Bowl	
6¼" d, blue	200.00
9⅜" d, shallow, scalloped rim, blue	100.00
10", sq, blue	325.00
Creamer, 5½" h, helmet shape, blue	450.00
Cup and Saucer, blue	
Set of 5	850.00
Set of 6	300.00
Dish	
5⅛" l, 5¼" w, scallop shell shape, c1770	275.00
7⅞", sq shape, rounded corners, blue	600.00
9½", sq, fluted, scalloped rim, blue	850.00
Garden Seat, 18¼" h, hexagonal, blue	5,000.00
Gravy Boat, blue, plain sides	100.00
Jug, 12½" h, blue	800.00
Pitcher	
6⅞" h, blue	850.00
7½" h, blue	850.00
8½" h, cov, blue	900.00

Platter	
16½" l, oval, blue, repaired rim edge	325.00
17¼", blue, cross shaped gray trap, well at one end, ftd	400.00
20" l, blue	550.00
Rice Bowl, pr, blue	75.00
Soap Dish, 5½" l, includes drain, blue	375.00
Sugar Bowl, cov	
5¼" h, blue	550.00
With undertray, blue, gold highlights	750.00
Teapot, cov	
5½" h, drum shape, blue	1,050.00
6½" h, blue	350.00
Tureen, cov, undertray, blue, pr	2,750.00
Vase, 13¼" h, beaker shape, blue, teakwood stand	1,250.00
Vegetable Dish, cov	
9½" l, oblong, blue	325.00
12½" l, rect, blue, liner	1,500.00
13" l, cov, oval, liner	1,050.00
Wine Bottle, 10⅞" h, blue	900.00

FLASKS

History: A flask is a container for liquids, usually having a narrow neck. Early American glass companies frequently formed them in molds which left a relief design on the front and/or back. Historical flasks with a portrait, building, scene, or name are the most desired.

A chestnut is hand blown, small, and has a flattened bulbous body. The pitkin has a blown globular body with vertical ribs with a spiral rib overlay. Teardrop flasks are generally fiddle shaped and have a scroll or geometric design.

Dimensions can differ for the same flask because of variations in the molding process. Color is important, with scarcer colors demanding more money. Aqua and amber are the most common colors. Bottles with "sickness," an opalescent scaling which eliminates clarity, are worth much less.

Reference: George L. and Helen McKearin, *American Glass,* Crown Publishers, 1941 and 1948.

Collectors' Club: The National Early American Glass Club, P.O. Box 8489, Silver Spring, MD 20907.

Blown, 5⅝" h, yellowish amber, twenty–four vertical rib pattern, open pontil, sheared and tooled lip	70.00
Historical	
Benjamin Franklin, McKearin GI–96, qt, bust, aqua, open pontil, sheared and tooled lip	230.00
Columbia–Kensington, Eagle, Union Co, McKearin GI–117, pint, bust of Columbia, aqua, open pontil, sheared lip	220.00
Columbian Exposition, McKearin GI–128, pint, bust of Columbus, amber,	

Pitkin, medium green, 14 right hand swirls, pontil, $375.00.

pumpkinseed shape, smooth base, tooled lip 1,000.00
Eagle
  McKearin GII–11, half pint, cornucopia, aqua, open pontil, sheared lip 175.00
  McKearin GII–21, pint, My Country, For Pikes Peak, Prospector, ice blue, smooth base, applied mouth 130.00
  McKearin GII–60, half pint, Liberty, oak tree, amber, open pontil, sheared lip 960.00
  McKearin GII–143, banner in beak, yellowish green calabash, iron pontil, applied mouth 110.00
Jenny Lind, bust
  McKearin GI–99
    Emerald green calabash, open pontil, applied mouth 690.00
    Light citron calabash, open pontil, applied mouth 160.00
  McKearin GI–104, sapphire blue with deeper wisps, iron pontil, applied mouth 1,050.00
Lafayette, McKearin GI–86, half pint, bust, olive amber, open pontil, sheared lip 330.00
Louis Kossuth, USS Steam Frigate, McKearin GI–112, aqua calabash, open pontil, applied mouth 250.00
Masonic Arch, McKearin GIV–1a, pint, eagle, bluish green, open pontil, sheared and tooled lip 130.00
Success To The Railroad, McKearin GV–6, pint, horse pulling cart, olive amber, open pontil, sheared lip . 160.00
Nailsea, 7⅜″ h, teardrop shape, milk glass, white and cranberry red loopings, pontil, sheared and tooled lip . 160.00
Pictorial
  Army Soldier, McKearin GXIII–15, daisy, aqua, green calabash tint, iron pontil, applied mouth 130.00
  For Pikes Peak, McKearin GXI–17, pint, eagle, yellow, amber overtones, smooth base, applied mouth 425.00
  Horseman–Hound, McKearin GXIII–16, qt, amber, open pontil, sheared and tooled lip 425.00
  Hunter–Fisherman, McKearin GXIII–4, aqua calabash, open pontil, applied mouth 70.00
  Merry Christmas and Happy New Year, half pint, woman sitting on barrel holding drink, clear, half barrel shape, smooth base, tooled lip 85.00
  Summer Tree, Winter Tree, McKearin GX–15, pint, aqua, open pontil, applied mouth 120.00
  Will You Take A Drink, McKearin GXIII–29, half pint, swimming duck, aqua, smooth base, tooled lip ... 350.00
Pitkin
  6¼″ h, thirty–one broken rib pattern, swirled, olive green to darker green, open pontil, sheared and tooled lip 275.00
  6½″ h, thirty–six broken rib pattern, swirled, olive green, open pontil, sheared and tooled lip 250.00
Scroll
  McKearin GIX–1, qt, aqua, iron pontil, rolled lip 55.00
  McKearin, GIX–2, qt, pontil, sheared and tooled lip 525.00
  McKearin GIX–3, qt, aqua, iron pontil, applied mouth 110.00
  McKearin GIX–10, pint, aqua, iron pontil, applied mouth 55.00
  McKearin GIX–42, half pint, aqua, open pontil, sheared lip 225.00
Sunburst
  McKearin GVIII–3a, pint, yellowish amber, open pontil, sheared and tooled lip 325.00
  McKearin GVIII–16, half pint, yellow olive, open pontil, sheared and tooled lip 300.00
Teardrop, 8½″ h, light green, emb fleur–de–lis on one side, diamond pattern on other, pontil, rolled lip 50.00

FLOW BLUE

History: Flow blue or flowing blue is the name applied to china of cobalt and white whose color, when fired in a kiln, produced a flowing or smudged effect. The blue varies in color from dark cobalt to a grayish or steel blue. The flow varies from very slight to a heavy blur where the pattern cannot be easily recognized. The blue color does not permeate through the china.

Flow blue was first produced around 1835 in the Staffordshire district of England by a large number of potters including Alcock, Davenport, J. Wedgwood, Grindley, New Wharf, Johnson Brothers, and many others. The early flow blue, 1830s to 1870s, was usually of the ironstone variety. The late patterns, 1880s to 1910s, and modern patterns, after 1910, usually were made of the more delicate semi-porcelain variety. Approximately 95% of the flow blue was made in England, with the remaining 5% made in Germany, Holland, France, and Belgium. A few patterns also were made in the United States by Mercer, Warwick, and Wheeling Pottery companies.

References: Susan and Al Bagdade, *Warman's English & Continental Pottery & Porcelain, 2nd Edition,* Wallace—Homestead, 1991; Mary F. Gaston, *The Collector's Encyclopedia Of Flow Blue China,* Collector Books, 1983, 1989 value update; Petra Williams, *Flow Blue China—An Aid To Identification, Revised Edition,* Fountain House East, 1981; Petra Williams, *Flow Blue China II, Revised Edition,* Fountain House East, 1981; Petra Williams, *Flow Blue China and Mulberry Ware—Similarity and Value Guide, Revised Edition,* Fountain House East, 1981.

Collectors' Club: Flow Blue International Collectors' Club, P.O. Box 205, Rockford, IL 61105.

Early, Sobroan, plate, 10″ d, $85.00.

EARLY PATTERNS: c1825–1850

Butter Dish, cov
Chusan, Podmore Walker & Co, c1845	120.00
Pelew, E Challinor, c1840	125.00

Creamer
Amoy, Davenport, c1844	225.00
Cashmere, Ridgway & Morley, c1840	275.00
Hong Kong, Charles Meigh, c1845	100.00
Indian Jar, Thomas Ford, c1840	175.00
Scinde, J & G Alcock, c1840	200.00

Sobraon, unknown English maker, c1845	200.00
Tonquin, W Adams & Son, c1845	100.00

Cup and Saucer, handleless
Amoy, Davenport, c1844	85.00
Chapoo, Wedgwood, c1850	125.00
Jeddo, Adams & Co, c1840	90.00
Kyber, Adams & Co, c1850	85.00
Scinde, J & G Alcock, c1840	125.00

Cup Plate
Oregon, T J & J Mayer, c1845, 4″ d	125.00
Rhine, Thomas Dimmock, c1844	50.00
Scinde, J & G Alcock, c1840	65.00

Gravy Boat
Daliah, E Challinor, c1850	100.00
Sobraon, unknown English maker, c1845	150.00

Pitcher, Cashmere, Ridgway & Morley, c1840, 7″ h, octagonal	325.00

Plate
Amoy, Davenport, c1844, 8¼″	50.00
California, Podmore Walker & Co, c1849, 7¾″	48.00
Chapoo, Wedgwood, c1850, 8½″	60.00
Chen–Si, John Meir, c1835, 8½″	80.00
Indian Jar, Jacob & Thos Furnival, c1843, 10½″	115.00
Jeddo, Adams & Co, c1840, 9″	65.00
Manilla, Podmore, Walker & Co, c1845, 9½″	100.00
Oregon, T J & J Mayer, c1845, 10″	115.00
Scinde, J & G Alcock, c1840, 7″	60.00
Tonquin, W Adams & Son, c1845, 7½″	65.00

Platter
Chen–Si, John Meir, c1835, 14 x 17″	250.00
Indian Jar, Jacob & Thos Furnival, c1843, 9¾ x 12⅜″	285.00
Kyber, Adams & Co, c1850, 17″	300.00
Manilla, Podmore, Walker & Co, c1845, 16″	400.00
Oregon, T J & J Mayer, c1845, 13½″	250.00

Sauce Dish
Amoy, Davenport, c1844, 5″	60.00
Indian Jar, Jacob & Thos Furnival, c1843	50.00
Oregon, T J & J Mayer, c1845, 5″	65.00
Scinde, Thomas Walker, c1847, 5″	60.00
Shell, Wood & Challinor, c1840	42.00
Tulip & Sprig, Thomas Walker, c1845	38.00

Soup Plate
Arabesque, T J & J Mayer, c1845	75.00
Oregon, T J & J Mayer, c1845, 9½″ d, flange rim	115.00
Sobraon, unknown English maker, c1845, 9″, flange rim	100.00

Soup Tureen
Chusan, Podmore Walker & Co, c1845	175.00
Scinde, J G Alcock, c1840, cov	600.00

Sugar, cov
Chen–Si, 7½ x 7″	200.00

Oregon, T J & J Mayer, c1845 . . . . 225.00
Scinde, J & G Alcock, c1840 . . . . . 350.00
Tea Set, cov teapot, creamer, and cov sugar
  California, Podmore Walker & Co, c1849 . . . . 300.00
  Oregon, T J & J Mayer, c1845 . . . . 900.00
Toddy Plate, Tonquin, W Adams & Son, c1845 . . . . 75.00
Vegetable Dish
  Covered
    Cashmere, Ridgway & Morley, c1840 . . . . 775.00
    Manilla, Podmore, Walker & Co, c1845, octagonal 445.00
  Open, Amoy, Davenport, c1844, 6 x 8" 175.00
Waste Bowl, Chen–Si, John Meir, c1835, 8½" 120.00

Middle, Temple, tea bowl and saucer, marked "P. W. & Co.," $115.00.

MIDDLE PATTERNS: c1850–1870

Charger, Tyrolean, Wm Ridgway & Co, c1850, 12¼" 125.00
Coffeepot, Simila, Elsmore & Forster, c1860 . . . . 165.00
Creamer
  Genevese, Edge Malkin, c1873 . . . . 100.00
  Honc, Petrus Regout, c1858 . . . . . . 148.00
Dish, Blossom, G L Ashworth & Bros, c1865, 9½" d 30.00
Pitcher, Temple, Podmore Walker & Co, c1850, 8" h 300.00
Plate
  Carlton, Samuel Alcock, c1850, 9½" 60.00
  Gothic, Jacob Furnival, c1850, 8¼" . 80.00
  Honc, Petrus Regout, c1858, 8" . . . 75.00
  Temple, Podmore Walker & Co, c1850, 10" 115.00
Platter
  Hindustan, 12 x 16" 220.00
  Shanghae, J Furnival, c1860, 13½" . 165.00
Soup Plate
  Blossom, G L Ashworth & Bros, 9", flange rim 20.00
  Carlton, Samuel Alcock, c1850, 10½", flange rim 80.00

Gothic, Jacob Furnival, c1850, flange rim 65.00
Sugar, cov, Temple, Podmore Walker & Co, c1850 . . . . 250.00
Syllaub Cup, Blossom, G L Ashworth & Bros 50.00
Teapot, cov, Gothic, Jacob Furnival, c1850, 7" h 525.00
Vegetable Dish
  Covered
    Asiatic Pheasants, John Meir & Son, c1865 . . . . 110.00
    Victor, J Maddock & Sons, c1850 . 115.00
  Open, Gothic, Jacob Furnival, c1850 90.00

LATE PATTERNS: c1880–1900s

Biscuit Jar, Watteau, Doulton, 1896–1930, metal top 325.00
Bone Dish
  Duchess, W H Grindley, c1891 . . . . 35.00
  Irdis, W H Grindley, c1910 . . . . 50.00
Bouillon Cup, underplate, Irdis, W H Grindley, c1910, two handles 48.00
Bowl
  Keswick, Wood & Sons, c1891, 9½" d 40.00
  Raleigh, Burgess & Leigh, c1906 . . 25.00
Butter Dish, cov
  Colonial, J & G Meakin, c1891, orig insert 110.00
  Kenworth, Johnson Bros, c1900 . . . 150.00
  Linda, John Maddock & Sons, Ltd, c1896 . . . . 75.00
  Oriental, Ridgway, c1891, orig patterned insert 150.00
Butter Pat
  Argyle, W H Grindley, c1896 . . . . . . 32.00
  Blue Danube, Johnson Bros, c1900 25.00
  Lugano, Ridgway, c1910 . . . . 22.00
Creamer, Richmond, Johnson Bros, c1900 . . . . 75.00
Cup and Saucer
  Duchess, W H Grindley, c1891 . . . . 40.00
  Lancaster, New Wharf Pottery, c1891 60.00
  Lugano, Ridgway, c1910 . . . . 70.00
  Oriental, Ridgway, c1891 . . . . 42.00
  Touraine, Stanley Pottery Co, c1898 45.00
Fruit Bowl, Jenny Lind, Arthur Wilkinson Ltd, Royal Staffordshire Pottery, c1895, 7½" d 125.00
Gravy Boat, attached underplate
  Kenworth, Johnson Bros, c1900 . . . 75.00
  Richmond, Johnson Bros, c1900 . . . 85.00
Ladle, Vermont, Burgess & Leigh, c1895 . . . . 85.00
Pitcher, Colonial, J & G Meakin, c1891, 6" 125.00
Plate
  Bentick, Cauldon, c1905, 8" 35.00
  Hamilton, John Maddock & Sons, c1896, 10½" 75.00

Holland, Johnson Bros, c1891, 8″	55.00
Kenworth, Johnson Bros, c1900, 10″	48.00
Lancaster, New Wharf Pottery, c1891, 9″	50.00
Linda, John Maddock & Sons, Ltd, c1896, small	20.00
Lorne, W H Grindley, c1900, 8″	48.00
Lugano, Ridgway, c1910, 10″	85.00

Platter

Argyle, W H Grindley, c1896, 15″	175.00
Kenworth, Johnson Bros, c1900, 12″	75.00
Keswick, Wood & Sons, c1891	75.00
La Belle, Wheeling Pottery, c1900, 12″	85.00
Lancaster, New Wharf Pottery, c1891, 9½″	90.00

Soup Plate

Lancaster, New Wharf Pottery, c1891, 9″, flange rim	48.00
Lugano, Ridgway, c1910, 9″	65.00
Rose, Ridgway, c1910, 9″, flange rim	20.00
Tulip, Johnson Bros, c1900, 9″, gilt	65.00

Sauce Dish, Richmond, Johnson Bros, c1900	20.00
Saucer, Lancaster, New Wharf Pottery, c1891	15.00
Teapot, cov, Oriental, Ridgway, c1891	245.00

Tureen, cov

Linda, John Maddock & Sons, Ltd, c1896	130.00
Lugano, Ridgway, c1910, 11½″	275.00

Vegetable Dish

Covered

Bentick, Cauldon, c1905, oblong	150.00
Oriental, Ridgway, c1891	145.00
Peach, Johnson Bros, c1891, 6 x 8″	50.00
Vermont, Burgess & Leigh, c1895	175.00

Open

Irdis, W H Grindley, c1910	110.00
Jenny Lind, Arthur Wilkinson Ltd, Royal Staffordshire Pottery, c1895, 7½″ d	125.00

FOLK ART

History: The definition of what constitutes folk art is still being vigorously debated among collectors, dealers, museum curators, and scholars. Some want to confine folk art to non-academic, handmade objects. Others are willing to include manufactured material. In truth, the term is used to cover objects ranging from crude drawings by obviously untalented children to academically trained artists' paintings of "common" people and scenery.

The folk art market is subject to hype and manipulation. Neophyte collectors are encouraged to read Edie Clark's "What Really Is Folk Art?" in the December 1986 *Yankee.* Clark's article provides a refreshingly honest look at the folk art market.

Finally, the folk art market is extremely trendy and fickle. What is hot today can become cool and passé tomorrow. Collecting folk art is not for the weak–of–heart or the cautious investor.

References: Kenneth L. Ames, *Beyond Necessity: Art In The Folk Tradition,* W. W. Norton, 1978; Robert Bishop and Judith Rieter Weissman, *Folk Art: The Knopf Collectors' Guides To American Antiques,* Alfred A. Knopf, 1983; Henry Niemann and Helaine Fendelman, *The Official Identification and Price Guide To American Folk Art,* House of Collectibles, 1988.

Museum: Museum of American Folk Art, New York, NY; Abby Aldrich Rockefeller Folk Art Center, Williamsburg, VA.

Train Station, wood, painted, maroon, gold, and green, gold painted pilasters, c1900, 16½″ l, 13″ d, 17″ h, $625.00.

Architectural Ornament, attributed to Julius Melchers, Detroit, mid 19th C, 23″ h, 24″ w, carved and painted, heads, half round, foliate and leaf surrounds, one with rosettes, other with curled horns, mounted on black metal base, orig polychrome, pr	7,700.00
Bird House, 7½″ h, pottery, tree trunk shape, incised bark and applied knots, old chips	25.00

Building Model, primitive, handmade

17″ h, church, tin and wood, old white paint, green roof and red chimney, light rust and wear, electric lighted int.	175.00
27¼″ h, 31″ l, farmyard, farmhouse, barn, outbuildings, gardens, trees, stream, pond, fenced sides, wood, stone, metal, fiber, paint, orig case and lid with red flame graining, paint dec paper cov int., minor damage	650.00
Embroidery, PA, early 19th C, 13½ x 14½″, crewel, still–life, pink, yellow, white, blue, and green, bouquet of garden blossoms arranged in crocheted basket, mounted on white cotton ground, framed	660.00

Figure, 25¾″ h, wood carver, holding mallet and chisel, old polychrome paint **525.00**
Fireboard, American, early 19th C, 25″ h, 37½″ w, painted pine, four combined boards, painted ftd compote with curling vines of pink flowers, lace trimmed red drapery swags on blue and red ground **1,100.00**
Jug, PA, 1830–60, 7¼″ h, grotesque, stoneware, salt glazed, cobalt blue dec, two protruding pouring spouts, applied arched handle, both sides with molded man's face, open mouth, incised teeth, applied stylized ears, incised inscription "IG...RJ...IA," back chipped **8,800.00**
Miniature Portrait, American School, 19th C
  3½ x 3″, dark haired young lady, tall comb, black dress, and frilled white collar, watercolor on jade green paper **1,980.00**
  4¾ x 3¼″, lady in eyelet cap and collar, gentleman in black frock coat, pencil on paper, sgd and dated on verso "J. M. Crowley, Delineator, Valatie, Jany 28–1836" **1,320.00**
  5¼ x 4½″, portrait of gentleman in black frock coat with gold buttons, lady in black dress with white fichu, c1880, orig black glass mats, watercolor on paper **770.00**
Painting, American School, 19th C, unknown artist
  14 x 20″, oil on canvas, The Sugar Run School, Pomeroy, Meigs County, Ohio, c1860, orig stretchers, contemporary frame **1,870.00**
  34½″ h, 20″ w, oil on wood panel, Miss Evelina Elmore Grace, dark haired little girl, printed yellow dress, green reticule, background with idealized view of Fort Edward, NY **11,000.00**
Scherenschnitte, PA German, 19th C
  7¾ x 9″, pr, one depicting abuse by man of animals in hunting, farming, and playing, second with animals taking their revenge, scissor–cut black paper, gray–green paper ground **880.00**
  11½ x 16″, pr, one with church in landscape of houses and trees, mill and fisherman, second with manor house with swan pond and garden gate, scissor–cut white paper, turquoise blue paper ground **1,100.00**
Ship's Figurehead, New England, c1900, 25½″ h, carved oak, bust portrait of young female angel, parted tresses, detached wings **2,200.00**

Theorem, American
  16½″ h, 19½″ w, velvet, painted basket of flowers, gilt frame **350.00**
  19¾″ h, 21½″ w, compote of fruit, mica flecks on compote base, watercolor on paper, framed **600.00**
Toy
  Doll, 10″ h, rag, whisk broom, black woman, embroidered face, hand–sewn clothes **30.00**
  Marble Shooter, 12″ h, soldier shape, wood, metal fittings, orig polychrome paint, damage to tin shoe **75.00**
Weather Vane, American, 20th C, 28″ l, 35½″ h, airplane, wood and metal, worn and weathered gray, red, and black paint, modern base **425.00**

FOOD BOTTLES

History: Food bottles were made in many sizes, shapes, and colors. Manufacturers tried to make an attractive bottle that would ship well and allow the purchaser to see the product, thus assuring him that the product was as good and as well made as home preserves.

Reference: Ralph & Terry Kovel, *The Kovels' Bottle Price List, 8th Edition,* Crown Publishers, Inc, 1984.

Periodical: *Antique Bottle and Glass Collector,* P.O. Box 187, East Greenville, PA 18041.

Additional Listings: See *Warman's Americana & Collectibles* for more milk bottle listings.

Milk Bottle, half pint, emb "Miller's Dairy," c1892, $12.00.

Catsup, Quickshank, paper label **5.00**
Celery Salt, Crown Celery Salt, Horton Cato & Co, Detroit, yellow amber, smooth base, ground lip, orig shaker type cap, 8″ h **165.00**

Ginger, Sanford's, orig label	**10.00**
Grape Juice, Bass Islands, 5″ h	**5.00**
Horseradish	
As You Like It, pottery, clamp	**25.00**
E T Caldren, aqua, paper label	**10.00**
Lemon Extract, Louis & Company . . .	**10.00**
Lime Juice, arrow motif, olive amber,	
smooth base, applied mouth, 10¼″ h	**80.00**
Milk	
Alta Crest Farms, Spencer, MA, yel-	
low green, smooth base, 9½″ h . .	**725.00**
Brighton Farm, Cramery, H Bahren-	
brug, 55 1st St, Hoboken, NJ, clear,	
smooth base, tooled lip, orig tin lid	
and wire closure	**65.00**
Farm Dairy Quality Products, yellow	**20.00**
Hebrew Dairy, three emb flags, qt . .	**30.00**
Palmer Dairy, dripless, qt	**25.00**
R F S Co, clear, tooled lip, orig tin lid	
and wire closure, qt	**25.00**
R M Deger, Phoenixville, PA, Pure	
Milk, clear, emb, 9½″ h	**5.00**
Ridgeview Farms, sq, pyro, pt	**45.00**
Peanut Butter, Bennett Hubba, 5″ h . .	**12.00**
Pepper Sauce, S & P Pat App For, teal	
blue, smooth base, tooled lip, 8″ h .	**50.00**
Pickle	
Hyman Pickle Co, Louisville, KY, yel-	
low olive, smooth base, applied	
mouth, 8″ h	**90.00**
Shaker Brand, olive yellow	**325.00**
Vinegar, Weso Biko Company Cider Vi-	
negar, jug shape	**40.00**

FOOD MOLDS

History: Food molds were used both commercially and in the home. For the most part, pewter
ice cream molds and candy molds were used on
a commercial basis; pottery and copper molds
were used in homes. Today, both types are collected largely for decorative purposes.

Pewter ice cream molds were made primarily by
two American companies: Eppelsheimer & Co.
[molds marked E & Co., N.Y.] and Schall & Co.
[molds marked S & Co.]. Both companies used a
numbering system for their molds. The Krauss Co.
bought out Schall & Co., removed the S & Co.
from some, but not all the molds, and added more
designs [marked K or Krauss].

The majority of pewter ice cream molds are individual serving molds. When used, one quart of
ice cream would make eight to ten pieces. Scarcer,
but still available, are banquet molds which used
two to four pints of ice cream per example. European pewter molds [CC is a French mold mark]
are available.

Chocolate mold makers are more difficult to determine. Unlike the pewter ice cream molds, maker's marks were not always on the mold or were
covered by frames. Eppelsheimer & Co. of New

York marked many of their molds, either with their
name or with a design resembling a child's toy top
with "Trade Mark" and "NY." Many chocolate
molds were imported from Germany and Holland
and were marked with the country of origin and,
in some cases, the mold maker's name.

Reference: Judene Divone, *Chocolate Moulds:
A History & Encyclopedia,* Oakton Hills Publications, 1987.

Additional Listings: Butter Prints.

CHOCOLATE MOLDS

Basket, 3½ x 6″, one cavity	**45.00**
Boy on bicycle, 8¾″ h, two parts	**375.00**
Chick and egg, 3½″ h, two parts, folding,	
marked "Allemagne," Germany	**40.00**
Circus Peanuts, 28 x 13″, tray type, 105	
cavities	**50.00**
Elephant, tin, three cavities	**75.00**
Jack O'Lantern, two pcs, wire clamp . .	**30.00**
Heart, 6½ x 6″, two cavities	**65.00**
Hen on basket, two pcs, clamp type,	
marked "E & Co/Toy"	**45.00**
Rabbit	
6″, two pcs, clamp type	**45.00**
14 x 10″, playing saxophone, tray	
type, six cavities	**45.00**
Skeleton, 5½″ h, pressed tin	**60.00**
Teddy Bear, two pcs, clamp type,	
marked "Reiche"	**275.00**
Turkey, 14 x 10″, tray type, eight cavities	**45.00**
Two Eggs, 3¼″, alligatored relief design	**35.00**
Witch, 4½ x 2″, four cavities	**55.00**

**Ice cream, Valentine, envelope shape,
pewter, marked "S & Co. 506," $45.00.**

ICE CREAM MOLDS

Banquet Size

Owl, four pints, marked "S & Co/7″ .	**550.00**
Pear, marked "S & Co, #17″	**250.00**

Ship, two quarts	**225.00**

Individual Size

Asparagus, 3⅝" h, pewter	**25.00**
Basket, pewter, replaced hinge pins	**18.00**
Cherub riding Easter Bunny, 4" h, pewter	**25.00**
Circle, pewter, marked "Kiwanis Club" and "E & Co, NY"	**20.00**
Easter Lily, pewter, 3 part	**57.50**
Egg, 2¾" d, marked "E & Co, NY" .	**25.00**
Flag, thirteen stars, pewter	**50.00**
Fruit, 2¾" d, marked "E & Co, NY" .	**25.00**
Kewpie, pewter, dated 1913	**145.00**
Man in the Moon, 5½" h, pewter, marked "E & Co, copyright 1888"	**75.00**
Pear, pewter, marked "CC849 Brevete"	**25.00**
Playing Cards with diamond, pewter, marked "E & Co, NY"	**25.00**
Rose, pewter, replaced hinge pins . .	**17.00**
Shoe, lady's, 5¾", pewter	**25.00**
Steamboat, pewter	**90.00**
Tulip, 4⅛" h, pewter, marked "E & Co, NY"	**35.00**

MISCELLANEOUS

Butter

4½ x 6⅞", rect cased, cherry, deep carved geometric design	**110.00**
5½ x 6", rect, cased, four part design, refinished	**65.00**
Cake, rabbit, Griswold	**245.00**
Cheese, 5 x 13", wood, relief carved design and "Bid," pinned, branded "Los," scratch carved date 1893 . . .	**45.00**

Pudding

5 x 5 x 6½", oval, pineapple, tin and copper	**65.00**
12½" h, tin, rabbit form, late 19th C, early 20th C	**125.00**

POTTERY (Center Design Indicated)

Ear of Corn, 6" l, yellowware, oval . . .	**40.00**
Grapes and leaf, 3 x 5 x 7", oval, Wedgwood Creamware	**110.00**
Rose, ironstone, marked "Alcock" . . .	**50.00**
Strawberries, 4"	**55.00**
Turk's Head, 9" d, redware, swirled fluting, brown sponged rim	**45.00**

FOSTORIA GLASS   FOSTORIA

History: Fostoria Glass Co. began operations at Fostoria, Ohio, in 1887, and moved to Moundsville, West Virginia, its present location, in 1891. By 1925 Fostoria had five furnaces and a variety of special shops. In 1924 a line of colored tableware was introduced. Fostoria was purchased by Lancaster Colony in 1983, and continues to operate under the Fostoria name.

Reference: Hazel M. Weatherman, *Fostoria, Its First Fifty Years*, published by author, c1972.

Collectors' Club: Fostoria Glass Society of America, P.O. Box 826, Moundsville, WV 26041.

Museum: Huntington Galleries, Huntington, WV.

Ashtray

Coin, light blue, frosted	**22.50**
Lafayette, Mayfair, 4" d	**30.00**
Baker, Versailles, yellow, oval, 9" l . . .	**60.00**

Bonbon

Chintz, three toes	**31.00**
Heirloom, green, opalescent	**16.00**

Bowl

Buttercup, handle, 10" d	**45.00**
Colony, low, ftd, 10½" d	**65.00**
Versailles, yellow, 5½" d	**20.00**

Butter Dish, cov

Baroque, blue	**275.00**
Fairfax, orchid	**350.00**
Cake Plate, Fairfax, blue, handle, 10" d	**37.50**
Candlesticks, pr, Lafayette, wisteria, 2" h	**65.00**

Candy Dish, cov

Baroque, blue, ftd, 9½" h	**70.00**
Coin, red, frosted	**50.00**
Candy Jar, cov, Camillia, 7" h	**65.00**
Celery, Buttercup	**35.00**

Champagne

Chintz	**16.00**
Fairfax, orchid	**25.00**
Cheese and Cracker Set, Versailles, yellow, #2375	**75.00**
Cheese Compote, Colony	**15.00**
Cocktail, Versailles, pink	**25.00**

Cordial

Fairfax, orchid	**55.00**
Lafayette, wisteria	**150.00**
Willowmere	**18.00**
Creamer, Versailles, green	**18.00**

Creamer and Sugar Set, matching tray, individual size

Camillia	**45.00**
Chintz	**67.00**
Cream Soup, Kashmir, blue	**60.00**
Cruet, orig stopper, Fairfax, pink	**125.00**

Cup and Saucer

Colony	**10.00**
Fairfax, blue	**12.50**
Navarre	**27.50**
Versailles, green	**22.00**
Decanter Set, Ring of Rings, six matching glasses	**65.00**
Demitasse Cup, Fairfax, blue	**15.00**
Dessert Bowl, Kashmir, blue, large . . .	**145.00**
Figure, mermaid	**225.00**

Goblet

America, 5½" h, 9 oz	**13.00**
Bouquet	**21.00**

Fairfax, blue	25.00		Midnight Rose, four parts	37.50
Mayflower	22.50		Minuet, yellow, four part, 2 handles	40.00
Willowmere	19.00		Salt and Pepper Shakers, pr, Versailles,	
Grapefruit, liner, Fairfax, orchid	75.00		pink	150.00

Fairfax, blue 25.00
Mayflower 22.50
Willowmere 19.00
Grapefruit, liner, Fairfax, orchid 75.00
Ice Bucket
  Baroque, blue 70.00
  Sunray 40.00
  Versailles, yellow 75.00
Iced Tea, ftd
  America, 12 oz 13.00
  Baroque, blue, 6" h 75.00
  Chintz 21.00
  Jamestown, blue 19.00
Juice Tumbler, ftd
  Chintz 17.50
  Lafayette, wisteria 37.50
Lemon Plate, Fairfax, blue 20.00
Mayonnaise, liner, ladle, Buttercup ... 55.00
Mint Tray, Baroque, yellow, ftd, 4¼" d . 18.00
Nappy, Coin, red 20.00
Olive Dish, cupped, Colony, 5½" d ... 20.00
Oyster Cocktail
  America 10.00
  Romance 22.50
Parfait, Fairfax, blue 31.00
Pickle Dish
  Bouquet, 8½" l 18.00
  Buttercup 25.00
  Midnight Rose 30.00
Pitcher
  Acanthus, amber 300.00
  Bouquet, 6⅛" h 75.00
Plate
  Kashmir, blue, 10¼" d 60.00
  Midnight Rose, 8½" d 14.00
  Minuet, yellow, 9" d 15.00
  Navarre, 7½" d 14.00
  Versailles, yellow, 7½" d 9.00
Platter, Minuet, yellow, 11" l 35.00
Punch Bowl, Baroque, crystal 400.00
Relish
  Baroque, blue, sq, two parts, 6" w .. 35.00
  Lido, three parts, 10" d 25.00

Midnight Rose, four parts 37.50
Minuet, yellow, four part, 2 handles . 40.00
Salt and Pepper Shakers, pr, Versailles,
  pink 150.00
Server, center handle
  Chintz 45.00
  Kashmir, blue 75.00
  Romance 35.00
Sherbet
  Chintz 16.00
  Jamestown, blue 15.00
  Versailles, yellow 22.00
Sugar, cov, June, yellow 225.00
Sweetmeat, Fairfax, blue, two handles 22.50
Tidbit, Chintz, three toes 31.00
Tray, Baroque, blue, 8" l 65.00
Tumbler
  Jamestown, blue 19.00
  Lafayette, wisteria 35.00
  Versailles, pink, 5¼" h 20.00
Vase
  America, sq, ftd, 10" h 40.00
  Buttercup, ftd, 7" h 135.00
Whipped Cream Bowl
  Fairfax, blue 24.00
  Versailles, yellow, 6" d 15.00
Whiskey, Fairfax, orchid 30.00
Wine
  America, hex foot, 2½ oz 15.00
  Buttercup, 3½ oz 29.50
  Chintz 40.00

FRAKTUR

History: Fraktur, the calligraphy associated with the Pennsylvania Germans, is named for the elaborate first letter found in many of the hand drawn examples. Throughout its history printed, partially printed-hand drawn, and fully hand drawn works existed side by side. Frakturs often were made by the school teachers or ministers living in rural areas of Pennsylvania, Maryland, and Virginia. Many artists are unknown.

Fraktur exists in several forms—geburts and taufschein (birth and baptismal certificates), vorschrift (writing example, often with alphabet), haus sagen (house blessing), bookplates and marks, rewards of merit, illuminated religious text, valentines, and drawings. Although collected for decoration, the key element in fraktur is the text.

Fraktur prices rise and fall along with the American folk art market. The key market place is Pennsylvania and the Middle Atlantic states.

References: Donald A. Shelley, *The Fraktur-Writings Or Illuminated Manuscripts Of The Pennsylvania Germans*, Pennsylvania German Society, 1961; Frederick S. Weiser and Howell J. Heaney (compilers), *The Pennsylvania German Fraktur Of The Free Library Of Philadelphia*, Pennsylvania German Society, 1976, two volumes.

Salt Shaker, rose in relief, 2" d, 3¼" h, $25.00.

Museum: The Free Library of Philadelphia, Philadelphia, PA.

HAND DRAWN

Blowsy (Flying) Angel Artist
Birth and baptismal certificate, Northampton County, dated 1800, 9½ x 13½", watercolor, pen, and ink on paper, center text block consumes lower two–thirds of paper, flanked by flowers above which are blowsy angels extending into center above text block, birth of Magdelena Gunziger **2,000.00**
Birth Letter, dated 1796, 13 x 15½", watercolor, pen, and ink, wove paper, red and yellow flying angels with tulips and hearts for Anna Maria Zollner **3,575.00**

Birth and Baptismal Certificate, Lancaster County, PA, hand drawn in imitation of printed form, 12¼ x 10", $900.00.

Crossed Legged Angel Artist, birth and baptismal certificate, Lancaster County, dated 1812, 14 x 17¼", watercolor, pen, and ink on laid paper, block format, floral motif on side borders, crossed legged angel in center of top panel, star burst in center of bottom panel, birth of Michael Klop . **2,500.00**
Eyer, Johann Adam, bookplate, dated 1781, 4¼ x 2½", watercolor, pen and ink, blue and yellow peacock perched on flowering tulip tree **4,125.00**
Gottschall, M., baptismal certificate, Bucks County, dated 1827, 12¾ x 16", watercolor, pen, and ink, hearts,

birds, pinwheels, and flying angels, for Rakel Stahr **24,200.00**
Heydrich, Baltzer, drawing, Montgomery County, 1845, pen, ink, and watercolor drawing on wove paper, checkerboard border, center with wall (altar) flanked by stylized flowers in a semi–circular motif, bird on branch of two of flowers, PA German inscription, "Baltzer Heydrich...1845...in his 83rd year," tones of red, black, green, blue, and yellow, minor stains, tears and damage at fold line, beveled frame with red graining, 16¼ x 20¼" **7,600.00**
Otto, Daniel (The Flat Tulip Artist), birth and baptismal certificate, Northumberland County, dated 1788, 11½ x 14¾", watercolor, pen, and ink on paper, central heart text, flanked at bottom by two large parrots with checkered wings facing outward and at top by two smaller parrots with plain wings facing inward, heart with border of attached flowers, red and yellow tones, birth of Catharina Lotz **13,250.00**
Seller, H., birth certificate, Dauphin County, PA, 1807, 16¼ x 19¼", pen, ink, and watercolor on laid paper, central heart flanked at base by large parrots above which is a tulip and peacock, tulip flanked by starburst across top, geometric circles along bottom with "H./Seiler", shades of red, green, blue, brown, yellow, and black, text is primarily in red ink, minor stains, short tears, large tulips have some holes caused by acid ink, bottom edge a bit ragged **12,000.00**
Spanenberg, John, double bookplate for Catharina Haupt, 5¾ x 6¼", pen, ink, and watercolor on laid paper, stylized horizontal floral bands across top and bottom, tones of red, blue, green, yellow, and brown, some stains, fading, and damage on fold line, gilt frame 8½ x 10½" **3,500.00**
Unknown
Bookplate
Southeastern PA, c1820, 3¾ x 5¾", fly leaf of Martin Luther's *Book of Catechisms,* published by Johann Bar, block motif, central block with heart from which flower radiates, starbursts in corner blocks, stemmed floral motifs in remaining blocks, shades of red, blue, yellow, and green, heart marked "Salome Beinhauer/1828," worn marbleized paper, leather binding for book . **2,350.00**
Southeastern PA, c1820–40, 5 x 5⅝", laid paper, central heart with

text, face from which radiates two stemmed tulips at top, bottom of heart decorated with fern–like leaves with two star floral motifs, heart contains name "Elizabeth Richter," dark shades of brown, olive, and reddish brown, minor stains, small edge damage, glued to lined paper, frame 10¾ x 11½" **1,650.00**

Southeastern PA, c1840s, 3 x 4¾", watercolor, pen, and ink on paper lining of cardboard book cover, heart with text from which ra- diates tulips and stems, bird sits on two of lesser tulips, shades of orange, yellow, lavender, and black, for "Georg Reiff," dated 1844, stains, frame 5 x 6¾" ... **425.00**

Drawing, southeastern PA, c1820– 40, laid paper, horizontal dec bands, top with two facing birds surrounded by flowers, block letters "REBECCA SNYDER," birds and flowers, bottom with man and dog flanking central flower, red, yellow, blue, pale green, and brown, stains and small tears, old black frame 8½ x 9¾" **3,700.00**

Reward of Merit, southeastern, PA, c1820–40, wove paper, 8 x 12¾", stylized vining plant with flowers and birds, initials "F/Z," green, brown, blue, and faded red, old damage and repairs, frame 12¾ x 16⅞" **1,600.00**

Song Book, southeastern PA, c1800– 10, possibly Bucks County, dated 1804, 6⅜ x 3¾", bookplate has cir- cular text flanked by vertical flower with multi–leaf stem, checkered border, belongs to "Abraham Landes," cover pulled loose from string binding but is not damaged **3,000.00**

HAND DRAWN–PRINTED

Brechall, Martin, birth and baptismal, printed form by Hütter, Easton, 1821, 13 x 16", central heart, borders hand painted with filigrees and flowers in red, yellow, blue, and green, for Lea Schull **950.00**

Dulheur, Henrich, birth and baptismal, 13 x 15¾" **950.00**

Otto, Heinrich, The Great Comet Of 1769, decorated with parrots and shooting stars **2,500.00**

Unknown Artist, birth certificate, Nor- thampton County, 1821, 7¾" x 12", German calligraphy, inscription within a keystone device, hand painted

paired birds and large flowering tulip plants, birth of Maria Margaretha Scherner **750.00**

PRINTED

Adam and Eve
  Bruckman, C. A., Reading **300.00**
  Dahlem, M., Philadelphia **400.00**
Birth and Baptismal
  Baumann and Ruth, Ephrata **350.00**
  Baumann, S., Ephrata **400.00**
  Blumer, A. & W., Allentown **175.00**
  Hartman, Joseph, Lebanon **250.00**
  Hanesche, J. G., Baltimore **150.00**
  Herschberger, Johann, Chambers- burg **325.00**
  Hütter, C. J., Easton **350.00**
  Lepper, Wilhelm, Hanover **300.00**
  Lippe, G. Ph., Pottsville **150.00**
  Puwelle, A., Reading **125.00**
  Saeger and Leisenring, Allentown, early form **150.00**
  Sage, G. A., Allentown **175.00**
  Scheffer, Theo. F., Harrisburg **75.00**
  Wiestling, Johann S., Harrisburg ... **200.00**
  Note: If signed by a scrivener, in- crease value by 25% to 40%

FRANKART

History: Arthur Von Frankenberg, artist and sculptor, founded Frankart, Inc., in New York City in the mid-1920s. Frankart, Inc., mass produced practical "art objects" in the Art Deco style into the 1930s. Pieces include aquariums, ashtrays, book- ends, flower vases, lamps, etc. Although Von Fran- kenberg used five female models as his subjects, his figures are characterized by their form and style rather than specific features. Nudes are the most collectible; caricatured animals and other hu- man figures were also produced, no doubt, to in- crease sales.

With few exceptions, pieces were marked Fran- kart, Inc., with a patent number or "pat. appl. for."

Pieces were cast in a white metal composition in the following finishes: cream–a pale iridescent white; bronzoid–oxidized copper, silver, or gold; french–a medium brown with green in the crevices; gun metal–art iridescent gray; jap–a very dark brown, almost black, with green in the crevices; pearl green–pale iridescent green; and verde–a dull light green. Cream and bronzoid were used primarily in the 1930s.

Note: All pieces listed are all original in very good condition unless otherwise indicated.

Advisor: Walter Glenn.

Aquarium, 10½" h, three kneeling nude figures encircle 10" d crystal glass aquarium bowl **675.00**

Lamp, nude figure with leg extended, sitting between two 6″ h, 2″ d amber glass cylinders, 8″ h, $725.00.

Ashtray
5″ h, stylized duck with outstretched wings supports green glass ash receiver	90.00
6″ h, nude figure kneels on cushion, holding 3″ d removable pottery ashtray	210.00
7″ h, caricatured monkey supports 3″ d glass ash receiver in in his tail .	85.00
9½″ h, seated nude figure on 3″ h column, leg extends over 5″ sq ceramic ashtray	385.00
12″ h, acrobatic nude figure balances 3″ d glass ashball on toes	365.00
25″ h, nude figure grows from tobacco plant to hold scalloped glass tray overhead	625.00

Bookends, pr
5″ h, horse heads with flowing manes	45.00
6″ h, seated cubist styled bears . . .	70.00
8″ h, nude figures peek around edge of books	245.00
10″ h, nude figures sit atop metal books	235.00

Candlesticks, pr, 12½″ h, nude figures standing on tiptoes, holding candle cup over heads	365.00
Cigarette Box, 8″ h, back to back nudes support removable green glass box .	425.00
Incense Burner, 10″ h, draped figure holds tray and cover for incense . . .	250.00

Lamp
8″ h, nude figure kneels before 4″ d crystal bubble ball	585.00
10½″ h, two nude figures stand on either side of geometrically shaped plate glass panel	1,150.00
13″ h, two back to back dancing nude figures support 11″ sq glass cylinder satin finished shade	750.00
18″ h, standing nude figure holds 6″ d round crackled rose glass globe	395.00
Wall Pocket, 12″ h, seated nude figure supported by wrought iron metal frame work, metal pan for flowers . .	285.00

FRANKOMA POTTERY

History: John N. Frank founded a ceramic art department at Oklahoma University in Norman and taught there for several years. In 1933 he established his own business and began making Oklahoma's first commercial pottery. Frankoma moved from Norman to Sapulpa, Oklahoma, in 1938.

A fire completely destroyed the new plant later the same year, but rebuilding began almost immediately. The company remained in Sapulpa and continued to grow. Frankoma is the only American pottery to be permanently exhibited at the International Ceramic Museum of Italy.

In September 1983 a disastrous fire struck once again, destroying 97% of Frankoma's facilities. The rebuilt Frankoma Pottery reopened on July 2, 1984. Production has been limited to 1983 production molds only. All other molds were lost in the fire.

Prior to 1954 all Frankoma pottery was made with a honey-tan colored clay from Ada, Oklahoma. Since 1954 Frankoma has used a brick red clay from Sapulpa. During the early 1970s the clay became lighter and is now pink in color.

There were a number of early marks. One most eagerly sought is the leopard pacing on the FRANKOMA name. Since the 1938 fire, all pieces have carried only the name FRANKOMA.

References: Phyllis and Tom Bess, *Frankoma Treasures,* published by authors, 1983; Susan N. Cox, *Collectors Guide To Frankoma Pottery,* Book I, published by author, 1979, and Book II, published by author, 1982.

Additional Listings: See *Warman's Americana & Collectibles* for more examples.

Advisor: Phyllis Bess.

Pitcher, green and bronze, 8″ h, $25.00.

Bookends, pr, 5¾″ h, Mountain Girl . .	60.00
Bottle Vase, V–2, 1970, sgd "John Frank"	50.00
Bowl, 10″ d, Cactus, carved	40.00
Candleholder, Oral Roberts	8.00

Christmas Card	
1952, Donna Frank	45.00
1960, Gracetone	75.00
1960, The Franks	55.00
1975, Grace Lee & Milton Smith	85.00
Coin, 1¾" d, Elect John Frank	15.00
Decanter, Fingerprint, stopper, 2 qt	25.00
Dish, leaf shape, Gracetone	15.00
Jar, carved, #70	25.00
Jewelry, earrings, clip, pr	20.00
Match Holder, 1¾" h, #89A	15.00
Mask	
Comedy	5.00
Tragedy	5.00
Mug	
American Airlines Eagle	35.00
Donkey, red and white, 1976	18.00
Elephant, Nixon–Agnew, desert gold and white, 1973	50.00
Pitcher	
Thunderbird, 5" h	50.00
Wagon Wheel, 2 qt	20.00
Plate	
Christmas	
1972	20.00
1986	12.00
Jesus The Carpenter, 1971	20.00
Liberty, 1986	15.00
Madonna of Love, 1978	15.00
Salt and Pepper Shakers, pr	
Monogrammed	25.00
Wagon Wheels	10.00
Sculpture	
Amazon Woman, 6¼" h	225.00
Buffalo, 3½" h	225.00
Clydesdale, 6¾" h, rearing position	55.00
Colt, 8" h, prancing	250.00
Dreamer Girl, Ada clay, prairie green	190.00
Fan Dancer, red clay	150.00
Gannet, 9" h	225.00
Greyhound, 14" l, peach glow	125.00
Indian Chief, Ada clay, brown high glaze	65.00
Mountain Girl, Ada clay, prairie green	210.00
Toby Mug	
Cowboy, 4½" h	8.00
Uncle Sam, 4½" h	8.00
Trivet	
Cattle Brands	10.00
Lazybone	30.00
Vase	
3½" h, Hobby Horse	75.00
9" h, Chinese Bottle, Chinese red glaze	90.00
11½" h, Flowerabrum, #58	70.00
17" h, Fireside	30.00
Wall Pocket	
Boot	15.00
Leaf, 8½" l	35.00
Ram's Head	50.00
Wreath, "With Our Love, Frankoma" on back	40.00

FRATERNAL ORGANIZATIONS

History: Benevolent and secret societies played an important part in American society from the late 18th to the mid-20th centuries. Initially the societies were organized to aid members and their families in times of distress or death. They evolved from this purpose into important social clubs by the late 19th century.

In the 1950s, with the arrival of civil rights, an attack occurred on the secretiveness and often discriminatory practices of these societies. The fraternal movement, with the exception of the Masonic organizations, suffered serious membership loss. Many local chapters closed and sold their lodge halls. This resulted in many fraternal items arriving in the antiques market.

Additional Listings: See *Warman's Americana & Collectibles* for more examples.

Masonic, pitcher, transfer printed, "Sailors' Farewell," splashed Sunderland luster border, 9" h, $435.00.

MASONIC

Apron	
Cotton, 16 x 17", blue printed design	12.00
Leather, 14 x 12", white, blue silk trim, white embroidery, silver fringe	25.00
Satin, 18 x 17", ivory, red fringe, polychrome painted insignia	45.00
Book, *History of the Most Ancient & Honorable Fraternity of Free & Accepted Masons in New York from the Earliest Date,* Charles T Mc-Clenachan, 1888, Grand Lodge, New York	20.00
Bowl, 5" d, brass, El Riad Temple 1911	30.00
Certificate, Third Degree Freemason, Penobscot Lodge, dated August 8, 1863	165.00
Chocolate Pot, cov, china, lodge name and officer roster dec, platinum color trim	110.00
Creamer, Ruby Thumbprint pattern, engraved "Masonic Temple 1893"	30.00
Flask, ½ pt, blue–green	200.00

Goblet, glass, 1908 St Paul 65.00
Ice Cream Mold, 3¾" d, pewter, symbol,
marked "E & Co, NY" 20.00
Lamp, 7½" h, light bulb with Masonic
symbol 45.00
Match Holder, 11", wall type, walnut,
pierce carved symbols 70.00
Mug, ceramic, marked "Lulu," Atlantic
City, dated 1904 . . . . 65.00
Shaving Mug, gold and blue symbol, red
"C A Beck," incised "Austria" 35.00
Sign, 29" d, wrought iron, hammered
wreath mounted with ribbon, encir-
cling calipers and triangle, three
hanging bells, 19th C 440.00
Watch Fob, 10k gold, raised emblem,
chain and ring 85.00

**Maccabees, advertising mirror, red let-
tering at top, green ground, 2" d,
$25.00.**

OTHERS

American Legion, cane, wood, Milwau-
kee, 1941 . . . . 25.00
Benevolent & Protective Order of the
Elks, B.P.O.E.
Ashtray, brass, three elks 20.00
Badge, 1920 Chicago 56th Annual
Reunion 15.00
Beaker, 5" h, cream, black elk head,
marked "Mettlach, Velleroy &
Boch" 100.00
Book, *National Memorial*, 1931, color
illus 30.00
Plaque, 10½" d, hp, elk head, BPOE,
Sioux City Lodge #112, c1895 . . 110.00
Plate, tin, litho Elk lodge, Mt Hood
and elk by river scene, 1912 . . . . 75.00
Shaving Mug, pink and white, gold elk
head, crossed American flags and
floral dec, marked "Germany" on
bottom 70.00

Tumbler, glass, marked "Philadelphia
1907" 15.00
Eastern Star
Demitasse Cup and Saucer, porcelain 18.00
Pendant, silverplated, rhinestones
and rubies 40.00
Ring, gold, Past Matron, star shape
stone with diamond in center 135.00
Grand Army of the Republic, G.A.R.
Badge, Wisconsin State Encamp-
ment, May 20–22, 1896 . . . . 20.00
Flask, 2½ x 2¾", china, Encampment
at Trenton, NJ, June 22 and 23,
1905, orig china, cork closure . . . 150.00
Souvenir Spoon, Philadelphia En-
campment, 1899 . . . . 20.00
Independent Order of Odd Fellows,
I.O.O.F.
Sign, 29½" h, 100" l, Phillipstown
Lodge 815, carved, painted, gilt let-
tering, three interlacing ropes,
c1830 . . . . 2,640.00
Watch Fob, 94th Anniversary, April
12, 1913 . . . . 25.00
Knights of Columbus, dress sword,
scabbard, detailed blade, marked
"The McLilley Co, Columbus, OH" . 50.00
Knights Templar
Plate, 8" d, china, Pittsburgh Com-
mandery, 1903 . . . . 45.00
Tumbler
3½" h, metal, 1901 Conclave 70.00
4" h, glass, 36th Conclave 75.00
Shrine
Cup and Saucer, china, Los Angeles,
1906 . . . . 70.00
Goblet, St Paul 1908, ruby stained
glass, pedestal foot 65.00
Ice Cream Mold, 4¼" l, pewter, cres-
cent with Egyptian head, marked
"E & Co, NY" 25.00
Liquor Measurer, cranberry and clear,
symbols and officers names, St
Louis, 1909 . . . . 295.00
Mug, Syria Temple, Pittsburgh 1895,
Nantasket Beach, gold figures . . . 120.00
Tumbler, milk glass, Pittsburgh 1916 110.00

FRUIT JARS

History: Fruit jars are canning jars used to preserve food. Thomas W. Dyott, one of Philadelphi-
a's earliest and most innovative glass makers, was
promoting his glass canning jars in 1829. John
Landis Mason patented his screw-type canning jar
on November 30, 1858. This date refers to the
patent date, not the age of the jar. There are thousands of types of jars in many colors, types of
closures, sizes, and embossings.
References: Alice M. Creswick, *The Red Book*

of Fruit Jars No. 6, published by author, 1990; Bill Schroeder, *1000 Fruit Jars: Priced And Illustrated, Revised 5th Edition*, Collector Books, 1987.

Mason, dark turquoise, emb "Pat'd No. 30, 1858," 5½" h, $35.00.

Adams & Co, Manufacturers, Pittsburgh, PA, aqua, applied mouth, orig stopper, qt 525.00

Advance, Pat Apld For, aqua, ground lip, qt 80.00

All Right–Patd Jan 28th 1868, aqua, ground lip, half gallon 90.00

Atlas Mason's Patent, medium yellow green, ABM lip, qt 45.00

Ball, Mason, yellow green, amber striations, qt 75.00

BBGMCO, aqua, ground lip, insert, zinc band, qt 70.00

Belle, Pat Dec 14th 1869, aqua, three raised feet, ground lip, lid, metal neck band, wire bail, qt 750.00

Clarke Fruit Jar Co, Cleveland, OH, aqua, ground lip, lid, metal cam lever closure, 1½ pt 160.00

Cohansey, aqua, ground lip, lid, wire clamp, pt 55.00

Crystal Jar, Patd Dec 17, 1878, clear, ground lip 70.00

Dodge Sweeney & Co's, California, Butter, aqua, ground lip, glass insert, zinc band, 1½ qt 425.00

Eagle, aqua, applied mouth, lid, cast iron yoke, qt 120.00

Excelsior, aqua, ground lip, insert, zinc band, qt 575.00

Fahnestock Albree & Co, aqua, applied mouth, qt 35.00

Flaccus Bros, yellow amber, ground lip, steer head motif 350.00

Franklin Fruit Jar, aqua, ground lip, zinc lid 210.00

Fruit Keeper, pale green aqua, ground lip, orig lid, GCCO monogram, pt . . 35.00

Gem aqua, ground lip, zinc band, CFJCO monogram 80.00

Gilberds Improved Jar, aqua, ground lip, wire band, qt 150.00

Globe, yellow amber, ground lip, lid, metal closure, half gallon 100.00

C K Halle & Co, 121 Water St, Cleveland, OH, aqua, applied mouth, qt . . 50.00

Helme's Railroad Mills, amber, ground lip, insert, zinc band, pt 70.00

High Grade, aqua, ground lip, zinc lid, qt 150.00

Howe, Scranton, PA, aqua, ground lip, lid, wire bail, qt 40.00

Johnson & Johnson, New York, cobalt blue, ground lip, orig insert, screw band, qt 325.00

Lafayette, aqua, tooled lip, orig 3 pc glass and metal stopper, qt 190.00

Mason
   Cross, patent Nov 30th 1858, yellowish amber, qt 160.00
   Crystal Jar, clear, ground lip, zinc lid 65.00
   Improved, aqua, ground lip, zinc band 40.00
   Patent Nov 30th 1858, medium yellow green, ground lip, qt 210.00
   Star, medium amber, ground lip, zinc lid, pt 300.00
   Union, shield, aqua, ground lip, qt . . 100.00

McMechens Always The Best Old Virginia Wheeling, WV, clear, black woman holding box, screw band, pt 55.00

Millville–Hitall's Patent, aqua, applied mouth, iron yoke, ½ pt 140.00

Ne Plus Ultra Airtight Fruit Jar, aqua, applied mouth, missing lid, half gallon 575.00

Peerless, aqua, applied mouth, iron yoke, half gallon 80.00

Pet, aqua, applied mouth, qt 55.00

Phoenix Surgical Dressing Co, Milwaukee, WI, amber, ground lip, wire closure, qt 275.00

Potter & Bodine, Air–tight Fruit Jar, Philada, aqua, pontil scar base, applied wax seal ring, half gallon 400.00

Protector, aqua, ground lip, orig metal lid, half gallon 40.00

Star, aqua, emb star, ground lip, zinc insert and screw band, qt 300.00

A Stone & Co, Philada, iron pontil, applied wax seal ring, qt 850.00

The Hero lne, aqua, ground lip, insert, screw band, qt 20.00

The Magic Fruit Jar, pale green, ground lip, metal clamp, qt 160.00

The Pearl, aqua, ground lip, screw band, qt 35.00

The Schaffer Jar, Rochester, NY, aqua, orig domed lid, qt 160.00

The Van Vliet Jar of 1881, aqua, ground lip, orig wire and iron yoke, qt 350.00

Tillyer, aqua, ground lip, lid, wire clamp,
qt **55.00**
Union N1, Beaver Falls Glass Co, Bea-
ver Falls, PA, aqua, applied wax seal
ring, half gallon **30.00**
Whitmore's Patent, Rochester, NY, 3,
aqua, ground lip, wire closure, qt . . **425.00**
B B Wilcox, Patd March 26th 1876, 18,
blue aqua, ground lip, qt **45.00**

FRY GLASS

History: The H. C. Fry Glass Co. of Rochester,
Pennsylvania, began operating in 1901 and continued until 1933. Their first products were brilliant
period cut glass. They later produced Depression
tablewares. In 1922 they patented heat resisting
ovenware in an opalescent color. This "Pearl Oven
Glass" was produced in a variety of oven and table
pieces including casseroles, meat trays, pie and
cake pans, etc. Most of these pieces are marked
"Fry" with model numbers and sizes.

Fry's beautiful art line, Foval, was produced only
in 1926–27. It is pearly opalescent, with jade green
or delft blue trim. It is rarely signed, except for
occasional silver overlay pieces marked "Rockwell." Foval is always evenly opalescent, never
striped like Fenton's opalescent line.

Reference: Fry Glass Society, *Collector's Encyclopedia of Fry Glass,* Collector Books, 1989.

Collectors' Club: H. C. Fry Glass Society, P.O.
Box 41, Beaver, PA 15009.

Reproduction Alert: In the 1970s, reproductions of Foval were made in abundance in Murano,
Italy. These pieces, including candlesticks, toothpicks, etc., have teal blue transparent trim.

Bowl, 8″ d, cut glass, pineapple design,
wheel cutting, sgd **100.00**

**Hot Water Server, individual size,
Foval, green handle and finial, 5¾″ h,
$225.00.**

Butter Dish, cov, Pearl Oven Ware . . . **65.00**
Canape Plate, 6¼″ d, 4″ h cobalt blue
center handle, Foval **160.00**
Candlesticks, 9″ h, Foval, blue threads,
cobalt blue neck and base rings, pr . **250.00**
Casserole, cov, Pearl Oven Ware **25.00**
Compote, 6¾″ d, Foval, jade green
stem **115.00**
Creamer, Foval, blue tinted loopings,
applied Delft blue handle **150.00**
Cruet, Foval, cobalt blue handle, orig
stopper **115.00**
Cup and Saucer, Foval, cobalt blue
stripe, pale blue opaline ground . . . **60.00**
Decanter, 9″ h, ftd, Foval, applied Delft
blue handle **165.00**
Ice Cream Tray, 14″ l, 7″ w, cut glass,
Nelson pattern variation, all over cut-
ting, sgd "Fry" **270.00**
Pitcher, cov, Crackle, clear, applied jade
green handle and finial **100.00**
Plate, 9½″ d, Foval, Delft blue rim . . **72.00**
Platter, Pearl Oven Ware, etched rim . **20.00**
Punch Cup, Crackle, clear, cobalt blue
ring handle **42.00**
Reamer, canary, fluted **200.00**
Sherbet, 4″ h, cut glass, Chicago pattern **72.00**
Teapot, Foval, cobalt blue spout, handle
and knob **215.00**
Tumbler, 5¼″ h, Crackle, green handle **65.00**
Vase
7½″ h, Foval, jade green, rolled rim
and foot **200.00**
10″ h, Foval, bud, cobalt blue foot . . **125.00**

FULPER POTTERY

History: The American Pottery Company of Flemington, New Jersey, made pottery jugs and hou-
sewares from the early 1800s. They made Fulper
Art Pottery from approximately 1910 to 1930.

Their first line of art pottery was called Vasekraft.
The shapes were primarily either rigid and controlled, being influenced by the arts and crafts
movement, or of Chinese influence. Equal concern
was given to the glazes which showed an incredible diversity.

Pieces made between 1910 and 1920 were of
the best quality, because less emphasis was put
on production output. Almost all pieces are
molded.

Reference: Robert Blassberg, *Fulper Art Pottery: An Aesthetic Appreciation,* Art Lithographers, 1979.

Bowl
    7½" h, Effigy, blue flambe glaze, speckled green matte glaze, vertical ink stamp, c1915, minor glaze base chips 465.00
    11½" d, emb fish swimming in waves, burgundy, beige, and green flambe int. glaze, matte green feathered ext. glaze, ink mark 825.00
    12" d, 4½" h, semi–matte raspberry glaze, early incised mark 150.00
    13" d, brown and caramel flambe glaze, ink mark, c1910 . . . . 275.00
Flask, 10" h, 7½" d, Chinese inspired vase, two curlicued handles, green–to–black flambe glaze, early ink mark 660.00
Perfume Lamp, 6½" h, ballerina, yellow, two part burner, hp accents 200.00
Urn, 11" h, 6" d, flaring lip, two scrolled handles, matte and glossy lapis blue glaze, early ink mark 550.00

Vase, c1905, marked "#164," 8½" h, $95.00.

Vase
    4" h, green, burgundy, and rose, semi–matte flambe,¼ glaze miss . 80.00
    4¾" h, squat bulbous, angular handles, green crystalline glaze, vertical ink stamp, c1915 . . . . 190.00
    5½" h, 7" d, bulbous, blue flambe ending into metallic cafe au lait flambe, incised mark 275.00
    6½" h, wide mouth, three reticulated handles at shoulder, tapering cylindrical body, mottled rust glaze dripping over rim and shoulder, taupe body 310.00

    6¾" h, 7½" d, short neck, bulbous, three loop handles, green crystalline glaze, imp mark, c1915 . . . . . 715.00
    8¼" h, sq, long neck, imp geometric dec, flaring towards base, rose and green glaze, ink mark 330.00
    9" h, 9" w, bulbous, two small handles, high glaze flambe, shading from ochre to periwinkle blue, early raised mark 770.00
    9½" h, graduated, flaring towards base, two handles, tiger's eye flambe, ink mark 440.00
    10" h, 4¼" d, cylindrical, mushroom, two sq windows, relief mushrooms at base, yellow to taupe flambe high glaze, early ink mark 925.00
    11¼" h, tapering, two sq handles, dark brown to blue flambe glaze, ink mark 350.00
    12" h, bulbous, two small handles, periwinkle blue flambe glaze, orig paper label 660.00
    16½" h, floor, flaring neck, smooth, mirrored gun–metal glaze, hairline at base, imp mark 725.00

FURNITURE

History: Two major currents dominate the American furniture marketplace–furniture made in Great Britain and furniture made in the United States. American buyers continue to show a strong prejudice for objects manufactured in the United States. They will pay a premium for such pieces and accept them above technically superior and more aesthetic English examples.

Until the last half of the 19th century formal American styles were dictated by English examples and design books. Regional furniture, such as the Hudson River Valley [Dutch] and the Pennsylvania German styles, did develop. A less formal furniture, often designated as the "country" or vernacular style, developed throughout the 19th and early 20th centuries. These country pieces deviated from the accepted formal styles and have a genre charm that many collectors find irresistible.

America did contribute a number of unique decorative elements to English styles. The American Federal period is a reaction to the English Hepplewhite period. American designers created furniture which influenced, rather than reacted to, world taste in the Gothic Revival style, Arts and Craft Furniture, Art Deco, and Modern International movement.

FURNITURE STYLES [APPROX. DATES]

William and Mary	1690–1730
Queen Anne	1720–1760
Chippendale	1755–1790

In the 1988 auction season, a Newport, Rhode Island, Chippendale desk–bookcase sold for 12.1 million dollars. Many other pieces broke the half million dollar barrier.

Country pieces, with the exception of Windsor chairs, seem to have stabilized and even dropped off slightly in value. The country–designer–look no longer enjoys the popularity it did during the American Bicentennial period.

Furniture is one of the few antiques fields where regional preferences are a factor in pricing. Victorian furniture is popular in New Orleans, and unpopular in New England. Oak is in demand in the Northwest, not so much in the Middle Atlantic states.

Prices vary considerably on furniture. Shop around. Furniture is plentiful unless you are after a truly rare example. Examine all pieces thoroughly. Too many furniture pieces are bought on impulse. Turn furniture upside down; take it apart. The amount of repairs and restoration to a piece has a strong influence on price. Make certain you know about all repairs and changes before buying.

Beware of the large number of reproductions. During the twenty–five years following the American Centennial of 1876, there was a great revival in copying furniture styles and manufacturing techniques of earlier eras. These centennial pieces now are over one hundred years old. They confuse many dealers and collectors.

The prices listed below are "average" prices. They are only a guide. High and low prices are given to show market range.

References: Joseph T. Butler, *Field Guide To American Furniture,* Facts on File Publications, 1985; E & R Dubrow *Furniture, Made In America, 1875–1905,* Schiffer Publishing, Ltd., 1982; Eileen and Richard Dubrow, *American Furniture of the 19th Century, 1840–1880,* Schiffer Publishing, Ltd., 1983; Rachael Feild, *Macdonald Guide To Buying Antique Furniture,* Wallace–Homestead, 1989; Benno M. Forman, *American Seating Furniture, 1630–1730,* Winterthur Museum, W. W.

Norton & Company, 1988; Don Fredgant, *American Manufactured Furniture,* Schiffer Publishing, Ltd., 1988; *Furniture Dealers' Reference Book, Zone 3, 1928–29,* reprint by Schiffer Publishing, Ltd., 1988; Phillipe Garner, *Twentieth–Century Furniture,* Van Nostrand Reinhold, 1980; Myrna Kaye, *Fake, Fraud, Or Genuine, Identifying Authentic American Antique Furniture,* New York Graphic Society Book, 1987; William C. Ketchum, Jr., *Furniture, Volume 2: Chests, Cupboards, Desks, & Other Pieces,* Knopf Collectors' Guides To American Antiques, Alfred A. Knopf, 1982; Kathryn McNerney, *Pine Furniture, Our American Heritage,* Collector Books, 1989; Kathryn Mc-Nerney, *Victorian Furniture,* Collector Books, 1981, values updated 1988; Milo M. Naeve, *Identifying American Furniture: A Pictorial Guide To Styles and Terms, Colonial to Contemporary, Second Edition,* American Association for State and Local History, 1989; Don & Carol Raycraft, *Collector's Guide To Country Furniture, Book II,* Collector Books, 1988; Charles Santore, *The Windsor Style in America, Volume II,* Running Press Book Publishers, 1987; Marvin D. Schwartz, *Furniture: Volume 1: Chairs, Tables, Sofas & Beds,* Knopf Collector's Guides To American Antiques, Alfred A. Knopf, 1982; Tim Scott, *Fine Wicker Furniture, 1870–1930,* Schiffer Publishing, 1990; Robert W. and Harriett Swedberg, *American Oak Furniture, Style and Prices, Book III, second edition,* Wallace–Homestead, 1991; —*Country Furniture and Accessories with Prices, Book 1,* 1983, *Book II,* 1984, Wallace–Homestead; —, *Collector's Encyclopedia of American Furniture, Volume 1 (1990) and Volume 2 (1991)* Collector Books; — *Country Pine Furniture,* Wallace–Homestead, 1983; —*Furniture of the Depression Era,* Collector Books, 1987; —*Victorian Furniture, Book I,* 1976, *Book II,* 1983, *Book III,* 1985, Wallace–Homestead; —*Wicker Furniture,* Wallace–Homestead, 1983; Gerald W. R. Ward, *American Case Furniture,* Yale University Art Gallery, 1988; Derita Coleman Williams and Nathan Harsh, *The Art and Mystery of Tennessee Furniture,* Tennessee Historical Society, 1988; Norman Vandal, *Queen Anne Furniture,* The Taunton Press, 1990; Lyndon C. Viel, *Antique Ethnic Furniture,* Wallace–Homestead, 1983.

There are hundreds of specialized books on individual furniture forms and styles. Two examples of note are: Monroe H. Fabian, *The Pennsylvania–German Decorated Chest,* Universe Books, 1978, and Charles Santore, *The Windsor Style In America, 1730–1830,* Running Press, 1981.

Additional Listings: Arts and Craft Movement, Art Deco, Art Nouveau, Children's Nursery Items, Orientalia, Shaker Items, and Stickley.

BEDS

Arts and Crafts, Gustav Stickley, three–
  quarter size, seven slats, butterfly

Bed, Sheraton, canopy, mahogany, turned and fluted posts, detailed carving, $5,000.00.

joints, orig medium finish, branded mark, 45½″ w, 48″ h **2,100.00**

Chinese, 19th C, opium bed, ivory and wood floral and figural inlay, 80½″ l, 50″ w, 92½″ h **2,200.00**

Chippendale, New England, c1770, daybed, carved mahogany, shaped crest, molded ears, pierced baluster splat, molded seat frame, cabriole legs joined by turned stretchers, pad feet, 74″ l **5,775.00**

Colonial Revival, Regency Style, inlaid rosewood, upholstered head and footboard, shaped framework, brass inlay and mounts, double mattress size, 56″ h **600.00**

Continental, 19th C, sleigh, fruitwood, shaped headboard, footboard, and side rails, 83″ l, 47″ d, 45″ h **385.00**

Daybed, rattan, mid 20th C, swept back ends, wrap around skirt, spring seat support, natural finish, 79″ w, 30″ h . **615.00**

Federal

American

Carved curly maple and mahogany, four post, ring and vase turned headposts, mahogany footposts waterleaf and plume carved and spirally reeded, tapered feet, casters, 72½″ w, 79″ l **4,125.00**

Walnut, tester, carved, reeded turned vase form posts, 80″ l, 56″ w, 74″ h **1,400.00**

New England

Birchwood and pine, c1810, tapered headposts, shaped headboard, reeded and crossbanded footposts, vase form feet, 55½″ w, 76¼″ h **2,750.00**

Birchwood and pine, c1880, pencil

post, faceted headposts, tapering centering arched pine headboard, faceted footposts, sq feet, later tester, 53″ w, 77″ l **3,850.00**

Mahogany, c1810, four post, turned headposts, shaped mahogany headboard, reeded and ring turned footposts, ring turned feet, tester, 57″ w, 81″ l **3,025.00**

Salem, MA, c1805, carving attributed to Samuel McIntire, carved mahogany, four post, tapered birchwood headposts, arched pine headboard with cyma–shaped cut–out, baluster form footposts with upper section reeded over acanthus leaf and waterleaf carved vase form mid section with draped grapes and leaves tied with bowknots against punchwork ground, turned feet, later tester, 58″ w, 77″ h **7,425.00**

German, pine, panel shaped headboard with painted lady and gentleman standing in landscape with floral and leaf motifs, inscribed "Johann and Maria Katharina" and "1824," turned footposts, overhead tester panel with painted landscapes within medallions, 50½″ w, 72½″ h **4,675.00**

Recamier, Classical, American, scrolled upholstered support, exposed seat rail, scrolled legs, ball feet, 77″ l . . . **1,980.00**

Rope

American

Curly maple, turned posts and finials, scrolled headboard with turned crest, turned blanket roll, replaced side rails, old refinishing, 75″ l, 54″ w, 48″ h **1,800.00**

Poplar, turned posts, peaked headboards, worn orig bluish–green paint, orig side rails, 46″ w, 69″ h **425.00**

New York State, c1830, turned, painted, and decorated poplar, paneled headboard with scrolled crest, center urn form finial, turned posts, turned footposts with center low footboard, headboard painted with grapes and floral motifs, reddish ground, varnished brown with yellow highlights, 55½″ w, 81½″ h **3,500.00**

Sheraton, late, c1825, tester, maple, acanthus carved foot posts, tester missing, refinished, 65″ h **1,300.00**

Victorian, Renaissance Revival, American, c1872, stained maple and burled maple, tester, arched headboard with center carved rosette above panel dec with opposed winged griffins and floral scrolls, panel of suspended palmettes below, gilt incised half round pilasters flanking the conforming footboard, side rails, posts, and rounded quarter canopy, minor restorations, 67" w, 72" h headboard **6,600.00**

Bench, single board top, 36" l, 11½" w, 18" h, $75.00.

BENCHES

Bucket, Ohio, Amish, ash, three shelves, old varnish finish, 37" w, 14" d, 32" h **250.00**
Cobbler, country, pine, top divided shelf, drawers, old nut brown patina, old repairs, 44" l **450.00**
Dresser, French style, carved wood frame, reupholstered gold plush seat, blonde finish, 35" l **150.00**
Garden, Gothic Revival, American, Philadelphia, mid 19th C, cast iron, scrolled back and arms, slat seat, marked "Wood & Perot, Makers Philad" **2,100.00**
Hall, George IV, English, c1850, mahogany, rect seat, turned legs, 42" l, 11¾" d, 17¼" h **770.00**
Kneeling, walnut, old dark finish, 39" l . **50.00**
Primitive, pine, legs mortised through top, old worn finish, traces of paint, 61" l, 12" d, 18" h **85.00**
Settle
  Arts and Crafts, Gustav Stickley, No. 225, five side slats, one broad horizontal back slat, orig color and finish, branded mark, 78" l, 31" d, 28" h **5,225.00**
  Country, scrolled arms, spindle back with turned posts, plank seat, plain turned tapering legs, old black repaint, minor repairs, 72½" l **250.00**
  Plank seat, arrow back, simple turnings, curved arms, brown refinishing, 90" l **610.00**
Water, country, poplar, one board bootjack ends, two shelves, sq nail construction, 36¼" l, 17⅜" d, 33½" h . . **350.00**
Window
  Federal, mahogany, S scroll end,

brass inlaid crest above pierced cornucopia slat, molded supports, plain seatrail foliage stenciled with gilt highlights, rect drop–in seat, saber legs, 45 x 32½" **4,950.00**
Italian, Neoclassical, pierced foliate carved over–scrolled sides, carved apron, gold textured upholstered seat, toupie feet, 41" l **835.00**
Regency style, stained wood, carved sides, needlepoint upholstered seat, circular turned legs, 52" l, 16" d, 30" h **210.00**

BENTWOOD

In 1856, Michael Thonet of Vienna perfected the process of bending wood by using steam. Shortly after, Bentwood furniture became popular. Other manufacturers of Bentwood furniture were Jacob and Joseph Kohn; Philip Strobel and Son; Sheboygan Chair Co.; and Tidoute Chair Co. Bentwood furniture is still being produced today by the Thonet firm and others.

Bed, c1900, scrolled and carved headboard, conforming footboard, double mattress size, 60" h **750.00**
Chair
  Arm, Thonet, c1900, scrolled back and arms, cane seat, splayed legs, orig label and stamp **300.00**
  Desk, c1890, arched crestrail, tightly woven cane back and rounded seat, scrolled bentwood arms, X–form base, adjustable pedestal . . **450.00**
  Side, J & J Kohn, c1900, oak, pressed wood seat insert, branded and paper label remnants, 36" h . **110.00**
Cradle, c1900, oval bentwood basket, shaped cradle, extended ornate scrolled support, 52" l, 36" h **750.00**
Easel, artist's **75.00**
Rack, spindle back, central mirror, overhead spindle shelf, bentwood hook on outside rails, spindle containers flank horizontal rack, bentwood frame, natural color, 48½" w, 17" d, 74¼" h . . **1,320.00**
Rocker, Thonet, sleigh type, sgd **850.00**
Settee, Kohn, three part scrolled back and arms, cane back and seat, splayed legs, 47" l **700.00**
Table, Austria, c1900, center, shaped oblong white marble top, narrow frieze, elaborate bentwood cruciform base with interlocking and overlapping scrolls centering on turned standard, 45½" l, 28½" h **300.00**

BLANKET CHESTS

Chippendale, New England, c1780, maple, molded lift top, case with two sim-

Blanket Chest, tulip wood, dovetailed, Ohio legs, 31½″ l, 17½″ d, 19¼″ h, $325.00.

ulated and two real thumbmolded drawers, bracket feet, old oval brass pulls, refinished, 40½″ w, 18″ d, 41½″ h **750.00**

Country, decorated

American, 1797, pine, rect lid, till, front polychrome painted with two rect panels enclosing vase with tulips, each vase inscribed "John Seltzer," one with date 1797, molded base, bracket feet, some restoration to background paint, feet reduced in height, 52″ w, 22¼″ d, 21¼″ h **4,950.00**

Maine, c1830, pine, oblong top, outset corners, till, well grained painted, front panel with two convex pilasters above dentil carved shaped skirt, bracket feet, painted brown and ochre on cream ground, 45″ w, 19¼″ d, 25¾″ h **6,000.00**

New England, early 19th C, pine, rect top, applied molded edge, plain int., top, front, and sides painted gray with black spots, 48½″ w, 19″ h . . **1,450.00**

Pennsylvania

Attributed to Berks County, 1773, pine, rect molded lid, till, top and front painted polychrome as two tombstone arched panels with pots of stylized flowers, third panel on front painted with potted tree and two stylized birds, inscription "Michael...DEN 19 DAIG/MERTZ AND 1773," arched panels with four birds perched on corners, side panels painted with hearts and flowers, two drawers painted with stylized tulips, scroll–cut bracket feet, orig wrought iron lock and heart strap hinges, 55½″ w, 22¼″ d, 29″ h **13,200.00**

Attributed to Centre County, pine,

dovetailed case, bracket feet, and till, orig wrought iron bear trap lock and strap hinges, worn orig painted dec, central panel of eagle, shield, banner, pinwheels, tulips, and compass stars, banner reads "Catarine Klinglibe 1816," traces of compass dec on lid and ends, replaced escutcheon, minor edge damage, 51½″ w, 22½″ d, 27″ h **3,500.00**

Pine, rect hinged lid, painted front with arch centered with flowers in urn, floral motifs and 1828, sides painted with geometric and diaper designs, molded base, bracket feet, blue, green, yellow, and tan, 43½ x 19¾ x 24½″ . . . **11,000.00**

Vermont, six board, pine and poplar, orig brown graining simulating figured wood with inlay, till with lid and secret drawer, scalloped apron, cutout feet, orig hinges reset, some damage, 43¾″ w, 17½″ d, 43¼″ h **1,700.00**

George III, early 19th C, mahogany, hinged rect top, storage well, front with two false drawers over deep drawer, ogee bracket feet, 37½″ l, 33″ h **1,980.00**

Pilgrim Century, carved, painted, and ebonized oak, attributed to Peter Blin, Wethersfield, CT, c1675–1710, rect hinged lid, well with till, front of case carved with two rect inset panels of stylized tulips and leaves, center octagonal panel carved with sunflowers, ebonized split balusters, mid molding, two long drawers with egg appliques, stiles form reduced feet, replaced lid, traces of orig red and black pigment, 47½″ w, 20 3 /4″ d, 34¼″ h **9,900.00**

Queen Anne, New England, mid 18th C, marriage chest, pine, upper half faced with false drawer fronts, hinged top, orig brown paint and hardware, 35″ w **3,500.00**

William and Mary, New England, early 18th C, pine and turned maple, molded lift top, well above case with two mock drawers over two working molded drawers, turned feet, 39¼″ w, 18½″ d, 37½″ h **1,760.00**

BOOKCASES

Art Deco, American, early 1900s, polished aluminum, tin plate, pr of leaded glass doors, bird's eye maple back panels, 58″ w, 17″ d, 65″ h . . . **7,500.00**

Art Nouveau, Majorelle, c1900, carved walnut, molded crest, carved splayed leaves, glazed door mounted with central textured purple glass panel, silvered bronze branch form spandrels, pr of narrow cupboards, molded base, carved feet, 64¼" w, 79" h **3,500.00**

Eastlake, American, c1870, carved walnut and burl walnut, three sections, broken pediment with architectural center ornament, plinth base over drawers **1,750.00**

Empire, mahogany, reeded top molding, three pairs of doors with Winthrop style glass dividers, rope twisted columns, paw feet **2,950.00**

Federal, New York, c1810, inlaid mahogany, two parts, upper section with flat top, molded cornice, pr of hinged glazed doors, int. with three adjustable shelves, projecting lower section with four cockbeaded inlaid drawers, shaped skirt, bracket feet, patches of molding and veneers, 46½" w, 22" d, 92" h **4,400.00**

George III, English, c1800, mahogany, stepped molded and Greek key carved cornice, blind–fret carved frieze, pr of geometrically glazed doors over sloping fall, fitted int. of drawers and pigeonholes, blind–fret carved cupboard flanked by document drawers, four long graduated drawers, ogee bracket feet, restorations, 37½" w, 84" h **2,750.00**

Georgian Style, mahogany, rect top, ovolo molded edge, straight frieze, canted glazed doors, four shelves, fluted stiles, plinth base, 47" w, 37" h **825.00**

Neoclassical, Italian, walnut, projected cavetto molded cornice, two grilled cupboard doors with shelf int., two paneled cupboard doors below, sq tapered legs, 62" w, 82" h **4,675.00**

Syrian, late 19th C, mother–of–pearl and bone inlaid, shaped rect top over case fitted with arched glass doors, int. shelves, series of drawers, 66½" w, 23" d, 95" h **3,300.00**

Victorian, American
    Gothic Revival, c1830, carved rosewood, architectural pediment, two glass doors, 45¾" w, 13¾" d, 86" h **3,800.00**
    Renaissance Revival, c1865, walnut, highly carved, three glass doors enclosing shelves, three cupboards below, 90" w, 17½" d, 118½" h .. **3,900.00**

BOXES

Ballot
    Maple, dovetailed, sliding top, 8" w, 6" d, 12" h **185.00**
    Walnut, wide dovetails, carved

Box, knife, inlaid mahogany, brass escutcheons, twenty slots, 9" w, 6" d, 13" h, $750.00.

wooden handles, 7½" w, 7" d, 18¼" h **125.00**

Band, New England, printed paper, rural country scene, 10½" w, 15" h **375.00**

Bible, Continental, late 17th C, oak chip work, rect molded top slanting above deep well, floral carved dec, 25" w, 16" d, 10" h **250.00**

Bonnet Box, PA, late 18th C, bentwood, fitted lid, dower chest type dec, green ground, large central red, yellow, black, and white stellate device, two large sprouting dark green feathered leaf forms, foliate and vines on lid, 21" oval, 11¾" h **5,775.00**

Bride's, Continental, 18th C, bentwood, fitted lid, painted Biblical scene, sides painted with large red and white tulips, black ground **900.00**

Candle
    Country, decorated, pine, sliding lid, old red paint, faded floral dec ... **275.00**
    George III, Provincial, oak, tapering rect form, wall hanging **165.00**
    Hanging, pine, one drawer, rounded back, scalloped front panel, natural weathered wood, 15¾" h **400.00**

Cigar, mahogany, striped inlay on lid and base, zinc lined, nickel plated hardware, 7½" w, 4" d, 12" h **150.00**

Desk, table top, poplar, dovetailed case, nailed drawer, lift top lid, dovetailed gallery, int. fitted with pigeonholes, old red paint, repairs, 26" sq, 15¾" h .. **200.00**

Document
    American, flame mahogany veneer, poplar secondary wood, bevel edge lid, divided two part int., orig brass bail handle, 13½" l **250.00**
    Pennsylvania, western, dec, dome top, poplar, orig black paint, yellow striping, well detailed polychrome floral design, 13½" l **150.00**

Hat, pine, domed top, strap handle, 16"
sq **200.00**

Knife

Federal, American, early 19th C, satinwood and inlaid mahogany, acorn
finial, domed lid, stepped pierced
cutlery support, urn shaped body,
sq base, ogee bracket feet, 7½" w,
24½" h, pr **7,150.00**

George III, English, 1791, mahogany,
serpentine front, sloping lid, inlaid
with central oval floral patera, reverse with stylized shell, fitted int.,
striped inlay, diamond shaped escutcheon suspending engraved
shield, George Braiser, London, silver mounts, minor losses and
cracks, set of three, two 14⅜" h,
one 13⅜" h **4,400.00**

Pantry, American

Decorated, mid 19th C, blue and
green dec, yellow, black, and putty
compass star on cov, 9¼" d **250.00**

Split Wood, orig dark stain, 14½" l . . **95.00**

Pipe, cherry, well scalloped top edge,
heart cut–out in front, circular crest,
dovetailed overlapping drawer, dovetailed base, applied edge molding, re-
finished, 22¼" h **4,000.00**

Salt, hanging, oak, dovetailed, cut–out
opening, 6½" w, 7½" d, 15" h **150.00**

Seaman's Chest, New England, c1850,
rect lid, fitted well with tiers of small
drawers incised on top with "C. B.
Fisher," top dec with compass star
motifs and center rect panel with "C.
B. Fisher," and a star, underside of
top painted with compass star motifs,
American flag, and applied paper engraving of man and machinery, front
with recessed panel pained with compass star, center applied American
shield, sides with applied shields and
carrying handles, painted in shades
of red, white, and blue, some restoration to paint, 39½" w, 20½" d, 19¾"
h **3,300.00**

Spice, American, 19th C, grained,
round, locking top, 9¾" h **195.00**

Trinket, New England, smoke grained,
basket of flowers motif on lid, brass
feet, 4½" h **600.00**

CABINETS

Buffet, Louis XIV, walnut, rect marble
top, two geometric fronted fielded
paneled doors, stepped molded
plinth, turnip front feet, 36¼" w, 48½"
h **3,300.00**

China

Colonial Revival, Chippendale Style,

c1940, walnut veneer, breakfront,
scrolled broken pediment, center
urn finial, pr of glazed doors and
panels, long drawer over two cup-
board doors, 44" w, 15" d, 76" h . . **600.00**

Hepplewhite, inlaid mahogany,
leaded glass, velvet lined int., 63"
w, 21" d, 75½" h **650.00**

Victorian, oak, bow front, leaded
glass, amber glass diamonds in top
panels, 37½" w, 14½" d, 61¾" h . **450.00**

Curio, French style, figured veneer, ormolu trim, curved crylic panels on
doors and ends, lighted, 40¾" w,
17½" d, 71¼" h **300.00**

Display

Napoleon III, mid 19th C, Continental,
lacquered, thumbmolded cornice
over pair of glazed doors, int.
shelves, front and sides inlaid in
mother–of–pearl, gilt dec of Oriental pavilions and figures, black
ground, bracket feet, wired for int.
illumination, 43½" w, 82½" h, pr . . **24,200.00**

Victorian, Renaissance Revival,
American, serpentine front, arched
projecting floral carved cornice and
frieze, conforming glazed sides and
door, female caryatids and floral
panels enclose shelves and mirror
back, caster feet, 55" w, 22" d, 77"
h **1,600.00**

Library, George IV, English, c1825, mahogany, superstructure of four graduated bookshelves on either side,
stand with two frieze drawers on one
side, false drawers on reverse, trestle
support with concentric bosses, down
swept legs joined by turned cylinder
stretcher, casters, 36" w, 59" h **5,225.00**

Parlor

Aesthetic Movement, American,
c1880, inlaid and ebonized cherry,
superstructure with arrangement of
shelves with floral pierced galleries
on turned baluster supports, beveled rect mirror panel surrounded
by floral emb red velvet, pr of
glazed doors below flanked by inlaid stylized floral sprigs, over two
cupboard doors carved with large
flowerheads, flanked by inlaid
sprigs, single shelf int., stylized
bracket feet, 36" w, 72½" h **2,200.00**

French Provincial, c1800, pine, rect
top, fielded door enclosing shelves
to one side, two glazed doors to the
right enclosing grilled shelf, two
drawers, and three cupboard doors
base, stiles continuing to form feet,
84" l, 81" h **3,300.00**

Pedestal, Empire, c1825, mahogany,

circular gray marble top, cylindrical body, door enclosing shelves, plinth base, 16″ d, 29″ h 770.00

Side

Continental, Neoclassical style, parquetry, crossbanded rect top, canted front, frieze drawer, two doors, scalloped apron with inlaid canted angles, block feet, 32″ w, 31″ h 825.00

Dutch, Rococo Style, 19th C, marquetry, rect top with inlaid central oval medallion reserved on trellis ground, tambour slide, inlaid bellflower pendants, exaggerated cabriole legs, 27¾″ w, 18″ h 610.00

Napoleon III, ebonized, breakfront top, door with central oval medallion, gilt metal mounted pilasters, plinth base, 40″ w, 38½″ h 610.00

Vitrine

Art Nouveau, Galle, c1900, marquetry, shaped rect top, chamfered corners, molded edge, rect cabinet, glazed door and sides, back inlaid with tall stalks of cow parsley, door inlaid with cow parsley and butterfly, reeded legs, 25¾″ w, 18″ d, 47¾″ h 5,225.00

Louis XV, ormolu mounted amaranth marble top, glass shelves, stamped on back "BOUDIN," capital intertwined script "ME," 37½ x 15″ . . . 3,750.00

Louis XVI style

Bow front, shaped incurved molded top, swag dec, glazed sides and door, pale lime silk lined shelf int., fluted tapered legs, 60 x 30¼ x 17″ 1,900.00

Mahogany, projected molded cornice, gilt metal dentil frieze, two glazed doors, foliate gilt metal mounted apron, toupie feet, 74½ x 48″ 4,125.00

Candlestand, cherry, eight sided top, 17¾″ w, 14¾″ d, 27½″ h, $500.00.

CANDLE SHIELDS

Country, cherry, replaced maple scrolled shield, turned column, snake feet, refinished, minor repairs, 15½″ w, 15″ d, 26½″ h 300.00

George III, mahogany, walnut and satinwood, shield form screen fitted with later embroidered and painted satin panel, adjusting on rect standard, entwined C−scroll base with ball feet, pr 8,500.00

Hepplewhite, mahogany, embroidered floral motif, 53″ h 600.00

CANDLESTANDS

Chippendale

Country, cherry and birch, one board top with cut−out corners, turned column, tripod base, cut−out feet, old reddish brown repaint, 17″ w, 15½″ d, 26¾″h 475.00

Philadelphia, c1750, carved mahogany, circular dished tilt and revolving top, bird cage support, ring turned and compressed ball standard, cabriole legs, claw and ball feet, repairs to three legs, 24¼″ d, 27¾″ h 7,700.00

Salem, MA, c1785, mahogany, tilt top with serpentine sides, urn standard, cabriole legs, snake feet, 20″ w, 19½″ d, 27½″ h 2,860.00

Empire Style, country, curly maple, tilt top, scrolled legs, turned column, two board top, refinished, repairs, 19″ d, 26¾″ h 600.00

Federal, New York, mahogany, octagonal top with crossbanded and brass inlaid border, reeded drum standard, molded down curved legs, carved paw feet, brass casters, 28″ h 9,350.00

George III, mahogany, circular dished top, baluster turned standard, three cabriole legs, snake feet, 28 x 18″ . . 610.00

Hepplewhite, country, cherry, tilt top, two board top, spider legs, turned column, replacements and refinishing, 20½ x 28″ 300.00

Hepplewhite Style, country, birch, tilt top, turned column, spider legs, repairs, 16″ w, 28½″ h 450.00

Queen Anne, American, mahogany, dish top, delicate base, carved snake feet 400.00

Sheraton, mahogany, hexagonal one board top, turned column, tripod base, spider legs, 17¾″ sq top, 28½″ h 350.00

Victorian, maple, circular tilt top with foliate marquetry and penwork, ring and

baluster turned standard, tripod base,
toupie feet, 16" d, 30" h **410.00**

CHAIRS

Art Deco, Vienna, side, walnut, black
stain, shaped back, scrolled side rails,
upholstered seat **350.00**
Art Furniture, c1810, side, bird cage
crest over seven bamboo turned uprights, saddle seat, bamboo turned
legs joined by stretchers, orig paint,
set of six **15,400.00**
Art Moderne
 Armchair and side, Luigi Tagliabue,
  light wood, vertical ebony stripes,
  black seats, 39" h, pr **500.00**
 Lounge
  Black wire frame seat and back,
   dec wooden arm rests, coiled
   spring seat support, four prong
   shaped splayed legs, c1955,
   32½" h, pr **990.00**
  Jens Risom, curvilinear seat frame,
   angular arm and leg supports,
   1952, 26" d, 30" h **165.00**
  Russel Wright, horizontal slatted
   back, deep seat, flat angular arm
   and leg supports, striped linen
   seat cushions, c1955, 32" d,
   29¾" h **330.00**
 Side, Charles Eames, manufactured
  by Herman Miller, natural finish
  laminated wood, backrest on metal
  frame, rod shape legs, paper label,
  17½" d, 30" h, set of six **500.00**
Art Nouveau, side, carved walnut,
 rounded crestrail over solid vertical

**Chair, high chair, oak, pressed back,
painted, c1905, 42" h, $95.00.**

splat, carved poppy sprigs, nail studded light brown simulated leather bow
front seat, channeled cabriole legs,
pointed toes, pr **800.00**
Arts and Crafts, American
 Armchair
  Harden and Co, c1910, double
   crestrail over wide central slat
   flanked by two narrow slats, bent
   arms over four vertical slats, pa-
   per label, 38" h **550.00**
  Mission, c1910, oak, wide concave
   crestrail, through tenons over
   two wide vertical slats, flat open
   arms with through tenons and
   corbel supports, spring cushion
   seat, 38¼" h **385.00**
  L. & J. G. Stickley, c1912, concave
   crestrail, two horizontal slats, flat
   open arms, spring cushion, seat,
   double side stretchers, branded
   "The Work of L. & J. G. Stickley,"
   37¼" h **220.00**
 Dining, Michigan Chair Co, c1912,
  concave crestrail over single wide
  vertical slat, black slip seat, paper
  label, 37⅜" h, set of four **360.00**
 Side, Gustav Stickley, c1907, shaped
  crestrail over five vertical slats,
  spring cushion seat, double side
  stretchers, dry finish, 35⅛" h **250.00**
Chinese Export, early 19th C, armchair,
 bamboo, rect back, down swept arms,
 caned seat, columnar legs joined by
 stretchers, fitted with cushion, minor
 losses, 34" h **880.00**
Chippendale
 Country
  Birch, repaired pierced splat, replaced rush seat, sq legs joined
   by stretchers, curl and old mel-
   low refinishing, 39" h **350.00**
  Hardwood, side, old black repaint,
   shaped crest, pierced splat, old
   worn rush seat, sq legs, 38½" h **625.00**
 Massachusetts, c1770, side, carved
  walnut, shaped crestrail, molded
  ears, scroll carved baluster form
  splat, upholstered seat, sq molded
  legs joined by stretchers **1,150.00**
 New York, side
  c1770, carved mahogany, shell and
   acanthus carved crest, scrolled
   ears, pierced and volute carved
   baluster form splat, molded seatrail, slip seat, shell and bellflower carved cabriole legs, claw
   and ball feet, minor repairs, pr **. 19,800.00**
  c1775, carved mahogany, shaped
   crest, pierced vase form splat,
   center diamond motif, molded
   seatrail, slip seat, cabriole legs,

claw and ball feet, some repairs to legs, feet, and stiles **1,870.00**

North Carolina, c1770, side, mahogany, shaped crest, pierced vase form splat with stylized quatrefoil design, molded seatrail, slip seat, sq molded legs joined by H–stretcher, pr **4,675.00**

Philadelphia

Armchair, c1780, carved mahogany, ladderback of four strapwork slats, shaped arms, scrolled handholds, molded seatrail, slip seat, sq legs joined by stretchers, minor patches and repairs **1,750.00**

Side, c1750, carved walnut, incised shaped crest, center volute carved shell device, volute carved terminals, vase form splat, molded seatrail with shell carved pendant, slip seat, shell and volute carved cabriole legs, claw and ball feet, metal braces at juncture of crest and stiles . . **9,625.00**

Portsmouth, NH, c1780, side, carved mahogany, shaped crest with incised edge, pierced vase form splat with Gothic arch, over–upholstered seat, sq molded legs joined by stretchers, pr **6,600.00**

Chippendale Style, 19th C, side, mahogany, pierced splat, sq legs joined by stretchers, slip seat, old finish, set of five **2,350.00**

Continental, late 18th C or early 19th C, corner, walnut, carved, needlepoint upholstery **440.00**

Eastlake, Victorian

Armchair, NY, c1876, George Hunzinger, arched crest with spindles, inlay cloth cov woven metal back and seat, marked "Hunzinger Ny Pat March 20, 1869, Pat April 18, 1876," 18" w, 17½" d, 38" h **1,250.00**

Side, walnut, small arms, cane seat **225.00**

Edwardian, English, c1900, side, rect pierced carved splat with gothic arches, rect figural painted panel, foliate and fluted circular stiles, rect caned seat, turned tapering legs, pr **660.00**

Empire Style, Dutch, 19th C, marquetry, side, gondola form, concave rect crestrail above down swept supports, drop–in seat, inlaid overall foliate sprigs, turned cylindrical legs **475.00**

Federal

Maryland, c1820, side, rect crestrail with painted sailing vessel and landscape, caned seat, turned tapering legs, classical motifs and gilt on pale yellow ground, pr **725.00**

New England, c1810, lolling, mahog-

any, arched crest, rect back, shaped arms, molded supports, frontal ring turned tapering legs, brass casters **2,750.00**

New York, c1790, side, mahogany, shaped and molded crest, three shaped, reeded, and acanthus carved uprights, upholstered seat, reeded tapering legs, spade feet, pr **1,650.00**

Philadelphia, c1805, side, carved and satinwood inlaid mahogany, molded shield back, pierced flowerhead and bellflower carved splat, satinwood inlaid fan, over–upholstered seat, sq molded tapering legs, feet extended, pr **4,125.00**

Rhode Island, Newport or Providence, c1880, side, carved mahogany, molded back, pierced splat carved at the center with calyx and swags, upholstered seat with serpentine front, molded sq legs joined by H–stretcher, minor repair to shoe **4,400.00**

George I Style, armchair, open waisted back with inset acanthus and tassel carved vase form splat, shepherd's crook arms, balloon seat, acanthus carved molded legs, claw and ball feet **720.00**

George II Style

Side, English, late 19th C, carved mahogany, foliate and ruffle carved crestrail over interlaced and pierced baluster splat, flared rect seat, cabriole legs carved at knees with ruffles and foliage, hairy animal paw feet **425.00**

Side, mahogany, arched backrest with pierced carved splat, upholstered drop–in seat, sq canted legs, set of eight **2,475.00**

George III

English, third quarter 18th C

Armchair, beechwood, molded crestrail, shaped upholstered back, serpentine seat, molded cabriole legs, scrolled feet, repairs, 37" h **660.00**

Armchair, carved mahogany, arched crestrail, pierced vertical splat over down swept arms, serpentine fronted seat, molded sq legs joined by stretchers, repairs **385.00**

Armchair and matching side chair, inlaid mahogany, arched crestrail centered by carved wheat sheaf, pierced splat with central inlaid patera, serpentine fronted seat, molded sq legs joined by stretchers, repairs, pr **550.00**

Dining, mahogany, serpentine

molded crestrail, pierced splat, bowed upholstered seat, sq tapering legs joined by stretchers, 36" h, pr 715.00

Library, armchair, mahogany, rect upholstered back, blind–fret carved arms, sq blind–fret carved legs joined by pierced stretchers, extensive restoration, 37" h, pr 1,650.00

Provincial, oak, arched crestrail, strapwork splat, plank seat, sq tapering legs joined with stretcher, pr 450.00

George III Style, English, 19th C

Armchair, library, mahogany, sq upholstered back, blind–fret carved arms, sq upholstered seat, blind–fret carved legs joined by stretchers, distressed upholstery, 38½" h 1,760.00

Armchair, mahogany, shield form backrest, pierced carved splat, Prince of Wales feathers above out scrolled arms, red velvet upholstered serpentine seat, sq tapering fluted legs, spade feet 440.00

Dining, carved mahogany, 19th C, armchair and six side chairs, serpentine crestrail above pierced ruffled foliate medallion over pierced and interlaced splat, flared rect drop–in seat, sq legs, restorations 3,025.00

Hepplewhite

Armchair, Martha Washington, string inlay, upholstered back and seat . 3,600.00

Side

American, cherry, curved crest, pierced splat with urn detail, slip seat, sq tapering legs, H–stretcher, refinished, pr 1,150.00

Connecticut, c1780, mahogany, pierced vase splat, urn finial, upholstered seat, straight tapering legs, replaced rear corner braces 650.00

Ladderback

Child's, Delaware River Valley, 18th C, back with four arched slats above rush seat, turned legs joined by stretchers, traces of red paint, once fitted with rockers 725.00

Highchair, country, three slats and turned finials, old red repair, woven splint seat, some edge damage, 38¾" h 650.00

Louis XV, French, Provincial, c1775, armchair, carved walnut, molded crestrail, center carved floral sprig, padded armrests, back, and seat, volute supports, serpentine fronted seat, cabriole legs, pr 2,750.00

Mission

Armchair, Gustav Stickley, c1910, oak, V shape back 450.00

Chair, ladderback, hardwood, rush seat, heavy bulbous turnings, $1,200.00.

Side, Charles Rohlf, 1900, octagonal, butterly pierced single back splat, shaped skirt, 37½" 1,500.00

Wing, L. & J. G. Stickley, c1910, oak, clamp decal mark 900.00

Moravian, side, scroll carved back, stylized flowers, shell crest, inlaid initials, relief carved "1830," plank seat, splayed tapering legs, old natural finish 125.00

Neoclassical

Italian

Armchair, c1800, walnut, caned back, molded frame above down swept arms, scrolled terminals, bow front seat raised on stop fluted tapering cylindrical legs, set of four 7,150.00

Side, scrolled upholstered backrest with channel molding, upholstered serpentine seat, tapering circular front legs, white leather upholstery, set of four 1,430.00

Swedish, parcel–gilt, side, oval upholstered back, beaded ribbon dec, bow front seat, leaf tip carved, fluted, tapering legs, peg feet . . . 440.00

Queen Anne

American, early 18th C, wing, walnut, rect upholstered back, incurved wings, out scrolled arms, shaped seat, cabriole legs, trifid feet, 43¾" h 2,420.00

Hudson River Valley, c1750–80, armchair, maple and ash, shaped crest, solid vase form splat, shaped arms, rush seat, turned tapering legs joined by stretchers, pad feet, later brass platforms **1,760.00**

Massachusetts, c1750, wing, carved walnut, arched upholstered back, ogival wings, out scrolled arms, upholstered bowed seat, loose cushion, cabriole legs joined by turned stretchers, pad feet **30,250.00**

New England, 1730–60, maple, shaped crest, vase form splat, rush seat, vase and block turned legs joined by stretchers, Spanish feet **1,200.00**

Philadelphia, c1740, armchair, walnut, molded and scrolled carved crestrail, vase form splat, cyma–curved rounded stiles, scooped arms ending in knuckle terminals, shaped arm supports, cyma–curved balloon seat, cabriole legs carved with shells and C–scrolls at the knee, shaped pad feet, rear legs flaring outward ending in sq pad feet, repairs to arms, rear legs pieced **22,000.00**

Regency

Armchair, English, mahogany, red leather seat, turned legs, old finish, 32″ h **175.00**

Desk, fruitwood, swivel type, brown leather upholstery, splayed legs, brass casters **375.00**

Rococo Revival

Armchair, oak, twisted arm supports and stretchers, intricate designed apron, striped upholstery, 46¾″ h . **200.00**

Side, walnut, balloon back, mounted scroll and foliate carved crest, carved splat, serpentine front seat rail, acanthus carved hipped saber legs, burgundy velvet upholstery, pr **250.00**

Rococo Style, Dutch, 19th C, armchair, marquetry, serpentine crestrail inlaid with floral sprigs over baluster form splat inlaid with bird perched on a swing, shaped arms with barberpole stringing, serpentine front drop–in seat, cabriole legs, stylized claw and ball feet **1,760.00**

Sheraton

Armchair, turned detail, shaped arms, gold striping dec, orig dark paint . **210.00**

Side, curly maple, scrolled slat, replaced rush seat, detailed turnings, refinished **625.00**

Victorian

Gothic Revival, American, mid 19th C, armchair, walnut, carved, upholstered arms and seat **5,250.00**

Renaissance Revival, American, attributed to John Jelliff, c1870, arm-

Chair, Victorian, Renaissance Revival, finger molded, nut carved crest, upholstered, $475.00.

chair, walnut and burl walnut, heavily carved, upholstered back, arms, and seat **600.00**

William and Mary

Connecticut River Valley, c1710, banister back, painted maple, shaped crestrail carved with incised flowerheads and leaves, four split banister uprights, shaped arms, splint seat, turned legs joined by stretchers, one finial restored **1,980.00**

Massachusetts, c1735, side, arched molded crest, serpentine over–upholstered leather back, upholstered leather seat, vase and clock turned legs, frontal bulbous stretcher, Spanish feet **5,500.00**

Windsor

Bow Back, New England, c1805–15

Child's, plank seat on raking and baluster turned legs joined by stretchers, painted green **650.00**

Side

Bowed crest, bamboo turned posts, shaped plank seat, bamboo turned splayed legs joined with turned stretchers, stamped "E Tebbets" under seat, c1820, set of six **2,475.00**

Maple and pine, seven turned spindles, horseshoe shaped seat, bamboo turned legs, H–stretcher, painted red over old black paint, pr **500.00**

Brace Back, side, saddle seat, turned back posts, shaped crest, splayed base, bulbous turnings and H–stretcher, black repaint **400.00**

Comb Back, New England, c1785, armchair, shaped crest, eight tapering spindles, U–shaped back continuing to scroll handholds, elliptical plank seat, turned legs joined by stretchers, later black paint **2,475.00**

Fan Back, American, c1790, side, shaped crest, seven tapering spindles and plank seat, turned legs joined by turned stretchers, pr . . . **2,000.00**

Low Back, PA, c1765, armchair, U–shaped back, slightly raised crest, thirteen spindles, elliptical plank seat, splayed turned legs joined by stretchers, arrow feet **6,325.00**

Highchair, bamboo, old worn reddish finish, repaired seat crack, 36½" h **725.00**

Writing, PA, c1800, armchair, spindle form back, plain crest, horseshoe back rest and writing arm, raking bamboo turned legs joined by stretchers, allover dark–green/brown stained surface, drawer restored **2,750.00**

Chest of Drawers, Hepplewhite, cherry, bow front, thumb molded top, four graduated drawers, applied bracket base, 36½" h, $4,200.00.

CHESTS OF DRAWERS

Arts and Crafts, L. & J. G. Stickley, two small drawers over four large drawers, paneled sides, 30 x 37½" w mirror, new medium finish, 37½" w, 19½" d, 47" h **1,375.00**

Baroque, South Germany, mid 18th C, oak, serpentine molded top, conforming case, three drawers, molded base, flattened bun feet, 41" w, 29½" d, 31" h **1,320.00**

Chinese, mid 19th C, campaign, teakwood, two pr of brass carrying handles, two part construction, fold–out writing desk with pigeonholes, marble top (later addition), as found, 37½" w, 19¾" d, 45" h **3,250.00**

Chippendale

Boston, Massachusetts, c1765, block front, carved mahogany, oblong top, thumbmolded edge, four graduated blocked drawers, cockbeaded surrounds, molded base, blocked bracket feet, 36" w, 20½" d, 30¼" h **19,800.00**

Country, American

Maple, dovetailed case, six overlapping dovetailed drawers, molded cornice, cut–out feet, replacements and refinishing, backboard dated 1801, 36¼" w, 58¾" h **1,600.00**

Poplar, old red repaint, molded cornice, five overlapping dovetailed drawers, applied base moldings, cut–out feet, 37" w . . **2,900.00**

Massachusetts, c1770

Block front, carved mahogany, oblong top with thumbmolded edge, four graduated molded drawers with cockbeading, molded base, claw and ball feet, 36¾" w, 20" d, 30½" h **12,650.00**

Block front, carved mahogany, rect molded top, four blocked and molded graduated long drawers, molded base, volute carved ogee bracket feet, formerly base to chest on chest, 43¼" w, 23½" d, 37½" h **10,450.00**

Oxbow front, mahogany, oblong top, reverse serpentine front, conforming case, four graduated long drawers, cockbeaded surrounds, molded base, bracket feet, rear feet restored, 36¼" w, 21¼" d, 32½" h **5,500.00**

Oxbow front, mahogany, oblong top, thumbmolded edge, four reverse serpentine graduated drawers with cockbeading, molded base with shaped pendant, ogee bracket feet, 39¼" w, 22½" d, 32¼" h **9,900.00**

Serpentine front, molded oblong top, four graduated cockbeaded drawers, molded base, shaped bracket feet, 41½" w, 21¾" d, 33⅞" h **9,900.00**

New England, c1785, birchwood, oxbow front, oblong thumbmolded top, reverse serpentine front, four conforming shaped molded graduated long drawers, claw and ball feet, skirt pendant missing, repairs to feet, 38" w, 21¼" d, 33½" h . . . **9,350.00**

Philadelphia, c1785, satinwood inlaid mahogany, bow front, oblong top, bowed front, four fan inlaid and crossbanded cockbeaded drawers, flanking fluted quarter columns, ogee bracket feet, minor restoration, 42" w, 23" d, 36½" h, pr **22,000.00**

Pennsylvania

Walnut, c1770, molded cornice, three short and five long graduated molded drawers, fluted quarter columns, ogee bracket feet, 44½" w, 23" d, 63½" h . . . **6,325.00**

Walnut, pine and poplar secondary wood, dovetailed case, eight overlapping dovetailed drawers, molded cornice with reeded frieze, fluted quarter columns, bracket feet, refinished, 39½" w, 62¾" h **4,850.00**

Continental, mahogany, three dovetailed drawers, molded edge top, rounded corners with fluting, scalloped apron, cabriole legs, repairs and replaced brasses, 42" w, 24" d, 35" h **2,000.00**

Empire, country

Cherry, curly maple facade with cherry drawer edge beading, seven dovetailed drawers, paneled ends, turned pilasters and feet, refinished, 41⅜" w, 21½" d, 49" h **950.00**

Curly maple, cherry, and figured walnut, seven dovetailed drawers and three step back handkerchief drawers, orig crest finials, turned feet and pilasters, alligatored varnish, 45" w, 46¼" h **675.00**

Curly maple, poplar secondary wood, four dovetailed drawers, cock beading, turned quarter columns, solid ends, turned feet, replaced brasses, old refinishing, 41" w, 18" d, 35¾" h **1,950.00**

Hardwood and poplar, red flame graining, six dovetailed drawers, scrolled feet and pilasters, 39" w, 47¾" h **400.00**

Mahogany, serpentine front, rect ovolo corner marble top, four graduated drawers, reeded three-quarter columns, turned feet, casters, 48" w, 43½" d, 24" h **880.00**

Federal

American

Cherry, bow front, figured walnut veneer drawers, reeded front edge, four dovetailed drawers, figured mahogany rails and shaped apron, reeded stiles, turned feet, replaced brasses, old refinishing, 40½" w, 23½" d, 41½" h **1,150.00**

Cherry, walnut, and curly maple, reeded edge top, three short and three long dovetailed drawers with applied edge beading, paneled ends, scalloped apron, turned feet, inlaid escutcheons, replaced brasses, old refinishing, 45" w, 21½" d, 49" h **1,950.00**

Massachusetts

Inlaid mahogany, c1810, bow front, four cockbeaded graduated and crossbanded long drawers, reeded three-quarter round stiles, turned feet, 44" w, 21" d, 40" h **2,420.00**

Inlaid mahogany and branch satinwood, c1805, bow front, top with inlaid edge, four beaded and bowed long drawers inlaid with oval feathered birch panels, ivory knobs, base with central sq inlaid pendant, flaring bracket feet, 39½" w, 20¾" d, 38½" h **6,500.00**

Maryland, c1810, mahogany, oblong top, bow front, bookend inlaid edge, four diamond and line inlaid graduated drawers, shaped skirt with fan inlaid pendant, bracket feet, 39½" w, 19" d, 36" h **4,400.00**

New England, c1810, cherry, bow front, oblong top with inlaid edge, four graduated line and fan inlaid drawers, flared bracket feet, 41½" w, 22" d, 37" h **4,400.00**

Pennsylvania, c1790, cherry, molded cornice, five short and five long molded graduated long drawers, quarter columns, ogee bracket feet, 43" w, 22" d, 70¼" h **5,225.00**

Southern, early 19th C, inlaid walnut, four cockbeaded and graduated long drawers flanked by inlaid canted corners, shaped apron, flaring bracket feet, 40" w, 18" d, 42" h **3,960.00**

George II, walnut, crossbanded rect top, three short and three long graduated drawers, shaped bracket feet, 38½ x 42½" **3,025.00**

George III, mahogany, serpentine, molded top, three graduated drawers, swept bracket feet, replaced top, repairs, 48" w, 23¼" d, 34" h **6,600.00**

George III Style, mahogany, bow front, rect top with rounded front and molded edge, four graduated cockbeaded drawers, shaped bracket feet, 34" w, 36" h **1,100.00**

Hepplewhite

Cherry, bow front, three board replaced top, pull-out shelf under top, four overlapping dovetailed drawers with applied edge beading, well shaped French feet, orig brasses, mellow refinishing, 34¾" w, 22¼" d, 41" h **2,550.00**

Cherry, poplar secondary wood, five overlapping dovetailed drawers, fluted inlaid stile, molded cornice, inlaid banded base, French feet, orig brasses, refinished, 36 x 43¾" **2,700.00**

Cherry and curly maple, country, poplar secondary wood, seven dovetailed drawers, applied edge beading, veneered top, curly maple cross banding, French feet, old refinishing, replaced brasses, 43¾" w **1,400.00**

Jacobean, third quarter 17th C oak, geometrical front, three drawers, bun feet **2,200.00**

Louis XV, French, Provincial, walnut, rect molded top, conforming case, three short drawers over two long drawers, fluted sides, cabriole legs, restoration, 44" l, 20¼" d, 33" h **1,650.00**

Louis XIV, French, Provincial, early 18th C, walnut, rect top, rounded corners, molded edge, three drawers flanked by foliate carved scrolled stiles continuing to form bracket feet, 50" w, 33" h **6,600.00**

Neoclassical, marquetry

Milanese, c1800, rect top with central oval reserve inlaid with scene of Abraham about to slay Isaac, angel above holding his arm, flanked by diamond reserves inlaid with marine scenes, three long drawers, sides with conforming dec, tapering sq legs, 48½" w, 34½" h **30,250.00**

North Italian, early 19th C, rect top, molded edge, inlaid central trophy surrounded by foliate scroll cartouche with flowering urns and perched birds, sides with similar inlay within rect reserves, slight serpentine front, two short over three long drawers, shallow bracket feet, age cracks to side, 54" w, 37½" h . **12,100.00**

Queen Anne, Massachusetts, c1760, walnut, block front, thumbmolded edge, four graduated blocked long drawers with cockbeading, shaped pendant, blocked bracket feet, 34¼" w, 20" d, 29¼" h **33,000.00**

Rococo, Dutch, mid 18th C, marquetry, bombe, serpentine front and top, molded edge, elaborate flowering urn, butterflies, and birds perched in foliate scrolls, sides dec en suite, four graduated cockbeaded drawers, scrolled feet, minor losses to top, age splits to side, minor repairs, 36" w, 31¾" h **5,500.00**

Sheraton

Country, curly maple, pine secondary wood, paneled ends, four overlapping dovetailed drawers, inlaid stiles, turned feet, refinished, replaced brasses, 43¼" w, 44¾" h . **1,800.00**

Curly maple, butternut, pine, and poplar secondary wood, four cockbeaded dovetailed drawers, paneled ends, turned feet, eagle brass handles, 41½" w, 43¼" h . . **2,700.00**

Victorian, American, 19th C, mahogany, bowed top, two short drawers, three graduated drawers, shaped apron, turned legs **385.00**

William and Mary, late 17th C, oak, two part, paneled sides, two paneled frieze drawers over geometrically molded cushion double fronted drawer, restored turnip feet, 38" w, 34½" h **3,300.00**

Chests, Other, highboy, Queen Anne, PA, c1750, two parts, walnut, five thumb molded and graduated drawers, base with single long drawer, three small drawers, shaped apron, cabriole legs, pad feet, 28" w, 30" d, 70" h, $70,000.00.

CHESTS, OTHERS

Apothecary, pine, forty dovetailed drawers, replaced frame to create freestanding drawers from former built–in unit, sponged red repaint, white painted labels, 51½" w, 10" d, 47½" h **500.00**

Bachelor, George III Style, walnut, molded rect top, writing slide, two short and three long graduated cockbeaded drawers, bracket feet, 30½ x 30" **1,430.00**

Butler's, Empire, American, c1835, mahogany, five drawers with brass escutcheons, fall front, fitted int., pr of cupboard doors, finely carved acanthus leaf and scroll designed columns, hairy paw feet, 53¼" w, 22¾" d, 53" h **1,700.00**

Chest on Chest

Chippendale

Connecticut, carved cherry, bonnet top, two sections, c1770, upper section with molded swan's neck cresting, three carved urn form finials, three short molded drawers, center drawer fan carved, four molded graduated long drawers below, stop–fluted pilasters flanking, lower section with four molded and graduated long drawers, molded base, scroll cut bracket feet, 39" w, 20½" d, 87½" h **31,900.00**

Connecticut, carved cherry, bonnet top, two sections, c1780, upper section with molded cornice, three turned finials, five small and four molded and graduated long drawers, lower section with four long molded drawers, fluted canted corners, ogee bracket feet, 44¾" w, 22½" d, 85" h . . . **22,000.00**

Philadelphia, c1760, carved mahogany, bonnet top, two parts, upper section with molded swan's neck crest, three urn and flame finials on fluted plinths, central short cockbeaded drawers with carved concave shell, applied leafage above five short cockbeaded drawers, four cockbeaded graduated long drawers, fluted canted corners, lower section with two long cockbeaded drawers over two long gradated cockbeaded drawers, fluted canted corners, molded base, canted ogee bracket feet, orig brasses, stamped "J. Stow," also inscribed "J. A. Alston," minor repair to feet and finial support, 46" w, 24" d, 101¾" h **41,800.00**

George III, English, late 18th C, mahogany

Cavetto molded cornice, two short cockbeaded drawers, three long graduated drawers over three long drawers, ogee bracket feet, 40¼" w, 68½" h **4,400.00**

Three short drawers over three long drawers, flanked by fluted canted stiles, base fitted with brushing slide over three long drawers, bracket feet, repaired age cracks to sides, handles replaced, 42" w, 72" h **3,300.00**

Late George III, English, early 19th C, mahogany, molded and dentil cornice, two short drawers and three long graduated drawers above base with three long drawers, cockbeaded borders, top lower drawer fitted with later leather inset writing slide, concealed swiveling drawer on right side, bracket feet, drawers partially relined, handles replaced, 40¼" w, 70" h **2,750.00**

Chest on Frame

Chippendale, c1755, walnut, flat top, molded cornice top with three short and four long molded graduated drawers, bottom with one long molded drawer, shaped skirt, cabriole legs, claw and ball feet, c1755, 43" w, 22" d, 65" h **6,600.00**

Queen Anne

American, walnut, molded cornice, five small and three long drawers, shaped apron, cabriole legs, trifid feet, 41½" w, 23" d, 65" h . **6,500.00**

Pennsylvania, c1760, walnut, two parts, upper section with molded cornice, five short and four long molded graduated drawers, lower section with projecting molding, shaped skirt, short angular cabriole legs, stylized trifid feet, 43½" w, 24¾" d, 70" h . . . **4,950.00**

William and Mary, Philadelphia, c1715, carved and turned walnut, two parts, upper section with molded cornice, two short and three graduated long drawers, lower section with mid–molding above long drawer, arched apron, six baluster and trumpet turned legs joined by shaped stretcher, ball feet, ink inscription on top board of lower section "Robert Pascall, Philadelphia, PA," repairs to four legs, two legs restored, 42" w, 22½" d, 61" h **12,650.00**

Commode

Louis XV Style

Bombe style, marquetry, variegated Sienna marble top, central frieze drawer, three drawers, gilt metal mask form design on corners, foliate cast feet, 64″ w, 38½″ h . **3,025.00**

Rosewood, crossbanded serpentine top, gilt metal banded edge, three line inlaid long drawers, sq cabriole legs, 22″ w, 32½″ h . . . **550.00**

Louis XVI, Provincial, walnut, rect thumbmolded top, three drawers, sq legs, 43″ w, 21″ d, 33½″ h **2,900.00**

Highboy

Chippendale, PA, c1760, carved walnut, flat top, two sections, upper section with molded cornice, five short and three long graduated molded drawers, fluted quarter columns flanking, lower section with projecting mid–molding above three short molded drawers, center drawer shell and volute carved, fluted quarter columns flanking, shaped skirt, center carved shell, scroll cut cabriole legs, claw and ball feet, some losses to feet and drawer lips, 42¼″ w, 24″ d, 66½″ h **14,850.00**

George I, Provincial, oak and walnut, top with projecting molded cornice, two short and three long crossbanded drawers, base with one short and two deep crossbanded drawers, cockbeaded scalloped apron, sq cabriole legs, 40 x 66″ . **1,540.00**

Queen Anne

American, country, curly maple, pine secondary wood, mismatched dovetailed top case with five drawers and molded cornice, base with four overlapping dovetailed drawers and scrolled apron, cabriole legs with duck feet and pads, refinished, 35¾″ w, 66½″ h **2,900.00**

Connecticut, attributed to Stonington Area, c1750, tiger maple, flat top, two parts, upper section with molded cornice, convex secret drawer, two short and three molded graduated long drawers, projecting molding, lower section with three short molded drawers, scroll cut shaped skirt, cabriole legs, pad feet, minor repair to front leg, 39¼″ w, 21½″ d, 96″ h **37,400.00**

Connecticut, c1765, carved cherry, flat top, two parts, upper section with projecting molded cornice, five molded and graduated long drawers, lower section with one long and three short molded drawers, center fan carved, shaped skirt, scrolled center pendant, cabriole legs, pad feet, re-

pair to rear leg and some moldings, 43¾″ w, 19¼″ d, 73½″ h . **6,600.00**

Massachusetts, 1730–50, maple and pine, flat top with molded cornice, two short and three long graduated molded drawers in upper section, lower section with three short molded drawers, allover japanned chinoiserie motifs with gilt highlights, shaped skirt, cabriole legs, pad feet **41,250.00**

New England, 18th C, carved maple, flat top, two sections, upper section with molded cornice, four graduated long drawers, lower section with one long drawer over triple fronted drawers, double carved fan, shaped apron, short cabriole legs, repairs, top and base may be married, 40½″ w, 74½″ h **2,200.00**

Newport, RI, Goddard–Townsend School, c1750, mahogany, flat top, two parts, upper section with molded cornice over three short and three long graduated molded drawers, projecting molding below, lower section with one long and three short molded drawers, scalloped skirt, removable angular cabriole legs, pointed slipper feet, orig brasses, incised initials "TB," 38¾″ w, 20½″ d, 71½″ h **34,100.00**

Lowboy, Queen Anne

Connecticut, c1765, cherry, rect molded top, one long and three short molded drawers, central fan carving, shaped skirt, cabriole legs, pad feet, 34⅞″ w, 21⅛″ d, 34″ h . **41,250.00**

Pennsylvania

c1750, carved cherry, rect thumbmolded top, notched front corners, case with one long drawer faced to simulate three short molded drawers over two short molded drawers, flanking fluted quarter columns, pierced and scroll cut skirt, scroll cut cabriole legs, paneled trifid feet, 40¼″ w, 25½″ d, 29⅛″ h **38,500.00**

c1750, curly maple, oblong top, thumbmolded edge, notched corners, one long and three short molded drawers, stop fluted pilasters, shaped skirt, shell carved cabriole legs, paneled pad feet, 34¼″ w, 19¾″ d, 29″ h **7,150.00**

c1760, walnut, rect thumbmolded top, one long and three short molded drawers, shaped skirt, cabriole legs, trifid feet, repairs and losses, 34″ w, 8¼″ d, 28½″ h **4,400.00**

c1770, cherry, rect molded top, notched corners, four molded small drawers, scroll cut skirt, cabriole legs, trifid feet, 34¾″ w, 22″ d, 30″ h **15,400.00**

Mule, decorated

Pine, two dovetailed drawers, hinged lid with molded edge, orig red and black graining with brown vinegar painting, green and yellow striping, gilt stenciled floral designs, 42″ w, 35¾″ h **750.00**

Pine and poplar, two dovetailed drawers, hinged lid, orig reddish brown flame graining, turned wood pulls, 38 x 36½″ **800.00**

Sea, attributed to China, c1800, camphor wood, slanted front and back, 38½″ l **1,050.00**

Spice, Chippendale, Pennsylvania

1763, walnut, projected molding, arched paneled door with inlaid flower head and initials "MF" and date 1763, opens to eleven small drawers, ogee bracket feet, 18¾ x 13 x 9½″ **60,500.00**

c1765, miniature, cherry, molded cornice above two short and two long drawers, scroll cut base, 6⅛″ w, 4¾″ d, 7¾″ h **4,675.00**

Tall

Chippendale, New England, late 18th C, carved curly maple, molded cornice, seven thumbmolded long drawers, bracket feet, 40½″ w, 17½″ d, 65½″ h **8,250.00**

Neoclassical style, Dutch, 19th C, marquetry, rect top, out–set drawer over five conforming long drawers, inlaid lyres, flowering vines, and birds grasping floral sprigs, saber legs, losses to veneer, 38½″ w, 64″ h **3,575.00**

Welsh Dresser, George III, early 19th C, pine, open back, two drawers in base, sq tapering legs **1,870.00**

CRADLES

Birch, hooded, dovetailed, cut–out rockers, scalloped ends, 41″ l **500.00**

Cherry, mortised sides, scrolled detail, sq corner posts, turned finials, scrolled rockers, old dark finish, nailed repairs, 40″ l **200.00**

Mahogany, dovetailed, scrolled sides and ends, old dark finish, 49½″ l ... **500.00**

Pine, American, late 18th or early 19th C, pine, hooded, scalloped hood sides, plain bonnet top, orig finish .. **400.00**

Cradle, bonnet top, spindles, 38″ l, 27¼″ h, $350.00.

Poplar, open, central cut–out sides and ends, hand holds, trestle rockers, old dark finish, 41″ l **250.00**

Walnut, dovetailed, scalloped sides, hand holds, brass knobs, heart cut–out in headboard, large rockers, 43½″ l **375.00**

CUPBOARDS

Armoire, Louis XV, French, Provincial, walnut, molded cornice, frieze with center stylized flowerhead in oval reserve, two doors with asymmetrically scroll carved panels, apron with center carved flowerhead, scrolled feet, 56″ w, 94½″ h **3,300.00**

China, Arts and Crafts, American

Gustav Stickley, No. 815, gallery top, two doors, eight glass panes in each, exposed tenons at top and bottom of sides, eight panes of glass in each side, straight apron, orig finish, double sgd, brand and paper label, 41″ w, 15″ d, 64″ h .. **4,125.00**

L. & J. G. Stickley, two large glass paned doors, four int. shelves, two small solid doors, strap hardware, orig dark brown finish, orig label "The Work of L. & J. G. Stickley," 70″ h, 49½″ w, 17¼″ d **17,600.00**

Corner

Country, one piece

Cherry, cove molded cornice, double top doors with 8 panes of glass, double paneled cupboard doors, scalloped apron, cut–out feet, replaced hinges, old repairs to cornice, old mellow refinishing, 48¼″ w, 83″ h **2,800.00**

Cupboard, walnut, projecting cornice, twelve-paned glass doors, three int. shelves, three drawers over two cupboard doors, brass hardware, 52" w, 18½" d, 84" h, $4,800.00.

Cherry, molded cornice, double doors with 3 panes of glass, one dovetailed drawer, paneled cupboard doors, simple scalloped feet, renailed backboards, rebuilt drawer, minor repairs, refinished, 46¾" w, 80¾" h 1,700.00

Curly Maple, poplar secondary wood, crown molded cornice, double top doors each with six panes of old glass, tapered mullions, arched top lights, two dovetailed overlapping drawers, orig brass thumb latches, arched panel doors, scalloped apron, cut–out feet, old golden color refinishing, 57¼" w, 84" h 6,500.00

Pine, Connecticut, c1770, architectural, molded projected cornice, flowerhead carved tympanum, carved shell above shaped shelves, fluted pilasters, hinged paneled door on bottom, painted, 54¾" w, 84½" h 17,600.00

Walnut, poplar secondary wood, cove molded cornice with dentilated frieze, paneled doors with dec scalloped panels, applied moldings, fluted stiles, bracket feet, refinished, minor repairs, back foot missing, 52" w, 95¾" h 3,500.00

Country, two pieces, dovetailed cases
Cherry, twelve pane door top with cove molded cornice, base with paneled door and bracket feet, refinished, 42 x 45¾ x 84" h . . . 2,300.00

Curly maple, cove molded cornice, single top door with twelve panes of old wavy glass, base with paneled doors, scalloped apron, orig turned cherry feet, refinished, 40¼" w, 88" h 7,250.00

Pine and tulip poplar, PA or NY, c1820, upper section with molded cornice, glazed cupboard door, shelved int., half round ring and spirally turned colonettes flanking, lower section with paneled cupboard door, ogee bracket feet, 50¾" w, 27¼" d, 82" h 1,980.00

Federal
American, walnut, top with molded cornice above carved arch with line and flower inlaid panel, line inlaid arched and glazed doors opens to shelved int., line inlaid pilasters, bottom with two short drawers, and pr doors, bracket feet, 96 x 58½ x 26¼" 9,075.00

Pennsylvania, c1795, inlaid cherry, upper section with triglyph–inlaid molded pitched pediment, turned urn finial, arched glazed hinged door, blue painted shelved int., lower section with three cockbeaded line inlaid drawers, pr of hinged paneled cupboard doors opening to shelf, scroll cut faceted bracket feet, 46" w, 27¼" d, 97" h 19,800.00

George III, English, c1760
Japanned, red, dentil molded pediment, frieze decorated with raised ellipses and gilt flowerheads, two glazed doors, scalloped shelves, fluted pilasters, lower section with pr of cupboard doors, decorated with gilt pavilions and Oriental figures, later plinth base, 43" w, 86" h 7,700.00

Pine, stepped and dentil cornice, arched aperture, blue painted int. of three shaped shelves, flanked by fluted stiles, base with pr of shallow fielded panel doors, paneled angled stiles, bracket feet, 59½" w, 81½" h 3,300.00

Neoclassical, Italian, walnut, quarter round top, straight frieze, one door, lobed sq feet, 37 x 30½" 660.00

Hanging
English, early 20th C, corner, mahogany, geometrical mullions and molded and dentiled cornice on door, old dark finish, 31" w, 43" h . 275.00

European, corner, mahogany, marquetry, tambour door, floral inlay, repaired, 17½ x 27" **525.00**

New York, Victorian, early 19th C, country, pine, shaped crest with three turned urn form finials, pr of hinged paneled cupboard doors, applied block corners, shelved int., geometric designs painted and dec in dark green and red, yellow ground, initials "JC," and date 1836 on topboard, 28½" w, 9½" d, 42½" h **4,675.00**

Pennsylvania, c1755, walnut, molded cornice, paneled hinged door with rattail hinges, shelved int., scroll cut sides, molded open transverse shelf, 27" w, 14" d, 36" h **4,070.00**

Jelly

Country, Pennsylvania, pine, shaped splashboard, two drawers, pr hinged doors, painted and grained, bracket feet, 41½" w, 22½" d, 47" h **1,650.00**

Empire, poplar, pine secondary wood, double door top with molded cornice and four dovetailed spice drawers, base with paneled doors, molded center stiles, paneled ends, and two dovetailed drawers, replaced brass drawer handles, 47" w, 18¾" d, 85½" h **2,600.00**

Kas, William and Mary, Hudson River Valley, 1730–70, gumwood, elaborately molded projecting cornice over pr of hinged paneled doors, removable shelves int., base with one long drawer faced to simulate two drawers, diamond molded reserves flanking, replaced ebonized ball feet, 72" w, 28½" d, 80" h **6,875.00**

Linen Press

George III, English, late 18th C, oak, rect molded cornice, pr of paneled doors, base with three false drawers over two working drawers . . . **2,800.00**

George III Style, bird's eye maple, projecting molded cornice with dentil frieze, two paneled doors above writing slide, three cockbeaded drawers, bracket feet, 61½ x 32" . **1,900.00**

Wall

Chippendale

American, attributed to PA, late 18th C, step back, walnut, two parts, upper section with molded cornice, two glazed doors, three grooved plate and spoon shelves, lambs' tongue chamfered corners, lower section with molded edge rect top over three beaded edge short drawers over

two paneled doors, shelved int., molded bracket feet, minor repairs, 80" w, 76" h **4,675.00**

Country, walnut, molded cornice, raised panel doors with beaded frame, replaced bracket feet, old refinishing, 41⅜" w, 14¾" d, 86¼" h **1,700.00**

Country, American, c1820, pine, one piece, molded cornice, pr of glazed hinged cupboard doors with four panes of glass each, white painted shelved int., flanking pilasters, hinged cupboard door below, painted green, 43¼" w, 21½" d, 87" h **1,980.00**

Dutch, marquetry, breakdown top with glass doors, convoluted crest, shaped shelves, and mirror back, Bombay style base with four drawers and turned feet, elaborate floral inlay, refinished, replaced brasses, 53" w, 88" h **5,000.00**

George III, English, 18th C, oak, projecting cavetto molded cornice, reeded frieze, two sets of paneled doors, reeded angles, plinth base, 51" w, 81" h **2,750.00**

Victorian, Renaissance Revival, American, c1872, parcel–gilt and stained burled maple, arched cornice dec and stained with opposed winged griffins flanked by foliate scrolls, canted corners with flanneted urn form finials, frieze incised and stained with stylized suspended palmettes, rounded rect beveled mirror door flanked by parcel–gilt fluted columns dec with leafy bands, base fitted with single drawer, circular disc feet, back inscribed in pencil "Mr. Latham," 48" w, 97½" h **6,600.00**

Wardrobe

Georgian Style, late 19th C, mahogany, breakfront, molded projecting cornice, paneled doors, two small and two large drawers, two paneled doors on each side, plinth base, 82 x 92 x 24" **2,750.00**

Victorian, c1880, mahogany, satinwood inlaid stepped and cavetto molded cornice, projecting tablet, satinwood banded sides and double doors, inlaid ribbon tied wreath upper panels, plinth base, 67½ x 45" **1,430.00**

DESKS

Art Nouveau, Austrian, gilt metal, repousse panels of country scenes,

glass top, brocade lining, matching
armchair **1,200.00**

Arts and Crafts, American

Lifetime, No. 8569, oak, drop front,
gallery top, two half drawers over
single wide drawer, lower median
shelf, marked, 1910, 34" w, 44" h . **935.00**

Limbert, c1910, oak, rect top, blind
drawer pulls, lift top compartment,
fitted pen tray and inkwell, four sq
post legs with tenons, branded
mark, cleaned finish, 24" w, 17½"
d, 29" h **470.00**

Desk, bookkeeper's, pine, three pieces, two cupboard doors, fitted int. with six slots, eighteen pigeon holes, lift top, slant front center section, six small drawers over two file type drawers, brass hardware, 49" w, 28" d, 90" h, $3,000.00.

Chippendale, American

Boston, MA, carved mahogany

c1765, block front, slant front, rect
molded hinged lid, stepped int.
with valanced pigeonholes over
small drawers, center prospect
section with hinged drop front
door opening to valanced drawer
and blocked small drawer, flanking document drawers, four
cockbeaded graduated long
drawers, molded base, shaped
pendant, blocked bracket feet,
patches to lid, 40" w, 19½" d,
42½" h **22,000.00**

c1775, oxbow slant front, rect
molded lid, int. fitted with drawers
over valanced pigeonholes,
block and fan carved prospect
section with three drawers, four
graduated reverse serpentine
drawers below, cockbeaded surround, molded base with fan and
volute carved pendant, ogee
bracket feet, repair to lid at
hinges, 42" w, 21½" d, 43¾" h . **10,450.00**

Country, slant front, dovetailed

Cherry, four overlapping drawers,
hinged lid, fitted int., bracket feet,
old worn dark varnish finish, repairs and replacements, 41" w,
19½" d, 43"h **2,200.00**

Maple, curly maple facade, pine
secondary wood, including most
of fitted int., stepped int. with
seven drawers, pigeonholes,
center door with raised tombstone panel, three int. drawers
with block carving, letter drawers
with turned pilasters, four overlapping drawers, bracket feet, replaced brasses, minor repairs,
old worn refinishing, 29¾" h writ-
ing surface, 38" w, 20" d, 41¾" h **6,500.00**

New England

c1760, curly maple, slant front,
hinged rect lid opens to fitted int.,
four graduated drawers, bracket
feet, 36¼" w, 19¼" d, 41¼" h . . **4,675.00**

c1775, Massachusetts or Rhode Island, carved mahogany, rect top,
thumbmolded edge, hinged front
flap above hinged fall front faced
to simulate two working drawers,
opening to pull–out stepped int.
of three fan carved and blocked
drawers, center valanced pigeonholes and small drawers below, case with one long drawer
with incised edges, molded skirt,
pierced leg brackets, stop fluted
sq legs, some restoration to plain
drawers, replaced pierced brack-
ets, 42½" w, 24¾" d, 41½" h . . **15,400.00**

c1780, maple and cherry, thumbmolded edge slant front, fitted int.
compartment with six valanced
pigeonholes, two center document drawers, two stepped
shelves of eight short drawers
above four thumbmolded graduated long drawers, lamb's tongue
chamfered corners, molded
bracket feet, restored int. and
feet, 40¼" w, 42" h **3,025.00**

Rhode Island, c1770, mahogany,
thumbmolded hinged lid, fitted int.
with valanced pigeonholes, shell
carved and scooped small drawers,
well below, four molded and grad-

uated long drawers, restored ogee bracket feet, 36" w, 19¼" d, 41½" h **6,325.00**

Colonial Revival

Chippendale Style, c1930, block front, solid walnut case, walnut veneered slant front lid, fitted int. with secret drawer, paw feet, 32" w, 18" d, 42" h **450.00**

Governor Winthrop Style, c1920, mahogany veneer, serpentine front, solid mahogany slant front, fitted int. with two document drawers, shell carved center door, four long drawers, brass pulls and escutcheons **400.00**

Queen Anne Style, c1940, walnut veneer top, sides, and front, crotch walnut veneer on two side drawers, shell carved cabriole legs, 44" w, 20" d, 31" h **450.00**

Edwardian, late 19th C

Mahogany and satinwood, lady's, reticulated galleried shelf and two drawers, rect tooled leather inset writing surface, frieze drawer, reeded edges, fluted sq tapered legs, inlaid and finished front, 42" l, 20¾" d, 37½" h **1,900.00**

Satinwood, Carlton House, U–shaped superstructure with drawers, pigeonholes, and letter slots, felt lined writing surface, floral inlay, two frieze drawers, sq tapering legs, spade feet, 39¼" l, 22" d, 40" h **4,950.00**

Federal

Boston, MA, c1800, lady's, inlaid mahogany, two parts, upper section with molded cornice above two hinged drawers, inlaid satinwood columns, int. with small drawers centering valanced pigeonholes, lower section with hinged baize lined writing flap above two cockbeaded drawers, rect inlaid dies, sq tapering legs ending in shaped angular vase form feet, 39" w, 20¼" d, 44" h **9,000.00**

Mid Atlantic States, c1820, curly maple, three sort drawers above retracting cylinder lid opening to short drawers over valanced pigeonholes, center tambour slide, retractable baize lined writing surface, two short drawers and long drawers, turned feet, 40½" w, 22" d, 50" h . **5,000.00**

New York, butler's, mahogany, oblong top, oval inlaid drawer, fall front opening with fitted int., three line inlaid long drawers on bottom, shaped skirt with central inlaid fan,

splayed bracket feet, c1805, 42" w, 22½" d, 46¼" h **3,850.00**

George I, English, early 18th C, slant front, walnut, rect crossbanded top, canted lid, shaped and stepped int. with small drawers and conforming cubbyholes, center prospect door, rect case with three short, two short and two full cockbeaded and crossbanded drawers, bracket feet, 37" w, 21" d, 40" h **6,500.00**

George III, English, c1800–10

Partner's, mahogany, gold tooled olive brown leather inset top, frieze drawer and two deep drawers, shallow arched kneehole, opposing with similar arrangement, replaced lion mask ring handles, ring turned tapering legs, inverted baluster feet, 42" l, 29" h **2,750.00**

Slant front, oak, valanced pigeonholes and drawers, four cockbeaded drawers, shaped bracket feet, c1800, 36" w, 39½" h **1,045.00**

George III Style, c1840, partner's, mahogany, two part rect tooled leather top, three frieze drawers on either side, pedestal fitted with three drawers on one side, cupboards on other side, plinth bases, 72" l, 30¾" h ... **3,300.00**

Napoleon III, Boston, c1870, ebonized and brass inlaid, rect top over two drawers, roll top, fitted writing surface, frieze drawer, tapering fluted legs joined by stretchers, orig paper label "Lawrence Wilde & Co, 38–48 Cornhill St, Boston" **1,760.00**

Neoclassical, Italian, walnut, kneehole, rect top with molded edge, gold tooled blue leather writing slide, three drawers, two cupboard doors, sq tapered legs, 54" w, 31" h **3,025.00**

Queen Anne, New England, child's, maple, slant front, hinged rect molded lid opens to fitted int., three graduated molded drawers, bracket feet, 24" w, 13" d, 28" h **4,950.00**

Regency, c1815, Davenport, rosewood, sliding sq writing surface, tooled brown leather inset, rect three quarter brass gallery, pull–out writing slide on either side fitted with pen and ink drawer, four long drawers, false drawers on other side, turned cylindrical feet, minor losses to molding, 30" h . **3,600.00**

Restoration, American, c1835–40, carved rosewood, fall front, well fitted line inlaid int., 30½" w, 57" h **2,400.00**

Victorian, Derby Desk Co, Boston, late 19th C, cherry, tambour roll top, fitted int., rect top, pedestals with drawers, plinth base, 54" l, 33" d, 50½" h ... **2,310.00**

DOUGH TROUGHS

Cherry, dovetailed, turned feet, white porcelain knobs, name "Hardin" scratched on base 265.00
Decorated, pine, American, late 18th C
  Orig blue paint, early train painted on one side in black, white, and faded red, sq nail construction, curved tin bottom, unpainted inner lid, worn leather hinges, 21 x 31" breadboard top, 15¼ x 25¾ x 28½" . . . 700.00
  Orig red paint, stretcher base, 46½ x 23 x 27⅜" 750.00
Maple, dovetailed, old replacement lid, traces of old red paint, 38 x 19¼ x 28¾" 450.00
Poplar, turned cherry legs, chestnut apron and hinged lid, refinished, 19 x 41 x 29½" 350.00
Walnut, dovetailed, splayed legs, 20 x 27 x 39" 450.00

Dry Sink, American, c1890, ash, one small drawer on top, two cupboard doors, wooden pulls, hand decorated, 46" l, 17" d, 45½" h, $600.00.

DRYSINKS

Cherry, Chippendale, two paneled doors on top, rect sink over two paneled doors in base, 46" l, 23½" w, 77" h 1,100.00
Curly Maple, poplar door panels, hard wood edge strips, replaced drawer front, re–cut top edge well, refinished, 55" l, 20¼" w, 34½" h 2,250.00
Pine, country, 19th C, shallow well top, two recessed paneled doors, bracket feet, 29" l, 22" w, 45" h 950.00
Pine and Poplar
  American, crest, paneled doors, one small nailed drawer, refinished, 34" l, 19¾" d, 62½" h 900.00

  Attributed to PA, c1825, shelf back with two small drawers, two base doors, refinished, minor restoration, 52" l, 22½" d, 50⅜" h 850.00
Poplar, country, paneled doors, dovetailed drawer, cut–out sides, shelf top, simple cut–out feet, old worn refinishing, 48" l, 19¾" d, 48¾" h 1,125.00

Hall Tree, Victorian, Renaissance Revival, walnut, beveled mirror, brown marble insert, 80" h, $2,000.00.

HAT RACKS AND HALL TREES

Art Nouveau
  French, c1900, carved walnut, thumbmolded cornice over shaped mirror plate, molded tendril border, serpentine projecting shelf, panel carved at sides with tendrils and leafy sprays, shaped feet, 50" w, 85" h 1,500.00
  Galle, c1900, oak, arched superstructure inlaid with three divided panels, sheep gracing scene, buildings, and rolling hills, paneled back with relief carving of branch, leaf, and pod motifs, flanked by glazed cupboard doors, int. shelves, rect seat above panels inlaid with floral sprigs, insects, and waterlilies, molded base, block feet, 77½" w, 79½" h 5,000.00
Arts and Crafts, Gustav Stickley, double, orig light finish, six black iron hooks, small version of Stickley No. 53, from Cleveholm Manor, CO, 13" w, 22" d, 66" h 1,870.00

Classical, New England, maple, turned and acanthus carved post, fifteen clothes supports, ball finial, scrolled legs, 79″ h **1,320.00**

Victorian, American

Gothic Revival, c1855, oak, ornate arched open cut upper frame, hooks at side, white marble shelf, ornate open cut base flanked by umbrella racks **10,000.00**

Renaissance Revival, c1870, walnut, orange carved cresting, shaped mirror within molded framework, drop columns at each side, candle sockets and candle shelves, white marble shelf, single drawer flanked by umbrella racks, orig brass pans **2,000.00**

Rococo Revival, walnut, intricate carving, six small and two large shelves, stained, mirror back, 46″ w, 14″ d, 90″ h **700.00**

Magazine Rack, American, walnut, one drawer, brass pull, acorn finials, brass castors, 22¾″ w, 17¼″ d, 23¼″ h, $600.00.

MAGAZINE RACKS

Arts and Crafts

Derby, oak, vertical double side stretchers, five shelves, rect legs, dark finish, remnants of paper label "Derby...Boston" **140.00**

Michigan Chair Co, oak, sq overhanging top, four open shelves, sides with two vertical slats, lower shelf with keyed tenons, 33⅛″ h, c1910 **500.00**

Stickley, L. & J. G., No. 47, trapezoidal sides, arched toe boards, four shelves, orig color and finish, decal "The Work of L. & J. G. Stickley," 20″ w, 15″ d, 42″ h **1,650.00**

Tobey Company, beveled overhanging top, slatted sides, orig dark finish, 16½″ sq, 33″ h **550.00**

George III, late 18th C, upper portion divided into three sections, full frieze drawer, turned legs, 18″ w, 13½″ d, 19″ h **1,500.00**

Regency Style, mahogany, rect, four partitions, one drawer, ring turned tapered legs, caster feet, 19½″ w, 13¾″d, 20″ h **425.00**

Victorian

Mahogany, c1840, divided top, turned cylindrical center posts, base with single drawer, turned tapered cylindrical legs on casters, 18″ l, 21½″ h **2,100.00**

Rosewood

American, c1850, single short drawer, turned feet, brass caps and casters, 18″ w, 16″ d, 19″ h **1,250.00**

English, early 19th C, upper portion divide into four sections, turned supports at corners, apron with full drawer, ring turned legs, 20″ w, 15″ d, 21″h **2,400.00**

William IV, c1835, rosewood, X–form dividers, baluster turned rails, bellflower wreaths above single long drawer, baluster turned legs, casters, 20″ l, 19¾″ h **1,800.00**

Mirror, Queen Anne, walnut, two part mirror, beveled glass, pierced heart and crown etching, $5,500.00.

MIRRORS

Architectural, country, two parts, pine, orig reverse glass painting of two story house with some flaking, old dark finish, 12½″ w, 19″ h **155.00**

Baroque Style

Continental

Mahogany and parcel–gilt, carved, rect mirror plate, conforming molded frame with floral and foliate spray, 61½″ l, 35″ h **725.00**

Oak, rect plate, carved pierced foliate mounted with cartouche and two putti, late 19th C, 44″ l, 26½″ h **1,870.00**

Italian, mid 19th C, parcel–gilt, ebonized, rect mirror plate, elaborate fruit and floral carved frame surmounted by figure of infant blackamoor holding large drapery swag aloft, polychromed blue, red, silver, and gilt foliate and floral scrolls, knotted at corners and interlacing the frame, corners with carved high relief blackamoor winged cherub heads, 42½″ w, 62″ h **6,050.00**

Chippendale

American

c1770, parcel–gilt mahogany, surmounted by giltwood phoenix finial flanked by swan's neck crest, rect mirror plate with gilt slip, shaped pendant, replaced finial, 19¾″ w, 39″ h **2,650.00**

c1770, parcel–gilt walnut, shaped crest, pierced gilt leaf reserve, shaped pendant, 24¼″ w, 45″ h **5,775.00**

c1780, parcel–gilt mahogany, shaped crest, rect mirror plate, gilt slip, shaped pendant below, restorations to side scrolls, 22½″ w, 44″ h **1,540.00**

Country, scroll

Mahogany, gilded composition eagle, gilded liner, orig mirror glass, one glued ear, old finish, 12½″ w, 21½″ h **650.00**

Pine, mahogany veneer, gilded liner, 19¾″ w, 37″ h **850.00**

Walnut, carved liner with traces of gilding, minor repairs, old refinishing, 14¼″ w, 28½″ h **325.00**

Classical, American, giltwood

c1795, wirework crest, central urn, scrolling vines, rect mirror plate, pierced flowerhead pendant, c1795, 28½″ d, 59½″ h **2,750.00**

c1820, mounted eagle flanked by C–scrolls, mirror plate surrounded with molded and pierced scroll carved border, shell carved pendant, 31½″ d, 49″ h **3,410.00**

Empire, two parts, turned pilaster frame, gold and black repaint, brass rosettes on corner blocks, orig reverse painting of lady dancing on red draped stage, 17″ w, 36¼″ h **400.00**

Federal, American

c1795, inlaid mahogany, urn with flower spray finial, swan's neck crest, shell inlaid tympanum, rect mirror plate with gilded slip, shaped pendant, 23″ w, 60½″ h **5,500.00**

c1800, NY, wall, inlaid mahogany, giltwood finial of urn with spray of leaves, molded swan's neck crest, conch shell inlaid tympanum, eglomise landscape panel with castle and birds, rect mirror plate, flowerhead and leaf filets flanking, shaped pendant, replaced finial, 23″ w, 59½″ h **9,350.00**

c1815, Philadelphia, girandole, classical carved giltwood, framework hung with gilt spherules, eagle perched on stylized leafage above and holding chains in its beak, circular flat mirror plate, ebonized slip, leafage flanking, leaf form pendant, 23″ w, 39½″ h **96,250.00**

c1820, dresser, bow front, inlaid mahogany, rect mirror plate pivots between turned uprights, case with three drawers, turned feet, 21″ w, 7½″ d, 21¾″ h **400.00**

Federal Style, mahogany, crested with urn filled with wheat sheaves and flowerheads, scrollboard with inlaid eagle, eglomise panel with landscape below, 22¾″ w, 52″ h **1,650.00**

George I, Continental, c1725, walnut, beveled two section rect plate

Raised molded border, scroll cut pierced cresting, carved giltwood foliage and scrolls, pomegranate, conforming apron, 16¾″ w, 38¾″ h **2,200.00**

Shaped upper border, tall arched pierced scroll cut cresting, circular aperture inset with gilt plume, matching plume on apron, re–gilt, 20″ w, 55″ h **3,300.00**

George II Style, 19th C, carved giltwood, vertical beveled plate, eared and mitred frame, interrupted scrolled pediment with center acanthus carved cartouche, applied molded cornucopia, C–scroll, husks, and foliage border on raised ovolo–carved frame with applied pendant acorns and oak leaves, apron with center basket of flowers, minor loss to gesso, repaired cresting, 35½″ w, 72″ h **3,575.00**

George III, American, late 18th C, inlaid mahogany, rect mirror plate tilting between two ring turned canted uprights, case with three drawers flanked by cruciform dies, turned ivory ball feet, knobs, and mounts, 29½″ w, 9″ d, 28″ h **880.00**

Louis XV Style, 19th C, rect carved giltwood and gesso frame, raised outer edge, mirrored oval reserves, center carved floral crest surrounded by sectioned inner mirrors, 66″ w, 86″ h, pr **26,500.00**

Louis XVI Style, 1889, cheval, mahogany, swiveling rect frame, inset oval mirror plate, gilt–bronze spandrels, floral sprays, and winged griffins, sq pilasters, candle arms and flame finials on each side, shaped cabriole legs, gilt–bronze sabots, 48″ w, 84″ h, stamped "Wararian" **11,000.00**

Regency, English, first quarter 19th C, giltwood, convex, circular mirror plate, ebonized border, spiral rope carved frame flanked by flames supporting scrolled candle arms, surmounted by spread winged eagle perched on rockwork, foliate pendant below, orig paper label "J. Del Vecchio, Jun. Carver, Gilder, Looking Glass & Composition Ornament Manufacturer,..." minor losses to gesso, restorations, 33″ w, 44″ h **3,300.00**

Renaissance, American, Herter Bros, NY, c1872, for Thurlow Lodge, Menlo Park, CA

Carved walnut, arched architectural pediment, center carved mask of Mercury flanked by seated putti, over central medallion of caduceus flanked by frieze of lionhead metopes and stylized flowering sprigs, large rect mirror plate with canted upper corners, flanked by simulated veined green marble columns with Ionic capitals, palmette carved bases, lower section with shaped simulated marble top over palmette carved frieze, tapering urn form supports with Ionic capitals joined by laurel swags, flanked by opposed winged lions, shaped plinth base, 130″ w, 186″ h **22,000.00**

Ebonized and inlaid maple, shaped cornice with central rounded section inlaid with opposed griffins, center urn over divided stylized sprig inlaid frieze, rounded rect mirror plate, flanked by palmette inlaid

Rocker, child's, ladderback, mixed woods, replaced rush seat, $150.00.

spandrels and stiles, outset platform with simulated gold veined marble top over conforming plinth base, 80″ w, 155″ h **15,400.00**

Rococo, Italian, c1770, giltwood, rect mirror plate, molded frame surmounted by pierced C–scroll, ruffle, and flowerhead crest and mirrored cartouche, sides with similar pendants, scrolled pendant below, 40″ w, 58″ h **4,950.00**

Sheraton, English, early 19th C, architectural, gilt finish, gesso flaking on columns, 27½″ h **75.00**

ROCKERS

Arrowback, bamboo turnings, red and black graining, stenciled floral designs on slats **200.00**

Art Furniture, Adirondack, American, early 20th C, bentrustic twigs and branches, interwoven latticework back and down swept arms, round seat, curlicue skirt **250.00**

Arts and Crafts, American

Harden & Co, concave crestrail over four vertical slats, flat arms with corbels over three vertical slats, spring cushion seat, 38½″ h, pr . . **450.00**

Limbert, c1910, No. 518, open flat arms, elongated corbels, adjustable back, orig upholstered spring cushion, branded mark, 36¾″ h . . **1,200.00**

Boston, American, mid 19th C, grain painted, gilt stencil dec, scenic dec rest, rosewood grained seat **600.00**

Eastlake, American, late 19th C, mahogany platform, incised and pierced cresting over sq panel back, center, padded reeded arms, velvet seat upholstered, reeded supports **225.00**

Ladderback

Armchair, short scrolled arms, turned supports, old woven splint seat, old worn dark graining, yellow striping, traces of floral dec, 38″ h **400.00**

Child's, armchair, old dark alligatored varnish, replaced blue and white tape seat, 27¼″ h **225.00**

Mission, L. & J. G. Stickley, c1910, arm, vertical back and side slats, decal mark **625.00**

Shaker, Mt Lebanon, NY, c1900, No. 7, arms, old brown wash finish, rush seat, 41½″ h **500.00**

Wicker, loom woven fiber, padded back, flattened down swept arms, loose cushion seat, turned and fiber wrapped legs, painted white **200.00**

Windsor, comb back, arm, old worn natural finished scrolled birch arms, bamboo turnings, arrow slats, old green repaint, yellow striping, stenciled vintage dec on crest, 38" h ... **300.00**

SECRETARIES

Chippendale
  Massachusetts, c1770, cherry, block front, top with molded cornice above pr arched and paneled doors, fitted int., carved pilaster with stylized scrolls, molded base with thumbmolded hinged lid opens to fitted int., four blocked and graduated drawers, bracket feet, 40½" w, 21¾" d, 96" h **11,550.00**
  Pennsylvania, c1765, walnut, bonnet top, two parts, upper section with swan's neck crest, carved rosettes, pr of arched hinged doors, int. adjustable shelves, small drawers, and pigeonholes, candle slides, lower section with hinged molded lid, int. with small pigeonholes and drawers, center prospect door opening to small drawer and pigeonhole, four molded graduated long drawers below, bracket feet, staining to int. drawers, 37½" w, 21" d, 96" h **18,700.00**
Empire, cherry and mahogany, removable bookcase top with freestanding brass trimmed columns, double doors with brass edge strip, molded and peaked cornice with turned medallions, turned and acanthus carved legs, one dovetailed drawer with fitted int., replaced clear blown glass drawer handles, 38¼" w, 23½" d, 81" h **1,000.00**
Federal
  Boston, MA, c1815, inlaid mahogany, two parts, upper section with molded cornice over pr of hinged glazed doors, shelved int., lower section with cylinder lid, int. fitted with small drawers, center valanced pigeonholes, one long drawer, pull-out writing surface, two short and one long cockbeaded drawers below, ring turned reeded tapering legs, 35¼" w, 21¾" d, 74½" h **5,500.00**
  Massachusetts, c1800, mahogany, top with cornice centering inlaid rect reserve, three ball and steeple finials, pr glazed hinged doors opens to shelf int. over valanced pigeonholes, bottom with hinged flap opening to lined writing surface, four graduated long drawers,

shaped skirt, slightly flared bracket feet, 42¼" w, 19" d, 75" h **8,100.00**
  New England, c1810, mahogany, removable pediment with central rect inlaid reserve surmounted with two brass ball and steeple finials on top with center brass eagle finial, middle with two glazed hinged doors with adjustable shelves, bottom with hinged flap opening to leather lined writing surface, three cockbeaded crossbanded drawers, shaped skirt, flared bracket feet, 40½" w, 20" d, 81¼" h **6,600.00**
George III, English
  Mahogany
    Broken dentil pediment, pierced foliate scroll and fretwork panels over two glazed doors, Chinese silk lined int. with shelves, lower section with slant front, fitted compartments and drawers, four graduated long drawers, bracket feet, late 19th C top, 42" w, 93¼" h **6,600.00**
    Molded cornice, crossbanded frieze, glazed doors, int. shelves, lower section with fitted secretary drawer over two long drawers flanked by cupboards, oval and quartered inlaid doors, plinth base, 85" l, 76" h **8,800.00**
  Walnut, double arched cornice, pr of mullioned glass doors, int. shelves, base with slant front, fitted int., pr of drawers over three long drawers, bracket feet **1,870.00**
Neoclassical
  Austrian, c1790, carved and inlaid walnut, two parts, superstructure with rect top, slant front opening to three suspended drawers flanked by shaped drawers with Gothic arch fret carved panels, two long drawers with corresponding fret carved panels, sides with brass handles, cabriole legs, pointed pad feet, 46" l, 39½" h **7,700.00**
  Italian, c1780, carved walnut, two parts, upper section with scrolled crest, center shell finial over pr of paneled doors, int. shelves, lower section with cylinder front opening, pull-out writing slide, drawers, and fitted compartments, three long drawers below flanked by shaped cupboard doors, shaped bracket feet, 62½" w, 108½" h **77,000.00**
Rococo
  Dutch, c1725, marquetry, two parts, upper section with double arched top over two doors inlaid with elab-

orate flowering urns and birds, cherubs among foliate scrolls, sides with putti holding foliate sprigs over flowering urns, int. shelves over floral sprig inlaid sharply serpentine drawers, lower section with slant front inlaid with foliate scrolls, flowering urns, and cornucopia, valanced compartments over floral sprig inlaid concave drawers, sliding compartment below flanked by stepped drawers, secret drawer on one side, over two short and two long drawers, later bun feet, minor losses to molding, 42″ w, 86″ h **33,000.00**

German, 1775, parquetry, two parts, upper section with C–scroll molded arched crest over central rounded rect cupboard door with penwork dec of classical walkway and arches, single drawer below flanked by banks of four drawers, lower section with tambour opening to pull–out writing slide and four drawers, two serpentine long drawers below, cabriole legs, 38½″ w, 69½″ h **7,150.00**

Rococo Style, Venetian, c1900, scrolled broken pediment, silver giltwood crest, two shaped foliate painted paneled doors, foliate painted paneled slant front with fitted int., three drawers center frieze drawer and kneehole, bracket feet, 38″ w, 77″ h **3,850.00**

Victorian, American, J & JW Meeks, c1845, mahogany and satinwood, molded cornice, pr of glazed doors, enclosing shelves, lower section with roll top, fitted compartments, pr of cabinet doors, molded block feet, stenciled inside drawer **3,850.00**

Wooton, American, c1880, walnut, standard grade, pierced three–quarter gallery above two arched doors opening to fall front secretary, door int. fitted on one side with pigeonholes, compartments on other, fall front, fitted compartments over four drawers flanked by horizontal and vertical file slats, trestle supports on casters, 42½″ w, 71″ h **5,500.00**

SETTEES

Classical Style, well shaped crest, plank seat, scrolled arms, turned spindles and legs, refinished, repairs, 80″ l . . **450.00**

Country, American, c1825, painted, three chair back, shaped crest, hori-

Settee, Hepplewhite, shield back, $1,750.00.

zontal splats and spindles, rect seat, turned legs, box stretchers, 72″ l . . . **1,400.00**

Decorated, American, c1830, painted green, polychrome dec, shaped and foliated painted crest, two horizontal splats, turned spindles and legs, box stretchers, 72″ l **400.00**

Federal, country, c1835, polychrome rose painted crest, spindle back, scrolling arms, turned legs, box stretcher, 72″ l **2,000.00**

George III, Provincial, early 19th C, oak, rect top rail, triple chairback, stylized baluster splats, drop in seat, sq legs joined by stretchers, 50″ l **2,125.00**

Hepplewhite, four shield shape chair back, upholstered seat, sq tapered legs **1,500.00**

Jacobean style, walnut, carved, high back, short cabriole legs, boldly scrolled acanthus feet, green velvet upholstery, 40″ l **440.00**

Rococo Style, Italian, walnut, serpentine upholstered backrest, molded crest, over scrolled arms, short cabriole legs, three cushions, 102″ l **1,100.00**

Victorian, American, c1860, floral dec, triple chair back, shaped crest, scrolling arms, caned back and seat, turned legs, 72″ l **1,600.00**

Windsor

American, c1810, arched crest, thirty–one bamboo turned spindles, plank seat, bamboo turned legs joined by stretchers, 77″ l **5,500.00**

Philadelphia, U–shape back, scrolled handholds, incised plank seat, vase and reel turned legs, turned stretcher, painted burnt orange over black, c1775, 76″ l **12,100.00**

SIDEBOARDS

Arts and Crafts

Limbert, Grand Rapids, MI, c1903, gallery top, three short drawers

Sideboard, Hepplewhite, American, c1800, inlaid mahogany, serpentine front, 75½" l, 40" h, $4,800.00.

over three cabinet doors, single long drawer, round copper and brass pulls, mirrored backboard with cut–outs flanked by elongated corbels, 59¼" w, 22½" d, 56" h .. **1,760.00**

L. & J. G. Stickley, c1910, No. 738, rect plate rack, conforming top, two long drawers flanked by cabinet doors, hammered copper hardware, 60" w, 21¾" d, 46¼" h **4,510.00**

Edwardian, English, c1900, Neoclassical taste inlaid and penwork dec, mahogany, inverted broken outline, maple crossbanded top with boxwood strung edges, dart and line inlaid border, concave fronted frieze drawer inlaid with ribbon tied swags of husks and flanked by simulated fluted end drawers and cupboards, each with penwork dec of classically robed maiden representing summer and music, lefthand cupboard enclosing three fitted drawers, plinth base, 83½" l, 33" h **4,675.00**

Empire, mahogany, elaborate carved backsplash, shaped rect top, two cushion molded drawers, three paneled doors, Corinthian columns, acanthus carved paw feet, 73" l, 22¾" d, 55½" h **700.00**

Federal

Boston, MA, c1810, attributed to John and/or Thomas Seymour, inlaid mahogany, oblong top, lunette inlaid edge, five short drawers, two bottle drawers, flanked by pr of hinged cupboard doors, reeded half round columns, lunette inlaid apron, ring turned reeded tapering legs, orig brasses, faint inscription on backboard, 68½" l, 23" d, 40¾" h **20,900.00**

Mid Atlantic, c1810, top with inlaid edge, one long drawer, four cupboard doors, line inlay, intersecting line and bellflower inlaid sq tapered legs, crossbanded cuffs, 68¼" l, 24" d, 40½" h **7,700.00**

New York, c1800

Bow front, painted and inlaid mahogany, oblong top, bowed front, case with two convex cupboard doors, two center convex drawers, bookend and line inlaid dies, line inlaid sq tapering legs, crossbanded cuffs, front painted in 19th C polychrome with classical motifs including griffins, bacchanalic figures, masks, and garlands, repair and losses to veneer, 68" w, 27½" d, 39¼" h ... **4,125.00**

Serpentine front, inlaid mahogany, oblong top, central serpentine long drawer faced to simulate two working drawers, two convex drawers flanking, pr of convex cupboard doors, pr of bottle drawers, recessed convex hinged cupboard door, line inlaid sq tapering legs, crossbanded cuffs, minor repair to inlay, 70½" l, 26½" d, 41¾" h **11,000.00**

Serpentine front, inlaid mahogany, oblong top, two convex small drawers, pr cupboard doors and bottle drawers, central hinged door, tombstone inlaid dies, line inlaid sq tapered legs, crossbanded cuffs, 73" l, 28" d, 44" h **16,500.00**

York, ME, 1810, flame birch inlaid mahogany, bow front, oblong top, bowed front, conforming shaped case, three convex drawers, two pr of hinged cupboard doors, center bottle drawers, rect inlaid dies on intersecting line, bellflower, and dot inlaid sq double tapering legs, crossbanded cuffs, orig brass knobs, penciled inscription "Made by Thomas Chandler, York, July 25 1810," 69" w, 26" d, 41½" h **38,500.00**

George III, English, late 18th C, mahogany

Bow Front, bowed top, frieze drawer, tambour slide, flanked by deep drawers, sq tapering legs, spade feet, 60" l, 23¼" d, 33" h **2,750.00**

Serpentine, top crossbanded in rosewood within boxwood strung borders, bowed center section with four drawers flanked on left by concave double fronted cellarette drawer over double fronted double drawer, on right by quadruple fronted cupboard, all divided and flanked by banded and strung sq stiles, tapering supports, spade feet, age splits and minor losses to stringing, 95¼" l, 37¼" h **2,475.00**

George III Style, c1880–1900, mahogany, carved, shallow gallery back, slightly broken outline front, two cupboard door centering drawers, sq tapered legs, 68″ l, 46″ h **660.00**

Hepplewhite, country, Southern, decorated, poplar and yellow pine, orig blue paint, black, red, and white geometric dec on drawer fronts, molded edge top, three dovetailed drawers, sq tapering legs, wear, replaced brasses, minor repairs, 50⅛″ w, 21¼″ d, 47¾″ h **9,500.00**

Louis XV, French, Provincial

Oak, mid 18th C, shaped rect molded top, conforming case, three central drawers, flanked by paneled doors, int. shelves, scrolled feet, 79″ l, 22¼″ d, 39½″ h **1,375.00**

Pine, molded cornice over frieze with center carved fruit and flower filled basket, two glazed doors opening to shelves, lower section with pr of cupboard doors, cabriole feet, restorations, 50½″ w, 90″ h **2,200.00**

Victorian, c1860, walnut, carved, serpentine Carrara marble top with molded edge, mirrored splash board with carved eagle, three paneled mirrored cupboard doors, scalloped plinth, 61″ w, 98″ h **1,870.00**

SOFAS

Chippendale, NY, c1770, mahogany, camel back, shaped crest, outward scrolling arm supports and seat, sq molded legs, flat stretchers, 80″ l . . **10,000.00**

Classical

American, NY, c1815–20, box style, carved mahogany and rosewood, carved eagle brackets, brass inlay, paw feet, cherry and pine secondary woods, slightly reduced, orig damaged brocade upholstery **2,000.00**

English, Adams, stylized foliage designs on base, sq tapered leg, mortised stretchers, brass casters, blue and white Apotheosis of Franklin print reupholstery, 78″ l **750.00**

Northern Europe, c1800, carved mahogany, scrolled crestrail, center plumed fan and opposed scrolls with foliate trailings, matching terminals, rect back flanked by out–scrolled arms, supports and feet finely carved with figures of spread winged eagles, 94″ l **5,225.00**

Empire

American, c1830, mahogany, carved cornucopias, acorns, oak leaves, and acanthus leaves, basket of flowers finial, refinished, gold brocade reupholstery, 83″ l **1,750.00**

New York, c1835, mahogany, acanthus carved shaped crest continuing to carved scrolled arms, rounded base, acanthus carved hairy paw feet, gilt feather returns, 78″ l **1,500.00**

Federal

American, c1805, mahogany, shaped crest, rect flame birch inlaid panel above upholstered back, down curved arms with reeded seatrail, reeded tapered front legs, alternating reeded and ring turned rear legs, 76″ l **33,000.00**

Philadelphia, c1815, carved mahogany, slightly arched crest, upholstered back flanked by leaf carved terminals, semi–exposed seatrail with flowerhead carved dies, reeded tapering legs, restoration to legs and crest, 74¾″ l **2,420.00**

Salem, MA, c1800, carved and inlaid mahogany, molded serpentine exposed crestrail, center carved basket of flowers and fruit, upholstered arms with acanthus carved front panels, serpentine over–upholstered seat, line inlaid sq tapering legs, crossbanded cuffs, feet extended, repairs to legs, 89″ l **16,500.00**

George III, 18th C, mahogany, camel back, upholstered serpentine crest, upholstered back flanked by outscrolling arms, serpentine upholster seat, molded sq tapered legs, casters, 83″ l **3,300.00**

Mission, L. & J. G. Stickley, c1910, oak, decal mark, 72″ l **1,450.00**

Restauration, American, NY, c1835–40, carved mahogany, scrolling back extends to form arms, orig upholstery removed **1,200.00**

Victorian, American, mid 19th C, carved mahogany, shaped crestrail, arched pediment, acanthus carved arm supports, later velvet upholstery **1,000.00**

SPINNING WHEELS

Flax Wheels (Saxony)

Maple, NE, c1830	**275.00**
Mixed woods, PA, c1810, nice turnings, incised heart dec	**450.00**
Mixed woods, PA, c1840, turned . . .	**350.00**
Oak, turned legs, chip carved back marked "A Knox," 36″ h	**250.00**

Wool Wheels (Walking)

Oak, cast iron parts, 30″ d wheel, 45″ h	**325.00**
Walnut, PA, mid 19th C	**450.00**

STANDS

Chinese, mother–of–pearl inlaid hardwood, sq inset marble top, 18″ d, 32″ h **385.00**

Coffin
21¾″ h, folding sawhorse type, turned legs, old black paint, pr **95.00**
29¾″ h, tripod, turned wooden legs and stretchers, old worn red and black paint, set of four **200.00**

Easel, Victorian, Gothic style, American, c1872, oak, swiveling pierced stand, tracery–carved top rail, rotating on platform base, molded sq legs joined by stretchers, adjustable racks missing, stamped 1738, 31″ w, 87″ h, pr . **4,950.00**

Etagere, Victorian
American, Gothic Revival, c1850, corner, mahogany, three arched fret carved shelves, base with doors and int. shelves, shaped plinth base **4,125.00**
English, late 19th C, turned maple, five galleried rect shelves flanked by brass capped ring turned supports, 10½″ w, 53″ h, pr **3,025.00**

Stand, shaving, Queen Anne style, mahogany, soap bowl, two drawers, tripod feet, $365.00.

Music
Arts and Crafts, Stickley, c1907, No. 670 type, four tapering posts, four shelves, gallery, 19¾″ w, 14¾″ d, 39″ h **1,100.00**
Eastlake, late 19th C, ebonized, rect top over floral inlaid fall front, folio compartment, sq legs, medial shelf above single drawer, 22½″ w, 15½″ d, 39″ h **325.00**

George III, English, early 19th C, mahogany
Lyre form angled music rests, adjustable brass support, hexagonal shaft, three downswept legs, minor repairs and losses, 13½″ w, 56½″ h **770.00**
Rect top, adjustable support, two swing candle holders, columnar form standard, three cabriole legs, snake feet, 24″ w, 43″ h . . **550.00**

Night
Arts and Crafts, Gustav Stickley, one drawer, one door, sq wooded faceted pulls, orig light finish, minor varnish alligatoring, red decal, from Cleveholm Manor, CO, 20″ w, 16″ d, 33½″ h **2,530.00**
Country, curly maple, two board top, one dovetailed beveled edge drawer, turned legs, refinished, 19¾″ w, 20″ d, 28½″ h **400.00**

Plant
Arts and Crafts, Paine Furniture Co, pedestal, circular top with orig leatherette cov, sides tacked, four long corbels, four slender legs, orig dark finish, metal tag, 12½″ d, 31″ h **450.00**
Edwardian, c1900, mahogany, hexagonal top with inlaid satinwood edge, paneled baluster form standard with bellflower inlay, three down scrolled supports, acanthus carved centerpiece, cylindrical feet, 15″ w, 42″ h **770.00**
Folk Art, wood, beaded trim, old gold repaint with black and red dec, repaired break on leg, 15¾″ sq, 31″ h **125.00**
George III Style, late 19th C, mahogany, octagonal dish top, acanthus carved ogee molded edge, baluster form reeded standard and fluted knop, foliate carved flaring plinth base, 16″ d, 64″ h **990.00**
Victorian, wire, three tiers, semicircular, wheels, old worn white paint, some damage and rust, 42″ w, 37½″ h **275.00**

Shaving, Victorian, walnut, canted rect top with molded edge, foliate carved crest and adjustable support, single tier with drawer, fluted standard supports bowl, tripod base, paw feet, 15″ d, 62″ h **550.00**

Wash Stand
Empire, cherry, flame mahogany veneer facade, gallery, two dovetailed round front drawers, turned feet and legs, base shelf, old refinishing, 32″ w, 20½″ d, 33½″ h **400.00**

Federal, double, mahogany, poplar secondary wood, scrolled dovetailed gallery, bowed front, cut–outs for two bowls in top scrolled sides, two dovetailed drawers in base, turned feet, replaced brasses, minor age cracks, old worn finish, 42¼" w, 21" d, 35½" h **750.00**

George III, 19th C, mahogany, corner, quarter round top with basin hole, circular splash board, lower tier with line inlaid drawer, down curved legs with shaped stretcher, 23" w, 44" h **330.00**

Regency Style, rect marble top, beveled mirror, shelf over marble backsplash, two raised panel doors, turned legs, caster feet, 42¼" w, 20¼" d, 59" h **375.00**

Victorian, walnut, marble top, shaped rect backsplash, two applied shelves, two short and one long drawer, cabinet door, 30¾" w, 15¾" d, 41" h **325.00**

What–Not, Victorian, English, third quarter 19th C, burl walnut, rect top, leather (distressed) inset over two shelves, spiral carved end supports, tapering cylindrical legs, later casters, 29" l, 30½" h **1,320.00**

Wig, Queen Anne, English, washbowl holder, mahogany, pine and oak secondary woods, turned ring supporting blue transfer Copeland Spode bowl, turned and carved columns, two dovetailed drawers, tripod base, snake feet, 31½" h **700.00**

Work, country, drop leaf, curly maple, walnut and poplar secondary wood, one board top, two dovetailed drawers, turned legs, old mellow refinishing, minor age cracks, 17½" w, 25" d, 10¾" leaves, 29" h **1,200.00**

STEPS

Bed
Regency, early 19th C, mahogany, three treads, inset tooled morocco leather surfaces, paneled risers, drawer, turned tapering fluted legs, 20½" w, 29" d, 28" h **2,400.00**

Victorian, English, c1840, mahogany, rect platforms with tooled red leather inset, two platforms open to storage area, turned cylindrical legs, 28¾" l, 28" h **1,870.00**

Library, Georgian, English, early 19th C, mahogany, four steps
Bench folds to steps, reupholstered seat **1,050.00**

Table folds to steps, emb green leather top, as found **700.00**

STOOLS

Choir, Louis XV, Provincial, oak, molded D–shaped top, sq legs joined by stretchers, 25¼" h, pr **440.00**

Foot
Chippendale, carved mahogany, rect upholstered top, shaped skirt, cabriole legs, claw and ball feet, 19¼" l, 8¼" h **990.00**

Continental, walnut, carved, scroll feet, black velvet upholstery, 13" l, 6½" h **150.00**

English, oak, foliate and scroll carved cabriole legs, shell carved knees, claw and ball feet, green damask upholstery, nailhead trim, 30" l, 18" d, 19" h **725.00**

Louis XVI Style, wood, petit–point upholstery, 4" h **175.00**

Neoclassical, Italian, c1800, carved walnut, tan suede upholstered sq feet, rail carved sides, elongated cartouche flanked by foliate dies, fluted tapering sq legs **1,980.00**

Victorian, Renaissance Revival, American, green velvet upholstery, 18" l, 13" h **170.00**

William and Mary, English, late 17th C, ebonized, rect upholstered wool crewelwork seat, turned feet, joined by H–form stretcher, 20" l, 15½" d, 16" h **1,100.00**

Gout, American, c1880, walnut, upholstered, rocking top, 19" l, 21" h **250.00**

Hinged, George III Style, mahogany, rect padded top, inlaid recessed panel sides, sq tapered legs, 18½" l, 20" h **225.00**

Milking, country, primitive, three legs, heart cut–out handle, relief carving of cow, old dark finish **275.00**

Organ, Victorian, circular, three fancy metal legs, ebonized stem, upholstered top **175.00**

Piano, Classical, late, American, c1840, rosewood, columnar, swivel top **250.00**

TABLES

Altar, Chinese, rosewood, carved, inset marble top, 49½" l, 21" w, 31½" h . . **850.00**

Banquet
Empire, American, c1840, mahogany, two sections, rect top, rounded corners, rect drop leaf, cushion molded frieze, ring turned tapering legs, 76" l extended, 30" h **935.00**

Sheraton, country, cherry, curly maple

drop leaf top, figured cherry veneer shaped aprons, turned and rope carved legs, casters, refinished, 44½″ w, 82″ l extended, 30½″ h, pr **4,000.00**

Breakfast

Empire, mahogany, rect top, two shaped drop leaves, single molded edge drawer, four turned drops at each corner, foliate carved pedestal, four down curving acanthus and lion paw carved legs, 38″ l, 28″ h . **660.00**

George III, English, c1800, mahogany, sq tilt top, reeded edge, ring turned vase form standard, high arched molded quadruple base, foliate and shell cast gilt bronze caps on casters, restored, 50½″ l, 27″ h **1,650.00**

George IV, English, c1825, mahogany, rect top with molded edge, multi–ring turned shaft, incised tripod base, plain brass cappings and casters, 28¾″ w, 49″ h **1,050.00**

Hepplewhite, walnut, drop leaf, rect round cornered top, line inlaid frieze, sq tapering legs, 46½″ l, 27½″ h **550.00**

Regency

Continental, mahogany, rect molded top, turned and reeded pedestal, four splayed legs, paw feet, casters, 59½″ l, 43″ w, 27¾″ h **1,045.00**

English, mahogany, round tilt top, turned column, tripod base, scroll carved legs, old finish, 52½″ d, 30¾″ h **1,250.00**

Card

Chippendale, Philadelphia

c1770, carved mahogany, turret top, oblong top, outset corners, conforming shaped hinged leaf,

Table, card, Sheraton, Philadelphia, c1810, mahogany, 36″ w, 29″ h, $950.00.

playing surface with later carving, conforming apron, cockbeaded frieze drawer, orig rococo brass, acanthus carved cabriole legs, claw and ball feet, 33″ l, 16″ w, 29″ h **23,100.00**

c1780, carved mahogany, rect top, skirt with cockbeaded frieze drawer, bracketed sq legs, Marlborough feet, orig brasses, brackets restored, 33¼″ l, 17½″ w, 28¾″ h **2,750.00**

Federal, New England, early 19th C

Flame birch and inlaid mahogany, North Shore, MA, c1805, oblong top with serpentine front and sides, conforming shaped hinged leaf, crotch figured frieze, inlaid dies, reeded tapering legs, elongated vase form feet, minor repair to two legs, 37½″ l, 18″ w, 29¾″ h **3,850.00**

Inlaid curly maple, bowed front bird's eye maple top, edge inlaid with patterned stringing, conforming apron, sq double tapering legs, 34½″ l, 17″ d, 29½″ h . **2,530.00**

Inlaid mahogany, c1805, D–shaped top, conforming shaped hinged leaf, line inlaid on frieze and sq tapering legs, 36″ l, 17½″ w, 29″ h **1,320.00**

Inlaid mahogany, oblong top, serpentine front, shaped hinged leaf, rect inlaid frieze, reeded tapering legs, tapered feet, 35¼″ w, 30″ h **1,320.00**

Federal Style, mahogany, serpentine front, fold top, 35½″ l, 17½″ d, 29¾″ h **1,900.00**

George II Style, burl walnut, carved, serpentine shape folding top with cable molded edge, acanthus carved cabriole legs, claw and ball feet, 31″ w, 31″ h **1,100.00**

George III, English, c1800, rosewood crossbanded mahogany, hinged rect top, rounded front corners, crossbanded playing surface, conforming apron, tapering sq legs, 38″ l, 30¼″ h **1,980.00**

George IV, English, c1825, carved mahogany, hinged rect top, rounded front corners, lotus carved baluster support with gadrooned border, four down swept reed legs, brass animal paw feet on casters, 37″ w, 29″ h **1,760.00**

Georgian Style, burl walnut, shaped rect crossbanded and acanthus leaf tip carved edge top, tooled leather inset, rosette and bellflower

carved cabriole legs, paw feet, 36"
l, 18" w, 29¼" h **1,700.00**
Hepplewhite, English, late 18th C
    Mahogany, demi–lune shape, inlaid
    banding **1,100.00**
    Walnut, line inlaid folded top, bell-
    flower inlaid sq tapering legs,
    shell inlaid medallions, 35¼" l,
    17" w, 29¼" h **625.00**
Queen Anne, mahogany, carved,
    folding rect top, straight frieze, four
    shell carved cabriole legs, trifid
    feet, 29" w, 29" h **1,870.00**
Center
Arts and Crafts, walnut, sq molded
    edge top, reeded reticulated frieze,
    shaped X–form base, turned
    stretcher, floral carved legs, caster
    feet, 26" w, 31" h **300.00**
Baroque
    German, mid 18th C, inlaid walnut,
    rect top, single frieze drawer, ta-
    pering legs, bun feet, flattened
    stretchers, 40¾" l, 26¼" d, 27¾"
    h **2,100.00**
    Italian, mid 18th C, walnut and burl-
    wood, shaped rect top, central
    burl inlay, frieze drawer, sq ta-
    pering legs, restorations to ve-
    neer, 39" l, 30¾" d, 29½" h . . . **1,980.00**
Neoclassical Style, Italian, walnut,
    rect top, frieze fitted with two draw-
    ers, fluted sq tapering legs, 72½" l,
    31" d, 31¼" h **2,200.00**
Queen Anne, Boston, 1730–50,
    carved walnut, rect marble top,
    shaped corners, projecting molding
    and apron with pendant on front
    and back rails, cabriole legs, plat-
    form pad feet, repairs to marble
    top, repairs to bracket returns and
    rear molding, 50" l, 26¼" w, 31½"
    h **52,250.00**
Victorian, Gothic Revival, New York,
    1840–50, rosewood, carved, hex-
    agonal marble top, six standards
    on shaped base, casters, 41¾" l,
    31" h **27,000.00**
William and Mary, oak, rect top,
    straight frieze, baluster turned legs
    joined with fluted box stretcher,
    38½" l, 29" h **1,540.00**
Console
Empire
    American, early 19th C, carved ma-
    hogany, circular tilt top, radiating
    crotch mahogany veneers, taper-
    ing triangular paneled pedestal,
    trefoil concave base, three
    winged eagle and lion paw feet,
    restoration to veneers, 47" d,
    28½" h **2,750.00**

Dutch, early 19th C, marquetry, cir-
    cular top, inlaid elaborate flow-
    ering vines, border of alternating
    floral sprigs and butterfly roun-
    dels, three foliate inlaid scrolled
    legs joined by shaped triangular
    platform stretcher, age cracks to
    top, 46½" d, 28" h **6,150.00**
George III, English, c1800, inlaid ma-
    hogany, D–shaped top, inset
    rounded corners inlaid with double
    banded borders of satinwood and
    rosewood, ebonized double string-
    ing lines, inlaid frieze, fluted and
    reeded turned tapering legs, slen-
    der tapered plain feet, 36" l, 33¾"
    h **3,575.00**
Gothic Style, wrought iron, gray mar-
    ble rect top, arched plate within
    scroll work, scrolled frieze, trestle
    base, 76" l, 43" h **1,650.00**
Louis XVI, late 18th C, oak, semi–oval
    marble top with molded edge,
    carved apron, tapering fluted legs,
    pendant swags, D–shaped plat-
    form base, 34½" l, 24" h **1,650.00**
Louis XVI Style, rect marble top with
    floral inlay, guilloche carved edge,
    frieze centers angel's head on
    front, rosettes on sides, fluted trum-
    pet legs, 59" l, 28" h **3,750.00**
Regency Style, 19th C, giltwood,
    carved, rect rouge marble top with
    molded edge, acanthus carved
    frieze, foliate carved scroll legs
    joined with X–shape stretcher
    mounted with bouquet, 41½" l,
    33½" h **4,675.00**
Rococo, Italian, c1775, parcel–gilt,
    silvered, false marble top, serpen-
    tine molded edge over elaborate
    ruffled C–scroll and foliate carved
    apron, ruffled C–scroll legs, con-
    forming stretcher, 60" l, 35" h **6,600.00**
Coffee, Art Moderne, Eero Saarien,
    c1956, circular mahogany top, cast
    metal pedestal base, white finish,
    42½" d, 15" h **310.00**
Corner, Chinese, rosewood, bow front,
    inset marble top with scalloped edge,
    reticulated floral and foliate carved
    frieze, carved cabriole legs joined
    with shaped medial shelf, claw and
    ball feet, 25" w, 18" d, 32" h **700.00**
Dining
Anglo–Indian, rosewood, circular top,
    carved and reticulated base, myth-
    ical reptile feet with casters, 54" l,
    32½" h **1,600.00**
Federal, New York, c1800–18, carved
    mahogany, D–shaped top, one
    drop leaf, plain veneered frieze,

rect veneered panel, ring turned and foliate carved legs, baluster turned feet, casters, 93″ l extended, 30″ h, pr **1,540.00**

George II Style, late 19th C, mahogany, rect top with rounded corners, ring and baluster turned standard, four fluted down swept legs, brass cuffs and casters, 80″ l extended, 28½″ h **2,200.00**

George III, English, c1800, mahogany, three parts

Drop leaf table, two D–shaped consoles, shaped top, molded sq legs, 47″ w, 107″ l extended, 28½″ h **3,300.00**

Rect top, rounded ends, reeded edges, three pedestals, baluster turned supports, four down swept legs, brass caps on casters, two leaves, 126″ extended, 29″ h **9,350.00**

Georgian Style, yew wood, rect crossbanded reeded edge top, two turned pedestals, three out swept legs, brass capped feet and casters, two leaves, 43½″ l, 30″ h . . . **1,500.00**

Queen Anne

American, walnut, rect top, two pedestals with baluster form standards, cabriole legs, pad feet and casters, two leaves, 46″ l, 30″ h **2,100.00**

New England, c1760, drop leaf, oblong top

Cherry, two rect hinged leaves, molded frieze, cabriole legs, pad feet, 42″ l, 41″ w extended, 27½″ h **2,200.00**

Curly maple, two D–shaped hinged leaves, plain skirt, circular tapered legs, pad feet, 43½″ w, 51¾″ l, 28″ h **2,310.00**

Rococo, Italian, carved walnut, serpentine top, molded edge, scalloped apron, cabriole legs, 58″ l, 29¼″ h **1,430.00**

Victorian, American

Gothic Revival, c1840, mahogany, hinged rect top with rounded corners and molded edge, four baluster turned swivel supports, reeded down swept legs, baluster turned stretchers, foliate cast brass feet, tapered sq and ball supports, 28½″ h **3,300.00**

Renaissance Revival, walnut, carved, rect plank top, gadrooned frieze, two foliate and scroll carved trifid supports, 100″ l, 30″ h **1,430.00**

William and Mary, PA, c1740, walnut,

oblong top, two hinged D–shaped leaves, molded frieze fitted at each end with a drawer, vase and reel turned gate legs joined by stretchers, flattened ball feet, top and frame restored, 48¾″ l, 56″ w extended, 29″ **4,400.00**

Dressing

George II, English, mid 18th C, oak, rect molded top, three drawers, cabriole legs, stylized pad feet, 28¼″ l, 18½″ d, 26½″ h **1,210.00**

George II Style, English, walnut, rect top, molded edge, frieze drawer over small blind drawer, recessed cupboard flanked by three cross banded drawers on either side, bracket feet, 28½″ l, 30″ h **1,100.00**

Neoclassical, Italian, early 19th C, burl walnut, parcel gilt, superstructure with retractable mirror, door flanked by four drawers over rect top, frieze fitted with slide, drawer, and basket, flanked by columns, shaped base, ball feet, 23″ l, 17¼″ w, 38½″ h **2,640.00**

Drum

Federal, mahogany and maple, circular star inlaid top, four frieze drawers, foliate carved vase form standard, reeded out swept legs, brass hairy paw caster feet, 22″ d, 28″ h **5,000.00**

Victorian, English, mahogany, circular top, four drawers alternating with false drawers, plain standard, four down swept reeded legs, casters, replaced top, 42″ d, 30″ h **770.00**

End

Arts and Crafts, American, Charles Rohlfs, rect top, four sq legs, sgd and dated 1905, 23¾″ l, 18″ w, 28½″ l **880.00**

Napoleon III Style, mahogany, ormolu mounted marquetry, shaped green marble top, floral marquetry one drawer frieze, sq fluted supports joined by medial shelf, cabriole legs ending with sabots, 24¾″ l, 13″ w, 29¾″, pr **1,700.00**

Games

George II, English, mid 18th C

Concertina, mahogany, shaped rect top, felt lined surface, circular turned legs, pad feet, 33″ l, 16″ d, 29″ h **3,575.00**

Triple Folding Top, walnut, plain playing surface, baize lined playing surface, and checkerboard inlaid surface, narrow Tunbridgeware borders, recessed well, lappet carved straight turned tapering supports, circular pad feet, repairs to all legs, replaced hinges, age cracks, 30" w, 30¾" h **4,125.00**

George III, English, c1800, rect folding top, shaped outset corners, int. with center painted checkerboard, four oval counter wells, plain frieze, end drawer, straight turned tapering legs, circular ovoid feet, later japanned and gilt work, cloud shaped reserves, landscape vignettes, scrollwork and bamboo sprays, black ground, 31½" l, 29½" h **990.00**

Louis XV Style, French, Provincial, oak, sq top, gilt dec red leather inset surface, shallow gallery, scalloped apron, cabriole legs, 32¼" l, 28¾" h **1,980.00**

Regency Style, English, c1830, kingwood, rect top with central reversible slide with crossbanded and inlaid chessboard, crossbanded frieze, ring turned trestle supports, down swept feet, 22" d, 29" h ... **1,430.00**

Gateleg

George III, English, first quarter 19th C, mahogany, rect top, cylindrical and block turned legs joined with turned stretchers, ball feet, 28" w, 31" h **2,200.00**

William and Mary, New England, c1725, maple, oblong top, two D–shaped hinged leaves, single drawer frieze, ring and vase and block turned legs, flattened ball feet, ring and vase turned stretcher, 28½" w, 41¾" h **13,200.00**

Lamp, Arts and Crafts, American, L. & J. G. Stickley, No. 575, round top, lower shelf, arched and pegged cross–stretchers, orig finish, decal, 29" h, 24" d **1,210.00**

Library

Arts and Crafts, American, Limbert

No. 121, four vertical slats on each side, flat medial stretcher ending in keyed through tenons, orig dark brown finish, branded mark, 30" h, 50" l, 36" d **1,870.00**

No. 146, library, long arched apron, long corbels, two sq end cut–outs, flat medial stretcher, orig medium brown finish, branded mark, 45" l, 30" w, 30" h **1,760.00**

Continental, rosewood, carved detail, conforming molded edge top, one dovetailed drawer, serpentine apron with carved shells, cabriole legs, old worn finish, 45¼" l, 27" d, 31½" h **2,025.00**

French Provincial, walnut, rect

molded edge top, recessed panel two drawer frieze, block and vase turned legs, disk feet, 70" l, 30½" d, 34" h **850.00**

Neoclassical, Italian, marquetry, walnut, rect egg and dart carved edge top, mythical figures above inlaid one drawer frieze, animal inlaid ring and tapering block legs joined by X–shape stretcher with urn finial, turnip feet, 30" l, 45" w, 27" h ... **2,750.00**

Victorian, English, top c1840, base c1820, mahogany, oval top with red leather writing surface, frieze fitted with drawer on both sides, ends with short drawers, ring turned support, four reeded down swept legs, brass animal paw feet on casters, leather distressed, 60" l, 30¼" h . **3,850.00**

Table, Pembroke, Chippendale, American, 18th C, carved mahogany, 38" l, 27½" h, $2,250.00.

Pembroke

Chippendale, Philadelphia, c1775, mahogany, rect top, two hinged leaves, single drawer frieze, molded skirt, sq legs, X–form stretcher, Marlborough feet, 31" l, 29" h **3,850.00**

Federal

Connecticut, c1805, inlaid cherry, oblong top, center inlaid patarae, flanked by two D–shaped hinged leaves with matching inlaid, frieze with line inlaid drawer at each end, flanked by bookend inlaid dies, line and icicle inlaid sq tapering legs, crossbanded cuffs, 40½" w extended, 28½" h **3,850.00**

New York, c1805, inlaid mahogany, rect top, two drop D–shaped leaves, single line inlaid drawer, reverse faced to simulate working drawer, line inlaid sq tapering

legs, crossbanded cuffs, 31½" l,
41¼" d, 28¾" h **4,675.00**
New York, c1825, mahogany, ob-
long top, two hinged shaped
leaves, single drawer frieze, ring
turned and spiral reeded legs, tapered feet, brass casters, 34½"
w, 28¾" h **1,210.00**
Philadelphia, c1790, mahogany,
rect top, two rect hinged leaves,
single drawer frieze, molded tapering sq legs, 30" l, 27¾" h . . **3,575.00**
Sheraton, country, walnut, pine and
poplar secondary wood, drop leaf
top, one dovetailed overlapping
drawer, slender turned legs, 35¾"
l, 17¼" w, 29¾" h **525.00**
Quartetto, George III, English, c1800,
mahogany, graduated rect top, shallow galleried border, simulated bamboo turned and blocked double standards, rect plinth base over ringed
feet, 20" w, 30" h, nested set of four **3,300.00**
Refectory, Italian Renaissance Style,
walnut, rect top, lozenge carved
molded edge, trestle supports carved
with lion form monopodia, center
carved cartouche, mask and foliate
carved stretcher, 74" l, 33" h **3,300.00**

**Table, sewing, Sheraton, cherry, glass
knob, brass escutcheon, 21½" w, 19½"
d, 29¼" h, $400.00.**

Sewing
Federal
American, curly maple and mahogany, octagonal crossbanded top,
frieze drawer, sq tapering ebony
inlaid legs, 20" l, 14½" w, 29½" h **6,000.00**
Massachusetts, c1820, mahogany,
oblong top, rounded outset corners, single cockbeaded drawer,
sewing bag drawer, carved flowerheads on each corner, reeded
tapering legs, ball feet, 18" l,
20¾" w, 28½" h **2,750.00**

George III, English, c1800, rosewood,
tulipwood, and satinwood, c1790,
octagonal top, three hinged compartments, slender sq tapering saber legs joined by X–form stretcher,
16" l, 12" w, 30¾" h **1,320.00**
Side
Baroque, Dutch, seaweed marquetry,
rect top, molded edge, inlaid central foliate medallion surrounded by
similar roundels and spandrels, single drawer, later spiral carved legs
joined by inlaid stretcher, later bun
feet, age cracks to top, 36¾" l,
28¼" h **4,675.00**
Chippendale, Philadelphia, c1780,
carved mahogany, rect top, single
drawer frieze, drawer with incised
edges, applied projecting molding
below, sq legs, orig brass handle
and escutcheon, 26¾" l, 18¼" w,
28" h **4,125.00**
Federal, Mid Atlantic States, c1820,
curly maple, sq top, single cockbeaded drawer, sq tapering legs,
19½" l, 19½" w, 29¾" h **1,320.00**
George III, Provincial, c1800, oak,
rect top with canted corners and
molded edge, crossbanded and
cockbeaded frieze drawer, scalloped apron, canted sq legs, 32" l,
27" h **2,750.00**
Late George III, English, c1810, pen-
work and brown japanning, octagonal top, Chinese figures with border of flowers and leaves dec, ring
turned baluster shaft, tripod base
dec with chains of leaves, minor
losses to borders, 14" w, 28" h . . . **825.00**
Queen Anne
Pennsylvania, c1750, walnut, rect
top, plain skirt, splayed turned tapering legs, pad feet, 20½" l,
19¾" w, 28½" h **6,700.00**
Rhode Island, c1760, mahogany,
molded oblong top, shaped skirt,
turned tapering legs, pad feet,
40¼" l, 21" w, 26" h **6,600.00**
William and Mary, late 17th C, walnut,
rect top with molded edge, frieze
drawer, ring and baluster turned
legs joined with waved cross
stretcher, ball feet, 27" l, 26" h . . . **3,300.00**
Sofa, George IV, mahogany, rosewood
inlay, rect crossbanded rounded corner top, two frieze drawers, baluster
form standard, four out swept legs,
brass paw caster feet, 34½" l, 29¾"
w, 29" h **2,200.00**
Tabouret, Arts and Crafts, American, L.
& J. G. Stickley, round top, through
tenon cross–stretchers, orig finish,

light water stain, conjoined "Craftsman" and "Handcraft" decal, 20" h,
18" d **825.00**

Tavern

Queen Anne, New England, c1750–
75, maple and birchwood, oval top,
arched skirt, turned legs, pad feet,
33¾" l, 26¾" h **5,500.00**

Spanish, wrought iron, marble top,
shaped rect top with beveled edge,
foliate trestle base, 30½" l, 21" w,
29" h **325.00**

William and Mary

New England, 1710–40, maple and
pine, oval top, molded skirt, vase
and reel turned splayed legs, box
stretcher, ball feet, 26¾" l, 22½"
h **6,000.00**

Pennsylvania, 1780–1810, walnut,
rect top, molded skirt, three
molded drawers, ring turned
legs, box stretcher, flattened ball
feet, 29" w, 30" h **5,500.00**

Tea

Chippendale, tilt top

New England, maple, circular tilt
top, molded edge, bird cage support, compressed ball standard,
cabriole legs, snake feet, 34½"
d, 26¼" h **3,850.00**

Philadelphia, c1775, carved mahogany, circular dished tilt and
revolving top, bird cage support,
ring turned and compressed ball
standard, cabriole legs, claw and
ball feet, restoration to top of bird
cage, 35½" d, 29¼" h **9,350.00**

Pennsylvania, c1780, carved walnut, circular tilt top, molded edge,
bird cage support, ring and ball
turned standard, arched tripod
base, snake feet, restoration to
cleats and standard, 34¼" d,
28¼" h **1,980.00**

Wilmington, NC, c1770, carved
mahogany, circular tilt and revolving top, bird cage support,
bulbous ring turned standard, cabriole legs, snake feet, 35" h,
30½" h **3,300.00**

Federal, New England, c1805, birchwood and mahogany, octagonal top
with inlaid edge, petal carved urn
standard, inlaid and shaped down
curving legs, 16" w, 30½" h **9,900.00**

George II Style, mahogany, circular
dished top, columnar standard, baluster knop on three down scrolled
fluted legs, 16" d, 25" h **375.00**

George III Style, mahogany, circular
dish tilt top, baluster turned stan-

dard, three cabriole legs, snake
feet, 21" d, 27½" h **990.00**

Oriental, black lacquer, gilded chino-
sierie dec, bird cage support,
turned column, tripod base, paw
feet, 23½" d, 30½" h **650.00**

Trestle, William and Mary, Hudson River
Valley, early 18th C, pine, rect cleated
top, scroll upright supports join with
molded board stretcher, trestle feet,
96" l, 30¾" h **8,250.00**

Work

Chippendale, country, one board top
with worn patina, one dovetailed
drawer, sq legs, molded outside
corners, hardwood base with
traces of old brownish red paint, old
reconstruction to apron, 43½" l,
27½" w, 28½" h **400.00**

Classical, European, marquetry, mahogany, lift top with fitted int., pull
out work bag, floral inlay, repairs
and restorations, 18½" l, 14½" w,
29¾" h **650.00**

Empire, early 19th C

American, country, figured mahogany veneer, drop leaf top, two
dovetailed drawers, four clear
lacy glass pulls, tapered pedestal
with edge beading, four legs,
acanthus carved knees, brass
paw feet with casters, minor repairs, two replaced pulls, old refinishing, 17" w, 20½" d, 8¾" l
leaves, 29¼" h **400.00**

New York, carved mahogany, rect
top, two drawers, twisted scroll
carved pedestal, four acanthus
carved curved hairy lion paw
feet, casters, repairs to side, veneer missing, repairs to two feet,
22½" w, 30½" h **550.00**

Empire Style, French, giltwood and
mahogany, circular lift top, molded
edge, fitted int., three winged monopodia and tripartite plinth base,
24" d, 17½" h **1,430.00**

Federal

Massachusetts, c1815, curly maple, oblong top, shaped corners,
octagonal frieze, molded edge,
ring turned pilasters, single cockbeaded drawer, ring turned tapering legs, tapered feet, 19¼" l,
18¾" w, 26" h **7,150.00**

Philadelphia, c1810, Hains–Con-
nelly School, carved mahogany,
oblong top, rounded outset corners above to cockbeaded drawers, upper drawer with divided
compartment, one side fitted with
drawer with hinged baize lined

writing flap, pencil compartments, case centering three-quarter round ring turned columns ball pendants below, spiral carved standard, acanthus carved down curving legs, brass animal paw feet, brass casters, 20″ l, 16″ w, 27¼″ h **2,475.00**

Philadelphia, c1825, carved mahogany, rect top, two cockbeaded drawers, acanthus carved panels, spiral turned legs, ball feet, 20″ w, 29¾″ h **4,950.00**

Hepplewhite, American, country, pine, one board top, one dovetailed drawer, sq tapering legs, old worn brown finish, 29¾″ l, 36″ w, 28¾″ h **650.00**

Writing

George II Style, walnut, brown tooled leather top, scalloped frieze with two drawers, fluted canted corners, carved trailing acanthus molded cabriole legs, claw and ball feet .. **3,575.00**

George III, English, c1800, mahogany, rect leather inset top, frieze fitted with drawers, false drawers on reverse, sq tapering legs, 51″ l, 41¾″ d, 30″ h **2,530.00**

Late George III, English, c1810, mahogany, gold and blind tooled faded green leather top, boxwood strung border, long frieze drawer, two short drawers flanking kneehole, sq tapering legs, brass caps and casters, 48″ l, 31″ h **4,675.00**

Renaissance Style, Italian, walnut, rect carved edge top, two aligned foliate carved frieze drawers, foliate and mask carved trestle base, 53″ l, 20″ w, 24½″ h **225.00**

William IV, mahogany, tooled green leather sq top, single drawer, four spiral twist columns, rect platform base, reeded scroll feet, 30″ w, 31¾″ h **1,540.00**

TEA WAGONS

Black lacquer finish, raised Chinese figures, landscape, D–shaped drop leaves, turned legs, support, two wheels **200.00**

Victorian, brass, glass top and shelf .. **700.00**

Wicker, serpentine edge, scrolled handle, removable glass serving tray top **325.00**

WAGON SEATS

Wagon seats cannot be classified with seats from a wagon. Early wagon seats were usually constructed with a double frame and a basketry–type seat. They served a dual purpose: in the

house and in the family wagon for additional seating.

Hickory spindle back and arms, leather basketweave seat, six legs, 18th C . **750.00**

Maple and oak, double chair back, flame turned finials, scrolled arms, rush seat, turned supports, box stretchers, 33″ l **1,200.00**

Painted

Ladderback, two slat back, turned stiles, splint seat, red paint, 35″ l . **600.00**

Spindle, two seater, turned arms, open back, five vertical turned spindles, double stretchers, red and green paint, 36″ l **800.00**

Pine, Windsor, primitive, shoe feet, 30¾″ l **500.00**

Walnut, Windsor, one board seat, trestle feet, natural finish, 33″ l, 28½″ h ... **250.00**

Wicker, ferner, painted white, $180.00.

WICKER

Bookcase, four oak shelves, turned wood frame, reed and wood fancy sunburst back, natural finish, c1890 . **550.00**

Carriage, c1890, serpentine edges, natural finish, orig velvet upholstery ... **475.00**

Chair

Armchair, Gustav Stickley, No. 88, c1913, high flat topped back, rect piercings, shallow wings continue to wide flat arms, conforming skirt, 39½″ h **800.00**

Armchair and Ottoman, Heywood Brothers and Wakefield, Chicago, IL, early 20th C, rounded back crestrail continues to arms, woven sides and apron, circular feet, upholstered pad seat, matching ottoman **825.00**

Corner, elaborate scrolling, bird cage arms and supports, natural finish . **650.00**

Highchair, c1880, shell design back,

set in cane seat, wooden footrest,
turned wooden legs, natural finish **285.00**
Side, Heywood Brothers and Wakefield Co, c1890, closely woven back
panel with center scalloped design,
closely woven shields over legs,
natural finish **350.00**
Foot Stool, upholstered seat, painted . **165.00**
Pedestal, 34½" h, 13" d top, sq top,
conforming tapered column, flared
base, natural, Heywood Wakefield . . **220.00**
Piano Chair, Heywood Brothers and
Wakefield Co, Wakefield, MA, No.
3901, tall arched back with ornate
scrolls and loops, round tightly woven
seat, cabriole front legs trimmed with
graduated scrolls, joined by stretchers with center turned drop, orig label,
43½" h **825.00**
Rocker, Wakefield Rattan Co, serpen-
tine edges, braided trim, wooden
rockers, painted white **250.00**
Settee, rect back, upholstered section
on back and seat, woven arms, scal-
loped skirt **425.00**
Stand, music, Wakefield Rattan Co,
c1883, three shelves, orig paper label **265.00**
Table, Karpen Guaranteed Construc-
tion Furniture, library, oval, orig paper
label **325.00**

Yarn Winder, hardwoods, chip carved base, $65.00.

YARN WINDERS

Floor Type, primitive, oak, mortised
frame, two reels, one stationary, other
adjustable, 51" h **125.00**
Niddy Noddy, hickory, turned, mortised
and pinned joints, 18" d **85.00**
Reel, hardwoods, turned detail and chip

carving at base, turned handle miss-
ing, traces of old red paint, 47" h . . **75.00**
Spoke Type
Four Spoke
Primitive, counter snap mecha-
nism, 27" d reel, 41" h **125.00**
Shaker, Sabbathday Lake, combi-
nation of hard and softwoods, sq
nail construction, geared side
counter needle, 26" d reel, 32" h **400.00**
Six Spoke, pine, maple, and bird's
eye maple, counter bell, 16" d reel,
40" h **200.00**
Twelve Spoke, pine, turned, wooden
gears, 45" h **175.00**

GAME PLATES

History: Game plates, popular between 1870
and 1915, are specially decorated plates used to
serve fish and game. Sets originally included a
platter, serving plates, and a sauce or gravy boat.
Many sets have been divided. Today, individual
plates are used for wall hangings.

Reference: Susan and Al Bagdade, *Warman's
English & Continental Pottery & Porcelain, 2nd
Edition,* Wallace–Homestead, 1991.

**Birds, multicolored snipes, magenta
border with gold overlay, sgd "Bir-
beck," marked "Crescent & Sons, England," 8¾" d, $38.00.**

BIRDS

Plate
9¼", wild geese, buffalo Pottery, 1908 **60.00**
9½", bird, scalloped edge, mauve
ground, gold trim, sgd "Vitet Lim-
oges" **125.00**
10", pheasant, Limoge, sgd "Max" . **90.00**
10½", game bird and two water span-

iels, crimped gold rim, sgd "RK
Beck" **75.00**
12½", flying game, hp, heavy gold,
rococo border, Limoges, artist sgd
"Rogin" **210.00**
13¼", game bird and pheasant,
heavy gold scalloped, emb rococo
border, Coronet Limoges, sgd
"Brussillon" **245.00**
Platter
16", quail, two handles, hp gold trim,
Limoges, France **125.00**
18 x 14¼", harvest scene, turkey cen-
ter, floral border, brown dec, Royal
Staffordshire **55.00**
Set
7 pcs, wild game birds, pastoral
scene background, molded edges,
shell dec, Fazent Mehlem, Bonn,
Germany **220.00**
9 pcs, 9¼" plates, hp, various birds,
gold scalloped edge, Haviland and
Co **350.00**
12 pcs, 10½" plates, game birds in
natural habitat, sgd "I Bubedi" . . .   **3,300.00**

DEER

Plate, 9", buck and doe, forest scene .   **50.00**
Set
5 pcs, Buffalo Pottery, artist sgd
"Beck" **275.00**
13 pcs, platter, 12 plates, deer, bear,
and game birds, yellow ground,
scalloped border, Haviland China,
sgd "MC Haywood" **3,000.00**

ELK

Plate, 9", two elk in natural setting, Buf-
falo Pottery **45.00**

FISH

Plate
8", bass, scalloped edge, gray–green
trim, fern on side of fish, Limoges   **50.00**
8½", hanging type, colorful fish swimming on green shaded background,
scalloped border, gold trim, sgd
"Lancy," "Biarritz, W. S. or S. W.
Co., Limoges, France" **35.00**
9", bass, Lenox, sgd "Morley" **70.00**
Platter
14", bass on lure, sgd "RK Beck" . .   **90.00**
23", hp, Charoone, Haviland **200.00**
Set
8 pcs, four plates, 24" platter, sauce
boat with attached plate, cov tur-
een, Rosenthal **350.00**
10 plates, artist sgd "Hammersley" .   **175.00**

11 pcs, 10 plates, serving platter, sgd
"Limoges" **350.00**
14 pcs, platter, 12 plates, gravy boat,
bass, blue beehive mark **250.00**
15 pcs, twelve 9" plates, 24" platter,
sauce boat with attached plate, cov
tureen, hp, raised gold design
edge, artist sgd, Limoges **750.00**

GAMES

History: Mass production of board games did
not take place until after the Civil War. Firms like
McLoughlin Brothers, Milton Bradley, and Selchow
and Righter were active in the 1860s, followed by
Parker Brothers, who began in 1883. Parker Brothers bought out the rights to the W. & S. B. Ives
Co., who had produced some very early games in
the 1840s, including the "first" American board
game, The Mansion of Happiness. All except
McLoughlin Brothers are giants in the game industry today.

McLoughlin Brothers's games are a challenge
to find. Not only does the company no longer exist
[Milton Bradley bought them out in 1920], but the
lithography on their games was the best of its era.
Most board games are collected because of the
bright, colorful lithography on their box covers. In
addition to spectacular covers, the large Mc-
Loughlin games often had lead playing pieces and
fancy block spinners, thus making them even more
desirable.

Common games like Anagrams, Authors, Jack-
straws, Lotto, Tiddledy Winks, and Peter Coddles
do not command high prices, nor do the games of
Flinch, Pit, and Rook, which still are being produced.

Games, with the exception of the common ones
stated above, generally are rising in price. However, interesting to note is the fact that certain
games dealing with good graphics on popular subject matter, e.g. trains, planes, baseball, Christmas
and others, often bring higher prices because they
are also sought by collectors in those particular
fields.

Condition is everything when buying. Do not buy
games that have been taped or that have price
tags stickered on the face of their covers. Also,
beware of buying games at outdoor flea markets
where weather elements can cause fading and
warping.

References: R. C. Bell, *The Board Game Book,*
The Knapp Press, 1979; Lee Dennis, *Warman's
Antique American Games, 1840-1940,* Wallace–
Homestead, 1991; Brian Love, *Great Board
Games,* 1895–1935, Macmillan Publishing Co.,
1979; Brian Love, *Play The Game: Over 40 Games
From The Golden Age Of Board Games,* Reed
Books, 1978.

Periodical: *Name of the Game,* Box 721, Plainville, CT, 06062.

Collectors' Club: American Game Collectors Association, 4628 Barlow Dr., Bartlesville, OK 74006.

Museum: Washington Dolls' House and Toy Museum, Washington, D.C.

Additional Listings: See *Warman's Americana & Collectibles*.

Milton Bradley, *American Boys, A Game*, #4644, rules on inside of lid, red and blue playing pieces, 11¼ x 16¼ x 1", $70.00.

An Exciting Motor Boat Race, No. 112, American Toy Manf'g Co, boxed board game, 1925, 11½ x 9¼", instructions on back of box cover, 4 colored wood counters, multicolored lithographed board has spinner superimposed, track game **75.00**

Bottoms Up, The Embossing Company, © 1934, 6½ x 3", instructions on back of box cover, pair of dice and 9 round domino–type counters with pigs' bottoms on their backs **15.00**

Cats and Mice, Gantlope, and Lost Diamond, McLoughlin Bros, c1890, 7½ x 14", wood "book" board game with slipcase, 3 different multicolored lithographed boards, instruction book, box of playing pieces including block spinner, 32 wood counters of assorted shapes **120.00**

Colors, Game Of, McLoughlin Bros, boxed board game, c1888, 8 x 15½", Gem Series, instructions on back of box cover, 23 pcs (spinner, red token, white token, 10 red counters, 10 white counters), multicolored lithographed board, pooling game **100.00**

Comic Conversation Cards, J. Ottmann Lith Co, card game, c1905, 5 x 7",

instruction sheet, numerous question and answer cards **40.00**

Glider Racing Game, Milton Bradley, boxed board game, 1930s, 14½ x 8¼", instructions printed on center of board, multicolored lithographed board pasted on box bottom, spinner, 4 round wood colored counters, track game **40.00**

Glydor, #423, All–Fair, 1931, 15½ x 12½", instructions on back of box cover, multicolored lithographed board with attached spinner and 4 gliders, track game **45.00**

Jack Straws, Crandall (of Montrose, PA), skill game, c1869, covered wood cylinder 6¼" h, 39 wood paddle letters, 2 hooks, Anagram game as well **100.00**

Jolly Darkie Target Game, Milton Bradley, skill game, c1905, 8 x 15½", instructions on back of box cover, multicolored lithographed board on platformed box, 3 wood balls, same picture on board, Black theme **200.00**

Leap For Life Game, Milton Bradley, boxed board game, 1930s, 8¼ x 14", instructions printed in center of board, 4 wood counters and spinner, multicolored lithographed board **25.00**

Limited Mail And Express Game, Parker Brothers, boxed board game, © 1894, 21 x 14", wood box, instructions on back of box cover, pack of route cards, 4 wood colored counters, 4 colored flat metal train tokens, board is multicolored lithographed map of U.S. pasted on box bottom **300.00**

Militac, Parker Brothers, card game, 1910, 5½ x 4", 52 cards, instruction card, and advertising card, cards show photographs of pre–WWI NCOs, Officers, and weaponry, red backs state "Tactics–The Military Game" **35.00**

Neutral Game of War, Peace And Indemnity, The, Biddle Corp, card game, 1916, 7¼ x 4", 104 cards, instruction card, light green backs depicting swords and cannon **35.00**

New Game Of Red Riding Hood, The, McLoughlin Bros, card game, c1888, 6¼ x 4½", 42 multicolored lithographed cards, instruction booklet .. **25.00**

New Premium Game of Logomachy, The, McLoughlin Bros, card game, 1887, 8½ x 6", wood box, 56 multicolored lithographed alphabet cards with bird on backs, instruction booklet, invented by F. A. Wright in 1874 **25.00**

Ocean To Ocean Flight Game, Wilder Mfg Co, boxed board game, c1927, 7½ x 12¼", spinner and 6 counters, multicolored lithographed board of U.S. map, directions in lower left corner of board **65.00**

Owl And The Pussy Cat, The, E. O. Clark, Tokalon Series, boxed board game, c1890, 19¼ x 10½″, wood box, instructions on back of box cover, spinner with 4 wood counters, multicolored lithographed board with turkey and pig **85.00**

Parker Brothers Post Office Game, educational play acting game, c1910, 9 x 12″, contains postman's mask, cancel stamp, sheets of stationery, envelopes, postcards, etc. **125.00**

Quartette Union War Game, E. G. Selchow, Civil War card game, 1874, 2½ x 3½″, 48 cards, instruction card, cards black on white, involves battles and Union generals **45.00**

Round The World, Milton Bradley, boxed board game, c1912, 21¼ x 14¼″, spinner with 4 round wood counters, multicolored lithographed board with instructions printed on it, track game **195.00**

Rummy, manufacturer unknown, card game, c1910, 5½ x 7½″, 48 cards, instruction sheet **12.00**

Setto, Game Of Syllables, Selchow and Righter, © 1882, 6 x 4″, 51 black and white cards, 5 illustrated "prize" cards, instruction booklet, invented by Charles P. Goldey **25.00**

Ski–Hi New York To Paris, Cutler & Saleeby Co., #2117, boxed board game, c1927, 12½ x 7½″, one die with 4 metal planes, multicolored lithographed board showing ocean, NYC, and Eiffel Tower, track game based on Lindbergh's crossing of the Atlantic **85.00**

Snake Eyes, Selchow & Righter, card game, c1930s, 11 x 7½″, 185 pcs (120 cards, dice cup, 2 wood dice, 62 chips), instructions on back of box cover, multicolored lithographed cards with "craps" expressions printed on them **55.00**

Teddy Bear's Trip, J. Ottmann Lith Co, card game, c1910, 7¼ x 11¼″, storybook, instructions on bottom of box cover together with legend of the storybook, numerous printed cards, played like Peter Coddles **28.00**

Telephone Game, The, J. H. Singer, card game, © 1898, 7½ x 6″, numerous question and answer cards, 2 black wood "receivers" connected to each other by a string **55.00**

Tiny Town Bank, The, Spear, boxed play acting game, c1910, 10½ x 7½″,

instructions on back of box cover, cardboard bank teller's front, 2 bank books, deposit slips, withdrawal slips, fake paper money and change **85.00**

Uncle Wiggily's New Airplane Game, Milton Bradley, board game with matching box of playing pieces, 1920s, instructions on back of box cover, numerous playing cards and counters, multicolored lithographed board opens to 16″ sq, track game . **45.00**

Ups And Downs Of School Life, Spear, boxed board game, c1910, 12½ x 6½″, instructions on back of box cover, 10 pcs (folding board, dice cup, 2 dice, 6 wood counters), multicolored lithographed board featuring amusing pictures of school life **45.00**

When My Ship Comes In, Parker Brothers, card game, © 1888, 5¼ x 4″, 84 non–illustrated cards, instruction sheet **25.00**

Wings, Parker Brothers, card game, © 1928, 5½ x 4″, 99 cards, instruction booklet, card backs are pink and white picturing airmail planes **20.00**

Witch–ee, Selchow & Righter, boxed board game, c1930s, 6½″ sq, instructions on back of box cover, chamois rubbing cloth and Witch–ee fortunes sheet, Halloween decor, multicolored lithographed deck of cards on box bottom with black witch tissue figure, game based on scientific principle of friction by rubbing **60.00**

Wonderful Game of Oz, Parker Bros, 1921, pewter playing pcs **70.00**

Wyhoo, Milton Bradley, card game ... **15.00**

GAUDY DUTCH

History: Gaudy Dutch is an opaque, soft-paste ware made between 1790 and 1825 in England's Staffordshire district. Most pieces are unmarked; marks of various potters, including the impressed marks of Riley and Wood, have been found on pieces.

The pieces first were hand decorated in an underglaze blue, fired, and then received additional decoration over the glaze. Many pieces today have the over glaze decoration extensively worn. Gaudy Dutch found a ready market within the Pennsylvania German community because it was inexpensive and intense with color. It had little appeal in England.

References: Susan and Al Bagdade, *Warman's English & Continental Pottery & Porcelain, 2nd Edition,* Wallace–Homestead, 1991; Eleanor and Edward Fox, *Gaudy Dutch,* published by author, 1970, out–of–print; John A. Shuman, III, *The Col-*

lector's *Encyclopedia of Gaudy Dutch & Welsh*, Collector Books, 1990.

Reproduction Alert: Cup plates, bearing the impressed mark "CYBRIS," have been reproduced and are collectible in their own right. The Henry Ford Museum has issued pieces in the single rose pattern, although they are of porcelain and not soft-paste.

Advisor: John D. Querry.

Plate, Single Rose pattern, blue rim, 7″ d, $300.00.

Butterfly
Coffeepot, high domed cov	10,000.00
Creamer	1,200.00
Cup Plate	975.00
Plate	
7¼″ d	775.00
9⅞″ d	850.00
Platter, oval, 14″ l	1,800.00
Sugar Bowl, rect	1,350.00
Tea Bowl and Saucer, Butterfly center	
position	875.00
Teapot, spout repair	650.00
Wash Basin, 13¾″ d, marked "Adams"	10,000.00

Carnation
Coffeepot, high domed cov	2,500.00
Creamer	750.00
Cup Plate	975.00
Plate	
9¾″ d	725.00
10″ d	1,100.00
Soup Plate	775.00
Sugar Bowl	850.00
Tea Bowl and Saucer	600.00
Teapot	850.00

Dahlia
Creamer	850.00
Plate, 8⅜″ d, double border	1,200.00
Sugar Bowl	1,200.00
Tea Bowl and Saucer	975.00

Double Rose
Creamer	850.00
Cup Plate	750.00
Jug, mask spout	1,550.00
Pitcher, 8¼″ h	1,300.00
Plate, 8¾″ d	775.00
Platter	
10½″ l	2,700.00
11⅝″ l	3,300.00
15″ l	3,300.00
Tea Bowl and Saucer	600.00
Teapot	1,800.00
Toddy Plate	625.00
Waste Bowl	675.00

Dove
Creamer	675.00
Plate, 8¼″ d	675.00
Sugar Bowl	750.00
Tea Bowl and Saucer	650.00
Teapot, knop restored on lid	625.00
Toddy Plate	675.00

Grape
Creamer	450.00
Cup Plate	725.00
Plate, 9¾″ d	525.00
Pitcher, 8″ h	2,200.00
Soup Plate, 8¾″ d	675.00
Teapot	650.00
Toddy Plate	450.00

Leaf
Bowl, unusual shape	975.00
Tea Bowl and Saucer	775.00

Oyster
Coffeepot, high domed lid	1,900.00
Creamer	375.00
Plate	
4½″ d	450.00
8½″ d	525.00
10″ d	650.00
Tea Bowl and Saucer	425.00
Teapot	625.00
Toddy Plate	625.00
Waste Bowl, rim chips	350.00

Primrose
Plate	
8¾″ d, imp "Riley"	650.00
9⅞″ d	2,400.00
Sugar Bowl	850.00
Tea Bowl and Saucer	675.00

Rose
Coffeepot, high domed cov	5,200.00
Creamer	550.00
Cup Plate	1,075.00
Plate	
7½″ d, imp mark	325.00
9½″ d	425.00
Sugar Bowl	650.00
Tea Bowl and Saucer	325.00
Waste Bowl	300.00

Straw Flower
Plate, 9¼″ d	2,500.00
Soup Plate	975.00

Sunflower
Coffeepot, high domed cov, restored
   spout 1,500.00
Creamer 775.00
Plate
   6½" d 750.00
   9¾" d 1,050.00
Tea Bowl and Saucer 775.00
Urn
Creamer 375.00
Cup Plate 1,075.00
Plate
   5½" d 775.00
   9⅞" d 600.00
Soup Plate 525.00
Tea Bowl and Saucer 375.00
Teapot 650.00
Waste Bowl 350.00
War Bonnet
Creamer 575.00
Cup Plate 950.00
Pitcher, 5¾" h, rim repair 200.00
Plate
   6⅜" d 575.00
   8¼" d 675.00
Soup Plate 775.00
Tea Bowl and Saucer 550.00
Water Lily, tea bowl and saucer, pink
   luster border 1,075.00
Zinnia, plate
   6⅜" d 550.00
   8½" d 575.00
   10" d, imp "Riley" 1,050.00

GAUDY IRONSTONE

History: Gaudy Ironstone was made in England
around 1850. Most pieces are impressed "Ironstone" and bear a registry mark. Ironstone is an
opaque, heavy body earthenware which contains
large proportions of flint and slag. Gaudy Ironstone
is decorated in patterns and colors similar to
Gaudy Welsh.

Reference: Susan and Al Bagdage, *Warman's
English & Continental Pottery & Porcelain, 2nd
edition,* Wallace–Homestead, 1991.

Butter Dish, octagonal, Seaweed pat-
   tern, three color, luster dec, orig insert   85.00
Creamer, Morning Glory pattern, under-
   glaze blue and luster 65.00
Cup and Saucer, handleless
   Seaweed, underglaze blue and luster,
     red and green enamel 48.00
   Strawberry, four color, luster dec . . . 65.00
Mug, underglaze blue stripes, luster,
   and red wavy lines 25.00
Pitcher, 9⅝" h, Vintage pattern 175.00
Plate
   8¾" d, stick spatter design, marked
     "Malkin" 35.00

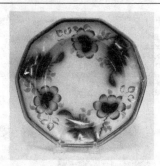

**Plate, blue, rust, green, and copper lus-
ter, 8½" d, $90.00.**

   9⅝" d, Strawberry, minor stains 35.00
Platter
   13¼" l, rose design, red, blue, green,
     and black, marked "England" . . . 75.00
   14¼" l, Berry pattern, Niagara shape,
     marked "E Walley" 75.00
   15" l, columbine, rosebud, and thistle
     dec, stick spatter rim 235.00
Soup Plate, 9¼" d, red, blue, and green
   floral dec 45.00
Sugar, cov, Urn of Flowers pattern, underglaze blue and luster, red and
   green enamel, emb lion head handles 75.00
Tea Set, Morning Glory, 9¼" h cov teapot, 6¼" h creamer, 8¼" h cov sugar,
   minor wear 350.00
Vegetable Dish, cov, 12½" l, black trans-
   fer floral dec, polychrome enameling,
   marked "Ashworth Bros, England" . 125.00

GAUDY WELSH

History: Gaudy Welsh is a translucent porcelain
that was originally made in the Swansea area of
England from 1830 to 1845. Although the designs
resemble Gaudy Dutch, the body texture and
weight differ. One of the characteristics is the gold
luster on top of the glaze.

In 1890, Allerton made a similar ware. These
wares are heavier opaque porcelain and usually
bear the export mark.

References: Susan and Al Bagdade, *Warman's
English & Continental Pottery & Porcelain, 2nd
Edition,* Wallace–Homestead, 1991; John A. Shu-
man, III, *The Collector's Encyclopedia of Gaudy
Dutch and Welsh,* Collector Books, 1990; Howard
Y. Williams, *Gaudy Welsh China,* Wallace–Home-
stead, out–of–print.

Daisy and Chain
Creamer 75.00

Cup and Saucer, Columbine pattern, pink flowers in white reserves, wide cobalt blue band, gold trim, $40.00.

Sugar, cov	125.00
Teapot, cov	165.00
Feather	
Cake Plate	45.00
Cup and Saucer	40.00
Plate, 5½" d	25.00
Flower Basket (also known as Urn or Vase)	
Bowl, 10½" d	175.00
Creamer	75.00
Cup and Saucer, handleless	65.00
Dinner Service, 56 pcs	1,500.00
Plate, 8½" d	45.00
Sugar, cov	90.00
Grape	
Bowl, 6⅜" d, pink luster rim	185.00
Creamer	35.00
Morning Glory	
Creamer	85.00
Cup and Saucer	50.00
Pitcher, 6½" h, Allerton, c1890	75.00
Plate, 8" d	70.00
Platter, 14½" l	135.00
Tea Set, teapot, creamer, sugar, six cups and saucers	750.00
Oyster	
Bowl, 6¼" d	50.00
Creamer	45.00
Cup and Saucer	65.00
Jug, 4½" h	70.00
Pitcher, 5½" h	95.00
Plate	
6" d	40.00
9½" d	100.00
Shanghai	
Plate, 5½" d	75.00
Sugar, cov, ftd	100.00
Strawberry	
Creamer	90.00
Mug, 4⅛" h	125.00
Plate, 8½" d	75.00
Spill Holder, pr, 4⅜" h	200.00
Teapot, cov	165.00
Tulip	
Cup and Saucer	50.00
Creamer, 5¼" h	75.00
Pitcher, milk	110.00

Plate	
6" d	30.00
9" d	45.00
Serving Dish, 9" d	40.00
Teapot, 8½" h	135.00
Waste Bowl, 6¾" d	50.00
Wagon Wheel	
Bowl, 7½" d	50.00
Cup and Saucer	65.00
Pitcher, 8" h	175.00
Plate	
5½" d	35.00
7½" d	50.00
Platter	100.00

GEISHA GIRL PORCELAIN

History: Geisha Girl porcelain is a Japanese export ware whose production commenced during the last quarter of the 19th century and continued heavily until WWII. The ware features kimono–clad Japanese ladies and children amidst Japanese gardens and temples. There are over 125 brightly colored scenes depicting the pre–modern Japanese lifestyle. Over 140 marks and almost 200 patterns and variations have been identified on pieces.

Geisha Girl ware may be totally hand painted, hand painted over a stenciled design, or occasionally decaled. The stenciled underlying design is usually red–orange, but also is found in brown, black, and green (rare).

All Geisha Girl items are bordered by one or a combination of blues, reds, greens, rhubarb, yellow, black, browns, or gold. The most common is red–orange. Borders may be wavy, scalloped, or banded and range from 1/16" to 1/4". The borders themselves often are further decorated with gold, white or yellow lacings, flowers, dots, or stripes. Some examples even display interior frames of butterflies or flowers.

Geisha Girl is found in many forms including tea, cocoa, lunch, and children's sets, dresser items, vases, serving dishes, etc. Large plates or platters, candlesticks, miniatures, and mugs are hardest to locate. Geisha Girl advertising items add to a collection.

Reference: Elyce Litts, *The Collectors Encyclopedia Of Geisha Girl Porcelain*, Collector Books, 1988.

Additional Listings: See *Warman's Americana & Collectibles* for more examples.

Reproduction Alert: Geisha Girl porcelain's popularity continued after WWII and it is being reproduced today. Chief reproduction characteristics are a red–orange border, very white and smooth porcelain, and sparse coloring and detail. Reproduced items include dresser, tea and sake sets, toothpick holders, small vases, table plates, and salt and pepper shakers.

Bouillon Cup and Saucer, lid, brown and gold, Rivers Edge 38.00

Bowl
6½" d, lobed, red, gold lacing, Flag . 23.00
9½" d, octagon shape, Geisha in Sampan E, red–orange, gold buds, Nippon 43.00

Celery Set, child's, 6 pc, master, five salts, Flower Gathering A, pine green, Made in Japan 40.00

Child's Dishes
Demitasse Set, 15 pcs, pot, creamer and sugar, six cups and saucers, Parasol C 65.00
Pitcher, 3⅝ x 1¾", cylindrical slenderizing towards top, almost indistinguishable pouring lip, Parasol B, red, Japan 15.00

Chocolate Pot, Parasol & Lesson, blue and gold, floral and butterfly ground 100.00

Creamer, cov, Garden Bench, hp, black, beige, and red–orange geometric border with gold diaper patterns, red–orange lid and spout with stylized chrysanthemums and gold lacings, marked "Ozan" 25.00

Cup and Saucer
After dinner, Parasol B, red–orange, gold buds, celadon ground, Japan 25.00
Tea, Kite A, brown and gold 12.00

Dresser Tray, Flower Gathering A, pine green, Made in Japan 35.00

Hair Receiver
Geisha in Sampan, sq, red, marked "t't' Japan" 18.00
Spider Puppet, round, blue and gold, fluted rim, marked 40.00

Nut Bowl, 6", nine lobed, three feet, Basket A, dark apple green 30.00

Olive Dish, 7", oval, Mother and Son C, red–orange, Kutani 25.00

Plate
6", Chinese Coin 15.00
8½", Geisha in Sampan A, brown and gold 25.00

Rice Bowl, Samurai Dance, red and gold 20.00

Sake Cup, Garden Bench B, red rim . 6.00

Salt and Pepper Shaker, pr
Pointing, sq, pine green 18.00
Visiting with Baby, individual, bulbous, blue and gold 20.00

Salt
Temple A, floral and turquoise border, pedestal, marked 25.00
To The Teahouse, red, fluted, handled, Kutani 20.00

Stein, 7½", Chrysanthemum Garden, red, gold buds, marked "Japan" ... 100.00

Sugar Bowl, Flower Gathering B, green, gold lacing 15.00

Teapot, Butterfly, apple green and gold, ftd, hairline on bottom 30.00

GIRANDOLES AND MANTEL LUSTRES

History: A girandole is a highly elaborate branched candleholder, often featuring cut glass prisms surrounding the mountings. A mantel lustre is a glass vase with attached cut glass prisms.

Girandoles and mantel lustres usually are found in pairs. It is not uncommon for girandoles to be part of a large garniture set. Girandoles and mantel lustres achieved their greatest popularity in the last half of the 19th century both in the United States and Europe.

GIRANDOLES, PR

11¾", gilt bronze, French, 19th C 630.00
13", tulip shape, cranberry, rect prisms,

Plate, Temple Vase, three borders, multicolored, unmarked, 6" d, $15.00.

Mantel Lusters, double cut overlay, white cut to emerald green, cut crystal prisms, 14" h, $250.00.

gilt dec, circular foot, Bohemian,
c1875 .... 310.00
15", Victorian, pink, enameled and colored wild flowers, notched prisms .. 275.00
16", two branch, cut glass, regency ormolu, bell shaped sockets, bobeches hung with beads, stepped oval base 1,000.00
18", oval base, ormolu mounted, gilt brass foliage, porcelain flowers, maroon parrots, oriental birds as girandoles, electrified 350.00
27", gilt bronze and cut glass, scrolling candle arms, faceted glass beads and pendant ropes electrified, French, early 20th C 850.00

MANTEL LUSTRES

9", pr, blue, enameled florals, gold trim, white beading, Waterford crystal prisms 225.00
10½", green, cut to crystal, ten cut glass prisms 290.00
12", opalene, green fold over top, white satin glass bodies, gold trim 225.00
13", pr, white cut to cranberry, scalloped flaring bowl, facet cut prisms 575.00
14", double cut overlay, white to emerald green, prisms of alternating lengths 250.00
15¾", Bohemian, cobalt blue, gilt scrollwork dec, colored floral sprigs, two rows of clear prisms, late 19th C ... 325.00

GLASS ANIMALS

History: It did not take glass manufacturers long to realize that there was a ready market for glass novelties. In the early nineteenth century, walking sticks and witch balls were two dominant forms. As the century ended, glass covered dishes with an animal theme were featured.

In the period between World War I and II, glass manufacturers such as Fostoria Glass Company and A. H. Heisey & Company created a number of glass animal figures for the novelty and decorative accessory markets. In the 1950s and early 1960s a second glass animal craze swept America led by companies such as Duncan & Miller Glass Company and New Martinsville - Viking Glass Company. A third craze struck in the early 1980s when companies such as Boyd Crystal Art Glass, Guernsey Glass, Pisello Art Glass, and Summit Art Glass began offering the same animal figure in a wide variety of collectible glass colors, with some colors in limited production.

There are two major approaches to glass animal collecting: (a) animal type and (b) manufacturer. Most collectors concentrate on one or more manufacturer, grouping their collections accordingly.

References: Everett Grist, *Covered Animal Dishes*, Collector Books, 1988; Frank L. Hahn and Paul Kikeli, *Collector's Guide to Heisey and Heisey By Imperial Glass Animals*, Golden Era Publications, 1991; Evelyn Zemel, *American Glass Animals A to Z*, A to Z Productions, 1978.

Price Note: Prices are for animal figures in clear (crystal) glass unless otherwise noted.

Rooster, Lalique, automobile mascot, amethyst, 7¼" h, $850.00.

Angel Fish, bookends, pr, clear
  American Glass Co, 8¼" h 45.00
  Heisey, wave base, 7" h 175.00
Bear, New Martinsville, clear, 3½" h .. 45.00
Bull, Heisey, 4" h 1,100.00
Cat, animal covered dish, milk glass, blue body, white head 75.00
Cockerel, frosted, circular base, block sgd "R Lalique, France," 8" h 800.00
Deer, Fostoria, blue, standing, 4½" h . 35.00
Dog
  Animal Covered Dish, milk glass
    Blue body, white head 75.00
    White head and body, wide rib base 45.00
  Scottie, caramel slag, Heisey by Imperial 200.00
Donkey, Heisey by Imperial, caramel slag 90.00
Duck
  Heisey, mallard, wings down 30.00
  Tiffin, green duck, white wavy base . 30.00
Eagle, Westmoreland, frosted, brown mist base 85.00
Elephant, Heisey 245.00
Fish
  Fostoria, vase
    Green 70.00
    Red 90.00
  Viking, bookends, pr 55.00
Frog, cov dish, amethyst slag, 5" d ... 55.00
Giraffe, Heisey, head turned, clear, 11" h 175.00
Goose, Heisey 75.00

Hen
 American Hen, milk glass **58.00**
 Atterbury, milk glass
  All white, eye sockets, 7" l **90.00**
  Blue and marble, lacy base **185.00**
  White body, blue head, lacy base . **145.00**
  Yellow and marble, lacy base . . . **150.00**
 Vallerystahl, milk glass, white, 5¾" w
  base **65.00**
 Westmoreland, milk glass, white,
  green trim, 1" h **20.00**
Hen and Chicks, New Martinsville, roos-
 ter, hen, and five chicks **175.00**
Horse, rearing, bookends, pr, LE Smith,
 green **65.00**
King Fish, LE Smith, green, 10" h **250.00**
Owl
 Doorstop, green slag **35.00**
 Paperweight, cobalt carnival, Summit
  Art Glass **15.00**
Penguin, decanter, Heisey, 8½" h **185.00**
Pigeon, Pouter, bookends, pr, Fenton . **175.00**
Pony, balking, caramel slag, Heisey by
 Imperial **135.00**
Ringed Neck Pheasant, Heisey **95.00**
Robin, on nest, milk glass
 Mint Green **65.00**
 White **50.00**
Rooster, head, cocktail shaker, Heisey **85.00**
Swan
 Cambridge, amber, 3½"h **25.00**
 Lalique, double, frosted, hand sgd,
  "Lalique, France," 3 x 3½" **120.00**
 Milk Glass, white
  Block, glass eyes, 8" h **195.00**
  Raised wing, eye sockets **140.00**
 New Martinsville, ebony, crystal neck,
  11" h **60.00**
Turtle, milk glass, white **105.00**

GLASS, EARLY AMERICAN

History: Early American glass covers glass made in America from the colonial period through the mid-19th century. As such it includes the early pressed glass and lacy glass made between 1827 and 1840.

Major glass producing centers prior to 1850 were Massachusetts with the New England Glass Company and the Boston and Sandwich Glass Company, South Jersey, Pennsylvania with Stiegel's Manheim factory and Pittsburgh, and Ohio with Kent, Mantua, and Zanesville.

Early American glass was collected heavily during the 1920 to 1950 period. It has now regained some of its earlier popularity. Leading sources for the sale of early American glass are the mail auctions of David and Linda Arman and the auctions of Richard A. Bourne, Early Auction Company, Garth's, and Skinners.

References: William E. Covill, *Ink Bottles and Inkwells*, 1971; Lowell Inness, *Pittsburgh Glass: 1797–1891*, Houghton Mifflin Company, 1976; George and Helen McKearin, *American Glass*, Crown, 1975; George and Helen McKearin, *Two Hundred Years of American Blown Glass*, Doubleday and Company, 1950; Helen McKearin and Kenneth Wilson, *American Bottles And Flasks*, Crown, 1978; Adeline Pepper, *Glass Gaffers of New Jersey*, Scribners, 1971; Jane S. Spillman, *American and European Pressed Glass*, Corning Museum of Glass, 1981; Kenneth Wilson, *New England Glass And Glassmaking*, Crowell, 1972.

Collectors' Club: The National Early American Glass Club, 7417 Allison Street, Hyattsville, MD 20784.

Additional Listings: Blown Three Mold, Cup Plates, Flasks, Sandwich Glass, and Stiegel Type Glass.

Keene, flask, half pint, eagle on one side, cornucopia on other, aqua, Mc-Kearin G2–18, $350.00.

Bakewell
 Lamp, fluid, 11¾" h, clear, blown pear
  shaped font, typical cut Pittsburgh
  pattern, large bulbous knops,
  heavy pressed ftd base, pewter col-
  lar **600.00**
 Window Pane, 6⅞ x 4⅞", clear,
  church, gothic arch design, sgd
  "Bakewell" on reverse, Innes Fig
  303–2 . . . . **2,000.00**
Engraved
 Celery Vase, 5⅛" d, 8½" h, clear,
  elaborate pattern of festoons, small
  flowers, and leaf band, twenty gadrooned ribs, applied foot with knob
  stem, early 19th C, slight crazing . **225.00**
 Mug, 3¾", clear, 24 wide ribs, applied
  strap handle with curl, copper
  wheel engraved tendrils, letter "P" **125.00**
 Wine, 5⅛" h, clear, blown, Pittsburgh

type engraved foliage, tapered stem and bowl, applied foot **50.00**

Keene (Marlboro Street) Glass Works, inkwell, 2½" d, olive–amber, blown three mold, McKearin GIII–29 . . . . . **145.00**

Lockport

Creamer, 4⅞" h, blue, free blown, solid applied handle and foot, folded rim, wide flaring mouth, pontil **600.00**

Vase, 3½" d, 7⅛" h, blue, free blown, three part vase, flared mouth, round base set onto solid baluster stem, thick solid circular foot, 5¼" d witch ball cov **600.00**

Mantua

Flask, 4⅛", chestnut, amber, 16 vertical ribs, terminal ring, attributed to Mantua or Kent **300.00**

Pan, 5½" d, 1½" h, brilliant aqua, free blown, 15 diamond, folded in rim, minor flakes at pontil **3,850.00**

Midwestern

Bowl, 5⅝" d, 3⅞" h, cobalt blue, lacy period, ftd, c1830, one moderate chip under rim, small rim chips and roughage **900.00**

Candlesticks, pr, 7⅛", clear, free blown sockets, lacy hairpin pattern base **5,250.00**

Sugar, cov, clear, lacy, Peacock Feather pattern, one foot scallop chipped **500.00**

Mt Vernon Glass Co

Lamp, fluid, 6⁷⁄₁₆", clear, blown three mold, cylindrical font, patterned from half pint decanter mold, mounted with wafer to heavy pressed base of two lion's paws on stepped and scalloped flat oval base **1,200.00**

Pitcher, 7¼", light aquamarine, blown three mold, quart, McKearin GIII–2, Type 1 . . . . **7,750.00**

New Jersey, South

Creamer, 5⅞" h, cobalt blue, applied crimped foot and solid curled handle, tooled rim, int. spall on side of spout **650.00**

Miniature

Compote, 2" d, 1⅞" h, brilliant green, circular, straight sides, hollow knop stem, applied circular foot, McKearin Plate 75, No. 20 . . . . **450.00**

Creamer, 1⅜" h, aquamarine, free blown, baluster shaped bowl, applied circular flat foot, applied solid ear shaped handle, lower end turned back **500.00**

Pitcher, 7⅝", aquamarine, opaque white loopings, double ribbed applied handle crimped at base, tooled lip, heavy circular applied foot **650.00**

New York

Compote, 8¼" d, tilted 4 to 4¾" h, bluish–aqua, applied lily pad dec, wide folded rim, heavy applied base **1,200.00**

Plate, 6⅝" d,¾" h, cobalt blue, free blown, attributed to Lancaster . . . **85.00**

Pittsburgh

Bowl, 4⅞" d, 2⅝" h, pattern molded, broken swirl, sixteen ribs to the right, folded rim, tooled foot, lead glass, sapphire blue, pontil scar . . **335.00**

Candlesticks, pr, 9", olive green, blown socket with bulbous base . . **1,800.00**

Compote, cov, 6½" h, lacy, Hairpin pattern, two large rim chips . . **2,750.00**

Creamer

4½" h, deep sapphire blue, applied solid handle, heavy crimped end, McKearin Plate 52, No. 3 . . . . . **1,300.00**

5⅛", opalescent blue, 8 rib pillar molded, short circular stem, circular foot, applied handle **4,500.00**

Inkwell, 5½", clear, free blown, egg shaped body, two reservoirs, applied rounded well, small cup for seals, short knop stem, circular foot, nine applied rosettes **1,000.00**

Pitcher, 8" h, eight pillar molded, blown, applied handle **350.00**

Plate

5¹⁵⁄₁₆" d, octagonal, clear, lacy, steamboat, Lee 170–3, minute roughage on upper rim **1,800.00**

6⅛" d, octagonal, clear, lacy, Constitution "Union," Lee 170–4, small rim flakes **1,400.00**

Sugar, cov, 7¼", deep sapphire blue, patterned in 12 rib mold and expanded, foot not pattern molded, McKearin Plate 52, No. 2 . . . . . . **2,500.00**

Redwood or Redford Glass Works, NY

Bowl, 14" d, 5⁷⁄₁₆ to 5⅞" h, brilliant aquamarine, wide flaring rim, heavy out folded edge, applied circular foot, superimposed lily pad dec, similar to McKearin Plate 15, c1831–50 . . . . **4,000.00**

Compote, 9" d, 4½" h, brilliant aquamarine, blown, circular bowl flaring to wide out folding rim, short cylindrical stem, circular stepped foot, superimposed gather of lily pad dec **9,000.00**

Pitcher, 10¼", light aquamarine, free blown, globular body, broad cylindrical neck with fine wide spaced applied threading extending to slightly flaring rim, tiny pinched lip, applied ear shaped aquamarine

handle, applied circular foot, superimposed gather tooled swooping
lily pad dec, McKearin Plate 20, No.
8 . . . . **19,000.00**
Vase, 4¾" h, free blown, brilliant
aquamarine, urn form, two applied
miniature handles **700.00**
Saratoga, NY
Creamer, 4" h, olive–green, yellow
tones, applied solid handle and
foot, attributed to Morris Holmes . **575.00**
Miniature, pitcher, 1¹³⁄₁₆", deep green,
blown, applied handle crimped at
base, McKearin Plate 69, No. 3 . . **700.00**
Sugar Bowl, cov, 7⅝" h, flaring lip,
applied threading extending to mid
body, thick strap handles, large medial ribs, blown ball shaped cov,
green–aqua, pontil scar, two small
pieces of threading missing, Mc-
Kearin Plate 69, lower right **2,900.00**
South Boston
Decanter, 9", pr, clear, free blown, two
bands of chain dec around bodies
and two around necks, period stop-
pers **700.00**
Sugar, cov, 5⅞" h, clear, free blown,
galleried rim, one band of applied
chain dec on base and one on
cover **3,250.00**
Stourbridge Flint Glass Works, salt,
dark blue, lacy, Innes Color Plate 6 . **1,200.00**
Wheeling
Compote, 7¼" d, 4¼" h, octagonal,
Oak Leaf pattern, bull's eye rim,
Roman Rosette pattern base **1,200.00**
Window Pane, 7 x 5", clear, portrait
of steamboat in center with name
"J & C Ritchie" above, c1833 . . . **5,000.00**
Whitney Works, Glassboro, NJ, pitcher,
6¹⁵⁄₁₆", medium sapphire blue, free
flown, horizontal threading around
neck, folded rim, small pinched lip,
heavy circular applied foot, solid ap-
plied handle crimped at lower end,
Joel Duffield, South Jersey c1835–
40, McKearin Plate 60, No. 6 . . . . . **1,300.00**
Zanesville, OH
Bottle, blown, 9" h, globular, amber,
24 swirled ribs **600.00**
Bowl, 8½" d, 3¾" h, amber, blown,
folded rim, minor broken blisters . **450.00**
Flip, 4⅛" d, 4⅝" h, blue–green, 24
ribs, broken swirl to left **350.00**
Pan, 6⅝" d, light green, blown, faint
impression of 24 ribs, folded rim . **250.00**

GOLDSCHEIDER

History: Friedrich Goldscheider founded a porcelain and faience factory in Vienna, Austria, in
1885. Upon his death, his widow carried on operations. In 1920 Walter and Marcell, Friedrich's
sons, gained control. During the Art Deco period,
the firm commissioned several artists to create
figural statues, among which were Pierrettes and
sleek wolfhounds. During the 1930s, the company's products were most traditional.

In the early 1940s, the Goldscheiders fled to the
United States and re–established operations in
Trenton, New Jersey. The Goldscheider Everlast
Corporation is listed in Trenton City directories be-
tween 1943 and 1950. Goldscheider Ceramics,
located at 1441 Heath Avenue, Trenton, New Jer-
sey, was listed in the *1952 Crockery and Glass
Journal Directory.* The firm was not listed in 1954.

**Dish, cov, multicolored, large modeled
bird finial, c1925, marked "Goldscheider Wein," 11" h, $400.00.**

Ashtray, 7½" l, German Shepherd . . . **45.00**
Bust
7" h, Madonna, crown **75.00**
26" h, finely molded face, downcast
eyes, long light brown hair looped
into chignon, narrow mauve head
band with oval irid glass jewel, gilt
draped gown, narrow mauve straps
set with matching jewel, incised
"Montenave," Goldscheider seal
molded in relief, imp "Reproduc-
tion/Reservee" and numerals **2,750.00**
Figure
4½" h, Madonna and Child, orig label **30.00**
4⅝" h, 4½" w, Springer Spaniel, sitting, orig paper label, sgd "Goldscheider, USA" **55.00**
4¾" h, terrier, orange, Art Deco **45.00**
6¾" h, Prince of Wales **75.00**
8½" h, lady with parasol, marked
"#817" **55.00**

10½" h, Southern Belle	85.00
11⅝" h, Butterfly Girl, winged cape with butterfly wing dec, burnt orange, cream, and brown, standing beside vase of flowers, imp "Goldscheider–Wien–Lorenzi," and "Made in Austria," factory numbers, c1930	1,550.00
13" h, flying duck, modeled by E Straub	100.00
14⅛" h, Negro gentleman sitting on rock, top hat and cane, brown suit	325.00
22" h, Bacchanalian woman dancing with leopard, multicolored, gray oval base	500.00
Music Box, 7" h, Colonial girl	100.00
Plaque, 13½" w, 25⅛" h, earthenware, rect, molded, maiden in profile, garland of blossoms and berries in hair, large blossom and cluster on left, earth tones, designer sgd "Lamassi," Goldscheider mark, c1900	1,000.00
Plate, mermaid pattern, multicolored	150.00
Wall Mask	
11¼" h, Art Deco, curly brown haired girl, red lips, aqua scarf	195.00
13½" h, girl, curly green hair, red lips, black mask	365.00

GONDER POTTERY

History: Lawton Gonder established Gonder Ceramic Arts, Inc., at Zanesville, Ohio, in 1941. He gained experience while working for other factories in the area. Gonder experimented with glazes, including Chinese crackle, gold crackle, and flambé. Lamp bases were manufactured under the name Eglee at a second plant location.

Gonder pieces are clearly marked. The company ceased operation in 1957.

Bowl, melon shape, turquoise ext., pink int., imp "E–12/Gonder/USA," 7" d, $20.00.

Bowl, 6½", ribbed, yellow	8.50
Candlestick, pr, 4¾", ext. turquoise, int. pink coral, marked "E–14, Gonder"	18.00
Creamer and Sugar, dark brown drip and brown spatter	24.00

Ewer	
6", mottled blue, pink int.	20.00
9", light green, matte finish, marked "Gonder, USA H34"	25.00
13", Shell and Star, green	50.00
Figure	
7", swan, shaded blue	12.00
10¹⁄₁₂", elephant with raised trunk, rose and gray	40.00
Flower Frog, 7¾ x 7", swirl pattern, blue and brown glossy glaze	18.00
Vase, 7½", flower shape, pink and mottled blue glaze	15.00

GOOFUS GLASS

History: Goofus glass, also known as Mexican Ware, Hooligan glass, and Pickle glass, is a pressed glass with relief designs. The back or front was painted. The designs are usually in red and green with a metallic gold ground. It was popular from 1890 to 1920 and was used as a premium at carnivals.

It was produced by several companies: Cresent Glass Company, Wellsburg, West Virginia; Imperial Glass Corporation, Bellaire, Ohio; LaBelle Glass Works, Bridgeport, Ohio; and Northwood Glass Co., Indiana, Pennsylvania, Wheeling, West Virginia, and Bridgeport, Ohio. Northwood marks include "N," "N" in one circle, "N" in two circles, and one or two circles without the "N."

Goofus glass lost its popularity when people found the paint tarnished or scaled off after repeated washings and wear. No record of its manufacture has been found after 1920.

Reference: Carolyn McKinley, *Goofus Glass*, Collector Books, 1984.

Additional Listings: See *Warman's Americana & Collectibles* for more examples.

Plate, adv., Old Rose Distilling Co., Chicago, 8¼" d, $60.00.

Bowl

9″, carnations	25.00
10½″ d, red roses, molded, gold ground	35.00

Cake Plate, 11″, Dahlia and Fan, red dec, gold ground — 32.00

Candle Holder, red and gold — 18.00

Candy Dish, red strawberries and green leaves, molded applied ring handle — 12.00

Compote, 9½″, strawberries and leaves, red and green dec, gold ground, ruffled — 45.00

Dish, 11″, chrysanthemum sprays, red and gold, scalloped rim — 70.00

Jar, butterflies, red and gold — 20.00

Pickle Jar, aqua, molded, gold, blue, and red painted floral design — 25.00

Pitcher, red rose bud, gold leaves — 45.00

Plate

7½″, apples, red dec, gold ground	18.00
8½″ d, red apples, molded, gold ground	20.00
11″, roses, red and gold, scalloped rim	25.00

Salt and Pepper Shakers, pr, 3″, Poppy — 35.00

Syrup, Strawberry — 32.50

Vase

7½″, brown, red bird	18.00
8″ h, red roses, molded, gold ground	15.00
12″ h, red roses, molded, gold ground	40.00

MARK

W H GOSS

GOSS CHINA AND CRESTED WARE

History: In 1858 William H. Goss opened his Henley factory and produced terra-cotta ware. A year later he moved to Stoke-on-Trent and added Parian ware to his line. In 1883 Adolphus, William's son, expanded on his father's idea of decorating small ivory pots and vases, with the coat of arms of schools, hospitals, colleges [especially Oxford and Cambridge], and other motifs to appeal to the souvenir seeking English "day-tripper." The forms used were copied from ancient artifacts in museums.

William died in 1906, his son in 1913. Following business setbacks, the firm was sold in 1929 to Geo. Jones & Sons Ltd., who had previously acquired Arcadian, Swan, and other firms that made crested wares. As late as 1931 the Goss name was still being used. In 1936–37 Cauldon Potteries purchased the Goss assets. Production ceased in 1940. In 1954 Ridgeway and Adderley acquired all Goss assets [molds, patterns, designs, and right to use the Goss name and trademark].

From 1883 to 1931 pieces carry the mark of GOSHAWK, with W. H. Goss beneath, and "England" on later pieces. Many early examples carry an impressed "W. H. Goss," either with or without the printed mark.

Other manufacturers of crested ware in England were: Arcadian, Carlton China, Grafton China, Savoy China, Shelley, and Willow Art. Gemma in Germany also made crested wares.

Crests are of little value unless they match, e.g., Shakespeare's jug with Shakespeare's crest. Collectors tend to collect one form (vase, ewer, jug, etc.), one particular crest, or one type of object (boat, cat, dog, etc.). Price is determined not by crest, but size, condition, and bottom mark.

References: Sandy Andrews, *Crested China: The History of Heraldic Souvenir Ware,* Milestone Publications [England]; John Galpin, *A Handbook Of Goss China,* Milestone Publications; Nicholas Pine, *The 1984 Price Guide To Goss China,* Milestone Publications, 1984; Nicholas Pine and Sandy Andrews, *The 1984 Price Guide To Crested China* (including revisions to *Crested China*), Milestone Publications; Roland Ward, *The Price Guide To The Models Of W. H. Goss,* Antiques Collectors' Club.

Collectors' Clubs: The Goss Collectors Club, 3 Carr Hill Gardens, Barrowford, Nelson, Lancashire England BB9 6PU; The Crested Circle, 26 Urswick Road, Dagenhem, Essex England RM9 6EA.

Pitcher, Stoke–Upon–Trent crest, multicolored, gold rim, marked "F Robinson, Victoria Porcelain," 2¼″ h, $15.00.

GOSS

Bottle

Canterbury, leather	20.00

Sunderland	25.00
Waterlooville Army Water	45.00
Bucket, Norwegian, Maldon	25.00

Building

First and Last House	145.00
Huers House	200.00
Look Out House	150.00
St Nicholas Chapel	200.00
Bust, parian, Dickens, 8"	150.00
Creamer, Yarmouth	25.00
Can, Welsh Mills	20.00
Carafe, Goodwin Sands	19.00

Ewer

Arundel, 4½"	20.00
Chichester, Roman, Beaulieu Abbey	20.00
Japan, Windsor	35.00
Jug, Spanish, Eddyston	30.00
Lamp, Hamworthy, Reigate Poole	30.00
Night Light, Manx Cottage	200.00
Nogen, Irish, wood	22.00

Pitcher

Cambridge	18.00
Leiston, Abbey	22.00
Pot, Roman, Painswick	20.00
Salt, Glastonbury, Wickford	30.00

Urn

Laxey, Huntington	28.00
Tewkesbury Saxon, Lizard	24.00

OTHER CRESTED WARE MANUFACTURERS

Arcadian

Bathing Wagon, Stockbridge	30.00
Ewer, Wembley, handled	20.00
Statue, Cinotaph, small	25.00
Toby Jug, Wantage	30.00
Warming Pan, Tesbury	30.00

Carlton

Bank, bell shape	20.00
Pot, handled, lid	25.00
Urn, Bourne	25.00

Coronet

Cottage, Tony Panda	25.00
Pot, Arms of Weymouth, two handles, three legs	15.00

Gemma

Cup, Aberystwyth	18.00
Helmet	30.00

Shelley

Common market Harbarcuth	30.00
Fish Basket, Fleetwood	30.00
Luggage, Portugal, #53	30.00
Olive Jar, Sussex	25.00
Rose Bowl, Stafford, silver, #147	35.00
Tea Caddy, Abbey of Glastonbury	25.00
Urn, #118, Roman, Chester	25.00
Victoria, Cheshire Cat, matching crest	25.00

Willow Art

Anvil, Saltash	25.00
Shakespeare Cottage	150.00

MADE IN

Zuid HolLAND

GOUDA POTTERY

History: Gouda and the surrounding areas of Holland have been one of the principle Dutch pottery centers for centuries. Originally the potteries produced a simple utilitarian Delft type earthenware with a tin glaze and the famous clay smoker's pipes.

When the pipe making portion declined in the early 1900s, the Gouda potteries turned to art pottery. Influenced by the Art Nouveau and Art Deco movements, artists expressed themselves with free form and stylized designs in bold colors.

Reference: Susan and Al Bagdade, *Warman's English & Continental Pottery & Porcelain, 2nd Edition,* Wallace–Homestead, 1991.

Periodical: *The Dutch Potter,* 47 London Terrace, New Rochelle, NY 10804.

Reproduction Alert: With the Art Nouveau and Art Deco revivals of recent years, modern reproductions of Gouda pottery currently are on the market. They are difficult to distinguish from the originals.

Bowl

8½" d, multicolored floral dec, two handles, Pelta mark	90.00
12" d, 3¼" h, flattened rim, emb Art Deco style black flowerhead dec, blue, orange, white, and gold geometric ground, matte finish, center flower holder, marked	175.00
Box, cov, 4¼" l, carved, black, gold, and white, glazed, Regina mark	160.00
Candlestick, 17" h, dark glaze	450.00
Charger, 12" d, white magnolias, teal petals, black stems, orange and amber speckled ground, marked "NV Kon Plazuid Unique Gouda Holland," artist's monogram "JVS," (J W Van Schaik,) c1930	440.00
Creamer, Verona pattern	45.00
Decanter, 10½" h, stopper, handle, Nadra pattern, orange, brown, and ochre floral dec, black base	150.00
Dish, 13" d, 7" h, ftd, shallow, polychrome foliage int., five black branched base supports, circular foot, painted factory marks, 1921	440.00
Dutch Shoe, high glaze	75.00
Ewer, 6½" h, cobalt blue, rust, and bright yellow design, marked "2960"	125.00
Inkwell, attached undertray, Kelat house mark	150.00

Lantern, green and brown earthtones, 9½″ h, $300.00.

Jar, cov, 5½″ h, Areo pattern, glossy finish, Royal Zuid mark	55.00
Lantern, 6″ h, Art Nouveau dec, Palzuid house mark	145.00
Pitcher, 9½″ h, orange, turquoise, and ochre stylized animal dec, ivory ground, marked "Distel Goedewaagen"	200.00
Planter, 5 x 7″, Art Nouveau, Royal Zuid mark, 1917	100.00
Plate, 12″ d, Nadra pattern	110.00
Powder Box, cov, 6″ d, round, stylized brown and rose florals, black ground, glossy finish, house mark	60.00
Tobacco Jar, cov, 5″ h, Verona pattern	90.00
Trivet, 4″ w, Damascus, c1895	185.00
Tumbler, 4⅜″ h, wide flaring rim, Art Deco style multicolored flowers and leaves, cream ground, black trim, matte finish, house mark	60.00
Vase	
7¼″ h, baluster, flared rim, brightly colored flowers, gray ground	80.00
12½″ h, Art Nouveau dec, blue and gold iris, green ground	330.00
16¾″ h, hp, lavender breasted birds, stylized brown, black, and green leaves, factory marks, monogram on base, W D Hartgring, c1908, mirror image pr	4,675.00

GRANITEWARE

History: Graniteware is the name commonly given to iron or steel kitchenware covered with enamel coating.

The first graniteware was made in Germany in the 1830s. Graniteware was not produced in the United States until the 1860s. At the start of World War I, when European manufacturers turned to the making of war weapons, American producers took over the market.

Colors commonly marketed were white and gray. Each company made their own special color, including shades of blue, green, brown, violet, cream, and red.

Older graniteware is heavier than new graniteware. Pieces with cast iron handles date from 1870 to 1890; wood handles date from 1900 to 1910. Other dating clues are seams, wood knobs, and tin lids.

References: Helen Greguire, *The Collector's Encyclopedia of Granite Ware: Colors Shapes and Values,* Collector Books, 1990; Vernagene Vogelzang and Evelyn Welch, *Granite Ware, Collector's Guide With Prices,* Wallace–Homestead, 1981; Vernagene Vogelzang and Evelyn Welch, *Granite Ware, Book II,* Wallace–Homestead, 1987.

Collectors' Club: National Graniteware Society, 4818 Reamer Road, Center Point, IA 52213.

Reproduction Alert: Graniteware still is manufactured in many of the traditional forms and colors.

Additional Listings: See *Warman's Americana & Collectibles* for more examples.

Coffeepot, blue, Moravian lion and shield mark and "18," 7″ d base, 11¾″ h, $95.00.

Bucket, 9 x 11″, gray, iron bail, wood handle	30.00
Canister Set, 4 pcs, robin egg blue . . .	130.00
Coffeepot, white, large	35.00
Flask, gray, missing lid	70.00
Food Mold, melon ribbed, gray, tin bottom with ring, marked "Extra Agate, etc"	70.00
Grater, mottled gray, marked "Ideal" . .	345.00
Kettle, 12½″ w, gray, iron bail, wood handle	25.00
Lunch Box, mottled gray, tray and cup, bail handle	75.00

Measure, qt, gray, emb "For Household Use Only" **40.00**
Milk Pan
  Crystolite green, swirled, small **32.00**
  Turquoise, swirl **25.00**
Muffin Pan, six sections, gray **12.00**
Pan, cov
  9" d, blue and white swirl **80.00**
  10¼" d, dark blue and white swirl, white int., black trim **45.00**
Pie Pan
  Cobalt blue and white swirl, 6" d ... **25.00**
  Crystolite green, swirled **18.00**
Pitcher, 7⅝" h, blue and white swirl .. **115.00**
Plate
  8½", mottled gray **12.00**
  10" d, blue and white swirl **8.00**
Preserving Kettle
  9" d, blue and white swirl, two handles **65.00**
  10½" d, shaded blue **50.00**
Roaster, cov, 15" l, mottled gray **40.00**
Salt, hanging, white, navy trim **125.00**
Skimmer, blue and white swirl **70.00**
Spoon, 9" l, mottled gray **15.00**
Tea Kettle, cobalt and white swirl, gooseneck spout **125.00**
Teapot, cov
  Bulbous, blue speckled, ornate pewter lid, collar, and spout, marked "Manning–Bowman" **175.00**
  Lighthouse shape, tapered, mottled gray, pewter rim, spout, and bracket handle with knob finial, domed cov with pointed finial, copper band around base, late 19th C **285.00**
Vegetable Pan, 13" l, Chrystolite green **80.00**
Washboard, cobalt blue insert **50.00**

GREENAWAY, KATE   K.G.

History: Kate Greenaway, or "K.G." as she initialed her famous drawings, was born in 1846 in London. Her father was a prominent wood engraver. Kate's natural talent for drawing soon was evident, and she began art classes at the age of 12. In 1868 she had her first public exhibition.

Her talents were used primarily in illustrating. She did cards for Marcus Ward, which are largely unsigned. China and pottery companies soon had her drawings of children appearing on many of their wares. By the 1880s she was one of the foremost children's book illustrators in England.

Reference: Ina Taylor, *The Art of Kate Greenaway: A Nostalgic Portrait of Childhood,* Pelican Publishing, 1991.

Collectors' Club: Kate Greenaway Society, P.O. Box 8, Norwood, PA 19074.

Reproduction Alert: Some Greenaway buttons have been reproduced in Europe and sold in the United States.

Napkin Ring, little girl and cat, marked "Meridan 199," 3¼" h, 3¼" l, $265.00.

Book
  Alphabet, 1885, London **90.00**
  Little Ann, Kate Greenaway, 1883 .. **75.00**
  Marigold Garden, illus and rhymes by Kate Greenaway, Frederick Warne & Co, 56 pgs **30.00**
  Toyland **100.00**
Butter Pat, boy and girl transfer print . **35.00**
Button,¾" d, girl with kitten on fence .. **10.00**
Children's Dishes, tea set, 15 pcs, multicolored scenes, gold trim **450.00**
Coffeepot, figures dec **175.00**
Cup and Saucer, girl doing laundry in wooden tub **35.00**
Dish, 11" l, oval, Jack Sprat and Sunbonnet girl dec **50.00**
Figure
  8½" h, boy with basket, satin, gold, pink, and blue trim, marked "1893" **525.00**
  9" h, girl with tambourine beside tree, marked "Royal Worcester" **400.00**
Hat, bisque, three girls sitting on brim, flowers **90.00**
Inkwell, bronze, two children, emb ... **200.00**
Jewelry Box, wooden, stenciled children on front **45.00**
Match Safe, pocket, SP, children, emb **50.00**
Mug, pink, children playing **60.00**
Napkin Ring, SS
  Boy holding books **165.00**
  Girl feeding yearling **150.00**
Pencil Holder, porcelain **18.00**
Perfume Bottle, 2" l, SS, girls in low relief, orig stopper **200.00**
Pin Tray, children playing seesaw **65.00**
Plate
  5" d, two girls playing ball **60.00**
  7" d, boy chasing rabbits **65.00**
Stickpin, figural, bronze, children playing ring around the rosy, c1900 .... **25.00**
Tape Measure, figural, girl holding muff **45.00**
Tapestry, 14½ x 56", children playing outdoors **265.00**

Teaspoon, SS, figural, girl handle, bowl
  engraved with Lucy Locket verse . . **50.00**
Tile, 6⅛" d, transfer print, four seasons,
  one spacer, brown and white dec,
  blue border, stamped mark, produced
  by T & R Boote, 1881, set of 5 . . . . **325.00**
Toothpick Holder, bisque, German
  Boy beside tree stump, 4" **60.00**
  Girl, playing, 5½" h **75.00**
Tray, girls playing, boy with hoop, silver
  frame **150.00**

GREENTOWN GLASS

History: The Indiana Tumbler and Goblet Co., Greentown, Indiana, produced its first clear, pressed glass table and bar wares in late 1894. Initial success led to a doubling of plant size in 1895 and other subsequent expansions, one in 1897 to allow for the manufacture of colored glass. In 1899 the firm joined the combine known as the National Glass Company.

In 1900, just before arriving in Greentown, Jacob Rosenthal developed an opaque brown glass, called "chocolate," which ranged in color from a dark, rich chocolate to a lighter "cream" coffee hue. Production of chocolate glass saved the financially pressed Indiana Tumbler and Goblet Works. The Cactus and Leaf Bracket patterns were made almost exclusively in chocolate glass. Other popular chocolate patterns are Austrian, Dewey, Shuttle, and Teardrop and Tassel. In 1902 National Glass Company bought Rosenthal's chocolate glass formula so other plants in the combine could use the color.

In 1902 Rosenthal developed the Golden Agate and Rose Agate colors. All work ceased on June 13, 1903, when a fire of suspicious origin destroyed the Indiana Tumbler and Goblet Company Works.

After the fire, other companies, e.g., McKee and Brothers, produced chocolate glass in the same pattern design used in Greentown. Later reproductions also have taken place, with Cactus among the most heavily copied pattern.

References: Brenda Measell and James Measell, *A Guide To Reproductions of Greentown Glass*, 2nd ed., The Printing Press, 1974; James Measell, *Greentown Glass, The Indiana Tumbler & Goblet Co.*, Grand Rapids Public Museum, 1979.

Collectors' Club: National Greentown Glass Association, 1807 West Madison, Kokomo, IN 46901.

Museums: Greentown Glass Museum, Greentown, IN; Grand Rapids Public Museum [Ruth Herrick Greentown Glass Collection], MI.

Additional Listings: Holly Amber and Pattern Glass.

Animal Covered Dish
  Dolphin, chocolate, chip on tail fin . . **195.00**

Rabbit, dome top, amber **250.00**
Bowl, 7¼" d, Herringbone Buttress,
  green **130.00**
Butter, cov
  Cactus, chocolate **175.00**
  Cupid, chocolate **575.00**
  Herringbone Buttress, green **200.00**
Celery Vase, Beaded Panel, clear . . . **90.00**
Compote, Geneva, 4½" d, 3½" h, choc-
  olate **145.00**
Cookie Jar, Cactus, chocolate **250.00**
Cordial, Austrian, canary **125.00**
Creamer
  Cactus, chocolate **70.00**
  Cupid, Nile green **400.00**
  Indian Head, opaque white **450.00**
  Shuttle, tankard, clear **35.00**
Cruet, orig stopper, Dewey, vaseline . . **165.00**
Goblet
  Overall Lattice **36.00**
  Shuttle, chocolate **500.00**

Berry Bowl, Geneva, chocolate, ftd, 4⅛" l, oval, $35.00.

Mug
  Elf, green **75.00**
  Herringbone Buttress **65.00**
  Overall Lattice **40.00**
Mustard, cov, Daisy, opaque white . . . **75.00**
Nappy, Masonic, chocolate **85.00**
Novelty, hairbrush, clear **55.00**
Paperweight, Buffalo, Nile green **600.00**
Pitcher, 8¾" h, Squirrel, clear **82.50**
Plate, Serenade, chocolate **85.00**
Punch Cup
  Cord Drapery, clear **20.00**
  Shuttle, chocolate **75.00**
Relish, Leaf Bracket, 8" l, oval, choco-
  late **75.00**
Salt and Pepper Shakers, pr, Cactus,
  chocolate **150.00**
Sauce, Cactus, chocolate, ftd **48.00**
Stein, 4⅜" h, outdoor drinking scene,
  Nile green **135.00**
Sugar, cov
  Cupid, opaque white **100.00**
  Dewey, cobalt blue **125.00**
Syrup
  Cactus, chocolate **125.00**
  Indian Feather, green **165.00**
Toothpick
  Cactus, chocolate **65.00**

Indian Head, chocolate	**140.00**
Tumbler	
Cactus, chocolate	**55.00**
Dewey, canary	**60.00**
Leaf Bracket, chocolate	**125.00**

Tile, turtle, brown shell, yellow ground, green leaves, 6″ sq, $450.00.

GRUEBY POTTERY

History: William Grueby was active in the ceramic industry for several years before he developed his own method of producing matte glazed pottery and founded the Grueby Faience Company in Boston, Massachusetts, in 1897.

The art pottery was hand thrown in natural shapes, hand molded, and hand tooled. A variety of colored glazes, singly or in combinations, were produced with green being the most prominent. In 1908 the firm was divided into the Grueby Pottery Company and the Grueby Faience and Tile Co., the latter making art pottery until bankruptcy forced closure shortly after 1908.

References: Paul Evans, *Art Pottery of the United States, 2nd Edition*, Feingold & Lewis Publishing Corp., 1987; Ralph and Terry Kovel, *The Kovels' Collector's Guide to American Art Pottery*, Crown Publishers, Inc., 1974.

Bowl

7″ d, green, high glaze	**425.00**
8″ d, 1¼″ h, swirled glossy green int. and ext. glaze	**285.00**
Lamp Base, 16″ h, wide cylindrical neck, ribbed bulbous base, mottled green glaze, sgd with logo and paper label "World's Fair St. Louis 1904," artist initials of Ruth Ericson, undrilled . . .	**5,200.00**
Paperweight, 2¾″ l, scarab, mottled green glaze, early 20th C	**150.00**
Pot, 10″ h, matte green, yellow flower bud dec	**4,400.00**
Tile	
3¾″ d, hexagonal, deer and tree, four colors	**145.00**
6″ d, grape cluster, four colors	**175.00**
8¼″ sq, complicated geometric cloisonne dec, brick red walls, early stamped mark	**520.00**
Vase	
4½″ h, short neck, wide shoulders tapering to narrow base, upright molded leaves, matte green glaze	**275.00**
4¾″ h, 5½″ d, bulbous, flaring neck, tooled and applied leaves, organic matte green glaze, imp mark	**800.00**
6¾″ h, 4″ w, tooled and applied leaves, yellow buds, organic matte green glaze, imp mark, minor rim restoration	**1,300.00**
7″ h, 4½″ d, bulbous base, flaring neck, tooled and applied leaves and buds, vegetable matte green glaze, rim chip restored, imp mark, orig paper label	**660.00**
8¼″ h, wide pinched rim, swollen cylindrical body, matte green glaze, broad leaves and bud, yellow glazed trailing stem dec, imp mark, artist Wilhelmina Post, c1898–07, rim chip	**1,210.00**
8¾″ h, wide mouth, tapering cylindrical form, overlapping blades, matte green glaze, partial paper label, c1904	**660.00**

HAIR ORNAMENTS

History: Hair ornaments, one of the first accessories developed by primitive man, were used to remove tangles and keep hair out of one's face. Remnants of early combs have been found in many archaeological excavations.

As fashion styles changed through the centuries, hair ornaments kept pace through design and use changes. Hair combs and other hair ornaments are made in a wide variety of materials, e.g., precious metals, ivory, tortoise shell, plastics, and wood.

Combs were first made in America during the Revolution when imports from England were restricted. Early American combs were made of horn and treasured as valued toiletry articles.

Reference: Evelyn Haetig, *Antique Combs and Purses*, Gallery Graphics Press, 1983.

Periodical: *Antique Comb Collector,* 3748 Sunray Drive, Holiday, FL 34691–3234.

Comb, faux tortoiseshell, pierced top, four prongs, 6″ l, $18.00.

Back Comb, Art Nouveau, tortoise shell, gilt brass and turquoise glass accents	125.00
Barrette, 4″, bar type, tortoise shell type with rhinestones	10.00
Bodkin	
Celluloid, Art Nouveau, imitation tortoise shell, sinuous contours, pique, rhinestones	8.00
Sterling Silver, emb Greek Key type design	40.00
Comb, ivory	
Art Nouveau, paste stones, French, c1910	45.00
Oriental, Victorian, c1860	145.00
Hairpin, Victorian, tortoise shell, 14K gold piercework, c1870	125.00
Ornament	
Plastic, 4½″, simulated stones, c1935	65.00
Rhinestones, 4¾″, simulated pearls, c1925	45.00
Ornamental Comb, 7¼ x 6″, plastic piercework, imitation blue stones, Art Nouveau	75.00
Pompadour Comb, pr, Art Nouveau, faux tortoise shell, gilt brass and turquoise glass accents	75.00

HALL CHINA COMPANY

History: Robert Hall founded the Hall China Company in 1903 in East Liverpool, Ohio. He died in 1904 and was succeeded by his son, Robert Taggart Hall. After years of experimentation, Robert T. Hall developed a leadless glaze in 1911,

opening the way for production of glazed household products.

The Hall China Company made many types of kitchenware, refrigerator sets, and dinnerware in a wide variety of patterns. Some patterns were exclusive, such as Heather Rose for Sears.

One of the most popular patterns was Autumn Leaf, an exclusive premium designed in 1933 for the Jewel Tea Company by Arden Richards. Still a Jewel Tea property, Autumn Leaf has not been listed in catalogs since 1978 but is produced on a replacement basis with the date stamped on the back.

References: Harvey Duke, *Superior Quality Hall China*, ELO Books, 1977; Harvey Duke, *Hall 2*, ELO Books, 1985; Harvey Duke, *The Official Price Guide To Pottery And Porcelain*, Collector Books, 1989; Margaret and Kenn Whitmyer, *The Collector's Encyclopedia of Hall China*, Collector Books, 1989, 1992 value update.

Periodical: *The Hall China Encore*, 317 N. Pleasant St., Oberlin, OH 44074.

Additional Listings: See *Warman's Americana & Collectibles* for more examples plus a separate section on Autumn Leaf.

Autumn Leaf, casserole, cov, 8½″ d, $25.00.

MISCELLANEOUS

Ashtray, advertising, Dresler Hotel, green, match stand	12.50
Bowl, cov, 7″ d, blue, Westinghouse	25.00
Coffeepot, Cube, ivory	30.00
Roaster, cov, canary, Westinghouse	20.00
Water Server, cov, blue, Westinghouse	45.00

PATTERNS

Autumn Leaf. Premium for Jewel Tea Co. Produced from 1933 until 1978.

Bean Pot	90.00
Cake Plate	14.00
Clock, electric	345.00
Coffeepot, electrical	240.00
Jug, ball	25.00
Mixing Bowl, 3 pcs	40.00

Pitcher, ear shaped handle	18.00
Plate	
7¼" d	4.00
9" d	7.50
Platter, 13½" l	15.00
Range Shakers and dripping jar, set . .	30.00
Sifter, metal	140.00
Vegetable, oval, cov	36.00

Heather Rose. Produced during the 1940s.

Bowl, oval	8.00
Coffeepot, "Terrace"	30.00
Fruit Dish, 5¼" d	3.00
Platter, 15½" l	14.00
Pitcher	12.00

Orange Poppy. Premium for Great American Tea Co. Produced from 1933 through 1950s.

Bean Pot	55.00
Drip Jar, cov	17.00
Jug, ball	32.00
Salad Bowl	13.00
Teapot, Boston	55.00

Rose Parade. Kitchenware line introduced in the 1940s.

Baker, French	15.00
Bean Pot, tab handle	35.00
Bowl, 7½" d, straight–sided #4	14.00
Drip Jar, tab handle	16.00
Jug, 7½" h, "Pert"	25.00

Springtime. Premium for Standard Tea Co. Limited production.

Ball jug, #3	27.00
Batter Bowl, Chinese red	47.00
Bowl	
6" d, cereal	6.00
9" d, round	14.00
Casserole, thick rim	25.00
Drip Coffee	75.00
Gravy Boat	18.00
Jug, Radiance, #6	25.00
Plate, 8¼" d	4.00
Platter, 14" l	9.00
Soup, flat	9.00

TEAPOTS

Aladdin, black and gold	40.00
Doughnut, ivory	125.00
Globe, dripless, cadet and gold	175.00
Los Angeles, brown and gold	40.00
Nautilus, yellow, 6 cup	65.00
Philadelphia, pink, gold label	35.00
Plume, pink	25.00

Windcrest, yellow	55.00
Windshield, maroon and gold	35.00

HAMPSHIRE POTTERY

History: In 1871 James S. Taft founded the Hampshire Pottery Company in Keene, New Hampshire. Production began with redwares and stonewares, followed by majolica decorated wares in 1879. A semi-porcelain, with the recognizable matte glazes plus the Royal Worcester glaze, was introduced in 1883.

Until World War I the factory made an extensive line of utilitarian and art wares including souvenir items. After the war the firm resumed operations, but only made hotel dinnerware and tiles. The company was dissolved in 1923.

Reference: Joan Pappas and A. Harold Kendall, *Hampshire Pottery Manufactured by J. S. Taft & Company, Keene, New Hampshire,* published by author, 1971.

Pitcher, transfer printed, Long Rock, Apostle Islands, Ashland, WI, red decal mark, 7¾" h, $120.00.

Bowl, 6½" d, 2½" h, blue, molded cattails	65.00
Candlestick, chamber type, mottled blue–gray and green, black glaze . .	175.00
Chocolate Pot, 9½" h, cream, holly dec	265.00
Compote, 13¼" d, ftd, two handles, ivy pattern, light green highlights, cream ground, red decal mark	150.00
Inkwell, 4⅛" d, 2¾" h, round, large center hole for ink, three holes for pens	90.00
Mug, East Hampton Library, scenic . . .	50.00
Nappy, 9" d, violets dec, ivory ground, artist sgd	75.00
Tankard, 8¼" h, cylindrical, imp abstract	

floral design, green matte, imp
"Hampshire" **165.00**
Vase
3½" h, narrow mouth, spherical body,
four raised leaves, mottled brown
matte glaze, imp mark, c1910 . . **260.00**
6" h, opalescent green glaze, raised
petal motif, marked "M" in circle . **90.00**
8" h, narrow rim, large bulbous body,
wavy leaf dec, mottled blue glaze,
imp marks, c1905 . . . . **375.00**
12¼" h, short neck, tapering cylindrical, matte blue glaze, imp mark and
"H" within circle, discolored paper
label, c1910 . . . . **415.00**

HAND PAINTED CHINA

History: Hand painting on china began in the
Victorian era and remained popular through the
1920s. It was considered an accomplished art form
for women in the upper and upper middle class
households. It developed first in England, but
spread rapidly to the Continent and America.

China factories in Europe, America, and the Orient made the blanks. Belleek, Haviland, Limoges,
and Rosenthal are among the European firms.
American firms include A. H. Hews Co., Cambridge, Massachusetts; Willetts Mfg. Co., Trenton,
New Jersey; and Knowles, Taylor and Knowles,
East Liverpool, Ohio. Nippon blanks from Japan
were used heavily during the early 20th century.

The quality and design of the blank is a key
factor in pricing. Some blanks were very elaborate.
Many pieces were signed and dated by the artist.

Aesthetics is critical. Value is added to a piece
when a decorator goes beyond the standard forms
and creates a unique and pleasing design.

Bread Tray, 12", oval, open handles,
roses, artist sgd **50.00**
Compote, 8⅞" d, 5½" h, shallow, pink

**Plate, red roses, sgd "Georgianna
Francis," 8¼" d, $15.00.**

roses, green leaves, artist sgd, dated
1907 . . . . **125.00**
Cup and Saucer, floral dec, marked
"Clairon Ohme, Silesia," c1870 . . . . **35.00**
Dish, 6½ x 10½", oval, strawberries and
leafy vines, gold trim, loop handle on
one edge, marked "Selb, Bavaria" . **55.00**
Hair Receiver, violet dec, blue and
white, Limoges blank **50.00**
Hatpin Holder, 5", blue forget–me–nots,
marked "Austria" **35.00**
Jug, 5¾", green and purple grapes,
green leaves, gold trim **90.00**
Milk Pitcher, 7" h, white, porcelain, basketweave, yellow flowers, green leaf
handle **17.50**
Plate
8½" d, pink roses, green ground, gold
border, Limoges **40.00**
9⅜" d, cavalier and lady scene, artist
sgd "D.L.R.L.," marked "Limoges,
France" **100.00**
9½" roses, Elite, France **20.00**
Platter, 23½", yellow roses, green
leaves, gold trim, artist sgd, marked
"Haviland" **240.00**
Sugar Shaker, 3½" d, 4½" h, blue and
white, pink roses, green leaves, gold
top and feet **45.00**
Tankard, 14½", green and purple
grapes, green leaves, Lenox blank . **175.00**
Teapot, 5", purple violets, green leaves,
gold trim, Lenox blank **125.00**
Tobacco Jar, 7¼" h, multicolored Indian
bust, gold trim and finial, artist sgd
"Florence Weaver, 1925," blank
marked "Favorite, Bavaria" **200.00**
Tray, 8⅝" l, floral dec, two handles, artist
sgd, marked "L. Haviland, France" . **55.00**
Trinket Box, 4½ x 3½ x 1½", yellow,
porcelain, couple and woodland setting, marked "JBH #121815, France" **75.00**
Vase, 5", black ground, white orchids,
artist sgd, marked "Rosenthal" **100.00**

HATPINS AND HATPIN HOLDERS

History: When the vogue for oversized hats developed around 1850, hatpins became popular.
Designers used a variety of materials to decorate
the pin ends, including china, crystal, enamel, gem
stones, precious metals, and shells. Decorative
subjects ranged from commemorative designs to
insects.

Hatpin holders are porcelain containers which
set on a dresser to hold these pins. The holders
were produced by major manufacturers, among
which were Meissen, Nippon, R. S. Germany, R.
S. Prussia, and Wedgwood.

Reference: Lillian Baker, *Handbook for Hatpins*

& *Hatpin Holders,* Collector Books, 1983; 1988 value update.

Collectors' Club: International Club for Collectors of Hatpins and Hatpin Holders, 15237 Chanera Avenue, Gardena, CA, 90249.

Museum: Los Angeles Art Museum, Costume Dept., Los Angeles, CA.

HATPINS

Amethyst, serpent around body, Victorian, 12″ l	85.00
Art Deco, plique–a–jour, two baroque pearls	385.00
Bakelite, black fluted disc with silver accents, rhinestone	35.00
Black Glass, faceted ball, painted top, 8″ l	25.00
Brass, openwork, amber setting	45.00
Carnival Glass, figural, rooster, amber	35.00
Garnet, Etruscean granulation, round, c1860	85.00
Hand Painted China, violets, gold trim	25.00
Ivory, ball shape, carved design	65.00
Jet, faceted top	25.00
Mercury Glass, elongated cased teardrop	70.00
Plique–a–jour, dome shape, green	675.00
Rhinestone, studded, 1½″ d	25.00
Satsuma	
Birds	245.00
Geisha Girls	245.00
Schafer & Vater, pink bisque on tan ground, relief molded lady's head on top, relief molded sphinx on base	185.00
Silverplated, tennis racquet shape	25.00
Sterling Silver	
Art Nouveau design, four sided, 12″ l	85.00
Charles Horner	55.00

Holder, violets, blue–green ground, marked "BT Co., Japan," 5″ h, $75.00.

HATPIN HOLDERS

Bavarian	
Floral twist ribs, marked "Z S & Co"	65.00
Irid luster, white ground, gold handles rising from bottom to top, marked "H & C Selb, Bavaria"	85.00
Mother–of–Pearl dec, marked "H & C Bavaria"	65.00
Belleek, 5¼″ h, relief pink and maroon floral dec with green leaves, gold top, marked "Willets Belleek," dated 1911	125.00
Hand Painted, 4″ h, violets, gold trim and beading	75.00
Limoges, grapes, pink roses, matte finish, artist sgd	60.00
Nippon, hp	
Clover dec	45.00
Pink florals, gold trim	75.00
Royal Bayreuth	
Figural, owl	400.00
Tapestry, portrait of lady wearing hat, blue mark	575.00
Schlegelmilch	
R S Germany, lily dec	75.00
R S Prussia, floral dec, gold trim, ftd	185.00

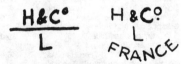

HAVILAND CHINA

History: In 1842, American china importer David Haviland moved to Limoges, France, where he began manufacturing and decorating china specifically for the U.S. market. Haviland is synonymous with fine, white, translucent porcelain, although early hand painted patterns were generally larger and darker colored on heavier whiteware blanks than are later ones.

David revolutionized French china factories by both manufacturing the whiteware blank and decorating it at the same site. In addition, Haviland and Company pioneered the use of decals in decorating china.

David's sons, Charles Edward and Theodore, split the company in 1892. Theodore opened an American division in 1936 which continues until today. In 1941 Theodore bought out Charles Edward's heirs and recombined both companies under the original name of H. and Co. The Haviland family sold its interests in 1981.

Charles Field Haviland, cousin of Charles Edward and Theodore, worked for, and then ran, the Casseaux Works after his marriage in 1857 until 1882. Items continued to carry his name as decorator until 1941.

Haviland patterns were not consistently named until after 1926. Pattern identification is difficult because of the similarity found in the over 66,000 patterns that have been made. Numbers assigned by Arlene Schleiger and illustrated in her books have become the identification standard for matching.

References: Mary Frank Gaston, *Haviland Collectibles & Art Objects*, Collector Books, 1984; Arlene Schleiger, *Two Hundred Patterns of Haviland China, Books I–V*, published by author, 1950–1977.

Bone Dish, Pansy, Ragged Robin, gray and pink, 1885 mark	25.00
Bouillon, matching saucer, Rajah pattern, marked "Theo Haviland"	20.00
Bowl	
6", oatmeal, scalloped edge with gold	18.00
7½", soup, "Troy," blue scroll, pink flower border	16.00
8", hp, yellow roses, marked "Haviland"	35.00
Butter Dish, Gold Band, Theo Hav	45.00
Butter Pat, sq, rounded corners, gold trim	10.00
Cake Plate, 10", gold handles and border	35.00
Celery Dish, scalloped edge, green flowers, pale pink scroll	45.00
Cream Soup and Saucer, scroll border in cranberry and blue	30.00
Creamer and Sugar	
Gold Band, 1930s, Theo Hav	45.00
Rajah pattern, marked "Theo Haviland"	20.00
Scalloped, small pink flowers, gold trim	65.00
Cup and Saucer	
Coffee, scalloped gold edge, deep pink flowers	30.00
Tea, small blue flowers, green leaves	25.00
Demitasse Cup and Saucer, 1885	30.00
Dinner Set	
Service of 8, pink flowers, 55 pcs, H and Co	900.00
Service of 12, Gold Band, 77 pcs, Theo Hav	1,200.00

Gravy Boat and Underplate, small pink and blue florals, red "Theodore Haviland, Limoges France" mark, 8″ l, $45.00.

Gravy Boat	
Oval, pink flowers, blue ribbon, H and Co	45.00
Round, tray, double handles and lips, navy and rust, Theo Hav	35.00
Ink Blotter, hp violets and foliage dec, marked "Haviland"	35.00
Oyster Plate, 9", blue and pink flowers, marked "Haviland & Co"	80.00
Plate	
6", bread and butter, Rajah pattern, marked "Theo Haviland"	5.00
7", salad, Rajah pattern, marked "Theo Haviland"	9.00
7½", bread and butter, gold scalloped edge, pink flowers	16.00
8½", gold, pink clover, ornate border, 1905	40.00
9", luncheon	
Frontenac	18.00
Whiteware, hp, pink rose, sgd H and Co	22.00
9½", dinner, "Princess," H and Co	22.00
9¾", dinner, white, scalloped edge	20.00
Platter	
12", turquoise morning glories, gold scalloped edge	35.00
16", gold band, scalloped end handles, Theo Hav	55.00
22", deep pink flowers, two wells, fancy gold edges	75.00
Relish Dish, blue and pink flowers	25.00
Soup Plate	
7½", Eden pattern, marked "Theo Haviland"	15.00
9½", olive and rust flowers, 1885 mark	22.00
Vegetable Dish, cov, small pink roses, gold edges	65.00

HEISEY GLASS

History: The A. H. Heisey Glass Co. began producing glasswares in April, 1896, in Newark, Ohio. Heisey was not a newcomer to the field, having been associated with the craft since his youth.

Many blown and molded patterns were produced in crystal, colored, milk (opalescent), and Ivorina Verde (custard) glass. Decorative techniques of cutting, etching, and silver deposit were employed. Glass figurines were introduced in 1933 and continued until 1957 when the factory ceased production. All Heisey glass is notable for its clarity. Not all Heisey glassware is marked with the familiar "H" within a diamond.

References: Neila Bredehoft, *The Collector's Encyclopedia of Heisey Glass, 1925–1938*, Collector Books, 1986; Mary Louise Burns, *Heisey's*

Glassware of Distinction, 2nd edition, published by author, 1983; Lyle Conder, *Collector's Guide To Heisey's Glassware for Your Table*, L-W Books, 1984; Tom Felt and Bob O'Grady, *Heisey Candlesticks, Candelabra, and Lamps*, Heisey Collectors of America, Inc, 1984; Frank L. Hahn and Paul Kikeli, *Collector's Guide to Heisey and Heisey by Imperial Glass Animals*, Golden Era Publications, 1991; Sandra Stoudt, *Heisey On Parade*, Wallace–Homestead, 1985.

Collectors' Club: Heisey Collectors of America, P.O. Box 4367, Newark, OH, 43055.

Museum: National Heisey Glass Museum, Newark, OH.

Reproduction Alert: Some Heisey molds were sold to Imperial Glass of Bellaire, Ohio, and certain items were reissued. These pieces may be mistaken for the original Heisey. Some of the reproductions were produced in colors which were never made by Heisey and have become collectible in their own right.

Examples include: the Colt family in Crystal, Carmel Slag, Ultra Blue, and Horizon Blue; the mallard with wings up in Carmel Slag; Whirlpool (Provincial) in crystal and colors; and Waverly, 7" oval footed compote in Carmel Slag.

Ashtray	
Empress, Alexandrite	140.00
Lariat, 4" d	12.00
Orchid, sq	30.00
Bonbon, Lariat, hp, 7½" d	95.00
Bowl	
Crystolite, 12" d	30.00
Empress, crystal, dolphin ftd, sterling floral overlay, 11" d	60.00
Lariat, centerpiece, crimped, 11" d	30.00
Orchid, 12" d	60.00
Queen Ann, etched, 9" d	70.00
Waverly, tea rose, 13" d	70.00
Butter Dish, cov	
Orchid, 6" d	178.00
Rose, etched	175.00
Cake Plate, Crystolite	325.00
Cake Stand, Plantation	80.00
Candlesticks, pr	
Artic Empress, round base	125.00
Charter Oak, Flamingo pink, three lights	155.00
New Era, crystal, 2 lights, bobeche	110.00
Old Williamsburg, 11" h	235.00
Orchid, triple light	85.00
Ridgeleigh, 4" d base	45.00
Candleblock, Crystolite, round	10.00
Candy Basket, Lariat, Moonglo cutting	45.00
Candy Dish, cov	
Continental	195.00
Crystolite, three toes	50.00
Celery Tray	
Greek Key, 9" l	24.00
King Arthur, diamond optic, hand dec, 11" l	24.00

Marigold	25.00
Champagne	
Colonial	12.00
Fairacre, Flamingo pink stem and foot	25.00
Penn Charter, Flamingo pink	30.00
Saturn	20.00
Stanhope, zircon blue–green	55.00
Cheese Dish, Empress, etched, pink, 6" d	15.00
Cheese Server, Rose, 14" d	150.00
Cigarette Set, Ridgeleigh, box, two matching ashtrays	35.00
Claret, Colonial	14.00
Coaster	
Colonial	10.00
Lariat	8.00
Cocktail	
Arcadia cut	17.00
Lariat, Moonglo cutting	18.00
Old Sandwich, Sahara	20.00
Orchid	40.00
Rooster stem, Moonglo cutting, pr	195.00
Seahorse stem, clear	140.00
Cocktail Shaker, Ipswich	275.00
Cologne Bottle, Winged Scroll, emerald	75.00
Cordial, Oxford	39.00
Creamer and Sugar	
Empress, Moongleam, matching tray	195.00
Old Dominion, Sahara	65.00
Orchid	65.00
Queen Ann, Minuet etching, dolphin feet	75.00
Cruet, stopper	
Crystolite, clear	25.00
Plantation	125.00
Provincal, clear	45.00
Victorian, diagonal cut stopper	30.00
Yeoman, Moongleam	85.00
Cup and Saucer, Empress, Sahara	43.00
Custard, Colonial	5.00
Egg Cup, Raised Loop	25.00
Floral Bowl, Twist, Sahara	60.00
Flower Holder, figural, kingfisher, Flamingo pink	200.00
Goblet	
Colonial	14.00
Crystolite, Arcadia cutting	20.00
Fairacre, Flamingo pink stem and foot	35.00
Pied Piper etching	18.00
Spanish	30.00
Ice Bucket, Twist, Moongleam, orig tongs	100.00
Iced Tea, Orchid	40.00
Jelly Compote	
Empress, Sahara, 6" h	30.00
Prince of Wales Plumes, crystal, gold trim	50.00
Waverly, 6½" d	40.00
Jug, Greek Key, three pints	175.00
Mayonnaise, liner, Rose	85.00
Mint Dish, Empress, etched, pink, 6" d	15.00
Oyster Cocktail, Ipswich, crystal, 4 oz	15.00

Parfait, Albermale, green base	35.00

Plate
Colonial, 4½" d	8.00
Crystolite, 7" d	7.00

Preserves Bowl, Empress, Sahara, two
handles, 5" d	30.00

Punch Bowl Set, Chrysanthemum, 15
pcs	495.00

Relish
Crystolite, five part, round, 10" d . . .	40.00
Lariat, three part, Moonglo cutting, 10" d	35.00
Orchid, three part	60.00
Ridgeleigh, two part	24.00

Salt and Pepper Shakers, pr
Empress, Sahara, ftd	130.00
Provincial, crystal	30.00
Sauce, 2 pcs, Rose	50.00

Server, center handle, King Arthur, dia-
mond optic, hand dec	40.00

Sherbet, Victorian pattern, ftd, sgd, $20.00.

Sherbet
Arcadia Cut, 4" h	15.00
Lariat, Moonglo cutting	18.00
Puritan, ruffled	12.00
Sherry, Colonial, 2 oz	10.00
Soup, Pleat and Panel, green	18.00
Sugar, Crystolite, individual	12.00

Tumbler
Old Sandwich	25.00
Orchid	50.00
Spanish cut, 12 oz, ftd	25.00
Water Bottle, Greek Key	200.00

Water Set, King Arthur, diamond optic,
hand dec, ftd pitcher, six matching
goblets	225.00

HOLLY AMBER

History: Holly Amber, originally called Golden Agate, was produced by the Indiana Tumbler and Goblet Works of the National Glass Co., Greentown, Indiana. Jacob Rosenthal created the color in 1902. Holly Amber is a gold colored glass with a marbleized onyx color on raised parts.

A new pattern, Holly [No. 450], was designed by Frank Jackson for Golden Agate. Between January 1903 and June 1903, more than 35 items were made in this pattern; the factory was destroyed by fire in June.

References: Brenda Measell and James Measell, *A Guide To Reproductions of Greentown Glass, 2nd Edition,* The Printing Press, 1974; James Measell, *Greentown Glass, The Indiana Tumbler & Goblet Co.,* Grand Rapids Public Museum, 1979.

Collectors' Club: National Greentown Glass Association, 1807 West Madison Street, Kokomo, IN 46901.

Museums: Greentown Glass Museum, Greentown, IN; Grand Rapids Public Museum [Ruth Herrick Greentown Glass Collection], MI.

Additional Listing: Greentown Glass.

Compote, 7⅜" d, 6¾" h, $875.00.

Bowl, 8½" d, berry	375.00
Butter, cov, 7¼ x 6¼"	1,200.00
Cake Stand	2,000.00

Compote
4¾" d, jelly, open	450.00
8½" d, 12" h, cov	1,800.00
Creamer, 4½" h	425.00
Cruet, 6½" h, orig stopper	2,100.00
Honey, cov	750.00
Match Holder	400.00
Mug, 4½" h, several heat lines on rim .	330.00
Nappy	375.00
Parfait	575.00
Relish, oval	275.00
Salt and Pepper Shakers, pr	500.00
Sauce	225.00
Spooner	425.00
Sugar, open	425.00
Syrup, 5¾" h, silverplated hinged lid . .	2,000.00
Toothpick Holder	375.00
Tumbler	350.00

HORN

History: For centuries horns from animals have been used for various items, e.g., drinking cups, spoons, powder horns, and small dishes. Some pieces of horn have designs scratched in them. Around 1880 furniture made from the horns of Texas longhorn steers was popular in Texas and the southwestern United States.

Additional Listings: Firearm Accessories.

Spoon, monogrammed "MBL, 1907," figural thistle terminal, hallmarked, 5½″ l, $45.00.

Calling Card Case, horn and ivory, floral
  design **40.00**
Comb Case, 7½ x 9″, pocket, diamond
  shape mirror **35.00**
Chair, arched back, brass acorn finial,
  splayed legs, upholstered seat miss-
  ing, American or German, late 19th
  C, pr **2,000.00**
Shoehorn, scratched carved, 1756 . . .   **65.00**
Spoon, 5½″, thistle, monogrammed
  "MBL, 1907," hallmarked **45.00**
Stand, Victorian, four horns form legs,
  American Southwest, 19th C **275.00**
Tea Caddy, 12¼ x 9¼ x 7½″, tapering
  ribbed sides and cov, wide plain bor-
  der, claw and ball feet, lobed domical
  flowerhead knop, dark stain, Anglo–
  Indian, c1815 . . . .   **900.00**

HULL POTTERY

History: In 1905 Addis E. Hull purchased the Acme Pottery Company, Crooksville, Ohio. In 1917 the A. E. Hull Pottery Company began making a line of art pottery, novelties, stoneware, and kitchenware, later including the famous Little Red Riding Hood line. Most items had a matte finish with shades of pink and blue or brown predominating.

After a disastrous flood and fire in 1950, J. Brandon Hull reopened the factory in 1952 as the Hull Pottery Company. New, more modern style molds, mostly with glossy finish, were produced. The company currently produces pieces, e.g. the Regal and Floraline lines, for sale to florists.

Hull pottery molds and patterns are easily identified. Pre–1950 vases are marked "Hull USA" or "Hull Art USA" on the bottom. Many also retain their paper labels. Post–1950 pieces are marked "Hull" in large script or "HULL" in block letters.

Each pattern has a distinctive number, e.g., Wildflower with a "W" and number, Waterlily with an "L" and number, Poppy with 600 numbers, Orchid with 300 numbers, etc. Early stone pieces have an H.

References: Brenda Roberts, *The Collectors Encyclopedia Of Hull Pottery,* Collector Books, 1980, 1989 value update; Joan Hull, *Hull: The Heavenly Pottery,* published by author, 1990; Mark E. Supnick, *Collecting Hull Pottery's "Little Red Riding Hood": A Pictorial Reference and Price Guide,* L–W Book Sales, 1989.

Additional Listings: See *Warman's Americana & Collectibles* for more examples.

Advisor: Joan Hull.

Vase, Wildflower, green shaded to pink, marked "Hull Art/U.S.A./W–12–9½," 9½″ h, $35.00.

PRE–1950 (MATTE)

Bowknot
  Basket, B–12, 10½″ h **495.00**
  Cornucopia, B–5, 6½″ h **95.00**
  Vase
    B–3, 6½″ h **75.00**
    B–9, 8½″ h **150.00**
  Wall Pitcher, B–26, 6″ h **125.00**
Calla Lily (Jack–in–the–Pulpit)
  Pitcher, 506/33, 10″ h **195.00**
  Vase
    500/33, 6″ h **65.00**
    510/33, 8″ h **95.00**
Dogwood (Wild Rose)
  Bowl, low, 521, 7″ d **85.00**
  Suspended Vase, 502, 6½″ h **135.00**
  Vase, 504, 8½″ h **85.00**
Iris
  Vase
    402, 4¾″h **45.00**
    405, 7″ h **85.00**
    414, 10½″ h **125.00**
Little Red Riding Hood, Pat. Des. No. 135889 USA
  Bank, standing, 7″ h **475.00**

Canisters, set	450.00
Creamer and Sugar, crawling, pr	400.00
Spice Jar	350.00

Magnolia

Pitcher, 18, 13½″ h	200.00

Vase

3, 8½″ h	60.00
8, 10½″ h	80.00
13, 4¾″ h	30.00

Open Rose (Camelia)

Cornucopia, 101, 8½″h	75.00
Jardiniere, ram's head	200.00
Pitcher, 105, 7″ h	95.00
Tea Set, 110, 111, 112	250.00

Orchid

Vase

301, 4¾″ h	50.00
303, 6″ h	70.00
304, 10½″ h	225.00

Poppy

Cornucopia Bowl, 602, 6½″ d	200.00

Vase

606, 8½″ h	125.00
607, 6½″ h	75.00

Rosella

Vase

R–1, 5″ h	25.00
R–6, 6½″h	60.00
R–15, 8½″ h	50.00

Stoneware

Jardiniere, 551H, 7″ h	60.00
Vase, 26H, 8″ h	40.00
Thistle, vase, 6½″ h	65.00

Tulip

Jardiniere, 115–33, 7″ h	175.00
Pitcher, 109–33, 8″ h	100.00
Vase, 101–33, 6″ h	55.00

Waterlily

Basket, L–14, 10½″ h	225.00
Pitcher, L–3, 5½″ h	40.00
Vase, L–10, 9½″ h	85.00

Wildflower

Cornucopia, W–7, 7½″ h	55.00

Vase

53, 8½″ h	125.00
56, 4½″h	55.00
W–5, 6½″ h	45.00
W–18, 12½″ h	125.00

Woodland

Cornucopia, double, W–23, 14″ h	225.00
Jardiniere, W–7, 5¼″ h	65.00
Vase, W–1, 5½″ h	40.00

POST 1950 (GLOSSY)

Blossom Flite

Basket, T–4, 8½″ h	35.00
Tea Set, T–14, 14, 16	125.00

Butterfly

Lavobo Set, B–24, 25	90.00
Vase, B–14, 10½″ h	40.00
Window Box, B–8, 12¾″ l	35.00

Capri

Ashtray, C–52	40.00
Flower Bowl, C–46	30.00

Continental

Basket, hanging, C–58, 13¾″ h	60.00
Vase, C–53, 8½″ h	35.00

Ebb Tide

Ashtray, mermaid, E–8	100.00
Vase, twin fish, E–2, 7″ h	45.00

Imperial

Planter

Dancing Lady	50.00
Goblet, F–3	5.00
Rectangular, A–4	50.00

Novelty

Figure, goose, large, F–23	50.00

Planter

Green	10.00
Kitten	40.00
Parrot, 60	30.00

Royal

Jardiniere, 75, 6″ h	20.00
Vase, W–4, 6¼″ h	25.00

Serenade

Vase

S 1, 6″ h	20.00
S 11, 10¼″ h	65.00
S 17, 8½″ h	35.00

Tokay/Tuscany

Basket, 6, 8″ h	65.00
Cornucopia, 1, 6½″ h	25.00
Vase, 8, 10″ h	75.00
Tropicana, vase, 54, 12½″ h	250.00

Woodland

Vase, W–4, 6½″ h	35.00
Wall Pocket, shell	40.00

HUMMEL ITEMS

History: Hummel items are the original creations of Berta Hummel, born in 1909 in Massing, Bavaria, Germany. At age 18, she was enrolled in the Academy of Fine Arts in Munich to further her mastery of drawing and the palette. Berta entered the Convent of Siessen and became Sister Maria

Innocentia in 1934. In this Franciscan cloister, she continued drawing and painting images of her childhood friends.

In 1935 W. Goebel Co. in Rodental, Germany, began reproducing Sister Maria Innocentia's sketches into three-dimensional bisque figurines. The Schmid Brothers of Randolph, Massachusetts, introduced the figurines to America and became Goebel's U.S. distributor.

In 1967 Goebel began distributing Hummel items in the U.S. A controversy developed between the two companies involving the Hummel family and the convent. Law suits and countersuits ensued. The German courts finally effected a compromise. The convent held legal rights to all works produced by Sister Maria Innocentia from 1934 until her death in 1946 and licensed Goebel to reproduce these works. Schmid was to deal directly with the Hummel family for permission to reproduce any pre–convent art.

All authentic Hummels bear both the signature M.I. Hummel and a Goebel trademark. Various trademarks were used to identify the year of production. The Crown Mark (CM) was used in 1935, Full Bee (FB) 1940–1959; Small Stylized Bee (SSB) 1960–1972; Large Stylized Bee (LSB) 1960–1963; Three Line Mark (3L) 1964–1972; Last Bee Mark (LB) 1972–1980, Missing Bee Mark (MB) 1979–1991. In 1991, a new Crown Mark was introduced which includes the restored name of Germany as a single country.

References: John F. Hotchkiss, *Hummel Art II*, Wallace–Homestead, 1981; Carl F. Luckey, *Luckey's Hummel Figurines and Plates, 8th Edition*, Books Americana, 1990; Lawrence L. Wonsch, *Hummel Copycats With Values*, Wallace–Homestead, 1987.

Collectors' Clubs: Hummel Collectors Club, P.O. Box 257, Yardley, PA 19067; M.I. Hummel Club, Goebel Plaza, P.O. Box 11, Pennington, NJ, 08534.

Additional Listings: See *Warman's Americana & Collectibles* for more examples.

Ashtray, Joyful, #33, CM, 3½ x 6" . . .	325.00
Bookends, pr	
Apple Tree Boy and Apple Tree Girl, #252A&B, SSB	250.00
Bookworms, #14/A&B, SSB	300.00
Strolling Along, #5, CM	275.00
Candleholder	
Silent Night, #54, LB	175.00
Watchful Angel, #194, FB	400.00
Candy Box	
Happy Pastime, #III/69, 3L	125.00
Joyful, #III/53, 3L	115.00
Figurine	
Adoration, #23/II, CM	750.00
Auf Widersehen, #153/0, LB	130.00
Baker, #128, SSB	85.00
Band Leader, #129, LB	120.00
Be Patient, #197/2/0, FB	125.00

Figure, Chick Girl, #57/0, stylized bee mark, $95.00.

Bird Duet, #169, 3L	90.00
Boy With Toothache, #217, 3L	110.00
Celestial Musician, #188	80.00
Chick Girl, #57/0, FB	100.00
Chicken Licken, #385, 3L	100.00
Chimney Sweep, 122/0, LB	70.00
Close Harmony, #336	100.00
Congratulations, #17/0 (no socks), FB	225.00
Doll Bath, #319, 3L	130.00
Easter Time, #384, LB	85.00
Farewell, #65, LB	80.00
Feathered Friends, #344	80.00
Going To Grandma's, #51/0, FB . . .	175.00
Heavenly Angel, #21/0, SSB	75.00
Heavenly Lullaby, #262, LB	110.00
Joyful, #52/0, 3L	135.00
Just Resting, #112/3/0, LB	85.00
Kiss Me, #311, 3L	145.00
Knitting Lessons, #256, 3L	350.00
Little Goat Herder, #200/0, SSB . . .	120.00
Little Hiker, #16/2/0, FB	80.00
Little Pharmacist, #322, FB	2,500.00
March Winds, #43, LB	75.00
Mother's Darling, #175, FB	225.00
Not For You, #317, LB	130.00
Playmates, #58/I, SSB	150.00
Postman, #119, FB	145.00
Puppy Love, #1, CM	425.00
School Girls, #177/I, LB	900.00
She Loves Me, She Loves Me Not, #174, FB	175.00
Smart Little Sister, #346, 3L	100.00
Stargazer, #132, LB	50.00
Surprise, #94/3/0, FB	165.00
The Artist, #304, 3L	350.00
The Builder, #305, 3L	140.00
The Photographer, #178, SSB	140.00
To Market, #49/3/0, FB	195.00
Umbrella Boy, #152/A/II, CM	2,000.00

Village Boy, #51/3/0, CM	115.00
Wayside Devotion, #28/III, CM	1,300.00
Which Hand?, #258, SSB	350.00
Font	
Angel Cloud, #206, LB, 2¼ x 4¾" .	40.00
Child With Flowers, #36/I, SSB . . .	100.00
Child Jesus, #26/0, 3L	30.00
Guardian Angel, #248, 3L, 2¼ x 5½"	50.00
Holy Family, #246, SB, 3 x 4"	65.00
Seated Angel, #167, FB, 3¼ x 4¼"	75.00
Music Box, Little Band, #388M, 3L . . .	250.00
Plaque	
Ba–Bee Rings, #30/OA&B, FB	250.00
Madonna, #48/0, CM, 3 x 4"	250.00
Mail Coach, #140, LB, 4½ x 6¼" . .	135.00
Merry Wanderer, #92, FB, 4¾ x 5⅛"	185.00
Table Lamp	
Culprits, #44/A, FB	350.00
Happy Days, #235, LB	280.00

IMARI

History: Imari derives its name from a Japanese port city. Although Imari ware was manufactured in the 17th century, the wares most commonly encountered are those made between 1770 and 1900.

Early Imari was decorated simply, quite unlike the later heavily decorated brocade pattern commonly associated with Imari. Most of the decorative patterns are an underglaze blue and overglaze "seal wax" red supported by turquoise and yellow.

The Chinese copied Imari ware. Important differences of the Japanese type include grayer clay, thicker glaze, runny and darker blue, and deep red opaque hues.

The pattern and colors of Imari inspired many English and European potteries, such as Derby and Meissen, to adopt a similar style of decoration for their wares.

Reference: Sandra Andacht, *Oriental Antiques & Art: An Identification And Value Guide*, Wallace-Homestead, 1987.

Reproduction Alert: Reproductions abound, and many manufacturers continue to produce pieces in the traditional style.

Bowl
    7¼" d, steep sides, low ring foot, central medallion of garden setting surrounded reserves of phoenix in flight and diaper patterns alternating with blue and gilt painted bands and floral shaped reserves, 19th C   **385.00**
    8" d, scalloped **140.00**
    9½" d, figural dec, brocade ground .   **275.00**
Charger
    17¾" d, painted underglaze blue and polychrome enamels, landscape scene, reserve ground of scattered floral and geometric pattern roun-

Vase, blue birds flying over water, white ground, blue rim border, 9½" h, $145.00.

    dels, linked diamond rim band, 19th C **715.00**
    18⅛" d, shaped reserve character encircled with radiating panels with alternating dragon, floral, and geometric motifs, precious emblems on underside, 19th C **1,210.00**
    25¾" d, sloping int., randomly scattered book and fan shape reserves int., cobalt blue flowers and scrolling tendrils ext., lappet band around ring foot, Meiji Period **3,850.00**
Creamer and Sugar, 5½" creamer, 5⅞" cov sugar, ovoid, dragon form handles, gilt and bright enamels, shaped reserves, dragon–like beasts, stylized animal medallions, brocade ground, high dome lid, knob, cipher mark of Mount Fuji and Fukagama Studio marks, Meiji period **500.00**
Jar, 27½", cov, ovoid, narrow foot, continuous scene of blossoming sakura shrouding pavilion complex, narrow neck band of interlocking foliage spirals, domed lid, shishi finial **715.00**
Jardiniere, 10", hexagonal, bulbous, short flared foot, alternating bijin figures and immortal symbols, stylized ground **250.00**
Plate
    9", wide everted rim, central medallion of Chinese scholars seated on garden terrace, blossoming plum tree, gilt highlights, Chinese, early 19th C **300.00**
    9⅝", gilt, multicolored enamels, and underglaze blue, irregular ho–o

and floral reserves, blue ground, foliate and cloud design, foliate edge, set of 6 . . . . **500.00**

Platter, 14", hexagonal, central reserve of flowers in vase, cavetto with floral reserves, scrolling branches, narrow blue band, Meiji period, pr **1,000.00**

Urn, 21" h, gilt bronze mounts, deep bowl, red, blue, and gilt floral dec, everted pierced collar, S scroll arms of leaves and cattails, mid band of plaited reeds, flaring porcelain base banded in bronze, pierced skirt interspersing four foliate clasps, pr **14,000.00**

Vase, 14½" h, lake and phoenix bird reserves, overall patterned ground, gilt highlights, Japanese, c1900 . . . **300.00**

IMPERIAL GLASS

History: Imperial Glass Co., Bellaire, Ohio, was organized in 1901. Its primary product was pattern (pressed) glass. Soon other lines were added including carnival glass, NUART, NUCUT, and NEAR CUT. In 1916 the company introduced "Free-Hand," a lustered art glass line, and "Imperial Jewels," an iridescent stretch glass that carried the Imperial cross trademark. In the 1930s the company was reorganized into the Imperial Glass Corporation and continues to produce a great variety of wares.

Imperial recently has acquired the molds and equipment of several other glass companies—Central, Cambridge and Heisey. Many of the "retired" molds of these companies are once again in use. The resulting reissues are marked to distinguish them from the originals.

References: Margaret and Douglas Archer, *Imperial Glass*, Collector Books, 1978; Frank L. Hahn and Paul Kikeli, *Collector's Guide to Heisey and Heisey by Imperial Glass Animals*, Golden Era Publications, 1991; National Imperial Glass Collector's Society, *Imperial Glass 1966 Catalog*, reprint, 1991 price guide, Antique Publications.

Collectors' Club: National Imperial Glass Collectors Society, P.O. Box 534, Bellaire, OH 43906.

Additional Listings: See Carnival Glass, Pattern Glass, and *Warman's Americana & Collectibles* for more examples of Candlewick.

Jack-In-The-Pulpit Vase, purple iridescent stretch glass, 10¼" h, $90.00.

ENGRAVED OR HAND CUT

Bowl, 6½" d, flower and leaf, molded star base **20.00**
Candlesticks, pr, 7" h, Amelia **32.00**
Celery Vase, three side stars, cut star base **25.00**
Nut Dish, 5½" d, Design No. 112 . . . . **15.00**
Pitcher, tankard, Design No. 110, flowers, foliage, and butterfly cutting . . . **50.00**
Plate, 5½" d, Design No. 12 . . . . **12.00**

JEWELS

Bowl, 6¼" d, purple Pearl Green luster, marked **75.00**
Candlesticks, blue luster, pr **50.00**
Compote, 7½" d, irid teal blue **60.00**
Rose Bowl, amethyst, green irid **75.00**
Vase, 6" h, irid pearl green and purple luster **135.00**

LUSTERED (FREE HAND)

Candlesticks, pr, 10¾" h, cobalt blue, white vine and leaf dec **325.00**
Hat, 9" w, ruffled rim, cobalt blue, embedded irid white vines and leaves **100.00**
Pitcher, 10" h, applied clear handle, pale yellow luster, white pulled loops . . . **225.00**
Rose Bowl, 6" d, irid orange, white floral cutting **75.00**
Vase
6" h, ovoid, tapering to short neck, flattened flared rim, orange irid int., white opal body, pulled blue and green leaf pads on vine, partial label **360.00**
10" h, gold luster neck, light green hearts and vines, white irid ground **300.00**

11¼" h, baluster, triangular pull-ups at mouth, opal opaque white ground, embedded irid blue trailing vines, orig paper label 325.00

NUART

Ashtray	18.00
Lamp Shade, marigold	50.00
Vase, 7" h, bulbous, irid green	125.00

NUCUT

Bowl, 4½" d, berry, handles	15.00
Celery Tray, 11" l	18.00
Creamer	17.50
Fern Dish, 8" l, brass lining, ftd	32.00
Orange Bowl, 12" d, Rose Marie	48.00
Punch Set, 13" d bowl, base, six cups, Rose Marie	175.00
Tumbler, flared rim, molded star	15.00

PRESSED

Ashtray, Cathay, jade	65.00
Bonbon, 5¼" d, D'Angelo, green, handle	18.00
Bowl, 9" d, satin irid, handles	20.00
Butter Dish, cov, Colonial, rose	50.00
Cheese Dish, cov, Monticello	35.00
Cordial, Wakefield, amber	20.00
Creamer and Sugar	
Cape Cod, clear	20.00
Flora, rose	15.00
Goblet, Cape Cod, red	15.00
Mayonnaise, underplate, Monaco, amber, orig spoon	20.00
Salt and Pepper Shakers, pr, Huckabee, aluminum tops	25.00
Sandwich Tray, black handle	25.00
Sweet Pea Vase, 4" h	15.00
Toothpick, ivory, orig label	18.00

INDIAN ARTIFACTS, AMERICAN

History: During the historic period there were approximately 350 tribes of Indians grouped into the following regions: Eskimo, Northeast and Woodland, Northwest Coast, Plains, and West and Southwest.

American Indian artifacts are quite popular. Currently the market is in a period of stability following a rapid increase of prices during the 1970s.

References: John W. Barry, *American Indian Pottery, 2nd Edition,* Books Americana, 1984; Harold S. Colton, *Hopi Kachina Dolls,* 15 printing, University of New Mexico Press, 1990; Robert Edler, *Early Archaic Indian Points & Knives,* Collector Books, 1990; Larry Frank, *Indian Silver Jewelry of the Southwest, 1868–1930,* Schiffer Publishing, Ltd., 1900; Lar Hothem, *Indian Artifacts of the Midwest,* Collector Books, 1991; Lar Hothem, *Arrowheads & Projectile Points,* Collector Books, 1983; Lar Hothem, *North American Indian Artifacts, 3rd Edition,* Books Americana, 1984; *North American Indian Points,* Books Americana, 1984; Noel D. Justice, *Stone Age Spear And Arrow Points Of the Midcontinental and Eastern United States,* Indiana University Press, 1987; Allan Lobb, *Indian Baskets Of The Pacific Northwest and Alaska,* Graphic Arts Center Publishing Co., 1990; Robert M. Overstreet and Howard Peake, *The Official Overstreet Price Guide to Indian Arrowheads, Second Edition,* House of Collectibles, 1991; Dawn E. Reno, *The Official Identification and Price Guide To American Indian Collectibles,* House of Collectibles, 1988; Sarah and William Turnbaugh, *Indian Baskets,* Schiffer Publishing, 1986.

Periodicals: *American Indian Basketry Magazine,* P.O. Box 66124, Portland, OR 97266; *Indian–Artifact Magazine,* RD #1 Box 240, Turbotville, PA 17772; *Prehistoric Antiquities & Archaeological News,* P. O. Box 88, Sunbury, OH 43074.

Note: American Indian artifacts listed below are objects made on the North American continent during the pre-historic and historic periods.

Pot, Acoma type, geometric earth toned dec, 4½" h, $125.00.

ESKIMO

Basket, coiled, baleen, pierced ivory disk in base, fitted lid	
2¾" d, 1¼" h, carved ivory seal head	440.00
3" d, 2" h, ivory tear drop shape finial	500.00
4¼" d, 3¾" h, carved ivory reclining seal on rect tab	990.00
Cribbage Board, 13¼" l, ivory, engraved, high relief carved walrus and reindeer dec, black pigment	220.00
Model	
Kayak, 12¾" l, wood, sinew sewn seal skin cov, mounted and cased	330.00
Umiak, 29" l, wood, cut sewn seal skin cov, paddles and ivory harpoon,	

three incised wood figures, black pigment detail 770.00

Painting, 8 x 12", ink, colored pencil, and watercolor on paper, sgd "Kivetoruk Moses, Nome, Alaska" 1,210.00

Pipe, 11" l, ivory, carved animal figures on top, black pigment animal dec on bowl and sides, yellow patina 1,760.00

Salt and Pepper Shaker, pr, 2½" h, ivory, carved, stylized polar bear, surmounted baby seal, baleen insets, red and black pigment details, inscribed "USID Alaskan Eskimo" . . . 110.00

NORTHEAST AND WOODLANDS

Bag, 15¼" l, corn husk, twined, aniline dyed wool, bow tie dec, green cloth edge, hide thong handle, Nez Perce 220.00

Box, 8 x 12 x 9¼", birchbark, natural dyed porcupine quill work dec, blue, sepia, pale green, and ivory, "MD" on dome lid 2,200.00

Club, 22" l, burl head, carved stylized animal heads, Penobscot 80.00

Jacket, 40" l, machine and hand sewn, smoke tanned, multicolored silk embroidered floral motif on yoke, pockets, and cuffs, black polished cotton lining, ten brass buttons, Cree 475.00

Ladle

9½" l, curly maple, shield form bowl, tapered cylindrical handle, carved and incised horse's head finial, brass nail head eyes 1,300.00

10¼" l, oval bowl, tapered handle with figural hooked termination, golden yellow patina, 19th C 175.00

Moccasins, pr, 7" l, hide, beaded dec, silk ribbon edge, bordered floral motif cuff 225.00

Sash, 138 x 6¼", wool yarn, finger woven, parallel zig–zag pattern, red ground, multicolored braided and twisted fringe on ends, Huron 800.00

NORTHWEST COAST

Basket, 3⅞" d, 3¼" h, cylindrical form, spruce, twined, embroidered dark brown and golden honey dyed grass, banded dec, Tlingit 710.00

Blanket, ceremonial, 65½ x 54", twined woven, natural and native dyed mountain goat wool, yellow, ivory, black–brown, and turquoise, heraldic design, fringed, Tlingit 8,000.00

Bowl, 13½" l, cedar, raven shape, carved and incised dec, black pigment, inlaid glass beads 520.00

Game Kit, crimson and black wood sticks, laced hide bag 550.00

Hat, 8" h, 15" brim, spruce root, twined, flaring conical form, painted black and vermilion crest emblem, skip–stitched rim, Tlingit/Haida 3,200.00

Mask, 11¼" h, wood, polychrome, cedar, carved and incised features, 20th C 600.00

Spoon, 10" l, horn, carved, pierced, bent and incised handle with totemic figure dec, copper pegs 1,760.00

PLAINS

Awl Case

13" l, leather, beaded and fringed, sinew sewn, German silver wrapped fringes, Kiowa, 19th C 500.00

14½" l, hide, sinew sewn, beaded, tin cone and German silver tab suspensions, Kiowa, 19th C 1,200.00

Bag, 8½ x 6¾", hide, beaded, quilled, and feathered, tin cone suspensions, Sioux, c1900 . . . . 200.00

Cradle

30" l, hide, beaded, sinew stitched, turquoise ground, boxed, banded, and forked triangles, diamonds, and squares, brass bells, fringed, cotton muslin lining, Sioux 2,300.00

33" l, wool broadcloth with cotton edge, parfleche hood support, wood framework, dec with blue cotton binding, cowrie shells, and clear and green glass tube beads, silk ribbon suspensions, hide thongs, brass hawk bells, Cheyenne, c1890 . . . . 4,000.00

Dance Stick, 36" l, wood wrapped with ochre rubbed cotton, attached feather and hide suspensions 100.00

Doll, 12" h, hide, beaded and fringed, wool coiffure 165.00

Gauntlets, 15¾" l, hide, beaded and fringed, stylized floral dec on cuff, pr 110.00

Leggins, pr

13" l, yellow ochre rubbed hide, polychrome and beaded, geometric design, white ground, beaded edge cuffs 600.00

16" l, hide, beaded, stitched stepped and feathered geometric design, white ground, brass buttons on hem, Sioux 325.00

Moccasins, pr,

9" l, boot type, hide, sinew and cotton sewn, beaded uppers and cuffs, stepped and banded geometric dec, white ground, laced domed German silver buttons, painted green ground, Kiowa/Cheyenne . . 880.00

10½" l, boot type, hide, sinew stitched, beaded, banded geomet-

ric designs, crystal green and opalescent ground, hard soles **275.00**
10¾" l, hide, sinew stitched, beaded uppers, cuffs, and forked tongue, hard soles, Sioux **800.00**
Pipe, 29¼" l, wood and stone, greenish–gray elbow type bowl, wood stem with carved spiral twists, golden honey patina, incised "Ma–Chu–Ta–Ga" **2,200.00**
Pipe Bag
18½" l, beaded and fringed, sinew sewn, stepped diamond and bar design, aqua background on one side, other white, brass wire wrapped fringe **1,600.00**
31" l, hide, beaded and quilled, sinew sewn, geometric design, white background, Sioux **900.00**
Pouch
7" l, hide, U shape, beaded and fringed, plaited beadwork handle . **550.00**
8 x 7½", beaded cross, bar, and hourglass dec, red wool binding on sides, black silk lining, white grosgrain cloth drawstring, Crow **385.00**
13" l, hide, beaded and fringed, twisted thong drawstring closure . **300.00**
Shirt, 30" l, hide, polychrome, beaded, and fringed, yellow ochre, red pigment, triangular neck flaps, U shape hem, silk ribbon suspensions, sinew, cotton thread, and hide laced construction, Arapaho/Kiowa, 19th C .. **1,400.00**
Spoon, 9¼" l, horn, handle forms bird's head on end, Sioux **100.00**
Vest
21" l, hide, beaded, stylized foliate dec on sky blue ground on front, yellow back with hide thong ties, beads, and faceted metallic dec, lined with cotton trade cloth, 19th C **850.00**
23" l, hide, beaded, stitched floral dec on front, calico print cotton lined . **200.00**

WEST AND SOUTHWEST

Basket
7½" l, oval, coiled, woven dark brown devil's claw and willow, Apache .. **410.00**
8" d, 2¾" h, coiled and beaded, compressed globular form, white clam shell disk attachment, Pomo **660.00**
13¾" d, flaring form, woven black bracken fern, redbud, and red wool dec, willow ground, Yoqut **660.00**
16½" d, coiled, flaring form, woven redbud dec, dark golden ground, Maidu **715.00**
Blanket
40 x 29½", wool, woven, brown, pur-

ple, green, and red, banded pattern, Navajo **440.00**
42½ x 62½", woman's, natural and aniline dyed homespun, woven nine spot pattern, red, black, white, and orange bar and concentric block dec, white and shaded black background stripe, Navajo **1,200.00**
51 x 39", child's, homespun, woven, golden yellow, indigo blue, orange, and dark salmon serrated zig–zag band dec, orange–red ground, Navajo **1,870.00**
Bow, 36" l, wood, polychromed, wool wrapped back curved ends, three metal tip arrows **275.00**
Bowl, 9½" d, polychrome, flared form, curved–out rim, dec int., black floral dec on ext., cream slip, Santo Domingo, c1910 .... **440.00**
Bracelet, 3" d, silver and turquoise, stamped openwork, five bezel set spider web stones, Navajo **425.00**
Concho Belt
31" l, silver, linked, stamp dec, attached charm, Navajo **325.00**
40⅛" l, tooled leather, seven silver oval conchos, open center buckle, stamped and repousse dec, Navajo **2,860.00**
43" l, silver and turquoise, seven silver conchos and eight butterfly shape dec, stamped and repousse dec, applied silver rope dec **3,080.00**
Doll
9¼" h, Kachina, wood, polychrome, Hopi **300.00**
9½" h, Deity, wood, polychrome, Hopi **165.00**
Figure, 5½" h, pottery, frog smoking cigar, beaded ear dec, red on buff, Mohave **600.00**
Jar
5" h
Blackware, matte painted water serpent dec, inscribed base "Tonita," San Ildefonso **250.00**
Polychrome, red and black painted dec, pale orange background, Hopi **350.00**
8½" h, low flaring body, tapered neck, indented base, creamy white slip dec, white background, orange and black painted banded block dec, painted brick red base and inner lip, Acoma **750.00**
14" h, polychrome, creamy ivory slip dec, red clay background, painted black stylized stepped designs, red painted base, Santo Domingo ... **3,300.00**
Moccasins, pr, 11¼" l, yellow pigment hide uppers, rawhide soles, repousse silver and coin button closure, Pueblo **165.00**

Necklace

12″ l, silver, single strand, tube and
globular beads, double barred sa-
cred heart style cross, Isleta, c1940 ... 100.00

13½″ l, silver and turquoise, squash
blossom, double strand, globular
beads, Navajo, c1940 .... 650.00

14½″ l, jet, turquoise, and gypsum,
Santo Domingo, c1910 .... 150.00

16″ l, silver, one strand of beads, hand
hammered engraved Roman cross,
Navajo, c1890 .... 950.00

18″ l, triple strand, shell, coral, and
turquoise, Pueblo 150.00

20″ l, triple strand, shell, coral, and
turquoise, two heishe jacla suspensions, Pueblo 1,000.00

Olla

9″ h, polychrome, globular form, tapered neck, grayish–white slip dec,
red and brown geometric dec,
Acoma/Laguna 300.00

10″ h, creamy ivory slip, red clay
body, painted black floral and bow
tie motifs, red painted base and inner lip, Santo Domingo 1,980.00

10½″ h, polychrome, flared sides,
creamy pink slip, red and black stylized horn dec, Zia 550.00

11″ d, 10¾″ h, polychrome, creamy
ivory slip dec, red clay ground,
painted brick and black banded
geometric and circular design, San
Ildefonso 1,210.00

17″ h, coiled basketry, woven brown
and yellow banded diamonds, willow background, Papago 165.00

Pin, 1⅜″ h, silver and turquoise, channel
work form, Zuni 165.00

Pouch, 6″ l, hide, flared rect, beaded
dec, tin cone suspension, Apache .. 165.00

Rug, Navajo

50 x 52″, Good Luck design, red, orange, black, tan, and white 750.00

53 x 64″, chief's, red, light brown, and
black 2,200.00

56 x 58″, bold red, black, and white,
brown squares 525.00

57 x 93½″, natural and aniline dyed
homespun, Third Phase Chief's
pattern, red, black, white, and indigo blue 2,090.00

59½ x 54″, blanket design, red, white,
and black 1,300.00

62 x 42½″, blanket design, red, black,
gray, and white 550.00

70 x 48″, red, black, yellow, tan, and
white 700.00

Saddle Blanket, 25½ x 25″, twill woven,
red, black, and white natural and aniline dyed wool 80.00

Tray, 13½″ d, coiled basket, Navajo .. 300.00

Vase, 8″, polychrome, red slip dotted
and swagged dec, handled, San Ildefonso 50.00

INDIAN TREE PATTERN

History: The Indian Tree pattern is a popular
pattern of porcelain made from the last half of the
19th century until the present. The pattern consisting of an Oriental crooked tree branch, landscape, exotic flowers, and foliage is found in pre-
dominantly greens, pinks, blues, and oranges on
a white ground. Several English potteries, including Burgess and Leigh, Coalport, and Maddock,
made wares with the Indian Tree pattern.

Reference: Susan and Al Bagdade, *Warman's
English & Continental Pottery & Porcelain, 2nd
Edition,* Wallace–Homestead, 1991.

**Plate, marked "Foley China," 6¼″ d,
$8.50.**

Berry Set, 10″ d master bowl, six 5″ d
serving bowls, Maddox 165.00
Bouillon, underplate, semi scalloped,
Coalport 20.00
Bowl, 8½″ d, ftd, Minton 48.00
Butter Dish, cov, Johnson Bros 45.00
Cake Plate, 10½″ d, Coalport 40.00
Creamer
Breakfast, Coalport 15.00
Large, semi scalloped, Coalport ... 25.00
Cup and Saucer, full scallop, Coalport 25.00
Demitasse Cup and Saucer, Coalport . 35.00
Egg Cup, 4″ h, Maddock & Sons 20.00
Fruit Bowl, full scallop, Coalport 12.00
Gravy Boat, Brownfield & Sons, c1856 35.00
Plate
6″ d, bread and butter, full scallop,
Coalport 8.00
9½″ d, dinner, KPM 15.00
Relish Dish, semi scalloped, Coalport . 20.00
Salt and Pepper Shakers, pr, Coalport 50.00
Sauce, 5″ d, Johnson Bros 8.00
Soup Plate, 7½″ d, Coalport 20.00

Soup Tureen, 10″ w, matching cov and ladle, Maddock & Sons	150.00
Sugar, open, semi scalloped, Coalport	20.00
Vegetable Bowl, oval, smooth edge, Coalport	60.00

INK BOTTLES

History: Ink was sold in glass or pottery bottles in the early 1700s in England. Retailers mixed their own formula and bottled it. The commercial production of ink did not begin in England until the late 18th century and in America until the early 19th century.

Initially, ink was supplied in pint or quart bottles, often of poor manufacture, from which smaller bottles could be filled. By the mid-19th century when writing implements were improved, emphasis was placed on making an "untippable" bottle. Shapes ranging from umbrella style to turtles were tried. Since ink bottles were displayed, shaped or molded bottles became popular.

The advent of the fountain pen relegated the ink bottle to the back drawer. Bottles lost their decorative design and became merely functional items.

References: Ralph & Terry Kovel, *The Kovels' Bottle Price List,* 8th edition, Crown Publishers, 1987; Carlo & Dot Sellari, *The Standard Old Bottle Price Guide,* Collector Books, 1989.

Periodical: *Antique Bottle and Glass Collector,* P. O. Box 187, East Greenville, PA 18041.

Additional Listings: See *Warman's Americana & Collectibles* for more examples.

Pottery, cone style, brown glaze, 2⅝″ h, $15.00.

Carter's Blak Writing Fluid, yellow amber, beveled corner, double collared mouth, label, 9¼″ h	190.00
Cottage Master Ink, aqua, smooth base, tooled lip, 5½″ h	450.00
Davids and Black, NY, emerald green, open pontil, applied mouth, 5¾″ h	110.00
E Waters, Troy, NY, aqua, open pontil, applied mouth, 2⅜″ h	220.00
Farley's Ink, yellow amber, eight sided, open pontil, flared lip, 3½″ h	325.00

Geometric, amber, open pontil, disc mouth, 1½″ h, 2¼″ d	100.00
Harrison's Columbian Ink, aqua, twelve sided, open pontil, applied mouth, 4⅞″ h	140.00
Hover, Phila, olive green, open pontil, tooled and flared lip, 5⅞″ h	200.00
J A Williamson Chemist, blue–green, cylindrical, applied mouth, spout, 9⅝″ h	125.00
L Poincelet, black amber, eight sided, pontil, flared lip, 2″ h	725.00
Maynard & Noyes, olive amber, three part mold, sloping collared mouth, spout, 8″ h	100.00
S Fine Black Ink, yellow–olive green, open pontil, rolled lip, 3″ h	300.00
Shepard & Allen's Writing Fluid, golden amber, cylindrical, red label, 6⅜″ h	85.00
Umbrella, eight sided	
Olive green, yellow tint, open pontil, rolled lip, 2½″ h	180.00
Yellow, smooth base, tooled lip, 2½″ h	550.00
Underwood's Ink, cobalt blue, smooth base, tooled lip, pour spout, 9¾″ h	100.00

INKWELLS

History: The majority of commonly found inkwells were produced in the United States and Europe from the early 1800s to the 1930s. The most popular materials were glass and pottery because these substances resisted the corrosive effects of ink.

Inkwells were a sign of the office or a wealthy individual. The common man tended to dip his ink directly from the bottle. The period from 1870 to 1920 represented a "golden age" when inkwells in elaborate designs were produced.

References: William E. Covill, Jr., *Inkbottles and Inkwells,* William S. Sullwold Publishing, 1971; Betty and Ted Rivera, *Inkstands and Inkwells: A Collector's Guide,* 2nd edition, Crown Publishers, Inc., 1973.

Collectors' Club: Society of Inkwell Collectors, 5136 Thomas Avenue, Minneapolis, MN 55410.

Additional Listings: See *Warman's Americana & Collectibles* for more examples.

CERAMIC

Flow Blue, 6 × 8 × 5¾″, floral, hinged, ornate brass stand	200.00
Nippon, 4″, sq, beige, gold, black flowers	130.00
Porcelain, pink luster, classical lady	75.00
Pottery, 3⅛″ h, 3¾″ l, sq, wide beveled corners, multicolored leaf and berry dec, white ground	135.00

French Faience, multicolored Oriental florals, yellow ground, marked "Aladin, France," 5" l, 3" h, $75.00.

Quimper, 5", round, scalloped edge, marked "Henriot Quimper France"	55.00
Royal Doulton, 2½" h, globular form, raised low relief dec, windmills, seated men and leaping dogs	35.00

GLASS

Blown Three Mold

1½" h, 2½" d, amber, cylindrical, disc mouth	150.00
1¾" h, 2¾" d, oliver amber, ringed base, pontil, flat collar, McKearin GII–18E	65.00
Cobalt Blue, 2⅛" h, 3¾" l, teakettle shape, eight sided, ground mouth	425.00
Cranberry, 4½" d, blown hemisphere, gold dec, brass hinged lid	500.00
Figural, 1⅝" h, 2⅝" l, snail, clear, ground mouth	330.00
Paperweight, 5¼" h, 4⅛" l, bulbous shape, clear, rose and green floral dec int., tooled mouth matching stopper	145.00
Pitkin Type, 1⅜" h, 2" d, conical cylinder, yellow olive funnel shaped mouth	725.00
Ruby Overlay, 3½" h, cut to clear cube, matching cut hinged lid	400.00
Tiffany type, 2" h, 5¼" d, Art Nouveau style, iridescent green, clear glass insert, brass closure	240.00

METAL

Brass, 11" l, Victorian style, pierced scrolled back plate, two ink pots, pen tray	110.00
Bronze, 11" l, three nude men retrieving chest from sea, c1920	1,210.00
Iron, 3" h, 8" l, revolving type, wheelbarrow shape, black, milk glass insert	325.00
Pewter, 7" d, wide flat base, ceramic insert	25.00
Sterling Silver, 5" d, circular, reeded band edge and hinged lid, marked "H M," Birmingham, England, 1906	170.00

IRONS

History: Ironing devices have been used for many centuries, with the earliest references dating from 1100. Irons from the Medieval, Renaissance, and early industrial era can be found in Europe, but are rare. Fine brass engraved irons and hand wrought irons dominated the period prior to 1850. After 1850 irons began a series of rapid evolutionary changes.

Between 1850 and 1910 irons were heated in four ways: 1) a hot metal slug was inserted into the body, 2) a burning solid, e.g., coal or charcoal, was placed in the body, 3) a liquid or gas, e.g., alcohol, gasoline, or natural gas, was fed from an external tank and burned in the body, and 4) conduction heating, usually drawing heat from a stove top.

Electric irons are just beginning to find favor among iron collectors.

References: Esther S. Berney, *A Collectors Guide To Pressing Irons And Trivets*, Crown Publishers, Inc., 1977; A. H. Glissman, *The Evolution Of The Sad Iron*, published by author, 1970; Brian Jewell, *Smoothing Irons, A History And Collector's Guide*, Wallace-Homestead, 1977; Judy (author) and Frank (illustrator) Politzer, *Early Tuesday Morning: More Little Irons and Trivets*, published by author, 1986; Judy and Frank Politzer, *Tuesday's Children*, published by author, 1977.

Collectors' Clubs: Friends of Ancient Smoothing Irons, Box 215, Carlsbad, CA 92008; Midwest Sad Iron Collectors Club, 3915 Lay Street, Des Moines, IA 50317.

Museums: Henry Ford Museum, Dearborn, MI; Shelburne Museum, Shelburne, VT; Sturbridge Village, Sturbridge, MA.

Additional Listings: See *Warman's Americana & Collectibles* for more examples.

Advisors: David and Sue Irons.

Fluting Machine, Eagle, cast iron and brass, orig inserts, marked "Pat. Nov 2, 1875," $100.00.

Charcoal, double spout, "Ne Plus Ultra," side vent, hand heat shield, removable top, 1902	85.00
Fluter, machine type, brass rolls, circu-	

lar cone base, paint dec, Tucker–New
Jersey **130.00**
Goffering, iron, round base, S shape
center post, 4" barrel, Kenrick **85.00**
Liquid Fuel
Alcohol, iron body, saw grip handle,
cylindrical tank, German, c1900 .. **110.00**
Natural Gas, "I Want For Comfort Gas
Iron," pie shape, wood handle, ex-
tension pipe c1910 .... **35.00**
Miniature
Flat, iron, strap handle, number on
top, 2–3" **30.00**
Swan, iron, paint dec more desirable,
various sizes 1¾–5", c1870 ..... **150.00**
Sad
Belgium Tear Drop, iron, rect handle,
raised numbers and letters, various
sizes and styles, c1850 .... **20.00**
Enterprise, two pointed or straight
back edge, removable C handle . **15.00**
Ober, flat, ribbing on arched handle,
weight number **18.00**
Slug, brass, wood handle, lift trap door,
turned posts, various sizes, c1850–
1900, English **120.00**
Speciality
Hat, flat wood tolliker for crown press-
ing, Cross, c1900 .... **45.00**
Polisher, iron, round bottom, Sidons,
England, c1900 .... **50.00**
Sleeve, Grand Union Tea Co, remov-
able bentwood handle **45.00**
Tailor, cast, narrow, raised weight
number, c1890 .... **25.00**

IRONWARE

History: Iron, a metallic element that occurs
abundantly in combined forms, has been known
for centuries. Items made from iron range from the
utilitarian to the decorative. Early hand-forged iron-
wares are of considerable interest to Americana
collectors.

References: Frank T. Barnes, *Hooks, Rings &
Other Things: An Illustrated Index of New England
Iron, 1600–1860*, The Christopher Publishing
House, 1988; Kathryn McNerney, *Antique Iron
Identification and Values*, Collector Books, 1984,
1991 value update; Herbert, Peter, and Nancy
Schiffer, *Antique Iron*, Schiffer Publishing Ltd.,
1979.

Additional Listings: Banks, Boot Jacks, Doorstops, Fireplace Equipment, Food Molds, Irons,
Kitchen Collectibles, Lamps, and Tools.

Andirons, pr
10½" h, wrought, scrolled finial, pitted **45.00**
24¾" h, wrought, scrolled feet, disk
shape finials, spit hooks on shaft,
black paint traces **175.00**

Skeleton key, 5½" l, $20.00.

Bank, penny, 6" h, cast, black mammy,
polychrome paint traces **55.00**
Basin, 12¼" d, cast, three short feet .. **10.00**
Boot Scraper, wrought, scrolled end, at-
taches to door frame **40.00**
Bottle Opener, cast
Donkey, 3⅝" h, polychrome traces . **65.00**
Pelican, 3½" h, polychrome **100.00**
Candlestick
6½" h, pushup with scrolled handle,
wrought iron spike hanger **135.00**
7" h, hog scraper, brass ring, lip hanger, stamped initials on underside
pushup **200.00**
Cigarette Dispenser, 8½" l, cast, figural,
elephant, bronze repaint **30.00**
Clothes Hook, 9" w, cast, eagle shape,
snake in talons forms hook, gold paint **40.00**
Dipper, 4¼" d, 12" l, cast, swivel lid,
wrought handle **85.00**
Door Handle, 13" l, wrought, thumb
latch **45.00**
Door Knocker, 3¾" l, cast, basket of
flowers, orig polychrome paint **30.00**
Door Stop, cast, figural
8¼" h, monkey, orig paint **175.00**
10½" h, rooster, painted **150.00**
12" h, rabbit, black repaint, pink and
white trim **125.00**
Dough Scraper, wrought iron, triangular
shape **25.00**
Figure, 5¼" l, frog, green paint **35.00**
Finials, 20¼" h, pr, cast, pineapple
shape, old repaint **300.00**
Fireplace Crane, 24" l, 16" h, wrought,
scroll work and three hooks **50.00**
Floor Lamp, 63" h, iron wrapped circular
column, scroll trifid base, flame finial
over carriage lamp **110.00**
Frame, 19 x 11½", reticulated scroll
crest, Cluette Peabody and Co **45.00**
Furniture
Bench, 41" l, kidney shape, ornate
trestle base joined with twist
stretcher, upholster top **175.00**
Garden, cast
Bench, 60½" l, vintage design,
worn black repaint, 20th C **130.00**

Settee, 45½″ l, old white repaint .	300.00
Side Chair, openwork back, circular seat, down curving legs, painted white	125.00
Table, 25″ l, 20″ w, 31″ h, wrought, rect top, lily pad base, twelve duck head legs, webbed feet	850.00
Garden Urn, cast	
13″ h, pr, old white repaint	450.00
28½″ h, removable ears, white repaint	290.00
Hinges, strap, wrought, pr	
31″ l	50.00
42″ l, made for two part bifold barn doors	55.00
Hitching Post, 62½″ h, cast, tree form, branch stubs, marked "Patent"	100.00
Lawn Ornament, cast, jockey, polychrome repaint	100.00
Lock, 13½″ h, wrought, violin shape, simple tooling, key	250.00
Masonry Ties, 13″ d, pr, cast, five point stars	50.00
Meat Hook, 8″ d, 13½″ h, wrought, crown shape, four hooks	210.00
Mortar and Pestle, 5½″ h, cast	20.00
Nut Cracker, 11″ l, cast, figural, dog, nickel finish, marked "The L A Althoff Mfg Co, Chicago"	45.00
Pan, spider type, cast	
8″ d, 7″ handle, deep bowl, pouring spout	25.00
9½″ d, 9½″ handle	20.00
10½″ d, 9½″ handle, mismatched lid	30.00
Peel, 28″ l, wrought, ram's horn finial .	110.00
Plant Stand, 38″ h, three twisted legs joined at base with floral finial, three acanthus leaf rings support copper planter	60.00
Porringer, 5″ d, marked "E & T Clark/1 pint," imp "Bellevue" on handle	60.00
Roaster, 22¾″ l, hooks fasten to open fire grate, adjustable tin pan with hood, wood handle	175.00
Sewing Clamp, 4″ l, table type, wrought	25.00
Sconce, wrought, 19th C	
41″ h, three scrolling arms, open work shield form body with scroll, reticulated flower form bobeches, ball and acanthus leaf motifs	300.00
58″ h, pr, scrolling floral form, spear shape leaves, flower form light sockets, electrified	110.00
Skewer Holder, 16″ l, four skewers, pitted	300.00
Skillet, 9¾″ d, cast, three short feet . .	40.00
Spatula, 18½″ l, wrought	45.00
Tea Kettle, cov, cast	
South Co–Op Foundry Co, Rome, GA, swing–out lid, sloped spout . .	50.00
Wagner No 0	125.00
Toaster, wrought	
7½″ l, one slice size	350.00

17″ l, heart dec, penny feet, pitted . .	1,550.00
Toy, wagon, 4⅝″ l, cast, Champion Express, red and blue, nickel wheels .	75.00
Trammel, wrought	
16″, hook and eye	30.00
28″ l, diamond tooling, marked "A S" and "A H," dated 1785	350.00
Trivet, 7¼″ l, wrought, heart shape . . .	150.00
Utensil Rack, 12″ l, wrought, scrolled dec	60.00

IVORY

History: Ivory, a yellowish–white organic material, comes from the teeth or tusks of animals and lends itself well to carving. It has been used for centuries by many cultures for artistic and utilitarian items.

Ivory from elephants shows a reticulated cross–cross pattern in a cross section. Hippopotamus teeth, walrus tusks, whale teeth, narwhal tusks, and boar tusks also are ivory sources. Vegetable ivory, bone, stag horn, and plastic are ivory substitutes which often confuse collectors.

For information on how to identify real ivory, see Bernard Rosett's "Is It Genuine Ivory," in Sandra Andacht's *Oriental Antiques & Art: An Identification and Value Guide* (Wallace–Homestead, 1987).

Note: Dealers and collectors should be familiar with The Endangered Species Act of 1973, amended in 1978, which limits the importation and sale of antique ivory and tortoise shell items.

Brush Pot, 4″ h, carved, figures and pavilions, Chinese, c1885	1,000.00
Bust, 8″ h, Madame Recamier, curly hair with wrapped band, arms hold shawl, raised on ebonized ivory fitted pedestal with crowned initial "R" & "J G," France, late 19th C	1,650.00
Cane, 36½″ l, bamboo form, horse foreleg shape handle, 19th C	250.00
Card Case, 4⅛″ l, carved, figures and pavilions, Chinese, 19th C	500.00
Cigarette Holder, carved	25.00
Crochet Hook, 6¼″ l, hand shape finial .	45.00
Figure	
2″, scholar, bearded man, scroll on staff, brocade robes	125.00
2¾″ l, seated man, carved, Japanese, sgd	275.00
5½″, man, two boys, and monkey on hurdy–gurdy, carved, stained, Japanese, c1900	400.00
9″ h, peasant, carved, low relief, hunched back, holding fishing rod and pipe, mounted on pedestal . .	880.00
11″ l, five elephants ascending in size on curved bridge, carved base, sgd "Yoneyama"	190.00

Gavel, 8¼", engraved scribe lines ... **250.00**
Jagging Wheel, 4¾" l, carved, heart
  shape handle, mid 19th C **170.00**
Ladle, 7⅛", African **100.00**

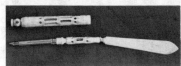

Letter opener and pen, Stanhope with map of Atlantic City, 9½" l, $75.00.

Memo Pad, 1½ x 2¾", silver fittings .. **25.00**
Model, 15¾" l, boat, carved zoomorphic
  figures on ends, wood oars on each
  side, cockswain on bow, Dutchman at
  stern, diaper pattern hull, carved
  cabin, 19th C **360.00**
Napkin Ring, 2" h, relief carved bird .. **12.00**
Pendant, 1 x 1½ x 2¼", double dragon
  design, orig silk chord **150.00**
Pie Crimper, 6¼" l, pewter wheel, wood
  handle **30.00**
Shoehorn, 8½", maiden and child **150.00**
Stand, 7", pierced relief, pink and cream
  flowers, peony and lotus flowers,
  green stones **425.00**
Tusk, 17½" l, carved, male and children,
  African **325.00**
Vase
  4" h, carved, four vertical ribs,
    Chinese, 18th C **500.00**
  10", ovoid, carved court ladies in mu-
    sical pursuits, domed cov with land-
    scape pines and figures, two ring
    handles **475.00**
  18½" h, pr, flattened cylindrical, in-
    dented neck, raised rect panel with
    figures above continuous scene of
    women and children in gardens,
    domed cov with Foo lion finial, ring
    handles, China, c1900 .... **1,050.00**

JACK-IN-THE-PULPIT VASES

History: Jack-in-the-Pulpit glass vases, made in the trumpet form, were in vogue during the late 19th and early 20th centuries. The vases were made in a wide variety of patterns, colors, and sizes.

Additional Listings: See specific glass categories.

Amberina, 7" h, honey amber stem and
  applied wafer base, ruby red top ... **475.00**
Amethyst shaded to clear ground, 23½"
  h, ribbed bulbous body, enameled
  pink and white poppies **1,210.00**

Cranberry shading to crystal, four molded petal feet, 8½" h, $150.00.

Burmese, Mt Washington
  6¾" h, ruffled, yellow pastel rust and
    tan ground, autumn leaves, blue
    berries, and tendrils dec **485.00**
  8" h, flesh tone to yellow, pink top,
    yellow refired border **585.00**
Cased
  6½" h, white ext., shaded maroon int.,
    ruffled **120.00**
  7¼" h, creamy opaque ext., white and
    yellow flowers, green leaves, gold
    trim, deep rose pink int., amber
    edge, ormolu leaf feet **125.00**
Iridescent amethyst and gold luster,
  feather veining **200.00**
Loetz, 12" h, green, silver–blue irid
  spots, c1900 .... **450.00**
Opalescent, 7½", chartreuse green, ruffled **75.00**
Peachblow, 7½" h, blue–gray, cherry
  blossom pink ruffled edge **2,450.00**
Spatter, 8½" h, white, green, and cranberry **110.00**
Stevens & Williams, 6¾" h, rainbow
  swirl, trefoil crimped top **485.00**
Vaseline, 6" h, clear bulging opalescent
  body, cranberry flared rim, ftd **145.00**
White blossom shading to peachblow
  pink base, 13" h, European **220.00**

JADE

History: Jade is the generic name for two distinct minerals, nephrite and jadeite. Nephrite, an amphibole mineral from Central Asia and used in pre-18th century pieces, has a waxy surface and ranges in hues from white to almost a black green. Jadeite, a pyroxene mineral found in Burma and used from 1700 to the present, has a glassy appearance and comes in various shades of white, green, yellow-brown, and violet.

Jade cannot be carved because of its hardness. Shapes are achieved through sawing and grinding with wet abrasives, such as quartz, crushed garnets, and carborundum.

Prior to 1800 few pieces are signed or dated. Stylistic considerations are used for dating. The Ch'ien Lung period (1736–95) is considered the "golden age" of Jade.

Reference: Sandra Andacht, *Oriental Antiques & Art: An Identification And Value Guide,* Wallace-Homestead, 1987.

Museum: Avery Brundage Collection, de Young Museum, San Francisco, CA.

Pendant, burial tomb type, $125.00.

Bowl
  5" d, translucent ivory to mottled white, russet striations, everted rim, ring foot **500.00**
  8¾" d, spinach green, hemispherical, ftd, polished surface, sgd "H Wolf" **1,045.00**
Box, cov, 3½ x 5½", rect, translucent dark gray–green, pale white streaking, ftd, wood stand, incised six–character Quianlong mark **2,090.00**
Brush Pot, 4¼", scrolling cloud pattern, Chinese, 19th C **310.00**
Candlestick, pr, 12⅞" h, dark green, carved low relief goose with outspread wings, stands on tortoise, head supports three tiered pricket, tripod bowl with int. carving, reticulated wood base with carved keyscroll motifs and floral scrolls **525.00**
Cup, 4½", white, boat shape, curved spout, dragon handles, Chinese ... **350.00**
Dish, 5½", octagonal, green spinach .. **140.00**
Figure
  6¾" h, grotto, wrinkled elephant and attendant on ledge beneath rocky outcrop and pine trees on front, reverse with gnarled pine and sage on flight of stairs with climbing monkey, China, late 17th C **16,500.00**
  7⅛" h, Meiren, standing holding

peach bough and hoe, mint green, China **1,980.00**
Inkstone, 3⅝" l, oval depression to one side, black and white mottling, incised rim band **175.00**
Lamp, 29" h, Goddess, Kuan Yin, standing, flowing cowl, robes, and jewels, child on one upraised arm, rosary and fly whisk in other **1,600.00**
Letter Opener, 10¾" l, carved interlocking C scrolls between keyfret bands handle, SS knife **250.00**
Pitcher, 5⅜" h, spiral and whirl circle bands, rope borders, angular strap handle **525.00**
Saucer, 4¼", flared rim, deep green, brown mottling, short ring foot **200.00**
Snuff Bottle
  Grayish–white, mottled russet skin on one side, rose quartz stopper ... **550.00**
  Greenish–white, sloping shoulder, oval foot, 1800–80, pr **600.00**
  Ovoid, carved leafy fruiting melon vines and rat, mottled grayish–white, russet inclusions, green glass twig and leaf form stopper, late 19th C **660.00**
Urn, 8" h, ovoid form, incised taotie mask dec, narrow neck, handles, domed lid with suspending carved chains, yoke shape hanger **700.00**
Vase
  7" h, ovoid, nephrite, animal headed ring handles, stork and lotus scroll on cov **500.00**
  8½" h, dark green, spade form, carved low relief dec, keyscroll band, russet inclusions, natural fissure cracks **610.00**

JAPANESE AND CHINESE CERAMICS

History: The Chinese pottery tradition has existed for thousands of years. By the sixteenth century, Chinese ceramic wares were being exported to India, Persia, and Egypt. The Ming dynasty (1368–1643) saw the strong development of glazed earthenwares and shapes. During the Ch'ing dynasty, the Ch'ien Lung period (1736–95) marked the golden age of interchange with the West.

Trade between China and the West began in the sixteenth century when the Portuguese established Macao. The Dutch entered the trade early in the seventeenth century. With the establishment of the English East India Company, all of Europe was seeking Chinese–made pottery and porcelain. Styles, shapes, and colors were developed to suit Western tastes. The tradition continued until the late nineteenth century.

Like the Chinese, the Japanese spent centuries developing their ceramic arts. Each region established its own forms, designs, and glazes. Individual artists added to the uniqueness.

Japanese ceramics began to be exported to the West in the mid–19th century. Their beauty quickly made them a favorite of the patrician class.

The ceramic tradition continues into the 20th century. Modern artists enjoy equal fame with older counterparts.

Reference: Sandra Andacht, *Oriental Antiques & Art: An Identification And Value Guide,* Wallace–Homestead, 1987.

Periodical: *The Orientalia Journal,* P.O. Box 94P, Little Neck, NY 11363.

Additional Listings: Canton, Fitzhugh, Imari, Kutani, Nanking, Rose Medallion, and Satsuma.

CHINESE

Bowl
6" d, pr, blue and white, floral, foliate, and crane dec 425.00
6¾" d, flared sides, cut foot, molded int. with twin fish medallion at well, pale crackled blue–green glaze, Song Dynasty 250.00
8⅜" d, stylized auspicious objects, lotus motifs, and two blue bands int., ext. with auspicious objects with circular blue band, Guangxu mark .. 330.00
Brushwasher, pr, 4¾" d, compressed circular form, splayed base, incurved rim, thick bluish–gray crackle glaze . 200.00
Censer, 3⅓" h, compressed globular form, splayed raised foot, everted rim, countersunk band dec, two scroll handles, white glaze, 19th C 385.00
Charger, 10¾" d, blue and white, crane and floral dec, Ming Dynasty 300.00
Cup, 4⅜" h, inverted bell form, raised on tapered cylindrical foot, thick copper red glaze with orange peel texture, six–character Qianlong mark .. 1,045.00
Dish, 6" d, central medallion of four children playing game int., ext. with children engaged in playing in scholar's garden, underglaze blue outline details, doucai enamels, six–character Yongzheng mark 825.00
Figure, 16" h, horse, standing, head band and draped with trappings and saddle, green, chestnut, and honey glaze, Tang style 470.00
Ginger Jar, 8" h, pr, butterfly dec 170.00
Plate, 8½" d, blue and white, Ming Dynasty 375.00
Sweetmeat Box, 16¼" sq, pr, polychrome lacquer dec, pavilion terrace, keyfret border, black lacquer ground, mid 19th C 770.00
Urn, 17" h, pr, baluster form, blue and white, scrolling foliate, floral, and shou dec 385.00
Vase
6" h, ovoid, rounded sides, long waisted neck, lavender–blue and speckled purple glaze, gilt lined flared rim 770.00
7" h, ovoid, flattened form, painted cloisonne enamel, gilt bronze rim and foot 175.00
8¾" h, gu form, raised mid–section, two countersunk bands, thick ivory colored glaze, 18th C 660.00
11¾" h, cong form, hollow splayed foot, short tapered neck, two applied mythical beast head simulated ring handles, thick dark blue glaze, six–character Tongzhi mark 660.00
12" h, baluster body, flared neck, fluted rim, incised scroll and applied imperial dragon dec, Sing Dynasty 500.00

Chinese Export, armorial charger, exported for the Dutch market, underglaze blue and famille verte dec, city of Utrecht coat of arms, flowers and birds dec, wide rim with blue diaper broken by reserve cartouches of sea creatures, Chinese figures and flowers, first quarter 18th C, 17" d, $2,600.00.

CHINESE EXPORT

Basket, oval, reticulated, fret pierced sides, reserve on front and back, brown and gold wheat border beneath dotted dentil and band borders, shell shape handles, matching stand, c1810 .... 1,100.00
Bowl
10¼" d, rose to pink and pale salmon petals, three reserve gilt edged

quatrefoil panels with iron–red edged gold hibiscus sprays, stylized floral sprigs on rim, central spray of iron–red edged gilt chrysanthemums and prunus with blossom and scroll border int., c1760 . **1,760.00**

11¼" d, pheasants perched on pierced rock with peonies and flowers in fenced garden, central peony sprig int., underglaze blue trellis diaper border, c1750 . . . . **1,430.00**

Dish, 10³⁄₁₆" d, center with painted rose, green, iron–red, blue, white, and gold peonies and flowers growing from stylized rockwork, iron–red edged gilt spearhead band, shaped and painted rim, c1760 . . . . **1,540.00**

Figure

8¼" h, pr, Fu lions, male with left paw on reticulated ball, female with pup, gilt pale pink, green, orange, light blue, and yellow painted, reticulated rect section plinth with floral spray dec, late 19th C **1,045.00**

9¼", pr, parrot, standing on blue glazed rockwork, green glaze, coral–red beak and feet **1,100.00**

9½" h, pr, cats grinning, ribbon collars, black painted eyes, one turquoise glaze, other coral glaze . . **450.00**

Mug, 5⅜" h, cylindrical, British Marine dec, brown, iron–red, gilded ship, iron–red chain border, entwined strap handle with iron–red floral terminals, 1785–90 . . . . **770.00**

Plate

6½" d, pr, Pseudo Tobacco Leaf dec, c1785 . . . . **990.00**

9" d, pr, Tobacco Leaf pattern, iron–red and gold pheasants with rose, blue, turquoise, and yellow wings, perched on gilt underglaze blue, turquoise, pale green, and rose tipped yellow leaves, green centered rose tobacco blossom, iron–red and gilt squirrel on fruited branch, 1770–85 . . . . **5,225.00**

10⁷⁄₁₆" d, leaping Pekinese dog, blue enamel delineated in black, reserved panels on brown and salmon trellis diaper border, blue enamel lined edge, c1740 . . . . . . **1,100.00**

Platter

12⅞" l, rect, Pseudo Tobacco Leaf dec, c1785 . . . . **2,475.00**

15" l, oval, Tobacco Leaf pattern, rose, blue, iron–red, yellow, and gold, scalloped edge **6,600.00**

15¼" d, iron red and gilt dec, scrolling leafy band and floral spray dec, central medallion with interwoven peonies, 19th C **250.00**

Punch Bowl

15⅛" d, famille rose palette ext. with gilded highlights, Oriental ladies and boys around table in garden scene, brown edged gilt spearhead border foot rim, painted rose, yellow, blue, and green floral spray center int., c1765 . . . . **4,125.00**

15½" d, three rows of petals shaded from rose to pale pink, four turquoise edged quatrefoil panels with painted iron–red and gold hibiscus sprays, gilt foliate sprigs between petal tips, rose, white, iron–red, brown, turquoise, green, and gilded chrysanthemum int. with gilt spearhead border, c1760 . . . . **8,250.00**

Sauceboat Stands, 8" l, Pseudo Tobacco Leaf dec, iron–red, chartreuse, brown, salmon, gilt edged rim, c1785 **1,430.00**

Teabowl and Saucer, set of 12, floral spray painted in underglaze blue, rose, iron–red, green, turquoise, and gold, underglaze blue trellis diaper int. border with four rose stylized blossom panels, 1765–75 . . . . **1,980.00**

Tureen

5½" l, pr, cov, floral dec, matching undertray **3,750.00**

12" l, rect, Famille Rose, landscape dec, animal mask handles, Qianlong **350.00**

Vase

4¼", beaker form, Imari palette dec . **130.00**

9⅛" h, baluster, Tobacco Leaf pattern, iron–red pheasants perched on flowering branch, enameled yellow, turquoise, green, and blue leaves, rose and yellow tobacco blossom, insects and floral sprigs on reverse, gilt ruyi lappet border with floral sprigs dec on iron–red hatchwork ground, gilt husk and dot band, ormolu pierced foliate scroll base, c1785 . . . . **1,550.00**

JAPANESE

Bowl, 6¾", painted iron–red, green, deep turquoise, black, gray, and gold int., chrysanthemum spray tied with tasseled gilt ribbon, molded base with incised petal border on ext., gold highlights, Arita, 18th C **1,150.00**

Dish, 8⅛" d, Nabeshima style, blossoming cherry branches on int., late 19th C **650.00**

Ewer, 10½", red and gilt motif, riverscape and figure dec, loop handle, dragon finial, Kaga, late 19th C **525.00**

Nodder, 5½", Fukujurojin, seated figure,

robe with knotted tie cord on chest,
polychrome dec, Banko **450.00**
Plate
  8½" d
    Kakiemon style, pr, blue and white,
      dragons among clouds dec, Ka-
      rakusa and Fugu mark, 19th C . **310.00**
    Nabeshima style, relief and under-
      glaze blue hibiscus dec, c1900 . **210.00**
  9¾" d, one relief carp and one un-
    derglaze blue carp dec, Fugu mark,
    c1900 . . . . **285.00**
Sake Bottle, 7¼", rect, underglaze blue,
  two pine trees and three pavilions,
  stylized landscape scene, sq top with
  leaf and cloud dec, sq spout and
  pierced hole, Arita, late 17th C **675.00**

JASPERWARE

History: Jasperware is a hard, unglazed porcelain with a colored ground, varying from the most common blues and greens to lavender, yellow, red, or black. The white designs are applied in relief and often reflect a classical motif. Jasperware was first produced at Wedgwood's Etruria Works in 1775. Josiah Wedgwood described it as "a fine terra-cotta of great beauty and delicacy proper for cameos."

Many other English potters, in addition to Wedgwood, produced jasperware. Two of the leaders were Adams, and Copeland and Spode. Several continental potters, e.g., Heubach, also produced the ware.

References: Susan and Al Bagdade, *Warman's English & Continental Pottery & Porcelain,* 2nd Edition, Wallace–Homestead, 1991; R. K. Henrywood, *Relief-Moulded Jugs, 1820–1900,* Antique Collectors' Club.

Reproduction Alert: Jasperware still is made today, especially by Wedgwood.

Note: This category includes all pieces of jasperware which were made by companies other than Wedgwood. Wedgwood jasperware is found in the Wedgwood listing.

Box
  2½ x 3 x 4½", blue, three white relief
    dancing cherubs on cov **55.00**
  6" d, white cameos of cherubs and
    lovebirds on cov, gray–green
    ground, ftd **175.00**
Cheese Dish, cov, white relief birds, insects, and ferns on cov with acorn
  finial, relief vintage grape border band
  on base, tan ground, Adams, En-
  gland, c1820 . . . . **350.00**
Creamer, 2½" h, pale pink frolicking
  Kewpies, sage green ground, sgd
  "O'Neill" **175.00**
Cruet, 6¾", white relief man and woman

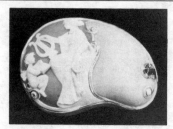

Box, cov, Art Nouveau style white cameo on light green jasper ground, blue jewel on pink jasper ground, imp "Schafer & Vater," 6" l, $100.00.

toasting each other, small cupid and
  word "Prosit," sage green ground,
  matching orig stopper, Germany . . . **100.00**
Cup and Saucer, dark blue, white clas-
  sical figures **100.00**
Dish, 4¼" d, white relief Indian with
  shield and hatchet, sheaf of wheat
  border, green ground, sgd "Heubach" **60.00**
Hatpin Holder, 4¼", deep blue, white
  figures, band of flowers at top,
  marked "Adams" **50.00**
Jar, 3½" h, white classical cameos, blue
  ground, SP lid and handle, marked
  "Adams, Tunstall, England" **110.00**
Jug, 7", blue, classical figures representing the four seasons, angular
  handles with foliage motif, silver rim,
  marked "Adams," late 18th C **225.00**
Pitcher
  5", white cameos of cherubs in roses,
    green ground **125.00**
  8", blue, white classical figures,
    marked "Copeland, England,"
    c1885 . . . . **225.00**
Planter, large, blue, white relief Apollo
  and four muses, c1850 . . . . **225.00**
Plaque
  5¾", white relief flowers, cupid with
    bow and woman, green ground . . **65.00**
  11¼", white raised figures of children
    at play, soft green ground, marked
    "Germany" **125.00**
  11½", white raised figures of putti,
    blue ground, marked "Germany" . **175.00**
Spill Vase, deep blue, white relief florals,
  trees, and muses representing poetry
  and drama **110.00**
Teapot, 6½", blue, white relief birds and
  bamboo, pewter top and finial,
  marked "Copeland–Spode" **150.00**
Tobacco Jar, cov, 6¼" h, cylindrical,
  white relief classical figures, dark blue
  ground, white relief band around
  base, silverplated rim, bail handle,

and cov with ivory finial, imp "Adams, Tunstall, England" **100.00**
Tumbler, 4", white classical cameos, brown ground **65.00**
Tureen, cov, 7½" d, blue, white relief bridge scene, floral dec, matching stand, marked "Copeland–Spode," c1820 . . . . **160.00**
Vase
  4", white cameos of man with spade, woman under tree, blue ground . . **25.00**
  7½" h, white relief Indian chief and owls, green, white, and pink ground, Germany **155.00**

JEWEL BOXES

History: The evolution of jewelry was paralleled by the development of boxes in which to store it. Jewel box design followed the fashion trends dictated by furniture styles. Many jewel boxes are lined.

German Silver, ftd, raised figures of man, woman, and animals, pink velvet lining, 4¾" w, 3" d, 3½" h, $100.00.

Art Nouveau, 10 x 8 x 7", ormolu, raised figural and floral dec, plaque dated 1903 . . . . **225.00**
Ebony, 11¾" l, allover scrolling flowering foliage dec, inlaid ivory, 19th C . **300.00**
German Silver, 6½" l, 13 oz, rect, heavily molded and bellied sides, winged dolphin form feet, early 19th C **850.00**
Gilt Bronze, 16" w, 9½" h, elaborate Moorish design, semi precious stones, enamel dec **900.00**
Glass
  Amethyst, 6 x 4⅞", enameled floral dec, silverplated rim and base . . . **125.00**
  Cranberry, 4½ x 2¾", enameled floral dec, silverplated rim **150.00**
Ivory, 8¾ x 5½ x 4¾", rect, hinged lid, delicate engraved and repousse mounts **200.00**

Malachite, 4½ x 2½", veneer, rect, raised feet, satin lining, Russian, 19th C **225.00**
Pewter, 5½ x 9½", engraved brass frame like ornament on top, oval mosaic work, purple velvet lining, marked "Marshall & Sons, Edinburgh, Scotland" **250.00**
Russian Silver, 4¾ x 8¾", rect, sky blue, deep red, and white enamel diapering pattern and stylized flower heads, raised studded bands, swing handles on lid and sides, pale blue padded satin lining, four bun feet **2,475.00**
Silverplated
  8" l, rococo floral design **85.00**
  8 x 5 x 3", oval, hinged lid, ftd emb cupids, daisy chain and roses, velvet lining, marked "Wilcox" **75.00**
Sterling Silver, 13 x 5 x 4", repousse sides, small petal–like beaded edges, fancy feet, red velvet lining, marked "Meridan" **150.00**
Wave Crest
  6 x 3", pale blue painted flowers, red banner mark **570.00**
  7 x 6½", puffy Egg Crate mold, hp lid, child with bow and arrow, satin finish, ftd, orig lining **1,200.00**

JEWELRY

History: Jewelry has been a part of every culture. It was a way of displaying wealth, power, or love of beauty. In the current antiques marketplace, it is easiest to find jewelry dating between 1800 to 1950.

Jewelry items were treasured and handed down as heirlooms from generation to generation. In the United States, antique jewelry is any jewelry one hundred or more years old, a definition linked to U.S. Customs law. "Heirloom/estate" jewelry, i.e., jewelry at least twenty–five years old and acquired new, used, or through inheritance, is used for old jewelry that does not meet the "antique" definition.

The jewelry found in this listing fits either the antique or "heirloom/estate" definition. The list contains no new reproduction pieces. The jewelry is made of metals and gemstones proven to endure over time. Inexpensive and mass–produced costume jewelry is covered in *Warman's Americana & Collectibles.*

Several major auction houses, especially Christie's, Doyle's, and Sotheby's in New York City, hold specialized jewelry auctions several times each year.

Note: The first step in determining the value of a piece of old jewelry is to correctly identify the metal and gemstones. Take into account the current value of the metal and gemstones plus the piece's age, identifying marks, quality, condition, construction, etc.

References: Lillian Baker, *Fifty Years of Collectible Fashion Jewelry, 1925–1975,* Collector Books, 1986, 1989 value update; David Bennett and Daniela Mascetti, *Understanding Jewellery,* Antique Collectors' Club, 1989; Shirley Bury, *Jewellery, 1789–1910, The International Era,* Antique Collectors' Club, 1991; Roseann Ettinger, *Popular Jewelry, 1840–1940,* Schiffer Publishing Co., 1990; Rose L. Goldemberg, *Antique Jewelry: A Practical And Passionate Guide,* Crown Publishers, Inc., 1976; *Jewelry Trade Mark Book, 1934 edition,* reprint, Golden Era Publications, 1991; Arthur Guy Kaplan, *The Official Identification Price Guide To Antique Jewelry, Sixth Edition,* House of Collectibles, 1990; Antoinette Matlins and A. C. Bonanno, *Gem Identification Made Easy,* Gemstone Press, 1988; Antoinette Matlins and A. C. Bonanno, *Jewelry & Gems: The Buying Guide,* Gemstone Press, 1987; Harrice Miller, *The Official Identification and Price Guide To Costume Jewelry,* House of Collectibles, 1990; Michael Poynder, *The Price Guide to Jewellery 3000BC–1950AD,* Antique Collectors' Club, 1990 reprint; Dorothy T. Rainwater, *American Jewelry Manufacturers,* Schiffer Publishing Ltd., 1988; Nancy N. Schiffer, *Handbook of Fine Jewelry,* Schiffer Publishing Ltd., 1991; Doris J. Snell, *Antique Jewelry With Prices, Updated Edition,* Wallace–Homestead, 1991; Ulrike von Hase–Schmundt, etal., *Theodor Fahrner, Jewelry...between Avant–Garde and Tradition,* Schiffer Publishing Ltd., 1991.

Periodical: *Vintage Fashions,* Hobby House Press, 900 Frederick Street, Cumberland, MD 21502.

Advisor: Elaine J. Luartes.

Dates:

Georgian	**1714–1837**
Victorian	**1837–1865**
Edwardian	**1885–1910**
Art Nouveau	**1880–1920**
Arts and Crafts	**1895–1915**
Art Deco	**1920–1930**
Art Retro	**1940–1950**

Bar Pin
- Art Deco, platinum, faceted citrine, round diamonds, and pearls **2,400.00**
- Edwardian, platinum, set with half pearls and rose diamonds **1,800.00**
- Victorian, name bar pin, carved Whitby jet **50.00**

Barrette, Edwardian, engraved 14K yg, lattice motif set with seed pearls ... **550.00**

Bead Necklace
- Art Deco, carved ivory, lotus motif, 32" l **450.00**
- Edwardian, seed pearl choker, 14 strands, 3 gold bars set with half pearls **1,900.00**
- Victorian
  - Coral, graduated beads, 14K yg ornate gold clasp **250.00**
  - Hollow bead, 18K yg beads, Etruscan granulation, 15" l **1,200.00**
  - Russian Amber, egg shaped beads, 42" l **600.00**

Bracelet
- Art Retro, 18K rose gold, wide honeycomb flexible mesh–link chain, large buckle style clasp set with diamonds **4,000.00**
- Edwardian
  - 10K yg, knife edge style, two heart–bow and cluster motifs, set with seed pearls and diamonds **700.00**
  - 14K white gold filigree, delicate flexible link, raised filigree center set with round diamonds **800.00**
- Victorian
  - 14K rose gold, link, graduated oval cabochon moonstone links **900.00**
  - 14K yg, mesh style, decorated clasp set with half pearls **1,200.00**
  - Gold filled, bangle, etched band dec **150.00**

Brooch, Victorian, cameo, Persephone motif, shell cameo, oval gold frame, artist sgd, $1,800.00.

Brooch, Arts and Crafts, gold, clover motif, enameled, pearl center, $300.00.

Brooch
  Art Deco
    Platinum, geometric design, set with sq cut rubies and round cut diamonds **2,200.00**
    Sterling, antelope motif **55.00**
  Art Nouveau, flower motif, poppy, gold, enameled, pearls **950.00**
  Art Retro, 14K rose gold, floral spray motif, set with rubies and diamonds **600.00**
  Arts and Crafts, sterling, hand hammered floral motif **75.00**
  Victorian
    Cameo, oval, shell, woman's head in profile, yg frame **400.00**
    14K yg
      Crescent shape, set with half pearls **100.00**
      Scroll motif, set with diamond and seed pearls **395.00**
      Starburst motif, pin/pendant, set with ruby and seed pearls . . . **185.00**

Brooch, Victorian, 14K yg, eagle motif, large and small mine cut diamonds, $1,600.00.

Chain Necklace
  Art Deco
    Platinum, fancy link spaced with diamonds, 2.5 cts TW, 32" l . . . **5,800.00**
    Sterling, enamel dec sterling links set with lapis color glass **165.00**
  Arts and Crafts, handmade, heavy link silver chain, mounted baroque pearl, dec large rect shaped frame set with one polished black opal from which suspend two more irregular shaped polished black opals **4,500.00**
  Victorian, woven hair, repousse gold clasp, 60" l **170.00**
Chatelaine, Victorian, ornate single purpose eyeglass case, sterling silver and tortoiseshell, English hallmarks . **650.00**
Cufflinks, pr
  Art Deco, platinum, set with mother-of-pearl and half pearls **250.00**
  Victorian, sterling, fancy shamrock motif **80.00**

Earrings, pr
  Art Deco, tear drop motif, white gold, black onyx, round diamonds **2,500.00**
  Art Retro, 18K rose gold, soft geometric sculpture and tassel motif, set with small round diamonds . . . **600.00**
  Georgian, bow and flower motif, silver, gold, large rose cut diamonds, small cushion cut diamonds **20,000.00**
  Victorian
    Acorn motif, 14K yg **300.00**
    Diamond drop style, silver and gold circular framed mounts set with mine cut diamonds, approx 1.25 cts TW **1,050.00**
    Teardrop circle, dangle, 15K yg . . **465.00**
    Urn motif, dangle, high carat yellow gold **750.00**
Lavaliere, Art Nouveau, 14K yg, set with opal and baroque pearl drop **300.00**

Locket, Victorian, 18K yg, oval, turquoise and pearl dec center design, $800.00.

Locket
  Art Deco, 14K white gold, geometric design **375.00**
  Art Nouveau, 14K yg, round swirl motif, set with one diamond **500.00**
Lorgnette, Art Nouveau, sterling silver, oval retractable lenses in ornate floral motif case **350.00**
Pendant
  Art Nouveau
    18K yg, cross, handmade, set with one diamond **850.00**
    Silver gilt, plique a'jour enamel, dragonfly motif, set with cabochon opals, baroque pearls, and diamonds **2,000.00**
  Victorian, yellow gold, heart motif, pave seed pearls **300.00**
Ring
  Art Deco, platinum, set with calibre

cut rubies surrounding round diamond, approx 1.20 cts **2,500.00**

Art Nouveau, sculptured child's face, two small baroque pearls, two tiny round rubies **1,200.00**

Art Retro, 14K rose gold, buckle motif, carved and calibre cut rubies, round diamonds **3,500.00**

Edwardian, platinum, filigree style, three diamond straight row set ... **2,000.00**

Victorian
  10K yg
    Cabochon opal surrounded by six rose cut diamonds **285.00**
    Two mine cut diamonds, ruby, and emerald **350.00**
  14K yg, hardstone cameo **500.00**
  18K yg, snake motif, set with rubies, English hallmarks **800.00**

Seal, Victorian, gold, flower motif amethyst intaglio **850.00**

Stick Pin, Art Nouveau, 18K yg, miniature Gibson Girl enameled portrait, set with diamonds **750.00**

Watch Fob, Victorian, 14K yg and mother–of–pearl horn motif **80.00**

JUDAICA

History: Throughout history, Jews have expressed themselves artistically in both the religious and secular spheres. Most Jewish art objects were created as part of the concept of "Hiddur Mitzva," i.e., adornment of implements involved in performing rituals both in the synagogue and home.

For almost 2,000 years, since the destruction of the Jerusalem Temple in 70 A.D., Jews have lived in many lands. The widely differing environments gave traditional Jewish life and art a multifaceted character. Unlike Greek, Byzantine, or Roman art which have definite territorial and historical boundaries, Jewish art is found throughout Europe, the Middle East, North Africa, and other areas.

Ceremonial objects incorporated not only liturgical appurtenances, but also ethnographic artifacts such as amulets and ritual costumes. The style of each ceremonial object responded to the artistic and cultural milieu in which it was created. Although diverse stylistically, ceremonial objects, whether for Sabbath, holidays, or the life cycle, still possess a unity of purpose.

Judaica has been crafted in all media, though silver is the most collectible. Sotheby's, Christie's, and Swann's hold several Judaica auctions in the United States, England, Amsterdam, and Israel.

References: Abraham Kanof, *Jewish Ceremonial Art*, Harry N. Abrams, n.d.; Cecil Roth, *Jewish Art—An Illustrated History*, Graphic Society of New York, 1971; Geoffrey Wigoder, (ed.), *Jewish Art and Civilization*, Chartwell Books, 1972.

Museums: B'nai B'rith Klutznick Museum,

Washington, DC; H.U.C., Skirball Museum, Los Angeles, CA; Jewish Museum, New York, NY; Judah L. Magnes Museum, Berkeley, CA; Maurice Spertus Museum of Judaica, Chicago, IL; National Museum of American Jewish History, Philadelphia, PA; Yeshiva University Museum, New York, NY.

Advisor: Arthur M. Feldman.

Diecut, Von Stufe zu Stufe, copyright Fuld & Co., NY, 3⅝″ w, 2⅞″ h, $10.00.

Beaker, 2¾″, silver, scale motif, German, c1800 .... **800.00**

Chalice, 13″ h, Continental silver, Herman Lang, Augsburg, 17th C, 29 oz **2,325.00**

Charger, 23″ d, Continental silver, repousse floral and figural dec, c1780, 48 oz **1,650.00**

Charity Box, 5″, cylindrical, sheet copper, German, 1800s **250.00**

Circumcision Cup, 5″, German, double, silver gilt, marked "Johanna Becker, Augsburg," c1755–57 ....**13,200.00**

Circumcision Knife
  6¾″, Continental brass handle, 1700s **700.00**
  7″, tortoise shell, SS, and steel, Continental, late 18th C **1,650.00**

Comb, Burial Society, 6″ w, brass, Hungarian, 1881 .... **5,775.00**

Esther Scroll, 10½″, cased, Austro–Hungarian silver, Vienna, 1846 .... **1,650.00**

Goblet, 4″, presentation, German silver, c1850 .... **660.00**

Hanukkah Lamp, 9¾″, Austrian 800 fine silver, scroll edge backplate surmounted by crown, facing emb facing with pair of tablets flanked by pair of griffins, Star of David cartouche, rect platform, contiguous row of eight urn form lamps on wire frame, four scrolled supports, servant's lamp missing, late 19th C, 22 oz 10 dwt . **1,800.00**

Kiddush Cup
  5¼″, silver gilt, Polish, mid 18th C .. **3,850.00**
  5½″, silver, tulip form, engraved, Polish, c1800 .... **950.00**

Knife, Burial Society, 3¾", wood, brass, and steel	**2,200.00**
Menorah Wall Sconce, 10½" l, Continental silver, heraldic repousse back shield, c1858, 18 oz	**2,860.00**
Mezuzah Case, 4½", American silver, Ludwig Wolpert, NY, stamped "Toby Pascher Workshop, The Jewish Museum, NY"	**650.00**
Passover Dish, 15¼", pewter, German, maker's initials "D.V.D.," c1768	**3,750.00**

Passover Plate

8¾", ceramic, Continental, 18th C	**500.00**
14", pewter, Continental, c1800	**225.00**
Plaque, 2¾ x 2", SS, rabbi, inscribed, after engraving by Boris Schatz, framed	**500.00**
Sabbath Candlesticks, pr, 16¼", Aaron Katz, London, 1894, Polish style	**1,000.00**

Spice Box

4¾", SS, Scandinavian, fish form, blurred marks on tail, articulated body, hinged head, green jeweled eyes, 19th C, 1 oz 10 dwt	**385.00**
5¼", SS, filigree, Bohemian, sgd "R. G., Prague, 1815"	**1,200.00**
8", tower shape, pewter, mounted wood, lion top, German, 1700s	**1,300.00**
Torah Binder, linen, embroidered silk, German, 1809	**650.00**
Torah Pointer, 10½", Polish silver, worn on index finger, 18th C	**825.00**

JUGTOWN POTTERY

History: In 1920 Jacques and Julianna Busbee left their cosmopolitan environs and returned to North Carolina to revive the state's dying craft of pottery making. Jugtown Pottery, a colorful and somewhat off-beat operation, was located in Moore County, miles away from any large city and accessible only "if mud permits."

Ben Owens, a talented young potter, turned the wares. Jacques Busbee did most of the designing and glazing. Julianna handled promotion.

Utilitarian and decorative items were produced. Although many colorful glazes were used, orange predominated. A Chinese blue glaze that ranged from light blue to deep turquoise was a prized glaze reserved for the very finest pieces.

Jacques Busbee died in 1947. Julianna, with the help of Owens, ran the pottery until 1958 when it was closed. After long legal battles, the pottery was reopened in 1960. It now is owned by Country Roads, Inc., a non-profit organization. The pottery still is operating and using the old mark.

Sugar Bowl, tobacco spit glaze, imp and stamped mark, $40.00.

Bowl, 6" d, 2" h, crimped, Chinese Translation, Chinese blue and red glaze	**85.00**
Candlesticks, pr, 3" h, Chinese Translation, Chinese blue and red, marked	**75.00**
Creamer, cov, 4¾" h, yellow	**50.00**
Finger Bowl, Chinese Translation, Chinese blue and red	**115.00**
Jar, cov, 6¾" h, bulbous, flaring rim, eared handles, redware, bright orange glaze	**75.00**
Pie Plate, 9½" d, orange ground, black concentric circles dec	**70.00**
Pitcher, 5" h, gray and cobalt blue salt glaze	**85.00**
Rose Jar, cov, 4½" h, blended olive green glaze	**50.00**
Teapot, cov, 5¼" h, Tobacco Spit glaze, sgd, c1930	**60.00**

Vase

4" h, Chinese Translation, thick flowing white glaze	**70.00**
8¾" h, 9" d, bulbous, two very small handles, mottled turquoise, semi–matte glaze over red underglaze, imp mark	**550.00**

KPM

History: The mark, KPM, has been used separately and in conjunction with other symbols by many German porcelain manufacturers, among whom are the Königliche Porzellan Manufactur in Meissen, 1720s; Königliche Porzellan Manufactur in Berlin, 1832–1847; and Krister Porzellan Manufactur in Waldenburg, mid-19th century.

Collectors now use the term "KPM" to refer to the high quality porcelain produced in the Berlin area in the 18th and 19th centuries.

Reference: Susan and Al Bagdade, *Warman's English & Continental Pottery & Porcelain, 2nd Edition,* Wallace–Homestead, 1991.

Vase, baluster, two handles, hp, multicolored florals, celery green ground, 8½″ h, $185.00.

Cheese Board, rose and leaf garland border, hole to hang, marked	45.00
Cup and Saucer, hunting scene, filigree, 18th C	50.00
Dinner Service, Art Deco style, gilt and jeweled in turquoise and pink, flowering plants on speckled gilt and iron red ground, sea green borders with molded gilt swags, blue scepter, iron red orb, KPM mark, c1880	8,000.00
Dish, 9½″, leaf shape, painted, birds on flowering branch, burgundy border, gilt drapery, blue scepter, iron red KPM and orb mark, c1860	250.00
Plaque	
7 x 5″, oval, Cupid portrait, sharpening arrow, sgd	2,600.00
8½ x 7″, dancing young woman, playing tambourine	100.00
12½ x 8″, Psyche sitting on rock, holding dragonfly on finger, orig gold shadowbox frame, imp "KPM"	11,500.00
Plate	
9″, hp, gold dec, wide scroll reticulated rims, orb mark, set of 4	125.00
10½″, Princess Royal	30.00

Scent Bottle, molded scrolls, multicolored painted bouquets of flowers, gilt trim, gilt metal C–scroll stopper, marked, mid 19th C	150.00
Teapot, 6″ h, oval, medallion with figural dec, gilt ground	70.00
Urn, cov, pr, cobalt blue and gilt, floral and cherub dec	300.00
Vase, cov, blue, painted floral bouquets with gilt foliage, flared foot, two loop handles, blue scepter and KPM mark, c1860	1,150.00

KAUFFMANN, ANGELICA

History: Marie Angelique Catherine Kauffmann was a Swiss artist who lived from 1741 until 1807. Her paintings were copied by many artists who hand decorated porcelain during the 19th century. The majority of the paintings are neo-classical in style.

Reference: Susan and Al Bagdade, *Warman's English & Continental Pottery & Porcelain, 2nd Edition,* Wallace–Homestead, 1991.

Clock, multicolored decal of classical scene, blue, red, and brown accents, cream ground, sgd "Chelsea, England," 14¾″ h, $200.00.

Box, 2¾ x 4½″, lilac, two maidens and child in woods on cov, brass hinges	85.00
Cake Plate, 10″, ftd, classical scene, two maidens and cupid, beehive mark	85.00
Compote, 8″, classical scene, beehive mark, sgd	80.00
Cup and Saucer, classical scene, heavy gold trim, ftd	90.00
Inkwell, pink luster, classical lady	75.00

Pitcher, 8½", garden scene, ladies, children, and flowers sgd **100.00**
Plaque, 8¾", classical scene, three maidens dancing **75.00**
Plate
  8", cobalt blue border, reticulated rim, classical scene with two figures . . **55.00**
  8¾", classical scene, three maidens dancing **60.00**
Tobacco Humidor, SP top, pipe on top, green ground, ladies and cupid **400.00**
Tray, 16½" d, round, classical figures in reserve, sgd, beehive mark **175.00**

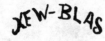

KEW BLAS

History: Amory and Francis Houghton established the Union Glass Company, Somerville, Massachusetts, in 1851. The company went bankrupt in 1860, but was reorganized. Between 1870 and 1885 the Union Glass Company made pressed glass and blanks for cut glass.

Art glass production began in 1893 under the direction of William S. Blake and Julian de Cordova. Two styles were introduced. A Venetian style consisted of graceful shapes in colored glass, often flecked with gold. An iridescent glass, labeled Kew Blas, was made in plain and decorated forms. The pieces are close in design and form to Quezel products, but lack the subtlety of Tiffany items.

The company ceased production in 1924.

Bowl, 14" d, pulled feather, red ground, sgd **1,200.00**
Candlesticks, pr, 8½" h, irid gold, twisted stems **725.00**
Compote, 7" h, twisted stem, ribbed bowl, irid gold, pink highlights **375.00**
Creamer, 3¼" h, irid gold, applied handle **225.00**
Finger Bowl and Underplate, 5" d bowl,

Tumbler, gold iridescent, dimpled, 3½" h, $245.00.

6" d plate, ribbed, scalloped border, metallic luster, gold and platinum highlights **465.00**
Pitcher, 4½" h, green pulled feather pattern, deep gold irid int., applied swirl handle, sgd "Kew–Blas" **800.00**
Rose Bowl, 3½" h, green and gold hooked dec, butterscotch ground, gold int. **525.00**
Salt, irid gold **200.00**
Sherbet, 5" h, irid gold **200.00**
Tumbler, 4" h, pinched sides, irid gold, sgd **185.00**
Vase
  5" h, spherical, rolled gold rim, green and gold pulled feather, white ground, sgd **475.00**
  6¼" h, cylinder, rolled rim, gold and green swags, pale orange ground, early 20th C, sgd, orig paper label **600.00**
  7" h, bulbous, flared, pulled feather, sgd **1,500.00**
Wine Glass, 4¾" h, curving stem, irid gold **185.00**

KITCHEN COLLECTIBLES

History: The kitchen was a central focal point in a family's environment until the 1960s. Many early kitchen utensils were handmade and prized by their owners. Next came a period of utilitarian products made of tin and other metals. When the housewife no longer wished to work in a sterile environment, color was added through enamel and plastic and design served both an aesthetic and functional purpose.

The advent of home electricity changed the type and style of kitchen products. Many items went through fads. The high technology field already has made inroads into the kitchen, and another revolution seems at hand.

References: Ronald S. Barlow, *Victorian Houseware: Hardware and Kitchenware*, Windmill Publishing Co., 1992; Jane H. Celehar, *Kitchens and Gadgets, 1920 to 1950*, Wallace–Homestead, 1982; Linda Campbell Franklin, *300 Hundred Years of Kitchen Collectibles, Second Edition*,, Books Americana, 1982; Kathryn McNerney, *Kitchen Antiques 1790–1940*, Collector Books, 1991; Gary Miller and K. M. Mitchell, *Price Guide To Collectible Kitchen Appliances*, Wallace–Homestead, 1991; Ellen M. Plante, *Kitchen Collectibles: An Illustrated Price Guide*, Wallace–Homestead, 1991; Glydon Shirley, *The Miracle in Grandmother's Kitchen*, published by author, 1983.

Additional Listings: Baskets, Brass, Butter Prints, Copper, Fruit Jars, Food Molds, Graniteware, Ironware, Tinware, and Woodenware. See *Warman's Americana & Collectibles* for more examples including electrical appliances.

Beater, Handy Maid, Torrington, T & S, green measuring cup base, $30.00.

Apple Peeler, cast iron, Reading Hardware Co 85.00
Butter Churn, 12½" h, wood, stave constructed, lid and dasher, old varnish finish 325.00
Cabbage Cutter, 9½ x 18", angled steel blade, cut-out heart handle 85.00
Cheese Sieve, 8" d, 7½" h, wood, stave construction, iron band 20.00
Cherry Stoner
  Cast Iron, Enterprise 48.00
  Hand Crank, 8½" l, marked "Pat'd Nov 17, 1863" 55.00
Colander, 10¾" d, 3" h, copper, punched star design 65.00
Cookie Board
  Beech, 9¾ x 16", carved basket of flowers on one side, bunch of grapes on other, scrubbed finish . 300.00
  Oak, 6¾ x 11", relief carved man and woman figures, brown patina . 250.00
Cranberry Scoop, 11½ x 17½", wood and tin, sheet metal teeth, refinished 85.00
Cutting Board, 6⅝ x 18", wood, round top, shaped base, metal blade 85.00
Food Chopper, 7" w, wrought iron, scalloped edge blade, turned wood handle 275.00
Fork, 11⅜" l, wrought iron 55.00
Griddle, cast iron, Griswold
  No 9 .... 25.00
  No 10 .... 50.00
Ice Shaver, nickelplated steel, marked "Enterprise", July 4, 1893 patent ... 40.00
Juice Reamer
  Handy-Andy, clear 30.00
  Sunkist, milk glass 25.00
Kettle, cast iron, Griswold No 4 ..... 70.00
Ladle, 15" l, wood, pot hook handle .. 45.00
Lemon Squeezer, iron, glass insert, marked "Williams" 45.00

Meat Tenderizer, 10¼" l, stoneware, sq head, wood handle, marked "Pat'd Dec 25, 1877" 110.00
Nutmeg Grater
  5¾" l, tin, marked "Boye" 85.00
  7" l, tin and cast iron, wood handle, marked "Edgar Mfg Co" 65.00
Pantry Box, 11½" d, 6½" h, cov, oak, bail handle 165.00
Pastry Board, wood, three sided 30.00
Potato Masher, 9" l, turned maple 30.00
Raisin Seeder, cast iron, marked "Enterprise," 1890s 50.00

Rolling Pin, white porcelain body, blue floral dec, turned wooden handles, 13¾" l, $20.00.

Rolling Pin
  15¼" l, blown, deep amber, knopped handles, 19th C 130.00
  15¾" l, blown, cobalt blue, tapered cylinder, knopped handles, America, 19th C 45.00
  22" l, milk glass, cylinder, turned wood handles, marked "Imperial Mfg Co, July 25, 1921" 35.00
  23½" l, curly maple 75.00
Sausage Stuffer, 17½" l, turned wood plunger 15.00
Sieve, 12" d, tin, bowl shape 8.00
Skillet
  Griswold, cast iron
    Erie No 8 .... 40.00
    No 3 .... 20.00
    No 14 .... 150.00
  Whitfield, 9" d, sheet iron, 10½" l wrought iron handle 125.00
Spatula, 14½" l, wrought iron, inlaid brass blade, initials "P M" 255.00
Spice Box, 15 x 9 x 11½", poplar, dovetailed case, slant top lid, divided drawer and int., worn brown finish .. 325.00
Toaster, 21" l, wrought, revolving, Queen Anne style, baluster form handle, 18th C 200.00
Trivet, 12" l, lyre form, wrought iron frame and turned handle, brass top, replaced foot, stamped marker's mark 35.00
Wafer Iron, cast iron, octagonal, church with steeple and trees dec on one side, pinwheel with plants and star flowers on other, wrought iron handles 400.00

KUTANI

History: In the mid 1600s Kutani originated in the Kaga province of Japan. Kutani comes in a variety of color patterns, one of the most popular being Ao Kutani, a green glaze with colors such as green, yellow, and purple enclosed in a black outline. Wares made since the 1870s for export are enameled in a wide variety of colors and styles.

Reference: Sandra Andacht, *Oriental Antiques & Art: An Identification And Value Guide*, Wallace-Homestead, 1987.

Vase, 9½" h, $225.00.

Beaker, 4½" h, hp florals and birds, red, orange, and gold, white ground, marked "Ao–Kutani"	85.00
Biscuit Jar, Geisha Girl, c1890	165.00
Bowl, 6⅝" d, gilt and bright enamel design, figural, animal, and floral reserves, kinrande ground, base inscribed "Kutani–sei," set of 10	385.00
Charger, 18⅜" d, pomegranate tree, chrysanthemums, and two birds on int., birds and flowers between scrolling foliate bands, irregular floral and brocade border, 11 character inscription	525.00
Dish, 10½" d, central scene, magpies in bamboo forest	250.00
Figure	
12" h, Bodhidharma, standing, long red robe, flywisk in right hand	175.00
14¼" h, Kannon, polychrome and gilt dec, standing, dragon mount, high coiffure, wind–swept robe, inscribed "Kutani–sei"	500.00
Garden Seat, 19" h, barrel shape, two large circular reserves of courtly figures in garden, small reserves with florals and landscape scenes, spiraling brocade ground, top pierced with circular florets, pr	2,000.00
Jar, 20½" h, ovoid, fan shaped reserves of warriors, molded ribbon tied tasseled ring handles, shippo–tsunagi ground, multicolored brocade patterned dome lid, pr	1,350.00
Mustard Pot, attached saucer, Nishikide diapering, figural raised gold reserves, marked	65.00
Tea Caddy, 6" h, bulbous, hexagonal, Nishikide diapering, figural raised gold reserves of children, red script mark	75.00
Teapot, cov, bulbous, One Thousand Faces	225.00
Tray, 14" l, polychrome and gilt, figural scene, red, orange, and gold border	325.00
Vase	
9¾" h, ovoid, waisted neck, recessed ring foot, upper portion with enameled reddish–brown wave pattern, underglaze blue wide band of archaistic keyfret design, raised borders, lower section with gilt painted stylized lotus blossoms, green enamel scrolling leafy tendrils, bluish–black ground	360.00
10¾" h, trumpet, shaped figural and floral reserves, kinrande patterned ground, base inscribed "Kutani 3 Kuma Zukuri"	250.00

LALIQUE

LALIQUE

History: Rene Lalique (1860–1945) first gained prominence as a jewelry designer. Around 1900 he began experimenting with molded glass brooches and pendants, often embellishing them with semiprecious stones. By 1905 he was devoting himself exclusively to the manufacture of glass articles.

In 1908 Lalique began designing packaging for the French cosmetic houses. He also produced many objects, especially vases, bowls, and figurines, in the Art Noveau style in the 1910s. The full scope of Lalique's genius was seen at the 1925 Paris International Exhibition of Decorative Arts. He later moved to the Art Deco form.

The mark "R. LALIQUE FRANCE" in block letters is found on pressed articles, tableware, vases, paperweights, and mascots. The script signature, with or without "France," is found on hand blown objects. Occasionally a design number is included. The word "France" in any form indicates a piece made after 1926.

The post–1945 mark is "Lalique France" without the "R"; there are exceptions to this rule.

References: Katherine Morrison McClinton, *Introduction to Lalique Glass*, Wallace-Homestead, 1978; Tony L. Mortimer, *Lalique*, Chartwell Books, 1989.

Reproduction Alert: Much faking of the Lalique signature occurs, the most common being the addition of an "R" to the post–1945 mark.

LAMP SHADES

History: Lamp shades were made to diffuse the harsh light produced by early gas lighting fixtures. These early shades were made by popular Art Nouveau manufacturers including Durand, Quezal, Steuben, Tiffany, and others. Many shades are not marked.

References: Dr. Larry Freeman, *New Lights on Old Lamps*, American Life Foundation, 1984; Jo Ann Thomas, *Early Twentieth Century Lighting Fixtures*, Collector Books, 1980.

Bonbon Box, Lily of the Valley, marked "Claire d'Lune," block sgd "R Lalique," 10⅛" d, $650.00.

Lustre Art, bell shaped, opalescent ground, gold feathers, gold iridescent int., 2½" d collar, 5¼" h, $175.00.

Ashtray, 5¾" d, lion, molded gargoyle form rim, extended mane ridges, engraved script sgd	**165.00**
Castor Set, 5½" h, two bottles, frosted, matching frosted glass holder, engraved script sgd	**220.00**
Center Bowl, 14" d, daisy, broad molded rim, clear, brown patina on floral border	**450.00**
Figure, 5½" h, Pan, dancing with wood nymph, c1950	**325.00**
Liqeur Glass, 2¼" h, frosted cherubs, clear ground, sgd "R Lalique"	**110.00**
Perfume Bottle 4" h	
Blue sphere, star design, quarter moon stopper, marked "Sans La Nuit"	**360.00**
Frosted urn, four faces molded at corners, marked "Guerlain Masques," orig black case	**550.00**
Powder Box, cov, sepia wash of two ladies, arms entwined, fancy scrolls and flowers on cov, sepia wash garlands of flowers on base, sgd on base "Coty" and "Lalique Depose," c1915	**500.00**
Powder Jar, 3¼" d, round, four moths on cov, pale green patina, molded trees base, sgd	**825.00**

Aladdin	
Cased, green	**850.00**
Satin, white, dogwood dec	**45.00**
Art Glass, 14" d, acid finish, white and green, lavender border, etched signature	**300.00**
Bradley and Hubbard, 18" d, leaded glass, geometric mottled green pattern	**350.00**
Cameo Glass, 8⅜" d, 5" h, white leaves, yellow ground	**225.00**
Cased Glass, 6⅞" d, 6⅜" h, shaded rose to pink, mushroom shape, emb swirl design, ruffled top	**225.00**
Custard Glass, 2" d fitter ring, brown nutmeg stain	**40.00**
Durand	
8" d, lily, irid threads, opal ground, sgd	**250.00**
9½", Gold Egyptian Crackle, blue and white overlay, bulbous, ruffled rim, sgd	**175.00**
Fenton, 4", white opal hobnails, blue ground	**90.00**
Fostoria	
5" d, white luster ground, gold, green leaves and vines	**150.00**
5½" d, zipper pattern, green pulled dec, opal ground, gold lining	**175.00**
Galle, 6½", cameo glass, floriform, milky	

sides with overlaid orange and olive, fired polished, sgd **475.00**

Handel, 24″ d, leaded glass, wisteria flower, foliage, and bamboo design, sgd "Handel" on shade and ring . . . **4,300.00**

Imperial Glass, marigold, NuArt **50.00**

Lalique

Amber, 12″, molded shells, sgd **560.00**

Crystal, 13″, molded ivy, green stain, sgd **750.00**

Leaded Glass, 28″ d, grape and foliage design, orig hanging hardware, sgd "Duffner and Kimberly, NY" **9,000.00**

Loetz, 8½″ d, irid, green oil spotting, ribbon work over white glass int., c1900 . . . . **225.00**

Luster Art, 5″ h, opal, blue pulled double hooked feather dec, gold border, gold iridescent int., acid etched signature **390.00**

Lutz Type, 8″ sq, 6¼″ h, opaque white loopings, applied cranberry threading, ribbon edge **175.00**

Monart Glass, 6½″ d, white opal **85.00**

Muller Freres, 6″ h, satin frosted white top, cobalt blue base, yellow highlights, set of 3 . . . . **225.00**

NuArt, irid, Carnival glass, marigold, pr **125.00**

Opalescent and amber, optic, Coinspot pattern, c1880 . . . . **55.00**

Opaque

7¾″ d, 6″ h, white, dome type **55.00**

9″ d, 4½″ h, white, gilt and gray dec, red lines **125.00**

Pairpoint, 7″ h, puffy, flower basket, reverse painted pink and yellow poppies and roses **400.00**

Quezal

Dark Green, 5½″, platinum feathering, gold lining **650.00**

Iridescent gold ground

Feather pattern, sgd, pr **200.00**

Opal snakeskin top, irid gold and green snakeskin base, corset shape, pr **275.00**

Opalescent Ground, 6⅞″ d, irid gold trellis design, gold lining, ruffled rim **765.00**

Rubena, 7¼″ d, 7⅝″ h, 3⅞″ fitter, cranberry shading to clear, frosted and clear etched flowers and leaves, ruffled **175.00**

Steuben

Aurene, irid brown, platinum applied border **425.00**

Calcite, etched dec, acorn shape . . **225.00**

Feather pattern, green, iridescent gold and white **100.00**

Tiffany

Bell shape, 5¼″, iridescent gold ground, set of 4 . . . . **1,000.00**

Yellow pulled feather dec, 1⅝″ d top, 1½″ d base, 3″ h, iridescent blue ground, soft blue, scalloped rim . . **250.00**

Verlys, 3⅝″ d, 5¾″ h, raised birds and fish dec **275.00**

LAMPS AND LIGHTING

History: Lighting devices have evolved from simple stone age oil lamps to the popular electrified models of today. Aimé Argand patented the first oil lamp in 1784. Around 1850 kerosene became a popular lamp burning fluid, replacing whale oil and other fluids. In 1879 Thomas A. Edison invented the electric light bulb, causing fluid lamps to lose favor and creating a new field for lamp manufacturers to develop. Companies like Tiffany and Handel developed skills in the manufacture of electric lamps, having their decorators produce beautiful aesthetic bases and shades.

References: James Edward Black, ed., *Electric Lighting of the 20s & 30s, Volume 2 with Price Guide*, L–W Book Sales, 1991; J. W. Courter, *Aladdin, The Magic Name in Lamps*, Wallace–Homestead, 1980; J. W. Courter, *Aladdin Collectors Manual & Price Guide #13*, published by author, 1990; J. W. Courter, *Aladdin Electric Lamps*, published by author, 1987; Robert De Falco, Carole Goldman Hibel, John Hibel, *Handel Lamps*, H & D Press, Inc., 1986; Larry Freeman, *New Light on Old Lamps*, American Life Foundation, 1984; Edward and Sheila Malakoff, *Pairpoint Lamps*, Schiffer Publishing, 1990; Nadja Maril, *American Lighting: 1840–1940*, Schiffer Publishing, 1989; Leland & Crystal Payton, *Turned On: Decorative Lamps of the 'Fifties*, Abbeville Press, 1989; Jo Ann Thomas, *Early Twentieth Century Lighting Fixtures*, Collector Books, 1980; Catherine M. V. Thuro, *Oil Lamps*, Wallace–Homestead, 1976; Catherine M. V. Thuro, *Oil Lamps II*, Thorncliffe House, Inc., 1983.

Collectors' Clubs: Aladdin Knights of the Mystic Light, Route 1, Simpson, IL 62985; Historical Lighting Society of Canada, P.O. Box 561, Postal Station R, Toronto, ON M4G 4E1; Rushlight Club, Old Academy Library, 150 Main Street, Wethersfield, CT 06109.

Museum: Winchester Center Kerosene Lamp Museum, Winchester Center, CT.

Additional Listings: See specific makers and Pattern Glass.

AMERICAN, EARLY

Betty Lamp, 5″ h, wrought iron, wire pick, hanger **175.00**

Hand

Cobalt Blue, Princess Feather pattern **125.00**

Lavender blue, applied handle, ftd . . **100.00**

Opalescent and blue, applied handle **550.00**

Hanging, 15″, aqua, flared rim, tin crown frame with applied knobs, tooling and

Early American, camphor, pewter, brass caps, 8⅜″ h, $190.00.

cut scallops, blown bell shape globe,
red paint traces 675.00
Kettle, 10½″, wrought iron, twisted stem
and pick on chain, spherical font,
whale oil burner, brass feet 200.00
Loom, 32″ l, wrought iron, hanging,
burns candles or splints 400.00
Marriage, 12¼″ h, opaque white base,
clambroth and blue opaque matching
holder and fonts, brass collars,
marked "D C Ripley & Co, Patd pend-
ing" 750.00
Miner's, 11¼″ h, brass and iron, 19th C 50.00
Peg
3¾″ h, cameo, cranberry cut to yellow–green, orig burner 120.00
5½″, brass, wood base, acorn shade 110.00
11″, amethyst cut to clear, Kosmos–
Brenner burner 250.00
Rushlight, 9″ h, wrought iron, candle
arm, mounted on block of wood . . . 65.00
Tole, 6¼″ h, saucer base, dark brown
japanning, whale oil burner 150.00
Whale Oil
7¼″ h, pr, pewter, Roswell Gleason . 200.00
8″ h, clear, sq pressed base, blown
font, pewter collar 110.00

BOUDOIR

Aladdin, 14½″ h, 8″ d reverse painted
bell shade, pine border, floral molded
polychromed metal base 200.00
Cut Glass, 9″ h, flared base, sunburst
design, mushroom shade 250.00
Handel
Reverse painted floral swag dome

shade, metal base, 14″ h, 7″ d, sgd
and numbered, stripped finish . . . 660.00
Tree trunk base, bronze finish 200.00
Pairpoint, bronze base with Art Nouveau design, domed shade with re-
verse painted poppy motif 2,000.00

Boudoir, custard glass shade, multi-colored floral dec, metal base, 16″ h, $85.00.

CHANDELIERS

Brass, 48″ d, sunburst design 200.00
French, 22″ h, 21″ d, Neoclassical style,
silver gilt metal, knopped and figural
mounted standard, four candle arms,
acanthus cast corona 495.00
Louis XV
32″ h, gilt bronze and rock crystal,
six–light, open cage form, suspending pear shape drops with ap-
plied floral prunts 3,025.00
47″ h waisted openwork cage form,
three tiers of C scrolls with faceted
citrine colored and plain glass pear
shape drops and fluted cylindrical
lusters, ribbed cane and bead
chains, applied floral prunts, spherical faceted globe supports a spire
and globular pendant, linked diagonal spiral reeded cane and bead
panels, mid 18th C 4,400.00
Regency Style, 45″ d, 42″ h, gilt bronze,
eighteen–light, c1900 . . . . 6,600.00
Sevres Style, 47″ h, 32″ w, inverted
dome base with twenty–four candle
arms, knobbed standard with foliate
dec, corona painted with putti 2,200.00
Venetian Glass
48″ d, 58″ h, threaded and blown
cranberry glass shaft, clear glass

scrolled rods suspends faceted
swags, fourteen scrolled candle
arms with molded drip pans **770.00**

DESK

Handel
6½" d, bronze base, overhanging
style, leaded glass green shade,
sgd **2,000.00**
17" h, paneled amber and red glass
cylinder piano shade, adjustable
carved bronze base, threaded label **825.00**
Louis XVI, 33", silverplated, four light,
circular dished stand with ribbed border, hexagonal molded and coved
standard, ribbed central knob, four S
scroll arms, hexagonal nozzles and
drip pans, beaded edges, black tole
painted shade **3,500.00**
Tiffany, 14" h, bronze base with verdi-
gris finish, opalescent green Nautilus
shade, marked "Tiffany Studios New
York" **4,250.00**

FLOOR

Bradley and Hubbard, 56" h, 7" d small
domed leaded glass shade, green
slag glass, gold key border, open
framework, adjustable standard,
domed circular foot **365.00**
Handel, harp base, bronze finish, two
parrots on yellow ground shade, sgd
"Handel #7073 G A" **8,000.00**
J Kuyken, 69" h, chromed metal, red
glass, c1930 . . . . **5,775.00**
Michael Taylor, 78" h, cast plaster, palm
tree, painted white, rising leaf molded
stem, fluted shallow cup, domical
base **2,750.00**

FLUID

Bristol Glass, 27" h, Victorian, high relief
foliate and cherub head dec, polychrome enamel painted floral re-
serves **425.00**
Hinks Duplex Patent, brass and cut
glass **150.00**
New England Glass Co, 9½" h, Acorn
and Drapery pattern, stepped
pressed base, three ring knob, free
blown font, pewter collar **255.00**
Ripley, 14½" h, opaque white and blue,
double fonts **475.00**
Sandwich
4½" h, Star and Punty pattern **150.00**
13" h, Onion pattern, opaque white,
c1840 . . . . **650.00**
Unknown Maker, 9" h, attributed to Pair-
point, pr, pear shape fonts, double cut

overlay, amethyst cut to clear, vintage
pattern, brass stems, marble bases . **400.00**

HANGING

Blown, 26½" h, hall type, clear, vintage
dec, globe with folded rims and
smoke bell, brass fittings, iron chain,
marked "Made in Austria" **225.00**
Brass, 11½", pierced globular vessel,
three suspending chains, 17th C . . . **375.00**
Handel
8" h, compressed ovoid form, painted
oasis scene, bronze mounts,
chipped ice surface **2,500.00**
10" d, hall type, spherical form, acid
cut, translucent white, brown vase
and foliate dec, ornate orig hard-
ware **4,100.00**
10" h, enameled birds in flight scene,
irid amber ground, orig fittings, sgd
"Handel #6885" **6,500.00**
27¾" l, angular strapwork, verdigris
finish, four cylindrical textured glass
shades, brown strapwork design,
marked "Handel 3410" **1,100.00**
Perzel, 40¼", chrome metal and glass **1,225.00**

STUDENT

Bradley and Hubbard, 21" h, brass, adjustable horizontal arm, rod form
standard, domed spreading foot,
opaque white glass shade, clear
glass chimney, vasiform oil reservoir
and matching burner, marked "Bradley & Hubbard Mfg Co" within trian-
gle, c1900 . . . . **250.00**
Brass, 23¼" h, double, replaced canary
shades, electrified, chimney rings
marked "Manhattan Brass Co" **700.00**
Handel, 8" h, Oriental gilded base,
pointed ovoid shade with parrot, yellow ground, sgd "Handel #7095 Co" **1,500.00**
Tiffany, 14" h, bronze, harp form, fluted
base, green patina, sgd "Tiffany Stu-
dios, New York 419" **650.00**

TABLE

Art Nouveau, leaded slag, domed
shade with wisteria design **750.00**
Astral style, 31" h, gilded brass and
marble, cut prisms, frosted and cut to
clear shade, electrified **375.00**
Bradley and Hubbard
14" d, octagonal paneled shade, patinated over variegated yellow,
matching base **800.00**
14" h, Art Nouveau, lily design, four
branch supports, green patina . . . **375.00**
18" d, patinated tapered base with re-

lief tulips, domed shade with re-
verse painted tulips, green ground **2,500.00**
23½" h, leaf cast baluster standard,
foliate fringed circular base, eight
panel domical shade with butterscotch and white striated glass overlaid with pierced foliate patinated
metal borders, imp "Bradley & Hub-
bard Mfg Co" **720.00**
Cameo Glass, Mt Washington, pink cut
to white, umbrella style shade, Pairpoint silverplated foot and font, orig
cleaning instruction label **6,500.00**

**Table, cameo glass, Galle, conical
shade, trumpet shaped base, translucent yellow glass overlaid in yellow—
orange, lime green, and brown, etched
oranges, branches, and leaves, cameo
sgd, 31" h, $24,500.00.**

Daum Nancy, 14" h, French, cameo
glass, mushroom cap shade with
amethyst overlay landscape scene on
blue—green ground, matching base . **4,500.00**
Durand, 29½" h, brass, blue glass standard, opaque white and clear feather
pattern **250.00**
Galle, 12" h, French, cameo glass, bul-
bous base, mushroom shape shade
with red overlay blossoms and foliage
design on soft yellow ground, orig fit-
tings **56,000.00**
Handel
23" h, 17¾" d reverse painted shade,
Teroma style, road scene, painted
brown, green, and orange trees,
golden sky, numbered "6230," sgd
"WR," urn shaped base **13,750.00**

23" h, 18" d shade
Leaded glass caramel slag panels
over green, pine needle border,
three socket bronzed base, sgd **1,540.00**
Reverse painted shade, grove of
orange and green maple trees,
golden ground, emb tree trunks
and branches on slender base,
orig patina, metal collar marked
"Handel Lamps Patent Number
979664," bronze base die
stamped "Handel" **8,800.00**
Jefferson, foliate base, green patina, reverse painted scene on domed
shade, sgd "Jefferson Co, 1012 L D" **900.00**
Miller, paneled glass, amber slag glass
panels, green over paint, applied
blossom molded gilt metal base . . . **330.00**
Moe Bridges, painted base, riverside
scene on shade **1,050.00**
Pairpoint
17½" d, tripod silver plated base, reverse painted flared shade with
four birds **5,000.00**
18" d, ftd baluster base with copper
finish, tapered shade with reverse
painted winter trees scene, orange
sky **3,700.00**
Tiffany
13" h, tripod base with three lily form
lights, stippled gold finish, sgd "Tiffany Studios" on base and "L C T"
on shade **3,400.00**
14" h, candlestick, favrile glass, ruf-
fled shade, twist baluster base,
gold iridescence, orig mounts, sgd
"LCT" **1,300.00**
16" d, slender baluster base, textured
gold finish, soft amber ten panel
linen fold shade **7,000.00**
21" h, Greek Model, three arm bronze
base with verdigris finish, green
and yellow acorn shade, marked
"Tiffany Studios, New York" **5,450.00**
21½" h, bronze, teardrop form tripod
base with turtle back tiles, domed
shade with green mosaic design
set with band of turtle back panels,
green patina **18,000.00**
Unknown Maker, 24" h, silvered cast
metal base, paneled shade with mot-
tled white and brown glass panels . . **350.00**

LANTERNS

History: A lantern is an enclosed, portable light
source, hand carried or attached to a bracket or
pole to illuminate an area. Many lanterns can be
used both indoors and outdoors and have a pro-
tected flame. Fuels used in early lanterns included

candles, kerosene, whale oil, coal oil, and later gasoline, natural gas, and batteries.

Reference: Anthony Hobson, *Lanterns That Lit Our World,* published by author, 1991.

Watchman's, tin, bull's eye lens, folding handle, whale oil burner, c1850, 6" h, $65.00.

Barn, 11" h, wood, four glass sides, hinged door 145.00
Candle
  10 x 9 x 14¼", pine, sliding panel, diamond shaped glass panes on sides, pierced, three openings, low strap handle 375.00
  9" h, tin, attributed to New England Glass Co, orig black paint 275.00
  16", sq, walnut, four glass sides, conical pierced tin top and ring handle, crimped pan and socket 625.00
Dark Room, 17" h, orig black paint, white striping, tin kerosene font and burner, "Carbutt's Dry Plate Lantern, PA April 25th 1882" label 55.00
Folding, 10", tin, glass sides, emb "Stonebridge 1908" 65.00
Japanese, Patterson Brothers adv, Lansing, MI, panels with General U S Grant, puppies, young girl, and wilderness scene 175.00
Kerosene
  9¾" h, brass, curved lens replaced . 40.00
  12", tin, pierced, brass burner, marked "Vortex" 150.00
  15", tin, pierced, orig kerosene burner and brass label "J. D. Brown/Patent/May 29, 1860," rusted surface 150.00
  24½" h, tin, orig black paint and kerosene burner, mercury reflector, stenciled label "C.T. Ham Mfg Co's New No. 8 Tubular Square Lamp, Label Registered 1886" 175.00
Miner's, tin, three part, leather fitting for head, adapter with brass plate for pole, two wire loop handles, adjustable reflector, hinged tin door, emb "Ferguson, NY 1878" 150.00
Nautical, masthead, 23" h, 11" d, copper

and brass, oil fired, orig burner, label reads "Ellerman, Wilson Line, Hull," mid 19th C 250.00
Political Rally, 67" h, gilded wrought iron, flat diamond shape with diamond shape windows outlined with gilding, amber glass panels, "1842" in gilt, acorn finials, pine carrying staff, mounted on wood base 1,800.00
Railroad, 16", tin, wide reflector, kerosene burner, marked "Buhol No. 100" 75.00
Ship's, 16" h, brass, orig whale oil burner, sgd on bottom, dated 1851 . 1,050.00
Skater's
  11" h, brass, clear bulbous globe, wire bail handle 125.00
  13½" h, cast iron, lacy base, bulbous clear globe, pierced tin top and wire bail handle 225.00
Wall, 24½", exterior, kerosene type, black painted metal sq frame, glass sides, pyramidal glass sided top, round metal finial, orig burner and mercury reflector, stenciled "C T Ham Mfg Co's New No 8 Tubular Square Lamp," c1886 .... 175.00

LEEDS CHINA

History: The Leeds Pottery in Yorkshire, England, began production about 1758. Among its products was creamware that was competitive with that of Wedgwood. The initial factory closed in 1820, but various subsequent owners continued until 1880. They made exceptional cream colored ware, either plain, salt-glazed, or painted with colored enamels, and glazed and unglazed redware.

Early wares are unmarked. Later pieces bear marks of "Leeds Pottery," sometimes followed by "Hartley-Green and Co." or the letters "LP". Reproductions also have these marks.

Reference: Susan and Al Bagdade, *Warman's English & Continental Pottery & Porcelain, 2nd Edition,* Wallace–Homestead, 1991.

Bowl, cov, floral panels dec, swan finial 160.00
Candlestick, 10" h, spreading sq pedestal pierced shaft, stylized flowers, balustrade nozzle, sq leaf sprig molded bobeche, sq coved leaf sprig molded and foliate reticulated base, imp "Leeds Pottery" 225.00
Charger, 15⅝", multicolored urn of flowers dec, blue feather edge 450.00

Creamer, 4½", gaudy flowers and
leaves, creamware 325.00
Cup and Saucer, handleless, multico-
lored floral design 200.00
Cup Plate, 3¾", gaudy blue and white
floral dec 250.00
Egg Cup, 2¾", creamware, reticulated   145.00
Jar, cov, 4¼" h, blue and yellow dec . .   175.00
Jug
5¾" h, sponge dec in shades of gray
and blue, entwined strap handle,
flower head and foliage terminals .   400.00
8¾" h, creamware, Mary and Eliza-
beth/William and Joseph, floral ter-
minal on handle 3,500.00
Miniature
Cup and Saucer, handleless, multicolored enameled flowers 125.00
Pitcher, 2" h, softpaste, multicolored
dec, emb leaf handle 85.00
Mug, 5", multicolored polychrome floral
dec 240.00
Nut Dish, 4¾", leaf shape, blue Oriental
dec 140.00

**Bowl, blue florals and rim, 4½" d, 3" h,
$75.00.**

Plate
6⅜", multicolored house scene,
sponged trees, blue feather edge .   325.00
7½", multicolored strawberry dec,
blue feather edge 300.00
8½", creamware, reticulated, emb . .   100.00
Platter, 19¼", blue flowers and leaves,
blue feather edge, minor staining . .   235.00
Sugar, softpaste
4¾" h, fluted ribs, multicolored floral
dec 200.00
6", gaudy floral, blue bands 250.00
Teapot
5½" h, gold, blue, green, and brown
garlands, spout repaired, disco-
lored 75.00
10" h, Queen Anne style, peafowl
dec, extensively repaired top and
lid 110.00

LENOX CHINA

History: In 1889 Jonathan Cox and Walter Scott
Lenox established The Ceramic Art Co. at Trenton,
New Jersey. By 1906 Lenox formed his own com-
pany, Lenox, Inc. Using potters lured from Belleek,
Lenox began making an American version of this
famous ware.

Older Lenox china has two marks: a green
wreath and a palette. The palette mark appears
on blanks supplied to amateurs who hand painted
china as a hobby. The Lenox Company still exists
and currently uses a gold stamped mark.

Reference: Mary Frank Gaston, *American Belleek,* Collector Books, 1984.

Additional Listings: Belleek.

Bouillon Cup and Saucer, gold band and
handles, monogrammed 25.00
Bowl, ftd, sterling silver overlay, blue
glazed ground, Art Deco 115.00
Chocolate Set, chocolate pot, cov, six
cups and saucers, Golden Wheat pat-
tern, cobalt ground, 13 pcs 275.00
Cigarette Box, white apple blossoms,
green ground, wreath mark 40.00
Cream Soup, Tuxedo, green mark . . .   35.00
Cup and Saucer
Alden 20.00
Golden Wreath 20.00
Honey Pot, 5" h, 6¼" underplate, ivory
beehive, gold bee and trim 75.00
Jug, 4" h, hp, grapes and leaves,
shaded brown ground, sgd "G Mor-
ley" 240.00
Mug
5¼" h, Harvard College dec, dated
1910 . . . .   85.00
6¼" h, monk, smiling, holding up
glass of wine, shaded brown
ground, SS rim 150.00

**Salt, shell motif, green wreath mark, 3"
d, 1" h, $35.00.**

Perfume Lamp, 9″ h, figural, Marie Antoinette, bisque finish, dated 1929	650.00
Plate	
Alden, dinner	15.00
Tuxedo, salad, gold mark	10.00
Salt, 3″ d, creamy ivory ground, molded seashells and coral, green wreath mark	35.00
Salt and Pepper Shakers, hp, green and gold bird dec, pr	65.00
Shoe, white, bow trim	185.00
Tea Set, teapot, creamer, and sugar, Hawthorne pattern, silver overlay	215.00
Tea Strainer, hp, small roses dec	65.00
Toby, William Penn, pink handle	150.00
Vase	
6″ h, roses dec, sgd "W Morley"	165.00
8″ h, tree stump, robin, glazed white	125.00
9¼″ h, hp, woodland scene, shaded brown ground, marked "Ceramic Art Co"	100.00

LIBBEY GLASS

History: In 1888 Edward Libbey established the Libbey Glass Company in Toledo, Ohio, after the closing of the New England Glass Works of W. L. Libbey and Son in East Cambridge, Massachusetts. The new Libbey company produced quality cut glass for the "Brilliant Period."

In 1930 Libbey's interest in art glass production was renewed. A. Douglas Nash was employed as a designer in 1931.

The factory continues production today as Libbey Glass Co.

Reference: Carl U. Fauster, *Libbey Glass Since 1818—Pictorial History & Collector's Guide,* Len Beach Press, 1979.

Additional Listings: Amberina Glass and Cut Glass.

Bowl	
8″ d, Regis pattern	230.00
9″ d	
Apple blossoms, sgd	135.00
Saber, hobstars, and crosshatching, notched prism, sgd	220.00
10″ d, 4″ h, amberina, fold down rim, sgd	825.00
Compote, 10½″ d, clear foot, clear ribbed crystal with pink optic swirl bowl, sgd	215.00
Cordial, American Prestige pattern, c1930	45.00
Ice Cream Tray, 10 x 14″, Gloria pattern	275.00
Pitcher, 10″ h, copper wheel cut leaves and butterfly design, sgd	140.00
Plate, 7″ d, Gloria pattern	165.00
Sherbet, silhouette stem, black rabbit, sgd	135.00

Vase, amberina, round base, flared rim, scalloped edges, sgd, 7⅞″ h, $1,000.00.

Tray, 15″ l, oval, saber, hobstars, cane, and central feather design, sgd	610.00
Vase	
8″ h, oviform, ribbed, waisted neck, wafer and ball stem	715.00
8¼″ h, tapered, optic fern and pink threaded design, clear foot, sgd	310.00
9″ h, bud, elongated, ribbed	610.00
12″ h, trumpet	
Amberina, fuchsia, ribbed	415.00
Cut glass, floral pattern, flutes and horizontal ladder, precise cutting, clear blank, 1906–19 trademark	295.00
13½″ h, baluster, emerald green cut flower panels, ftd, sgd base	700.00
14″ h, amberina, tapered, ribbed, fuchsia flared rim, ftd	880.00

LIMITED EDITION COLLECTOR PLATES

History: Bing and Grondahl made the first collector plate in 1895. Royal Copenhagen issued their first Christmas plate in 1908.

In the late 1960s and early 1970s, several potteries, glass factories, mints, and artists began issuing plates commemorating people, animals, events, etc. Christmas plates were supplemented by Mother's Day plates, Easter plates, etc. A sense of speculation swept the field, fostered in part by flamboyant ads in newspapers and flashy direct mail promotions.

Collectors often favor the first plate issued in a series above all others. Condition is a prime factor. Having the original box also increases price.

Limited edition collector plates, more than any other object in this guide, should be collected for design and pleasure and only secondarily as an investment.

References: *The Bradford Book of Collector Plates, 12th Edition,* published by Bradford Exchange, 1987; Diane Carnevale and Susan K. Jones, *Collectibles Market Guide & Price Index To Limited Edition Plates, Figurines, Bells, Graphics, Christmas Ornaments, and Dolls, Eighth Edition,* Collectors' Information Bureau, 1991; Gene Ehlert, *The Official Price Guide To Collector Plates, Fifth Edition,* House of Collectibles, 1988; Paul Stark, *Limited Edition Collectibles, Everything You May Ever Need To Know,* New Gallery Press, 1988.

Periodicals: *Collector Editions,* 170 Fifth Ave, New York, NY 10010; *Collectors Mart, Inc.,* 15100 W. Kellogg, Wichita, KS 67235; *Plate World Publication,* 9200 N. Maryland Ave., Niles, IL 60648.

Collectors' Clubs: Foxfire Farm (Lowell Davis) Club, 55 Pacella Park Drive, Randolph, MA 02368; M.I. Hummel Club, P.O. Box 11, Rte, 31, Pennington, NJ 08534; Lalique Society of America, 11 East 26th Street, New York, NY 10010; Llardo Collectors Society, 43 West 57th Street, New York, NY 10019; Precious Moments Collectors' Club, 1 Enesco Plaza, Elk Grove Village, IL 60009.

Museum: Bradford Museum, Niles, IL.

Additional Listings: See *Warman's Americana & Collectibles* for more examples of collector plates plus many other limited edition collectibles.

BAREUTHER (Germany)

Christmas Plates, Hans Mueller artist, 8″ d

1967 Stiftskirche, FE	90.00
1969 Christkindlemarkt	20.00
1971 Toys For Sale	20.00
1973 Christmas Sleigh Ride	20.00
1975 Snowman	25.00
1977 Story Time (Christmas Story)	30.00
1979 Winter Day	40.00
1981 Walk In The Forest	40.00
1983 The Night Before Christmas	45.00
1985 Winter Wonderland	42.50
1987 Decorating The Tree	46.50
1989 Sleigh Ride	50.00

Father's Day Series, Hans Mueller artist, 8″ d

1969 Castle Neuschwanstein	48.00
1971 Castle Heidelberg	24.00
1973 Castle Katz	30.00
1975 Castle Lichtenstein	35.00
1977 Castle Eltz	30.00
1979 Castle Rheinstein	30.00
1981 Castle Gutenfels	40.00
1983 Castle Lauenstein	40.00

Mother's Day

1969 Mother & Children	75.00
1971 Mother & Children	20.00
1973 Mother & Children	22.00
1975 Spring Outing	25.00
1977 Noon Feeding	28.00
1979 Mother's Love	38.00
1981 Playtime	40.00

Bing and Grondahl, Christmas Plate, 1899, $900.00.

BING AND GRONDAHL (Denmark)

Christmas Plates, various artists, 7″ d

1895 Behind The Frozen Window	3,400.00
1896 New Moon Over Snow Covered Trees	1,975.00
1897 Christmas Meal Of The Sparrows	725.00
1898 Christmas Roses And Christmas Star	700.00
1899 The Crows Enjoying Christmas	900.00
1900 Church Bells Chiming In Christmas	800.00
1901 The Three Wise Men From The East	450.00
1902 Interior Of A Gothic Church	285.00
1903 Happy Expectation Of Children	150.00
1904 View Of Copenhagen From Frederiksberg Hill	125.00
1905 Anxiety Of The Coming Christmas Night	130.00
1906 Sleighing To Church On Christmas Eve	95.00
1907 The Little Match Girl	125.00
1908 St Petri Church Of Copenhagen	85.00
1909 Happiness Over The Yule Tree	100.00
1910 The Old Organist	90.00
1911 First It Was Sung By Angels To Shepherds In The Fields	80.00
1912 Going To Church On Christmas Eve	80.00
1913 Bringing Home The Yule Tree	85.00

1914 Royal Castle Of Amalienborg, Copenhagen	75.00
1915 Chained Dog Getting Double Meal On Christmas Eve	120.00
1916 Christmas Prayer Of The Sparrows	85.00
1917 Arrival Of The Christmas Boat	75.00
1918 Fishing Boat Returning Home For Christmas	85.00
1919 Outside The Lighted Window	80.00
1920 Hare In The Snow	70.00
1921 Pigeons In The Castle Court	55.00
1922 Star Of Bethlehem	60.00
1923 Royal Hunting Castle, The Hermitage	55.00
1924 Lighthouse In Danish Waters	65.00
1925 The Child's Christmas	70.00
1926 Churchgoers On Christmas Day	65.00
1927 Skating Couple	110.00
1928 Eskimo Looking At Village Church In Greenland	60.00
1929 Fox Outside Farm On Christmas Eve	75.00
1930 Yule Tree In Town Hall Square Of Copenhagen	85.00
1931 Arrival Of The Christmas Train	75.00
1933 The Korsor–Nyborg Ferry	70.00
1935 Lillebelt Bridge Connecting Funen With Jutland	65.00
1937 Arrival Of Christmas Guests	75.00
1939 Ole Lock–Eye, The Sandman	150.00
1941 Horses Enjoying Christmas Meal In Stable	345.00
1943 The Ribe Cathedral	155.00
1945 The Old Water Mill	135.00
1947 Dybbol Mill	70.00
1949 Landsoldaten, 19th Century Danish Soldier	70.00
1951 Jens Bang, New Passenger Boat Running Between Copenhagen And Aalborg	115.00
1953 Royal Boat In Greenland Waters	95.00
1955 Kalundborg Church	115.00
1957 Christmas Candles	155.00
1959 Christmas Eve	120.00
1961 Winter Harmony	115.00
1963 The Christmas Elf	120.00
1965 Bringing Home The Christmas Tree	65.00
1967 Sharing The Joy Of Christmas	48.00
1969 Arrival Of Christmas Guests	30.00
1971 Christmas At Home	20.00
1973 Country Christmas	25.00
1975 The Old Water Mill	24.00
1977 Copenhagen Christmas	25.00
1979 White Christmas	30.00
1981 Christmas Peace	50.00
1983 Christmas In Old Town	55.00
1985 Christmas Eve At The Farmhouse	55.00
1987 The Snowman's Christmas Eve	60.00
1989 Christmas Anchorage	65.00

Mother's Day Plates, Henry Thelander, artist, 6″ d

1969 Dog And Puppies	400.00
1971 Cat And Kitten	24.00
1973 Duck And Ducklings	20.00
1975 Doe And Fawns	20.00
1977 Squirrel And Young	25.00
1979 Fox And Cubs	30.00
1981 Hare And Young	40.00
1983 Raccoon And Young	45.00
1985 Bear And Cubs	40.00
1987 Sheep With Lambs	42.50
1989 Cow With Calf	48.00

Haviland and Parlon, Tapestry Series, 1972, $70.00.

HAVILAND & PARLON (France)

Christmas Series, various artists, 10″ d

1972 Madonna And Child, Raphael, FE	80.00
1974 Cowper Madonna And Child, Raphael	55.00
1976 Madonna And Child, Botticelli	50.00
1978 Madonna And Child, Fra Filippo Lippi	65.00

Lady And The Unicorn Series, artist unknown, 10″ d

1977 To My Only Desire, FE	60.00
1978 Sight	40.00
1980 Touch	110.00
1982 Taste	80.00

Tapestry Series, artist unknown, 10″ d

1971 The Unicorn In Captivity	145.00
1972 Start Of The Hunt	70.00
1974 End Of The Hunt	120.00
1976 The Unicorn Is Brought To The Castle	55.00

LALIQUE (France)

Annual Series, lead crystal, Marie–Claude Lalique, artist, 8½" d

1965 Deux Oiseaux (Two Birds), FE	800.00
1966 Rose de Songerie (Dream Rose)	215.00
1968 Gazelle Fantaisie (Gazelle Fantasy)	70.00

Lalique, 1969, Papillon, $80.00.

1970 Paon (Peacock)	50.00
1972 Coquillage (Shell)	55.00
1974 Sous d'Argent (Silver Pennies)	65.00
1976 Aigle (Eagle)	100.00

LENOX (United States)

Boehm Bird Series, Edward Marshall Boehm, artist, 10½" d

1970 Wood Thrush, FE	175.00
1972 Mountain Bluebird	65.00
1974 Rufous Hummingbird	50.00
1976 Cardinal	58.00
1978 Mockingbirds	60.00
1980 Black–Throated Blue Warblers	75.00

Boehm Woodland Wildlife Series, Edward Marshall Boehm, artist, 10½" d

1973 Raccoons, FE	80.00
1974 Red Foxes	50.00
1976 Eastern Chipmunks	60.00
1978 Whitetail Deer	60.00
1980 Bobcats	90.00
1982 Otters	100.00

LLARDO (Spain)

Christmas, 8" d, undisclosed artists

1971 Caroling	30.00
1973 Boy & Girl	50.00
1975 Cherubs	60.00
1977 Nativity	70.00

1979 Snow Dance	80.00

Mother's Day, undisclosed artists

1971 Kiss Of The Child	75.00
1973 Mother & Children	35.00
1975 Mother & Child	55.00
1977 Mother & Daughter	60.00
1979 Off to School	90.00

REED & BARTON (United States)

Christmas Series, Damascene silver, 11" d through 1978, 8" d 1979 to present

1970 A Partridge In A Pear Tree, FE	200.00
1971 We Three Kings Of Orient Are	65.00
1973 Adoration Of The Kings	75.00
1975 Adoration Of The Kings	65.00
1977 Decorating The Church	60.00
1979 Merry Old Santa Claus	65.00
1981 The Shopkeeper At Christmas	75.00

ROSENTHAL (Germany)

Christmas Plates, various artists, 8½" d

1910 Winter Peace	550.00
1911 The Three Wise Men	325.00
1912 Shooting Stars	250.00
1913 Christmas Lights	235.00
1915 Walking To Church	180.00
1917 Angel Of Peace	210.00
1919 St Christopher With The Christ Child	225.00
1921 Christmas In The Mountains	200.00
1923 Children In The Winter Wood	200.00
1925 The Three Wise Men	200.00
1927 Station On The Way	200.00
1929 Christmas In The Alps	225.00
1931 Path Of The Magi	225.00
1933 Through The Night To Light	190.00
1935 Christmas By The Sea	185.00
1937 Berchtesgaden	195.00
1939 Schneekoppe Mountain	195.00
1941 Strassburg Cathedral	250.00
1943 Winter Idyll	300.00
1945 Christmas Peace	400.00
1947 The Dillingen Madonna	975.00
1949 The Holy Family	185.00
1951 Star Of Bethlehem	450.00
1953 The Holy Light	185.00
1955 Christmas In A Village	190.00
1957 Christmas By The Sea	195.00
1959 Midnight Mass	195.00
1961 Solitary Christmas	225.00
1963 Silent Night	185.00
1965 Christmas In Munich	185.00
1967 Christmas In Regensburg	185.00
1969 Christmas In Rothenburg	220.00
1971 Christmas In Garmisch	100.00
1973 Christmas In Lubeck–Holstein	110.00

ROYAL COPENHAGEN (Denmark)

Christmas Plates, various artists, 6″ d 1908, 1909, 1910; 7″ 1911 to present

1908 Madonna And Child	1,750.00
1909 Danish Landscape	150.00
1910 The Magi	120.00
1911 Danish Landscape	135.00
1912 Elderly Couple By Christmas Tree	120.00
1913 Spire Of Frederik's Church, Copenhagen	125.00
1914 Sparrows In Tree At Church Of The Holy Spirit, Copenhagen	100.00
1915 Danish Landscape	150.00
1916 Shepherd In The Field On Christmas Night	85.00
1917 Tower Of Our Savior's Church, Copenhagen	90.00
1918 Sheep and Shepherds	80.00
1919 In The Park	80.00
1920 Mary With The Child Jesus	75.00
1921 Aabenraa Marketplace	75.00
1922 Three Singing Angels	70.00
1923 Danish Landscape	70.00
1924 Christmas Star Over The Sea And Sailing Ship	100.00
1925 Street Scene From Christianshavn, Copenhagen	85.00
1926 View Of Christmas Canal, Copenhagen	75.00
1927 Ship's Boy At The Tiller On Christmas Night	140.00
1928 Vicar's Family On Way To Church	75.00
1929 Grundtvig Church, Copenhagen	100.00
1930 Fishing Boats On The Way To The Harbor	80.00
1931 Mother And Child	90.00
1932 Frederiksberg Gardens With Statue Of Frederik VI	90.00
1933 The Great Belt Ferry	110.00
1934 The Hermitage Castle	115.00
1935 Fishing Boat Off Kronborg Castle	145.00
1936 Roskilde Cathedral	130.00
1937 Christmas Scene In Main Street, Copenhagen	135.00
1938 Round Church In Osterlars On Bornholm	200.00
1939 Expeditionary Ship In Pack–Ice Of Greenland	180.00
1940 The Good Shepherd	300.00
1941 Danish Village Church	250.00
1943 Flight Of Holy Family To Egypt	425.00
1945 A Peaceful Motif	325.00
1947 The Good Shepherd	210.00
1949 Our Lady's Cathedral, Copenhagen	165.00
1951 Christmas Angel	300.00
1953 Frederiksborg Castle	120.00
1955 Fano Girl	185.00
1957 The Good Shepherd	115.00
1959 Christmas Night	120.00
1961 Training Ship Danmark	155.00
1963 Hojsager Mill	80.00
1965 Little Skaters	60.00
1967 The Royal Oak	45.00
1969 The Old Farmyard	35.00
1971 Hare In Winter	80.00
1973 Train Homeward Bound For Christmas	85.00
1975 Queen's Palace	85.00
1977 Immervad Bridge	75.00
1979 Choosing The Christmas Tree	60.00
1981 Admiring The Christmas Tree	55.00
1983 Merry Christmas	60.00
1985 Snowman	55.00
1987 Winter Birds	58.00
1989 The Old Skating Pond	50.00

Mother's Day Plates, various artists, 6¼″ d

1971 American Mother	125.00
1973 Danish Mother	60.00
1975 Bird In Nest	50.00
1977 The Twins	50.00
1979 A Loving Mother	30.00
1981 Reunion	40.00

SCHIMD (Japan)

Disney Christmas Series, undisclosed artists, 7½″ d

1973 Sleigh Ride, FE	400.00
1975 Caroling	20.00
1977 Down The Chimney	25.00
1979 Santa's Surprise	20.00
1981 Happy Holidays	18.00

Disney Mother's Day Series

1974 Flowers For Mother, FE	80.00
1976 Minnie Mouse And Friends	20.00
1978 Flowers For Bambi	20.00
1980 Minnie's Surprise	20.00
1982 A Dream Come True	20.00

Peanuts Christmas Series, Charles Schulz, artist, 7½″ d

1972 Snoopy Guides The Sleigh, FE	90.00
1974 Christmas Eve At The Fireplace	65.00
1976 Woodstock's Christmas	30.00
1978 Filling The Stocking	20.00
1980 Waiting For Santa	50.00
1982 Perfect Performance	35.00

Peanuts Mother's Day Series, Charles Schulz, artist, 7½″ d

1972 Linus, FE	50.00
1974 Snoopy And Woodstock On Parade	40.00
1976 Linus And Snoopy	35.00
1978 Thoughts That Count	25.00
1980 A Tribute To Mom	20.00
1982 Which Way To Mother?	20.00

WEDGWOOD (Great Britain)

Christmas Series, jasper stoneware, 8″ d

1969 Windsor Castle, FE	225.00
1970 Christmas In Trafalgar Square	30.00
1972 St Paul's Cathedral	40.00
1974 The Houses Of Parliament	40.00
1976 Hampton Court	46.00
1978 The Horse Guards	55.00
1980 St James Palace	70.00
1982 Lambeth Palace	80.00
1984 Constitution Hill	80.00
1986 The Albert Memorial	80.00

Mothers Series, jasper stoneware, 6½″ d

1971 Sportive Love, FE	25.00
1972 The Sewing Lesson	20.00
1974 Domestic Employment	30.00
1976 The Spinner	35.00
1978 Swan and Cygnets	35.00
1980 Birds	48.00
1982 Cherubs With Swing	55.00
1984 Musical Cupids	55.00
1986 Anemones	55.00

Queen's Christmas, A Price artist

1980 Windsor Castle	30.00
1981 Trafalgar Square	25.00
1982 Piccadilly Circus	35.00
1983 St Pauls	32.50
1984 Tower Of London	35.00
1985 Palace Of Westminister	35.00
1986 Tower Bridge	35.00

LIMOGES

History: Limoges porcelain has been produced in Limoges, France, for over a century by numerous factories other than the famed Haviland. One of the most frequently encountered marks is "T. & V. Limoges" which is the ware made by Tressman and Vought. Other identifiable Limoges marks are A. L. (A. Lanternier), J. P. L (J. Pouyat, Limoges), M. R. (M. Reddon), Elite and Coronet.

References: Susan and Al Bagdade, *Warman's English & Continental Pottery & Porcelain, 2nd Edition,* Wallace–Homestead, 1991; Mary Frank Gaston, *The Collector's Encyclopedia Of Limoges Porcelain, 2nd Edition*, Collector Books, 1991.

Additional Listings: Haviland China.

Berry Set, 9½″ master bowl, eight 8″ serving bowls, hp, purple berries on ext., white blossoms on int., marked "T & V"	250.00
Bowl, 4½″ h, ftd, hp, wild roses and leaves, sgd "J E Dodge, 1892"	75.00
Box, 4¼″ sq, cobalt and white ground, cupids on lid, pate–sur–pate dec	170.00
Cache Pot, 7½″ w, 9″ h, male and female pheasants on front, mountain scene on obverse, gold handles and four ball feet	225.00
Cake Plate, 11½″ d, ivory ground, brushed gold scalloped rim, gold medallion, marked "Limoges T & V"	70.00
Chocolate Pot, 13″ h, purple violets and green leaves, cream ground, gold handle, spout, and base, sgd "Kelly, JPL/France"	325.00
Chocolate Set, 9½″ h chocolate pot, four cups and saucers, light green, floral dec, gold trim	250.00
Creamer, 3¼″ h, purple flowers, white ground, gold handle and trim	40.00
Cup and Saucer, hp, flowers and leaves, gold trim, artist sgd	75.00
Dresser Set, pink flowers, pastel blue, green, and yellow ground, large tray, cov powder, cov rouge, pin tray, talc jar, and pr candlesticks, 7 pcs	395.00
Dinner Service, twelve dinner plates, eleven salad plates, eight dessert plates, ten tea cups, eleven saucers, gilt geometric panels, white ground, stamped factory mark "J P, L France," incised numbers, 52 pcs	365.00
Figure, 25″ h, 13″ w, three girls, arms entwined, holding basket of flowers, books, and purse, marked "C & V" and "L & L"	450.00
Fish Service, twelve sq form plates, six different fishing scenes in center, gilt dec cobalt blue border, matching rect two handled sauce boat, underglaze green mark "CFH/GDM," Gerad Defraissein et Morel, late 19th C, 13 pcs	275.00
Hair Receiver, blue flowers and white butterflies, ivory ground, gold trim, marked "JPL"	75.00
Lemonade Pitcher, matching tray, water lily dec, sgd "Vignard Limoges"	335.00

Oyster Plate, multicolored florals, white ground, gold trim, marked "G. D. & Co.," 10½″ d, $75.00.

Mug, corn motif, sgd "T & V Limoges France" **60.00**
Nappy, 6″ d, curved gold handle, gold scalloped edges, soft pink blossoms, blue–green ground **30.00**
Oyster Plate, 8″ d, six wells, ribbed molded, gold tracery, cream and yellow ground **85.00**
Plaque, 9½″ w, 7″ h, hp, landscape, curved roadway, tall trees, setting sun, green, blue, orange, and brick red, T & V printed mark, framed, c1915 .... **275.00**
Perfume Tray, 9½″ d, hp, apple blossoms, blue shaded to pink to gray ground, pierced handles **50.00**
Pitcher, 8 x 6½″, hp, russet yellow apples, multicolored shaded ground, beaded handle, artist sgd "JPL" ... **115.00**
Plate
  8½″ d, hp, pink roses, leaves, gold trim, scalloped rim **25.00**
  9″ d, hp, pastel florals, Art Nouveau enameled gold dec, ornate gold scalloped rim **30.00**
Presidential China, 8½″ d plate, cup, and saucer, William Henry Harrison, made for firm of M W Beveridge, Washington, DC, marked "Harrison 1892," 3 pcs **1,150.00**
Punch Bowl, 13″ d, scalloped gold rim, fruit blossom dec, gold band pedestal base **225.00**
Sauce Bowl, hp, fish, baskets, and sailing ships, shell motif, c1895 ...... **95.00**
Snuff Box, hp, wildflowers and gold tracery, pink ground, artist sgd, dated 1800 .... **200.00**
Strawberry Dish, artist sgd, factory mark **95.00**
Tankard Set, 14″ h tankard, four mugs, hp, grape dec, gold and green ground, 5 pcs **300.00**
Tray, 14⅛″ d, scenic, thatched cottages, bridge, and stream, two people on path, emb leaf border, pink and gold trim **225.00**
Vase, 11″ h, flamingo, sgd "WG Limoges France," c1890 .... **135.00**

LINENS

History: The term linen now has become a generic designation for household dressings for table, bed, or bath, whether made of linen, cotton, lace, or other fabrics.

Linen, as a table cover, is mentioned in the Bible and other writings of an early age. We see "borde cloths" in early drawings and paintings with their creases pressed in sharply. It was a sign of wealth and social standing to present such elegance.

During the period before the general use of forks when fingers were the accepted means of dining, napkins were important. They usually were rectangular and large in size. In the early 18th century, napkins lost their popularity. The fork had become the tool of the upper classes who apparently wished to show off their new found expertise in the use of the fork. After diners did much damage to tablecloths, finicky hostesses decided that the napkin was a necessity. It soon reappeared on the table.

The Victorian era gave us the greatest variety of household linens. The lady of the house had time to sit and sew a fine seam. Sewing became a social activity. Afternoon callers brought their handwork with them when they came to gossip and take tea. Every young girl was expected to fill her hope chest with fine examples of her prowess. In the late 19th century these ladies made some very beautiful "white work," using white embroidery of delicate stitchery, lace insertions, and ruffles on white fabrics. These pieces are highly sought after today.

The 20th century saw a decline in that type of fine stitchery. The social pace quickened. Household linens of that period show more bright colors in the embroidery, the designs become more light-hearted and frivolous, and inexpensive machine-made lace was used. Kitchen towels were decorated with animals or pots and pans. Vanity sets dominated the bedroom; the Bridge craze put emphasis on tablecloths and napkin sets. To fill the desire for less expensive lace cloths and bedspreads, women of the Depression started crocheting. Many examples of this craft are available.

With the advent of World War II, more women went to work. The last remnant of fine stitchery quickly diminished. Technological advances in production and fibers lessened the interest in hand made linens.

Collecting And Use Tips: Most old linens are fragile, some are age stained from being stored improperly for years. Unless you have a secret for removing these stains without damaging the fabric, look for those items in very good or better condition.

Linens which are not used frequently are best stored unpressed, rolled Boy Scout style, and tucked away in an old pillowcase out of bright light. Be sure the linens and pillowcases have been rinsed several times to remove all residue of detergent.

For laundered pieces which are used often, wrap in acid free white tissue or muslin folders. If the tissue is not acid-free, it will cause the folded edges to discolor. If possible, store on rollers to prevent creasing. Creased areas become weak and disintegrate in laundering. Acid–free wrapping material can be purchased from Talas, 104 Fifth Avenue, New York, NY 10011.

References: Virginia Churchill Bath, *Lace*, Henry Regnery Co., 1974; Alda Horner, *The Offi-*

cial *Price Guide Linens, Lace and Other Fabrics,* House of Collectibles, 1991; Frances Johnson, *Collecting Antique Linens, Lace, and Needlework,* Wallace–Homestead, 1991; Lois Markrich and Heinz Edgar Kiewe, *Victorian Fancywork,* Henry Regnery Co., 1974; *McCall's Needlework Treasury,* Random House, 1963; Francis M. Montgomery, *Textiles In America, 1650–1870,* W. W. Norton & C. (A Winterthur/Barra Book); Patricia Esterbrook Roberts, *Table Settings. Entertaining And Etiquette. A History And Guide,* Viking Press, 1967.

Collectors' Clubs: International Old Lacers, Box 1029, West Minster, CO 80030; Lace Guild of New York, P.O. Box 1249, Gracie Street Station, New York, NY 10028.

Museums: Metropolitan Museum of Art, New York, NY; Museum of Early Southern Decorative Arts (MESDA) Winston–Salem, NC; Museum Of Fine Arts, Boston, MA; Rockwood Museum, Wilmington, DE; Shelburne Museum, Shelburne, VT; Smithsonian Institution, Washington, D.C.

Bedspread
   Crochet, double size, small medallion motif, crocheted together with fine webbing, pale green, green fringed, three sides **250.00**
   Victorian, 104 x 112″, white work, bleached muslin, one third tucking and embroidered eyelet dec, eyelet edges, c1890 .... **225.00**
Bolster Case, white linen, ends open, embroidered garland of white flowers with script letter "P" in center, crocheted edging, c1920 .... **50.00**
Bridge Set
   Irish Linen, double damask, allover floral and swirl pattern, wide hand hemstitched border, four matching napkins, set **35.00**
   Madeira, white linen, drawn and embroidery work, embroidered flower basket corners, scalloped edges, four matching napkins, set **25.00**
Curtain Panel, each panel 36 x 84″, pr, appliqued linen and re–embroidered floral and scroll design, scalloped outer edge and bottom, net background, machine made, ... **75.00**
Doily
   Crochet, 10 x 13″, rooster center, white **24.00**
   Filet Net, 14″ d, ecru, re–embroidered flowers and leaves **3.50**
Dresser Scarf
   Madeira, cut work, hand embroidered satin stitch, pointe lace insets each end, filet lace borders on four sides, c1930 .... **30.00**
   Victorian, 122 x 36″, white linen, white work, floral design ends, heavy

   padded satin stitch, scalloped edges, c1890 .... **25.00**
Napkin
   Cocktail, cotton, pale yellow, one corner elephant embroidered, fringed edges, c1930, set of 8 .... **7.50**
   Dinner, linen
      20″ sq, double damask, ½″ hand hemstitched border, wreath motif center, set of 4 .... **24.00**
      22″ sq, double damask, rose pattern, hand rolled hem, set of 8 . **36.00**
      24″ sq, double damask, satin stripe border, hand hemstitched, set of 8 .... **40.00**
   Luncheon, 14″ sq, white Swiss linen, one corner flower basket embroidered, c1920, set of 4 .... **12.00**
Pillow Case
   Cotton, embroidered girl with umbrella, bright colors, machine made lace edge, from stamped kit, c1935, pr **15.00**
   Linen, 22 x 15″, cut work and embroidery, filet lace showing mythological marine theme in center and filet lace corner, edged in machine made lace, button back **65.00**
   Madeira, linen, pointe lace surrounded by embroidered cut work, pale blue floral and swirl design, scalloped end opening, pr **45.00**
   Percale, 19 x 12″, scalloped and eyelet border **15.00**
Pillow Sham
   48 x 34″, single size, white muslin, wide border of machine tucking, machine made lace edge **35.00**
   50 x 35″, double size, muslin, Victorian white work, narrow machine tucking on border, cut and embroidered edges, c1890 .... **65.00**
Placemat Set, cotton, white, Battenberg, lavish corners and edging, napkins to match, c1940, set of 8 ..... **75.00**
Runner
   10½ x 105″, Pointe de Venise, cartouche and circle design, handmade, early 20th C **275.00**
   16 x 50″, cotton, white, Chinese hand drawn work, early 20th C **18.00**
   26 x 148″, irish linen, white, double damask, allover small flower design, hand rolled ends, early 20th C **75.00**
Sheet, linen, white
   44 x 100″, floral and spray motif cut work top, scalloped sides, machine hemmed bottom **100.00**
   86 x 101″, madeira, bridal, 18″ deep embroidered cut work, filet lace insets, 2″ filet lace border top, narrow

hemstitching bottom, pr matching pillow cases, set **250.00**

Tablecloth

54 x 54", tea cloth, Chinese cotton, hand drawn central star motif, deep drawn work borders sides, hand hemstitched border **15.00**

60" d, white linen, heavy padded satin stitch, roses and open work, 4" machine made lace border **50.00**

66 x 128", banquet cloth, ecru, allover handmade Pointe de Venise lace, central five medallions motif with floral and foliate design set in panel, bordered swirls of medallion of flowers, interspersed flower vase forms with flowers, floral design outside border, scalloped edges, twelve cream napkins with motif in one corner and 1" matching lace edge, pre 1935, napkins unused . **3,500.00**

Table Cloth, natural color linen, Richelieu, all handmade cutwork and embroidery, floral and scroll motif, early 20th C, 68 x 100", $575.00.

68 x 98", Irish linen, double damask, Queen Victoria Royal Jubilee 1887, portrait of Queen circular motif center, surrounded by symbols of countries of Realm interspersed with thistles motif, Royal Jubilee and 1887 ribbon motif, fleur–de–lis, maltese crosses, and small bellflowers background border, 19th C **950.00**

68 x 100", hemstitched, lavish blue Madeira embroidery, twelve matching napkins, 13 pcs **225.00**

72 x 58", crochet, tobacco string, filet lace sq motifs, c1930–40 . . . . **50.00**

76 x 116", linen, cut work and filet lace inserts, twelve large napkins, 13 pcs **325.00**

92 x 105", cotton, cut work with blue apenzell type cut work and embroidery design center, scalloped edges **75.00**

Towel, hand

23 x 15", linen huck, cut work and filet lace inserts on both ends, late 19th C **8.00**

24 x 40", white linen, double damask, gold color woven border leaf pattern, satin stitch monogram "MW", 6" hand tied fringe **18.00**

Tray Cover, pale blue linen, embroidered small pink flowers, "Good Morning" upper left corner, 2 matching napkins, set **12.00**

LITHOPHANES

History: Lithophanes are highly translucent porcelain panels with impressed designs. The design is formed by the difference in thickness of the plaque. Thin parts transmit an abundance of light while thicker parts represent shadows.

Lithophanes were first made by the Royal Berlin Porcelain Works in 1828. Other factories in Germany, France, and England later produced them. The majority of lithophanes on the market today were made between 1850 and 1900.

Collectors' Club: Lithophane Collectors Club, P.O. Box 4557, Toledo, OH 43620.

Museum: Blair Museum of Lithophanes and Carved Waxes, Toledo, OH.

Candle Shield, 9" h, panel with scene of two country boys playing with goat, castle in background **260.00**

Cup and Saucer, blue Oriental lady with nude lady **150.00**

Fairy Lamp, 9" h, three panels, lady leaning out of tower, rural romantic scenes **1,200.00**

Lamp

Night, 5¼" h, sq, four scenes, irid green porcelain base, gold trim, electrified **600.00**

Table

8" h, 8" d five panel shade, 4½ x 6¼" panels with scenes of children, lovers, emb floral brass frame, panels sgd "PPM" **400.00**

20¾" h, colored umbrella style shade, four panels of outdoor

Victorian scenes, bronze and slate standard, German **675.00**

Lamp Shade, 13″ d, dome, three genre scenes, scrolling designs **425.00**

Panel
  KPM
    2½ x 3¼″, view from West Point . **175.00**
    3⅞ x 5¼″, lake setting, ship and windmill **150.00**
    4¾ x 6½″, man kneeling, mosque type building **225.00**
  PPM
    3¼ x 5¼″, view of Paterson Falls . **175.00**
    4 x 6″, boy with drum **400.00**
  P.R. Sickle, 4¼ x 5″
    Cupid and girl fishing **150.00**
    Scene of two women in doorway, dog, and two pigeons, sgd, #1320 .... **115.00**
  Unmarked
    6 x 7½″, Madonna and Child **175.00**
    7¾ x 6″, Paul and Virginia, scene of young man holding bird's nest and lemon, young woman, tropical setting **100.00**

Plaque, classical woman in garden, imp "1308/52," c1860, 4¼″ w, 5¼″ h, $125.00.

Pitcher, puzzle type, Victorian scene, nude on bottom **165.00**

Stein, ½ liter
  Floral front, soldier bidding farewell on reverse **150.00**
  Negro Boy, 5″ h **175.00**
  Regimental **190.00**

Tea Warmer, 5⅞″ h, one pc cylindrical panel, four seasonal landscapes with children, copper frame, finger grip and molded base **225.00**

LIVERPOOL CHINA

History: Liverpool is the name given to products made at several potteries in Liverpool, England, between 1750 and 1840. Among the early potters who made tin enameled earthenwares were Seth and James Pennington and Richard Chaffers.

By the 1780s tin-glazed earthenware gave way to cream colored wares decorated with cobalt, enamel colors, and blue or black transfers.

The Liverpool glaze is characterized by bubbles and most often there is clouding under the foot rims. By 1800 about 80 potteries were working in the town producing not only creamware, but soft paste, soapstone, and bone porcelain.

Reference: Susan and Al Bagdade, *Warman's English & Continental Pottery & Porcelain, 2nd Edition,* Wallace–Homestead, 1991.

Dish, blue and white, three spur feet, c1765, 5″ w, $450.00.

Jug
  6″, orange transfers, compass with label "Come box the compass" on one side, sailor's farewell scene on other, three rim chips and minor roughage **300.00**
  8″ h
    Orange transfers, ship on one side, Britannia weeping loss of Lord Nelson and banner "Trafalgar" on other, repaired around top .. **400.00**
    United States arms and banner with "May Success Attend Our Agriculture Trade and Manufactures" on one side, other with ship portrait labeled "The True Blooded Yankee," old repairs and imperfections **400.00**
  9¼″ h, American ship portrait on one

side, black transfer rural scene on other side, wreath under spout with "J Purinton," small nicks on spout and upper rim **1,600.00**

10" h, black transfer of American ship on one side, heraldic eagle on other, gold highlighting on top and sides, transfer titled "Peace, Plenty and Independence," worn dec . . . **1,800.00**

10¼" h, American ship *Caroline* portrait on one side, black transfer "The Shipwrights' Arms" on other, wreath below spout with "James Leech" and heraldic eagle in black, repaired spout, chip on bottom . . **600.00**

Mug, 3¾", dark brown transfer, Hope, allover luster trim, c1820–30 . . . . . . **125.00**

Pitcher

5¼", creamware, brown transfer of two classical women in large oval, brown transfer of flowers on ext. rim, pseudo brown transfer Fitzhugh border on int. rim, floral transfer on handle, highlighted with applied green, red, blue, and magenta, small base chip, minor restoration to spout **150.00**

6½", polychromed black transfer of Hope and man waving frantically at two ships, transfer verse "Hope as an Anchor firm and sure/Hold fast the Christian Vessel/And defies the blast," green, yellow, and red highlights **350.00**

8"

Creamware, black transfer, Peace, Plenty, and Independence, American flag sailing vessel . . . **1,150.00**

Washington Apotheosis, grieving Liberty and Indian seated in foreground, Father Time raises Washington from his tomb towards rays emanating from heaven, words on tomb "Sacred to the Memory of Washington Ob 14 Dec AD 1977 Ae 68," United States seal and ribbon under spout, transfer of American flag frigate, three pinhead size flakes **3,500.00**

LOETZ

History: Loetz is a type of iridescent art glass made in Austria by J. Loetz Witwe in the late 1890s. Loetz was a contemporary of L. C. Tiffany and worked in the Tiffany factory before establishing his own operation; therefore, much of the wares are similar in appearance to Tiffany. Some pieces are signed "Loetz," "Loetz, Austria," or "Austria." The Loetz factory also produced ware with fine cameos on cased glass.

Bowl, 12" d, deep cranberry to mottled green to clear irid, ruffled rim, sgd . . **400.00**

Compote, 10⅝" d, 5¼" h, bright orange int., deep black ext., wide flaring circular rim, three ball feet, c1920 . . . . **300.00**

Cracker Jar, 7¾" h, irid green–blue, brown oil spot dec, blown–out teardrops, silverplate lid and mountings . **625.00**

Inkwell

Amethyst, 3½" h, sq, irid, web design, bronze mouth **100.00**

Cobalt and irid gold, angular quatraform, conforming Art Nouveau hinged metal cov, ceramic well . . **360.00**

Lamp, table, 17¾" h, irid mushroom glass shade, pinched and tooled dec, hexagonal bronze base **4,000.00**

Pitcher, 8⅝" h, pinched bulbous body, purple green irid, applied handle, gilt metal mount with cast foliate motif . . **600.00**

Rose Bowl, 6½", ruffled purple irid raindrop dec **200.00**

Sweetmeat Jar, cov, 5" h, irid silver spider web dec, green ground, sgd . . . **400.00**

Urn, 9¼", ovoid, irid, blue oil spot dec, inscribed "Loetz, Austria" **1,500.00**

Vase, green irid ground, applied blue irid ribbon swirls, acid sgd "Loetz, Austria," 5" h, $250.00.

Vase

3¼" h, gold, blue zig–zag dec, ftd bronze leaf holder **360.00**

3½" h, ovoid, pinched rim, gold iridescence, silver floral overlay . . . **600.00**

5½" h

Bottle shape, bluish–gold, platinum pulled dec **440.00**

Tooled quatraform lip, metallic green and silver–blue, cased orange int. **1,045.00**

6" h, 2¼" w, triangular, two applied

shells, rippled free form drips on each side and ends, textured ground **500.00**

7" h, silvery turquoise oil spot dec, tobacco ground, four dimples **1,750.00**

7¼" h, flared, orange cased, black vertical striping, rim, and knop ... **660.00**

8" h, rainbow oil spot dec, pull-up opal and green leaves **200.00**

9" h, elongated, long blue drips, irid oil spot ground, bronze Art Nouveau double handle holder **330.00**

11¼", oval, dark red, four silver-blue pulled feather dec, ftd, sgd with circular arrow mark and "Austria" .. **2,750.00**

12" h

Amber to purple irid, bluish-gold pulled leaves, polished pontil .. **1,430.00**

Blue iridescent, pear shape, quilted pattern, gilded bronze mounts, ftd **300.00**

Flared fan shape, opal and mottled green, gold iridescent spotted dec, red-orange satin finish rim **1,650.00**

13" h

Pear shape, gold oil spot dec, wide everted rim, sgd with circle and crossed arrows **850.00**

Quatraform, rib molded, amber, maroon and gold iridescent swirl striations, folded rim, fitted bronzed metal curvilinear mount **660.00**

LOTUS WARE CHINA

History: Knowles, Taylor and Knowles Co., East Liverpool, Ohio, made a translucent, thinly potted china between 1891 and 1898. It compared favorably to Belleek. It first was marked "KTK." After being exhibited at the 1893 Columbian Exposition in Chicago, Col. John T. Taylor, company president, changed the marking to Lotus Ware because the body resembled the petals of the lotus blossom.

Blanks also were sold to amateurs who hand painted them. Most artist-signed pieces fit this category.

Bowl

4" d, raised floral dec, filigree handles **200.00**

7½" d, boat shape, pink and gold openwork, cherry blossoms, marked "KTK" **500.00**

9" w, 5" h, twig handles, floral dec, artist initials **1,300.00**

Creamer, 3¾" h, white ground, undecorated **200.00**

Cup and Saucer, hp violets, white ground, marked "KTK" **100.00**

Dish, shell shape, shell pink and pale green, small green florals, gilt coral feet, marked "KTK" **400.00**

Ewer, 7½" h, pierced, jeweled, pastel panels, Lotus mark **500.00**

Pitcher, 7" h, bulbous, fish net dec, gold, marked "KTK" **450.00**

Sugar, 4" d, fish net dec, florals, white ground, handles **350.00**

Teapot, emb flowers, gold trim, white ground, marked "KTK" **350.00**

Vase, green foliage, blue flowers, gold insect and trim, gold ball feet, white ground, 8" h, $675.00.

Vase

8" h, cylinder, ball feet, green fish net pattern, orange flowers **520.00**

10¼" h, applied white floral dec, dark green ground, Lotus mark **1,000.00**

LUSTER WARE

History: Lustering on a piece of pottery creates a metallic, sometimes iridescent, appearance. Josiah Wedgwood experimented with the technique in the 1790s. Between 1805 and 1840 luster earthenware pieces were created in England by makers such as Adams, Bailey and Batkin, Copeland and Garrett, Wedgwood, and Enoch Wood.

Luster decorations often were used in conjunction with enamels and transfers. Transfers used for luster decoration covered a wide range of public and domestic subjects. They frequently were accompanied by pious or sentimental doggerel as well as the humors of everyday life.

Copper luster was created by the addition of a copper compound to the glaze. It was very popular in America during the 19th century and experienced a collecting vogue from the 1920s to the 1950s. Today it has a limited market. The market stagnation can partially be attributed to the large number of reproductions, especially creamers and the "polka" jug, which fool many new buyers. Reproductions are heavier in appearance and weight than the earlier pieces.

Pink luster was made by using a gold mixture. Silver luster was first covered completely with a thin coating of a "steel luster" mixture, containing a small quantity of platinum oxide. An additional coating of platinum, worked in water, was applied before firing.

Sunderland is a coarse type of cream colored earthenware with a marbled or spotted pink luster decoration which shades from pink to purple. A solution of gold compound applied to the white body developed the many shades of pink.

The development of electroplating in 1840 created a sharp decline in the demands for metal-surfaced earthenware.

Reference: Susan and Al Bagdade, *Warman's English & Continental Pottery & Porcelain, 2nd Edition,* Wallace–Homestead, 1991.

Additional Listings: English Softpaste.

Copper Luster, pitcher, multicolored English wildflowers dec, copper luster oak leaves, 7½" h, $155.00.

COPPER

Creamer
3⅛" h, two rect panels, Hope transfers, red, green, blue, and purple enamel highlights, pink luster dec handle and mouth int. 70.00
3⅜" h, three bands of copper luster alternating with two bands of mustard, round blue flowers 25.00
4" h, polychrome floral dec, French, 19th C 75.00
Figure, 8", spaniels, pr 110.00

Goblet, 4½" h, 3½" d, pink luster band, floral resist dec, copper luster int. . . 45.00
Jug, 8", three transfers of mother and child playing badminton and writing letters on canary yellow band 175.00
Mug
4", raised green and white flowers on tan luster band 50.00
4¾", leaves and berries on orange luster band 60.00
Pepper Shaker, 4¼", cream colored band 40.00
Pitcher
5" h, compressed baluster, polychrome floral band, white ground . 75.00
6" h, two narrow white bands with pink luster house and trees dec, wide copper luster bands 50.00
7", green and white flowers raised dec on broad blue band 90.00
10", wide blue band around body, emb greyhound, bull, and urn of flowers in polychrome enamel, pink and purple luster 200.00
Teapot
5½" h, oblong, blue enamel band, relief molded gadrooning 50.00
6", emb ribs, polychrome enameled floral dec 125.00

PINK

Child's Mug, 2" h, pink luster band, reddish hunter and dogs transfer, green highlighted foliage transfer 50.00
Creamer, 4⅜" h, stylized flower band, pink luster highlights and rim, ftd . . . 55.00
Cup and Saucer, magenta transfers, Faith, Hope, and Charity, applied green enamel highlights, pink luster line borders 45.00
Dish, 12⅝" x 7½", shell shape, imp "Wedgwood–DUF–I–R," black underglaze "R. PHOLAS EASTATUS" . . . 85.00
Jug
5½" h, bulbous, gadrooned rim, molded berry vine border highlighted in purple–pink and lime green luster 75.00
5¾", bulbous, applied scroll handle, green glazed ground, luster spotted tracking dogs, luster spout, rim, and handle 85.00
8", church, white toned to tan 150.00
Mug, 2⅞", overall pink splash luster dec, handled 35.00
Pitcher
5½" h, ornate pink luster dec, single and double house 100.00
5⅝" h, hunting scenes, deep relief, pink luster, green enamel 55.00

Plate

6¼", relief figures of dogs running on rim, highlighted with green, red, and pink luster, red, green, and blue stylized floral dec in center . . **50.00**

7⅝" d, King's Rose pattern, red, green, and yellow, double pink luster band border **25.00**

Teapot, 12" h, House pattern, Queen Anne style, repaired finial on lid . . . **275.00**

Toddy Plate, 5¹⁄₁₆", pink luster House pattern, emb flowers sprigs border . **40.00**

Waste Bowl, 6", House pattern **125.00**

SILVER

Creamer, 4¼" h, band of scrolling flowering foliage, iron–red and silver luster, Wedgwood, 19th C **85.00**

Jug, 4½", ribbed, Staffordshire, 19th C **75.00**

Mustard Pot, 3⅞", vertical ribbed design, emb body, matching cov, ftd . . **70.00**

Pepper Pot, 5" h, standing toby form, round hollow base, pouring holes . . **85.00**

Pitcher, 6¼", Sawtooth pattern, canary and silver luster, late 18th C **375.00**

Shaker, 3⅝", ringed circumference, pedestal base **48.00**

Tea Set, pot, dome cov, sugar and creamer, oval, bulbous body, standard handles **135.00**

Vase, 5¼", flared top, painted red and silver luster nasturtium vine, c1810 . **110.00**

Sunderland Luster, pitcher, black motto, 4" h, $175.00.

SUNDERLAND

Bowl, 10", House pattern **125.00**

Celery Dish, scene of couple courting, sgd "Bucher" **120.00**

Cup and Saucer, black transfer, farm scene, handleless **85.00**

Dish, pink splash, black transfer, mother playing with son **22.00**

Gravy Boat, House pattern **150.00**

Jug

5½", black and white transfer of Mariners Arms on front, Cast Iron Bridge on back **140.00**

9", black transfer, "A Frigate in Full Sail," verse, sailor and maid, French and English coat of arms joined with "Cremea" **200.00**

17¼", heroic, pink luster int. and ext. **850.00**

Mug, 5", Foresters Arms transfer on front, Mariner's Compass on back . . **175.00**

Pitcher, 9⅛", black transfer, farmer's arms, "Cast Iron Bridge over the River Wear at Sunderland...," polychrome enameling, marked "Dixon Austin & Co, Sunderland" **475.00**

Plate

7", pink splash **15.00**

8", floral center, luster border **50.00**

Salt, master **60.00**

Sugar, House pattern **75.00**

Syrup, cov, 5" **100.00**

Tumbler, 2¾" h **60.00**

Vase, 7", trumpet shape **100.00**

LUTZ TYPE GLASS

History: Lutz type glass is an art glass attributed to Nicholas Lutz. He made this type of glass while at the Boston and Sandwich Glass Co. from 1869 until 1888. Since Lutz type glass was popular, copied by many capable glass makers, and unsigned, it is nearly impossible to distinguish genuine Lutz products.

Lutz is believed to have made two distinct types of glass, striped and threaded glass. This style often is confused with a similar style Venetian glass. The striped glass was made by using threaded glass rods in the Venetian manner. Threaded glass was blown and decorated by winding threads of glass around the piece.

Finger Bowl, white dec, red rim, clear baby face handles, 5" w, 2⅜" h, $275.00.

Compote, 8⅞ x 6½", DQ, threaded, amberina, clear hollow stem **500.00**

Epergne, three pcs, pink threads **250.00**

Finger Bowl, 7" d, ruffled edge, amber

swirls, amethyst latticino, gold metallic borders, matching underplate ... 150.00
Lamp Shade, 8" sq, 6¼" h, 2½" fitter,
sq top, opaque white loopings, applied cranberry threading, ribbon
edge 175.00
Punch Cup, 3 x 2⅝", cranberry threading, clear ground, circular foot, applied clear handle 85.00
Tumbler, 3¾", white and amethyst latticino, goldstone highlights 75.00

MAASTRICHT WARE

History: Maastricht, Holland is where Petrus
Regout founded the De Sphinx Pottery in 1836.
The firm specialized in transfer printed earthenwares. Other factories also were established in the
area, many employing English workmen and their
techniques. Maastricht china was exported to the
United States in competition with English products.

Reference: Susan and Al Bagdade, *Warman's
English & Continental Pottery & Porcelain, 2nd
Edition,* Wallace–Homestead, 1991.

Periodical: *The Dutch Potter,* 47 London Terrace, New Rochelle, NY 10804.

**Plate, design spatter, red flowers,
green leaves, blue border, marked, 9⅛"
d, $65.00.**

Bowl, 8", Oriental scene 40.00
Chocolate Pot, transfer of children,
marked 75.00
Cup and Saucer
Blue Willow, handleless 25.00
Stick spatter and gaudy polychrome
floral dec 35.00

Mug, 3" h, stick spatter and gaudy polychrome floral dec, marked 65.00
Pitcher, 4½", Oriental scene 65.00
Plaque, 10", decal of realistic pears,
shaded rust border, back pierced for
hanging 35.00
Plate
9", gaudy stick spatter dec, polychrome floral enameling 25.00
11", red and blue flower border, gold
stick spatter flowers, marked
"Maastricht, Holland" 65.00
14½", children skating, windmill in
background, blue transfer, sgd ... 65.00
Platter, 11½", gaudy polychrome florals
in red, yellow, and green, white
ground 50.00

MAJOLICA

History: Majolica, an opaque, tin glazed pottery,
has been produced by many countries for centuries. It originally took its name from the Spanish
Island of Majorca, where figuline (a potter's clay)
is found. Today majolica denotes a type of pottery
which was made during the last half of the 19th
century in Europe and America.

Majolica frequently depicted elements in nature:
leaves, flowers, birds, and fish. Human figures
were rare. Designs were painted on the soft clay
body using vitreous colors and fired under a clear
lead glaze to impart the rich color and brilliance
characteristic of majolica.

Among English majolica manufacturers who
marked their works were Wedgwood, George
Jones, Holdcraft, and Minton. Most of their pieces
can be identified through the English Registry
mark and/or the potter-designer's mark. Sarreguemines in France and Villeroy and Boch in
Baden, Germany, produced majolica that compared favorably with the finer English majolica.
Most Continental pieces had an incised number
on the base.

Although 600 plus American potteries produced
majolica between 1850 and 1900, only a handful
chose to identify their wares. Among these manufacturers were George Morely, Edwin Bennett,
the Chesapeake Pottery Company, the New Milford–Wannoppee Pottery Company, and the firm
of Griffen, Smith, and Hill. The others hoped their
unmarked pieces would be taken for English examples.

References: Susan and Al Bagdade, *Warman's
English & Continental Pottery & Porcelain, 2nd
Edition,* Wallace–Homestead,1991; Nicholas M.
Dawes, *Majolica,* Crown Publishers, 1990; Marilyn
G. Karmason with Joan B. Stacke, *Majolica: A
Complete History And Illustrated Survey,* Abrams,
1989; Mariann K. Marks, *Majolica Pottery: An
Identification And Value Guide,* Collector Books,
1983; M. Charles Rebert, *American Majolica*

1850–1900, Wallace–Homestead, 1981; Mike Schneider, *Majolica*, Schiffer Publishing, 1990.

Biscuit Jar, 8⅜ x 7⅝″, mottled green, brown, and aqua int., attached SP ftd base, hinged SP cov, sphinx finial, c1875 . . . . 250.00
Bowl
  6″, Grape, oval, lavender int., George Jones 175.00
  9″, Shell, figural, blue int., brown ext., Holdcroft 150.00
Bread Plate
  13″, Oak Leaf, green and aqua, pink edge, Etruscan 140.00
  14″, Twin Shells on Wave 185.00
Cake Stand, Geranium, pedestal, Etruscan 145.00
Cheese Dish, 8″, Rope and Fern 250.00
Compote, Morning Glory, Etruscan . . . 275.00
Creamer, 3″, Butterfly and Bamboo . . . 125.00
Cup and Saucer, Shell and Seaweed, Etruscan 150.00
Dish, Picket Fence and Morning Glory, brown mottled center 75.00
Jardiniere, 33″ h, 16″ d, C–scroll and foliage dec, shaped pedestal 275.00
Oyster Plate, 9″, six multicolored shells, plain band rim, Etruscan 125.00
Pitcher
  4¾″, Pineapple 75.00
  6½″, Basketweave, turquoise and brown, lavender int. 50.00
  7″, Pond Lily, yellow petal rim 165.00
  8¼″, Rustic, molded leaves, tree trunk body, Etruscan 200.00
  9½″, Stork in Marsh, eel figural handle 250.00
Plate
  6¾″, rect, Lily of the Valley, leaf center 70.00

Plate, raised red raspberries and green leaves, gray ground, imp leaves, marked "Keller & Guerin," 8¼″ d, $65.00.

8″
  Begonia Leaf 85.00
  Fern and Floral 75.00
9″, Morning Glory, blue, yellow lobed edge 85.00
Platter, 11¾″, Raspberry, mottled center 100.00
Relish, Onion and Pickle, cobalt ground 185.00
Sardine Box, 9½″, Pineapple, fish finial, attached underplate 300.00
Sauce Dish
  Pineapple, 5″ 35.00
  Wicker and Begonia Leaf, 5″ l, Etruscan 60.00
Spooner
  Bamboo 95.00
  Bird and Fan 90.00
  Shell and Seaweed, Etruscan, Albino, rust trim 75.00
Strawberry Server, 10½ x 6¾″, pale green, lavender border, two brown baskets, yellow flowers, green leaves, English 425.00
Sugar, cov
  Bird and Fan, marked "Wedgwood, England" 125.00
  Shell and Seaweed, Etruscan 250.00
Syrup
  Bamboo, Etruscan, pewter lid 285.00
  Blackberry, metal lid 150.00
  Sunflower, cobalt ground, Etruscan . 300.00
Teapot
  Basketweave and Flora, cream ground, pink and green, brown handle 150.00
  Cauliflower, Etruscan 195.00
  Holly and Berries, blue and green, bark handle and spout 160.00
  Shell and Seaweed, Etruscan 350.00
Toast Rack, 8½″ l, four slice, emb basketweave, mottled green, brown, and blue 300.00
Tray, 11½ x 14″, oval, shallow, cream weave, flowers, leaves, and birds in flight, green bamboo border, marked "Wedgwood" 350.00
Umbrella Stand, 24¼″ h, cylindrical, band of carnations above stylized floral dec, band of leaf tips 550.00

MAPS

History: Maps provide one of the best ways to study the growth of a country or region. From the 16th to the early 20th century, maps were both informative and decorative. Engravers provided ornamental detailing which often took the form of bird's eye views, city maps and ornate calligraphy and scrolling. Many maps were hand colored to enhance their beauty.

Maps generally were published in plate books.

Many of the maps available today result from these books being cut apart and sheets sold separately.

In the last quarter of the 19th century, representatives from firms in Philadelphia, Chicago, and elsewhere traveled the United States preparing county atlases, often with a sheet for each township and a sheet for each major city or town. Although mass produced, they are eagerly sought by collectors. Individual sheets sell for $25 to $75. The atlases themselves can usually be purchased in the $200 to $400 range. Individual sheets should be viewed solely as decorative and not as investment material.

Collectors' Club: The Association of Map Memorabilia, 8 Amherst Road, Pelham, MA 01002.

Canada, "Plan of City of Quebec," Andrews, c1771, engraved, vignettes, 33 x 24 cm **125.00**

England, "Lower Saxony...Tho. Kitchin, Geographer," hand colored, matted and framed, 14½" h, 15" w **85.00**

Mexico, "Hispaniae Novae," Ortelius, 1579, uncolored, Latin text, 53 x 42 cm **350.00**

North America, "A New And Correct Map Of North America, With The West India Islands, Divided According To The Last Treaty Of Peace Concluded At Paris 10 February 1763...," Pownall, London, 1777, two sheets, 20½ x 46½" at platemarks, full margins, from Thomas Jeffreys *American Atlas* **750.00**

North and South America, "Totius Americae Septentrionalis et Meridionalis novissima repraesantatio," Johann Baptist Homann, Nuremberg, c1720, engraved, partially hand colored in outline, lower cartouche colored in full, matted, framed, and glazed, 22 x 19½" **1,650.00**

United States
"A General Atlas, Improved And Engraved Being A Collection Of Maps Of The World And Quarters, Their Principal Empires, Kingdoms, & c.," Mathew Carey, third edition, Philadelphia, 1814, Maryland, 12½ x 17¾" **375.00**

"Boston, Cape Cod, and New York Canal," wall chart, description info, maps, insect damage near top, 37¼" w, 24" h **300.00**

Florida, "A Map of Part of West Florida, from Pensacola to the Mouth of the Iberville River, with a View to show the Proper Spot for a Settlement on the Mississippi," London, J. Lodge, 1772, engraving, hand colored, inset of Plan for a New Settlement, 7½ x 13½" **250.00**

Idaho, "Railroad And County Map Of Idaho," Cram, Chicago, 1880, 19¾ x 16¾", lithograph, outline color . . **100.00**

New Hampshire and Vermont, "A Map Of The States Of New Hampshire And Vermont," Denison, Boston, 1796, 7½ x 9" **185.00**

New York, "A Map of the Province of New York. . . ," New Jersey added by topographical observation, Claude–Joseph Sauthier, London, 1776, engraved 29 x 25", framed . **700.00**

San Diego River, survey to build levee–canal, 1853, 12 x 15" **50.00**

South Carolina, "State of South Carolina From The Best Authorities," Samuel Lewis, 15 x 18" **475.00**

Virginia, "A Map Of The Most Inhabited Part Of Virginia Containing The Whole Province of Maryland With Part of Pensilvania, New Jersey and North Carolina," engraved by Joshua Fry and Peter Jefferson, printed for R Sayer and T Jefferys, 1775, London, hand colored in outline and wash, four sheets joined in two dimensions, matted, framed, and glazed, 32½ x 48½" **13,200.00**

World
"A Chart Of The World According To Mercator's Projection Showing The Latest Discoveries Of Capt. Cook," Dilly and Robinson, 1785, 14½ x 19", colored borders and outlines . **100.00**

"A Map Of The World In Three Sections Describing The Polar Regions To The Tropics In Which Are Traced The Tracts Of Lord Mulgrave And Captain Cook ...," Bell, c1776, 9 x 16½", twin hemisphere, uncolored **125.00**

MARBLEHEAD POTTERY

History: This hand thrown pottery had its beginning in 1905 as a therapeutic program introduced by Dr. J. Hall for the patients confined to a sanitarium located in Marblehead, Massachusetts. In 1916 production was removed from the hospital to another site. The factory continued under the directorship of Arthur E. Baggs until it closed in 1936.

Most pieces found today are glazed with a smooth, porous, even finish in a single color. The most desirable pieces are decorated with conventionalized design in one or more subordinate colors.

Bowl, 7″ d, green stylized leaves, blue petaled flowers, brown trim, ochre ground, imp mark, c1910 . . . . **725.00**

Bowl, blue, matte finish, ship mark, 5″ d, 3¼″ h, $70.00.

Bookends, pr, 5¾″ h, sq tile form side, stylized cut back and incised panel of galleon on sea, dark blue glaze, incised mark and paper label **195.00**
Bulb Bowl, 6″ d, slate gray glaze, c1915 **150.00**
Honey Pot, 3½″ h, light yellow–green ground, painted stylized grapevine with clusters of blue grapes, green leaves and vines, marked **465.00**
Pitcher, 6⅛″ h, scenic band, brown bands, designed by Arthur Baggs, imp artist's marks, c1915 . . . . **1,760.00**
Tile, 4¾″ sq, high relief oyster white sailing ship, blue ground, marked **125.00**
Vase
  4½″ h, inverted bell shape, red berries and green leaves on wide neck border, brown tree trunk dec, oatmeal yellow ground, c1915 . . . . **1,000.00**
  5¼″ h
    6¼″ d, bulbous, banded dec of brown abstract geometric patterns, smooth matte green glaze, imp ship mark, incised artist initials, stilt pull on base **2,310.00**
    7⅛″ d, flared rim, tapering cylindrical body, circular foot, matte blue glaze, imp mark, c1901 . . . . . . **300.00**
  5⅜″ h, wide mouth, swollen cylindrical form, blue rhododendron leaves band, slate–blue ground, imp mark, artist initials for Hanna Tut, c1915 **425.00**
  6″ h, ovoid tapering to flared rim, wide band of stylized hanging flowers in shades of blue, matte gray ground, imp mark, paper label, and artist's initials **935.00**

MARY GREGORY TYPE GLASS

History: The use of enameled decoration on glass, an inexpensive imitation of cameo glass, developed in Bohemia in the late 19th century. The Boston and Sandwich Glass Co. copied this process in the late 1880s.

Mary Gregory (1856–1908) was employed for two years at the Boston and Sandwich Glass Co. factory when the enameled decorated glass was being manufactured. Some collectors argue that Gregory was inspired to paint her white enamel figures on glass by the work of Kate Greenaway and a desire to imitate pate–sur–pate. However, evidence for these assertions is very weak. Further, a question can be raised whether or not Mary Gregory even decorated glass as part of her job at Sandwich.

The result is that ''Mary Gregory Type'' is a better term to describe this glass. Collectors should recognize that most examples are either European or modern reproductions.

Box, 5¼″ d, 4¾″ h, sapphire blue, white enameled young girl holding basket of flowers on lid, multicolored enamel dec on base, fancy wire legs, hinged lid **630.00**
Cruet, 8½″ h, sapphire blue, sq, dimpled sides, white enameled two girls facing each other, blue handle and orig stopper **485.00**
Decanter, 5″ d, 10⅝″ h, cranberry, white enameled young girl with hat by fence **365.00**
Dresser Set, 6 pcs, tray, two perfume bottles, powder box, ring tree, and pin tray, cranberry **1,100.00**
Jewel Box, 3 x 3½″, cranberry, hinged lid **400.00**
Mug, 4½″ h, amber, ribbed, girl praying **55.00**

Tumbler, blue, white enameled boy, gold bands, pedestal foot, 5¾″ h, $140.00.

Pitcher
  6⅝" h, 4¼" d, lime green, bulbous, optic effect, round mouth, white enameled boy, applied green handle 125.00
  7½ x 9½", medium green, white enameled boy with bird and trees and girl with bowl and brush dec, pr 250.00
Plate, 6¼" d, cobalt blue, white enameled girl with butterfly net 125.00
Rose Bowl, 3" h, 3¼" d, 8 crimp top, cranberry, white enameled young girl 225.00
Salt Shaker, 5" h, blue, paneled, white enameled girl in garden, brass top . 180.00
Stein, 4" h, pr, smoked amber, boy and girl, pewter and glass lids 110.00
Toothpick Holder, cranberry, white enameled girl and floral sprays 55.00
Tumbler, 1¾" d, 2½" h, cranberry, white enameled boy on one, girl on other, facing pr 100.00
Vase
  8" h, cranberry, white enamel dec .. 165.00
  9" h, 4" d, frosted emerald green, white enameled girl holds flowers in her apron and hand 150.00
  11¼" h, 3⅞" d, cranberry, white enameled young boy with tam holding sprig, cut scalloped top 325.00
  13" h, 6⅞" d, scalloped top, applied clear reeded snail handles, cranberry, white enameled girl with flowers in her apron 400.00

MATCH HOLDERS

History: After 1850 the friction match achieved popular usage. The early matches were packaged and sold in sliding cardboard boxes. To facilitate storage and to eliminate the clumsiness of using the box, match holders were developed.

The first examples were cast iron or tin, the latter often having advertising on them. A patent for a wall hanging match holder was issued in 1849. By 1880 match holders also were being made from glass and china. Match holders lost popularity in the late 1930s and 1940s with the advent of gas and electric heat and ranges.

Advertising
  New Process Gas Range, hanging, tin, gray stove, red ground 55.00
  Sharples Separator Co, tin, mother and daughter, farm scene 85.00
Brass
  2 x 2½", fire department, copper colored, hinged lid, Reading, PA Fire Hall cello insert in lid, early 1900s 40.00
  2¾" h, owl, glass eyes, cast 60.00
  3" h, bear chained to post, cast, orig fire gilt 225.00

Advertising, Old Judson, J. C. Stevens, Kansas City, MO, 3⅝" w, 5" h, $65.00.

Bronze, 3", shoe, mouse in toe, 19th C 120.00
Cast Iron, figural
  Bird 45.00
  High Button Shoe, 5½" h, black paint, c1890 .... 40.00
  Horseshoe, antlered stag crest, hanging type, cov box at base with knob finial 35.00
Glass, 4¼" h, cobalt blue, SP brass trim, cylindrical 40.00
Majolica, 2½ x 2¼", drum shape, yellow and green, striker on base 40.00
Metal, 2 x 2¼", black enamel paint, hinged lid, inside striking surface, "The Original Teddy" photo in lid, red inscription "Theodore Bear, 149 Market St., Chicago," c1910 .... 75.00
Papier Mache, 2¾" h, black lacquer, Oriental dec 15.00
Porcelain, girl, seated, feeding dog on table, sgd "Elbogen" 125.00
Silver
  Plated, 3" h, devil's head, brass insert 40.00
  Sterling, 1¾ x 2½", hinged lid, diecut striking area, cigar cutter on one corner, lid inscription "H. R." and diamond, inside lid inscription "Made For Tiffany & Co/Pat 12, 09/Sterling" 75.00
Tin
  ¾ x 1½ x 2¼", cigar, wrap–around red, white, and blue cello, Davenport Cigars 50.00
  2⅜" h, top hat, hinged lid, orig green paint, black band 60.00

MATCH SAFES

History: Match safes are small containers used to safely carry matches in one's pocket. They were first used in the 1850s. Match safes are often figural with a hinged lid and striking surface.

Reference: Audrey G. Sullivan, *A History of Match Safes In The United States,* published by author, 1978.

Note: While not all match safes have a striking surface, this is one test, besides size, to distinguish a match safe from a calling card case.

Padlock, sterling silver, English, patent date "6/1882," 1¾" h, $250.00.

Advertising
Minnesota State Firemen's Association 1916 Tournament, silvered brass, wrap–around cello, winged nude lady angel illus on button, issued 1915 . . . . 100.00
National Supply Co, Boston, silvered brass, wrap–around cello, horse head illus, black and white design and text, early 1900 . . . . 45.00
San Felice Cigars, pocket, man and woman, "For Gentleman of Good Taste," dated 1912 . . . . 65.00
United Hatters Union, 1½ x 2¾", silvered brass, black and white cello insert panels, union text, 1900–01 75.00
Vacuum Oil Co, Rochester, NY, silvered brass, lighthouse with beam and floating barrel of marine oil on one side, 1⅜ x 2¼" 50.00
Art Nouveau stylized flowers, loop, 1⅜ x 1⅝", German (800 silver) 75.00
Brass
Billiken, watch chain loop, 1908 . . . 275.00
Dragon, Chinese 175.00
Metamorphic, skull changes to rooster 275.00
Milk Pail 185.00
Walnut 200.00
Copper and Brass, figural, baby in shirt 150.00

Gunmetal, three miniature rose diamond horseshoes, twenty seven diamonds, sapphire, gold button 325.00
Lapis, 2⅝ x ⅞" cylindrical, hinged top, brass accents 350.00
Nickel Plated, figural
Cigar 115.00
Shoe 125.00
Pewter, figural, pig, silvered 175.00
Silver
Plated, playing card dec, King of Hearts, two score keeping dials, marked "Gorham" 200.00
Sterling, Art Nouveau, repousse, lady, long flowing hair, flowers, marked "Sterline" 70.00

McCOY POTTERY

History: The J. W. McCoy Pottery Co. was established in Roseville, Ohio, in September, 1899. The early McCoy Co. produced both stoneware and some art pottery lines, including Rosewood. In October, 1911, three potteries merged creating the Brush–McCoy Pottery Co. This company continued to produce the original McCoy lines and added several new art lines. Much early pottery is not marked.

In 1910, Nelson McCoy and his father, J. W. McCoy, founded the Nelson McCoy Sanitary Stoneware Co. In 1925, the McCoy family sold their interest in the Brush–McCoy Pottery Co. and started to expand and improve the Nelson McCoy Co. The new company produced stoneware, earthen ware specialities, and artware. Most of the pottery marked McCoy was made by the Nelson McCoy Co.

References: Sharon and Bob Huxford, *The Collectors Encyclopedia of McCoy Pottery,* Collector Books, 1991 value update; Harold Nichols, *McCoy Cookie Jars: From The First To The Latest,* Nichols Publishing, 1987.

Periodical: *Our McCoy Matter,* 12704 Lockleven Lane, Woodbridge, VA 22192.

Additional Listings: See *Warman's Americana & Collectibles* for more examples.

Basket, Rustic, pine cone dec, 1945 . . 25.00
Bowl, Mt Pelee, lava type, charcoal irid, 1902 . . . . 325.00
Clothes Sprinkler, turtle 15.00
Cookie Jar
Apple Basket 35.00
Cat 35.00
Clown 35.00

Cook Stove, black	40.00
Ducks, yellow	40.00
Frontier Family	30.00
Mammy	70.00
Penguins	27.50
Pineapple	30.00
Strawberry	30.00
Train Engine, yellow	35.00
Wish I Had A Cookie	25.00
Creamer and Sugar, Daisy, brown and green	17.50
Decanter	
Apollo Missile, c1968	185.00
Pierce Arrow, Sport Phantom	35.00
Jardiniere	
4", Blossomtime	20.00
9", Rosewood, brown glaze, orange streaks	65.00
Lamp, Arcanture, bird and foliage dec	275.00
Pitcher, watering, 9½", turtle, green, twig handle	20.00

McKEE GLASS

History: The McKee Glass Co. was established in 1843 in Pittsburgh, Pennsylvania. In 1852 they opened a factory to produce Pattern Glass. In 1888 the factory was relocated to Jeannette, Pennsylvania, and began to produce many types of glass kitchenwares, including several patterns of Depression Glass. The factory continued until 1951 when it was sold to the Thatcher Manufacturing Co.

McKee named its colors Chalaine Blue, Custard, Seville Yellow, and Skokie Green. McKee glass may also be found with painted patterns, e.g., dots and ships. A few items were decaled. Many of the canisters and shakers were lettered in black to show the purpose for which they were intended.

References: Gene Florence, *Kitchen Glassware of the Depression Years, 4th Edition,* Collector Books, 1990; Lowell Innes and Jane Shadel Spillman, *M'Kee Victorian Glass,* Dover Publications, 1981.

Additional Listings: See *Warman's Americana & Collectibles* for more examples.

Planter, bust of Uncle Sam, green, 7¼" h, $30.00.

Candy Dish, orange ground, gold trim on lid, gold finial, clear base, 7¾" h, $20.00.

Planter	
Cat, green bow	8.75
Cradle	8.00
Dog, light green	12.00
Lamb, blue bow	8.00
Swan, white	7.50
Triple Lily, 1953	45.00
Spittoon, 4½", pansies, marked "Loy–Nel Art"	100.00
Tankard, corn, marked "J.W. McCoy"	80.00
Tea Set, English Ivy pattern, vine handles, 3 pcs	40.00
Vase	
9", iris dec, marked "Loy–Nel–Art"	100.00
12", handles, Olympia	175.00
15", fan, glossy, browns and yellows	200.00
Wall Pocket	
Clock	24.00
Orange	15.00

Animal Dish, dove, round base, beaded rim, vaseline, sgd	350.00
Birdhouse	85.00
Berry Set, Hobnail with Fan pattern, blue, master berry and eight sauce dishes	150.00
Bowl, 9½" d, flower band, jade	12.00
Butter Dish, Wiltec pattern, Pres–cut Ware, frosted	50.00
Candlesticks, pr, 9" h, Rock Crystal	140.00
Candy Dish, nude, lid	225.00
Cheese and Cracker Set, red, Rock Crystal	165.00
Clock, amber, tambour art	300.00
Cookie Jar, Patrician Crystal	80.00
Cruet, stopper, amber, Rock Crystal	185.00
Egg Cup, ivory	5.00

Ice Bucket, cov, black 55.00
Lamp, nude, green 150.00
Measuring Pitcher, half pint, red ships
  dec 25.00
Pitcher, 8" h, Wild Rose and Bowknot,
  frosted, gilt dec 50.00
Punch Bowl Set, bowl, twelve mugs,
  Tom and Jerry, red scroll dec 45.00
Reamer, Jadite 20.00
Refrigerator Dispenser, Jadite, 5 x 10" 95.00
Ring Box, cov, Jadite 15.00
Server, center handle, red, Rock Crystal 125.00
Toothbrush Holder, Jadite 15.00
Tumbler
  Bottoms Up
    Caramel 60.00
    Jadite 50.00
    Opalescent, green coaster 45.00
  Gladiator pattern, green, gold trim . . 30.00
  Rock Crystal, red 45.00
Vase, 8½" h, nude, Chalaine 165.00
Water Cooler, 21" h, spigot, vaseline, 2
  pc 300.00

MEDICAL AND PHARMACEUTICAL ITEMS

History: Medicine and medical instruments are well documented for the modern period. Some instruments are virtually unchanged since their invention. Others have changed drastically.

The concept of sterilization phased out decorative handles. Early handles of instruments were often carved and can be found in mother–of–pearl, ebony, and ivory. Today's sleekly designed instruments are not as desirable to collectors.

Pharmaceutical items include items commonly found in a drugstore and pertain to the items used to store or prepare medications.

References: Bill Carter, Bernard Butterworth, Joseph Carter, and John Carter, *Dental Collectibles & Antiques*, Dental Folklore Books of K.C., 1984; Douglas Congdon–Martin, *Drugstore and Soda Fountain Antiques*, Schiffer Publishing, 1991; Don Fredgant, *Medical, Dental & Pharmaceutical Collectibles*, Books Americana, 1981; Keith Wilbur, *Antique Medical Instruments,* Schiffer Publishing, 1987.

Museums: National Museum of History and Technology, Smithsonian Institution, Washington, DC; Waring Historical Library, Medical University of South Carolina, Charleston, SC.

APOTHECARY

Advertising
  Calendar, The Owl Drug Co, Dr Miles,
    weather, 1937 . . . . 55.00
  Sign, 12 x 7", The Owl Drug Co, owl

on pestle and interlaced TODCO,
  orange, brown, and gray, 1908–20 185.00
Capsule Filler, 8 x 16", Sharp and
  Dohme, chrome, orig wood box and
  instruction booklet, 1920–30 . . . . . . 150.00
Cough Drop Container, Lutted's S P
  Cough Drops, figural, cabin, clear
  with amethyst tin, American, 1910–20 260.00
Jar, 24½" h, clear, reverse painting coat
  of arms style, gold, black, and red
  paint, ground pontil base, 1880–90 . 575.00
Measuring and Cutting Tablet, 9¾ x 10",
  stoneware, glazed, black incised
  measurements, 1860s 55.00
Mortar and Pestle, 9", ash burl, turned,
  wide turned foot, plain birch pestle . 125.00
Pill Maker, 12" l, brass, iron, and wood,
  American, c1900 . . . . 130.00
Scale, counter top, marble top, wood
  base, two brass pans, orig weights . 175.00
Sign, Cosmos Medical Healer, neon . . 300.00
Window Display, bottle, bulbous, clear,
  1850–70
  35" h, engraved cross–hatched de-
    sign 375.00
  37" h, engraved leaf and grape clus-
    ter design, pontiled base 350.00

Prescription Scale, traveling, Dr. C. H. Fitch, brass top case, nickel plated scale and box base, mfg. by N. V. Randolph & Co., Richmond, VA, orig spatula, 3" l, 1½" h, $175.00.

DENTAL

Advertising
  Mirror, "Your 32 Teeth Are 32 Reasons For Using Calox, The Oxygen
    Tooth Powder," pocket, tin, oval,
    blue and yellow design, white
    ground, 1890–1910 . . . . 110.00
  Sign, 18½ x 7½", Plus De Maux De
    Dents/Le Meilleur Elixir Dentrifical/

Dontophile, green, gold, red, and
black, French **450.00**
Cabinet, oak, door with two rect win-
dows, pull out shelves, ceramic
drawer pulls **1,500.00**
Forceps, extracting, SP, handle design,
F Arnold **50.00**
Guide, *Mould Guide For Trubyte New
Hue Teeth,* The Dentists' Supply
Company of New York, American,
1920s **125.00**
Pliers, nerve canal **15.00**

MEDICAL

Advertising
Mirror, Smiths Green Mountain Ren-
ovator...Health Is Yours If You Will
Use, pocket, tin, round, bust of
woman, multicolored, 1890—1910 **175.00**
Tray, 10″ d, Hicks Capudine Cure For
All Headaches, tin, yellow and
shades of blue, 1900–20 . . . . **325.00**
Anesthesia Mask, folding, brass, c1870 **75.00**
Amputation Saw, bow blade, ebony
handle **125.00**
Book, *Gunn's New Family Physician,*
1884, illus, 1,230 pgs **25.00**
Box, wood, black print, stenciled
Dr Greene's Nervura Nerve tonic,
10½ x 11 x 8½″ **60.00**
Goff's Cough Syrup, 16½ x 14⁹/₁₆ x 9″ **55.00**
Hall's Catarrh Cure, 12½ x 8¾ x 6½″ **90.00**
Dose Glass
Royal Pepsin Stomach Bitters, clear,
American, 1900–10 . . . . **40.00**
The Owl Drug Co, 1⅞″, amethyst, owl
motif **45.00**
Todd's Best Tonic In The World, clear,
American, 1900–10 . . . . **50.00**
Hearing Aid, silk tubing **85.00**
Inhaler, Doctor Copeland's New Steam
Inhaler, The Copeland Medical Insti-
tute, 210 State Street, Chicago, box
lid with instructions, 1900s **250.00**
Model, anatomical, "Smith New Outline
Map of Human System," lithograph
on cardboard, mounted on tin, de-
tachable organs and muscles, wood
carrying case, copyright 1888 . . . . . **260.00**
Nasal Douche Cup, The Ideal Nasal
Douche Cup, emb, handle **225.00**
Paperweight, 4½″ h, Phrenologist bust,
brown, 1880–1900 . . . . **200.00**
Scalpel, set of 3, ebony, c1860 . . . . . . **400.00**
Shock Box, The Beekman Home Med-
ical Aparatus, black, orig oak box, in-
cludes battery, 1890–1900 . . . . **100.00**
Stethoscope, monatural, metal **110.00**
Surgical Set, contains saw, pliers, four
knives, tongs, and two probes, wood
case with green velvet, plaque read

"Dec 25, Randolph Campbell Hurd
1899" **650.00**
Vaporizer
Dr Geo Leininger's Formaldehyde
Generator, 5″ h, metal, alcohol
burning lamp on stand, orig box
and instructions, American, 1900–
10 . . . . **120.00**
Vapo–Cresolene, 6½″ h, metal stand
with glass oil burning lamp, orig box
and instructions, American, c1900 **130.00**

OPTICAL

Advertising Mirror, pocket, Get Your
Eyes Fitted At Schearer's Drug Store,
round, multicolored **35.00**
Eyelid Retractor, ivory handle, marked
"Hills King St," c1853 . . . . **125.00**
Opthalmoscope, cased, Morton **100.00**

MEDICINE BOTTLES

History: The local apothecary and his book of
formulas played a major role in early America. In
1796 the first patent for a medicine was issued by
the United States Patent Office. Anyone could apply for a patent. As long as the dosage was not
poisonous, the patent was granted.

Patent medicines were advertised in newspapers and magazines and sold through the general
store and by "medicine" shows. In 1907 the Pure
Food and Drug Act, requiring an accurate description of contents of medicine on the label, put an
end to the patent medicine industry. Not all medicines were patented.

Most medicines were sold in distinctive bottles,
often with the name of the medicine and location
in relief. Many early bottles were made in the glass
manufacturing area of southern New Jersey. Later
companies in western Pennsylvania and Ohio
manufactured bottles.

References: Joseph K. Baldwin, *A Collector's
Guide To Patent And Proprietary Medicine Bottles
Of The Nineteenth Century,* Thomas Nelson, Inc.,
1973; Ralph & Terry Kovel, *The Kovels' Bottle
Price List, 8th Edition,* Crown Publishers, 1987;
Carlo & Dot Sellari, *The Standard Old Bottle Price
Guide,* Collector Books, 1989.

Periodical: *Antique Bottle And Glass Collector,*
P.O. Box 187, East Greenville, PA 18041.

Amaryllis Val Schmidt & Co Chemists,
San Francisco, cobalt blue, tooled
top, 5¾″ h **130.00**
Bennet's Wild Cherry Stomach Bitters,
amber, applied top, smooth base,
1871–79 . . . . **245.00**
Burns Indian Physical Bitters, rect, bev-

eled edges, aqua, applied tapered lip, open pontil, 9⅜" h **150.00**

Cullen's Remedies Rowand & Walton Philada, rect, indented panels, aqua, tapered collar lip, open pontil, 5⅞" h **75.00**

Dr Browder's Compound Syrup Indian Turnip, rect, beveled edges, aqua, tapered collar lip, open pontil **190.00**

Dr Duncan's Expectorant Remedy, rect, beveled edges, aqua, tapered collar lip, open pontil, 6⅜" h **80.00**

Dr Fitch's Female Specific To Restore Monthly Sickness, aqua, open pontil, 3⅓" h, c1840 .... **250.00**

Dr Hoofland Balsamic Cordial CM Jackson Philadelphia, rect, rounded shoulders, indented panels, aqua, sq collar lip, open pontil, 6¾" h, c1850 . **100.00**

Dr J F Churchill's Hypophosphites of Lime Soda & Potash A Specific Remedy for Consumption, rect, indented panel, aqua, sq collar lip, open pontil, 7¾" h **300.00**

Dr. Kilmer's Female Remedy, Binghamton, NY, aqua, 8¾" h, $18.00.

Dr Kilmer's Ocean Weed Heart Remedy, The Blood Specific, aqua, double collar lip, smooth base, 8" h, c1890 . **110.00**

Dr Mintie's Nephretiucm, aqua, applied top, smooth base, 6⅞" h, 1877–80 . **210.00**

Dr Petzold's Genuine German Bitters, yellow amber, sloping collared mouth with ring, smooth base, 10½" h **110.00**

Dr R Goodales/American/Catarrh Remedy, rect, beveled edges, aqua, tapered collar lip, open pontil **110.00**

E G Lyons & Co, Ess Jamaica Ginger, lime green, applied top, smooth base, 6" h, 1866–75 .... **260.00**

Eureka Hair Restorative, aqua, applied top, smooth base, 7¼" h, 1868–73 . **750.00**

From The Laboratory of G W Merchant Chemist Lockport NY, rect, yellow–

green, applied tapered lip, open pontil, c1850 .... **400.00**

Germ Bacteria or Fungus Destroyer, amber, tooled top, smooth base, 10¼" **120.00**

Gibb's Bone Liniment, six–sided, medium olive–green, applied tapered lip, open pontil, 6¼" h, c1840 .... **625.00**

Grandjean's, New York, pyramid shape, rect base, aquamarine, rolled mouth, pontil scar, button feet, 11¼" h **120.00**

Hall's Balsam For The Lungs, sapphire blue, tooled top, smooth base, 7⅝" h **90.00**

Hall's Hair Renewer, peacock blue, tooled top, includes box and pamphlet, 7¼" h, 1900–1910 .... **130.00**

Hampton's V Tincture Mortimer & Mowbray Balto, oval, deep red–amber, applied sq collar lip, pontil, c1850 .... **600.00**

Howlands Ready Remedy/Columbia, sq, indented panels, aqua, tapered lip, open pontil, 5" h, c1850 ...... **120.00**

McClellan's Diphtheria Remedy, aqua, tooled top, smooth base, 8¼" h, 1875–85 .... **90.00**

Opium Habit Cured by Dr S B Collins Laporte Inda, cylindrical, sq collar lip, smooth base, 8" h, c1890 .... **240.00**

Rhodes Fever & Ague Cure, aqua, tapered collar lip, open pontil, 8¼" h, c1850 .... **180.00**

Rohrer's Wild Cherry Tonic Expectoral, pyramid shape, roped corners, golden amber, sloping collared mouth with ring, iron pontil mark, 10½" h .. **150.00**

Sanford's Radical Cure, rect, indented panels, sapphire blue, applied sq collar lip, emb, 1880s **150.00**

Sarracenia Life Bitters, amber, sloping collared mouth with ring, smooth base, 9¼" h **175.00**

Sun Drug Co, Los Angeles, amber, tooled top, smooth base, 8¾" h **375.00**

USA Hosp Dept, round, forest green, applied sq collar lip, smooth base, 6" h, c1865 .... **220.00**

Warner's Safe Rheumatic Cure Rochester NY USA, amber, blob top, smooth base, 9½" h, c1880 ...... **100.00**

Wing & Sisson's Magic Liniment for the cure of spavin, rect, indented panels, aqua, applied double collar lip, open pontil, 7⅜" h, c1850 .... **150.00**

Yerba Buena Bitters, flask shape, amber, tooled mouth, smooth base, 9¾" h **65.00**

MERCURY GLASS

History: Mercury glass is a light bodied, double walled glass that was "silvered" by applying a solution of silver nitrate to the inside of the object through a hole in the base of the formed object.

F. Hale Thomas, London, patented the method in 1849. In 1855 the New England Glass Co. filed a patent for the same type of process. Other American glass makers soon followed. The glass reached the height of its popularity in the early 20th century.

METTLACH

History: In 1809 Jean Francis Boch established a pottery at Mettlach in Germany's Moselle Valley. His father had started a pottery at Septfontaines in 1767. Nicholas Villeroy began his pottery career at Wallerfanger in 1789.

In 1841 these three factories merged. They pioneered in underglaze printing on earthenware, using transfers from copper plates, and in using coal fired kilns. Other factories were developed at Dresden, Wadgassen, and Danischburg.

The castle and Mercury emblems are the two chief marks. Secondary marks are known. The base also contains a shape mark and usually a decor mark. Pieces are found in relief, etched, prints under the glaze, and cameo.

Prices are for print under glaze unless otherwise specified.

References: Susan and Al Bagdade, *Warman's English & Continental Pottery & Porcelain, 2nd Edition,* Wallace–Homestead, 1991; Gary Kirsner, *The Mettlach Book, Second Edition,* Glentiques, 1987; R. H. Mohr, *Mettlach Steins, Ninth Edition,* published by author, 1982.

Additional Listings: Villeroy & Boch.

Vases, frosted palm trees, flowers, paneled sides, gold luster int., pr, $120.00.

Bowl, 4¾", enameled floral dec, gold int.	**50.00**
Cake Stand, 8" d, pedestal base, emb floral dec	**75.00**
Candlesticks, pr, 12¾", baluster, domed circular foot, amber, enameled floral sprigs, pr	**300.00**
Cologne Bottle, 4¼ x 7½", bulbous, flashed amber panel, cut neck, etched grapes and leaves, corked metal stopper, c1840	**150.00**
Creamer, 6½" h, etched ferns, applied clear handle, Sandwich	**125.00**
Garniture, 14", baluster, raised circular molded foot, everted rim, enameled foliate motif	**215.00**
Goblet, 6⅞" h, silver, etched Vintage pattern, gold int.	**50.00**
Pitcher, 5½ x 9¾", bulbous, panel cut neck, engraved lacy florals and leaves, applied clear handle, c1840 .	**200.00**
Tiebacks	
3¼", etched grapes, vines, and leaves, pewter shanks, pr	**65.00**
4", etched budding iris and scrolls, pr	**90.00**
Sugar, 4¼ x 6¼", cov, low foot, enameled white foliage dec, knob finial . .	**35.00**
Vase, 9¾", cylindrical, raised circular foot, everted rim, bright enameled yellow, orange, and blue floral sprays and insects, pr	**225.00**

Beaker, 2781, ¼ L, cameo, couple, man seated	**230.00**
Charger, 1044, 12½" d, discolored glaze	**50.00**
Compote, 346, 5½", relief, grapes and leaves, flake on base	**70.00**
Creamer and Sugar, 3321, etched . . .	**150.00**
Cup and Saucer, relief, cupids, blue, gray, and silver	**75.00**
Jar, cov, 1324, 5", glazed mosaic	**175.00**
Mug, 3287, ½ L, "Sons of the Revolution, Feb. 22, 1910"	**65.00**
Mustard, cov, 3¼", relief, floral	**85.00**
Pitcher, 8" h, applied brown floral and leafy vine dec, gray shell motif body, ftd, brown seal on base	**120.00**
Plaque	
1044/147, 14", Liechtenstein castle .	**375.00**
1044/165, 12" Meissen/Elbe	**250.00**
1048/11, 16" d, etched, brown, tan, and gray border, teal highlights, cream and black center scene of Opening Crypt of Carl the Great by Order of Otto III, castle mark	**600.00**
2013, 27" d, German eagle, names and crests of cities, eye bolts, chain hanger, imp castle mark	**6,600.00**

2112, 16″, etched, dwarf in nest holding wine bottles, sgd "H. Schlitt," rim flake ... 1,025.00
2332, 18″ d, green and white, Trojan warriors on boat, sgd "Stahl," castle mark ... 1,195.00
2625, 7½″, etched, mandolin player . 300.00
Punch Bowl, 16¼″ h, ovoid, high shouldered, tapered, domed spreading foot, applied dolphin type handles, two panels with cavaliers drinking, smoking, and playing lute with lady and servant girl, molded scroll frame, lattice ground, applied bunch of grapes on cov, includes stand with bearded dwarf seated in flowering tree drinking from wine cup, blue, green, chocolate brown, and pale pink, matte gilded highlights, castle mark, 1898–99 ... 1,450.00

Stein, 1/2 L, beige ground, green and brown dec, gilt trim, imp "2051," c1896, $700.00.

Stein
675, ½ L, relief, 6″ h ... 170.00
1467, ½ L, relief, harvest scene ... 225.00
1508, ½ L, etched, tavern scene, sgd, "Gorig" ... 435.00
1526/598, 1 L, man with rifle scene . 305.00
1526/1108, ½ L, ram and dancers scene, sgd "Hein Schlitt" ... 265.00
1909/726, ½ L, comical scene, walking beer stein ... 360.00
1909/1143, ½ L, Schlitt scene, 4 men in early dress drinking, exceptional relief pewter lid ... 250.00
1940, 3 L, etched, keeper of the wine, sgd "Warth" ... 1,500.00
2001, ½ L ... 375.00
2134, ½ L, etched, dwarf in nest ... 1,440.00
2530, ½ L, boar hunt ... 850.00

2772, ½ L, Brown University seal, owl thumb piece ... 225.00
2893/1197, 2L, PUG, Hessen shield 450.00
Tea Service, Art Nouveau dec, 16 pcs 1,200.00
Tile, 3¼ x 5¾″, blue warrior ... 225.00
Tobacco Jar, 1323, 7″ h ... 125.00
Tray, 8 x 12″, frame and handles, flying geese and large flowers ... 275.00

MILITARIA

History: Wars always have been part of history. Until the mid–19th century, soldiers often had to fill their own needs, including weapons. Even in the 20th century a soldier's uniform and some of his gear are viewed as his personal property, even though issued by a military agency.

Conquering armed forces made a habit of acquiring souvenirs from their vanquished foes. They brought their own uniforms and accessories home as badges of triumph and service.

Saving militaria may be one of the oldest collecting traditions. Militaria collectors tend to have their own special shows and view themselves outside the normal antiques channels. However, they haunt small indoor shows and flea markets in hopes of finding additional materials.

References: Ray A. Bows, *Vietnam Military Lore 1959–1973*, Bows & Sons, 1988; Robert Fisch, *Field Equipment of the Infantry 1914–1945*, Greenberg Publication, 1989; *North South Trader's Civil War Collector's Price Guide, 5th Edition*, North South Trader's Civil War, 1991; *Official Price Guide To Military Collectibles*, House of Collectibles, 1985; Jack H. Smith, *Military Postcards 1870–1945*, Wallace-Homestead, 1988; Sydney B. Vernon, *Vernon's Collectors' Guide To Orders, Medals, and Decorations*, published by author, 1986.

Periodicals: *Military Collectors' News*, P.O. Box 702073, Tulsa, OK 74170; *North South Trader's Civil War*, P.O. Drawer 631, Orange, VA 22960.

Collectors' Clubs: American Society of Military Insignia Collectors, 1331 Bradley Avenue, Hummelstown, PA 17036; Association of American Military Uniform Collectors, 446 Berkshire Rd, Elyria, OH 44035; Company of Military Historians, North Main Street, Westbrook, CT, 06498; Imperial German Military Collectors Association, 82 Atlantic St, Keyport, NJ 07735; Orders and Medals Society of America, P.O. Box 9791, Alexandria, VA 22304.

Reproduction Alert: Pay special attention to Civil War and Nazi material.

Additional Listings: Firearms and Swords. See World War I and World War II in *Warman's Americana & Collectibles* for more examples.

WAR OF 1812

Button, set of 15 buttons, coat and vest, Army, General Service, pewter 1808–

30, Infantry, pewter 1812–15, Regiment of Artillerists 1811–13, Artillery 1813–14, Light Artillery 1808–21, Artillery Corps 1814–21 . . . . 250.00

Civil War, Lt. Col. George Armstrong Custer, 6th Michigan Calvary, flag, $99,000.00.

CIVIL WAR

Bayonet, Confederate, Boyle, Gamble & MacFee 900.00
Box
 Cap, Federal, lambs wool, vent pick, die stamped US letters 100.00
 Cartridge, leather, oval brass plate emb "US" outer flap, inner flap marked "H.H. Hartzell/US/Ord Dep'/Sub Inspector," and "E. Metzger, Phila" 275.00
 Pistol, Federal, .44 cal Colt 75.00
Bullet Mold, brass, Merrill carbine 175.00
Buttons, Confederate, set of 35 buttons, coat and vest, initials, states 925.00
Canteen, 8", tin, cloth cov, stopper and carrying strap, stamped "Wadden, Porter & Booth, Phila" on pewter spout 150.00
Epaulets, officer's, gilded brass, attaching bars with silver stars, emb eagle, shield, olive branches, and arrows button, pr 200.00
Flag
 Confederacy, red, white, and blue Battle Flag, white background, inscription 5.00
 Grand National Confederate, 5 x 10', used at the 4th Encampment 225.00
Fuse Pouch
 Confederate, marked "P Darrah, Augusta, GA" 2,500.00
 Federal, marked "Navy Yard, Phila 1862" 125.00
Medical Instrument
 Amputating Knife 100.00
 Microscope, Army doctor's, mobile, brass tweezers, mahogany case, 6" h 35.00

Surgical Kit, pocket type 425.00
Plate, 8½" d, tin 35.00
Slouch Hat, Confederate cavalry 650.00
Sword
 Confederate Cavalry, curved 36" steel blade, black steel scabbard, brass basket handle, initialed and serial numbered, marked "R" & "S" . . . 175.00
 Federal, cavalry saber, scabbard, M–1840, stamped "US" 400.00

INDIAN WARS

Bayonet, Model 1873, 3½" w blade . . 75.00
Belt Buckle, Naval officer, brass, stamped "Horstman, Phila" 100.00
Broadside, Ohio massacre, Nov 4, 1791, printed in Boston, 1792, foxed, water stained, modern frame, 60¾" w, 22" h 900.00
Insignia, hat, cavalry, brass, crossed sabers, 3" w 50.00
Medical Patch, sleeve, Army, dark blue wool backing, 4 x 4" 8.00

FRANCO–PRUSSIAN WARS

Badge, bronze, Emperor Josef under eagle with crown, maker's mark "Wien" 50.00
Bayonet, black anodized scabbard, 22½", curved blade, solid brass handle, marked "MRE d'Armes Je St. Etienne, 1873" 50.00
Helmet, Prussian General Officer, spiked, silver grade star, enameled black Eagle Order on breast of Heraldic Eagle, gilt chin strap and rosettes, silk lining 1,500.00
Medal, Order of the House of Hohenzollen Knight, badge with swords, silver gilt and enameled breast badge 350.00

SPANISH AMERICAN WAR

Badge, hat, infantry, brass, crossed krag rifles, 2" l 50.00
Cartridge Box, US Army 125.00
Pinback Button
 Remember The Maine, battleship scene, patent 1896 . . . . 20.00
 We Didn't Want To Fight, But, By Jingo, Now We Do, We'll Show The Proud Old Spaniard What A Yankee Dude'll Do, white cello, black lettering 25.00
Spy Glass, pocket, Naval, brass, round holder, brown leather grip, 16" 100.00

World War I, divisional helmet, American, orig liner, $45.00.

WORLD WAR I

Badge, wound, silver, crossed silver
swords stickpin **10.00**
Bandolier, rifle cartridge, cotton, khaki,
brad arrow within C, marked "50 Ball
.303 Mark 7 D D 1916" **25.00**
Bayonet, Erzatz style, Mauser, 12" steel
blade, green painted handle, scabbard, Serial #7979 .... **30.00**
Binoculars, French Officer's, leather
carrying case, 8 x 32", excellent op-
tics **30.00**
Button
French General Joffre, black and
white portrait, yellowish color uniform **8.00**
Liberty 1776–1917, Liberty Bell,
tinted pink, white background, title
inscription and "Portland–Army–
Navy Auxiliary" **12.00**
Cartridge Pouch, leather, green, single
pocket **25.00**
Coat, officer's, wool, black scrolls on
sleeves **30.00**
Compass, British **90.00**
Dog Tag, aluminum, engraved name,
corps, and company of US Infantry,
serial number on back **8.00**
Mess Kit, tin plated steel, lid **25.00**
Parade Bar, 5 medals, includes EK 2nd
Class, nine year service silver medal
3rd class, Hindenburg cross with
swords, Leopold Bavarian 1905
medal, and Bavarian reserves medal **75.00**
Photo Album, Field Artillery Unit #27
under General Hindenburg, 34 photos, dated 1907 .... **135.00**
Propeller, US, wood, four blade **325.00**
Shoes, field, British, leather, black pebble grained, taps on toes, steel horseshoes on heels, punched broad arrow on ankle **65.00**
Sword, officer's, German, brass lion
head handle with ruby eyes, detailed

mane and mouth holding oak leaf
guard, helmeted women on back of
handle, 33" engraved blade, black
scabbard with brass ring **275.00**

WORLD WAR II

Banner, window, stitched fabric patch,
blue star center, white background,
red border **5.00**
Belt Buckle, German, DAK Luftwaffe
Em, tan web belt, marked "#85" ... **75.00**
Blanket Roll, 72" l, khaki duck, white
cloth lining, set of 3 tie tapes, Japanese **55.00**
Boots, pr
Combat, light brown, unused **12.00**
German, leather, felt wool tops, sewn
leather reinforcement straps **30.00**
Bracelet, Air Crew Member, SS, curved
wings **25.00**
Coat, Navy, flier's, leather and wool,
marked "Bu–Aero–US Navy" **50.00**
Desk Stand, prisoners, handmade,
metal, 6½" h, iron cross, eagle top,
dated 1940 & 1941, hand scratched
by Air Force Pilot in POW camp from
11/44 to 11/45 .... **15.00**
Flag, window, US Merchant Marine, 8½
x 12" **20.00**
Flying Cross, ribbons with attached
bronze oak leaves, cased **50.00**
Helmet, Tanker's, football style, leather
liner, green, snaps for earphones,
made by Wilson Ath Goods **65.00**
Knapsack, 13½" h, 12½" w, canvas,
khaki, woven light green–brownish
tapes, double friction rings, Japanese **85.00**
Knife, diver's, deep sea demolition,
solid brass scabbard, ribbed oak han-
dle with brass guard, 8" steel blade . **120.00**
Leggins, Japanese, straps, hooks,
brought back from Guam **42.00**
Medal, soldier's, parade ribbon, enameled lapel bar, black leather case .. **20.00**
Pin, Remember Pearl Harbor, brass, eagle, soldier and sailor standing attention, red, white, blue enamel inscription **8.00**
Recognition Book, Naval Forces Ship,
70 pgs, some entries, marked "Restricted", separate wall chart **10.00**
Swagger Stick, US, officer's, brass shell
casings, copper bullet tip, 22" l **20.00**

VIETNAM

Ammo Box, steel, M5-20A1, dated ... **12.00**
Helmet, flight, South Vietnam Officer's,
sun visor, white poly lining, attached
black muffed earphones, marked
"Maker Gentax Corp" **65.00**

Medal, parade type, Air Force Commendation, ribbon and lapel bar, case **20.00**

Parachute, cargo, camouflage, nylon straps, hooks, etc, American manufacturer **30.00**

Tunic, US Army, Sgt, 5th Division, green gold stripes, red diamonds insignia . **25.00**

MILK GLASS

History: Opaque white glass attained its greatest popularity at the end of the 19th century. American glass manufacturers made opaque white tablewares as a substitute for costly European china and glass. Other opaque colors, e.g., blue and green, were made. As the Edwardian era began, milk glass expanded into the novelty field.

The surge of popularity in milk glass subsided after World War I. However, milk glass continues to be made in the 20th century. Some modern products are reissues and reproductions of early forms. This presents a significant problem for collectors, although it is partially obviated by patent dates or company markings on the originals and by the telltale signs of age.

Collectors favor milk glass from the pre–World War I era, especially animal covered dishes. The most prolific manufacturers of these animal covers were Atterbury, Challinor–Taylor, Flaccus, and McKee.

References: E. McCamley Belknap, *Milk Glass,* Crown Publishers, 1949, out–of–print; Regis F. and Mary F. Ferson, *Yesterday's Milk Glass Today,* published by author, 1981; Regis F. and Mary F. Ferson, *Today's Prices For Yesterday's Milk Glass,* privately printed, 1985; S. T. Millard, *Opaque Glass,* Wallace–Homestead, 1975, 4th edition.

Collectors' Club: National Milk Glass Collectors Society, 1113 Birchwood Drive, Garland, TX, 75043.

Museum: Houston Antique Museum, Chattanooga, TN.

Notes: There are many so–called McKee animal covered dishes. Caution must be exercised in evaluating pieces because some authentic covers were not signed. Further, many factories have made, and many still are making, split rib bases with McKee–like animal covers or with different animal covers. There also is disagreement among collectors on the issue of flared vs. unflared bases. The prices for McKee pieces as given are for authentic items with either the cover or base signed.

Pieces are cross referenced to the Ferson's and Belknap's books by the (F—) or (B—) marking at the end of a listing.

Animal Dish, cov
  Dog, setter, white base, sgd "Flaccus," repair to tail **145.00**
  Fish, 8¾" l, walking, divided horizontally, five central fins support body, detailed scales, red glass eyes (B167b) **175.00**
  Hen, 7½" l, marbleized, head turned to left, lacy base, white and deep blue, Atterbury (F8) **150.00**

Bowl, 8¼" d, Daisy, allover leaves and flower pattern, repeated on inner base, open scalloped edge (F165) . **80.00**

Butter Dish, cov, 4⅞" l, sq, ftd base, curves outwards toward top, Roman Cross pattern, cube shape finial (F240) **50.00**

Calling Card Receiver, bird, back view, wings extended over fanned tail, head resting on leaf, detailed feather pattern (F669) **130.00**

Celery, 6⅝" h, scalloped rim, plain band above vertical surface, Blackberry pattern, low stem rising from circular base, Hobbs Brockunier (F317) **95.00**

Compote, Atlas, lacy edge, blue **180.00**

Creamer, 4⅜" h, row of paneled sunflowers above row of paneled lilies of the valley, long lip, heavy handle, purple slag, Atterbury (F288a) **60.00**

Egg Cup, 4¼" h, bird, cov, round, fluted, Atterbury (F130) **130.00**

Lamp, 11" h, Goddess of Liberty, bust, three stepped hexagonal base, clear and frosted font, brass screw connector, patent dated, Atterbury (F329) . . **200.00**

Match Safe, 4½" h, baby in hat, corrugated striker, black hat, match design (F534) **310.00**

Mug, 3" h, Ivy in Snow **32.00**

Plate, 6" d, two cats form upper edge, bracketed dog head, open work swirled leaves, emb "He's all right" (B20d) **90.00**

Platter, Retriever **70.00**

Spooner, 5⅛" h, monkey, cylinder

Sugar Shaker, Waffle pattern, metal top, emb "Pat'd Appl. For" on base, 7" h, $35.00.

shape, scalloped top, seated monkeys molded around circumference (F275) **115.00**

Sugar, cov, Trumpet Vine, fire painted, sgd "SV" **65.00**

Sugar Shaker, Royal Oak **75.00**

Syrup, 6" h, Bellflower pattern, single vine, dated, Collins & Wright (F155C0) **225.00**

Tumbler, Royal Oak, orig fired paint, green band **45.00**

Whimsey, rowboat, patent date, Atterbury **37.50**

Wine, Feather **35.00**

MILLEFIORI

History: Millefiori (thousand flowers) is an ornamental glass composed of bundles of colored glass rods fused to become canes. The canes were pulled while still ductile to the desired length, sliced, arranged in a pattern and again fused together. The Egyptians developed this technique in the first century B.C.; it was revived in the 1880s.

Reproduction Alert: Millefiori items, such as paperweights, cruets, toothpicks, etc., are being made by many modern companies.

Miniature Lamp, cobalt blue, orange, and ochre canes, brass trim, electrified, 12" h, $600.00.

Bowl, 8", tricorn, scalloped, folded sides, amethyst and silver deposit .. **125.00**

Cabinet Vase, 3½", waisted, ruffled top, light blue, cobalt blue, medium blue, and white canes, four applied knob handles **35.00**

Creamer, 3 x 4¼", white and cobalt blue canes, yellow centers, satin finish .. **100.00**

Cruet, bulbous, multicolored canes, applied camphor handle, matching stopper **100.00**

Cup and Saucer, white and cobalt blue canes, yellow centers, satin finish .. **85.00**

Door Knob, 2½", paperweight, center cane dated 1852, New England Glass Co **375.00**

Goblet, 7½" h, multicolored canes, clear stem and base **150.00**

Pitcher, 6½", multicolored canes, applied candy cane handle **165.00**

Rose Bowl, 6", crimped top, cased, white lining **145.00**

Slipper, 5", camphor ruffle and heel .. **135.00**

Sugar, cov, 4 x 3½", white canes, yellow centers, satin finish **115.00**

Vase, 4", multicolored canes, applied double handles **100.00**

MINIATURE LAMPS

History: Miniature oil and kerosene lamps, often called "night lamps," are diminutive replicas of larger lamps. Simple and utilitarian in design, miniature lamps found a place in the parlor (as "courting" lamps), hallway, children's rooms, and sickrooms.

Miniature lamps are found in many glass types from amberina to satin glass. Miniature lamps measure 2½ to 12 inches in height with the principle parts being the base, collar, burner, chimney, and shade. In 1877 both L. J. Atwood and L. H. Olmsted patented burners for miniature lamps. Their burners made the lamps into a popular household accessory.

Study a lamp carefully to make certain all parts are original; married pieces are common. Reproductions abound.

References: Ann Gilbert McDonald, *Evolution of the Night Lamp*, Wallace–Homestead, 1979; Frank R. & Ruth E. Smith, *Miniature Lamps*, Schiffer Publishing Ltd., 1981, 6th printing; Ruth E. Smith, *Miniature Lamps - II*, Schiffer Publishing Ltd., 1982; John F. Solverson, *Those Fascinating Little Lamps*, Antique Publications, 1988; John F. Solverson (comp.), *"Those Fascinating Little Lamps"/Miniature Lamps*, (includes prices for Smith numbers) *Value Guide*, Antique Publications, 1988.

Note: The numbers given below refer to the figure numbers found in the Smith books.

#11–I, milk glass pedestal base and shade, clear pressed font, Sandwich, 6¾" h **245.00**

#25–II, cranberry, Berger Lamp **125.00**

#29–I, cobalt blue glass font, emb "Nutmeg," narrow brass band forming handle, nutmeg burner, clear glass chimney, 2¾" d base **100.00**

Smith 229–II, cobalt blue, emb shade, $225.00.

#49–I, cobalt blue, Little Butter Cup, 2″
h, pr 250.00
#59–II, clear, emb "Vienna" 125.00
#68–I, pewter base, emb rococo de-
sign, burner marked "Stellar, E M &
Co," 3½″ h 85.00
#78–I, nickel plated, wall type, emb
"Comet," blue glass beehive chimney
shade, 7¼″ h 75.00
#89–I, brass, double student lamp, orig
opaque white shades, 9¾″ h 500.00
#109–I, green, Beaded Heart pattern,
acorn burner, clear glass chimney,
5½″ h 190.00
#112–I, amber, Bull's Eye pattern, nut-
meg burner, clear glass chimney, 5″
h 100.00
#116–I, amber, Fishscale pattern, nut-
meg burner, clear glass chimney ... 135.00
#118–I, amber, Buckle pattern, 8½″ h 125.00
#125–I, red paint, ball shaped shade,
emb flowers and designs, acorn
burner, clear glass chimney, 7¼″ h . 135.00
#154–II, brass, pedestal, saucer base 80.00
#156–I, milk glass, emb flower and
scrolls, 8″ h 115.00
#184–I, milk glass, beaded and emb
design, blue painted highlights on
base and globe–chimney shade, hornet burner 200.00
#190–I, milk glass, Block and Dot pat-
tern, 7¾″ h 135.00
#192–I, clear, Block pattern, hp blue
and green flowers, acorn burner, 6½″
h 60.00
#204–II, blue, camphor shade 100.00
#213–I, red, stain, Chrysanthemum and
Swirl pattern base and globe, hornet
burner, 9″ h 425.00
#215–I, milk glass, emb beaded panels
and boats, windmill and lighthouse on

base, vertical roses of beading on
globe–chimney shade, hornet burner,
7¾″ h 325.00
#230–I, milk glass, Acanthus pattern,
fired on yellow dec, base marked
"Buc. PA/1898," 8½″ h 175.00
#231–I, green, satin, Drape pattern,
globe shade, nutmeg burner, clear
glass chimney, 8½″ h 315.00
#267–II, Pairpoint, all orig, sgd "Dres-
den" on base 400.00
#285–II, all brass, three colored jew-
eled inserts, beading on rim, engraved flowers and leaves, 6″ d
shade, 13″ h 200.00
#287–I, apricot shaded to clear, over-
shot glass, tulip molded base and
shade, nutmeg burner, clear glass
chimney, 8½″ h 650.00
#289–II, brass, pedestal, handle 100.00
#317–I, milk glass, pink and yellow
flowers, shaded green ground 300.00
#369–I, spatter, tortoiseshell, 8¼″ h .. 250.00
#393–I, white, satin, emb ribbing, hp
pink, yellow, and green florals, nutmeg burner, clear glass chimney ... 285.00
#394–I, blue, satin, puffy DQ pattern
base and umbrella shade, nutmeg
burner, clear glass chimney, 8″ h ... 475.00
#400–I, pink, satin, Gone with the Wind,
Beaded Drape pattern, 10″ h 385.00
#459–II, red shaded to pink, satin, emb
scrolled leaves and swirl, 10″ h 1,650.00
#477–I, sapphire blue, hobnail, 7¼″ h 375.00
#482–I, clear, Daisy and Cube pattern,
nutmeg burner, 8″ h 225.00
#538–I, amberina, paneled, amber feet,
9¼″ h 1,500.00
#546–I, blue, Swirl pattern, 8½″ h ... 500.00

MINIATURES

History: There are three sizes of miniatures:
doll house scale (ranging from ½ to 1″), sample
size, and child's size. Since most earlier material
is in museums or extremely expensive, the most
common examples are 20th century.

Many mediums were used for miniatures: silver,
copper, tin, wood, glass, and ivory. Even books
were printed in miniature. Prices are broad ranged,
depending on scarcity and quality of workmanship.

The collecting of miniatures dates back to the
18th century. It remains one of the world's leading
hobbies.

References: Lillian Baker, *Creative and Collectible Miniatures*, Collector Books, 1984; Flora Gill
Jacobs, *Dolls Houses in America: Historic Preservation in Miniature*, Charles Scribner's Sons,
1974; Flora Gill Jacobs, *History of Dolls Houses*,
Charles Scribner's Sons; Constance Eileen King,
Dolls and Dolls Houses, Hamlyn; Eva Stille, *Doll*

Kitchens, 1800–1980, Schiffer Publishing, Ltd., 1988; Von Wilckens, *Mansions in Miniature,* Tuttle.

Periodicals: *Miniature Collector,* Collector Communications Corp., 170 Fifth Ave, New York, NY 10010; *Nutshell News,* Clifton House, Clifton, VA 22024.

Collectors' Clubs: International Guild Miniature Artisans, P.O. Box 842, Summit, NJ 07901; National Association of Miniature Enthusiasts, 123 N. Lemon St., Fullerton, CA 92632.

Museums: Kansas City Doll House Museum, Kansas City, MO; Margaret Woodbury Strong Museum, Rochester, NY; Mildred Mahoney Jubilee Doll House Museum, Fort Erie, Canada; Toy Museum of Atlanta, Atlanta, GA; Washington Dolls House and Toy Museum, Washington, DC.

Additional Listings: See Doll House Furnishings in *Warman's Americana & Collectibles* for more examples.

Table and Chairs, multicolored courting scenes painted on porcelain, bronze frames, Austrian, c1890, 2″ h, $900.00.

DOLL HOUSE SIZE

Armoire, tin litho, purple and black	20.00
Bathroom, wood, painted white, Strombecker	35.00
Bedroom	
French Provincial style, antique white, includes dressing table and bench, bed, night stands	150.00
Victorian style, metal, veneer finish, bed, night stand and commode with faux marble tops, armoire and mirror, cradle, Biedermeier clock, metal washstand	650.00
Bench, wood, rush seat	20.00
Breakfront, Renwal	15.00
Buffet, stenciled, three shelves, columns supports, 6″ h, Biedermeier	400.00
Chair	
Golden Oak, center splat, upholstered seats, German, c1875, pr	70.00
Ivory, high pointed back, ornately pierced, 2″ h, 19th C	175.00
Ormolu, ornate, 3″ h, c1900, pr	75.00
Couch, wood frame, floral design seat,	

blue painted back, six legs, 6″ h, Tynietoy stamp ... 70.00

Cradle, cast iron, painted green, 2″ l, 2½″ h ... 40.00

Curio Cabinet, maple, four graduated shelves, fancy carved sides, 7″ h ... 50.00

Desk
Chippendale style, slant top, drawers open	50.00
Roll top, oak, office chair, drawers open	75.00

Dining Room
Edwardian style, dark red stain, extension table, chairs, marble top cupboard, grandfather clock, chandelier, candelabra, 5″ h bisque head and shoulder maid doll, table service for six, Gebruder Schneegrass, Waltershausen, Thuringia, c1915	1,200.00
French style, gilded wood, round pedestal table, six matching chairs, damask upholstered settee, pier mirror, fireplace, table with faux marble top	800.00

Hall Rack, walnut, carved, fretwork, arched mirror back shelves, umbrella holder ... 450.00

Kitchen Stove, Petite Princess ... 70.00

Living Room
Empire style, sofa, fainting couch, two side chairs, upholstered tapestry, matching drapery	350.00
Tudor style, settee, two chairs, footstool, upholstered, fringe trim, marble topped table, candle stand	250.00
Victorian style, upholstered red velvet, settee, two parlor chairs, footstool, two plant stands, two gilt filigree tables, three panel screen, Gone with the Wind style lamp	500.00

Lounge, Victorian style, minor upholstery wear ... 100.00

Piano, grand, wood, eight keys, 5″ h ... 30.00

Rocker, Victorian style, faded upholstery ... 50.00

Sewing Table, golden oak, drawer, c1880 ... 100.00

Side Chairs, Victorian, pr ... 125.00

Table, tin, painted brown, white top, floral design, 1½″ l, ¾″ h, ornate ... 20.00

Tea Cart, Petite Princess ... 20.00

Vanity, Biedermeier ... 90.00

ACCESSORIES

Ashtray, stand, c1910	30.00
Bird Cage, brass, bird, stand, 7″ h	60.00
Candelabra, Petite Princess	20.00
Carpet Sweeper, gilt, Victorian	65.00
Chamber Pot, 1¾″ h, yellow ware, white and brown stripes	55.00

Coffee Grinder, wooden base, tin, cast iron handle and drawer, 5″ h, $65.00.

Christmas Tree, with accessories	**40.00**
Clock, metal	**25.00**
Coffeepot, brass	**20.00**
Cup and Saucer, china, flower design, 1″ scale, c1940	**8.00**
Decanter, two glasses, Venetian, c1920	**25.00**
Dust Pan and Broom, pewter, German, c1890	**30.00**
Fireplace, tin, Britannia metal fretwork, draped mantle, carved grate	**75.00**
Fireplace Tools, metal, stand, c1930 .	**50.00**
Mirror, wood, Tynietoy, c1930	**45.00**
Radio, Strombecker, c1930	**25.00**
Refrigerator, Petite Princess	**75.00**
Sewing Machine, copper, treadle	**50.00**
Silhouettes, Tynietoy, c1930, pr	**15.00**
Tea Set, teapot, cream and sugar, two cups and saucers, tray, green and white floral pattern, two handles repaired	**100.00**
Telephone, wall, oak, speaker and bell, German, c1890	**30.00**
Towel Stand, golden oak, turned post .	**45.00**
Umbrella Stand, brass ormolu, sq, emb palm fronds	**50.00**
Urn, silver, handled, ornate	**100.00**

SAMPLE SIZE

Bed, mahogany, poster, canopy top, turned posts, arched headboard . . .	**275.00**
Blanket Chest, Victorian, country, pine, 19th C, 19″ w, 9½″ d, 26″ h	**300.00**
Chest of Drawers	
Empire, pine, orig graining in imitation of curly maple, ends have face turned design, five drawers, sq nail construction, unpainted later crest, 9″ w, 6″ d, 10″ h	**300.00**

Federal, cherry, rect top, reeded edge, four graduated drawers with incised edges, slightly splayed bracket feet, 11½″ w, 5½″ d, 15″ h	**2,475.00**
Sheraton, mahogany, top with simple inlay, four dovetailed drawers with flame grain veneer facade, edge veneer, inlaid ivory escutcheons, rope carved corner columns with biscuit corners, turned front feet, old refinishing, 12¾″ w, 8¼″ d, 12¾″ h	**1,100.00**
Victorian, American, mid 19th C, mahogany, rect top, conforming case, two short and three long drawers, bracket feet, 23″ w, 11″ d, 23″ h . .	**700.00**
Clock, wag–on–the–wall, brass gears, wooden plates, wooden case, painted face, weights and pendulum, 7″ h .	**475.00**
Sleigh, poplar, worn green and red paint, yellow and white striping, polychrome floral dec, floral flocked velvet lining, wear, steel rod runners, 14¼″ l	**525.00**
Cradle, pine, orig blue paint, 16″ l	**120.00**
Desk, Chippendale, country, pine, slant front, three long drawers, molded base, bracket feet, 22″ w, 13″ d, 21″ h	**2,600.00**
Plow, pine and steel, splayed handles, projecting plow support, gilt dec, red painted ground, inscribed "South Bend Chilled Plow Co, Pat May 25, 1886, No. 15 trademark," South Bend, IN, c1886, 23½″ l	**2,000.00**
Trunk, leather bound, brass tack trim and bale handle, iron lock and hasp, orig red marbleized paper lining and label "Nath'l. E. March, Saddle, Harness and Trunk Maker, Portsmouth, New Hampshire," 9″ l	**200.00**

CHILD SIZE

Blanket Chest, William and Mary, walnut, dovetailed, turnip feet, inset initials "EB" made with cut–off nails, green paper lining, 14¾ x 7¼ x 7½″	**275.00**
Chair, ladderback, side, rabbit ear posts, worn paper rush seat, old dark finish, 25¼″ h	**45.00**
Chest of Drawers	
Chippendale, Centennial, mahogany, four drawers, bracket base, Victorian bail brass, 10⅝ x 6½ x 16¼″	**350.00**
Georgian, burl walnut, band inlay, 15½ x 8¼ x 16⅜″	**700.00**
Hepplewhite, English, late 19th C, select mahogany with some curl, pair of small drawers at top, three graduated full width drawers, French splayed bracket base, brass pulls	

with engraved flowers, 11⅞ x 7¾ x 15⅝" 550.00

Cupboard, country style, pine, two glazed doors, two drawers and doors in base, white porcelain knobs, 24½ x 23 x 13" 400.00

Desk, Chippendale, MA, c1770, painted and dec maple, slant front, rect hinged lid, int. of valanced pigeonholes, center two blocked and concave carved drawers, prospect drawers flanking, three graduated long drawers below, bracket feet, painted black on reddish–brown ground, 23 x 12½ x 28" 30,000.00

Dresser, Eastlake style, stenciled design, mirror panel, one drawer, two cabinets, 31" h 125.00

Rocker
Eastlake style, folding, bamboo turnings, tapestry seat and back, 27" h 150.00
Empire style, mahogany, vase shaped splat, rush seat, scrolled arms, 22" h 200.00
Victorian, American, late 19th C, painted black, wooden arms, caned back and seat 300.00

Side Chair, country style, pine plank seat, crest rail, turned legs, 22½" h . 150.00

Table, country style, drop leaf, walnut, turned legs, 24 x 28 x 21" 150.00

MINTON CHINA

History: In 1793 Thomas Minton and others formed a partnership and built a small pottery at Stoke–on–Trent, Staffordshire, England. Production began in 1798 with blue printed earthenware, mostly in the Willow pattern. In 1798 cream colored earthenware and bone china were introduced.

A wide range of styles and wares was produced. Minton introduced porcelain figures in 1826, Parian wares in 1846, encaustic tiles in the late 1840s, and Majolica wares in 1850. Many famous designers and artists in the English pottery industry worked for Minton.

Many early pieces are unmarked or have a Sevres type marking. The "ermine" mark was

used in the early 19th century. Date codes can be found on tableware and Majolica. Between 1873 and 1911 a small globe signed Minton with a crown on top was used.

In 1883 the modern company was formed and called Mintons Limited. The "s" was dropped in 1968. Minton still produces bone china tablewares and some ornamental pieces.

References: Paul Atterbury and Maureen Batkin, *The Dictionary of Minton*, Antique Collectors' Club; Susan and Al Bagdade, *Warman's English & Continental Pottery & Porcelain*, 2nd Edition, Wallace–Homestead, 1991.

Plate, Vermont pattern, 7¾" d, $7.50.

Centerpiece, 16" l, elongated parian vessel, molded scroll handles and feet, pierced rim, two brown reserves, white pate–sur–pate amorini, gilding, dec attributed to Lawrence Birks, marked "Minton," retailer's marks of Thomas Goode & Co, Ltd, London, c1889 .... 1,300.00

Dessert Service, Pattern G3439, fruits, twelve plates, three stands, light wear, imp mark, 1880 date code ... 825.00

Dresser Set, pin box, 5½" h pitcher, 11" d tray, pink roses dec, gold trim, incised maker and potter marks, c1898 250.00

Dish, 10¾" d, earthenware, artist sgd "W S Coleman," imp mark, 1869 ... 685.00

Ewer, 21¼" h, majolica, heron and fish, after model by J Protat, imp mark, 1869 date code 2,300.00

Figure, 7½" h, two nude children holding oval trays, pierced baskets, circular base, white, imp mark, c1882 ..... 225.00

Garden Seat, 20¾" h, majolica, streaky turquoise glaze, imp "Minton, 1896" 550.00

Jardiniere, 7" h, molded wooden planks, white vines, lilac int., majolica, matching stands, pr 425.00

Jug, 9⅞" h, majolica, bright yellow,

green, blues, aubergine, and white, imp mark "437," and 1873 date code **2,345.00**

Oyster Stand, 10″ d, majolica, revolving base, glazed green, brown, and white, imp mark, 1869 . . . . **2,225.00**

Plaque, 7⅝″ d, pate–sur–pate, matching pr, one with maiden and cupid spinning web, other with maiden seated on bench with whip in one hand, sunflowers stalked with humanistic snail in other, artist sgd "Louis Solin," both marked on back, framed **2,000.00**

Plate, 9″ d, portrait panels, multicolored, gilt tracery, reticulated border **70.00**

Soup Plate, 10⅜″ d, printed and painted famille rose style, Orientals, molded floral band border, ironstone, c1825 . **50.00**

Sweetmeat Dish, 8″ d, majolica, blue titmouse on branch, leaf shaped dish, imp mark, 1868 . . . . **665.00**

Tea Service, salt glazed, polychrome dec, Botanical pattern, 15 pcs **450.00**

Vase, 8½″ h, Oriental style, pierced scroll formed ivory ground body, raised ribbon, enameled and gilt dec, raised and ftd black ground base, printed and imp marks, c1888 . . . . . **935.00**

MOCHA

History: Mocha decoration usually is found on utilitarian creamware and stoneware pieces and is produced through a simple chemical action. A color pigment of brown, blue, green, or black is made acidic by an infusion of tobacco or hops. When the acidic colorant is applied in blobs to an alkaline ground, it reacts by spreading in feathery, seaplant–like designs. This type of decoration usually is supplemented with bands of light colored slip.

Types of decoration vary greatly, from those done in a combination of motifs, such as "Cat's Eye" and "Earthworm," to a plain pink mug decorated with green ribbed bands. Most forms of mocha are hollow, e.g., mugs, jugs, bowls, and shakers.

English potters made the vast majority of the pieces. Marked pieces are extremely rare. Collectors group the ware into three chronological periods: 1780–1820, 1820–1840, and 1840–1880.

Reference: Susan and Al Bagdade, *Warman's English & Continental Pottery & Porcelain, 2nd Edition,* Wallace–Homestead, 1991.

Bowl

4⅛″ d, black and white checkered band on rim, medium blue glaze . **70.00**

5¼″ d, black seaweed dec, blue stripes, yellow ochre band **450.00**

Caster, 4⅞″ h, black and white check-

Bowl, brown, cream, and orange earthworm dec, tan ground, raised green border, c1790–1820, 6¼″ d, $600.00.

ered band, medium blue speckled glaze **75.00**

Creamer, 5¼″ h, black and white checkered band on shoulder, medium blue glaze **200.00**

Cup and Saucer, black and white checkered band on top, fluted band on bottom, medium blue glaze **125.00**

Jug

6⅝″ h, blue and white raised earthworm dec, two blue bands **675.00**

8¼″ h, dark brown seaweed dec, blue bands enclosing gray band on top and bottom, gallon **350.00**

8½″ h, two black and white checkered bands, blue glaze, foliate handle and spout **325.00**

Measure, 4¾″ h, black seaweed dec, emb black stripe rim, emb leaf handle, applied crest "Imperial" **130.00**

Mug

2¾″ h

Black and white checkered band on top, white fluted band on bottom, medium blue glaze **100.00**

Brown and orange marbleized band, ribbed handle **55.00**

3½″ h, black and white checkered bands top and bottom, white vertical bar band on middle, medium blue glaze **170.00**

3¾″ h, barrel shape, black and white checkered bands on top and bottom, medium blue glaze **175.00**

4″ h, brown marbleized, black striping **70.00**

4¾″ h, black and white checkered body, blue rings on top and bottom **225.00**

5⅞″ h, blue, orange, tan, black, and white geometric design and stripes, emb leaf handle **700.00**

Mustard Pot, 2¾ x 2¼″, reddish brown band with seaweed dec, dark brown line borders **175.00**

Pitcher
6¾" h, earthworm design, gray, green, and yellow ochre, emb spout, band and leaf handle **500.00**
7½" h
 Blue, orange, tan, black, and white geometric design and stripes, emb leaf handle, crow's foot in bottom **1,450.00**
 Earthworm design, blue, blue green, and black emb band with stripes and bands, emb leaf handle **900.00**
8" h, medium blue, white fluted band on bottom, black and white checkered band in middle **110.00**
Salt, 3" d, 2" h, earthworm design, tan band **300.00**
Shaker, 4⅝" h, white, emb band and blue and white stripes **80.00**
Sugar Bowl, cov, 4⅛" d, black and white checkered band on rim, medium blue glaze **425.00**
Tea Canister
4" h, blue, black, and white band on shoulder, white fluted band on bottom, medium blue glaze **70.00**
4¼" h, black and white checkered band on shoulder, medium blue speckled glaze **80.00**
Teapot
5½" h, globular, medium blue, black and white checkered band on shoulder, acorn finial on cov **200.00**
5⅞" h, oval shape, medium blue, fluted band on bottom, black and white checkered band on top, acorn finial on top **550.00**
Waste Bowl
4½" d, blue bands with black, tan, and white cat's eye dec, black stripes . **475.00**
5¼" d, black seaweed dec, blue stripes, yellow ochre **450.00**

MONART GLASS

History: Monart glass is a heavy, simple shaped art glass in which colored enamels are suspended in the glass during the glass-making process. This technique was originally developed by the Ysart family in Spain in 1923. John Moncrief, a Scottish glassmaker, discovered the glass while vacationing in Spain, recognized the beauty and potential market, and began production in his Perth glassworks in 1924.

The name "Monart" is derived from the surnames Moncrief and Ysart. Two types of Monart were manufactured: a "commercial" line which incorporated colored enamels and a touch of aventurine in crystal, and the "art" line in which the suspended enamels formed designs such as feathers or scrolls. Monart glass, in most instances, is not marked. The factory used paper labels.

Basket, brown to light tan opal vertical striations, Cluthra type **585.00**
Bowl, 11½" d, mottled orange and green **185.00**
Candlestick, two shades of green, goldstone mica, paper label **95.00**
Lamp Shade, 6½" d, white opal **85.00**

Vase, bulbous body, tapered extended neck, flared rim, blue shaded to pink, Cluthra type, gold highlights, 14" h, $625.00.

Vase
6½" h, mottled shades of red and blue, white lining **190.00**
8½" h, blue, silver, mica, orange streaks, small bubbles **250.00**
16" h, green, flecked neck, orange body, dark inclusions, gold Cluthra centers **450.00**

MONT JOYE GLASS

History: Mont Joye is a type of glass produced by Saint-Hilaire, Touvier, de Varreaux & Company at their glassworks in Pantin, France. Most pieces were lightly acid etched to give them a frosted appearance and decorated with enameled floral decorations. All pieces listed are frosted, unless otherwise noted.

Pitcher, 10", amethyst, enameled flowers, aqua, blue, pink, and gold, sgd . **250.00**
Rose Bowl, 3¾" h, 4¼" d, pinched sides, acid etched, enameled purple violets, gold stems and dec **145.00**
Vase
4" h, pink enameled poppy and gold leaves, frosted textured ground, marked **180.00**

Rose Bowl, acid etched, enameled purple violets, gold stems, gold dec, pinched sides, 3¾" h, 4¼" d, $145.00.

6½", green, cut poppies, crimson and gilt enameling, sgd 250.00
7½" h, cameo, burgundy poppies, leafy stems, gilt highlights, frosted textured ground, dark rainbow iridescence 355.00
10", bulbous, narrow neck, clear to opalescent green, natural color thistle dec, gold highlights 275.00
18", green, enameled purple flowers, gold leaves, sgd 250.00
25¾", flared waisted bottle form, overlaid foliate dec, MOP beads, green metallic flaked ground, base stamped "Mont Joye," c1910 . . . . 1,200.00
Bulbous, raised gold spider mums, green textured finish 480.00

MOORCROFT

History: William Moorcroft was first employed as a potter by James Macintyre & Co., Ltd. of Burslem in 1897. He established the Moorcroft pottery in 1913. The company initially used an impressed mark, "Moorcroft, Burslem"; a signature mark, "W. Moorcroft," followed.

The majority of the art pottery wares were hand thrown, resulting in a great variation among similarly styled pieces. Color and marks are keys to determining age.

Walker, William's son, continued the business upon his father's death and made the same style wares. Modern pieces are marked simply "Moorcroft" with export pieces also marked "Made in England."

Reference: Susan and Al Bagdade, *Warman's English & Continental Pottery & Porcelain, 2nd Edition*, Wallace–Homestead, 1991.

Bowl
10", octagonal, grape dec 200.00
12½" d, grapes and leaves, green ground, Walter Moorcroft facsimile signature, factory mark, c1945 . . . 440.00
Candlesticks, pr, 10", tree dec, shades of yellow, cobalt blue ground, script sgd 150.00
Coffeepot, cov, Sicilian pattern, sgd "Moorcroft–MacIntyre" 250.00
Ginger Jar, cov, 11½", pomegranate dec 520.00
Loving Cup, 4¼", tulip and cornflower dec, green, blue, and red, three handles, printed and painted signature, c1900 . . . . 340.00
Marmalade Jar, blue flowers, attached stand, sgd "MacIntyre" 150.00
Pitcher, 7", red poppies, pewter lid, sgd "MacIntyre" 250.00
Plate
7¼" d, toadstool, blue–ground, imp "Moorcroft Claremont" 615.00
8½", pr, Natural Ware, green and blue glaze 150.00
Teapot, 8", orchid dec, cobalt blue ground 200.00

Vase, Spanish pattern, dark colors, 6½" h, $600.00.

Vase
3" h, pansy dec, high glaze, script sgd 500.00
4" h, cobalt blue ground, purple and yellow plums, c1918–29 . . . . 260.00
7" h
Red florals, green to blue ground, green mark 180.00
Wide mouth, tapering cylindrical, green tree landscape, blue ground, fitted hammered pewter circular foot, stamped "H Made In England, Tudric, Moorcroft 01359, Made by Liberty & Co" . 935.00
7½" h, blue and red clematis, yellow green ground, marked "Walter Moorcroft" 310.00

10″, yellow tulip **200.00**
10¼″, purple and blue wisteria, cream ground, sgd "Moorcroft–MacIntyre" **550.00**
11 ¾″, Florian Ware, baluster, poppy and leaf dec, shades of blue, printed and painted signature, c1900 . . . . **425.00**
12″, Anemone **275.00**

MORIAGE, JAPANESE

History: Moriage refers to applied clay (slip) relief motifs and decorations used on certain classes of Japanese pottery and porcelain.

This decorating was done by three methods: 1) handrolling and shaping, which was applied by hand to the biscuit in one or more layers; the design and effect required determined thickness and shape, 2) tubing or slip trailing, which applied decoration from a tube, like decorating a cake, and 3) hakeme which is reducing the slip to a liquid and decorating the object with a brush. Color was applied either before or after the process.

Vase, floral pattern, green ground, 10″ h, $240.00.

Bowl, 7″ d, orange flowers and leaves, green wreath mark **135.00**
Chocolate Pot, 9″ h, green ground, four floral medallions, heavy moriage . . . **225.00**
Demitasse Set, pot, two ftd cups and saucers, white wisteria flowers, green trim **400.00**
Manicure Set, three tools, buffer, and cov trinket box, heavy dec **175.00**
Planter, 3¾″ h, 3¾″ l, swan, figural, multicolored enamel dec **95.00**
Powder Box, 5″ d, light green, raised turquoise beading, hp flowers **75.00**
Tea Set, teapot, creamer, cov sugar, five cups and saucers, mauve

ground, red roses, delicate white slipwork, unmarked **650.00**
Vase
9¼″ h, pedestal base, green ground, white overall slipwork, floral medallions **250.00**
12½″ h, tan ground, light green bands, pink and blue flowers, three panels of multicolored Bird on Limb dec, Japanese **250.00**

MOSER GLASS

History: Ludwig Moser (1833–1916) founded his polishing and engraving workshop in 1857 in Karlsbad (Karlovy Vary), Czechoslovakia. He employed many famous glass designers, e.g., Johann Hoffmann, Josef Urban, and Rudolf Miller. In 1900 Moser and his sons, Rudolf and Gustav, incorporated Ludwig Moser & Söhne.

Moser art glass included clear pieces with inserted blobs of colored glass, cut colored glass with classical scenes, cameo glass, and intaglio cut. Many inexpensive enameled pieces also were made.

In 1922 Leo and Richard Moser bought Meyr's Neffe, their biggest Bohemian rival in art glass. Moser executed many pieces for the Wiener Werkstätte in the 1920s. The Moser glass factory continues to produce new items.

References: Gary Baldwin and Lee Carno, *Moser–Artistry In Glass: 1857–1938,* Antique Publications, 1988; Mural K. Charon and John Mareska, *Ludvik Moser, King of Glass: A Treasure Chest of Photographs And History,* published by author, 1984.

Atomizer, 4½″ h, melon ribbed body, sapphire blue, small gold florals, leaves, and swirls, orig gold top and bulb **250.00**
Basket, 8″, brilliant cut, sgd **375.00**
Bowl
3¾″ h, cranberry, gold flowers and gilded insects dec, two handles, ftd **330.00**
6¾″ d, quatraform, heavy scrollwork and floral designs, conforming undertray, gilt enameling **1,450.00**
Box, 6 x 3¾″, cranberry, white enamel woman carrying cornucopia and grapes, enameled gold vine and berries **650.00**
Calling Card Holder, cranberry, turquoise jewels, gold prunts, four scrolled feet **350.00**

Bowl, etched forest scene with deer, amethyst shading to clear pedestal, script sgd, 9½" h, 5⅛" h, $795.00.

Chalice, 13" h, amber bowl with cut leaves and gold enamel flowers and birds dec, multicolored enamel on clear stem and foot 1,200.00
Compote
   4" h, pale amber, electric blue rigaree and four applied dec, twelve painted leaves on int., brown branches, gold leaves, white cherries, matching branch on hollow base 645.00
   5⅝" h, clear cut, diamond point, gilded ship on bowl, sgd 65.00
   9½" h, pr, quatraform, enameled gold scrolled reserves, pedestal foot, gilt enamel 425.00
   11¼" h, cov, clear, cut, diamond point, gilded dec, sgd 50.00
Dresser Jar, 5" d, cobalt blue, gilded band and ship on lid, sgd 110.00
Ewer, 10¾", cranberry, gold oak leaves, lacy gold foliage, small applied glass acorns, pedestal foot, ruffled top, applied clear handle, unsigned 750.00
Goblet, pr, 5¾", deep amethyst, gold figure dec 175.00
Mug, 3¼", green, multicolored oak leaves and bee, applied acorns 300.00
Pitcher, 8½", amber, multicolored floral enamel 200.00
Plate, 7⅜", amberina, gold dec 125.00
Scent Bottle, 5", green, multicolored leaves and berries, ball stopper . . .   165.00
Sherbets, 5" h, set of 12, cranberry, clear cut stems, gold dec, sgd 1,055.00
Sweetmeat Dish, round, cranberry, engraved, gold band 225.00
Tumbler
   Blue, sgd 110.00
   Lavender, vines, leaves, berries, and floral work, heavy gilting, 4" 175.00
   Ruby cut to clear, gold dec, octagonal, 3½" 60.00
Vase
   6½" h, amber, applied fish dec 600.00
   7" h, cut green to clear, raised gold scroll dec 180.00

8¼", pr, quatraform, bulbous, Baroque scrolling design, blue forget–me–nots and monogram detail, gilt enameling 1,090.00
8½" h, free form, amber, enamel dec, applied feet, prunts, and rim 285.00
8¾" h, malachite, simulated green stone molded nude women, vineyard background, faceted borders   545.00
9¾" h, overlay, green cut to pale amber, sgd 75.00
10½" h, clear, cut, pressed, and etched, gilded dec, sgd 100.00
11¼" h, emerald green, ribbed, gold band on top with warriors, marked "Made in Cecho–Slovakia–Moser Carlsbad" 250.00
12" h, triangular baluster, ruby, gold enameled children dec 250.00

MOSS ROSE PATTERN CHINA

History: Several English potteries manufactured china with a Moss Rose pattern in the mid-1800s. Knowles, Taylor and Knowles, an American firm, began production of a Moss Rose pattern in the 1880s.

The moss rose was a common garden flower grown in English gardens. When American consumers tired of English china with oriental themes, they purchased the Moss Rose pattern as a substitute.

Cup and Saucer, marked "Winterling/ Bavaria/Germany," $12.00.

Butter Pat, sq, marked "Meakin" 15.00
Coffee Mug and Saucer, marked "Meakin" 40.00
Coffeepot, 9", marked "E. C. & Co" . .   75.00
Cup and Saucer, marked "Edwards" . .   25.00
Dessert Set, 28 pcs, cake plate, eight 7½" plates, eight cups and saucers, creamer and sugar, marked "Fr Haviland" 250.00
Gravy Boat, with underplate, marked "Green & Co, England" 40.00
Nappy, 4½", marked "Edwards" 10.00

Plate

7½", pink edge, marked "Haviland" .	**16.00**
8½", marked "KTK"	**20.00**
9½", marked "Haviland"	**12.00**
Platter, 10 x 14", rect, marked "Meakin"	**26.00**
Salt and Pepper Shaker, pr, 5", SS top and base, marked "Rosenthal"	**50.00**
Sauce Dish, 4½", marked "Haviland" .	**15.00**
Soup Plate, 9", marked "Meakin"	**16.00**
Syrup, 8½", pewter top, marked "KTK," c1872	**165.00**
Tea Service, 3 pcs, teapot, 5½" creamer, and 6¼" sugar bowl, marked "Meakin"	**200.00**
Teapot, 8½", bulbous, gooseneck spout, basketweave trim, marked "T & V"	**40.00**
Tureen, cov, 12", gold trim	**70.00**

MOUNT WASHINGTON GLASS COMPANY

History: In 1837 Deming Jarves, founder of the Boston and Sandwich Glass Company, established for George D. Jarves, his son, the Mount Washington Glass Company in Boston, Massachusetts. In the following years the leadership and the name of the company changed several times as George Jarves formed different associations.

In the 1860s the company was owned and operated by Timothy Howe and William L. Libbey. In 1869 Libbey bought a new factory in New Bedford, Massachusetts. The Mount Washington Glass Company began operating again there under its original name. Henry Libbey became associated with the company early in 1871. He resigned in 1874 during the general depression, and the glass works was closed. William Libbey had resigned in 1872 to work for the New England Glass Company.

The Mount Washington Glass Company opened again in the fall of 1874 under the presidency of A. H. Seabury and the management of Frederick S. Shirley. In 1894 the glass works became a part of the Pairpoint Manufacturing Company.

Throughout its history the Mount Washington Glass Company made a great variety of glass including pressed glass, blown glass and art glass, lava glass, Napoli, cameo, cut glass, Albertine, and Verona.

References: George C. Avila, *The Pairpoint Glass Story,* Reynolds–DeWalt Printing, Inc., 1968; Leonard E. Padgett, *Pairpoint Glass,* Wallace–Homestead, 1979; John A. Shuman III, *The Collector's Encyclopedia of American Art Glass,* Collector Books, 1988.

Collectors Club: Mount Washington Art Glass Society, P.O. Box A2038, New Bedford, MA 02741.

Museum: The New Bedford Glass Museum, New Bedford, MA.

Additional Listings: Burmese, Crown Milano, Peachblow, and Royal Flemish.

Biscuit Jar, 7" d, squatty, tan, gold poppies and leaves, raised floral and scroll bottom, emb scroll bail and cov, marked "M W #4426"	**330.00**
Bowl, 10" d, cameo, pink, ruffled rim, Griffin and floral band, acid stamp . .	**1,090.00**
Bride's Basket, 8¼", sq, cased, deep rose and white ext., white int., dragon, floral, and leaf dec, ruffled edge . . .	**650.00**
Center Bowl, 11½" h, 13" l, swan, cranberry, clear curved neck and head, polished beak	**330.00**
Condiment Set, Burmese	
3 pcs, two fluted shakers and matching cruet with orig stopper, orig Pairpoint quadruple silverplated base, 8½" h	**900.00**
3 pcs, cruet, shaker, and barrel shape condiment, silverplated base, 7" h	**300.00**
4 pcs, cruet, two shakers, barrel shaped condiment with coin silver ladle, Pairpoint quadruple silverplated base, 8⅛" h	**425.00**
Cracker Jar, 6⅜" h, floral dec, pale yellow ground, silverplated lid, handle, and rim, marked "MW"	**250.00**
Creamer and Sugar, satin finish, opaque white lid on sugar, silverplated mountings	**110.00**
Ewer, 9½" h, wading stork dec, raised gold aquatic plants, satin white to peach ground, autumn green spout, gold handle	**630.00**
Lamp, table	
15" h, Burmese, squatty cylindrical base with desert scene and men riding camels dec, satin finish, 10" d shade	**1,090.00**
17" h, bulbous base, pansy dec, satin finish, 10" d shade	**725.00**

Salt Shaker, Egg and Blossom, 2½" h, $125.00.

Muffineer, 4″ h, egg shape	
Green satin, pink flowers	145.00
White satin, green Maiden Hair ferns	150.00
Pitcher, 8″ h	
Rose Amber, four matching tumblers	385.00
Verona, bulbous, maiden hair fern dec, gold highlights, applied D-shaped clear reeded handle	225.00
Plate, 12″, twin cupids, leaf and floral border	120.00
Rose Bowl, 5½″ d, pale blue ground, life–like pansy dec, numbered "617" on bottom	565.00
Salt and Pepper Shaker, pr	
Fig, one with pansies, other with green enameled ferns and orange flowers	200.00
Tomato, Burmese and cream, daisy dec	110.00
Sugar Shaker	
4″ h	
Egg shape, floral dec, orig top	160.00
Melon ribbed, blue and white for-get–me–not dec, yellow ground	210.00
5½″, IVT, lighthouse shape, blue, orig metal top	270.00
Sweetmeat, 6″ d, squatty, oak leaves with acorns, yellow ground, gold or-nate rim, bail, and cov, marked "M W #4417"	550.00
Talc Shaker, 3″ h, Erie Twist, pink, gray florals, blue and raised gold scrolls	450.00
Toothpick Holder, satin, Brownie Police-man, holding billy club in one hand, Brownie by scruff of neck in other, sitting Brownie on back	550.00
Tumbler, 3¾″ h, floral dec, Thomas Hood verse	650.00
Vase	
6″ h, white, ribbed, acid finish	120.00
6½″ h, cameo, cylinder, red scrolled design, white ground, ftd	990.00
7¼″ h, Burmese, mounted on quad-ruple plated base	300.00
8¼″, lily shape, peachblow, satin fin-ish	1,800.00
9″ h, gold flowers, green leaves, gold highlights, cream ground, double gold handled, numbered	380.00
Lava, black ground, blue, pink, green, and white inclusions, applied reeded han-dles, pr	2,530.00

MULBERRY CHINA

History: Mulberry china, made primarily in the Staffordshire district of England between 1830 and 1850, is porcelain whose transfer pattern is the color of mulberry juice. The potters that manufac-tured Flow Blue also made Mulberry china; the ware often has a flowing effect similar to Flow Blue.

References: Susan and Al Bagdade, *Warman's English & Continental Pottery & Porcelain*, 2nd Edition, Wallace–Homestead, 1991; Petra Wil-liams, *Flow Blue China and Mulberry Ware–Sim-ilarity and Value Guide*, Revised Edition, Fountain House East, 1981.

Plate, Bochara pattern, marked "J. & E.," 10¼″ d, \$45.00.

Coffeepot, Jeddo, Adams	175.00
Creamer	
Beehives in Garden	140.00
Foliage, Edward Walley	85.00
Jeddo, Adams	100.00
Marble, Wedgwood	65.00
Tavoy	100.00
Temple, Podmore, Walker	125.00
Cup and Saucer, handled cup	
Genoa, Davenport, 1852	40.00
Roselle, J M & Son, England	40.00
Cup and Saucer, handleless cup	
Castle Scenery, Jacob Furnival	50.00
Pelew, Edward Challinor	60.00
Temple, Podmore Walker	40.00
Washington Vase, Podmore Walker	60.00
Cup Plate	
Allegheny, Thomas Goodfellow	45.00
Corean, Podmore Walker	45.00
Gravy Boat	
Jeddo, Adams	65.00
Pelew	85.00
Pitcher, 9½″, Vincennes, J Alcock	135.00
Plate	
7″, Genoa	20.00
8″, Temple	25.00
9½″	
Corea, Clementson	65.00
Ning Po	40.00
10½″	
Bochara, Edwards	35.00
Cyprus, Davenport	60.00
Vincennes	45.00

Platter
8 x 10", Lucerne, Parkhurst mark	35.00
12½ x 9½", Abbey, Adams, c1900	100.00
15½", Rhone Scenery	150.00
15¾ x 12¼", Washington Vase, Podmore Walker	135.00
16", Peruvian	125.00
Relish, Percy, Morley, shell shape	35.00
Sauce Dish, 5", Corea, Clementson	18.00
Sauce Tureen, cov, Bochara, Edwards	125.00
Soup Bowl, 10½", Scinde	30.00
Sugar, cov, Jeddo, Adams	75.00
Teapot, Strawberries	175.00
Vegetable Bowl, cov, octagonal, pedestal base	
Cyprus, Davenport	75.00
Jeddo	100.00

MUSIC BOXES

History: Music boxes were invented in Switzerland around 1825 and include a broad field of automatic musical instruments from a small box to a huge circus calliope.

A cylinder box consists of a comb with teeth which vibrate when striking a pin in the cylinder and producing music from light tunes to opera and overtures.

The first disc music box was invented by Paul Lochmann of Leipzig, Germany, in 1886. It used an interchangeable steel disc with pierced holes bent to a point which hit the star–wheel as the disc revolved, and thus produced the tune. Discs were easily stamped out of metal, allowing a single music box to play an endless variety of tunes. It reached the height of its popularity from 1890 to 1910. The phonograph replaced it.

Music boxes also were put into many items, e.g., clocks, sewing and jewelry boxes, steins, plates, toys, perfume bottles, and furniture.

Reference: H. A. V. Bulleid, *Cylinder Musical Box Design and Repair*, Almar Press, 1987.

Collectors' Club: Musical Box Society, International, Rt. 3, Box 205, Morgantown, IN, 46160.

Museums: Bellms Cars and Music of Yesterday, Sarasota, FL; Lockwood Matthews Mansion, Norwalk, CT.

Additional Listings: See *Warman's Americana & Collectibles* for more examples.

CYLINDER–TYPE

5" cylinder, L'Epee, France, four tune, simple case	350.00
5⅛" cylinder, Junod, four tune, inlaid rosewood case, tune indicator, two bells, dec figural tune card, inner glass lid	1,000.00
6" cylinder, Ducommon Girod, six tune, case, tune sheet, c1880	750.00

Bird's eye maple case, litho of children playing instruments on lid, 3⅜ x 5⅜ x 2½", $60.00.

7¾" cylinder, four tune, key wind, simple case style	750.00
8½" cylinder, Imhof and Mukle, spring driven movement, rosewood and ebony case, marquetry dec, trade label, c1880	400.00
10¾" cylinder, Paillard, eight tune, lever wind, rosewood case, floral dec, c1860	800.00
11" cylinder, ext. handle wind, inlaid rosewood case, maker's initials "JB" in butterfly, six extra cylinders in burlwood case, Swiss, c1900	4,750.00
12¾" cylinder, time card, inlaid burl and ebonized case, plays eight airs, Swiss, c1900	825.00
13" cylinder, walnut case, inlaid musical trophies on lid and front, strung and banded borders, zither attachment, six engraved brass bells, drum with eight strikers, Swiss, late 19th C	3,630.00
15" cylinder, twelve tune, lever wind, rosewood with floral dec	1,250.00

DISC–TYPE

7" h, 10" l, Regina, single exposed comb, handle wound, eleven discs, Japanese lacquer case with birds and flowers, 8" discs, early 20th C	950.00
7½" disc, sq mahogany case, lid int. shows little girls at play, crank wound, single comb, Germany, c1900	275.00
8¾" disc, Criterion, table model, mahogany case, figural litho inside lid	750.00
9" disc, Britannia, simple case, table model, c1900	900.00
9¼" disc, six bells, walnut case, floral inlay lid, figural litho inside cov	950.00
10½" disc, Perfection, table model, ma-	

hogany case, scenic litho inside lid, zinc discs **1,400.00**
14″ d discs, Polyphon, two exposed combs, twelve bells, metal bed imp "744," walnut case, one disk case, c1900 .... **3,850.00**
15¼″ w, walnut case, single comb movement, lithograph label on lid, matching stand with pressed palmette median border, fitted single drawer, includes twenty–three discs, Philadelphia, c1897 .... **1,810.00**
17¼″ disc, Stella Grand, carved front panel of base with drawer, oak **2,500.00**
21″ w, carved and incised oak case, coffered lid, paneled sides, inset corner with fluted baluster columns, lea tip carved base, scroll cast bracket feet, includes thirty–six discs, Regina ... **6,000.00**

MISCELLANEOUS

Bird in Cage, 9″ h, domed cage on sq base, cast and enameled geometric dec **275.00**
Coin Operated, 25¼″ w, 36¾″ h, Polyphon Style 104, walnut case, arched glazed door, circular panel flanked by engaged columns, ovoid turned front feet, includes one disc **5,750.00**
Figural, 13½″ h, heavily carved man, elaborate bow tie, bowler hat, hands in pockets, whistles "How Dry I Am," c1920 .... **525.00**
Floor Model, 37¾″ h, 29½″ w, Stella, double comb movement, mahogany case, double panel door with applied neoclassical husk and swag dec, angled three–quarter round reeded stiles, ring turned feet with casters, includes thirty–seven discs **3,025.00**
Roller Organ
Automatic Melodia, Bates & Co, 11½ x 9½ x 8½″, sliding tremolo stop, gilt stencil dec case, four paper rolls **500.00**
Barrel Organ, 20½ x 11 x 11¼″, six air, paper roll, lid stamped Archibald Campbell, imp line border, scroll spandrels, German **950.00**
Gem, 14¼ x 12 x 8″, gilt stenciled floral case, twenty–three cobs ... **425.00**

MUSICAL INSTRUMENTS

History: From the first beat of the prehistoric drum to the very latest in electronic music makers, musical instruments have provided popular modes of communication and relaxation.

The most popular antique instruments are violins, flutes, oboes, and other instruments associ-
ated with the classical music period of 1650 to 1900. Many of the modern instruments, such as trumpets, guitars, drums, etc., have value on the "used" rather than antiques market.

The collecting of musical instruments is in its infancy. The field is growing very rapidly. Investors and speculators have played a role since the 1930s, especially in early string instruments. Sotheby's and Christie's hold annual auctions of fine musical instruments.

References: Tom and Mary Anne Evans, *Guitars: From the Renaissance To Rock; The Official Price Guide To Music Collectibles, Sixth Edition,* House of Collectibles, 1986.

Collectors' Club: Fretted Instrument Guild of America, 2344 South Oakley Avenue, Chicago, IL 60608.

Museum: The Museum of the American Piano, New York, NY.

Piccolo, 12″ l, $35.00.

Bagpipe, Scottish, rosewood chanters, late 17th C **4,500.00**
Banjo, Edgemere, nickel shell, wood lined, seventeen nickel plated hexagon brackets, raised frets, birch neck finished in imitation mahogany, c1900 **325.00**
Clarinet, Laube, A, thirteen nickel silver keys, two joints, graduated bore, low pitch, c1920 .... **325.00**
Flute, 22⅜″, ivory, one keyed, French, mid 18th C **6,500.00**
Harp, 68″ h, Lyon & Reily, Chicago, No 701, parcel gilt satinwood, late 19th C **3,500.00**
Mandolin, Joseph Bohmann, Chicago, spruce, rosewood, mahogany, ebony, tortoise shell, abalone, ivory, inlaid, paper label, engraved brass plate, orig worn leather case, patent date 1890 .... **125.00**

Oboe, Italian, c1840 . . . . **700.00**

Organ, Victorian, portable, five stops, grained pine and ebonized case, 23¾" l **400.00**

Piano

Baldwin, grand, ebonized case, sq legs, includes bench **5,225.00**

Bluthner, grand, satinwood, triple line inlaid borders, strung and cross-banded lid, inlaid oval panels, sq tapered legs, bronze caps and casters, includes bench **6,050.00**

Starch, baby grand, ebonized case, sq tapered legs, includes bench . . **1,320.00**

Steinway & Sons, NY

Model B, c1911, ebonized, sq tapering legs, 43" h, 83¾" l **2,750.00**

Model L, grand, ebonized case, incised sq tapered legs, spade feet **7,700.00**

Pianoforte

Loud and Brothers, Philadelphia, mahogany, Empire, rect case, turned round tapered legs, 1835–40 . . . . **550.00**

Royal Patent/Longman & Broderip/ Musical Instrument Makers, No 26 Cheapside & No 13 Haymarket/ London, mahogany, orig battersea label, 63 x 22½ x 33½" **1,400.00**

Saxophone, Bantone, bee front, three valves, lacquer bore **1,200.00**

Trumpet, Holton, four valve **1,500.00**

Ukulele, birch, black rings around sound hole, white celluloid binding, c1920 . **55.00**

Viola

Collin–Mezin Fils, two piece narrow curl back, light curl ribs and scroll, orange color varnish, includes case and bow, labeled "Ch JB Collin–Mezin Fils, Maitre–Luthier 1950 Medaille D'Or–Exposition Universelle 1900 Paris" **1,210.00**

Hans Nebel, 15¹⁵/₁₆", one piece broad curl back, medium curl ribs and head, gold–brown varnish, includes case and bow, labeled "Hans Nebel Mittenwalder Geigenbau, N 18 Anno 1956" **2,320.00**

Hans Zölch, 14⅝", one piece light curl back, strong curl ribs, scroll plain, orange color varnish, includes case and two bows, stamped "HZ" . . . **550.00**

Matthew Hardie, 16⅛", one piece light curl back, plain scroll, brown color varnish, labeled "Made by Mat Hardie & Son, Edinburgh, 1821" **825.00**

Maxwell Weaner, 16⅝", one piece strong curl back, medium curl ribs and scroll, medium grain top, yellow–brown color varnish, includes case, nickel mounted bow, and silver mounted bow, labeled "Maxwell Weaner, Lake Carmel NY 1968" . **610.00**

Verne Swan, one piece light curl back, medium curl ribs and scroll, irregular grain top, yellow–brown color varnish, labeled "Made by Verne Swan, Utica, New York 1940" **385.00**

Violin

Andrea Guarnerius, 13¹⁵/₁₆", two piece narrow curl back, wide to fine grain top, orange–brown color varnish, includes case and three bows, labeled "Nicolaus Amati Cremonensis Hieronymi Fili Ac Antoni Nepos Fecit Anni" **63,800.00**

George Gemunder, 14", two piece broad curl back, fine to medium grain top, red color varnish, case, labeled "George Gemunder Fecit, Astoria L I Anno 1881 IHS" **8,800.00**

Giuseppe Martini, 13¹⁵/₁₆", one piece broad curl back, fine to wide grain back, red–brown color varnish, case, labeled "Giuseppe Martino, Maker, Boston Mass," 1931 . . . . . **1,540.00**

Hawkes and Son, 14⅛", two piece strong curl back, plain scroll, fine grain top, orange color varnish, case, labeled "The Concert Violin Registered, 1920 Hawkes & Son, Denman St Piccadilly Circus London W" **1,100.00**

Jerome Bonaparte Squier, two piece medium curl back, medium grain top, red color varnish, includes case, labeled "Jerome B Squier, Maker, Boston, 1891" **2,750.00**

Joannes Tononi, 13¹³/₁₆", two piece medium curl back, broad curl scroll, medium grain top, red gold color varnish, canvas cov case, labeled "Joannes De Tononis Fecit Bononiae, In Via S Mamuli Anno 1716" **27,500.00**

John Morse, 14⅛", two piece plain back, plain ribs and scroll, wide grain top, brown color varnish, includes case and silver mounted bow, labeled "John A Morse, Maker, Putnam Connecticut, No 151 AD" **660.00**

John Smith, 14", faint curl one piece back, medium grain top, red color varnish, labeled "Made By John Smith, Teddingon, London, W" . . **825.00**

Nicolas Vuillaume, 14⅛", two piece medium curl back, medium grain top, red color varnish, case, labeled "Nicolas Vuillaume", branded bottom bout "N Vuillaume" **10,120.00**

William Knaggs, 13¾", two piece medium curl back, light curl ribs and scroll, wide grain top, red–brown color varnish, case, labeled "Made by Wm Knaggs, Toronto, 1914 No 92" **1,100.00**

Violincello

German, 29⅜", two piece medium curl back, medium grain top, red color varnish, includes case and bow **2,310.00**

Plumerel, 28⁹⁄₁₆", two piece light curl back, wide grain top, orange color varnish, stamped "Al A Ville, De Cremonne Plumerel" **1,045.00**

MUSIC RELATED

Ashtray, 3¼ x 4", cast iron, figural, bearded black man playing banjo, c1920 . . . . **65.00**

Book, *The Hawley Collection Of Violins,* Chicago, 1904, limited edition **550.00**

Music Stand, Duet type, rosewood, pierced lyres, brass candleholders, adjustable baluster support, raised trefoil base, ball shape feet **1,600.00**

Poster, Metropolitan Opera House, illus, 1920s **125.00**

Violoncello Case, W E Hill and Sons, London, 19th C

50⁹⁄₁₆", wood, black finish, brass mountings and hardware **440.00**

51⅜", figured oak, brass mountings and hardware **1,320.00**

MUSTACHE CUPS AND SAUCERS

History: Mustache cups and saucers were popular in the late Victorian era, 1880–1900. They were made by many companies in porcelain and silver plate. The cups have a ledge across the top of the bowl of the cup to protect a gentleman's mustache from becoming soiled while drinking.

Reference: Susan and Al Bagdade, *Warman's English & Continental Pottery & Porcelain,* 2nd Edition, Wallace–Homestead, 1991.

PORCELAIN

Carlsbad, floral dec, ring handle **35.00**

German, "Papa," pink and green florals, gold trim **40.00**

Hand Painted, pink and white flowers, green leaves, pale green ground, gold trim **45.00**

Haviland, white, gold trim **90.00**

Limoges, hp pastel flowers, rococo molded scrolls, all–over gold dec . . **45.00**

Majolica

Bird and Fan pattern **135.00**

Cup and Saucer, yellow and brown florals, unmarked, $35.00.

Shell and Seaweed, pink and gray, Estruscan **265.00**

Onion Meissen, c1890 . . . . **85.00**

Pink Luster, gold leaves, beaded edges **65.00**

Royal Worcester, hp, flowers, peach ground **125.00**

White Patterned Ironstone, copper luster dec, c1850 . . . . **250.00**

SILVER-PLATED

Barbour Bros Co, cut floral design . . . **60.00**

Derby Silver Co, engraved floral design, crimped rim **50.00**

Tufts, band of flowers, strawberries, leaves within border, matching design on saucer, marked **125.00**

NAILSEA TYPE GLASS

History: Nailsea type glass is characterized by swirls and loopings, usually white, on a clear or colored ground. One of the first areas where this glass was made was Nailsea, England, 1788–1873, hence the name. Several other glass houses, including American factories, made this type of glass.

Bottle

8¾" l, gemel, cranberry, white looping, applied rigaree **165.00**

10½" l, bellows, white, rose loopings, applied rigaree, stand **250.00**

Candlestick, 10" h, clear, white loopings, folded socket rim, hollow blown socket drawn out to a double knop, bulb shaped stem, and two additional knops, inverted cone shaped base, early 19th C **375.00**

Fairy Lamp, 6" h, blue shade, matching ruffled trifold rim base, clear pressed insert **710.00**

Finger Bowl, 4¼" d, ftd, clear body, swirled streaks of deep blue and white, foot drawn from body, applied clear handles imp with cherub's face **60.00**

Flask, clear ground, white loopings, orig stopper, 7½" h, $125.00.

Flask, cranberry, white zig–zag allover loopings	165.00
Lamp, 10" h, pear shaped font, swirl base stem, sq marble base	200.00
Pitcher, 4" d, 6½" h, clear, white loopings, ftd, solid applied base, triple ribbed solid handle with curled end, flaring formed mouth, attributed to South Jersey, c1840–60	1,125.00
Powder Horn, 13" l, clear, white loopings and red stripes, stand	250.00
Rolling Pin, 18" l, clear, pink and white loopings	250.00
Tumbler, white, blue loopings	115.00
Vase, 5" d, 8" h, cylindrical, flared mouth and base, clear, white loopings, plain sheared rim–pontil, attributed to South Jersey	175.00
Witch Ball, 5¼" d, clear, opaque white casing, red loopings, attributed to Pittsburgh	250.00

NANKING

History: Nanking is a type of Chinese porcelain made in Canton, China, from the early 1800s into the 20th century for export to America and England. It is often confused with the Canton pattern.

Three elements help distinguish Nanking from Canton. Nanking has a spear and post border, as opposed to the scalloped line style of Canton. The blues may tend to be darker on the Nanking ware. Second, in the water's edge or Willow pattern, Canton usually has no figures. Nanking features a standing figure with open umbrella on the bridge. Finally, Nanking wares often are embellished with gold.

Green and orange variations of Nanking survive, although scarce.

Reference: Sandra Andacht, *Oriental Antiques & Art: An Identification And Value Guide*, Wallace–Homestead, 1987.

Reproduction Alert: Copies of Nanking ware currently are being produced in China. They are of inferior quality and decorated in lighter rather than the darker blues.

Bowl, 9", fruit, oval, reticulated, blue and white, matching underplate	700.00
Cup and Saucer, loop handle	50.00
Dish, 7¾", leaf shape, blue and white, c1795	185.00
Ewer, 11", small spout, blue and white, mid 19th C	300.00
Jug, 9½", blue and white, c1800	450.00
Pitcher	
7¼" h, blue	200.00
9½" h, blue and white, Liverpool shape, cov	550.00
Plate, 9½", water's edge scene, c1780–1800	85.00

Platter, 11½ x 14½", $400.00.

Platter	
11½ x 14½", blue and white, pagoda in foreground	400.00
14¾", oval, blue and white, landscape, stylized dragons on cavetto, geometric patterned bands, base inscribed "Da Nihon Tatebayashi–sei," Meiji period	275.00
Teapot, 5¾ x 4⅜", scenic, gold dec, matching stand, 18th C	565.00
Tureen, 14½ x 10½", oval, dome cov, flower finial, ftd base, twisted strap handles, early 19th C	1,300.00

NAPKIN RINGS, FIGURAL

History: Gracious home dining during the Victorian era meant each household member had their personal napkin ring. Figural napkin rings were first patented in 1869. The remainder of the 19th century saw most plating companies, e.g., Cromwell, Eureka, Meriden, Reed and Barton, etc., manufacturing figural rings, many copying with slight variations the designs of other companies.

Values are determined today by the subject matter of the ring, the quality of the workmanship, and the condition.

Reference: Victor K. Schnadig, *American Victorian Figural Napkin Rings,* Wallace–Homestead, 1971, out–of–print.

Reproduction Alert: Quality reproductions do exist.

Additional Listings: See *Warman's Americana & Collectibles* for a listing of non–figural napkin rings.

Cupid, ring on back, 3¼″ h, 2¾″ l, $295.00.

Baby in cradle, James W Tufts, Boston	300.00
Bird, wings spread over nest of eggs .	145.00
Boy	
Pulling wheeled cart	245.00
Sitting on bench, holding drumstick .	180.00
Brownie, climbing up side of ring, Palmer Cox	175.00
Butterfly, perched on pair of fans	100.00
Cat, glass eyes, ring on back	260.00
Cherries, stems, leaf base, ball feet . .	70.00
Cherub, sitting cross legged on base, candleholder and ring combination .	175.00
Chicken, nesting beside ring	160.00
Child, crawling, ring on back	295.00
Dachshund, supporting ring on back . .	160.00
Dog, figural dog sitting next to barrel shaped ring, round base, sgd "Tufts #1531"	110.00
Deer, standing next to fence	175.00
Dutch Boy, pulling on boots, resilvered	125.00
Fox, standing erect, dressed	225.00
Frog, holding drumstick, pushing drum–like ring	300.00
Girl, Kate Greenaway type, detailed dress and bonnet, pushing ring, orig silver finish	195.00
Goat, pulling wheeled flower cart	245.00
Horse, standing next to elaborate ring	175.00
Man, walking uphill, ring on shoulders	190.00
Owl, sitting on leafy base, owls perched on upper limbs	250.00
Parrot, on wheels, Simpson, Hall, Miller & Co	175.00
Rabbit, sitting alertly next to ring	175.00

Roman Centurion, stands next to ring, sword drawn	130.00
Sailor Boy, anchor	210.00
Schoolboy with books, feeding begging puppy	225.00
Sheep, resting on base near ring	165.00
Squirrel, eating nut, log pile base	125.00
Swan, one each side of ring, separate bases	120.00
Turtle, crawling, ornate ring on back . .	200.00

NASH GLASS

History: Nash glass is a type of art glass attributed to Arthur John Nash and his sons, Leslie H. and A. Douglas. Arthur John Nash, originally employed by Webb in Stourbridge, England, came to America and was employed in 1889 by Tiffany Furnaces at its Corona, Long Island, plant.

While managing the plant for Tiffany, Nash designed and produced iridescent glass. In 1928 A. Douglas Nash purchased the physical facilities of Tiffany Furnaces. The A. Douglas Nash Corporation firm remained in operation until 1931.

Vase, ftd, irid gold, marked "544Nash," 4¼″ h, $325.00.

Bowl, 7¾ x 2½″, Jewel pattern, gold phantom luster	275.00
Candlestick, 4″ h, Chintz pattern, ruby and gray, sgd	440.00
Compote, 6 x 2″, fold over rim, Chintz pattern, green–blue bowl, clear pedestal foot, sgd	175.00
Cordial, 5½″ h, Chintz pattern, green and blue	75.00
Goblet, 6¾″ h, feathered leaf motif, gilt dec, sgd	275.00
Plate, 8″ d, Chintz pattern, green and blue	175.00
Sherbet, bluish–gold texture, ftd, sgd, #517	275.00

Tumbler, 5″ h, conical, Chintz pattern,
blue and silver, low pedestal foot, sgd   **115.00**
Vase
   9¼″ h, vertical orange and clear
striped body, pale green knob, ftd   **240.00**
   11½″ h, tapered, bluish–gold, molded
leaf dec, sgd **450.00**
   12″ h, Chintz pattern
     Clear, blue and green design, sgd   **330.00**
     Ruby and chartreuse stripe, sgd .   **1,090.00**
Wine, Chintz pattern, red and green,
sgd **200.00**

NAUTICAL ITEMS

History: The seas that surround us have fascinated man since time began. The artifacts of sailors have been collected and treasured for years. Because of their environment, merchant and naval items, whether factory or handmade, must be of quality construction and long lasting. Many of these items are aesthetically designed as well.

Richard Bourne, Hyannis, Massachusetts, and Chuck DeLuca, York, Maine, regularly hold auctions of marine items.

References: Alan P. Major, *Maritime Antiques*, A. S. Barnes & Co., 1981; Jean Randier, *Nautical Antiques*, Doubleday and Co., 1977.

Periodicals: *Conklin's Guide: Maritime Auction Annual*, Leeward Shore Press, P.O. Box 838–20, Brisbane, CA 94005; *Nautical Brass* P.O. Box 3966, North Ft. Myers, FL 33918.

Museums: Burgess Mariner's Museum, Newport News, VA; Museum of Science and Industry, Chicago, IL; Mystic Seaport Museum, Mystic, CT; National Maritime Museum, San Francisco, CA.

Advertising, poster, Frank E Brown Co,
New Bedford, bomb guns, bombs,

Horn, cast iron and steel, wood base, orig Makrofon, serial no. on metal case, 24″ h, $130.00.

harpoons, and whaling gear, framed,
13⅝ x 6½″ **1,000.00**
Binnacle, brass
   11½″ h, Victorian, lanterns and compass, late 19th C **1,000.00**
   12″ h, compass, six panes of glass .   **850.00**
   28″ h, compensating balls, compass,
and lanterns **1,000.00**
   36″ h, Victorian, orig compass and
lamps, engraved "Julia" **3,850.00**
   51″ h, compensating balls and compass, wood base, made by Lionel
Corp, New York **440.00**
Book
   Maritime History of Maine, William
Hutchinson, Rowe, New York, 1948   **60.00**
   *Masting, Mast–making and Rigging
of Ships,* Robert Kipping, N A Fourteenth Edition, London, 1877, orig
cov **90.00**
   New Bedford Fairhaven and Dartmouth Signal Book, 1853, Charles
Taber & Co, New Bedford, orig
cloth cov, leather spine **650.00**
   *Ship Registers and Enrollments of
Machias, Maine 1780–1930,* Rockland, Maine, 1942, heavy pasteboard textured cov **100.00**
   *The Peabody Museum Collection of
Navigating Instruments,* M V Brewington, Salem, Ma, 1963 . . . . . .   **250.00**
   *The Sailing Ships of New England
Series Two,* John Robinson and
George Francis Dow, Salem, MA,
1924 . . . .   **60.00**
Certificate, American Seamen's Friend
Society, engraved harbor scene, Victorian frame, stained, 19th C **25.00**
Chest
   27 x 6¾ x 35¼″, apothecary, mahogany, mirrored door, reverse painted
panels, late 19th C **770.00**
   37⅜″ l, work, fitted int., includes tools,
painted green, mid 19th C **3,800.00**
   45½″ l, dovetailed, orig grained finish,
black and gold molding, compartment int., American, mid 19th C . .   **575.00**
   47½″ l, pine, dovetailed, carved top
and front panel, eagle with American flag shield and banner, full
rigged ship passing lighthouse,
early 19th C **650.00**
   50½″ l, chart, canvas covered, black
paint, "Charts" in broad headed
tacks, 19th C **385.00**
   54¾″ l, chart, orig green paint, includes Mediterranean charts, early
to mid 19th C **330.00**
Clock, ship's
   Chelsea, navigation, 5¼″ d **385.00**
   Howard & Co, Boston, Propeller Log,

double wind movement, second bit,
12½" d **1,750.00**

Seth Thomas, nickel plated, time and
strike movement, bell mounted on
top, orig label, 6¼" dial **935.00**

Dagger, 7¾" l, sailor's, animal bone
handle, 19th C **250.00**

Deck Spade
56¼" l, pike extension, pitted **110.00**
65" l, mounted, pitted **220.00**

Diorama, two schooners under full sail,
lighthouse, cased, 25 x 19 x 19" . . . **2,200.00**

Document, allowing ship *Ganges* passage, sgd by President Martin Van-
Buren, printed on vellum, framed and
engraved, 1839 . . . . **625.00**

Figurehead
Man wearing gray coat and red vest,
gold watch chain, 43" h **11,000.00**
Plumed Knight, nose chip, flaking
paint, 31" h **3,750.00**

Flare Gun, brass, International Flare
Co, incised name Easter Steamship
Lines **175.00**

Harpoon
Darting, brass, includes bomb,
stamped 1882 on top, Eben, 28¾"
l **660.00**
Double flue, long shaft, incised "WIS"
on one side, other with circle and
four dots, repainted black, 45" l . . **600.00**
Single flue, pitted, 36" l **440.00**

Lamp, 4¾" h, ship's, wall, gimbal, double camphene burner and caps,
weighted base, 19th C **145.00**

Lance, 99⅝" l, mounted on green
stained pole, pitted **110.00**

Lantern
11½" h, starboard, brass, orig oil fix-
ture **90.00**
31½" h, German **330.00**

Log Book
Bark *Black Eagle,* May 5, 1862 thru
September 25, 1863, 129 pgs,
whale stamps provision list, sgd of
John Kehew's navigational store on
front and back cov **1,870.00**
Bark *Pamela,* May 4, 1859 thru Sep-
tember 5, 1861, whale stamps and
entries **3,900.00**

Model
Ocean Liner *Trent,* built by ship's captain Clifton Taylor, cased **6,600.00**
Sloop, plank on frame construction,
66" l, 19th C **2,200.00**
USS Constitution, plank on frame,
copper sheathing, planked deck,
good detail, glass case with inlaid
mahogany base **3,025.00**
Steam Tug *Champion,* scale, painted
off white, deep red and green accents, mounted in brass and glass

case, inlaid mahogany base, 22 x
7 x 11" **1,100.00**

Steamship *Nantucket,* paddle wheel,
mounted on inlaid mahogany case,
40 x 10 x 18" **1,750.00**

Whaleship *Charles W Morgan,* plank
on frame, copper sheathing,
planked cherry dec, mounted in
plexiglas case with wood base, 47
x 14 x 38" **3,300.00**

Navigational Circle, G Dollond, London,
brass, two mahogany cases, silver in-
lay in scale, label on cov **4,500.00**

Octant
Ebony, ivory scales and brass radial
arm, 18" l **500.00**
Rosewood, brass radial arm, ivory
scales, 19⅞" l **440.00**

Painting
British School, *Shipping Off The
Coast,* 25 x 30", oil on canvas, active marine scene with six vessels,
orig gilt frame, unsigned **1,050.00**
Broe, Vern, American, 20th C, *A New
England Catboat,* oil on artist's
board, sailing among islands, sgd
lower right, orig gilt frame, 18 x 24" **1,150.00**
Burns, Milton Jewett, *Three Winds,*
mixed media on heavy pasteboard,
black and white, sgd lower left
"Bruns/99," titled on mat, 14⅞ x
16⅝" **550.00**
Cameron, H., British, 19th C, *Portrait
of the Grain Clipper "Stoneleigh,"*
24 x 30", oil on canvas, framed, sgd
lower left **2,780.00**
Gardener, Derek G M, British, 20th C,
A Clipper Putting Out to Sea, 36 x
42", oil on canvas, three–masted
clipper, orig frame, sgd lower right **3,750.00**
Jacobsen, Antonio, American, 1850–
1921
Portrait of the Belmont at Sea, oil
on heavy pasteboard, sgd lower
right and dated 1919, orig frame,
20 x 36" **12,000.00**
The Advance At Sea, oil on can-
vas, sgd lower right "A Jacobsen," West Hoboken address
and dated 1885, 22 x 36" **6,500.00**
Pringle, Joseph Fulton, British/Amer-
ican, 19th C, ship *Mississippi,* oil
on canvas, sgd lower left on floating log "J Pringle NY 1834," 28 x
36" **6,500.00**
Tufnell, E, American or British, 20th
C, *Sovereign of the Sea 1852,* watercolor on paper, sgd lower right,
titled lower left, 14½ x 20¾" **1,000.00**

Quadrant, 12" l, ebony, Richard Le
Keux, London, 19th C **410.00**

Reverse Painting on Glass, *Titanic*, oil
paint, orig frame, 16 x 20," 19th C . . **165.00**
Sailing Card, A1 clipper ship *St John
Smith*, New York to San Francisco,
personal account record **170.00**
Sextant, brass
J Hughes, London, ivory scale, 19th
C **355.00**
La Precision Moderne, Paris, No
2362, orig mahogany case, 19th C **1,100.00**
W & L Jones, London, silver en-
graved scales, orig case **385.00**
W Desitua, Liverpool, Captain James
Martin Tukey on brass nameplate
on case, captain of clipper ship *Cri-
terion*, c1860 . . . . **660.00**
Speaking Trumpet, captain's, 17" l,
brass **240.00**
Telegraph, Chadburns, Liverpool
42" h **1,000.00**
50" h **825.00**
Tool, ship's, carpenter's
Gouging Plane, 15" l, cherry, double
blades separated with whalebone,
19th C **190.00**
Trailboard, 92¼" l, *A W Cook*, carved
tassels, cannon, cannonballs, and foliate dec, orig paint, 19th C **990.00**
Weathervane, 36" l, wood, Whaleship
form **275.00**
Wheel
14¾" d, brass, cast iron hub, orna-
mented, American, 19th C **110.00**
50" d, brass hub, inlaid, 19th C **1,320.00**
Work Box, 14¼ x 10½ x 4⅞", sailor's,
laminated various woods, inlaid eagle, trophy of flag shield, flags, and
arrow on cov, 19th C **330.00**

NAZI ITEMS

History: The National Socialist Party came to
power in the 1920s during a period of severe economic depression in Germany. Under the leadership of Adolph Hitler, the party assumed first political control and then social control over Germany.
National socialism dominated all aspects of German life. World War II was launched in 1939 to
achieve a military conquest of Europe. The Nazi
era ended in 1945 when Germany surrendered at
the end of World War II.

References: John M. Kaduck, *World War II German Collectibles*, published by author, 1978, 1983
price update; *The Official Price Guide To Military
Collectibles, Fifth Edition*, House of Collectibles,
1985; Sydney B. Vernon, *Vernon's Collectors'
Guide To Orders, Medals, and Decorations (With
Valuations)*, published by author, 1986.

Periodicals: *Military Collectors News*, P. O. Box
702073, Tulsa, OK, 74170; *The MX Exchange*,
P. O. Box 3, Torrington, CT 06790.

**Medal, Iron Cross, 2nd Class, orig rib-
bon, $25.00.**

Badge
Breast, tank battle, bronze, Panzer
Grenadier Personnel, dated 1943 **50.00**
Cap, RAD, silver finish, enameled,
wreath **25.00**
Banner, 16 x 21", Artillery Regt #27,
black embroidered eagle on wine red
field, reverse side white embroidered
FR 27 on blue field, three sided white
fringe, tie ropes **275.00**
Bayonet, police, dress, 13" blade, stag
handle, attached police insignia,
black leather scabbard, silvered fit-
tings, orig black frog, guard marked
"S. MG. 415" and matching numbers **165.00**
Belt Buckle
Prison Official's, round, eagle holding
sword and bolts, swastika on breast **50.00**
SA, rotated swastika, brass body, SP
faceplate, 2 pcs **45.00**
Car Pennant, 8½ x 11½", Teno, printed
on both sides, white eagle on blue
field, two tie strings **75.00**
Cigarette Case, presentation, steel,
painted, brass plate, emb heads of
Mussolini and Hitler, "Vincere" above
heads, eagle embracing wreath of
swastikas, wreath with emblem of It-
aly **175.00**
Correspondence Card, 5 x 8", raised
gold eagle and Adolf Hitler, Mujnchen,
Den address, orig gilt stamped, 2 pcs **45.00**
Dagger, orange and yellow celluloid
grip, SP fittings and scabbard,
marked "E & F Horstaer" **110.00**
Document, 6 x 8", Kriegsurlaubsschein,
seal, unissued **10.00**
Emblem, 27 x 16", train engine, eagle
with swastika **250.00**

Fez, SS 175.00
Flag, sport, 58 x 31″, double sided, sports eagle and swastika 50.00
Flag Pole Top, 8½″, nickel plated, round gear with swastika int. 45.00
Hat
    Panzer Officer, cloth, black, eagle and wreath, silver wire bullion, WWII . 15.00
    Police Officer, back visor, bright eagle and wreath device, green–blue wool, silver cord, leather chin strap, pebbled side buttons 150.00
Helmet, Luftwaffe pilot's, summer, throat mikes 250.00
Holster, P–38, black leather, Nazi acceptance mark, pouch for extra clip . 50.00
Invitation, 4½ x 7″, gold gilt heading, black printed German script, Hitler engraved, orig 35.00
Knee Pads, paratrooper, pr, cotton, tan, padded, elastic straps 175.00
Knife, paratrooper 100.00
Lamp, table, 16″ h, figural, eagle, Munich party headquarters, plaster, gold leaf, marbleized stand 100.00
Meat Fork, 10″ l, SS, Runes engraved in handle 150.00
Mess Kit, steel, large spoon, fork, knife, can opener, steel handle, hallmarked, standing eagle and swastika, 1942 . 75.00
Passbook, D. R. Arbeitsbuch, Weimer eagle, dated 1936, some entries ... 15.00
Patch, Air Force, 7″ 15.00
Post Card, celebrating 700 years of Berlin, seven city and state shields, gold letter inscription, dated 18.8.37, special anniversary cancellation, sent to London 20.00
Shot Glass, Pioneer Battalion, SS ... 30.00
Shooting Medal, Kreisschiessen Kofstein, 1942, silver finish 25.00
Shoulder Boards, police, Wachtmeister Rank, black and silver cord, pink piping, removable style 10.00
Stationery, 8½ x 11½″, NSDAP eagle and Der Fuhrer in raised gold, orig singe sheet 40.00
Stickpin, SS, NSDAP, swastika 20.00
Street Sign, "Juden Gasse," enameled metal, historical piece, orig 650.00
Sword
    Dress, eagle and Swastika, engraved brass handle, black wire wrapped plastic grip, black painted scabbard 100.00
    Officer's, dove head, scabbard, NSDAP eagle on guard 65.00
Tab, collar, rank of Zollwachtmeister .. 10.00
Tunic
    Parade, Panzer NCO Waffenrock, wool, pink piped collar, shoulder boards with machine stitched "2,"

left side with silver tank breast badge, 1938 .... 425.00
Police, green piping, removable shoulder boards, Bevo collar tabs, Bevo green police eagle arm shield on left sleeve, silver pebbled buttons, tailored cuffs, dark brown trim 185.00
Wine Glass, 4″ h, white Nazi eagle on side 70.00

NETSUKES

History: The traditional Japanese kimono has no pockets. Daily necessities such as money, tobacco supplies, etc., were carried in leather pouches or *inros* which hung from a cord with a netsuke toggle. Netsuke comes from "ne" (to root) and "tsuke" (to fasten).

Netsukes originated in the 14th century and initially were associated with the middle class. By the mid-18th century all levels of Japanese society used them. Some of the most famous artists, e.g., Shuzan and Yamada Hojitsu, worked in the netsuke form.

Netsukes average 1 to 2 inches and are made from wood, ivory, bone, ceramics, metal, horn, nutshells, etc. The subject matter is broad based, but always portrayed in a lighthearted, humorous manner. A netsuke must have no sharp edges and balance so it hangs correctly on the sash.

Value depends on artist, region, material, and skill of craftsmanship. Western collectors favor *katabori*, pieces which represent an identifiable object.

Reference: Sandra Andacht, *Oriental Antiques & Art: An Identification And Value Guide*, Wallace-Homestead, 1987.

Collectors' Club: Netsuke Kenkyukai Society, Box 11248, Torrance, CA 90510.

Reproduction Alert: Recent reproductions are on the market. Many are carved from African ivory.

Chrysanthemum, boxwood, carved, etched and curved petal, rect gold plaque sgd "Kosei, Hideyuki" 1,210.00

Ivory, carved, 19th C, $125.00.

Dragon, carved openwork, flaming clouds, 19th C **880.00**

Duck, ivory, carved, sitting, Hakusen . . **150.00**

Man, carved

Holding boy, ivory, 1¾" h **30.00**

Wearing robe, wood and ivory, 2½" h **90.00**

Matchlock Gun, iron, movable hammer, lacquered case, brass ring, 19th C . **330.00**

Monkey, boxwood, male, seated, hunched body, inlaid horn eyes, sgd "Ikkan" **1,000.00**

Okame, standing with basket of mushrooms above head, oval cartouche with "Yoshitomo" on reverse, ivory . **880.00**

Oni, walking in kimono, ivory, sgd "Tomomasa" **340.00**

Rabbit, boxwood, feeding on blossom clusters, inlaid eyes, sgd "Tomokazu," 19th C **1,200.00**

Sage, standing, holding staff in right hand, supporting bird in other, ivory . **470.00**

Snail, ivory, spiral form shell, mollusk turned head, overlaid lacquer and aogai beetle, 19th C **300.00**

Turtle, ivory, pouring water from gourd into bowl held by man, Mitsu Hide, late 18th C **275.00**

Whistle, pottery, bulbous shaft, band of phoenix birds, scrolling foliage, green, blue, and purple glaze, yellow glazed ground, deep green bowl and mouth piece, 19th C **475.00**

NEWCOMB POTTERY

History: William and Ellsworth Woodward, two brothers, were the founders of a series of businesses which eventually merged into the Newcomb pottery effort. In 1885 Ellsworth Woodward, a proponent of vocational training for women, organized a school from which emerged the Ladies Decorative Art League. In 1886 the brothers founded the New Orleans Art Pottery Company with the ladies of the league serving as decorators. The first two potters were Joseph Meyer and George Ohr. The pottery closed in 1891.

William Woodward was on the faculty at Tulane. Ellsworth taught fine arts at the Sophie Newcomb College, a women's school which eventually merged with Tulane. In 1895 Newcomb College developed a pottery course in which the wares could be sold. Some of the equipment came from the old New Orleans Art Pottery.

Mary G. Sheerer joined the staff to teach decoration. In 1910 Paul E. Cox solved many of the technical problems connected with making pottery in a southern environment. Other leading figures were Sadie Irvine, Professor Lota Lee Troy, and Kathrine Choi. Pottery was made until the early 1950s.

Students painted a quality art pottery with a distinctive high glaze. Designs have a decidedly southern flavor, e.g., myrtle, jasmine, sugar cane, moss, cypress, dogwood, and magnolia motifs. Later matte glazed pieces usually are decorated with carved back floral designs. Pieces depicting murky, bayou scenes are most desirable.

References: Suzanne Ormond and Mary E. Irvine, *Louisiana's Art Nouveau: The Crafts Of The Newcomb Style,* Pelican Publishing Company, 1976; Jessie Poesch, *Newcomb Pottery: An Enterprise for Southern Women,* Schiffer Publishing, Ltd, 1984.

Collectors' Club: American Art Pottery Association, 9825 Upton Circle, Bloomington, MN 55431.

Museum: Newcomb College, Tulane University, New Orleans, LA.

Bowl, tricorn, Joseph Meyer potter, artist sgd "Sadie Irvine," 6¼" d, 3¾" h, $675.00.

Bowl, 8¼" d, pink and blue matte body, pink floral relief dec rim, artist sgd . . **825.00**

Candlestick

4" h, 5" d, high glaze, incised, motto at rim "In Winter I Get Up At Night & Dress by Yellow Candle–light," white blossoms in wax plate, decorated by Sadie Irvine, incised "NC," "JM," and "SI," small repair at top **1,045.00**

9½" h, 5¼" d, flaring, semi–matte glaze, band of stylized white blossoms at top, long green stems, blue ground, Sadie Irvine, incised "NC," "S," "JM," and "B," painted "DP92," repair to small chip at bobeche . . **825.00**

Mug, 4½" h, 5" d, high glaze, devil's mask dec, motto "Pile up the coals/

Fill the red bowl/Drink every one" in blue, neutral ground, decorated by Gertrude Roberts Smith, painted "G.R.S." and die–stamped "New-comb College" **2,530.00**

Pitcher, 6¾" h, 4½" d, high glaze, paper whites with green leaves, natural and black ground, decorated by Amelie Roman, incised "AR," "NC," and "JM" **5,325.00**

Plaque, 5¾" d, scenic, matte glaze, landscape of green pine trees, deep blue ground, decorated by Sadie Irvine, incised "NC," "JH," "SV68," orig paper label **1,210.00**

Tile, 4" sq, birds in maple tree, blue and green matte glazes, decorated by Cynthia Littlejohn, ink marks "NC," "FW19," and "CL" **1,100.00**

Vase

3¾" d, squatty, wide mouth, low relief band of flowers, Sadie Irvine decorator, J Meyer potter **470.00**

5" h

5" d, bulbous, upright rim, high glaze, incised bunches of purple grapes and green leaves, ivory ground, decorated by Sara Bloom Levy, painted "S.B.L.," "FF47," stamped "JM" and "NC" **4,400.00**

5½" d, bulbous, high glaze, incised wide band of stylized blue trees, ivory ground, decorated by Marie de Hoa Le Blanc, marked "NC," "MHLB," "JM," minor chip at base **4,950.00**

5½" h, 4½" d, Spanish moss and moon scene, blue trees, green moss carved against light blue ground, decorated by Anna Simpson, stamped "NC," "QK21" and "86" **1,870.00**

6½" h, 4¼" d, corset, band of green bats and yellow crescent moons, artist sgd "F.P.," painted "AQ44" . **4,400.00**

7¼" h, 5" d, corset, clusters of pink pine cones, blue ground, decorated by Henrietta Bailey, imp "NC," "HB," "R284/80" **1,550.00**

7½" h, inverted rim, tapering cylindri-cal, three V–shaped panels, low molded relief dec, blue, white, and green stylized tree tops and open petaled flowers, matte glaze, imp factory mark, artist initials Corinne Chalaron, New Orleans, 1928 . . . **825.00**

10¼" h, 5" d, high glazed, incised or-ange iris blossoms, green leaves, neutral and deep blue ground, dec-orated by Sabina Elliot Wells, painted "S.E.W.," "NC," and "FF9" **18,700.00**

10¾" h, 4½" d, Spanish moss and moon landscape, decorated by

Anna Simpson, incised "NC," "150," "QC35," "AFS" **6,325.00**

NILOAK POTTERY, MISSION WARE

History: Niloak Pottery was made near Benton, Arkansas. Charles Dean Hyten experimented with native clay, trying to preserve its natural colors. By 1911 he perfected Mission Ware, a marbleized pottery in which the cream and brown colors pre-dominate. The pieces were marked Niloak (kaolin spelled backwards).

After a devastating fire, the pottery was rebuilt and named Eagle Pottery. This factory included the space to add a novelty pottery line which was introduced in 1929. This line usually was marked Hywood–Niloak until 1934 when the name Hy-wood was dropped from the mark. Mr. Hyten left the pottery in 1941. In 1946 operations ceased.

Additional Listings: See *Warman's Americana & Collectibles* for more examples, especially the name novelty pieces.

Note: Prices listed below are for Mission Ware pieces.

Bowl, 7½", marbleized swirls **65.00**

Candlesticks, pr, 8", marbleized swirls, blue, cream, terra cotta, and brown . **250.00**

Toothpick Holder, marbleized swirls, tan and blue **100.00**

Urn, 4½", marbleized swirls, brown and blue **35.00**

Vase, Mission Ware, yellow, blue, and brown swirls, imp mark, 5¼" h, $60.00.

Vase
  4½", marbleized swirls, red and
    brown **55.00**
  5½", bulbous, marbleized swirls, rust,
    blue, and cream **65.00**
  6", marbleized swirls, cream, tur-
    quoise blue, rust, and brown **70.00**

NIPPON CHINA, 1891–1921

History: Nippon, Japanese hand painted porcelain, was made for export between 1891 and
1921. In 1891, when the McKinley tariff act proclaimed that all items of foreign manufacture be
stamped with their country of origin, Japan chose
to use "Nippon." In 1921 the United States decided
the word "Nippon" no longer was acceptable and
required that all Japanese wares be marked with
"Japan." The Nippon era ended.

There are over 220 recorded Nippon backstamps or marks. The three most popular are the
wreath, maple leaf, and rising sun marks. Wares
with variations of all three marks are being reproduced today. A knowledgeable collector can easily
spot the reproductions by the mark variances.

The majority of the marks are found in three
different colors: green, blue, and magenta. Colors
indicate the quality of the porcelain used: green
for first grade porcelain, blue for second grade,
and magenta for third grade. Marks were applied
by two methods, decal stickers under glaze and
imprinting directly on the porcelain.

References: Gene Loendorf, *Nippon Hand
Painted China*, McGraw Color Graphics, 1975;
Joan Van Patten, *The Collector's Encyclopedia Of
Nippon Porcelain, Series One*, Collector Books,
1979; Joan Van Patten, *The Collector's Encyclo-
pedia Of Nippon Porcelain, Series Two*, Collector
Books, 1982; Joan Van Patten, *The Collector's
Encyclopedia Of Nippon Porcelain, Series Three*,
Collector Books, 1986.

Collectors' Clubs: Great Lakes Nippon Collectors Club, Rt. 2, Box 81, Peotone, IL 60468; International Nippon Collectors Club, P.O. Box 230,
Peotone, IL 60468; Long Island Nippon Collectors
Club, P.O. Box 88, Jericho, NY 11753; New England Nippon Collectors Club, 22 Mill Pond, North
Andover, MA 01845.

Additional Listings: See *Warman's Americana
& Collectibles*.

Advisor: Kathy Wojciechowski.

Ashtray, triangular shape, dog's head
  medallion center, moriage trim, maple
  leaf mark **225.00**
Basket, 8¾" h, pastoral tapestry scene,
  ducks and pond **790.00**
Berry Set, master, five matching smaller
  bowls, lavender and purple colum-
  bines, gold outlining, Wreath, 6 pcs . **95.00**

Bowl
  7" d, red and pink roses, green
    leaves, gold flowers on edge, gold
    trim, green M in Wreath mark ... **65.00**
  10" d, hp, flowers, scrolls, and center
    medallion dec, open handles,
    green "M" in wreath mark **85.00**
Bread Tray, gaudy, green and gold, pink
  asters **225.00**
Calling Card Tray, 7¾ x 6", mythical
  dragon and bird, blue Maple Leaf
  mark **45.00**
Candle Lamp, bisque, sailing ships,
  pastel blue, Wreath, pr **3,200.00**
Candlestick
  6" h, Wedgwood and rose nosegay
    design, Jasperware, Wreath mark,
    pr **235.00**
  10" h, Galle scene, moriage trees,
    Maple Leaf mark, pr **400.00**
Candy Dish, scalloped edge, pink roses,
  gold trim, twisted handle **50.00**
Celery Set, 11½" l tray, four matching
  salts, hp, garland of red wild roses
  and daisies dec, lime green border,
  blue Rising Sun mark **75.00**
Children's Dishes
  Mug, 3¾" h, clowns and rabbit, white,
    Rising Sun mark **75.00**
  Tea Set, teapot, creamer and sugar,
    four cups, saucers, and plates, gold
    flowers and beading, white back-
    ground, Rising Sun **235.00**
Chocolate Pot, cov, white and caramel
  marbleized ground, allover gold design, Maple Leaf mark **135.00**
Compote, 4¾" h, 8½" d, Wedgwood and
  rose nosegay dec, Wreath mark ... **200.00**
Cracker Jar, melon ribbed, bisque background, Indian in canoe shooting
  moose on river edge, ftd, Wreath
  mark **425.00**
Decanter, 8" h, blue and pink background, pink and lavender roses, gold
  overlay designs and trim, Maple Leaf
  mark **180.00**
Doll
  11" h, boy, bisque head, brown hair
    and eyes, teeth, composition body,
    FY Nippon mark **275.00**
  12" h, bisque head, sleep eyes, dark
    brown hair, composition body,
    Christening gown, FY Nippon mark **175.00**
Dresser Set, woodland scene, tray, hatpin holder, powder box, and hair receiver, Maple Leaf mark **950.00**
Dutch Shoe, 3" l, bisque, scenic design,
  Wreath mark **125.00**
Egg Warmer, holds four eggs, stopper,
  sailboat scene, Rising Sun mark ... **110.00**
Ewer, 6" h, multicolored moriage design,

enameling technique, floral bouquet
medallions front and back, unmarked ... 90.00
Ferner, 6″ w, floral dec, gold beading,
four handles, green M in Wreath mark ... 125.00
Hair Receiver, 5″ d, yellow and red
roses, black ground, blue Maple Leaf
mark 60.00
Hatpin Holder, 5″ h, serpent in relief,
mottled ground 165.00
Jam Jar, floral dec, gold trim 45.00
Lazy Susan, 10″ d, floral dec, pastel
shades, heavy gold overlay, orig papier mache box 175.00
Mayonnaise Dish, 4½″ d, ladle, multicolored floral dec, gold trim 60.00
Mug, 5½″ h, gray bisque background,
moriage dragon, blue enameled
eyes, green M in Wreath mark 225.00
Napkin Ring, 4″ h, figural, owl on tree
stump, Wreath mark 375.00
Nappy, 5″ d, scalloped, cobalt, red flowers, elaborate gold allover design .. 127.50
Nut Set, 7″ d, master bowl, six cups,
relief molded, nut shell shape 225.00
Pitcher, 7″ h, slate gray ground, moriage
sea gulls, Leaf mark 250.00
Planter, 7″ d, Egyptian designs, gold
outlining, supported by three columns
forming Egyptian heads 225.00
Plaque, relief molded, Wreath mark
10½″ d, collie and terrier 950.00
12″ d, farmer sowing seeds 2,100.00
Plate
8½″ d, lake, house, and roses scene,
cobalt and gold trim, Leaf mark .. 185.00
10″ w, gold center, cobalt and gold
trim, Maple Leaf mark 150.00
Powder Box, cov, 5¼″ d, portrait on cov,
green and white base, heavy gold
scrolling, gold feet, blue Maple Leaf
mark 125.00
Punch Bowl and Stand, 12½″ d, 6½″ h,

**Vase, two gold handles, hp lake scene,
green wreath mark, 8¾″ h, $225.00.**

bisque, bouquet of roses scene, wide
rim decorated with gold and jewels,
Wreath mark 295.00
Ring Tree, gold, beading, green M in
Wreath mark 40.00
Scent Bottle, 4¼″ h, cream, pink and
red roses, green raised lattice with
white dots 125.00
Serving Tray, 11″ d, gold and burgundy
medallions inside gold fluted rim, multicolored roses and leaves center,
gold open pierced handles, Royal
Kinran mark 195.00
Shaving Mug, shaded green, floral dec,
gold beading, gold handle 225.00
Spittoon, lady's hand, violets, turquoise
beading, green M in Wreath mark .. 150.00
Stein, relief molded, dog heads, leash
handle, green M in Wreath mark ... 950.00
Stick Pin Holder, 1½″ h, multicolored
roses, gold trim, Wreath mark 100.00
Sugar Shaker, 4¼″ h, cobalt, floral, Maple Leaf mark 145.00
Tankard, 13¼″ h, cobalt, red roses,
gold, sgd 250.00
Tea Set, teapot, creamer, and sugar,
melon ribbed shape, gold handles
and trim, gold overlay design, pink
roses, Leaf mark 250.00
Tea Strainer, pink roses 50.00
Tea Tile, scenic, cow, pasture 45.00
Toothpick Holder, 2½″ h, fruit and floral
dec, Rising Sun mark 65.00
Trivet, octagonal, portrait, Egyptian
lady, shaded red ground, blue trim . 140.00
Urn
9½″ h, white flowers, gold outline,
fancy handles, dome lid, pedestal
base, Royal Kinran mark 425.00
16″ h, medallion in center with cow
drinking from pond, gold floral overlay, gold stand–up handles,
bolted base, Wreath mark 575.00
Vase
6″ h, scenic cartouche front, beading
allover, handled, sgd 100.00
8¼″ h, abstract brown and pink pine
cones and needles, olive green
ground, gold leaf trim, matte glaze,
double scroll handles 275.00
8½″ h, red roses, moriage design,
loop handles and rim, green M in
Wreath mark, pr 400.00
9¼″ h, woodland and water scene,
shaded ground, gold handles,
green M in Wreath mark 150.00
12″ h, red flowers, gold neck and
base, jeweling, blue Maple Leaf
mark 275.00
13″ h, mums in medallions, gold handles, blue Maple Leaf mark 225.00
Wall Pocket, 6″ l, molded dog, floral dec ... 65.00

NODDERS

History: Nodders are figurines with heads and/ or arms attached to the body with wires to enable them to move. They are made in a variety of materials—bisque, celluloid, papier-mâché, porcelain, and wood.

Most nodders date from the late 19th century with Germany being the principal source of supply. Among the American made nodders, those of Disney and cartoon characters are most eagerly sought.

Child, seated, white dress, yellow basket, 4½″ h, $125.00.

Baby, 4½″, bisque, pink and white gown, pulling off blue sock	175.00
Black, 5½″, bisque, school boy, seated in chair, white shirt, blue, white, and tan plaid pants, holding slate	125.00
Brownie, 10″, policeman, blue, Palmer Cox	275.00
Bulldog, 10 x 6½″, brown, sanded finish	60.00
Buttercup, bisque, German	175.00
Colonial Woman, 7½″, bisque	185.00
Couple, pr	
African, bisque, black man and woman, pr	575.00
Oriental, 8¾″, bisque, pink robes, gilding, seated before keyboard and music book, Continental, 19th C	500.00
Daddy Warbucks, bisque	100.00
Donald Duck, plastic, Louis Marx & Co	25.00
Elephant, 8½ x 6½″, gray felt, canvas blanket, wood base	150.00
Girl, Turkish, 6 x 6″, bisque, white beading	300.00
Happy Hooligan, 6″, papier mache, red jacket, blue pants	90.00
Indian Princess, 3¾″, bisque, seated, holding fan, pale blue, gold trim	115.00
Japanese Boy and Girl, pr, 5½″, papier mache	35.00
Kayo, bisque, marked "Germany"	125.00
Monk, 5¾″, bisque, standing, holding wine pitcher, German	140.00
Orphan Annie, bisque, German	100.00
Rabbit, 8″, papier mache, sitting, light brown	80.00
Santa Claus, 10″, papier mache, candy container, mica glitter trim, German	100.00
Shriner, 7″, papier mache	85.00

NORITAKE CHINA

History: Morimura Brothers founded Noritake China in 1904 in Nagoya, Japan. They made high quality chinaware for export to the United States and also produced a line of china blanks for hand painting. In 1910 the company perfected a technique for the production of high quality dinnerware and introduced streamlined production.

During the 1920s the Larkin Company of Buffalo, New York, was a prime distributor of Noritake China. Larkin offered Azalea, Briarcliff, Linden, Modjeska, Savory, Sheridan, and Tree In The Meadow patterns as part of their premium line.

The factory was heavily damaged during World War II; production was reduced. Between 1946 and 1948 the company sold their china under the "Rose China" mark, since the quality of production did not match the earlier Noritake China. In 1948, expansion saw the resumption of quality production and the use of the Noritake name once again.

There are close to 100 different marks for Noritake, the careful study of which can determine the date of production. Most pieces are marked "Noritake" and have a wreath, "M," "N," or "Nippon." The use of the letter "N" was registered in 1953.

References: Aimee Neff Alden and Marian Kinney Richardson, *Early Noritake China: An Identification And Value Guide To Tableware Patterns*, Wallace-Homestead, 1987; Joan Van Patten, *Collector's Encyclopedia of Noritake*, Collector Books, 1984.

Additional Listings: See *Warman's Americana & Collectibles* for price listings of the Azalea pattern.

Ashtray	
4¾″ w, triangular, figural pipe in center, shades of brown and tan, green mark	75.00
5″ d, circular, horses dec, green border, red cigarette rests, red mark	65.00
Bouillon Cup and Saucer, Azalea pattern	24.00
Bowl, 8½″ d, gold, wood scene border	65.00
Bread Plate, 14″ l, 6¼″ w, white, pale green and gold floral border, open handles	24.00

Dish, hp, brown, gold, green, gray, nuts in bowl, three legs, green mark, $75.00.

Candy Dish, 6½" d, round, black luster, orange flowers, gold trim 135.00
Children's Dishes, white, gold trim, six cups and saucers, plates, teapot, creamer, sugar, cookie plate, platter, cov casserole, orig box, 1922 . . . . . 250.00
Cigarette Holder, 5" h, bell shaped, floral dec, bird finial, red mark 100.00
Condiment Set, salt and pepper shakers, mustard, and round tray, red ground, blue and yellow birds on perch 75.00
Cup and Saucer, 3" d cup, 5" d saucer, white, pink and blue flowers, gold trim 25.00
Demitasse Cup and Saucer, orange and blue florals 18.00
Dresser Doll, figural, gold luster 185.00
Ferner, 6" w, triangular 75.00
Hatpin Holder, 4½" h, gold luster, black band at top with multicolored flowers 45.00
Lemon Dish, 6" d, relief molded, lemon, hp blossoms and leaves, M in wreath mark 50.00
Mustard Jar, underplate, orange luster finish, blueberries finial 45.00
Nut Set, figural, peanut shape, 7¼" d master bowl, six 3" d individual figural dishes 175.00
Perfume, orange luster bottle, blue flower stopper 85.00
Plaque
8½" d, silhouette of girl in bouffant dress, looking into hand mirror, green M in wreath mark 100.00
10" d, hp, cottage, trees, and pastel flowers, brown rim 65.00
Powder Box, desert scene, Arab on camel, cobalt blue ground, ornate gold beading 300.00
Punch Bowl Set, banquet size, eight matching cups, scenic, swans, cottage, island, and trees, heavy raised gold, green M in wreath mark 675.00

Shaving Mug, 3¾" h, hp, scene of stalking tiger, green M in wreath mark . . 200.00
Tile, hp, scenic, water, willow tree, rushes, and man in boat 38.00
Tobacco Jar, 6½" h, hp, golfer, red jacket and cap, black and white checkerboard knickers, green M in wreath mark 190.00
Tray, 8" l, two handles, hp, blue violets, red M in wreath mark 40.00
Vase
5¼" h, relief molded, squirrel on berried leafy branch, multicolored, shaded brown ground 150.00
7" h, bulbous, figural red birds on rim, orange and pale blue luster, red and black floral dec 150.00
10" h, hp, two bluebirds, apple blossoms, handles 275.00
11½" h, cylindrical, two gold trimmed handles, hp, white and pink poppies, green leaves, gold foliate design on shoulder and base 150.00
Vegetable Bowl, Wild Ivy pattern 12.00
Wall Pocket, 6¾" l, bulbous, blue luster, exotic bird dec 60.00

NORITAKE: TREE IN THE MEADOW PATTERN

History: Tree In The Meadow is one of the most popular patterns of Noritake china. Since the design is hand painted, there are numerous variations of the scene. The basic scene features a large tree (usually in the foreground), a meandering stream or lake, and a peasant cottage in the distance. Principal colors are muted tones of brown and yellow.

The pattern is found with a variety of backstamps and appears to have been imported into the United States beginning in the early 1920s. The Larkin Company distributed this pattern through its catalog sales in the 1920–1930 period.

Reference: Joan Van Patten, *Collector's Encyclopedia of Noritake,* Collector Books, 1984.

Ashtray, 5¼" d, green mark 35.00
Berry Set, large bowl, pierced handles, six small bowls 68.00
Bowl, 6½" d, green mark 25.00
Cake Plate, 10" d, pierced handles . . . 30.00
Condiment Set, mustard pot, ladle, salt and pepper shakers, tray 40.00
Creamer 25.00
Dish, 6" d, pierced handles, blue luster border 40.00
Jam Jar, underplate, and spoon 65.00
Lemon Dish, 5½" d, center ring handle 15.00
Plate
6½" d 10.00

Bowl, hp, beige ground, purple, orange, and brown dec, three legs, marked "Noritake, Made In Japan," 6¼" d, $27.50.

7½" d	12.00
8½" d	15.00
Platter	
12" l	30.00
14" l	35.00
Relish, divided	40.00
Salt and Pepper Shakers, marked "Made In Japan," pr	30.00
Sauce Dish, underplate, and spoon, green mark	50.00
Shaving Mug, 3¾" h, green mark	85.00
Sugar, cov	25.00
Tea Set, teapot, creamer, and cov sugar, six cups and saucers	135.00
Tea Tile, 5" w, chamfered corners, green mark	25.00
Toothpick Holder	55.00
Vase, 7" h, fan shape	120.00
Vegetable Dish, 9⅜" l, oval, Noritake mark	30.00
Waffle Set, sugar shaker and syrup jug	70.00
Wall Plaque, 8½" l, green mark	75.00

NORTH DAKOTA SCHOOL OF MINES

History: The North Dakota School of Mines was established in 1890. Earle J. Babcock, an instructor in chemistry, was impressed with the high purity of North Dakota potter's clay. In 1898 Babcock received funds to develop his finds. He tried to interest commercial potteries in North Dakota clay, but had limited success.

In 1910 Babcock persuaded the school to establish a Ceramics Department. Margaret Cable, who studied under Charles Binns and Frederick H. Rhead, was appointed head. She remained until her retirement in 1949.

Decorative emphasis was placed on native themes, e.g., flowers and animals. Art Nouveau, Art Deco, and fairly plain pieces were made.

The pottery is marked in cobalt blue underglaze with "University of North Dakota/Grand Forks, N.D./Made at School of Mines/N.D. Clay" in a circle. Some earlier pieces only are marked "U.N.D." or "U.N.D./Grand Forks, N.D." Most pieces are numbered (they can be dated with University records) and signed by both the instructor and student. Cable signed pieces are most desirable.

Reference: *University Of North Dakota Pottery, The Cable Years,* Knight Publishing Company, 1977.

Vase, squatty bulbous shape, white shading to light green ground, circular dec and imp leaf dec, stamp mark, 4½" d, 4" h, $165.00.

Bowl	
4" d, carved turkeys, shaded green to brown, sgd "Mattson"	275.00
5½" d, carved florals, gray–green matte	150.00
Curtain Pull, Indian head, turquoise, marked "Homecoming 1939," orig box	115.00
Paperweight, 3½" d, "Parent's Day, 1938," deep blue	100.00
Tile, 3½" w, high relief dec, "R" for Rebekah Assemblies	120.00
Vase, 3½" h	
3¾" d, band of coyotes, ivory ground, blue semi–matte glaze, ink stamp and "934," "JM"	550.00
4½" d, band of buffalo, ivory ground, caramel semi–matte glaze, ink stamp and "JM"	725.00

NUTTING, WALLACE

History: Wallace Nutting (1861–1941) was one of America's foremost photographers in the first third of the twentieth century. Between 1897 and his death, he took over 50,000 pictures, kept approximately 10,000, destroyed the rest because they did not meet his standards, and commercially marketed over 2,500 of the 10,000 that he retained. Of the remaining 7,500 views, some were sold in limited numbers and the others used personally for lectures, research, or simply entertaining friends.

Millions of Nutting's hand–colored platinotype pictures were sold. Nutting opened his first studio in New York City in 1904. In 1905 he moved to a larger studio in Southbury, Connecticut. A Toronto branch office followed in 1907. In 1911–1912 Nutting sold his business and house, Nuttinghame, in Southbury. The person who purchased the business backed out, leaving Nutting without a home.

Nutting moved his entire operation, including twenty employees, to Framingham, Massachusetts. His business blossomed. At its peak, it provided employment for over two hundred people in positions ranging from colorists and support staff to salesmen and framers.

Wallace Nutting began actively collecting antiques sometime around 1912. In 1917 he published his first book on furniture, *American Windsor*. In 1928 the first two volumes of *The Furniture Treasury* appeared. Volume 3 followed in 1933.

In 1917–1918 Wallace Nutting began offering reproduction furniture for sale. During the early 1920s the business prospered. However, by 1927–1928 the business was in decline. The Depression brought further decline. Nutting laid off employees, but refused to allow the business to fold. It was operating on a very limited basis at the time of his death.

During his lifetime Nutting had a close relationship with Berea College in Kentucky. Upon his wife's death, Berea was given the remains of the furniture business. After copying the blueprints and patterns at the Framingham factory for their records, Berea sold the business to Drexel Furniture Company.

References: Michael Ivankovich, *The Alphabetical & Numerical Index to Wallace Nutting Pictures*, Diamond Press, 1988; Michael Ivankovich, *The Guide To Wallace Nutting Furniture*, Diamond Press, 1990; Michael Ivankovich, *The Guide To Wallace–Nutting Like Photographers of the Early 20th Century*, Diamond Press, 1991; Michael Ivankovich, *The Price Guide To Wallace Nutting Pictures, Fourth Edition*, Diamond Press, 1989; Wallace Nutting, *The Wallace Nutting Expansible Catalog* (reprint of 1915 catalog), Diamond Press; Wallace Nutting, *Wallace Nutting General Catalog, Supreme Edition* (reprint of 1930 catalog), Schiffer Publishing.

BOOKS

American Windsors	165.00
England Beautiful	85.00
Furniture Treasury, three volumes, 1st edition	600.00
Pathways Of The Puritans	150.00
Pennsylvania Beautiful	45.00
Photographic Art Secrets	220.00
The Clock Book	80.00
The Cruise of the 800, 1904	115.00
Wallace Nutting's Biography, 1st edition, dust jacket	80.00

FURNITURE

Chair, side, Style #361, maple, old nut brown finish, paper rush seat, branded label on bottom rack rung, 41¼″ h, pr	1,150.00
Chest, oak, single drawer	2,585.00
Table, tavern, pine top, maple turned legs, block branded signature	1,250.00

Picture, *To Slumberland,* 1915 copyright, 14 x 17″, $1,450.00.

PICTURES

A Face Of The Falls, 14 x 17″	440.00
A Maine Farm Entrance, 16 x 20″	285.00
An Old Time Romance, 16 x 20″	425.00
Anxious To Please, 12 x 14″	550.00
Between The Spruces, 16 x 20″	200.00
Cosmos and Larkspur, 13 x 16″	965.00
Evangeline Lane, 16 x 20″	345.00
Fireside Contentment, 14 x 17″	375.00
Four O'Clock, 14 x 17″	1,450.00
Gloucester Cloister, 16 x 20″	665.00
Honeymoon Stroll, 11 x 14″	200.00
In Bright Array, 15 x 18″	245.00

In The Midst Of Her China, 14 x 17" ..	330.00
Lorna Doone, 14 x 17"	880.00
Mending, 18 x 22"	365.00
Off For The Legislature, 13 x 16"	2,035.00
Slack Water, 15 x 22"	220.00
Stepping Heavenward, 13 x 16"	220.00
The Harvest Fiend, 13 x 16"	1,320.00
The Meeting Place, 18 x 22"	2,750.00
The Stream of Peace, 13 x 16"	235.00
Upper Winooski, 11 x 17"	220.00

SILHOUETTES

Girl, wearing long dress	
Arranging flowers on pedestal, 4 x 4"	50.00
Playing piano, 7 x 8"	65.00
Lincoln, Abe and Mary Todd, pr, 4 x 5"	200.00
Nutting, Mr and Mrs, Christmas Card	
type, 6 x 8"	110.00
Washington, George, 4 x 5"	85.00

OCCUPIED JAPAN

History: At the end of World War II, the Japanese economy was devastated. To secure needed hard currency, the Japanese pottery industry produced thousands of figurines and other knick-knacks for export. From the beginning of the American occupation until April 28, 1952, these objects were marked "Japan," "Made in Japan," "Occupied Japan," and "Made in Occupied Japan." Only pieces marked with the last two designations are of strong interest to Occupied Japan collectors. The first two marks also were used at other time periods.

The variety of products is endless—ashtrays, dinnerware, lamps, planters, souvenir items, toys, vases, etc. Initially it was the figurines which attracted the largest number of collectors; today many collectors focus on non–figurine material.

References: Gene Florence, *The Collector's Encyclopedia Of Occupied Japan Collectibles, 1st Series* (1976, 1982 revision), *2nd Series* (1979, 1982 revision), *Third Series* (1987), *4th Series* (1990), Collector Books.

Collectors' Clubs: Occupied Japan Collectors Club, 18309 Faysmith Avenue, Torrance, CA 90504; O.J. Club, 29 Freeborn Street, Newport, RI 02840.

Additional Listings: See *Warman's Americana & Collectibles* for more examples.

Bisque	
Ashtray, 2¼" w, heart shape, hp, floral	
sprays, white ground	12.00
Creamer, figural cow	20.00
Figure	
3" h, girl, bright dress	10.00
3½" h, girl sitting on bench	10.00
6½" h, boy standing by fence ...	20.00

8" h, Victorian Man, playing instru-	
ment	40.00
Miniature, pitcher, multicolored ap-	
plied floral spray, pink ground ...	8.00
Planter, figural, peasant girl standing	
beside leaf covered planter	35.00
Shelf Sitter, 4¾" h, Oriental girl, green	12.00
Vase, 7" h, ftd, emb floral dec	18.00
Wall Pocket, 5" h, cuckoo clock, or-	
ange luster, pine cone weights ...	12.00
Celluloid	
Doll Carriage, 2¾" h, pink and blue,	
movable hood, Acme	24.00
Figure, 6" h, Betty Boop, blond hair,	
movable arms	24.00
Toy, wind–up	
Boy with tin suitcase	45.00
Lion	32.00

Figure, woman in green dress, man in maroon coat and blue pants, 4¾" h, $15.00.

Metal	
Ashtray, 6¾" d, chrome plated,	
pierced floral rim	10.00
Binoculars, Egyptian figures, emb ..	32.00
Candy Dish, pedestal base	10.00
Cigarette Lighter, 4" h, cowboy, head	
flips back	25.00
Harmonica, butterfly shape	20.00
Nut Dish, 6" d, floral borders	10.00
Pincushion, figural, shoe, silver finish,	
red velvet cushion	15.00
Plate, 4½" d, pierced scalloped fancy	
rim, silvered metal	12.00
Vase, 6" h, SP, Art Deco style, stylized	
blossoms, ftd	25.00
Papier Mache	
Nodder, rabbit, sitting	35.00
Tray, 10½" l, rect, floral dec	50.00
Plastic, necklace, 25" l, hp, football and	
baseball players, other figural charms	65.00

Porcelain

Child's Tea Set, 24 pcs, white, floral
dec **100.00**
Creamer and Sugar, rose, pink, and
white **24.00**
Dish, 5″ d, triangular, handle, gold trim **20.00**
Figure

3″ h, cherub, playing drum, pierced
pedestal base **10.00**
6¾″ h, lady, Art Deco style dress . **25.00**
Honey Pot, 4½″ h, black Mammy,
head lifts off, spoon as tongue,
holding spoon and frying pan **35.00**
Incense Burner, cobalt blue, floral
dec, gold trim **18.00**
Lamp, figural, Colonial man and
woman, pr **65.00**
Planter, figural, shoe, floral dec **18.00**
Plaque, ducks in flight **18.00**
Plate, 7½″ d, Ambassador pattern . . **8.00**
Rice Bowl, 6″ d, emb dragon **25.00**
Salt, master, figural, swan **18.00**
Salt and Pepper Shakers, pr, negro
chiefs **30.00**
Tea Set, cov teapot, four cups and
saucers, white, small pink roses,
green leaves **65.00**

G.E.OHR, BILOXI.

OHR POTTERY

History: Ohr pottery was produced by George E. Ohr in Biloxi, Mississippi. There is some discrepancy as to when he actually established his pottery. Some suggest 1878, but Ohr's autobiography indicates 1883. In 1884 Ohr exhibited 600 pieces of his work, indicating that he had been working for some time.

Ohr's techniques included twisting, crushing, folding, denting, and crinkling thin walled clay into odd, grotesque, and sometimes graceful forms. Much of his early work is signed with an impressed stamp of his name and location in block letters. His later work, often marked with the flowing script designation "G E Ohr," was usually left unglazed.

In 1906, Ohr closed the pottery and stored over 6,000 pieces as his legacy to his family. He hoped it would be purchased by the U.S. Government, which never happened. The entire collection remained in storage until it was rediscovered in 1972.

Today Ohr is recognized as one of the leading potters in the American Art Pottery movement. Some greedy individuals have taken the later unglazed pieces and covered them with poor quality glazes, in hopes of making them more valuable. These pieces, usually with the flowing script mark, do not have "stilt marks" on the bottom.

Reference: Garth Clark, Robert Ellison, Jr., and Eugene Hecht, *The Mad Potter of Biloxi: The Art & Life of George Ohr,* Abbeville Press, 1989.

Candleholder, puzzle mug, pink, mottled green glaze, 4⅝″ h, $800.00.

Bowl, 2″ d, 3½″ h, bulbous, closed, vibrant orange and mottled brown and
green high glaze, die–stamped mark **495.00**
Candlestick

3⅞″ h, dark and light green mottled
glaze, marked **175.00**
4½″ h, twisted body, handles, gunmetal black **425.00**
Creamer, 5″ h, pinched cylinder, open
handle, deep violet and mottled blue
glaze, imp "G. E. OHR Biloxi, Miss" **5,000.00**
Inkwell, 2″ h, 5½″ l, 5″ w, artist's palette,
green high glaze inkwell, brown high
glaze base, die–stamped mark **1,980.00**
Jug, 5″ h, bisque, tapered, script sgd . **350.00**
Mug

Single handle, gunmetal gray **350.00**
Three handles, green, brown, and
gray **700.00**
Novelty

Log Cabin, 2½″ h, 2½″ l, white clay,
bisque fired, die–stamped mark . . **330.00**
Puzzle Mug, 3½″ h, mottled green
high glaze, pressed rope and leaf
handle, screw under handle, script
sgd "G E Ohr" **375.00**
Pitcher

2¾″ h, 8″ d, collapsed, blue, green,
red, and gunmetal mottled glaze,
some restoration to stilt pull on
base, die–stamped mark **2,750.00**
5″ h, bulbous, off center handle,
brown irid, imp mark **415.00**
8¼″ h, black speckled dark mustard,
handle, imp mark **600.00**
Shelf, 6″ h, 6″ w, 3″ d, corner, ceramic,
curving sides, beehive pattern, two

factory holes for hanging, khaki–
green high glaze, die–stamped mark,
imp "JHP," minor chip at base **525.00**
Teapot, 4⅛" h, unglazed bisque, shading orange to cream, marked **85.00**
Vase
3" h, 4¼" d, bulbous, deep in–body
twist, bisque fired red clay, incised
mark, dated "06" **525.00**
3½" h, 2½" d, pedestal base, flared
rim, metallic green and black high
glaze, die–stamped twice **385.00**
3½" h, 2¾" d, cylindrical, bulging center, green and brown high glaze
flambe, die–stamped mark **330.00**
4½" h
2¼" d, bud, rose–pink high glaze,
band of purpled sponged pattern
at top and base, die–stamped
mark, small kiln bruise on side . **550.00**
3" d, flaring neck, hammered shoulder, black lustrous glaze, die–
stamped twice **600.00**
5½" h, 2" d, bud, pinched waist, semi–
matte lapis blue glaze, die–
stamped mark **440.00**
6" h, 4½" h, bulbous base, cylindrical
neck, bulbous rim, bisque fired,
script mark **300.00**
12½" h, 4" d, bulbous top, flared circular base, bisque fired, die–
stamped mark **470.00**
Water Jug, 8" h, 6½" d, bulbous, two
spouts, ring handle, bisque fired, unmarked **300.00**

OLD IVORY
84

OLD IVORY CHINA

History: Old Ivory derives its name from the
background color of the china. It was made in
Silesia, Germany, during the second half of the
19th century. Marked pieces usually have a pattern
number (pattern names are not common) and the
crown Silesia mark.

Reference: Susan and Al Bagdade, *Warman's
English & Continental Pottery & Porcelain*, 2nd
Edition, Wallace–Homestead, 1991.

Bowl
6½" d, #15 .... **40.00**
9½" d, #28 .... **95.00**
Buffet Tray, #200 .... **80.00**

Cake Plate, #84, open handles **85.00**
Celery Tray, #84 .... **80.00**
Chocolate Pot, #11 .... **350.00**
Creamer, #8 .... **65.00**
Cup and Saucer, #10 .... **48.00**
Mustard Pot, #16 .... **90.00**
Nappy, #28, 6 x 4", self handle **75.00**

**Cake Plate, Pattern #X, Clarion, Ger-
many, 11" w handle to handle, $70.00.**

Plate
7½" d, #11, Clarion **24.00**
8" d, #16 .... **35.00**
9½" d, #6, Elysee **100.00**
Platter, #84, 11½" l **150.00**
Relish Tray, #200 .... **60.00**
Salt and Pepper Shakers, pr
#15 .... **100.00**
#28 .... **110.00**
Soup Plate, #84 .... **45.00**
Sugar, cov
#15 .... **50.00**
#84 .... **35.00**
Teapot, #84 .... **285.00**
Toothpick, #10 .... **135.00**
Vegetable Dish, #84 .... **60.00**

OLD PARIS CHINA

History: Old Paris china is fine quality porcelain
made by various French factories located in and
about Paris during the 18th and 19th centuries.
Some pieces were marked, but the majority was
not. Characteristics of this type of china include
fine porcelain, beautiful decorations, and gilding.
Favorite colors were dark maroon, deep cobalt
blue, and a deep green.

Reference: Susan and Al Bagdade, *Warman's
English & Continental Pottery & Porcelain*, 2nd
Edition, Wallace–Homestead, 1991.

Additional Listing: Continental China and Porcelain (General).

Bust, 14″ h, man and woman, elaborate
Empire dress, pr **600.00**
Cachepot, 6″ h, Neo–classical style, gilt
ornaments, sepia bands, center polychrome summer flower spray, early
19th C, pr **1,150.00**
Clock Case, 20″ h, surmounted by
group of lovers, richly dec clothes, minor damage, c1830 .... **525.00**
Dessert Set
8 pcs, cov tureen, six plates, gilt
leaves and devices on lilac banding, polychrome center panel of exotic and domestic animals, early
19th C **1,500.00**
33 pcs, thirteen plates, two compotes,
sauce tureen and stand, seven
cups, eight saucers, pierced compote, specimen botanical center,
cobalt border, gilt vermicelli ornament **3,800.00**
Dinner Service, partial, rect platter,
three luncheon plates, six dinner
plates, floral dec, blue ground, c1850 **150.00**
Figure, 6″ h, recumbent lion, faux lapis
glaze, gilded base, pr **1,800.00**
Jardiniere and Stand, portraits, green
ground, small chips, gilding rubbed,
mid 19th C, pr **1,650.00**
Inkwell, 4¾″ h, fountain shape **1,200.00**

**Tray, multicolored floral center, white
ground, yellow–cream border, gilt
edge, 10″ l, $600.00.**

Tray, 13½″ w, sq, mythological, iron–red
Duc d'Angouleme, factory mark,
c1800 .... **450.00**
Urn
9½″ h, two sections, gilded bands of
griffins and anthemions, mottled
turquoise ground, shallow bowl socle, early 19th C **900.00**
12″ h, octagonal baluster, caryatid
handles, pedestal base, figural
scenes, gilt accents, one cracked,
pr **1,100.00**
15½″ h, European landscape on ob-

verse, reverse with romantic figural
scene, winged maiden figural handles, matte and burnished gilt
ground, pr **5,000.00**

OLD SLEEPY EYE

History: Sleepy Eye, a Sioux Indian chief who
reportedly had a droopy eye, gave his name to
Sleepy Eye, Minnesota, and one of its leading flour
mills. In the early 1900s Old Sleepy Eye Flour
offered four Flemish gray heavy stoneware premiums, decorated in cobalt blue: a straight–sided
butter crock, curved salt bowl, stein, and vase. The
premiums were made by Weir Pottery Company,
later to become Monmouth Pottery Company, and
finally to emerge as the present–day Western Stoneware Company of Monmouth, Illinois.

Additional pottery and stoneware pieces were
issued. Forms included five sizes of pitchers (4,
5½, 6½, 8, and 9 inches), mugs, steins, sugar
bowls, and tea tiles (hot plates). Most were cobalt
blue on white, but other glaze hues, such as
browns, golds, and greens, were used.

Old Sleepy Eye also issued many other items,
including bakers' caps, lithographed barrel covers,
beanies, fans, multicolored pillow tops, postcards,
trade cards, etc. Production of Old Sleepy Eye
stoneware ended in 1937.

In 1952 Western Stoneware Company made a
22 and 40 ounce stein in chestnut brown glaze
with a redesigned Indianhead. From 1961 to 1972
gift editions, dated and signed with a Maple Leaf
mark, were made for the Board of Directors and
others within the company. Beginning in 1973,
Western Stoneware Company issued an annual
limited edition stein, marked and dated, for collectors.

Reference: Elinor Meugnoit, *Old Sleepy Eye*,
published by author, 1979.

Collectors' Club: Old Sleepy Eye Collectors
Club, Box 12, Monmouth, IL 61462.

Reproduction Alert: Blue and white pitchers,
crazed, weighted, and often with a stamp or the
word "Ironstone" are the most copied. The stein
and salt bowl also have been made. Many reproductions come from Taiwan.

A line of fantasy items, new items which never
existed, includes an advertising pocket mirror with
miniature flour barrel label, small glass plates, fruit
jars, toothpick holders, glass and pottery miniature
pitchers, and salt and pepper shakers. One mill
item has been made, a sack marked as though it
were old but of a size that could not possibly hold
the amount of flour indicated.

MILL ITEMS

Bread Board Scraper **625.00**
Calendar, 1904 .... **200.00**
Cookbook, loaf of bread shape **120.00**

Pitcher, cobalt blue dec, cream ground, Indian head handle, 6¼″ h, $155.00.

Demitasse Spoon	130.00
Postcard	
Monument	45.00
Picture of mill	17.50
Stationery, envelope	65.00
Teaspoon, silverplate	90.00

POTTERY AND STONEWARE

Creamer, #1, all white, pottery	900.00
Mug	
Brush–McCoy, green and brown, cream ground	255.00
Stoneware	420.00
Pitcher, pottery	
#2, blue rim	580.00
#4, blue rim	425.00
#5, blue rim	420.00
Standing Indian, blue dec, gray ground	850.00
Salt Bowl, stoneware	465.00
Stein	
Blue dec, white ground	475.00
Directors, 1968	185.00
Stoneware, 7¾″ h, brown, Western Stoneware, 1950s	350.00
Sugar Bowl, blue dec, white ground	510.00
Vase, stoneware, blue dec	240.00

ONION MEISSEN

History: The blue onion or bulb pattern is of Chinese origin and depicts peaches and pomegranates, not onions. It was first made in the 18th century by Meissen, hence the name Onion Meissen.

Factories in Europe, Japan, and elsewhere cop-

ied the pattern. Many still have the pattern in production, including the Meissen factory in Germany.

Note: Prices given are for pieces produced between 1870 and 1930. Many pieces are marked with a company's logo; after 1891 the country of origin is indicated on imported pieces. Early Meissen examples bring a high premium.

Soup Plate, scalloped edge, marked "Meissen" with star, late, 9¾″ d, $42.00.

Bouillon Cup and Underplate	42.00
Bowl	
6″	40.00
9″	135.00
Butter Dish, cov	40.00
Butter Pat	90.00
Candle Snuffer, 10¼″, SP handle	62.00
Cheese Board	45.00
Cheese Dish, cov	150.00
Coffeepot, 9½″	160.00
Compote, 9″ h, 9″ d, reticulated rim	350.00
Creamer, 3½″	50.00
Cup and Saucer	
Coffee	40.00
Tea	30.00
Darner, wooden handle	75.00
Dinner Set, 29 pcs, eight dinner plates and bread plates, seven tea cups, six saucers	825.00
Dipper, wood handle	100.00
Dish, 10½″, round, deep, imp mark	55.00
Egg Cup	225.00
Fish Plate, pierced drain insert	225.00
Fruit Knives, set of 6	85.00
Funnel, 4¾″	85.00
Knife Rest	30.00
Ladle, 4 x 2″, wood handle	135.00
Lemon Dish	35.00
Match Holder	35.00
Mustache Cup	85.00
Pastry Wheel	135.00
Plate	
6″	35.00
9″	48.00
10½″	70.00

Platter
12", oval, marked	160.00
17"	225.00
19"	250.00
Pot de Creme	50.00

Relish Dish
6½ x 4¾", oblong, octagonal	45.00
11¾ x 7¼", scalloped edge	85.00
Rolling Pin	150.00
Salt Box	135.00
Salt Dip, crossed swords mark	48.00
Sauce Dish, 4¾"	30.00
Soup Bowl, 9"	60.00
Soup Tureen, cov, 10½ x 14", rose finial	250.00
Spill Vase, 5½", scroll feet	65.00
Stein, ½ L, matching conical lid, dwarf thumb lift	500.00
Sugar, cov, melon ribbed, late 19th C	100.00
Tea Strainer, 5", l, handle	65.00
Teapot, 10", rose finial, 19th C	200.00

Vegetable Dish
Covered
8½"	90.00
10", sq	130.00
Divided, 14"	225.00
Vinegar Jar, stopper	225.00
Water Pitcher, 7", rococo molded, c1860	225.00

OPALESCENT GLASS

History: Opalescent glass is a clear or colored glass with milky white decorations which shows a fiery or opalescent quality when held to light. The effect was achieved by applying bone ash chemicals to designated areas while a piece was still hot and then refiring it at tremendous heat.

There are three basic categories of opalescent glass: (1) Blown (or mold blown) patterns, e.g., Daisy & Fern and Spanish Lace; (2) Novelties, pressed glass patterns made in limited pieces which often included unusual shapes such as Corn or Trough; and (3) Pattern (pressed) glass.

Opalescent glass was produced in England in the 1870s. Northwood began the American production in 1897 at its Indiana, Pennsylvania, plant. Jefferson, National Glass, Hobbs, and Fenton soon followed.

References: William Heacock, *Encyclopedia of Victorian Colored Pattern Glass, Book II, Opalescent Glass from A to Z, Second Edition,* Antique Publications, 1977; William Heacock and William Gamble, *Encyclopedia of Victorian Colored Pattern Glass, Book 9, Cranberry Opalescent from A to Z,* Antique Publications, 1987; William Heacock, James Measell and Berry Wiggins, *Harry Northwood: The Early Years 1881–1900,* Antique Publications, 1990.

Barber Bottle, Stars and Stripes, cranberry	150.00
Basket, bushel, blue, Northwood	55.00

Sugar Shaker, Spanish Lace, vaseline, Northwood, 3¼" h, $115.00.

Berry Set
Chrysanthemum Base Swirl, cranberry, master bowl, six serving bowls	325.00
Scroll with Acanthus, 9½" d bowl, twelve serving bowls	200.00
Biscuit Jar, Spanish Lace, vaseline	275.00
Bottle, Bull's Eye, blue	115.00

Bowl
Beatty Rib, rect	35.00
Consolidated Criss–Cross, cranberry, 8" d	150.00
Beaded Stars, green, 8½" d	40.00
Jolly Bear, white	75.00
Meander, 9" d, ftd, fluted	46.00
Roman Rosette, lacy, Sandwich, 6¾"	200.00
Seaweed, white, 9"	60.00
Bushel Basket, blue	75.00

Butter Dish, cov
Argonaut Shell	275.00
Spanish Lace, blue	250.00

Celery Vase
Chrysanthemum Base Swirl, cranberry, satin finish, 6¾" h	160.00
Consolidated Criss–Cross, Rubena, satin finish	250.00
Daffodils, blue	95.00
Ribbed Coin Spot, cranberry	150.00
Compote, Dolphin, vaseline	85.00

Creamer
Intaglio	65.00
Reverse Swirl, blue	75.00

Cruet
Christmas Pearls	250.00
Fern, blue	250.00
Hobbs Hobnail, cranberry, polished pontil	350.00
Ribbed Opalescent Lattice, blue	235.00
Curtain Tie Back, 5¾", fiery, lacy, young woman seated holding straw hat, Boston & Sandwich Glass Co	150.00
Epergne, 9½ x 19½", four lilies, green, ruffled base, applied glass spiral trim	325.00

Finger Bowl
Hobbs Hobnail, cranberry	50.00

Spanish lace, blue	48.00

Lamp

Christmas Snowflake, cranberry	300.00
Reverse Swirl, cranberry, satin base	425.00
Snowflake, cranberry, hand type	500.00

Miniature Lamp

Coin Spot, Smith #510	625.00
Spanish Lace, blue	225.00
Mustard, Reverse Swirl, vaseline	50.00

Pickle Castor, Daisy and Fern, cranberry, swirl mold body, ornate metal frame and cov ... 365.00

Pitcher, water

Arabian Nights, cranberry	325.00
Buttons and Braids, blue	80.00
Christmas Snowflake, cranberry	375.00
Coin Spot, cranberry, star crimped top, applied clear handle	245.00
Daisy in Criss–Cross, cranberry	600.00
Hobbs Hobnail, cranberry, heavy opalescent, opal handle	200.00
Poinsettia, blue, tankard, 13"	200.00
Spanish lace, ruffled rim, blue	250.00
Stripe and Swirl, sq top	285.00
Plate, Tokyo, green, ftd	40.00

Rose Bowl

Daisy and Fern, blue	50.00
Fancy Fantails, cranberry, four clear applied feet	650.00
Leaf Chalice, green pedestal	50.00
Salt Shaker, Consolidated Criss–Cross, cranberry, orig top	85.00

Spooner

Consolidated Criss–Cross, cranberry	125.00
Fluted Scrolls, vaseline	65.00
Spanish Lace, cranberry	75.00
Wreath and Shell, blue	125.00

Sugar, cov

Bubble Lattice, cranberry	125.00
Fluted Scrolls, vaseline	110.00
Reverse Swirl, blue	125.00
Stripe, cranberry	80.00

Sugar Shaker, orig top

Bubble Lattice, blue	135.00
Fern, white	100.00
Opalescent Windows, blue, swirled	235.00
Poinsettia, blue	165.00
Reverse Swirl, cranberry	150.00

Syrup Pitcher, orig top

Bubble Lattice, canary yellow	150.00
Coin Spot & Swirl, white	65.00
Daisy in Criss–Cross, blue	250.00
Poinsettia, blue	450.00

Toothpick

Swirl, blue	100.00
Windows, cranberry	115.00

Tumbler

Arabian Nights, blue	60.00
Consolidated Criss–Cross, white	50.00
Herringbone, cranberry	75.00
Poinsettia, green	35.00
Spanish Lace, cranberry	45.00

Swirl, cranberry	40.00
Vase, Piasa Bird, blue, 10" h	50.00

Water Set, water pitcher and six tumblers, 7 pcs

Arabian Nights, blue	400.00
Button and Braids, blue	300.00
Daffodils, blue	650.00
Poinsettia, blue	250.00

OPALINE GLASS

History: Opaline glass was a popular mid- to late-19th century European glass. The glass has a certain amount of translucency and often is found decorated in enamel designs and trimmed in gold.

Toothpick Holder, ruffled top, cased, pink int., blown, 3⅜" h, $75.00

Biscuit Jar, white ground, hp, florals and bird dec, brass lid and bail handle	150.00
Box, 5½" d, white ground, brass fittings	125.00
Chalice, white ground, Diamond Point pattern	25.00
Cheese Dish, cov, white ground, gold enamel dec	180.00
Cologne Bottle, 8¾" h, jade green ground, gold ring dec, orig stopper	85.00
Creamer, shaded yellow to white ground, pink roses and blue forget–me–nots, SP rim and handle	125.00
Dresser Jar, 5½" d, egg shape, blue ground, heavy gold dec	200.00
Ewer, 13¼" h, white ground, Diamond Point pattern	125.00
Finger Bowl, matching underplate, powder blue ground	125.00
Perfume Bottle, 4" h, blue ground, gold, white, and yellow dec, matching stopper	65.00
Pitcher, 4¼" h, pink ground, applied white handle	70.00

Posy Holder, 8" h, blue ground, figural
hand holding small vase, ruffled rim **75.00**

Rose Bowl, 4" h, opaque green ground,
gilt strawberries, flowers, and leaves
dec **50.00**

Sugar, cov, shaded yellow to white
ground, pink roses and blue forget—
me—nots, SP cover, rim, and handle **150.00**

Toothpick, lavender ground, small ball
feet **75.00**

Tumble–Up, carafe, tumbler, and underplate, pale green ground, gold
beading, black and white jeweled
dec, 3 pcs **300.00**

Tumbler, white ground, enameled pink
rose **25.00**

Urn, 13" h, flared rim, blue ground,
enameled blue flowers, gilt trim, pr . **335.00**

ORIENTAL RUGS

History: The history of oriental rugs or carpets
dates back to 3,000 B.C.; but it was in the 16th
century that they became prevalent. The rugs originated in the regions of Central Asia, Iran (Persia),
Caucasus, and Anatolia. Early rugs can be classified into basic categories: Iranian, Caucasian,
Turkoman, Turkish, and Chinese. Later India, Pakistan, and Iraq produced rugs in the oriental style.

The pattern name is derived from the tribe which
produced the rug, e.g., Iran is the source for Hamadan, Herez, Sarouk, Tabriz, and others.

When evaluating an oriental rug, age, design,
color, weave, knots per square inch, and condition
determine the final value. Silk rugs and prayer rugs
bring higher prices.

References: Murray Eiland, *Oriental Rugs: A
New Comprehensive Guide,* Little, Brown and
Company, 1981; Linda Kline, *Beginner's Guide To
Oriental Rugs,* Ross Books, 1980; Ivan C. Neff
and Carol V. Maggs, *Dictionary of Oriental Rugs,*
Van Nostrand Reinhold Company, 1979.

Periodical: *Oriental Rug Review,* Beech Hill
Road, R.F.D. 2, Meredith, NH 03253.

Reproduction Alert: Beware! There are repainted rugs on the market.

Afshar, South Persia, early 20th C, bagface, 3' x 2', midnight blue field, real-
istically drawn roses and small
sprays, shades of red, navy blue,
apricot, green, and dark teal, narrow
ivory meander border **880.00**

Agra, 18' x 10', allover rust and green
floral dec, ivory field, conforming
green band border **1,600.00**

Baluch, Northeast Persia, mid 19th C,
prayer, 5' 4" x 3' 10", navy blue field,
Dokhtor–e–Ghazi design, staggered
rust–red, blue, and brown floral mo-

**Sarouk, ivory field, directional floral
motifs, midnight blue main border, 4'
2" x 6' 4", $725.00.**

tifs, rust–red spandrels, tiled design
border **1,760.00**

Baktiari, 9' 8" x 5', red, green, and blue
floral center medallion, floral bouquets and vases of flowers, ivory field,
red, blue, and yellow floral border . . **880.00**

Bidjar

7' x 4' 6", Northwest Persia, early 20th
C, dark red field, overall large–scale
Herati design, shades of royal and
sky blue, rose, red–brown, and teal,
dark red turtle border **1,320.00**

11' 8" x 8' 7", multicolored stylized
floral motif, ivory field, floral band
border **550.00**

Chi–Chi, Northeast Caucasus, late 19th
C, 5' 10" x 4', midnight blue field, alternating rows of octagons and
hooked polygons, shades of red,
royal blue, gold, green, and teal,
black rosette and diagonal bar border,
small areas of wear, patches **2,200.00**

Daghestan, Northeast Caucasus,
c1875, prayer, 3' 8" x 2' 8", ivory field,
diamond lattice of flowering plants,
shades of red, midnight blue, sky
blue, gold, aubergine, and pale teal,
red interrupted vine border, even side,
sides slightly reduced, reovercast . . **2,310.00**

Ferreghan

12' x 7', multicolored stylized floral
motif, dark blue field **550.00**

13' 2" x 6' 8", multicolored stylized
floral motif, dark blue field, green
band border **1,650.00**

13' 3" x 10' 3", multicolored stylized
floral motif, dark blue field, red
band border **2,100.00**

17' x 14', allover stylized floral motif,
dark blue field, wide band border . **5,060.00**

Gorovan, 10'10" x 8' 4", ivory and pumpkin center medallion, allover blue floral field, rust corner pockets, ivory
band border **2,310.00**

Hamadan, 3' 3" x 8', floral geometric design **800.00**

Heriz

11' 10" x 8' 2", bold multicolored geometric design, red field, wide green blue band border **2,530.00**

12' x 8' 6", bold multicolored geometric design, brick red field **3,630.00**

12' x 8' 10", multicolored geometric design, brick red field, blue band border **825.00**

Kashan

4' 9" x 3' 7", Central Persia, early 20th C, red field, circular lobed royal blue and rose medallion, blossoms royal blue spandrels, midnight blue palmette and arabesque vine border **660.00**

10' x 8' 2", green, rose, and ivory center, rose floral field, ivory corner pockets, wide floral band border . **1,210.00**

Kazak

Northwest Persia, Kurd, late 19th C, 7' 8" x 4' 6", red field, column of four sawtooth edge diamond medallions flanked by half medallions, shades of midnight blue, sky blue, gold, aubergine, and teal, ivory rosette border **4,950.00**

Southwest Caucasus, late 19th C, 7' 3" x 4' 9", red field, three navy blue, royal blue, pale gold, aubergine, and teal hooked diamond medallions, ivory crab border, wear creases, stain, machine overcast edges **2,310.00**

Keshan, 14' 8" x 10' 9", red flowering vine dec field, matching dark blue border **4,075.00**

Lesghi, Northeast Caucasus, late 19th C, 4' 2" x 3' 2", royal blue field, two large light brown and red Lesghi star medallions, abrashed dark green quatrefoil motif border **1,760.00**

Mahal

11' 5" x 8' 10", multicolored floral motif, brick red field, blue band border **630.00**

16' 5" x 10', blue, ivory, and red floral center medallion, red floral field, conforming floral band border ... **550.00**

Marasali, East Caucasus, c1875, 4' 8" x 3' 10", midnight blue field, staggered rows of rayed boteh, shades of red, sky blue, gold, and light green, ivory striped boteh border, small areas of wear, creases **2,200.00**

Pakistan, 6' 2" x 4' 2", architectural and animal motif **385.00**

Perepedil, Northeast Caucasus, late 19th C, 4' 5" x 3' 5", midnight blue field, ram's horn motifs, small medallions, bird figures, shades of red,

navy blue, ivory, and deep gold, red flowerhead and vine border **1,980.00**

Qashqai Kelim, Southwest Persia, late 19th C, 10' 2" x 5', light red field, two concentric stepped diamond medallions flanked by half medallions, shades of blue, gold, brown, and light green, stepped reciprocal border ... **2,530.00**

Sarouk

11' 8" x 8' 10", multicolored floral motif, dark blue field, red band border **7,590.00**

16' 4" x 8' 9", floral red field, matching border **1,100.00**

Shahsavan Soumak, Northwest Persia, South Caucasus, mid 19th C, bagface, 19" x 11", dark blue field, center red hooked medallion, pale blue hooked motif, pale blue border with ivory, red, and blue star and cross border **2,310.00**

Shirvan

East Caucasus, late 19th C

5' x 3' 3", abrashed medium blue field, three red, tan, and rose stepped diamond medallions, red interrupted vine border, even wear, slight end fraying **2,200.00**

5' 4" x 3' 2", abrashed navy blue field, three red and gold indented diamond medallions flanked by four aubergine cruciform medallions, other geometric motifs, ivory flowerhead and vine border **1,760.00**

Pakistan, 8' 2" x 5' 1", lozenge shape rust medallion rows alternating with geometric medallions rows, dark blue field, narrow border **300.00**

Sultanabad, West Persia, early 20th C, 6' 4" x 4' 4", ivory and gold lattice field, allover light rose flowerheads and teal vines, stepped rose spandrels, narrow navy floral meander border, even wear, slight end fraying **2,310.00**

Tabriz, Northwest Persia, early 20th C, 6' x 4' 5", ivory field, allover design of rust, rose, and dark gold rosettes, curved serrated leaves, rose rosette and blossoming vine border, even wear, faded colors **770.00**

Turkish, 14' 7" x 12', allover pastel floral motif, ivory filed **2,975.00**

Yagcibedir, West Anatolia, late 19th C, prayer rug, 3' 10" x 3' 3", midnight blue field, rows of red and ivory stars, midnight blue spandrels and cross panel, burnt orange indented flowerhead border, slight moth damage .. **1,320.00**

Yomud Asmalyk, West Turkestan, late 19th C, 3' 4" x 2', compartmented red and royal blue field inset with midnight blue, red, soft brown, apricot,

ivory, and teal pole trees, ivory Syrga border, slight moth damage **2,100.00**
Yomud Ensi, West Turkestan, late 19th C, 5' 4" x 4' 4", quartered mahogany field of red and blue oval motifs, ivory border of connected floral motifs, upper elem multicolored pole tree motifs, dark brown lower elem **2,310.00**

ORIENTALIA

History: Orientalia is a term applied to objects made in the Orient, which encompasses the Far East, Asia, China, and Japan. The diversity of cultures produced a variety of objects and styles.

References: Sandra Andacht, *Oriental Antiques & Art: An Identification And Value Guide,* Wallace–Homestead, 1987; Lea Baten, *Japanese Animal Art: Antique & Contemporary,* Charles Tuttle, 1989; Carl Crossman, *The Decorative Arts of The China Trade,* Antique Collectors Club, 1991; John Esten (editor), *Blue and White China,* Little, Brown, and Company, 1987.

Periodical: *The Orientalia Journal,* P. O. Box 94, Little Neck, NY 11363.

Additional Listings: Canton, Celadon, Cloisonné, Fitzhugh, Nanking, Netsukes, Rose Medallion, Japanese Prints, and other categories.

Basket, Chinese, hanging, ivory, carved, teak stand, 10¼" h **275.00**
Birdcage, Chinese, domed wirework body, two tiered quatrefoil finials with brass hook suspension, ornate carved apron, three spade feet with conforming carving, int. with two blue and white porcelain feeders, 30" h . **440.00**
Bookends, pr, Buddha, cast metal, bronze finish, 7¾" h **65.00**
Box
  Japanese, rect, scarlet lacquer, rising top relief with gilt and colored cranes with foliage and flower dec, 19th C, 12" **140.00**
  Korean, rect, wood, allover horn inlaid rectangle dec, polychrome pigments on red ground, hinged lid, etched metal fittings, fish form lock, 7¼ x 11 x 7" **440.00**
Brush Pot, pr, Meiji Period, Shibayama style, ivory, curved tusk, scene of small birds, butterflies, and two cranes among flowering wisteria vines, leafy bamboo stalks, blossoming peony, wild pinks and flowers, reverse with long tailed bird beneath fruiting loquat tree, gold and silver hir–amaki–e, takamaki–e, and gold gyobu, additional inlay of carved and incised coral, mother of pearl, aogai,

tortoise shell, and semi–precious hardstone, 7⅝" h **2,750.00**
Candlestick, Japanese, bronze, gull and wave base, wide circular dish form holder, 19th C, 9½" h **250.00**
Charger, Chinese, porcelain, polychrome enameled floral and leaf dec, gold highlighting, sgd, 18" d **225.00**
Compote, Japanese, bronze, circular tray, cloud dec, tripod base, 7¼" d . **55.00**
Ewer, Korean, Koryo Dynasty, globular, short shaped spout, double loop handle, short cylindrical neck, brown slip under gray celadon glaze, scroll of stylized flowering branch below wide shoulder petal border **1,250.00**
Fan, Japanese, paper and ivory, people and landscape scene, orig fitted lacquered box, late 19th C, 11" l **410.00**
Figure
  Ivory, Chinese, carved, Quan Yin holding herb branch, standing on lotus blossom, teak base, cloth cov box, 13½" h **880.00**
  Jade, Chinese, carved, Quan Yin with fruit, 8½" h **300.00**
  Marble, Chinese, carved, Hotei, teak stand, 4" h **360.00**
  Porcelain, woman, holding fan, polychrome enamel and gilt, 12" h ... **220.00**
  Wood, Shou Lao, carved, old finish, 16" h **120.00**
Frame, 10⅞" h, 8⅜" w, jade like stone, pale green, teak dec, marked "China" **140.00**
Furniture
  Altar Table, rect, rosewood, inset panel top, down scrolled ends with carved ruyi head form dec, pierced and carved fretwork apron, rect legs, cross braces, 34 x 46 x 16¼" **880.00**
  Blanket Chest, Korean, rect, hinged fall front top, two small drawers, two hinged doors, shaped apron, bracket feet, brass hinges, lockplates, and bail handles, 39 x 37 x 17½" **970.00**
  Cabinet
    Curio, rect, glazed doors with glass shelf int., two drawers with carved dec and brass pulls above two paneled doors with carved bat suspending a chime, fretwork border, shaped and carved apron, straight feet, 70¾ x 34½ x 15½" **900.00**
    Display, rect, central glazed door, staggered shelves, two hinged paneled doors, beaded apron, stylized hoof feet, 20th C, 78 x 36 x 14" **600.00**
  Side, Chinese, hardwood, rect top, upscrolled ends, two drawers

flanked by lingzhi shape spandrels, two hinged doors, carved shou medallions, shaped and carved apron, rect stiles form feet, brass hinges and pulls, 33½ x 40 x 17" **600.00**

Chair

Chinese, pr, arm, teak, carved, shaped crest rail, circular bird carved medallion splat, plank seat, shaped apron, cabriole legs, 19th C **960.00**

Ming Style, arm, horseshoe back, U shape crestrail, out scrolled handgrips, S curved splat with carved opposing dragons, curved rear legs joined to arms supported by brass posts, rect seat with carved scrolling vine **1,100.00**

Chair, carved rosewood, solid back, carved birds, trees, and dragons, $600.00.

Chest, Chinese, teak, mortised and paneled construction, black painted dec, one drawer, lift lid with well, 35 x 22½ x 34" **350.00**

Desk, kneehole, black lacquer, rect top, central drawer, two small hinged and two large hinged doors, gilt dec, allover pavilion scene, scrolling vine borders, diaper ground, 32 x 56 x 18½" **850.00**

Settee, Chinese, teak, carved, open arm, dragon form back splat, dragon arm supports, leaf carved apron, scroll feet, 19th C, 50" l . . **525.00**

Storage Chest, rosewood, carved, rect hinged top with carved central

dragon roundel flanked by shou characters, brass corner mounts, two carved dragon roundels front and back, carved ruyi scepters on sides, brass foliate form lockplate, brass bail handles, separate base with carved and shaped apron and spandrels, four short legs with stylized scroll feet, c1900, 25 x 24½" **1,090.00**

Table

Low, blackwood, rect inset panel top, open apron with rect spindles, rect supports with stylized hoof feet, 20¼ x 71 x 23" **1,090.00**

Side, lacquered, sq black top with chamfered corners, red shaped apron with carved and pierced scrolling flowering vines, four S scroll legs joined with X form fretwork stretcher, 32¼" h **850.00**

Ginger Jar, pr, enameled floral dec, dark blue ground, 9¾" h **110.00**

Incense Pot, bronze, Foo dog finial, 6¾" h **125.00**

Inro, five case, elegant peacock on branch of blossoming sakura overlooking companion below, leaves overlaid in silver hiramaki–e, tortoise accents, gold highlights, reverse with group of chidori in flight, bright kinji surface **2,500.00**

Jar

9½" h, brass, cloisonne type enameling **75.00**

10⅜" h, cov, porcelain, polychrome dec, yellow ground **40.00**

15" h, bronze, dragon dec **200.00**

23¾" h, bronze, four legs, bird handles, old dark finish **500.00**

29¾" h, bronze, dragons and lion dec, dark two–tone finish **800.00**

Jardiniere, Chinese, porcelain, coral dragon, black ground, 14" h **110.00**

Lantern, Korean, garden, granite, carved sections, pagoda form capital with drop form finial, octagonal lamp box supported with conforming leaf tip carved section, circular column, sq base, circular leaf tip plinth, 74" h . . **970.00**

Mirror

Chinese, 19th C, rect, giltwood, carved and pierced frieze of flowers and scrolls, columns, flame finials, drawer, carved feet, 20" h, 15" w . **160.00**

Japanese, rect, shaped base with fitted drawers, dark wavy grain veneer, golden color ground, 44½" h **900.00**

Planter, Japanese, rect, bronze, bullet chased sides, stylized elephant head handles, short round feet, 16¾" l . . . **190.00**

Pot, 11½" h, 18" d, green foliage design white craquelle glaze **30.00**

Robe, priest's, Chinese, Daoist emblems, cloud scrolls and roundels of figural scenes, coral ground, medallion with cranes, spheres, and geometric designs, yellow ground hem and sleeves, front opening with navy blue ground border, 19th C, 53" l .. **1,650.00**

Screen, folding

Kano School, two panels, two peacocks perched on ornamental rockwork, flowering red and white peony, meandering stream silhouetted on gold ground, 18th C, each panel 39 x 20¼" **1,540.00**

Nihonga School, six panels, meandering stream with various types of birds, winter willow and flowering camellia, applied gold flecked mist, sgd "Minamoto Gensho," two seals, Meiji Period, each panel 63 x 24½" **3,575.00**

Seal, Chinese, sq, jade, pale green, carved dragons, horned beasts, pierced, 4¼" **1,600.00**

Stand

Bronze, reticulated, round, lobed sides, stylized ruyi lappet head with floral motifs on each side, six out curled feet, 18th C, 10½" d **715.00**

Teak, carved

32" h, marble insert **260.00**
35½" h, marble insert, bamboo detail **300.00**
36" h, soapstone insert, shelved base **375.00**

Textile, Chinese

Panel, silk batik, port scene, 20 x 48" **50.00**
Pillow, Qianlong, Imperial, yellow brocade, central metallic gold dragon striding drawings on floral ground, peach, blue, and green, 26½" ... **1,250.00**

Tray, Meiji/Taisho Period, rect, short everted sides, chamfered corners, four cabriole shape legs, rooster and hen feeding under leafy bamboo, gilt lacquer, nashiji ground, 26¼" l **440.00**

Tree Ornament, stone, carved, 19¼" h **275.00**

Urn, Japanese, bronze, ovoid, relief reserves of hawk and trees, domed cov with mounted hawk finial, hawk and tree handles, pedestal base, 39" h . **2,300.00**

Vase

Chinese, pr, polychrome dec, flowers and butterflies, salmon ground, 14¼" h **110.00**
Japanese, bronze, two applied dragon handles, 19th C, 9¾" h .. **715.00**
Yongzheng, pr, ovoid, allover powder blue glaze, molded rim, six character Yongzheng mark, 19th C, 6¾" h **300.00**

OVERSHOT GLASS

History: Overshot glass was developed in the mid–1800s. A gather of molten glass was rolled over the marver upon which had been placed crushed glass to produce overshot glass. The piece then was blown into the desired shape. The finished effect was a glass that was frosted or iced in appearance.

Early pieces were mainly made in clear. As the demand for colored glass increased, color was added to the base piece and occasionally to the crushed glass.

Pieces of overshot generally are attributed to the Boston and Sandwich Glass Co., although many other companies also made it as it grew in popularity.

Pitcher, amber, clear dark amber applied handle, attributed to Boston & Sandwich, $295.00.

Compote

9 x 8⅞", applied gold dec cranberry serpent around stem **100.00**
9 x 14", rubena overshot bowl, white metal bronze finished figural standard **150.00**

Custard Cup, pink, applied clear handle, Sandwich **50.00**

Dish, 6¼", crimped edge, canary yellow, cranberry overshot **160.00**

Ewer, 13½", trefoil top, clear, twisted rope handle, Sandwich **250.00**

Ice Bucket, silver rim and handle **75.00**

Milk Pitcher, 6" h, light blue, amber reeded handle, roughness on top .. **65.00**

Mug, 3", clear, applied clear handle .. **20.00**

Pitcher

6", bulbous, cranberry **115.00**
7½", bulbous, clear **100.00**
8", heavy enamel dec of white roses, blue forget–me–nots, and green leaves **125.00**

Vase, 7½" h, pr, amethyst to clear, applied petal feet **80.00**

OWENS POTTERY

History: J. B. Owens began making pottery in 1885 near Roseville, Ohio. In 1891 he built a plant in Zanesville and in 1897 began producing art pottery. Not much art pottery was produced by Owens after 1907, when most of their production centered on tiles.

Owens Pottery, employing many of the same artists and designs of its two crosstown rivals, Roseville and Weller, can appear very similar to that of its competitors (i.e. Utopian—brown glaze; Lotus—light glaze; Aqua Verde—green glaze, etc.).

There were a few techniques used exclusively at Owens. These included Red Flame ware (slip decoration under a high red glaze) and Mission (over-glaze, slip decorations in mineral colors) depicting Spanish Mission scenes. Other specialities included Opalesce (semi-gloss designs in lustred gold and orange) and Coralene (small beads affixed to the surface of the decorated vases).

References: Paul Evans, *Art Pottery of the United States, 2nd Edition,* Feingold & Lewis Publishing Corp., 1987; Ralph and Terry Kovel, *The Kovels' Collector's Guide to American Art Pottery,* Crown Publishers, Inc., 1974.

Vase, matte glaze, spring flowers dec, numbered, imp torch mark, 5½" h, $245.00.

Creamer, 3½", Aqua Verdi, green matte, imp mark	65.00
Inkwell, 3¾", Light Weight, lime leaves, brown ground, sgd	100.00
Jardiniere, 9¼", orange and cream	

swirls, green ground, marked "JB Owens/Art Nouveau/1005"	175.00
Jug, handled, tomato dec	175.00
Mug, 4½", Utopian, cherries	75.00
Pitcher, 12", tankard, Utopian, gooseberries, artist sgd	275.00
Tile, 6", relief foliage dec, matte green, sgd	115.00
Vase	
5", Chinese Translation, white flowing glaze, marked	100.00
6¾", incised profile of woman's head, chocolate brown ground, artist sgd "Henri Deux"	200.00
8", bud, Utopian, floral design, artist sgd "Martha Gray"	100.00
11", Lotus, morning glories dec, artist sgd "Charles Fouts"	150.00
14", Art Nouveau, frolicking nudes and flowers, green, white, and orange, brown ground, raised gold base, two handles	500.00

PAIRPOINT

History: The Pairpoint Manufacturing Co. was organized in 1880 as a silverplating firm in New Bedford, Massachusetts. The company merged with Mount Washington Glass Co. in 1894 and became the Pairpoint Corporation. The new company produced speciality glass items, often accented with metal frames.

Pairpoint Corp. was sold in 1938 and Robert Gunderson became manager. He operated it as the Gunderson Glass Works until his death in 1952. From 1952 until the plant closed in 1956, operations were maintained under the name Gunderson-Pairpoint. Robert Bryden reopened the glass manufacturing business in 1970, moving it back to the New Bedford area.

References: Edward and Sheila Malakoff, *Pairpoint Lamps,* Schiffer Publishing, 1990; Leonard E. Padgett, *Pairpoint Glass,* Wallace–Homestead, 1979; John A. Shumann III, *The Collector's Encyclopedia of American Art Glass,* Collector Books, 1988.

Collectors' Club: Pairpoint Cup Plate Collectors, Box 52D, East Weymouth, MA 02189.

Bowl	
7" l, white opaque, silverplate rim and lid	125.00
8½", peppermint stick, satin, clear, overlay rose rim cut to clear stripes, engraved	125.00
8½ x 3½", Ambero, heavy, textured ext., int. painted with trailing vines, three pink lotus blossoms, lush green leaves floating on pool of lime green water, sgd "Ambero L"	745.00

Bride's Basket, pink and white, ornate
ruffled edge 325.00
Box, 7¼ x 6″, hinged lid, enameled gold
and silver iris and foliage, buff
ground, sgd 450.00
Candlesticks, pr
4″, amethyst, clear controlled bubble
ball connector 100.00
6″, Blue Swirl pattern, clear controlled
bubble ball connector 185.00
Calling Card Receiver, 5″ d, engraved
floral dec, clear controlled bubble ball
connector to saucer base 125.00
Centerpiece Bowl, 11½″ d, 16½″ h, red
cranberry, attached clear trumpet
vase, controlled bubble ball pedestal
base 310.00
Champagne, 5⅛″, Flambo pattern, crystal 50.00
Compote
6½″ d, amber, clear bubble stem ... 145.00
9¼″, cov, ruby, clear controlled bubble
ball connector, ruby base, steeple
bubble finial 125.00

**Condiment Set, salt and pepper shak-
ers, cov mustard, amber glass, hammered SP holder, 7″ h, 4½″ w, $225.00.**

Decanter, 10″, Old English pattern,
quart, matching stopper 1,250.00
Hat, 4¼″, deep red, white with controlled bubbles, orig paper label ... 75.00
Inkwell, 4″ d, clear, all–over controlled
bubbles, SS cap 200.00
Jack in the Pulpit Vase, 7¾″, ruby,
enameled bird on pine bough 165.00
Jewelry Box, 10″, Viscaria pattern, opal
flowers, cut, hinged, thumbprint base 225.00
Lamp
Boudoir
14½″ h, gilt metal baluster base,

closed top, blown out Papillon
shade, rose blossoms clusters
and four butterflies, ftd, shade
marked "The Pairpoint Corp"
and "Patented July 9, 1907,"
base marked "Pairpoint" 3,390.00
15″ h, gold urn shape base with
raised torch and wreath motif,
puffy sq domed shade, florals
surrounded with rays of floral and
green ribbon motif with blown out
red roses on two ends, marked
"Pairpoint Mfg Co, #B3051" ... 5,750.00
Table
22″ h, puffy ribbed shade, multicolored floral rim with two hummingbirds, pink stippled ground,
silver tripod base, shade marked
"Pairpoint Corp," base marked
"Pairpoint #D3070" 10,890.00
23″ h, bronze color ribbed cone
shape base, reverse painted
beehive shade with blossoms
dec on white stippled ground,
shade marked "Pairpoint Corp,"
base marked "Pairpoint D3058" 4,235.00

Napkin Ring, 5¼″, SP, figural, seated
Cupid, posy holder, marked 325.00
Punch Cup, cylindrical, flaring rim and
low foot, vaseline, engraved grapes 30.00
Rose Bowl, 6½″, egg shape, enameled
blue windmill scene, white opaline
ground, c1890 .... 575.00

Talc Shaker, twelve panels, emb, robin's egg blue background with florals 145.00
Tazza, 8″ d, 7¼″ h, green, etched
leaves, ferns, and grain, controlled air
trap knob, sgd 175.00
Tobacco Humidor, 6¾″ h, gold mums
dec, metal base, hinged lid, base
marked "Pairpoint" 1,000.00
Urn, 14″, cov, Vintage pattern, amethyst 225.00
Vase
8½″ h, blood red, turned down collar,
clear controlled bubbles in ball
stem 200.00
9″, Ambero, painted scene of couple
strolling down country lane int., textured finish 750.00
11½″ h, ruby, flared rim, clear controlled bubble knob and wafer stem 275.00
14¾″ h, opal glass cylinder, blue blossoms, gilt tracery, silverplate swag
dec holder, draped cherub pedestal, sgd "Pairpoint" 330.00
15″, winged cherub in flowing pink
drape with tray of peonies, multicolored poppy spray on reverse,
gold borders, powder blue rim
shading to cobalt blue ground, applied cobalt blue openwork handles 1,250.00

PAPER EPHEMERA

History: Maurice Rickards, author of *Collecting Paper Ephemera*, suggests that ephemera are the "minor transient documents of everyday life," material destined for the wastebasket but never quite making it. This definition is more fitting than traditional dictionary definitions that stress length of time, e.g., "lasting a very short time." A driver's license, which is used for a year or longer, is as much a piece of ephemera as is a ticket to a sporting event or music concert. The transient nature of the object is the key.

Collecting ephemera has a long and distinguished history. Among the English pioneers were John Seldon (1584–1654), Samuel Pepys (1633–1703), and John Bagford (1650–1716). Large American collections can be found at historical societies and libraries across the country, and museums, e.g., Wadsworth Antheneum, Hartford, CT, and the Museum of the City of New York.

When used by collectors, "ephemera" usually means paper objects, e.g., billheads and letterheads, book plates, documents, labels, stocks and bonds, tickets, valentines, etc. However, more and more ephemera collectors are recognizing the transient nature of some three dimensional material, e.g., advertising tins and pinback buttons. Today's specialized paper shows include dealers selling both two and three dimensional material.

References: Anne F. Clapp, *Curatorial Care of Works of Art on Paper*, Nick Lyons Books, 1987; Joseph Raymond LeFontaine, *Turning Paper To Gold*, Betterway Publications, 1988; John Lewis, *Printed Ephemera*, Antique Collectors' Club, 1990; Maurice Rickards, *Collecting Paper Ephemera*, Abbeville Press, 1988; Demaris C. Smith, *Preserving Your Paper Collectibles*, Betterway Publications, 1989.

Periodical: *The Check Collector*, P.O. Box 71892, Madison Heights, MI 48071.

Collectors' Club: Ephemera Society of America, Inc., P.O. Box 37, Schoharie, NY 12157.

BLOTTERS

Badger Soap, You Want The Best, attached advertising card, multicolored	**15.00**
Kellogs Corn Flakes, multicolored	**6.00**
None Such Mince Meat, factory illus, multicolored	**6.00**
None Such Novelty Mask, multicolored	**15.00**
Prudential Insurance Co, battleship, blue and white	**5.00**
Sundial Shoes, Bonnie Laddie, multicolored	**6.50**
Wayne Oakland Bank, Santa	**6.00**

BOOKMARKS

Reference: A. W. Coysh, *Collecting Bookmarks*, Drake Publishers, 1974, out–of–print.

Stock Certificate, Adelaide Consolidated Silver Mining Company, New Mexico, 1864, 2,400 shares, \$330.00.

Periodicals: *Bookmark Collector*, 1002 West 27th Street, Erie, PA, 16502; *Bookmark Quarterly*, Route 10, Box 120, Morgantown, NC 28655.

Advertising

Austin Young & Co Biscuits, multicolored, 2 x 7"	**3.00**
Bell Pianos, Art Nouveau woman, multicolored	**10.00**
Crown Piano, Clapsaddle, girl with holly	**12.00**
Eastmans Extract, silver gild, multicolored	**7.50**
Hoyt's German Cologne, multicolored	**1.50**
Palmer Violets Bloom Perfume, gold trim	**10.00**
Pears Soap, diecut, multicolored, 1 x 7"	**2.50**
Youth's Companion, 1902, multicolored, 2¾ x 6"	**5.50**
Cross Stitched on Punched Paper	
Black Emancipation, black couple dancing, 1860s, 3⅞ x 1½"	**25.00**
Ever Constant–Ever True, young girl with bouquet of flowers, diecut paper attached, 2⅝ x 7"	**5.00**
Holy Bible, Brother, Jan 1873, silk ribbon attached	**20.00**
In God We Trust	**6.00**

BUSINESS CARDS

Atlis Brewing Co, Detroit, MI, printed, multicolored	**10.00**
Commercial Hotel, Grand Rapids, MI, \$1.00 A Day, printed, black and white	**7.50**
E. H. Moore, Fancy Pigeons, Milrose, MA, Erdmann Del, Printer, red and black pigeons	**10.00**
F. A. Howe, Jr., Contracting Freight Agent, MI, Central RR & Blue Line Chicago, blue on white	**10.00**
H. H. Howe, Collins, MI, Lumber, printed, black and white	**5.00**
Pfeiffer Brewing Co, Detroit, MI, printed, multicolored	**14.50**
Silverthaw & Sons Dealers In Diamonds	

& Watches, New Haven, CT, gold lettering, black ground, 1880s, printed . **10.00**
Stephen McCrath, Wines and Ales, Hartford, CT, green **10.00**

CALENDARS

1882, Canada First, The Great Literary–Political Journal, broadside calendar, 8 x 12″ **55.00**
1891, Scotts Emulsion, May Blossoms, Knapp Litho, months missing **10.00**
1893, Benton Hall Dry Goods, Palmyra, NY, 2½″ **10.00**
1894, Hoyt's, lady's, perfumed **10.00**
1896, Singer Sewing Machines **40.00**
1898, La Belle Jardiniere, 8 x 10″, twelve loose sheets in wrappers . . . **75.00**
1889, Pansies Bright, Taber Prang Art Co, six parts, pansy dec on each part **30.00**
1900, Hood's, full pad, two girls **45.00**
1901, Colgate, miniature, flower **15.00**
1903, Franco American, miniature . . . **15.00**
1906, Deering Harvesters, lady seated on farm wall, 13 x 20″ **150.00**
1908
  A J Russlow, Livery & Feed Stable, Randolph, VT, 14¼ x 10″ **15.00**
  Moose Jaw, three scenes **35.00**
1909, Bank of Waupun, emb lady **30.00**
1912, Anti–Kammia Tablets, young girl **10.00**
1914, Youth's Companion, marching scene, easel back **6.00**
1915, Hoosier **18.00**
1916
  Putnam Dyes **40.00**
  The Robert W Service Calendar, service verse and drawings **55.00**
1919
  McLaughlin Carriages, 20 x 30″, five buggy illus **75.00**
  Woodrow Wilson **10.00**
1922, Warren National Bank, Norman Rockwell illus **300.00**
1928, Hudson's Bay Company, color graphics **70.00**
1929, Clothesline **60.00**
1930, Lydia E Pinkham, little girl holding medicine box, 8 x 15″ **650.00**
1940, Columbian Rope **40.00**
1941, Pepsi, complete pad **200.00**
1944, Sinclair Gasoline, twelve color wildlife pictures **20.00**
1957, Sun Crest Cola **28.00**
1961, TWA, six sheets, 16 x 24″ **15.00**

CHECKS

Collectors' Club: *American Society of Check Collectors,* Charles Kemp, 2075 Nicholas Court, Warren, MI 48092.

1857, Albany City Bank, drawn to the Treasurer of the State of New York on account of the Canal Fund, deposited by H H Martin **15.00**
1865, vignette of boat, farmer, two cent bank check stamp, printed, black and white **7.50**
1875, Masonic Savings Bank, sgd by Simon Bolivar Buckner, CSA general, revenue stamp on upper left corner . **195.00**
1906, First National Bank of Liverpool, PA, yellow ground, sq photograph marked "Old Canal Boat Days, Liverpool, Pennsylvania, 1906," photograph of boats on Cheaspeake and Ohio Canal near Williamsport, MD, check unissued **5.00**
1920, sgd by George W. Carver **450.00**
1934, Harry Truman, sgd as presiding Judge, Jackson County, Kansas City, MO, 8 x 3″ **375.00**
1962, sgd by George Lincoln Rockwell, assassinated leader of American Nazi Party, printed "American Nazi Party" above signature **200.00**

COLORING BOOKS

Annie Oakley, Whitman, 11 x 14″, 1955, unused **18.00**
Batman and Robin, Whitman, 31002, 8 x 11″, 1967, unused **15.00**
Blondie, Dell Publishing, 8½ x 11″, 1954, unused **20.00**
Blyth, Ann, 1952, unused **35.00**
Charlie Chaplin, Donohue & Co, 10 x 17″, 1917 copyright **80.00**
Dick Tracy, Saalfield, #2536, 8¼ x 11″, 1946 copyright **25.00**
Donald Duck, Whitman, 7½ x 8½″, 1946, unused **20.00**
Eve Arden, 1953, unused **30.00**
Green Hornet, Watkins–Strathmore, 8 x 11″, copyright 1966, unused **30.00**
Hopalong Cassidy, Samuel Lowe Co, 5¼ x 5¼″, 48 pgs, 1951 copyright . . **25.00**
Lone Ranger, Whitman, 8½ x 11″, Cherrios premium, 1956 . . . . **75.00**
Pinky Lee's Health and Safety Cut–Out Coloring Book, Pocket Books, copyright 1955 . . . . **15.00**
Rin Tin Tin, Whitman, #1257, 8¼ x 11″, 1955 . . . . **15.00**
Roy Rogers and Dale Evans, 15 x 11″, 1952 . . . . **20.00**
Superman, Whitman, 8 x 11″, unused, 1966 National Periodical Publications copyright **25.00**
Tom Mix, Whitman, 11 x 14″, 1935 . . . **50.00**
Walt Disney's Disneyland, Whitman, 8 x 11″, copyright 1965 . . . . **20.00**

Wyatt Earp, Hugh O'Brien on cov, unused **35.00**

DIECUTS

Advertising
Aber Shoes, Lansing, girl with dog, basket of flowers, 9¼" **20.00**
Great Japan & China Tea Co, two children with jack in the box, 9" .. **30.00**
New Century Bells, girl ringing bells, calendar under bell top, 12½" ... **75.00**
Bird Feeder surrounded by birds, one in–slot bird, wall pocket, German, 16" **65.00**
Child, halo, tree, German **10.00**
Girls giving medicine to cats, multicolored, 10½ x 13" **75.00**
Greenhouse, woman feeding fish, 1884, 7½ x 10" **12.00**
Happy Easter, chickens and chicks, easel back, 8" **25.00**
Man carrying billboard, dogs biting, 7" **8.00**
Santa, Christmas ornament, bag of toys, cotton batting, red crepe paper **110.00**
School Teacher, open book, add on stick, emb, multicolored, glossy finish, 17" h **150.00**
Snowman, two boys, glossy finish, wall pocket, 14" **75.00**
Star, hand colored, engraved "Farmstead," Robinson Eng. Co., Boston, 1881, 4¾" **15.00**
Uncut Sheet, emb, multicolored
Animals, rabbits, chicks, and lambs, doing human type things, German, 4 x 5½" **6.50**
Hands, flowers, ships, three different designs, 5½ x 7" **4.00**
Hearts, six different designs **3.00**

GREETING CARDS

Assortment, Lil Abner, seven different designs, boxed set, 1950s **35.00**
Birthday
Amos 'n' Andy, brown portraits, message includes song title "Check and Double Check," inked birthday note, Rust Craft **20.00**
Blondie, Dagwood illus, full color, Hallmark, 1939 copyright **15.00**
Golliwog, c1930 .... **10.00**
Snow White and the Seven Dwarfs, c1938 .... **40.00**
Space Patrol Man, diecut, full color, green transparent helmet, orig envelope **20.00**
Christmas
A Merry Christmas, three children huddled beneath umbrella, Wolf & Co, NY **2.50**

Christmas Greetings, emb holly, silver background, The Art Lithographic Co **6.00**
Hearty Greetings, cut out emb border, holly on front **4.00**
Wishing You A Happy Christmas, two birds on branches, sepia tones, Raphael Tuck & Sons, London **4.00**
Get Well, Amos 'n' Andy, black and white photo, Hall Bros, 1951 copyright **30.00**
Mother's Day, Cracker Jack, diecut, full color, puppy, c1940 .... **40.00**
Valentine
Diecut, Felix the Cat, full color, Pat Sullivan copyright, c1920 .... **15.00**
Easel Back, 6 x 9", fancy cutwork border, 1900 .... **10.00**
Embossed, handmade, layered, lacy, c1865 .... **8.00**
Mechanical
R Tuck, paper doll, 1900 .... **25.00**
Train, German, 1914 .... **45.00**
Stand–up, To My Sweetheart, white dog with envelope in mouth, 6" h, marked "Germany" **4.00**

INVITATIONS AND PROGRAMS

Caledonia Ball, Majestic Hotel, Shanghi, 1928, blue and white **6.00**
Camp On White River Col Dance Program, Nov 24, 1881, scrap dec, hand written **10.00**
D. W. Griffith Presents Way Down East, 1920, 4 pgs, 5½ x 8½" **10.00**
Eddie Cantor, "How To Make A Quack–Quack," program on back, portrait on cov, printed, black and white, four part fold–out **10.00**
First Commencement of the Portland High School, MI, 1882, printed, black and white **12.00**
Grand Masquerade Ball, Marion Hose Co, NY, 1901, gold trim **8.50**
Invitation and Program for Carnival in Honor of George Washington, Request at Opera House, 1893, multicolored cover **10.00**
Jackson Glacers, Grand Excursion, Bawbeese Lake Park, 1893, four pages, adv from U. S. Baking Co .. **7.50**
Leap Year Party By Young Ladies, 1888, opens, dance program inside, printed, black and white **10.00**
Pre–Lenten Dance, Given by the United Gunmen, 1914, printed, black and white **5.00**
Roy Rogers Official Souvenir Program, photographs **7.50**
Sonja Henie Program, white cov, orig tissue cov, 1949 .... **10.00**

St. Patricks Ball, Lusks Hall, Jacobs City, UT, 1878, red lettering, blue ground, emb, opens **12.00**

LABELS

References: Jerry Chicone, Jr., *Florida's Classic Crates*, privately printed, 1985; Gordon T. McClelland and Jay T. Last, *Fruit Box Labels, A Collector's Guide*, Hillcrest Press, Inc., 1983; John Salkin and Lauri Gordon, *Orange Crate Art, The Story of Labels That Launched A Golden Era*, Warner Books, 1976.

Collectors' Club: Citrus Label Society, 16633 Ventura Blvd., No. 1011, Encino, CA 91436.

Apple

Bird Valley, blue crown perched on shield, orange background **2.00**
Snow Owl, snowy owl, blue background **2.00**
Yakima Chief, Indian chief wearing headdress **3.00**
Asparagus, King O'Hearts, playing card, red heart on black background   **1.00**
Broom, Dixie, black man seated on bench, playing banjo **1.00**
Butter, Wilson's Clearbrook Butter, yellow, black, white, and red, farm scene   **2.00**
Cigar
Buzzer, ornate butterfly, cigar as body   **3.00**
Traveler, fancy design, gilt, black, and red **1.00**
Cosmetic
Fairy Cream, emb, gilt, florals . . . . .   **.75**
Violet Ammonia, purple flowers, white background, York, PA . . . .   **.75**
Cranberry, Rancocas, Indian village, green valley, river, horses, and tepees   **3.00**
Grape
Mirador, ranch scene, red grapes, Uncle Sam's hat **1.00**
Valley Beauty, girl, bunch of purple grapes, two hands holding wine glasses, red background . . . .   **.50**
Lemon
El Merito, lemons, blue, green, and yellow background, Santa Paula .   **1.00**
Kaweah Maid, Indian girl wearing turquoise beads, brown background, Lemon Cove **3.00**
Ocean Spray, glass lemonade, red roses, blue vase, Santa Paula . . .   **5.00**
Vesper, people going to church, maroon background, Porterville **1.00**
Orange
Altissimo, pink, aqua, and blue mountains, dated 1918, Placentia **1.00**
Bronco, cowboy swinging lariat, riding galloping brown horse, western desert scene, Redlands **2.00**

Golden Trout, trout leaping out of water, Orange cov **25.00**
Lincoln, Honest Abe portrait, oranges, and leaves, Riverside **2.00**
Royal Knight, brave knight in armor, castle, yellow background, Redlands **2.00**
Symbol, California poppies, maple leaf, wrapped Sunkist orange, Riverside **2.00**
Pear
Duckwall, wood duck standing by brick wall **2.00**
Lady of the Lake, lady in green gown, lake scene, holding pear **2.00**
Mopac, Modoc Indian portrait, blue background **1.00**
Summit, snowy mountains, forest scene **2.00**
Tomatoes
Award, farmer holding box of tomatoes, ranch background . . . .   **.25**
Sun Prince, tomato background . . .   **.25**
Yam
Coon, raccoon holding large yam . .   **3.00**
Sunset Packers, two yams, deco look design . . . .   **.50**

LETTERHEADS AND BILLHEADS

A. J. Weidener, Lamps, Chandeliers, Champion Lamps, Philadelphia, 1866, black and white, used **15.00**
D. S. Erb & Co, Keystone Cigar Factory, Boyertown, PA, 1893, C. Jourgensen, NY, black and white, used, 6 x 9" . .   **8.00**
F. W. Carpenter, Manuf. of Toys, Novelties, Harrison, NY, c1880, billhead, printed, black and white **10.00**
John P. Lovell & Sons, Manuf & Wholesale Dealers In Fire Arms, Boston, 1879, black and white, used **12.00**
J. W. H. Mann, Charlton, MA, 1883, receipt for 44 quarts of milk, printed, black and white **10.00**
Fort Scott Foundry & Machine Works, Fort Scott, KS, 1883, billhead, black and white, used **8.00**
Geo. W. Gilliatt, Sweet Grass Baskets and Indian Goods, Portland, ME, 1927, billhead, used **10.00**
National Sewing Machine Co, Belvedere, IL, Manuf. of High Grade Bicycles, Wilmanns Bros. Litho., 1896, billhead, black and white, used **12.00**
Pontiac Gazette Co., Pontiac, MI, 1873, receipt, printed, black and white . . .   **5.00**
The Champion Blower & Forge Co, Lancaster, PA, 1891, Craig Finley & Co. Litho, black and white **6.00**
United States Cigar Co, York, PA, 1933, two color **8.00**

MAGAZINES

References: Marjorie M. and Donald L. Hinds, *Magazine Magic*, The Messenger Book Press, 1972; Denis Jackson, *Men's 'Girlie' Magazines: The Only Price Guide!: Newstanders, 3rd Edition*, The Illustrator Collector's News, 1991; *Official Price Guide To Paperbacks and Magazines*, House of Collectibles, 1986.

American, Dec 1926, Earl C Christy cov	10.00
American Golfer, Dec 1932	10.00
Antiques, Oct 1931	7.50
Atlantic Monthly, Nov 1907, anniversary edition	18.00
Bonzanza, Vol #1, 1965	25.00
Breed's Gazette, The, April, 1885	6.50
Child's Life, 1930	3.00
Children's Play Mate, Oct, 1954	5.00
Collier's, June 1938	7.00
Cosmopolitan, 1910	6.50
Esquire, Sept 1935	14.00
Farmer's Wife Magazine, June 1936	2.00
Hobbies, August 1942	2.00
Ladies Home Journal, 1917	12.00
Look, Nov 17, 1964, John F Kennedy memorial issue	20.00
McCall's, 1925	15.00
Movie Star Parade, Jan 1947	22.00
National Geographic, June 1926	3.00
Needlecraft, 1927	3.00
New Yorker, 1948	2.50
Pictorial Review, March 1915	12.50
Prairie Farmer, Feb 1867	4.00
Radford's American Builder, 1920s	6.00
Saturday Evening Post 1923, Pearl Harbor cov	10.00
1936, Springtime, Norman Rockwell cov	7.50
1938, Christmas, Leyendecker cov	5.00
Spinning Wheel, July 1960	30.00
Stage and Screen, 1926	4.50
Time, 1940, Mickey Rooney cov	10.00
Travel, 1915, Santa cov, Murad	25.00
Vogue, March, 1935	12.00
Wild West Weekly, 1915	7.00
Woman's Home Companion, 1925	20.00
Working Craftsman, winter, 1977	4.00
Youth's Companion, bound year, 1907	125.00

MATCHBOOKS

References: Yosh Kashiwabara, *Matchbook Art*, Chronicle Books, 1989; Bill Retskin, *The Matchcover Collectors Resource Book and Price Guide*, published by author, 1988; H. Thomas Steele, Jim Heimann, Rod Dyer, *Close Cover Before Striking, The Golden Age of Matchbook Art*, Abbeville Press, 1987.

Periodical: *The Front Strike Bulletin*, 3417 Clayborne Avenue, Alexandria, VA 23306–1410.

Collectors' Clubs: Rathkamp Matchcover Society, 1359 Surrey Road, Vandalia, OH 43577; Trans–Canada Matchcover Club, Box 219, Caledonia, Ontario, Canada NOA–1A0. There are 33 regional clubs throughout the United States and Canada.

Dr Pepper, Universal Match Corp	25.00
Heilman's Old Style Lager, Ohio Match Co, Wadsworth, OH	25.00
Joe Louis & Max Schmeling Championship Fight, Giant	18.00
Petty Girl, Snug As A Bug, Martins Tavern, Chicago, late 1940s	4.00
Political	1.00
Presidential Yacht, *Patricia*	10.00
Pull for Willkie, Pullquick Match	28.00
Stoeckle Select Beer, Giant, Stoeckle Brewery	6.00

MENUS

Banquet To The Western Michigan Press, Reed City, 1883, foldover, Robinson Engraving Co, 1882, printed, black and white	15.00
Francaise, 5 x 9″, Art Nouveau design, sgd "Mucha," dated 5 Janvier 1913	340.00
Johnson Line	10.00
Metropolitan Hotel, 4 pgs, c1874	35.00
SS City of Omaha, Christmas 1940	5.00
SS Oakwood American Export Lines, Christmas, 1939	5.00
United States Hotel, Saratoga Springs, NY, 1882, 7 x 10″	12.00

NEWSPAPERS, HEADLINE EDITIONS

References: Harold Evans, *Front Page History*, Salem House, 1984; Robert F. Karolevitz, *From Quill To Computer: The Story of American's Community Newspapers*, National Newspaper Foundation, 1985.

1865, April 15, Lincoln Assassinated	375.00
1886, Oct 28, Statue of Liberty Dedicated	55.00
1901, Sept 14, McKinley Dies	40.00
1903, Dec 17, Wright Bros Fly	255.00
1912, April 15, Titanic Sunk	185.00
1919, June 28, Peace Treaty Signed	25.00
1921, July 14, Sacco & Vanzette Convicted	10.00
1933, Dec 5, Prohibition Repealed	27.00
1941, Dec 7, Japan Attacks Pearl Harbor	45.00
1945, May 7, War In Europe Ends	27.00
1948, Nov 3, Dewey Defeats Truman, Chicago Tribune error headline	650.00
1955, May 17, Court Bans School Segregation	15.00
1963, Nov 22, Kennedy Assassinated	27.00
1969, July 20, Man Walks On The Moon	23.00

1986, Jan 28, Challenger Explodes . .	**5.00**
1989, Nov 10, Berlin Wall Falls	**5.00**

POST CARDS

References: Diane Allmen, *The Official Price Guide To Postcards,* House of Collectibles, 1990; Frederic and Mary Megson, *American Advertising Postcards–Set and Series: 1890–1920,* published by authors, 1985; Cynthia Rubin and Morgan Williams, *Larger Than Life; The American Tall–Tall Postcard, 1905–1915,* Abbeville Press, 1990; Dorothy B. Ryan, *Picture Postcards In The United States, 1893–1918,* Clarkson N. Potter, 1982, paperback edition; Jack H. Smith, *Postcard Companion: The Collector's Reference,* Wallace–Homestead Book Company, 1989; Jane Wood, *The Collector's Guide To Post Cards,* L–W Promotions, 1984, 1987 values updated.

Periodicals: *Barr's Postcard News,* 70 S. 6th Street, Lansing, IA 52151; *Postcard Collector,* Joe Jones Publishing, P. O. Box 337, Iola, WI 54945.

Special Note: An up–to–date listing of books about and featuring post cards can be obtained from Gotham Book Mart & Gallery, Inc., 41 West 47th Street, New York, NY, 10036.

Collectors' Clubs: *Barr's Postcard News* and the *Postcard Collector* publish lists of over fifty regional clubs in the United States and Canada.

Advertising

American Soda Fountain Co, smiling sphinx	**25.00**
Berry Brothers Varnishes	**4.50**
Diamond Expansion Bolt Co, Garwood, NJ	**4.00**
Elgin Watch Co	**3.50**
Hotel Astor, NY	**3.50**
Johnson's Corn Flour	**8.50**
New York Life Insurance, NY	**2.00**
Pacific Mall Steamship Co	**2.50**
Rogers Brothers Silverplate	**3.00**
Sugar Creek Creamery	**2.00**
Troy Detachable Collars	**3.25**
United Cigar Stores	**2.00**
Wilson's Supply Co, Long Island . . .	**5.00**
Wrigley's Chewing Gum	**2.00**

Artist Signed

Attwell, Mabel Lucie, early, Tuck . . .	**8.00**
Browne, Tom, American baseball series	**9.00**
Brundage, Francis, early chromolithograph	**30.00**
Carmichael, comic	**3.00**
Christy, Howard Chandler	**10.00**
Clapsaddle, Ellen, children	**9.00**
Daniell, Eva, Art Nouveau	**100.00**
Fisher, Harrison	**6.00**
Gibson, Charles Dana	**5.00**
Greiner, M, blacks	**8.00**
Gutmann, Bessie Pease	**17.50**
Kirchner, Raphael, third period	**40.00**

Mucha, Alphonse, Art Nouveau, months of the year	**125.00**
O'Neill, Rose, Kewpies	**30.00**
Outcault, Yellow Kid, calendars	**55.00**
Price, Mary Evans	**4.50**
Remington, Frederic	**25.00**
Smith, Jessie Wilcox	**15.00**
Thiele, Arthur, cats, action	**15.00**
Upton, Florence, Golliwogs, Tuck . .	**35.00**
Wall, Bernhardt, sunbonnets	**15.00**

Greetings

April Fools, comic	**1.50**
Birthday, florals	**5.00**
Christmas, Santa, German, highly embossed	**20.00**
Easter, chick or rabbits	**1.50**
Fourth of July, Uncle Sam	**4.50**
Halloween, children	**3.50**
New Years, Father Time	**2.50**
Saint Patrick's Day, children	**4.50**
Thanksgiving	**1.00**

Photographic

American Steel Posts & Wire Co, Monches, WI, detailed view of story and stockyard, 1924 postmark . . .	**22.00**
Auctioneer, Col. Casey Selling A $3,400 Case Steam Tractor, South Dakota, c1910	**55.00**
Black Machine Gun Crew, American Lake, WA, well posed view, three black US soldiers and white commanding officer manning gun, 1910 postmark	**30.00**
Brandon Inn Coach, Brandon, VT, stagecoach, c1920	**37.00**
Canalos Bros. Pool Room, Lorain, OH, 1914 postmark	**38.00**
Cook Of The North Pole, whistle stop view, Dr Cook, Discoverer of the North Pole, Litchfield, IL, 1909 . . .	**27.00**
Highwood Ice Cream Parlor, Highwood, IL, soda fountain foreground, 1920s	**65.00**
Indian Family At Home Near Watersmeet, MI, A J Kingsbury #82X, 1908	**30.00**
Juneau Alaska Fire Department, group posed outside of fire station, 1919	**45.00**
Liberty Theatre, Seattle, WA, large crowd gathered in front of building, night scene, c1912	**25.00**
Loyal Order Of The Moose Brass Band, detailed studio view of large band, c1910	**15.00**
President Taft, Breaking Ground At Panama–Pacific Expo	**28.50**
Ringling Bros Circus Band, Al Sweet's Concert Band, 1909 Season, promo by Conn's Band Instrument Factory, detailed view of band	**65.00**
Roller Coaster, Rothchild's Park,	

Wausau, WI, close up view of car in motion, 1910 postmark	**32.00**
Sod House, unidentified location, c1910	**22.00**
Sundance of the Acoma Indian, Southwest pueblo, #93, c1912 . .	**27.50**
World War I, 4th Liberty Loans, ext. of American Exchange Nat'l Bank, New York City, huge banners, Underwood and Underwood, c1917 .	**72.00**
Yale Motorcycle, detailed broadside, 1913 postmark	**45.00**

REWARDS OF MERIT

A Testimonial of Approbration..., 1872, printed, black and white, 8½ x 10¼"	**12.00**
Bank of Industry, five honors, 1852, used, hand colored children, printed by A. C. Beaman, rounded corners .	**18.50**
Knowledge In Power, girl with hand on head, green and beige	**8.00**
Music Award Card, Theo. Presser Co., Philadelphia, green printing, unused	**12.00**
Our Motto Truth, boy with flag, beige and blue	**8.00**
Reward of Merit, flowers, multicolored, 1880, unused, 4"	**3.50**

SHEET MUSIC

References: Debbie Dillon, *Collectors Guide To Sheet Music,* L–W Promotions, 1988; Daniel B. Priest, *American Sheet Music with Prices,* Wallace–Homestead, 1978.

Collectors' Clubs: National Sheet Music Society, 1597 Fair Park, Los Angeles, CA 90041; New York Sheet Music Society, P. O. Box 1126, East North 67th Ave., Suite 103–306, Glendale, AZ 85301; The Sheet Music Exchange, P. O. Box 69, Quicksburg, VA 22847.

America To–Day, Woodrow Wilson and Statue of Liberty, 1917	**10.00**
American Legion Song–Five Million Strong!, J H Benson, 1919	**4.00**
Birds Fly Over White Cliffs of Dover, Glenn Miller, 1941–42	**8.00**
Break the News to Mother, 1897	**15.00**
Colorado Moon, Baby Rose Marie, 1933	**8.00**
Evacuation Day March, George Washington drawing sword, 1883	**4.00**
Full Moon & Empty Arms, Frank Sinatra, 1946	**10.00**
General Pershing Song, 1918	**4.00**
He's Coming Home on the 8 O'Clock Train, Kendall, 1912	**15.00**
Kokomo, IN, Betty Grable, 1947	**5.00**
Little Alabama Coon, Black illus, 1893	**25.00**
Little Sweetheart of the Ozarks, Sandy Williams, 1937	**5.00**

Moonlight & Shadows, Dorothy Lamour and Ray Milland, 1936	**8.00**
Mrs. Casey Jones, Newton, 1915	**25.00**
My Ozark Mountain Home, Maple City Four–WLS Chicago, 1933	**8.00**
Normandy Chimes, Powell, 1913	**3.00**
Oh Why, Oh Why, Did I Ever Leave Wyoming, Jerry Colonna cartoon portrait, 1946	**8.00**
Over the Rainbow, cast on cov	**25.00**
Pennsylvania Polka, Andrew Sisters, 1942	**5.00**
Red River Valley, Gene Autry photo, 1935	**10.00**
Sierra Sue, Ray Herbeck, 1940	**5.00**
Sioux City Sue, Bing Crosby, 1945 . . .	**5.00**
Song For Me, Bromo–Seltzer, c1890 .	**12.00**
Spirit of America, Patriotic Patrol, 1917–18	**10.00**
Those Ragtime Melodies, Hodgkins, 1912	**6.00**
Up In My Flying Machine, Saxby, 1910	**15.00**
Won't You Let Me Take You Home, Doeer, 1912	**5.00**

STEREOGRAPHS

References: William C. Darrah, *Stereo Views, A History Of Stereographs in America And Their Collection,* published by author, 1964, out–of–print; William C. Darrah, *The World of Stereographs,* published by author, 1977, out–of–print. (Copies available from N. S. A. Book Service); John Waldsmith, *Stereo Views: An Illustrated History and Price Guide,* Wallace–Homestead, 1991.

Collectors' Club: National Stereoscopic Association, Box 14801, Columbus, OH 43214.

Animal

Cat, Keystone #2314	**4.00**
Dog, Universal #3231	**4.50**
Horses, Schreiber & Sons, Jarvis and sulky, early	**18.00**
Zoo, London Stereo Company, animals in London Zoo	**9.00**
Aviation, air mail plane, Keystone #29446, Cleveland	**25.00**
Circus, Universal & Universal, Chicago	**20.00**
Civil War, Taylor & Huntingdon #458, Confederate fortifications	**25.00**
Dirigible, Keystone #17397, *Los Angeles* at Lakehurst	**45.00**
Disaster, Lovejoy & Foster, Chicago Fire, 1871, ruins	**9.00**
Fireman, Proctor, hook–ladder, horse drawn	**35.00**
Hot Air Balloon, Anthony #4114, Prof Lowe's flight from NYC	**100.00**
Humor, Keystone #2346–7, before and after marriage	**7.00**
Lindbergh, Keystone #28029	**45.00**
Luray Caverns, Universal & Universal .	**8.00**

Niagara Falls, Barker, ice bridge 2.00
Railroad, Kilburn #432, locomotive . . .   30.00
Romance, Weller #353, Unexpected .   4.00
Ship, cruise, White #7422, *USS New
    York* 10.00
Spanish American War, Universal &
    Universal 8.50
Wedding Set, White #5510–19, getting
    ready, wedding, reception, alone in
    bedroom 40.00
Whaling, Keystone #14768 . . . .   7.50
World's Fairs and Expositions
    1872, World Peace Jubilee, Boston,
        Pollock, int. view of Coliseum . . .   8.00
    1901, Pan American, Buffalo, Kilburn   5.00
    1908, West Michigan State Fair, Key-
        stone #21507 . . . .   12.00
    1933, Century of Progress, Chicago,
        Keystone #32992 . . . .   15.00
Yellowstone, Wm Jackson 15.00

**Certificate of Deposit, Albany, NY, Me-
chanics and Farmers Bank, 1885, 7⅛ x
3¼", $5.00.**

STOCK AND BOND CERTIFICATES

References: Bill Yatchman, *The Stock & Bond
Collectors Price Guide,* published by author, 1985.
    Periodical: *Bank Note Reporter,* 700 East State
Street, Iola, WI 54990.
    Collectors' Club: Bond and Share Society, 24
Broadway, New York, NY 10004.

Anglo–California Trust Co, capital stock,
    vignette of eagle and shield at top,
    brown and white, unissued 5.00
Atchison, Topeka & Santa Fe Railroad,
    blue $1000 bond, two vignettes of
    railroad station int., issued 18.00
California Street Cable Railroad Co, ca-
    ble car vignette, punch canceled . . .   125.00
Chicago Cotton Manufacturing Co, or-
    nate design in brown, place for reve-
    nue stamp, factory vignette, 1870, un-
    used 10.00
Egypt Silver Mining Co, Franklin, ME,
    vignette of miners working, 1880s,
    unissued 10.00
First National Bank of Chicago, IL, 1864
    certificate, three vignettes, early sol-

dier carrying stars and stripes, two
    eagles, affixed revenue stamp, pen
    canceled 35.00
Ford International Capital Corporation,
    1968, $1000 bond, blue, black, and
    white 12.00
Foremost Dairy Products, Inc., Colum-
    bian Bank Note Co, 1933, blue and
    white, issued 10.00
New York Central Railroad, brown cer-
    tificate, vignette of Commodore Van-
    derbilt, 1940s, issued 10.00
Northampton Brewery Corp, orange
    certificate, engraved, vignette featur-
    ing woman, ship, and city skyline, PA,
    1930s, issued 15.00
Penn National Bank & Trust Co of
    Reading, gray certificate, vignette,
    PA, 1930, issued but not canceled .   15.00
Pepsi–Cola United Bottlers, orange or
    green certificate, vignette, Pepsi bot-
    tle in oval medallion, issued 10.00
Submarine Signal Co, green certificate,
    vignette of ship on ocean, 1940, is-
    sued 15.00
United Air Lines, 1970s, $100 share,
    olive 6.00
Wilys Overland Co, Fractional Share of
    Common Stock, American Banknote
    Co, non–pictorial, orange and white   6.00

TICKETS

Boxing, World's Heavyweight Champi-
    onship, Dempsey vs. Gibbons, July 4,
    1923, O'Toole County American Le-
    gion, Shelvy, MT, full ticket 50.00
Lottery
    Kansas State Lottery Co, 1894, mul-
        ticolored 8.00
    State of New York Medical Science
        Lottery Promotion, 1915, orange
        and white, used 8.00
    Washington City Canal Lottery, prize
        drawn for cutting the Canal through
        the city of Washington to Eastern
        Branch Harbour, black and white,
        used 15.00
Members, Board of Trade, City of Chi-
    cago, 1930, printed, black and white   6.00

PAPERWEIGHTS

    History: Although paperweights had their origin
in ancient Egypt, it was in the mid–19th century
that this art form reached its zenith. The classic
period for paperweights was 1845–55 in France
where the Clichy, Baccarat, and Saint Louis factories produced the finest examples of this art.
Other weights made in England, Italy, and Boh-

emia during this period rarely matched the quality of the French weights.

In the early 1850s, the New England Glass Co. in Cambridge, Massachusetts, and the Boston and Sandwich Glass Co. in Sandwich, Massachusetts, became the first American factories to make paperweights.

Popularity peaked during the classic period and faded toward the end of the 19th century. Paperweights were rediscovered nearly a century later in the mid–1900s. Contemporary weights still are made by Baccarat, Saint Louis, Perthshire, and many studio craftsmen in the U.S. and Europe.

References: Paul Hollister, Jr., *The Encyclopedia of Glass Paperweights,* Paperweight Press, 1969; Leo Kaplan, *Paperweights,* published by author, 1985; George N. Kulles, *Identifying Antique Paperweights–Lampwork,* Paperweight Press, 1987; James Mackay, *Glass Paperweights,* Facts on File, 1973; Edith Mannoni, *Classic French Paperweights,* Paperweight Press, 1984; L. H. Selman Ltd, *Collector's Paperweights: Price Guide and Catalogue,* Paperweight Press, 1986.

Collectors' Club: Paperweight Collectors Assoc. Inc., P.O. Box 1059, East Hampton, MA 01027.

Periodicals: *Paperweight Gaffer,* 35 Williamstown Circle, York, PA 17404; *Paperweight News,* 761 Chestnut Street, Santa Cruz, CA 95060.

Additional Listings: See *Warman's Americana & Collectibles* for examples of advertising paperweights.

ANTIQUE

Baccarat
Double Cut Overlay, 2¾", ruby cut to clear, interlaced strings of fine green and white canes encircling center group of circular set up canes, star cut base, minute edge nicks 900.00
Faceted Overlay, 3", nineteen windows, blue to white to clear, flower cane setups in center 550.00
Floral, 3", five petal red and white primrose on stem, single bud and eight green leaves enclosed by outer circle of alternating red, white, and green, red and white canes, star cut base 1,650.00
Millefiori, 3¼", close millefiori mushroom, two silhouette canes of horse and monkey, blue and white torsade, star cut base 700.00
Primrose, 3¼", white flower, red center cane, petals outlined in blue, green leaves and stem, star cut base 600.00
Clichy
Garland, 3", twenty–eight green and pink rose canes, encircles six ruby

and white canes, green, red, and white pastry mold center encloses pink and white concentric rings, medium blue ground 3,190.00
Pansy, 2⅝", soft purple upper and lower petals shaded lighter at edges, lower with purple–striped yellow centers, nodding bird, clear 1,400.00
Rose, 1¾", pink and white, encircled with eight green and white floral canes, pink and blue floral canes around circumference 385.00
Sodden Snow, 3", multicolored pastry mold canes, opaque white ground 950.00
Swirl, 2⅝", alternating opaque pink and white ribbons, green and red pastry mold center cane 770.00
Dupont, 2⅜", concentric rings of pastel canes encircle date 1851 . . . . 135.00

New England Glass Company
Clematis, 2⅞", double pink flowers with striated petals, white center, five green leaves, swirling white latticinio 1,700.00
Floral, 2½", three yellow, red, and white flowers, air trap centers, three multicolored canes surrounding pink, blue, and white center cane, six green leaves, white latticinio ground 1,400.00
Fruit, 3", five pears, four cherries, three green leaves, white latticinio ground 475.00
Mushroom, 3³⁄₁₆", concentric circle, faceted with quatrefoils, multicolored, shamrocks, hearts, and millefiori canes, white torsade 325.00
Poinsettia, 3⅜", ten petals, five pale blue dots, and dew drops on petals, pebble ground 325.00
Pantin, Lilies of the Valley, 2⅝", pink spray, thin pale amber stems, green leaves, clear 6,000.00
Sandwich
Bouquet, 2½", red center flower, two flowers on either side, green leaves, clear ground, white torsade 900.00
Floral and Fruit, 3⅞", red, white, and blue flowers, three pears, and two cherries, twenty green leaves, white latticinio ground 13,000.00
Pansy, 3", clear, bull bloom, two pink, two cobalt, and one white and blue striped petal encircling a blue, pink, and white center cane, three green leaves, single stem 250.00
Poinsettia, 2½", blue, ten petal blossom, five jeweled green leaves, white latticinio ground 475.00
Wild Rose, 3", white, blue and pink striping, eight leaves on green stem 500.00

Saint Louis
Bouquet, 2⅞", three blue flowers with
yellow centers surrounded by garland of multicolored canes, clear
ground 2,500.00
Chrysanthemum, 2¾", pink with
striped petals, four green leaves
and stem, swirling white latticinio . 1,850.00
Crown, 2⅞", center animal silhouette
cane dated 1825, red, blue, green,
and white 1,150.00
Lizard, 3½", opaque white, deep blue
overlay, gold lizard on top 2,200.00
Posy, 2⅝", five florets, pink, ochre,
pale and dark blue, and white, five
green leaves, strawberry cut base 490.00
Whitefriars, 3⅛", concentric rings of
pastel canes, mid 19th C 80.00

**Modern, Baccarat, Candy pattern, mul-
ticolored, sgd, $285.00.**

MODERN

Ayotee, Rick
Cockatoo, yellow sulfur crest, deep
blue translucent ground 350.00
Snow Owl, perched on pine branch,
moon on midnight ground, sgd . . 400.00
Baccarat, sulfide
John F. Kennedy, 2⅞", bust, black
amethyst ground 90.00
Mount Rushmore, 4⅛", red over white
overlay, clear blue base, dated
1976 . . . . 100.00
Charles Kaziun
Faceted, 2½", single pink and yellow
flowers, star cut base, signature
cane in center of three green
leaves 1,950.00
Millefiori, 2", seven multicolored millefiori canes with fish, turtle, duck,
and heart silhouettes, white filigree
with "K" initial, light green ground
shot with gold, sgd "K" on base . . 500.00
Miniature, 1⅞", set up canes in center, surrounded by pink and white
spiral ring, cobalt ground shot with
gold 800.00

Overlay
2⅜", triple cut overlay, blood red to
white to clear 4,500.00
2¼", double cut overlay, plum cut
to white cut to clear, six side windows, single window on top, multicolored center cane with "K"
signature surrounded by two
concentric circles of green, red,
and white canes, raised black
ground 1,200.00
Perthshire, penguin in hollow bubble,
ice blue flash overlay 350.00
St Louis
Bust, Queen Elizabeth, 3", faceted,
encircled in pink and white ring,
green and white alternating setup
canes, sgd, dated 2/6/53 . . . . 100.00
Pansy, 3", faceted, white muslin
ground, sgd S.L./1980 in red cane
on back 250.00
Stankard, Paul
Cactus, two yellow flowers and buds,
stem, translucent dark blue ground 950.00
Violets, wood, bouquet, purple and
white flowers, green leaves and
stem, clear ground 1,000.00
Whittemore, F. D.
Rose, 2¾", pink, four green leaves,
yellow and black signature cane,
pedestal base 150.00
Paul Ysart
Butterfly, 3", single blue flower with
white center, long green stem, eight
leaves, mottled pink and white
ground 250.00
Oval rings of pastel canes, 2⅞", signature cane center surrounded by
five pink canes 415.00

PAPIER-MÂCHÉ

History: Papier-mâché is made from a mixture
of wood pulp, glue, resin, and fine sand which is
subject to great pressure and then dried. The finished product is tough, durable, and heat resistant.
Various finishing treatments are used, such as
enameling, japanning, lacquering, mother-of-
pearl inlaying, and painting.

During the Victorian era papier-mâché articles
such as boxes, trays, and tables were in high fashion. Papier-mâché also found use in the production
of banks, candy containers, masks, toys, and other
children's articles.

Candy Container
9", rabbit, glass eyes 45.00
10", angel, fur, wax face, German . . 575.00
12¾" h, belsnickle holding green
feather tree, red wool trim hat,

white coat with mica flakes, orig polychrome paint, Germany 500.00
Case, 5" h, 4" w, book shape, gilded floral dec, orig polychrome paint, tin type soldier inside 125.00
Figure, 13¾" h, owl, molded body, worn orig paint, glass eyes 35.00
Hand Screen, 10" w, 15¼" h, cartouche shape, enameled chinoiserie figural group in garden, crest with lyre and foliate forms, black ground, turned black wood handles, pr 200.00
Jack–O–Lantern, 7" h, orange, printed tissue paper screen, electric lamp, bracket for battery 55.00
Mask, 24" h, donkey head, brown, white, nose, upright ears, teeth, shoulder cut–outs, polychrome paint 100.00
Pip–Squeak
2¾" h, elephant, worn orig polychrome paint, cloth cov bellows, silent 55.00
4" h, animated girl and lamb, orig polychrome paint and flocking, loose leather on bellows, lamb's ears missing 375.00
4⅜" h, dog, seated, orig black paint, polychrome trim, replaced leather on bellow, wear and damaged ears 45.00
4⅞" h, rooster, orig polychrome paint, loose leather on bellows, faint squeak, minor edge damage 45.00
5¾" h, peafowl, orig dark blue paint, red and green, white polka dots, silent bellow base 250.00
8" h, rooster, spring legs, orig polychrome paint and gilt, faint squeak, cracked seam, old repairs 250.00
Plate, 12" d, primitive cat painting, marked "Patented August 8, 1880" . 35.00
Powder Box, lady, bouffant skirt, French 45.00
Roly Poly, clown, 4⅛" h, orig white and

blue paint, polychrome trim, green ribbon around neck 60.00
Snuff Box
2¾" d, girl in dressing gown holding mirror painted on lid 150.00
3⅝" d, naval battle on lid, chipped .. 35.00
Tray, 25¾" l, black and gold, gilded brass handles, imp mark, English .. 975.00

PARIAN WARE

History: Parian ware is a creamy white, translucent, marble–like porcelain. It originated in England in 1842 and was first known as "Statuary Porcelain." Minton and Copeland have been credited with its development. Wedgwood also made it. In America, parian ware was manufactured by Chistopher Fenton in Bennington, Vermont.

At first parian ware was used only for figures and figural groups. By the 1850s it became so popular that a vast range of wares were manufactured.

Figure, young girl with bird on shoulder, imp "Copeland," 13½" h, $300.00.

Box, 5¾" l, 4¼" h, oval, full figured sleeping child on lid, Bennington ... 165.00
Bust
10" h, Ulysses S Grant, civilian dress, inscribed on back "Broome, Sculp. 1876," and "Ott and Brewer Manufacturers, Trenton, New Jersey," hairlines 2,640.00
12" h, maiden, socle base 150.00
12¾" h, Shakespeare, raised circular base, Robinson and Leadbeater mark, c1875, minor chip to hair .. 715.00
13¼" h, Shakespeare, imp "R Monti SC, Crystal Palace Art Union,

Roly Poly, German, 6½" h, each, $115.00.

Copeland," raised circular base, c1860, nicks to base rim **715.00**

15" h, Sir Walter Scott, raised circular base, Copeland, c1860, imp mark **500.00**

15½" h, Abraham Lincoln, raised circular base, English, c1860 . . . . . **275.00**

16" h, maiden, garland in hair, black pedestal base **150.00**

Creamer, 5" h, Tulip pattern, relief dec **90.00**

Ewer, 10¼" h, blue and white, applied grapes dec, Bennington, c1850 . . . . **215.00**

Figure

15½" h, Columbus, young man seated atop mooring post, waves splashing at feet, imp title on base, incised on back, "copyright applied for M. F. Libby," English, mid 19th C, repair to ring on mooring **500.00**

21" h, John A Andrews, full modeled figure standing on cut–corner sq base, printed verse on back, imp marks "M Milmore SC, publishers," and "J McD & S Boston, copyright," c1867, chips to base **1,210.00**

21¾" h, Maidenhood, classical style figure, standing, round base, imp Copeland mark and publishing date, 1861, chips and hairline to base **250.00**

26" h, The Bather Surprised, standing bather, cut–corner rect base, imp Royal Worcester mark, inscribed "T Brock, Sc, London, 1868," right arm restored **385.00**

Loving Cup, 8¾" h, relief figures of Bacchus and woman, grapes, and vines, Charles Meigh, c1840 . . . . **300.00**

Pastile Burner, 8¼" sq, relief molded, bird and human figures, raised on turned columns, stepped sq base, pr **190.00**

Pitcher, 9¾" h, hanging game scene, flake on spout **75.00**

Statue, 18" h, young Apollo, finely modeled **200.00**

Vase

7⅛" h, eagle, enameled blue and red, gilt trim, Bennington, slight hairlines in base **45.00**

10" h, applied white monkey type creatures, grape clusters at shoulders, blue ground, c1850, pr **250.00**

PATE–DE–VERRE

History: Pate–de–Verre can be translated simply as glass paste. It is manufactured by grinding lead glass into a powder or crystal form, making it into a paste by adding a 2% or 3% solution of sodium silicate, molding, firing, and carving. The Egyptians discovered the process as early as 1500 B.C.

In the late 19th century, the process was rediscovered by a group of French glassmakers. Amalric Walter, Henri Cros, Georges Despret, and the Daum brothers were leading manufacturers.

Contemporary sculptors are creating a second renaissance, lead by the technical research of Jacques Daum.

Dish, shallow, molded vine and leaf dec, dark orange, purple, and black, 3½" d, $850.00.

Ashtray, 5", circular, brown beetle surmount, Almeric Walter **1,200.00**

Atomizer, 5¾", red berries, green leaves, sgd "H Berge" **1,000.00**

Bookend, 5¾" h, yellow fox leaping from leaf molded green ground to trellis hung with green and purple grapes and foliage, sgd "A Walter Nancy," c1925 . . . . **850.00**

Bowl

2¾", molded sprays of red berries, green–brown branches, body lightly streaked with purple, c1920 **850.00**

10¼", ftd, molded with concentric blossoms, long necked birds rim, gray sides streaked with lavender and rose **4,000.00**

Clock, 4½", sq, stars within pentagon and tapered sheaves motif, orange and black, molded sgd "G Argy–Rousseau," clock by J E Caldwell . . **2,650.00**

Dagger, 12" l, frosted blade with relief design, green horse head handle, script sgd "Nancy, France" **1,100.00**

Jewelry, pendant, circular, molded green mistletoe leaves encircling purple berried center, amethyst translucent ground trimmed in blue, green knotted silk cord and hanging tassel **600.00**

Sculpture

7⅛" l, wave washing over fish, black, rust, pale sea green, and emerald green, shaped ovoid dish on one side, sgd "A Walter/Nancy and Berge SC" **4,400.00**

9⅝" l, crab in sea grasses, lemon yellow, chocolate brown, pale mauve, and sea green, sgd "A Walter/Nancy and Berge/SC" 8,250.00

10⅝" l, leaf form, relief lizard on one side, bee perched on opposite side, lime green, emerald green, midnight blue, and lemon yellow, sgd "A Walter/Nancy and Geno" 9,900.00

Tray, 6 x 8", apple green, figural green and yellow duck with orange beak at one end, sgd "Walter, Nancy" 750.00

Vase

8⅝" h, flaring trumpet form, pale lemon–yellow shaded to deeper yellow, molded stem with green mottled lizard, molded "A Walter/Nancy and Berge/SC," c1920 . . . 9,900.00

9", tapered cylindrical, border of rose faun, satyr, girl among amber waves, framed by purple morning glories, green ground 3,600.00

PATE–SUR–PATE

History: Pate–sur–Pate, paste on paste, is a 19th century porcelain form featuring relief designs achieved by painting successive layers of thin pottery paste one on top of the other.

About 1880 Marc Solon and other Sevres artists, inspired by a Chinese celadon vase in the Ceramic Museum at Sevres, experimented with this process of porcelain decoration. Solon migrated to England at the outbreak of the Franco–Prussian War and worked at Minton, where he perfected the pate–sur–pate process.

Box, cov, white slip design, blue ground, blue, white, and gold rings, Limoges, c1890, 5½" d, $215.00.

Box, 4¼ x 4", blue and white, cupids, artist sgd, marked "Limoges" 200.00

Demitasse Cup and Saucer, roses, gold trim, Coalport 350.00

Dessert Plate, 8¾" d, alternating paneled borders, three panels decorated with classical figures and cupids

in white on pale medium blue ground, three larger panels with gilt scrolling foliate dec, narrow bead borders, gilded rims, inscribed "Mintons," gilt painted factory and retailer's mark, decorated by R Bradbury, retailed by Tiffany & Co, New York, set of twelve 2,750.00

Flask, 8⅞", sunrise, sunset, two white figures floating above horizon, deep olive green parian body, sgd "Frederick Schenk," mounted as table lamps, pr 600.00

Pitcher, 8", mythical figures, bearded mask handle, white and pink 225.00

Plaque

4", white relief pastoral scene with couple courting beneath tree, blue ground, wooden frame, marked "F M Limoges, France" 300.00

7⅝ x 7", pr, one with maiden and cupid spinning web, other with maiden seated on bench with whip in one hand, sunflower stalk with humanistic snail in other, artist sgd "Louis Solin", marked "Mintons" on back, framed 2,000.00

Plate, 10⅝" d, alternating paneled borders, three panels decorated with classical figures and cupids in white on pale medium blue ground, three larger panels with gilt scrolling foliate dec, narrow bead borders, gilded rims, inscribed "Mintons," gilt painted factory and retailer's mark, decorated by R Bradbury, set of twelve 3,575.00

Sardine Dish, 2½ x 5½ x 4½", fish and seaweed dec, deep brown ground, SP cov, sgd "Jones" 500.00

Vase

10", pilgrim bottle shape, white relief cupids, one armed with large net, other with arrow, frolicking in tall weeds and flowers, chasing butterflies, gilding on neck, shoulder, and handles, marked "Mintons," c1880 900.00

10⅝", flattened oviform, obverse dec of classical maidens on swing suspended from leafy tree, enhanced with gold, upper and lower frieze of stylized blossoms and leaves, olive green ground, clear overglaze, pr 1,500.00

PATTERN GLASS

History: Pattern glass is clear or colored glass pressed into one of hundreds of patterns. Deming Jarves of the Boston and Sandwich Glass Co. invented the first successful pressing machine in 1828. By the 1860s glass pressing machinery had been improved, and mass production of good quality matched tableware sets began. The idea of a matched glassware table service (including goblets, tumblers, creamers, sugars, compotes, cruets, etc.) quickly caught on in America. Many pattern glass table services had numerous accessory pieces among which were banana stands, molasses cans, water bottles, etc.

Early pattern glass (flint) was made with a lead formula, giving it a ringing quality. During the Civil War lead became too valuable to be used in glass manufacturing. In 1864 Hobbs, Bruckunier & Co., West Virginia, developed a soda lime (non–flint) formula. Pattern glass also was produced in colors, milk glass, opalescent glass, slag glass, and custard glass.

The hundreds of companies which produced pattern glass experienced periods of development, expansions, personnel problems, material and supply demands, fires, and mergers. In 1899 the National Glass Co. was formed as a combine of nineteen glass companies in Pennsylvania, Ohio, Indiana, West Virginia, and Maryland. U. S. Glass, another consortium, was founded in 1891. These combines resulted as attempts to save small companies by pooling talents, resources, and patterns. Because of this pooling, the same pattern can be attributed to several companies.

Sometimes the pattern name of a piece was changed from one company to the next to reflect current fashion trends. U. S. Glass created the States series by issuing patterns named for a particular state. Several of these patterns were new issues, others were former patterns renamed.

References: E. M. Belnap, *Milk Glass,* Crown Publishers, Inc., 1949; Regis F. and Mary F. Ferson, *Yesterday's Milk Glass Today,* published by author, 1981; William Heacock, *Toothpick Holders from A to Z, Book 1, Encyclopedia of Victorian Colored Pattern Glass,* Antique Publications, 1981; William Heacock, *Opalescent Glass from A to Z, Book 2,* Antique Publications, 1981; William Heacock, *Syrups, Sugar Shakers & Cruets, Book 3,* Antique Publications, 1981; William Heacock, *Custard Glass From A to Z, Book 4,* Antique Publications, 1980; William Heacock, *U. S. Glass From A to Z, Book 5,* Antique Publications, Inc. 1980; William Heacock, *Oil Cruets From A to Z, Book 6,* Antique Publications, 1981; William Heacock, *Ruby Stained Glass From A To Z, Book 7* Antique Publications, Inc., 1986; William Heacock, *More Ruby Stained Glass, Book 8,* Antique Publications, 1987; William Heacock and William Gamble, *Cranberry Opalescent From A to Z, Book 9,* Antique Publications, 1987; William Heacock, *Old Pattern Glass,* Antique Publications, 1981; William Heacock, *1000 Toothpick Holders: A Collector's Guide,* Antique Publications, 1977; William Heacock, *Rare and Unlisted Toothpick Holders,* Antique Publications, 1984.

Bill Jenks and Jerry Luna, *Early American Pattern Glass–1850 to 1910: Major Collectible Table Settings with Prices,* Wallace–Homestead Book Co, 1990; Minnie Watson Kamm, *Pattern Glass*

Pitchers, Books 1 through 8, published by author, 1970, 4th printing; Ruth Webb Lee, *Early American Pressed Glass,* Lee Publications, 1966, 36th edition; Ruth Webb Lee, *Victorian Glass,* Lee Publications, 1944, 13th edition; Bessie M. Lindsey, *American Historical Glass,* Charles E. Tuttle Co., 1967; Robert Irwin Lucas, *Tarentum Pattern Glass,* privately printed, 1981; Mollie H. McCain, *Pattern Glass Primer,* Lamplighter Books, 1979; Mollie H. McCain, *The Collector's Encyclopedia of Pattern Glass,* Collector Books, 1982; George P. and Helen McKearin, *American Glass,* Crown Publishers, 1941; James Measell, *Greentown Glass,* Grand Rapids Public Museum Association, 1979; James Measell and Don E. Smith, *Findlay Glass: The Glass Tableware Manufacturers, 1886-1902,* Antique Publications, Inc, 1986; Alice Hulett Metz, *Early American Pattern Glass,* published by author, 1958; Alice Hulett Metz, *Much More Early American Pattern Glass,* published by author, 1965.

Dori Miles and Robert W. Miller, *Wallace–Homestead Price Guide To Pattern Glass, 11th Edition,* Wallace–Homestead, 1986; S. T. Millard, *Goblets I,* privately printed, 1938, reprinted Wallace–Homestead, 1975; S. T. Millard, *Goblets II,* privately printed, 1940, reprinted Wallace–Homestead, 1975; Arthur G. Peterson, *Glass Salt Shakers: 1,000 Patterns,* Wallace–Homestead, 1970; Jane Shadel Spillman, *American and European Pressed Glass in the Corning Museum of Glass,* Corning Museum of Glass, 1981; Jane Shadel Spillman, *The Knopf Collectors Guides to American Antiques, Glass Volumes 1 and 2,* Alfred A. Knopf, Inc., 1982, 1983; Doris and Peter Unitt, *American and Canadian Goblets,* Clock House, 1970; Doris and Peter Unitt, *Treasury of Canadian Glass,* Clock House, 1969, 2nd edition; Peter Unitt and Anne Worrall, *Canadian Handbook, Pressed Glass Tableware,* Clock House Productions, 1983; Dina von Zweck, *The Woman's Day Dictionary of Glass,* The Main Street Press, 1983.

Museums: Corning Museum of Glass, Corning, NY; National Museum of Man, Ottawa, Ontario, Canada.

Periodical: *Glass Collector's Digest,* Richardson Printing Corp., P. O. Box 663, Marietta, OH 45750.

Additional Listings: Bread Plates, Children's Toy Dishes, Cruets, Custard Glass, Milk Glass, Sugar Shakers, Toothpicks, and specific companies.

Abbreviations:
ah—applied handle
GUTDODB—Give Us This Day Our Daily Bread
hs—high standard
ls—low standard
os—original stopper

We continue to be fortunate in assembling a panel of prestigious pattern glass dealers to serve as advisors in reviewing the pattern glass listings found in this edition. Their dedication is symbolic of those dealers and collectors who view price guides as useful market tools and contribute their expertise and time to make them better.

Research in pattern glass is continuing. As in the past, we have tried to present patterns with correct names, histories, and pieces. Catagories have been changed to reflect the most current thinking of all patterns alphabetically. Colored, opalescent, and clear patterns now are included in one listing, avoiding duplication of patterns and colors.

Pattern glass has been widely reproduced. We have listed reproductions with an *. These markings are given only as a guide and clue to the collector that some reproductions may exist in a given pattern.

Advisors: John and Alice Ahlfeld, Mike Anderton, William Jenks, and Darryl K. Reilly.

ACTRESS (Theatrical)

Made by LaBelle Glass Co., Bridgeport, Ohio, and Crystal Glass Co., c1870. All clear 20% less. Some items have been reproduced in clear and color by Imperial Glass Co.

	Clear and Frosted		Clear and Frosted
Bowl		Dresser Tray.	60.00
6", ftd	45.00	Goblet, Kate Claxton (2	
7", ftd	50.00	portraits)	85.00
9½, ftd	85.00	Marmalade Jar, cov.	125.00
8", Miss Neilson.	85.00	Mug, HMS Pinafore.	50.00
Bread Plate		Pickle Dish, Love's Request	
7 x 12", HMS Pinafore . . .	90.00	is Pickles.	45.00
9 x 13", Miss Neilson	72.00	Pickle Relish, different actresses	
Butter, cov	90.00	tresses	
Cake Stand, 10"	150.00	4½ x 7"	35.00
Candlesticks, pr	250.00	5 x 8"	35.00
Celery Vase		5½ x 9"	35.00
Actress Head.	130.00	Pitcher	
HMS Pinafore, pedestal . .	145.00	Milk, 6½", HMS Pinafore. .	275.00
Cheese Dish, cov, The Lone		Water, 9", Romeo & Juliet.	250.00
Fisherman on cov, Two		Salt, master	70.00
Dromios on base	250.00	Salt Shaker, orig pewter top .	42.50
Compote		Sauce	
Cov, hs, 12" d	300.00	Flat.	15.00
Open, hs, 10" d	90.00	Footed	20.00
Open, hs, 12" d	120.00	Spooner	60.00
Open, ls, 5" d	45.00	Sugar, cov	100.00
Creamer.	75.00		

ALABAMA (Beaded Bull's Eye and Drape)

Made by U. S. Glass Co., c1898. One of the States patterns. Also found in green (rare).

	Clear	Ruby Stained		Clear	Ruby Stained
Bowl, berry, master .	30.00	—	Compote, cov		
Butter, cov	50.00	150.00	7"	100.00	—
Cake Stand	55.00	—	8"	125.00	—
Castor Set, 4 bottles,			Compote, open, 5",		
glass frame	125.00	—	jelly.	65.00	—
Celery Vase	35.00	110.00	Creamer.	45.00	60.00

	Clear	Ruby Stained		Clear	Ruby Stained
Cruet, os	65.00	—	Sauce	18.00	—
Dish, rect	20.00	—	Spooner	30.00	—
Honey Dish, cov	60.00	—	Sugar, cov	48.00	—
Nappy	25.00	—	Syrup	125.00	250.00
Pitcher, water	72.00	—	Toothpick	60.00	150.00
Relish	24.00	35.00	Tray, water, 10½″	50.00	—
Salt & Pepper	65.00	—	Tumbler	45.00	

ALL-OVER DIAMOND (Diamond Splendor, Diamond Block #3)

Made by George Duncan and Sons, Pittsburgh, Pennsylvania, c1891 and continued by U.S. Glass Co. It was occasionally trimmed with gold, and had at least 65 pieces in the pattern. Biscuit jars are found in three sizes; bowls are both crimped and non-crimped; and nappies are also found crimped and non-crimped in fifteen sizes. Also made in ruby stained.

	Clear		Clear
Biscuit Jar, cov	60.00	Ice Tub, handles	35.00
Bitters Bottle	30.00	Lamp, Banquet, tall stem	150.00
Bowl		Nappy	
7″	20.00	4″	15.00
11″	35.00	9″	35.00
Cake Stand	35.00	Plate	
Candelabrum, very ornate, 4 arm with lusters	175.00	6″	15.00
		7″	15.00
Celery Tray, crimped or straight	20.00	Pickle Dish, long	15.00
Claret Jug	50.00	Pitcher, water, bulbous, 6 sizes	45–60.00
Compote, cov	40.00	Punch Bowl	50.00
Condensed Milk Jar, cov	25.00	Salt Shaker	15.00
Cordial	35.00	Spooner	20.00
Creamer	20.00	Sugar	
Cruet, patterned stopper		Cov	35.00
1 oz	50.00	Open	18.00
2 oz	45.00	Syrup	55.00
4 oz	45.00	Tray	
6 oz	25.00	Ice Cream	30.00
Decanter		Water	30.00
Pint	45.00	Wine	30.00
Quart	45.00	Tumbler	15.00
Egg Cup	20.00	Water Bottle	35.00
Goblet	25.00	Wine	15.00

ALMOND THUMBPRINT (Pointed Thumbprint, Finger Print)

An early flint glass pattern with variants in flint and non-flint. Pattern has been attributed to Bryce, Bakewell, and U. S. Glass. Sometimes found in milk glass.

	Flint	Non-Flint		Flint	Non-Flint
Bowl, 4½" d, ftd . . .	—	20.00	Decanter	70.00	—
Butter, cov	80.00	40.00	Egg Cup.	45.00	25.00
Celery Vase	50.00	25.00	Goblet	30.00	12.00
Champagne	60.00	35.00	Punch Bowl	—	75.00
Compote			Salt		
Cov, hs, 4¾", jelly	60.00	40.00	Flat, large	25.00	15.00
Cov, hs, 10".	100.00	45.00	Ftd, cov.	45.00	25.00
Cov, ls, 4¾".	55.00	30.00	Ftd, open	25.00	10.00
Cov, ls, 7"	45.00	25.00	Spooner	20.00	15.00
Open, hs, 10½" . .	65.00	—	Sugar, cov	60.00	40.00
Cordial	40.00	30.00	Sweetmeat Jar, cov.	65.00	45.00
Creamer.	60.00	40.00	Tumbler	60.00	20.00
Cruet, ftd, os.	55.00	—	Wine	28.00	12.00

AMAZON (Sawtooth Band)

Non-flint; made by Bryce Brothers, Pittsburgh, Pennsylvania, late 1870s–1880 and also by the U. S. Glass Co., c1890. Mostly found in clear, either etched or plain. Heacock notes pieces in amber, blue, vaseline, and ruby stained. Over 65 pieces made in this pattern, including a toy set. Add 200% for color, e.g., pedestalled amber cruet with maltese cross stopper ($165.00) and pedestalled blue cruet with hand and bar stopper ($200.00). An amethyst cruet with a hand-bar stopper ($275.00) also is known.

	Etched	Plain		Etched	Plain
Banana Stand.	95.00	65.00	Cordial	40.00	25.00
Bowl			Creamer.	30.00	28.00
4", scalloped	—	10.00	Cruet, os	50.00	45.00
4½", scalloped. . .	—	10.00	Egg Cup.	—	14.00
5", scalloped	—	15.00	Goblet		
6", scalloped	—	25.00	4½".	30.00	—
6½", cov, oval . . .	—	50.00	5"	25.00	—
7", scalloped	—	20.00	6"	30.00	—
8", scalloped	—	25.00	Pitcher, water	60.00	55.00
9", cov	30.00	25.00	Relish.	28.00	25.00
Butter, cov	65.00	50.00	Salt & Pepper, pr. . .	50.00	40.00
Cake Stand			Salt		
Large	—	50.00	Individual.	—	15.00
Small	—	40.00	Master	—	18.00
Celery Vase	35.00	30.00	Sauce, ftd	10.00	10.00
Champagne	—	35.00	Spooner	25.00	20.00
Claret	35.00	30.00	Sugar, cov	55.00	45.00
Compote			Syrup	50.00	42.50
Cov, hs, 7"	—	65.00	Tumbler	25.00	20.00
Open, 4½", jelly . .	45.00	35.00	Vase	30.00	25.00
Open, hs, 9½", sawtooth edge	—	45.00	Wine	25.00	20.00

ARCHED OVALS

Made by U. S. Glass Co., c1908. Found in gilt, ruby stained, green, and rarely in cobalt blue. Popular pattern for souvenir wares.

	Clear	Cobalt	Green	Ruby Stained
Bowl, berry	12.50	—	18.00	—
Bowl, cov, 7"	40.00	—	—	—
Butter, cov	45.00	—	50.00	80.00
Cake Stand	35.00	—	—	—
Celery Vase	15.00	40.00	20.00	—
Compote				
Cov, hs, 8", belled	42.00	—	—	—
Open, hs, 8"	30.00	—	—	—
Open, hs, 9"	35.00	—	—	—
Creamer				
Ind	20.00	—	—	—
Regular.	30.00	—	—	25.00
Cruet	35.00	—	45.00	—
Goblet	20.00	—	30.00	35.00
Mug	18.00	30.00	20.00	25.00
Pitcher, water	30.00	—	40.00	—
Plate, 9"	20.00	—	25.00	—
Punch Cup	8.00	—	—	—
Relish, oval, 9"	20.00	—	—	—
Salt & Pepper, pr. . .	45.00	—	50.00	—
Sauce	7.50	—	—	—
Saucer	—	—	—	30.00
Syrup	35.00	—	—	—
Spooner	20.00	—	25.00	35.00
Sugar, cov	35.00	—	40.00	—
Toothpick	18.00	50.00	25.00	35.00
Tumbler	12.00	25.00	18.00	30.00
Wine	15.00	—	20.00	30.00

ARGUS

Flint, thumbprint type pattern made by Bakewell, Pears & Co. in Pittsburgh, Pennsylvania, in the early 1870s. Copiously reproduced, some by Fostoria with raised "HFM" trademark for Henry Ford Museum.

	Clear		Clear
Ale Glass	75.00	Goblet	40.00
Bitters Bottle	60.00	Lamp, ftd	75.00
Bowl, 5½"	50.00	Mug, ah	65.00
Butter, cov	85.00	Pitcher, water, ah	225.00
Celery Vase	90.00	Salt, master, open	30.00
Champagne	65.00	Spooner	48.50
Compote, open, 6" d, 4½" h	50.00	Sugar, cov	65.00
Creamer, applied handle . . .	100.00	Tumbler, bar	65.00
Decanter, qt	70.00	Whiskey, ah	75.00
Egg Cup	30.00	Wine	45.00

ART (Job's Tears)

Non-flint produced by Adams and Co., Pittsburgh, Pennsylvania, in the 1870s. Reissued by U. S. Glass Co. in the early 1890s. A milk glass covered compote is known.

	Clear	Ruby Stained		Clear	Ruby Stained
Banana Stand.....	95.00	175.00	Regular........	55.00	60.00
Biscuit Jar	135.00	175.00	Cruet, os	125.00	250.00
Bowl			Goblet..........	58.00	—
6" d, 3¼" h, ftd ..	30.00	—	Mug............	35.00	50.00
7", low, collar			Pitcher		
base	35.00	—	Milk..........	115.00	150.00
8", berry, one end			Water, 2½ qt	85.00	—
pointed	50.00	55.00	Plate, 10"	40.00	—
Butter, cov	60.00	100.00	Relish..........	20.00	65.00
Cake Stand			Sauce		
9".............	55.00	—	Flat, round, 4" ...	15.00	—
10¼"..........	65.00	—	Pointed end.....	18.50	—
Celery Vase	42.50	65.00	Spooner.........	25.00	55.00
Compote			Sugar, cov	45.00	85.00
Cov, hs, 7".....	55.00	185.00	Tumbler	45.00	—
Open, hs, 9"	50.00	—	Vinegar Jug, 3 pt. ..	75.00	—
Open, hs, 9½" d	60.00	—			
Open, hs, 10" ...	65.00	—			
Creamer					
Hotel, large, round					
shape	45.00	55.00			

ASHBURTON

A popular pattern produced by Boston and Sandwich Glass Co. and McKee Brothers from the 1850s to the late 1870s with many variations. Originally made in flint by New England Glass Co. and others and later in non-flint. Prices are for flint. Also reported is an amber handled whiskey mug and a scarce emerald green wine glass ($200.00). Some items known in fiery opalescent.

	Clear		Clear
Ale Glass, 5"............	90.00	Honey Dish............	15.00
Bar Bottle		* Jug, qt	90.00
Pint...............	55.00	Lamp	75.00
Quart	75.00	* Lemonade Glass.........	55.00
Bitters Bottle............	55.00	Mug, 7"	100.00
Bowl, 6½".............	75.00	Pitcher, water	450.00
Carafe	175.00	Plate, 6⅝"...........	75.00
Celery Vase, scalloped top..	125.00	Sauce	10.00
Champagne, cut	75.00	* Sugar, cov	90.00
Claret, 5¼" h	50.00	Toddy Jar, cov	375.00
Compote, open, ls, 7½"....	65.00	Tumbler	
Cordial, 4¼" h..........	75.00	Bar................	75.00
Creamer, ah	210.00	Water	75.00
Decanter, qt, cut and		Whiskey	60.00
pressed, os	250.00	Whiskey, ah	125.00
Egg Cup		Water Bottle, tumble up	95.00
Double	95.00	* Wine	
Single...............	25.00	Cut	65.00
Flip Glass, handled	140.00	Pressed	40.00
* Goblet	40.00		

ATLANTA (Square Lion, Clear Lion Head)

Produced by Fostoria Glass Co., Moundsville, West Virginia, c1895. Pieces are usually square in shape. Also found in milk glass, ruby and amber stain.

	Clear	Frosted		Clear	Frosted
Bowl			Goblet	50.00	60.00
7", scallop rim . . .	60.00	75.00	Marmalade Jar	75.00	85.00
8", low collar			Pitcher, water	125.00	175.00
base	55.00	85.00	Relish, oval.	35.00	40.00
Butter, cov	85.00	125.00	Salt & Pepper, pr. . .	100.00	125.00
Cake Stand, 10" . . .	95.00	110.00	Salt		
Celery Vase	45.00	75.00	Individual.	30.00	40.00
Compote			Master	50.00	70.00
Cov, hs, 7".	90.00	125.00	Sauce, 4"	22.00	25.00
Cov, hs, 8" d,			Spooner	50.00	60.00
9½" h.	110.00	150.00	Sugar, cov	85.00	100.00
Open, hs, 5", jelly	55.00	65.00	Toothpick	55.00	60.00
Creamer.	50.00	65.00	Tumbler	45.00	55.00
Cruet	125.00	150.00	Wine	40.00	65.00
Egg cup	25.00	30.00			

ATLAS

Non-flint glass pattern occasionally ruby stained and etched. Made by Adams and Co., U. S. Glass Co. in 1891, and Bryce Brothers, Mt. Pleasant, Pennsylvania, in 1889.

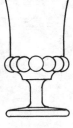

	Clear	Ruby Stained		Clear	Ruby Stained
Bowl, 9"	20.00	—	Pitcher, water	50.00	—
Butter, cov, regular	45.00	75.00	Salt		
Cake Stand			Master	20.00	—
8"	35.00	—	Individual.	15.00	—
9"	40.00	95.00	Salt & Pepper, pr. . .	20.00	—
Celery Vase	28.00	—	Sauce		
Champagne, 5½" h	35.00	45.00	Flat.	10.00	—
Compote			Footed	15.00	20.00
Cov, hs, 8".	65.00	—	Spooner	30.00	35.00
Cov, hs, 5", jelly. .	50.00	65.00	Sugar, cov	40.00	65.00
Open, ls, 7"	40.00	—	Syrup, molasses		
Cordial	35.00	—	can	65.00	—
Creamer			Toothpick	20.00	50.00
Table, ah.	30.00	55.00	Tray, water	75.00	—
Tankard	25.00	—	Tumbler	28.00	—
Goblet	45.00	65.00	Whiskey	20.00	45.00
Marmalade Jar	45.00	—	Wine	25.00	—

AURORA (Diamond Horseshoe)

Made in 1888 by the Brilliant Glass Works, which only existed for a short time. Taken over by the Greensburg Glass Co. who continued the pattern. Also found etched.

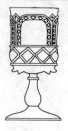

	Clear	Ruby Stained		Clear	Ruby Stained
Bread Plate, 10", round, large star in center	30.00	35.00	Relish Scoop, handle	10.00	25.00
Butter, cov	45.00	90.00	Salt & Pepper, pr	45.00	80.00
Cake Stand	35.00	85.00	Sauce, flat	8.00	18.00
Celery Vase	32.50	42.50	Spooner	25.00	48.00
Compote, cov, hs	65.00	110.00	Sugar, cov	45.00	65.00
Creamer	35.00	50.00	Tray, water	45.00	60.00
Goblet	30.00	45.00	Tray, wine	35.00	60.00
Mug, handle	50.00	65.00	Tumbler	25.00	45.00
Olive, oval	18.00	35.00	Waste Bowl	30.00	45.00
Pitcher, water	40.00	100.00	Wine	25.00	35.00
			Wine Decanter, os	75.00	150.00

AUSTRIAN (Finecut Medallion)

Made by Indiana Tumbler and Goblet Co., Greentown, Indiana, 1897. Experimental pieces were made in cobalt blue, nile green, and opaque colors.

	Amber	Canary	Clear	Emerald Green
Bowl				
8", round	—	150.00	55.00	—
8¼", rect	—	145.00	50.00	—
Butter, cov	185.00	300.00	90.00	—
Compote, open, ls	—	150.00	75.00	—
Cordial	145.00	150.00	50.00	150.00
Creamer	120.00	125.00	40.00	120.00
Goblet	—	150.00	40.00	—
Nappy, cov	—	135.00	55.00	—
Pitcher, water	—	350.00	100.00	—
Plate, 10"	—	—	40.00	—
Punch Cup	150.00	150.00	18.00	125.00
Rose Bowl	—	150.00	50.00	—
Sauce, 4⅝" d	—	50.00	20.00	—
Spooner	—	100.00	40.00	—
Sugar, cov	—	175.00	45.00	—
Tumbler	175.00	85.00	25.00	—
Wine	175.00	150.00	30.00	150.00

BALTIMORE PEAR (Gipsy)

Non-flint, originally made by Adams and Company, Pittsburgh, Pennsylvania, in 1874. Also made by U. S. Glass Company in 1890s. There are 18 different size compotes. Given as premiums by different manufacturers and organizations. Heavily reproduced. Reproduced in cobalt blue.

	Clear		Clear
Bowl		* Celery Vase	50.00
6"	30.00	Compote	
9"	35.00	Cov, hs, 7"	80.00
Bread Plate, 12½"	70.00	Cov, ls, 8½"	45.00
* Butter, cov	75.00	Open, hs	30.00
* Cake Stand, 9"	65.00	Open, jelly	28.50

	Clear		Clear
* Creamer	30.00	Relish	25.00
* Goblet	35.00	* Sauce	
Pickle	20.00	Flat	15.00
* Pitcher		Footed	20.00
Milk	80.00	Spooner	40.00
Water	95.00	* Sugar, cov	50.00
Plate		Tray, 10½"	35.00
8½"	30.00		
10"	40.00		

BANDED PORTLAND (Virginia #1, Maiden's Blush)

States pattern, originally named Virginia, by Portland Glass Co. Painted and fired green, yellow, blue, and possibly pink; ruby stained, and rose-flashed (which Lee notes is Maiden's Blush referring to the color, rather than the pattern, as Metz lists it). Double flashed refers to color above and below the band, single flashed refers to color above or below band only.

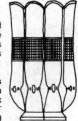

	Clear	Color Flashed	Maiden's Blush Pink
Bowl, 9"	30.00	—	40.00
Butter, cov	50.00	165.00	85.00
Cake Stand	55.00	—	90.00
Candlesticks, pr	80.00	—	125.00
Carafe	80.00	—	90.00
Celery Tray	25.00	—	40.00
Celery Vase	35.00	—	45.00
Cologne Bottle	50.00	65.00	85.00
Compote			
Cov, hs, 7"	95.00	—	125.00
Cov, jelly, 6"	40.00	65.00	90.00
Creamer			
Individual, oval	25.00	35.00	38.00
Regular, 6 oz.	35.00	45.00	50.00
Cruet, os	60.00	90.00	125.00
Decanter, handled	50.00	—	100.00
Dresser Tray	50.00	—	65.00
Goblet	40.00	55.00	65.00
Lamp			
Flat	45.00	—	—
Tall	50.00	—	—
Nappy	15.00	55.00	65.00
Olive	18.00	—	35.00
Pin Tray	16.00	—	25.00
Pitcher, tankard	75.00	95.00	240.00
Pomade Jar, cov	35.00	45.00	65.00
Punch Bowl, hs	110.00	—	300.00
Punch Cup	20.00	—	30.00
Relish			
6½"	25.00	30.00	20.00
8¼"	20.00	35.00	40.00
Ring Holder	75.00	—	125.00
Salt & Pepper, pr.	45.00	75.00	75.00
Sardine Box	55.00	—	90.00
Sauce, round, flat, 4 or 4½"	12.00	—	20.00

	Clear	Color Flashed	Maiden's Blush Pink
Spooner	28.00	—	45.00
Sugar, cov	48.00	75.00	75.00
Sugar Shaker, orig top	45.00	—	85.00
Syrup	50.00	—	135.00
Toothpick	40.00	45.00	45.00
Tumbler	25.00	35.00	45.00
Vase			
6″	20.00	—	38.00
9″	35.00	—	50.00
Wine	35.00	—	75.00

BARBERRY (Berry)

Non-flint made by McKee Glass Co. and the Boston and Sandwich Glass Co. in the 1860s and 1880s. 6″ plates are found in amber, canary, pale green, and pale blue; they are considered scarce. Also alleged to have been made at Iowa City. Pattern comes in "9 berry bunch" and "12 berry bunch" varieties.

	Clear			Clear
Bowl		Creamer		30.00
6″, oval	20.00	Cup Plate		15.00
7″, oval	25.00	Egg Cup		18.00
8″, oval	28.00	Goblet		25.00
8″, round, flat	30.00	Pickle		10.00
9″, oval	32.00	Pitcher, water, ah		100.00
Butter		Plate, 6″		20.00
Cov	50.00	Salt, master, ftd		25.00
Cov, flange, pattern on		Sauce		
edge	100.00	Flat		10.00
Cake Stand	125.00	Footed		15.00
Celery Vase	40.00	Spooner, ftd		30.00
Compote		Sugar, cov		45.00
Cov, hs, 8″, shell finial	85.00	Syrup		150.00
Cov, ls, 8″, shell finial	75.00	Tumbler, ftd		25.00
Open, hs, 8″	35.00	Wine		30.00

BARLEY

Non-flint, originally made by Campbell, Jones and Co., c1882, in clear; possibly by others in varied quality. Add 100% for color which is hard to find.

	Clear		Clear
Bowl		Celery Vase	25.00
8″, berry	15.00	Compote	
10″, oval	15.00	Cov, hs, 6″	45.00
Bread Tray	30.00	Cov, hs, 8½″	60.00
Butter, cov	42.50	Open, hs, 8½″	35.00
Cake Stand		Cordial	50.00
8″	28.00	Creamer	30.00
10″	32.00	Goblet	35.00

	Clear
Honey, ftd, 3½"	8.00
Marmalade Jar	65.00
Pickle Castor, SP frame. . . .	85.00
Pitcher, water	
Applied handle.	100.00
Pressed handle	45.00
Plate, 6"	35.00
Platter, 13" l, 8" w	30.00

	Clear
Sauce	
Flat.	8.50
Footed	10.00
Spooner	21.50
Sugar, cov	35.00
Vegetable Dish, oval	15.00
Wine	30.00

BASKETWEAVE

Non-flint, c1880. Some covered pieces have a stippled cat's head finial.

	Amber or Canary	Apple Green	Blue	Clear	Vaseline
Bowl.	22.00	—	25.00	18.00	—
Bread Plate, 11" . . .	35.00	—	35.00	10.00	—
Butter, cov	35.00	60.00	40.00	30.00	40.00
Compote, cov, 7". . .	—	—	—	35.00	—
Cordial	25.00	40.00	28.00	20.00	30.00
Creamer.	30.00	50.00	35.00	28.00	36.00
Cup & Saucer.	35.00	60.00	35.00	30.00	38.00
Dish, oval	12.00	20.00	15.00	10.00	16.00
Egg Cup.	18.00	30.00	20.00	15.00	25.00
* Goblet	28.00	50.00	35.00	20.00	30.00
Mug	25.00	40.00	25.00	15.00	30.00
Pickle.	18.00	30.00	20.00	15.00	22.00
Pitcher					
Milk.	40.00	60.00	45.00	35.00	50.00
* Water	60.00	75.00	80.00	45.00	85.00
Plate, 11", handled .	25.00	38.00	25.00	20.00	30.00
Sauce	10.00	10.00	12.00	8.00	12.00
Spooner	30.00	36.00	30.00	20.00	30.00
Sugar, cov	35.00	60.00	35.00	30.00	40.00
Syrup	50.00	75.00	50.00	45.00	55.00
* Tray, water, scenic					
center	35.00	45.00	40.00	30.00	55.00
Tumbler, ftd	18.00	30.00	20.00	15.00	20.00
Waste Bowl.	20.00	36.00	25.00	18.00	25.00
Wine	30.00	50.00	30.00	25.00	30.00

BEADED ACORN MEDALLION (Beaded Acorn)

Made by the Boston Silver Glass Co., East Cambridge, Massachusetts, c1869.

	Clear
Butter, cov, acorn finial.	65.00
Champagne	65.00
Compote, cov, hs	50.00
Creamer.	40.00
Egg Cup.	25.00
Goblet	30.00
Pitcher, water	150.00

	Clear
Plate, 6"	30.00
Relish.	15.00
Salt, master	30.00
Sauce, flat	12.00
Spooner	25.00
Sugar, cov	45.00
Wine	45.00

BEADED BAND

Attributed to Burlington Glass Co., Hamilton, Ontario, Canada, c1884. Limited production and scarce pattern. May have been made in light amber and other colors.

	Clear		Clear
Butter, cov	35.00	Relish	
Cake Stand, 7⅝".	25.00	Double	30.00
Compote, cov		Single	15.00
hs, 8"	55.00	Sauce, ftd.	10.00
ls, 9"	50.00	Spooner	25.00
Creamer	30.00	Sugar, cov	40.00
Goblet	30.00	Syrup	95.00
Pickle, cov	45.00	Wine	30.00
Pitcher, water, applied strap handle	75.00		

BEADED GRAPE MEDALLION

Non-flint made by Boston Silver Glass Co., Cambridge, Massachusetts, c1868. Also found in flint; add 40%.

	Clear		Clear
Bowl, 7"	25.00	Honey Dish, 3½".	10.00
Butter, cov, acorn finial.	45.00	Pitcher, water, ah	115.00
Cake Stand, 11"	150.00	Plate, 6".	30.00
Celery Vase	50.00	Relish	
Castor Set, 4 bottles	110.00	Cov.	140.00
Compote		Open, mkd "Mould Pat'd	
Cov, collared base	85.00	May 11, 1868"	40.00
Cov, hs	75.00	Salt	
Open, hs, 8"	35.00	Individual, flat	20.00
Creamer, ah	48.00	Master, ftd.	25.00
Egg Cup.	30.00	Spooner	40.00
Goblet		Sugar, cov, acorn finial.	60.00
Buttermilk	30.00	Vegetable, cov, ftd.	75.00
Lady's	30.00	Wine	55.00

BEADED SWIRL (Swirled Column)

Made by George Duncan & Sons, c1890. The dual names are for the two forms of the pattern. Beaded Swirl stands on flat bases and is solid in shape. Swirled Column stands on scrolled (sometimes gilded) feet, and the shape tapered towards the base. Some pieces trimmed in gold and also in milk white.

	Clear	Emerald Green		Clear	Emerald Green
Bowl			Celery Vase	30.00	55.00
Berry, 7"	10.00	20.00	Compote		
Flat.	15.00	25.00	Cov, hs	40.00	50.00
Footed, oval	18.00	24.00	Open, hs.	35.00	45.00
Footed, round	18.00	24.00	Creamer		
Butter, cov	35.00	45.00	Flat.	25.00	35.00
Cake Stand	35.00	45.00	Footed	30.00	40.00

	Clear	Emerald Green			Clear	Emerald Green
Dish	10.00	15.00	Sugar, cov			
Egg Cup	14.00	15.00	Flat	35.00	45.00
Goblet	30.00	25.00	Footed	35.00	45.00
Mug	10.00	12.00	Sugar Shaker	35.00	60.00
Pitcher, water	40.00	65.00	Syrup	48.00	100.00
Sauce			Tumbler	20.00	30.00
Flat	8.00	12.00	Wine	25.00	35.00
Footed	10.00	14.00			
Spooner					
Flat	25.00	40.00			
Footed	30.00	45.00			

BEAUTIFUL LADY

Made by Bryce, Higbee and Co. in 1905.

	Clear		Clear
Banana stand, hs	30.00	Goblet	35.00
Bowl		Pitcher, water	40.00
8″, low collared base	15.00	Plate	
9″, flat	18.00	7″, sq	15.00
Bread Plate	15.00	8″	18.00
Cake Plate, 9″	25.00	9″	25.00
Cake Stand, hs	35.00	11″	27.50
Compote		Salt and Pepper, pr	60.00
Cov, hs	35.00	Spooner	15.00
Open, hs	25.00	Sugar, cov	25.00
Open, jelly	15.00	Tumbler	15.00
Creamer	25.00	Vase, 6½″	15.00
Cruet	30.00	Wine	20.00

BELLFLOWER

A fine flint glass pattern first made in the 1830s and attributed to Boston and Sandwich. Later produced by McKee Glass Co. and other firms for many years. There are many variations of this pattern - single vine and double vine, fine and coarse rib, knob and plain stems, and rayed and plain bases. Type and quality must be considered when evaluating. Very rare in color. Prices are for high quality flint. Reproductions have been made by the Metropolitan Museum of Art.   Abbreviations: DV - double vine; SV - single vine; FR - fine rib; CR - coarse rib.

	Clear		Clear
Bowl		Compote	
6″ d, 1¾″ h, SV	75.00	Cov, hs, 8″ d, SV-FR	375.00
8″, all types	75.00	Cov, ls, 7″ d, SV	200.00
Butter, cov, SV-FR	100.00	Cov, ls, 8″ d, SV	225.00
Castor Set, 5 bottle, pewter		Open, hs, 8″, SV	225.00
stand	225.00	Open, ls, 7″, DV-FR	90.00
Celery Vase, SV-FR	165.00	Open, ls, 7″, SV	100.00
Champagne		Open, ls, 8″, SV	100.00
DV-FR, cut bellflowers	225.00	Open, ls, 9″, SV-CR	125.00
SV-FR, knob stem, rayed		Cordial, SV-FR, knob stem,	
base, barrel shape	100.00	rayed base, barrel shape	115.00

	Clear		Clear
Creamer, DV-FR	135.00	Plate, 6", SV-FR	125.00
Creamer, SV-FR	135.00	Salt, master	
Decanter		SV-FR, ftd	60.00
Pint, DV-FR, bar top	225.00	DV-FR	35.00
Quart		Sauce, flat, SV-FR	15.00
DV-FR, orig patterned		Spooner	
stopper	275.00	DV	45.00
SV-FR, bar top	185.00	SV-FR	35.00
Dish, SV-FR, 8", round, flat,		Sugar	
scalloped top	65.00	Cov, DV	100.00
Egg Cup		Cov, SV-CR	95.00
CR	35.00	Open, DV-CR	45.00
SV-FR	40.00	Sweetmeat, cov, hs, 6", SV	300.00
Goblet		Syrup, ah	
DV-FR, cut bellflowers	230.00	Ftd, 10 sides	750.00
SV-CR, barrel shape	45.00	SV-FR	550.00
SV-CR, straight sides	40.00	Tumbler	
SV-FR, knob stem, barrel		DV-CR	95.00
shape	55.00	SV-FR, ftd	90.00
* SV-FR, plain stem, rayed		* SV-FR, cut bellflowers	250.00
base, barrel shape	30.00	Whiskey, 3½", SV-FR	150.00
Hat, SV-FR, made from tum-		Wine	
bler mold, rare	350.00	DV-FR, cut bellflowers,	
Honey Dish, SV-FR, 3"	35.00	barrel shape	250.00
Lamp, whale oil, SV-FR,		SV-FR, knob stem, rayed	
brass stem, marble base	175.00	base, barrel shape	90.00
Mug, SV-FR	250.00	SV-FR, plain stem, rayed	
Pitcher		base, straight sides	75.00
Milk, DV-FR	500.00		
Milk, DV, pint	175.00		
Milk, SV-CR, quart	175.00		
Water, DV-CR	350.00		
* Water, SV-FR	250.00		

BIRD AND STRAWBERRY (Bluebird)

Non-flint, c1890. Made by Beatty and Indiana Glass Co., Dunkirk, IN. Pieces occasionally highlighted by the coloring of birds blue, strawberries pink, and leaves green, plus the addition of gilding.

	Clear	Colors		Clear	Colors
Bowl			Cup	25.00	35.00
5"	25.00	45.00	Goblet	200.00	300.00
9½", ftd	50.00	85.00	Nappy	40.00	65.00
10½"	55.00	95.00	Pitcher, water	235.00	350.00
Butter, cov	100.00	175.00	Plate, 12"	125.00	175.00
Cake Stand	65.00	125.00	Punch Cup	25.00	35.00
Celery Vase	45.00	85.00	Relish	20.00	45.00
Compote			Spooner	50.00	120.00
Cov, hs	125.00	200.00	Sugar, cov	65.00	125.00
Open, ls, ruffled	65.00	125.00	Tumbler	45.00	75.00
Jelly, cov, hs	150.00	225.00	Wine	70.00	100.00
Creamer	55.00	135.00			

BLEEDING HEART

Non-flint, originally made by King & Son, Pittsburgh, PA, c1870, and by U. S. Glass Co., c1898. Also found in milk glass. Goblets are found in six variations. Note: A goblet with a tin lid, containing a condiment (mustard, jelly, or baking powder) was made. It is of inferior quality compared to the original goblet.

	Clear		Clear
Bowl		Dish, cov, 7″	55.00
7¼″, oval.	30.00	Egg Cup.	45.00
8″	35.00	Egg Rack, cov, 3 eggs.	350.00
9¼″, oval, cov	65.00	Goblet, knob stem.	35.00
Butter, cov	75.00	Honey Dish.	15.00
Cake Stand		Mug, 3¼″.	40.00
9″	60.00	Pickle, 8¾″ l, 5″ w	30.00
10″	85.00	Pitcher, water, ah	150.00
11″	90.00	Plate	75.00
Dessert slots	125.00	Platter, oval.	65.00
Compote		Relish, oval, 5½ x 3⅝″.	35.00
Cov, hs, 8″.	75.00	Salt, master, ftd.	60.00
Cov, hs, 9″.	95.00	Salt, oval, flat	20.00
Cov, ls, 7″	60.00	Sauce, flat	15.00
Cov, ls, 7½″.	60.00	Spooner.	25.00
Cov, ls, 8″	75.00	Sugar, cov	60.00
Open, ls, 8½″	30.00	Tumbler, ftd	80.00
Creamer		Wine	165.00
Applied Handle	60.00		
Molded Handle	30.00		

BLOCK AND FAN

Non-flint made by Richard and Hartley Glass Co., Tarentum, PA, late 1880s. Continued by U. S. Glass Co. after 1891.

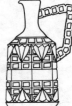

	Clear	Ruby Stained		Clear	Ruby Stained
Biscuit Jar, cov	65.00	150.00	Ice Tub.	45.00	50.00
Bowl, 4″, flat	15.00	—	Orange Bowl.	50.00	—
Butter, cov	50.00	85.00	Pickle Dish	20.00	—
Cake Stand			Pitcher		
9″	35.00	—	Milk.	35.00	—
10″	42.00	—	Water	48.00	125.00
Carafe	50.00	95.00	Plate		
Celery Tray.	30.00	—	6″	15.00	—
Celery Vase	35.00	75.00	10″	18.00	—
Compote, Open, hs,			Relish, rect	25.00	—
8″	40.00	165.00	Rose Bowl	25.00	—
Condiment Set, salt,			Salt & Pepper	30.00	—
pepper & cruet on			Sauce		
tray.	75.00	—	Flat, 5	8.00	—
Creamer			Ftd, 3¾″	12.00	25.00
Individual.	—	35.00	Spooner	25.00	—
Regular.	25.00	45.00	Sugar, cov	50.00	—
Large	30.00	100.00	Sugar Shaker	40.00	—
Small	35.00	75.00	Syrup	75.00	95.00
Cruet, os	35.00	—	Tray, ice cream, rect	75.00	—
Dish, large, rect. . . .	25.00	—	Tumbler	30.00	40.00
Finger Bowl	55.00	—	Waste Bowl.	30.00	—
Goblet	48.00	120.00	Wine	45.00	80.00

BROKEN COLUMN (Irish Column, Notched Rib, Rattan)

Made in Findlay, Ohio, c1891, by Columbia Glass Co., c1892, and later made by U. S. Glass Co. May also have been made at Portland, ME. Notches may be ruby stained. A cobalt blue cup is known. The square covered compote has been reproduced. Some items have been reproduced for the Metropolitan Museum of Art. Some items are reproduced by the Smithsonian Institution with a raised "SI" trademark.

	Clear	Ruby Stained		Clear	Ruby Stained
Banana Stand.....	110.00	—	Open, ls, 5" d, 6" h, flared......	65.00	135.00
Basket, applied handle, 12" h, 15" l ..	125.00	—	Creamer.........	42.50	125.00
Biscuit Jar	85.00	165.00	Cruet, os	85.00	150.00
Bowl			Decanter	85.00	—
4", berry	15.00	20.00	Finger Bowl	30.00	—
6", berry	20.00	45.00	* Goblet	50.00	100.00
8".............	35.00	—	Marmalade Jar	85.00	—
9"..............	40.00	—	Pickle Castor, sp frame	150.00	450.00
Bread Plate	60.00	125.00	Pitcher, water	90.00	230.00
Butter, cov	85.00	175.00	Plate		
Cake Stand			4".............	25.00	40.00
9".............	70.00	225.00	5"..............	35.00	—
10"............	80.00	245.00	7½"..........	40.00	95.00
Carafe, water	75.00	150.00	Punch Cup	15.00	—
Celery Tray, oval...	35.00	85.00	Relish..........	25.00	—
Celery Vase	50.00	135.00	Salt Shaker.......	45.00	65.00
Champagne	100.00	—	* Sauce, flat	15.00	20.00
Claret...........	75.00	—	* Spooner	35.00	85.00
Compote			Sugar, cov	70.00	135.00
Cov, hs, 5¼" d, 10¼" h......	90.00	200.00	Sugar Shaker	85.00	200.00
Cov, hs, 7" d, 12"h.........	85.00	—	Syrup...........	130.00	400.00
Cov, hs, 10".....	110.00	350.00	Tumbler	40.00	50.00
Open, hs, 7" d ...	—	150.00	Vegetable, cov	90.00	—
Open, hs, 8" d ...	75.00	175.00	Wine	80.00	125.00

BUCKLE

Flint and non-flint pattern. Sandwich Glass Co. in Massachusetts is attributed to the flint production. The non-flint production was made by Gillinder and Sons in Philadelphia, PA, in the late 1870s.

	Flint	Non-Flint		Flint	Non-Flint
Bowl			Egg Cup.........	38.00	28.00
8".............	60.00	50.00	Goblet	40.00	25.00
10"............	65.00	50.00	Pickle...........	40.00	15.00
Butter, cov	65.00	60.00	Pitcher, water, ah ..	500.00	85.00
Cake Stand, 9¾"...	—	30.00	Salt, flat, oval	30.00	15.00
Champagne	60.00	—	Salt, footed.......	20.00	18.00
Compote			Sauce, flat	10.00	8.00
Cov, hs, 6" d	95.00	40.00	Spooner.........	35.00	27.50
Open, hs, 8½"..	40.00	35.00	Sugar, cov	75.00	55.00
Open, ls	40.00	35.00	Tumbler	55.00	30.00
Creamer, ah	110.00	40.00	Wine	75.00	32.00

BUCKLE WITH STAR (Orient)

Non-flint made by Bryce, Walker and Co. in 1875, U. S. Glass Co. in 1891. Finials are shaped like Maltese crosses.

	Clear		Clear
Bowl		Relish.	15.00
6", cov	25.00	Salt, master, ftd.	20.00
7", oval	15.00	Sauce	
8", oval	15.00	Flat.	8.00
9", oval	15.00	Footed	10.00
10", oval	18.00	Spill holder	55.00
Butter, cov	40.00	Spooner	25.00
Cake Stand, 9"	35.00	Sugar	
Celery Vase	30.00	Cov.	45.00
Compote		Open	25.00
Cov, hs, 7".	60.00	Syrup	
Open, hs, 9½".	30.00	Applied handle, pewter or	
Creamer.	35.00	Brittania top, man's head	
Cruet	45.00	finial	80.00
Goblet	30.00	Molded handle, plain tin	
Mug.	60.00	top.	60.00
Mustard, cov.	75.00	Tumbler	55.00
Pickle.	15.00	Wine	35.00
Pitcher, water, applied			
handle.	70.00		

BULL'S EYE

Flint made by the New England Glass Co. in the 1850s. Also found in colors and milk glass, which doubles the price.

	Clear		Clear
Bitters Bottle	80.00	Lamp	100.00
Butter, cov	150.00	Mug, 3½", ah	110.00
Carafe	45.00	Pitcher, water	285.00
Castor Bottle.	35.00	Relish, oval.	25.00
Celery Vase	85.00	Salt	
Champagne	95.00	Individual.	40.00
Cologne Bottle	85.00	Master, ftd	100.00
Cordial	75.00	Spill holder	85.00
Creamer, ah	125.00	Spooner	40.00
Cruet, os	125.00	Sugar, cov	125.00
Decanter, qt, bar lip	120.00	Tumbler	85.00
Egg Cup		Water Bottle, tumble up	125.00
Cov.	165.00	Whiskey	70.00
Open	48.00	Wine	50.00
Goblet	65.00		

BULL'S EYE AND FAN (Daisies in Oval Panels)

Made by U.S. Glass, c1910. Also made in blue; prices same as emerald green.

	Amethyst Stain	Clear	Emerald Green	Pink Stain	Sapphire Blue Stain
Bowl					
5", pinched ends	—	—	18.00	—	—
8", berry	—	15.00	20.00	—	30.00
Butter, cov	—	45.00	65.00	—	—
Cake Stand	—	25.00	—	—	—
Creamer					
Individual.	—	10.00	—	—	—
Regular.	—	25.00	30.00	—	35.00
Custard Cup	—	10.00	—	—	—
Goblet	25.00	22.50	45.00	25.00	45.00
Lemonade Mug, 5"	—	20.00	—	—	—
Pitcher					
Lemonade, ftd . . .	—	55.00	—	—	—
Water, tankard . . .	55.00	40.00	100.00	50.00	100.00
Relish.	20.00	15.00	35.00	20.00	35.00
Sauce	25.00	10.00	20.00	25.00	30.00
Spooner	25.00	21.50	45.00	25.00	45.00
Sugar, cov	40.00	35.00	60.00	30.00	35.00
Toothpick	—	35.00	40.00	65.00	—
Tumbler	55.00	15.00	45.00	40.00	35.00
Wine	22.00	20.00	40.00	40.00	25.00

BUTTON ARCHES

Non-flint, made by Duncan and Miller Glass Co. in 1885. Pieces have frosted band. Some pieces, known as "Koral," usually souvenir type, are also seen in clambroth, trimmed in gold. The toothpick holder comes in both a smooth scallop and beaded scallop variety. They have the same value. In the early 1970s souvenir ruby stained pieces, including a goblet and table set, were reproduced. Scarce in other colors.

	Clambroth	Clear	Ruby Stained
Bowl, 8"	—	20.00	50.00
Butter, cov	—	48.00	100.00
Cake Stand, 9"	—	35.00	180.00
Compote, jelly.	—	48.00	50.00
Creamer.	25.00	20.00	45.00
Cruet, os	—	55.00	175.00
* Goblet	40.00	25.00	40.00
Mug	30.00	25.00	30.00
Mustard, cov, underplate	—	—	100.00
Pitcher			
Milk.	—	35.00	100.00
Water, tankard . . .	—	75.00	125.00
Plate, 7"	—	10.00	25.00
Punch Cup	—	15.00	25.00
Salt, ind	—	15.00	—
Salt Shaker, three types.	—	15.00	30.00
Sauce, flat	—	8.00	22.00

	Clambroth	Clear	Ruby Stained
Spooner	—	25.00	40.00
Sugar, cov	—	35.00	75.00
Syrup	—	65.00	175.00
Toothpick	30.00	20.00	35.00
Tumbler	20.00	24.00	35.00
Wine	25.00	15.00	35.00

CABBAGE ROSE

Non-flint made by Central Glass Co, Wheeling, WV, c1870. Reproduced in colors.

	Clear		Clear
Basket, handled, 12″	125.00	Cov, ls, 7½″	100.00
Bitters Bottle, 6½″ h	125.00	Cov, ls, 8½″	110.00
Bowl, Oval		Open, hs, 7½″	75.00
7½″	32.50	Open, hs, 9½″	100.00
8½″	38.00	Creamer, applied handle	55.00
9½″	40.00	Egg Cup	45.00
Bowl, Round		* Goblet	42.50
6″	25.00	Mug	60.00
7½″, cov	65.00	Pitcher	
7½″, open	35.00	Milk	150.00
Butter, cov	60.00	Water	125.00
Cake Stand		Relish, 8½″ l, 5″ w, rose-filled	
11″	40.00	horn of plenty center	38.00
12½″	50.00	Salt, master, ftd	25.00
Celery Vase	48.00	Sauces, six sizes	10–20.00
Champagne	50.00	Spooner	25.00
Compote		Sugar, cov	55.00
Cov, hs, 7½″	110.00	Tumbler	40.00
Cov, hs, 8½″	120.00	Wine	40.00
Cov, ls, 6″	95.00		

CABLE

Flint, c1850. Made by Boston and Sandwich Glass Co. to commemorate the laying of Atlantic Cable. Also found with amber stained panels and in opaque colors (rare).

	Clear		Clear
Bowl		Creamer	200.00
8″, ftd	45.00	Decanter, qt, ground stopper	295.00
9″	70.00	Egg Cup	
Butter, cov	100.00	Cov	225.00
Cake Stand, 9″	100.00	Open	60.00
Celery Vase	70.00	Goblet	70.00
Champagne	250.00	Honey Dish	15.00
Compote, open		Lamp, 8¾″	
hs, 5½″	65.00	Glass Base	135.00
ls, 7″	50.00	Marble Base	100.00
ls, 9″	55.00	Pitcher, water, rare	500.00
ls, 11″	75.00	Plate, 6″	75.00

	Clear		Clear
Salt, ind, flat	35.00	Syrup	225.00
Sauce, flat	15.00	Tumbler, ftd	200.00
Spooner	40.00	Wine	175.00
Sugar, cov	120.00		

CALIFORNIA (Beaded Grape)

Non-flint made by U. S. Glass Co., Pittsburgh, PA, c1890. Also with gold trim. Many pieces reproduced.

	Clear	Emerald Green		Clear	Emerald Green
Bowl			Cruet, os	65.00	125.00
5½", sq	17.50	20.00	* Goblet	35.00	50.00
5½ x 8"	—	30.00	Olive, handle	20.00	35.00
6" sq	—	25.00	Pickle	20.00	30.00
7½", sq	25.00	35.00	Pitcher		
8", round	28.00	35.00	Milk	75.00	—
Bread Plate	25.00	45.00	Water	85.00	120.00
Butter, cov	65.00	85.00	* Plate, 8¼", sq	28.00	40.00
Cake Stand, 9"	65.00	85.00	Salt & Pepper	45.00	65.00
Celery Tray	30.00	45.00	* Sauce, 4"	15.00	18.00
Celery Vase	40.00	60.00	Spooner	35.00	45.00
Compote			Sugar, cov	45.00	55.00
Cov, hs, 6½"	65.00	95.00	Sugar Shaker	75.00	85.00
Open, hs, 5", sq	55.00	75.00	Toothpick	40.00	65.00
Open, hs, 7"	45.00	80.00	* Tumbler	32.50	45.00
Open, hs, jelly	55.00	75.00	* Wine	35.00	65.00
Creamer	40.00	50.00			

CANADIAN

Non-flint, made by Burlington Glass Works, Hamilton, Ontario, Canada, c1870.

	Clear		Clear
Bowl, 7" d, 4½" h, ftd	65.00	Goblet	45.00
Bread Plate, 10"	45.00	Mug, small	45.00
Butter, cov	85.00	Pitcher	
Cake Stand, 9¼"	85.00	Milk	90.00
Celery Vase	65.00	Water	125.00
Compote		Plate, 6", handles	32.50
Cov, hs, 6"	90.00	Sauce	
Cov, hs, 7"	100.00	Flat	15.00
Cov, hs, 8"	110.00	Footed	20.00
Cov, ls, 6"	50.00	Spooner	45.00
Open, ls, 7"	35.00	Sugar, cov	90.00
Creamer	65.00	Wine	45.00

CAPE COD

Non-flint, attributed to Boston and Sandwich Glass Co., c1870.

	Clear		Clear
Bowl, 6", handled	30.00	Marmalade Jar, cov	85.00
Bread Plate	45.00	Pitcher	
Butter, cov	50.00	Milk	65.00
Celery Vase	45.00	Water	75.00
Compote		Plate	
Cov, hs, 6" d	50.00	5", handles	30.00
Cov, hs, 8"	100.00	10"	45.00
Cov, hs, 12"	175.00	Platter, open handles	45.00
Cov, ls, 6"	50.00	Sauce, ftd	12.50
Open, hs, 7"	50.00	Spooner	30.00
Creamer	35.00	Sugar, cov	35.00
Decanter	160.00	Wine	35.00
Goblet	45.00		

CARDINAL

Non-flint, c1875, attributed to Ohio Flint Glass Co., Lancaster, OH. There were two butter dishes made, one in the regular pattern and one with three birds in the base—labeled in script Red Bird (cardinal), Pewit, and Titmouse. The latter is less common. Goblet and creamer reproduced.

	Clear		Clear
Butter, cov		Pitcher, water	150.00
Regular	65.00	Sauce	
Three birds in base	100.00	Flat, 4"	10.00
Cake Stand	75.00	Footed, 4½" or 5½"	15.00
* Creamer	40.00	Spooner	38.00
* Goblet	30.00	Sugar, cov	60.00
Honey Dish, 3½"			
Cov	45.00		
Open	20.00		

CATHEDRAL (Orion)

Non-flint pattern made by Bryce Bros., Pittsburgh, PA., in the 1880s and by U. S. Glass Co. in 1891. Also found in ruby stained, add 50% to clear prices.

	Amber	Amethyst	Blue	Clear	Vaseline
Bowl, berry, 8"	48.00	60.00	50.00	25.00	42.50
Butter, cov	60.00	110.00	62.00	45.00	60.00
Cake Stand	50.00	75.00	60.00	40.00	68.00
Celery Vase	35.00	60.00	40.00	30.00	38.00
Compote					
Cov, hs, 8"	80.00	125.00	100.00	70.00	90.00
Open, hs, 9½"	50.00	85.00	65.00	55.00	—
Open, ls, 7"	45.00	80.00	35.00	25.00	48.00
Open, jelly	—	—	—	25.00	—
Creamer					
Flat, sq	50.00	82.00	—	35.00	48.00
Tall	45.00	80.00	50.00	30.00	45.00

	Amber	Amethyst	Blue	Clear	Vaseline
Cruet, os	80.00	—	—	45.00	—
Goblet	48.00	70.00	50.00	40.00	60.00
Lamp, 12¾" h	—	—	185.00	—	—
Pitcher, water	75.00	110.00	75.00	60.00	100.00
Relish, fish shape . .	40.00	50.00	50.00	—	45.00
Salt, boat shape . . .	20.00	30.00	24.00	15.00	24.00
Sauce					
Flat	16.00	30.00	20.00	12.00	16.00
Footed	18.00	35.00	22.00	15.00	20.00
Spooner	40.00	65.00	50.00	35.00	45.00
Sugar, cov	70.00	100.00	60.00	50.00	60.00
Tumbler	32.50	40.00	35.00	25.00	40.00
Wine	40.00	60.00	55.00	28.00	50.00

CHAIN WITH STAR

Non-flint, made by Portland Glass Co, Portland, ME, and U. S. Glass Co., c1890.

	Clear		Clear
Bread Plate, 11", handles . .	30.00	Pickle, oval	12.50
Butter, cov	35.00	Pitcher, water	55.00
Cake Stand		Plate, 7"	25.00
8¾"	30.00	Relish	10.00
10½"	35.00	Salt Shaker	25.00
Celery Vase	25.00	Sauce flat	10.00
Compote		Spooner	24.00
Cov, hs	50.00	Sugar, cov	35.00
Open, hs	30.00	Syrup	45.00
Creamer	25.00	Wine	25.00
Goblet	25.00		

CHANDELIER (Crown Jewel)

Non-flint, O'Hara Glass Co., Pittsburgh, PA, c1880, continued by U. S. Glass Co. Also attributed to Canadian manufacturer. Sauce bowls made in amber, $35.00.

	Etched	Plain		Etched	Plain
Banana Stand	—	100.00	Pitcher, water	125.00	115.00
Bowl, 8" d, 3¼" h . .	35.00	37.50	Salt, master	—	30.00
Butter, cov	85.00	65.00	Salt & Pepper	75.00	65.00
Cake Stand, 10" . . .	85.00	65.00	Sauce, flat	—	15.00
Celery Vase	40.00	40.00	Sponge Dish	—	30.00
Compote			Spooner	30.00	35.00
Cov, hs	80.00	75.00	Sugar, cov	75.00	85.00
Open, hs, 9½" . . .	70.00	68.00	Sugar Shaker	125.00	110.00
Creamer	60.00	45.00	Tray, water	70.00	50.00
Finger Bowl	40.00	30.00	Tumbler	45.00	35.00
Goblet	60.00	65.00	Violet Bowl	—	40.00
Inkwell, dated hard					
rubber top	—	85.00			

COLORADO (Lacy Medallion)

Non-flint States pattern made by U. S. Glass Co. in 1898. Made in amethyst stained, ruby stained, and opaque white with enamel floral trim, all of which are scarce. Some pieces found with ornate silver frames or feet. Purists consider these two are separate patterns, with the Lacy Medallion restricted to souvenir pieces. Reproductions have been made.

	Blue	Clear	Green
Banana Stand	45.00	25.00	40.00
Bowl			
6″	35.00	25.00	30.00
7½″, ftd	40.00	25.00	35.00
8½″, ftd	65.00	45.00	60.00
Butter, cov	200.00	60.00	125.00
Cake Stand	70.00	55.00	65.00
Celery Vase	65.00	35.00	75.00
Compote			
Open, ls, 6″	45.00	20.00	42.00
Open, ls, 9¼″ . . .	95.00	35.00	65.00
Creamer			
Individual.	45.00	30.00	40.00
Regular	95.00	45.00	70.00
Mug	40.00	20.00	30.00
Nappy	40.00	20.00	35.00
Pitcher			
Milk.	145.00	—	100.00
Water	375.00	95.00	185.00
Plate			
6″	50.00	18.00	45.00
8″	65.00	20.00	60.00
Punch Cup	30.00	18.00	25.00
Salt Shaker.	65.00	30.00	40.00
Sauce, ruffled	30.00	15.00	25.00
Sherbet	50.00	25.00	45.00
Spooner	65.00	40.00	60.00
Sugar			
Cov, regular.	75.00	60.00	70.00
Open, individual. .	35.00	24.00	30.00
Toothpick	60.00	30.00	45.00
Tray, Calling Card . .	45.00	25.00	35.00
Tumbler	35.00	18.00	30.00
Vase, 12″	85.00	35.00	60.00
Violet Bowl	60.00	—	—
Wine	—	25.00	40.00

CORDOVA

Non-flint made by the O'Hara Glass Co., Pittsburgh, Pa. It was exhibited for the first time at the Pittsburgh Glass Show, December 16, 1890. Toothpick has been found in ruby stained, valued at $35.00.

	Clear	Emerald Green		Clear	Emerald Green
Bowl, Berry, cov . . .	30.00	—	Cologne Bottle	20.00	—
Butter, cov, handled	50.00	—	Compote		
Cake Stand	45.00	—	Cov, hs	40.00	—
Celery Vase	45.00	—	Open, hs	35.00	—

	Clear	Emerald Green		Clear	Emerald Green
Creamer	35.00	45.00	Punch Cup	15.00	30.00
Finger Bowl	16.00	—	Salt Shaker	20.00	—
Inkwell, metal lid	80.00	—	Spooner	35.00	45.00
Mug, handled	17.50	30.00	Sugar, cov	40.00	80.00
Nappy, handled, 6"d	12.00	—	Syrup	125.00	40.00
Pitcher			Toothpick	15.00	20.00
Milk	30.00	—	Tumbler	18.00	—
Water	48.00	—	Vase	12.00	—
Punch Bowl	87.50	—			

CRYSTAL WEDDING

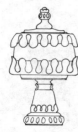

Non-flint made by Adams Glass Co., Pittsburgh, PA, in the late 1880s and U. S. Glass Co. in 1891. Also found in frosted, amber stained, and cobalt blue (rare). Heavily reproduced in clear, ruby stained, and milk with enamel trim.

	Clear	Ruby Stained		Clear	Ruby Stained
Banana Stand	95.00	—	Pitcher		
Bowl			Milk, round	110.00	125.00
4½", ind berry	15.00	—	Milk, sq	125.00	200.00
6", sq, cov	65.00	75.00	Water, round	110.00	210.00
7", sq, cov	75.00	85.00	Water, sq	165.00	225.00
8", sq, master			Plate, 10"	25.00	40.00
berry	50.00	85.00	Relish	20.00	40.00
8", sq, cov	60.00	95.00	Salt		
Butter, cov	75.00	125.00	Individual	25.00	40.00
Cake Plate, sq	45.00	85.00	Master	35.00	65.00
Cake Stand, 10"	65.00	—	Salt Shaker	65.00	75.00
Celery Vase	45.00	75.00	Sauce	15.00	20.00
Compote			Spooner	30.00	60.00
Cov, hs, 7 x 13"	100.00	110.00	Sugar, cov	70.00	85.00
Open, hs, 7", sq	60.00	65.00	Syrup	150.00	200.00
Open, ls, 5", sq	50.00	55.00	Tumbler	35.00	45.00
Creamer	50.00	75.00	Vase		
Cruet	125.00	200.00	Footed, twisted	25.00	—
Goblet	55.00	85.00	Swung	25.00	—
Nappy, handle	25.00	—	Wine	45.00	70.00
Pickle	25.00	40.00			

CUPID AND VENUS

Non-flint made by Richards and Hartley Glass Co., Tarentum, PA, in the late 1870s. Also made in vaseline, rare.

	Amber	Clear		Amber	Clear
Bowl			Cake Stand	—	60.00
8", cov, ftd	—	35.00	Celery Vase	—	40.00
9", oval	—	32.00	Champagne	—	90.00
Bread Plate	75.00	40.00	Compote		
Butter, cov	—	55.00	Cov, hs, 8"	—	100.00
Cake Plate	—	45.00	Cov, ls, 7"	—	90.00

	Amber	Clear		Amber	Clear
Cov, ls, 9″	—	100.00	Pitcher		
Open, ls, 8½″,			Milk.	175.00	75.00
scalloped	135.00	35.00	Water	195.00	65.00
Open, hs, 9¼″ . . .	—	45.00	Plate, 10″, round . . .	75.00	40.00
Cordial, 3½″	—	85.00	Sauce		
Creamer.	—	36.50	Flat.	—	10.00
Cruet, os	—	135.00	Footed, 3½″, 4″		
Goblet	—	75.00	and 4½″.	—	15.00
Marmalade Jar, cov	—	85.00	Spooner	—	35.00
Mug			Sugar, cov	—	65.00
Miniature.	—	40.00	Wine, 3¾″.	—	85.00
Medium, 2½″. . . .	—	35.00			
Large, 3½″	—	40.00			

CURRIER AND IVES

Non-flint made by Bellaire Glass Co. in Findlay, OH, in 1890. Known to have been made in colors, but rarely found. A decanter is known in ruby stained.

	Clear		Clear
Bowl, oval, 10″, canoe		Plate, 10″	20.00
shaped	30.00	Relish.	18.00
Butter, cov	50.00	Salt Shaker.	30.00
Cake Stand, 10″	75.00	Sauce, oval	12.00
Compote		Spooner	30.00
Cov, hs, 7½″	95.00	Sugar, cov	45.00
Open, hs, 7½″, scalloped	50.00	Syrup.	75.00
Creamer.	30.00	Tray	
Cup and saucer	30.00	Water, Balky Mule	65.00
Decanter	35.00	Wine, Balky Mule.	50.00
Dish, oval, boat shaped, 8″	27.50	Tumbler	45.00
Goblet, knob stem.	30.00	Water Bottle, 12″ h, os.	55.00
Lamp, 9½″, hs	75.00	Wine, 3¼″.	18.00
Pitcher			
Milk.	65.00		
Water	70.00		

DAHLIA

Non-flint, made by Portland Glass Co, Portland, ME, c1865, and Canton Glass Co., c1880. Also attributed to a Canadian manufacturer.

	Amber	Apple Green	Blue	Clear	Vaseline
Bowl.	30.00	25.00	25.00	18.00	30.00
Bread Plate	55.00	50.00	60.00	45.00	55.00
Butter, cov	80.00	70.00	85.00	40.00	80.00
Cake Plate	60.00	45.00	60.00	24.00	60.00
Cake Stand, 9″	72.50	50.00	50.00	25.00	72.50
Champagne	65.00	85.00	75.00	55.00	75.00
Compote					
Cov, hs, 7″.	90.00	85.00	85.00	55.00	80.00
Open, hs, 8″	60.00	45.00	45.00	30.00	60.00

	Amber	Apple Green	Blue	Clear	Vaseline
Cordial	55.00	50.00	50.00	35.00	55.00
Creamer	40.00	35.00	35.00	25.00	40.00
Egg Cup					
Double	80.00	65.00	65.00	50.00	80.00
Single	55.00	40.00	40.00	25.00	55.00
Goblet	55.00	85.00	75.00	40.00	65.00
Mug					
Large	55.00	55.00	55.00	35.00	55.00
Small	50.00	45.00	40.00	30.00	50.00
Pickle	35.00	30.00	30.00	20.00	35.00
Pitcher					
Milk	70.00	55.00	55.00	45.00	70.00
Water	100.00	90.00	90.00	55.00	90.00
Plate					
7"	45.00	40.00	40.00	20.00	45.00
9", handles	35.00	45.00	50.00	18.00	50.00
Platter	50.00	45.00	45.00	30.00	50.00
Relish, 9½" l	20.00	20.00	20.00	15.00	25.00
Salt, ind, ftd	35.00	30.00	30.00	5.00	35.00
Sauce					
Flat	15.00	12.00	15.00	10.00	15.00
Footed	20.00	15.00	15.00	10.00	20.00
Spooner	50.00	45.00	50.00	35.00	50.00
Sugar, cov	75.00	60.00	60.00	40.00	75.00
Syrup	75.00	—	—	55.00	—
Wine	45.00	40.00	45.00	25.00	45.00

DAISY AND BUTTON

Non-flint pattern made in the 1870s by several companies in many different forms. In continuous production since inception. Also found in amberina, amber stain, and ruby stained.

	Amber	Apple Green	Blue	Clear	Vaseline
Bowl, triangular	40.00	45.00	45.00	25.00	65.00
Bread Plate, 13" . . .	35.00	60.00	35.00	20.00	40.00
Butter, cov					
Round	70.00	90.00	70.00	65.00	95.00
Square	110.00	115.00	110.00	100.00	120.00
Butter Pat	30.00	40.00	35.00	25.00	35.00
Canoe					
4"	12.00	24.00	15.00	10.00	24.00
8½"	30.00	35.00	30.00	25.00	35.00
12"	60.00	35.00	28.00	20.00	40.00
14"	30.00	40.00	35.00	25.00	40.00
Castor Set					
4 bottle, glass std	90.00	85.00	95.00	65.00	75.00
5 bottle, metal std	105.00	100.00	110.00	100.00	95.00
Celery Vase	48.00	55.00	40.00	30.00	55.00
Compote					
Cov, hs, 6"	35.00	50.00	45.00	25.00	50.00
Open, hs, 8"	75.00	65.00	60.00	40.00	65.00
Creamer	35.00	40.00	40.00	18.00	35.00
Cruet, os	100.00	80.00	75.00	45.00	80.00
Egg Cup	20.00	30.00	25.00	15.00	30.00

	Amber	Apple Green	Blue	Clear	Vaseline
Finger Bowl	30.00	50.00	35.00	30.00	42.00
Goblet	40.00	50.00	40.00	25.00	40.00
Hat, 2½″.	30.00	35.00	40.00	20.00	40.00
Ice Tub.	—	35.00	—	—	75.00
Inkwell	40.00	50.00	45.00	30.00	45.00
Parfait	25.00	35.00	30.00	20.00	35.00
Pickle Castor	125.00	90.00	150.00	75.00	150.00
Pitcher, water					
Bulbous, reed					
handle	125.00	95.00	90.00	75.00	90.00
Tankard	62.00	65.00	62.00	60.00	65.00
Plate					
5″, leaf shape . . .	20.00	24.00	16.00	12.00	25.00
6″, round	10.00	22.00	15.00	6.50	24.00
7″, square	24.00	35.00	25.00	15.00	35.00
Punch Bowl, stand	90.00	100.00	95.00	85.00	100.00
Salt & Pepper	30.00	40.00	30.00	20.00	35.00
Sauce, 4″	18.00	25.00	18.00	15.00	25.00
Slipper					
5″	45.00	48.00	50.00	45.00	50.00
11½″	40.00	50.00	30.00	35.00	50.00
Spooner	40.00	40.00	45.00	35.00	45.00
Sugar, cov	45.00	50.00	45.00	35.00	50.00
Syrup	45.00	50.00	45.00	30.00	45.00
Toothpick					
Round	40.00	55.00	25.00	40.00	45.00
Urn	25.00	30.00	25.00	15.00	30.00
Tray	65.00	65.00	60.00	35.00	60.00
Tumbler	18.00	30.00	35.00	15.00	25.00
Vase, wall pocket . .	125.00	—	—	—	—
Wine	15.00	25.00	20.00	10.00	45.00

DAISY AND BUTTON WITH V ORNAMENT (Van Dyke)

Made by A. J. Beatty & Co., 1886–1887.

	Amber	Blue	Clear	Vaseline
Bowl				
9″	30.00	40.00	25.00	35.00
10″	30.00	40.00	25.00	35.00
Butter, cov	75.00	95.00	50.00	85.00
Celery Vase	50.00	55.00	30.00	55.00
Creamer	30.00	50.00	30.00	50.00
Finger Bowl	28.50	45.00	22.50	55.00
Goblet	35.00	45.00	25.00	50.00
Mug	20.00	30.00	20.00	35.00
Pickle Castor	120.00	120.00	60.00	100.00
Pitcher, water	65.00	90.00	40.00	60.00
Punch Cup	12.00	20.00	12.50	25.00
Sauce, flat	20.00	20.00	12.00	30.00
Spooner	40.00	38.50	35.00	45.00
Sugar, cov	50.00	75.00	45.00	65.00
Toothpick	32.50	40.00	28.50	35.00
Tray, water	55.00	65.00	20.00	55.00
Tumbler	25.00	28.00	15.00	35.00

DAKOTA (Baby Thumbprint, Thumbprint Band)

Non-flint made by Ripley and Co., Pittsburgh, PA, in the late 1880s and early 1890s. Later reissued by U. S. Glass Co. as one of the States patterns. Prices listed are for etched fern and berry pattern; also found with fern and no berry, and oak leaf etching, and scarcer grape etching. Other etchings known include fish, swan, peacock, bird and insect, bird and flowers, ivy and berry, stag, spider and insect in web, buzzard on dead tree, and crane catching fish. Sometimes ruby stained with or without souvenir markings. There is a four piece table set available in a "hotel" variant, prices are about 20% more than the regular type.

	Clear Etched	Clear Plain	Ruby Stained
Basket, 10 x 2"	250.00	225.00	275.00
Bottle, 5½"	45.00	35.00	—
Bowl, berry	45.00	30.00	—
Butter, cov	65.00	40.00	125.00
Cake Cover, 8"	300.00	200.00	—
Cake Stand			
9½"	58.00	35.00	—
10½"	65.00	45.00	—
Celery Tray	35.00	25.00	—
Celery Vase	40.00	30.00	—
Compote			
Cov, hs, 5"	60.00	—	—
Cov, 6", jelly	65.00	50.00	—
Open, hs, 7"	55.00	40.00	—
Condiment Tray . . .	—	75.00	—
Creamer	55.00	30.00	60.00
Cruet	90.00	55.00	135.00
Goblet	35.00	25.00	75.00
Pitcher			
Milk	100.00	80.00	200.00
Tankard	125.00	95.00	225.00
Water	95.00	75.00	190.00
Plate, 10"	85.00	—	—
Salt Shaker	65.00	50.00	125.00
Sauce			
Flat	20.00	10.00	—
Footed	25.00	15.00	—
Spooner	30.00	25.00	65.00
Sugar, cov	65.00	55.00	85.00
Tray, water	100.00	75.00	—
Tumbler	35.00	30.00	55.00
Waste Bowl	75.00	45.00	—
Wine	30.00	20.00	55.00

DEER AND PINE TREE (Deer and Doe)

Non-flint pattern, made by Belmont Glass Co., and McKee Glass Co. 1883. Souvenir mugs with gilt found in clear and olive green. Also made in canary (vaseline). The goblet has been reproduced.

	Amber	Apple Green	Blue	Clear
Bread Plate	100.00	125.00	125.00	75.00
Butter, cov	125.00	425.00	125.00	95.00
Cake Stand	—	—	—	75.00

	Amber	Apple Green	Blue	Clear
Celery Vase	—	—	—	75.00
Compote				
Cov, hs, 8″, sq . . .	—	—	—	100.00
Open, hs, 7″	—	—	—	45.00
Open, hs, 9″	—	—	—	55.00
Creamer.	95.00	85.00	90.00	65.00
Finger Bowl	—	—	—	55.00
Goblet	—	—	—	55.00
Marmalade Jar	—	—	—	90.00
Mug	40.00	45.00	50.00	40.00
Pickle.	—	—	—	24.00
Pitcher				
Milk.	—	—	—	90.00
Water	125.00	125.00	125.00	125.00
Platter, 8 x 13″	—	—	80.00	60.00
Sauce				
Flat.	—	—	—	18.50
Footed	—	—	—	25.00
Spooner	—	—	—	65.00
Sugar, cov	—	—	—	85.00
Tray, water	100.00	—	90.00	60.00

DELAWARE (Four Petal Flower)

Non-flint pattern made by U. S. Glass Co. c1899. Also found in amethyst (scarce), clear with rose trim, custard, and milk glass. Prices are for pieces with perfect gold trim.

	Clear	Green w/gold	Rose w/gold
Banana Bowl	40.00	55.00	65.00
Bowl			
8″	30.00	40.00	50.00
9″	25.00	60.00	75.00
Bottle, os	80.00	150.00	185.00
Bride's Basket, SP frame	—	115.00	165.00
Butter, cov	50.00	115.00	150.00
Claret Jug, tankard shape	110.00	195.00	200.00
Celery Vase, flat . . .	75.00	90.00	95.00
Creamer.	45.00	65.00	70.00
Cruet, os	90.00	200.00	250.00
Finger Bowl	25.00	50.00	75.00
Lamp Shade, electric	—	—	100.00
Pin Tray	30.00	55.00	95.00
Pitcher, water	50.00	150.00	125.00
Pomade Box, jeweled	—	250.00	350.00
Puff Box, bulbous, jeweled	—	200.00	315.00
Punch Cup	18.00	30.00	35.00
Sauce, 5½″, boat . .	15.00	35.00	30.00
Spooner	45.00	50.00	55.00
Sugar, cov	65.00	85.00	100.00
Toothpick	35.00	125.00	150.00

	Clear	Green w/gold	Rose w/gold
Tumbler	20.00	40.00	45.00
Vase			
6″............	—	45.00	70.00
8″............	—	55.00	75.00
9½″............	—	80.00	85.00

DIAMOND POINT

Flint, originally made by Boston and Sandwich Glass Co., in the 1830-1840 period, and by the New England Glass Co. Many other companies manufactured this pattern throughout the 19th century.

	Flint	Non-Flint		Flint	Non-Flint
Bowl			Egg Cup.........	40.00	20.00
7″, cov	60.00	20.00	Goblet	45.00	35.00
8″, cov	60.00	20.00	Honey	15.00	—
8″, open	45.00	15.00	Mustard, cov......	28.50	—
Butter, cov	95.00	50.00	Pitcher		
Cake Stand, 14″ ...	185.00	—	Pint..........	185.00	—
Candlesticks, pr ...	145.00	—	Quart	275.00	—
Celery Vase	75.00	30.00	Plate		
Champagne	85.00	—	6″............	30.00	—
Claret..........	90.00	—	8″............	50.00	—
Compote			Salt, master, cov ...	75.00	—
Cov, hs, 8″......	135.00	—	Sauce, flat	14.00	—
Open, hs 10½″, flared........	100.00	—	Spillholder	45.00	—
Open, hs, 11″, scalloped rim ..	110.00	—	Spooner.........	45.00	25.00
			Sugar, cov	65.00	—
Open, ls, 7½″ ...	50.00	40.00	Syrup...........	150.00	—
Cordial	165.00	—	Tumbler, bar......	65.00	35.00
Creamer, ah	115.00	—	Whiskey, ah	85.00	—
Decanter, qt, os. ...	165.00	—	Wine	75.00	30.00

DIAMOND THUMBPRINT

Flint, attributed to Boston and Sandwich Glass Co., and other factories from 1840 to 1850s. Compotes are being reproduced for Sandwich Glass Museum.

	Clear		Clear
Bitters Bottle, orig pewter pourer, applied lip, polished pontil...........	450.00	Champagne	285.00
		Compote	
Butter, cov	200.00	Cov, hs, 8″............	150.00
Celery Vase, scalloped top..	185.00	Open, ls, scalloped, 8″ ...	50.00
		Cordial	325.00

	Clear		Clear
Creamer	225.00	Sauce, flat	15.00
Decanter		* Spooner	85.00
Pint, ns	175.00	* Sugar, cov	150.00
Quart, os	225.00	Tray, rect, 11 × 7″	100.00
Finger Bowl	100.00	Tumbler, bar	125.00
* Goblet	350.00	Whiskey, ah	300.00
Honey Dish	25.00	* Wine	250.00
Pitcher, water	650.00		

ESTHER (Tooth and Claw)

Non-flint made by Riverside Glass Works, Wellsburg, WV, c1896. The green has gold trim. Also found in ruby stained and amber stained with enamel decoration.

	Clear	Green	Ruby Stained
Bowl, 8″	25.00	50.00	—
Butter, cov	65.00	100.00	150.00
Cake Stand, 10½″	60.00	80.00	—
Celery Vase	40.00	90.00	—
Compote, jelly, hs	30.00	75.00	—
Cracker Jar	—	—	200.00
Creamer	45.00	70.00	75.00
Cruet, os	45.00	245.00	—
Goblet	40.00	95.00	75.00
Jam Jar, cov	—	125.00	—
Pitcher, water	65.00	165.00	250.00
Plate, 10″	—	60.00	—
Relish	20.00	25.00	40.00
Salt & Pepper	50.00	100.00	—
Spooner	35.00	50.00	60.00
Sugar, cov	55.00	70.00	100.00
Syrup	—	200.00	—
Toothpick	48.00	85.00	—
Tumbler	25.00	48.50	55.00
Wine	35.00	—	—

EXCELSIOR

Flint made by several firms, including Sandwich and McKee, from 1850s-1860s. Quality and design vary. Prices are for high quality flint.

	Clear		Clear
Bar Bottle	85.00	Cordial	40.00
Bowl, 10″, open	125.00	Creamer	85.00
Bitters bottle	95.00	Egg Cup	
Butter, cov	100.00	Double	55.00
Candlestick	125.00	Single	40.00
Celery Vase, scalloped top	85.00	Goblet, Maltese Cross	50.00
Champagne	60.00	Lamp, hand	95.00
Claret	45.00	Mug	30.00
Compote		Pickle Jar, cov	45.00
Cov, ls	125.00	Pitcher, water	350.00
Open, hs	85.00	Salt, master	30.00

	Clear			Clear
Spillholder	75.00	Tumbler, bar		50.00
Spooner	60.00	Whiskey, Maltese Cross		65.00
Sugar, cov	90.00	Wine		45.00
Syrup	125.00			

FEATHER (Doric)

Non-flint made in Indiana in 1896 and by McKee Glass. Later the pattern was reissued with variations and quality differences. Also found in amber stain (rare).

	Clear	Emerald Green		Clear	Emerald Green
Banana Boat, ftd	75.00	175.00	Open, ls, 6″	20.00	—
Bowl, oval			Open, ls, 7″	30.00	—
8½″	25.00	—	Open, ls, 8″	35.00	—
9¼″	18.00	75.00	Cordial	125.00	—
Bowl, round			Creamer	40.00	85.00
4″	15.00	—	Cruet, os	45.00	250.00
4½″	15.00	—	Dishes, nest of 3: 7″,		
6″	20.00	—	8″, and 9″	40.00	—
7″	25.00	75.00	Goblet	55.00	150.00
8″	30.00	85.00	Honey Dish	15.00	—
Bowl, sq			Marmalade Jar	125.00	—
4½″	15.00	—	Pickle Castor	145.00	—
8″	30.00	—	Pitcher		
Butter, cov	55.00	150.00	Milk	50.00	165.00
Cake Plate	65.00	—	Water	75.00	250.00
Cake Stand			Plate, 10″	35.00	—
8″	40.00	125.00	Relish	18.00	—
9½″	50.00	125.00	Salt Shaker	35.00	70.00
11″	70.00	175.00	Sauce	12.00	—
Celery Vase	35.00	85.00	Spooner	25.00	60.00
Champagne	65.00	—	Sugar, cov	45.00	80.00
Compote			Syrup	125.00	300.00
Cov, hs, 8½″	125.00	250.00	Toothpick	85.00	165.00
Cov, ls, 4¼″,			Tumbler	45.00	85.00
jelly	100.00	150.00	Wine		
Cov, ls, 8¼″	150.00	—	Scalloped border	40.00	—
Open, ls, 4″	15.00	—	Straight border	25.00	—

FINECUT AND PANEL

Non-flint pattern made by many Pittsburgh factories in the 1880s. Reissued in the early 1890s by U. S. Glass Co. An aqua wine is known.

	Amber	Blue	Clear	Vaseline
Bowl				
7″	28.00	35.00	15.00	30.00
8″, oval	40.00	—	18.00	30.00
Bread Plate	50.00	45.00	30.00	—
Butter, cov	65.00	75.00	40.00	60.00
Cake Stand, 10″	50.00	75.00	30.00	50.00
Compote				
Cov, hs	125.00	135.00	75.00	130.00
Open, hs	65.00	65.00	35.00	60.00

	Amber	Blue	Clear	Vaseline
Creamer.........	35.00	50.00	25.00	40.00
Goblet	40.00	48.00	20.00	35.00
Pitcher				
Milk...........	65.00	—	—	50.00
Water	85.00	85.00	40.00	45.00
Plate, 6"........	12.00	20.00	10.00	15.00
Platter	30.00	50.00	25.00	30.00
Relish..........	20.00	25.00	15.00	20.00
Sauce, ftd........	15.00	25.00	8.00	15.00
Spooner.........	35.00	45.00	20.00	30.00
Sugar, cov	37.50	42.50	30.00	32.50
Tray, water	60.00	55.00	30.00	60.00
Tumbler	25.00	30.00	20.00	38.00
Waste Bowl.......	30.00	35.00	20.00	35.00
Wine	30.00	35.00	20.00	35.00

FLAMINGO HABITAT

Maker unknown, etched pattern.

	Clear		Clear
Bowl, 10", oval	35.00	Creamer...............	40.00
Celery Vase	45.00	Goblet	45.00
Champagne	45.00	Sauce, ftd.............	15.00
Cheese Dish, blown	110.00	Spooner	25.00
Compote		Sugar, cov	50.00
Cov, 4½"..............	75.00	Tumbler	30.00
Cov, 6½"..............	95.00	Wine	42.50
Open, 5", jelly	35.00		
Open, 6".............	40.00		

FLORIDA (Emerald Green Herringbone, Paneled Herringbone)

Non-flint made by U. S. Glass Co., late 1880s-1890s. One of States patterns. Reproduced in green and other colors.

	Clear	Emerald Green		Clear	Emerald Green
Berry Set	75.00	110.00	Pitcher, water	50.00	75.00
Bowl, 7¾"........	10.00	15.00	Plate		
Butter, cov	50.00	85.00	7½"...........	12.00	18.00
Cake Stand			9¼"...........	15.00	25.00
Large	60.00	75.00	Relish		
Small	30.00	40.00	6", sq	10.00	15.00
Celery Vase	30.00	35.00	8½", sq	15.00	22.00
Compote, open, hs,			Salt Shaker.......	25.00	50.00
6½", sq........	—	40.00	Sauce	5.00	7.50
Creamer.........	30.00	45.00	Spooner.........	20.00	35.00
Cruet, os	40.00	110.00	Sugar, cov	32.00	50.00
*Goblet	25.00	40.00	Syrup...........	60.00	175.00
Mustard Pot, attach-			Table set	125.00	185.00
ed underplate, cov	25.00	45.00	Tumbler	20.00	30.00
Nappy	15.00	25.00	Wine	25.00	50.00

GALLOWAY

Non-flint made by U. S. Glass Co., 1904. Clear glass with and without gold trim; also known with rose stain and ruby stain.

	Clear w/gold	Rose Stained		Clear w/gold	Rose Stained
Basket, no gold....	75.00	—	Pitcher		
Bowl			Milk..........	60.00	—
6½"..........	25.00	—	Tankard	75.00	—
8½", oval......	25.00	—	Water, ice lip....	65.00	175.00
8½", round	25.00	—	Plate, 8", round....	40.00	65.00
9¾"..........	35.00	50.00	Punch Bowl	160.00	—
11" d, 3" h......	45.00		Punch Bowl Plate,		
Butter, cov	65.00	125.00	20"............	80.00	—
Cake Stand	65.00	90.00	Punch Cup	10.00	15.00
Carafe, water	55.00	85.00	Relish...........	20.00	30.00
Celery Vase	35.00	75.00	Rose Bowl	25.00	—
Champagne	65.00	—	Salt Dip	25.00	—
Compote			Salt & Pepper, pr...	35.00	—
Open, hs, 4¼"...	35.00	—	Sauce		
Open, hs, 10",			Flat...........	10.00	—
scalloped	85.00	—	Footed	12.00	—
Creamer.........	30.00	50.00	Sherbet	25.00	—
Cruet	45.00	—	Spooner.........	30.00	80.00
Egg Cup.........	35.00	—	Sugar, cov	55.00	75.00
Finger Bowl	40.00	—	Sugar Shaker	40.00	—
Goblet	80.00	—	Syrup..........	65.00	135.00
Lemonade	35.00	—	Toothpick	30.00	55.00
Mug............	38.00	50.00	Tumbler	25.00	—
Nappy, tricorn	—	50.00	Vase, swung......	30.00	—
Olive, 6".........	20.00	30.00	Waste Bowl.......	38.00	—
Pickle Castor, sp			Water Bottle	40.00	—
holder and lid ...	65.00	—	Wine	45.00	—

GEORGIA (Peacock Feather)

Probably Richards and Hartley, but reissued by several glass companies, including U. S. Glass Co. in 1902 as part of their States series. Rare in blue. (Chamber lamp, pedestal base, $275.00.) No goblet known in pattern.

	Clear		Clear
Bon bon, ftd	25.00	Decanter	70.00
Bowl, 8"	25.00	Lamp	
Butter, cov	45.00	Chamber, pedestal......	85.00
Cake Stand, 10"	50.00	Hand, oil, 7"	80.00
Celery Tray, 11¾"	35.00	Mug..................	22.50
Compote		Nappy	28.00
Cov, hs, 8".	50.00	Pitcher, water	70.00
Open, hs, 7"	30.00	Plate, 5¼".............	15.00
Open, hs, 8"	42.50	Relish................	15.00
Open, ls, 10"	30.00	Salt Shaker...........	40.00
Open, jelly............	20.00	Sauce	6.00
Condiment Set, tray, oil cruet,		Spooner..............	35.00
salt and pepper	75.00	Sugar, cov	45.00
Creamer...............	35.00	Syrup, metal lid.........	65.00
Cruet, os	55.00	Tumbler	35.00

HAND (Pennsylvania #2)

Made by O'Hara Glass Co., Pittsburgh, Pennsylvania, c1880. Covered pieces have a hand holding bar finial, hence the name.

	Clear		Clear
Bowl		Goblet	45.00
9″	30.00	Marmalade Jar, cov	90.00
10″	40.00	Pickle	20.00
Butter, cov	85.00	Pitcher, water	75.00
Cake Stand	55.00	Sauce	
Celery Vase	48.00	Flat	12.00
Compote		Footed	15.00
Cov, hs, 7″	60.00	Spooner	30.00
Cov, hs, 8″	95.00	Sugar, cov	75.00
Open, hs, 7¾″	35.00	Syrup	125.00
Cordial, 3½″	85.00	Tumbler	85.00
Creamer	40.00	Wine	55.00

HEART WITH THUMBPRINT (Bull's Eye in Heart)

Non-flint, made by Tarentum Glass Co. 1898. Some emerald green pieces have gold trim. Made experimentally in custard, blue custard, opaque nile green and cobalt. Some pieces are found with ruby stain. (Creamer $175.00.)

	Clear	Emerald Green		Clear	Emerald Green
Banana Boat	75.00	—	Mustard, SP cov . . .	95.00	100.00
Barber Bottle	115.00	—	Nappy, triangular . . .	30.00	60.00
Bowl			Pitcher, water	200.00	—
7″ sq	35.00	—	Plate		
9½″ sq	35.00	—	6″	25.00	75.00
10″ scalloped	45.00	—	10″	35.00	—
Butter, cov	125.00	175.00	Powder Jar, SP cov	65.00	—
Cake Stand, 9″	150.00	—	Punch Cup	20.00	35.00
Carafe, water	100.00	—	Rose Bowl		
Card Tray	20.00	45.00	Large	60.00	—
Celery Vase	65.00	—	Small	30.00	—
Compote, open, hs			Salt & Pepper, pr . . .	95.00	—
7½″, scalloped . . .	150.00	—	Sauce, 5″	20.00	35.00
8½″	100.00	—	Spooner	50.00	—
Cordial, 3″ h	125.00	—	Sugar		
Creamer			Ind	28.00	35.00
Ind	30.00	45.00	Regular, cov	85.00	90.00
Regular	60.00	110.00	Syrup	95.00	—
Cruet	75.00	—	Tray, 8¼″ l, 4¼″ w . .	30.00	—
Finger Bowl	45.00	—	Tumbler	45.00	—
Goblet	58.00	125.00	Vase		
Hair Receiver, lid . . .	60.00	—	6″	35.00	65.00
Ice Bucket	60.00	—	10″	65.00	—
Lamp			Wine	45.00	—
Finger	65.00	115.00			
Oil, 8″	50.00	160.00			

HOLLY

Non-flint made by Boston and Sandwich Glass Co., late 1860s, early 1870s.

	Clear		Clear
Butter, cov	150.00	Salt	
Cake Stand, 11″	135.00	Flat, oval	65.00
Celery Vase	85.00	Ftd	60.00
Compote, cov, hs	165.00	Sauce, flat	20.00
Creamer, ah	125.00	Spooner	60.00
Egg Cup	65.00	Sugar, cov	125.00
Goblet	100.00	Tumbler	125.00
Pitcher, water, ah	225.00	Wine	125.00

HONEYCOMB

A popular pattern made in flint and non-flint glass by numerous firms, c1850–1900, resulting in many minor pattern variations. Rare in color.

	Flint	Non-Flint		Flint	Non-Flint
Ale Glass	50.00	25.00	Honey, cov	—	25.00
Barber Bottle	45.00	25.00	Lamp		
Bowl, cov, 7¼″ pat'd			All Glass	—	45.00
1869, acorn finial	100.00	45.00	Marble base	—	40.00
10″	—	40.00	Lemonade	40.00	20.00
Butter, cov	65.00	45.00	Mug, half pint	25.00	15.00
Cake Stand	55.00	35.00	Pitcher, water, ah	165.00	60.00
Castor Bottle	25.00	18.00	Plate, 6″	—	12.50
Celery Vase	45.00	20.00	Pomade Jar, cov	48.00	20.00
Champagne	50.00	—	Relish	30.00	—
Claret	35.00	—	Salt, master, cov,		
Compote, cov, hs			ftd	35.00	30.00
6½″ x 8½″ h	100.00	50.00	Salt & Pepper	—	40.00
9¼ x 11½″ h	110.00	65.00	Sauce	12.00	7.50
Compote, open, hs			Spillholder	24.00	—
7 x 5″ h	35.00	25.00	Spooner	65.00	35.00
7 x 7″ h	60.00	40.00	Sugar		
7½″, scalloped	42.00	—	Frosted rosebud		
8 x 6¼″ h	65.00	—	finial	—	50.00
11 x 8″ h	135.00	—	Regular	75.00	45.00
Compote, open, ls,			Tumbler		
7½″, scalloped	40.00	—	Bar	35.00	—
Cordial, 3½″	25.00	—	Flat	—	12.50
Creamer, ah	35.00	20.00	Footed	—	15.00
Decanter			Vase		
Pint	55.00	18.50	7½″	45.00	—
Quart, os	70.00	65.00	10½″	75.00	—
Egg Cup	20.00	15.00	Whiskey, handled	125.00	—
Finger Bowl	48.00	—	Wine	35.00	15.00
Goblet	25.00	15.00			

HORN OF PLENTY

A fine flint glass pattern reputed to have been first made by Boston and Sandwich Glass Co. in the 1850s. Later made in flint and non-flint by other firms. Rare in color.

	Clear Flint		Clear Flint
Bar Bottle, pewter spout, 8"	135.00	Egg Cup	40.00
Bowl, 8½"	145.00	* Goblet	75.00
Butter, cov		* Lamp	200.00
Conventional finial	125.00	Mug, small, applied handle	150.00
Shape of Acorn	130.00	Pepper Sauce Bottle, pewter	
Butter Pat	20.00	top	200.00
Cake Stand	350.00	Pitcher, water	600.00
Celery Vase	150.00	Plate, 6"	100.00
Champagne	145.00	Relish, 7" l, 5" w	45.00
Compote		Salt, master, oval, flat	75.00
Cov, hs, 6¼"	175.00	Sauce, 4½"	15.00
Cov, hs, 8¼" d, 5¾" h,		Spillholder	65.00
oval	350.00	Spooner	45.00
Open, hs, 7"	130.00	Sugar, cov	175.00
Open, hs, 8"	125.00	Tumbler	
Open, hs, 9¼"	200.00	Bar	85.00
Open, hs, 10½"	140.00	Water	75.00
Open, ls, 8"	55.00	Whiskey	
Open, ls, 9"	85.00	Applied handle	235.00
Cordial	150.00	Shot glass, 3"	100.00
Creamer, ah		Wine	125.00
5½"	225.00		
7"	175.00		
Decanter, os			
Pint	150.00		
Quart	165.00		

HORSESHOE (Good Luck, Prayer Rug)

Non-flint made by Adams & Co. and others in the 1880s.

	Clear		Clear
Bowl, cov, oval		Goblet	
7"	150.00	Knob Stem	40.00
8"	195.00	Plain Stem	38.00
Bread Plate, 14 x 10"		Marmalade Jar, cov	110.00
Double horseshoe handles	65.00	Pitcher	
Single horseshoe handles	40.00	Milk	110.00
Butter, cov	95.00	Water	85.00
Cake Plate	40.00	Plate	
Cake Stand		7"	45.00
9"	70.00	10"	55.00
10"	80.00	Relish, 5 x 7"	20.00
Celery Vase, knob stem	40.00	Salt	
Cheese, cov, woman		Ind, horseshoe shape	20.00
churning	275.00	Master, horseshoe shape	100.00
Compote		Sauce	
Cov, hs, 7", horseshoe		Flat	10.00
finial	95.00	Footed	15.00
Cov, hs, 8 x 12¼"	125.00	Spooner	35.00
Cov, hs, 11"	135.00	Sugar, cov	65.00
Creamer, 6½"	55.00	Vegetable Dish, oblong	35.00
Doughnut Stand	75.00	Waste Bowl	45.00
Finger Bowl	80.00	Wine	150.00

ILLINOIS

Non-flint. One of the States patterns made by U. S. Glass Co., c1897. Most forms are square. A few items are known in ruby stained, including a salt, $50.00, and a lidless straw holder with the stain on the inside, $95.00.

	Clear	Emerald Green		Clear	Emerald Green
Basket, ah, 11½"...	100.00	—	Salt		
Bowl, 8"	35.00	—	Ind	15.00	—
Butter, cov	60.00	—	Master	25.00	—
Candlesticks, pr ...	80.00	—	Salt and Pepper, pr	40.00	—
Celery Tray, 11" ...	40.00	—	Sauce	15.00	—
Cheese, cov	75.00	—	Spooner.......	35.00	—
Creamer			Straw Holder, cov ..	175.00	400.00
Ind	30.00	—	Sugar		
Regular........	40.00	—	Ind	30.00	—
Cruet	65.00	—	Regular, cov	55.00	—
Marmalade Jar	135.00	—	Sugar Shaker	65.00	—
Olive	18.00	—	Syrup, pewter top ..	95.00	—
Pitcher, milk, round,			Toothpick		
SP rim	175.00	—	Adv emb in base	45.00	—
Pitcher, water			Plain..........	30.00	—
Square	65.00	—	Tray, 12 x 8", turned		
Tankard, round,			up sides	50.00	—
SP rim........	75.00	135.00	Tumbler	30.00	40.00
Plate, 7", sq	25.00	—	Vase, 6", sq	35.00	45.00
Relish			Vase, 9½"........	—	125.00
7½" x 4"	18.00	—			
8½ x 3"........	18.00	—			

IOWA (Paneled Zipper)

Non-flint made by U. S. Glass Co. c1902. Part of the States pattern series. Available in clear glass with gold trim (add 20%) and ruby or cranberry stained. Also found in amber (goblet $65.00), green, canary, and blue. Add 50% to 100% for color and amber stained.

	Clear		Clear
Bowl, berry.............	12.00	Lamp	125.00
Bread Plate, motto	80.00	Olive	15.00
Butter, cov	40.00	Pitcher, water	50.00
Cake Stand	35.00	Punch Cup	15.00
Carafe	35.00	Salt Shaker, single	24.00
Compote, cov, 8".........	40.00	Sauce, 4½".............	6.50
Corn Liquor Jug, os.......	60.00	Spooner	30.00
Creamer...............	30.00	Sugar, cov	35.00
Cruet, os	30.00	Table Set, 4 pc	125.00
Cup	15.00	Toothpick	20.00
Decanter	40.00	Tumbler	25.00
Goblet	28.00	Wine	30.00

JACOB'S LADDER (Maltese)

Non-flint made by Portland Glass Co, Portland, ME, and Bryce Bros, Pittsburgh, PA, in 1876, and U. S. Glass Co in 1891. A few pieces found in amber, yellow, blue, pale blue, and pale green.

	Clear
Bowl	
6" x 8¾"	15.00
6¾" x 9¾"	20.00
7½" x 10¾"	20.00
9", berry, ornate SP holder, ftd	125.00
Butter, cov	65.00
Cake Stand	
8" or 9"	50.00
11" or 12"	60.00
Castor Bottle	18.00
Castor Set, 4 bottles	100.00
Celery Vase	45.00
Cologne Bottle, Maltese cross stopper, ftd	85.00
Compote	
Cov, hs, 6"	60.00
Cov, hs 7½"	60.00
Cov, hs, 9½"	125.00
Open, hs, 7½"	35.00
Open, hs, 8½", scalloped	30.00
Open, hs, 9½", scalloped	38.00
Open, hs, 10"	40.00

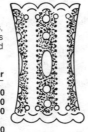

	Clear
Creamer	35.00
Cruet, os, ftd	85.00
Goblet	60.00
Honey, 3½"	10.00
Marmalade Jar	75.00
Mug	100.00
Pitcher, water	150.00
Plate, 6¼"	20.00
Relish, 9½ x 5½"	15.00
Salt, master, ftd	20.00
Sauce	
Flat, 4", or 5"	8.00
Footed, 4"	12.00
Spooner	35.00
Sugar, cov	60.00
Syrup	
Knight's Head finial	125.00
Plain top	100.00
Tumbler, bar	85.00
Wine	35.00

KANSAS (Jewel With Dewdrop)

Non-flint originally produced by Co-Operative Flint Glass Co., Beaver Falls, Pennsylvania. Later produced as part of the States pattern series by U. S. Glass Co. in 1901 and by Jenkins Glass Co, c1915–25. Also known with jewels stained in pink or gold. Mugs have been reproduced in vaseline, amber, and blue.

	Clear
Banana Stand	90.00
Bowl	
7", oval	35.00
8½"	45.00
Bread Plate, ODB	45.00
Butter, cov	65.00
Cake Plate	45.00
Cake Stand	
7⅝"	45.00
10"	85.00
Celery Vase	45.00
Compote	
Cov, hs, 8"	125.00
Open, hs, 6½", jelly	50.00
Open, ls, 6½"	45.00

	Clear
Creamer	40.00
Goblet	55.00
Mug, regular	45.00
Pitcher	
Milk	50.00
Water	60.00
Relish, 8½", oval	20.00
Salt Shaker	50.00
Sauce, flat, 4"	12.00
Sugar, cov	65.00
Syrup	125.00
Toothpick	65.00
Tumbler	45.00
Whiskey	15.00
Wine	65.00

KENTUCKY

Non-flint made by U. S. Glass Co., c1897, as part of the States pattern series. The goblet is found in ruby stained ($50.00). A footed, square sauce ($30.00) is known in cobalt blue with gold. A toothpick holder is also known in ruby stained ($150.00).

	Clear	Emerald Green		Clear	Emerald Green
Butter, cov	50.00	—	Plate, 7″, sq	15.00	—
Cake Stand, 9½″	40.00	—	Punch Cup	10.00	15.00
Creamer	25.00	—	Salt & Pepper, pr.	50.00	—
Cruet, os	45.00	—	Sauce, ftd, sq	8.00	12.00
Cup	10.00	20.00	Spooner	35.00	—
Goblet	20.00	50.00	Sugar, cov	30.00	—
Nappy	10.00	15.00	Toothpick, sq	35.00	85.00
Olive, handle	25.00	—	Tumbler	20.00	30.00
Pitcher, water	55.00	—	Wine	28.00	38.00

KING'S CROWN (Ruby Thumbprint; X.L.C.R.)

Known as Ruby Thumbprint when pieces are ruby stained. A non-flint pattern made by Adams and Co., Pittsburgh, Pennsylvania, in the 1890s and later. Made in clear and with the thumbprints stained amethyst, gold, green, and yellow, and in clear with etching and trimmed in gold. It became very popular after 1891 as ruby stained souvenir ware. Cobalt blue pieces reported as very rare. Approximately 87 pieces documented. NOTE: Pattern has been copiously reproduced for the gift-trade market. New pieces are easily distinguished: in the case of Ruby Thumbprint, the color is a very pale pinkish red; green and blue pieces have an off-color. Reproduced in milk glass. Available in amethyst stained in goblet ($30.00) and wine ($10.00) and in green stained in goblet ($25.00) and wine ($15.00). Add 30% for engraved pieces.

	Clear	Ruby Stained		Clear	Ruby Stained
Banana Stand, ftd	85.00	135.00	Honey, cov, sq	100.00	175.00
Bowl			Goblet	30.00	45.00
9¼″, pointed	35.00	90.00	Lamp, oil, 10″	135.00	—
10″, scalloped	45.00	95.00	Mustard, cov	35.00	75.00
Butter, cov	50.00	90.00	Pickle, lobed	18.00	40.00
Cake Stand			Pitcher		
9″	68.00	125.00	Milk, tankard	75.00	100.00
10″	75.00	125.00	Water, bulbous	95.00	225.00
Castor Bottle	45.00	70.00	Water, tankard	110.00	200.00
Castor Set, glass			Plate, 7″	20.00	45.00
stand, 4 bottles	175.00	325.00	Punch Bowl, ftd	275.00	300.00
Celery Vase	40.00	60.00	Punch Cup	15.00	30.00
Claret	35.00	50.00	Salt, master, sq	25.00	60.00
Compote			Salt, ind, oblong	16.00	30.00
Cov, hs, 8″	55.00	245.00	Salt & Pepper	40.00	70.00
Cov, ls, 12″	90.00	225.00	Sauce, 4″	15.00	20.00
Open, hs, 8¼″	75.00	95.00	Spooner	45.00	50.00
Open, ls, 5¼″	30.00	45.00	Sugar, cov	50.00	85.00
Cordial	45.00	—	Toothpick	20.00	35.00
Creamer, regular	50.00	65.00	Tumbler	20.00	35.00
Cup & Saucer	55.00	70.00	Wine	25.00	40.00
Custard Cup	15.00	25.00			

KING'S #500

Made by King Glass Co. of Pittsburgh, Pennsylvania in 1899. It was made in clear, frosted, and a rich, deep blue, known as Dewey Blue, both trimmed in gold.

Continued by U. S. Glass Co. in 1891 and made in a great number of pieces. A clear goblet with frosted stem ($50.00) is known. Also known in dark green and a ruby stained sugar is reported ($95.00).

	Clear w/gold	Dewey Blue w/gold		Clear w/gold	Dewey Blue w/gold
Bowl			Lamp		
7"	10.00	30.00	Hand	45.00	—
8"	12.00	35.00	Stand	65.00	—
9"	14.00	45.00	Pitcher, water	55.00	200.00
Butter, cov	65.00	125.00	Relish	20.00	30.00
Cake Stand	40.00	60.00	Rose Bowl	20.00	45.00
Celery Vase	20.00	—	Salt Shaker, single	15.00	40.00
Compote			Sauce	15.00	35.00
Covered	45.00	—	Spooner	30.00	70.00
Open	30.00	—	Sugar, cov	45.00	75.00
Creamer	30.00	50.00	Syrup	55.00	225.00
Cruet	45.00	175.00	Tumbler	25.00	35.00
Cup	15.00	15.00			
Decanter, locking top	100.00	—			

LILY OF THE VALLEY

Non-flint pattern made by Boston & Sandwich, Sandwich, Massachusetts, in the 1870s. Shards have also been found at Burlington Glass Works, Hamilton, Ontario. Lily of the Valley on Legs is a name frequently given to those pieces having three tall legs. Legged pieces include a covered butter, covered sugar, creamer and spooner. Add 25% for this type.

	Clear		Clear
Butter, cov	70.00	Pitcher	
Buttermilk Goblet	35.00	Milk	125.00
Cake Stand	65.00	Water	135.00
Celery Tray	40.00	Relish	15.00
Celery Vase	55.00	Salt, master	
Champagne	80.00	Cov	125.00
Compote		Open	50.00
Cov, hs, 8½"	85.00	Sauce, flat	12.00
Open, hs	50.00	Spooner	35.00
Creamer, ah	65.00	Sugar, cov	75.00
Cruet, os	110.00	Tumbler	
Egg Cup	40.00	Flat	50.00
Goblet	55.00	Footed	65.00
Honey	10.00	Vegetable Dish, oval	30.00
Nappy, 4"	20.00	Wine	100.00
Pickle, scoop shape	20.00		

LION

Made by Gillinder and Sons, Philadelphia, Pennsylvania, in 1876. Available in clear (20% less). Many reproductions.

	Frosted		Frosted
Bowl, oblong		Cordial	175.00
6½ x 4¼"	55.00	* Creamer	75.00
8 x 5"	50.00	Egg Cup, 3½" h	65.00
Bread Plate, 12"	90.00	* Goblet	70.00
Butter, cov		Marmalade Jar, rampant	
Lion's head finial	90.00	finial	85.00
Rampant finial	125.00	Pitcher	
Cake Stand	85.00	Milk	375.00
Celery Vase	85.00	Water	300.00
Champagne	175.00	Relish, lion handles	38.00
Cheese, cov, rampant lion		Salt, master, rect lid	250.00
finial	400.00	* Sauce, 4", ftd	25.00
Compote		* Spooner	75.00
Cov, hs, 7", rampant finial	150.00	Sugar, cov	
* Cov, hs, 9", rampant finial,		Lion head finial	90.00
oval, collared base	150.00	Rampant finial	110.00
Cov, 9", hs	185.00	Syrup, orig top	350.00
Open, ls, 8"	75.00	Wine	200.00

LOG CABIN

Non-flint made by Central Glass Co. Wheeling, West Virginia, c1875. Also available in color, but rare. Creamer, spooner, and covered sugar reproduced in clear and cobalt blue.

	Clear		Clear
Bowl, cov, 8 x 5¼ x 3⅝" . . .	400.00	Pitcher, water	300.00
Butter, cov	300.00	Sauce, flat	75.00
Compote, hs, 10½"	275.00	* Spooner	120.00
* Creamer	100.00	* Sugar, cov	275.00
Marmalade Jar, cov	275.00		

MAGNET AND GRAPE (Magnet and Grape with Stippled Leaf)

Flint first made by Boston and Sandwich Glass Co., c1860. Later non-flint versions have grape leaf in either clear or stippled. Reproduced by Metropolitan Museum, New York with frosted leaf.

	Flint Frosted Leaf	Non-Flint Stippled or Clear Leaf		Flint Frosted Leaf	Non-Flint Stippled or Clear Leaf
Bowl, cov, 8"	175.00	75.00	Compote		
Butter, cov	185.00	40.00	Cov, hs, 4½"	125.00	—
Celery Vase	150.00	25.00	Open, hs, 7½" . . .	110.00	65.00
Champagne	135.00	45.00	Cordial, 4"	125.00	—

	Flint Frosted Leaf	Non-Flint Stippled or Clear Leaf		Flint Frosted Leaf	Non-Flint Stippled or Clear Leaf
* Creamer	175.00	40.00	Relish, oval	35.00	15.00
Decanter, os			Salt, ftd	50.00	25.00
Pint	150.00	75.00	Sauce, 4"	20.00	7.50
Quart	200.00	85.00	Spill	65.00	—
Egg Cup	75.00	20.00	Spooner	95.00	30.00
* Goblet			* Sugar, cov	125.00	80.00
American Shield	300.00	—	Syrup	125.00	55.00
Low Stem	75.00	—	* Tumbler, water	110.00	30.00
Regular stem	70.00	30.00	Whiskey	140.00	25.00
Pitcher			* Wine	90.00	50.00
Milk, ah	—	75.00			
Water, ah	350.00	75.00			

MARDI GRAS (Duncan and Miller #42, Paneled English Hobnail with Prisms)

Made by Duncan and Miller Glass Co., c1898. Available in gold trim and ruby stained.

	Clear	Ruby Stained		Clear	Ruby Stained
Bowl, 8", berry	18.00	—	Plate, 6"	10.00	—
Butter, cov	65.00	145.00	Punch Bowl	200.00	—
Cake Stand, 10"	65.00	—	Punch Cup	10.00	—
Celery Tray, curled			Relish	12.50	—
edges	25.00	—	Sherry, flared or		
Champagne, saucer	32.00	—	straight	35.00	—
Claret	35.00	—	Spooner	25.00	—
Compote			Sugar, cov	35.00	65.00
Cov, hs	55.00	—	Syrup, metal lid	65.00	—
Open, jelly, 4½"	30.00	55.00	Toothpick	35.00	125.00
Cordial	35.00	—	Tumbler		
Creamer	35.00	60.00	Bar	25.00	—
Finger Bowl	25.00	—	Champagne	20.00	—
Goblet	35.00	—	Water	30.00	40.00
Lamp Shade	35.00	—	Wine	30.00	65.00
Pitcher					
Milk	50.00	—			
Water	75.00	200.00			

MARYLAND (Inverted Loop and Fan; Loop and Diamond)

Made originally by Bryce Brothers, Pittsburgh, Pennsylvania. Continued by U. S. Glass Co. as one of their States patterns.

	Clear w/gold	Ruby Stained		Clear w/gold	Ruby Stained
Banana Dish	35.00	85.00	Bread Plate	25.00	—
Bowl, berry	15.00	35.00	Butter, cov	65.00	95.00

	Clear w/gold	Ruby Stained		Clear w/gold	Ruby Stained
Cake Stand, 8″	40.00	—	Plate, 7″, round. . . .	25.00	—
Celery Tray.	20.00	35.00	Relish, oval.	15.00	55.00
Celery Vase	28.00	65.00	Salt Shaker, single	30.00	—
Compote			Sauce, flat	10.00	15.00
Cov, hs	65.00	100.00	Spooner.	30.00	55.00
Open, jelly.	25.00	45.00	Sugar, cov	45.00	60.00
Creamer.	25.00	55.00	Toothpick	125.00	175.00
Goblet	30.00	48.00	Tumbler	25.00	50.00
Olive, handled.	15.00	—	Wine	40.00	75.00
Pitcher					
Milk.	42.50	135.00			
Water	50.00	100.00			

MASSACHUSETTS (Geneva #2, M2-131)

Made in 1880s, maker unknown, and continued in 1898 by U. S. Glass Co. as one of the States series. The vase ($45.00) and wine ($45.00) are known in emerald green. Some pieces reported in cobalt blue and marigold carnival glass. Reproduced in clear and colors.

	Clear		Clear
Bar Bottle, metal shot glass		Plate, 8″	32.00
for cover	75.00	Punch Cup	15.00
Basket, 4½″, ah	50.00	Relish, 8½″.	25.00
Bowl		Rum Jug	90.00
6″, sq	17.50	Spooner	22.00
9″, sq	20.00	Sugar, cov	40.00
* Butter, cov	50.00	Syrup.	65.00
Celery Tray	28.00	Toothpick	40.00
Cologne Bottle, os.	37.50	Tumbler	
Compote, open	35.00	Champagne or Juice	25.00
Cordial	55.00	Water	30.00
Creamer.	28.00	Whiskey (shot).	15.00
Cruet, os	45.00	Vase	
Goblet	45.00	6½″, trumpet	25.00
Mug	20.00	7″	25.00
Olive	8.50	9″, trumpet	35.00
Pitcher, water	65.00	Wine	40.00

MINNESOTA

Non-flint made by U. S. Glass Co., late 1890s. One of the States patterns. A two-piece flower frog has been found in emerald green ($46.00).

	Clear	Ruby Stained		Clear	Ruby Stained
Basket	65.00	—	Celery Tray, 13″ . . .	25.00	—
Biscuit Jar, cov	55.00	150.00	Compote		
Bowl, 8½″, flared. . .	30.00	100.00	Open, hs, 10″,		
Butter, cov	50.00	—	flared.	60.00	—
Carafe	35.00	—	Open, ls, 9″, sq . .	55.00	—

	Clear	Ruby Stained			Clear	Ruby Stained
Creamer			Relish	20.00	—
Individual	20.00	—	Sauce, boat shape	10.00	28.50
Regular	30.00	—	Spooner	25.00	—
Cruet	35.00	—	Sugar, cov	35.00	—
Cup	18.00	—	Syrup	65.00	—
Goblet	35.00	50.00	Toothpick, 3 handles	30.00	150.00
Hair Receiver	30.00	—	Tumbler	20.00	—
Mug	25.00	—	Wine	40.00	—
Olive	15.00	25.00			
Pitcher, water, tank-ard	85.00	200.00			
Plate					
5", turned up edges	25.00	—			
7⅜" d	15.00	—			

MISSOURI (Palm and Scroll)

Non-flint made by U. S. Glass Co. c1899, one of the States pattern series. Also made in amethyst and canary.

	Clear	Emerald Green			Clear	Emerald Green
Bowl, berry, 8"	15.00	35.00	Pitcher		
Butter, cov	45.00	65.00	Milk	40.00	85.00
Cake Stand, 9"	35.00	45.00	Water	75.00	85.00
Celery Vase	30.00	—	Relish	10.00	12.50
Cordial	55.00	—	Salt Shaker, single	35.00	45.00
Creamer	25.00	40.00	Sauce, flat, 4"	10.00	16.00
Cruet	55.00	130.00	Spooner	25.00	48.00
Dish, cov 6"	65.00	—	Sugar, cov	50.00	65.00
Doughnut stand, 6"	40.00	—	Syrup	85.00	—
Goblet	50.00	60.00	Tumbler	30.00	38.00
Mug	35.00	45.00	Wine	40.00	45.00
Pickle Dish, rectangular	18.00	27.50			

MOON AND STAR (Palace)

Non-flint and frosted (add 30%). First made by Adams & Co., Pittsburgh, Pennsylvania, in 1874 and later by several manufacturers, including Pioneer Glass who probably decorated ruby stained examples. Six different compotes documented. Also found with frosted highlights. Heavily reproduced in clear and color.

	Clear			Clear
Banana Stand	90.00	Butter, cov	70.00
Bowl		Cake Stand, 10"	50.00
6"	20.00	Carafe	42.50
8", Berry	25.00	Celery Vase	35.00
12½", Round	42.00	Champagne	75.00
Bread Plate, rect	45.00	Claret	47.50

	Clear		Clear
Compote		Relish.	20.00
Cov, hs, 10".	68.00	Salt, ind	10.00
Cov, ls, 6½".	55.00	Salt & Pepper, pr.	70.00
Open, hs, 9"	35.00	Sauce	
Open, ls, 7½"	25.00	Flat.	8.50
Creamer, ah	55.00	Footed	12.00
Cruet	125.00	Spooner	45.00
Egg Cup.	35.00	Sugar, cov	65.00
Goblet	45.00	Syrup	150.00
Lamp	140.00	Tray, water	65.00
Pickle, oval.	20.00	Tumbler, ftd	50.00
Pitcher, water, ah	175.00	Wine	60.00

NEW HAMPSHIRE (Bent Buckle, Modiste)

Non-flint made by U. S. Glass Co. in the States Pattern series. There is a large ruby mug ($50.00), 5½" bowl ($25.00), syrup ($48.00), toothpick ($40.00), and tumbler ($40.00). A vase is known in green stain ($30.00).

	Clear w/gold	Rose Stained		Clear w/gold	Rose Stained
Bowl			Goblet	25.00	45.00
Flared, 8½"	15.00	25.00	Mug, large	20.00	45.00
Round, 8½"	18.00	30.00	Pitcher, water, tank-		
Square, 8½"	25.00	35.00	ard	70.00	90.00
Butter, cov	45.00	70.00	Relish.	18.00	—
Cake Stand, 8¼". . .	30.00	—	Sugar		
Carafe	60.00	—	Cov.	45.00	60.00
Celery Vase	35.00	50.00	Ind, open.	20.00	25.00
Compote, open	38.00	55.00	Syrup	75.00	—
Creamer			Toothpick	25.00	40.00
Ind	20.00	30.00	Tumbler	20.00	35.00
Regular.	30.00	45.00	Vase	35.00	50.00
Cruet	55.00	135.00	Wine	25.00	50.00

NEW JERSEY (Loops and Drops)

Non-flint made by U. S. Glass Co. in States Pattern series. Items with perfect gold are worth more than those with worn gold. An emerald green 11" vase is known, value $75.00.

	Clear w/gold	Ruby Stained		Clear w/gold	Ruby Stained
Bowl			Compote		
8", flared	25.00	50.00	Cov, hs, 5", jelly. .	45.00	55.00
9"	32.50	65.00	Cov, hs, 8".	75.00	—
10", oval	30.00	—	Open, hs, 6¾" . . .	30.00	—
Bread Plate	30.00	—	Open, hs, 8"	60.00	—
Flat.	75.00	100.00	Creamer.	35.00	60.00
Footed	125.00	—	Cruet	50.00	—
Cake Stand, 8" . . .	65.00	—	Goblet	40.00	—
Celery Tray, rect . . .	25.00	—	Olive	18.50	—

	Clear w/gold	Ruby Stained		Clear w/gold	Ruby Stained
Pickle, rect	15.00	—	Sauce	10.00	30.00
Pitcher			Spooner	27.00	75.00
Milk, ah	75.00	—	Sugar, cov	60.00	80.00
Water			Sweetmeat, 8"	45.00	
Applied handle	80.00	210.00	Syrup, no gold	90.00	—
Pressed handle	50.00	185.00	Toothpick	55.00	225.00
Plate, 12"	30.00	—	Tumbler	30.00	50.00
Salt & Pepper			Wine	40.00	60.00
Hotel	50.00	—			
Small	35.00	55.00			

O'HARA DIAMOND (Sawtooth and Star)

Non-flint, made by O'Hara Glass Co. in 1928 and by U. S. Glass Co. in 1898.

	Clear	Ruby Stained		Clear	Ruby Stained
Bowl, berry			Lamp, Oil	50.00	—
Individual	—	25.00	Pitcher, water,		
Master	25.00	75.00	tankard	—	165.00
Butter, cov, ruffled			Plate		
base	45.00	125.00	7"	20.00	—
Compote			8"	30.00	—
Cov, hs	40.00	185.00	10"	40.00	—
Open, hs, jelly	48.00	145.00	Salt, master	15.00	35.00
Condiment Set, pr			Salt Shaker	20.00	35.00
salt and pepper,			Spooner	20.00	55.00
sugar shaker, tray	—	250.00	Sugar, cov	35.00	90.00
Creamer	30.00	60.00	Sugar Shaker	55.00	150.00
Cruet	55.00	150.00	Syrup	55.00	200.00
Cup and Saucer	40.00	60.00	Tumbler	30.00	45.00
Goblet	25.00	50.00			

OREGON #1 (Beaded Loop)

Non-flint. First made in the 1880s. Reissued in 1907 as one of the States series. Reproduced in clear and color by Imperial.

	Clear		Clear
Berry Set, master, 6 sauces	72.00	Celery Vase	30.00
Bowl		Compote	
7"	15.00	Open, hs, 8"	50.00
8"	15.00	Open, ls, 9"	40.00
9", berry, cov	25.00	Creamer	
Bread Plate	35.00	Flat	30.00
Butter, cov		Footed	35.00
English	65.00	Cruet	50.00
Flanged	50.00	Goblet	35.00
Flat	40.00	Honey Dish	10.00
Cake Stand	35.00	Mug	35.00
Carafe, water	35.00	Pickle Dish, boat shape	15.00

	Clear			Clear
Pitcher		Sugar, cov		
Milk	40.00	Flat		25.00
Water	60.00	Footed		30.00
Relish	15.00	Syrup		55.00
Salt, master	20.00	Toothpick		55.00
Sauce		Tumbler		25.00
Flat, 3½ to 4"	5.00	Wine		50.00
Footed, 3½"	10.00			
Spooner				
Flat	24.00			
Footed	26.00			

PANELED THISTLE (Delta)

Non-flint made by J. P. Higbee Glass Co., Bridgeville, Pennsylvania, in the early 1900s. The Higbee Glass Co. often used a bee as a trademark. This pattern has been heavily reproduced with a similar mark. Occasionally found with gilt. A covered sugar in ruby stained is known.

	Clear		Clear
Basket, small size	65.00	Plate	
Bowl		7"	20.00
8", bee mark	25.00	10", bee mark	30.00
9", bee mark	30.00	Punch Cup, bee mark	20.00
Bread Plate	40.00	Relish, bee mark	24.00
Butter, cov,	60.00	Rose Bowl, 5"	50.00
Cake Stand, 9"	35.00	Salt, ind	20.00
Candy Dish, cov, ftd	30.00	Sauce	
Celery Tray	20.00	Flared, bee mark	12.00
Celery Vase	40.00	Footed	20.00
Champagne, bee mark	40.00	Spooner	25.00
Compote		Sugar, cov	45.00
Open, hs, 8"	30.00	Toothpick, bee mark	45.00
Open, hs, 9"	35.00	Tumbler	25.00
Open, ls, 5", jelly	30.00	Vase	
Creamer, bee mark	40.00	5"	25.00
Cruet, os	50.00	9¼"	25.00
Doughnut Stand, 6"	25.00	Wine, bee mark	30.00
Goblet	35.00		
Honey, cov, sq, bee mark	80.00		
Pitcher			
Milk	60.00		
Water	70.00		

PAVONIA (Pineapple Stem)

Non-flint made by Ripley and Co. in 1885 and by U. S. Glass Co. in 1891. This pattern comes plain and etched.

	Clear	Ruby Stained		Clear	Ruby Stained
Bowl, 9"	20.00	—	Cake Stand	55.00	—
Butter, cov, flat	75.00	125.00	Celery Vase, etched	45.00	75.00

	Clear	Ruby Stained		Clear	Ruby Stained
Compote			Salt		
Cov, hs, 8″	75.00	—	Ind	15.00	50.00
Open, jelly, etched	38.00	—	Master	28.00	50.00
Creamer, etched . . .	48.00	65.00	Salt Shaker.	25.00	—
Cup and Saucer . . .	35.00	—	Sauce, ftd, 3½″ or		
Finger Bowl, ruffled			4″	15.00	—
underplate.	48.00	110.00	Spooner, pedestal . .	45.00	50.00
Goblet, etched	35.00	60.00	Sugar, cov, flat	55.00	75.00
Mug	—	50.00	Tray, water, etched .	75.00	—
Pitcher			Tumbler, etched		
Lemonade.	125.00	135.00	bellflowers.	35.00	50.00
Water	75.00	195.00	Waste Bowl.	60.00	—
Plate, 6½″, etched	17.50	—	Wine, etched	35.00	40.00

PENNSYLVANIA (Balder)

Non-flint issued by U. S. Glass Co., 1898. Also known in ruby stained. A ruffled jelly compote documented in orange carnival.

	Clear w/gold	Emerald Green		Clear w/gold	Emerald Green
Biscuit Jar, cov	65.00	100.00	Juice Tumbler.	10.00	20.00
Bowl			Pitcher, water	60.00	—
8″, berry	25.00	35.00	Punch Bowl	175.00	—
8″, sq	20.00	40.00	Punch Cup	10.00	—
Butter, cov	60.00	85.00	Salt Shaker.	10.00	—
Carafe	45.00	—	Sauce	7.50	—
Celery Vase	45.00	—	Spooner	24.00	35.00
Cheese Dish, cov . .	65.00	—	Sugar, cov	40.00	55.00
Compote, hs, jelly . .	50.00	—	Syrup	50.00	—
Creamer.	25.00	50.00	Toothpick	35.00	90.00
Cruet, os	45.00	—	Tumbler	28.00	40.00
Decanter, os	100.00	—	Whiskey	15.00	—
Goblet	24.00	—	Wine	15.00	40.00

PORTLAND

Non-flint pattern made by several companies c1880–1900. An oval pintray in ruby souvenir ($20.00) is known, and a flat sauce ($25.00).

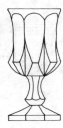

	Clear w/gold		Clear w/gold
Basket, handled	85.00	Compote	
Biscuit Jar, cov	90.00	Cov, hs, 6″.	60.00
Bowl		Open, hs, 8¼″	40.00
Berry.	20.00	Open, hs, 9½″	45.00
Small, flat, cov.	30.00	Open, ls, 7″	45.00
Butter, cov	50.00	Creamer.	30.00
Cake Stand, 10½″.	45.00	Cruet, os	48.00
Carafe, water	45.00	Decanter, qt, handled	50.00
Celery Tray.	25.00	Goblet	35.00

	Clear w/gold		Clear w/gold
Lamp base, 9"	75.00	Spooner	30.00
Pitcher, water, straight sides	55.00	Sugar, cov	45.00
Pomade Jar, SP top	30.00	Sugar Shaker	40.00
Puff Box, glass lid	35.00	Syrup	50.00
Punch Bowl, 13⅝", ftd	150.00	Toothpick	25.00
Punch Cup	10.00	Tumbler	18.00
Relish.	15.00	Vase	25.00
Salt Shaker.	16.00	Water Bottle	40.00
Sauce	8.00	Wine	30.00

PRINCESS FEATHER (Rochelle)

Non-flint made by Bakewell, Pears & Co. in the late 1870s. Occasional pieces made in flint. Later by U. S. Glass Co. in the 1890s. Also made in milk glass. A rare blue opaque tumbler has been reported.

	Clear		Clear
Bowl		Goblet	45.00
7", cov, pedestal	35.00	Pitcher, water	75.00
7", oval	20.00	Plate	
8", oval	25.00	6"	30.00
9", oval	30.00	7"	35.00
Butter, cov	50.00	8"	40.00
Cake Plate, handled	35.00	9"	45.00
Celery Vase	40.00	Relish.	20.00
Compote		Sauce	8.00
Cov, hs, 7".	50.00	Spooner	30.00
Cov, hs, 8".	50.00	Sugar	
Open, ls, 8"	35.00	Cov.	55.00
Creamer, ah	55.00	Open	25.00
Dish, oval	20.00	Wine	45.00
Egg Cup.	40.00		

QUEEN ANNE (Bearded Man)

Non-flint made by LaBelle Glass Co., Bridgeport, Ohio, c1879. Finials are Maltese cross. At least 28 pieces documented. A table set and water pitcher are known in amber.

	Clear		Clear
Bowl, cov		Egg Cup.	45.00
8", oval	45.00	Pitcher	
9", oval	55.00	Milk.	75.00
Bread Plate	50.00	Water	85.00
Butter, cov	65.00	Spooner	40.00
Celery Vase	35.00	Sugar, cov	55.00
Compote, cov, ls, 9"	75.00	Syrup	100.00
Creamer.	40.00		

RED BLOCK (Late Block)

Non-flint with red stain made by Doyle and Co.; later made by five companies plus U. S. Glass Co. in 1892. Prices for clear 50% less.

	Ruby Stained		Ruby Stained
Bowl, 8″	75.00	Rose Bowl	75.00
Butter, cov	110.00	Sauce, flat, 4½″	20.00
Celery Vase, 6½″	85.00	Salt Dip, ind	50.00
Creamer		Salt Shaker, single	75.00
Individual.	45.00	Spooner	45.00
Regular.	70.00	Sugar, cov	90.00
Decanter, 12″, os, variant. . .	175.00	Tumbler	40.00
*Goblet	35.00	Water Set, pitcher, 6	
Mug	50.00	tumblers	285.00
Pitcher, water, 8″ h	175.00	*Wine	40.00

REVERSE TORPEDO (Bull's Eye Band, Bull's Eye with Diamond Point #2, Pointed Bull's Eye)

Made by Dalzell, Gilmore & Leighton Glass Co., Findlay, Ohio, c1888–1890. Also attributed to Canadian factories. Sometimes found with etching.

	Clear		Clear
Banana Stand, 9¾″	100.00	Open, hs, 7″	65.00
Biscuit Jar, cov	135.00	Open, hs, 8⅜″ d	45.00
Bowl		Open, hs, jelly	50.00
8½″, shallow	30.00	Open, ls, 9¼″, ruffled	85.00
9″, fruit, pie crust rim	70.00	Goblet	85.00
10½″, pie crust rim.	75.00	Honey Dish, sq, cov	145.00
Butter, cov	75.00	Pitcher, tankard, 10¼″	160.00
Cake Stand	85.00	Sauce, flat, 3¾″	10.00
Celery Vase	55.00	Spooner	30.00
Compote		Sugar, cov	85.00
Cov, hs, 7″.	80.00	Syrup	165.00
Cov, hs, 10″.	125.00	Tumbler	30.00
Cov, hs, 6″.	80.00		
Open, hs, 10½″ d, V shape bowl	90.00		

SAWTOOTH (Mitre Diamond)

An early clear flint-glass pattern made in the late 1850s by the New England Glass Co., Boston and Sandwich Glass Co., and others. Later made in non-flint by Bryce Brothers and U. S. Glass Co. Also known in milk glass, clear deep blue, and canary yellow.

	Flint	Non-Flint		Flint	Non-Flint
Butter, cov	75.00	45.00	Compote		
Cake Stand, 10″ . . .	85.00	55.00	Cov, hs, 9½″	85.00	48.00
Celery Vase, 10″ . . .	60.00	30.00	Open, ls, 8″, saw-		
Champagne	65.00	30.00	tooth edge	50.00	30.00

	Flint	Non-Flint		Flint	Non-Flint
Cordial	50.00	30.00	Plate, 6½"	45.00	30.00
Creamer			Pomade Jar, cov	50.00	35.00
Applied handle	75.00	40.00	Salt		
Pressed handle	—	30.00	Cov, ftd	65.00	40.00
Cruet, acorn stopper	100.00	—	Open, smooth		
Egg Cup	45.00	25.00	edge	25.00	20.00
Goblet	50.00	20.00	Spooner	70.00	30.00
Pitcher, water			Sugar, cov	65.00	35.00
Applied handle	150.00	95.00	Tumbler, bar	50.00	25.00
Pressed handle	—	55.00	Wine, knob stem	35.00	20.00

SNAIL (Compact, Idaho, Double Snail)

Non-flint made by George Duncan & Sons, Pittsburgh, Pennsylvania, c1880, and by U. S. Glass Co. in the States Pattern series. Ruby stained pieces date after 1891. Add 30% for engraved pieces.

	Clear	Ruby Stained		Clear	Ruby Stained
Banana Stand	145.00	225.00	Finger Bowl	50.00	—
Basket, cake or fruit			Goblet	65.00	95.00
9"	85.00	—	Marmalade, cov	90.00	125.00
10"	95.00	—	Pitcher		
Bowl			Milk, tankard	100.00	—
4"	20.00	90.00	Water, bulbous	125.00	—
4½"	20.00	—	Water, tankard	135.00	250.00
7", cov	60.00	45.00	Plate		
7", oval	28.00	45.00	5"	35.00	—
7", round	28.00	45.00	6"	35.00	—
8", cov	60.00	45.00	7"	40.00	—
8", oval	28.00	45.00	Punch Cup	35.00	—
8", round	28.00	45.00	Relish, 7", oval	25.00	—
9", oval	30.00	—	Rose Bowl		
9", round	30.00	—	3"	50.00	—
10"	35.00	45.00	5"	45.00	—
Butter, cov	75.00	160.00	6"	45.00	—
Cake Stand			7"	50.00	—
9"	85.00	—	Salt		
10"	95.00	—	Ind	35.00	—
Celery Vase	35.00	85.00	Master	35.00	75.00
Cheese, cov	95.00	—	Salt Shaker		
Compote			Bulbous	65.00	90.00
Cov, hs, 6"	50.00	—	Straight sides	60.00	90.00
Cov, hs, 7"	50.00	100.00	Sauce	25.00	45.00
Cov, hs, 8"	80.00	135.00	Spooner	45.00	75.00
Cov, hs, 10"	125.00	—	Sugar		
Open, hs, 6"	30.00	—	Ind, cov	50.00	—
Open, hs, 7"	45.00	—	Regular, cov	60.00	100.00
Open, hs, 8"	35.00	—	Sugar Shaker	85.00	200.00
Open, hs, 9", twisted stem, scalloped	75.00	—	Syrup	125.00	225.00
Cracker Jar, cov	85.00	—	Tumbler	55.00	65.00
Creamer	65.00	75.00	Vase	50.00	—
Cup, Custard	30.00	—	Violet Bowl, 3"	50.00	—
Cruet, os	100.00	275.00	Wine	65.00	—

SPRIG

Non-flint made by Bryce, Higbee & Co., Pittsburgh, Pennsylvania, mid-1880s.

	Clear		Clear
Bowl, 10″, scalloped	35.00	Pitcher, water	50.00
Bread Plate	40.00	Relish	12.00
Butter, cov	65.00	Salt, master	55.00
Cake Stand, 8″	35.00	Sauce	
Celery Vase	40.00	Flat	10.00
Compote		Ftd	15.00
Cov, hs	60.00	Spooner	25.00
Open, hs	45.00	Sugar, cov	40.00
Creamer	30.00	Wine	40.00
Goblet	30.00		

STATES, THE (Cane and Star Medallion)

Non-flint made by the U. S. Glass Co. in 1908. Also found in emerald green; add 50%.

	Clear w/ gold		Clear w/ gold
Bowl		Plate, 10″	25.00
7″, round, 3 handles	25.00	Punch Bowl, 13″ d.	75.00
9¼″, round	30.00	Punch Cup	8.00
Butter, cov	65.00	Relish, diamond shape	35.00
Celery Tray	20.00	Salt & Pepper	40.00
Cocktail	25.00	Sauce, flat, 4″, tub shape	10.00
Compote		Spooner	25.00
Open, hs, 7″	30.00	Sugar, cov	45.00
Open, hs, 9″	40.00	Syrup	65.00
Creamer		Toothpick, flat, rectangular,	
Ind, oval	18.00	curled lip	45.00
Regular, round	30.00	Tray, 7¼″ l, 5½″ w	18.00
Goblet	35.00	Tumbler	22.00
Pitcher, water	45.00	Wine	30.00

TENNESSEE (Jewel and Crescent; Jeweled Rosette)

Made by King Glass Co., Pittsburgh, Pennsylvania, and continued by U. S. Glass Co., in 1899, as part of the States series.

	Clear	Colored Jewels		Clear	Colored Jewels
Bowl, berry	20.00	30.00	Compote		
Bread Plate	40.00	75.00	Cov, 5″, jelly	40.00	55.00
Butter, cov	55.00	—	Open, hs, 8″	45.00	—
Cake Stand			Open, hs, 9″	45.00	—
9½″	38.00	—	Open, hs, 10″	45.00	—
10½″	45.00	—	Open, ls, 7″	35.00	—
Celery Vase	35.00	—	Creamer	30.00	—

	Clear	Colored Jewels		Clear	Colored Jewels
Goblet	40.00	—	Spooner	35.00	—
Mug	40.00	—	Sugar, cov	45.00	—
Pitcher			Syrup	90.00	—
Milk	55.00	—	Toothpick	75.00	85.00
Water	65.00	—	Tumbler	35.00	—
Relish	20.00	—	Wine	65.00	85.00

TEXAS (Loop with Stippled Panels)

Non-flint made by U. S. Glass Co., c1900, in the States Pattern series. Occasionally pieces found in ruby stained. Reproduced in solid colors.

	Clear w/gold	Rose Stained		Clear w/gold	Rose Stained
Bowl			Pickle, 8½"	25.00	—
7"	20.00	40.00	Pitcher, water	125.00	—
9", scalloped	35.00	50.00	Plate, 9"	35.00	60.00
Butter, cov	75.00	125.00	Sauce		
Cake Stand, 9½"	60.00	80.00	Flat	10.00	18.00
Celery Tray	30.00	—	Footed	20.00	—
Celery Vase	40.00	—	Spooner	35.00	—
Compote			Sugar		
Cov, hs, 6"	60.00	—	Individual, cov	45.00	—
Cov, hs, 8"	75.00	—	Regular, cov	65.00	—
Open, hs, 5"	40.00	—	Toothpick	25.00	95.00
Creamer			Tumbler	25.00	—
Individual	20.00	—	Vase		
Regular	40.00	—	6½"	25.00	—
Cruet, os	60.00	165.00	9"	35.00	—
Goblet	85.00	95.00	Wine	50.00	100.00

THOUSAND EYE

The original pattern was non-flint made by Adams Glass Co, Tarentum, PA, 1875, and by Richards and Hartley, 1888. (Their Pattern No. 103). It was made in two forms: Adams with a three knob stem finial, and Richards and Hartley with a plain stem with a scalloped bottom. Several glass companies made variations of the original pattern and reproductions were made as late as 1981. Crystal Opalescent was produced by Richards and Hartley only in the original pattern. (Opalescent celery vase $70.00; open compote, 8", $115.00; 6" creamer, $85.00; ¼ gallon water pitcher, $140.00; ½ gallon water pitcher, $180.00; 4" footed sauce, $40.00; spooner, $60.00; and 5" covered sugar, $80.00). Covered compotes are rare and would command 40% more than open compotes. A 2" mug in blue is known.

	Amber	Apple Green	Blue	Clear	Vaseline
ABC Plate, 6", clock center	50.00	55.00	52.00	45.00	52.00
Bowl, large, carriage shape	85.00	—	85.00	—	85.00
Butter, cov					
6¼"	65.00	75.00	70.00	45.00	90.00

	Amber	Apple Green	Blue	Clear	Vaseline
7½"	65.00	75.00	70.00	45.00	90.00
Cake Stand					
10"	50.00	78.00	55.00	30.00	84.00
11"	50.00	78.00	55.00	30.00	84.00
Celery, hat shape . .	50.00	65.00	60.00	35.00	55.00
Celery Vase, 7"	50.00	60.00	52.00	45.00	55.00
Christmas Light	27.00	45.00	35.00	25.00	40.00
Cologne Bottle	25.00	45.00	35.00	20.00	45.00
Compote, cov, ls, 8", sq	—	100.00	100.00	—	—
Compote, open					
6"	35.00	40.00	38.00	25.00	38.00
7"	38.00	44.00	40.00	30.00	40.00
8", round	40.00	50.00	44.00	35.00	48.00
8", sq, hs	39.00	50.00	48.00	38.00	55.00
9"	48.00	56.00	52.00	40.00	52.00
10"	55.00	65.00	60.00	45.00	60.00
Cordial	35.00	52.00	40.00	25.00	58.00
Creamer					
4"	32.00	40.00	36.00	25.00	38.00
6"	38.00	75.00	55.00	35.00	72.00
Creamer & Sugar Set	—	—	—	100.00	—
*Cruet, 6"	40.00	58.00	47.00	35.00	60.00
Egg Cup	65.00	85.00	70.00	45.00	90.00
*Goblet	37.00	42.00	38.00	35.00	45.00
Honey Dish, cov, 6 × 7¼"	85.00	95.00	90.00	70.00	92.00
Inkwell	45.00	—	75.00	35.00	80.00
Jelly Glass	20.00	25.00	22.00	15.00	23.00
Lamp, Kerosene					
hs, 12"	120.00	150.00	130.00	100.00	140.00
hs, 15"	125.00	155.00	135.00	110.00	150.00
ls, handled	110.00	115.00	110.00	90.00	120.00
Mug					
2½"	23.00	30.00	25.00	20.00	32.00
3½"	23.00	30.00	25.00	20.00	32.00
Nappy					
5"	34.00	—	39.00	30.00	45.00
6"	39.00	—	44.00	35.00	52.00
8"	45.00	—	50.00	42.00	60.00
Pickle	25.00	30.00	27.00	20.00	29.00
Pitcher					
Milk, cov, 7"	85.00	110.00	105.00	70.00	105.00
Water, ¼ gal	70.00	85.00	80.00	55.00	80.00
Water, ½ gal	80.00	92.00	84.00	65.00	85.00
Water, 1 gal	90.00	100.00	95.00	85.00	95.00
*Plate, sq, folded corners					
6"	24.00	28.00	26.00	20.00	26.00
8"	26.00	30.00	28.00	22.00	30.00
10"	34.00	50.00	36.00	25.00	34.00
Platter					
8 × 11", oblong . .	40.00	48.00	42.00	38.00	45.00
11", oval	75.00	80.00	55.00	40.00	75.00
Salt Shaker, pr					
Banded	60.00	68.00	62.00	58.00	62.00
Plain	50.00	60.00	55.00	40.00	56.00
Salt, ind	80.00	95.00	90.00	50.00	90.00

	Amber	Apple Green	Blue	Clear	Vaseline
Salt, open, carriage shape	65.00	—	—	50.00	—
Sauce					
Flat, 4"	10.00	22.00	12.00	8.00	15.00
Footed, 4"	12.00	25.00	15.00	10.00	20.00
Spooner	32.00	48.00	40.00	27.00	45.00
*String Holder	35.00	60.00	45.00	30.00	42.00
Sugar, cov, 5"	52.00	70.00	54.00	45.00	55.00
Syrup, pewter top	80.00	100.00	70.00	55.00	70.00
Toothpick					
Hat	35.00	52.00	58.00	30.00	45.00
Plain	35.00	50.00	55.00	25.00	40.00
Thimble	55.00	—	—	—	—
Tray, water					
12½", round	64.00	78.00	65.00	55.00	60.00
14", oval	65.00	80.00	75.00	60.00	74.00
*Tumbler	26.00	62.00	34.00	21.00	30.00
*Wine	35.00	50.00	40.00	20.00	40.00

THREE-FACE

Non-flint made by George E. Duncan & Son, Pittsburgh, Pennsylvania, c1872. Designed by John E. Miller, a designer with Duncan, who later became a member of the firm. Companies in the Pittsburgh area produced many patterns in expectation of the 1876 Philadelphia Centennial Exposition. It has been heavily reproduced.

	Clear		Clear
Biscuit Jar, cov	300.00	Cov, ls, 4"	150.00
Butter, cov	140.00	Open, hs, 7"	75.00
Cake Stand		Open, hs, 8"	85.00
9"	150.00	Open, hs, 9"	135.00
10"	160.00	Open, ls, 6"	75.00
11"	165.00	Open, jelly, paneled "Huber" top	85.00
Celery Vase		Creamer	135.00
Plain	95.00	Goblet	85.00
Scalloped	95.00	Lamp, Oil	150.00
Champagne		Marmalade Jar	200.00
Hollow stem	250.00	Pitcher, water	375.00
Saucer type	150.00	Salt Dip	35.00
Claret	100.00	Salt & Pepper	75.00
Compote		Sauce, ftd	25.00
Cov, hs, 7"	165.00	Spooner	80.00
Cov, hs, 8"	175.00	Sugar, cov	125.00
Cov, hs, 9"	190.00	Wine	150.00
Cov, hs, 10"	225.00		
Cov, ls, 6"	160.00		

THREE PANEL

Non-flint made by Richards & Hartley Co., Tarentum, Pennsylvania, c1888, and by U. S. Glass Co. in 1891.

	Amber	Blue	Clear	Vaseline
Bowl				
7"	25.00	40.00	20.00	45.00
8½"	25.00	40.00	20.00	45.00
10"	40.00	50.00	35.00	48.00
Butter, cov	45.00	50.00	40.00	50.00
Celery Vase, ruffled top	55.00	65.00	35.00	55.00
Compote, open, ls, 7"	35.00	55.00	25.00	40.00
Creamer.........	40.00	45.00	25.00	40.00
Cruet	250.00	—	—	—
Goblet	30.00	40.00	25.00	35.00
Mug	35.00	45.00	25.00	35.00
Pitcher, water	100.00	125.00	40.00	110.00
Sauce, ftd........	15.00	15.00	10.00	15.00
Spooner.........	42.50	45.00	30.00	40.00
Sugar, cov	55.00	60.00	45.00	70.00
Tumbler	35.00	40.00	20.00	30.00

U. S. COIN

Non-flint frosted, clear, and gilted pattern made by U. S. Glass Co. in 1892 for three or four months. Production was stopped by U. S. Treasury because real coins, dated as early as 1878, were used in the molds. 1892 coin date is the most common.

	Clear	Frosted		Clear	Frosted
Bowl			Cruet, os	375.00	500.00
6"	170.00	220.00	Epergne	—	1,000.00
9"	215.00	325.00	Goblet	250.00	400.00
Bread Plate	175.00	325.00	Goblet, dimes	—	550.00
Butter, cov, dollars and halves	250.00	450.00	Lamp		
Cake Stand, 10" ...	225.00	400.00	Round font	275.00	450.00
Celery			Square font	300.00	—
Tray	200.00	—	Mug, handled	185.00	300.00
Vase, quarters ...	135.00	350.00	Pickle	200.00	—
Champagne	—	400.00	Pitcher, water, dollars...........	400.00	800.00
Compote			Sauce, ftd, 4", quarters.......	100.00	185.00
Cov, hs, 7"......	300.00	500.00	Spooner, quarters ..	225.00	325.00
Cov, hs, 8", quarters and dimes	—	415.00	Sugar, cov	225.00	350.00
Open, hs, 7", quarters and dimes .	200.00	300.00	Syrup, dated pewter lid............	—	525.00
Open, hs, 7", quarters and halves	225.00	350.00	* Toothpick	180.00	275.00
Open, 8⅜" d, 6½" h.	—	240.00	Tray, water, 8", rect .	275.00	—
Creamer.........	350.00	500.00	Tumbler	135.00	235.00
			Waste Bowl.	225.00	—
			Wine	225.00	375.00

UTAH (Frost Flower, Twinkle Star)

Non-flint made by U. S. Glass Co. in 1901 in the States Pattern series. Add 25% for frosting.

	Clear		Clear
Bowl		Creamer	30.00
Cov, 6"	20.00	Goblet	25.00
Open, 8"	18.00	Pickle	12.00
Butter, cov	35.00	Pitcher, water	45.00
Cake Plate, 9"	20.00	Salt & Pepper, in holder	45.00
Cake Stand		Sauce, 4"	8.50
8"	20.00	Spooner	15.00
10"	30.00	Sugar, cov	35.00
Celery Vase	20.00	Tumbler	15.00
Compote		Wine	25.00
Cov, ls, 6", jelly	25.00		
Open, ls, 6", jelly	18.00		

VERMONT (Honeycomb with Flower Rim; Inverted Thumbprint with Daisy Band)

Non-flint made by U. S. Glass Co., 1899–1903. Also made in custard (usually decorated), chocolate, caramel, and novelty slag, milk glass, and blue. Toothpick has been reproduced in clear and opaque colors.

	Clear w/gold	Green w/gold		Clear w/gold	Green w/gold
Basket, handle	30.00	45.00	Pitcher, water	50.00	125.00
Bowl, berry	25.00	45.00	Sauce	15.00	20.00
Butter, cov	40.00	75.00	Spooner	25.00	75.00
Celery Tray	30.00	35.00	Sugar, cov	35.00	80.00
Creamer	30.00	55.00	*Toothpick	30.00	50.00
Goblet	40.00	50.00	Tumbler	20.00	40.00

VIKING (Bearded Head)

Non-flint, made by Hobbs, Brockunier, and Co. in 1876 as their centennial pattern. No tumbler or goblet originally made.

	Clear		Clear
Apothecary Jar, cov	55.00	Creamer, 2 types	50.00
Bowl		Cup, ftd	35.00
Cov, 8", oval	55.00	Egg Cup	40.00
Cov, 9", oval	65.00	Marmalade Jar	85.00
Bread Plate	70.00	Mug, ah	50.00
Butter, cov	75.00	Pitcher, water	100.00
Celery Vase	45.00	Relish	20.00
Compote		Salt, master	40.00
Cov, hs, 9"	95.00	Sauce	15.00
Cov, ls, 8", oval	75.00	Spooner	35.00
Open, hs	60.00	Sugar, cov	65.00

WASHINGTON (Early)

Flint made by New England Glass Co., c1869.

	Clear		Clear
Ale Glass	125.00	Egg Cup	75.00
Bowl, 6 x 9″, oval	45.00	Goblet	110.00
Bottle, bitters	85.00	Honey Dish, 3½″	30.00
Butter, cov	175.00	Lamp	150.00
Celery Vase	95.00	Pitcher, water	375.00
Champagne	125.00	Plate, 6″	60.00
Compote		Salt, individual	20.00
Cov, hs, 6″	125.00	Sauce	25.00
Cov, hs, 10″	175.00	Spooner	75.00
Cordial	150.00	Sugar, cov	125.00
Creamer	200.00	Tumbler	85.00
Decanter, os	150.00	Wine	125.00

WESTWARD HO! (Pioneer)

Non-flint, usually frosted, made by Gillinder & Sons, Philadelphia, Pennsylvania, late 1870s. Molds made by Jacobus who also made Classic. Has been reproduced.

	Clear		Clear
Bread Plate	175.00	Marmalade Jar, cov	200.00
Butter, cov	185.00	Mug	
Celery Vase	125.00	2″	225.00
Compote		3½″	175.00
Cov, hs, 5″	225.00	Pitcher, water	250.00
Cov, hs, 9″	275.00	Sauce, ftd, 4½″	35.00
Cov, ls, 5″	150.00	Spooner	85.00
Open, hs, 8″	125.00	Sugar, cov	185.00
Creamer	95.00	Wine	200.00
Goblet	90.00		

WILDFLOWER

Non-flint made by Adams & Co., Pittsburgh, Pennsylvania, c1874, and by U. S. Glass Co., c1898. This pattern has been heavily reproduced.

	Amber	Apple Green	Blue	Clear	Vaseline
Bowl, 8″, sq	25.00	35.00	35.00	18.00	20.00
Butter, cov					
Collared base	40.00	50.00	50.00	35.00	45.00
Flat	35.00	45.00	45.00	30.00	40.00
Cake Stand, 10½″	50.00	80.00	75.00	45.00	50.00
Champagne	40.00	55.00	50.00	25.00	45.00
Celery Vase	55.00	60.00	55.00	35.00	55.00
Compote					
Cov, hs, 8″, oblong	80.00	85.00	85.00	50.00	75.00
Cov, ls, 7″	—	—	70.00	—	—
Open, hs	80.00	—	—	—	—
Creamer	35.00	50.00	45.00	40.00	48.00

	Amber	Apple Green	Blue	Clear	Vaseline
* Goblet	30.00	40.00	40.00	25.00	40.00
Pitcher, water	55.00	95.00	65.00	40.00	70.00
Plate, 10", sq	30.00	30.00	45.00	25.00	30.00
Platter					
10", oblong	40.00	45.00	40.00	30.00	30.00
11 x 8", deep scal-					
loped edges	—	—	45.00	—	—
Relish	20.00	22.00	20.00	18.00	20.00
* Salt, turtle	45.00	50.00	50.00	30.00	40.00
Salt Shaker	35.00	55.00	40.00	20.00	45.00
Sauce, ftd, 4",					
round	17.50	18.00	18.00	12.00	17.50
Spooner	30.00	35.00	30.00	20.00	40.00
Sugar, cov	45.00	45.00	50.00	30.00	45.00
Syrup	125.00	150.00	140.00	65.00	150.00
Tray, water, oval	50.00	60.00	60.00	40.00	55.00
Tumbler	40.00	35.00	35.00	25.00	35.00
Wine	45.00	45.00	45.00	25.00	45.00

WILLOW OAK (Wreath)

Non-flint made by Bryce Bros. Pittsburgh, Pennsylvania, c1880, and by U. S. Glass Company in 1891.

	Amber	Blue	Canary	Clear
Bowl, 8"	25.00	40.00	48.00	20.00
Butter, cov	55.00	65.00	80.00	40.00
Cake Stand, 8½"	60.00	65.00	70.00	45.00
Celery Vase	45.00	60.00	75.00	35.00
Compote				
Cov, hs, 7½"	50.00	65.00	80.00	40.00
Open, 7"	30.00	40.00	48.00	25.00
Creamer	40.00	50.00	60.00	30.00
Goblet	40.00	50.00	60.00	30.00
Mug	35.00	45.00	54.00	30.00
Pitcher				
Milk	50.00	60.00	72.00	45.00
Water	55.00	60.00	72.00	50.00
Plate				
7"	35.00	45.00	50.00	25.00
9"	32.50	35.00	40.00	25.00
Salt Shaker	25.00	40.00	55.00	20.00
Sauce				
Flat, handle, sq	15.00	20.00	24.00	10.00
Footed, 4"	20.00	25.00	30.00	15.00
Spooner	35.00	40.00	48.00	30.00
Sugar, cov	68.50	70.00	75.00	40.00
Tray, water, 10½"	35.00	50.00	60.00	30.00
Tumbler	30.00	35.00	45.00	25.00
Waste Bowl	35.00	40.00	40.00	30.00

WISCONSIN (Beaded Dewdrop)

Non-flint made in Pittsburgh, Pennsylvania, in the 1880s. Later made by U. S. Glass Co. in Indiana, 1903. One of States patterns. Toothpick reproduced in colors.

	Clear		Clear
Banana Stand	75.00	Goblet	65.00
Bowl		Marmalade Jar, straight	
4½ x 6½"	20.00	sides, glass lid	125.00
6", oval, handled, cov	40.00	Mug	35.00
7", round	42.00	Pitcher	
8", oblong, preserve	42.00	Milk	55.00
Butter, flat flange	75.00	Water	70.00
Cake Stand		Plate, 6¾"	25.00
8½"	45.00	Punch Cup	12.00
9½"	55.00	Relish	25.00
Celery Tray	40.00	Salt Shaker, single	30.00
Celery Vase	45.00	Spooner	30.00
Compote		Sugar, cov	55.00
Cov, hs, 6"	45.00	Sugar Shaker	90.00
Open, hs, 6", triangular . .	35.00	Sweetmeat, 5", ftd, cov	40.00
Condiment Set, SP, horse-		Syrup	110.00
radish on tray	100.00	*Toothpick	55.00
Creamer	50.00	Tumbler	40.00
Cruet, os	80.00	Wine	75.00
Cup & Saucer	50.00		

WYOMING (Enigma)

Made by U. S. Glass Co., in the States Pattern series, 1903.

	Clear		Clear
Bowl, 8"	15.00	Mug	40.00
Butter, cov	50.00	Pitcher, water	75.00
Cake Plate	55.00	Relish	15.00
Cake Stand	70.00	Spooner	30.00
Compote, cov, hs, 8" d	85.00	Sugar, cov	45.00
Creamer		Syrup, small	65.00
Covered	50.00	Tumbler	55.00
Open	35.00	Wine	85.00
Goblet	65.00		

X-RAY

Non-flint made by Riverside Glass Works, Wellsburg, West Virginia, 1896 to 1898. Prices are for pieces with gold trim. A toothpick holder is known in amethyst ($125.00). Also, a toothpick holder with marigold iridescence is known ($35.00).

	Clear	Emerald Green		Clear	Emerald Green
Bowl, berry, 8", beaded rim	25.00	45.00	Butter, cov	40.00	75.00
			Celery Vase	—	50.00

	Clear	Emerald Green		Clear	Emerald Green
Compote			Pitcher, water	40.00	75.00
Cov, hs	40.00	65.00	Salt & Pepper, pr. . .	25.00	45.00
Jelly	—	40.00	Sauce, flat	8.00	10.00
Creamer			Spooner	25.00	40.00
Individual.	15.00	30.00	Sugar		
Regular.	30.00	60.00	Ind, open.	20.00	32.50
Cruet	—	140.00	Regular, cov	35.00	45.00
Cruet Set, 4 leaf clover tray	125.00	350.00	Syrup	—	265.00
Goblet	20.00	35.00	Toothpick	25.00	50.00
			Tumbler	12.00	25.00

S.E.G.

PAUL REVERE POTTERY

History: Paul Revere Pottery, Boston, Massachusetts, was an outgrowth of a club known as "The Saturday Evening Girls." The S.E.G. was a group of young female immigrants who met on Saturday nights for reading and crafts such as ceramics.

Regular production began in 1908. The name Paul Revere was adopted because the pottery was located near the Old North Church. In 1915 the firm moved to Brighton, Massachusetts. Known as the "Bowl Shop," the pottery grew steadily. In spite of popular acceptance and technical advancements, the pottery required continual subsidies. It finally closed in January, 1942.

Items produced range from plain and decorated vases to tablewares to illustrated tiles. Many decorated wares were incised and glazed either in an Art Nouveau matte finish or an occasional high glaze.

In addition to the impressed mark, paper "Bowl Shop" labels were used prior to 1915. Pieces also can be found dated with P.R.P. or S.E.G. painted on the base.

References: Paul Evans, *Art Pottery of the United States, Second Edition*, Feingold & Lewis Publishing Corp, 1987; Ralph and Terry Kovel, *The Kovels' Collector's Guide to American Art Pottery*, Crown Publishers, Inc., 1974.

Collectors' Club: American Art Pottery Association, 9825 Upton Circle, Bloomington, MN 55431.

Bowl, 8" d, 3" h, band of incised and surface decorated green leaves, earthen ground, painted on base "S.E.G. 9.13" and "S.G.," for Sara Galner	880.00
Child's Feeding Set, cup, bowl, and plate, navy blue, light border, chick in landscape centers, inscribed name "Mary Phillipa Elwes," 1928	500.00
Creamer, 3½" h, mountains, trees, and sky, beige ground, marked "S.E.G." .	175.00
Egg Cup, matching underplate, yellow chick dec, blue ground, marked "S.E.G."	175.00

Mug, juvenile, yellow–brown ground, rabbit in medallion, marked "David/His Jug," 4½" h, $185.00.

Mug, 4" h, motto, "In The Forest Must Always Be A Nightingale and In The Soul A Faith So Faithful That It Comes Back Even After It Has Been Slain," forest landscape, green, blue, cream, and black, artist initials "AM," SEG mark, 1918	880.00
Pitcher, 7" h, bulbous, angled handle, circular medallion, initials "E.L.C." on	

blue ground, sgd "S.E.G.," dated
1923 . . . . **85.00**
Plate, 7¾" d, motto, "Nor the Battle to
the Strong" and "Betty," yellow and
cream matte glaze, rabbit and turtle
border, artist sgd "FR, 4–26–10,"
marked "SEG" **525.00**
Tile, 4⅛ x 6⅛", tree landscape, blue and
yellow, harbor pictorial reverse, verse
"The Bay Where Lay the Somerset
British Man of War" **415.00**
Vase, 4¼" h, 4" d, continuous band of
green trees, rolling hills, blue sky,
deep blue semi–gloss ground,
stamped circular mark, painted "C.E." **660.00**

PEACHBLOW

History: Peachblow, an art glass which derives its name from a fine Chinese glazed porcelain, resembles a peach or crushed strawberries in color. Three American glass manufacturers and two English firms produced peachblow glass in the late 1880s. A fourth American firm renewed the process in the 1950s. The glass from each firm has its own identifying characteristics.

Hobbs, Brockunier & Co., Wheeling peachblow: Opalescent glass, plated or cased with a transparent amber glass; shading from yellow at the base to a deep red at top; glossy or satin finish.

Mt. Washington "Peach Blow": A homogeneous glass, shading from a pale gray–blue to a soft rose color. Pieces may be enhanced with glass appliqués, enameling, and gilting.

New England Glass Works, New England peachblow [advertised as "Wild Rose," but called "Peach Blow" at the plant]: Translucent, shading from rose to white; acid or glossy finish. Some pieces enameled and gilted.

Thomas Webb & Sons and Stevens and Williams, England: Around 1888 these two firms made a peachblow style art glass marked "Peach Blow" or "Peach Bloom." A cased glass, shading from yellow to red. Occasionally found with cameo–type designs in relief.

Gunderson Glass Co.: About 1950 produced peachblow type art glass to order; shades from an opaque faint tint of pink, which is almost white, to a deep rose.

Reference: John A. Shuman III, *The Collector's Encyclopedia of American Glass,* Collector Books, 1988.

Note: All pieces listed below are satin finish unless otherwise noted.

GUNDERSON

Creamer and Sugar **420.00**
Cruet, 6½" h **175.00**
Goblet **140.00**

Vase, bulbous bottom, extended neck, Wheeling, 10″ h, $975.00.

Sugar, open, ftd **65.00**
Tumbler, 4" h **125.00**

MT WASHINGTON

Pitcher, 6⅞" h, bulbous, sq handle . . . **3,700.00**
Toothpick, DQ, sq mouth, enamel floral
and berry dec **6,350.00**
Vase
7" h, ruffle top, acid finish **3,810.00**
8" h, bulbous, blue and white enamel
forget–me–not dec, acid finish . . . **3,875.00**
8¼", lily form, satin finish **1,800.00**

NEW ENGLAND

Celery Vase
6" h, celery, Wild Rose, squared
shape **375.00**
6¼", crimped top, glossy finish **800.00**
6½" h, celery, squared shape, satin
finish **200.00**
Darner, 6" l **100.00**
Finger Bowl, 5¼" d, wide ruffled top . . **335.00**
Punch Cup, applied frosted ribbed han-
dle **700.00**
Salt and Pepper Shaker, pr, metal
holder, orig tops **850.00**
Toothpick, 2" h, tri–corn, shiny finish . . **480.00**
Vase
5½" h, pinched sides, sq rim, shiny
finish **550.00**
8¼" h, stick, gold prunus dec **360.00**
10" h, white to deep pink, wafer base,
crimson three petal rim **950.00**

WEBB

Cologne, 5" h, bulbous, raised gold floral branches, silver hallmarked dome
top **900.00**
Creamer, satin finish, Coralene dec,
rolled rim, flat base **660.00**

Epergne, 7½" h, three clear glass
   leaves, shiny finish, mirror base . . .   **785.00**
Finger Bowl, 4½" d, cased **185.00**
Vase
   2½" h, ruffled top, pine cone dec,
     shiny finish, marked "Webb &
     Sons–Queen's Burmese–Patent" .   **785.00**
   6½" h, stick, gold prunus flowers,
     leaves, and insect dec, propeller
     mark **550.00**
   8" h, stick, raised gold floral and
     branches dec **465.00**

WHEELING

Cruet, bulbous, amber reeded handle
   and cut faceted stopper **970.00**
Decanter, 9" h, amber, faceted stopper,
   satin reeded handle **3,140.00**
Fairy Lamp, 5" h, wide ruffled base . .   **650.00**
Lamp, 8" h, tapered, cut–out floral foot,
   missing font **360.00**
Pitcher
   6½" h, bulbous, sq rim, shiny finish . **1,375.00**
   9½" h, tankard, shiny finish **4,730.00**
   9¾" h, tankard, firing line near handle   **425.00**
Salt Shaker, bulbous, orig silverplate top   **200.00**
Tumbler, 3¾" h **150.00**
Vase
   4¼" h, bulbous, light to dark color
     shoulder and rim **325.00**
   8" h, Morgan
     Acid finish
       Amber glass, Griffin holder **2,200.00**
       Green glass Griffin holder **2,640.00**
     Shiny finish **825.00**
   8½" h, stick, ring of amber rigaree
     around base of neck **350.00**

PEKING GLASS

History: Peking glass is a type of cameo glass
of Chinese origin. Its production began in the
1700s and continued well into the 19th century.
The background color of Peking glass may be a
delicate shade of yellow, green, or white. One style
of white background is so delicate and transparent
that it often is referred to as the "snowflake"
ground. The overlay colors include a rich garnet
red, deep blue, and emerald green.

Bowl
   4⅜" d, pr, sq, flared sides, everted
     rim, light blue translucent **610.00**
   6¾" d, U–shape, raised foot, flared
     lip, opaque pale blue **300.00**
   7" d, pr, sq, flared sides, lipped rim,
     raised foot, greenish–white **660.00**
Jar, 5⅛", pr, cov, globular form, red ov-
   erlay, opaque white, four shaped
   medallions with flower sprigs, ruyi

**Snuff Bottle, blue ground, flowers and
birds dec, 3¼" h, 2½" w, $215.00.**

   band on shoulders, floriform knops,
   late 19th C **800.00**
Snuff Bottle
   Blue and white, dragon dec, silver
     top, 2⅞" h **225.00**
   Red and white, horses and branches
     dec, 3¼" h **120.00**
   White
     Flattened form, translucent, mot-
       tled, dark green stopper **360.00**
     Ovoid form, enameled scene on
       front and back, rose quartz stop-
       per **1,100.00**
     Tapered cylindrical form, lemon–yel-
       low, carved mask, ring handles,
       carnelian stopper **1,045.00**
Vase
   5⅛" h, pr, ovoid, rounded shoulders,
     waisted neck, translucent white . .   **360.00**
   7" h
     Blue, flowers and trees dec, white
       ground **800.00**
     Red, fruit tree dec, white ground,
       two handles **700.00**
   8" h, ovoid, two cranes on leafy veg-
     etation, green overlay, white
     ground **150.00**

PELOTON

History: Wilhelm Kralik of Bohemia patented
Peloton art glass in 1880. Later it was also patented in America and England.

   Peloton glass is found with both transparent and
opaque grounds with opaque being more common. Opaque colored glass filaments (strings) are
applied by dipping or rolling the hot glass. Generally, the filaments (threads) are pink, blue, yellow, and white (rainbow colors) or a single color.
Items also may have a satin finish and enamel
decorations.

Biscuit Jar, 6¾" h, ribbed body, pale
   blue ground, multicolored filaments,

white lining, SP rim, cover, and bail
handle **500.00**
Bowl, 3½" d, 2½" h, pinched top, ribbed
sides, clear ground, white, pink, blue,
and olive green filaments, fiery opal
pastel orchid lining **175.00**
Finger Bowl, clear, multicolored filaments **65.00**
Punch Cup, turquoise ground, multicolored filaments, enameled florals, set
of six **300.00**
Rose Bowl, 2½" d, 2¼" h, crimped top,
opaque white ground, pink, yellow,
blue, and white filaments **250.00**
Toothpick
2½" h, clear ground, green filaments **100.00**
3" h, clear, white filaments **125.00**

**Tumbler, yellow, pink, red, light blue,
and white, 3¾" h, $125.00.**

Tumbler, 3¾" h, clear ground, yellow,
pink, red, light blue, and white filaments **125.00**
Vase
3¼" h, 3" d, ball shape, flared ruffled
top, orchid pink ground, blue, pink,
yellow and white filaments **175.00**
4¼" h, 4¾" d, squat, ribbed, tricorn
folded down rim, clear ground,
rose, yellow, blue and white filaments, white lining **300.00**
6¾" h, 3" d, stick, yellow ground,
white, rose, blue, and yellow filaments, white lining **225.00**
Water Set, blown water pitcher, polished
pontil, five tumblers, light yellow amber ground, multicolored filaments .. **650.00**

PERFUME, COLOGNE, AND SCENT BOTTLES

History: Decorative bottles to hold scents have
been made in various shapes and sizes. They
reached a "golden age" during the second half of
the 19th century.

An atomizer is a perfume bottle with a spray
mechanism. Cologne bottles usually are larger and
have stoppers which also may be used as appli-
cators. A perfume bottle has a stopper that often
is elongated and designed as an applicator.

Scent bottles are small bottles used to hold a
scent or smelling salts. A vinaigrette is an ornamental box or bottle with a perforated top used to
hold aromatic vinegars or smelling salts. Fashionable women of the late 18th and 19th centuries
carried them in purses or slipped them into gloves
in case of a sudden fainting spell.

References: Hazel Martin, *A Collection Of Figural Perfume & Scent Bottles*, published by author, 1982; Jacquelyn Jones–North, *Commercial
Perfume Bottles*, Schiffer Publishing, 1987; Jacquelyn Jones–North, *Czechoslovakian Perfume
Bottles & Boudoir Accessories*, Antique Publications, 1990; Jacquelyn North, *Perfume, Cologne,
and Scent Bottles,* Schiffer Publishing, 1987; Jean
Sloan, *Perfume and Scent Bottle Collecting With
Prices, Second Edition,* Wallace–Homestead,
1989.

Collectors' Club: Perfume and Scent Bottle
Collectors, 2022 East Charleston Blvd., Las Ve-
gas, NV 89104.

ATOMIZERS

Amber, etched floral, marked "De Vil-
biss" **150.00**
Cameo, 9" h, tapered, red wisteria,
frosted citron ground, sgd "Galle" .. **1,100.00**
DeVilbiss, black amethyst art glass,
goldstone spiderweb dec, bulb missing **80.00**
Moser, 4½" h, melon ribbed body, sapphire blue, gold florals, leaves, and
swirls, orig gold top and bulb **250.00**

COLOGNES

Amethyst, swirled pattern, sheared
mouth, pontil scar, 5¼" h **135.00**
Baccarat, 7" h, frosted rosette ground,
gold flower and bow swag dec, cut
faceted stoppers, pr **330.00**
Burmese, 5" h, bulbous, raised gold floral branch dec, satin finish, silver hallmarked screw–on dome top, Webb . **880.00**
Cameo Glass, 3⅜" h, round body, white
florals and butterfly, frosted vaseline
ground, hallmarked silver hinged cap,
English **800.00**
Cobalt Blue, tooled mouth with neck
ring, pontil scar, 12¾" h, 1840–60 .. **40.00**
Cut, 7" h, cranberry to clear, cane cut,
matching stopper **250.00**
Midnight Blue, 11¼" h, tapered cylinder,
paneled shoulder and base, sheared
mouth with ring, ground pontil mark . **275.00**

Nash Glass, Chintz pattern, paper-
weight stopper **225.00**
Pairpoint, 8″ h, applied vertical cran-
berry ribbing, elaborate flower form
cranberry and clear stopper **110.00**
Peachblow
4¾″ h, floral dec, acid finish, cut stop-
per **355.00**
5″ h, bulbous, raised gold floral
branches and butterfly dec, satin
finish, hallmarked gold wash
screw–on dome top, Webb **800.00**
Quezal, 8¼″ h, bluish gold, tapered, sgd **525.00**
Silver Overlay, clear ground, marked
"Sterling" **150.00**
Verre–de–Soie, 5½″ h, intaglio cut floral
sprays, sterling and blue enameled
top with cherubs, marked "Hawkes" **385.00**

PERFUMES

Art Deco, 3¾″ h, triangular shape, brass
collar, intaglio stopper **80.00**
Black Jade, 6¾″ h, long stem, pink opa-
lescent petal top **1,155.00**
Bohemian, 2½″ h, cut stopper **75.00**
Bristol, 8¾″ h, yellow, pointed stopper . **440.00**
Cameo
3″ h, bulbous, serpent weaving
through textured design, hallmarked silver swirl hinged top,
Webb **770.00**
4½″ h, pear shape, red, white star
flower and leaf dec, hallmarked
sterling hinged lid **1,045.00**
Lalique, 5″ h, black glass, molded, low
relief standing female figure on each
corner, flattened sq stopper with
molded low relief florets, molded "Lalique" and "Ambre D'Orsay" **1,870.00**
Mary Gregory, 4⅝″ h, cranberry, white
enameled girl dec, clear ball stopper **165.00**

Scent, sterling silver, fiddle case, enameled roses, yellow ground, orig dauber, marked "Webster Co, North Attleboro, MA," 1⅝″ h, $75.00.

Pairpoint, 5½″ h, heavy crystal, con-
trolled bubbles **60.00**
Steuben
Aurene, 6½″ h, gold, black jade flat
top, clear dauber **275.00**
Rosa, black jade stopper **660.00**
Verre–de–Soie, 4¾″ h
Celeste blue **470.00**
Jade Green **300.00**

SCENTS

Blown, clear
2¹⁄₁₆″ h, circular, cut design **55.00**
2⅜″ h, coiled tail, applied rigaree . . **65.00**
3″ l, swirled ribs, coiled tail **65.00**
Clear, 2⅞″ h, sheared and polished lip,
pontil, 1840–60 . . . . **60.00**
Czechoslovakian, lay down type, multicolored jewels, enameled top **100.00**
Frosted and cut glass, 2¾″ l, cylindrical,
light to dark blue, flared base, gold
plated cap and chain, orig dauber . . **150.00**
Ivory, 5½″ h, figural, robed Oriental
man, teakwood base **225.00**
Opalescent, blown, cast pewter lid . . . **165.00**
Powder Blue, 2⅛″ h, transparent, gold
bands and stars, polished pontil, silver top stamped "GWI," 1840–50 . . **225.00**
Ruby Glass, cylindrical, SS cap dated
1884 . . . . **90.00**
Sabino Glass, five nudes, missing stop-
per **120.00**

VINAIGRETTES

Cut Glass, 3⅞″ l, cobalt glass, yellow
flashing, SS overlay, emb SS cap . . **125.00**
Gold, 2½″ l, flattened cartouche shape,
putto playing lute, another playing
with hound, carnelian intaglio base
with two lovebirds and chaplet, inscribed "Vivons Fidelle," English, mid
18th C **650.00**
Silver
Purse Shape, engraved basketwork
body, florals at clasp, hallmarks for
John Lawrence & Co, Birmingham,
England, 1819 . . . . **450.00**
Rectangular, vermeil int., George III,
John Shaw Birmingham, 1808 . . . **240.00**

PERSONALITY COLLECTIBLES

History: While a host of fictional characters orig-
inate from the comics, movies, radio, and television, a group of "stars" who retained their own
identity are also a by–product. Hopalong Cassidy
is a fictional character; Gene Autry and Roy Rogers are real life personalities. Real life drama also

produces "heroes" honored for a heroic moment or a unique personal achievement.

The fame achieved by stars and heroes has attracted the attention of promoters and manufacturers for over a century. From Buffalo Bill's Wild West Show to Michael Jackson's Coca–Cola commercial, star power has shown itself to be a proven value. Little wonder the advertising and toy industry has produced so many products featuring stars and heroes.

This category includes only objects related to real life personalities. Sometimes the line can become very blurred. Does Edgar Bergen and Charlie McCarthy belong under character collectibles or personality collectibles? We have chosen to list them in this category.

References: Richard DeThuin, *The Official Identification and Price Guide To Movie Memorabilia*, House of Collectibles, 1990; Ted Hake, *Hake's Guide To TV Collectibles*, Wallace–Homestead, 1990; John Hegenberger, *Collector's Guide to Treasures From The Silver Screen,*, Wallace–Homestead, 1991; Jefferson Graham, *Come On Down !!! – The TV Game Show Book*, Abbeville Press, 1988; Richard O'Brien, *Collecting Toys, A Collector's Identification & Value Guide, No. 5*, Books Americana, 1990; Patricia Smith, *Shirley Temple Dolls and Collectibles*, (1977, 1992 value update), *Second Series*, (1979, 1992 value update); Collector Books; John R. Warren, *Warren's Movie Poster Price Guide*, Overstreet Publications, 1986; Dian Zillner, *Hollywood Collectibles*, Schiffer Publishing, 1991.

Periodicals: *Big Reel*, Route #3, P.O. Box 83, Madison, NC 27025; *Classic Images*, P.O. Box 809, Muscatine, IA 52761; *Movie Collectors' World*, P.O. Box 309, Fraser, MI 48026.

Additional Listings: See Character Collectibles in *Warman's Antiques and Their Prices* and Cowboy Collectibles, Movie Personalities, Radio Characters and Personalities, Shirley Temple, and TV Personalities & Memorabilia in *Warman's Americana & Collectibles*.

Amos 'N Andy
    Autograph, 8 x 10" black and white
        photo, inscribed in blue ink **150.00**

Bing Crosby, box, Valley Farms Ice Cream, pint size, cardboard, $5.00.

Toy, Fresh Air Taxi, litho tin windup,
    Marx, 1929 .... **395.00**
Ball, Lucille
    Magazine, Life, April 6, 1953, five
      page article, full color cover of Lucy,
      Desi Arnaz, Desi IV, and Lucy De-
      siree **25.00**
    Movie Lobby Card, 11 x 14", full color,
      1949 Columbia Picture "Miss Grant
      Takes Richmond" **20.00**
Bernhardt, Sarah, cabinet photo, 4¼ x
    6½", sepia portrait, c1910 .... **30.00**
Blyth, Ann, coloring book, 1952, some
    pages colored **12.00**
Cantor, Eddie
    Big Little Book, *Eddie Cantor In An
      Hour With You*, Whitman, #774,
      1934, 154 pages, 4½ x 5¼" **40.00**
    Children's Book, *Eddie Cantor In
      Laughland*, Goldsmith Publishing
      Co, 1934, 5 x 5¼" soft cover, 122
      page story, art by Henry Vallely,
      foreword with endorsement by Ju-
      venile Educations League **35.00**
Captain Kangaroo
    Puzzle, 10 x 14", frame tray, Captain
      and nursery rhyme characters,
      1956 K— Enterprises copyright,
      Milton Bradley **18.00**
    Whisk Broom, 7" h, wood handle,
      blue and fleshtones, black, white,
      red, and yellow accents, copyright
      R.K.A., c1960 .... **35.00**
Cassidy, Hopalong
    Barrette, 2" l, diecut brass, bright lus-
      ter, initials outlined in bright red,
      black and red portrait, c1950 .... **27.50**
    Bed Spread, chenille, beige and
      brown **225.00**
    Bottle Cap, 1¼" stiff cardboard disk,
      green image, words "Play Money"
      and "1¢", slight browning, c1950 . **25.00**
    Notebook Filler Paper, Hoppy pic-
      tured on wrapper, unopened, mint **18.00**
    Pinback Button, 1⅛" d, litho, black
      picture, bright yellow ground,
      c1950 .... **35.00**
    Radio, red, tin saddle back, orig tin
      tag on bottom, Hoppy on reared
      Topper, mint, working condition .. **475.00**
    Record Album, Hoppy & Square
      Dance Hold Up, two record set .. **65.00**
Crawford, Joan, tin, 7", plaid design,
    young MGM Studios portrait **235.00**
Dionne Quintuplets
    Advertisement, 5 x 7", Quintuplet
      Bread, Schulz Baking Co, diecut
      cardboard, loaf of bread, brown
      crust, bright red and blue letters,
      named silhouette portraits, text on
      reverse **60.00**
    Fan, 8¼ x 8¾" diecut cardboard, ti-

tled "Sweethearts Of The World," full color tinted portraits, light blue ground, 1936 copyright, name of funeral director 20.00

Evans, Dale
  Jewelry Set, child's, orig wrist watch Ring, litho tin, Post's Raisin Bran premium, copyright 1952 . . . . 20.00 / 25.00

Flynn, Erroll, pin, 1" d, litho tin disk, black and white photo, silver rim, reverse with name and fold over tab with straight pin, English, c1950 . . . 20.00

Garland, Judy, sheet music, On The Atchison, Topeka, and the Sante Fe, from 1945 MGM movie "The Harvey Girls," sepia photo on purple, light pink, and brown cov 20.00

Gleason, Jackie
  Coloring Book, "Jackie Gleason's Dan Dan Dandy Color Book," Abbott, 1956 copyright, unused 17.50
  Magazine, TV Guide, May 21, 1955, Philadelphia edition, three page article on Honeymooners 15.00

Haley, Bill, pinback button, 7/8" d, light blue litho, browntone portrait, marked on back "A Decca Recording Star" . 35.00

Houdini, Harry, big little book, *Houdini's Big Little Book Of Magic,* Whitman, 1927, premium for American Oil and Amoco Gas, 192 pages 20.00

Leigh, Vivian, pin, 1" d, litho tin disk, black and white photo, silver rim, reverse with name and fold over tab with straight pin, English, c1950 . . . 20.00

Lloyd, Harold, playing card, 2½ x 3½", white, black, red, and fleshtone image as Jack of Hearts, white lady, black maid playing card game, promoting comedy movie "Dr Jack," 1922 . . . . 15.00

Marx Brothers
  Book, *Beds,* hardbound 40.00
  Sheet Music, 9½ x 12¼", Alone, MGM musical "A Night At The Opera," 1935, orange, blue, and white cover, blue photos of Groucho, Chico, Harpo, Allan Jones, and Kitty Carlisle 20.00

Maynard, Ken
  Big Little Book, *Ken Maynard & The Gun Wolves of the Gila* 25.00
  Pinback Button, 1¾" d, "Cole Bros Circus/Ken Maynard," black, white, and gray, c1930 . . . . 90.00

Monroe, Marilyn
  Calendar, 1953, colorful, complete . . 225.00
  Magazine, Life, April 7, 1952, cover article, black and white photo cover, 172 pages 35.00

Peck, Gregory, pin, 1" d, litho tin disk, black and white photo, silver rim, re-

verse with name and fold over tab with straight pin, English, c1950 . . . 20.00

Presley, Elvis, pin, 1¾" l brass guitar, simulated white mother–of–pearl inlay on face, yellow paint, six tiny green rhinestones, small brass frame with black and white photo inscribed "Best Wishes From Elvis Presley," c1950 . . . . 125.00

Rogers, Roy
  Bank, Roy on reared Trigger, porcelain, sgd "Roy Rogers and Trigger" 250.00
  Clothing, sweat shirt, child's, Roy and Trigger graphics, c1950 . . . . 65.00
  Toy, Roy Fit It Stagecoach, figure, Bullet, two horses, and complete accessories 75.00
  Yo–Yo, illus of Roy and Trigger on side, unplayed with 15.00

Rogers, Will, rolled penny, portrait, star designs, issued c1935 to commemorate death in plane crash 20.00

Rooney, Mickey
  Postcard, showing home, c1940 . . . 7.50
  Washboard, wood and tin 20.00

Sinatra, Frank, pin, 2½" h, diecut wood, brass pin, black and white face, red accents, c1940, minor wear 25.00

Temple, Shirley
  Children's Book, *Shirley Temple's Birthday Book,* Dell Publishing Co, c1934, soft cover, 24 pages, unused condition 100.00
  Handkerchiefs, Little Colonel, boxed set of three 195.00
  Magazine, Hollywood, June 1936, full color cov of Shirley holding bouquet of flowers, article titled "Is Shirley A Poor Little Rich Girl," 74 pages, other mid 1930s movie stars 35.00

Turner, Lana
  Autograph, black and white glossy photo, 8 x 10", c1940, black ink inscription 35.00
  Pin, 1" d, litho tin disk, black and white photo, silver rim, reverse with name and fold over tab with straight pin, English, c1950 . . . . 18.00

Vallee, Rudy, adv, clapper, wood 50.00

Valentino, Rudy, book, *Sons of the Sheik,* Photo Play movie edition, orig dust jacket 50.00

Williams, Esther, adv, box, Quick Oats 38.00

PETERS AND REED POTTERY

History: J. D. Peters and Adam Reed founded their pottery company in South Zanesville, Ohio, in 1900. Common flowerpots, jardinieres, and cooking wares comprised their early major output.

Occasionally art pottery was attempted, but it was not until 1912 that their Moss Aztec line was introduced and widely accepted. Other art wares included Chromal, Landsun, Montene, Pereco, and Persian.

Peters retired in 1921 and Reed changed the name of the firm to Zane Pottery Company. Marked pieces of Peters and Reed Pottery are unknown.

Vase, yellow ground, brown drip glaze, 11⅜" h, $75.00.

Bookends, pr, 5", Pereco, stylized dec, matte green glaze	**45.00**
Candlesticks, pr, 10" h, mirror black glaze	**24.00**
Ewer, 11" h, brown, raised grapes, orange and yellow dec	**40.00**
Jardiniere, 6½ x 7½", green lion's head dec, beige ground	**75.00**
Jug, bulbous, grape clusters and vine dec, standard glossy brown glaze, handled	**50.00**
Mug, 5½", grape clusters and vine dec, standard glossy brown glaze	**35.00**
Pitcher, 4", man with banjo, standard glossy brown glaze	**35.00**
Rose Bowl, wreath and vine dec, standard glossy brown glaze, ftd	**40.00**
Vase	
6 x 4", hexagonal, pinched sides, floral medallion dec, standard brown glaze	**60.00**
8½", Shadow Ware, blue and cream drip glaze, olive green ground . . .	**40.00**
9¾", pine cones and needles, green wash glaze, terra cotta ground . . .	**65.00**
13", chromal scene, Mt Fujiyama . .	**200.00**
Wall Pocket	
7¾", Pereco, Egyptian dec	**70.00**
8", Moss Aztec, emb grape cluster dec, sgd "Ferrell"	**50.00**

PEWTER

History: Pewter is a metal alloy consisting mostly of tin with small amounts of lead, copper, antimony, and bismuth added to improve forma-

bility and hardness. The metal can be cast, formed around a mold, spun, easily cut, and soldered to form a wide variety of utilitarian articles.

Pewter ware was known to the ancient Chinese, Egyptians, and Romans. English pewter supplied the major portion of the needs of the American colonies for nearly 150 years before the American Revolution. The Revolution ended the embargo on raw tin and allowed the small American pewter industry to flourish. This period lasted until the Civil War.

The listing concentrates on the American and English pewter forms most often encountered by the collector.

Reference: Donald L. Fennimore, *The Knopf Collectors' Guides to American Antiques, Silver & Pewter,* Alfred A. Knopf, Inc., 1984.

Collectors' Club: Pewter Collector's Club of America, 29 Chesterfield Road, Scarsdale, NY 10583.

Tobacco Jar, cov, Continental, 7" h, $215.00.

Basin	
Graham & Wardrop, Glasgow, Scotland, pitted int., 10" d	**150.00**
Hamlin, Samuel, Providence, RI, 1769–1810, 5¾" d	**700.00**
Jones, Gershom, Providence, RI, 1774–1809, 7¾" d	**850.00**
Townsend & Compton, London, 1785–1801, 11½" d, hammered booge	**300.00**
Unmarked, American, rampant lion touch mark of Thomas Danforth II, 7⅞" d	**250.00**
Beaker	
Boardman and Hart, NY, c1830, 5¼" h	**850.00**
Flagg, Asa F, and Henry Homan, Cincinnati, OH, whiskey size	**225.00**
Yale, Hiram, Wallingford, CT, 1820–30, sgd "Yale" and "Britannia," 3" h	**300.00**

Bedpan
  Boardman, Thomas Danforth, missing handle, 12″ d 60.00
  Hamilin, Samuel, Sr and Jr, Providence, RI, 10½″ d 250.00
Box, Coldwell, George, New York, NY, 1787–1811, oval, hinged engraved lid, 2⅞″ l 575.00
Candlestick
  Hopper, Henry, New York, 1842–47, trumpet shape, straight line touch, 9⅞″ h 350.00
  Unmarked
    American, orig insets, pr, 9⅜″ h .. 325.00
    Dutch, c1700, provision for snuffer, weighted base, 6½″ h 225.00
    English, 1800–25, pr, push up ejectors, 8¾″ h 375.00
Chalice, Leonard, Reed & Barton, Taunton, MA, 1835–40, 7″ h 175.00
Chamber Basin, unmarked, Continental, flat rim, minor scratches, 13⅛″ d 200.00
Charger
  Austin, Richard, Boston, MA, c1800, cleaned and polished, 13⅜″ d ... 230.00
  Boyd, Parks, Philadelphia, PA, c1800, knife marks and pitting, 12″ d ... 125.00
  Hamlin, Samuel, Sr, Providence, RI, c1790, heavy pitting on upper surface, 13½″ d 225.00
  Spackman & Grant, London, c1715, repair in center, knife marks and denting, 15″ d 125.00
  Townsend and Reynolds, London, 18th C, small dents, 15″ 450.00
Coffeepot
  Boardman & Hart, NY, c1935, bulbous, finial resoldered, 11″ h 415.00
  Dunham, Rufus, Westbrook, ME, 1837–61, lighthouse shape, 10¾″ h 350.00
  Gleason, Roswell, Dorchester, MA, 1822–71, 10¼″ h, lighthouse shape 450.00
  Porter, Allen, Westbrook, ME, 1830–40, bulbous, bold straight line "A. Porter" touch in rect on bottom, 11¾″ h 600.00
  Putnam, James, Malden, MA, 1830–35, pear shape, cleaned, 11″ h .. 350.00
  Simpson, Samuel, Yalesville, CT, 1835–52, minor pitting in foot ring, 11¼″ h 500.00
  Smith & Co, Boston, MA, c1840, restoration at base and top of handle, handle repainted, 9½″ h 150.00
Communion Plate
  Calder, William, Providence, RI, 1817–56, minor scratches, 11⅜″ d 300.00
  Gleason, Roswell, Dorchester, MA, c1850, 10¾″ d 250.00
Cuspidor, Gleason, Roswell, Dorchester, MA, c1850, well preserved, few minor dents, 8″ d 200.00
Dish, deep
  Boyd, Parks, Phila, PA, 1795–1819, large eagle touch, 12″ d 800.00
  Griswold, Ashbil, Meriden, CT, 1802–42, double struck with large eagle touch, 11⅛″ d 250.00
  Townsend, John and Thomas Giffin, London, 1777–1801, hammered booge, numerous knife marks, 12″ d 250.00
Flagon
  Boardman & Co, New York, c1825, lighthouse shape 900.00
  Calder, William, Providence, RI, 1817–56, 11″ h 850.00
  Trask, Oliver, Boston, MA, c1830, 10⅞″ h 550.00
Funnel, unmarked, English, c1800, 3½″ d, 4½″ l 175.00
Goblet, unmarked, American, attributed to Israel Trask, early 19th C, 5⅛″ h . 200.00
Haystack Measure, Austen and Son, Irish, 1828–33, set of 7 .... 1,600.00
Hot Water Plate
  Compton, Thomas, London, 18th C, fine hallmarks, minor dent, 7⅞″ d 125.00
  Ellis, Samuel, Longon, 18th C, one dent, knife marks, 9⅛″ d 125.00
  King, Richard, London, c1750, minor flaking, 9½″ d 75.00
Inkwell, unmarked, c1800, circular, ironstone china inset with slight blue discoloration, lid, age and glaze cracks, 3¼″ d 100.00
Ladle
  Hall & Cotton, Middlefield, CT, c1840, straight line rect touch, 12¾″ l ... 300.00
  Kruiger, Lewis, Phila, PA, c1830, turned wood handle, 14″ l 250.00
  Lee, Richard, early 19th C, punchwork dec on int. and ext. of bowl, turned hardwood handle, 13⅜″ l . 300.00
  Palethrop, John H, Phila, PA, 1820–40, soup, double rect straight line touch 350.00
  Stedman, S, Eastern CT or RI, c1800, curved wood handle with finely turned finial, marked "N" on shank, 14″ l 450.00
  Unmarked, American, turned wood handle, minor damage, 16″ l 100.00
  Yates, John, England, mid 19th C, soup, fiddle handle, 14¼″ l 200.00
Lamp
  Chamber, unmarked, American, attributed to Meriden Brittania Co, c1840, pr, whale oil burners, 5¾″ h 350.00
  Gimball, unmarked, American, double camphene burner and ring handle, one cap missing, 8″ h 300.00

Hand
  Morey & Smith, Boston, c1850,
    double whale oil burners, strong
    touch marks, bell shaped, "C"
    shaped handle, 3½" h **150.00**
  Unmarked American
    Boston, c1850, bell shape, cam-
      phene burner, 3½" h **125.00**
    New England or New York,
      c1840, double whale oil
      burner, bell shaped lamp, "C"
      shaped handle, resoldered
      handle, 2⅝" h **100.00**
Sparking, whale oil
  Putnam, James, Malden, MA,
    1830–65, straight line "Putnam"
    touch, saucer base with ring han-
    dle, minor denting, 2⅝" h **125.00**
  Unmarked, American, c1850, sau-
    cer base with ring handle, cylin-
    drical font, 2¾" h **100.00**
Whale Oil
  Dunham, Rufus, Westbrook, ME,
    1837–61, c1840, straight line
    "Dunham" touch, brass double
    whale oil burner, cylindrical foot,
    several small base holes, 5½" h **100.00**
  Gleason, Roswell, Dorchester, MA,
    c1840, unmarked, weighted
    base, single plated silver over
    copper bull's eye lens, 8½" h ... **225.00**
  Putnam, James, Malden, MA,
    1830–65, straight line "Putnam"
    touch, minor resoldering at
    seam, 6" h **175.00**
  Taunton Britannia Mfg Co, Taun-
    ton, MA, 1830–35, straight line
    touch "T. B. M. Co.," brass dou-
    ble whale oil burner, acorn font,
    resoldered under font, minor
    denting, 7¼" h **275.00**
  Unmarked, semi–saucer base, cy-
    lindrical font, bulbous bottom,
    double drop burner, 8" h **175.00**

Loving Cup, James Dixon & Sons, England, two handles, 7" h **125.00**

Miniature
  Porringer, Lee, Richard, Springfield,
    VT, late 18th C, 2⅜" d **700.00**
  Tea Service, child's, attributed to
    James Tufts, Boston, MA, c1870,
    cov 4" h teapot, sugar, creamer,
    waste bowl, six cups and saucers **275.00**

Mug
  Austin, Nathaniel, Charlestown, MA,
    late 18th C, 6" h **1,350.00**
  Bassett, Frederick, NY, c1780, 4½" h **1,600.00**
  Kilbourn, Samuel, Baltimore, MD,
    early 19th C, 4" h **750.00**
  Unmarked American
    Attributed to Thomas Danforth

Boardman, Hartford, CT, c1820,
  one gill, 2¹¹⁄₁₆" h **325.00**
Attributed to Samuel Danforth,
  Hartford, CT, 1795–1816, pint,
  4½" h **650.00**
Unmarked, English, mid 19th C, own-
  er's name inscribed on front, quart **100.00**
Pitcher
  Boardman, Thomas Danforth, CT,
    1840, two quarts, cider type, "X"
    quality mark, minor denting and re-
    soldering, 6¼" h **500.00**
  Curtis, Daniel, Albany, NY, c1830, 8"
    h **725.00**
  Dunham, Rufus, Westbrook, ME,
    c1850, straight line touch, two
    quarts **400.00**
  Gleason, Rosewell, Dorchester, MA,
    1822–71, minor repairs, cleaned . **550.00**
  McQuilkin, William, Phila, PA, balus-
    ter shape, scrolled handle, 10" h . **950.00**
Plate
  Austin, Nathaniel, Charlestown, MA,
    1763–1800, incised X in brim, 8" d **300.00**
  Austin, Richard, Boston, MA, 1792–
    1815, allover pitting, 8½" d **350.00**
  Badger, Thomas, Boston, MA, 1787–
    1815, 8½" d **350.00**
  Barns, Blakslee, Phila, PA, 1812–17,
    second touch of straight line touch
    "B Barnes/Philad'a," stamped
    "DM" in rim, 7⅞" d **225.00**
  Belcher, Newport, RI, 1769–84, 8" d **350.00**
  Billings, William, Providence, RI,
    c1800, 11½" d **775.00**
  Calder, William, Providence, RI,
    1817–56, eagle touch, 7⅞" d **350.00**
  Curtis, Daniel, Albany, NY, 1822–40,
    "X" quality mark, faint touch, pitted,
    7⅞" d **150.00**
  Danforth, Edward, Middletown and
    Hartford, CT, 1788–94, 8" d **150.00**
  Danforth, John, Norwich, CT, 1773–
    95, smooth brim, pitted, touch
    marks, 9" d **250.00**
  Duncombe, Samuel, Birmingham,
    1740–80, smooth brim, set of 4, 9"
    d **425.00**
  Jones, Gershom, Providence, RI,
    1774–1809, few knife marks and
    gouges on back, 8⁵⁄₁₆" d **300.00**
  Lightner, George, Baltimore, MD,
    1808–1815, cleaned, 7⅞" d **200.00**
  Melville, David or Thomas, Newport,
    RI, 1790–95, 8¼" d **200.00**
  Pierce, Samuel, Sr, Greenfield, MA,
    earliest eagle touch, 8" d **250.00**
  Whitmore, Jacob, Middletown, CT,
    1758–90, two small areas of pitting,
    7⅞" d **200.00**
  Will, Henry, NY, late 18th C, 15" d .. **1,450.00**

Porringer, New England, Thomas Danforth Boardman, 5″ d, $390.00.

Platter, Thomas Compton, London, oval, 20 x 15⅜″ 500.00
Porringer
  Boardman, Thomas D and Sherman, Hartford, CT, 1830, old English style handle, straight line touch, 4″ d 550.00
  Danforth, Samuel, Hartford, CT, 1795–1816, basin type, old English style handle, 3⅝″ d 850.00
  Gleason, Roswell, Dorchester, MA, c1850, heart and crescent handle, 3¼″ d 425.00
  Green, Samuel, Boston, 1790–1810, crown handle, reverse "SG" signature, 5⁷⁄₁₆″ d 200.00
  Hamlin, Samuel E, Providence, RI, 1790–1810, 5¼″ d 600.00
  Hamlin, Samuel E, Jr, Providence, RI, 1801–56
    5¼″ d, flower handle, bold touch on top of handle 550.00
    5⅜″ d, flower handle, strong eagle touch on top of handle 700.00
  Lee, Richard, Springfield, VT, late 18th C, 3¾″ d 800.00
  Melville, David, Newport, RI, 1755–93, geometric handle, Newport style bracket, 5″ d 500.00
  Unmarked, New England, c1800, crown handle, "IC" signature on back of handle, 4¼″ d 225.00
Salt, English, pedestal, octagonal base, candlestick standard, 3⅜″ d 185.00
Sugar Bowl
  Boardman, Thomas Danforth, Hartford, CT, baluster shape, scrolled handles, 5¾″ h 500.00
  Will, William, double bellied, beaded rim and foot, 4¾″ h 3,500.00
  Unmarked, New England, c1825–40, cov, strap handles, 6¾″ h 100.00
Syrup Pitcher, unmarked, American,

lighthouse shape, reversed "C" handle, old resoldering on spout, 5⅞″ h **75.00**
Tankard
  Griffin, Thomas, London, late 18th C, 7½″ h **475.00**
  Redhead, Anthony, English, Stuart, flat lid, wriggle work engraving, 6½″ h **485.00**
  Young, Peter, cylindrical, molded base, flat top, 6¾″ h **4,500.00**

Teapot, American, G. Richardson, 9½″ h, $350.00.

Teapot
  Boardman & Hart, New York, 1830–40, "X" quality mark, 8¼″ h **225.00**
  Calder, William, Providence, RI, c1825, globular, minor surface scratches, some int. pitting, 8¼″ h **275.00**
  Curtiss, Edwin and Lemuel, Meriden, CT, c1840, inverted mold, resoldered hinge, minor denting, 6″ h . . **200.00**
  Gleason, Roswell, Dorchester, MA, c1830–40, inverted mold, minor pitting, 7″ h **250.00**
  Graves, H. H., c1850, inverted mold, minor dents, resoldered hinge, 8″ h **150.00**
  Locke, J D, New York, NY, 1835–60, c1840, good touch mark, minor pitting and denting, 7½″ h **125.00**
  Richardson, George, Sr, Cranston, RI, 1828–45, tapered, 8″ h **400.00**
  Smith, Eben, Beverly, MA, 1813–56, pear shape, Queen Anne style, 7″ h **1,550.00**

PHOENIX BIRD CHINA

History: Phoenix Bird pattern is a blue and white china exported from Japan during the 1920s to 1940s. A limited amount was made during the "Occupied Japan" period.

Initially it was available at Woolworth's 5 & 10, through two wholesale catalog companies, or by selling subscriptions to needlecraft magazines.

Myott Son & Co., England, also produced this pattern under the name "Satsuma," c1936. These earthenware items were for export only.

Once known as "Blue Howo Bird China," the Phoenix Bird pattern is the most sought after of seven similar patterns in the Hō–ō bird series. Other patterns are: Flying Turkey (head faces forward with heart–like border); Howo (only pattern with name on base); and Twin Phoenix (border pattern only, center white). The Howo and Twin Phoenix patterns are by Noritake and are occasionally marked "Noritake." Flying Dragon (bird–like), an earlier pattern, comes in green and white as well as the traditional blue and white and is marked with six oriental characters. A variation of Phoenix Bird pattern has a heart–like border and is called Hō–ō.

Phoenix Bird pattern has over 500 different shapes and sizes. Also varying is the quality found in the execution of design, shades of blue, and shape of the ware itself. All these factors must be considered in pricing. The maker's mark tends to add value; over 90 marks have been cataloged.

Post-1970 pieces were produced in limited shapes with precise detail, but are on a milk white ground and usually don't have a maker's mark. When a mark does appear on a modern piece, it appears stamped in place.

Reference: Joan Collett Oates, *Phoenix Bird Chinaware*, published by author, *Book One*, 1984, *Book Two (A Through M)*, 1985, *Book Three (N through Z and Post-1970)*, 1986; *Book Four (With A Section On Flying Turkey)*, 1989.

Collectors' Club: Phoenix Bird Collectors of America, 5912 Kingsfield Drive, West Bloomfield, MI 48322.

Additional Listings: See *Warman's Americana & Collectibles* for more examples.

Advisor: Joan Oates.

Butter Pat	8.00
Cake Tray, #3	48.00
Children's Dishes, tea set, #4, 3 pcs	65.00
Chocolate Pot, scalloped, tall	125.00
Coffeepot, post 1970	35.00
Condensed Milk Holder	75.00
Creamer and Sugar, #20	50.00

Ice Cream Dish, individual serving size, superior border, 6¾ x 4 x 1½", $35.00.

Custard Cup	15.00
Egg Cup, double	18.00
Fruit Dish, 5½" d, scalloped, wide border	10.00
Gravy Boat, attached plate	60.00
Hair Receiver	65.00
Pitcher, buttermilk	55.00
Plate	
9¼" d, breakfast	30.00
9¾" d, dinner	45.00
Platter	
7¾ x 5", scalloped	25.00
12¼ x 9"	45.00
15 x 9¾"	60.00
Rice Bowl, "A"	10.00
Rice Tureen, #3–A	85.00
Salt and Pepper Shaker, pr	25.00
Sauce Boat, with underplate, #2	65.00
Soup Bowl, 7¼"	20.00
Syrup, #1	35.00
Teapot, pre-1970	45.00

PHOENIX GLASS

History: Phoenix Glass Company, Beaver, Pennsylvania, was established in 1880. Known primarily for commercial glassware, the firm also produced a molded, sculptured, cameo–type line from the 1930s until the 1950s.

Reference: Jack D. Wilson, *Phoenix & Consolidated Art Glass, 1926–1980*, Antique Publications, 1989.

Vase, pillow shape, turquoise, peach colored carp, 8" w, 9" h, $115.00.

Bowl, 9½" d, 5½" h, bittersweet, white ground	150.00
Canoe, 13½" l, sculptured blue love-birds, opal ground	325.00
Charger, 18" d, relief of white dancing nudes, blue ground	525.00
Compote, 8½" d, dragonflies and water lilies dec, butterscotch ground	80.00

Console Bowl, diving ladies, blue figures, white ground 235.00
Lamp, table
   17½" h, green peacock feather pattern, irid blue, sgd "Phoenix Studios, Tom Arnold, #197" 185.00
   20" h, red cardinals on tree branches, green berries, ivory ground 225.00
Plate
   6¾" d, dancing nudes, frosted and clear 38.00
   8½" d, cherries, frosted and clear . . 55.00
Powder Box, cov
   6¾" d, sculptured roses, humming bird, amethyst 125.00
   7¼" d, sculptured white violets, pale lavender ground 100.00
Vase
   6½" h, rect, opal sculptured lovebirds on branch, white ground 100.00
   7½" h, blown out pearlized white fern fronds and narrow leaves, salmon pink ground, orig label 250.00
   8⅜" h, fan shape, sculptured praying mantis, foliage, pearlized and frosted, pale blue–gray ground . . 150.00
   9" h, Canada geese in flight, opal white birds, pastel blue ground, remnants of paper label 165.00
   9½" h, heavily gilted roses, white ground 125.00
   10" h, dogwood, blue, white ground, partial paper label 80.00
   10¼" h, Madonna, blue ground, sculptured head, white irid 240.00
   11" h, sculptured, coral, green, and brown dogwoods, white ground . . 275.00
   18" h, pearlized white thistles, blue ground, orig paper label 495.00

PHONOGRAPHS

History: Early phonographs were commonly called "talking machines." Thomas A. Edison invented the first successful phonograph in 1877. Other manufacturers followed with their variations.

Collectors' Club: Antique Phonograph Collectors Club, 502 E. 17th Street, Brooklyn, NY 11226.

Periodical: *Horn Speaker,* Box 53012, Dallas, TX 75253.

Apollo, oak case, blue fluted metal horn, crank wind 400.00
Boston Talking Machine, Little Wonder Disc Phonograph, cast iron case and horn, single spring, 1909–12 . . . . . . 250.00
Brunswick, Model 105, mahogany case, two headed reproducer, oval fretwork grill, crank wind 275.00
Columbia
   Baby Regent, square mahogany ta-

Edison, Gem, orig horn, 1904–06, $350.00.

   ble, four carved cabriole legs, drawer in turntable int., louvered speaker horn 1,150.00
   Graphophone, oak case, nickelplated and black painted metal parts, gold and red dec, belled horn, black reproducer, decal 400.00
   Home Grand, oak case, nickelplated works, six spring motor 1,400.00
Decca Junior, portable, leather cov case, carrying handle 190.00
Edison
   Excelsior, coin operated, spring wound 1,700.00
   Gem Model D, two and four minute K reproducer, early 1900s 1,250.00
   Opera, stationary reproducer and moving mandrel, wood horn 2,500.00
   Standard Model A, short black brass bell horn, orig banner decal 450.00
   Harvard, trumpet style horn 300.00
Kalamazoo Duplex, reproducer, orig horns and decals, patent date 1904 3,300.00
Odeon Talking Machine Co, table model, crank wind, brass bell horn, straight tone arm 500.00
Silvertone, Sears & Roebuck, two reproducers, 1914 . . . . 200.00
Sonora Disc Console Phonographs
   Gothic Deluxe, Normandy, walnut case, triple spring, goldplated metal parts, automatic stop, storage for eighty records 350.00
   Luzerne, Renaissance style case, storage for eighty records 200.00
Talk–O–Phone Company, The Brooke, table model, oak case, beaded dec, triple spring, steel horn with brass bell, detachable metal horn bracket,

combination brake and speed regulator **550.00**
Victor
Monarch, table model, corner columns, brass bell horn, reproducer **1,400.00**
VI, mahogany case, fluted Corinthian corner columns, carved capitals, gold dec, reproducer, triple spring, bell brass morning glory horn ... **1,500.00**
Wizard, cylinder, table model, oak case, morning glory horn **850.00**

PHOTOGRAPHS

History: A vintage print is a positive image developed from the original negative by the photographer or under the photographer's supervision at the time the negative is made. A non–vintage print is a print made from an original negative at a later date. It is quite common for a photographer to make prints from the same negative over several decades. Changes between the original printing and subsequent prints usually can be identified. Limited edition prints must be clearly labeled.

References: Stuart Bennett, *How To Buy Photographs,* Salem House, 1987; O. Henry Mace, *Collector's Guide To Early Photographs,* Wallace–Homestead, 1990; Lou W. McCulloch, *Card Photographs, A Guide to Their History And Value,* Schiffer Publishing Ltd., 1981; Floyd and Marion Rinhart, *American Miniature Case Art,* A. S. Barnes and Co., Inc., 1969; John Waldsmith, *Stereoviews, An Illustrated History and Price Guide,* Wallace–Homestead, 1991.

Collectors' Clubs: American Photographic Historical Society, P.O. Box 1775, Grand Central Station, New York, NY 10163; National Stereoscopic Association, P.O. Box 14801, Columbus, OH 43214.

Additional Listings: See *Warman's Americana & Collectibles* in the categories of Carte de Visite and Cabinet Cards and Stereographs.

Album
Civil War
Cartes–De–Visite, group of 33, military figures, clipped signature of Jefferson Davis, image of General OO Potter signed on image, rest identified on window mount, two tintypes of men posing with rifles, 8vo, gilt lettered morocco, worn, gilt edges, 1860s **1,210.00**
Photographs, Jimmy Hare, group of 57, titled "Gettysburg Reunion," Brig Gen Hunter Liggett, General Leonard Wood, many aging veterans, scenes of parades, parties, views of battlefield and camp, 4½ x 6½" silver prints, oblong 4to, faux–alligator, gilt let-

Daguerreotype, gentleman, orig velvet lined case, 3¼" h, $45.00.

tered, leaves chipped, signed by photographer on last page, 1913 **880.00**
Class Album, Harvard College 1874, 183 photographs by William Notman, 4¼ x 3" oval albumen cabinet photographs of faculty and students, each identified on mount recto, 9 large (7 x 9½") group portraits of baseball team, telegraph group, society group, glee club, boating team, and other student activities, thick folio, gilt lettered morocco, edges worn, spine torn, brass clip, gilt edges **825.00**
Albumen Print
Barnard, George N, Scene of General McPherson's Death, titled "Photographic Views of the Sherman Campaign, plate 35," penciled notions on mount recto, 10¼ x 14¼", 1864 .... **850.00**
Carroll, Lewis, portrait of Xie Kitchen, child holding daisy, oval, 2½ x 2", c1873 .... **660.00**
Gardner, Alexander, Lincoln and McClellan, seated together inside tent, penciled notations on mount verso, 3½ x 4½", 1862 .... **605.00**
Smith, W Morris and Alexander Gardner, Dedication of Monument on Bull Run Battlefield, two toned sketchbook mount, printed with photographer's credit, copyright, title, number "100," and "June, 1865," with accompanying text, 7 x 9", 1865 .... **315.00**
Unknown Photographer
Augustus Saint–Gaudens, view of sculptor, chisel in hand, NY studio, 6½ x 8¾", 1870s **300.00**
Fire steam engine, mounted, 17 x 22¼", c1855 .... **360.00**
Ambrotype, occupational, quarter–plate, cased, 1860s
Framer in studio **605.00**
Shoemakers, tinted **605.00**

Tinsmiths, rows of pots and pans behind them **465.00**

Cabinet Card, Napoleon Sarony, Oscar Wilde, studio imprint, identification on mount recto, 1882 . . . . **475.00**

Carte–De–Viste, Alexander Gardner, portrait of president elect Abraham Lincoln, Brady/Anthony imprint on mount verso, 1861 . . . . **1,100.00**

Daguerreotype

Portrait, children, George and Charles T Thomas, quarter–plate, cased, hand colored, hand written label identifies boys, 1840s **195.00**

Serial, medical, Dr George Frederick Shrady, Intern at NY Hospital, name plate inserted in brass preserver, sixth–plate, double case, images of intern with arm and scalpel, c1859 . . . . **6,600.00**

Photogravure, Frederick H Evans, portrait of Aubrey Beardsley, photographer's credit in plate below image, 5 x 4″, 1904 . . . . **990.00**

Platinum Print

Evans, Frederick H, portrait of W Herbert Grant, tipped to the mount, hand ruled in ink and wash, titled and signed by photographer in pencil on mount recto, 7½ x 5″, early 1900s **550.00**

Rinehart, FA, photographer's identification, title, copyright date and number in negative, 9 x 7″

Cocadah, Burn Some Man, (North American Indian), 1899 . . . . . . **250.00**

Portrait of Two Little Braves, Sac & Fox, hand colored, 1898 . . . . . **525.00**

White Face–Sioux, 1899 . . . . **360.00**

Stereograph

Albee, SV, publisher, group of 42 views of railroad war at Pittsburgh, July 21–22, 1877, each scene identified on verso **1,870.00**

Hiller, John and J Fennimore, group of 16 view from Powell Geological Survey of the Colorado River of the West, each with descriptive label on mount verso, 1875 . . . . **600.00**

O'Sullivan, Timothy H and William Bell, group of 41 views of American West, genre scenes, scenic views, 11 with Indians in native surroundings, all captioned, on "War Department Corps of Engineers Geographical Explorations and Surveys West of the 100th Meridian" mounts **1,320.00**

Underwood & Underwood, group of 63 views of President William McKinley, scenes from inauguration through 1900 campaign and fu-

neral, captions on mount recto, 1896–1891 . . . . **500.00**

Tintype, sixth plate, cased

Civil War Soldier **185.00**

Musicians, black trio, one holding banjo, second with guitar, and third with large lute, thermoplastic frame, 1860s **220.00**

Portrait, young black woman, white frilled bonnet, seated, double elliptical mat, 1850s **1,430.00**

Vintage Print

Abbott, Berenice, silver print

Fulton Street Dock, photographer's "Changing New York" handstamp and notations on verso, 8 x 10″, 1935 . . . . **1,100.00**

Greenwich Avenue, pencil photographer's signature on verso, 10 x 8″, 1940s **1,870.00**

Adams, Ansel, Church in Spanish–American Town, Cordova, NM, silver print, photographer's handstamp, 9¼ x 12¼″, late 1940s . . . **660.00**

Alland, Alexander, Grand Central Station, silver print, ink photographer's signature, 9¾ x 8″ **1,100.00**

Bingham, Katherine, The Easter Lily, platinum print, tipped to orig mount, pencil photographer's initials, 9¼ x 5¼″, 1910 . . . . **330.00**

Chislett, John, Woods in Winter, platinum print, 7½ x 9½″, c1910 . . . . **470.00**

Cunningham, Imogen, Mother and Child, platinum print, photographer's Seattle studio label, 6½ x 4½″, c1912 . . . . **880.00**

Curtis, Edward S, Out of the Canyon, toned silver print, photographer's signature, orig frame, 5½ x 7½″, c1906 . . . . **880.00**

Eagle, Arnold, In The Synagogue, toned silver print, photographer's studio handstamp and notations, also sgd in pencil on mat, 12 x 9¾″, 1935 . . . . **330.00**

Hammitt, Howard, Day Lilies, tricolored bromoil print, 13½ x 10¼″, c1927 . . . . **250.00**

Hartsook Studio, Portrait of Americans and Nationals in front of the Continental Hotel, bromide print, wearing baseball uniforms, photograph studio's handstamp, 9¼ x 15¼″, c1915 . . . . **275.00**

Harvey, Harold, Buildings, New York City, toned silver print, pencil photographer's signature, 10 x 8″, 1930s **330.00**

Johnston, Alfred Cheney, Mary Pickford, toned silver print, ink photographer's notation, 12½ x 9½″ **660.00**

Nelson, Lusha, Alfred Stieglitz at Lake George, silver print, ink photographer's signature, 7 x 9", 1935 .... **600.00**

Post, William B, Snowy Field, platinum print, pencil photographer's signature, 9½ x 5", c1905 ...... **500.00**

Steichen, Edward, Portrait of Rabbi Stephen Wise, silver print, Conde Nast identification number and title in negative, 10 x 8", 1939 ...... **735.00**

Sunami, Soichi, Portrait of Martha Graham, toned silver print, photographer's blindstamp, 9½ x 7¼", c1928 .... **1,045.00**

Underhill, Irving, View over Sixth Avenue, NY, silver print, typed caption on verso, 9 x 6", c1937 .... **300.00**

Zwart, Piet, Tinsel Icicles Composition, silver print, ink photographer's signature, handstamp, 6¾ x 5", c1933 .... **715.00**

PICKARD CHINA

History: The Pickard China Company was founded by Wilder Pickard in Chicago, Illinois, in 1897. Originally the company imported European china blanks, principally from the Havilands at Limoges, which they then hand painted. The firm presently is located in Antioch, Illinois.

Bowl, 10½" d, ruffled, poppies and leaves, gold trim, artist sgd, 1905 .. **175.00**

Plate, pastel scenic view of Yosemite Valley, gold rim, Nippon blank, orig paper label, artist sgd "E. Challinor," 10½" d, $400.00.

Cake Plate, violets, trees with pink blossoms, lake and mountains background, two handles, artist sgd "Felix" **350.00**

Chocolate Pot, cov, 9" h, conical, pink carnations, green leaves, gold arches, pink and white flowers, scrolling, gold handle, rim band, and knob **235.00**

Coffee Set, cov coffeepot, creamer, and sugar, artist sgd, 3 pcs **300.00**

Creamer and Sugar, birds, butterflies, and flowers, artist sgd **140.00**

Dinnerware, five piece place setting, Grandeur pattern **40.00**

Hatpin Holder, allover gold design of etched flowers, c1925 .... **45.00**

Lemonade Set, tankard pitcher, five tumblers, bluebells and foliage, lemon colored ground **100.00**

Marmalade Jar, 6" h, matching cov and underplate, hp, dogwoods and leaves, gold trim, artist sgd **85.00**

Perfume Bottle, yellow primroses, shaded ground, artist sgd and dated 1905, Limoges blank, gold stopper . **200.00**

Pitcher
  6½" h, peaches dec, artist sgd "Seidel" **575.00**
  6⅝" h, red carnations, daisies, and green leaves, artist sgd "E Challinor" **595.00**
  8½" h, bulbous, hexagonal, colored fruit, blossoms, and foliage, silver bands, gold trim, artist sgd, c1912 **285.00**

Plate
  7½" d, hp, currants, 1898 .... **75.00**
  8¼", poppies, gold leaves and rim, artist sgd "Challinor" **150.00**

Platter, 12" d, hp, landscape, artist sgd "Marker" **225.00**

Powder Box, 4" d, roses, artist sgd ... **100.00**

Punch Bowl, 12" d, orange grapes and plums design, artist sgd "F Walton" . **1,295.00**

Relish Dish, 9½" l, 4¼" w, pink and green leaves, open handles, maple leaf mark **70.00**

Stein, 7", large bunches of grapes and leaves, black ground, gold handle, rim, and base, artist sgd, c1898 ... **275.00**

Tea Set, ftd cov teapot with dolphin's head spout, tankard creamer, cov sugar, 11" d tray, pearlized ground, turquoise blue, pink, and rose tulips, gold tracery and trim on rims and handles, artist sgd **650.00**

Tray, 11" d, circular, bisque, teal blue, gold grapes and leaves, engraved, artist sgd "Coufall," 1905 mark **200.00**

Urn, 11½" h, allover gold, 3" band of grapes and strawberries, artist sgd, Belleek blank **500.00**

Vase

  7¾″, cylindrical, moonlight lake and pine forest scene, artist sgd "Challinor," Nippon blank **250.00**

  9″ h, large golden yellow, pink, and deep rose chrysanthemums and green leaves, soft turquoise blue shaded to green ground, gold trim, artist sgd, 1898 . . . .   **300.00**

  12″ h, hp, gold dec, scenic medial band with rose bushes at riverside, artist sgd "Marken" **330.00**

PICKLE CASTORS

History: A pickle castor is a table accessory used to serve pickles. It generally consists of a silver-plated frame fitted with a glass insert, matching silver-plated lid, and matching tongs. Pickle castors were very popular during the Victorian era. Inserts are found in pattern glass and colored art glass.

Double, pressed glass insert, Block & Star pattern, Viking feet, Meridan, c1884, 10½″ h, 6¾″ w, $295.00.

Amber, Bag Ware pattern, silver frame with relief masks, tongs, and cov . .   **230.00**
Blue, finecut design, tongs and frame .   **210.00**
Burmese, hobnail, fuchsia amberina, silverplate frame and cov, 11½″ h . . . **1,100.00**
Cranberry, 13″, thumbprint, enameled daisies, twig feet, elaborate floral cut– out sides, top and tongs **325.00**
Crown Milano, forget–me–not dec, sil- verplate finish frame, orig tongs . . .   **985.00**
Mount Washington, Rubina Crystal, enameled floral dec, wild roses, bleeding hearts, and daisies, green floral, silverplate frame, orig tongs, 10½″ h **875.00**

Northwood, Netted Apple Blossom in- sert, ornate SP ftd frame **275.00**
Pattern

  Daisy & Button, clear, quadruple plate holder, cov, and tongs **130.00**

  Paneled and Diamond Point, clear, tri- ple plate holder, cov, and tongs . .   **80.00**

Pigeon Blood, Beaded Drape insert, Consolidated Glass Co, orig cov and frame **425.00**
Rubena, vertical optic pattern insert, Pairpoint, ornate ftd fretwork frame and bail handle **225.00**

PIGEON BLOOD GLASS

History: Pigeon blood refers to the deep oran- gish-red colored glassware produced around the turn of the century. Do not confuse it with the many other red glasswares of that period. Pigeon blood has a very definite orange glow.

Salt Shaker, Bulging Loops pattern, 3¼″ h, $95.00.

Berry Bowl, 9″, master, Torquay, SP rim   **110.00**
Butter Dish, cov, Venecia, enameled dec **350.00**
Celery, 6″, Torquay, SP rim **225.00**
Cooler, 5″ l, hand, cut panels, two com- partments with silver fittings **135.00**
Creamer, Venecia, enameled dec **125.00**
Decanter, 9½″, orig stopper **75.00**
Pickle Castor, Beaded Drape insert, SP cov and frame, Consolidated Glass Co **425.00**
Pitcher, water

  Diamond Quilted, 10½″, tankard shape **185.00**

  Torquay, SP trim **325.00**

Salt and Pepper Shaker, pr, Bulging Loops, orig top **145.00**
Sugar Shaker, Bulging Loops, orig top   **150.00**
Syrup, Beaded Drape, Consolidated Glass Co, orig hinged lid **245.00**

Toothpick, Bulging Loops **125.00**
Tumbler, 3¼", alternating panel and rib **75.00**

PINK SLAG

History: True pink slag is found only in the molded Inverted Fan and Feather pattern. Quality pieces shade from pink at the top to white at the bottom.

Reproduction Alert: Recently, pieces of pink slag made from molds of the now defunct Cambridge Glass Company have been found in the Inverted Strawberry and Inverted Thistle pattern. This is not considered "true" pink slag and brings only a fraction of the Inverted Fan and Feather pattern prices.

Punch Cup, Inverted Fan and Feather pattern, ftd, $285.00.

Berry Bowl
   Individual, ftd, set of 6 . . . . **825.00**
   Master, 10" d, ftd **740.00**
Butter, cov **650.00**
Compote, jelly **375.00**
Creamer **450.00**
Cruet, 6¾" h **950.00**
Jam Jar **875.00**
Pitcher, water **750.00**
Punch Cup, 2½" h, ftd **275.00**
Salt Shaker **300.00**
Sauce Dish, 4½" w, 2½" h, four ball feet **285.00**
Sugar, cov **550.00**
Toothpick **400.00**
Tumbler **450.00**

PIPES

History: The history of pipe making dates as early as 1575. Almost all types of natural and man–made materials, some which retained smoke and some that did not, were used to make pipes. Among the materials were amber, base metals, clay, cloisonné, glass, horn, ivory, jade, meerschaum, parian, porcelain, pottery, precious metals, precious stones, semi–precious stones, assorted woods, *inter alia*. Chronologically the four most popular materials and their generally ac-

cepted introduction dates are: clay, c1575; woods, c1700; porcelain, c1710; and meerschaum, c1725.

National pipe styles exist around the globe, wherever tobacco smoking is custom or habit. Pipes reflect a broad range of themes and messages, e.g., figurals, important personages, commemoration of historical events, mythological characters, erotica and pornographica, the bucolic, the bizarre, the grotesque, and the graceful.

Pipe collecting began in the mid–1880s; William Bragge, F.S.A., Birmingham, England, was an early collector. Although firmly established through the efforts of free–lance writers, auction houses, and museums (but not the tobacco industry), the collecting of antique pipes is an amorphous, maligned, and misunderstood hobby. It is amorphous because there are no defined collecting bounds; maligned because it is conceived as an extension of pipe smoking, now socially unacceptable [many pipe collectors are avid non–smokers]; and misunderstood because of its association with the "collectibles" field.

References: R. Fresco–Corbu, *European Pipes*, Lutterworth Press, 1982; E. Ramazzotti and B. Mamy, *Pipes et Fumeurs des Pipes. Un Art, des Collections, Sous le Vent*, 1981; Benjamin Rapaport, *A Complete Guide To Collecting Antique Pipes*, Schiffer Publishing, 1979.

Collectors' Club: Pipe Collectors International, Inc., P. O. Box 22085, Chattanooga, TN 37422.

Periodicals: *Pipe Collectors Of The World*, Box 11652, Houston, TX 77293; *Universal Coterie of Pipe Smokers*, 20–37 120th Street, College Point, NY 11356.

Museums: Museum of Tobacco Art and History, Nashville, TN; National Tobacco–Textile Museum, Danville, VA; U.S. Tobacco Museum, Greenwich, CT.

Man with bulldog, amber stem, 4⅜" l, $160.00.

PIPES

Briar
   Man, 7" l, bearded, tasseled hat and
     pipe, carved, marked "G.B.D." . . . **55.00**
   Queen Victoria, 6¼", head, carved,
     silver trim, case, hallmarked **75.00**

Clay, 18" l, figural, young man with curly
hair, wooden slim stem, french, Gam-
bier **65.00**
Glass, large ovoid bowl, long shaped
stem, red and ivory dec **75.00**
Meershum
Boy with mandolin, 12", carved **200.00**
Carved man on lid, 6" **50.00**
Dog, long hair, amber stem, case .. **45.00**
Horses, 14", carved **100.00**
Maiden, 7¾" l, full figural, seated,
flowing gown, garlands of roses,
basket weave bowl, amber stem,
orig case **185.00**
Negro, 8", figural, cream, bust bowl . **900.00**
Wild Animal, 17", carved, dated 1800 **150.00**
Opium, 7¾", cranes, reed stem, brass
fittings, Oriental, c1800 .... **85.00**
Porcelain
Character, 10", man under barrel .. **60.00**
Family Crest 1847, 30", marked
"Made by Cmielow Factory, Po-
land" **75.00**
Floral, 12", relief **125.00**
Graf Zeppelin, 9", P.O.G. **125.00**
Hunter, 24", sleeping **125.00**
Stag, 12", marked "P.O.G." **75.00**
Pottery
Man with pipe, set on lid, post war . **60.00**
Monk, post war **45.00**
Ram, post war **65.00**
Regimental
4 Field Art. Regt. Magdellburg 1896–
98, 36" l **260.00**
149 Inft. Regt. 1881, 10" l, blacksmith
tools in rear **85.00**
Soapstone, Eskimo man, 9", skinning
animal, late 19th C **140.00**

TAMPS

Brass
Napoleon, 2⅜" **25.00**
Robin Hood, 2¼", marked "England" **35.00**
Wood, 1½", boot **35.00**
Ivory, 2¾", column **15.00**
Silverplated, 1⅝", man bending at waist,
marked "E.P.N.S." **25.00**

POCKET KNIVES

History: Alcas, Case, Colonial, Ka–Bar, Queen,
and Schrade are the best of the modern pocket
knife manufacturers, with top positions enjoyed by
Case and Ka–Bar. Knives by Remington and Winchester, firms no longer in production, are eagerly
sought.

Form is a critical collecting element. The most
desirable forms are folding hunters (1 and 2
blades), trappers, peanuts, Barlows, elephant
toes, canoes, Texas toothpicks, Coke bottles, gun

stocks, and Daddy Barlows. The decorative aspect
also heavily influences prices. Values are for
pocket knives in mint condition.

References: James F. Parker, *The Official Price
Guide to Collector Pocket Knives, 9th Edition*,
House of Collectibles, 1987; Jim Sargent, *Sar-
gent's American Premium Guide To Pocket
Knives: Identification and Values*, Books Ameri-
cana, 1986; Ron Stewart and Roy Ritchie, *The
Standard Knife Collector's Guide*, Collector
Books, 1986.

Periodical: *Knife World*, P.O. Box 3395, Knox-
ville, TN 37917.

Collectors' Clubs: American Blade Collectors,
P.O. Box 22007, Chattanooga, TN 37422; Cana-
dian Knife Collectors Club, 3141 Jessuca Court,
Mississauga, ON L5C1X7; The National Knife Col-
lectors Association, P.O. Box 21070, Chattanooga,
TN 37421.

Museum: National Knife Museum, Chattanooga, TN.

Additional Listings: See *Warman's Americana
& Collectibles* for more examples.

CASE

Case uses a numbering code for its knives. The
first number (1–9) is the handle material; the second number (1–5) designates the number of
blades; the third and fourth number (0–99) the
knife pattern. Stage (5), pearl (8 or 9), and bone
(6) are most sought in handle materials. The most
desirable patterns are 5165—folding hunters,
6185—doctors, 6445—scout, muskrat—marked
muskrat with no number, and 6254—trappers.

In the Case XX series a symbol and dot code
are used to designate a year.

1920–40
6111½, green bone, long pull,
stamped "Tested XX" **400.00**
6265, green bone, 5¼", flat blade,
stamped "Tested XX" **300.00**
6465, green bone, 5¼", saber blade,
bail in handle stamped "Tested
XX" **1,750.00**
9265, imitation pearl, 5¼", flat blade,
stamped "Tested XX" **400.00**
1940–65
3254, yellow composition 4⅛",
stamped "XX" **125.00**
42057, white composition, 3⅜"
marked on handle "OFFICE
KNIFE" **90.00**
6246R, green bone, 4⅜", bail in handle, stamped "Tested XX," rigger's
knife **150.00**
6265, red bone, 5¼", flat blade,
stamped "XX" **250.00**
8271, genuine pearl, 3¼", long pull
stamped "XX" **220.00**

Fly Fisherman 150.00
1965–70
    4200, white composition, 5½", serrated master blade, stamped "USA," melon tester 125.00
    5265, stag, 5¼", saber ground, bolsters drilled stamped "USA" 85.00
    62009, bone, 3⁵⁄₁₆", master blade in front, stamped "USA," Barlow . . . 35.00
    6265, red bone, 5¼", flat blade, stamped "XX" 225.00
1970–80 (Number of dots indicate year)
    5111½, genuine stag, 4⁷⁄₁₆", lockback, Cheetah, large stamp 175.00
    62009, bone stag, 3⁵⁄₁₆", Barlow . . . 35.00
    6265, stag, 5¼", saber ground, bolsters drilled, 10 dot 75.00
    Fly Fisherman 100.00
    Muskrat bone, 3⁷⁄₈", 10 dot 40.00

KA–BAR (Union Cut. Co., Olean, New York)

The company was founded by Wallace Brown at Tidioute, PA in 1892. It was relocated to Olean, NY, in 1912. The products have many stampings including Union [inside shield]; U–R Co. Tidoute [variations]; Union Cutlery Co. Olean, NY; Alcut Olean, NY; Keenwell, Olean, NY; and Ka–Bar. The larger knives with a profile of a dog's head on the handle are the most desirable. Pattern numbers rarely appear on a knife prior to the 1940s.

24107 . . . . 1,000.00
31187, 2 blades 150.00
61161, light celluloid handle 100.00
61126L, dog's head 850.00
61187, Daddy Barlow 150.00
6191L 600.00
6260KF 100.00

Simons Keencutter, Christmas tree handle, $100.00.

KEEN KUTTER (Simons Hardware, St. Louis, MO)

K1881, Barlow 70.00
K1920 . . . . 300.00
6354, Scout 100.00

REMINGTON, last made in 1940

R293, Field and Stream Bullet, bone, long pull, 5¼" 1,750.00
R953, toothpick, bone, 5" 225.00
R3273, Cattle, brown bone, equal end, 3¾" 235.00
R4233, Junior Scout, brown bone, scout shield, pinched bolsters, 3⅜" 200.00

RUSSELL, Turner Fall, MA

55, 2 blades 125.00
600, Daddy Barlow 200.00

WINCHESTER

1621, Budding, ebony, 4¾" 130.00
1920, Folding Hunter, bone, 5⅜" 1,000.00
2337, Senator, pearl, 3¼" 100.00
2703, Barlow, brown bone, 3½" 140.00
3944, Whittler, bone, 3¼" 225.00
4961, Premium Stockman, bone, 4" . . 285.00

OTHER MANUFACTURERS

Elephant Toe
    Kutwell, Olean, NY 200.00
    Primble, John 250.00
Folding Hunter
    Case, Nantucket Sleigh Ride 125.00
    Marble Arms Co 350.00
    Neft Saftey 220.00
    New York Knife Co. 400.00
    Novelty Cutlery Co., pictured handle 125.00
    Queen Cutlery Co. Titusville, PA, buffalo horn 200.00
    Robeson 175.00
    Schrade, Trail of Tears 150.00

POISON BOTTLES

History: Poison bottles were designed to warn and prevent accidental intake or misuse of their poisonous substances, especially in the dark. Poison bottles generally were made of colored glass, embossed with "Poison" or a skull and crossbones, and sometimes were coffin–shaped.

John H. B. Howell of Newton, New Jersey, designed the first safety closure in 1866. The idea did not become popular until the 1930s when bottle designs became simpler and the user had to read the label to identify the contents.

References: Ralph and Terry Kovel, *The Kovels' Bottle Price List, 8th Edition,* Crown Publishers, Inc., 1987; Carlo and Dorothy Sellari, *The Standard Old Bottle Price Guide,* Collector Books, 1989.

Periodical: *Antique Bottle and Glass Collector,* P.O. Box 187, East Greenville, PA 18041.

Poison Tingt Iodine, skull and crossbones, sq, amber, machine made, 3³⁄₁₆″ h, $7.50.

Cash Boots Chemist, green, emb "Not To Be Taken," 4⅛″ h	12.00
Durfee Embalming Fluid Co, amethyst, 8¾″ h	25.00
Irregular hexagon, tooled top	
5″ h, emerald green, 1900–10	60.00
6¼″ h, cobalt blue, 1900–10	100.00
Lin Saponis, green, 6¾″ h	20.00
Norwich, 16A, coffin shape, emb diamond design, cobalt blue, tooled mouth, smooth base, 7⅜″ h, 1880–1900	1,300.00
Quilted	
Cobalt blue, tooled top, smooth base, poison stopper, 5½″ h, 1890–1910	60.00
Teal green, cylindrical, tooled flared mouth, smooth base, emb "U S P H S," 1870–1900	1,325.00
Spirits, milk glass, silver, 9″ h	20.00
The Owl Drug, Poison, owl motif, cobalt blue, tooled top	
2¾″ h, c1892–1900	75.00
3¼″ h, 1892–95	55.00
5⅛″ h, 1895–1910	110.00
7⅞″ h, 1895–1905	400.00
Tinct Opii, cobalt, poison on base, 7″	40.00

POLITICAL ITEMS

History: Since 1800 the American presidency has always been a contest between two or more candidates. Initially souvenirs were issued to celebrate victories. Items issued during a campaign to show support for a candidate were actively being distributed in the William Henry Harrison election of 1840.

Campaign items cover a wide variety of materials—buttons, bandannas, tokens, pins, etc. The only limiting factor has been the promoter's imagination. The advent of television campaigning has reduced the emphasis on individual items. Modern campaigns do not seem to have the variety of materials which were issued earlier.

References: Herbert Collins, *Threads of History*, Smithsonian Institution Press, 1979; Stan Gores, *Presidential and Campaign Memorabilia With Prices, Second Edition*, Wallace–Homestead, 1988; Theodore L. Hake, *Encyclopedia of Political Buttons, United States, 1896–1972*, Americana & Collectibles Press, 1985; Theodore L. Hake, *Political Buttons, Book II, 1920–1976*, Americana & Collectibles Press, 1977; Theodore L. Hake, *Political Buttons, Book III, 1789–1916*, Americana & Collectibles Press, 1978; Ted Hake, 1991 Revised Prices for three books above, Hake's Americana & Collectibles, 1990; Ted Hake, *Hake's Guide to Presidential Campaign Collectibles*, Wallace–Homestead, 1992; Edmund B. Sullivan, *American Political Badges and Medalets, 1789–1892*, Quarterman Publications, Inc., 1981. (Note: Theodore L. Hake issued a revised set of prices for his three books in 1984.)

Collectors' Club: American Political Items Collectors, P.O. Box 340339, San Antonio, TX 78234.

Periodical: *Political Collector*, P.O. Box 5171, York, PA 17405.

Museum: Smithsonian Museum, Washington, D.C.

Note: The abbreviation "h/s" is used to identify a head and shoulder photo or etching of a person.

Additional Listings: See *Warman's Americana & Collectibles* for more examples.

Advisor: Theodore L. Hake.

Diecut, Harrison and Morton, 1888, adv premium from Samuel Clarke, Lancaster, PA, 11 x 7″, $25.00.

Ashtray, china, white, gold band, "Vote Republican In '52" inscription, man hitchhiking next to exhausted Democratic donkey with GOP elephant lumbering down road cartoon, "My Ass Is Tired" caption, 5″ d	15.00

Badge

1896, McKinley–Hobart, ribbon, celluloid jugate attached, "Sound Money/No Repudiation/Republican/Traveling Men's/Club/Peoria, Ill," 8 x 2½" **50.00**

1910, Taft, Wisconsin Republican Convention, inscribed on black ribbon "We oppose men who are Republicans for office and Democrats in office," Taft medal on bottom, delegate label on top, 5 x 2" **45.00**

1949, Truman, Truman–Barkley inauguration jugate, gray ribbon attached, "Democrats from Cambria, Indiana, Armstrong, Somerset Counties, Johnstown, PA," 4 x 2" . **175.00**

Bandanna

1896, Bryan, cotton, black and white, jugate of Bryan and Sewall, eagle and shield at top, coin and rooster in center, White House at bottom, numerous slogans, 17¾ x 18¼" .. **80.00**

1928, Hoover, linen, white ground, blue oval bust portrait in center, "Our President," surrounded by state seals in red, 17 x 18" **60.00**

1957, red, white, and blue, "I Like Ike" slogan repeated four times, white stars on red and white elephants on blue border, 29" sq ... **35.00**

Bank, Roosevelt, c1908, cast iron, still, "Teddy" on one side, orig gold paint, 1½ x 3½ x 2½" **80.00**

Blotter, Willkie, black and white, campaign slogans, inscription "Contributed By A Citizen Of Amsterdam NY 1940," 4 x 9" **15.00**

Bookmark, Taft, diecut, aluminum, teddy bear shape, portrait on cutout heart, back Sherman portrait, The Bear–Still In Evidence–But In Charge Of A New Keeper" slogan, 2½ x 2¾" .. **75.00**

Bumper Sticker, orange and black, license plate design, inscribed "Elect JFK–60 President," 4 x 7" **8.00**

Button

1896, sepia portrait of Bryan, St Louis Button Company, 1¾" **30.00**

1900, jugate, McKinley and TR, black and white portraits on red, white, and blue flag motif, gold border, 2⅛" **50.00**

1900, McKinley and Roosevelt, blue and gold, 1¼" **25.00**

1904, Parker–Davis, jugate, multicolor, ribbon center, 1¼" **50.00**

1912, Progressive, head of moose, "Progressive," white and gold on light blue **15.00**

1916, Wilson, black and white portrait, blue rim with "Progressive

Policies Become Law Under Wilson," ⅞" **15.00**

1920, Coolidge–Dawes, jugate, black and white, text above and below oval portrait, ⅞" **45.00**

1924, Smith, gray tone, h/s, rim "For President/Alfred E. Smith," ⅞" ... **20.00**

1924, Hoover, oval, red, white, and blue, "100%/HOOVER/AMERICAN" **10.00**

1932, Roosevelt–Garner, jugate, black and white, "Return our country to the People" **200.00**

1940, "I'M FOR WILLKIE AND McNARY," jugate, black and white, ⅞" **55.00**

1948, Dewey–Warren, jugate, ⅞" .. **20.00**

1952, Stevenson, brown and white, portrait, name across bottom, 1¾" **10.00**

1968, Goldwater, black, white, and blue, bust portrait, "I'll Back Barry," 1⅝" **6.00**

Cabinet Card, Horatio Seymour, (opposed Grant for Pres) New Bedford, MA, sewing machine dealer adv on back, c1868, 4 x 6½" **20.00**

Car Attachment, silvered metal holder, tin plate with black and white portrait and slogan "Keep Coolidge", threaded shaft, 2½" d **250.00**

Carte De Visite, James Garfield's assassin, titled "Charles Jules Guiteau, The Murderous Assassin of President Garfield, July 2nd, 1881," 2¼ x 4" .. **35.00**

Cigar, 1928, Al Smith, black, white, gold, red, and green label picturing Smith, orig box, 8½" l **30.00**

Cigarettes, 1952, Eisenhower, h/s, "I Like Ike," red, white, and blue stripes **15.00**

Election Ticket, Horace Greely, 1872, Liberal Republican Ticket, paper, image of Greely between figures of Justice and Liberty, lists MA presidential elector and other state candidates, 6 x 12" **55.00**

Gearshift Knob, Woodrow Wilson, solid amber celluloid, metal ring surrounds rubber disk with Wilson's portrait, c1916, 2" d **75.00**

Glass, clear, etched

1896, McKinley–Hobart, tumbler, etched pictures in wreath, names below, 3¾" h **45.00**

1902, Roosevelt, punch cup, etched "President Roosevelt/1902/Oyster Bay," on bottom "Bloomingdales New York," 2¾" h **35.00**

Inaugural Item

Invitation, 1885, Cleveland–Hendricks, ball, 7 x 9¾" **45.00**

Periscope, white and green cardboard box, JFK's name and picture on two sides, capitol on other two sides, two built in mirrors, 3 x 4 x 16″ **50.00**

Program

1881, Garfield–Arthur, 16 pgs ... **35.00**

1957, Eisenhower, Rockwell cov, 50 pgs **15.00**

Letter Opener, plastic, white, blue image and red lettering, "Vote Demo! Hubert Humphrey For President!", 1968, 1¾ x 8″ **7.00**

License Plate

1940, Willkie, white key on composition, "Good/Willkie/to White House/ 1940," made by Kuleness Co, Paulding, OH, 5½ x 10″ **30.00**

1952, Eisenhower–Nixon, jugate, "I Like/Ike/and Dick," h/s of both red, white, and blue, 5¼ x 12″ **25.00**

Medal, copper, Buchanan, buck leaping over cannon and "Ans/Breckinridge," reverse with portrait of Washington and slogan, 1⅞″ **150.00**

Megaphone, cone shape, plastic, white, blue inscription "President Nixon, Now More Than Ever," 1972, 7½″ l . **10.00**

Mirror, Taft, black and white, bust of Taft, "Its Up To The Man On The Other Side To Put This Tried & Safe Man At The Head Of The Government," 2¼″ d **200.00**

Mug

1896, Bryan, milk glass, oval transfer of h/s with name on right shoulder, floral dec border, 3¾″ h **60.00**

1928, Hoover, toby, face with seating posture base, cream color, facsimile signature on side, 7″ h **50.00**

Note Pad, Cleveland picture of front with wife, Baldwin & Gleason 1886 copyright, 2 x 2¾″ **10.00**

Notebook, celluloid, 1927 calendar on back, "Vote The Straight Republican Tickets–Republican State Committee Women's Division" slogan, 2 x 3″ .. **10.00**

Pen, dark blue, silver inscription "Businessmen For Humphrey/Thank You/ Hubert H. Humphrey," 5½″ l **8.00**

Pencil, mechanical, light gray point end, transparent plastic covering JFK portrait clip end, diecut "109″ PT boat that floats back and forth, skyline background scene, 5½″ l **30.00**

Pennant

1912–16, Wilson, h/s to left with "Our/ President," name in center, white and flesh tones, blue ground, 8½ x 21″ **25.00**

1948, Truman, oval with Truman h/s and name on left "For President" in center, white, red ground, 4½ x 12″ **25.00**

Pin

1896, McKinley, Nose Thumber, gold color, push heels to reveal Mckinley thumbing nose, on reverse "McKinley to Democrats and Populists," 1⅞″ **200.00**

1936, Landon, brass, sunflower, "Landon/Knox" in pedals **12.00**

1956, Eisenhower, bar, "IKE" above, "volunteer" inscribed, and "56″ in relief **7.50**

Pinback Buttons, left, Willkie, red, white, and blue, 1″ d, $12.00; right, The Constitutionalists, No Third Term, red, white, and blue, ⅞″ d, $10.00.

Plate, china

1884, Blaine, black on white, floral motif, 9″ d **35.00**

1912, Wilson, White House in center, oval h/s of all presidents up to Wilson on border, 9½″ d **35.00**

Platter, oval, china, jugate portraits of W. H. Taft and JS Sherman, surrounded by red, white and blue flags, and purple roses, eagle with shield below, gold floral design border, 9 x 11½″ **35.00**

Post Card

1896–1900, Bryan, speaking from train platform label reads "Much Ado Abt Nothing," multicolored .. **15.00**

1908, Hopefuls, "Watching the Presidential Game," Hughes, Foraker, Cannon, Taft, and Fairbanks on one side of fence, T. Roosevelt on other, cartoon, multicolored **20.00**

1908, Taft, mechanical, black, white, and yellow elephant with rope tail, black and white portrait slides out when pulled by tail, October 24, 1908 postmark, brief message ... **25.00**

Print, N. Currier

Jackson Memorial, hand colored, titled "General Andrew Jackson, The Hero, The Sage, and the Patriot We Mourn Our Loss," professionally framed, 9½ x 13½" 60.00

Polk, titled "The Presidents of the United States," each president from Washington thru Polk, center Declaration of Independence scene, 1844 copyright, walnut veneer period frame, 12 x 16½" 150.00

Washington, George, hand colored, professionally framed, 9½ x 13½" 100.00

Ribbon

1832, George Washington Centenary Anniversary, black illus, white silk, laurel wreath, sailing ships above portrait 200.00

1880, Hancock and English, jugate, black and white, beige cloth, marked "Junior/Hancock/Club/of Chambersburg," 2¾ x 6" 125.00

1888, Cleveland, center "Cleveland/ And/Truman," bandanna design top and bottom, red on white, 5 x 1¾" 50.00

1904, Roosevelt, h/s of Roosevelt, above "For President/1904," signature at base, black on white, 4¼ x 2" 65.00

Salt and Pepper Shakers, pr, ceramic, beige and tan, Ike's head lifts off for one shaker, body serves as other, c1952 .... 15.00

Sheet Music

1856, "Fremont's Great Republican March," woodcut of h/s, black on white, 6 pgs 40.00

1912, Wilson, "Its Woodrow Wilson, That's All," side h/s etching of Wilson imposed on Capitol dome, 6 pgs 20.00

1952, Eisenhower, "For Eisenhower," h/s photo, peach, orange, and black, 4 pgs 7.50

Soap, 1964, Goldwater, bath size, wrapper with black, silver, and white on gold 7.50

Stereocard, McKinley And His Eight Chosen Advisors–Cabinet Room, Executive Mansion, 1900 .... 5.00

Stickpin

Blaine, 1884, cardboard photo 50.00

Coolidge, 1920, green and silver license plate logo, "Cal/24/Coolidge," ¼ x 1" 15.00

Benjamin Harrison, brass, 2" l 15.00

McKinley, 1" d gold and silver engraved dish, mounted, c1896, 2" l 20.00

Stud, 1896, "How The Farmer Loves Gold Bugs," lapel, three insects impaled on points of pitchfork, black ground 150.00

Tape Measure, gold glass case, metal measure, red, white, and blue inscription "President Nixon Now More Than Ever," orig plain gold box, 1¾" d ... 5.00

Tapestry, JF Kennedy with American flag and US Capitol, inscribed back "Made In Italy," 19½ x 38" 20.00

Tab

1928, "HOOVER–CURTIS," white letters on blue metal tab 7.00

1936, Landon–Knox, diecut elephant 10.00

Tie, 1936, Landon, "For President/h/s/ Alfred M. Landon," brown ground, white lettering, round picture 25.00

Tie Clip, brass, hat shape, "LBJ" in black lettering, orig dark blue card .. 5.00

Token

1838, Hard Times Token, copper, front tortoise and safe, black donkey, 28mm 8.00

1860, Lincoln, copper, h/s on front, Lincoln as rail splitter and log cabin on back, 28mm 40.00

1893, Grover Cleveland, brass, luster, inscription "United States Mint Exhibit/World's Columbian Exposition Chicago/1893," 1" 12.00

1881, James Garfield, brass, White House and canal boat, inscription "Canal Boy 1845/President 1881" inauguration souvenir, 1" 10.00

T–Shirt, 1956, Eisenhower, children's size, h/s, "I'm Safe With Ike," gray picture, red letters, white shirt 20.00

Watch Fob, Cox and Roosevelt, brass, 1920, $175.00.

Watch Fob

William J Bryan, 1¼" black and white celluloid, mounted, black leather fob with strap 30.00

Taft, silvered brass, red and blue enamel pennant design, 1908 patent date on back 25.00

POMONA GLASS

History: Pomona glass, produced only by the New England Glass Works and named for the Roman goddess of fruit and trees, was patented in 1885 by Joseph Locke. It is a delicate lead, blown art glass which has a pale, soft beige ground and a top one–inch band of honey amber.

There are two distinct types of backgrounds. First ground, made only from late 1884 to June 1886, was produced by fine cuttings through a wax coating followed by an acid bath. Second ground was made by rolling the piece in acid resisting particles and acid etching. Second ground was made in Cambridge until 1888 and until the early 1900s in Toledo where Libbey moved the firm after purchasing New England Glass works. Both methods produced a soft frosted appearance, with fine curlicue lines more visible on first ground pieces. Designs are used on some pieces, which were etched and then stained in color. The most familiar design is blue cornflowers.

Do not confuse Pomona with "Midwestern Pomona," a pressed glass with a frosted body and amber band.

Reference: Joseph and Jane Locke, *Locke Art Glass: A Guide For Collectors,* Dover Publications, 1987.

Bowl, first grind, flint, ruffled amber ribbon, crimped foot, ground pontil, 5½" d, 3" h, $115.00.

Bowl, ruffled, first grind, amber edge .	65.00
Carafe, second grind, Cornflower	200.00
Celery, first grind, Cornflower	300.00
Creamer, second grind, Daisy and Butterfly, applied clear handle, three applied clear feet	275.00
Cruet, 5½", first grind, Blueberry, gold leaves, applied clear handle, clear ball stopper	285.00
Lemonade Glass, 4½" h, first grind, blue cornflower dec	175.00
Pitcher, milk, second grind	
Blueberry	200.00
Cornflower, sq top	225.00
Punch Cup, 2½" h, first grind, amber scalloped rim and handle	85.00

Toothpick, first grind, Cornflower	245.00
Tumbler	
3½" h, second grind, acanthus leaf dec	125.00
3⅝", first grind, Cornflower, blue flowers	200.00
Vase	
10⅞", lily form, second grind	400.00
14½" h, trumpet, DQ, second grind, clear base	330.00

PORTRAIT WARE

History: Plates, vases, and other articles with portraits on them were popular in the second half of the 19th century. Although male subjects, such as Napoleon or Louis XVI, were used, the ware usually depicted a beautiful woman, often unidentified.

A large number of English and Continental china manufacturers made portrait ware. Because most ware was hand painted, an artist's signature often is found.

Additional Listings: KPM and Royal Vienna.

Charger, 12½" d, gypsy woman with tambourine, polychrome and gilt, Victorian bronzed metal circular frame, imp "Montreal B & Cie"	350.00
Ewers, oval portraits of maidens, one with diaphanous red gown, floral sash, standing before classical architecture, flowing brown hair, titled "Sehnsucht," other with red dress, holding white shawl, dark hair, titled "Echo," elaborate palmette and Greek key gilt tooled reserves, shaded brown to copper luster ground, three large foliate scroll and	

Plate, Napoleon, multicolored, white ground, gold scalloped rim, marked "J. P. L. France," 8½" d, $150.00.

spray registers, molded scrolled handle and leaf tip spout, socle base, circular plinth, scrolled feet, obscured factory mark, blue pseudo Vienna shield mark, black titles, artist sgd "Wagner," pr **4,125.00**

Plaque, 5½" w, 6½" h, King George IV, self framed, polychrome enamels, imp title "Welcome King George IV," Scotland, c1882 . . . . **615.00**

Plate
  9½" d

    Apfelbluthen, young woman, vase of flowering branches, green and gilt border, small rim chip, Vienna, 19th C **330.00**

    Cleopatra, enameled turquoise cabochons rim on gilt ground, raised floral and foliate dec on inner rim, mottled teal and lavender ground, sgd "Wagner" . . **1,800.00**

    Duchess of Devonshire, raised gilt motif on rim, five polychrome floral reserves, sgd "Wagner" . . . **1,700.00**

    Empress Josephine, raised gilt border, scrolling arabesques and polychrome urn dec, white ground, sgd "Wagner" **1,600.00**

    Madame de Lamballe, raised gilt border, scrolling arabesques and polychrome urn dec, white ground, sgd "Wagner" **1,700.00**

    Odalisque, raised gilt dec rim, cobalt ground, sgd "Wagner" **1,700.00**

    Young Girl, multicolored, six flowered wells, scalloped gold border, open handles, Schegelmilch, marked "ES Germany" **170.00**

  9⁵⁄₁₆", pr, lady, cobalt and light blue and gold border, Rabot **450.00**

  9⅞"

    Hebe, green irid and gold border, sgd "Wagner" **1,700.00**

    Una Gitana, two tone irid and gold border, sgd "Wagner" **1,500.00**

Urn, cov, 30" h, elongated waisted cylindrical neck painted in reserve with bust portrait of Marie Antoinette on one, Louis XVI on other, gilt border with foliage scrollwork, drum form body painted with continuous landscape frieze depicting aristocratic ladies and gentlemen in 18th C costumes, waisted lobed base and foot, gilt highlights and rims, pierced dome cov with gilded pineapple knob, blue celeste ground, marked "Serves," pr **1,250.00**

Vase
  3½" h, lady portrait, raised gold floral dec, blue luster ground, Royal Vienna, sgd "Wagner" **450.00**

  5" h, lady portrait, raised gold floral

dec, purple luster ground, Royal Vienna, sgd "Wagner" **400.00**

  6⅜", bud, cylindrical, oval self portrait, after Vigee Librun, flanked by molded gilt scrolls, green ground, gilt vertical banding, floral sprigs, and foliate scrolls, gilded asymmetrical rim and foot, crowned Dresden mark, "34927" in black, c1900 . . . . **250.00**

POSTERS

History: The poster was an extremely effective and critical means of mass communication, especially in the period before 1920. Enormous quantities were produced, helped in part by the propaganda role posters played in World War I.

Print runs of two million were not unknown. Posters were not meant to be saved. Once they served their purpose, they tended to be destroyed. The paradox of high production and low survival is one of the fascinating aspects of poster history.

The posters of the late 19th century and early 20th century represent the pinnacle of American lithography printing. The advertising posters of firms such as Strobridge or Courier are true classics. Philadelphia was one center for the poster industry.

Europe pioneered in posters with high artistic and aesthetic content. Many major artists of the 20th century designed posters. Poster art still plays a key role throughout Europe today.

References: John Barnicoat, *A Concise History of Posters*, Harry Abrams, Inc., 1976; Tony Fusco, *The Official Identification and Price Guide To Posters, First Edition*, House of Collectibles, 1990; George Theofiles, *American Posters of World War I: A Price and Collector's Guide*, Dafram House Publishers, Inc.; Walton Rawls, *Wake Up, America!: World War I and The American Poster*, Abbeville Press, 1988; Stephen Rebello and Richard Allen, *Reel Art: Great Posters From The Golden Age of The Silver Screen*, Abbeville Press, 1988.

Collectors' Club: Poster Society, 138 West 18th St., New York, NY 10011.

Additional Listings: See *Warman's Americana & Collectibles* for more examples.

Advisor: George Theofiles.

ADVERTISING

American Beauty, 13 x 20", c1938, Standee, Adjustable automatic electric iron...with thermoscope," tinted photomontage, yellow, red, black, and gray, corner bumps **65.00**

Arm & Hammer Baking Soda, 17 x 25", c1912, matched pair, Birds of America, stone litho, multicolored, orig metal ribs **125.00**

Card Seed Grows, F. Earl Christy, 15 x 22″, c1913, Fredonia, NY, seed company, full color litho of pretty girl holding large bouquet of daisies, orig metal ribs 350.00

Hoffman Brewing Co, Oriental Brewery, J Ottmann, NY, 31 x 21″, c1900, multicolored floral arrangement, white ground 220.00

Ivory Soap, 11 x 21″, Art Deco, two women inspecting garment 90.00

James Montgomery Flagg, Uncle Sam scowling, vivid colors, 20 x 30″, $150.00.

Peter Paul Mounds/Dreams, 29 x 45″, c1940, chocolate bars shown floating over coconut palm, native climber, full color 150.00

Raleigh Cigarettes, 12 x 18″, c1935, gentleman with cigarette against jet black ground 70.00

Satin Skin Powder, 28 x 42″, 1903, pretty girl with fan, detailed packages, full color 95.00

Zenith Radios, 42 x 58″, c1935, uncut proof sheet, Susi Lanner and Alice Eyland models, full color 175.00

CIRCUS, SHOWS, AND ACTS

Barnum and Bailey, combined shows, Presenting 150 Horses In The Fete Of Garlands, 30 x 40″, c1919–20 .. 175.00

Christiani Bros Circus, 28 x 49″, c1950, elephant with leggy trainer posed at ear, full color 75.00

Christy Bros Big 5 Ring Wild Animal Shows, The Wonder Show, 27 x 41″, litho, camels in foreground with trained bison, oxen and deer, Christy Bros in vignette at upper left, c1925 150.00

Ringling Bros and Barnum & Bailey, Bill Bailey, 28 x 21″, c1945, clown tips hat towards viewer, red ground 110.00

Wallace Bros Circus, 28 x 41″, c1950, full color, snarling tiger and lion 75.00

MOVIE

One Sheet, Silent
Chase Me, Otis litho, Fox Sunshine Comedy, Arbuckle at beach with two ladies 300.00

Dawn Of Revenge, 1922, 41 x 27″, Richard Travers, Otis litho, linen backed 150.00

Second Hand Line, Charles Jones, c1915, man in boat wooing girl .. 135.00

One Sheet, 27 x 41″
A Hard Days Night, 1964, The Beatles 200.00

Head Over Heels In Love, 1936, Jessie Matthews, litho, blue, yellow, brown, green, black 90.00

Most Precious Thing In Life, 1934, Jean Arthur, Richard Cromwell, litho, bust portraits, red, blue, orange, flesh tones, brown, and gray, yellow background 125.00

The Glass Webb, 1955, Edward G. Robinson 70.00

Three Sheets
Leave It To Me, 42 x 80″, c1916, William Russell and woman 175.00

The Stowaway, 40 x 80″, 1936, Shirley Temple, close–up 450.00

THEATRICAL

Bunco In Arizona, 30 x 40″, 1907, saloon scene, man shooting pistol from hand of another 200.00

Child Slaves Of New York, 20 x 30″, Strobridge Litho, Arab holding man in front pointing Kaldah The Mystic, frightened Victorian beauty, 1903 .. 165.00

Nip and Tuck, Detectives Out Of The Window Into The Water, 28 x 21″, J. M. Jones Co, man falling from up–ended rain barrel into jaw's of ferocious mastiff, c1880 .... 225.00

The Beautiful Indian Maidens, 20 x 27″, Enquirer Co, fourteen Victorian ladies dressed in tights and head dresses, catching duck dressed in tuxedo, lobster with smiling man's face, 1898 200.00

The Gambler Of The West, Strobridge,
20 x 30″, 1906, comedic bad man . . **190.00**
The New Fogg's Ferry, Enquirer Job
Printing, 27 x 41″, c1905, The Farew-
ell, multicolored **135.00**

TRANSPORTATION

American Airlines–San Francisco, E.
McKnight Kauffer, 30 x 40″, 1948,
Cubist Golden Gate Bridge and citys-
cape, blue night sky, yellow full moon,
paper loss to upper left border **175.00**
Cadillac–For Carefree Driving In The
Months Ahead, 28 x 42″, 1954, dark
blue sedan, autumn leaf setting, logo
at left, vivid colors, reverse archival
repairs to left margin **325.00**
Furness Caribbean Cruises, Adolph
Treidler, 40 x 50, c1950, multicolored
silkscreen, high fashion tourists play-
ing games and deck scenes of *Ocean
Monarch,* 3″ repair to right border . . **200.00**
Majestic, White Star Line, W. J. Aylward,
Brussels, 41 x 28″, multicolored,
ocean liner approaching dock **1,320.00**
Take The Union Pacific Railway To
Denver and San Francisco, Omaha
Republican Print, 9 x 24″, two huge
letters U and P with names of towns
serviced, 1883 . . . . **135.00**

WORLD WAR I

All Together. Enlist In The Navy, 40 x
29″, sailors of all nations beckon
standing beside each other **165.00**
Be A US Marine, 29 x 40″, marine
image, no–nonsense pose, loom-
ing stars and stripes **375.00**
First Call–I Need You In The Navy This
Minute!, 10 x 11″, Uncle Sam, full
color, Navy recruiting use **275.00**
I Want You For The US Navy, 27 x 41″,
appealing blonde in Navy jacket looks
seductively to viewer, 1917 . . . . **500.00**
Men Wanted For The Army, 30 x 40″,
chromolithograph, fortress, gun crew,
and sergeant preparing to fire toward
distant sea **175.00**
Over There! Skilled Workers On The
Ground Behind The Lines In The Air
Service, 30 x 38″, three color lithograph, American Doughboy with hand
in air beckoning to silhouette of biplane near hanger, 3″ black and gray
bottom border, rebuilt **375.00**
You–Help My Boy Win The War, Buy A
Liberty Bond, 21 x 11″, close–up of
mother in front young Doughboy . . . **100.00**

WORLD WAR II

Buy War Bonds, N. C. Wyeth, 22 x 14″,
patriotic image, Uncle Sam holding
billowing flag in one hand, pointing
sternly toward unseen enemy with
other **150.00**
Enlist In The Waves/Release A Man To
Fight At Sea, 42 x 28″, recruiting im-
age **100.00**
From Mine to Firing Line/More Produc-
tion, 40 x 28″, stylized image, coal
dust proceeded from mine to artillery
shell casings **80.00**
Nurses Are Needed Now, 1944, 19 x
13″, recruiting registered nurses,
Army Nurse Corps **60.00**
Our Fighters/Deserve Our Best, 1942,
40 x 29″, US Army Ordinance, defiant
soldier helping wounded buddy, flam-
ing and devastated landscape **85.00**
The United Nations Fight For Freedom,
28 x 20″, colorful image, flags of Allied
Nations surrounding Statue of Liberty **125.00**

POT LIDS

History: Pot lids are the lids from pots or small
containers which originally held ointments, po-
mades, or soap. Although a complete set of pot
and lid is desirable to some collectors, lids are the
most collectible. The lids frequently were decorated with multicolored underglaze transfers of rural and domestic scenes, portraits, florals, and
landmarks.

The majority of the containers with lids were
made between 1845–1920 by F. & R. Pratt, Fenton, Staffordshire, England. In 1920, F. & R. Pratt
merged with Cauldon Ltd. Several lids were reissued by the firm using the original copper engraving plates. They were used for decoration and
never served as actual lids. Reissues by Kirkhams
Pottery, England, generally have two holes for
hanging and often are marked as reissues. Cauldon, Coalport, and Wedgwood were other firms
making reissues.

References: Susan and Al Bagdade, *Warman's
English & Continental Pottery & Porcelain, 2nd
Edition,* Wallace–Homestead, 1991; A. Ball, *The
Price Guide to Pot–Lids And Other Underglaze
Multicolor Prints On Ware, Second Edition,* An-
tique Collectors' Club, 1991 value update; Ronald
Dale, *The Price Guide To Black and White Pot–
Lids,* Antique Collectors' Club; Barbara and Sonny
Jackson, *American Pot Lids,* published by authors,
1987.

Note: Sizes are given for actual pot lids; size of
any framing not included.

Artic Expedition, multicolored, T J & J
Mayer, 3″, rim chip **320.00**

Bloater Paste, black label, white ironstone, 4½", marked "England"	25.00
Dr Hassall's Hair Restorer, 1¾"	250.00
Dr. Johnson, multicolored, 4"	125.00
Dublin Industrial Exhibition, multicolored, 3¾"	50.00
Embarking For The East, multicolored, Pratt, 4⅛", orig jar	100.00
Lady Brushing Hair, multicolored, 3"	220.00
Linaleton's Eye Ointment, 1⅝"	210.00
Morris's Imperial Eye Ointment	200.00
Mrs Ellen Hale's Celebrated Heal All Ointment, black on white, 4"	350.00
Napirima, Trinidad, T J & J Mayer, c1853, medium	165.00
No By Heaven I Exclaimed..., multicolored, 4½"	175.00
Persuasion, multicolored, 4⅛"	150.00
Picnic On The Banks Of The River, Gothic Ruins, Pratt, 4¾"	90.00

Pratt type, multicolored transfer, titled "Strathfieldsay," orig jar, 4¼" d, $125.00.

Prepared Only By Hooks Windsor Ointment, bird on branch	120.00
Residence of the Late Sir Robert Peel, Pratt	150.00
Roman Eye Balsam, purple, glass base	210.00
Tam O'Shanter and Souter Johnny, 4", framed	275.00
Trouchet's Corn Cure Safe Reliable, light house	125.00
Trysting Place, The, small	165.00
Queen Victoria on Balcony, T J & J Mayer, large	265.00
View of Windsor Castle, Pratt, 6½"	150.00
Village Wedding, The, multicolored, Pratt, 4¼"	80.00
Ville De Strasbourg, Pratt type	75.00
Walmer Castle, Kent, Tatnell & Son, 4½"	200.00
Washington Crossing the Delaware, Pratt, orig jar	225.00
Wellington, T J & J Mayer, c1850, medium	100.00
Wood's Areca Nut Tooth Paste	100.00

PRATT

PRATT
FENTON

PRATT WARE

History: The earliest Pratt earthenware was made in the late 18th century by William Pratt, Lane Delph, Staffordshire, England. In 1810–1818, Felix and Robert Pratt, William's sons, established their own firm, F. & R. Pratt, in Fenton in the Staffordshire district. Potters in Yorkshire, Liverpool, Sunderland, Tyneside, and Scotland copied the ware.

The wares consisted of relief molded jugs, commercial pots and tablewares with transfer decoration, commemorative pieces, and figure and animal groups.

Much of the early ware is unmarked. The mid–19th century wares bear several different marks in conjunction with the name Pratt, including "& Co."

References: Susan and Al Bagdade, *Warman's English & Continental Pottery & Porcelain, 2nd Edition,* Wallace–Homestead, 1991; John and Griselda Lewis, *Pratt Ware 1780–1840,* Antique Collectors' Club, 1984.

Additional Listing: Pot Lids.

Jug, polychrome on cream ground, c1800, 8" h, $575.00.

Bowl, 9⅞" d, 3½" h, dark brown int., green transfer of Dr Syntax Drawing After Nature, polychrome	100.00
Creamer	
4⅞" h, orange, blue, green, and yellow, sailor's farewell scene, 18th C	110.00
5¼" h, cow, milkmaid, underglaze enamels, yellow and black sponged cow, translucent green stepped rect base, horns chipped	440.00
Cup Plate, 3⅛" d, white Dalmatian, black spots	65.00
Figure	
Four Seasons, 9½" h, matched set of four, late 18th C	1,700.00

Mother and her children, 8½" h, late
18th C 300.00
St. Mark, 9" h, late 18th C 275.00
Flask, 7¾" h, The Late Duke of Wellington on front, Rt Hon Sir Robt Peel on
reverse, multicolored print, reserved
on malachite ground, gilt borders,
c1865 .... 400.00
Jar, 7¾" h, molded oval panels of peacocks in landscapes, blue, brown,
green, and ochre, lower section with
vertical leaves, band of foliage on rim,
c1790 .... 600.00
Jug, 11" h, figural, Bacchus and Pan,
sea lion handle, 1800 .... 685.00
Mug, 4¼" h, multicolored scenes, maroon ground 135.00
Mustard Jar, dark blue hunt scene, tan
ground 55.00
Pipe, 8" l, neatly coiled in concentric
circles, 1800 .... 1,100.00
Pitcher, 7¼" h, yellow, blue, brown, and
green, raised couple, mother, children, and trees dec, 18th C 340.00
Plaque, pierced for hanging
5¾" d, relief of bird with insect
perched on cherry branch, brown,
ochre, and green, c1775 .... 350.00
11" l, oval, relief of two recumbent
lions, yellow ochre, brown, and
green, blue border, c1800 ...... 570.00
Plate, 9" d, Haddon Hall, classical figure
border 100.00
Tea Caddy, 6¼" h, rect, fluted and yellow trimmed lid, raised figural panels
front and back, blue, yellow, orange,
and green dec 330.00
Toby Jug, 7¾" h, underglazed enamels,
red face, molded caryatid handle, attributed to Yorkshire Pottery, c1810 . 825.00
Watch Holder, 10" h, figural, tall case
clock, attended by two figures, early
19th C 700.00
Whistle, figural, bird 500.00

PRINTS

History: Prints serve many purposes. They can
be a reproduction of an artist's paintings, drawings,
or designs. Prints themselves often are an original
art form. Finally, prints can be developed for mass
appeal as opposed to aesthetic statement. Much
of the production of Currier & Ives fits this latter
category. Currier & Ives concentrated on genre,
urban, patriotic, and nostalgia scenes.

Prints are beginning to attract a wide following.
This is partially because prices have not matched
the rapid rise in oil and other paintings.

References: Frederic A. Conningham and Colin
Simkin, *Currier & Ives Prints, Revised Edition,*
Crown Publishers, Inc., 1970; Victor J. W. Christie,

Bessie Pease Gutmann: Her Life and Works, Wal-
lace–Homestead, 1990; William P. Carl and Wil-
liam T. Currier, *Currier's Price Guide to American
and European Prints at Auction, First Edition,* Cur-
rier Publications, 1989; Denis C. Jackson, *The
Price & Identification Guide to J. C. Leyendecker
& F. X. Leyendecker,* published by author, 1983;
Robert Kipp and Robert Weiland, *Currier's Price
Guide to Currier & Ives Prints, First Edition,* Currier
Publications, 1989; Craig McClain, *Currier & Ives:
An Illustrated Value Guide,* Wallace–Homestead,
1987; Rita C. Mortenson, *R. Atkinson Fox, His
Life and Work,* Revised, L–W Book Sales, 1991;
Ruth M. Pollard, *The Official Price Guide To Col-
lector Prints, 7th Edition,* House Of Collectibles,
1986.

Collectors' Clubs: American Historical Print
Collectors Society, Inc., P.O. Box 1532, Fairfield,
CT 06430; *Imprint*; Prang–Mark Society, Century
House, P.O. Box 306, Old Irelandville, Watkins
Glen, NY 14891.

Periodical: *The Illustrator Collector's News,*
P.O. Box 1958, Sequim, WA 98392.

Reproduction Alert: Reproductions are a problem, especially Currier & Ives prints. Check the
dimensions before buying any print.

Additional Listing: See Wallace Nutting.

**Louis Icart, Venetian Nights, unframed,
$875.00.**

Audubon, John James, after, hand colored etching, engraving, and aquatint
by R Havell & Son, London, watermark of J Whatman Turkey Mill
Carolina Turtle Dove, Plate XVII,
1933, large margins, faint mat
stain, framed, 37⅝ x 25⅞" 9,350.00
Great Northern Diver Or Loon, Plate
CCCVI, long tear, faded, paper

tone slightly discolored, backboard stain, framed, 25⅝ x 38″ sheet size **2,200.00**

Mocking Bird, Plate 21, 1837, full sheet, 39¼ x 26¼″ sheet size ... **3,850.00**

Rice Bird, Plate LIV, 1936, full sheet, 39¾ x 26⅛″ **770.00**

Wood Ibis, Plate CCXVI, 1834, full margins, glued to backmat in margin edges, 38⅛ x 25¼″ **6,600.00**

Baumann, Gustave, American, 1881–1971, Farmyard with Chickens, color woodcut, sgd in pencil lower right, 9⅛ x 13″ **600.00**

Bennett, William J, Megarey's Views In The City Of New–York, set of three aquatints, c1826 and c1828, fine impressions, published by Henry I Megarey, NY, issued c1834, full margins, slight soiling, foxing, and discoloration in the margins, orig text, orig blue paper wrappers, each sheet 14⅛ x 20⅞″, set **26,400.00**

Benton, Thomas Hart, American, 1889–1975, Jessie and Jake, litho, sgd in pencil lower right and "Benton" in pencil lower right, annotated "To Kitsie..." in pencil lower left, wove paper, framed, 13⅜ x 9¹⁵⁄₁₆″ **1,100.00**

Bontecou, Lee, American, b1931, untitled, etching and aquatint in black and brown, sgd in pencil lower right, dated 1967, numbered 133/144, 26 x 17⅛″ **300.00**

Calder, Alexander, American, 1898–1976, Spider's Nest, color litho, sgd in pencil lower right, numbered 25/95, 29½ x 43¼″ **500.00**

Cartwitham, John, A South–East View Of The City Of Boston In North America, hand colored engraving, fourth (final) state, published by Bowles & Carver, c1764, wove paper with watermark "J. Whatman 1764," trimmed within the platemark, two tears at left, creases, other minor damage, framed, 11¾ x 17½″ **6,600.00**

Chagall, Marc, Russian–French, 1887–1985

He Wrote In The Tables The Words Of The Covenant..., color litho, 1966, from the "Story of Exodus," set no. 142 of 250 edition, 18 x 13″ **900.00**

Kopekne et Napoleon, etching, from series "Les Ames Mortes," 11 x 8¼″ **300.00**

Table Fleurie, color litho, 1933, sgd in pencil lower right, numbered 46/50, printed on white wove paper with watermark Arches, 16 x 20⅞″ **5,200.00**

The Four Seasons, color litho, 1974, sgd and numbered edition of 100, 35⅜ x 23½″ **200.00**

Cheney, Philip, American, b1897, Western Landscape, litho, sgd in pencil lower right, 9⅝ x 13⅝″ **90.00**

Church, Frederick Stuart, American, 1842–1923, Dissertation On A Roast Pig, etching, sgd and dated in plate lower left, "F. S. Church/NY 83," titled in pencil on mat, 4¾ and 6¼″, matted and framed **50.00**

Copley, William, American, b1919, Think, serigraph, sgd in pencil lower right, dated '67, numbered 48/100, 20¾ x 25¾″ **50.00**

Currier and Ives, publishers

Clipper Ship "Red Jacket" In The Ice Off Cape Horn, after drawings by JB Smith & Son, Brooklyn, hand colored litho, fresh impression on stone by C Parsons, 1855, lower publication line, water stains, framed, 16⅛ x 23¾″ **4,675.00**

The Express Train, hand colored litho, touches of gum arabic, 1870, red pencil inscription in lower left margin corner, slight soiling, 10 x 14″ sheet size **1,760.00**

View On The Harlem River, N.Y.: The Highbridge In The Distance, after the painting by F F Palmer, hand colored litho with gum arabic, 1852, two sharp handling creases, soiling, pale discoloration in margins and verso, framed, 18⅛ x 24″ sheet size **990.00**

Winter In The Country, The Old Grist Mill, after the painting of George H Durrie, hand colored litho, 1864, lower publication line, slight discoloration, framed, 22⅛ x 30″ sheet size **6,600.00**

Currier, Nathaniel, publisher

American Winter Scenes, Evening, after the painting by FF Palmer, hand colored litho, 1854, paper tone discolored, foxing, soiling, water staining, framed, 20½ x 28⅛″ sheet size **3,025.00**

Camping Out: Some Of The Right Sort, after the painting by L Maurer, hand colored litho, gum arabic, 1856, paper tone slightly darkened, 22 x 30″ sheet size **3,575.00**

Degas, Edgar, French, 1834–1917, Mary Cassatt At The Louvre: The Paintings Gallery, etching, aquatint, soft–ground, and drypoint, 1879–80, impression from canceled plate, printed edition of 150, published by Ambroise Vollard in 1919–20, 12 x 5″ **600.00**

Dow, Arthur Wesley, American, 1857–1922, Sunset Bayberry Hill, color woodblock, sgd and dated in pencil lower left and lower right, title on inner mat, framed, 4 x 6⅞″ sight size **2,970.00**

Fantin–Latour, Henri, French, 1936–1904, La Nymphe, litho, 1903, plate of 11 illustrations, published edition of 633, 7⅞ x 5½″ **225.00**

Gag, Wanda, American, 1893–1946, Blacksmith's Shop, litho, sgd in pencil lower right, annotated lower left, wove paper, framed, 11½ x 13¾″ **385.00**

Gifford, Robert Swain, American, 1840–1905, Coal Dock, New Bedford, Mass, etching, sgd in plate lower right, 6¾ x 4¾″, matted and framed **70.00**

Golinken, Joeseph W., American, b1896 Prize Fight, litho, sgd in pencil lower right, 10⅝ x 9¼″ **190.00**
Sumo Wrestlers, litho, sgd in pencil lower right, 13¼ x 11⅞″ **130.00**

Hagerman, Kurt, Kentucky Tradition–The Derby, Churchill Downs, etching, sgd in pencil lower right, titled in pencil lower left, 6½ x 9″ **50.00**

Heap, George, attributed to, An East Perspective Of The City Of Philadelphia, In The Province Of Pennsylvania, In North America, hand colored etching and line engraving, 1731, fine first state impression, "engraved from the Original Drawing sent over from Philadelphia in the possession of Carrington Bowles...printed for and sold by Carrington Bowles...published as the Act directs, 1 Jany., 1778," cream laid paper, Gaylord watermark, large margins, deckle on three sides, slight discoloration, soiling, slight creases, old hinge stains in upper corner verso, framed, 10⅞ x 16⅞″ plate size **23,100.00**

Helleu, Paul Cesar, French, 1859–1927, Madame Letellier, drypoint, sgd in pencil lower right, fair condition, laid down, framed, 21⅛ x 12⅞″ image size **1,540.00**

Homer, Winslow, American, 1836–1910, The Army Of The Potomac—A Sharp–Shooter On Picket Duty, engraving done for Harper's Weekly, Nov 15, 1862, sgd "Homer" in illustration lower right, titled lower center, faded, several repaired tears, 9 x 13½″, matted and framed **20.00**

Hornor, Thomas, New York From Brooklyn, hand colored engraving, c1836–39, printed by William Neale, plate margins, touched–in vertical and horizontal folds, tears, losses, and abrasions in the margins, colors revised, Japan–backed, 20¼ x 32″ plate size **3,850.00**

Icart, Louis, French, 1888–1950 Girl in Crinoline, color aquatint, 1937, sgd in pencil lower right, artist's

stamp lower left, artist's label on frame backing, 23¼ x 19½″ **1,800.00**
Nude, soft–ground and aquatint, black and red, sgd in pencil lower right, 10½ x 8¼″ **1,000.00**

Kelly, Ellsworth, American, b1923, Yellow, color litho, sgd in pencil lower right, numbered 39/75, printed on white Rives paper, 23¼ x 15¼″ **400.00**

Kent, Rockwell, American, 1882–1971, Climbing The Bars, transfer printed, 1928, sgd in pencil lower right, stamped "Oct 11, 1929" on verse, edition of 110, printed by George Miller, tan paper, framed, 11 x 8″ ... **275.00**

Kingman, Doug, American, 20th C, Spirit of July 4th 1976, litho, sgd in pencil lower right, titled on reverse, numbered 451/500 in pencil lower left, 20½ x 31¾″, matted and framed **100.00**

Klinger, Max, German, 1857–1920, Intermezzi, etching, roulette, and stipple on heavy wove paper, inscribed in plate with artists name lower left and "II" lower right, titled and dated on mat, scattered foxing, matted, 9 x 16″ **220.00**

Lautrec, Henri de Toulouse, French, 1864–1901
Adieu, litho, 1895–96, first in series "Melodies de Desire Dihau," 10⅜ x 7⅞″ **300.00**
Ballade de Noel, litho, 1895–96, second in series "Melodies de Desire Dihau," 10¼ x 7⅜″ **300.00**
Ce Que Dit la Pluie, litho, 1895–96, third in series "Melodies de Desire Dihau," 10⅛ x 7⅝″ **300.00**
La Gage, litho, 1897, 13⅝ x 9⅞″ ... **1,200.00**

Liebermann, Max, German, 1847—1935, Girl With Dachshund, transfer litho, sgd in pencil lower right, 13¼ x 7½″ **550.00**

Lindenmuth, Tod, American, 1885–1976, Dory Fisherman, color woodblock, sgd in pencil lower right, titled in pencil lower left, metal frame, 11¼ x 14″ **550.00**

Miro, Joan, Spanish, 1893–1983, Composition, etching and carborundum, sgd in white pencil lower right and numbered 35/50 .... **1,000.00**

Moran, Thomas, American, 1837–1926, The White Squadron, after Edward Moran, etching, 1891, sgd in pencil lower right, also sgd lower left by Edward Moran, third state, 22¾ x 32⅝″ **400.00**

Morisot, Berthe, French, 1841–95, Jeune Fille, drypoint, impression from canceled plate, 3¼ x 4⅝″ **90.00**

Mucha, Alphonse, Czechoslovakia, 1860–1939, Le Lys, color litho, 1897, sgd in the stone, 40 x 16¼″ **1,000.00**

Picasso, Pablo, Spanish, 1881–1973, Papiers/Colles/1910–1914, litho, unsigned, numbered 68/300, 24 x 17½", matted and framed **200.00**

Rembrandt Van Rijn, Dutch, 1606—69

A Peasant In A High Cap Standing Leaning On A Stick, etching, 1939, Basan impression, 3¼ x 1¾", unframed **2,000.00**

Cornelis Claez Ansio, Mennonite Preacher, etching, 1641, later impression from reworked plate, 7¼ x 6" **2,000.00**

Jan Lutma, Goldsmith, etching and drypoint, 1656, impression of Nowell–Usticke's second state, 7⅝ x 5¾" **1,000.00**

Man Standing In Oriental Costume and Plumed Fur Cap, etching, 1632, 18th C impression, 4¼ x 3" **400.00**

Peter and John At The Gate Of The Temple, etching, 1659, impression of Nowell–Usticke's fifth or sixth state, 7⅛ x 8⅜" **450.00**

Rembrandt In Velvet Cap and Plume, etching, 1636, impression of Nowell–Usticke's third state, 5¼ x 4" . **1,500.00**

Rembrandt's Mother In Oriental Headdress, etching, 1631, impression of Nowell–Usticke's fourth state, 5¾ x 5" **300.00**

Remington, Frederic Sackrider, American, 1861–1909,

Cold Winds On The Plains, litho, published in 1901 by Robert Howell Russell sgd and dated in plate lower right, 1901, very minor foxing at edges, 19½ x 14½", matted and framed **450.00**

The Retreat, litho, sgd and dated in plate, 1889, 20¼ x 35½", matted and framed **75.00**

The Scout, litho, published in 1901 by Robert Howell Russell sgd and dated in plate lower right, several scratches upper left, small water stain lower left, mat water stained, 19½ x 14½", matted and framed . **450.00**

The Smoke Signal, litho, sgd in plate lower left, 22¼ x 33¼", matted and framed **275.00**

Victory Dance, litho, sgd in plate lower right, 19¼ x 20½", matted and framed **125.00**

Renoir, Pierre–Auguste, French, 1841–1919

Femme Nue Couchee, Tournee a Droite, etching, 1906, 5⅜ x 7⅝" . . **425.00**

La Danse a la Campagne, soft–ground etching, c1890, stamped sgd lower right, printed on cream wove paper, 12⅜ x 9⅜" **9,000.00**

Trois Esquisses de Maternites, heliogravure, printed on cream wove paper, 9¾ x 12¾" **1,500.00**

Ripley, Aiden Lassell, American, 1896–1969, Partridge Eating Grapes, drypoint, sgd in pencil lower right, cream wove paper, framed, fair, laid down to board, light staining, 6 9/16 x 8 7/16" . . . **110.00**

Salathe, after the painting by H Sebron, Les Chutes Du Niagara, Le Fer A Cheval, Niagara Falls, The Horse Shoe, hand colored etching and engraving, published by Goupil & Co, 1852, margins beyond platemark, minor damage, laid down, framed, 28⅜ x 42⅜" **1,100.00**

Steinlen, Theophile Alexandre, Swiss, 1859–1923, Femme de Trois Quarts se Coiffant, soft–ground and aquatint on zinc, June 1902, sgd in pencil lower right, from edition of 25 plus 4 trial proofs, printed in brown ink, 14 x 9½" **700.00**

Tanner, Robin, British, b1904, Spring, engraving, sgd in pencil lower right, inscribed "Trial W Slate" in pencil lower left, 6¾ x 8¾", matted and framed **60.00**

Thorne, Diane, American, b1895, Russians, etching, sgd in pencil lower right and lower center, 6 x 7¾", matted **55.00**

Thornton, Dr Robert John, British, 1768–1837, after P Henderson, engraved by William Ward, The Dragon Arum From The Temple Of Flora, mezzotint and aquatint, printed in color, hand finishing, heavy wove paper, inscriptions below image, framed, 17⅜ x 13¾" **475.00**

Tittle, Walter Ernest, American, 1883–1960, Golfer, drypoint, sgd in pencil lower right, and in the plate lower left, framed, 11¾ x 9¾" **315.00**

Walker, Bernard Eyre, British, b1886, Dove Cottage, Grosmire, Wordsworth's Home, etching, sgd in pencil lower right, titled in pencil lower left, 4¾ x 6¾", matted and framed **25.00**

Wengenroth, Stow, American, 1906–1977, Summer Shadows Wiscasset Maine, litho, sgd in pencil lower right, annotated "Ed/85" lower left, titled in pencil lower left, wove paper, framed, extensive foxing in margins, mount staining, 8⅜ x 15⅜" **360.00**

Whistler, James Abbott McNeill, American, 1834–1903

Early Morning, lithograph, 1878, monogrammed on the plate lower left, wove paper, framed, 6½ x 10¼" . **715.00**

The Little Pool, etching, 1961, 3½ x
  4⅝" **500.00**
Zorn, Anders, Swedish, 1860–1920
  Djos Mats, etching, 1911, sgd in pen-
    cil lower right, 7 x 4½" **600.00**
  Sapho, etching, 1917, mono-
    grammed and dated in the plate
    lower left, framed, 8 x 7⅛" **330.00**

PRINTS—JAPANESE

History: Buying Japanese woodblock prints requires attention to detail and skilled knowledge of
the subject. The quality of the impression (good,
moderate, or weak), the color, and condition are
critical. Various states and strikes of the same print
cause the price to fluctuate. Knowing the proper
publisher and censor's seals are helpful in identifying an original print.

Most prints were recopied and issued in popular
versions. These represent the vast majority of the
prints found in the marketplace. These popular
versions should be viewed solely as decorative
since they have little value.

A novice buyer should seek expert advice before
buying. Talk with a specialized dealer, museum
curator, or auction division head.

The listings below concentrate on details to
show the depth of data needed for adequate pricing. Condition and impression are good, unless
indicated otherwise.

O = Oban, 10 x 15"   C = Chuban, 7 x 10"
t = tat-e,   H = Hosoban,
  large in width   5½ x 13"
y = yoke-e,   T = Triptyck
  large in length
Reference: Sandra Andacht, *Oriental Antiques
& Art: An Identification And Value Guide,* Wallace-
Homestead, 1987.

Buncho, courtesan *Nishikigi* of the Kan-
  aya standing before a *tokonoma* with
  a spray of plum blossoms in her hand,
  scroll on wall sgd *Ippitsusai* and seal

**Hiroshige, Hodogaya/Shimachi Bridge,
c1838, $200.00.**

Mori uji, minor fading, one set of three
  titled *Wrestling Match or Battle of
  Flowers,* H **3,500.00**
Eisen, *Ukiyo nijuyonko* series, Yang
  Hsiang shown teasing cat, sgd *Keisai
  Eisen–ga,* with *kiwame* and publisher's seal, good impression, slight
  wrinkling, Ot **725.00**
Eizan, Kakemono–E, humorous tiger
  emerging from behind large stalk of
  bamboo, sgd *Kikugama Eizan hitsu,*
  good impression, fair color, good condition **375.00**
Gakutei, seated geisha playing the
  biwa, from *Hanazo bantsuki* series,
  sgd *Gakutei,* color slightly faded, C . **950.00**
Harunobo, courtesan showing the neck
  of her kamoro before a screen dec
  with farmers harvesting rice, titled *Jin,
  Virtue,* from *The Five Cardinal Virtues*
  series, sgd *Suzuki Harunobo ga,* Ct **7,750.00**
Hashimoto, Oklie, Rocks in a Garden,
  color woodcut, sgd in pencil lower
  right, 1960, numbered 47/60, inscribed in Japanese, artist's chop
  mark, 21¼ x 16¾" **275.00**
Hiroshige
  Fishing boats at Tsuikudajima in
    Buyp Province, *Shokoku meisho*
    series, "Famous Places in Various
    Provinces," sgd *Hiroshiga ga,* pub-
    lished by Dansendo, *unchima–e*
    center fold, margins slightly soiled,
    backed **5,750.00**
  Kanagawa–Dai no tei, hilltop view,
    from *Tokaido Gojusan–tsugi* se-
    ries, sgd *Hiroshige–ga,* red gourd
    shaped seal with *kiwame* and *Tak-
    enouchi* seals, fair impression,
    good color, backed, left margin
    trimmed, Oy **125.00**
  Mishima asagiri, "Morning Mist,
    Mishima," from *Toto meisho* series,
    "Famous Places of the Eastern
    Capital," sgd *Hiroshege ga,* with
    Hoseido/Senkakudo, publisher's
    seals, margins trimmed, slightly
    rubbed, and soiled, Oy **675.00**
Hiroshige II, Chuban Album, complete
  set of series *Edo meisho yonju hak-
  kei/Forty–eight famous Sights of Edo,*
  each sgd *Hiroshige–ga,* some margins with *aratame/negetsu* (c1860)
  and publisher *Tsuta–ya Kichizo*
  seals, good states, laid down, Ct ... **1,350.00**
Hokusai
  Sinsho Suwa–ko, "Lake Suma in
    Shinano Province," from *Fugaku
    sanjurokkei* series, "Thirty–six
    views of Mt Fuji," sgd *Zen Hokusai
    Iitsui hitsu,* publisher's seal *Eijudo,*
    Oy **4,250.00**

Uki–e depicting the Oji Inari Shrine, sgd *Hokusai ga,* slightly faded and trimmed, Oy 300.00

Kawase Hasui
Ebisu Harbor, Sado Island in Winter, Tabi miyage dinishi series, sgd *Hasui,* seated *kawase,* dated Taishi 10 (1921), *Watanabe* publisher's seal, Oy 1,200.00

Okayamajo no Asahi/Dawn at Okayama Castle, dated Showa 30 (1955), misty view of castle, sgd *Hasui,* circular *Watanabe Shosaburo* seal, good impression, color, and state, Ot 350.00

Kikumaro, courtesan seated by hibachi, surrounded by female attendants, blossoming prunus and sparrow, sgd *Kikumaro hitsu,* fair impression, poor color, stained, Ot 275.00

Kunisada, Kakemono–e, high ranking courtesan walking in elaborate kimono, sgd *Kochoro Kunisada hitsu,* with *aratame/negetsu* seal, c1865, good impression, fair color, faded, toned, trimmed, backed 225.00

Kotondo, Beauty in sudden shower, sgd *Genjin ga,,* dated Showa 4 (1929), numbered 84/200, published by Sakai–Kawaguchi, large Ot 1,000.00

Kuniyoshi
Giyu hakken–den series, depicting *Inyuama Dosetsu,* sgd *Ichiyasi Kuniyoshi–ga,* two *naushi* and publisher seals, fair impression and color, faded, fair state, Ot 100.00

Oda Kazuma, titled *Matsue Ohashi/ The Great Bridge of Matsue,* group of figures crossing bridge in snow storm, sgd *Kazuma hitsu,* red artist's seal, right margin with title and dated Taisho 13 (1924), very good impression and color, Oy 850.00

Maekawa, Sempan, Bird in Hand, color woodcut, 1955, sgd in pencil lower right, artist's red chop, unframed, 11¼ x 16⅝" 750.00

Nakayama, Tadashi, Three Zebras, color woodcut, sgd in pencil lower left, 1959, numbered 30/50, 28 x 22" ... 1,200.00

Saito, Kiyoski
Buddha, color woodcut, sgd in ink within the image, 1962, titled and numbered 96/200, artist's red chop, 20¾ x 15" 900.00

Hut In The Forest, color woodcut, sgd in ink lower right, artist's red chop, 15¼ x 20¾" 2,500.00

Sekino, Junichiro
My Daughter, color woodcut, 1952, sgd in pencil lower right, numbered

and annotated 98/100 lle etat, artist's red chop, 18 x 14½" 900.00

Portrait, woodcut, sgd in pencil lower right, numbered 28/30, unframed, 29 x 18¼" 1,900.00

Shinagawa, Takumi, Stone Buddha, color woodcut, sgd in pencil lower right, 1974, unframed, 19½ x 22½" . 375.00

Toyokuni I, three courtesans and their attendants strolling on busy street, sgd *Toyokuni–ga, kiwame* and *Iwato–ya Kisaburo* publisher's seal, fair impression, poor color, faded, fair state, Ot 400.00

Utamaro, one courtesan standing over another in front, sgd *Utamaro hitsu,* with *kiwame, negetsu, (1806)* and publisher's seals, fair impression, poor color, faded, wrinkled, Ot 300.00

Utamaro II, Beauty, half length, holding up her baby who plays with ball, sgd *Utamaro hitsu, kiwame* seal, publisher's seal *Iwatoya Kisaburo,* and censor's seal of Kisabura, Ot 2,000.00

Yakamura Koko (Toyonari), three quarter view of actor *Matsumoto Koshiro* as *Sekibei,* sgd *Koka–ga,* publisher's seal and blind printed date Taisho 8 (1919), good impression and color, Ot 900.00

Yoshida, Toshi
Irozaki Morning, color woodcut, sgd in pencil unframed, 9½ x 13½" .. 50.00

Silver Pavilion, color woodcut, sgd in pencil, 14½ x 9¾" 150.00

Yoshitoshi
Diptych Set, from series *Shinsen Azuma Nishiki–e/Newly Selected Edo Color Prints,* titled *Tamiya Botaro no Hanashi/the Story of Tamiya Botaro,* sgd *Yoshitoshi,* one seal reading *Taiso,* left margin dated Meiji 19 (1886) and publisher *Tsunanshima Kamekichi* cartouche, good impression and colors, margins partially trimmed, Ot 650.00

Triptych Set, titled *Taiheiki Sengatake honjun no zu,* showing samurai *Takuma Morimasa* bound in ropes held by warriors, sgd *Ikahaisai Yoshitoshi hutsu* with *aratame/negetsu (c1867)* and publisher *Tsunajima Kamekuchi* seals, fair impression and color, fair state, Ot 300.00

PURPLE SLAG (MARBLE GLASS)

History: Challinor, Taylor & Co., Tarantum, Pennsylvania, c1870s–80s, was the largest producer of purple slag in the United States. Since the quality of pieces varies considerably, there is no doubt other American firms made it as well.

Purple slag also was made in England. English pieces are marked with British Registry marks.

Other color combinations, such as blue, green, or orange, were made, but are rarely found.

Additional Listings: Greentown Glass (chocolate slag) and Pink Slag.

Reproduction Alert: Purple slag has been heavily reproduced over the years and still is reproduced at present.

Miniature Lamp, Button Arches pattern, $100.00.

Bread Plate, 12″ l, 8½″ w, oval, Tam O'Shanter, Tam holds glass, Soutar Johnny balances pitcher on knee	250.00
Cake Stand, Flute	75.00
Compote, 4½″, crimped top	65.00
Creamer, Flower and Panel	85.00
Goblet, Flute	40.00
Match Holder, Daisy and Button	40.00
Mug, rabbit	65.00
Plate, 10½″, closed lattice edge	100.00
Salt, 2½ x 4″	50.00
Spooner, Scroll with Acanthus	65.00
Sugar, cov, Flute	200.00
Toothpick, Inverted Fan and Feather	65.00

PUZZLES

History: The jigsaw puzzle originated in the mid–18th century in Europe. John Silsbury, a London map maker, was selling dissected map jigsaw puzzles by the early 1760s. The first jigsaw puzzles in America were English and European imports and aimed primarily at children.

Prior to the Civil War, several manufacturers, e.g., Samuel L. Hill, W. and S. B. Ives, and McLoughlin Brothers included puzzle offerings as part of their line. However, it was the post–Civil War period that saw the jigsaw puzzle gain a strong foothold among the children of America.

In the late 1890s and first decade of the twentieth century, puzzles designed specifically for adults first appeared. Both forms have existed side by side ever since. Adult puzzlers were responsible for two twentieth century puzzle crazes: 1908–09 and 1932–33.

Prior to the mid–1920s the vast majority of jigsaw puzzles were cut using wood for the adult market and composition material for the children's market. In the 1920s the die–cut, cardboard jigsaw puzzle evolved. By the time of the puzzle craze of 1932–33, it was the dominant puzzle medium.

Jigsaw puzzle interest has cycled between peaks and valleys several times since 1933. Mini–revivals occurred during World War II and in the mid–1960s when Springbok entered the American market.

References: Linda Hannas, *The Jigsaw Book*, Dial Press, 1981, out of print; Harry L. Rinker, *Collector's Guide To Toys, Games and Puzzles*, Wallace–Homestead, 1991; Anne D. Williams, *Jigsaw Puzzles: An Illustrated History and Price Guide*, Wallace–Homestead, 1990.

Additional Listings: See *Warman's Americana & Collectibles* for an expanded listing.

Collectors' Club: American Game Collectors Association, 4628 Barlow Drive, Bartlesville, OK 74006.

Seymour Lyman, New York, NY, Tally Ho, copyright 1878, 30 sliced cardboard pieces, 6¾ x 9¾″ cardboard box, 13¼ x 28½″, $225.00.

ADULT

Wood

Milton Bradley, Springfield, MA, Premier Jig Saw Puzzle, No. 65–99, "A Scene in Brussels," 7¾ x 5¾″, 66 pcs, bridge over stream, c1930, cardboard box, 4½ x 8¼ x 1¾″	15.00
C. L. Loomis, "The Glistening Sheen," 20 x 16″, 419 pcs, snow covered forest scene, stream in center, 1931, cigar box (Keller Cigar Company's Factory Secrets), 17½ x 5½ x 2¾″	35.00

Jigsaws by Jane, "Napoleon From Eagle in the Sky," 18 x 26", 414 pcs, irregular shaped edge, custom made wooden box with hinged lid, 9⅝ x 9⅝ x 5¼" **50.00**

Madmar Quality Co., Utica, NY, Madmar Interlox Puzzle, "Scene of the Orient," 5¾ x 7½", about 100 pcs, ox drawn cart with Buddha in mountain setting, cardboard box, 4¼ x 8¼ x 1⅛" **15.00**

Par Company, New York, NY, Par Picture Puzzle, "Never Too Hurried," about 250 pcs, English hunters finishing breakfast before hunt, 1960s, cardboard box, 9¾ x 7¼ x 2¾" **100.00**

Harry E. Pulver, New Hartford, CT, "Idle–Hour" Jig–Saw Puzzles – Novelties, No. 557, "A Hunting Morn," 16 x 12", 355 pcs, hunters getting ready to depart English village, c1930, cardboard box, 4¼ x 8¼ x 3" **25.00**

S. & H. Novelty Co., Atlantic City, NJ, Spare Time Jig Saw Puzzles, "Sulgrove Manor: Home of George Washington," 8 x 6", 75 pcs, figurals, cardboard box, 8¼ x 6⅜ x ⅞" **15.00**

Sear's Jig–Saw Puzzle, No. 1235, "The Pirates Treasure," 9¾ x 11¾", approx 150 pcs, 3 ply, composition material as center ply, pin–up pirate girl inspecting treasure trunk on ship's deck, dark blue tones in background, Pressler artist, cardboard box, 8¼ x 7¼ x 1½" **25.00**

Raphael Tuck & Sons, Ltd., Tuck's Sweetheart Zag–Zaw Picture Puzzle, "A Midsummer Night's Dream," 7 x 10¾", about 115 pcs, fairy awakes sleeping girl at base of tree by dropping floral petals on face, figural pcs including script "Sweetheart," Howard Davis artist, cardboard box, 8⅛ x 4¾ x 1⅞" **40.00**

Unknown cutter, "Ironing Table," 14 x 12", 271 pcs, solid wood, cut on color lines, domestic scene of woman ironing, cigar box (Doria, Puritanos Finos), 6⅜ x 5⅛ x 3" **60.00**

Unknown cutter, rural grist mill, 20 x 16", color photograph, 1940s or 50s, housed in modern Bernardo shoe box **15.00**

U–Nit Puzzles, West Caldwell, NJ, "Marina at Capri," 21½ x 18", 600 pcs, fishing village, cardboard box, 5¾ x 8¼ x 4" **40.00**

E. T. White, Hillside, NJ, White House Jig Saw Puzzle, No. 52, "The Old Windmill," 12 x 9", 214 pcs, irregular edges of puzzle tabs, cardboard box, 5⅛ x 7⅛ x 1¾" **30.00**

Wilder Corporation, St. Louis, MO, No. 20, "The Betrothal Puzzle," 10 x 11¾", over 250 pcs, 18th C Dutch scene of young man on knees proposing to seated lady, non–interlocking, cardboard box, 9 x 7¾ x 1¼" . . **20.00**

Die–Cut, Cardboard

Note: Cardboard puzzles from the post–1945 period sell between fifty cents and two dollars depending on company and subject matter.

Milton Bradley, Marlboro Jig Picture Puzzle, No. 10, "Father Neptune's Kingdom," 17 x 12", over 275 pcs, ocean waves crash on rocky shore, late 1930s, cardboard box, 8 x 5 x 1¾" **4.00**

Milton Bradley, Mayfair Jig Picture Puzzle, No. 4934, "The Charmer," 11⅞ x 14¾", over 200 pcs, jeweled Arabic beauty admires herself in mirror, Pressler artist, late 1930s, cardboard box, 9 x 7 x 1½" **20.00**

Built–Rite Interlocking Picture Puzzle, "Curtiss P40 War Hawk," 15¾ x 19¾", over 350 pcs, formation of six planes banking right, cardboard box, 7⅛ x 10⅝ x 1⅞", guide picture **15.00**

Columbian Offset Company, Chicago, IL, De Luxe Jig Puzzle of A Famous Painting, "Fortune Teller," 12 x 15½", over 280 pcs, cardboard box, 9⅛ x 7⅛ x 1¼" **3.00**

Consolidated Paper Box Company, Perfect Picture Puzzle, No. 1410, "Tough Luck," 10⁵⁄₁₆ x 13⁹⁄₁₆", over 250 pcs, two part scene of boy running in front of car and boy sitting in wheel chair looking out window as group of boys play baseball, cardboard box, 4⅝ x 6⅝ x 2", guide picture **12.50**

Detroit Gasket & Mfg. Co., Detroit, MI, Dee–Gee Picture Puzzle, It's A Corker (puzzle on cork, not cardboard), "Daughter of Setting Sun," 7¾ x 9⅞", over 125 pcs, Indian princess reaching toward sky in mountain setting, R. Atkinson Fox artist, cardboard box, 6¼ x 6¼ x 1½" **20.00**

Einson–Freeman, Every Week Jig–Saw Puzzle, No. 20, "Jungle Killers," 14⁵⁄₁₆ x 10⁷⁄₁₆", over 160 pcs, two tigers fighting, cardboard box, 7 x 7 x ¾", guide picture on back of box **10.00**

Santway Photo–Craft Company, Watertown, NY, The Muddle: The New Jig Puzzle, Fine Art Series E, "Happy Days," 14⅞ x 11⅛", over 300 pcs, peasant family brings new baby to visit grandparents, E. Zampighi artist, cardboard box, 8 x 8 x 1" **8.00**

Transogram Company, NY, Fine Art Picture Puzzle, "A Good Story by a Bad Shot," 16 x 12", over 200 pcs, English hunters gathered around fireplace after hunt, Mobltе artist, mid–1930s, cardboard box, 7¼ x 5¼ x 1½" **3.00**

Tuco Work Shops, Tuco Picture Puzzle, "Colorful Venice," 15 x 19," approx 350 pcs, copyright 1933, cardboard box with black, blue, red, and white jigsaw puzzle pieces motif and silhouette vignette of young couple assembling puzzle in upper right quadrant of lid **8.00**

University Distributing Company, Jig of the Week Puzzle, No. 21, "Picket's Charge at Gettysburg," 13¼ x 10", over 300 pcs, notched along top and bottom borders, view from Union lines, cardboard box, 7¼ x 7¼ x 1" . **15.00**

Unknown Manufacturer, "A Scene from RKO Radio Picture *The Half–Naked Truth* Starring Lupe Velez and Lee Tracy," 13¼ x 10", approx 135 pcs, couple watching detective inspect telephone **30.00**

CHILDREN

Pre–1940

Louis Marx & Co., New York, Genuine Jig–Saw Puzzle, wood, No. 5 from set of 12, "No Time To Lose," 3⅝ x 5⅜", 32 pcs, hunters shooting across canyon at deer, c1930, cardboard box, 6 x 4 x ⅝" **6.00**

Parker Brothers, Fairy Land Picture Puzzle, No. 0756, The Clock Struck One, wood, 6 x 8", 35 pcs, young girl stands on stool as mouse runs up tall case clock about to strike one, M. L. Kirk artist, c1920, cardboard box, 6⅜ x 8⅜ x ⅞", guide picture **25.00**

Saalfield Publishing Company, No. 909, four puzzle set, Bringing Up Father, die–cut, cardboard, each puzzle 9⅝ x 7⅝", early 1930s, cardboard box, 9⅞ x 8⅛ x 1", guide picture for one of puzzles on lid **30.00**

Selchow & Righter, NY, "Buster Brown's Christmas Puzzle," die–cut, cardboard, 13 pcs, 12¾ x 12", sliced format, c1920, cardboard box, 9¼ x 11¼ x 1" **225.00**

G. N. Tackabury & Co., Canastota, NY, "KINDERGARTEN, GEOGRAPHY, NEW AND IMPROVED DISSECTED MAP OF THE UNITED STATES," wood, 17⅞ x 11⅜", 51 pcs, early 1880s, multicolored, wooden box with sliding lid, green, yellow, and black checkered pattern paper on box

sides, label with gold printing on black ground **150.00**

Post–1940

Baron Scott Enterprises, Silver Spring, MD, "Sugar Ray Leonard," die–cut, cardboard, 11¼ x 15¾", 275 pcs, picture of Leonard wearing World Welterweight Champion belt, 1980, cardboard box, 8½ x 11 x 1¼", orig shrink wrap, guide picture **7.50**

Consolidated Paper Box Company, No. 521, Big 4 Circus Puzzles, three puzzle set, Set No. 1, die–cut, cardboard, each puzzle 9⅜ x 7½", 50 pcs, cardboard box, 9⅞ x 7⅝ x ¾", four sets in series **15.00**

Jaymar Specialty Company
"Mr. I. Magination," No. 2060, die–cut, cardboard, 19¼ x 14", 414 pcs, Mr. I. Magination and friend on train at Imagination Town train station, 1951, cardboard box, 10⅛ x 6⅞ x 1¾", guide picture **15.00**

"The Little King," Have Fun with Funnies Jigsaw Puzzle, Series No. 3, die–cut, cardboard, 9¼ x 14", cartoon format, mid–1940s, cardboard box showing cartoon characters in series **20.00**

Whitman, A Big Little Book Jigsaw Puzzle, No. 4657–1, "Lassie," die–cut, cardboard, 10 x 13", 99 pcs, 1967, cardboard box, 5⅛ x 6⅜ x 1½", book format, guide picture **10.00**

Frame Tray

Milton Bradley, No. 4508–X12, Helicopter Puzzle, 35 pcs, scene on aircraft carrier deck, 35 pcs, copyright 1960 **8.00**

Whitman, No. 2982, Roy Rogers working at blacksmith's anvil, cartoon background, 9¼ x 11½", 1952 .... **17.50**

Whitman, No. 4559, Hanna–Barbera's Space Kidettes Frame–Tray Puzzle, Kidettes flying in open space craft from space capsule "Klub House" to planet surface, copyright 1967 .... **10.00**

ADVERTISING

Chase & Sanborn, Chase & Sanborn's Puzzle Picture, Picking Coffee Berries, one of series of four, cardboard, 8 x 6", 63 pcs, c1910, cardboard box, 3¼ x 2½ x 1" **17.50**

College Inn Food Products Co., Hotel Sherman, Chicago, No. 1 of series of four, At Anchor, cardboard, 7⅜ x 9⅜", two two–masted sailing ships moored beside each other in harbor, early 1933, paper envelope, 7⅞ x 9½" . . . 12.00

Dunlop Tire & Rubber Corporation, Dunlop Circular Picture Puzzle, cardboard, 19" diameter, approx 650 pcs, outer border is a Dunlop tire, center is picture looking up through the hole on a tee at group of golfers, one of which is removing Dunlop golf ball from hole, c1970, cardboard box, 10½ x 7½ x 1½" . . . 30.00

Goodrich Tire, Akron, OH, The Goodrich Silver Fleet at Niagara Falls, cardboard, 9¾ x 7½", approx 50 pcs, paper envelope, 10 x 8", no adv on envelope except Stock No. 4091–GT 25.00

Greyhound, Jig Saw Puzzle Cartoon Map of the United States, The Greyhound Lines, cardboard, 20 x 13½", over 300 pcs, 250 four color illus on map plus historical data, c1950, cardboard box, 8½ x 6¼ x 1½" . . . 25.00

International Salt Co., A Family Reunion, cardboard, 12 x 9", approx 125 pcs, central figure of young boy holding puppy, puppy's mother in front of dog house on left, Alfred Guilloy artist, c1933, paper envelope, 12⅜ x 9⅜" . . . 15.00

McKesson & Robbins, McKesson's "Our Gang" Jig–Saw Puzzle, cardboard, 14 x 10¾", chamfered corners, drugstore and soda fountain scene, copyright 1932, paper envelope, 11 x 14", guide picture . . . 85.00

C. F. Sauer Co., Richmond, VA, Sauer's Vanilla and Duke's Home Made Mayonnaise, Sauer's Gardens, cardboard, 8 x 10¼", colored picture of garden setting, blue border, c1933, paper envelope, 8½ x 10½" . . . 15.00

Standard Oil Company of Ohio, Radio Jig Saw Puzzle No. 3, A Bully Time in Spain, cardboard, 14½ x 11", 252 pcs, double sided, observe shows Lena fighting bull in Spanish bullring, reverse head and shoulder portrait of Gene and Glenn, advertising sheet with guide picture, cardboard box, 6¾ x 8¼" . . . 12.50

John Wanamaker, New York, cardboard, 7 x 9½", 40 pcs, double sided, obverse shows E. J. Meeker etching of Grace Church and Wanamaker's New York City, reverse is twenty–five line description of Wanamaker store entitled "THE GREAT STORES OF THE WORLD," c1933, orig packaging missing . . . 50.00

Wausau Insurance Company, The Famous Wausau Depot, unopened can measuring 4" d and 5$\frac{7}{16}$" high, guide picture on can . . . 15.00

Weinberger's Cut Rate Drugs, cardboard, 3¼ x 4¾", 15 pcs, Co–operation, baking scene of young Dutch boy and girl in kitchen, c1930, paper envelope labeled "WEINBERGER'S Gift Picture Puzzle for Boys and Girls" . . . 20.00

Pearl Publishing Co., Brooklyn, NY, Mystery Puzzle of the Month, No. 2, Case of the Duplicate Door, 19402, 208 diecut pieces, cardboard box, 16 page story booklet with solution to mystery, 11½ x 13½", $15.00.

MULTIPURPOSE PUZZLES

E. J. Curtis, Inc, Pittsfield, MA, JIG SAW PUZZLE ENLARGEMENT from your negative, wood, 7¾ x 9¾", 128 pcs, Mildred Carlson taken at Suffield Academy in CT about 1931, cardboard box measures 5⅜ x 6¾ x 1" . 20.00

Squirrel Brand Co., Cambridge, MA, Squirrel Jig Puzzles, "ONE FREE with every Penny Purchase," cut out pieces from card and assemble into puzzle, four different cards (No. 1–Queer Fellow [clown face]; No. 2–Singing Sam from the Sunny South; No. 3–A Fine Old Ship; No. 4–Squirrel), individual card, 3½ x 5⅜", c1930

Box of one hundred, twenty–five of each view, cardboard box, 8⅛ x 6⅛ x 1" . . . 175.00

No. 2 . . . 5.00

No. 4 . . . 2.00

Unidentified Maker, Christmas Greeting, wood, partially interlocking, 5⅝ x 4$\frac{7}{16}$", 26 pcs, families arriving home for Christmas, separate verse sheet, orig cardboard mailer, 1944 Christmas Seal . . . 15.00

Quezal

QUEZAL

History: The Quezal Art Glass Decorating Company, named for the "quetzal," a bird with brilliantly colored feathers, was organized in 1901 in Brooklyn, New York, by two disgruntled Tiffany workers, Martin Bach and Thomas Johnson. They soon hired two more Tiffany workers, Percy Britton and William Wiedebine.

The first products, unmarked, were exact Tiffany imitations. In 1902 the "Quezal" trademark was first used. Quezal pieces differ from Tiffany pieces in that they are more defined and the decorations are more visible and brightly colored. No new techniques came from Quezal.

Johnson left in 1905. T. Conrad Vahlsing, Bach's son–in–law, joined the firm in 1918, but left with Paul Frank in 1920 to form Lustre Art Glass Company which copied Quezal pieces. Martin Bach died in 1924 and by 1925 Quezal ceased operations.

Wares are signed "Quezal" on the base of vases, bowls and rims of shades. The acid-etched or engraved letters vary in size and may be found in amber, black, or gold. A printed label of a quetzal bird was used briefly in 1907.

Vase, trumpet, green feather dec, gold border, opal ground, highly irid gold, stretched int., sgd, 6½" h, $1,400.00.

Candlesticks, pr, 7¾" h, blue irid, sgd	550.00
Cruet, green pulled feather design, clear yellow stopper and applied handle, white opal ground	2,300.00
Finger Bowl, gold, underplate	330.00
Lamp, 16" d, hanging, green and gold pulled feather design, light green ground, allover iridescence, dome shade, gold metal fixture, sgd	1,650.00
Lamp Shade, pr	
Pulled feather, calcite and gold	185.00
Opal, ribbed, irid gold liners, 5" h, 2¼" fitting, sgd "Quezal"	165.00
Perfume Bottle, 5" h, flattened teardrop form, bulbous stopper, Gorham SS monogrammed foliate mounts	585.00
Salt, 2¾" h, ribbed, irid gold	175.00
Toothpick, 2¼" h, melon ribbed, pinched sides, irid blue, green, purple, and gold, sgd	190.00
Vase	
4½" h, double hooked and pulled feathers, opal ground, amber with green and gold irid, Martin Bach design, sgd "Quezal P 507"	1,320.00
6⅝" h, ivory and green, platinum pulled feather design, sgd "Quezal 739"	1,100.00
6⅞", irid blue, abstract gold threading, opaque white hearts, sgd	500.00
Wall Sconces, pr, arrow in sheath form, gold metal, double arms, green ribbed lily shades with gold int. sgd "Quezal," electrified	850.00

QUILTS

History: Quilts have been passed down as family heirlooms for many generations. Each is an individual expression. The same pattern may have hundreds of variations in both color and design.

The advent of the sewing machine increased, not decreased, the number of quilts which were made. Quilts still are being sewn today.

The key considerations for price are age, condition, aesthetic beauty, and design. Prices are now at a level position. Exceptions are the very finest examples which continue to bring record prices.

References: American Quilter's Society, *Gallery of American Quilts, 1849–1988,* Collector Books, 1988; Suzy McLennan Anderson, *Collector's Guide to Quilts,* Wallace–Homestead, 1991; Barbara Brackman, *Clues in the Calico: A Guide To Identifying and Dating Antique Quilts,* EPM Publications, 1989; Alda Leake Horner, *The Official Price Guide to Linens, Lace and Other Fabrics,* House of Collectibles, 1991; William C. Ketchum, Jr., *The Knopf Collectors' Guides to American Antiques: Quilts,* Alfred A. Knopf, Inc., 1982; Jean Ray Laury and California Heritage Quilt Project, *Ho For California: Pioneer Women and Their Quilts,* E. P. Dutton, 1990; Lisa Turner Oshins, *Quilt Collections: A Directory For The United States And Canada,* Acropolis Books, Ltd., 1987; Rachel and Kenneth Pellman, *The World of Amish Quilts,* Good Books, 1984; Schnuppe von Gwinner, *The History of the Patchwork Quilt,* Schiffer Publishing Ltd, 1988.

Collectors' Club: The American Quilter's Society, P.O. Box 3290, Paducah, KY 42001.

Periodical: *Quilter's Newsletter Magazines,* Box 394, Wheat Ridge, CO 80033.

Album
  Pieced
    Calico, red and various shades of yellow, blue field, each white center sq with pen and ink signature and date 1858, white homespun backing, minor age stains, 76 x 89" 500.00
    Prints, shades of brown, blue, green, and white, center intersecting crosses with ink signatures, 1846 dates, including "Lexington, Goshen, Salem, Marlbrough, Damascus, Ohio," sgd by maker "Ann Coppock Quilt," minor damage, 94 x 105" 400.00
    Pierced, Appliqued, Reverse Appliqued, and Trapunto, red, green, yellow, and pink cotton patches, series of squares on point, each with different floral, fruit, or geometric motif, sgd "Mrs. Roy Hindman, Sayles Park, 1863," diagonal line and cube quilting, minor stains, 80" sq 4,950.00
  Alphabet, pieced, cotton, red and white, diamond and diagonal line field, 65 x 76" 3,300.00
Amish
  Appliqued, crib, cotton, four geometric cross motifs in pale gray, black ground, pale gray primary border, subsidiary large black border, pale gray edge, chain, foliate vine, and

Birds and Flowers, presentation type, rings of flowers, four inward facing peafowl, double headed bird in center, c1880, 86″ sq, $1,100.00.

vertical bar quilting, Ohio, c1930, 45 x 37" 350.00
Pieced, cotton, central large six pointed star, lavender and pale lavender, black ground, lavender and black borders, concentric feathered wreath, leaf, potted plant, and chain quilting, Lancaster County, PA, late 19th C, 77 x 84" 3,850.00
Bar, pieced, alternating bars of lemon yellow and blue, squares of multicolored prints, feather quilted, pencil pattern intact, goldenrod binding and backing, 69 x 83" 400.00
Baskets, pieced and applique, red print, medium solid green and white, trapunto baskets and circles, wear, stains, fading, 86 x 100" 500.00
Bear Paw, pieced, cotton, white geometric and printed orange and blue squares, chintz floral patterned border with blue piping, diagonal bar quilting, 85 x 76" 1,150.00
Bird In Hand, pieced, red and white, feather quilted circles, compass stars in white squares, very slight bleeding of red, machine sewn binding, 83" sq 650.00
Blossom, Bud, and Berry pattern, pieced and appliqued, cotton, red, bright green, and yellow, white cotton field, feather wreath, diamond, and outline quilting, PA, 19th C, 80 x 88" 900.00
Bouquet of Spring Flowers, pieced and appliqued, blue, yellow, green, rose, lavender, and light blue, rose blossom clusters and bud tendrils center, circle of Black–eyed Susans and berries within twisted swag ribbon border, corners with cactus lyres filled with roses, white cotton ground, dark blue border, 84 x 83" 4,675.00
Bride's, pieced, multicolored prints, teal blue print grid, white squares sgd in ink, some inscriptions and place names of Salem, NH, Concord, Cornish, presentation inscription "J. T. Foster, Salem, Dec 6th 1845," later paper label "Quilt given to Isreal Thorndike Foster when he was married to Lydia Cluff in Sept 1847," cut out for posts, 88 x 90" 350.00
Carolina Lily
  Applique, red and blue calico, white field, machine applique, hand quilted, minor stains, 73" sq 350.00
  Pieced and applique, green calico, solid goldenrod flowers, wear, fading, machine sewn binding, 78" sq 395.00
Carpenter's Wheel, pieced, calico, blue, yellow, green, and red, cube quilted field, 86½ x 85" 1,650.00
Christmas Cactus, pieced, cotton, red

and white, leaf and bud border, diamond and feather wreath quilting, 90 x 88″ **2,200.00**

Clock, pieced, wool, silk, and rayon, red, beige, purple, and dark green, metallic threading, light and dark diagonal stripe border, 67 x 84″ **1,980.00**

Crazy, pieced, random patches of velvet, satin, cotton, and calico, shades of yellow, blue, green, brown, red, purple, white, and black, fifty-six squares joined by turkey work stitching, embroidered floral sprigs, flowerheads, and foliage, brown border, Victorian, 75 x 69″ **425.00**

Crib, pieced, Star, pink calico and white, wear and stains, 28½ x 31½″ **375.00**

Double Anvil, Mennonite, pieced, wool and cotton, dark red and black, cube and diagonal line quilting, yellow, blue, and brown gingham checked backing, 71½″ sq **4,950.00**

Double Irish Chain, pink and green, white field, c1920 . . . . **185.00**

Eagle, pieced and appliqued, calico, red, green, and brown, four spread winged American eagles grasping berries and leaves, undulating berry and leaf borders, white ground, feather, wreath, and diagonal line quilting, red and green piped binding, 84 x 81″ **14,300.00**

Feathered Star
Pieced
    Blue and white cotton, white field, feather wreath, leaf, and diagonal line quilting, 79¾ x 82¼″ . . **3,300.00**
    Olive green and yellow calico, white cotton field, tulips, hearts, wreaths, and meandering vines quilting, American, 19th C, 96″ sq **2,650.00**
    Pieced and Trapunto, cotton, blue and white, stuff work floral and fruit motifs, white ground, diagonal line quilting, 91 x 86½″ **5,775.00**

Feather Wreath, pieced and applique, bright red wreaths, navy blue ground, red meandering vine border, outline and diagonal line quilting, brown and white printed cotton back, 84 x 88″ . **3,300.00**

Floral, pieced and appliqued, yellow, green, slate blue, brown, orange, and white concentrical ringed oval with bold flower blossom, vines and dots, layered and pieced corner flowers, bright yellow ground, herringbone, shell, vine, and floral quilting, 79 x 84″ **7,975.00**

Grandma's Fan, multicolored prints, 1930 . . . . **170.00**

Grandmother's Flower Garden, pieced, multicolored prints, some wear, 78 x 84″ **200.00**

Heart and Star, pieced and appliqued, cotton, slate blue, yellow, green, and red, calico, hearts, jagged leaf sprays, and pineapples, birds perched on leafy branches, white ground, cube and diagonal line quilting, 89 x 88½″ **4,400.00**

Honeycomb Star, patchwork, 96″ sq, American, 19th C **950.00**

Monkey Wrench, pieced
    Solid red, beige floral print, faded blue, lavender homespun backing, small patch on back, 69 x 75″ . . . **125.00**
    Yellow stylized pinwheel motif, cotton, white ground, square, stylized floral sprig and berry, and triangular quilting, yellow edge, Missouri, 1930, 78 X 59″ **675.00**

Nine Patch Variant, pieced, multicolored prints, predominately browns, cut out for bedposts, corner ties, 100 x 114″ **150.00**

Ocean Waves, pieced, multicolored triangular calico patches, printed red and white borders, Missouri, early 20th C **500.00**

Optical Star, pieced, white, yellow, and purple, lavender machine sewn binding, 72 x 82″ **200.00**

Paper Dolls, pieced, calico, blue and white, white field, meandering border, leaf, star, and heart quilting, 100 x 80″ **1,980.00**

Pennsylvania Volunteers No 62, pieced and appliqued, cotton, red, green, orange, and beige hearts, triangles, circles, crosses, and stars, American flags top and bottom, white ground, diagonal line and channel quilting, 88 x 92″ **3,300.00**

Pinwheel, applique, four large pinwheels and vining border, red and yellow–green, 96″ sq **600.00**

Postage Stamp, pieced
    Cotton, red, yellow, green, orange, and blue, cube quilting, brown and green clover leaf printed backing, 79″ sq **4,400.00**
    Cotton and calico, green, black, blue, brown, and gray diamond patches, diamond quilting, Iowa, third quarter 19th C, 81 x 67″ **850.00**

Princess Feather, pieced and appliqued
    Bright green and orange patches, white field, wreath, flowerhead, and blossom quilting, swag leaf border, PA, 19th C, 84″ sq **1,500.00**
    Olive green and brown patches, yellow ground, pinwheel star center, sawtooth borders, cube and cable quilting, red, white, and blue backing, 88½ x 91½″ **4,950.00**

Rainbow, pieced, cotton, bright blue, orange, and red fabric, scalloped overlapping arches, striped borders, white cotton ground, fine diagonal line and feathered wreath quilting, minor stains, PA, mid 19th C, 64″ sq **7,700.00**

Reel Variation, pieced and appliqued, cotton, printed red, white, and blue reels alternating with white squares, green, red, beige, and black floral chintz border, 92″ sq **1,690.00**

Sailboat, pieced, cotton, blue and white, diamond and diagonal line quilting, red thread initials JMD on left corner, 67 x 80″ **2,475.00**

Schoolhouse, pieced, cotton
Four rows of pink schoolhouse squares, white trim, blue band borders, white intersecting squares, concentric semi–circle quilting, minor wear, late 19th C, 65 x 74″ . . **725.00**
Four rows of red schoolhouse squares, white cotton ground, leaf and cable quilting, 64 x 85″ **6,050.00**

Star Flower, applique, vining floral border, red, blue, and goldenrod, red and goldenrod puffed berries and circles, machine stitched vine on border, red binding very worn, 68 x 78″ **500.00**

Star Medallion, pieced, twelve stars in solid green and goldenrod, pink calico, white field, feather wreath and meandering vine quilting, minor wear, 84 x 85″ **475.00**

Star within Frame, pieced and applique, red, navy blue, brown, beige, and black printed calico patches, white cotton field, interlacing circles and petal quilting, minor stains and discoloration, New England, 19th C, 84 x 92″ **2,200.00**

Tree of Life, pieced, cotton, five rows of four green, brown, and white stylized diagonal tree motifs within red bar borders, green intersection squares, triangular, bar, and band quilting, minor fading and patches, c1875, 81 x 69″ **500.00**

Wrench, pieced, multicolored prints, pink calico field, 64 x 72″ **250.00**

QUIMPER

History: Quimper faience, dating back to the 17th century, is named for Quimper, a French town where numerous potteries were located. Several mergers resulted in the evolution of two major houses—the Jules Henriot and Hubaudiébre–Bousquet factories.

The peasant design first appeared in the 1860s, and many variations exist. Florals and geometrics, equally popular, also were produced in large quantities. During the 1920s the Hubaudiébre–Bousquet factory introduced the Odetta line which utilized a stone body and Art Deco decorations.

The two major houses merged in 1968, each retaining its individual characteristics and marks. The concern suffered from labor problems in the 1980s and recently was purchased by an American group.

Marks: The HR and HR Quimper marks are found on Henriot pieces prior to 1922. The Henriot Quimper mark was used after 1922. The HB mark covers a long span of time. The addition of numbers or dots and dashes refers to inventory numbers and are found on later pieces. Most marks are in blue or black. Pieces ordered by department stores, such as Macy's and Carson Pirie Scott, carry the store mark along with the factory mark, making them less desirable to collectors. A comprehensive list of marks is found in Bondhus's book.

References: Susan and Al Bagdade, *Warman's English & Continental Pottery & Porcelain, 2nd Edition,* Wallace–Homestead, 1991; Sandra V. Bondhus, *Quimper Pottery: A French Folk Art Faience,* published by author, 1981; Millicent Mali, *Quimper Faience,* Airon, Inc., 1979; Marjatta Taburet, *La Faience de Quimper,* Editions Sous le Vent, 1979, French text.

Museums: Musee des Faiences de Quimper, Quimper, France; Victoria and Albert Museum, French Ceramic Dept., London, England.

Advisors: Susan and Al Bagdade.

Basket, male peasant on one side, female on reverse, red, green, and blue flowers, four dot design, blue sponged rim and handle, "Henriot Quimper France" mark, 4¾″ h, $225.00.

Bank, 3¾″ h, figural, pig, female peasant on one side, pink daisy with blue, green, pink, and yellow scattered flowers on reverse, pink shaded head, tail, and feet, reglued chip, "HB Quimper" mark 165.00

Basket, 7½" h, 8" w, handle formed from two kissing swans, yellow beaks, green heads, yellow–gold dot and blue sponging, body with molded blue and gold feathers, male peasant on one side, single strike flowers on reverse, "Henriot Quimper France" mark 850.00

Bowl, 6¼" d, male peasant, green blouse, blue pantaloons, flanked by flowers, single stroke flowers border band, blue outlined scalloped rim, "Henriot Quimper France" mark . . . 104.00

Box, cov, 4¾" l, 3½" w, rect, stoneware, bust of peasant woman, brown shades, white coif and streamers, blue–green ground, "HB Quimper, Odetta" mark 250.00

Bucket, 6" h, 6" d, green, blue, and orange bird on flowers, scattered florals, woven wicker handle, "HB Quimper France" mark 75.00

Butter Dish, cov, 7¼" d, seated peasant woman on cov, lavender bodice, blue skirt, rose apron, holding cup, blue dec riche borders, gold scalloped rims, small gold–yellow flowers, blue striped handle, "HB Quimper" mark 357.00

Bookends, Modern Movement, male in black shirt, gold embroidery, brown pants, female in black blouse, gold vest, blue skirt, brown bases, sgd "C. Millard, Henriot Quimper" mark, pr, 5½" l, 4¼" w, 8⅝" h, $575.00.

Charger, 12¼" d, male peasant bust, green hat, smoking pipe, female peasant, yellow coif, blue decor riche border outlined with gold and yellow stripes, "HB Quimper" mark 250.00

Cheese Dish, cov, 10¼" l, 8" w, 4¾" h,

bagpipe shape, seated peasant man with horn, blue decor riche borders, figural brown pipe handles, green and blue bows at top and bottom 1,000.00

Chocolate Cup and Saucer, peasant, single stroke floral border, ribbed ext., "Henriot Quimper" mark, pr 135.00

Cup and Saucer
Female peasant, multicolored florals, red chain motif border, yellow ground, "Henriot Quimper France" mark 125.00

Male and female peasant, scattered flowers, blue forget–me–nots, green dolphin handle, red chain border on saucer, "Henriot Quimper France" mark, pr 35.00

Male peasant, floral dec, blue and yellow banded borders, "Henriot Quimper France" mark 25.00

Dish, 10½" d, three sections, detailed male peasant with pipe, female holding bouquet, large cabbage rose, mustard feathered rim, figural blue swan handle 440.00

Egg Cup, 3½" h, male and female peasant, typical floral designs, red, blue, and green, blue banded rim, yellow and blue banded base, "HR Quimper" marks, pr 125.00

Figure
8½" h, standing female peasant, pink, green, yellow, and blue costume, wheat sheaf in one hand, scythe in other, "Marik" on oct base, "Henriot Quimper" mark 325.00

13½" h, standing Breton woman, light orange shirt, dark blue jacket, tan skirt, green apron, light green basket in right hand, walking stick in left, light green mound base, repairs, "Porquier Beau Quimper" mark 450.00

15¾" h, center dancing male peasant, black suit, gold embroidery, female peasant dancer on each arm in black dress, blue blouse, gold embroidered vest, white apron with gold designs, rect base, sgd "Micheau–Vernez, Henriot Quimper" mark 1,600.00

Fish Platter
21" l, 9½" w, male and female peasants, facing each other, green, blue, yellow, and orange scattered flowers and border design, scattered four blue dot design, "HR Quimper" mark on front 2,000.00

23⅝" l, molded fish head, male and female peasant in center, blue and green outlined fins and tails, "HB Quimper" mark 190.00

Holy Water Font, 9½" l, figural, ermine tail, kneeling boy with scattered flowers, four blue dot design, bowl with black ermine tails, blue sponged rim, "Henriot Quimper" mark 165.00

Inkwell, 3¼" h, 4¼" d, trefoil shape, seated orange, green, and blue male peasant playing horn, green, blue, and orange floral sprays, three small feet, repaired insert, "Henriot Quimper France" mark 190.00

Jardiniere
9¾" l, 4" w, 5" h, front panel with two boys playing with toy sailboat, back panel with pink and blue botanical, green decor riche side panels, pale blue glaze, "Porquier Beau" mark 1,300.00

11" handle to handle, 3⅛" h, front panel with seated male peasant playing horn, female in meadow, light green, burnt orange, and blue scattered flowers, dark green handles and rim, four small feet, repair to handle, "Henriot Quimper France" mark 425.00

19⅝" handle to handle, 9¹⁄₁₆" h, multicolored scene, female peasant laying in meadow, male playing horn, gold outlined cartouche, reverse with floral design, blue decor riche sections, Brittany crest, oval foot, gold demi–loops, figural dragon handles, "Henriot Quimper" mark 1,800.00

Jug, 3⅜" h, male peasant under spout, scattered green, red, and blue flowers, blue outlined rim and base, blue and gold handle, "HB Quimper" mark 75.00

Knife Rest, 3¼" l, triangular shape, female peasant, blue dashes, orange, blue, and green flower sprays, "Henriot Quimper" mark 40.00

Menu Card, 4¼" h, 2¼" w, shield shape, male fisherman peasant, yellow, brown, blue, and gray, net in left corner, blue chain border, yellow rim, repaired stand, "HB Quimper" mark . . 170.00

Petite Dejeuner Set, 3¼" h, 9½" l, frontal view of male peasant on cup, female peasant with distaff on tray, single stroke flowers, four blue dot design, "HB" mark 250.00

Pitcher
4" h, male peasant with pipe, floral branches on reverse, watery blue glaze, "HR Quimper" mark 85.00

6¼" h, male peasant, gold shirt, blue pantaloons, yellow stockings, red, green, and blue flowers, blue dash handle, "Henriot Quimper France" mark under handle 175.00

8" h
Female peasant on side, single stroke flower designs, blue and yellow banding, blue sponged handle, "Henriot Quimper France" mark 250.00

Modern Movement, figural female peasant with hands in apron pockets, blue skirt, plaid apron, embroidered bodice, rose garnet handle, sgd "C. Maillard, Henriot Quimper" mark 550.00

Plate, 8½" d, green blouse, yellow skirt, orange apron, red, green, and blue flowers, blue chain rim, "Henriot Quimper France" mark on front, 8½" d, $250.00.

Plate
6¾" d, blue, yellow, rose, and green stylized rooster, burnt orange and blue flower chain border 155.00

8⅛" d, gold, blue, burnt orange, and light green flowers in stylized basket, rose sponged border, "Henriot Quimper France" mark 66.00

8½" d, female peasant, green blouse, yellow skirt, orange apron, red, green, and blue flowers, blue chain rim, "Henriot Quimper France" mark on front 250.00

9" d, oct, female peasant, pink, orange, and blue, pink and green bud border, four blue dot designs, blue sponged rim, "HB Quimper" mark on front 215.00

9¼" d
Gold and yellow fleur–de–lis, black ermine tails, blue and green swirls, "Porquier Beau" mark, hairline 250.00

Male peasant, playing bagpipe, standing on knoll, blue, green, gold, and red costume, fenced house in background, blue decor riche on light yellow border, crest of Brittany at top, shaped rim, chip on reverse, "Porquier Beau Quimper" mark **1,200.00**

9⅝″ d, seated peasant woman with distaff, foot on stool, small blue and yellow flowers at sides, blue, red, and green bouquets on border with four blue dot design, shaped rim, "HB" mark **250.00**

10″ d

Bird of Paradise, yellow, blue, and burnt orange, limb, dark green insect, shaped rim, "Porquier Beau Quimper" mark **357.00**

Female peasant with basket and umbrella, male peasant blowing curved horn, dark blue decor riche border on light blue ground, gold outlines, "HB Quimper" mark, pr **550.00**

Platter, 21¼″ l, 13¾″ w, rect, center scene of twelve peasants and animals on country road, pink, green, white, and orange Breton broderie enameled border, cream, blue, and brown ground, "HB Quimper" mark . **2,750.00**

Porringer, 7″ w, male peasant flanked by flowers, blue and yellow banded border, pierced for hanging, "Henriot Quimper France" mark **92.00**

Snuff, 3″ d, blue, green, yellow, and red geometric on one side, blue, yellow, and red criss–cross on reverse, blue banded border **475.00**

Spoon Rest, 5″ l, fish shape, portrait bust of female peasant, blue sponged circles with red dot chains, ivory ground, "Henriot Quimper" mark . . . **42.00**

Sugar Bowl, 6″ h, 6½″ w, male peasant on front, female peasant on back, scattered single stroke flowers, four blue dot design, green sponged handles and ring finial, "Henriot Quimper France" mark **145.00**

Teapot

7″ h, Art Deco style, cream ground, blue, black, and gold accents, figural male peasant seated on handle, "HB Quimper" mark **550.00**

8½″ h, hex body, male peasant with bagpipes on side, female with bouquet on reverse, blue bands and four blue dot design, green sponged handle, green finial, chips "HR Quimper" mark **650.00**

Tray, 8½″ l, 4½″ w, male peasant with staff, blue, red, and green scattered flowers, four blue dot border, blue shaped rim, "HB" mark **500.00**

Vase

5″ h, sq shape, stylized frontal view of male peasant, arms folded, light green, orange, and blue floral sprays on three sides, blue and gold frames **198.00**

10½″ h, fleur–de–lis shape, blue, yellow, and green blonde female peasant on front, green, blue, orange, and yellow flowers on reverse, green, blue, and yellow sides, black ermine tail shields on base **475.00**

13¼″ h, tricorn shape, Art Deco style bust of male peasant, black shirt, gold accents, purple brimmed black hat, pink and gold flowers, yellow ground, "HB Quimper" mark **950.00**

14½″ h, male peasant playing horn, female peasant with jug on head, single stroke flowers, gold double handles, "Henriot Quimper France" marks, pr **2,400.00**

14⅞″ h, bulbous, flared lip, dancing peasant couple on front, yellow and pink flowers and green foliage on back, vertical blue decor riche bands, lip outlined with blue decor riche and green band, "Henriot Quimper" mark **1,000.00**

Wall Pocket

7½″ h, 5½″ w, bagpipe shape, male peasant smoking pipe, green molded pipe horns, yellow–orange and blue molded bows at top and base, "HR Quimper" mark **275.00**

12″ h, molded overlapped body, female child holding bird on hand, cage at feet, crouching male peasant smoking pipe, green decor riche border outlined in orange, "Porquier Beau" mark, repaired, pr **2,200.00**

RADIOS

History: The radio was invented over 100 years ago. Marconi was the first to assemble and employ the transmission and reception instruments that permitted sending electric messages without the use of direct connections. Between 1905 and the end of World War I many technical advances were made to the "wireless," including the invention of the vacuum tube by DeForest. By 1920 technology progressed. Radios filled the entertainment needs of the average family.

Changes in design, style, and technology brought the radio from the black boxes of the 1920s to the styled furniture pieces and console models of the 1930s and 1940s, to midget models of the 1950s, and finally to the high–tech radios of the 1980s.

References: Robert F. Breed, *Collecting Tran-*

sistor *Novelty Radios,* L–W Book Sales, 1990; Marty & Sue Bunis, *Collector's Guide To Antique Radios,* Collector Books, 1991; Philip Collins, *Radios: The Golden Age,* Chronicle Books, 1987; Alan Douglas, *Radio Manufacturers of the 1920s, Volume 1,* (1988), *Volume 2* (1989), *Volume 3* (1991), Vestal Press, Ltd.; David and Betty Johnson, *Guide To Old Radios, Pointers, Pictures, And Prices,* Wallace-Homestead, 1989; Harry Poster, *The Illustrated Price Guide To Vintage Televisions and Deco Radios 1991 Edition,* published by author, 1991; John Sideli, *Classic Plastic Radios of the 1930s and 1940s: A Collector's Guide to Catalin Radios,* E. P. Dutton, 1990.

Periodicals: *Antique Radio Classified,* 9511 Sunrise Boulevard, Cleveland, OH 44133; *Antique Radio Topics & The Classic Radio Newsletter,* Box 28572, Dallas, TX 75228; *Radio Age,* 636 Cambridge Road, Augusta, GA 30909; *Sight, Sound, Style,* P.O. Box 2224, South Hackensack, NJ 07606.

Collectors' Clubs: Antique Radio Club of America, 81 Steeplechase Road, Devon, PA 19333; Antique Wireless Association, Main St., Holcomb, NY 14469.

Museums: Antique Wireless Museum, East Bloomfield, NY; Caperton's Radio Museum, Louisville, KY; Muchow's Historical Radio Museum, Elgin, IL; Museum of Wonderful Miracles, Minneapolis, MN; New England Museum of Wireless and Steam, East Greenwich, RI; Voice of the Twenties, Orient, NY.

Additional Listings: See *Warman's Americana & Collectibles* for more examples.

Fada, Model 1001, Universal Superheterodyne, wood, restored, $45.00.

Atwater Kent, Model 318, table model, dome	100.00
Columbia, table model, oak	135.00
Crosley	
Model 4–29, battery operated, 1926	110.00
Model 10–135	45.00
Fada, two color bakelite case	
115, bullet shape, deep ochre, red trim, 10½ x 5¼ x 6″	990.00
625, round end, rect caramelized body, red knobs, slide rule dial cracked	440.00
General Electric, Model 81, 8 tube, 1934	195.00
Metrodyne Super 7, 1925	250.00
Philco	
Model 37–84, Cathedral, schematic design, 1937	85.00
Model 551, 1928	125.00
RCA, Radiola 20, 1925	135.00
Spartan, Model 5218	85.00
Stromberg Carlson, Model 636A, console, 1928	120.00
Westinghouse, Model WR–602	45.00
Zenith, Zephyr, 6–S–147, multiband	85.00

RAILROAD ITEMS

History: Railroad collectors have existed for decades. The merger of the rail systems and the end of passenger service made many objects available to private collectors. The Pennsylvania Railroad sold its archives at public sale.

Railroad enthusiasts have organized into regional and local clubs. Join one if interested. Your local hobby store can probably point you to the right person. The best pieces pass between collectors and rarely enter the general market.

References: Stanley L. Baker, *Railroad Collectibles: An Illustrated Value Guide, 4th Edition,* Collector Books, 1990; Phil Bollhagen, *The Pictorial Value Guide to Railroad Playing Cards,* published by author, 1987; Arthur Dominy and Rudolph A. Morgenfruh, *Silver At Your Service,* published by authors, 1987; Richard Luckin, *Dining On Rails,* published by author, 1983, reprint 1991; Douglas W. McIntrye, *The Official Guide To Railroad Dining Car China,* Walsworth Press Company Inc., 1990.

Collectors' Clubs: Railroad Enthusiasts, 456 Main Street, West Townsend, MA 01474; Railroadiana Collectors Association, 795 Aspen Drive, Buffalo Grove, IL 60089; Railway and Locomotive Historical Society, P.O. Box 1418, Westford, MA 01886.

Periodicals: *Key, Lock and Lantern,* P.O. Box 15, Spencerport, NY 14559; *U.S. Rail News,* P.O. Box 7007, Huntington Woods, MI 48070–7007.

Museums: Baltimore and Ohio Railroad, Baltimore, MD; Museum of Transportation, Boston, MA; New York Museum of Transportation, Albany, NY; California State Railroad Museum, Sacramento, CA.

Additional Listings: See *Warman's Americana & Collectibles* for more examples.

Ashtray, Norfolk & Western, Dogwood, 3¾″, no backstamp, Syracuse China	65.00
Baggage Checks, 4¾ x 2¼″, brass	
B & O Southwestern Railroad, man-	

China, platter, stamped insignia, gold band, black scrolls, marked "Warwick," 11" l, $24.00.

ufactured by American Railway Supply	65.00
Missouri Kansas & Texas Railway	70.00
Bell, steam type, brass	425.00

China
Butter Pat, 3¼" d, Atchinson, Topeka & Santa Fe, Black Chain, no backstamp, Sterling China 20.00
Celery Tray, 10¾" l, Chicago, Burlington & Quincy, Violet & Daisies, no backstamp, Syracuse China 75.00
Cup and Saucer
Baltimore and Ohio, Capital, both pieces have top logo, no backstamp, Shenango China 225.00
Southern Pacific, Prairie Mountain Wildflower, backstamp, Syracuse China 75.00
Plate
6¼" d, Chesapeake and Ohio, Greenbrier, no backstamp, Shenango China 25.00
9" d, Baltimore and Ohio, Derby, no backstamp, Shenango China .. 65.00
Platter, 10½ x 7¼", oval, Missouri Pacific, Eagle, top logo, backstamp, Syracuse China 65.00
Sauce Dish, 5" d, Great Northern, backstamp, Syracuse China 35.00
Soup
8" d, Reading RR, Bound Brook, backstamp, Lamberton China .. 350.00
9" d, Southern RR, Pelican, no backstamp, Lamberton China .. 100.00
Document, sgd letter, Pennsylvania Railroad stationery, Office of Superintendent, 1860, orig envelope 40.00
Fire Grenades, pr, 18" l, Northwestern RR, c1870 .... 125.00
Glassware
Cordial, 4½" h, stemmed, gold oval logo NEW YORK CENTRAL 50.00
Water, 4½" h, black and gold diesel engine and cars, "NEW YORK

CENTRAL SYSTEM" in black log, "ROUTE TO THE WORLD'S FAIR NEW YORK WORLD'S FAIR 1964–1965" in black and gold ... 25.00
Wine, 4" h, Baltimore & Ohio, stemmed, gold line around top, series of train cars running around glass, "B & O" on side of one gold and one white train car 35.00
Handbook, *Railroad Handbook for Track Foreman*, 1902 .... 5.00
Hat, cap badges
Delaware & Hudson, old style hat with two gold bands running around outside, enameled badge with circle at top with "The D&H" and "CONDUCTOR" in gold at bottom 175.00
Louisville & Nashville, old style hat with two gold buttons marked "L&N" with cord running between buttons, domed style badge with red "L&N" in rect box and black enamel "CONDUCTOR" at bottom 100.00
Seaboard Airline, old style hat with two "SEABOARD" buttons and silver band running between buttons, cap badge with silver "SEABOARD AIRLINE" at top and "FLAGMAN" at bottom 75.00
Lantern, tall globe
Colorado & Southern Railway, frame marked with large letters, double horizontal wire guards, twist–off pot and burner, cobalt blue globe, Adams & Westlake Company, last patent date Nov 30, 1897 .... 250.00
Lehigh Valley Railroad, frame marked with large letters, single horizontal wire guard, extended base globe, Keystone Lantern Co "The Casey," last patent date June 2, 1903 ... 350.00

Lantern, Adlake Non Sweating Lamp, Chicago, painted yellow, red, blue, yellow and clear lights, 17½" h, $150.00.

Lantern Globe, 5⅜" h

Canadian National Railroad, clear cast, extended base, globe has cast "CNR" in serifs **85.00**

Louisville & Nashville, amber, etched "L&N RR," manufactured by MacBeth Pearl Glass 220 ...... **210.00**

Northern Pacific, amber, etched "N.P.R.R.," etched "SAFETY AL-WAYS" on backside **150.00**

Union Pacific, amber, etched "Southern Ry" **65.00**

Silver, Flatware

Fork, dinner, Missouri Pacific, top and bottom marked with logo, Century, International Silver **12.00**

Knife

Dinner, Northern Pacific, top and bottom marked with logo, Embassy, Reed & Barton **18.00**

Steak, Soo Line, bottom marked with logo, Vasser, Reed & Barton **28.00**

Spoon

Grapefruit, California Zephyr, bottom marked with logo, Century, International Silver **15.00**

Teaspoon, Union Pacific, bottom marked "U.P.R.R.," Zephyr, International Silver **8.00**

Serving, Rock Island Lines, top marked, Empire, Gorham **18.00**

Silver, Holloware

Bouillion Cup Holder, Lehigh Valley, 4", hammered mounts, side logo is raised "LVRR" in diamond, Barth . **135.00**

Change Tray, Western Pacific, 6½", #05090, backstamp with name of railroad, International Silver **65.00**

Creamer, Great Northern, 4 oz, #05082, side logo is incised over "G" and "N," International Silver . **50.00**

Gravy Boat, Pullman, 2 oz, #SL0688, backstamp with name of railroad, International Silver **65.00**

Ice Bucket, double handled, Southern, 7½", #1833–S, side logo incised "Southern," Reed & Barton . **400.00**

Switch Key

MK&TRY, Slaymaker, 28928, fat barrel **35.00**

SANTA FE ROUTE, A & W, football hallmark **28.00**

WP&BRR, C, tapered barrel **175.00**

Tablecloth, Baltimore & Ohio **20.00**

RAZORS

History: Razors date back several thousand years. Early man used sharpened stones. The Egyptians, Greeks, and Romans had metal razors. Razors made prior to 1800 generally were crudely stamped WARRANTED or CAST STEEL, with the maker's mark on the tang. Until 1870 almost all razors for the American market were manufactured in Sheffield, England. Most blades were wedge shaped; many were etched with slogans or scenes. Handles were made of natural materials: various horns, tortoise shell, bone, ivory, stag, silver, and pearl. All razors were handmade.

After 1870 razors were machine made with hollow ground blades and synthetic handle materials. Razors of this period usually were manufactured in Germany (Solingen) or in American cutlery factories. Hundreds of molded celluloid handle patterns were produced.

Cutlery firms produced boxed sets of two, four, and seven razors. Complete and undamaged sets are very desirable. Most popular are the 7-Day sets with each razor etched with a day of the week.

The fancier the handle or more intricately etched the blade, the higher the price. Rarest handle materials are pearl, stag, sterling silver, pressed horn, and carved ivory. Rarest blades are those with scenes etched across the entire front. Value is increased by certain manufacturer's names, e.g., H. Boker, Case, M. Price, Joseph Rogers, Simmons Hardware, Will & Finck, Winchester, and George Wostenholm.

hgb = hollow ground blade
wb = wedge blade

References: Robert A. Doyle, *Straight Razor Collecting, An Illustrated Price Guide*, Collector Books, 1980, out-of-print; Phillip L. Krumholz, *Value Guide For Barberiana & Shaving Collectibles*, Ad Libs Publishing Co., 1988.

Periodical: *Blade Magazine*, P.O. Box 22007, Chattanooga, TN 37422.

Additional Listings: See *Warman's Americana & Collectibles* for more examples.

J. R. Terry & Co., Worcester, MA, fully etched blade, tortoise shell handle, $50.00.

AMERICAN BLADES

Case Brothers, Little Valley, NY, blade stamped "Tested XX," yellow wrapped rope pattern handle **30.00**

Golden Rule Cutlery Co, Chicago USA, blade ground slightly out of shape, four beautiful women in bathing suits on handle **65.00**

Ontario Cutlery Co, Geneva, NY, blade etched with two crossed American flags, crown above and "The Mighty" below, black and white striped handle — 25.00

Schrade Cutlery Co, Walden, NY, hg, etched "Everlasting Sharp," green swirl handle with German silver ends, gray and green orig box with model number 158–R — 135.00

Waterville Cutlery Co, Waterville, CT, blade "Waterville Hand Forged," black celluloid handle with raised floral pattern, oak leaf and acorn scroll — 65.00

ENGLISH BLADES, SHEFFIELD

Cutler, Turniss & Stacey Sheffield, pressed horn handle, two intertwined snakes, maker's mark on blade — 615.00

Johnson, Chris, wide hgb, plated brass handle — 55.00

Rodgers, Joseph & Sons, wb, stag handle with inlaid rect escutcheon plate — 125.00

Wade & Butcher, hg, etched in ribbon "Wade & Butcher," Art Nouveau handle stamped "Sterling," raised scroll across front and back, monogrammed — 320.00

Wostenholme, Geo, etched adv on blade, emb ivory handle — 30.00

GERMAN BLADES

Cosmos Mfg Co, hgb, ivory handle, raised nude picking purple grapes, green leaves — 100.00

Henckels, corn, rounded and shaped bone handle, plain blade, orig box with silver emb adv "J A Henckels Twin Works, Germany" — 50.00

Imperial Razor, blade etched with ship US Battleship Oregon scene, dark blue celluloid handle — 40.00

Koch, F A & Co, Made In Germany, ivory handle, colored scene of branches, oak leaves, and deer dec — 45.00

Lewis Razor Co, hgb, celluloid handle, stork eating fish and standing in cattails — 50.00

Scott, Chas T, hgb, marbleized green celluloid handle — 12.00

Wadsworth Razor Co, semi wb, carved bone handle, c1870 — 55.00

Zartina Cutlery Works, hgb, floral SS handle — 275.00

SWISS BLADE

Engstrom, Joh, frameback, seven interchangeable wafer blades, black horn handle, c1880 — 65.00

Tornablom, hgb, ivory handle — 27.00

SETS OF RAZORS

Pair, G W Ruff's Peerless, hg, ivory handles, leather over wood case with "Gentlemen's Companion Containing 2 Razors Special Hollow Ground," red lining — 55.00

7–Day Set, Crown and Sword, blades etched "The Crown & Sword Razor Extra Hollow Ground," black handles with raised "Crown and Sword," homemade felt lined wood case, plaque with "RAZORS" emb on top — 45.00

RECORDS

History: With the advent of the more sophisticated recording materials, such as 33⅓ RPM long playing records, 8–track tapes, cassettes, and compact discs, earlier phonograph records became collectors' items. Most have little value. The higher priced examples are rare (limited production) recordings. Condition is critical.

References: L. R. Docks, *1915–1965 American Premium Record Guide, 3rd Edition,*, Books Americana, 1986; Fred Heggeness, *Country Western Price Guide,* FH Publishing, 1990; Jerry Osborne, *The Official Price Guide To Movie/TV Soundtracks and Original Cast Albums,* House of Collectibles, 1991; Jerry Osborne, *The Official Price Guide To Records, Ninth Edition,* House of Collectibles, 1990; Neal Umphred, *Goldmine's Price Guide To Collectible Record Albums, 1950–1979, Second Edition,* Krause Publications, 1991; Neal Umphred, *Goldmine's Rock 'n Roll 45 RPM Record Price Guide,* Krause Publications, 1990.

Collectors' Clubs: Association For Recorded Sound Collectors, P.O. Box 75082, Washington, DC 20013; International Association of Jazz Record Collectors, Box 10208, Oakland, CA 94610.

Periodicals: *Discoveries,* P.O. Box 255, Port Townsend, WA 98368; *Goldmine,* 700 E. State Street, Iola, WI 54990.

Additional Listings: See "Records" in *Warman's Americana & Collectibles* for those recordings in the $5.00 to $25.00 price range.

Note: Most records, especially popular recordings, have a value of less than $3.00 per disc. *The records listed here are classic recordings of their type and in demand by collectors.*

Barlett, Slim & His Orchestra, Asphalt Walk, Superior 2692 — 75.00

Beasley, Irene, You'll Come Back To Me Someday, Victor 40173 — 10.00

Blue Rhythm Orchestra, Keep Your Temper, Pathe–Actuelle 36364 — 30.00

California Poppies, What A Wonderful Time, Sunset 506/507 — 80.00

Carlton, Bud & Orchestra, Rainy Weather Rose, 81308 — 10.00

Clifford's Louisville Jug Band, Dancing
Blues, Okeh, 8221 . . . . 60.00
Davis, Julia, Black Hand Blues, Para-
mount 122498 . . . . 25.00
Down Home Serenaders, Cootie
Stomp, Champion 15399 . . . . 75.00
Erwing Brothers' Orchestra, The Erwing
Blues, Vocalion 2564 . . . . 15.00
Herman, Woody & His Orchestra, The
Goose Hangs High, Decca, 1056 . . 10.00
The Ink Spots, Your Feets Too Big, Vic-
tor 24851 . . . . 25.00
Jolson, Al, That Haunting Melody, Victor
17037 . . . . 10.00
Keppard's, Freddie Jazz Cardinals,
Stock Yards Strut, Paramount 12399 80.00
Lewis, Alfred, Friday Moan Blues, Vo-
calion 1498 . . . . 25.00
Lombardo, Guy & His Royal Canadians,
So This Is Venice, Gennett 5416 . . 30.00
The Melody Sheiks, Mighty Blue, Okeh
40484 . . . . 20.00
Oliver, Joe "King," King Porter, Auto-
graph 617 . . . . 350.00
Original Tuxedo Jazz Orchestra, Black
Rag, Okeh 8198 . . . . 100.00
Red Onion Jazz Babies, Terrible Blues,
Gennett 5607 . . . . 150.00
Richie, Bud & His Boys, Slappin' The
Bass, Champion 16109 . . . . 40.00
Savoy Bearcats, Senegalese Stomp,
Victor 20182 . . . . 25.00
Sissle, Noble, Slow River, Okeh 40824 10.00
Trent, Alphonse & His Orchestra,
Louder and Funnier, Gennett 6664 . 60.00
Tucker, George & His Novelty Band,
Doin' The New Low Down, Champion
15638 . . . . 40.00
The Wanderers, I Ain't Got Nobody,
Bluebird 5869 . . . . 10.00
Welk, Lawrence & His Orchestra,
Shanghai Honeymoon, Gennett
20341 . . . . 40.00

REDWARE

History: The availability of clay, the same used
to make bricks and roof tiles, accounted for the
great production of red earthenware pottery in the
American colonies. Redware pieces are mainly
utilitarian—bowls, crocks, jugs, etc.

Lead glazed redware retained its reddish color,
but a variety of colored glazes were obtained by
the addition of metals to the basic glaze. Streaks
and mottled splotches in redware items resulted
from impurities in the clay and/or uneven firing
temperatures.

"Slipware" is a term used to describe redwares
decorated by the application of slip, a semi–liquid
paste made of clay. Slipwares were made in England, Germany, and elsewhere in Europe for dec-

ades before becoming popular in the Pennsylvania
German region and elsewhere in colonial America.
Reference: Kevin McConnell, *Redware: Amer-
ica's Folk Art Pottery*, Schiffer Publishing, 1988.

Bottle, 5½" l, keg shaped, bung hole,
gray glaze, brown and green spots,
hairlines and minor chips 250.00
Bowl
5¼" d, crown like molded handles,
mottled brownish black glaze, minor wear and small edge flakes . . 375.00
9¼" d, flared, scalloped rim and
tooled lines, mottled brownish amber glaze, black spots, wear and
edge chips 300.00
Charger, 11½" d, yellow slip crossed
wavy lines, worn and chipped 475.00
Coffeepot, 11¼" h, molded and tooled
dec, dome top, English 385.00
Creamer, 3¾" h, strap handle, running
black splotches, clear glaze, minor
wear, small flakes, close fitting mismatched lid 175.00

Crock, green slip, Strasburg, VA emb
mark, $150.00.

Cup, 3¾" h, flared lip, applied handle,
clear glaze with mottled amber, minor
wear and glaze flakes 85.00
Cup and Saucer, dark brown glaze,
small flakes, handle glued 50.00
Cuspidor, 8 x 4¼", tooled bands, brown
and green running glaze with brown
dashes, some wear and edge chips 250.00
Dish
6¼" d, brown sponged glaze with
flecks 220.00
7" d, brown sponged glaze with flecks 220.00
Flask, 6½" h, tooled lines and brown
splotched glaze, old hairline in side,
chip on lip 220.00
Flower Pot
4⅝" h, tooled lines, crimped lip, brown

flecked glaze, brown sponging, attached saucer, wear and edge chips **155.00**

5¼" h, wheel turned foot, applied crimped dec on base and rim, yellow slip and running dark glaze with mottled black, edge wear and small chips, drainage hole in bottom ... **115.00**

8½" h, edge tooling on rim and attached saucer base, yellow slip int., ext. with yellow slip and splotches of brown and green, clear shiny glaze, Shenandoah, some wear and chips **500.00**

Food Mold, Turk's head

8 x 2¼", scalloped rim, greenish amber glaze, brown sponging, wear and small flakes **115.00**

9¼", scalloped rim and black sponged glaze, some filled in rim chips and small flakes **65.00**

Jar

5⅝" h, well shaped, tooled lines, flaring lip, mottled greenish glaze, brown sponging, rim chips **200.00**

6" h, ovoid, dark brown sponging, greenish glaze **135.00**

7" h, sloping shoulder, tooled lip, dark green glaze, brown splotching, bottom incised "Pickle," wear and edge chips **425.00**

9½" h, flared lip, yellow slip stripes, green highlights, brown wavy lines, rim hairline and small rim chips, two old chips on base **1,350.00**

Jug

6¾" h, ovoid, tooled lines at shoulder, green glaze, red highlights, strap handle **80.00**

10¾" h, ovoid, shiny green glaze, orange spots, applied strap handle, Galena **200.00**

Loaf Pan, 9½ x 13½", coggled edge, four line yellow slip dec, old surface and edge flakes **825.00**

Milk Bowl, 10½" d, pouring spout **35.00**

Milk Pan, 17" d **60.00**

Mug

4½" h, rich brown sponging, imp "John Bell" **775.00**

5¼" h, butter print style applied star design, strap handle and tooled lip, clear glaze with greenish highlights, good patina, minor glaze flakes and wear **125.00**

Pie Plate

6⅞" d, yellow slip X and O design, brown spots, old edge chips **675.00**

7⅝" d, coggled edge, yellow slip double tulip, highlighted in rich green, old chips **1,625.00**

8⅛" d, yellow slip wavy lines, imp "W.

Smith, Womelsdorf," two old rim chips **500.00**

8⅞", three line yellow slip dec, small edge flakes **325.00**

9¾", coggled edge, wear and small chips **250.00**

Pitcher

6¼" h, squat, ovoid, tooled dotted line, ribbed strap handle, slightly greenish glaze, three brown vertical slashes, wear and glaze flakes, mismatched lid **150.00**

6¾" h, tooled lines and strap handle, dark brown sponged glaze, bottom incised "10," wear and old chips . **250.00**

7¾" h, applied handle, tooling at rim and shoulder, clear slightly greenish glaze, sponged brown vertical bands, edge wear and flakes **250.00**

Plate

11" d, slip dec, red ground, serrated border, New England, c1830 .... **660.00**

12" d, yellow slip dec, red ground, serrated border, New England, c1830 .... **770.00**

Preserving Jar

7", tooled lines, wide vertical brushed brown bands, some wear, small chips **200.00**

10" h, cov, green, orange spots, Galena **110.00**

Salt, 3" l, scroddle ware, marbleized yellow slip with brown and green, cast from lacy salt **325.00**

RED WING POTTERY

History: The Red Wing pottery category covers several potteries from Red Wing, Minnesota. In 1868 David Hallem started Red Wing Stoneware Co., the first pottery with stoneware as its primary product and with a red wing stamped under the glaze as its mark. The Minnesota Stoneware Co. started in 1883. The North Star Stoneware Co., 1892–1896, used a raised star and the words Red Wing as its mark.

The Red Wing Stoneware Co. and the Minnesota Stoneware Co. merged in 1892. The new company, the Red Wing Union Stoneware Co., made stoneware until 1920 when it introduced a pottery line which it continued until the 1940s. In 1936 the name was changed to Red Wing Potteries, Inc. During the 1930s it introduced several popular lines of hand painted pattern dinnerware which were distributed through department stores, Sears, and gift stamp centers. Dinnerware declined in the 1950s, being replaced with hotel and restaurant china in the early 1960s. The plant closed in 1967.

References: Stanley Bougie and David Newkirk, *Price Guide & Supplement for Red Wing Dinnerware (1990–1991 Edition)*, published by authors, 1990; Dan and Gail DePasquale and Larry Peterson, *Red Wing Collectibles*, Collector Books, 1983, 1992 value update; David A. Newkirk, *A Guide To Red Wing Markings*, Monticello Printing, 1979; Dolores Simon, *Red Wing Pottery With Rumrill*, Collector Books, 1980; Gary and Bonnie Tefft, *Red Wing Potters and Their Wares, Second Edition*, Locust Enterprises, 1987; Lyndon C. Viel, *The Clay Giants, The Stoneware of Red Wing, Goodhue County, Minnesota, Book 2* (1980), *Book 3*, (1987), Wallace–Homestead.

Collectors' Club: Red Wing Collectors Society, Route 3, Box 146, Monticello, MN 55362.

Additional Listings: See *Warman's Americana & Collectibles* for more examples.

Vase, green-blue, marked "Redwing, USA 1563," 10″ h, $30.00.

Bean Pot, cov, Saffron	75.00
Beater Jar, H L Sander, Arlington, MN adv, marked "Red Wing Saffron Ware"	90.00
Bowl	
7″ d, four blue stripes, T C Johnson, Latimer, IA adv	50.00
10″ d, two blue stripes, marked "10 Red Wing USA"	70.00
11″ d, stoneware, paneled, sponged rust and blue ext. dec	115.00

Butter Churn, molded blue elephant ear leaves, 3 gal, sgd "Minnesota" oval on bottom	400.00
Butter Jar, deep blue lettering, 20 lb	200.00
Canteen, stoneware, 1900–08	350.00
Casserole, cov, allover sponge dec	150.00
Clock, figural, wall, electric, marked "Tik–Tok Baker"	40.00
Crock, 20 gal, marked "Red Wing Union Stoneware"	225.00
Cuspidor, brown and white, mold seam, unsigned	100.00
Jar, ball lock, self–sealing, 3 gal	75.00
Jug	
1 gal, salt glaze, funnel top, marked "Minnesota"	70.00
4 gal, shoulder, birch leaf, molded, sgd	125.00
5 gal, beehive, large wing	135.00
Nappy, white, marked "Minnesota"	60.00
Pitcher, cherry band, medium size	30.00
Salt Box, cov, hanging, sponge band	450.00
Snuff Jar, white glaze, 1 qt, marked "RW"	75.00
Spittoon, salt glaze, "Red Wing Stoneware Company" stamped on side	275.00
Umbrella Stand, blue sponge dec, unsigned	500.00
Vase	
6½″ h, Art Pottery, paper label, pr	35.00
9¾″ h, four relief panels with brown semi–glaze trees, gray matte ground, marked	45.00
Wash Bowl and Pitcher, blue and white, lily	350.00
Water Cooler, marked "Ice Water," #4, orig cork	265.00

RELIGIOUS ITEMS

History: Objects for the worshipping or expression of man's belief in a superhuman power are collected by many people for many reasons.

Icons are included since they are religious mementos, usually paintings with a brass encasement. Collecting icons dates from the earliest period of Christianity. Most antique icons in today's market were made in the late 19th century.

Reproduction Alert: Icons are heavily reproduced.

Altar Stick, pr, 15″ h, Gothic Revival, mounted turrets and angels, late 19th C	140.00
Bible Box	
17¼″ l, pine, simple chip carved design on facade, rose head wrought iron nail construction, old dark patina	120.00
23$^{1}/_{12}$ x 15½ x 8″, oak, slant lid, carved	

front panel dec, butterfly hinges, orig lock and hasp, dated 1703 . . **350.00**

Communion Items

Chalices, pr, pewter, Leonard, Reed & Barton, 1835–40 . . . . **350.00**

Flagon, 14½" h, pewter, silver plating, marked "Reed & Barton" **45.00**

Token, 1" d, pewter, marked "A. C. of Hebron" on one side, "J.I. 1824" on other **25.00**

Cross, 3¼" h, Russian Orthodox, brass, early 19th C **175.00**

Crucifix, 19" h, wood, Gesso and polychrome repaint **200.00**

Figure, 10½", Madonna and child, glass, luminary wood base, sgd "Erroadom" **55.00**

Icon, Russian, Our Lady of Kazanskaya, silvered metal, repousse riza, gilt, pseudo 19th C marks, 12¼ x 10¾", $500.00.

Icon

Greek

5⅝ x 7½", St George and dragon, wood, polychrome **225.00**

6¾ x 9", wood, polychrome paint, gold leaf **525.00**

10 x 7½", Virgin Mother and child, gilded ground **355.00**

12⅓ x 10½", Virgin Mother and child **325.00**

Russian

8½ x 7", Saints Peter and Paul, repousse silver oklad, applied raised enameled halos **770.00**

12 x 9½", Smolensk mother of God,

repousse metal oklad, applied raised enameled halo **410.00**

12⅓ x 10⅓", metal repousse, flanked with angels and Mary Magdalene, Mary Mother of God, and Saints John and James . . . **330.00**

Painting, 27½ x 19½", Polish Icon Triptych, oil on panel, Jozef Borkowski, 20th C **200.00**

REVERSE PAINTING ON GLASS

History: The earliest examples of reverse painting on glass were produced in 13th century Italy. By the 17th century the technique had spread to Central and Eastern Europe. It spread westward as the glass industry center moved to Germany in the late 17th century.

The Alsace and Black Forest region developed a unique portraiture style. The half and three–quarter portraits often were titled below the portrait. Women tend to have general names. Most males are of famous men.

The English used a mezzotint method, rather than free–style, to create their reverse paintings. Landscapes and allegorical figures were popular. The Chinese began working in the medium in the 17th century, eventually favoring marine and patriotic scenes.

Reverse painting was done in America. Most were by folk artists, unsigned, who favored portraits, patriotic and mourning scenes, floral compositions, landscapes, and buildings. Known American artists include Benjamin Greenleaf, A. Cranfield, and Rowley Jacobs.

In the late 19th century commercially produced reverse paintings, often decorated with mother–of–pearl, became popular. Themes included the Statue of Liberty, the capitol in Washington, D.C., and various world's fairs and expositions.

PORTRAITS

George and Martha Washington, bust portrait, white wig, frilled stock, white shawl, shaded brown ground, 19th C, 28 x 24", pr **350.00**

La Belle Polonaise, orig frame, 11¾ x 9¼" **330.00**

Mandarin, seated, smoking, attendant standing, Chinese Export, 19 x 21" . **3,200.00**

Napoleon, three quarter length portrait, white uniform, gold and red, green oval, black rect background, gilt flowers, beveled frame, worn black paint, 12½ x 14½" **1,000.00**

Nikolaus, Kaizer Aller Russina, green uniform, blue sash, gold highlights, brown ground, orig frame, 9½ x 12" **225.00**

Scene of stream, cottages, and trees, gold frame, 16½ x 20″, $35.00.

SCENES

Flowers, large cream white peonies and buds, green leaves, blue ground, later gilt gesso carved frame, artist sgd "Drian," 17¾ x 15½″ 4,400.00

H.M.S. Marlborough, Victorian, three masted ship, sails furled, small boat approaching, oval border, four pierced and dec corners, gilt lined rect outer border, ogee maple frame, 13½ x 12¼″ 220.00

Perry's Lake Erie Victory, Sept 10th, 1813, naval battle scene, multicolored, 7 x 9″ 250.00

Picnic Scene, three couples discovering bird's nest, 4½ x 6″ 250.00

RIDGWAY

History: Throughout the 19th century the Ridgway family, through a series of partnerships, held a position of importance in Shelton and Hanley, Staffordshire, England. The connection began with Job and George, two brothers, and Job's two sons, John and William. In 1830 John and William separated with John retaining the Cauldon Place factory and William the Bell Works. By 1862 the porcelain division of Cauldon was carried on by Coalport China Ltd. William and his heirs continued at the Bell Works and the Church [Hanley] and Bedford [Shelton] works until the end of the 19th century.

Many early pieces are unmarked. Later marks include the initials of the many partnerships.

References: Susan and Al Bagdade, *Warman's English & Continental Pottery & Porcelain, 2nd Edition,* Wallace–Homestead, 1991; G. A. Godden, *Ridgway Porcelains,* Antique Collectors' Club, 1985.

Additional Listings: Staffordshire, Historical, and Staffordshire, Romantic.

Cup and Saucer, green transfer, children at play 85.00

Dish, 10¼″ d, Oriental scenes, blue ground 25.00

Jug, 5″ h, soft paste, white griffins and cherubs, brown body, mask spout . . 150.00

Pitcher, 10″ h, salmon and gilt shell dec, gilt foliage dec on shoulder, cobalt blue border 80.00

Plate

7½″ d, gray transfer, Columbian Star pattern, imp "John Ridgway" 25.00

9″ d, Coaching Days 25.00

Platter, 17″ l, Asiatic Places, dark blue, two people on mound in foreground scene, vase with flowers to left, temple background, cartouche enclosing label "Ridgways Asiatic Places" . . . 155.00

Saucer, 5¼″ d, blue, small child petting lamb, imp "Ridgway" on back 90.00

Soup Tureen, 13½″ d, black transfer, Indus pattern, marked "Ridgway, Sparks & Ridgway" 145.00

Relish Dish, Mankin Jar pattern, green, gold trim, c1842–45, marked "Ridgway & Morley," 9¾″ l, $48.00.

Teapot

4¾″ h, molded formal and fluted borders, mid 19th C 30.00

6″ h, President Harrison Log Cabin, blue transfer, hexagonal shape, spreading foot, missing lid, marked "Columbia Star, October 22, 1840, John Ridgway" 70.00

Tray, 12½″ d, Pickwick Series, Mr Pickwick at the Election, black transfer, caramel ground, silver scalloped edge 100.00

RING TREES

History: A ring tree is a small, generally saucer shaped object made of glass, porcelain, metal, or wood with a center post in the shape of a hand, branches, or cylinder for hanging or storing finger rings.

GLASS

Cranberry, 3¾" h, 3¾" d, enameled blue, yellow, and white flowers, green leaves, clear post	85.00
Cut Glass, tapering center post, diamond cut saucer	40.00
Fenton, turtle	20.00
Opaline, 4½" h, blue, hp gold, blue, and white floral dec, ftd	70.00
Ruby Stained, Button Arches pattern .	50.00
Spatter, 3¾" h, yellow, white, and clear	65.00

Porcelain, hp, tree standard, forest scene with road and pasture, 3" h, $20.00.

PORCELAIN

Child's hand, 4" h, fingers extended, Parian Ware	45.00
German, hand on saucer, dec	22.50
Limoges, multicolored blossoms, white ground, marked "T & V Limoges" . .	40.00
Minton, 3" h, pastel flowers on top, gold edge and knob, marked "Minton, England"	40.00
Nippon, gold hand, rim dec	35.00
Schlegelmilch, RS Poland, violets, pearlized finish	90.00

POTTERY

Irid gold, 3½" h, Zsolnay	75.00
Jasper, 2¾" h, center post, panels of white cameos of classical ladies, floral border, blue ground, marked "Wedgwood"	145.00
Pink and green flowers, gold, hp, marked "M Z Austria"	65.00

WOOD

Tramp Art, carved fruitwood, hand shape	25.00

ROCK 'N' ROLL

History: Rock music can be traced back to early rhythm and blues music. It progressed and reached its golden age in the 1950s and 1960s. Attention and most of the memorabilia issued during that period focused on individual singers and groups. The two largest sources of collectibles are items associated with Elvis Presley and The Beatles.

In the 1980s two areas—clothing and guitars—associated with key Rock 'n' Roll personalities received special collector attention. Sotheby's and Christie's East regularly feature Rock 'n' Roll memorabilia as part of their collectibles sales. At the moment, the market is highly speculative and nostalgia driven.

It is important to identify memorabilia issued during the lifetime of an artist or performing group as opposed to material issued after they died or disbanded. This latter material is identified as "fantasy" items and will never achieve the same degree of collectibility as its period counterparts.

References: Jeff Augsburger, Marty Eck, and Rich Rann, *The Beatles Memorabilia Price Guide*, Branyan Press, 1988; Rosalind Cranor, *Elvis Collectibles*, Collector Books, 1983; L. R. Docks, *1915–1965 American Premium Record Guide, Third Edition*, Books Americana, 1986; Barbara Fenick, *Collecting The Beatles: An Introduction and Price Guide To Fab Four Collectibles, Records and Memorabilia, Volume 1* (1984) and *Volume 2*, Perian Press; Alison Fox, *Rock & Pop*, Boxtree Ltd. (London), 1988; Paul Grushkin, *The Art of Rock—Posters From Presley To Punk, Revised Edition*, Abbeville Press, 1991; Jerry Osborne, Perry Cox, and Joe Lindsay, *The Official Price Guide to Memorabilia of Elvis Presley And The Beatles*, House of Collectibles, 1988; Neal Umphred, *Goldmine's Price Guide To Collectible Record Albums, 1949–1989, 2nd Edition*, Krause Publications, 1991; Neal Umphred, *Goldmine's Rock 'n Roll 45 RPM Record Price Guide*, Krause Publications, 1991.

Collectors' Club: Beatles Fan Club of Great Britain, Superstore Productions, 123 Marina St., Leonards on Sea, East Sussex, England TN 38 0BN.

Periodicals: *Beatlefan*, P. O. Box 33515, Decatur, GA 30033; *Good Day Sunshine*, Liverpool Productions, 397 Edgewood Avenue, New Haven, CT 06511.

Reproduction Alert: Records, picture sleeves, and album jackets, especially for The Beatles, have been counterfeited. Sound may be inferior. Printing on labels and picture jackets usually is inferior to the original. Many pieces of memorabilia also have been reproduced, often with some change in size, color, and design.

Additional Listings: See The Beatles, Elvis Presley, and Rock 'n' Roll in *Warman's Americana & Collectibles*.

Buddy Holly Stage Jacket, red with black stitched dots, $4,000.00. Glasses, black plastic, marked "Japan" on inner right arm, $7,000.00.

Belt Buckle, Kiss, 2 x 4", bronzed metal, late 1970s 25.00

Book

  The Beatles Yellow Submarine, copyright 1968 King Features Syndicate, Signet Books, 128 pgs 18.00

  The Elvis Presley Story, Hillman Books, paperback, 4 x 6", 160 pgs, 1960 . . . .   30.00

  The Monkees Annual, Century 21 Publishing Ltd, 96 pgs, 1968 . . . .   25.00

  Woodstock 69 Summer Pop Festivals, Scholastic Book Services, copyright 1970, Joseph J Sia, 128 pgs 20.00

Bracelet, 7" l, metal, link, four metal chars, orig cardboard card marked "Elvis Presley Exclusive RCA Victor Recording Star," 1956 Elvis Presley Enterprises copyright 110.00

Costume, Gene Simmons, one–piece vinyl suit, molded thin plastic mask, Collegeville Costumes, copyright 1978 Aucoin Management Inc 50.00

Doll

  Boy George, 12", poseable, LJN, copyright 1984 Sharpegrade Ltd .   75.00

  Kiss, set of 4, 13" h, poseable, Mego, copyright 1978 Aucoin Management Inc 200.00

Figure, Dave Clark 5, 3" h, hard plastic, set of 4, Remco, c1964 . . . .   75.00

Flag, Beatles, 8 x 10", blue and white rayon, group's heads above Beatles name, marked "LTE," c1960 . . . . . .   75.00

Folder, Culture Club, 9½ x 12", Boy George photo, Popfolios, copyright 1984 Zebra Marketing 12.00

Game

  Jackson Five Action Game, Shindana Toys, copyright 1972 Motown Record Corp 25.00

  The Monkees Game, Transogram, copyright 1967 Rayburt Productions Inc 110.00

Guitar, Monkees, plastic, black, full color paper label, black and yellow logo, orig black and white shoulder strap, Mattel, copyright 1966 Raybert Productions 30.00

Lunch Box

  Beatles, metal, emb, color illus, Aladdin, copyright 1965 Nems Enterprises Ltd 200.00

  Kiss, red plastic thermos, yellow plastic cup, King–Seeley Thermos Co, copyright 1977 Aucoin Management Inc, unused 75.00

  The Osmonds, metal, emb, color illus, Aladdin Industries, copyright 1973 Osbro Productions 45.00

Pennant, 11 x 29", felt, black and yellow, black and white photo, late 1970s . .   50.00

Pinback Button, I Love Freddy and the Dreamers, 3½" d, red and white lettering, black and white photos, Premier Talent Associates Inc copyright, c1960 . . . .   25.00

Photo Album, 8½ x 11", 12 pgs, sepia photos, copyright 1956 Elvis Presley Enterprises 55.00

Photograph

  James Dean, 8 x 10", color, blue signature "Sincerely James Dean," c1955 . . . .   45.00

  Smokey Robinson, 8 x 10", glossy, black and white, black felt tip signature "To William/God Bless/You/ Smokey Robinson" 15.00

Poster

  Chubby Checker, 21 x 27", red, white, and purple, July 15–21, Atlantic City Steel Pier, c1970 . . . .   40.00

  Cream, 11 x 15½", Nov 4, 1969, Rhode Island Auditorium 110.00

  Family Dog, 14 x 20", Aug 3–6, 1967, Avalon Ballroom 50.00

  Ike and Tina Turner, 14 x 22", Tampa Curtis–Hixon Hall, early 1970s . . .   75.00

  James Brown, 14 x 22½", Rhode Island Auditorium, c1960 . . . . 200.00

  Janis Joplin, 14 x 19", 1967, Mt Tamalpias Outdoor Theater, San Francisco, marked "Copyright Also–Gut–67" 150.00

  The Doors, 13 x 22½", Kacy and Jim Salzer, Aug 5, 1967, Earl Warren Showgrounds, Santa Barbara, CA   50.00

  The Grateful Dead, 21 x 27½", Oct 22–31, 1980 Radio City Music Hall   75.00

Woodstock, 24 x 36½″, Aug 15–17, 1969, white dove, blue and green guitar held by yellow hand, red background 400.00

Program

Kiss, 1979 Dynasty Tour, 16 pgs, copyright 1979 Aucoin Management 25.00

The Doors, 8½ x 11″, 4 pgs, Saturday, May 11, Detroit, MI, Cobo Arena, c1967 .... 200.00

Puppet, finger, Monkees, Davey, 5″ h, vinyl, soft molded head, black hair, orig plain brown box marked "Davey," late 1960s 25.00

Puzzle

Bee Gees, group in white suits, APC, copyright 1979 Bee Gees 15.00

Donny and Marie, frame tray, 8 x 11″, color photo, Whitman, copyright 1977 Osbro Productions Inc 12.00

Record

Bill Haley and His Comets, Dim, Dim The Lights, Happy Baby, Birth of the Boogie, Mambo Rock, 45 rpm, Decca label, 1955 .... 50.00

Little Richard, Good Golly Miss Molly, Lucille, 33⅓ rpm, Specialty label, 1957 .... 55.00

Orlons, South Street, 33⅓ rpm, Cameo label 25.00

The Shirelles, Baby It's You, 33⅓ rpm, Cameo label 25.00

Record Player, Beatles, wood case, blue vinyl covering, black plastic carrying handle, metal clasp, c1964 ... 800.00

Sheet Music

Heartbreak Hotel, Elvis Presley, 9 x 12″, 2 pgs, words and music, copyright 1956 Tree Publishing Co Inc 25.00

Like a Rolling Stone, Bob Dillan, 9 x 12″, 4 pgs, copyright 1965 M Whitmark & Sons 50.00

Mrs Brown You've Got A Lovely Daughter, Herman's Hermits, 9 x 12″, 28 pgs, words and music, 1965 Big Top Records Inc 20.00

Sunglasses, Monkees, gold wire frames, yellow lenses, attached gold link chain, orig bag, Teen International, c1960 .... 25.00

Ticket

Elvis, San Antonio Convention Center, Oct 8, 1974, purple, black and red lettering, unused 25.00

Woodstock, Saturday, Aug 16, 1969, unused 75.00

Thermos, 6½″ h, metal, color photos, blue background, white plastic cup, King–Seely Thermos Co, copyright 1967 Raybert Productions Inc 30.00

Wallet, Elvis Presley, vinyl, two illus, attached gold key chain handle, copyright 1956 Elvis Presley Enterprises 250.00

ROCKINGHAM AND ROCKINGHAM BROWN GLAZED WARES

History: Rockingham ware can be divided into two categories. The first consists of the fine china and porcelain pieces made between 1826 and 1842 by the Rockingham Company of Swinton, Yorkshire, England, and its predecessor firms: Swinton, Bingley, Don, Leeds, and Brameld. The Bramelds developed the cadogan, a lidless teapot. Between 1826 and 1842 a quality soft paste body with a warm, silken feel was developed by the Bramelds. Elaborate specialty pieces were made. By 1830 the company employed 600 workers and listed 400 designs for dessert sets and 1,000 designs for tea and coffee services in their catalog. Unable to meet its payroll, the company closed in 1842.

The second category of Rockingham ware includes pieces produced in the famous Rockingham brown glaze, that became an intense and vivid purple–brown when fired. It had a dark, tortoise shell mottled appearance. The glaze was copied by many English and American potteries. American manufacturers who used Rockingham glaze include D. & J. Henderson of Jersey City, New Jersey; United States Pottery in Bennington, Vermont; potteries in East Liverpool, Ohio; and several potteries in Indiana and Illinois.

Reference: Susan and Al Bagdade, *Warman's English & Continental Pottery & Porcelain, 2nd Edition,* Wallace–Homestead, 1991.

Additional Listings: Bennington and Bennington–Type Pottery.

Bowl
  8¾″ d, shallow 30.00
  10½″ d 90.00
  12⅜″ d 115.00
  14″ d 75.00
Creamer, 6¼″, cow shape, brown Rockingham glaze 100.00
Cuspidor, 6½″, sq, molded, emb American eagles 65.00
Dish, 11½″ l, oval, flaked glaze 35.00
Figure, 9½″ h, seated dog, oblong base 85.00
Food Mold, 8½″ d, turk's head 35.00

Foot Warmer, brown Rockingham glaze	85.00
Inkwell, 4⅛″ l, shoe shape	55.00
Jar, 12″ h, cov, chipped lid	175.00
Pie Plate	
8¾″ d	55.00
9⅝″ d	85.00
Pitcher	
8¼″ h	
Molded peacock	65.00
Paneled	65.00
9″ h, molded tulips	55.00
9¼″ h	
Molded oval hanging fish design, cov	135.00
Paneled	100.00

Bowl, mocha and gold dec, 7⅜″ d, 3¼″ h, $65.00.

Platter, 15″ l, emb scalloped rim, Rockingham glaze	350.00
Soap Dish	
4⅛″ d	50.00
4¾″ l, oval	55.00
Spittoon	
7½″ d, raised medallions dec on sides	25.00
8″ d, twelve raised scallop shells around shoulder	30.00
Tea Service, part, 6¼″ h teapot, dolphin form spout, scroll handle, dome cov, rosebud finial, two handled sugar bowl with dome cov, rosebud finial, matching creamer, waste bowl, nine tea cups, five coffee cups, twelve saucers, transfer printed, beige acanthus leaves, polychrome floral sprays, gilt, white ground	425.00
Teapot	
8⅜″ h, molded fern and foliage designs	75.00
9¾″ l, figural, duck, emb detail, rect lid, Rockingham glaze	225.00
Tobacco Jar, cov	
7½″ h, cylindrical, molded alternate ribs, "1849" Bennington mark . . .	60.00
9″ h, emb dec, Gothic Arches pattern, Rockingham glaze	225.00
Vegetable Dish, oval	
7⅞ x 10¼″	50.00
10 x 11¾″	75.00

ROCKWELL, NORMAN

History: Norman Rockwell (February 3, 1894–November, 1978) was a famous American artist and illustrator. During the time he painted, from age 18 until his death, he created over 2,000 works.

His first professional efforts were illustrations for a children's book. He next worked for *Boy's Life*, the Boy Scout magazine. His most famous works were used by *Saturday Evening Post* for their cover illustrations.

Norman Rockwell painted everyday people in everyday situations, mixing a little humor with sentiment. His paintings and illustrations are treasured because of this sensitive approach. Rockwell painted people he knew and places with which he was familiar. New England landscapes are found in many of his illustrations.

References: Denis C. Jackson, *The Norman Rockwell Identification And Value Guide To: Magazines, Posters, Calendars, Books, 2nd Edition*, published by author, 1985; Mary Moline, *Norman Rockwell Collectibles, Sixth Edition*, Green Valley World, 1988.

Museums: Corner House, Stockbridge, MA; Norman Rockwell Museum, Northbrook, IL.

Reproduction Alert: Because of the popularity of his works, they have been reproduced on many objects. These new collectibles should not be confused with original artwork and illustrations. However, they do allow a collector more range in collecting interests and prices.

Additional Listings: See *Warman's Americana & Collectibles* for more examples.

Print, *Saturday Evening Post* cover, titled "Before the Shot," sgd, 11 x 14″, $45.00.

HISTORIC

Book, *The Adventures of Tom Sawyer*, Mark Twain, 1936	50.00
Calendar, 1922, Warren National Bank, Music Master	300.00
Poster, 22 x 28", The Saturday Evening Post 100th Year of Baseball, 1939 .	175.00
Tray, 17½ x 12¾", Green Giant adv, c1940	48.00

MODERN

Bell, Royal Devon, Butter Girl, 1976 . .	40.00
Coin, Ford Motor Co, 50th Anniversary	35.00
Figure	
Gorham Fine China	
Batter Up	50.00
Four Seasons, Childhood, 1973, set of four	500.00
Pride of Parenthood	60.00
Grossman Designs, Inc.	
Barbershop Quartet, 1975	125.00
Tom Sawyer, Series No. 1, 1976 .	100.00
Ingot, Franklin Mint, tribute to Robert Frost, 1974	275.00
Plate	
Ages of Love, Gorham Fine China, 1973, Four Seasons series, set of 4	300.00
Doctor and Doll, Royal Devon, 1975, Mother's Day	90.00
Scotty Gets His Tree, Rockwell Society of America, 1974, Christmas	175.00
Under The Mistletoe, Franklin Mint, SS, 1971	175.00
Print	
Circle Fine Arts, limited edition, sgd and numbered	
Dressing Up, pencil sgd	2,800.00
Icabod Crane	5,000.00
Music Hath Charms	3,000.00
Wet Paint, 24 x 30", collotype . . .	1,550.00
Eleanor Ettinger, Inc.	
After The Prom, 24 x 26¾", litho .	4,500.00
Gilding The Eagle, 21 x 25½", litho	3,225.00
The Swing, 20 x 21", litho	4,750.00

ROGERS & SIMILAR STATUARY

History: John Rogers, born in America in 1829, studied sculpturing in Europe and produced the first plaster-of-paris statue, "The Checker Players," in 1859. It was followed by "The Slave Auction" in 1860.

His works were popular parlor pieces of the Victorian era. He produced at least 80 different subjects and the total number of groups made from the originals is estimated to be over 100,000.

Casper Hennecke, one of Rogers' contemporaries, operated C. Hennecke & Company from 1881 until 1896 in Milwaukee, Wisconsin. His statuary often is confused with Rogers' work since both are very similar.

It is difficult to find a statue in undamaged condition and with original paint. Use the following conversions: 10% minor flaking; 10% chips; 10–20% piece or pieces broken and reglued; 20% flaking; 50% repainting.

References: Paul and Meta Bieier, *John Rogers' Groups of Statuary*, published by author, 1971; Betty C. Haverly, *Hennecke's Florentine Statuary*, published by author, 1972; David H. Wallace, *John Rogers: The People's Sculptor*, Wesleyan Univ., 1976.

Periodical: *Rogers Group*, 4932 Prince George Avenue, Beltsville, MD 20705.

Council of War, Type C, Rogers, 24" h, $475.00.

ROGERS

Courtship in Sleepy Hollow, 16½" h, 2/8/1870	750.00
Council of War	
Type A, 24½" h, 3/31/1868	875.00
Type B, 3/31/1868, orig paint, flaked, chair cov chipped, document cracked	500.00
Type C, 24" h, minor flaking	475.00
Faust & Marguerite–Leaving The Garden, 25½" h, 1890	400.00
Mail Day, 16" h, 1864	650.00
One More Shot, 24" h, 1865	425.00
Referee, The, 22" h, 1880, repainted .	350.00
School Days, 21½" h, 1877	700.00
The Balcony, 32½" h, 11/4/1879, orig paint, some flaking, violin repaired .	600.00
Union Refugees, spelter, 1864, one of	

seven known, hammer of rifle
chipped **1,200.00**

ROGERS TYPE

After The Case, 20″ h **110.00**
By Jingo, 17″ h, orig paint, minor chip-
ping **125.00**
Can't You Talk, 10½″ h **135.00**
First Love, 13″ h, repainted **165.00**
Holy Family, 18″ h **225.00**
Romeo and Juliet, 16″ h **150.00**

ROOKWOOD POTTERY

History: Mrs. Marie Longworth Nicholas Storer,
Cincinnati, Ohio, founded Rookwood Pottery in
1880. The name of this outstanding American art
pottery came from her family estate "Rookwood,"
named for the rooks (crows) which inhabited the
wooded grounds.

There are five elements to the Rookwood marking system—the clay or body mark, the size mark,
the decorator mark, the date mark, and the factory
mark. Rookwood art pottery can best be dated
from factory marks.

In 1880–1882 the factory mark was the name
"Rookwood" incised or painted on the base. Between 1881 and 1886 the firm name, address, and
year appeared in an oval frame. Beginning in
1886, the impressed "RP" monogram appeared
and a flame mark was added for each year until
1900. After 1900 a Roman numeral, indicating the
last two digits of the year of production, was added
at the bottom of the "RP" flame mark monogram.
This last mark is the one most often found on
Rookwood pottery today.

Though the Rookwood pottery filed for bankruptcy in 1941, it was soon reorganized under new
management. Efforts at maintaining the pottery
proved futile, and it again was sold in 1956 and in
1959. The pottery was moved to Starkville, Mississippi, in conjunction with the Herschede Clock Co.
It finally ceased operation in 1967.

Rookwood wares changed with the times. The
variety is endless, in part because of the great
variations in glazes and designs due to the creativity of the many talented artists.

References: Herbert Peck, *The Book of Rookwood Pottery*, Crown Publishers, Inc., 1968; Herbert Peck, *The Second Book of Rookwood Pottery*, published by author, 1985.

Collectors' Club: American Art Pottery Association, 9825 Upton Circle, Bloomington, MN
55431.

Candleholder, 3½″ h, pr, water lily form,
white, matte finish, dated 1956 . . . . **120.00**
Ewer
8¾″ h, wild rose dec, standard glaze,
red clay base, sgd Albert R Valen-
tien, dated 1888 . . . . **825.00**
9½″ h, blueberry and leaf dec, stan-
dard glaze, artist sgd Amelia B
Sprague, dated 1900 . . . . **715.00**
10¾″ h, fern dec, incised geometric
dec bands, bisque finish, sgd W H
Breuer, dated 1882 . . . . **550.00**
Figure, 7″ h, cat, yellow matte glaze, sgd
Louise Abel, 1930 . . . . **150.00**
Flower Boat, 13″ l, branch and leaf dec,
standard glaze, artist sgd dated 1894 **1,045.00**
Humidor, 7½″ h, floral and leaf dec, wax
matte, sgd Catherine Covalenco,
dated 1922 . . . . **525.00**
Jar, 4″ h, leaf and berry dec, ruffled rim,
two loop handles, sgd S J, dated
1902 . . . . **325.00**
Loving Cup
4⅝″ h, Indian portrait, standard glaze,
three handles, sgd Sadie Markland,
dated 1898 . . . . **550.00**
6¾″ h, woodland scene, canopy of
trees, vellum glaze, three handles,
artist sgd Ed Diers, dated 1908, in-
cised X **550.00**
Mug, standard glaze
4½″ h, cavalier holding mug of beer
portrait, sgd Emma D Foertmeyer **770.00**
4¾″ h, Sertenta, Kiowa, Indian portrait, sgd Sturgis Laurence, dated
1899 . . . . **825.00**
4⅝″ h, portrait
Child chasing butterfly, hat in hand,
sgd Harriet E Wilcox, dated 1892 **660.00**
Child on horse, sgd Harriet E Wil-
cox, dated 1892 . . . . **660.00**
Child pouring liquid out of pitcher,
sgd Grace Young, dated 1891 . **1,045.00**
5″ h, Peter Iron Shell–Sioux, Indian
portrait, sgd Jeannette Swing,
dated 1900 . . . . **1,210.00**
6″ h, floral dec, curved handle, sgd
Marianne Mitchell, dated 1901 . . . **440.00**
Pitcher
5″ h, compressed body, yellow blossoms dec, glazed, sgd Carl
Schmidt, dated 1898 . . . . **240.00**
8⅛″ h, three ears of corn, standard
glaze, sgd Bruce Horsfall, dated
1895 . . . . **825.00**
10½″ h, floral dec, standard glaze,
sgd M A Daly, dated 1886 . . . . . . **880.00**

Plaque

5 x 8¾", Early Autumn, woodland scene, vellum glaze, sgd Ed Diers 3,025.00

5¼ x 9¼", A Quiet Stream, sun setting behind trees, vellum glaze, sgd C Schmidt 4,400.00

6 x 6", Weasaw–Shoshonie, Indian portrait, imp "REM 2.14.1902" ... 2,910.00

6 x 7⅞", Ships Anchored in the Lagoon, vellum glaze, sgd Carl Schmidt, dated 1921 .... 3,190.00

6 x 8", Venetian canal scene, vellum glaze, sgd Carl Schmidt 3,960.00

9¾ x 8", National Glacier Park, snow capped mountains, sgd Fred Rothenbusch, dated 1929 .... 4,125.00

Portrait Vase, 8" h, male with long white hair and beard, standard glaze, sgd Anna M Valentien, dated 1894 .... 1,925.00

Tankard

7½" h, corn and tassel dec, standard glaze, sgd Lenore Asbury, dated 1898 .... 410.00

7¾" h, cavalier portrait, standard glaze, sgd M A Daly, dated 1897 . 660.00

Teapot, 4½" h, blue shading to light green, clover dec, high glaze, sgd Ed Diers, dated 1902, marked X on bottom 550.00

Tile, 5½" sq, polychromed relief dec, dated 1919 .... 1,800.00

Tobacco Humidor, standard glaze

5½" h, corn cob pipe, matches, and holly dec, sgd Carrie Steinle, dated 1903 .... 550.00

6½" h, male wearing hat and cape, sgd Edith R Felten, dated 1902 .. 1,100.00

6¾" h, clear pink cone, needle, and branch dec, sgd Carrie Steinle, dated 1907 .... 660.00

7" h, pipes, cigars, matches, and flower dec, sgd Fred Rothenbusch, dated 1899 .... 880.00

Vase

3¼" h, ovoid, crocus dec, sgd Laura E Lindeman, 1903 .... 175.00

4¼" h, Art Deco, white, floral relief, matte glaze, dated 1938 .... 70.00

5¾" h

Daisy dec, vellum glaze, sgd Fred Rothenbusch, dated 1926 .... 525.00

Dimpled surface, purple high glaze, gray and purple splotches, dated 1926 .... 550.00

Iris dec, double handles, sgd Mary Nourse, dated 1891 .... 880.00

6" h, ovoid, deep red flowers, rose ground, ftd, sgd Margaret Helen McDonald, dated 1927 .... 350.00

6¼" h, cherry blossom dec, vellum glaze, sgd Lenore Asbury, dated 1928 .... 550.00

Vase, wax resist, ducks, blue tones, 1910, #1659E, artist sgd "Kath–Van Horne," 7⅜" h, $1,200.00.

6⅜" h, detailed floral and leaf dec, standard glaze, sgd Bruce Horsfall, dated 1893 .... 660.00

6⅝" h, holly dec, standard glaze, sgd Leona Van Briggle, dated 1904 .. 470.00

6¾" h, three carved butterflies, purple to pink mottled ground, matte glaze, sgd C S Todd, dated 1913 440.00

7½" h

Berry and leaf dec, glazed, artist sgd Rose Fechheimer, dated 1901 .... 550.00

Stylized purple grapes and leaf clusters, high glaze, sgd W E Hentschel, dated 1945 .... 470.00

8¼" h, stylized design, matte glaze, artist sgd Cecil A Duell, dated 1907 330.00

8½" h

Art Deco flowers, high glaze, drip glazed neck, artist sgd Elizabeth Barrett, dated 1931 .... 410.00

Trumpet flower dec, standard glaze, sgd O Geneva Reed, dated 1897 .... 575.00

8¾" h, holly dec, wax matte glaze, sgd Sallie E Coyne, dated 1927 .. 715.00

9" h

Hollyhock dec, high glaze, artist sgd Elizabeth Barrett, dated 1944 .... 385.00

Mum dec, standard glaze, sgd Carrie Steinle, dated 1907 .... 710.00

9¼" h, flowering wild rose, silver overlay, standard glaze, sgd Hattie Horton, dated 1902 .... 1,650.00

9½" h, canal scene, vellum glaze, sgd Carl Schmidt, dated 1921 ...... 3,300.00

9¾" h

Bird and floral dec, high glaze, mottled liner, sgd Lorinda Epply, dated 1925 .... 825.00

Crocus dec, sterling band on top, iris glaze, sgd Carl Schmidt, dated 1908, imp "W" **3,575.00**

10" h

Indian portrait, Buffalo Hunter–Shoshonie, standard glaze, sgd O Geneva Reed, dated 1899 . . **4,400.00**

Stylized flowers, alternating broad leaves, matte glaze, artist sgd John D Wareham **440.00**

10¾" h, incised geometric dec, mottled mustard body, matte glaze, sgd C S Todd, dated 1928 . . . . **250.00**

11" h, floral dec, flaring rim, wax matte, sgd Sallie E Coyne, dated 1925 . . . . **525.00**

11½" h, detailed trumpet vine flowers, standard glaze, sgd M A Daly, dated 1902 . . . . **1,100.00**

11⅝" h, floral dec, mottled blue ground, wax matte glaze, sgd Louise Abel, dated 1927 . . . . **770.00**

12" h, ovoid, Japanese style, painted butterflies and bamboo, gilded neck and foot, sgd Albert R Valentien, dated 1883 . . . . **1,150.00**

12¼", cascading cluster of cherries and leaves dec, vellum glaze, sgd Sara Sax, dated 1914 . . . . **770.00**

12⅝" h, splashy woodbine floral dec, pink to green mottled ground, wax matte glaze, sgd Elizabeth N Lincoln, dated 1922 . . . . **630.00**

13" h, Venetian scene, vellum glaze, sgd Carl Schmidt, dated 1918 . . . **4,070.00**

13⅛" h, multicolored floral dec, vellum glaze, sgd Elizabeth F McDermott, dated 1919 . . . . **1,100.00**

13⅜" h, bold lotus blossom dec, wax matte glaze, sgd Sallie E Coyne, dated 1925 . . . . **1,155.00**

13½" h, floral and leaf motif, mottled bulbous body, matte glaze, sgd Charles S Todd, dated 1928 . . . . **600.00**

14" h, blue to green, wax matte finish, sgd Elizabeth N Lincoln, dated 1925 . . . . **500.00**

15⅝" h, trees in bloom dec, vellum glaze, sgd Ed Diers, dated 1916 . **1,430.00**

16½" h, floral and leaf dec, standard glaze, sgd M A Daly, dated 1891 . **1,650.00**

Whiskey Jug

6" h, standard glaze

Corn dec, sgd Lenore Asbury, dated 1895 . . . . **385.00**

Two ears of corn dec, one husk opened, sgd O Geneva Reed, dated 1893 . . . . **550.00**

7½" h, corn and tassel dec, standard glaze, orig stopper, sgd Josephine Zettel, dated 1898 . . . . **740.00**

8" h

Ear of corn and tassel dec, standard glaze, sgd Josephine E Zettel, dated 1897 . . . . **470.00**

Indian portrait dec, Feather Wolf–Cheyenne, standard glaze, sgd Sadie Markland, dated 1899 . . . **2,970.00**

8¾" h, ear of corn, detailed tassel, standard glaze, stopper, sgd Josephine E Zettel, dated 1895 . . . . . **710.00**

ROSE BOWLS

History: A rose bowl, a decorative open bowl with a crimped, pinched, or petal top, held fragrant rose petals or potpourri which served as an air freshener in the late Victorian period. Practically every glass manufacturer made rose bowls in a variety of patterns and glass types, including fine art glass.

Additional Listings: See specific glass categories.

Opalescent, Pearl and Scale, green, ftd, 4¾" d, $60.00.

Burmese, miniature, dec, acid finish . . **330.00**

Cameo, miniature

Cobalt blue foliage trees and distant mountains, pink to yellow sky and water, scalloped rim, 3½" d, sgd "deVez" **550.00**

Enamel floral dec, acid finish **235.00**

Cased, 3½" d, pink fold down rim, shiny finish **40.00**

Cranberry, 6" d, opalescent, hobnail . . **60.00**

Mother–of–Pearl

4½" d, DQ, striped blue and white, marked "Patent" **355.00**

7" d, DQ, white, red leafy branched apple blossoms **1,825.00**

Mount Washington, 4¼" d, pr, peachblow coloring **155.00**

Opalescent
Pink florals, 7″ d, applied amber
branch and leaves 130.00
Swirl pattern, blue 75.00
Peachblow, 4″ d, six crimp top 125.00
Satin Glass
4½″ d, beige, mauve pull–up feathers,
soft blue–green int., close crimped
top 900.00
5¼″ d, DQ, shaded peach ground,
dimpled sides, eight crimp top,
white int. 275.00
5½″ d, DQ, MOP, dimpled sides,
peach to ivory shading, white int.,
eight crimp top 275.00
Spangled, 6″ d, cased, lavender, silver
veining, attributed to Cape Cod Glass
Works 90.00

ROSE CANTON, ROSE MANDARIN, ROSE MEDALLION

History: The pink rose color has given its name
to three related groups of Chinese export porcelain. Rose Mandarin was produced from the late
18th century to approximately 1840. Rose Canton
began somewhat later extending through the first
half of the 19th century. Rose Medallion originated
in the early 19th century and was made through
the early 20th century.

Rose Mandarin derives its name from the Mandarin figure(s) found in garden scenes with women
and children. The women often feature gold decorations in their hair. Polychrome enamels and
birds separate the scenes.

Rose Medallion has alternating panels of figures
and birds and flowers. The elements are four in
number, separated evenly around the center medallion. Peonies and foliage fill voids.

Rose Canton is similar to Rose Medallion except
the figure panels are replaced by flowers. People
are present only if the medallion partitions are
absent. Some patterns have been named—Butterfly and Cabbage, Rooster, etc. The category
actually is a catchall for all pink enamel ware not
fitting into the first two groups.

Reference: Sandra Andacht, *Oriental Antiques
& Art: An Identification And Value Guide,* Wallace-
Homestead, 1987.

Reproduction Alert: Rose Medallion is still
made, although the quality does not match the
earlier examples.

ROSE CANTON

Bowl, 11½″ d, green, alternating sections of florals and figures 285.00
Brush Pot, 4½″ h, scenic, ladies, reticulated, gilt trim 265.00
Charger, 13″ d, floral panels, 19th C .. 200.00

Creamer, helmet shape, hog snout,
c1860, 3½″ h, 4″ d, $235.00.

Compote, flower and butterfly medallions, pedestal base 300.00
Plate, 8½″ d, floral dec 75.00
Soup Tureen, cov, lozenge shape, gilt
floral ground, figural scenes 300.00
Sugar, cov, handle 100.00
Teapot, 5″ h, flowers and butterflies .. 135.00

ROSE MANDARIN

Bough Vase, 7″ h, elongated, flaring,
hexagonal section over stepped foot,
panels of figures, birds, and landscape, red, black, and gilt fish scale
ground, five apertures on cov 2,000.00
Brush Box, cov, 7¾″ l, rect, allover figural courtyard scene on cover, fruits
and butterflies on sides, c1840, int.
rim chip 880.00
Cup and Saucer, scenic panels, butterfly and floral border 150.00
Flask, Pilgrim, 9¾″ h, lizard form handles, figural scenes, birds and peacock dragon borders, c1840, pr 3,575.00
Fruit Platter, 14½″ l, shaped rim, central
figural courtyard scene, Rose Canton
border, c1840, rim chip repair 880.00
Plate, 7¾″ d, central figural courtyard
scenes, mid 19th C, minor wear, assembled set of 24 .... 2,530.00
Punch Bowl
15⅞″ d, paneled figural courtyard
scenes, birds, flowers, fruits, and
precious ornaments, c1840 ..... 2,750.00
21¼″ d, panels of figural courtyard
scenes, Rose Canton field, c1840,
hairlines 3,410.00
Serving Dish, 9¼″ sq, central figural
courtyard scene, floral, bird, butterfly,
and fruit borders, c1840, pr 1,870.00
Shrimp Dish, 10¾″ l, lobed rims, extended ends, central figural scenes,
Rose Canton border, c1840, chips, pr 1,870.00
Vase, 9½″ h, figures and precious ornaments below Rose Canton floral
designs, c1860, crazed ground, one
rim repaired, pr 495.00

Vegetable Dish, 11″ l, central figural panel, Rose Canton borders, c1840, pr **1,540.00**

Wash Basin, 17¼″ d, typical palette, figural courtyard scene within panels, surrounded by fruits, flowers, and ornaments, mid 19th C, wear and rim chip **910.00**

Water Bottle, 15½″ h, typical palette, figural courtyard scene within panels, surrounded by fruits, flowers, and ornaments, mid 19th C, rim chip, neck hairline **500.00**

ROSE MEDALLION

Bouillon Cup and Saucer, cov, handle . **75.00**
Bowl
9½″ d, int. painted with reserve panel of flowers and figures, gilt floral ground, ext. with unusual frieze of figures, 19th C, pr **1,500.00**
10″ d, notched sq form, int. single rose spray, ornate border, ext. figural vignettes, 19th C **400.00**
Dish
11¼″ l, reticulated sides and rim, underplate, marked "Made in China" **425.00**
11½″ l, oval, orange peel glaze **150.00**
14¼″ l, almond shape, raised foot, marked "China" **135.00**
Ginger Jar, 10½″ h, pr, figural reserve dec **200.00**
Pomade Jar, 2½ x 2¼″, cylindrical, scenic lid, man and woman at window . **125.00**
Punch Bowl, 16″ d, alternating floral and figural panels, c1880 .... **1,430.00**
Sauce Boat, 4¼″, int. border with rose and butterfly dec, ext. with household scenes, orange glaze **150.00**
Teapot Set, 5½″ h teapot, three handleless cups, wicker cozy **130.00**
Tray, 15″ l, twin strap handles, 19th C . **900.00**
Vase, 9¼″ h, pr, lion head ring handles **460.00**
Vegetable Dish, cov, 10½″ l, orange peel glaze, marked "China" **200.00**

MARKE

Rosenthal

ROSENTHAL

History: Rosenthal Porcelain Manufactory began operating at Selb, Bavaria in 1880. Specialities were tablewares and figurines. The firm is still in operation.

Reference: Susan and Al Bagdade, *Warman's English & Continental Pottery & Porcelain, 2nd Edition,* Wallace–Homestead, 1991.

Bowl, 10″ d, multicolored, classical woman, paint brush and easel, cobalt blue rim **30.00**
Cake Plate
10¼″ d, open handles, hp, multicolored roses, cobalt blue ground, gold border, artist sgd **50.00**
12″ w, hp, three color grapes, scalloped ruffled edge, open ruffled handles **65.00**
Chocolate Set, chocolate pot, cov, 10″ d plate with handle, four cups and saucers, transitional Art Deco–Art Nouveau dec, brown shaded to beige, cream ground, gold trim, artist sgd, 1922, 10 pcs **135.00**
Creamer and Sugar, pate–sur–pate cherries dec **85.00**

Cup and Saucer, Donatello pattern, light green, dark green, and gold, $10.00.

Cup and Saucer
Donatello pattern, light green, dark green, and gold, white ground ... **10.00**
Portrait, woman, gold trim, artist sgd **50.00**
San Souci pattern, white **12.00**
Demitasse Cup and Saucer, medallion portrait **45.00**
Figure
6″ h, young boy frolicking with lamb, artist sgd **200.00**
10½″ h, group of birds, bright blue, green, orange, yellow, and brown, underglaze green factory mark, imp "J Feldtmann," numbered **425.00**
14″ h, nude, kneeling, sgd "Klimsch" **775.00**
15″ h, nude, standing, sgd "Davmiller" **650.00**
Model
6″ h, Dachshund, seated **150.00**
8 x 8″, Poodle, standing, white, green collar, artist sgd **235.00**
10 x 6 x 5″, reclining deer **350.00**
Planter, 7½″ l, 4″ w, tree bark textured surface, knot holes front and back, unglazed white ext., glazed int. **90.00**

Plate

4" d, white glaze, SS rim	**10.00**
8¾" d, bearded Dutch fisherman, lavender trousers and cap, pale blue ground	**38.00**
10½" d, Maria pattern	**35.00**
Platter, 15" l, Greenblume pattern	**48.00**
Portrait Plate, 9⅞" d, lady, head and shoulder portrait, pale yellow and white ground, faux green, turquoise, blue, and red hardstone jewels	**342.00**
Urn, cov, 10½" h, portrait of woman, garden setting, multicolored	**240.00**

Vase

7" h, shaded tan and rust foliage, crackle glaze, artist sgd, 1946 ...	**90.00**
8" h, blue and white Dutch scene ..	**80.00**
10¼" h, Copenhagen series, SS overlay, marked, c1890	**385.00**
Vegetable Dish, cov, 10¾" w, Maria pattern	**65.00**

Roseville
u. s. a.

ROSEVILLE POTTERY

History: In the late 1880s a group of investors purchased the J. B. Owens Pottery in Roseville, Ohio, and made utilitarian stoneware items. In 1892 the firm was incorporated and joined by George F. Young who became general manager. Four generations of Youngs controlled Roseville until the early 1950s.

A series of acquisitions began: Midland Pottery of Roseville in 1898, Clark Stoneware Plant in Zanesville (formerly used by Peters and Reed), and Muskingum Stoneware (Mosaic Tile Company) in Zanesville. In 1898 the offices also moved from Roseville to Zanesville.

In 1900 Roseville introduced its art pottery—Rozane. Rozane became a trade name to cover a large series of lines. The art lines were made in limited amounts after 1919.

The success of Roseville depended on its commercial lines, first developed by John J. Herald and Frederick Rhead in the first decades of the 1900s. In 1918 Frank Ferrell became art director and developed over 80 lines of pottery. The economic depression of the 1930s brought more lines including Pine Cone.

In the 1940s a series of high gloss glazes were tried to revive certain lines. In 1952 Raymor dinnerware was produced. None of these changes brought economic success. In November 1954 Roseville was bought by the Mosaic Tile Company.

References: Sharon and Bob Huxford, *The Collectors Encyclopedia Of Roseville Pottery*, Collector Books, 1976, 1991 value update; Sharon and Bob Huxford, *The Collectors Encyclopedia Of Roseville Pottery, Second Series*, Collector Books, 1980, 1991 value update.

Collectors' Clubs: American Art Pottery Association, 9825 Upton Circle, Bloomington, MN 55431; Roseville's of the Past, P.O. Box 1018, Apopka, FL 32704–1018.

Additional Listings: See *Warman's Americana & Collectibles* for more examples.

Ashtray, Meteor, #1981	**15.00**

Basket

Freesia, brown, 7½ x 8½", flat loop handle	**70.00**
Magnolia, 12½ x 12", green ground, pink and white flower, green leaves, large loop handle	**160.00**
Bookends, pr, Pine Cone, brown	**200.00**

Bowl

Cosmos, 15", blue, II/132/2/2	**185.00**
Dahlrose, 10", I/79/1/3	**150.00**
Primrose, 4", pink	**58.00**
Water Lily, 6 x 10", two handles, tan to brown ground, creamy water lily, green leaves, rim crack	**60.00**
Coffee Set, 3 pcs, Wincraft, lime green	**250.00**
Conch Shell, Foxglove, blue, 426–6 ..	**60.00**

Console Bowl

Apple Blossom, pink	**80.00**
Freesia, green, 469–14, 2/139/3/2 ..	**85.00**
Topeo, blue	**150.00**
White Rose, blue	**80.00**

Cornucopia

Gardenia, double, gray, 622–8	**60.00**
Snowberry, rose	**35.00**
Creamer, child's, Juvenile Chicks, 3" h, 2/64/3/2, uncrazed	**85.00**
Ewer, Silhouette, brown, 716–6	**40.00**
Flower Frog, Ferrella, 3½", red, II/186/15	**125.00**

Hanging Basket

Apple Blossom, 8", blue, I/129/1/2 ..	**200.00**
Bittersweet, gray	**175.00**
Clematis, brown	**80.00**
Dahlrose, 8½"	**175.00**
Fuchsia, 5", blue	**300.00**
Gardenia, gray	**145.00**
Jonquil, 7"	**275.00**

Peony

Pink	**120.00**
Yellow	**125.00**
Pine Cone, green	**185.00**
Primrose, 8", pink	**225.00**
Snowberry, blue	**125.00**
Sunflower, 6½"	**325.00**
Water Lily, brown	**110.00**
Zephyr Lily, green	**125.00**

Jardiniere

Apple Blossom, 8", pink, #302–8 ..	**165.00**
Imperial I, 8 x 9"	**65.00**
Jonquil, 5 x 7", 2/101/2/1	**135.00**
Persian	**295.00**

Mug, child's, Juvenile Chicks, 3½" h . . **65.00**
Pitcher
  Fuchsia, 8", blue **325.00**
  Pine Cone, 8", blue, ice lip **350.00**
Planter, Columbine, 5", brown **60.00**
Strawberry Pot, Jonquil, 7¼", 2/101/3/4 **150.00**
Toothbrush Holder, Colonial **65.00**
Tray
  Pine Cone, 7", green, #497 . . . . . . **45.00**
  Snowberry, blue **45.00**
Umbrella Stand, Dogwood II, 19½",
  crack in base **225.00**

Vase, blue, marked "#649–3," 3" h, $45.00.

Vase
  Blackberry
    4" **225.00**
    10" **425.00**
  Clematis
    Blue, #755/9 . . . . **175.00**
    Green, 9½" **225.00**
    Tan, 12½" **250.00**
  Corinthian, 8" **60.00**
  Futura, pillow **175.00**
  Ixia, 12", yellow **185.00**
  Laurel, 9½", green mottled ground,
    raised pink flowers, green leaves,
    c1934 . . . . **75.00**
  Morning Glory, beige **165.00**
  Mostique, high glaze, 9" **75.00**
  Russco, 7¼" **75.00**
  Topeo, 8"
    Blue, #659/8 . . . . **225.00**
    Red **235.00**
  Tuscany, 9", pink II/94/2/2 . . . . **150.00**
  White Rose, 15", blue **300.00**
  Wincraft, 12", tan, #286/12 . . . . **95.00**
Wall Plate, Pine Cone, green **285.00**
Wall Pocket
  Apple Blossom, 8", pink, II/169/2/1 . **175.00**
  Dahlrose, 10" **135.00**
  Donatello, high gloss, 11½" **135.00**
  La Rose, 7½", II/165/1/4 . . . . **125.00**
  Magnolia, blue–green, #1294 . . . . . **145.00**

Moss, pink, 8", pink, repaired **175.00**
Pine Cone, 8½", brown **275.00**
Poppy, 8½", green **300.00**
Thorn Apple, 8", brown **200.00**
Tuscany, 8½", pink **100.00**
Wincraft, 5", tan **100.00**
Zephyr Lily, brown **110.00**
Window Box, Ming Tree, 10", green . . **70.00**

ROYAL BAYREUTH

History: In 1794 the Royal Bayreuth factory was founded in Tettau, Bavaria. Royal Bayreuth introduced their figural patterns in 1885. Designs of animals, people, fruits, and vegetables decorated a wide array of tablewares and inexpensive souvenir items.

Tapestry ware, rose and other patterns, were made in the late 19th century. The surface of the ware feels and looks like woven cloth. Tapestry ware was made by covering the porcelain with a piece of fabric tightly stretched over the surface, decorating the fabric, glazing the piece, and firing.

The Royal Bayreuth crest mark varied in design and color. Many wares were unmarked. It is difficult to verify the chronological years of production due to the lack of records.

Royal Bayreuth still manufactures dinnerware. It has not maintained production of earlier wares, particularly the figural items.

Reference: Susan and Al Bagdade, *Warman's English & Continental Pottery & Porcelain*, 2nd Edition, Wallace–Homestead, 1991.

Corinthian, classical figures dec, black
  ground
    Creamer and Sugar **75.00**
    Pitcher, 6" h, yellow bands, leaf dec
      around neck and base **125.00**
    Toothpick, three handles **75.00**
Devil and Cards
  Ashtray **125.00**
  Creamer, 4" h **120.00**
  Demitasse Cup and Saucer **135.00**
  Humidor, 7¾" h, winged finial **675.00**
  Mug, beer **450.00**
  Pitcher, milk, green mark **235.00**
  Salt, master **325.00**
  Wall Pocket, figural **200.00**

Devil and Cards, tankard, black and red dec, cream ground, $435.00.

Grape Cluster, mother of pearl luster
Creamer, white, marked "Germany"	85.00
Mustard, pink, Tettau mark	100.00
Relish, white	80.00

Lobster
Ashtray, 6¼" l	50.00
Creamer, 4" h	50.00
Humidor	625.00
Pitcher, 7" h	375.00
Sugar, cov	115.00

Miscellaneous Patterns
Ashtray
Clown, white	800.00
Eagle	500.00
Bread Plate, figural, oak leaf, white satin finish	175.00
Candleholder, farm scene, ring handle	80.00
Candy Dish, oval, Bavarian women and horses	60.00
Chocolate Pot, dome shaped lid, ornate handle, floral and fruit dec	175.00
Cigarette Set, box and matching holder, musicians dec	150.00

Creamer, figural
Apple	170.00
Bear	300.00
Chick	325.00
Crow, black, tan beak, blue mark	200.00
Dachshund	140.00
Duck, marked "Deponiert"	90.00
Eagle, blue mark	275.00
Fish, open mouth, blue mark	160.00
Geranium	130.00
Iris, unmarked	290.00
Lamplighter	165.00
Rooster, multicolored	350.00
Seal	225.00
Water Buffalo, black, blue mark	95.00
Marmalade Jar, cov, figural, strawberry	175.00
Milk Pitcher, white, figural red parrot handle	525.00

Mustard, Lemon, cov, orig spoon	75.00
Pitcher, Coachman	850.00
Powder Dish, cov, figural, elk	85.00
Relish, figural, poinsettia, 7½" l	100.00

Toothpick
Colonial dining room scene, three handles, blue mark	125.00
Elk, figural, blue mark	125.00

Vase
3¼" h, 2⅜" d, brown and tan ground, multicolored musicians, hallmarked silver top, two handles	45.00
3½" h, 2½" d, Goose Girl, natural scene, peasant girl and geese, blue mark	60.00
Wall Pocket, figural, strawberry	225.00

Murex Shell
Cigarette Vase	90.00
Creamer	50.00
Match Holder, hanging, MOP, green and gold	60.00
Pitcher, water, blue mark	375.00
Toothpick, spikes, blue mark	58.00

Nursery Rhyme
Creamer, Little Jack Horner	55.00
Jug, 6½" h, Babes in Woods, two little girls talking to troll	300.00
Match Holder, girl and dog	200.00
Mug, Little Jack Horner, blue mark	125.00
Vase, 3¼", girl with candle, silver rim, green mark	50.00

Poppy
Biscuit Jar, red, blue mark	650.00
Bowl, 6"	85.00
Creamer, red	160.00
Demitasse Creamer and Sugar, red	150.00
Match Holder, wall, red	115.00
Mustard, spoon, Deponiert and green mark	100.00
Plate, 5¾"	50.00
Teapot	175.00

Sand Babies
Dresser Tray	150.00
Planter, 3" h, two handles	100.00
Sugar	75.00
Vase, 2¾" h, brown ground, ball feet	100.00
Wall Pocket	175.00

Snow Babies
Cereal Set, sledding	150.00
Creamer and Sugar	185.00
Plaque, 9" d, pierced	175.00
Plate, babies on ice	75.00
Trinket Box, cov, 3" l, 3" h, kidney shape	135.00

Sunbonnet Babies
Candlesticks, pr, washing	325.00
Cereal Set, bowl, 7" d underplate, washing and ironing	385.00
Creamer, babies cleaning, pinch spout, blue mark	275.00
Cup and Saucer, sewing	145.00

Dish

Diamond shape, sewing		155.00
Heart shape, farming		165.00

Hair Receiver, babies sweeping,
three high gold legs, blue mark . . 450.00
Milk Pitcher, babies cleaning, 5¼" h,
blue mark 375.00
Plate

7" d, cleaning	100.00
8" d, washing	100.00

Relish, 8" l, open handle, fishing . . . 175.00
Vase, 3¼" h, washing clothes 100.00
Tomato

Biscuit Jar	265.00
Box, cov, 4½" l, 3¾" h	50.00
Pitcher, water	275.00
Plate, 8¾" d	30.00
Tea Set, leaf base	185.00

ROSE TAPESTRY

Box, cov, 4" w, 1¾" h, pink and yellow
roses 285.00
Cake Plate, 10½" d, pink roses 200.00
Creamer, 3½" h, pinched spout, blue
mark 225.00
Cup and Saucer 525.00
Dresser Tray, blue mark 350.00
Fernery, flared, three color roses, pink,
white, and yellow, tiny gold handles,
orig insert, blue mark 245.00
Flower Pot, drainer, three color roses . 165.00
Hair Receiver, blue mark 250.00
Mustard Jar, spoon, pink and white
roses 225.00
Pitcher, 3½" h, gold trim 165.00
Plate, 6" d, three colored roses, gold rim 150.00
Powder Box, blue mark 250.00
Ring Tree, saucer base 425.00
Vase, 5½" h, four color roses, soft green
ground, apricot, yellow, pink, and
white roses, narrow base, bulbous
center, narrow top 300.00

TAPESTRY, MISCELLANEOUS

Box, cov, 2½" d, five sheep 185.00
Cake Plate, 10" d, handles, mountain
goats among aspens 140.00
Chocolate Pot, mountain goats, pastoral
scene 415.00
Clock, Christmas Cactus pattern,
dresser type, blue mark 400.00
Humidor, 6¾" h, scenic, gold trim,
mushroom finial 350.00
Pitcher, court lady and cavalier, formal
garden setting 425.00
Toothpick, woman in large hat, fur coat
and muff, four gold feet, gold handles 350.00
Trinket Box, 3½" d, Colonial couple,
multicolored dec 235.00
Vase, 4½" h, polar bear, gold handle . 250.00

ROYAL BONN

Bonn

History: In 1836 Franz Anton Mehlem founded a Rhineland factory that produced earthenware and porcelain, including household, decorative, technical, and sanitary items. In 1890 the name Royal was added to the mark. All items made after 1890 include the name "Royal Bonn." The firm reproduced Hochst figures between 1887 and 1903. These figures, produced in both porcelain and earthenware, were made from the original molds from the defunct Prince-Electoral Mayence Manufactory in Hochst. The factory was purchased by Villeroy and Boch in 1921 and closed in 1931.

Reference: Susan and Al Bagdade, *Warman's English & Continental Pottery & Porcelain, 2nd Edition,* Wallace–Homestead, 1991.

Vase, multicolored garden flowers, cream ground, enamel dots, lime green base, gold handles, 13¼" h, $75.00.

Bowl, 10" d, hp rose dec, heavy gold
trim 200.00
Cake Plate, 10¼" d, dark blue floral
transfer 20.00
Celery Tray, floral dec, gilt trim 80.00
Cheese Dish, cov, multicolored floral
dec, cream ground, gold trim 75.00
Cracker Jar, multicolored enamel floral
dec 100.00
Ewer, 12" h, pink, yellow, and blue flow-
ers, cream ground, gold trim 175.00

Jardiniere, 15" d, 12" h, hp, multicolored
flowers 365.00
Marmalade Jar, 5" h, floral dec, beige
ground, SP cov and bail handle ... 65.00
Plate, 9" d, floral dec, gilt tracery 60.00
Relish, 10" l, handle, three sections, hp,
florals, gold trim 125.00
Teapot, 4½" h, red, black, and light blue,
gilding, marked "1755" in cartouche
with crown 75.00
Urn, cov, 13" h, hp, multicolored flowers,
green and yellow ground, two gold
handles, artist sgd 100.00
Vase
8¼" h, 8" d, gold emb dec, portrait of
lady with wreath of roses in hair,
cream dress, brown and gold
shaded ground, artist sgd "G
Muller" 550.00
9" h, floral dec 375.00
10½" h, 5" d, gold emb dec, gold handles, portrait of lady in purple dress
and scarf, light brown hair, brown
and gold shaded ground, artist sgd
"G Muller" 550.00

ROYAL COPENHAGEN

History: Franz Mueller established a porcelain factory at Copenhagen in 1775. When bankruptcy threatened in 1779, the Danish king acquired ownership, appointing Mueller manager and adopting the name "Royal Copenhagen." The crown sold its interest in 1867; the company remains privately owned today.

Blue Fluted, Royal Copenhagen's most famous pattern, was created in 1780. It is of Chinese origin and comes in three styles: smooth edge, closed lace edge, and perforated lace edge (full lace). Many other factories copied it. Flora Danica, named for a famous botanical work, was introduced in 1789 and remained exclusive to Royal Copenhagen. Botanical illustrations were done free hand; all edges and perforations were cut by hand.

Royal Copenhagen porcelain is marked with three wavy lines (which signify ancient waterways) and a crown (added in 1889). Stoneware does not have the crown mark.

Reference: Susan and Al Bagdade, *Warman's*

English & Continental Pottery & Porcelain, 2nd Edition, Wallace–Homestead, 1991.

Additional Listings: Limited Edition Collectors' Plates.

Figure, couple dressed in period clothes, gray and cream, dated 1925, marked "R. C. Denmark," 12" h, $750.00.

Butter Pat, Symphony pattern, set of 6 20.00
Candle Bobeches, 3½" d, Full Lace pattern, blue, pr 65.00
Candlesticks, 7" h, white and gilt, circular columns molded with foliate
swags suspended from tied ribbons
enriched in gilding, lower and upper
parts with shallow grooves, bases
with stylized foliage, matched set of
four 1,000.00
Cup and Saucer, Half Lace pattern,
blue, fluted 25.00
Dinnerware, Flora Danica pattern, pink
and green, botanical specimen, gilt
dentil rim, underglaze blue triple wave
mark, numbered, printed mark, green
painter's mark, black botanical inscription
Chocolate Cup and Saucer, 5½" d,
gilt highlighted scalloped reticulated border, molded beading, gilt
roundels, buds, and leaves on rim,
inscribed numbers, set of 8 ..... 3,575.00
Compote, 6" d, pink and gold molded
beadwork border, pr 1,250.00
Creamer and Sugar, branch handles 900.00
Fish Plates, 10⅛" d, various fish species in aquatic setting, green and
gold molded beadwork border, set
of 12 .... 4,500.00
Fruit Bowl, 5⅝" d, set of 6 .... 1,760.00
Pickle Dish, 6" l, shaped, everted rect
handle 300.00
Plate, set of 12
5⅝" d, bread and butter 2,200.00
7⅝" d, salad 3,575.00
10⅛" d, dinner 4,125.00

Platter

14" d, round	825.00
16⅛" l, oval	1,125.00
17¼" l, oval	1,650.00
Salad Bowl, 9½" d	900.00
Soup Plate, 8¾" d, set of 6	2,000.00

Vegetable Dish, cov, 9½" l, twig handles with flowerhead terminals, molded rim, inscribed artist's ciphers, black inscription 1,550.00

Wine Cooler, 6½" h, oval, twig handles with flowerhead terminals, inscribed artist's ciphers 1,775.00

Figure

5½" h, cat, sitting, gray and white, green eyes	125.00
7¼" h, boy with teddy bear	200.00
8½" h, fawn, perched on half columns, holding pipes, rabbit at base, No. 433	125.00
11" h, polar bear, hunting	250.00

Inkwell, 6" w, 8½" l, Blue Fluted pattern, matching undertray 125.00

Jar, 16½" h, flat sided circular shape, rocky seascape dec, bronze cov, oval bronze base, knop feet 450.00

Pitcher, 4" h, cobalt blue ground, floral dec 50.00

Plate, 8" d, hp, fruit center 35.00

Tureen, cov, 18" l, Blue Fluted pattern, c1897 .... 275.00

Vase, 6" h, bulbous, celadon green, molded leaves, applied frog, 19th C 200.00

ROYAL CROWN DERBY

History: Derby Crown Porcelain Co., established in 1875 in Derby, England, had no connection with earlier Derby factories which operated in the late 18th and early 19th centuries. In 1890 the company was appointed "Manufacturers of Porcelain to Her Majesty" (Queen Victoria) and from that date has been known as "Royal Crown Derby."

Derby porcelains from 1878 to 1890 carry only the standard crown printed mark. After 1891 the mark carries the "Royal Crown Derby" wording. In the 20th century "Made in England" and "English Bone China" were added to the mark.

A majority of these porcelains, both tableware and figures, were hand decorated. A variety of printing processes were used for additional adornment. Today, Royal Crown Derby is a part of Royal Doulton Tableware, Ltd.

References: Susan and Al Bagdade, *Warman's English & Continental Pottery & Porcelain, 2nd Edition,* Wallace–Homestead, 1991; John Twitchett and Betty Bailey, *Royal Crown Derby,* Antique Collectors' Club, 1988.

Vase, cobalt blue, dark red, and gold Oriental design, Pattern #6299, c1905, 10" h, $250.00.

Cake Basket, 12" h, rect, meandering roses, polychrome and gilt, ftd, marked, c1830 .... 150.00

Creamer, 1⅛" h, miniature, cobalt blue, orange, and white floral dec, marked 110.00

Cup and Saucer, Imari pattern, iron red, cobalt blue, burnished gilt, set of 22 1,200.00

Dinner Set, Japanese pattern, Imari palette, marked, c1870, 30 pcs 1,400.00

Dish, 9" d, scattered rose sprays, floral border, late 18th C 150.00

Entree Dish, cov, lozenge form, Imari pattern, iron red, cobalt blue, burnished gilt, set of 3 .... 1,500.00

Ewer, 7½" h, cobalt blue, profuse gold gilt dec and floral, sgd 200.00

Plate

8½" d, #2451 pattern	60.00
10¼" d, Imari pattern, iron red, cobalt blue, burnished gilt, set of 48	9,500.00

Sauce Dish, pr, Imari pattern, iron red, cobalt blue, burnished gilt, matching stand 1,200.00

Soup Plate, 10" d, Imari pattern, iron red, cobalt blue, burnished gilt, set of 16 .... 3,250.00

Toothpick Holder, 3½" h, green, hp floral reserve 135.00

Urn

7" h, apple green, scenic reserve, figures, landscape, handles terminat-

ing at masks, sq pedestal base,
c1880 .... **300.00**
11½" h, cobalt blue, red, and gold
floral pattern, painted red crown
mark **400.00**
Vase
4¼" h, pink, gold floral, two gold handles **200.00**
7" h, dark red and gold, two handles,
c1884 .... **185.00**
13" h, pr, raised gold florals and
scrolls, blue and red ground, double gold handles, ftd, marked
"Royal Crown Derby" **410.00**

ROYAL DOULTON FLAMBE

ROYAL DOULTON

History: Doulton pottery began in 1815 under the direction of John Doulton at the Doulton & Watts pottery in Lambeth, England. Early output was limited to salt-glazed industrial stoneware. John Watts retired in 1854. The firm became Doulton and Company, and production was expanded to include hand decorated stoneware such as figurines, vases, dinnerware, and flasks. In 1872 the firm began marking their ware "Royal Doulton."

In 1878, John's son, Sir Henry Doulton, purchased Pinder Bourne & Co. in Burslem and the companies became Doulton & Co., Ltd. in 1882. Decorated porcelain was added to Doulton's earthenware production in 1884. The Royal Doulton mark was used on both wares.

Most Doulton figurines were produced at the Burslem plants from 1890 until 1978, when they were discontinued. A new line of Doulton figurines was introduced in 1979.

Beginning in 1913, an "HN" number was assigned to each new Doulton figurine design. The "HN" numbers refers to Harry Nixon, a Doulton artist. "HN" numbers were chronological until 1940, after which blocks of numbers were assigned to each modeler. From 1928 until 1954, a small number appeared to the right of the crown mark; this number added to 1927 gives the year of manufacture of the figurines.

Dickens ware, in earthenware and porcelain, was introduced in 1908. The ware was decorated with characters from Dickens' novels. The line was withdrawn in the 1940s, except for plates which continued until 1974.

Character jugs, a 20th century revival of early Toby models, were designed by Charles J. Noke

for Doulton in the 1930s. They come in 4 major sizes and feature fictional characters from Dickens, Shakespeare and other English and American novelists, as well as historical heroes.

Doulton's Rouge Flambee (also Veined Sung) is a highly glazed, strong colored ware noted most for the fine modeling and exquisite colorings, especially in the animal items. The process used to produce the vibrant colors in this ware is a Doulton secret.

Production of stoneware at Lambeth ceased in 1956; production of porcelain continues today at Burslem.

References: Susan and Al Bagdade, *Warman's English & Continental Pottery & Porcelain, 2nd Edition,* Wallace—Homestead, 1991; Jean Dale, *The Charlton Standard Catalogue of Royal Doulton Figurines, Second Edition,* The Charlton Press, 1991; Jean Dale, *The Charlton Standard Catalogue of Royal Doulton Jugs, First Edition,* The Charlton Press, 1991; Jocelyn Lukins, *Collecting Royal Doulton Character & Toby Jugs,* Venta Books, 1985; Kevin Pearson, *The Character Jug Collectors Handbook, 5th Edition,* Kevin Francis Publishing Ltd, 1991; Kevin Pearson, *The Doulton Figure Collectors Handbook, 3rd Edition,* Kevin Francis Publishing Ltd, 1991; Ruth M. Pollard, *The Official Price Guide To Royal Doulton, Sixth Edition,* House of Collectibles, 1988; Princess and Barry Weiss, *The Original Price Guide to Royal Doulton Discontinued Character Jugs, Sixth Edition,* Harmony Books, 1987.

Periodicals: *Collecting Doulton,* BBR Publishing, 2, Strattford Avenue, Elsecar, Barnsley, S. Yorkshire, S74 8AA, England; *Jug Collector,* P.O. Box 91748, Long Beach, CA 90809.

Collectors' Club: Royal Doulton International Collectors Club, P.O. Box 1815, Somerset, NJ 08873.

Animal Mold
Mallard, HN 807 .... **45.00**
Setter with Pheasant, HN 2529, sgd
"JB" **325.00**
Character Jug, large
Barleycorne **140.00**
Cardinal **140.00**
Cook and Cheshire Cat **85.00**
Guy Fawkes, Canadian **165.00**
Jarge **350.00**
Peel **140.00**
Poacher, D6781 .... **75.00**
Romeo **75.00**
Sam Weller **140.00**
Veteran Motorist **120.00**
Yachtsman, D6820 .... **75.00**
Character Jug, miniature
Apothecary **50.00**
'Arry **75.00**
Blacksmith **50.00**
Gone Away **60.00**
Night Watchman **50.00**

Pickwick	60.00
Toby Philpots	50.00
Tony Weller	50.00
Walrus and Carpenter	60.00

Character Jug, small

Auld Mac	50.00
Blacksmith	50.00
Jarge	160.00
Mephistopheles	750.00
Old King Cole	125.00
Paddy	75.00
Pearly King	30.00
Pearly Queen	30.00
Punch and Judy	400.00
Sairey Gump	60.00
Toby Philpots	75.00
Turpin, mask up	75.00

Child's Feeding Dish, boy pushing wheelbarrow at beach, c1908 ..... 60.00

Coaching Days Series

Biscuit Jar, 6½" d, 5½" h, SP cov, rim and handle 225.00

Pitcher, 5½" h 85.00

Plate

6¾" d	60.00
7¾" d	65.00
8" d, scalloped edge	80.00

Dickens Ware

Bowl, 7¾" d, 3⅞" h, three characters, marked 145.00

Demitasse Cup and Saucer, Mr Pickwick on 2⅛" h cup, Sam Weller on 4" d saucer 55.00

Pitcher, pottery, sq shape

6⅝" h, 3¼" d, Trotty Veck	115.00
7⅜" h, 3½" d, Alfred Jingle	125.00

Sandwich Tray, 5⅝" w, 11" l, rect shape, Bill Sykes 85.00

Sauce Dish, Fat Boy, 5¼" d 45.00

Vase, 7⅝" h, 5" d, Alfred Jingle, sq flattened shape, two handles 135.00

Figure

Balloon Man, HN 1954	130.00
Biddy Penny Farthing, HN 1843	130.00
Bridget, HN 2070	210.00
Granny's Heritage, HN 2031	300.00
Joker	112.00
Partners	150.00
Old Balloon Seller, HN 1315	130.00
Owd William, HN 2042	200.00
Sairey Gump, HN 1896	250.00
Tiptoe	112.00
Tumbling	112.00

Flambe Ware

Animal Mold, 12½" l, fish	800.00

Bowl, 9¾" d, 3" h, Oriental style, handled 225.00

Jardiniere, blue and white, woman playing guitar scene 210.00

Plate, 6" d, landscape scene 45.00

Hannah B Barlow Ware

Jardiniere, 7¾" h, incised frieze of

Flask, stoneware, Mr. & Mrs. Candle, Miss Pretty Maid, imp marks, 5⅝" h, $225.00.

coach pulled by team of horses, grazing sheep and cattle, stylized leaf borders, imp mark, sgd, dated 1883 .... 1,870.00

Pitcher

6½" h, incised dog standing in tall grass, stippled ground, imp mark, sgd, c1890 .... 1,100.00

9¼" h, incised cat frieze, light blue enamel, stippled ground, stylized leaf frame, imp mark, sgd, c1895 2,860.00

9" h, shaped panels, incised hounds and pate–sur–pate quail on stippled ground, imp mark, sgd "Hannah B Barlow" and "Florence E Barlow," c1895 ... 2,090.00

9½" h, bottle shape, incised running goats, dog tied to base of handle, stiff leaf borders, imp mark, sgd, dated 1876 .... 1,540.00

Tankard, 9½" h, pewter hinged lid, incised frieze of herons among reeds, blue slip enamel, imp mark, sgd, c1875, int. rim chip 1,430.00

Teapot, cov, 5½" h, formed spout, incised frieze of goats, blue dec stiff leaf and floret border, imp mark, sgd, dated 1880 .... 1,540.00

Tobacco Jar, 8" h, plated rim, handle, and cov, incised frieze of cattle, goats, and donkeys, imp mark, sgd, dated 1880, worn plating 990.00

Vase

11" h, incised frieze of sheep with stippled clouds, flower, and foliage borders, imp Lambeth mark, sgd "Hannah B Barlow" and "Florence C Roberts," c1895 .. 990.00

13⅞" h, slender, incised frieze of cattle and horses, dog resting

nearby, scrolled slip borders, imp
mark, sgd, c1905 . . . . **1,100.00**

14½" h, bulbous, incised dec of
young girl surrounded by goats,
donkeys, cattle, and geese, blue
enamel leaf borders, imp mark,
sgd, dated 1880 . . . . **3,740.00**

15¼" h, incised frieze, scene of
sheep grazing, relief molded foliage border, imp mark, sgd
"Hannah B Barlow" and "Flor-
ence C Roberts," c1905 . . . . . . **3,520.00**

Isaac Walton Ware, cuspidor, 7" h, polychrome dec, transfer printed, fisherman on ext., verses on int. lip,
printed mark **315.00**

Silicon Ware, candlesticks, pr, tan and
brown **145.00**

Stoneware

Tazza, 8" h, 8¾" d, two parts, incised
blue leaf designs, green to brown
ground, imp Lambeth marks, sgd
"Edith D Lupton," dated 1876, mi-
nor chip, firing line to dish **935.00**

Umbrella Stand, 23½" h, enamel dec,
applied floral medallions within diamond formed panels, framed by
button motifs, imp mark, c1910,
glaze crazing **500.00**

Vase

7¾" h, Arts and Crafts style, blue,
green, and pink, imp marks,
c1910, rim roughage, chips, pr . **165.00**

12¾" h, Pilgrim, multicolored body,
incised flowers and seed pods,
serpent handles, imp Lambeth
marks, sgd "Frank A Butler,"
c1885, firing line to base rim . . **1,210.00**

24½" h, Slater's Patent, chine–gilt
style, allover floral dec, enamel
and gilt dec, imp marks, base rim
chips, c1885 . . . . **165.00**

ROYAL DUX

History: Royal Dux porcelain was made in Dux,
Bohemia (Czechoslovakia) by E. Eichler at the
Duxer Porzellan-Manufaktur, established in 1860.
Many items were exported to the United States.
By the turn of the century Royal Dux figurines,
vases, and accessories were captivating consum-
ers, especially Art Nouveau designs.

A raised triangle with an acorn and the letter
"E" plus Dux, Bohemia was used as a mark between 1900 and 1914.

Reference: Susan and Al Bagdade, *Warman's
English & Continental Pottery & Porcelain, 2nd
Edition,* Wallace–Homestead, 1991.

**Vase, beige, green, and red matte fin-
ish, cream ground, acorn and pink triangle mark, 14" h, $385.00.**

Bust, 6½" h, Art Deco style woman, gold
wide brimmed hat, cobalt blue scarf,
sgd "E Strobach" **225.00**

Centerpiece

7¾" h, 4¼" d, 11" l, Art Deco, off
white, two nudes kneeling by center vase, cobalt blue and gold trim,
raised pink triangle, marked "Royal
Dux Bohemia" **475.00**

11½" h, 11" d, beige, maiden over-
looking pool **525.00**

Figure

7¾" h, woman, getting dressed,
#3396, sgd "E Strobach" **125.00**

9" h, Victorian Couple, lady in gold
brown dress, wrap around pink
sash, holding flower, man in gold
brown toga with sash holding palette and ewer, brown sandals, pink
triangle mark, minor chips **350.00**

10" h, Art Deco lady, soft blue–green
dress, tam, and gloves, gold ac-
cents, sgd "Strobach" **275.00**

14" h, young Greek athlete standing
on backs of two horses **500.00**

14¾" h, 4½" d, shepherdess, rose
toga, beige sheepskin robe, green
turban, two white and tan goats on
green grass, semi–gloss finish,
marked "Royal Dux Bohemia" . . . **575.00**

18" h, fisherman, carrying net, over
the knee boots and hat, green and
brown, pink triangle mark **635.00**

21" h, harvester and wife, cobalt blue

and white, gold trim, both holding
  sheath of wheat, man with sickle,
  pink triangle mark, paper label, pr   **725.00**
Flower Bowl, 9" h, 9½" d, kneeling girl
  pouring water out of jug, water lily
  bowl, pink dress, pink triangle and
  acorn mark **650.00**
Jardiniere, 10¼" h, figural boy and girl,
  hanging drapery from bowl, poly-
  chrome matte finish, repairs **250.00**
Mantle Set, 12½" d double handled
  bowl, two 12½" h vases, applied pink
  roses, yellow and green ground . . .   **145.00**
Tray, figural, irid blue, center maiden
  holding basket on her back **300.00**
Vase
  9" h, hourglass shape, pink and green
    florals **110.00**
  15½" h, classical maiden climbing
    tree trunk **450.00**

ROYAL FLEMISH

History: Royal Flemish was produced by the
Mount Washington Glass Co., New Bedford, Mas-
sachusetts. The process was patented by Albert
Steffin in 1894.

Royal Flemish has heavy raised gold enamel
lines on frosted transparent glass that separates
areas into sections, often colored in russet tones.
It gives the appearance of stained glass windows
with elaborate floral or coin medallions in the design.

Advisors: Clarence and Betty Maier.

**Vase, lower panels of alternating pale
blue and tan, dark blue circles on cer-
ise field, central light blue crosses,
raised gold separation lines, chrysanthemum blossoms, and foliage, 11½" h,
$4,000.00.**

Biscuit Jar, 7" h, multicolored wild roses,
  frosted ground, marked Pairpoint lid   **6,000.00**
Ewer, 9" h, bulbous, raised gold stylized
  flowers and swirl medallions, various
  shield dec on shoulder, gold rope
  handle **4,510.00**
Jar, cov, 9½" h, olive green and gold
  sections, Roman motif medallions,
  gold scrolls and leaves, fancy pointed
  swirled finial, unsigned **2,250.00**
Vase
  7½" h, squatty, clear, frosted, pansy
    dec, gold dec collar **1,950.00**
  10¼" h, black cross on one side,
    winged creatures on other, gold
    and tan ground **6,000.00**
  12" h, bulbous, stick, ornate raised
    gold perched peacock with floral
    branches and scrolls, base aper-
    ture **3,025.00**
  13" h, ornate gold dec, cupids fighting
    griffins, pastel green, blue, and yel-
    low ground, raised gold sections,
    double handles **4,290.00**

GERMANY

RW

RUDOLSTADT

ROYAL RUDOLSTADT

History: Johann Fredrich von Schwarzburg–
Rudolstadt was the patron of a faience factory
located in Rudolstadt, Thuringen, Germany, from
1720 to c1790. The pottery's mark was a hayfork
and later crossed two–prong hayforks in imitation
of the Meissen mark.

In 1854 Ernst Bohne established a factory in
Rudolstadt. His pieces are marked "EB."

The "Royal Rudolstadt" designation originated
with wares imported by Lewis Straus and Sons
(later Nathan Straus and Sons) of New York from
the New York and Rudolstadt Pottery between
1887 and 1918. The factory's mark was a diamond
enclosing the initials "RW" and which was surmounted by a crown. The factory manufactured
several of the Rose O'Neill (Kewpie) items.

Reference: Susan and Al Bagdade, *Warman's
English & Continental Pottery & Porcelain*, 2nd
Edition, Wallace–Homestead, 1991.

Cake Plate, 12" d, pink, white roses,
  gold handles and trim **75.00**
Candlesticks, pr, 7" h, ivory, emb acan-

ing, elaborate gold handles, flower
form opening, cobalt ground **155.00**

ROYAL VIENNA

History: Production of hard paste procelain in
Vienna began in 1720 with Claude Innocentius du
Paquier, a runaway employee of the Meissen factory. In 1744 Empress Maria Theresa brought the
factory under royal patronage; subsequently the
ware became known as Royal Vienna. The firm
went through many administrative changes until it
closed in 1864. The quality of its workmanship
always was maintained.

Many other Austrian and German firms copied
the Royal Vienna products, including the use of
the "Beehive" mark. Many of the pieces on today's
market are from these firms.

Reference: Susan and Al Bagdade, *Warman's
English & Continental Pottery & Porcelain, 2nd
Edition,* Wallace–Homestead, 1991.

**Vase, cream ground, floral dec, gold
handle, relief vine dec, marked "RW"
in diamond within crown, 11⅝″ h,
$175.00.**

**Plate, hp, gilded, maroon and yellow
border, raised enamel dec, 9¼″ d,
$325.00.**

thus leaves, petal shape cups, crown
  mark on base **50.00**
Celery Dish, 13″ d, hp yellow rose, gold
  trim, handled, artist sgd **80.00**
Child's Tea Set, teapot, creamer and
  sugar with lid, four cups, saucers, and
  plates **275.00**
Dresser Set, 6 pcs, tray, hatpin holder,
  hair receiver, ring tree, cov jar, rose
  dec **250.00**
Ewer, 10″, ivory, floral dec, gold handle
  and trim **100.00**
Figure, 5½″ h, beggar girl holding tam-
  bourine, white, c1905 . . . . **100.00**
Hair Receiver, 4¼″ d, yellow roses,
  green leaves, shaded yellow ground,
  gold trim **75.00**
Hatpin Holder, lavender and roses . . . **25.00**
Inkwell, 6 x 3½″, cream, multicolored
  flowers, attached saucer, sgd **60.00**
Nut Set, master bowl, six small bowls,
  white and green roses, fluted, ftd, B
  under crown mark **250.00**
Pin Tray, 5″ l, clover dec **25.00**
Pitcher
  8″ h, cream, gray and gold birds, coral
    and pink leaves, raised mark **75.00**
  11″ h, bulbous, floral dec, gold handle **125.00**
Plate, 8½″ d, pink, yellow, and white
  roses, gold pie crust molded rim . . . **30.00**
Relish Dish, 8¾″ d, hp floral dec **25.00**
Teapot, cov, 5½″ h, ivory, pink, lavender,
  and green hp floral dec **95.00**
Urn, cov, 10″ h, mythological scene,
  •Hector and Andro crowning maiden,
  gold handled, cobalt blue ground, includes stand, artist sgd **125.00**
Vase
  4″ h, floral dec, elephant handles . . **90.00**
  6½″ h, enameled florals, gold bead-

Charger, 13⅜″ d, octagonal, gilding,
  center scene of maiden and companion being crowned, paneled ground,
  blue shield mark, c1900 . . . . **660.00**
Chocolate Pot, bust of lady, burgundy
  and gold, beehive mark **185.00**
Desk Set, 3 pcs, 6″ d tapered inkwell
  with high relief hinged cover and double handles, 5″ d tapered hinged cov
  stamp box, 9″ h candle stand with
  metal holder, panels of painted figures and gold outdoor scenes on
  each, ftd metal bases **600.00**
Demitasse Cup and Saucer, portrait,

lady and dog, scalloped green border
with gold design, blue beehive mark   **75.00**
Ewer, 6¼" h, maiden and cupid in reverse, gold, maroon, and dark green,
sgd "Kauffmann," beehive mark . . .   **195.00**
Fernery, 6½" h, bathing nudes dec,
elaborate gold daffodils, leaves, and
raised scrolls, ruby luster ground, ftd,
titled Nixen Geschichten, artist sgd
"Wagner"   **2,200.00**
Figure, 7" h, young boy, period dress,
enameled colors, imp beehive mark   **285.00**
Jug, 8½" h, portrait, mother and small
child, mask shape lip, sgd "LCF,"
c1920 . . . .   **275.00**
Luncheon Set, 31 pcs, eleven 7½" d
plates, nine cups, ten saucers, and
10" d double handled cake plate, ladies and cupids in garden settings,
cobalt rims with gold, artist sgd **525.00**
Milk Jug, cov, 8" h, floral spray dec . . .   **300.00**
Plaque, 12" d, portrait, woman with
child, gilt tracery, raised gold and jewels, pink border, artist sgd, beehive
and "Flora" mark **425.00**
Plate
9½" d, portrait, Reflexion, downcast
gaze, brown flowing curls, claret
cov drapery, gilt band, luster pink
border with reserves of shaped
claret panels, gilded, late 19th C .   **900.00**
10½" d
Flower Seller, two women with bas-
kets of flowers, artist sgd **290.00**
On The Hay, two peasant women
with sheep, artist sgd **280.00**
Tray, 8¼ x 12", pale green, hp violet
dec, gold trim **175.00**
Urn
5¼" h, crimson and green, gold bordered cartouche on front, handles,
beehive mark **265.00**
13" h, cov, man and woman in classic
garden setting, cupid on reverse,
multicolored, sgd "Wagner" **550.00**
13¼" h, cov, two maidens and six
cupids dec, powder blue and gold
field, handled **660.00**
Vase
3½" h, flattened teardrop form, shepherdess, sheep, and goat in
woods, gold glazed rim and foot   **290.00**
7" h, portrait, Terra Sita, bottle shape,
gold, brown, and blue, sgd "Wag-
ner," beehive mark **500.00**

ROYAL WORCESTER

History: In 1751 the Worcester Porcelain Company, led by Dr. John Wall and William Davis, acquired the Bristol pottery of Benjamin Lund and

moved it to Worcester. The first wares were
painted blue under the glaze, followed closely by
painting on the glaze in enamel colors. Among the
most famous 18th century decorators were James
Giles and Jefferys Hamet O'Neale. Transfer–print
decoration was developed by the 1760s.

A series of partnerships took over upon Davis's
death in 1783: Flight (1783–93), Flight & Barr
(1793–1807), Barr, Flight & Barr (1807–13), and
Flight, Barr & Barr (1813–40). In 1840 the factory
was moved to Chamberlain & Co. in Diglis. Decorative wares were discontinued. In 1852 W. H.
Kerr and R. W. Binns formed a new company and
revived the ornamental wares.

In 1862 the firm became the Royal Worcester
Porcelain Co. Among the key modelers of the late
19th century were James Hadley and his three
sons and George Owen, expert at pierced clay
pieces. Royal Worcester absorbed the Grainger
factory in 1889 and the James Hadley factory in
1905. Modern designers include Dorothy Boughty
and Doris Lindner.

References: Susan and Al Bagdade, *Warman's
English & Continental Pottery & Porcelain, 2nd
Edition,* Wallace–Homestead, 1991; David, John,
and Henry Sandon, *The Sandon Guide To Royal
Worcester Figures, 1900–1970,* The Alderman
Press, 1987.

Museum: Charles William Dyson Perrins Museum, Worcester, England.

Basket, 5¾" h, caneweave base,
twisted reed handle, tan, gold highlights, purple mark, Reg #26402/
1080, c1891 . . . .   **450.00**
Biscuit Jar, 7" h, 5¾" d, cobalt blue
leaves, white bamboo ground, match-
ing lid **355.00**
Bone Dish, 5¾" l, cream, blue floral dec   **55.00**
Bowl
4½" d, cov, multicolored florals, ivory
ground, dated 1862 . . . .   **75.00**
7¾" l, boat shape, pedestal base,
gold handles, floral dec, gilt trim,
date mark 1918 . . . .   **385.00**
8½" w, sq, reticulated basketweave,
burnt orange, yellow, rose, olive
green, blue florals, and leaves, gilt
int. and border **775.00**
9" d, beige, emb basketweave, large
pink and green grape leaves, gold
trim, c1896 . . . .   **350.00**
Candle Snuffer, white, pink plume . . .   **60.00**
Candlesticks, pr, 11⅜" h, 3¾" d, figural,
classic lady wears gold laurel wreath,
semi–gloss, cream, gold trim, 1862,
pr **900.00**
Candy Dish, 10" h, majolica glazed par-
ian ware, girl, turquoise coat, pink
skirt, holding two baskets, pedestal
base, pale pink int., turquoise ext. . .   **995.00**
Cologne, 3¾" h, pansies, lavender, rust,

and pale yellow, green leaves, SP
cap, sgd, 1887 . . . . 220.00
Creamer, 2⅞" h, wren in leaves, twig
handle, sgd "Powell" 35.00
Cup and Saucer, polychrome Imari dec,
matching 8¾" d plate, imp "FBB" with
crown 115.00
Demitasse Cup and Saucer, blue and
white, crescent mark 95.00
Dish, 5½" l, shell, blue and white, bird
on rockwork, flowering plants and insects, foliage border, c1755 . . . . . . 350.00
Ewer
  6" h, floral sprays, gold coiled handle,
  c1889 . . . . 140.00
  6½" h, flowers, gold trim, horn handle,
  white ground 180.00
Figure
  6⅞" h, John Bull, beige, satin finish,
  marked, 1891 . . . . 400.00
  7½" h, 6½" w, boy and girl getting
  water from cistern, Hadley, dated
  1882 . . . . 350.00
  15¾" h, The Bather Surprised, parian,
  ivory ground figure, gilt dec, draped
  cloth, tree trunk, oval base, printed
  mark, small chips 615.00
Jug, 10" h, mask spout, floral dec, gold
trim 375.00
Lamp, figural, 13" Elizabethan era
woman playing lute, 18" tree base,
supports 14" brass arm that holds two
Clarke Cricklites, orig inserts and
shades, dated 1898, marked "Clarke
and Worcester" 2,475.00
Pitcher
  8" h, fluted top, gold handle, florals,
  artist sgd, 1889 . . . . 200.00
  8½" h, rose and yellow Oriental florals, gold trim, cream satin ground,
  horn handle, purple mark 66.00
Plate, 9½" d, man fishing in pond, trees,
and castled mountain top scene . . . 250.00
Rose Jar, 4⅜" h, cov, pink, gold outline,
purple mark 125.00

**Urn, ivory, reticulated, brown scroll
feet, 4½" h, $295.00.**

Serving Dish, 11" l, oval, Imari dec, gilt . . . 175.00
Spill Vase, 5¼", emb full figures of girls,
sunflowers and cattails, 1908, pr . . . 450.00
Sugar Bowl, 5¼" h, porcelain, swirled
ribs, purple and green enameled foliage with gilt, imp "BFB" with crown . . 75.00
Tankard, 10" h, gold mask face under
spout, gold handle, floral dec 350.00
Teapot, 5" h, pastel floral sprays, gold
leaves, purple mark 265.00
Urn, 12" h, hp, bird, white ground, reticulated handle and top 965.00
Vase
  6½" h, bud, reticulated handles, sgd
  "#982" 225.00
  7⅛" h, hexagonal, Sabrina Ware,
  golden green trees dec, blue
  ground, marked, c1910 . . . . 150.00
  7½" h, pierced, simulate bamboo,
  ivory body, gilt and enamel trim,
  molded crane and prunus dec,
  scalloped base rim, printed and imp
  marks, c1872, pr 935.00
  10" h, multicolored floral dec, sgd
  "#1053" 325.00
  10¼" h, robin's egg, blue, raised gilt
  daisies, slender ivory neck, mask
  handles, marked, c1902 . . . . 375.00
  15¼" h, sheep in mountainous landscape, gilt foliage, handles terminating in lotus flowers, pierced cov,
  crown finial, green mark, early 20th
  C 900.00

ROYCROFT

History: Elbert Hubbard founded the Roycrofters in East Aurora, New York, at the turn of the
century. Considered a genius in his day, he was
an author, lecturer, manufacturer, salesman, and
philosopher.

Hubbard established a campus which included
a printing plant where he published *The Philistine*,
The Fra, and *The Roycrofter*. His most famous
book was *A Message to Garcia*, published in
1899. His "community" also included a furniture
manufacturing plant, a metal shop, and a leather
shop.

References: Nancy Hubbard Brady, *The Book
of The Roycrofters*, House of Hubbard, 1977;
Nancy Hubbard Brady, *Roycroft Handmade Fur-*

niture, House of Hubbard, 1973; Charles F. Hamilton, *Roycroft Collectibles*, A. S. Barnes & Company, Inc., 1980; Kevin McConnell, *Roycroft Art Metal*, Schiffer Publishing, 1990; Paul McKenna, *A New Pricing Guide For Materials Produced by The Roycroft Printing Shop*, Tona Graphics, 2nd edition, 1982.

Additional Listing: Arts and Crafts Movement and Copper.

Chest of drawers, three drawers, 44″ w, 20″ d, 47¼″ h, $950.00.

Book, *Sesame and Lilies,* John Ruskin, Roycroft Publications, 1897	175.00
Bookends, pr	
6″ h, leather, tooled design, orb mark on back	150.00
10″ h, copper, fleur–de–lis design, large orb mark	120.00
Candlesticks, pr, 20½″ h, hammered copper, twisted standard, two applied candleholders, orb mark	300.00
Furniture	
Bench	
Ali Baba, oak slab seat, some exposed bark underneath, plank ends, long center stretcher, exposed keyed tenons, sgd orb and carved initials "WFG," 42″ l, 15″ d, 17″ h, c1910, weathered, nicks	1,650.00
Piano, No. 71, flat top, flat medial stretcher, four tapered legs, recent dark finish, branded orb mark, 36″ w, 16″ d, 21″ h	2,090.00
Desk, oak, four drawers on left, 60″ l, 30″ d, 30″ h	700.00
Hall Chair, oak, wood seat, carved orb mark, 46″ h	475.00
Library Table, oak, two drawers, 52″ l, 33″ d, 30″ h	750.00
Magazine Pedestal, No. 080, 1906, overhanging sq top, canted sides, keyed tenons, five shelves, carved	

oak leaf design, maker's mark on sides, minor damage, 18″ w, 64″ h	3,520.00
Inkwell, 2½″ h, No. 3574–2, Sheffield plate, hammered finish	125.00
Letter Opener, hammered copper	40.00
Platter, 22″ l, oval, hammered copper, handles	175.00
Vase	
5″ h, No. 3573–2, Sheffield plate, hammered finish	100.00
15½″ h, No. 241, flared rim, long neck, squatty base, orb mark, pitted finish, c1910	325.00
19″ h, 8″ d, American Beauty, hammered copper, elongated cylindrical neck, rolled rim, flaring to two part riveted bulbous base, stamp on base	880.00
Wall Sconces, pr, 8¾″ h, rect, copper, No. 402, marked	175.00

RUBENA GLASS

History: Rubena crystal is a transparent blown glass which shades from clear to red. It also is found as the background for frosted and overshot glass. It was made in the late 1800s by several glass companies, including Northwood and Hobbs, Brockunier & Co. of Wheeling, West Virginia.

Rubena was used for several patterns of pattern glass including Royal Ivy and Royal Oak.

Vase, bud, enameled floral dec, 6″ h, $45.00.

Bowl, 4½″ d, Daisy and Scroll	60.00
Celery Vase, threaded, Northwood	75.00
Compote, 9″ d, 14″ h, rubena overshot bowl, white metal bronze finished figural standard	150.00
Creamer, Medallion Sprig, applied clear handle	160.00
Decanter, 9″ h, bulbous base, narrow neck, applied clear handle	140.00

Marmalade Jar, cov, enamel dec, sgd "Moser"	315.00
Perfume, 3¼" h, SP top rim, cranberry cut stopper	125.00
Pickle Castor, vertical optic insert, fancy fretwork on ftd Pairpoint SP frame	225.00
Sugar, cov, Royal Ivy, frosted	135.00
Sugar Shaker, 5½" h, 2⅝" d, Coin Spot, tapered body	310.00
Tumbler, Royal Ivy, 3¾" h	48.00
Vase	
6" h, bud, bank of cut diamonds, enameled floral dec	60.00
9½" h, six crimp gold trim top, chrysanthemum dec, gold foliage, pr	265.00
Water Set, Hobnail, opalescent, pitcher with applied clear handle, six matching tumblers	750.00

RUBENA VERDE GLASS

History: Rubena Verde, a transparent glass that shades from red in the upper section to yellow-green in the lower, was made by Hobbs, Brockunier & Co., Wheeling, West Virginia, in the late 1880s. It often is found in the inverted thumbprint (IVT) pattern, termed "Polka Dot" by Hobbs.

Bride's Basket, 4½" d, 6½" h, $90.00.

Bowl, 9" d, Honeycomb, ftd, rolled rim	100.00
Butter Dish, cov, Daisy and Button base, Thumbprint cov	225.00
Celery Vase, 6¼" h, IVT	225.00
Compote, 6" h, Honeycomb	125.00
Creamer, IVT, bulbous, reeded handle	265.00
Cruet, 6" h, Hobnail, clear faceted stopper	250.00
Pitcher, 7½" h, Hobnail, bulbous base, sq mouth, Hobbs, Brockunier & Co	400.00
Salt and Pepper Shakers, orig tops, pr	200.00
Sugar Shaker, enameled floral dec, metal lid, Hobb's Coloratura series	295.00
Syrup, 6¾" h, IVT, orig hinged pewter cov	300.00
Tumbler, 3¾" h, 2¾" d, IVT, cranberry shading to vaseline	65.00
Vase	
4" h, threaded dec	225.00

7" h, bulbous, scalloped rim, enameled floral dec	225.00
Wine Glass, 6" h, drape motif, stemmed, set of four	210.00

RUBY STAINED GLASS, SOUVENIR TYPE

History: Ruby stained glass was produced in the late 1880s and 1890s by several glass manufacturers, primarily in the area of Pittsburgh, Pennsylvania.

Ruby stained items were made from pressed clear glass which was stained with a ruby red material. Pieces often were etched with the name of a person, place, date, or event and sold as souvenirs at fairs and expositions.

In many cases one company produced the pressed glass blanks and a second company stained and etched them. Many patterns were used, but the three most popular were Button Arches, Heart Band, and Thumbprint.

Reference: William Heacock, *Encyclopedia of Victorian Colored Pattern Glass, Book 7: Ruby-Stained Glass From A to Z*, Antique Publications, Inc., 1986.

Reproduction Alert: Ruby staining is being added to many pieces through the use of modern stain glass coloring kits. A rash of fake souvenir ruby stained pieces was made in the 1960s, the best known example is the "bad" button arches toothpick.

Mug, Blairsville, PA, 3¼" h, 2⅝" d, $25.00.

Bell, Button Arches, Elkhorn Fair, 1913, clear paneled handle, 6½" h	65.00
Bread Tray, Triple Triangle, Cape Cod	65.00
Butter Dish, Button Arches, Atlantic City, 1919	75.00
Candy Dish, cov, Columbia Expo, 1893	65.00
Goblet	
Royal, My Mother 1894	35.00
Ruby Thumbprint, Mother	30.00
Triple Triangle, 1906	30.00

Miniature, creamer
Arched Ovals, Lakemont Park, 1908	**24.00**
Heart Band, Union City	**22.00**

Mug
Diamond Point Band, 1897 Raymond	**30.00**
Heart, World's Fair, 1904	**20.00**

Napkin Ring, Diamond with Peg, 1907	**85.00**
Pitcher, Button Arches, tankard, Pittsburgh	**125.00**
Punch Cup, Button Arches, Chicago . .	**20.00**
Sauce Dish, Cathedral, Niagara Falls .	**18.00**
Spooner, York Herringbone, World's Fair, 1893	**45.00**

Toothpick Holder
King's Crown, Atlantic City, 1899 . . .	**25.00**
Shamrock, Coney Island	**30.00**

Tumbler
Inverted Strawberry pattern, Deshler, OH	**30.00**
Red Block, World's Fair, 1893	**35.00**

Whiskey Glass, Ruby Thumbprint, 1907	**25.00**

Wine
Asbury Park, NJ	**35.00**
Button Arches, World's Fair	**25.00**
Honeycomb, Lydia	**28.00**
Triple Triangle, Christmas	**35.00**

RUSSIAN ITEMS

History: During the late 19th and early 20th centuries Russia contained skilled craftsmen in lacquer, silver, and enamel wares. Located mainly in Moscow during the Czarist era (1880–1917), were a group of master craftsmen, led by Faberge, who created exquisite enamel pieces. Faberge also had an establishment in St. Petersburg and enjoyed the patronage of the Russian Imperial family and royalty and nobility throughout Europe.

Almost all enameling was done on silver. Pieces are signed by the artist and the government assayer.

The Russian Revolution in 1917 brought an abrupt end to the century of Russian craftsmanship. The modern Soviet government has exported some inferior enamel and lacquer work, usually lacking in artistic merit. Modern pieces are not collectible.

Advisor: Barbara and Melvin Alpren.

ENAMELS

Casket, 3 x 2″, domed, lid with en plein enamel cabbage roses, Ivan Saltykov, Moscow, 1895–1900	**3,900.00**
Charka, 2⅞″, silver gilt, Pan Slavic style enameling, pointed prow, Gregory Sbitnev, Moscow, 1890–1900	**1,250.00**
Kovsh, 3″, silver gilt, Art Nouveau style enameling, pointed prow, hooked handle, Marie Semenova, Moscow, c1900	**1,900.00**

Bowl, blue flowers, yellow centers, dark rose–pink ground, Moscow, 6½″ d, $75.00.

Letter Opener, 10½″ l, cylindrical handle with enameled translucent green guilloche ground, overlaid gilt trellis dec, horse head finial with red cabochon eyes and seed pearl border, agate blade	**855.00**
Salt, 1½″, open, silver gilt, shaded enamel, four ball feet, Vasili Aga, Moscow, c1900	**795.00**
Serving Spoon, 7½″, silver gilt, shaded enamel, scrolling foliage, pink enamel background, Marie Semenova, Moscow, 1895–1900	**1,500.00**
Sugar Basket, 4½″, round, open, silver gilt, shaded enamel, swing handle, Nokolai Alekseev, Moscow, c1900 . .	**2,400.00**
Sugar Shovel, 5″, silver gilt, champleve enamel, Anton Kuzmichev, Moscow, 1895–1900	**600.00**
Tea Glass Holder, 5″, silver gilt, reticulated edges, pastel enamel floral motifs, 20th Masters Artel, Moscow, 1900	**1,800.00**
Trinket Box, oval, silver gilt, en plein enameling, slip–on lid, Moscow, c1900	**1,950.00**
Wine Beaker, 3½″, Art Nouveau style, pastel enamel, ftd, Fedor Ruckert, Moscow, 1900	**1,900.00**

MISCELLANEOUS

Box
4 x 4″, birch, gilded imperial eagle on lid, Karehan	**115.00**

5″
Black lacquer, sgd "Koianeb," Palek, 1937	**250.00**
Polychrome egg tempera painted fairy tale dec, rect Palek	**150.00**

Creamer, 4½″, porcelain, gilt scrolling foliage dec, cobalt blue ground, Kuznetsov	**165.00**
Egg Warmer, 10″, brass, egg form, tripod base, eagle finial, marked "Gebr–Buch, Warsaw"	**200.00**

Plate
7¼″, neoclassical Mars and Venus	

scene center, polychrome, Kuznetsov 175.00
10″, cobalt blue, gilt dec, four hp floral
panels, Alexander III, dated 1893 . 200.00
Punch Bowl, 14″, 2 pcs, glass, floral and
leaf cut 550.00
Samovar, 19″, brass, sgd 200.00
Snuff Box, 3½″, papier mache, figural
dec 220.00

**Spoon, red, blue, green, pink, navy
blue, and white enamels, made by Ni-
kolai Alekseev, Moscow, 1890, orig
box, 5¾ x 2 x 1″, $525.00.**

Tea Set, 4 pcs, 6½″ teapot, hot water,
creamer and cov sugar, floral gilt
bands on handles, spout, and trim,
Popov, Moscow, 19th C 1,265.00
Teapot
3½″, medallion with floral dec, cobalt
blue ground, double headed eagle
mark, Kuznetsov 190.00
5½″, medallion with floral dec, blue
ground 145.00
Treen Bowl, 9¼″, hp dec, marked
"Hand painted in USSR" 30.00

SILVER

Beaker, 3″, inverted tapered form, engraved stylized dec, beaded border . 500.00
Cake Basket, 11¾″, Art Nouveau, oval,
engraved daisies on collar, swing
handle, marked "Cyrillic HPN," 14 oz,
4 dwt 275.00
Goblet, 3″, mid 19th C 75.00
Soup Ladle, Fiddle pattern, Moscow,
1891–96 .... 150.00
Teaspoon, 5⅓″, set of 6, twisted handles, enameled terminals with foliage
and stylized dec 880.00
Toasting Mug, Slavic design, marked
"St George and the Dragon," 1885 . 475.00

Tray, 22½″, oval, raised pierced edge,
two handle, Cyrillic maker's mark "Ya
P," Assaymaster Mikhail Karpinski,
Moscow, 1806 .... 1,875.00

SABINO GLASS

History: Sabino glass, named for its creator Ernest Marius Sabino, originated in France in the
1920s and is an art glass which was produced in
a wide range of decorative glassware: frosted,
clear, opalescent, and colored glass. Both blown
and pressed moldings were used. Hand sculpted
wooden molds that were cast in iron were used
and are still in use at the present time.

In 1960 the company introduced a line of figurines, one to eight inches high, plus other items in
a fiery opalescent glass in the Art Deco style. Gold
was added to the batch to attain the fiery glow.
These pieces are the Sabino that is most commonly found today. Sabino is marked with the
name in the mold, an etched signature, or both.

**Scent Bottle, classical ladies, frosted,
inscribed "Sabino, France," 5″ h,
$10.00.**

Ashtray, shell, 5½″ w 30.00
Bird, 3″ h, two chubby baby birds
perched close on twig with berries
and leaves, opal, oval molded base,
relief molded "Sabino" 22.00
Blotter, 6″ l, rocker type, crossed Amer-
ican and French flags 275.00
Butterfly, opal, relief molded "Sabino" . 20.00
Cat, 2″ h 20.00
Chick, drinking 45.00
Dog
Collie, 2″ h 50.00
Pekingese, 1¼″ h, sitting up begging,
opal, relief molded "Sabino" 24.00
Elephant 25.00
Fox 25.00

Hand, left	200.00
Hen	30.00
Knife Rest, duck	20.00
Mouse, 3″ h	50.00
Napkin Ring, birds, opal	45.00
Owl, 4½″ h	65.00
Powder Box, small	40.00
Rooster, large	400.00
Scent Bottle, Petalia	50.00
Snail, opal, relief molded "Sabino" . . .	22.00
Squirrel, 3½″ h, opal, oval molded base, relief molded "Sabino"	24.00
Statue, Venus de Milo, large	65.00
Vase, Art Deco, topaz, 12″ h	500.00

ℂ 𝕊 SALOPIAN

SALOPIAN WARE

History: Salopian ware was made at Caughley Pot Works, Salop, Shropshire, England, in the 18th century by Thomas Turner. The ware is polychrome on transfer. One time classified as Polychrome Transfer, it retains the more popular name of Salopian. Wares are marked with an "S" or "Salopian" impressed or painted under the glaze. Much of it was sold through Turner's Salopian warehouse in London.

Plate, blue and white Oriental design, gold inner and outer rim, 8″ d, $185.00.

Charger, 11″ d, Bird on Branch pattern, blue transfer	400.00
Coffeepot, 9½″ h, multicolored stag scene, woodland setting	1,000.00
Creamer, 5¼″ h, milkmaid and cow scene	180.00
Cup and Saucer, handleless	
Bird on Branch pattern, 2⅞″ d cup, 4¾″ d saucer	175.00

Cottage scene, 3⅝″ d cup, 5⅞″ d saucer	120.00
Cup Plate, 4½″ d, double deer	350.00
Dish, 10″ d, oval, milkmaid and cow scene, scalloped edge, blue transfer	200.00
Mug, 2½″ h, double deer, five colors . .	400.00
Plate, 8⅝″ d	
Country house and deer dec, pr, c1800	290.00
Fishermen on bank, painted centers, dark blue and gold borders, palmettos, scrolls and loops, imp "Salopian"	120.00
Punch Bowl, 9⅝″ d, 4¼″ h, Willow pattern, brown monochrome, wide border of flowers and leaves on int. and ext., applied blue enamel rim	175.00
Sauce Dish, 4⅝″ d, polychromed scene of woman and two children, manor house background, brown transfer with yellow, blue, pink, and green applied highlights	150.00
Sugar Bowl, cov, 5″ h, yellow bird, blue, yellow, and orange dec	325.00

SALT AND PEPPER SHAKERS

History: Collecting salt and pepper shakers, whether late 19th century glass forms or the contemporary figural and souvenir types, is becoming more and more popular. The supply and variety is practically unlimited; the price for most sets is within the budget of cost conscious young collectors. Finally, their size offers an opportunity to assemble a large collection in a small amount of space.

One can specialize in types, forms, or makers. Great art glass artisans such as Joseph Locke and Nicholas Kopp designed salt and pepper shakers in the normal course of their work. Arthur Goodwin Peterson's *Glass Salt Shakers: 1,000 Patterns* provides the reference numbers given below. Peterson made a beginning; there are hundreds, perhaps thousands, of patterns still to be cataloged.

The clear colored and colored opaque sets command the highest prices, clear and white sets the lowest. Although some shakers, e.g., the tomato or fig, have a special patented top and need it to hold value, it is not detrimental to the price to replace the top of a shaker.

The figural and souvenir type is often looked down upon by collectors. Sentiment and whimsy are prime collecting motivations. The large variety and current low prices indicate a potential for long term price growth.

Generally older shakers are priced by the piece, figural and souvenir types by the set. The pricing method is indicated at each division. All shakers are assumed to have original tops unless noted. Identification numbers are from Peterson's book.

References: Gideon Bosker, *Great Shakes: Salt and Pepper For All Tastes*, Abbeville Press, 1986; Melva Davern, *The Collector's Encyclopedia of Salt & Pepper Shakers: Figural And Novelty*, Collector Books, 1985, 1991 value update; Melva Davern, *The Collector's Encyclopedia of Salt and Pepper Shakers, Second Series*, Collector Books, 1990; Helene Guarnaccia, *Salt & Pepper Shakers*, Collector Books, 1984; Helene Guarnaccia, *Salt & Pepper Shakers III: Identification & Values*, Collector Books, 1991; Mildred and Ralph Lechner, *The World of Salt Shakers, 2nd Edition*, Collector Books, 1992; Arthur G. Peterson, *Glass Salt Shakers: 1000 Patterns*, Wallace–Homestead, 1970.

Collectors' Clubs: Antique and Art Glass Salt Shaker Collectors Society, 2832 Rapidan Trail, Maitland, FL 32751; Novelty Salt & Pepper Shakers Club, 581 Joy Road, Battle Creek, MI 49017.

Additional Listings: See *Warman's Americana & Collectibles* for more examples.

Amethyst, gold trim, SP holder marked "Meridan," New England Glass Co., $235.00.

ART GLASS (PRICED INDIVIDUALLY)

Barrel, ribbed, Mt Washington, Burmese, floral motif, satin finish, 2 pc pewter top with finial, Peterson 154–A 200.00
Egg, shiny finish, lay down type, Pairpoint type windmills dec, orig lids, pr ... 195.00
Fig, enameled pansy dec, satin, orig prong top, Mt Washington 110.00
Inverted Thumbprint, reverse amberina, pewter top 165.00
Knobby, heavy opaque white, hp pastel flowers, shading to pale yellow, orig pewter top 42.50

Lob #5, satin, hp, orange floral spray, pewter top with finial, Mt. Washington, 33–C 62.50
Melon, squatty, enameled daisy dec, satin, orig two piece top, Mt Washington 55.00
Medallion Sprig, 3¼", shaded cobalt blue to white, orig brass top, 33–S . 67.50

FIGURAL AND SOUVENIR TYPES (PRICED BY SET)

Black Cooks, man in white hat, lady in white apron and turban, pottery, red and white underglaze dec, stove size 25.00
Ducks, 2½", sitting, glass, clear bodies, blue heads, sgd "Czechoslavakia" . 35.00
Lobsters, 3", marked "Made in Japan" 15.00
Nipper, RCA Dog, marked "Lenox" ... 35.00
Refrigerator, 2⅞", old G.E. refrigerator shape, white opaque glass, black trim, chrome plated top, 36–N 30.00
Squirrels, 3½", standing, metal, SP top 37.50

OPALESCENT GLASS (PRICED INDIVIDUALLY)

Argonaut Shell, Northwood, blue 55.00
Circle Scroll, Northwood, blue, tin top, 5", 156–S 72.00
Fluted Scrolls, Northwood, vaseline .. 40.00
Jewel and Flower, Northwood, blue, 164–J, replaced top 35.00
Ribbed, 3", white, brass top, 36–W ... 42.50
Seaweed, Hobbs, cranberry 45.00
Twelve Panel, 2⅞" h, robin's egg blue ground, pink carnations, blown mold, Pairpoint, c1895–1900, orig lid 95.00
Windows, Hobbs, blue, pewter top ... 45.00

OPAQUE GLASS (PRICED INDIVIDUALLY UNLESS OTHERWISE NOTED)

Acorn, Hobbs, shaded pink to white, tin top, 3", 21–A 45.00
Apple Blossom, milk glass 25.00
Brownie, 2⅜" h, rounded cube, four vertical sides, Palmer–Cox Brownies in different postures on each (F448) .. 75.00
Creased Waist, yellow, milk glass 30.00
Diamond Point and Leaf, 2¾" h, blue, diamond point ground broken by compound leaf extending up side of shaker (F489) 35.00
Everglades, Northwood, purple slag, white, gold highlights, pewter top, 160–K 70.00
Melon Ribbed, red, floral dec, pewter top 72.50
Punty Band, Custard 42.50
Sunset, Dithridge, white, 3", 40–U ... 30.00
Winged Scroll, Custard 87.50

PATTERN GLASS (PRICED INDIVIDUALLY)

Actress, pewter top	40.00
Beautiful Lady, Bryce, Higbee and Co, 1905, clear	20.00
Block and Fan, US Glass Co, 1891, clear	15.00
Cane, Gillinder Glass Co, c1885, apple green, non–flint	25.00
Crown Jewel, O'Hara Glass Co, c1880, etched	35.00
Croesus, McKee Glass, 1899, amethyst, gold trim	75.00
Diamond Horseshoe, Brilliant Glass Works, 1888, ruby stained	40.00
Diamond Point, Boston and Sandwich Glass Co, 1830–40, clear, flint	25.00
Francesware, Hobbs, Brockunier & Co, c1880, hobnail, frosted, amber stained	30.00
Mikado, Richards and Hartley, c1888, vaseline, non–flint	20.00
Whirligig, US Glass Co, clear, tin top, 3½", 177–A	15.00

SALTGLAZED WARES

History: Saltglazed wares have a distinctive "pitted" surface texture, made by throwing salt into the hot kiln during the final firing process. The salt vapors produce sodium oxide and hydrochloric acid which react on the glaze.

Many Staffordshire potters produced large quantities of this type of ware during the 18th and 19th centuries. A relatively small quantity was produced in the United States. Saltglazed wares still are made today.

Reference: Susan and Al Bagdade, *Warman's English & Continental Pottery & Porcelain, 2nd Edition,* Wallace–Homestead, 1991.

Cache Pot, 7½" d, taupe, applied classical dec, c1830	400.00
Cream Jug, 5¼" h, pear shape, drapery below raised rose branch band, lamb finial on lid	500.00
Creamer	
3" h, pear shape, shield design, circular foot, lyre handle, 18th C . . .	500.00
3¼" h, pear shape, raised leaf and putti dec, lyre handle, claw feet, 18th C	740.00
Dish	
9" d, circular, scroll and latticinio dec	290.00
14" d, pr, white, scroll edged diaper panel borders, basketwork ground, shaped rim, mid 18th C	925.00
Fruit Basket, 9½" l, circular, open work and scroll dec, loop handles	1,265.00
Fruit Stand, 14¾" l, oval, open work scroll and latticinio dec, glazed	1,650.00

Jug, blue and white griffins, cherubs, mask spout, English, mid-19th C, 7" h, $145.00.

Jug	
5⅛" h, baluster, three shell and paw feet, restored	500.00
7" h, Silenus, gray, raised No 16 mark, Minton, c1840	575.00
Loving Cup, 4¼" h, white raised US seal and two gold initials on front, Britannia on reverse, handles outlined in blue, Castleford	225.00
Plate, shaped rim	
8½" d, emb and reticulated border .	550.00
9¾" d, emb diaper and reticulated border	300.00
Platter	
13½" l, oval serpentine, scroll and latticinio border, 18th C	385.00
16¾" d, molded diaper work panels, scalloped rim, 18th C	200.00
Salt, helmet shape, latticinio star and lion, bird and shell dec, claw feet, 18th C	880.00
Sauceboat, 3⅛" l, oval, relief molded diaper, ozier, and scrolling panels, loop handle	370.00
Soup Tureen, 9⅜" l, cov, oval, three mask and claw feet with latticinio and scroll dec, loop handles on lid and ends, glazed	1,375.00
Tea Caddy, 4¼" h, pear shape, latticinio dec, knob finial, 18th C	355.00
Teapot, 7" h, ball shape, raised branch dec, bird finial on lid, 18th C	2,860.00
Tray, 7¾" l, oval, scalloped, latticinio dec	300.00

SALTS, OPEN

History: When salt was first mined, the supply was limited and expensive. The necessity for a receptacle in which to serve the salt resulted in the first open salt, a crude, hand-carved, wooden trencher.

As time passed salt receptacles were refined in style and materials. In the 1500s both master and individual salts existed. By the 1700s firms such as Meissen, Waterford, and Wedgwood were making glass, china, and porcelain salts. Leading manufacturers in the 1800s included Libbey Glass Co., Mount Washington, New England Glass Company, Smith Bros., Vallerysthal, Wavecrest, Webb, and many outstanding silversmiths in England, France, and Germany.

Open salts were used as the only means of serving salt until the appearance of the shaker in the late 1800s. The ease of procuring salt from a shaker greatly reduced the use and need for the open salts.

References: William Heacock and Patricia Johnson, *5,000 Open Salts: A Collectors Guide*, Richardson Printing Corporation, 1982, 1989 value update; L. W. and D. B. Neal, *Pressed Glass Dishes Of The Lacy Period 1825–1850*, published by the author, 1962; Allan B. and Helen B. Smith have authored and published ten books on open salts beginning with *One Thousand Individual Open Salts Illustrated* (1972) and ending with *1,334 Open Salts Illustrated: The Tenth Book* (1984). Daniel Snyder did the master salt sections in Volumes 8 and 9. In 1987 Mimi Rudnick compiled a revised price list for the ten Smith Books.

Collectors' Club: New England Society of Open Salt Collectors, 587 Dutton Road, Sudbury, MA 01776.

Note: The numbers in parenthesis refer to plate numbers in the Smith's publications.

CONDIMENT SETS WITH OPEN SALTS

Metal, collie pulling rickshaw, salt, pepper, and mustard, blown glass liners, Oriental (461)	**350.00**
Porcelain, Limoges, double salt and mustard, sgd "JM Limoges" (388)	**75.00**
Pottery, Quimper, double salt and mustard, white, blue and green floral dec, sgd "Quimper" (388)	**100.00**

INDIVIDUALS

China
Noritake, oval, blue and gold int. dec (382)	**38.00**
Royal Bayreuth, lobster claw (87)	**75.00**

Colored Glass
Cambridge, amber, Decagon pattern (468)	**35.00**
Galle, cameo, green pedestal, enamel dec, sgd, early (205)	**275.00**
Irish, cobalt blue liner, round sterling silver hallmarked holder, marked "Made in Dublin, Ireland 1795" (412)	**225.00**
Moser, cobalt blue, pedestal, gold bands, applied flowers, sgd (380)	**60.00**
Purple Slag, 3″ d, 1¼″ h, emb shell pattern	**55.00**
Webb, 2¼″ d, 1¾″ h, pink, overlay, cream int., plated metal rim	**110.00**

Cut Glass, 2″ d, 1½″ h, cut ruby ovals, allover dainty yellow enameled scrolls, clear ground, gold trim, scalloped top	**50.00**

Double Salt
China, boat shaped bowls, anchor handle, floral dec (392)	**185.00**
Glass, Baccarat, pedestal, paneled and frosted sides, sgd (395)	**125.00**

Metal
German Silver, dolphin feet, 1890–1910 (353)	**100.00**
Silverplate, pot, hallmarked "Wilcox Silver Plate Co" (414)	**45.00**
Sterling Silver, Georg Jensen, Denmark, porringer (238)	**200.00**
Opalescent Glass, 2″ d, 1½″ h, pink striped ext., gold luster int., Monot Stumpf, Pantin, French	**65.00**

Pattern Glass
Crystal Wedding	**25.00**
Fine Rib, flint	**35.00**
Hawaiian Lei, Higbee (477)	**35.00**
Mt Vernon, Cambridge (80)	**30.00**
Pineapple and Fan, Heisey	**25.00**
Three Face	**35.00**

Figural, bird, purple slag, Degenhart Glass, 3″ l, $25.00.

FIGURALS

Boat, lacy, clear, New England, Neal BT–9, slight rim roughage	**150.00**
Bucket, 2½″ d, 1⅝″ h, Bristol glass, turquoise, white, green, and brown enameled bird, butterfly, and trees, SP rim and handle	**75.00**
Peacock, glass, amethyst wings, green base (462)	**70.00**
Seahorse, Belleek, brilliant turquoise, white base, supports shell salt, first black mark (458)	**350.00**

INTAGLIOS

Niagara Falls, scene (368)	**75.00**
Tree, six intaglios, Venus and Cupid (423)	**115.00**

Master, Sunderland Luster, 3″ d, 2⅛″ h, $30.00.

MASTERS

China, pedestal, girl sitting on grass, marked "Printemps, Monbijou Germany" (387) 60.00
Colored Glass
  Cranberry, 3″ d, 1¾″ h, emb ribs, applied crystal ruffled rim, silverplated holder with emb lions' heads 150.00
  Green, light, dark green ruffled top, open pontil (449) 80.00
  Raspberry, heavy, sq, Pairpoint (444) 70.00
  Vaseline, 3″ d, 2¼″ h, applied crystal trim around middle, silverplated stand 125.00
Cut Glass, 2″ d, 2″ h, green cut to clear, silverplated holder 110.00
Lacy
  Eagle, Providence, clear, Neal EE–5 100.00
  New England Glass Co
    Heart, clear, Neal OG–2, small chip at bottom corner, light roughage to corners 30.00
    Rect, green, Neal NE–6 .... 375.00
  Pittsburgh, Peacock Eye, clear, ftd, Neal PP–1 .... 275.00
  Sandwich Glass Co
    Neal EE–8, Eagle/Constitution, chip on bottom of foot, slight roughage, tiny annealing checks on rim 200.00
    Neal PO–6a, Peacock Eye, clear, tiny upper rim flake 225.00
    Neal RP–9, round, pedestal, clear 100.00
Metal
  Gold, pedestal, marked "1880" (349) 80.00
  Pewter, pedestal, cobalt blue liner (349) 62.00
  Sterling Silver, boy with bow and arrow, holding salt on head, Simpson Hall Miller & Co (312) 400.00
Pattern Glass
  Bakewell Pears 25.00

Barberry, pedestal 35.00
Basketweave, sleigh (397) 110.00
Cathedral, boat shape, amethyst ... 30.00
Diamond Point, cov 75.00
Excelsior 30.00
Fine Rib, cov, pedestal 85.00
Sawtooth Circle 30.00
Snail, ruby stained 75.00
Sunflower, pedestal 35.00
Viking 25.00

SAMPLERS

History: Samplers served many purposes. For a young child they were a practice exercise and permanent reminder of stitches and patterns. For a young woman they demonstrated her skills in a "gentle" art and preserved key elements of family genealogy. For the mature woman they were a useful occupation and functioned as gifts or remembrances, e.g., mourning pieces.

Schools for young ladies of the early 19th century prided themselves on the needlework skills they taught. The Westtown School in Chester County, Pennsylvania, and the Young Ladies Seminary in Bethlehem, Pennsylvania, are two examples. These schools changed their teaching as styles changed. Berlin work was introduced by the mid-19th century.

Examples of samplers date back to the 1700s. The earliest ones were long and narrow, usually done only with the alphabet and numerals. Later examples were square. At the end of the 19th century, the shape tended to be rectangular.

The same motifs were used throughout the country. The name is a key element in determining the region. Samplers are assumed to be on linen unless otherwise indicated.

References: Ethel Stanwood Bolton and Eva Johnston Coe, *American Samplers*, Dover, 1987; Glee Krueger, *A Gallery of American Samplers: The Theodore H. Kapnek Collection*, Bonanza Books, 1984 edition; Betty Ring, *American Needlework Treasures; Samplers and Silk Embroideries From The Collection of Betty Ring*, E. P. Dutton, 1987; Anne Sebba, *Samplers: Five Centuries of a Gentle Craft*, Thames and Hudson, 1979.

1760, Rachel McClure, New York, blue, green, yellow, and brown silk threads, linen ground, alphabets, verse, figures, tree with snake, and birds, 16 x 14″ 4,250.00
1768, Phebe Smith, blue, green, yellow, red, brown, and black silk threads, alphabet, scenic panel with tree, flower, and birds, "Phebe Smith her sampler marked the year of our Lord 1768," framed, 20 x 7¾″ 310.00

Maria Catherine Zimmerman, aged 11, rows of alphabets, numbers, meandering floral border, 15¾ x 12½", $275.00.

1792, Polly Shores, Warren, RI, green, white, blue, rose, yellow, and brown silk stitches, linen ground, alphabets, house, trees, verse, arched columns, outer border with shepherds, rose blossoms, and trumpeting angels, stylized bud border, 22 x 17" **5,225.00**

1795, Anna Brynbergs, Philadelphia, PA, blue, green, yellow, peach, cream, and black silk threads, gauze ground, four verses, "Anna Brynbergs work done in the Eleventh Year of Her Age 1795," 15¼ x 17½" **5,500.00**

1799, Sally Johnson, Newburyport, MA, blue, green, pink, yellow, cream, and black silk threads, linen ground, central panel with alphabets, verse, and signature cartouche, servants, sugar cane field buildings, windmill, slave quarters, one story house, 19 x 27" . **33,000.00**

1801

Cane, Sally, Hagarstown, NJ, shades of brown, green, blue, and white, scene of girl and two lambs beside river, sailboats, large pinnacled building with trees, inscribed below "Sally Cane is my name/America is my nation/Hagarstown is my dwelling place/and Christ is my salvation/Finished this September 17 1801," zigzag border with flowerhead and buds, faded, giltwood frame, 8 x 9½" **1,870.00**

Hannah Headher, homespun, alphabets, yellow house, "Hannah Headher Sampler the year 1801," dark linen with wear, stains, repairs, fading, and puckering, framed, 22" h, 14" w **180.00**

1802, Elizabeth Dursee, green, white, pink, blue, and yellow silk stitches, linen ground, alphabet bands, house, trees, ladies, gentlemen, and "Elizabeth Dursee's Sampler Wrought in the 9 year of her age AD 1802," stylized floral border, 24¾ x 17½" **3,300.00**

1805, Hannah Davis, blue, green, rose, yellow, beige and black silk stitches, linen ground, bands of alphabets, men seated on river banks fishing, men in boats, verse and "Hannah Davis AE 11 years Roxbury September 27, 1805" **26,400.00**

1808

Harrington, Sally, green, yellow, pink, blue, and sienna silk threads, linen ground, alphabets, verse, house, trees, and "Sally Harringtons Work 1808," 25 x 19½" **2,100.00**

Wiley, Hannah and Eliza, green, blue, black, and pink silk stitches, linen ground, alphabet bands, flowers, pots of flowers, verse, and "The above wrought by Eliza Wiley now dec, Hannah Wiley, aged 13, 1808," birds perched in trees border, 17¼ x 13" **1,980.00**

1811, Mary Ann M Holtzbecher, green, blue, yellow, rose, and white silk stitches, linen ground, alphabet bands, tulips, leaping rabbits, and "Mary Ann M. Holtzbecher's work, Anno Domini, 1811," rose spray outer border, framed, 14¾ x 15" **6,050.00**

1812, Rachel Borton, blue, gold, pink, and rose silk stitches, linen ground, alphabet bands, lower twined wreath, blue birds, roses, and basket of fruit, strawberry border, 18 x 12¼" **1,320.00**

1814, Sarah Wells, olive green stitches, linen ground, random octagonal cartouches, birds, swan, roses, stars, tulips, snowflakes, carnations, "Sarah Wells, 1813," and "Token of Love SW to EW, 1814," framed, 17 x 21" **1,980.00**

1818

Gibson, Hannah, colorful alphabets, house, birds, plants, and "Hannah Gibson aged 9 years, Thorp School," framed, 16¼" h, 20" w .. **700.00**

Jackson, Mary, homespun, birds, flowers, animals, angels, ship, house design, and "By this work of mine, you may plainly see, what pains my parents took with me. Mary Jackson worked this in the 8th year of her age 1818.," minor wear, framed, 18" h, 23½" w **800.00**

1821

Bellows, Mary W, MA, silk stitches, linen ground, family tree, tree with large fruit stitched with name and birth date, two entwined hearts at bottom inscribed with parents names, and "Family Record wrought by Mary W Bellows aet 11 1821," framed, 19½ x 16" **4,125.00**

Stoy, Mary, PA, rose, pink, white, green, and blue silk stitches, linen ground, girl carrying basket, house, dog, flock of sheep, leaping stag, and "Mary Stoy, The Daughter of William and Mary Stoy Her Work Done In the 19th year of her age at Mrs Ross School in 1821," carnation border, quilled silk ribbon outer border, orig walnut veneered frame, 13½ x 15" **3,300.00**

1822

Brett, Fanny, silk threads, linen ground, rows of alphabets, stylized house, flowers, trees, verse "The Rose," and "Fanny Brett aged twelve years, March sixth day 1822," faded colors, minor stains, one row of letters incomplete, framed, 18½" h, 13" w **450.00**

Tupper, Harriet, Sandwich, MA, alphabets, verses over center house, meandering vine border, dated March 1822, framed, 12¾ x 10" .. **1,000.00**

1823, Mary Martin, blue, white, pink, green, yellow, and brown wool, black ground, crewel embroidered compote filled with roses and lilies, cross stitched "Mary Martin, aged 10 years, 1823," stenciled frame, 10⅜ x 9" ... **990.00**

1824

Noel, Elizabeth, red, yellow, purple, magenta, green, and orange silk stitches, linen ground, house, shepherd, polka dot stags, trees, parrots, and "Elizabeth Noel, Her Work Aged 11 Years, 1824," meandering pink carnation border, 25 x 17" **16,500.00**

Owston, Mary Ann, age 11, Adam and Eve in the Garden of Eden, numbers, alphabets, and flowers, framed, 12" sq **300.00**

Pader, Catharine A, homespun, floral dec and verse "Admonition...Catherine A. Pader, aged–years, New York Bethel School No 2, A.D. 1824," vine border, tear, stains, and fading, 18" sq **210.00**

Unidentified Maker, homespun, colorful alphabets, verse, and "Hannah—-ton, April 28, 1824," animal

border, framed, bleeding and fading, 12½" sq **435.00**

1826

Noyes, Sarah M, MA, shades of blue, green, white, and yellow silk threads, linen homespun ground, alphabets, house, trees, and "Sarah M Noyes was born Jan. 15th 1817," dated 1826, vining floral border, minor fading, brown stains, minor damage to silk floss and linen ground, back has label identifying maker as living in Scituate, MA, died in 1831, framed .. **800.00**

Pryer, Hannah Ann, NY, age 7, green, gold, blue, and white silk stitches, linen ground, religious verse, undulating strawberry vine flanked by bellflowers, second inscription with name and date, flower filled urns above and below, framed, 17⅛ x 13⅞" **1,210.00**

1827

Bridge, Katharine H, green, blue, yellow, and bittersweet silk threads, alphabet, sentimental verse, and "Katharine H. Bridge born February the twentieth 1813 aged 14 Windsor Vt August the ninth 1827," 16½ x 17" **500.00**

Gove, Mary B, Weare, NH, green, white, gold, rose, and blue silk stitches, linen ground, upper register with pair of spread winged birds, leafy tree, blue and white checkered basket filled with rose and carnation blossoms, central panel with bands of alphabets, pious verse, and "Mary B Gove, sgd 13 Dec 15, 1827, P.H. Chase, Instructuress," outer borders with large, full blossoms, small landscape scene, sheep grazing in meadow, small white house, sponge painted and stenciled landscape scene painted on paper, orig pine, maple and mahogany veneer frame, 23 x 17" **20,900.00**

Squire, Clarissa, green, blue, white, and pink silk stitches, linen ground, alphabet bands, verse, family genealogy, and memorial, trees and flower border, 17¼ x 18" **2,200.00**

1828

Montaqu, Mary L, black, green, blue, and tan silk threads, "Mary L Montaqu, A D 1828 AE 11 yrs," framed, 18¾ x 13¾" **150.00**

Robb, Christina C, red, green, yellow, and blue stitches, woven homespun, alphabet bands, central star, and inscription, flowering trees in corners, 17½ x 16½" **1,980.00**

1829

Perkins, Mary J, Jaffrey, NH, green, blue, white, pink, and gold silk stitches, linen ground, cut-out and applied figures of mother, father, three young boys, and four young girls dressed in mourning clothes, standing beside monument with three urns and three oval paper plaques each inscribed with member of Perkins family, stitched weeping willow trees, borders of meandering rose blossom vine, sgd in upper right hand corner "Mary J Perkins, 13 yrs, Jaffrey, Aug 6, 1829," orig frame, 17½ x 18¾" **13,200.00**

Sargeant, Julia, blue, green, yellow, white, and pink silk stitches, linen ground, alphabet bands, landscape scene, verse, and "Julia Sargeant wrought in her 9 year 1829," meandering bud border, 17 x 16½" . . . **7,700.00**

1830

Brown, Sarah Stanley, Honeybrook, PA, silk stitches, linen ground, pious verse above red brick two story house with green roof and blue and white picket fence, paired birds, rose garlands, tulips, and butterflies, stylized grape clusters and leaf border, framed, 17 x 23¼" **4,400.00**

Deputron, Ann S, red, pale blue, navy blue, beige, and green stitches, linen ground, basket of flowers center, red and yellow birds, mother with infant in arms, child, dog, strawberry border, and verse, 15½ x 20" **2,420.00**

1831, Mary A Fawcett, green, pink, white, blue, and yellow silk stitches, house, pine trees, birds, baskets of fruit, and verse with names "Mary A. Stanford, Mary A. Ross, Eliza Fawcett, John Fawcett, Joseph Fawcett, and Elanor Fawcett," fruit and flower border, 22 x 17¼" **13,200.00**

1835

Bassett, Ida, homespun, alphabets, simple floral design, old faded colors, wear and holes, modern frame, 11¾" h, 16" w **245.00**

Wild, Jane, green, brown, red, and tan threads, sq linen panel, birds in flight, trees, recumbent stag, animals, figures, and three story brick manor house, religious verse above, some discoloring to borders, mahogany frame, 20¼ x 21" **1,760.00**

1842, Esther Beaulah, shades of red

and rose threads, homespun, finely detailed, parrot, dog, swans, flowers, verse, and "Esther Beaulah her work aged 11 years, 1842," flowering border, old faded colors, wear, primitive sewn repair, bird's eye maple veneer frame, 26" h, 24" w **1,250.00**

1846, M A Bottomley, red, green, blue, yellow, and green silk stitches, linen ground, red carnations, urns with flowers, baskets of fruit, paired birds and tulips, blue roofed house, verse, maker's name, and "Aged 8 1846," strawberry border, 16 x 15½" **2,310.00**

1850, Sarah Ann Cooper, Sherborne, Dorset, silk stitches, finely woven linen, pots of flowers and verse, stylized floral border, holes in linen, stains, puckering, framed, 18⅜" h, 14½" w **500.00**

1853, wool and silk threads, flowers, building, alphabets, and "Anne Lindemuth, Sampler made in the year of our Lord 1853," several backwards letters, good colors, minor stains, framed, 21¼ x 23¼" **450.00**

1856, red, blue, green, and yellow threads, homespun, alphabet, numerals, stylized birds and flowers, and hearts, wear, minor soiling, fading, framed, 15 x 12½" **270.00**

1873, Emma Arnold, homespun, rows of alphabets, faded colors, modern frame, 12 x 9" **225.00**

Undated

8¾" sq, homespun, alphabets and "Nancy Stones Ae 9," very faded, modern frame **100.00**

14 x 15½", homespun, alphabets, angel, crucifixion, Adam and Eve, figures, animals, and flowers, wear, fading, small holes, gold gilded frame with "Winchester, Mass" label **350.00**

15 x 17", homespun, dark blue, shades of gold and brown, red, green, and yellow threads, homespun, alphabets, numbers, stylized floral design, and "Emeline Bagleys Sampler," stains, framed **200.00**

15¾ x 14¾", red, olive green, shades of blue, and white threads, linen ground, stylized flowers, birds, and animals, vining border, minor stains, damaged rosewood veneer frame **375.00**

22 x 24", dark olive brown threads, natural linen ground, family register, alphabets, listing of Lilly family parents and children, old gilt frame **325.00**

SANDWICH GLASS

History: In 1818 Deming Jarves was listed in the Boston Directory as a glass factor. The same year he was appointed general manager of the newly formed New England Glass Company. In 1824 Jarves toured the glass-making factories in Pittsburgh, left New England Glass Company, and founded a glass factory in Sandwich.

Originally called the Sandwich Manufacturing Company, it was incorporated in April 1826 as the Boston & Sandwich Glass Company. From 1826 to 1858 Jarves served as general manager. The Boston & Sandwich Glass Company produced a wide variety and quality of wares. The factory used the free-blown, blown three-mold, and pressed glass manufacturing techniques. Clear and colored glass both were used.

Competition in the American glass industry in the mid-1850s forced a lowering of quality of the glass wares. Jarves left in 1858, founded the Cape Cod Glass Company, and tried to maintain the high quality of the earlier glass. At the Boston & Sandwich Glass Company emphasis was placed on mass production. The development of a lime glass (non-flint) led to lower costs for pressed glass. Some free-blown and blown-and-molded pieces, mostly in color, were made. Most of this Victorian era glass was enameled, painted, or acid etched.

By the 1880s the Boston & Sandwich Glass Company was operating at a loss. Labor difficulties finally resulted in the factory closing on January 1, 1888.

References: Raymond E. Barlow and Joan E. Kaiser, *The Glass Industry In Sandwich*, Vol. 2, Vol. 3 and Vol. 4, distributed by Schiffer Publishing, Ltd.; George S. and Helen McKearin, *American Glass*, Crown Publishers, Inc., 1941 and 1948; Ruth Webb Lee, *Sandwich Glass. The History Of The Sandwich Glass Company*, Charles E. Tuttle, 1966; Ruth Webb Lee, *Sandwich Glass Handbook*, Charles E. Tuttle, 1966; L. W. and D. B. Neal, *Pressed Glass Dishes Of The Lacy Period 1825–1850*, published by author, 1962; Catherine M. V. Thuro, *Oil Lamps II: Glass Kerosene Lamps*, Wallace–Homestead, 1983.

Museum: Sandwich Glass Museum, Sandwich, MA.

Additional Listings: Blown Three Mold and Cup Plates.

Salt Shaker, Christmas Pearl, agitator top, $110.00.

Basket, 6¼″ d, ribbed, ruffled top, clear loop handle	**180.00**
Bowl, 9¼″ d, Gothic Arches, clear, lacy, Lee 129	**150.00**
Candlestick, 9″ h, dolphin, clear, dolphins and shells on socket, McKearin 204–65	**800.00**
Celery Vase, 8½″ h, flint, clear, Diamond Thumbprint	**125.00**
Cologne Bottle, amber, gilded floral dec, orig gilded lily stopper	**400.00**
Compote	
7¼″ d, 5″ h, Waffle pattern, clear, flint, minute under rim roughage	**50.00**
8½″ d, 6¼″ h, Excelsior pattern, clear, flint	**100.00**
Creamer	
Amberina, 3¼″ h, Coin Spot pattern, rope handle, sq top	**190.00**
Lacy, Fish Scale pattern, clear	**75.00**
Cup Plate, Lee–Rose 440–B, deep blue, heart	**325.00**
Decanter, 12″ h, 1½–2 pint capacity, Sandwich Star, canary yellow, period stopper, pr	**3,300.00**
Dish, 12″ l, 9″ w, 1¾″ h, oblong, Peacock Eye	**800.00**
Ewer, 10″ h, amber overshot, clear twist handle and collar	**135.00**
Jewel Casket, cov, 6½″ l, oblong, clear, lacy, Lee 162	**1,100.00**
Lamp	
4⅛″ h, sparking, tin burner, clear, globular, minor roughage to base .	**300.00**
9¾″ h, whale oil, clear, blown teardrop font, heavy pressed triangular paw foot base, slight base roughage . .	**1,200.00**
Lamp Shade, 8½″ d, 5½″ h, 3¾″ fitter ring, white, allover ruby threading, 4″ ruby threaded floral band, ruffled trim	**250.00**
Miniature	
Bowl, cov, 1⅝″ d, pattern around base	**100.00**
Cup and Saucer, handleless, lacy, Lee 80–7	**250.00**
Flat Iron, blue–green	**600.00**
Plate, opal, lacy, Lee 81–5	**150.00**
Tureen, cov, matching undertray, clear, lacy, Lee 180–12, minimal roughage	**250.00**
Wash Bowl and Pitcher, clear, Lee 80–3	**350.00**
Ointment Jar, 3″ d, opaque white, orig pewter lid, oval, concave panels . . .	**125.00**
Plate, 7⅛″ d, Peacock Eye, translucent moonstone, lacy, Lee 108–2	**150.00**
Salt, cov, Neal CD–2, clear, lacy, minor	

chips on underside of cov and one
corner **400.00**
Scent Bottle
Deep emerald green, violin shape,
orig pewter screw top, McKearin
241–31 .... **225.00**
Medium purple–blue, McKearin 241–
55 .... **130.00**
Sugar, cov, Gothic Arches, electric blue,
slight roughage, two minor upper rim
flakes, Lee 158–4 .... **1,500.00**
Sweetmeat, cov, Waffle pattern, clear,
flint, one scallop rim chipped **90.00**
Tray, 10" l, Butterfly, clear, lacy, Lee 95–
3 .... **300.00**
Vase
7¼" h, Bull's Eye and Ellipse, dark
emerald green, gauffered rims, pr **3,000.00**
9½" h, tulip, amethyst, McKearin
201–40, tiny flake under point of
one foot, pr **2,300.00**
Vegetable Dish, cov, 10½" l, clear, lacy,
grape border, Lee 151–1 .... **5,500.00**
Whiskey Glass, 2⅜" h, hexagonal, deep
cobalt blue, flint **225.00**

SARREGUEMINES CHINA

History: Sarreguemines ware is a faience porcelain, i.e., tin–glazed earthenware. The factory was established in Lorraine, France, in 1770, under the supervision of Utzcheider and Fabry. The factory was regarded as one of the three most prominent manufacturers of French Faience. Most of the wares found today were made in the 19th century. Later wares are impressed Sarreguemines and Germany due to a change of boundaries and location of the factory.

Reference: Susan and Al Bagdade, *Warman's English & Continental Pottery & Porcelain, 2nd Edition,* Wallace–Homestead, 1991.

Box, 6", multicolored children in Kate
Greenaway type dress dec **60.00**
Compote, 9½", majolica, five different
raised fruits series, natural colors .. **65.00**
Creamer, 5", row of ducks, frog, flower
border **48.00**
Dish, cov, 8½", majolica, basketweave,
white egg lid finial **175.00**
Pitcher, 8", shoemaker scenes **145.00**
Plate
7½", multicolored French comic
scene **20.00**
8½", majolica, strawberries and floral
trim, aqua ground **70.00**
Toby Jug
6½", majolica, shaded beige flesh
tones, ruddy cheeks **85.00**

Plate, multicolored tinsmith scene, cream ground, 8½" d, $55.00.

8", majolica, The Scotsman **125.00**
Vase, pr, 20", pyriform, pearlware,
Moorish influence, shaped panel with
painted cavaliers in tavern scene,
painted fortress on river banks on reverse, emerald green ground, multicolored enamels, gilted, printed mark **2,750.00**

SARSAPARILLA BOTTLES

History: Sarsaparilla refers to a number of tropical American, spiny, woody vines of the lily family whose roots are fragrant. An extract was obtained from these dried roots and used for medicinal purposes. The first appearance in bottle form dates from the 1840s. The earliest bottles were stoneware, later followed by glass.

Carbonated water often was added to sarsaparilla to make a soft drink or to make consuming it more pleasurable. For this reason, sarsaparilla and soda became synonymous even though they were two different entities.

References: Ralph & Terry Kovel, *The Kovels' Bottle Price List, 8th Edition,* Crown Publishers, 1987; Carlo & Dot Sellari, *The Standard Old Bottle Price Guide,* Collector Books, 1989.

Periodical: *Antique Bottle and Glass Collector,* P. O. Box 187, East Greenville, PA 18041.

Additional Listings: See *Warman's Americana & Collectibles* for a list of soda bottles.

Allen's, Warren Sarsaparilla Beer, tan,
pottery **125.00**
Bull's Extract Of Sarsaparilla, beveled
corner, 7 x 2" **385.00**
Compound Extract Of Sarsaparilla, amber, gallon **125.00**
Dr Green's **15.00**
Dr Ira Belding's, Honduras Sarsaparilla,
clear, 10½" **20.00**
Dr Townsend's Sarsaparilla, olive
green, pontil **80.00**

Foley's Sarsaparilla 15.00
Guysott's Yellow Dock & Sarsaparilla . 35.00
Lancaster Glassworks, barrel, golden
amber 120.00
Murray's, Burnham, ME, aqua 20.00
Riker's Compound Sarsaparilla, rect,
beveled corners, aqua 30.00
Skoda's Sarsaparilla, amber 20.00

SATIN GLASS

History: Satin glass, produced in the late 19th century, is an opaque art glass with a velvety matte (satin) finish which was achieved through treatment with hydrofluoric acid. A large majority of the pieces were cased or had a white lining.

While working at the Phoenix Glass Company, Beaver, Pennsylvania, Joseph Webb perfected Mother-of-Pearl (MOP) satin glass in 1885. Similar to plain satin glass in respect to casing, MOP satin glass has a distinctive surface finish and an integral or indented design, the most common being diamond quilted (DQ).

The most common colors are yellow, rose, or blue. Rainbow coloring is considered choice. Satin glass, both plain and MOP, has been widely reproduced.

Additional Listings: Cruets, Fairy Lamps, Miniature Lamps, and Rose Bowls.

Vase, bud, double, blue, Mount Washington, 5″ w, 3″ h, $235.00.

Basket, 9½″ d, Herringbone, MOP, pink
shaded to salmon ext., tightly crimped
edge, clear frosted twisted thorn han-
dle 650.00
Bowl, 5¼″ d, DQ, MOP, tricorn, blue,
applique crystal edge, marked "Pat-
ent" 750.00
Bride's Basket, 15½″ h, deep rose,
enamel swan and floral dec, heavy
bronze holder with birds perched at
top 415.00
Cologne Bottle, 5½″ h, globular, peach,
SS top 250.00
Ewer, 8″ h, 3½″ d, Herringbone, MOP,
shaded blue, white lining, frosted applied handle, rose petal satin finish . 195.00

Jar, cov, 6¼″ h, DQ, MOP, salmon, clear
applied flower finial 325.00
Miniature Lamp, 8½″ h, DQ, MOP, pink
shaded to rose, frosted applied han-
dle 1,325.00
Pitcher, 8¼″ h, Coinspot, MOP, blue,
frosted applied handle 160.00
Rose Bowl
2¾″ h, 4½″ d, Rivulet pattern, MOP,
shaded pink, eight crimp top 245.00
3¾″ h, 5″ d, Herringbone, MOP, deep
rose shaded to pink, white int., six
crimp top, rose petal finish 300.00
Toothpick, 2½″ h, DQ, MOP, yellow . . 165.00
Tumbler, DQ, MOP, deep blue to pearly
white, heavy enameled pink blos-
soms, multicolored foliage 285.00
Vase
4¾″ h, 6″ d, Ribbon, MOP, pouch,
blue, three petal top, white int. . . . 495.00
5″ h, 3″ d, DQ, MOP, shaded apricot,
white int., ruffled top, frosted binding, five frosted applied wishbone
feet 225.00
5½″ h, 4″ d, DQ, MOP, blue, frosted
binding around ruffled edge, white
lining 185.00
8″ h, 3½″ d, Drape pattern, MOP,
shaded rose, ruffled top, white lin-
ing, pr 495.00
9¾″ h, 4½″ d, Herringbone, MOP,
blue, white int., frosted applied
thorny handles and feet, ruffled
tops, pr 750.00

SATSUMA

History: Satsuma, named for a war lord who brought skilled Korean potters to Japan in the early 1600s, was a hand-crafted Japanese faience glazed pottery. It is finely crackled, has a cream, yellow-cream, or gray-cream color, and is decorated with raised enamels in floral geometric and figural motifs.

Figural satsuma was made specifically for export in the 19th century. Later satsuma, referred to as satsuma-style ware, is Japanese porcelain also hand decorated in raised enamels. From 1912 to the present, satsuma-style ware has been mass produced. Much of the ware on today's market is of this later period.

References: Sandra Andacht, *Oriental Antiques & Art: An Identification And Value Guide*, Wallace-Homestead, 1987; Sandra Andacht, *Treasury of Satsuma*, Wallace-Homestead, 1981.

Bowl
4¼″ d, cov, flat 325.00
5″ d, figures, pavilion, and mountain
landscape dec, ftd, Showa period 165.00

6¼" d, Kwannon surrounded by Arhats scene 175.00

7⅞" d, bulbous form, finch on snow covered flowering hawthorn branches, late 19th C 475.00

8⅜" d, floriform, shaped rim, wisteria blossom int., imp and enameled signatures 2,000.00

9⅞" d, deities and attendants dec, landscape background, black reserve with gilt sgd "Dai Nihon, Hattori Gyokuzan," 19th C 1,400.00

10" d, women, boys, and landscape scene int., figural panels ext., blue ground, sgd "Kinkozan Zo," 19th C 1,800.00

Box

3½" l, cov, melon form, shaped reserves, sgd 600.00

5" d, cov, spherical, dragon and saints dec, ftd, sgd 410.00

Bucket, 12" h, fan and floral dec 165.00

Cup and Saucer, bird and floral motif, cobalt blue borders, sgd "Kinkozan" 110.00

Flask, moon

6½" h, battling samurai scene, reserve verso, sgd "Satsuma," 19th C 1,800.00

11¾" h, pr, floral and figural dec, stylized dragons on shoulder, early 20th C 300.00

Inkwell, 3" h, scenic reserves, gold trim, Mon mark and signature, missing lid and insert 100.00

Jar, cov, maroon, white, gold leaf trim, c1830, 8½" h, $135.00.

Jar

7" h, bulbous, figural reserves 800.00

8", globular body, three applied figures holding bowl and ladle, 19th C 1,200.00

Jardiniere, 11" h, baluster form, figural scenes, diaper patterns, late 19th C 175.00

Plate, 9⅝" d, brocaded pattern, polychrome and gold floral bands and medallions, sgd "Kizan," 19th C . . . 325.00

Tea Bowl, 3¼" d, cylindrical, figural reserves, diaper pattern ext., butterflies int., inscribed, 19th C 4,000.00

Tea Set

9 pcs, teapot, cov sugar and creamer, six cups and saucers, ovoid form, polychrome floral, net, and butterfly dec, late 19th C 250.00

15 pcs, teapot, creamer and sugar, twelve cups and saucers 275.00

Tray, 7½" l, rect, Mt Fuji with procession beneath, millefiori border, Meiji period, Yabu Meizan 5,500.00

Umbrella Stand, 24⅝" h, cylindrical, applied dragon and painted nobleman and attendants scene, eight character signature, Kyoto, 19th C 300.00

Urn, 24" h, ovoid, warrior, scholar, and official dec, molded handles, ftd, sgd "Kyoto Yasuda zo Kore," 19th C . . . 1,400.00

Vase

3⁵⁄₁₆" h, pr, hexagonal, baluster form, figural reserve dec, inscribed "Gosuido," 19th C 225.00

5" h, baluster, dragon and saints dec, Imperial Satsuma signature 500.00

6" h, pr, bottle form, figural reserves, sgd, 19th C 500.00

7¾" h, globular baluster form, bird and floral dec, sgd, c1900 . . . . . . 250.00

8" h, bottle form, four medallions with figural dec, four molded gilt bows, Meiji period 220.00

9" h, flask form, moon shape, polychrome and gilt children playing game dec 60.00

9¾" h, pr, cobalt blue, polychrome dec and gilt 310.00

10" h, baluster, dragon and figural motifs, bronze scroll pattern ground, sgd "Fuzan," 19th C 2,400.00

11½" h, ovoid, Samurai and figures in waterfall reserves, 19th C 1,000.00

14½" h, ovoid, stylized chrysanthemums and foliate borders, sgd, Shimazu crest and seal, 19th C 3,100.00

18" h, baluster, two scholars and immortals reserves, imp "Kozan," 19th C 800.00

18½" h, jewel type enamel colors . . 130.00

19½" h, ovoid, waisted neck, flowering branch dec 150.00

75½" h, pr, ovoid, four figures dec, 19th C 1,500.00

SCALES

History: Prior to 1900 the simple balance scale commonly was used for measuring weights. Since then scales have become more sophisticated in design and more accurate. A variety of styles and types include beam, platform, postal, and pharmaceutical.

Collectors' Club: International Society of Antique Scale Collectors, 176 W. Abram St., Suite 1706, Chicago, IL 60603.

Fairbanks, marked "IZ8," 50% of the orig paint, 15½" l, 8¾" h, $50.00.

Baby, wicker	45.00
Balance	
Cast Iron, 14" l, orig red paint with black and yellow trim, nickel plated brass pans, marked "Henry Troemner, Phila, No 5B, Baker's"	100.00
Glass and mahogany, marked "Chainomatic, Christian Becker Inc, New York," c1919	220.00
Wrought Iron, 22" h, cast iron base, tin pans	60.00
Candy	
Dayton, metallic orange, brass pan	300.00
National Store Co, tin pan, c1910	85.00
Coin Operated, 69" h, floor model, porcelain top and bottom, mirrored front, wood back, marked "National Weighing Machine, NY"	175.00
Counter, blue, chrome with tan, marked "Toledo"	165.00
Computing, 15¼" h, 17½" w, merchant's, Computing Scale Co, Dayton	220.00
Egg, Oaks Mfg Co	7.50
Grain, brass	235.00
Hand Held, wide side gauge, unusual cylinder, marked "Chatillon, NY"	20.00
Jeweler, brass pans, brass standard, ten brass weights, green velvet lined box	150.00
Photographer, brass pans, brass weights, marked "Made in Germany"	145.00
Postal, 4¼" h, desk, SS, cased, monogram, marked "Shreve & Co," c1900–22	250.00
Steelyard, wood, weighted bulbous end, turned shaft, 18th C	200.00
Store	
Hanson Weighmaster, 6 x 14 x 10",	

cast iron, gold case with ground, black lettering and indicator	25.00
Howe, cast iron, red base, gold highlights, brass pan, five weights, patent June 18, 1867	80.00
National Store Specialty Co, green base	175.00

SCHLEGELMILCH PORCELAINS

History: Erdmann Schlegelmilch founded his porcelain factory in Suhl in the Thuringia region in 1861. Reinhold, his brother, established a porcelain factory at Tillowitz in Upper Silesia in 1869. In the 1860s Prussia controlled Thuringia and Upper Silesia, both rich in the natural ingredients needed for porcelain.

By the late 19th century an active export business was conducted with the United States and Canada due to a large supply of porcelain at reasonable costs achieved through industrialization and cheap labor. Both brothers marked their pieces with the RSP mark, a designation honoring Rudolph Schlegelmilch, their father. Over 30 mark variations have been discovered.

The Suhl factory ceased production in 1920, unable to recover from the effects of World War I. The Tillowitz plant, located in an area of changing international boundaries, finally came under Polish socialist government control in 1956.

References: Susan and Al Bagdade, *Warman's English & Continental Pottery & Porcelain, 2nd Edition,* Wallace–Homestead, 1991; Mary Frank Gaston, *The Collector's Encyclopedia Of R.S. Prussia and Other R.S. and E.S. Porcelain, First Series,* (1982, 1990 value update) and *Second Series,* (1986), Collector Books; George W. Terrell, Jr., *Collecting R.S. Prussia Identification and Values,* Books Americana, 1982; Clifford S. Schlegelmilch, *Handbook Of Erdmann And Reinhold Schlegelmilch, Prussia–Germany And Oscar Schlegelmilch, Germany, 3rd Edition,* published by author, 1973.

Reproduction Alert: Many "fake" Schlegelmilch pieces are appearing on the market. These reproductions have new decal marks, transfers, or recently hand painted animals on old, authentic R.S. Prussia pieces.

R. S. GERMANY

Biscuit Jar, 6" h, loop handles, roses dec, satin finish, gold knob	95.00
Bonbon Dish, 7¾" l, 4½" w, pink carnations, gold dec, silver–gray ground, looped inside handle	30.00
Bread Plate, Iris variant edge mold, blue and white, gold outlined petal and rim, multicolored center flowers, steeple mark	115.00
Bride's Bowl, ornate, floral center, ftd	45.00

E. S. Germany, plate, 11″ w, multicolored fruit center, green leaves and grapes border, crown mark, $175.00.

Cake Plate, deep yellow, two parrots on hanging leaf vine, open handle, green mark **225.00**

Celery Tray, 11″ l, 5¾″ w, lily dec, gold rim, open handles, blue label **100.00**

Cheese and Cracker Dish, 8½″ d, two tiers, pink orchid dec **125.00**

Chocolate Pot, white rose florals, blue mark **85.00**

Creamer and Sugar, pedestal, sheepherder scene, overall dec, red mark **650.00**

Cup and Saucer, plain mold, swan, blue water, mountain and brown castle background, red mark **235.00**

Demitasse Cup and Saucer, 3″ h, pink roses, gold stenciled design, satin finish, blue mark **55.00**

Hatpin Holder **75.00**

Inkwell, 3″ h, pink roses, gold scroll, hp, artist sgd, blue mark **70.00**

Napkin Ring, green, pink roses, white snowballs **45.00**

Nut Bowl, 5¼″ d, 2¾″ h, cream, yellow roses, green scalloped edge **55.00**

Pin Tray, woman with oxen scene, attached powder box **200.00**

Pitcher, 5¾″, light blue, chrysanthemums, pink roses, gold trim **65.00**

Plate

6½″ d, dessert, yellow and cream roses, green and rich brown shades, set of 6 . . . . **125.00**

9¾″ d, white flowers, gold leaves, gilded edge, green ground, marked "RS Germany" in dark green, script sgd "Reinhold Schlegelmilch/Tillowitz/Germany" in red **40.00**

10″ d, hp flowers **40.00**

Powder Box, cov, green poppies, green mark **45.00**

Salt and Pepper Shakers, pr, shaded green, peach floral dec, gold trim . . **45.00**

Sauce Dish, underplate, green, yellow roses, blue mark **40.00**

Tea Tile, peach and tan, greenish white snowballs, red mark over faint blue mark **150.00**

Toothpick Holder, White Rose, three handles **55.00**

Vase, 4″, bottle shape, shaded green to cream, cottage scene, marked **65.00**

R. S. POLAND

Candleholder, floral dec, marked **115.00**

Creamer, soft green, chain of violets, applied fleur–de–lis feet, red mark . **100.00**

Flower Holder, pheasants, brass frog insert **675.00**

Vase

8½″ h, 4¾″ d, large white and tan roses, shaded brown and green ground **165.00**

10″ h

Cottage scene, woman with sheep in foreground, ornate handles, gold rim **640.00**

Mill scene, woman with sheep in foreground, ornate handles, gold rim **640.00**

12″ h, 6¼″ d, white poppies, cream shaded to brown ground, pr **750.00**

R. S. Prussia, box, cov, raised florals on rim, white lobed body, sgd and marked, 5″ l, 1½″ h, $350.00.

R. S. PRUSSIA

Berry Set, poppies, iris mold, master bowl, four serving bowls **300.00**

Biscuit Jar, Sunflower mold, red mark . **400.00**

Bowl

9″ d, green, scalloped, gold beading, melon ribbed int., white flowers, gold tracing **95.00**

11″ d, medallion mold, high gloss finish, sgd **225.00**

Butter Dish, porcelain insert, cream,

gold shading, pink roses, raised
enamel, red mark 700.00
Cake Plate
9½" d, Mold #209, irid green border,
white dogwood flowers, red berries,
green leaves, satin finish 150.00
11" d, plume mold, brown, gold, and
cream ground, peach, pink, maroon, and white roses in wicker
basket, gold trim 275.00
Celery Tray, 12" l, flowers in bowl dec 125.00
Chocolate Set, chocolate pot, four cups
and saucers, dark green, pink Bachelor Button type flowers, fancy handles, red mark, 10 pcs 900.00
Creamer, floral 225.00
Demitasse Cup and Saucer, dainty flow-
ers 100.00
Dresser Tray, poppies, Carnation mold,
satin finish, blown–out, red mark . . . 330.00
Ewer, 8¼" h, small roses, gold leaves,
pedestal base, red mark, satin finish 400.00
Fruit Bowl, 10½" d, circular, gilt border,
three int. floral sprays 275.00
Hairpin Box, hidden image, multicol-
ored, star mark 200.00

**R. S. Prussia, hair receiver, floral dec,
gold trim, 3½" d, 2¾" h, $200.00.**

Hair Receiver, green Lilies of the Valley,
white ground, red mark 110.00
Hatpin Holder, hexagonal, paneled,
hexagonal attached saucer base,
roses and lilac florals, green band,
gold traced roses around top of
holder and saucer rim 145.00
Plate
8¾" d, poppies dec, raised molded
edge and gilding 65.00
10" d, scalloped, gold beading and
chain, satin finish, green foliage
and white flowers, open handles,
red mark 180.00
Relish Dish, 9" d, blown–out mold, lavender and pink gloss finish, pink and
white roses, two handles, red mark . 80.00

Spoon Holder, 14" l, pink and white
roses 200.00
Sugar Shaker, 5" h, scalloped base,
pearl finish, roses, red mark 235.00
Teapot, brown cottage scene, red mark 450.00
Toothpick Holder, green shadows, pink
and white roses, six ftd jeweled, red
mark 250.00
Vase
6" h, pearl jeweled, satin finish, pink
and white roses, purple bottom,
shadow leaves at top, solid gold
handles, red mark 325.00
9" h, 3½" d, gold and green ground,
pink poppy like flowers, gold dec
handles 275.00
9½" h, six sheepherders, pink flow-
ering trees, red mark 700.00

R. S. SUHL

Coffee Set, 9" h coffeepot, creamer,
sugar, six cups and saucers, figural
scenes dec, some marked "Angelica
Kauffmann" 1,675.00
Jar, cov, 7" h, tapestry dec 135.00
Pin Tray, 4½" d, round, Nightwatch . . . 375.00
Plate, 8½" d, windmill scene and water,
green mark 100.00
Vase, 8" h, four pheasants, green mark 265.00

R. S. TILLOWITZ

Bowl, 7¾" d, slanted sides, open handles, four leaf shape feet, matte finish,
pale green ground, roses and violets,
gold flowered rim, marked 100.00
Creamer and Sugar, soft yellow and
salmon roses 50.00
Plate, 6½" d, mixed floral spray, gold
beading, emb rim, brown wing mark 100.00
Relish Tray, 8" l, oval, hp, shaded green,
white roses, green leaves, center
handle, blue mark 35.00
Syrup, pastel pink snowballs, blue mark 35.00
Teapot, creamer and sugar, stacking,
yellow, rust, and blue flowers, gold
trim, ivory ground, marked "Royal Silesia," and green mark in wreath . . . 75.00
Vase, 10" h, pheasants, brown and yellow, two curved handles 115.00

SCHNEIDER GLASS

History: Brothers Ernest and Charles Schneider, founded a glassworks at Epiney-sur-Seine,
France, in 1913. Charles, the artistic designer, previously had worked for Daum and Galle.

Although Schneider art glass is best known, the firm also made table glass, stained glass, and lighting fixtures. The art glass exhibits simplicity of design; bubbles and streaking often are found in larger pieces. Other wares include cameo cut and hydrofluoric acid etched designs.

Schneider signed their pieces with a variety of script and block signatures, "Le Verre Francais," or "Charder." Robert, son of Charles, assumed art direction in 1948. Schneider moved to Loris in 1962.

Vase, fluted, light amber, sgd, 7½" h, 7" d, $130.00.

Bowl
6" d, amethyst, shallow, sgd	175.00
9¼" d, mottled, red and purple, sgd	**175.00**

Compote
8¼" d, deep amethyst, knobbed stem and pedestal, sgd	**115.00**
11½" h, shallow clear cobalt blue mottled bowl with lemon yellow int., red standard, wrought iron circular foot, applied leaves and spherical glass berries, scrolling feet, intaglio sgd, c1925	**1,430.00**
15" d, purple and red, sgd	**275.00**

Dish, 13½ x 5½", mottled orange and dark blue, amethyst with white ribbing pedestal base ... **260.00**

Ewer, 15½" h, ovoid, pointed spout, thick cushion foot, mottled white frosted ground, mottled orange and green overlay, etched floral bands, applied purple angled handle at shoulder, engraved "Charder Le Verre Francais" ... **1,100.00**

Lamp Base, 12" h, orange, pink floral cut top, turquoise cut base, Candy Cane RK mark ... **650.00**

Lamp Shade, 18" d, Art Deco style, sgd **1,050.00**

Pitcher
6" h, raspberry body, mottled handle and spout	350.00
7½" h, maroon, white, and pink, sgd	**325.00**

Plate, 4" d, mottled, deep pink ... **75.00**

Vase
5½" h, cased, blue, black, and clear, orange lining, wrought iron ftd base, c1925, sgd ... **250.00**

7¼" h, globular, clear sides, random bubbles, neck overlaid in tangerine, wheel carved stylized blossom band, intaglio sgd, acid stamped, c1920 ... **3,850.00**

8" h, variegated orange, ftd ... **110.00**

8¾" h, 7" w, brown and orange randomly mixed, thick crystal, various sized air bubbles, pulled sq top ... **765.00**

9½" h, round, handles, orange with lavender and lemon pulls at raised neck, sgd ... **325.00**

14³⁄₁₆" h, trumpet, clear body, streaked pink and pale lime green, wrought iron mounting of spiky berried leaves, circular domed foot, intaglio sgd, c1920 ... **2,475.00**

17" h
Baluster, mottled orange and white glass, black handles, ftd, engraved signature ... **1,100.00**
Trumpet, ftd, clear with streaks of pink and raspberry, controlled bubbles, sgd ... **325.00**

SCHOENHUT TOYS

History: Albert Schoenhut, son of a toymaker, was born in Germany in 1849. In 1866 he ventured to America to work as a repairman of toy pianos for Wanamaker's in Philadelphia, Pennsylvania. Finding the glass sounding bars inadequate, he perfected a toy piano with metal sounding bars. His piano was an instant success, and the A. Schoenhut Company had its beginning.

From that point, toys seemed to flow out of the factory. Each of his six sons entered the business. The business prospered until 1934 when misfortune forced the company into bankruptcy. In 1935 Otto and George Schoenhut contracted to produce the Pinn Family Dolls.

At the same time, the Schoenhut Manufacturing Company was formed by two other Schoenhuts. Both companies operated under a partnership agreement that eventually led to O. Schoenhut, Inc., which continues today.

Some dates of interest: 1872-toy piano invented; 1903-Humpty and Dumpty and Circus patented; 1911–1924-wooden doll production; 1928–1934-composition dolls.

Reference: Richard O'Brien, *Collecting Toys, 5th Edition,* Books Americana, 1990.

Animal
Bear, 4¼", brown, glass eyes, twine tail, missing ears	200.00
Buffalo, 5½", cloth fur, glass eyes, cord tail	330.00
Camel, 8", painted eyes, two humps	175.00

Lion, painted eyes, $130.00.

Cat, 7", glass eyes, leather ears . . .	215.00
Donkey, small, painted eyes	50.00
Elephant, jointed hooves, glass eyes, rope tail, Howdah blanket, triangular headdress	385.00
Goat, 7½", leather horns, ears, and beard, painted eyes, replaced tail, missing one ear	180.00
Hippopotamus, glass eyes	250.00
Leopard, 5½", spotted, painted eyes, cord tail	230.00
Lion, 9", glass eyes	165.00
Ostrich, painted eyes	250.00
Poodle, 5½", grooved fur, twine tail, painted eyes, cracked neck	45.00
Sea Lion	480.00
Tiger, glass eyes	185.00
Building Blocks, orig box	175.00

Circus

Accessories

Barrel	20.00
Chair	20.00
Platform	18.00
Set, includes chair, ladder, barrel, tub, and whip	65.00
Tent, 25 x 35"	350.00

Performer

Acrobat, 8½", lady	550.00
Bare back rider on white horse, 6½"	200.00
Clown, 6¾"	120.00
Lion Tamer, wooden head	175.00
Ringmaster, 7", orig whip	265.00

Doll, carved wooden socket head and painted facial features, wooden spring jointed body, marked "Schoenhut Doll Pat. Jan 17, 1911, USA"	
13", Nature Baby, domed head, bent limb baby body, painted baby hair, almond shaped green eyes, c1915	375.00
19", blonde mohair wig, blue painted intaglio eyes, closed pouty mouth, 2 pc linen suit, c1915	325.00

Farm Characters

Farmer	135.00
Goat, painted eyes	150.00
Goose, painted eyes	200.00
Horse, 10", painted eyes	150.00
Lamb, painted eyes	150.00
Milkmaid	75.00
Pig, glass eyes	160.00
Movie Camera, marked "Spirit of Hollywood," orig box	75.00

Personalities

Barney Google	175.00
Felix, 4", 7 pc ball jointed body, Patent 1925	200.00
Golfer, orig skirt	375.00
Hobo	125.00
Jiggs and Maggie, pr	750.00
Teddy Roosevelt, 8"	485.00
Piano, 8½ x 9½ x 16", fifteen keys . . .	125.00

SCIENTIFIC INSTRUMENTS

History: Chemists, doctors, geologists, navigators, and surveyors used precision instruments as tools of their trade. Such objects are well designed and beautifully crafted. The principal medium is brass. Fancy hardwood cases also are common.

References: Crystal Payton, *Scientific Collectibles Identification & Price Guide*, published by author, 1978; Anthony Turner, *Early Scientific Instruments, Europe 1400–1780*, Sotheby's Publications, 1987.

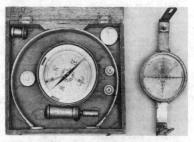

Surveyor's Instrument, cased, orig paper label reads "Made by W. & L. E. Gurley Co. Manuf. of Engineers & Surveyors' Instruments, Troy, New York," 13¼ x 12¼", $1,100.00.

Barometer, 17¼" h, standing, thermometer, German, H Richter, Berlin, late 19th C	130.00
Chronometer, 5" d, ship, orig case, Hamilton	400.00

Compass

Ship's, 10", sq, gimbeled mahogany box, Ritchie, Boston, mid 19th C .	220.00

Surveyor's, 3½", sq, wood case, French, 19th C 110.00

Heeling Error Instrument, orig case, marked "Pratt No. 5" 100.00

Inclinometer, cased, French, marked "Made by H Bellieni of Nancy," dated 1900 .... 125.00

Navigational Device, wood, brass hub, Index Hora Noctis, sgd "G Reynolds Fecit" 130.00

Octant
12¾" l, ebony, brass arm, ivory scales and label, orig black paint, label with "Spencer Browning & Co London," early 19th C 500.00
13" l, ebony, brass arm, ivory scales and label, label with "H Duren New York," mahogany case with "A Stowell" label, early 19th C 500.00
17¾" l, rosewood, ivory scales, brass radial arm, ivory nameplate with incised "Joseph Clark 79" 600.00

Protractor, 23¼" l, brass and steel, Crane & Vinton, Brattleboro, VT, dated 1858 .... 165.00

Quadrant
12" l, ebony
Crichton Brothers, London, ivory scales and label 355.00
Frye & Shaw, New York, cased, ivory nameplate and scales, brass radial arm, orig label "Costigan, South Street, New York" . 800.00
13¼" l, ebony, brass radial arm, ivory scales, ivory label with "John Martin," J Bassnett, Liverpool 410.00
14⅞" l, rosewood, engraved brass radial arm and scale, brass nameplate with "Cornelis Willemsz Junior/fait a FOHR," Dutch 1,150.00
20¼" l, ebony, engraved brass radial arm, brass and ivory scales 500.00

Sextant, brass, cased, silver scales, unmarked, 19th C 275.00
Stadimeter, cased 50.00
Surveyor's Compass, 4¾" sq case, removable handle, 19th C 225.00

Telegraph, ship's, brass
17" h, includes lamps 630.00
50" h, Chadburn, Liverpool 900.00

Telescope
13⅛" l closed, five draw, brass, twine wrapped barrel, mid 19th C 220.00
25" l, brass, directs artillery, includes tripod, dated 1924 .... 1,250.00
36¾" l, single draw, orig sailor ropework cov, Daniel James, London, early 19th C 165.00

Thermograph, cased, USD Navy Mark 2, Barth 200.00

SCRIMSHAW

History: Norman Flayderman defined scrimshaw as "the art of carving or otherwise fashioning useful or decorative articles as practiced primarily by whalemen, sailors, or others associated with nautical pursuits." Many collectors expand this to include the work of Eskimos and War of 1812 French POWs.

Collecting scrimshaw was popularized during the presidency of John F. Kennedy.

References: E. Norman Flayderman, *Scrimshaw, Scrimshanders, Whales And Whalemen,* N. Flayderman & Co., 1972, out–of–print; Richard C. Malley, *Graven By The Fishermen Themselves,* Mystic Seaport Museum, Inc., 1983.

Periodical: *Whalebone,* P. O. Box 2834, Fairfax, VA 22031.

Museums: Cold Spring Harbor Museum, Long Island, NY; Kendall Whaling Museum, Sharon, MA; Mystic Seaport Museum, Mystic, CT; National Maritime Museum, San Francisco, CA; Old Dartmouth Historical Society, New Bedford, MA; Whaling Museum, Nantucket, MA.

Reproduction Alert: The biggest problem in the field is fakes. A very hot needle will penetrate the common plastics used in reproductions. Ivory will not generate static electricity when rubbed, plastic will. Patina is not a good indicator; it has been faked with tea, tobacco juice, burying in raw rabbit hide, and other ingenious ways. Usually an old design will not be of consistent depth of cut as the ship rocked and tools dulled; however, skilled forgers have even copied this.

Basket, 8⅛" l, oval, reticulated panbone, swing handle, pine bottom, coin silver rivets 3,100.00

Bodkin, 3⅞" l, whale ivory, carved and crosshatched, 19th C 130.00

Cane
33¾" l, lady's, fluted whalebone shaft, twist carved, clenched hand holding baton knob, 19th C 850.00
34" l, coconut wood shaft, wood and whale ivory upper shaft, carved whale ivory clenched hand knob, mid 19th C 400.00
35" l, rope and diamond carved whalebone shaft, whale ivory and wood separators, whale ivory turk's head knot knob, mid 19th C 850.00
36¾" l, rope and flute carving, abalone inlays, faceted whale ivory knob, American, 19th C 1,400.00

Carpenter's Level, 26½" l, walnut, geometric wood inlays and border, brass bound, nameplate with "WT," 19th C 400.00

Coat Rack
29½" l, wood, three whale teeth hooks mounted on panbone, mid 19th C 800.00

35½" l, walnut, four sperm whale teeth hooks mounted on panbone, mid 19th C **1,600.00**

Corset Busk

12½" l, engraved hearts and potted plants, 19th C **325.00**

12⅝" l, engraved ship *Cape Cod* flying flag, two Victorian lovers, and young man presenting basket of flowers to girl, mid 19th C **1,400.00**

13⅛" l, engraved geometric design and foliage, back marked "Corset Stay Came From Sandwich Islands in the Year 1818" **550.00**

Cradle, bonnet type, incised line dec, bone peg construction, two quarter moon rockers, 6" l, 5" h, $475.00.

Dipper, coconut shell bowl

14½" l, octagonal whalebone handle, brass and copper connectors, mid 19th C **100.00**

15" l, wood and whalebone handle, mid 19th C **250.00**

15½" l, bowl with whalebone rim, mahogany and whale ivory handle with baleen and whale ivory rings, 19th C **1,100.00**

Ditty Box, cov

6⅜" l, panbone, wood top and bottom, engraved scene **550.00**

7⅞ x 5¾ x 4⅛", oval, panbone, mahogany bottom, engraved American ship on cov, mid 19th C **2,400.00**

Figure, 5¼" h, bird, mounted on whale tooth section with carved swans, 19th C **225.00**

Jagging Wheel, 6½" l, whale's tooth, 3–tined fork and wheel, mid 19th C . . **425.00**

Jewelry Box, 9⅜" l, wood, whale ivory and mother–of–pearl geometric inlays, fitted velvet lined tray, 19th C . **250.00**

Knife Box, 14⅜" l, wood and whale ivory inlays, includes thirteen pieces of bone handled flatware, 19th C **500.00**

Knitting Needles, 14¾" l, whalebone, fitted whale ivory clenched hands, ebony and whale ivory separators, mid 19th C **1,400.00**

Mantel Ornament, 12½" l, 5¼" h, whale ivory and whalebone, two mounted birds, carved wings, glass eyes, engraved colored flowers on stands, 19th C **550.00**

Mirror, 13¼" l, hand, wood frame, whalebone, animal bone, baleen and mother–of–pearl inlay, mid 19th C . . **250.00**

Model

Schooner, 6½" l, whale ivory and whalebone, mid 19th C **400.00**

Ship, 7" l, full rig, bone and ivory, 19th C **400.00**

Needle Holder

2⅛" l, whalebone, heart shape, mid 19th C **280.00**

3" h, whale ivory, pierced, mounted on green velvet, c1840 . . . . **600.00**

Pastry Tool, 6¾" l, whale ivory, 3–tined fork, crimper, and pinned hanger, early 19th C **450.00**

Plaque, 12¼" h, mounted whalebone Neptune figure on whale vertebrae, English **1,400.00**

Pointer

24¼" l, whalebone shaft, whale ivory and wood separators, clenched fist form handle **250.00**

29½" l, carved and inlaid whalebone shaft, hook shape whale ivory handle, mid 19th C **300.00**

35¾" l, whalebone shaft, turned whale ivory head with red, blue, and black scribe lines, mid 19th C **110.00**

Powder Horn

10" l, engraved panoramic whaling scenes and hunting scene, ship, whaleboat, and Indian tepee around bottom, 19th C **880.00**

13" l, engraved band around bottom, American ship and two Mediterranean vessels, marked "James Waterhouse of Bath 1805" **400.00**

Rolling Pin, 19½" l, hardwood, whale ivory turned handles, mid 19th C . . . **275.00**

Salt, master, 2" d, whale ivory, turned, 19th C **80.00**

Sewing Basket, 8¾ x 9¼", hexagonal shape, whale ivory and whalebone, reticulated, acorn finial, mid 19th C . **4,400.00**

Shelf, 19¼ x 9¼ x 30", wood and whale ivory inlays, drawer with turned whale ivory pull, 19th C **500.00**

Stool

10" l, rect, panbone, four wood legs, engraved "Mary Mace Fellows/ March 8, 1851" **375.00**

18" h, whalebone, Nantucket, mid 19th C **1,600.00**

Swift
  18½" h, whale ivory spools, whale-
    bone molding on double edges,
    mounted on circular wood base,
    19th C 1,750.00
  27" l, engraved coin silver inlays,
    plaque with initials, orig box with
    whalebone inlays and urn en-
    graved center plaque 6,000.00
Vase, pr, 6¾" h, whale's tooth, mounted
  on whale ivory base, engraved sailing
  ship, 19th C 500.00
Watch Holder, 10" h, building form,
  wood, fitted whalebone and whale
  ivory mountings, rectangular abalone
  over doorway engraved with 1839
  date, contains later Elgin pocket
  watch 2,200.00
Whale's Tooth, engraved
  4½" l, Scottish soldier holding shield,
    standing on castle wall, mid 19th C   250.00
  6" l, carousing pirates on beach
    scene on one side, Victorian lady
    on other, mid 19th C 1,100.00
  6⅜" l, engraved fisherman on beach
    on one side, building and beached
    vessel on other, 19th C 1,050.00
  7¼" l, sperm whale on one side, girl
    in red dress entitled "In the Sulks"
    on other, 19th C 500.00
Yardstick, 35¾" l, engraved numerals,
  marked in quarter inch segments,
  American, 19th C 625.00

SEBASTIAN MINIATURES

History: Sebastians are hand painted, lightly
glazed figurines of characters from literature and
history. They range in size from 3 to 4 inches.
Each figurine is made in limited numbers. Other
series include children and scenes from family life.

Prescott W. Baston, the originator and designer
of Sebastian figures, began production in 1938 in
Marblehead, Massachusetts. Sebastian Studios
are located in Hudson, Massachusetts. Prescott
Baston died on May 25, 1984.

Each year a Sebastian Auction is held in Box-
borough, Massachusetts, at the Sebastian Collector's Society meeting. Prices are determined from
this source plus the work of the Sebastian Exchange Board which develops a price list that is
the standard reference for the field.

References: Dr. Glenn S. Johnson, *The Sebastian Miniature Collection & A Guide To Identifying,
Understanding, and Enjoying Sebastian Miniatures,* Lance Corp., 1982; Paul J. Sebastian,
(comp.), *1991–92 Value Register Handbook For
Sebastian Miniatures,* The Sebastian Exchange,
1990.

Collectors' Club: Sebastian Collector's Society, 321 Central Street, Hudson, MA 01749.

**Cleopatra, Queen of Egypt, #359, early
mark, 3" h, $115.00.**

Abraham Lincoln, seated 125.00
Andrew Jackson, #159–A 250.00
Baby Buggy of 1850 .... 85.00
Betsy Ross, #129 .... 85.00
Colonial Carriage 75.00
Davy Crockett, #249 .... 225.00
Evangeline, #12 .... 125.00
Family Sing, #371 .... 200.00
Gabriel, #11 .... 135.00
George Washington, pen holder, sgd
  "PW Baston, 1961" 22.50
Gibson Girl, #316–A 85.00
Henry Hudson, #311 .... 175.00
House of Seven Gables, #111 ...... 100.00
Kennel Fresh, ashtray, #239 ...... 300.00
Mark Twain, #315 .... 100.00
Mary Had A Little Lamb, #137 ..... 100.00
Parade Rest, #216 .... 100.00
Peggotty, #52–A 85.00
Santa Claus, #123 .... 100.00
Shaker Man, #1 .... 150.00
St Joan of Arc, bronzed 275.00
Thomas Jefferson, #124 .... 85.00
Victorian Couple, #89–B 85.00

SEVRES

History: The principal patron of the French porcelain industry in early 18th century France was
Jeanne Antonette Poisson, Marquise de Pompa-

dour. She supported the Vincennes factory of Gilles and Robert Dubois and their successors in their attempt to make soft paste porcelain in the 1740s. In 1753 she moved the porcelain operations to Sevres near her home, Chateau de Bellevue.

The Sevres soft paste formula used sand from Fontainbleau, salt and saltpeter, soda of alicante, powdered alabaster, clay, and soap. Louis XV allowed the firm to use the "double L's." Many famous colors were developed, including a cobalt blue. The great scenic designs on the ware were painted by such famous decorators as Watteau, La Tour, and Boucher. In the 18th century Sevres porcelain was the world's foremost diplomatic gift.

In 1769 kaolin was discovered in France, and a hard paste formula developed. The baroque gave way to rococo, a style favored by Jeanne du Barry, Louis XV's next mistress. Louis XVI took little interest in Sevres. Many factories began to turn out counterfeit copies. In 1876 the factory was moved to St. Cloud and was eventually nationalized.

Reference: Susan and Al Bagdade, *Warman's English & Continental Pottery & Porcelain, 2nd Edition,* Wallace–Homestead, 1991.

Reproduction Alert.

Bowl, 11½" d, painted bouquets and sprays, molded double handles, blue line and gilt dash crenelated rim, blue interlaced L mark, c1765 . . . . **2,640.00**

Bust, pr, 18 and 19½" h, portraits of George Washington and Benjamin Franklin, white biscuit, Washington with pronounced forehead and receding hairline, shoulder drapery over blouson, Franklin with long curling hair, furrowed brow, buttoned vest and cravat, imp "Sevres S1914, Presented to Whitney Warren By The French Government MCDXV," white biscuit socle bases **18,700.00**

Cache Pot, 12¼" h, cylindrical, molded foot, two rect reserves, one painted with two maids and shepherd in 18th C costumes, obverse with large spray of flowers, gilt borders, gros bleu ground, four scroll feet, gilt bronze acanthus and scroll mounts with lion mask terminal, pierced rim, beaded collar, restoration to base, blue crossed L's mark **1,450.00**

Cup, pr, painted bouquets and sprays, blue line and gilt dash border, gilt dentil rim and metal stands, blue interlaced L mark, c1763 . . . . **1,430.00**

Urn

24" h, pr, ovoid, one with bust portrait of Marie Antoinette wearing straw hat, other with Mme Elizabeth holding a bouquet of flowers, pastel shades, wide gilt border, white

Urn, cov, cobalt blue, gold, and turquoise, courting scenes, bouquet of summer flowers, c1870, 17½" h, pr, $1,500.00.

ground dec with trophies and pr of flanking putti holding drapery, reverse with musical trophy or dove, pale green and gilt circular base, mounted as lamp, c1900 . . . . **1,870.00**

28½" h, pr, cov, amorous couple in garden, obverse with landscape and architectural monuments, two gilt bronze handles cast with beading and foliate scroll terminals, circular gilt bronze cast base, painted by Marant, sgd, c1900 . . . . **11,000.00**

29" h, ovoid, heart shaped gilt bordered panel with young couple in Grecian costume, classical landscape background, gros bleu ground, gilt foliate scrollwork borders, diapered cartouches, foliate cast handles headed by female bust, waisted pedestal with molded gilt line borders, reticulated gilt bronze spreading circular cast base, c1900 . . . . **3,850.00**

30½" h, cov, cylindrical, historical frieze sgd "E Lattermann," two colorful scenes of mid 16th C triumphal entry into European city, reverse with int. scene of presentation before bishop, applied molded guilloche border above, acanthus below, swirl molded porcelain socle and sq base, painted panels of Venus and cupids in landscape, gros bleu ground, swirl molded domed cov, large gilded pineapple knop, extensive cracking and restoration to base, c1900 . . **2,250.00**

Vase

5⅛" h, oviform, narrow waisted neck, white ground, pale green line dec, allover honeycomb pattern, gray sunbursts with yellow centers, shaded yellow neck band with overlapping leaf tips, printed date mark for 1911, decorator's mark for 1912, inscribed monogram in iron– red **100.00**

16" h, pr, silvered classical reserves, dark red ground, ormolu mounts . **1,500.00**

SEWING ITEMS

History: As late as 50 years ago, a wide variety of sewing items were found in almost every home in America. Women of every economic and social status were skilled in sewing and dress making. Even the most elegant ladies practiced the art of embroidery with the aid of jeweled gold and silver thimbles. Sewing birds, an interesting convenience item, were used to hold cloth (in the bird's beek) while sewing. Made of iron or brass, they could be attached to table or shelf with a screw-type fixture. Later models featured a pincushion.

References: Joyce Clement, *The Official Price Guide To Sewing Collectibles,* House of Collectibles, 1987; Victor Houart, *Sewing Accessories: An Illustrated History,* Souvenir Press (London), 1984; Gay Ann Rogers, *American Silver Thimbles,* Haggerston Press, 1989; Gay Ann Rogers, *An Illustrated History of Needlework Tools,* John Murray (London), 1983; Estelle Zalkin, *Zalkin's Handbook Of Thimbles & Sewing Implements, First Edition,* Warman Publishing Co., 1988.

Collectors' Club: Thimble Collectors International, 6411 Montego Bay Dr., Louisville, KY 40228.

Periodical: *Thimbletter,* 93 Walnut Hill Road, Newton Highlands, MA 02161.

Museums: Fabric Hall, Historic Deerfield, Deerfield, MA; Museum of American History, Smithsonian Institution, Washington, D.C.; Shelburne Museum, Shelburne, VT.

Additional Listings: See *Warman's Americana & Collectibles* for more examples.

Scissors, folding, adv, "Compliments of the Home Insurance Co, NY," sterling silver case, 2¼" l closed, $85.00.

Bodkin, 4½" l, three rings of dark wood separators, carved clenched hand end, 19th C **250.00**

Box, 4½" l, straw work, abstract design on sides, cottage on cov, English, 19th C **150.00**

Darning Egg, 5¾" l, ebony egg, SS handle with raised floral and scroll dec . **45.00**

Embroidery Hoop, 5¼" d, SS **35.00**

Hem Gauge, cast iron, marked "Pelouze," c1894 .... **30.00**

Needle Case

5⅝" l, animal bone, engraved whaling scene, 19th C **110.00**

7⅜" l, sailmaker's, wood, includes needles, 19th C **175.00**

Needle Holder

2⅛" l, whalebone, scrimshaw, heart shape, mid 19th C **280.00**

3" h, 1¾" w, ivory, pierced, mounted on green velvet, c1840 .... **600.00**

Needle Threader, metal, Champion Oil adv **10.00**

Pincushion

4", doll, flapper, porcelain head **75.00**

4½ x 5 x 8", figural, red, beaded, two strawberries, thimble pocket **150.00**

Scissors

Embroidery, 3", silverplated, emb floral dec on handles, patent 1864 .. **20.00**

Tailor's, 10", steel, japanned handles, bent trimmers **15.00**

Seam Rubber, wood

4½" l, carved handle, early 29th C . **100.00**

5⅜" l, carved hearts and diamonds rosettes, and initials "CS" on handle, rubber with "WS," early 19th C **225.00**

6½" l, carved "R" and "H" on rubber, carved handle, early 19th C **250.00**

Sewing Basket, 11" l, oval, baleen and wood, early 19th C **330.00**

Sewing Bird

Iron, one pincushion, bird with long sweeping curved tail which turns under **290.00**

Silver Plated, double pincushion, emb bird and clamp **165.00**

Sewing Box

11½ x 8½ x 6½", sailor made, various woods and ebony inlays, paper lining, 19th C **500.00**

12½" h, wood, two tiers, canted corners, ftd, mounted with swift, 19th C **1,100.00**

Sewing Knife, 3" l, scrimshaw, nude lady with upswept hairstyle, 19th C **325.00**

Sewing Machine

Singer, hand operated, japanned, gold trim, c1820 .... **175.00**

Wilcox and Gibbs, portable, orig booklet **75.00**

Sewing Stand, 8½" h, scrimshaw, re-

volving tiers, holds twelve spools of
thread, orig pincushion, 19th C **700.00**
Sewing Table, bird's eye maple, walnut
pedestal base, two drawers, pull out
slide, glass knobs, carved foliate
scrolls with floral band around stem,
Baltimore, early 19th C, 22 x 17 x 33" **4,200.00**
Spool Cabinet
  Brooks, two drawer, reversed glass
  insert **265.00**
  Clark's Christmas, six drawer **650.00**
Tape Measure
  Advertising, Lydia Pinkham Medi-
  cines **30.00**
  Brass, pig, tail turns to pull out tape **95.00**
Thimble
  China, floral dec, hp, artist sgd **15.00**
  Gold, engraved leaf border, 14K . . . **85.00**
Whalebone
  2⅜" d, circular, mid 19th C **190.00**
  2½" l, teardrop shape, 19th C . . . **175.00**
Thimble Case, crochet, basket shape,
handle and cov **20.00**

SHAKER

History: The Shakers, so named because of a
dance used in worship, are one of the oldest com-
munal organizations in the United States. This religious group was founded by Mother Ann Lee who
emigrated from England and established the first
Shaker community near Albany, New York, in
1784. The Shakers reached their peak in 1850
with 6,000 members.

The Shakers lived celibate and self–sufficient lives.
Their philosophy stressed cleanliness, order, simplicity, and economy. Highly inventive and moti-
vated, the Shakers created many utilitarian household forms and objects. Their furniture reflected a
striving for quality and purity in design.

In the early 19th century, the Shakers produced
many items for commercial purposes. Chairmak-
ing and the packaged herb and seed business
thrived. In every endeavor and enterprise, the
members followed Mother Ann's advice: "Put your
hands to work and give your heart to God."

References: Michael Horsham, *The Art of the
Shakers*, The Apple Press, 1989; Charles R.
Muller and Timothy D. Rieman, *The Shaker Chair*,
The Canal Press, 1984; Don and Carol Raycraft,
Shaker, A Collector's Source Book II, Wallace–
Homestead, 1985; June Sprigg and David Larkin,
Shaker Life, Work, and Art, Stewart, Tabori &
Chang, 1987.

Periodical: *The Shaker Messenger*, P.O. Box
1645 Holland, MI 49422.

Museums: Hancock Shaker Village, Pittsfield,
MA; Shaker Museum Foundation, Old Catham,
NY; Shaker Historical Museum, Shaker Heights,
OH.

**Sap Bucket, sgd "N. F. (North Family)
Shakers/Enfield, N. H.," 11½" d, 9⅛" h,
$125.00.**

Bonnet, dark brown palm and straw,
black ribbons, 9" flounce, KY **385.00**
Bottle, 9" h, aqua, emb "Shaker Pic-
kles," base labeled "Portland, Maine,
E. D. P. & Co" **90.00**
Brush, 10¾" l, horsehair, turned wood
handle **85.00**
Carpet Beater, 41½" l, bent willow,
turned beech handle **85.00**
Dough Scraper, 4½", wrought iron . . . **40.00**
Display Case, 8 x 10 x 10", pine, red
stain, sliding lid, dovetailed, Mt Leb-
anon **375.00**
Dress, homespun linen, pale brown,
wide double collar, twelve later but-
tons, late 19th C **200.00**
Furniture
  Apothecary Cabinet, 66 x 13", stained
  wood, rect, front fitted with twelve
  small drawers, molded white
  glazed porcelain handles, identification labels, drawer sides inscribed with various content titles,
  New England, 19th C **400.00**
  Blanket Chest, 37 x 24¾", red painted
  wood, hinged rect top with molded
  edge, int. till, paneled front and
  sides raised on tapering cylindrical
  legs, lid int. inscribed in pencil
  "Bloomsburg, C B Hutton, Box 105,
  Orangeville," midwestern, 19th C . **1,000.00**
Chair
  Counter, painted and dec, single
  arched slat back, rush seat,
  turned legs, turned stretchers,
  ochre dec, stamped "FW" on top
  right front leg, Freegift Wells, Wa-
  tervliet, NY, c1845 . . . . **8,800.00**
Clothes Rack, 36½" w, 72" h, red

painted wood, three horizontal bars, top bar mounted on either side with three hooks, rect uprights continuing to form arched feet, New England, late 19th C **2,500.00**

Rocker, curly maple, lemon form finials, four arched graduated back slats, mushroom capped arms, rush seat, turned legs and stretchers, rockers, Enfield, CT, first half 19th C **14,300.00**

Table

Dining, 34¾ x 35½ x 28", maple, drop leaf, rect top, hinged rect leaves, single drawer, sq tapering legs, first half 19th C **6,600.00**

Side

42 x 23 x 28", birchwood, rect top, frieze with molded drawer, slightly turned circular tapering legs, New Lebanon Community, c1830, painted red **6,600.00**

36 x 28⅞", cherry, red stained, two board scrubbed rect top, single drawer, turned wood pull, tapering sq legs, 19th C **1,250.00**

Work, 37½ x 23 x 25½", painted birchwood and pine, rect top and splash board, single molded drawer, circular tapering legs, orig red paint, New Lebanon Community, first half 19th C . . . **8,800.00**

Yarn Winder, 18" l, 20¼" h, movable winder with rect bars joined by block and cylindrical shaft, slightly arched trestle base joined by stretchers, dark green paint, late 19th C **350.00**

Hanger, 24", bentwood, chestnut **65.00**

Measure, 14½" d, 7¾" h, pine, cylindrical bentwood body, nailed end, metal band rim, cast iron semi–circular handles, int. with stenciled Shaker label, late 19th C **175.00**

Pantry Box, bentwood, oval, lappet construction

Blue painted, 6 x 2¼", single lappet on rim and body, off–white painted int. **325.00**

Matched set of four, 4⅝", 7⅞", 11½", and 13½", sgd "S. Marmouth Kegsilk, August 1848," New England . **3,575.00**

Scoop, 11¾", walnut **275.00**

Sewing Box, pink cotton lining and pin cushion, stamped "Shaker Goods, Alfred, Maine" **100.00**

Sock Stretcher, 26" l, wood **20.00**

Utility Box, cov

7½ x 3½", painted chrome yellow, oval bentwood form, lid, printed paper label inscribed "Isaac N. Youngs," first half 19th C **6,600.00**

10¾ x 4½", painted green, oval bentwood form, 19th C **2,000.00**

Whisk, 14½" l, wood, primitive **45.00**

SHAVING MUGS

History: Shaving mugs hold the soap, brush, and hot water used to prepare a beard for shaving. They come in a variety of materials including tin, silver, glass, and pottery. One style is the scuttle, so called because of its "coal scuttle" shape, with separate compartments for water and soap.

Shaving mugs were popular between 1880 and 1925, the period of the great immigration to the United States. At first barbershops used a common mug for all customers. This led to an epidemic of a type of eczema, known as barber itch.

Laws were passed requiring each individual to have his own mug. Initially names and numbers were used. This did not work well for those who could not read. The occupational mug developed because illiterate workers could identify a picture of their trade or an emblem of its tools. Fraternal emblems also were used and were the most popular of the decorative forms. Immigrants especially liked the heraldry of the fraternal emblems since it reminded them of what they knew in Europe.

European porcelain blanks were decorated by American barber supply houses. Prices ranged from fifty cents for a gold name mug to two dollars and fifty cents for an elaborate occupational design. Most of the art work was done by German artists who had immigrated to America.

The invention of the safety razor by King C. Gillette, issued to three and one–half million servicemen during World War I, brought an end to the shaving mug era.

References: Susan and Al Bagdade, *Warman's English & Continental Pottery & Porcelain*, 2nd Edition, Wallace–Homestead, 1991; Phillip L. Krumholz, *Value Guide For Barberiana & Shaving Collectibles*, published by author, 1988; Robert Blake Powell, *Occupational & Fraternal Shaving Mugs of The United States*, published by author, 1978.

Collectors' Club: National Shaving Mug Collectors Association, 818 South Knight Avenue, Park Ridge, IL 60068.

Advisor: Edward W. Leach.

BARBER SHOP: FRATERNAL

B.L.E.E., Brotherhood of Locomotive Eng, "BLE" monogram **90.00**

Elks, B.P.O.E., double emblem, Dr. title **300.00**

Fraternal Order of Eagles, eagle holding F.O.E. plaque **250.00**

International Brotherhood of Paper Makers, paper making machine, clasped hands, IB of PM **265.00**

International Order of Mechanics, ark
ladder, I.O.M. 250.00
Jr. Order United American Mechanics,
arm, hammer, compass, square, and
crossed flags 275.00
Loyal Knights of America, eagle, flags,
and six pointed star 275.00
Retail Clerks Union, red star, clasped
hands, initials, ARCIP 175.00

**Fraternal, K of P, gold trim, multico-
lored dec, marked "Austria," $125.00.**

BARBER SHOP: OCCUPATIONAL

Barber, hp, pair of hair clippers, worn
name 125.00
Bartender, hp, bartender pouring drink,
mirrored back bar, two patrons drink-
ing and smoking 400.00
Butcher, man standing with prize steer 500.00
Caboose, B.R.R.T. 400.00
Chicken Farmer, rooster crowing 225.00
Coal Miner, man in mine shoveling coal
into cart 350.00
Cooper, man working on wooden barrel 400.00
Dentist, upper false teeth 350.00
Hand Car Operator on track, two men
pumping 350.00
Hotel Clerk, clerk at desk, guest signing
register 375.00
Ice Cream Parlor, metal dish of straw-
berry ice cream with spoon, worn gold
trim 250.00
Livery Stable, horse drawn wagon with
driver in front of stable 275.00
Marksman, crossed rifles, target eagle
wreath 225.00
Musical, banjo, owner's name 350.00
Oyster House Proprietor, hp, oysters
and clams in foreground, sailing ships
and birds in background, gilt vines
and name, marked "Royal China International," 1929 adv for oyster
house 1,200.00
Painter, two men on scaffold painting
house 385.00

Phonograph, outside horn phono 350.00
Photographic, man with beard 250.00
Plasterer, hp, mortar board and two
trowels, gilt sprigs, marked "TECD
Co, Semovit" 150.00
Poultry Farmer, rooster, hen, and
chicks, worn gold trim 100.00
Shepherd, sheep standing in field 350.00
Shoemaker, tapering cylindrical body,
spreading gilt foot, gilt swags around
name, hp colored scene of shoe-
maker in shop 75.00
Theater Owner, movie entrance scene,
patrons on side walk, hand bills . . . 750.00
Trolley Repair Wagon, horse drawn,
scaffolding 1,250.00
Truck, chain driven, early 375.00
Tugboat in water, crew and captain, title 750.00

BARBER SHOP: OTHER

Drape and Flowers, purple drape, pot
of flowers, gold name 85.00
Flowers, purple, wheatheads, gold
name 65.00
Horses In Storm, white and black
horses, copied from painting 100.00

GOLDEN SPORTSMAN MUGS

The Bartender, three customers, saloon
scene 75.00
The Dentist, pulling teeth, patient in
chair 100.00
The Engineer, locomotive tender 75.00

**Scuttle, figural, dolphin, irid glaze,
marked "Germany 1," $85.00.**

SCUTTLES

Character
    Fish shape, green and brown 45.00
    Skull shape 75.00
Rose Decoration, mirror, R.S. Prussia . 175.00
Ribbed, multicolored flowers, gold dec 65.00

SHAWNEE POTTERY

History: The Shawnee Pottery Co. was founded in 1937 in Zanesville, Ohio. The company acquired a 650,000 square foot plant that formerly housed the American Encaustic Tiling Company. Shawnee produced as many as 100,000 pieces of pottery per day until 1961, when the plant closed.

Shawnee limited its chief production to kitchenware, decorative art pottery, and dinnerware. Distribution was primarily through jobbers and chain stores.

Shawnee can be marked "Shawnee," "Shawnee U.S.A." "USA #—," "Kenwood," or with character names, e.g., "Pat. Smiley," "Pat. Winnie," etc.

Reference: Mark Supnick, *Collecting Shawnee Pottery: A Pictorial Reference And Price Guide,* L-W Book Sales, 1989.

Advisor: Mark Supnick.

Sugar Bowl, Corn King, marked "U.S.A.," 5¼" h, 4¼" d, $20.00.

Bank, Bulldog	48.00
Casserole, cov, Corn Queen, large	38.00
Creamer	
Corn Queen	18.00
Elephant	20.00
Puss N Boots, gold trim, decals, marked "Pat. Puss N Boots"	110.00
Cookie Jar	
Clown, seal	75.00
Dutch Girl	125.00
Winnie The Pig, marked "Pat. Winnie USA"	80.00
Figure	
Bear	25.00
Gazelle	35.00
Puppy	25.00
Squirrel	20.00
Rabbit	25.00
Fruit Bowl, Corn Queen	22.00
Mug, Corn King	25.00
Pitcher	
Bo Peep, marked "Pat. Bo Peep"	35.00
Smiley Pig, marked "Pat. Smiley"	48.00
Planter	
Doe, seated next to log	24.00
Train engine	12.00
Wishing Well, Dutch boy and girl	18.50
Relish	
Corn King	17.00
Corn Queen	17.00
Salt and Pepper Shakers, pr	
Milk Cans	8.00
Wheelbarrow	10.00
Winking Owl	10.00
Teapot, 8½" h, 7½" w, Granny Anne, blue bowl, gold apron, white ground	30.00
Utility Jar, Corn King	48.00
Wall Pocket, Bird House	18.00

SILHOUETTES

History: Silhouettes (shades) are shadow profiles produced by hollow cutting, mechanical tracing, or painting. They were popular in the 18th and 19th centuries.

The name came from Etienne de Silhouette, a French Minister of Finance, who tended to be tight with money and cut "shades" as a pastime. In America the Peale family was one of the leading silhouette makers. An impressed stamp marked "PEALE" or "Peale Museum" identifies their work.

Silhouette portraiture lost popularity with the introduction of daguerreotype prior to the Civil War. In the 1920s and 1930s a brief revival occurred when tourists to Atlantic City and Paris had their profiles cut as souvenirs.

Reference: Blume J. Rifken, *Silhouettes in America, 1790–1840, A Collectors' Guide,* Pardigm Press, 1987.

Book, *Philadelphia Peale's Museum Silhouette Book,* sgd by Isaac Collins, dated 1830, sixty hollow cut silhouette portraits, mounted on blue or black paper, bound into small book, red leather bindings, marbled board covers, portraits of Elizabeth Sellers, Eliza Vaux, Susan Vaux, Susan and Samuel Emlen, Susan and Trotter Parrish, members of the Morris family, some paper loss and stain, 4" w, 6½" h	2,200.00
Children	
5" h, 4⅝" w, girl, ink and watercolor, blue dress, white collar, gilded brass and ebonized wood frame	325.00
6½" h, 10¼" w, two children, full length, gilded details, ink wash ground, labeled "Master Hubbard," framed	220.00
12½" h, 15" w, boy, full length, black paper, gilt details, ink wash ground, labeled "D. W. R. Buchanan 1847," gold frame	225.00

Gentleman, full length, top hat and cane, ink details, artist sgd "White," 10½ x 6½", $265.00.

Couple
2¾" h, 3½" w, oval, watercolor and cut paper, mounted on black fabric, inscribed on reverse "Samuel Fish and Mrs. Elvira Fish, Gov Wentworth's family, NH," repousse brass frames, c1825 . . . . 4,000.00
5¼" h, 4½" w, hollow cut, ink details, man and woman, orig emb brass frames, worn gilding, slight damage, pr 900.00
Gentlemen
4¾" h, 3¾" w, ink silhouette, old black reeded frame 175.00
5⅝" h, 4¾" w, hollow cut, pencil detail, old gilt frame 150.00
6⅜" h, 5¾" w, standing, gilded frame 100.00
7¼" h, 5" w, full length, frock coat, ink details, stains and paper damage, old gilt frame 150.00
Group
13½" h, 15½" w, family, brushed white highlights, black backing, white ink wash ground, room int., fireplace, titled "The Lesson 1840," printed paper label "Clay Turner, Profiles From Life," inscription "George Walters and his family, Jan 7th, 1840" on back, bird's eye veneer ogee frame 900.00
17" h, 13" w, seven reverse painted glass silhouettes of James Loader family, silk backing, orig wooden frame, names and dates on back, deaths from 1830 to 1856, orig wood frame, old gilding, repainted black ground 1,200.00

Women
3⅞" h, 2⅜" w, young woman, emb signature of Peales Museum, framed 85.00
5¼" h, 4¼" w, cut silhouette, old woman wearing bonnet, old black reeded frame 150.00
5¾" h, 3¾" w, cut silhouette, young woman, ink detail, old black reeded frame 90.00
6" h, 5⅜" w, hollow cut, pen work details, one titled "Miss Julia Wood," other titled "Miss Eliza Esther Wood," rosewood veneer frames, pr 250.00

SILVER

History: The natural beauty of silver lends itself to the designs of artists and craftsmen. It has been mined and worked into an endless variety of useful and decorative items. Pure silver is too soft to be fashioned into strong, durable, and serviceable utensils. Therefore, a way was found to give silver the required degree of hardness by adding alloys of copper and nickel.

Silversmithing in America goes back to the early 17th century in Boston and New York. It began in the early 18th century in Philadelphia. Boston was influenced by the English styles, New York by the Dutch.

References: Frederick Bradbury, *Bradbury's Book of Hallmarks*, J. W. Northend, Ltd, 1987; Louise Bilden, *Marks Of American Silversmiths In the Ineson–Bissell Collection*, Univ. of VA Press, 1980; Rachael Feild, *Macdonald Guide To Buying Antique Silver and Sheffield Plate*, Macdonald & Co., 1988; Donald L. Fennimore, *The Knopf Collectors' Guides To American Antiques: Silver & Pewter*, 1984; *Jewelers' Circular Keystone Sterling Flatware Pattern Index, 2nd Edition*, Chilton Book Company, 1989; Benton Rabinovitch, *Antique Silver Servers For The Dining Table*, Joslin Hall Publishing, 1991; Dorothy T. Rainwater, *Encyclopedia of American Silver Manufacturers, 3rd Edition*, Schiffer Publishing Ltd., 1986; Dorothy T. and H. Ivan Rainwater, *American Silverplate*, Schiffer Publishing, Ltd., 1988; Jeri Schwartz, *The Official Indentification And Price Guide To Silver and Silver-Plate, Sixth Edition*, House of Collectibles, 1989; Peter Waldon, *The Price Guide To Antique Silver, 2nd Edition*, Antique Collectors' Club, 1982 (price revision list 1988); Seymour B. Wyler, *The Book Of Old Silver, English, American, Foreign*, Crown Publishers, Inc., 1937 (available in reprint).

Periodicals: *Silver*, P. O. Box 1243, Whittier, CA 90609; *Silver Collector*, 170 Fifth Avenue, 12th Floor, New York, NY 10010.

Additional Listing: See Silver Flatware in *War-*

man's Americana & Collectibles for more examples in this area.

AMERICAN, 1790–1840
Mostly Coin

Coin silver is slightly less pure than sterling silver. Coin silver has 900 parts silver to 100 parts alloy. Sterling silver has 925 parts silver. American silversmiths followed the coin standards. Coin silver is also called Pure Coin, Dollar, Standard, or Premium.

Bailey & Kitchen, Philadelphia, PA, 1833–46, creamer, spheroid body, scrolled handle, flaring open concave spout, conforming circular stepped base, monogrammed **350.00**
Bancker, Adrian, New York, NY, c1760, lemon strainer, 3⅝″ d, hemispherical bowl, flowerhead pattern piercing below lozenge border, single incised line rim, side applied with scrolled strap clip, 2 troy oz **1,750.00**
Boelin, Joseph, New York, NY, c1720, tablespoon, upturned midrib handle, fluted rattail bowl, terminal engraved with initials, marked on back of stem, 2 troy oz **385.00**
Farnam, R & H, Boston, MA, c1807, teapot, 12″ l, Federal style, oval body, banded design engraved on shoulder, hinged lid, urn finial, wood handle . . **650.00**
Farrington & Hunnewell, Boston, MA, 1835–85, cake slice, medallion, 6 troy oz **100.00**
Harding & Co, Newel, Boston, MA, 1822–32
  Ladle, bright cut design, 7 troy oz . . **165.00**
  Tray, 21″ l, engraved with Bates family coat of arms, wide wreath of oak leaves and acorns, conforming cast border, raised on cast and pierced feet, marked at base, 103 troy oz . **4,400.00**
Hurd, Jacob, Boston, MA, 1740–50
  Cann, clear mark, 12½ troy oz **4,000.00**
  Sugar Nippers, 4¼″ l, scissor form, spurred ring grips, shaped arms, shell tips, circular hinged with engraved initials, marked on inside tip, 10 dwts **3,250.00**
Jones Ball & Poor, Boston, MA, c1850, goblet, 7″ h, chased overall, birds among grapevines, stippled ground, 8 troy oz **385.00**
Moulton, Ebenezer, Newburyport, MA, c1810, beaker, 4¼″ h, two S–scroll handles, monogrammed, 5 troy oz . **475.00**
Myers, Myer, New York, NY, 1723–95, teaspoon, engraved initials on handle **225.00**
Targee, John and Peter, New York, NY,

1811–25, porringer, 7½″, pierced handle, deep bowl, 9 ozs, 2 dwts . . **1,500.00**
Tisdale, B H, Newport, RI, 1824, ladle, 6 troy oz **150.00**
Wittberger, Christian, Philadelphia, PA, c1795
  Bowl, 6¼″ d, circular, pedestal base, beaded borders, marked twice on base **1,750.00**
  Soup Ladle, 13¼″ l, circular bowl, curved flaring handle engraved with bright cut floral border, pointed oval grip, roulette work border, monogram, 5 troy oz **1,000.00**

American, Sugar Basket, red liner, Reed & Barton, c1868, 4″ h, 4¼″ w, $85.00.

SILVER, AMERICAN, 1840–1920
Mostly Sterling

There are two possible sources for the origin of the word sterling. The first is that it is a corruption of the name Easterling. Easterlings were German silversmiths who came to England in the Middle Ages. The second is that it is named for the starling (little star) used to mark much of the early English silver.

Sterling silver has 925/1000 parts pure silver. Copper comprises most of the remaining alloy. American manufacturers began to switch to the sterling standard about the time of the Civil War.

Adams, W, New York, c1842, water pitcher, 17″ h, urn shape, allover floral and scroll repousse dec, C–shape handle with ram's head and leaf dec, circular plinth with loop and dart dec, 48 oz **1,810.00**
Bailey, Banks & Biddle Co, basket, 9½″, Art Nouveau, oval, pierced, flared sides, swing handle, monogram, 11 ozs, 11 dwts **365.00**
Ball, Black & Co, New York, NY, c1870, tea set, 6″ h, teapot, creamer, and sugar, oval cylindrical, beaded border,

engraved foliage, marked "E&S" and "Old Silver," 57 troy oz **660.00**

Barbour Silver Co, Hartford, CT, box, cov, 7¼" sq, Rococo style rose and foliate dec, handle set with green stone, four thread edge feet, gilt int., monogram, 19 troy oz **350.00**

Black, Starr & Frost, New York, NY
Bowl, 13" d, everted rim, putto flanked by flowers, 30 troy oz **1,650.00**
Cake Basket, 11" l, shaped octagonal, pierced rim, sides, and handle, 27 troy oz **825.00**

Caldwell, J E, Philadelphia, PA, late 19th C, bowl, 11" d, pierced everted rim, chased int., scrolling flowers, monogram, 25 troy oz **880.00**

Davis and Galt, Philadelphia, PA, c1900, bowl, 9" d, chased scrolling leafy vine, molded foot, 22 troy oz .. **357.50**

Dimes, Richard Co, Boston, MA, candy bowl, 5¾" d, circular serpentine shape, 10 oz, pr **175.00**

Dominick & Haff, New York
Asparagus Fork, 9¼" l, Renaissance pattern, enamel accents, 5 troy oz **330.00**
Entree Dish, 1891, 12" l, rect, scrolled rim and feet, foliate handles, 64 troy oz **2,970.00**

Duhme Co, Cincinnati, OH, 1898–1907, punch bowl, 14" d, chased and pierced, floral rim border and feet, 76 troy oz **3,000.00**

Durgin Co, William B, Concord, NH, cake basket, lobed hexagonal form, scroll and flower rim swing handle, 22 troy oz **770.00**

Elgin Silversmith Co, Inc, candelabra, 9¾" h, chamfered flaring central shaft supporting arm with nozzle on either side, circular base with engraved cypher monogram, c1945, pr **175.00**

Fletcher and Gardiner, Philadelphia, PA, c1820, hot water kettle on stand, 15½" h, domed cov, chased vine band, ovoid body with leafy band, scrolled legs, sq base, paw feet, later Tiffany burner, monogram, dents, 103 troy oz **3,190.00**

Gorham, Providence, RI
Bowl, 1873, 10½" d, hexagonal rim, strawberries, raspberries, and cherries, monogram, minor dents, 13 troy oz **385.00**
Butter Dish, cov, c1860, 10½" l, oval, guilloche rim, Renaissance style handles, conforming cov, cow finial, pierced insert, 22 troy oz **715.00**
Dresser Set, c1910, ten pcs, hand mirror, whisk broom, hair brush, shoehorn, button hook, nail file,

tray, powder jar, comb brush, and clothes brush, minor dents **600.00**
Epergne, 23¼" h, Rococo style, aprons of scrolling foliage centering leafy spray, supporting platform with collet base for large cut glass bowl, four leaf capped scrolling arms with smaller matching cut glass bowls, four multiple scrolled feet, 85 troy oz **4,125.00**
Fruit Bowl, 9" d, reverse design, 25 oz **200.00**
Ladle, 12" l, Maryland pattern, gilt bowl, monogram, 7 oz **220.00**
Teapot, scroll feet with engraved wreath and scroll design, 23 oz .. **350.00**
Tureen, 11½" h, 1878, oval, deer finial, grotesque mask ring handles, spreading base, monogram, 94 troy oz **4,400.00**
Tea Set, 1869, teapot, sugar, and waste bowl, wide pear form, engraved oval reserves, beaded moldings, handle damage, 52 troy oz **525.00**

Graff, Washbourne & Dunn, New York, NY
Bowl, 12" d, everted rim, chased and applied scrolls and foliate, plated liner, 22 troy oz **500.00**
Inkstand, pierced three–quarter gallery, scrolled feet, two cut glass bottles, 17 troy oz **770.00**
Service Plate, 11½" d, French border, hand chased, retailed by Theodore B Starr, Inc, NY, 221 ozs, 12 dwts, set of eleven **6,000.00**

Kalo Shops, Park Ridge, IL
Compote, 10⅝" d, 5¼" h, shallow bowl, scalloped border, five floriform sections, slender neck, circular base, slightly peened finish, marked "Sterling/Hand Wrought/ At/The Kalo Shop," c1920, 23 ozs, 12 dwts **1,250.00**
Platter, 12" w, 19½" l, oval, folded over border, convex moldings form handles, applied crescent borders, peened surface, marked "Kalo Shops, Sterling/Hand Beaten," c1905, 34 ozs, 8 dwts **5,500.00**

Kirk, S, Baltimore, MD
Bud Vase, 8" h, repousse, everted, tapering, 8½ troy oz **440.00**
Flatware Service, Repousse pattern, service for twelve, serving pieces, baby fork and spoon, 136 troy oz . **2,310.00**

Lebkuecher, Newark, NJ, 1896–1909, cake plate, applied and chased grape, interlaced design, monogram, 18 troy oz **220.00**

Lebolt, Chicago, IL, early 20th C, salad

servers, fork and spoon, hand hammered design, monogram, 8 troy oz ... **330.00**

Matthews Co, Newark, NJ, 1907–30, child's set, three pcs, 5½″ d plate, mug, and brush, acid etched with scenes and names of nursery rhymes, 6 troy oz **250.00**

Meriden Britannia Co, Meriden, CT

Dessert Plate, 10½″ d, shaped circular form, wide applied cast reticulated border with winged masks, foliate scrolls, and flowers, 19 troy oz **200.00**

Flower Basket, 14½″, cylindrical body, wavy open mouth, threaded rim, swelling shoulder, swinging strap handle, pierced with flat chased floral design, monogrammed, 62 troy oz **1,650.00**

Nydl and Goodron, New Orleans, LA, vase, 8″ h, goblet form, ornate bacchanalian repousse dec, 13 oz **1,430.00**

Pepper, Henry J, Philadelphia, PA c1825, creamer, urn shape, ribbed rim, loop, and dart mid band and base, lyre handle, monogrammed "EHR," 8 oz **255.00**

Schofield Co, Baltimore, MD, shakers, set of four, 5″ h, pear form, chased C–scrolls and foliage, 20 troy oz ... **825.00**

Shreve & Co, San Francisco

Bowl, 4½″ d, 7½″ d underplate, hammered, strapwork rim border, imp San Francisco marks 4091 and 5100 .... **412.50**

Cocktail Shaker, 10½″ h, cylindrical body, peened surface, fish tail removable pourer, side set with gilt and enameled medallion, bell mark, 20 ozs, 4 dwts **500.00**

Garniture, Art Nouveau, 15½″ h cov center vase, two 11¼″ h flanking vases, inverted pyriform bodies, domed circular feet, flaring lip, domed lids, upright stiff leaf finial, applied chased bearded iris dec on shoulder, three pcs, c1909, bell mark, 75 ozs, 12 dwts **2,500.00**

Ice Bucket, Arts and Crafts, 6″ h, flaring cylindrical body, applied horizontal staves, swing handle, finger strap below at back, hammered surface, applied monogram on spout, c1910, 17 ozs, 6 dwts **400.00**

Teapot, Art Nouveau, 9½″ h, undulating vines, 19 ozs, 10 dwts **400.00**

Spaulding & Co, Chicago, 1888–1920, dish, 11″ l, grape leaf form, tendril and leaf handle, 25 troy oz **415.00**

Starr, Theodore, New York, NY, 1900–24, claret jug, 12″ h, sterling mounts, globular clear glass body, peach cut to clear, palmettes, floral repousse rim and stopper, slight base chip ... **3,190.00**

Tiffany & Co, New York, NY

Bowl, 9″ d, octagonal, molded vertical rim, 1907–38, 18 troy oz **425.00**

Cake Slice, English King pattern ... **265.00**

Fruit Bowl, 8⅜″ d, circular, Revere design, three fan and block feet, 21 oz **440.00**

Meat Fork, etched morning glories, 3 troy oz **475.00**

Soup Tureen, 16½″ l, oval, chased edges and foot, ornate scroll handles on lid and sides, 81 oz **7,150.00**

Unger Bros, Newark, NJ

Basket, 20th C, 12″ h, waisted octagonal, pierced ribbon and leaf panels, repaired, 12 troy oz **330.00**

Warner, A E, Baltimore, MD, c1880, coffeepot, 12″ h, baluster, repousse, overall chased roses, stippled ground, ram's head mask handle, 35 troy oz **825.00**

Whiting Manufacturing Co, Providence, RI, 1840–1926, fruit bowl, 11″ d, hexagonal, shell and floral chasings, 15 oz **385.00**

Willard, A, Utica, NY, c1810, soup ladle, fiddle handle **550.00**

Wood & Hughes, NY, c1870, hot water urn, Renaissance Revival style, 20″ h, trumpet shaped body, pressed band of leaves and berries, lid engraved with scrolling design on matted surface, twisted post finial, handles with foliate ends and capped with figure of putto on each side, spigot handle topped with bust of female beauty, attached stand with cast openwork foliage on legs, orig burner, 82 ozs, 10 dwts **975.00**

Woodside Sterling Co, Richard M Woods, New York, NY, bowl, 11″ d, serpentine octagonal rim, heavily chased roses, fluted int., 16 troy oz . **525.00**

SILVER CONTINENTAL

Continental silver does not have a strong following in the United States. The strong feeling of German silver cannot compete with the lightness of the English examples. In Canada, Russian silver finds a strong market.

Austrian, hot water kettle, 10¾″ h, inverted pyriform, scrolling handle, hinged lid, ivory finial, matching stand with heating pan, ivory handle, three extra ivory knobs, M & K, Vienna, 1862, 66 ozs, 10 dwts **1,500.00**

Belgium, cruet stand, 13½″ h, baluster standard, swan handle, rect base,

Neoclassical motif dec, repairs, later bottles with German silver stoppers, mid 19th C, 19½ troy oz **330.00**

Continental

Bowl, 9" l, lobed crescent, acanthus, floral border, repousse floral dec, mask and scrolled feet, 19th C, 48 troy oz, set of four **1,700.00**

Plate, 10½" d, Neoclassical, center bust and putti, pierced rim, Neoclassical motifs, 14 troy oz **440.00**

Tobacco Box, 6" l, oval, portraits of Frederick II of Prussia and Ferdinand of Brunswick, inscriptions commemorating victory at Minden in 1759, marks "C" crowned and "IR" in oval, 19th C, 7 troy oz ... **525.00**

Danish

Bowl, 8" d, Model #19B, openwork leaf and berry support, ftd, Jensen, Georg Jensen, early 20th C, 41 troy oz **2,750.00**

Compote

4¼" h, Model #574C, shallow bowl, laurel leaf and berry support, import mark, Jensen, Georg Jensen, c1950, 8 troy oz **825.00**

12½" h, bowl applied with threaded band alternating with leaves, bulbous pedestal engraved with band of foliage, cushion foot with circular medallions in repousse encircled with strapwork and foliage, Michelsen, Copenhagen, 1851, assayer's mark for P R Hinnerup, zodiac marks for Libra and Scorpio, 39 ozs **800.00**

Flatware Service, Cactus pattern, service for twelve, serving pieces, Jensen, Georg Jensen, 164 troy oz .. **7,700.00**

Tea Set, 6" h teapot, sugar and creamer, oval, chased leaf and gadroon kylix dec, grape and leaf band dec **630.00**

Water Pitcher, 9" h, Model #432A, ovoid hammered body, angled mouth, Jensen, Georg Jensen, designed by Johan Rohde, 18 troy oz **1,320.00**

Dutch

Marrow Scoop, 9¼" l, plain design, double ends, Amsterdam, 19th C, 1 troy oz **375.00**

Stuffing Spoon, repousse tavern bowl scene, Rotterdam, 19th C, attributed to maker H Vrigman, 5 troy oz **110.00**

French

Asparagus Tongs, 10" l, engine turned dec, 950 standard, marked "JG," late 19th C **215.00**

Dessert Bowl, 4¼ x 2¾", plain, threaded bands at rim and circular ftd base, monogram, Paris, 950

standard, 82 ozs, 6 dwts, set of twelve **1,750.00**

Wine Taster, 19th C, maker "EP" in lozenge, circular, chased vine dec, inset Louis XV 1737 coin, 4" d, 3 troy oz **385.00**

German

Bowl, 13½" l, Nuremberg, c1900, repousse, oval, chased fruit and putti, leaf handles, marks "N" in oval, 14 troy oz **360.00**

Box, sq, 5" l, chamfered corners, repousse, musical putti and swags, imp "Menner Stuttgart, 925," 20th C, 12 troy oz **550.00**

Bread Basket, 15", oval, pierced openwork and repousse ornaments, floral garland borders entwining flower filled baskets at ends holding agricultural implements, draped over ribbons tied in French knots, alternating with cartouche at either side with scene of kneeling suitor and intended in Alpine landscape, each scene spaced with facing pair of birds and flowers, base with medallion of two infants playing with baby ducks, 19th C, 800 standard, 15 ozs **525.00**

Cup, 17" h, domed cov, globular cup, knopped stem, overall Renaissance style design, gilt int., imp "Heisler 800M," c1887, 22 troy oz **1,100.00**

Ewer and Basin, 17" d, fluted oval, hand raised marks of Voight, cross and crowned quarter shield with griffin and two stars mark, handle repair, 18th C, 53 troy oz **3,300.00**

Salver, 10" d, 2¾", circular piecrust molded border with plain center, flaring standard, molded foot, Augsburg, mid 18th C, 16 ozs ... **3,600.00**

Table Ornament, owl, 9¼" h, chased plumage, glass eyes, marked sterling, retailed by I F and Son, Ltd, 30 ozs, 4 dwts **1,100.00**

Tea and Coffee Service, silver gilt, pyriform bodies and domed tops, elaborately chased allover with panels of scrolling foliage and flowers, pricked ground, floral swags centering cartouche on either side, scrolling finial, domed spreading feet, 14½" h hot water kettle on stand with burner, 12" h coffeepot, teapot, two handled sugar and creamer, marked W W H, post 1888, 160 ozs, 14 dwts, coffeepot handle loose **5,500.00**

Italian

Candlestick, 9½" h, Neoclassical, attributed to Naples, early 19th C, knopped shaft, spreading base, engraved diaper bands, marked "GP," city mark head of woman with N over 8, 20 troy oz, pr **2,090.00**

Tea and Coffee Service, Flli. Peruzzi, 20th C, teapot, coffeepot, creamer, sugar, 26" l tray, twist–fluted pear form, chased rococo finials, 800 fine, 178 troy oz **1,760.00**

Norwegian

Coffee Set, 3 pcs, engine turned, cobalt blue enamel, gilt int., ivory handle on 7" coffeepot, David Andersen **800.00**

Liqueur Goblets, 3¾" h, set of twelve, engine turned and enameled, stems and feet of plain silver, gilt bowl **465.00**

English, Spoon Warmer, nautilus shell, seaweed base, c1840, hallmarked, 5½" h, 6" w, $165.00.

SILVER, ENGLISH

From the seventeenth century to the mid–nineteenth century, English silversmiths set the styles which American silversmiths copied. The work from the period exhibits the highest degree of craftsmanship. Active collection of English silver takes place in the American antiques marketplace.

Charles I

Goblet, London, 1633–34, tapering cylindrical, engraved crest, spreading molded foot, silver–gilt int., marked on rim, scallop maker's mark, 8¾" h, 17 troy oz **9,900.00**

Spoon, Apostle, London, 1633, fig shaped bowl, surmounted by saint figure, 7½" l, 3 troy oz **1,600.00**

Charles II, tumbler, hammered sides, slightly convex bottom, marks rubbed, 3" d, 2 ozs **250.00**

Edwardian

Center Bowl, Mapin and Webb, London, c1903, Baroque style, trun-

cated baluster form, repousse with acanthus leaf tips, scrolling acanthus form lug handles, stepped socle base, 10" d, 10" h, 72 troy oz . **2,200.00**

Dish Ring, Carrington & Co, London, 1910–11, waisted cylinder, pierced and engraved, 7½" d, 14 troy oz . **440.00**

Edward VII

Asparagus Tongs, W. W. BT. London, 1903, crested Fiddle, Thread, and Shell pattern, 9" l, 6 oz **175.00**

Epergne, Birmingham, 1909–10, central narrow flared vase, six arms supporting alternating conforming vases and condiment bowls, flared base, C–scroll rims, maker "TL" and "EM" in quatrefoil, minor dents, 16" h, 86 troy oz **3,190.00**

Serving Spoon, W Hutton & Sons, Ltd, London, 1910–11, C–scroll and flower design, 6 troy oz **140.00**

Elizabeth II, tray, Birmingham, 1952, A & Bro Ltd, octagonal, molded border, 27½" l, 133 troy oz **2,420.00**

George I

Caudle Cup, London, c1725, plain lip, cast S–scroll handles, reeded and gadrooned body, socle base, maker's mark rubbed, 5" h, 9 troy oz . **200.00**

Pepper Pot, John Albright, London, 1721–22, cylindrical, molded borders, domed engraved cov, 3" h, 3 troy oz **525.00**

Tankard, cov, William Fleming, London, 1714, molded domed hinged cov, scrolled and reeded thumbpiece, S–scrolled handle, cylindrical body, banded waist, rounded molded foot, 7" h, 22 troy oz **4,300.00**

George II

Candlesticks, Thomas England, London, c1725–39, segmented shafts on circular convex shaped feet, maker's mark stamped twice, 27 ozs, 4 dwts, lacking nozzles, pr . . **900.00**

Coffeepot, Henry Brind, London, 1749–50, tapering cylindrical, domed cov, chased overall with C–scrolls and flowerheads, monogram, wood handle repair, 9 troy oz **2,090.00**

Creamer, London, c1753, baluster, S–scrolled handle with later floral repousse dec, 4" h **100.00**

Inkstand, Magdeline Feline, London, c1758, oblong tray, gadrooned edge, baluster form inkwell and pounce pot, tapered stand of differing origin, raised on ball and claw feet, 8 " l, 14½ troy oz **900.00**

Pitcher, 7¾" h, pear shape, allover hunt scene and floral repousse dec, floral repousse domical lid, pierced thumb grip, C–scroll handle, vermeil int., 25 troy oz **2,300.00**

Sauce Boat, helmet form, floral and scroll repousse dec, lyre handle, shell feet, 16.5 oz **2,200.00**

Tankard, Robert Albin Cox, London, 1754, baluster, S–scrolled handle, overall floral repousse, center C–scroll and acanthus cartouche, 5¼″ h, 12 troy oz **400.00**

Waiter, Hugh Mills, London, 1749–50, shell and scroll border, hoof feet, 6½″ d, 7½ troy oz **440.00**

George III

Basin, William Simmons, London, c1809, oval, gadrooned lip quartered by shell form clasps, plain body, engraved coronet, 16½″ w, 3½″ h, 50 ozs **3,250.00**

Basket, Peter and Anne Bateman, London, 1795, oval, threaded swing handle, scalloped rim, threaded with pierced border, oval pierced foot, bright cut armorial and monogram on face, 14½ x 3½″, 22 ozs, 18 dwts **1,320.00**

Calling Card Tray, attributed to Edward Capper, London, c1768, shell and S scroll molded border enclosing plain surface, raised on double C scroll legs, pad feet, 6¾″ d, 7 ozs **175.00**

Candlestick, John Winter & Co, Sheffield, 1782–5, flared nozzle, tapering fluted column, beaded base, imperfections, weighted, 11″ h, set of four **4,730.00**

Center Bowl, Paul Storr, London, 1805, shallow, applied rim with branches and flowers, Victorian dec on sides in repousse of flowers and foliage, monogram in central cartouche, domed ring foot, caryatid handles, 8½ x 3½″, 18 ozs, 10 dwts **665.00**

Chocolate Pot, Robert Gray & Son, Glasgow, Edinburgh mark, 1804, pyriform, leaf capped scroll handle, hinged lid, foliate finial, circular foot, body engraved with cartouches centered by scrolling foliate medallions, one inscribed 1847, 11½″ h, 23 ozs, 4 dwts, foot repaired **800.00**

Compote, Matthew Boulton, Birmingham, 1809–10, oval cut glass dish, egg and dart rim, four molded legs, paw feet, center foliate finial, two date letters, glass chipped, 10½″ h, 32 troy oz **1,540.00**

Cup, Edinburgh, Scotland, 1801–02, urn form, high handles, urn finial and waisted cov, maker's mark "M

& F" in rect, minor dents, 12½″ h, 30 troy oz **550.00**

Hot Water Urn, John Edwards, London, c1810, heavily molded lid with gadrooned border, loop handles with acanthus terminals, projecting reeded spout, sq base, angled monopodia, 15″ h, 122 ozs **4,500.00**

Ladle, rubbed Irish maker's marks, Dublin, c 1775, 3 ozs **250.00**

Salt, William Simmons, London, 1784 and 1786, boat form, beaded rim and molded feet, repairs, minor dent, set of four, 9 troy oz **360.00**

Salver, Hester Bateman, London, 1781, shaped piecrust top, beaded border, three claw and ball feet, chased armorial of later date, 10″ d, 18 ozs **1,540.00**

Sauce Tureen, James Young, London, 1792–93, oval, spreading base, loop handles, urn finial and base molding, engraved arms, 9″ l, 43 troy oz **4,950.00**

Serving Spoon, John Pittar, Dublin, Ireland, 1780, engraved crest, wavy border, 12¼″ l, 4 troy oz . . . **220.00**

Skewer, Hester Bateman, London, 1782–93, ring and cartouche handle, engraved birdhead crest, 11½″ l, 3 troy oz **420.00**

Snuff Box, Joseph Willmore, Birmingham, c1818, oblong lid, cast floral rim, engraved turned surface above conforming case, band of scrolling floral engraving, 3½″ l, 3½ ozs **285.00**

Sugar Stand, Samuel Taylor, London, c1769, inverted slightly compressed dome form, stepped socle with gadrooned edges, 3″ h, contemporary armorial, 6 ozs **500.00**

Tea Caddy, Henry Chawner, London, 1794–95, oval section with reeded sides, engraved wrigglework and crest with motto, 5½″ h, 12 troy oz **1,430.00**

Teapot on Stand, Henry Chawner, London, 1793–94, oval section with reeded sides, engraved wrigglework and crest with motto, conforming stand, finial damage, 7″ h, 22 troy oz **1,540.00**

George III, late, tea set, Samuel Hennell, London, 1810–12, teapot, creamer, and sugar, sq handles, guilloche band, ball feet, 34 troy oz **1,430.00**

George IV

Fruit Basket, Robert Hennell, London, 1820, pierced basket with applied border chased with scrolls and fluted garlands, sides of fluted swirls terminating in acanthus leaves, swing openwork handle, pierced band of flowers and scrolls base, central face engraved with rampant cat, inscribed below "Touch Not The Cat Bot A Glove," 14¾" l, 45 ozs, 16 dwts **5,000.00**

Grape Shears, Jonathan Hayne, London, 1822, gilt handles, shells, flowers, and fruit on matte ground, 6" l, 3 oz, 10 dwts **500.00**

Salt, Charles Price, London, 1822, double border of scrolls and flowers, tripod hoof feet, gilt int., 3¾" d, 15 ozs, set of 4 .... **375.00**

Stand, London, c1824, rect, rounded corners, scrolling gadrooned border, bellied body heavily repoussed with scrolling foliage and flower heads, center armorial within foliate clasps, paw feet, treen base, marker's mark "AK," 8½" l, 14 ozs ... **200.00**

Tea Set, Edward Power, Dublin, Ireland, 1825–26, teapot, creamer, and sugar, fluted pear shape, chased florals, stippled ground, engraved griffin reserve, 7" h, 59 troy oz **1,100.00**

Toast Rack, John Cope Folkard, London, 1820, oval gadrooned and shell dec handle, seven slice rack, gadrooned stand with floral and shell corners, lion paw feet, 6½" h, 13 troy oz **100.00**

Tray, Philip Rundell, London, 1820, incised center field, coat of arms surrounded by rocaille and leaf scrolls, repousse rocaille, grapes, leaves, and scrolls on rim, shell feet, 24" d, 180 troy oz **6,800.00**

George V

Entree Dish, Crichton Bros, London, 1933–34, low cylindrical form, domed cov, 9" d, 67 troy oz, pr .. **1,980.00**

Muffineer, Birmingham, 1934, oct Queen Anne style, acorn finial, maker "TS" in two ovals, 8" h, 7 troy oz **275.00**

Tea and Coffee Service, Crichton Bros, London, 1933–34, 10" tea kettle on stand, coffeepot, teapot, cov sugar, creamer, and waste bowl, fluted, floral, and shell dec body, 179 troy oz **4,600.00**

James I, spoon, Apostle, London, 1616, fig shaped bowl, hexagonal engraved stem, surmounted by saint figure, 7" l, 2 troy oz **1,600.00**

Queen Anne

Caster, Charles Adam, London, 1705, partly fluted baluster body, foliate pierced cov, ball finial, 6¼" h, 6 troy oz **880.00**

Chocolate Pot, London, c1709, hinged knop finial, domed hinged cov, reeded rolled thumb piece, flaring cylindrical body, treen S–scrolled handle, side spout, 10" h, 24 troy oz **4,400.00**

Victorian

Cake Basket, Joseph and John Angel, London, 1840–41, shaped circular rim, foliage chased flutes, spreading base, matching swing handle by S LeBass, Dublin, 1870, 12" d, 30 troy oz **1,210.00**

Clock, mantel, W Comyns, London, 1900–01, Louis XV style, waisted case, scroll feet, finial dent, replaced movement, 14" h **880.00**

Cruet Stand, James Edwards, London, 1845, boat shaped bulging body, spiral gadrooned border, four scrolled leafy feet, segmented columnar handle with heart shaped handle, cut plate to hold bottles, wooden platform below, monogram on body, six glass bottles, diaper cut band **900.00**

Dressing Spoon, Samuel Hayne & Dudley Cater, London, 1844, Fiddle, Thread, and Shell pattern, 6 oz, 10 dwts **350.00**

Standish, London, 1869, etched and wrigglework dec, two crystal bottles, taper stick, 14 troy oz **225.00**

Tea Kettle, Foligno, London, 1867, indented ovoid shape, highly worked emb, chased, and engraved surface, Elizabethan figures in village dec, hinged lid with male sitting on keg, leaf capped spout terminating in bearded mask, matching stand applied with cast and reticulated floral swags headed by female masks, three cabriole legs, leafy feet, strut branching from each leg to support fuel container, 14" h, 80 ozs, 10 dwts **1,450.00**

Tea Service, Charles T Fox and George Fox, London, 1839, 10½" h hot water pot, teapot, creamer, and sugar, repousse, floral spray and leaf scrolls, leaf scrolled handles, 86 troy oz **2,800.00**

Wine Cooler, Barnard, London, Greek vase shape, bulging lobed body with acanthus leaves, emb and chased border of English rose, Scotch thistle, and Irish shamrock at top, overhanging lip with alternating leaves, squat stem with border of tongues and leaves, circular foot chased with acanthus on matted ground, S–curved handles end-

ing in acanthus leaf terminals, 9½
x 11½", date letter rubbed, c1840s,
74 ozs **3,850.00**

Wine Ewer, John S Hunt, London,
1857, Ascos form, leaf scrolled
handle, goat figural terminal, 8½"
h, 64 troy oz, pr **5,500.00**

William III, candlesticks, Wm Denny and
John Bache, London, 1698–99, gadrooned nozzle, stop–fluted column,
spreading stepped molded oct base,
marked "Britannia," "DB" and "EA"
crossed in quatrefoil, 7½" h, 20 troy
oz, pr **9,350.00**

SILVER, ENGLISH, SHEFFIELD

Sheffield Silver, or Old Sheffield Plate, was
made by a fusion method of silver plating used
from the mid–18th century until the mid–1880s
when the silver electroplating process was introduced.

Sheffield plate was discovered in 1743 when
Thomas Boulsover of Sheffield, England, accidentally fused silver and copper. The process consisted of sandwiching a heavy sheet of copper
between two thin sheets of silver. The result was
a plated sheet of silver which could be pressed or
rolled to a desired thickness. All Sheffield plate
articles were worked from those plated sheets.

Most of the silver plated items found today
marked "Sheffield" are not early Sheffield plate.
They are later wares made in Sheffield, England.

Biscuit Box, 6½" h, sq, hinged lid, lion
mask and loose ring handles, faux
tray base with paw supports, gadroon
borders, 19th C, replated **250.00**

Candelabra, tapering turned column
form, heavily gadrooned banding,
surmounted by twin scrolling candle
arms, 19½" h, pr **950.00**

Candlesticks, Victorian, Hawksworth,
Eyre & Co, Ltd., 5" h, columnar, spiral
bands of acorns, beaded borders,
weighted, 1890–91 .... **467.50**

Cruet Stand, Victorian, 1870, C–scroll
handle, eight pierced caster holders,
cut crystal bottles, ball and claw feet,
12" h, 25 oz **425.00**

Entree Dish, cov, 12½ x 9", gadrooned
borders, shells and flowers at corners, covs with fluted borders and
conforming borders, detachable handle with double bound branch terminating on calyx of acanthus leaves,
armorial engraved on side, pr **1,320.00**

Inkstand, 9" l, rect tray, twin pen channels, faceted crystal pounce pot and
inkwell, central chamberstick, 19th C **425.00**

Meat Dish and Cov, Regency, oval,
domed cov, engraved Prince of Wales

plumes and motto "Royal Welch (sic)
Fusiliers," shaped oval tray, well and
tree surface, overall gadrooned moldings, minor dents, base repair, 22" w,
11½" h, first quarter 19th C **1,540.00**

Plateau, 17½", Rococo style, mirror
plate in shell and scroll border, conforming spreading border, spreading
shell form sides, mask, and scroll
feet, possibly T J Creswick, mid 19th
C, feet cut down **625.00**

Sauce Dish, cov, 5½ x 6½", form of cov
calyx craters, disc shaped lids with
gadrooned handles, spoon openings
on rim, bowl with spiral gadrooned
border, hot water reservoir, pair of
double threaded handles, lobed
sides, conforming circular foot with
spiral gadrooned ring, early 19th C,
pr **715.00**

Tea Urn, 16" h, heavily gadrooned lid,
flattened urn form body, everted leaf
tip collar, scrolling hand fitted with
molded petcock, sq molded base with
ruffled foliate feet **700.00**

Tureen, cov, 14 x 20", turtle shape, detachable hinged lid **1,760.00**

Wine Cooler, pr, 9½" h, campana form,
broad bands of acanthus leaves, loop
handles, 19th C **1,800.00**

SILVER, PLATED

Plated silver production by an electrolytic
method is credited to G. R. and H. Ekington, England, in 1838.

In electroplating silver, the article is completely
shaped and formed from a base metal and then
coated with a thin layer of silver. In the late 19th
century, the base metal was Britannia, an alloy of
tin, copper, and antimony. Other bases are copper
and brass. Today the base is nickel silver.

In 1847 the electroplating process was introduced in America by Rogers Bros., Hartford, Connecticut. By 1855, a number of firms were using
the method to mass produce silver plated items in
large quantities.

The quality of the plating is important. Extensive
use or polishing can cause the base metal to show
through. The prices for plated silver items are low,
making it a popular item with younger collectors.

Bowl, 17¾ x 6¾", Neoclassical style,
plain body, four paw feet with acanthus terminals, lion mask ring handles, band of spiral gadrooning, unmarked **600.00**

Butler's Tray, 18½ x 28", crescent
shape, threaded edge, solid galleried
sides imp with repeating rect band of
flowers and leaves, face bright cut in
Egyptianizing floral motif, large cir-

cular medallion with traces of acid etched design of Athena drawn in chariot in reserve at center, large bracket handles with lotus terminals, unmarked, late 19th C **665.00**

Butter Dish, three pcs, base, lid, insert, delicate tiny double rows of beading around base, on edges, and dome lid, cut glass drip tray, Meriden Silver Plate Co **50.00**

Candelabra, pr, 20″ h, Neoclassical style, fluted pedestal shaft, draped urn supporting four lights, scrolling reeded branches and urn form nozzles, molded and reeded base **1,500.00**

Champagne Bucket, 9″, cylindrical, bracket handles, applied scroll border band, monogrammed, Simpson, Hall, Miller & Co **250.00**

Cheese Ball Frame, 5″ d, mechanical, vitriculture border, E G Webster & Sons **75.00**

Coffeepot, 11⅞″ h, George III design, pseudo hallmarks **3,525.00**

Decanter Set, 10½″ h, Victorian, figural, three whiskey barrels on four wheeled cart **1,100.00**

Desk Set, four pcs, inkstand, letter holder, letter opening, and half moon blotter, raised design of Rococo flowers, scrolls, trellis, and stork, marked J B **75.00**

Egg Caddy, emb floral platform holding six egg cups, dec prongs, feet with raised lion's masks, heart shaped bail handle, six egg spoons with shell shaped bowls, marked Simpson Hall Miller **225.00**

Epergne, 18½″ h, figural, central shaft with globe supporting spread winged eagle carrying partially draped maiden holding cornucopia with glass dish, two plated petal form dishes on either side rising from curvilinear foliate tendrils, domed base chased with applied flowers, four feet of curving elongated leaves, Art Nouveau, English, c1895 .... **2,750.00**

Frame, 9¾ x 17½″, 2″ wide border with raised figures, dancing and seated peasants, trees, houses, and fences in village scene, rough textured finish **90.00**

Fruit Stand, 16″ d, slightly dished shaped circular bowl, emb with vitricultural dec, four ftd base, International **200.00**

Goblet, Victorian, floral and leaf repousse dec, inscribed, pr **310.00**

Ice Bucket, cov, Baroque pattern, thermos lined, Wallace **225.00**

Jardiniere, 25½″, Baroque style, oblong, pair of leaf capped scroll handles,

body emb with broad band of acanthus leaves and foliate scrollwork, supported by pair of griffins, stepped oval platform base, metal liner **1,200.00**

Jelly Stand, Victorian, center handle, tongs, two glass jars **225.00**

Kettle on Stand, 8″ h, Ellis–Barker Silver Co, Birmingham, 20th C, modern design, basket form stand, scallop mark **200.00**

Meat Cover, 18 x 10½″, domed body, bright cut with panel of foliage swags and roses, beaded base edge, twisted branch handle, monogrammed, maker's marks, Victorian . **225.00**

Pitcher on Stand, 18″ h, Simpson Hall Miller & Co, c1880, tapering cylinder, Greek Revival designs, rosetted banded moldings, swivel stand, dented **220.00**

Plateau, 18″ l, Georgian style, oval, acanthus and shell border, center mirror plate **375.00**

Punch Bowl Set, 20¼ x 8″ punch bowl, twelve cups, circular waiter, Harvest pattern, Wallace **250.00**

Sardine Box, small Greek key border on box, lid with figural fish finial, fancy feet, monogrammed, glass liner ... **75.00**

Serving Dish, 15¾″ l, 10¾″ d, 2½″ h, rect, deep vertical sides, flanged everted border with double grooves on ends and sides, peened finish, four ivory ball feet, marked "Dirk Van Erp, San Francisco," Arts and Crafts, c1930 .... **1,760.00**

Serving Set, 20th C, cov tureen, four cov vegetable dishes, two salts, rotating hot 29″ d tray, gadrooned moldings **770.00**

Sweet Meat, 7″ h, Victorian, peasant carrying basket, pr **1,350.00**

Tea and Coffee Service, Art Nouveau, Argentor for Weiner Werkstatte, Vienna, Austria, c1900, angular form, four large cup and saucers, six small cup and saucers, two tiered stand, tray **15,500.00**

Teapot, circular, floral repousse dec, glass handle **120.00**

Tea Tray, 35″ l, oval, heavily cast border, engraved scrollwork center, Victorian **750.00**

Tea Urn, 16″ h, Regency, oblong stepped lid with fan form finial, conforming bowl with scrolling handles, slender reeded legs, paw feet, plinth base with ball feet **1,300.00**

Tray, 25¼″, Winthrop pattern, shaped rect, Rococo form, flat chased surface, bracket handles, Reed & Barton **200.00**

Umbrella Stand, 20½″, elongated trumpet shape, interlaced flowering

branches, H Wilkinson & Co, copper
showing **225.00**
Vegetable Dish, 15" l, cov, oval, Empire
design, bar handles, double shell feet **145.00**
Watch Holder, 6", cherub holds bird
aloft, stands on raised base, emb trim
around edge, Meriden Co **125.00**
Wine Coasters, pr, 5¾", sides emb with
repeating repousse frieze of female
mask crowned with grapes, scrolling
grape vines and leaves on pricked
ground, base of wood, engraved armorial central plug, English **550.00**
Wine Cooler, 10" h, German, WMF, late
19th C, bombe form, rococo scrolls,
cartouches, lion mask ring handles . **550.00**

SILVER DEPOSIT GLASS

History: Silver deposit glass, consisting of a thin
coating of silver actually deposited on the glass by
an electrical process, was popular at the turn of
the century. The process was simple. The glass
and a piece of silver were placed in a solution. An
electric current was introduced which caused the
silver to decompose, pass through the solution,
and remain on those parts of the glass on which
a pattern had been outlined.

Creamer, crystal, 2¾" h, $18.00.

Bowl, 10½" d, cobalt blue, flowers and
foliage, silver scalloped edge **85.00**
Cologne Bottle, 3⅜" h, bulbous, floral
and flowing leaf motif **165.00**
Compote, 7" d, clear, floral dec **75.00**
Decanter, 13¼" h, crystal, Continental
silver mounts, grape clusters and
leaves dec, orig stopper **80.00**
Ice Tub, closed tab handles, floral and
foliage dec, matching sterling silver
ice tongs **125.00**
Perfume Bottle, 4½" h, clear, vine and
grape leaf dec **40.00**
Plate, 12" d, crystal, floral dec **75.00**
Relish Tray, 12" l, three part, fruit tree
springs, bottom emb frosted grape
leaves and fruit **40.00**

Stemware, 90 pcs, ten water goblets,
eleven white wine, twelve red wines,
twelve champagne, twelve dessert
wines, nine cordials, twelve dessert
bowls and underplates **740.00**
Sugar Shaker, vine and grape leaf dec,
silver plate top **60.00**
Tray, 11" d, cobalt blue, vine and grape
leaf dec **100.00**

SILVER OVERLAY

History: Silver overlay is silver applied directly
to a finished glass or porcelain object. The overlay
is cut and decorated, usually by engraving, prior
to being molded around the object.

Glass usually is of high quality, either crystal or
colored. Lenox used silver overlay on some porcelain pieces. The majority of design motifs are
from the Art Nouveau and Art Deco periods.

**Compote, amethyst, overlay sgd
"Rockwell," 5½" d, 3¼" h, $130.00.**

Bowl, 8¼" d, 5¾" h, green, etched floral
dec, cut silver overlay applied rim and
swag border, three winged scroll feet **300.00**
Box, cov, 6¼" d, 3" h, frosted amethyst,
silver overlay mistletoe dec on top
and sides, silvered metal mountings **265.00**
Cologne Bottle, 6" h, green spherical
body, short neck, flared rim, hallmarked silver overlay of carved
scrolls and blossoms, orig overlaid
ball stopper **990.00**
Cruet, 5¾" h, squatty, waisted neck,
clear, silver overlaid foliate scrollwork,
cartouche, silver cased handle, neck,
and stopper neck, factory stamp
"Hemming Company, Montreal, Canada" **330.00**
Decanter, 7⅝" h, bulbous, ruby cut
glass, Art Nouveau floral silver overlay, faceted silvered ball stopper ... **360.00**
Pitcher, 5½" h, clear, geometric silver
overlay design, faceted stopper **130.00**

Vase

6½" h, baluster, transparent green, diamond airtrap design, satin finish, silver overlay cut in swirling florals, c1900	385.00
7¼" h, squat, flared, red glass body, silver overlay cut in scrolling floral design, star-cut base, imp numbers and hallmarks, minor damage to silver	1,045.00
8" h, baluster, red, silver overlay trelliswork and scrolling foliate vines, imp "999 Fine 946"	415.00
9¼" h, black amethyst glass body, silver wrap and applied rose, marked "925," sgd	522.50
9¾" h, squatty, bulbous, emerald green, outwardly tapering neck, inverted rim, silver overlay of poppies, continuous scrolling stems and leaves, imp "Sterling 29"	880.00

SILVER RESIST

History: Silver resist ware was first produced about 1805. It is similar to silver luster in respect to the silvering process and differs in that the pattern appears on the surface.

The outline of the pattern was drawn or stenciled on the ware's body. A glue or sugar-glycern adhesive was brushed over the part not to be lustered, causing it to "resist" the lustering solution which was applied and allowed to dry. The glue or adhesive was washed off. When fired in the kiln, the luster glaze covered the entire surface except for the pattern.

Pitcher, Wedgwood, dog handle, c1942, imp marks, 4" h, $55.00.

Child's Mug, girl reading, floral dec	100.00
Cup and Saucer, flower and vine dec	85.00
Flower Horn, 6⅝" h, three spouts, floral design	355.00
Goblet, 4½" h, vintage design	90.00
Jug, 4⅜" h, shield shape, painted floral dec, blue ground, c1820	260.00

Pitcher

5⅞" h, emb ribs and floral rim, polychrome enamel highlights	150.00
6¼" h, floral dec, putty ground, white int.	225.00
7⅜" h, floral dec	450.00
Pot, 8½" l, 5⅛" h, semicircular, vintage design	200.00
Teapot, 5½" h, flower and vine dec	290.00
Vase, 7½" h, ovoid, flared rim, flowering vines and foliage dec, rect base, Leeds, c1810	300.00

SMITH BROS. GLASS

History: After establishing a decorating department at the Mount Washington Glass Works in 1871, Alfred and Harry Smith struck out on their own in 1875. Their New Bedford, Massachusetts, firm soon became known worldwide for its fine opalescent decorated wares, similar in style to those of Mt. Washington.

Their glass often is marked on the base with a red shield enclosing a rampant lion and the word "Trademark."

Reproduction Alert: Beware of examples marked "Smith Bros."

Vase, SP holder, 8½" h, c1884, $195.00.

Bowl, 8½" d, leaves and acorn dec, silverplated rim, Rampant Lion mark	375.00
Cracker Jar	
Crab dec, sea plants and shells, cream background, sgd	1,850.00
Pansy dec, ribbed	475.00
Creamer and Sugar, individual size, 2¾" h creamer, 3¼" d, 3½" h cov sugar, slightly ribbed satin glass, tiny yellow and orange flowers, silverplated trim, sugar marked	410.00
Mustard Jar, 2" h, ribbed, gold prunus dec, white ground	300.00

Potpourri Vase, 10″ h, enameled chrysanthemums and leaves, gold outlines, satin ground, sgd 950.00

Rose Bowl, 4¼″ h, pink and rose pansies, green leaves, cream ground, sgd 300.00

Salt, open, melon ribbed, gold florals and beaded rim, sgd Rampant Lion mark 110.00

Sweetmeat Jar, cov, 5¼″ d, 5¼″ h, melon ribbed body and lid, tiny blue flowers, white satin ground, silverplated collar and braided bail handle 625.00

Toothpick Holder, columned ribs, pansies dec, blue enameled dots around rim, white ground 115.00

Vase

5¼″ h, 3″ d, opaque pink ground, white, brown, and black heron standing in pond 95.00

5¾″ h, 2½″ d, opaque gray ground, white, black, and brown heron, bug on front and back of ornate silverplated stand 95.00

7¼″ h, 8″ d, double pilgrim, lavender wisteria traced in gold dec, gold top beading 1,220.00

8½″ h, melon ribbed, satin, wisteria and leafy vine, gold highlights, emb scrolled neck 760.00

SNOW BABIES

History: Snow babies, small bisque figurines spattered with glitter sand, were made originally in Germany and marketed in the early 1900s. There are several theories about their origin. One is that German doll makers copied the designs from the traditional Christmas candies. Another theory, the most accepted, is that they were made to honor Admiral Peary's daughter who was born in Greenland in 1893 and was called the "Snow Baby" by the Eskimos.

Reference: Ray and Eilene Early, *Snow Babies*, Collector Books, out–of–print.

Babies

Pair, ice skating, boy and girl, 2″ . . . 250.00

Riding bear, 2⅞″, red, blue, and maroon 150.00

Seated

2″, one leg tucked under 30.00

3½″, one arm extended, black face, googly eyes, marked "Germany" 200.00

Seven babies playing musical instruments, 2″ 325.00

Sledding, pulled by huskies, 2¾″ . . . 75.00

Figure

Elf, 1½″ 55.00

Kitten, 1½″ 50.00

Baby riding polar bear, $150.00.

Snow Man 50.00

Sheep, 2″ 45.00

Match Holder, 3½″ 125.00

Planter, 8″ 175.00

Tree Ornament, snow angel, 1¾″ 200.00

SNUFF BOTTLES

History: Tobacco usage spread from America to Europe to China during the 17th century. Europeans and Chinese preferred to grind the dried leaves into a powder and sniff it into their nostrils. The elegant Europeans carried their snuff in boxes and took a pinch with their finger tips. The Chinese upper class, because of their lengthy fingernails, found this inconvenient and devised a bottle with a fitted stopper and attached spoon.

In the Chinese manner, these utilitarian objects soon became objets d'art. Snuff bottles were fashioned from precious and semi-precious stones, glass, porcelain and pottery, wood, metals, and ivory. Glass and transparent stone bottles often were enhanced further with delicate hand paintings, some done on the interior of the bottle.

Reference: Sandra Andacht, *Oriental Antiques & Art, An Identification and Value Guide*, Wallace-Homestead, 1987.

Collectors' Club: International Chinese Snuff Bottle Society, 2601 North Charles Street, Baltimore, MD 21218.

Amethyst, 2¼″ h, pear shape, carved, matching stopper, flat foot 175.00

Bronze, 2⅝″ h, circular, flask form, silver thread inlay 90.00

Ceramic

2¼″ h, two lions, green 75.00

2⅜″ h, pink and blue flowers, yellow ground, blue top 35.00

2½″ h, octagonal, white roses and blue flowers, carnelian top, stand . 90.00

Famille Rose, 2½″ h, 2″ w, $150.00.

3″ h, military procession design, blue underglaze, red coral top	190.00
3¼″ h, dragon dec, blue underglaze, white quartz top	75.00
3½″ h, relief Lohan dec, bright red top	110.00
Cinnabar, 2¾″ h, deep blood red, carved figures and scenic design, matching stopper, apocryphal seal of Chien Lung, 20th C	110.00
Enamel, 2½″ h, painted noble ladies design, gold top	65.00
Glass	
2¾″ h, painted int., green top	40.00
3⅛″ h, red, green top	135.00
Ivory	
2¾″ h, red floral motif on one side, brown figures on reverse	90.00
2⅞″ h, painted landscape on one side, relief figure on reverse	90.00
Malachite, 2½″ h, carved roses	265.00
Oriental, 4½″ h, two ivory panels with landscape dec, dipper with jade half beads, gilt metal frame, 19th C	220.00
Peking Glass, 2¼″ h, red, animal dec, green top	110.00
Porcelain, 3¼″ h, raised figure dec, ivory top	120.00
Quartz	
2⅜″ h, brown, orange top	110.00
2⅝″ h, red and dark green	45.00
2¾″ h, purple gray, carved pine tree design	350.00
2⅞″ h, brown, incised bird on pine design, poem on reverse	65.00
3⅜″ h, smoky	50.00
Turquoise, 2¼″	90.00

SOAPSTONE

History: The mineral steatite, known as soapstone because of its greasy feel, has been utilized for carving figural groups and designs by the Chinese and others. Utilitarian pieces also were made. Soapstone pieces were very popular during the Victorian era.

Jar, cov, 5½″ h, 3¾″ d, $25.00.

Bowl, 11½″ d, irregular oval, carved figure dec, carved teak stand, Chinese, 19th C	225.00
Candlestick, pr, 5⅛″ h, red tones, flowers and foliage	80.00
Figure	
3½ x 3¼″, geisha, kneeling, Chinese, c1880	125.00
6¾″ h, bird in flowering tree, carved	45.00
8½″ h, loon, carved, green, sgd "Pauloosie"	300.00
10″ l, 8¾″ h, polar bear carrying a seal, mounted on turntable, dated	1,300.00
11″ l, walrus, carved, green, sgd "Nooveya Ipeelie"	400.00
Plaque, 9½″ h, birds, trees, flowers, and rocks	115.00
Sculpture, 11″ h, four dancing figures in circle	110.00
Teapot, 5″ h, carved, figures, vines, and flowers	350.00
Toothpick Holder, two containers with carved birds, animals, and leaves	80.00
Vase	
4¾″ h, double, carved animals	110.00
6″ h, carved floral and bird dec	60.00

SOUVENIR AND COMMEMORATIVE CHINA AND GLASS

History: Souvenir, commemorative, and historical china and glass includes those items produced to celebrate special events, places, and people.

Among the china plates, those by Rowland and Marcellus and Wedgwood are most eagerly sought. Rowland and Marcellus, Staffordshire, England, made a series of blue and white historic plates with a wide rolled edge depicting scenes beginning with the Philadelphia Centennial in 1876 and continuing to the 1939 New York World's Fair. Wedgwood collaborated in 1910 with Jones, McDuffee and Stratton to produce a series of historic dessert–sized plates depicting scenes throughout the United States.

Many localities issued plates, mugs, glasses, etc., for anniversary celebrations or to honor a local historical event. These items seem to have greater value when sold in the region from which they originated.

Commemorative glass includes several patterns of pressed glass which celebrate persons or events. Historical glass includes campaign and memorial items.

References: Bessie M. Lindsey, *American Historical Glass*, Charles E. Tuttle Company, Inc., 1967; Frank Stefano, Jr., *Wedgwood Old Blue Historical Plates And Other Views Of The United States Produced For Jones, McDuffee & Stratton Co., Boston, Importer; A Check–List with Illustrations*, published by author, 1975.

Periodical: *Travel Collector*, P.O. Box 40, Manawa, WI 54949.

Collectors' Club: Souvenir China Collectors Society, Box 562, Great Barrington, MA 01230.

Additional Listings: Cup Plates, Pressed Glass, Political Items, and Staffordshire, Historical. Also see *Warman's Americana & Collectibles* for more examples.

Views of Asbury Park, NJ, Rowland and Marcellus, Heath Novelty Co., Asbury Park, NJ, 8½″ d, $20.00.

CHINA

Creamer, 6″ h, white ground, blue illus of Williamsburg, VA scenes, English	25.00

Pitcher

Masonic Hall, Chester, PA, blue and white transfer, tankard shape	225.00
William Penn, coral Indian handle, Lenox	150.00

Plate

Rowland and Marcellus, 10½″ d, Atlantic City, NJ	45.00
Staffordshire, 10″ d, Lewis & Clark Centennial Expo 1905, flow blue, marked	50.00
Unknown Maker	
Lincoln Sesquicentennial, 10″ d, white ground, black illus, 1959	20.00
Pennsylvania Turnpike, George Washington	35.00
Wedgwood, 7½″ d, blue	
King Edward VII Coronation, dated June 26, 1902	50.00
Marietta College 125th Anniversary, 1960	20.00
Signing of the Declaration of Independence, blue	45.00
Vase, 6½″ h, scrolled enameled panel of Niagara Falls with scenic background, allover enameled pink apple blossoms, purple highlights, brass base	425.00

GLASS

Butter Dish, Liberty Bell	140.00
Creamer and Sugar, breakfast size, Georgia Gem, custard glass, marked "Illinois State Pentientiary–Joliet"	85.00
Dish, cov, Remember the *Maine*, green	125.00
Goblet, G. A. R., 1887, 21st Encampment	100.00
Mug	
Bryan, William Jennings, milk glass	30.00
Independence Hall	70.00
Washington and Lafayette, milk glass	50.00
Paperweight	
Plymouth Rock, clear	65.00
Washington Monument, 5½″ h, deep blue, sq base, bust of Washington on oval medallion sq and compass medallion on opposite corner, top inscribed "Cornerstone, July 4th–48, Dedicated Feb 21, '85"	165.00
Pitcher, Garfield Drape	75.00
Plate	
Columbus, 9″ d, emb "1892"	50.00
Grant, 9½″ sq, emb "Patriot & Soldier," amber	50.00
Old Glory, 5½″ d	25.00
Washington Centennial, 7″ d, center emb "Centennial Exhibition 1876"	250.00
Platter, clear and frosted, three presidents, remembrance center	55.00
Tile, 4″ d, Detroit Women's League, multicolored irid	130.00

Tumbler
  Dewey, Banded Icicle pattern, portrait
    base **50.00**
  McKinley, William and Theodore Roo-
    sevelt, prosperity and protection
    slogan **75.00**

SOUVENIR AND COMMEMORATIVE SPOONS

History: Souvenir and commemorative spoons have been issued for hundreds of years. Early American silversmiths engraved presentation spoons to honor historical personages or mark key events.

In 1881 Myron Kinsley patented a Niagara Falls spoon, and in 1884 Michael Gibney patented a new flatware design. M. W. Galt, Washington, D.C., issued commemorative spoons for George and Martha Washington in 1889. From these beginnings a collecting craze for souvenir and commemorative spoons developed in the late 19th and first quarter of the 20th century.

References: Dorothy T. Rainwater and Donna H. Fegler, *American Spoons, Souvenir and Historical,* Schiffer Publishing, 1990; Dorothy T. Rainwater and Donna H. Fegler, *A Collector's Guide To Spoons Around The World,* Everybodys Press, Inc., 1976; *Sterling Silver, Silverplate, and Souvenir Spoons With Prices,* L–W Inc., 1988.

Collectors' Club: American Spoon Collectors, 4922 State Line, Westwood Hills, KS 66205.

Periodical: *Spoony Scoop Newsletter,* 84 Oak Avenue, Shelton, CT 06484.

Additional Listings: See *Warman's Americana & Collectibles* for more examples.

Louisana Purchase Exposition, Festival Hall and Cascades in bowl, demitasse size, Ball, marked "1904" on back, $30.00.

Atlantic City, NJ, Steel Pier, chased flo-
  ral handle, demitasse **32.00**
Bar Harbor, emb bowl, fish handle, She-
  pard mark **35.00**
Boulder, CO, name in bowl, Indian head
  handle **34.00**
California, Golden Gate emb in bowl,
  bear handle, marked "Watson" **15.00**
Decatur, IL, SS **40.00**
Denver, mule handle, SS **15.00**

Fort Dearborn, SS **12.00**
Grand Army of Republic, engraved bowl **65.00**
Huron, SD, Ralph Voorhees Hall **35.00**
Jamestown Expo **35.00**
King Cotton **30.00**
Lake Okaboji, cut out Indian head han-
  dle **45.00**
Memorial Arch, Brooklyn, round oak
  stove **30.00**
Nebraska, Omaha, high school emb in
  bowl, SS, Watson **25.00**
New Orleans, SS **35.00**
Palm Springs Aerial Tramway, SP, John
  Brown, marked "Antico" **100.00**
Pasadena, Golden Gate, diecut bear fi-
  nial **40.00**
Philadelphia, SS **35.00**
Portland, Oregon, SS **25.00**
Prophet, veiled **135.00**
Queen Elizabeth, 1953 Coronation ... **15.00**
Richmond, MO, SS **25.00**
Rip Van Winkle **30.00**
Rushville, IL, SS **30.00**
Salem, witch **40.00**
San Antonio, TX, SS **35.00**
San Francisco, CA, SS **35.00**
Silverton, CO, SS **25.00**
Statue of Liberty, NY **40.00**
Teddy Roosevelt, riding horse, full fig-
  ure handle **85.00**
Thousand Islands, fish handle, en-
  graved bowl, SS, Watson **40.00**
Williamsport, emb shield, knight's head
  on handle, teaspoon **35.00**
Winona Hotel, IN, SS **35.00**
World's Fair, Chicago 1893, SS **50.00**

SPANGLED GLASS

History: Spangled glass is a blown or blown molded variegated art glass, similar to spatter glass, with the addition of flakes of mica or metallic aventurine. Many pieces are cased with a white or clear layer of glass. Spangled glass was developed in the late 19th century and still is being manufactured.

Originally spangled glass was attributed only to the Vasa Murrhina Art Glass Company of Hartford, Connecticut, which distributed the glass for Dr. Flower of the Cape Cod Glassworks, Sandwich, Massachusetts. However, research has shown that many companies in Europe, England, and the United States made spangled glass, and attributing a piece to a specific source is very difficult.

Basket, 7½" h, 5¼" d, oxblood red and
  opaline, swirled together, splotches of
  gold aventurine, thick crystal casing,
  crystal handle, gold enamel dec ... **285.00**
Beverage Set, bulbous pitcher, six
  matching tumblers, rubena, opales-

cent mottling, silver flecks, attributed to Sandwich, c1850–60 . . . . **250.00**

Bowl, 5" sq, 3" h, ruffled, rainbow spatter, mica flecks **285.00**

Bride's Bowl, 10⅜" d, multicolored, ruby, cranberry, and green, ivory–yellow ground, silver flecks **100.00**

Candlesticks, 8⅝" h, pink and white spatter, green Aventurine flecks, cased white int., pr **110.00**

Cruet, Leaf mold pattern, cranberry, mica flecks, white casing, Northwood **450.00**

Ewer, 11" h, clear, cased pink, mica flecks, twisted applied handle **120.00**

Fairy Lamp, 6⅜" h, multicolored, gold mica flecks, Clarke insert **200.00**

Pitcher, 7½" h, bulbous, four sided top, apricot, gold mica flecks form diamond pattern, white casing, pontil . . **165.00**

Rose Bowl, 3⅜" d, 3½" h, eight crimp top, cased deep rose, heavy mica coral like dec, white int. **110.00**

Sugar Shaker, cranberry, mica flecks, white casing, Northwood **115.00**

Tumbler, pink and ivory stripes, silver flecks, 3¾" h, $100.00.

Tumbler, 4" h, pink, white, orange, red, yellow, and silver spangles **75.00**

Vase
8" h, modified baluster, tulip shaped lip, deep cranberry casing, clear casing with gold foil flecks in wide vertical swath, brown, green, yellow, and red spatter **225.00**

9½" h, cased pink and white spatter, silver mica flecks, clear applied handles **150.00**

SPATTER GLASS

History: Spatter glass is a variegated blown or blown molded art glass. It originally was called "End-of-Day" glass, based on the assumption that it was made from leftover batches of glass at the end of the day. However, spatter glass was found to be a standard production item for many glass factories.

Spatter glass was developed at the end of the 19th century and still is being produced in the United States and Europe.

Reference: William Heacock, James Measell and Berry Wiggins, *Harry Northwood: The Early Years 1881–1900,* Antique Publications, 1990.

Reproduction Alert: Many modern examples come from Czechoslovakia.

Miniature Lamp, green and brown spatter, clear ground, emb beaded swirl pattern, wick burner marked "P & A Hornet," 8½" h, $275.00.

Basket
7" h, 5" d, maroon, pink, yellow, green, and white spatter, white cased int., emb swirl pattern, applied clear thorn handle **175.00**

7¾" h, 4¼" d, maroon, white, yellow, and green spatter, white cased int., applied clear twisted handle **145.00**

Box, 7½ x 4½", egg shaped, hinged, white casing, yellow and blue flowers, gold and white leaves, three applied clear feet **275.00**

Candlestick, 7½" h, yellow, red, and white streaks, clear overlay, vertical swirled molding, smooth base, flanged socket **50.00**

Creamer, 4¾" h, pink and white, applied clear handle, Northwood **45.00**

Cologne Bottle, 8½" h, etched adv "Rich Secker Sweet Cologne, New York," applied clear handles **60.00**

Darning Egg, multicolored, attributed to Sandwich Glass **125.00**
Ewer, cranberry spatter, applied clear handle **50.00**
Fairy Lamp, 3¾" h, 3" d, deep rose ground, white spatter, satin glass, pyramid, clear Clarke base **125.00**
Jack–in–the–Pulpit Vase, 9¼" h, ruffled, DQ, white and peach spatter top, green base **115.00**
Pitcher, 8⅛" h, emb rosette swirl pattern, pink, yellow, and white spatter, applied clear handle **135.00**
Salt, 3" l, maroon and pink, white spatter, applied clear feet and handle . . **125.00**
Tumbler, 3¾" h, emb Swirl pattern, white, maroon, pink, yellow, and green, white int. **50.00**
Vase, 7" h, ring neck, shaded pink, white, and yellow patter, white int., pontil mark **50.00**

SPATTERWARE

History: Spatterware is made of common earthenware, although occasionally creamware was used. The earliest English examples were made about 1780. The peak period of production was 1810–1840. Marked pieces are rare. Firms known to have made spatterware are Adams, Barlow, and Harvey and Cotton.

The amount of spatter decoration varies from piece to piece. Some objects simply have decorated borders. These often are decorated with a brush, requiring several hundred touches per square inch to achieve the spatter effect. Other pieces have the entire surface covered with spatter. Aesthetics of the final product are a key to value.

Collectors today focus on the patterns—Cannon, Castle, Fort, Peafowl, Rainbow, Rose, Thistle, Schoolhouse, etc. On flatware the pattern is in the center. On hollow pieces it occurs on both sides.

Color of spatter is another price key. Blue and red are the most common. Green, purple, and brown are in a middle group. Black and yellow are scarce.

Like any soft paste, spatterware was easily broken or chipped. Prices are for pieces in very good to mint condition.

References: Susan and Al Bagdade, *Warman's English & Continental Pottery & Porcelain, 2nd Edition,* Wallace–Homestead, 1991; Kevin McConnell, *Spongeware and Spatterware,* Schiffer Publishing, 1990; Carl and Ada Robacker, *Spatterware and Sponge,* A. S. Barnes & Co., 1978.

Reproduction Alert: "Cybris" spatter is an increasing collectible ware made by Boleslow Cybris of Poland. The design utilizes the Adams type peafowl and was made in the 1940s. Many con-

temporary craftsmen also are reproducing spatterware.

Bowl, blue spatter
  Peafowl, 5⅞" d **275.00**
  Tulip, 18¾" d **300.00**
Chamber Pot, rose dec in red, green, and black, blue spatter, 8½" d **250.00**
Creamer
  Peafowl, blue spatter **400.00**
  Rainbow, red and blue, 5½" h **265.00**
Cup and Saucer
  Acorn, blue spatter **250.00**
  Castle, purple spatter **185.00**
  Peafowl, red, blue, yellow, and black, handleless **130.00**
  Schoolhouse, multicolored **550.00**
  Thistle, purple spatter **245.00**
Honey Pot, Schoolhouse, red, yellow, and blue **3,000.00**
Mustard Pot, Peafowl, green spatter . . **785.00**
Pitcher, Rainbow, green and red spatter **475.00**

Plate, blue, green, and red florals, cream ground, imp "Edge Malkin & Co," 9" d, $90.00.

Plate
  Dahlia, red, blue, and green, blue spatter, 8⅜" d **275.00**
  Flora, purple floral transfer, enameling, 10" d, marked "T. Walker, Flora" **125.00**
  Fort, blue spatter, 5⅛" d **175.00**
  Peafowl, blue spatter, 8¼" d **300.00**
  Rainbow
    5⅛" d, blue and red spatter **200.00**
    9½" d, blue and purple **125.00**
    Star, red and black, 8¾" d **75.00**
    Tulip, purple spatter, 6¼" d **275.00**
Platter, Rainbow, red and blue spatter . **500.00**
Sugar, cov
  Dahlia, red, blue, and green, 4½" h, mismatched lid **90.00**
  Peafowl, blue, yellow, red, and black, 4½" h **750.00**

Tea Bowl and Saucer
Coxcomb, red, blue spatter	**235.00**
Peafowl, three color rainbow spatter	**175.00**

Teapot
Peafowl, blue, green, yellow, and black, red spatter, 7" h	**150.00**
Tulip, blue and purple, 10" h	**175.00**
Toddy Plate, Acorn, brown and black, green and purple spatter, 5⅛" d . . .	**375.00**
Wash Bowl and Pitcher, Peafowl, red, blue, green, yellow, and black	**1,000.00**
Waste Bowl, Rainbow, red and blue . .	**250.00**

SPONGEWARE

History: Spongeware is a specific type of decoration, not a type of pottery or glaze.

Spongeware decoration is found on many types of pottery bodies—ironstone, redware, stoneware, yellow ware, etc. It was made in both England and the United States. Marked pieces indicate a starting date of 1815, with manufacturing extending to the 1880s.

Decoration is varied. In some pieces the sponging is minimal with the white underglaze dominant. Other pieces appear to be sponged solidly on both sides. Pieces from 1840–1860 have sponging which appears in either a circular movement or a streaked horizontal technique.

Examples are found in blue and white, the most common colors. Other prevalent colors are browns, greens, ochres, and a greenish–blue. The greenish–blue results from blue sponging which has been overglazed in a pale yellow. A red overglaze produces a black or navy color.

Other colors are blue and red (found on English creamware and American earthenware of the 1880s), gray, grayish–green, red, dark green on stark white, dark green on mellow yellow, and purple.

References: Susan and Al Bagdade, *Warman's English & Continental Pottery & Porcelain, 2nd Edition,* Wallace–Homestead, 1991; Kevin McConnell, *Spongeware and Spatterware,* Schiffer Publishing, 1990; Earl F. and Ada Robacker, *Spatterware and Sponge,* A. S. Barnes & Co., 1978.

Batter Bowl, 7½ x 4¼", blue sponging, yellow ware ground, pour spout, replaced wire bail handle	**120.00**
Bean Pot, cov, green, brown, and ochre sponging	**150.00**

Bowl
6½" d, blue and rust sponging, cream ground, Iowa adv	**50.00**
6¾" d, brown and green sponging, cream ground	**40.00**
10¾" d, light blue sponging, tan ground, arch molded sides	**210.00**
13¾" d, blue and white sponging spatter	**275.00**

Creamer, 4", green sponging, corset shape	**65.00**
Cup and Saucer, blue and white sponging, straight sides	**110.00**
Cuspidor, blue sponging, molded basketweave dec, white ground	**150.00**
Inkwell, green sponging	**180.00**
Jar, cov, 6" h, blue sponging, cream ground, wire handle	**215.00**

Jug
3" h, green, brown, and ochre sponging	**125.00**
7¼" h, flared top, blue sponged bands, cream ground, applied handle	**125.00**
Mug, 1¾" h, red sponging, cream ground	**125.00**
Nappy, 8½" d, rect, blue sponged int., white ground	**175.00**

Pitcher
8⅞" h, blue and white sponging . . .	**325.00**
9⅝" h, blue and white sponging spatter	**425.00**
11¼" h, baluster form, blue sponging	**120.00**

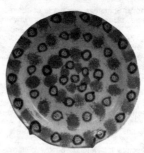

Plate, yellow, ochre, and blue sponged circles, English Delft, early 18th C, $2,000.00.

Plate, 10¼" d, blue sponging, white ground, scalloped rim	**120.00**
Soap Dish, blue and cream sponging .	**60.00**
Sugar, blue and red sponging, cream ground	**175.00**
Wash Bowl and Pitcher, blue and olive green sponging, blue bands, white ground	**325.00**

SPORT CARDS

History: Baseball cards date from the late 19th century. By 1900 the most common cards, known as "T" cards, were those produced by tobacco companies such as American Tobacco Co., with the majority of the tobacco–related cards being produced between 1909 and 1915. During the 1920s American Caramel, National Caramel, and York Caramel candy companies issued cards identified in lists as "E" cards.

From 1933 to 1941 Goudey Gum Co. of Boston, and in 1939, Gum Inc., were the big producers of baseball cards. Following World War II, Bowman Gum of Philadelphia (B.G.H.L.I.), the successor to Gum, Inc., lead the way. Topps, Inc., (T.C.G.) of Brooklyn, New York, followed. Topps bought Bowman in 1956 and enjoyed almost a monopoly in card production until 1981.

In 1981 Topps was challenged by Fleer of Philadelphia and Donruss of Memphis. All three companies annually produce sets of cards numbering 600 cards or more.

Football cards have been produced since the 1890s. However, it was not until 1933 that the first bubble gum football card appeared in the Goudey Sport Kings set. In 1935 National Chickle of Cambridge, Massachusetts, produced the first full set of gum cards devoted exclusively to football.

Both Leaf Gum of Chicago and Bowman Gum of Philadelphia produced sets of football cards in 1948. Leaf discontinued production after their 1949 issue. Bowman Gum continued until 1955.

Topps Chewing Gum entered the market in 1950 with its college stars set. Topps became a fixture in the football card market with its 1955 All–American set. From 1956 thorough 1963 Topps printed a card set of National Football League players, combining them with the American Football League players in 1961.

Topps produced sets with only American Football League players from 1964 to 1967. The Philadelphia Gum Company made National Football League card sets during this period. Beginning in 1968 and continuing to the present, Topps has produced sets of National Football League cards, the name adopted by the merger of the two leagues.

References: James Beckett, *The Official 1992 Price Guide To Baseball Cards, Eleventh Edition*, House of Collectibles, 1991; James Beckett, *Sports Americana Baseball Card Price Guide, No. 10*, Edgewater Book Co., 1988; James Beckett and Denis W. Eckes, *The Sport Americana Football, Hockey, Basketball and Boxing Card Price Guide, No. 5*, Edgewater Books, 1987; Gene Florence, *The Standard Baseball Card Price Guide, Fourth Edition*, Collector Books, 1992; Jeff Kurowski, (ed.), *Baseball Card Price Guide, 6th Edition*, Krause Publications, 1992; Jeff Kurowski, (ed.), *Standard Catalog Of Baseball Cards, Second Edition*, Krause Publications, 1990; Troy Kirk, *Collector's Guide To Baseball Cards*, Wallace–Homestead Book Company, 1990; Sports Collectors Digest, *Football, Basketball, & Hockey Price Guide*, Krause Publications, 1991.

Periodicals: *Baseball Card News*, 700 East State Street, Iola, WI 54490; *Beckett Baseball Monthly*, P.O. Box 1915, Marion, OH 43305; *Current Card Prices*, P.O. Box 480, East Islip, NY 11730; *Malloy's Sports Collectibles,* 17 Danbury Rd., Ridgefield, CT 06877; *Sports Collectors Digest* 700 East State Street, Iola, WI 54990; *Tuff Stuff*, P.O. Box 1637, Glen Allen, VA 23060.

Baseball, Bowman, Richie Asburn, #10, 1953, $4.50.

BASEBALL

BOWMAN ERA

1948 Bowman (black and white)	
Complete set (48)	525.00
Common player (1–36)	5.00
Common player (37–48)	7.50
9 Walker Cooper	7.00
29 Joe Page	16.00
45 Hank Sauer	16.00
1949 Bowman	
Complete set (240)	2,975.00
Common player (1–144)	5.00
Common player (145–240)	20.00
31 Dick Kokos	14.00
36 Pee Wee Reese	50.00
1950 Bowman	
Complete set (252)	1,825.00
Common player (1–72)	10.00
Common player (73–252)	5.00
35 Enos Slaughter	40.00
232 Al Rosen	22.50
248 Sam Jethroe	7.50
1952 Bowman (color)	
Complete set (252)	475.00
Common player (1–216)	1.00
Common player (217–252)	2.00
1 Yogi Berra	30.00
101 Mickey Mantle	600.00
196 Stan Musial	200.00
218 Willie Mays	400.00
1953 Bowman (color)	
Complete set (160)	1,200.00

Common player (1–112)	10.00
Common player (113–128)	16.00
Common player (129–160)	12.00
46 Roy Campanella	110.00
117 Duke Snider	250.00
146 Early Wynn	55.00
153 Whitey Ford	175.00

1954 Bowman

Complete set (224)	450.00
Common player (1–128)	2.00
Common player (129–224)	2.40
55 Jim Delsing	3.00
132 Bob Feller	32.50
181 Les Moss	3.50
224 Bill Bruton	5.00

TOPPS ERA

1951 Topps, blue backs

Complete set (52)	625.00
Common player (1–52)	10.00
3 Richie Ashburn	20.00
30 Enos Slaughter	16.00
50 Johnny Mize	20.00

1952 Topps

Complete set (407)	3,800.00
Common player (1–80)	11.00
Common player (81–252)	6.00
Common player (253–310)	12.00
Common player (311–407)	25.00
26 Monte Irvin	50.00
48 Joe Page (error)	150.00
88 Bob Feller	60.00
175 Billy Martin	150.00
191 Yogi Berra	175.00
407 Eddie Mathews	500.00

1954 Topps

Complete set (250)	1,675.00
Common player (1–50)	3.50
Common player (51–75)	3.00
Common player (76–250)	3.50
17 Phil Rizzuto	27.50
94 Ernie Banks	300.00
132 Tom Lasorda	75.00
250 Ted Williams	150.00

1956 Topps

Complete set (340)	1,260.00
Common player (1–180)	1.50
Common player (181–260)	2.50
Common player (261–340)	3.00
20 Al Kaline	32.50
31 Hank Aaron	80.00
79 Sandy Koufax	110.00
130 Willie Mays	110.00
166 Brooklyn Dodgers	75.00

1958 Topps

Complete set (495)	975.00
Common player (1–110)	1.25
Common player (111–440)	1.00
Common player (441–495)	.60
1 Ted Williams	100.00
30A Hank Aaron	65.00
52A Roberto Clemente	45.00
187 Sandy Koufax	50.00

1960 Topps

Complete set (572)	875.00
Common player (1–506)	.75
Common player (507–572)	2.25
148 Carl Yastrzemski	175.00
300 Hank Aaron	40.00

1961 Topps

Complete set (589)	1,260.00
Common player (1–522)	.50
Common player (523–589)	7.50
10 Brooks Robinson	12.50
260 Don Drysdale	9.00
287 Carl Yastrzemski	75.00
417 Juan Marichal	40.00

FOOTBALL

Bell Brand

1960, Common card	4.50
Gene Selawski	120.00

Bowman Gum Company

1948
Common card	2.25
Harry Gilmer	15.00

1953
Common card	1.20
Frank Gifford	18.00

1955
Common card	1.00
Norm VanBrocklin	8.00

Fleer Gum Company

1960
Common card	.35
Sammy Baugh	6.50

1962
Common card	.25
George Blanda	5.50
Jack Kemp	4.75

Leaf Gum

1948
Common card	2.00
Jackie Jensen	18.00

1949
Common card	2.00
Bobby Layne	9.00

Philadelphia Gum Company

1964
Common card	.25
Jim Brown	18.00

1966
Common card	.20
Fran Tarkenton	5.25

Topps Chewing Gum Inc

1950
Common card	2.25
Joe Paterno	20.00

1951
Common card	1.25
Bill Wade	5.00

1955
Common card	1.00
Knute Rockne	10.00

1958
- Common card .... **.30**
- John Unitas **5.00**

1960
- Common card .... **.30**
- Y A Title **5.00**

1963
- Common card .... **.25**
- Don Meredith **6.00**

SPORTS COLLECTIBLES

History: Individuals have been saving sports related equipment since the inception of sports. Some was passed down from generation to generation for reuse. The balance occupied dark spaces in closets, attics, and basements.

In the 1980s two key trends brought collectors' attention to sports collectibles. First, decorators began using old sports items, especially in restaurant decor. Second, card collectors began to discover the thrill of owning the "real" thing. Although the principal thrust was on baseball material, by the beginning of the 1990s all sport categories were collectible with golf and football especially strong.

References: Mark Baker, *Sport Collectors Digest Baseball Autograph Handbook*, Krause Publications, 1991; James Beckett, *The Sport Americana Price Guide To Baseball Collectibles*, Edgewater Book Co., 1986; James Beckett and Dennis W. Eckes, *The Sports Americana Baseball Memorabilia and Autograph Price Guide*, Edgewater Book Co., 1982; Peter Capano, *Baseball Collectibles*, Schiffer Publishing, 1989; Ralf Coykendall, Jr., *Coykendall's Sporting Collectibles Price Guide*, Lyons & Burford, 1991; Ted Hake & Roger Steckler, *An Illustrated Price Guide To Non-Paper Sports Collectibles*, Hake's Americana & Collectibles Press, 1986; Buck Kronnick, *The Baseball Fan's Complete Guide To Collecting Autographs*, Betterway Publications, 1990; John M. and Morton W. Olman, *Encyclopedia of Golf Collectibles: A Collector's Identification and Value Guide*, Books Americana, 1985; Don Raycraft and Stew Salowitz, *Collector's Guide To Baseball Memorabilia*, Collector Books, 1987.

Periodical: *Sports Collectors Digest*, 700 East State Street, Iola, WI 54990.

Collectors' Club: Golf Collectors' Society, P. O. Box 491, Shawnee Mission, KS 66202.

BASEBALL

Game, Walter Johnson Baseball Game, 10 x 14″ panel, yellow baseball diamond on green playing field, inscribed metal spinning top, boxed .. **200.00**

Glass, 1956 Phillies, 5½″ h, clear, weighted bottom, red cap symbol .. **20.00**
Pencil, 6½″, plastic, baseball bat shape, orange, Charles Gehringer signature above Detroit Tigers, Hillerich & Bradsby Co, late 1930s **25.00**
Pennant, felt
- Boston Red Sox, Fenway Park, 29″, red, white inscriptions, 1955–58 .. **50.00**
- Brooklyn Dodgers, 27″, blue, white inscriptions **75.00**
- Pittsburgh Pirates, 29″, black, white inscription, yellow trim strip **25.00**
Pinback Button, 3½″ d
- Baltimore Orioles, black, white, and orange, c1950 .... **12.00**
- Cleveland Indians, red with black and white accents, 1940–50 .... **15.00**
Program, Cleveland Indians, 5½ x 9″, includes scorecard, 1946 .... **15.00**
Roster, Philadelphia Athletics, 3½ x 8″, 4 pgs, 1953 .... **15.00**
Rug, Cleveland Indians, 24″ d, chenille, black baseball symbols and stitched "Indians" **25.00**
Ruler, Baltimore Oriole 1958 Home Schedule, 12″, tin, white litho design **20.00**
Toy, squeaker, Cleveland Indian mascot, 7″, soft rubber, blue axe head, Rempel Mfg Co, c1949 .... **150.00**
Wiffle Ball, plastic, box with black and white photo, early 1970s
- Pete Rose, 3″ **20.00**
- Thurman Munson, 2½″ **15.00**
Yearbook, 1943 Baseball Pictorial, 8½ x 11½″, 98 pgs, Street & Smith Publications **15.00**

BASKETBALL

Game, Bas-ket, Cadaco–Ellis, boxed, 1956 .... **25.00**
Program
- 1954 All–Americans vs Globetrotters, 8 x 11″, 28 pgs **15.00**
- 1965 Harlem Globetrotters, Magicians of Basketball Tour, 8 x 10½″, 30 pgs **15.00**

BODY BUILDING

Certificate, American Continental Weight Lifters Association, 10¾ x 12¾″, black print, c1930 .... **12.00**
Photo, John Grimek, 11 x 12½″, tinted fleshtone **20.00**
Program, Body Builder, 8½ x 11″, 4 pgs, March 11, 1951 Olympic Fund Strength Show, Chicago, black and white John Grimek photo on front cov **15.00**

BOXING

Autograph, 3 x 5″, white index card, blue
ink signature "9–8–80/Muhammad
Ali/Serve God, He is the Goal" **100.00**
Book, *1944 Official Boxing Guide*, 4½
x 6½″, 96 pgs, National Collegiate
Athletic Association, Barnes & Co .. **15.00**
Boxing Gloves, Jack Dempsey, brown,
white vinyl trim, orig box, Everlast,
c1950 .... **35.00**
Clock, Joe Louis/World Champion, 12″
h, portrait, white metal with copper
finish, United Clock Corp, 1938–39 . **400.00**
Exhibit Card, 3½ x 5½″, biography on
back
   Gene Tunney, black and white, copy-
   right 1923 .... **10.00**
   James Jeffries, light color tint, copyright 1921 .... **15.00**
Game, Championship Fight Game,
Frankie Goodman, U S National & In-
tercollegiate Champion, box with boxing illus, 1940–50 .... **25.00**
Magazine, *Life,* Cassius Clay, March 6,
1964, cover article **12.00**
Pennant, Muhammad Ali vs Joe Frazier,
Oct 1, 1975, 29″, felt, black, white lettering, red trim strip **75.00**

FOOTBALL

Clock, New York Jets, desk, alarm, plastic, figural, football, brown vinyl base,
gold colored dial case, boxed,
marked "Japan" **25.00**
Game, Junior Quarterback, Warren
Built–Rite, boxed, 1950s **25.00**
Magazine
   1943 Illustrated Football Annual, 8½
   x 11½″, Fiction House, 96 pgs ... **15.00**
   1952 Collier's All–American Football
   Team Issue, Dec 6, 1952, Don
   McAuliffe on front cov **12.50**
Nodder
   Cincinnati Bengals, 7¼″ h, composition, round gold base, Sports Spe-
   cialties sticker, 1968 copyright ... **40.00**
   Washington Redskins, 6″ h, composition, maroon sq base, 1961–62 . **50.00**
Pennant, felt
   Houston Oilers, 29″, red, light blue
   inscription, late 1960s **12.00**
   Kansas City Chief, 29″, red, late
   1960s **15.00**
   Miami Dolphins, 29″, white with aqua
   blue and orange inscription, late
   1960s **18.00**
   New York Giants, 29″, dark blue,
   white stadium and title inscription,
   dark pink football player, red trim
   bands, late 1960s **15.00**

Philadelphia Eagles, 29½″, white,
green team name, full color helmet
illus, NFL Official Licensed Product,
c1970 .... **20.00**
Puzzle, Joe Namath, 500 pcs, full color
action photo, American Publishing
Corp, copyright 1971, boxed **18.00**
Tie Clip, 2″, NFL, metal, gold, raised
symbol with white accents, orig box,
1960s **18.00**

**Golf, match safe, sterling, 2¼ x 1¼″,
$225.00.**

GOLF

Badge, pr, Woman's Golf Association,
67th Western Open, red and black,
1970 .... **8.00**
Book, *Guide To Good Golf*, James
Barnes **25.00**
Cigarette Lighter, figural, golf bag **45.00**
Press Badge, Chicago Area Golf Tour-
nament, 1950–60 .... **12.00**
Score Pad, 2½ x 4″, cell cov, unused,
1900s **15.00**

MISCELLANEOUS

Book, *The Spectacle of Sports from
Sports Illustrated*, 1957, 320 pgs .. **25.00**
Catalog
   1880 Lawn Sports, 5½ x 8″, 16 pgs,
   illus, Horace Partridge & Co **25.00**
   1958 Parker's, 5½ x 8″, 128 pgs,
   hunting and fishing equipment ... **15.00**
Dispenser, figural, bowling ball, marbleized plastic, chrome push top, figural bowler handle, includes six
glasses **60.00**
Handbook, women's, *Handbook of
Light Gymnastics*, Lucy B Hunt, 1887,
92 pgs **50.00**
Magazine, Field and Steam, November
1914, 7 x 10″, 136 pgs **8.00**

Photo, Evel Knievel, 8½ x 11", glossy, Harley–Davidson sales brochure, purple ink autograph "To Auburn! Happy Landings' Evel Knievel" 12.00

Ribbon, 1904 Dog Show, fabric, white, sepia cello photo, gold inscription "Winner/Madison, NJ 1904" 12.00

OLYMPICS

Book, 1936, text review of Germany Summer and Winter Olympics, 166 pgs 110.00

Glass, 1932 Olympics, 5½", clear, frosted white illus 50.00

Postcard, 1912, 3½ x 5½", photo, Swedish crest on back and inscription "Swedish for 1912 Olympics in Stockholm," unused 18.00

Program
    1948 Summer Olympic Trials, 8 x 10½", 20 pgs 15.00
    1952 Olympic Tryouts, July 3–5, 72 pgs 20.00

RACING

Paperweight, Churchill Downs, 2¼ x 2½", metal, horseshoe image, brass finish, early 1900s 25.00

Pennant, Derby Day, 18", felt, red and white design with pink accents, white lettering, red ground, 1939 .... 15.00

Program, Kentucky Derby, May 4, 1963, 4 x 9" 15.00

Ticket, Kentucky Derby, Saturday May 2, 1936, 2¼ x 3½", general admission 10.00

STAFFORDSHIRE, HISTORICAL

History: The Staffordshire district of England is the center of the English pottery industry. There were eighty different potteries operating there in 1786, with the number increasing to 179 by 1802. The district includes Burslem, Cobridge, Eturia, Fenton, Foley, Hanley, Lane Delph, Lane End, Longport, Shelton, Stoke, and Tunstall. Among the many famous potters were Adams, Davenport, Spode, Stevenson, Wedgwood, and Wood.

In historical Staffordshire the view is the most critical element. American collectors pay much less for non-American views. Dark blue pieces are favored. Light views continue to remain undervalued. Among the forms, soup tureens have shown the highest price increases.

References: David and Linda Arman, *Historical Staffordshire: An Illustrated Check List,* published by authors, 1974, out–of–print; David and Linda Arman, *First Supplement, Historical Staffordshire: An Illustrated Check List,* published by authors, 1977, out–of–print; Susan and Al Bagdade, *War-*man's English & Continental Pottery & Porcelain, 2nd Edition,* Wallace–Homestead, 1991; Ada Walker Camehl, *The Blue China Book,* Tudor Publishing Co., 1946, (Dover, reprint); A. W. Coysh and R. K. Henrywood, *The Dictionary Of Blue And White Printed Pottery, 1780–1880,* Antique Collectors' Club, 1982; Ellouise Larsen, *American Historical Views On Staffordshire China, 3rd Edition,* Dover Publications, 1975.

Notes: Prices are for proof examples. Adjust prices by 20% for an unseen chip, a faint hairline, or an unseen professional repair; by 35% for knife marks through the glaze and a visible professional repair; by 50% for worn glaze and major repairs.

The numbers in parentheses refer to items in the books by Linda and David Arman, which constitute the most detailed list of American historical views and their forms.

W.ADAMS & SONS   ADAMS

ADAMS

The Adams family has been associated with ceramics from the mid 17th century. In 1802 William Adams of Stoke–upon–Trent produced American views.

In 1819 a fourth William Adams, son of William of Stoke, became a partner with his father and was later joined by his three brothers. The firm became William Adams & Sons. The father died in 1829 and William, the eldest son, became manager.

The company operated four potteries at Stoke and one at Tunstall. American views were produced at Tunstall in black, light blue, sepia, pink, and green in the 1830–40 period. William Adams died in 1865. All operations were moved to Tunstall. The firm continues today under the name of Wm. Adams & Sons, Ltd.

Adams, plate, Mitchell & Freeman's China & Glass Warehouse, Chatham Street, Boston, dark blue, c1804–40, (444), 10" d, $425.00.

Log Cabin, medallions of Gen. Harrison on border, teapot, pink (458) **450.00**

Seal of United States, dark blue, pitcher, 7½" (443) **1,200.00**

U.S. Views

Lake George, U.S., brown, vegetable dish (448) **375.00**

Shannondale Springs, Virginia, U.S., pink, 8" plate (451) **75.00**

CLEWS

From sketchy historical accounts that are available, James Clews took over the closed plant of A. Stevenson in 1819. His brother Ralph entered the business later. The firm continued until about 1836 when James Clews came to America to enter the pottery business at Troy, Indiana. The venture was a failure because of the lack of skilled workmen and the proper type of clay. He returned to England but did not re–enter the pottery business.

Clews, States plate, (5), 8¾" d, $225.00.

Cities Series, dark and medium blue

Albany, 10" plate (16) **375.00**

Chillicothe, 10½" platter (20) **3,500.00**

Washington, 7¾" plate (30) **325.00**

Doctor Syntax, dark blue

Doctor Syntax setting out on his first tour, 12" covered dish (35) **1,200.00**

Doctor Syntax and the gypsies, soup tureen (51) **2,200.00**

Doctor Syntax turned nurse, 7¾" plate (56) **125.00**

Don Quixote Series, dark blue

Don Quixote's Library, vegetable dish (68) **750.00**

Sancho Panza's debate with Teresa, 9" plate (78) **150.00**

Landing of Lafayette at Castle Garden, dark blue (1)

Cup Plate, 3½", oval medallion **400.00**

Pitcher, 5½" **800.00**

Plate, 7½" **175.00**

Platter, 21¾", well and tree **1,200.00**

Teapot **700.00**

Picturesque Views Series

Bakers Falls, Hudson River, pink, 9" plate (101) **75.00**

Fort Edward, Hudson River, light blue, 4⅛" cup plate (102) **75.00**

Hudson, Hudson River Gravy Tureen, black (107) **275.00**

Penitentiary in Allegheny, near Pittsburgh, pink, 15½" tray (117) **425.00**

Troy From Mount Ida, light blue, 6" pitcher (120) **225.00**

Peace and Plenty, dark blue (34)

Cup Plate, 4½" **1,200.00**

Platter, 17" **750.00**

Pittsfield Elm, dark blue, soup, 10½" (33) **275.00**

States or America and Independence Series, dark blue

Building, Deer on Lawn, 10½" plate (2) **225.00**

Dock, large building and ships, 19½" platter (4) **1,700.00**

Mansion, small boat with flag in foreground, 13½" bowl (12) **1,750.00**

J.&J. JACKSON

J. & J. JACKSON

Job and John Jackson began operations at the Churchyard Works, Burslem, about 1830. The works formerly were owned by the Wedgwood family. The firm produced transfer scenes in a variety of colors, such as black, light blue, pink, sepia, green, maroon and mulberry. Over 40 different American views of Connecticut, Massachusetts, Pennsylvania, New York, and Ohio were issued. The firm is believed to have closed about 1844.

American Scenery Series, all colors

Albany, NY, 20" platter (462) **350.00**

At Richmond, VA, 7" plate (465) ... **75.00**

Bunker Hill Monument, 6½" plate (468) **125.00**

Hartford, CT, 10" soup (476) **75.00**

Iron Works at Saugerties, 12″ platter
   (478) **275.00**
Water Works, Phila, 9″ plate (487) . . **75.00**
Yale College, deep dish (493) **175.00**

THOMAS MAYER

In 1829, Thomas Mayer and his brothers, John and Joshua, purchased Stubbs' Dale Hall Works of Burslem. They continued to produce a superior grade of ceramics.

Arms of the American States, dark blue
   CT, gravy tureen (498) **3,000.00**
   DE, 17″ platter (499) **1,700.00**
   PA, 21″ platter (506) **7,500.00**
Lafayette at Franklin's Tomb, dark blue,
   sugar bowl (510) **850.00**

CHARLES MEIGH

Job Meigh began the Meigh pottery in the Old Hall Pottery, in 1780. Later his sons and grandsons entered the business. The firm's name is recorded as Job Meigh & Sons, 1823; J. Meigh & Sons, 1829; Charles Meigh, 1843.

The American Cities and Scenery series was produced by Charles Meigh between 1840 and 1850. The colors are light blue, brown, gray, and purple. Sometimes the colors appear in combination.

Albany, 7½″ pitcher (544) **175.00**
Baltimore, wash bowl (546) **275.00**
Capitol at Washington, tureen, round,
   cover (550) **650.00**
City Hall, New York, 10¼″ plate (551) . **75.00**
Hudson City, 10¼″ soup (552) **75.00**
Utica, cup plate (556) **75.00**
Village of Little Falls, 8¼″ plate (558) . **75.00**
Yale College, New Haven, 9½″ plate
   (560) **75.00**

MELLOR, VENEABLES & CO.

Little information is recorded on Mellor, Veneables & Co. except that they were listed as potters in Burslem in 1843. Their Scenic Views series with the Arms of the States Border does include the arms for New Hampshire. This state is missing from the Mayer series. However, the view was known in England and collectors search for a Mayer example.

Arms of States, white body, light color
   transfers (529)
   MD, teapot **300.00**
   PA, sugar bowl **300.00**
Scenic Views, Arms of States Border,
   light blue, pink, brown, purple
   Albany, 15″ platter (516) **250.00**
   The President's House from the
   River, 14″ pitcher (520) **300.00**
   Tomb of Washington, Mt. Vernon,
   7½″ plate **90.00**
   View of Capitol at Washington, 11″,
   vegetable dish (526) **300.00**

J. W. R.

Stone China

W. RIDGWAY

J. & W. RIDGWAY AND WILLIAM RIDGWAY & CO.

John and William Ridgway, sons of Job Ridgway and nephews of George Ridgway who owned Bell Bank Works and Couldon Place Works, produced the popular Beauties of America series at the Couldon plant. The partnership between the two brothers was dissolved in 1830. John remained at Couldon.

William managed the Bell Bank works until 1854. Two additional series were produced based upon the etchings of Bartlett's American Scenery. The first series had various borders including narrow lace. The second series is known as Catskill Moss.

Beauties of America is in dark blue. The other series are found in the light transfer colors of light blue, pink, brown, black, and green.

American Scenery
   Albany, wash bowl (279) **325.00**
   Columbia Bridge on the Susque-
   hanna, soup tureen (281) **650.00**
   Peekskill Landing, Hudson River, tea-
   pot (287) **275.00**
   Valley of the Shenandoah from Jef-
   ferson's Rock, 7″ plate (289) **75.00**
   Wilkes–Barre, Vale of Wyoming, cof-
   feepot (294) **350.00**
Beauties of America, dark blue
   Almshouse, Boston, soup tureen
   (254) **3,000.00**
   Bank, Savannah, gravy tureen (257) **1,500.00**
   City–Hall, New York, 10″ plate (260) **150.00**
   Exchange, Charleston, vegetable
   dish (265) **1,200.00**

Octagon Church, Boston, 10″ soup
(271) **225.00**
Catskill Moss
  Anthony's Nose, 6″ plate (295) **75.00**
  Caldwell, Lake George, 5″ sauce dish
  (298) **50.00**
  Kosciusko's Tomb, 10″ plate (305) . **75.00**
  Valley of Wyoming, cup (317) **40.00**
Columbia Star, Harrison's Log Cabin
  End View, plate (276) **125.00**
  Side View, cup with handles (277) . . **70.00**

ROGERS

ROGERS

John Rogers and his brother George established a pottery near Longport in 1782. After George's death in 1815, John's son Spencer became a partner and the firm operated under the name of John Rogers & Sons. John died in 1816. His son continued the use of the name until he dissolved the pottery in 1842.

Boston Harbor, dark blue (441)
  Cup Plate **1,400.00**
  Cup and Saucer **650.00**
  Waste Bowl **900.00**
Boston State House, dark blue (442)
  Creamer **500.00**
  Platter, 19″ **650.00**
  Soup Tureen **3,500.00**

STEVENSON

As early as the 17th century the name Stevenson has been associated with the pottery industry. Andrew Stevenson of Cobridge introduced American scenes with the flower and scroll border. Ralph Stevenson, also of Cobridge, used a vine and leaf border on his dark blue historical views and a lace border on his series in light transfers.

The initials R. S. & W. indicate Ralph Stevenson and Williams are associated with the acorn and leaf border. It has been reported that Williams was Ralph's New York agent and the wares were produced by Ralph alone.

Acorn and Oak Leaves Border, dark
blue
  Columbia College, New York, 7½″
  plate (350) **500.00**

Stevensons, platter, Alms House, Boston, vine border, dark blue, (365), 12 x 16¼″, $1,250.00.

State House, Boston, 5″ plate (360)   **750.00**
Water Works, Phila, 10″ soup (363) .   **375.00**
Floral and Scroll Border, dark blue
  Almshouse, New York, 10″ plate (394)   **750.00**
  Catholic Cathedral, New York, 7½″
  plate (395) **1,000.00**
  Troy from Mt. Ida, 9¾″ platter (402) .   **1,500.00**
  View of New York From Weekawk,
  soup tureen (404) **10,000.00**
Lace Border
  Erie Canal at Buffalo, 10″ soup (386)   **100.00**
  New Orleans, Sugar Bowl (387) . . .   **150.00**
  Riceborough, GA, wash bowl (388) .   **375.00**
Vine Border
  Almshouse, New York, 7″ pitcher
  (366) **750.00**
  Battery, New York, 7¾″ plate (367) .   **450.00**
  Columbia College, New York, 8″ plate
  (372) **500.00**
  Hospital, Boston, 9″ plate(378) **325.00**
  Pennsylvania Hospital, Phila, soup
  tureen (383) **8,500.00**

STUBBS

In 1790 Stubbs established a pottery works at Burslem, England. He operated it until 1829 when he retired and sold the pottery to the Mayer brothers. He probably produced his American views about 1825. Many of his scenes were from Boston, New York, New Jersey and Philadelphia.

Rose Border, dark blue

Boston State House, 7″ pitcher (335)	**700.00**
City Hall, New York, plate, 6″ (336) .	**400.00**

Spread Eagle Border, dark and medium blue

City Hall, New York, 6½″ plate (323)	**400.00**
Fair Mount Near Phila, platter, 22″ (324)	**900.00**
Highlands, North River, 10″ plate (325)	**2,500.00**
Hoboken in New Jersey, salt shaker (326)	**700.00**
State House, Boston, 14½″ platter (331)	**750.00**

Upper Ferry Bridge over the River Schuylkill (332)

Dish, round	**750.00**
Platter, 19″	**800.00**
Vegetable Dish	**750.00**
Wash Pitcher	**750.00**

S. TAMS & CO.

The firm operated at Longton, England. The exact date of its beginning is not known, but believed to be about 1810–15. The company produced several dark blue American views. About 1830 the name became Tams, Anderson, and Tams.

Capitol, Washington

Bowl, deep (514)	**1,500.00**
Wash Pitcher (514)	**1,500.00**

United States Hotel, Phila, soup, 10″ (515) **1,000.00**

BURSLEM

WOOD

Enoch Wood, sometimes referred to as the Father of English Pottery, began operating a pottery at Fountain Place, Burslem, in 1783. A cousin Ralph Wood was associated with him. In 1790 James Caldwell became a partner and the firm was known as Wood and Caldwell. In 1819 Wood and his sons took full control.

Enoch died in 1840. His sons continued under the name of Enoch Wood & Sons. The American views were first made in the mid 1820s and continued through the 1840s.

It is reported that the pottery produced more signed historical views than any other Staffordshire firm. Many of the views attributed to unknown makers probably came from the Woods.

Marks vary, although always with the name Wood. The establishment was sold to Messrs. Pinder, Bourne & Hope in 1846.

Enoch Wood, cup and saucer, English Scenery, blue transfer, marked "Wood & Sons, England," $25.00.

Celtic China, light transfer colors

Columbus, GA, 3⅞″ cup plate (238)	**450.00**
Shipping Port on the Ohio, KY, 12″ platter (249)	**500.00**
Transylvania University, Lexington, KY, 10″ soup (250)	**125.00**
West Point, Military Academy, open-work dish (252)	**350.00**

Floral Border, irregular, dark blue

Commodore MacDonnough's Victory (154)

Coffeepot	**1,500.00**
Cup and Saucer	**450.00**

Entrance of the Erie Canal into the Hudson at Albany (156)

Plate, 6″	**750.00**
Soup, 10″	**825.00**

Erie Canal, Aqueduct Bridge at Rochester, pitcher, with first canal view, 5½″ (157) **1,500.00**
Wadsworth Tower, sugar bowl (155) **550.00**

Four Medallion, Floral Border Series, light transfers

Castle Garden, 8″ plate (225)	**75.00**
Monte Video, 7½″ plate (229)	**75.00**
Race Bridge, Phila, gravy tureen (233)	**300.00**

General Jackson (224)

Cup Plate	**750.00**
Pitcher, luster, 4″	**1,500.00**
Plate, 7″	**900.00**

Shell Border, circular center, dark blue

Belleville on the Passaic River, soup tureen (159) **6,000.00**

Castle Garden Battery, New York, 18½" platter (160)	1,500.00
Catskill Mountains, Hudson River, custard cup with handle (162)	600.00
City of Albany, State of New York, 10" plate (163)	450.00
Highland, Hudson River, vegetable dish (167)	1,200.00
Mount Vernon, 5¾" plate (173)	700.00
Railroad, Baltimore and Ohio, incline, 9" plate (182)	750.00
West Point Military Academy, 12" platter (188)	1,500.00
White House, Washington, cup plate (189)	2,500.00
Shell Border, irregular center, dark blue Cadmus, 10" soup (125)	450.00
Commodore MacDonnough's Victory, coffeepot (130)	1,500.00
Constitution and Guerriere, 10" plate (131)	800.00
Erith on the Thames, vegetable dish (136)	800.00
Union Line, 10" soup (144)	450.00
Wadsworth Tower (147)	
Coffeepot	1,200.00
Cup and Saucer	400.00
Waste Bowl	500.00
Washington's Tomb, dark blue (190B)	
Creamer	700.00
Soup, 10"	900.00
Sugar Bowl	700.00
Teapot	900.00

UNKNOWN MAKERS

Anti–slavery, light blue, 9¼" plate (608)	150.00
Erie Canal inscription (597)	
Cup Plate, 3¾"	1,500.00
Pitcher, 5¼"	1,000.00
Famous Naval Heroes	
Pitcher, 7" (604)	800.00
Washbowl (604)	1,200.00
Franklin Flying a Kite, light blue, 3¾" platter, miniature (603)	100.00
Great Fire, City of New York, series, plates, each (605–607)	125.00
Mount Vernon, Washington's Seat, 8" pitcher (600)	800.00

STAFFORDSHIRE ITEMS

History: A wide variety of ornamental pottery items originated in England's Staffordshire district, beginning in the 17th century and extending to the present. The height of production was from 1820 to 1890.

These naive pieces are considered folk art by many collectors. Most items were not made carefully; some were even made and decorated by children.

The types of objects are varied, e.g., animals, cottages, and figurines (chimney ornaments). The key to price is age and condition. The older the piece, the higher the price is a general rule.

References: Susan and Al Bagdade, *Warman's English & Continental Pottery & Porcelain, 2nd Edition,* Wallace–Homestead, 1991; Pat Halfpenny, *English Earthenware Figures, 1740–1840,* Antique Collectors' Club; P. D. Gordon Pugh, *Staffordshire Portrait Figures Of The Victorian Era,* Antique Collectors' Club; Charles Kenyon Kies, *Collecting Victorian Staffordshire Pottery Figures,* Antique Publications, 1989; Dennis G. Rice, *English Porcelain Animals Of The 19th Century,* Antique Collectors' Club, 1989.

Sauce Tureen, blue Oriental transfers, c1825, 7" l, 7½" h, $325.00.

Bust	
8" h, George Washington, yellow floral coat, marked "Wood/Caldwell"	750.00
8½" h, clergyman, black marbleized plinth	200.00
12" h, John Wesley, soft paste, multicolored, minor edge flakes	300.00
Chimney Ornament	
Cat, 5½" h, black spotted white bodies, orange cushions, green collars, mid 19th C, pr	1,200.00
Dog	
4" h, poodle, cole–slaw coat, standing, ftd plinth	125.00
8" h, pr, King Charles Spaniels, black and brown–gray, c1820–30	450.00
Commemorative Cup, 4⅜" h, Admiral Hood, black–gray, green, and flesh tones, brown eyes, c1780–90	550.00
Cow Creamer, 5½" h, spotted ochre and indigo glazes, hobbled back legs, green milkmaid on base, orig cov, c1785–1800	1,500.00
Figure	
3⅞" h, ewe, reclining, relief textured, pale blue eyes, green glazed base, c1780–90	300.00

4" h, ram and ewe, relief textured, sponged blue manganese and yellow, green glazed bases, c1780–90, pr 3,200.00

5¾" h, cat, enamel sponged yellow and brown, oval blue banded base, c1775–85 .... 1,800.00

6" h, pr, deer, bocage, naturalistic colors, stag missing antlers, c1820–35 .... 225.00

7" h, group, Tenderness, bocage, man and woman in front of tree, titled, naturalistic colors, sgd "John Walton," c1820, repairs 325.00

7¾" h, owl, cream ware, raised wings, molded relief feathers, sponged manganese dec, possibly by Thomas Whieldon, c1770–80 ... 13,000.00

8⅝" h, cupid astride lioness, Ralph Wood, restored 2,000.00

8¾" h, female fish peddler, glazed enamel gaudy dec, carries basket with sign "Haddies," c1800 ..... 275.00

10½" h, hound, chasing hare, multicolored 300.00

11½" h, Widow of Zarephath, Obadiah Sherratt 500.00

12½" h, shepherd, sheep and harp, white 120.00

14" h, Benjamin Franklin, dark blue jacket, gold trim 750.00

15" l, Death of Monrow, Obadiah Sherratt, restored 1,600.00

Flower Pot, 6¾" h, pearl ware, emb leaves and acorns, matching saucer 250.00

Inkstand

3½" h, swan, cole–slaw dec, wings with pink highlights 175.00

4½" l, dog, red–brown whippet, cobalt blue base 200.00

5½" l, greyhound, cobalt blue base . 150.00

Mantel Vase, 8" h, pearl ware, cov, diapered pattern with medallions of Chinese scenes, polychrome enamels, c1790–1810 .... 950.00

Mug

3½" h, pearl ware, underglaze blue dec "Beer," and floral sprays, c1800 .... 500.00

5½" h, cream ware, hand colored transfer printed dec of gentry on outing, c1790–1810 .... 300.00

Pastile Burner, 4½" h, two part, porcelain, four gilt edge windows and door in front, heavily encrusted multicolored blossoms, pink roses, single leaf painted inside base, c1835, repairs to flowers 2,000.00

Sauce Tureen, 8" l, 4" h, cov, pearl ware, duck, relief textured, feathers, green, yellow, blue, and brown, c1770–80 .... 1,300.00

Tea Service, 20 pcs, strawberry luster, cov teapot, creamer, spill bowl, large dish, eight cups and saucers, c1820–40 .... 475.00

Teapot, cov, 5" h, cream ware, floral finial, blue, green, yellow, and rose stylized leaves, splattered iron–red ground, chinoiserie scenes, c1780–1800 .... 500.00

Spill Vase, eagle perched above sleeping child, multicolored, mid 19th C, 7½" h, $225.00.

Toy Figure, 2½" h

Cat, agate ware, c1740–50 .... 450.00

Lion, pink, iron–red, and black, green base, c1800 .... 325.00

Vase, 8" h, boy and maiden with basket 100.00

STAFFORDSHIRE, ROMANTIC

History: The Staffordshire district of England produced dinnerware with romantic scenes between 1830 and 1860. A large number of potters were involved and over 800 patterns have been identified.

The dinner services came in a variety of colors with light blue and pink perhaps being the most popular. Usually the pattern is identified on the back of the piece. It was not uncommon for two potters to issue pieces with the same design. Therefore, check the pattern name as well as the maker's name.

It would be impossible to list all patterns. A representative selection follows. Some price ranges to keep in mind are: cups and saucers (handleless) $35–50; cup plates $40–75; plates, 9–10", $15–50; platters $35–75.

References: Petra Williams, *Staffordshire: Romantic Transfer Patterns,* Fountain House East, 1978; Petra Williams, *Staffordshire II,* Fountain House East, 1986.

Asiatic Plants, maker unknown

Cup and Saucer	65.00
Plate, 10½"	85.00
Vegetable Bowl, cov, ornate handles, finial, light blue, 12 x 9½"	135.00

Canova, Thomas Mayer, c1834–1848

Cup and Saucer	45.00
Plate, 7½", pink	20.00
Platter, 18 x 11½"	85.00
Soup Plate	35.00
Vegetable Bowl, 8½", blue, cov with floral finial	120.00
Waste Bowl, 4"	40.00

Corinthian, E Challinor

Bowl, 5½"	45.00
Gravy Boat, attached underplate	95.00
Plate	40.00
Sauce Dish, 4"	20.00
Saucer	15.00
Vegetable Dish, open	45.00

Plate, Oriental, red transfer, marked "Baker & Co, Ltd," 10¼" w handle to handle, $12.00.

Damascus, blue and white, Wm Adams and Sons

Bowl, 4"	20.00
Creamer, paneled	125.00
Cup Plate	50.00
Custard Cup	30.00
Plate	
8½"	60.00
9¾"	65.00
Tureen, cov, oval	130.00

Friburg, Davenport, c1844

Bowl	45.00
Cup and Saucer, handleless	60.00
Plate, 10½"	55.00
Platter	100.00
Teapot, tall, paneled, fruit finial	200.00
Tureen, matching underplate	150.00

Medici, Mellor, Veneables & Co., 1834–1851

Bowl	30.00

Cup and Saucer	40.00
Gravy Boat	80.00
Plate, twelve sided	37.50
Platter	75.00
Sugar Bowl, tab handles	80.00

Palestine, John Ridgway, c1830–1855

Creamer	55.00
Cup and Saucer, handleless	50.00
Plate	45.00
Platter, 16½ x 10"	65.00
Sugar, cov	80.00
Vegetable Bowl, open, matching underplate	130.00

Rhone Scenery, T. J. & J. Mayer, c1850

Dish, 5½", oblong	40.00
Plate	
8½"	48.00
9¼", twelve sided, brown	35.00
Platter, 7 x 5"	45.00
Toothbrush Holder	50.00

Siam, J. Clementson, c1839–1864

Bowl	35.00
Creamer	55.00
Cup and Saucer	35.00
Gravy Boat	60.00
Plate, 9"	45.00
Sauce Dish, 4"	27.00
Sugar, cov	75.00
Tureen, cov, matching underplate	125.00

STAINED AND/OR LEADED GLASS PANELS

History: American architects in the second half of the 19th century and the early 20th century used stained and leaded glass panels as a chief decorative element. Skilled glass craftsmen assembled the designs, the best known being Louis C. Tiffany.

The panels are held together with soft lead cames or copper wraps. When purchasing a panel, check the lead and have any repairs made to protect your investment.

Collectors' Club: Stained Glass Association of America, 4050 Broadway, Suite 219, Kansas City, MO 64111.

Periodicals: *Glass Art Magazine*, P.O. Box 1507, Broomfield, CO 80038; *Glass Patterns Quarterly*, P.O. Box 131, Westport, NY 40077.

Leaded

Gothic, 30¼" h, 13¼" w, interlocking arch motif, etched design inside arched sections, beveled orig frame	200.00
Prairie School, 96" h, 20" w, rect panel of textured, rippled, and opaque glass, turquoise, white, and avocado, clear glass ground, stylized flowering plant motif, set of six panels, c1910	6,000.00

Tiffany, 29" h, 27½" w, central tiny white blossoms radiating towards larger mottled brown and white pebbled blossoms, pink and green stamens, amber glass surround, geometric green glass border   . . . **18,000.00**

Window, multicolored, tree and leaf motif, 19 x 19⅛", $100.00.

Stained
  Alice D Laughlin, 96" h, American, Gloucester, MA, divided into eight panels depicting scenes of medieval clergy, surrounded by multicolored foliate border **850.00**
  John LaFarge, 36" h, 144" w, central rect panel finely plated with overflowing cornucopia, three winged cherubs, painted features, sinuous blossoms, stems, and leaves, rect jeweled panel set with six fractured glass reserves, identical flanking panels with jeweled diamond, surrounded by ornate wreaths, c1885 **35,000.00**

STANGL POTTERY BIRDS

History: Stangl ceramic birds were produced from 1940 until the Stangl factory closed in 1972. The birds were produced at Stangl's Trenton plant and shipped to their Flemington, New Jersey, plant for hand painting.

During World War II the demand for these birds and Stangl pottery was so great that 40 to 60 decorators could not keep up with the demand. Orders were contracted out to private homes. These orders then were returned for firing and finishing. Colors used to decorate these birds varied according to the artist.

As many as ten different trademarks were used. Almost every bird is numbered; many are artist signed. However, the signatures are used only for

dating purposes and add very little to the value of the birds.

Several birds were reissued between 1972 and 1977. These reissues are dated on the bottom and valued at approximately one half of the older birds.

References: Harvey Duke, *The Official Identification And Price Guide To Pottery And Porcelain, Seventh Edition,* House of Collectibles, 1989; Joan Dworkin and Martha Horman, *A Guide To Stangl Pottery Birds,* Willow Pond Books, Inc., 1973; Norma Rehl, *The Collectors Handbook of Stangl Pottery,* Democrat Press, 1982.

Additional Listings: See Stangl pottery in the American Dinnerware category in *Warman's Americana & Collectibles* for more examples.

Bird, #3276, blue and yellow, $70.00.

3276D Double Bluebirds, 7½" h	140.00
3402–D Orioles	85.00
3404 Lovebirds, pr	100.00
3405 Cockatoo, 6¼" h	45.00
3406 Kingfisher	60.00
3408 Bird of Paradise	80.00
3431 Duck, standing, 8" h	300.00
3443 Duck, flying, 9" h	220.00
3444 Cardinal	75.00
3445 Rooster, gray, 9" h	135.00
3446 Hen, 7" h	145.00
3447 Prothonotary Warbler	60.00
3448 Blue Headed Vireo	40.00
3453 Key West Quail Dove	225.00
3582 Parakeets	100.00
3583 Parula Warbler	38.00
3589 Indigo Bunting	35.00
3595 Bobolink	125.00
3598 Kentucky Warbler	40.00
3626 Broadtail Hummingbird, 6" h . . .	90.00
3629 Broadbill Hummingbird, 6" h . . .	85.00
3635 Goldfinch family, 12" l, 4½" h . . .	150.00
3634 Allen Hummingbird	48.00
3747 Canary, facing left, blue flower, 6¼" h	155.00
3754D White Wing Crossbill, 8¾" h . .	325.00
3810 Blackpoll Warbler	100.00
3811 Chestnut Backed Chickadee . . .	80.00
3813 Evening Grosbeak	120.00
3815 Western Bluebird	145.00
3848 Golden Crowned Kinglet, 4" h . .	50.00

STATUES

History: Beginning with primitive cultures, man produced statues in the shape of people and animals. During the Middle Ages most works were religious and symbolic in character and form. The Renaissance rediscovered the human and secular forms.

During the 18th and 19th centuries it was fashionable to have statues in the home. Many famous works were copied for popular consumption.

Statuette or figurine denotes smaller statues, one-fourth life size or smaller.

Reference: Lynee and Fritz Weber, (eds.), *Jacobsen's Eleventh Painting and Bronze Price Guide,* Jacobsen's Publications, 1990.

Cupid and Psyche, Italian, carved marble, from Thurlow Lodge, Menlo Park, $176,500.00.

Bronze
   25″, seated philosopher, draped man holding tablet and pen, rich brown patina, inscribed "P DuBois, F. Barbedienne Fondeur Paris 337," stamped "Reduction Mechanique" seal, France, late 19th C **8,250.00**
   44½″, Sophocles Celebrating the Victory at Salamis, nude, holding tortoiseshell and horn lyre, rect plinth base inscribed in Greek, brown patina, inscribed "F. Barbedienne Fondeur, Paris," c1900 . . . . **44,000.00**
Cast Iron, 27″, Victory, winged figure wearing swirling tunic, resting on marble sphere, sienna marble plinth, French, early 19th C **850.00**
Ivory, 7″, three Grecian nude women embracing each other, sgd "G.R." . .   **85.00**

Ivory and gilt bronze, 14½″, woman, carved ivory head and forearms, lace and ribbon dec bodice and wide skirt with train, hat with wide, undulating brim, incised "Armand Quenard," mounted on shaped sq black and white striated marble plinth, c1900 .   **725.00**
Marble, young maiden
   36″, revealing robes, holding bunch of wheat in left hand, leaning on wheat bundle resting on tree stump, late 19th C, weathered . . . **1,425.00**
   45″, partially draped figure resting on rocky base, floral garland in her hair, circular base, weathered . . . **2,250.00**
Porcelain, 7⅜″, blacksmith, pale green vest under brown apron, Meissen, attributed by J. J. Kaendler, incised "99," c1750, hammer and sword repaired **1,200.00**
Silvered Bronze, 32½″, Cupid and Psyche, naked figure with draped cloth, winged cupid gazing over her shoulder, circular base **3,000.00**
Silvered Gilt, patinated bronze, and carved marble, 24½″, girl lifting skirt stepping across stream, carved white marble face and hands, ruffled bonnet, laced bodice beneath shawl, oval base, inscribed "Monginot," French, c1900 . . . . **2,250.00**

STEIFF

History: Margarete Steiff, GmbH, established in Germany in 1880, is known for very fine quality stuffed animals and dolls as well as other beautifully made collectible toys. It is still in business, and its products are highly respected.

The company's first products were wool-felt elephants made by Margaret Steiff. In a few years the elephant line was expanded to include a donkey, horse, pig, and camel.

By 1903 the company also was producing a jointed mohair Teddy Bear, whose production dramatically increased to over 970,000 units in 1907. Margarete's nephews took over the company at this point. The bear's head became the symbol for its label, and the famous "Button in the Ear" round, metal trademark was added.

Newly designed animals were added: Molly and Bully, the dogs, and Fluffy, the cat. Pull toys and kites also were produced, as well as larger animals on which children could ride or play.

Become familiar with genuine Steiff products before purchasing an antique stuffed animal. Plush in old Steiff animals was mohair; trimmings usually were felt or velvet. Unscrupulous individuals have attached the familiar Steiff metal button to animals that are not Steiff.

References: Peggy and Alan Bialosky, *The*

Teddy Bear Catalog, Workman Publishing, 1984, revised edition; Shirley Conway and Jean Wilson, *Steiff Teddy Bears, Dolls, and Toys With Prices*, Wallace–Homestead, 1984, 1991 value update; Margaret Fox Mandel, *Teddy Bears And Steiff Animals*, Collector Books, 1984; Margaret Fox Mandel, *Teddy Bears, Annalee Animals & Steiff Animals, Third Series*, Collector Books, 1990; Christel & Rolf Pistorius, *Steiff: Sensational Teddy Bear, Animals & Dolls*, Hobby House Press, 1991; Jean Wilson, *Steiff Toys Revisited*, Wallace–Homestead, 1989.

Periodical: *Steiff Collectors' Anonymous*, 1308 Park Avenue, Piqua, OH 45356.

Additional Listings: Teddy Bears. See Stuffed Toys in *Warman's Americana & Collectibles* for more examples.

Bambi, 1939, 39″ h, $400.00.

Bear, 10″, shoe button eyes, plain button in ear, ribbon sgd by Otto Steiff, 1907	140.00
Cat	
Siamese, 9″, mohair, jointed neck, orig leg tag, c1950	125.00
Tom, 5″, black velvet body, mohair tail, glass eyes, sewn nose and mouth, c1960	85.00
Dog	
Collie, 20½ x 10″, long and short mohair, glass eyes, sewn nose, felt mouth	125.00
Poodle, 8″, Snobby, long and short mohair, jointed glass eyes, c1960	90.00
Duck, Mallard, 8″, pull toy, felt and velvet, metal wheels	275.00
Fish, 14″, mohair body, glass eyes, felt fins, tail, and mouth	85.00
Frog, 4″, felt, orig neck tag	45.00
Goat, 5 x 6″, mountain, gray mohair, glass eyes, felt horns, c1950	50.00
Lion, 45″, Leo, mohair, reclining, orig tag, c1955	600.00
Monkey, 19″, white mohair, felt face, hands, and feet, green glass eyes, c1905	700.00

Panda, 6″ h, orig tag, 1920–30	440.00
Polar Bear, 6½″, stands on all four, orig box	175.00
Seal, 6″, Floppy Robby, buff Dralon, soft stuffing, sewn eyes, c1950	65.00
Teddy Bear	
11″, Zotty, tan curly mohair, jointed body, glass eyes, sewn nose, felt mouth, c1950	150.00
19″, straw stuffed, jointed arms and legs, applied eyes	250.00
Tiger, 16″, mohair, reclining, orig button, #0910/60	400.00
Turtle, 5″, mohair, vinyl shell, glass eyes, c1950	65.00

STEINS

History: A stein is a mug especially made to hold beer or ale, ranging in size from the smaller ³⁄₁₀ liters and ¼ liters to the larger 1, 1½, 2, 3, 4, and 5 liters, and in rare cases to 8 liters. (A liter is 1.05 liquid quarts.)

Master steins or pouring steins hold 3 to 5 liters and are called krugs. Most steins are fitted with a metal hinged lid with thumblift. The earthenware character–type steins usually are German in origin.

References: Susan and Al Bagdade, *Warman's English & Continental Pottery & Porcelain, 2nd Edition*, Wallace–Homestead, 1991; John L. Harrell, *Regimental Steins*, published by author, 1984; Gary Kirsner and Jim Gruhl, *The Stein Book*, Glentiques, Ltd., 1984; Dr. Eugene Manusov, *Encyclopedia of Character Steins*, Wallace–Homestead, 1976; Eugene V. Manusov and Mike Wald, *Character Steins: A Collector's Guide*, Cornwall Books, 1987; James R. Stevenson, *Antique Steins: A Collector's Guide, Second Edition*, Cornwall Books, 1989; Mike Wald, *HR Steins*, SCI Publications, 1980.

Collectors' Club: Stein Collectors International, 8113 Bondage Dr., Gaithersburg, MD 20879.

Additional Listing: See Mettlach.

Advisor: Ron Fox.

Brass, 17½″ h, relief, coins and faces, fancy figural handle, rampant lion finial	1,150.00
Glass	
Blown	
1/2 L, enameled floral and verse, c1850	275.00
1 L, cut circle design, stag under prism lid, pewter base rim	320.00
Blown with pewter, ½ L, amber glass, elaborate pewter faces, serpent handle	575.00
Mold Blown, ½ L, flashed cranberry panels, porcelain inlay, turquoise inset thumblift	210.00

Skull, ½ L, pewter top, tan, brown, and white, Germany, 7" h, 5¾" w, $195.00.

Ivory, 9½" h, hand carved, three scenes, reattached finial, sgd "B. Rudolph Stuttgart"	2,475.00
Lithophane, ½ L, clown	350.00
Pewter, ½ L, relief, eagles and angels faces, eagle finial	155.00
Porcelain	
Bohne, ½ L, bisque, Indian	275.00
Regimental, 1 L, Naval S.M.S. Von Der Tann 1909–12, four Naval scenes, bolt hinge, rear roster	1,290.00
Schierholz, ½ L, rabbit E.C.S. #62	2,255.00
Pottery, relief, 1 L, cavaliers drinking	115.00
Russian Enamel, 6½" h, on silver, turquoise, light and dark blue, violet, white, and red enamel, gold wash, silver marks on base and lid, Silversmith Gustau Klingert, Moscow, 1889	6,000.00
Stoneware	
Character, ½ L, monk, E.C.S. #357	115.00
Dreihausen, 13" h, red metallic glaze, minor rim chips, thumblift missing	600.00
Print Over Glaze, ½ L, Munich child and city side scenes	175.00
Relief, ½ L, Occupational, fireman, strap repair	80.00

STEUBEN GLASS

History: Frederick Carder, an Englishman, and Thomas G. Hawkes of Corning, New York, established the Steuben Glass Works in 1904. In 1918 the Corning Glass Co. purchased the Steuben company. Carder remained with the firm and designed many of the pieces bearing the Steuben mark. Probably the most widely recognized wares are "Aurene," "Verre De Soie," and "Rosaline," but many other types were produced.

The firm continues operating, producing glass of exceptional quality.

References: Paul Gardner, *The Glass of Frederick Carder*, Crown Publishers, 1971; Paul Perrot, Paul Gardner, and James S. Plaut, *Steuben: Seventy Years Of American Glassmaking*, Praeger Publishers, 1974.

Museum: The Corning Museum of Glass, Corning, NY.

ACID CUT BACK

Bowl, 13¼" d, jade green, Oriental design, peonies and paulownia leaves, flared rim, ftd	800.00
Lamp, 14" h, baluster form, high shouldered, gold overlay flowers and buds, gilded bronze mounts	1,600.00
Vase	
7½" h, double, moths above leaves, floral motif on shoulder, Rosaline to Alabaster	1,430.00
9" h, green jade, birds among floral brances, Alabaster foot	1,100.00
13" h, dark amethyst flying ducks and foliaged trees, pale frost pink sky, double handles	2,970.00

AURENE

AURENE

Atomizer, 7" h, tapered	
Blue	525.00
Gold	410.00
Bulb Bowl, 10" d, gold	325.00
Compote	
6¼" d	
Irid blue, stretch bowl, twist stem, sgd "Steuben Aurene #686"	880.00
Irid gold, ruffled rim, twist stem, sgd "Aurene #172"	525.00
6¾" d, irid blue, twist and prunt stem, sgd "Aurene #2604"	880.00
8" h, gold, stemmed, #2642	440.00
Finger Bowl, gold, underplate with stretch border, sgd, #171	300.00
Vase	
3½" h, DQ, irid gold, sgd "Aurene #216"	385.00
6" h, trumpet type, irid blue, ruffled rim, sgd "Aurene #346"	935.00

CALCITE

Bowl	
5½" d, gold, stretch rolled rim	275.00

9¾" d, gold 300.00
Finger Bowl, pr, 5" d, gold 165.00
Lighting Bowl, pr, 14" d, hanging, acid
  etched acanthus leaves 550.00
Sherbet
  3¾" h, gold, 6" d underplate 250.00
  4½" d, gold, ruffled rim, marked ster-
    ling holder 210.00

CLUTHRA

Bowl, 11" d, rosaline to white 660.00
Vase, 11" h, classical form, rosaline . . 1,375.00

IVORINE

Bowl, 5¾" d, blue irid int. 325.00
Corncucopia, 6" h, ribbed, ftd, sgd
  "Steuben" 550.00
Jack–in–the–Pulpit Vase, 6½" h 330.00
Vase, 6" h, sq form, grotesque 440.00

JADE

Demitasse Cup and Saucer, dark blue 440.00
Lemonade, set of 4, green, swirled, Alabaster handles 240.00
Vase
  7" h, lion mounts, ribbed 110.00
  8½" h, pr, green, ribbed, Alabasater
    knob stem, marked "Steuben" in
    block letters 300.00
  10" h, green, Alabaster loop handles,
    makred "Steuben" with fleur–de–lis 770.00

Lamp Shade, pulled feathers, white ground, silver stamped mark, 5½" h, $200.00.

MISCELLANEOUS

Bowl
  7¾" d, reddish–gold, ftd 265.00
  8" d, clear, swirl design, sgd "Steu-
    ben" in script 275.00
  10" d, flared form, yellow, swirled . . 45.00
  11" d, amber, ribbed, fold–over rim,
    marked "Steuben" in block letters 165.00

Candlestick, pr, 9¾" h, yellow ribbed,
  double bulb stems 275.00
Cocktail Set, 6 pcs, 10" h, pitcher, five
  ftd and handled cups, clear, ribbed,
  black stopper 410.00
Vase
  7" d, flared, applied handles 100.00
  7½" h, DQ, clear, green threaded rim 80.00

ROSALINE

Dish, 6" d, alabaster, ftd 150.00
Goblet, 7" h, cone shape, Alabaster
  twist stem, makred "Steuben" with
  fleur–de–lis 140.00

VERRE DE SOIE

Bowl, 10" d, green cast, Celeste blue
  border, sgd 300.00
Dish, 5¼" d, cov, two blue handles, pear
  finial on lid 250.00
Vase, 12" h, ruffle top 525.00

STEVENGRAPHS

History: Thomas Stevens of Coventry, England, first manufactured woven silk designs in 1854. His first bookmark was produced in 1862, followed by the first Stevengraphs, perhaps in 1874, but definitely in 1879 at the York Exhibition. The first "portrait" Stevengraphs (of Disraeli and Gladstone) were produced in 1886, and the first postcards incorporating the silk woven panels in 1903. Stevens offered many other items with silk panels, including valentines, fans, pin cushions, needle cases, etc.

Stevengraphs are miniature silk pictures, matted in cardboard, and usually having a trade announcement, or "label," affixed to the reverse. Thomas Stevens' name appears on the mat of the early Stevengraphs directly under the silk panel. Many of the later "portraits" and the larger silks (produced initially for calendars) have no identification on the front of the mat other than the phrase "woven in pure silk" and have no label on the back. Other companies, notably W. H. Grant of Coventry, copied this technique. Their efforts should not be confused with Stevengraphs.

American collectors favor the Stevengraphs of American interest, such as "Signing of the Declaration of Independence," "Columbus Leaving Spain," "Landing of Columbus." Sports related Stevengraphs such as "The First Innings" (baseball), and "The First Set" (tennis) are also popular, as well as portraits of Buffalo Bill, President and Mrs. Cleveland, George Washington, and President Harrison.

The bookmarks are longer than they are wide, have mitered corners at the bottom, and are finished with a tassel. Originally, Stevens' name was woven into the fold-over at the top of the silk, but soon the identification was woven into the fold-under mitered corners. Almost every Stevens bookmark has such identification, except the ones woven at the World's Columbian Exposition in Chicago, 1892–93.

Postcards with very fancy embossing around the aperture in the mount almost always have Stevens' name printed on them. Embossed cards from the "Ships" and "Hands Across The Sea" series generally are not printed with Stevens' name. The most popular postcard series in the United States are "Ships" and "Hands Across the Sea," the latter incorporating two crossed flags and two hands shaking. Seventeen flag combinations have been found, but only seven are common. Stevens produced silks that were used in the "Alpha" Publishing Co. cards. Many times the silks were the top or bottom half of regular bookmarks.

References: Geoffrey A. Godden, *Stevengraphs and Other Victorian Silk Pictures*, Associated University Presses, Inc., 1971; Chris Radley, *The Woven Silk Postcard*, privately printed, 1978; Austin Sprake, *The Price Guide to Stevengraphs*, The Antique Collectors' Club, Baron Publishing, 1972.

Collectors' Club: Stevengraph Collectors' Association, 2103–2829 Arbutus Road, #2103, Victoria, British Columbia, V8N 5X5, Canada.

Museum: Coventry, England.

Note: Prices are based on pieces in mint or close to mint condition.

Advisor: John High.

Post Card, The First Train, black and brown wagons, orig mat, $185.00.

BOOKMARK

For A Good Boy, I had a little doggy . .	60.00
For A Good Girl, Sweet Maggie had a little bird	60.00
Little Bo–Peep	50.00
Little Jack Horner	50.00
Little Red Riding Hood	50.00
The Late Earl Of Beaconsfield, Peace With Honour	25.00

POST CARD

Anne Hathaway's Cottage	40.00
Hands Across The Sea, man and woman's hands	
R.M.S. Carmania, GB and USA flags	40.00
U.S.M.S. Philadelphia, USA and Norway flags	100.00
Houses Of Parliament	60.00
Princes Street, Edinburgh	60.00
R.M.S. Lusitania	70.00
R.M.S. Saxonia	40.00

STEVENGRAPH

Are You Ready?	150.00
John L. Sullivan, story label	100.00
Rt. Hon. J. Chamberlain, M.P., flower spray	125.00
The Final Spurt	175.00
The First Innings	300.00
The First Over	250.00

STEVENS AND WILLIAMS

History: In 1824 Joseph Silvers and Joseph Stevens leased the Moor Lane Glass House at "Briar Lea Hill" (Brierley Hill), England, from the Honey-Borne family. In 1847 William Stevens and Samuel Cox Williams took over, giving the firm its present name. In 1870 the firm moved to its Stourbridge plant. In the 1880s the firm employed such renowned glass artisans as Frederick C. Carder, John Northwood, other Northwood family members, James Hill, and Joshua Hodgetts.

Stevens and Williams made cameo glass. Hodgets developed a more commercial version using thinner-walled blanks, acid etching, and the engraving wheel. Hodgetts, an amateur botantist, was noted for his brilliant floral designs.

Other glass products and designs manufactured by Stevens and Williams include intaglio ware, Peach Bloom (a form of peachblow), moss agate, threaded ware, "jewell" ware, tapestry ware, and Silveria. Stevens and Williams made glass pieces covering the full range of late Victorian fashion.

After WWI the firm concentrated on refining the production of lead crystal and achieving new glass colors. In 1932 Keith Murray came to Stevens and Williams as a designer. His work stressed the pure nature of the glass form. Murray stayed with Stevens and Williams until WWII and later followed a career in architecture.

Reference: R.S. Williams-Thomas. *The Crystal Years*, Stevens and Williams Limited, England, Boerum Hill Books, 1983.
Additional Listings: Cameo Glass.

Vase, bulbous, pleated undulating rim, applied opaque white flowers and clear leaves, white ground, pink int., 7½″ h, $400.00.

Basket, 5″ l, oblong, ribbed, cased, cranberry int., canary thorn handle, mask prunts and rigaree rim 180.00
Biscuit Jar, cov, 7¾″ h, 5½″ d, cream opaque, large amber and green applied ruffled leaves, rich pink int., SP rim, lid, and handle 275.00
Bowl
  3¾″ d, 3½″ h, box pleated top, plain panels alternating with raised emb beaded panels, white shaded to cranberry, frosted cranberry lining, satin finish 185.00
  6″ d, 7½″ h, opaque white, blue int., enamel floral dec, four amber spade feet, amber rim 350.00
Calling Card Receiver, 10″ l, applied amber handle, rolled edge, translucent opalescent ground, three applied berries, blossoms, and green leaves, three applied amber feet 725.00
Cruet, 9½″ h, 3½″ d, amber, opaque Arboresque pattern, applied amber handle, amber pedestal foot, orig flattened amber stopper 165.00
Jar, cov, 6½″ h, alabaster, rolled rim, ftd base, sgd 275.00
Pitcher, 7″ h, amber, applied fruit, leaves, and thorny stem 480.00
Plate, 4¾″ d, ruffled shell shape, Swirl pattern, shaded pink to green, MOP satin finish 175.00
Rose Bowl, 5″ h, 3½″ d, egg shape, shaded brown ground, rich cream lining, gold prunus blossoms and branches dec, box pleated top 475.00

Vase
  7½″ h, bulbous, MOP, blue and pink swirl design, pr 990.00
  10″ h, slender refined shape, six medallions of applied clear glass, trailing stems swirling to base, engraved ornate stylized petals and foliate, pontil sgd "Frederick Carder," Stevens and Williams logo . . 750.00
  12″ h, double gourd, cameo, bright turquoise blue, white layer cut with nasturium blossoms, medial and rim borders of repeating stylized floral borders, stamped mark "Stevens & Williams Art Glass Stourbridge" 3,575.00

STICKLEYS

History: There were several Stickley brothers: Albert, Gustav, Leopold, George, and John George. Gustav often is credited with creating the Mission style, a variant of the Arts and Crafts style. Gustav headed Craftsman Furniture, a New York firm, much of whose actual production took place near Syracuse. A characteristic of Gustav's furniture is exposed tenon ends. Gustav published *The Craftsman*, a magazine supporting his anti–machine points of view.

Originally Leopold and Gustav worked together. In 1902 Leopold and John George formed the L. and J. G. Stickley Furniture Company. This firm made Mission style furniture and cherry and maple early American style pieces.

George and Albert organized the Stickley Brothers Company, located in Grand Rapids, Michigan.

References: David M. Cathers, *Furniture Of The American Arts and Crafts Movement*, New American Library, 1981; Bruce Johnson, *The Official Identification And Price Guide To Arts And Crafts*, House of Collectibles, 1988.

Periodical: *Arts and Crafts Quarterly,* P.O. Box 3592, Station E, Trenton, NJ 08629.

Book, *Craftsman Homes,* 1909, orig buckram cov 175.00
Chandelier, hammered copper and glass dome, orig hanging chain, 20¼″ l, c1910 . . . . 6,675.00
Furniture
  Bed, No. 923, double, tapering vertical posts, five wide center slats, sgd "Gustav Stickley," 57½″ w, 48″ h 3,300.00
  Chair
    No. 306½, side, horizontal slats, slip seat, wide front rail, double side stretchers, branded mark, 36⅛″ h 215.00
    No. 308, dining, H–back, slip seat, branded mark, 39¼″ h, c1912 . 315.00

No. 346, Morris, mahogany, open rounded and bulging arms, loose seat cushion, woven seat, orig dark alligatored varnish finish, small decal, 41" h, 30" w, 32" d ... **1,320.00**

No. 471, adjustable back, flat arms, six vertical slats, spring cushion seat, branded "The Work of L & JG Stickley," 31¾" w, 35" d, 40½" h, c1912 .... **1,200.00**

No. 800, three concave horizontal rails, spring cushion seat, branded mark, 36½" h, c1912, one No. 802 arm chair, five side **2,200.00**

Chest of Drawers

No. 902, reverse V–splashboard, two half drawers over four graduated drawers, sq wooden pulls, V–groove paneled sides, large red Gustav Stickley decal, 40" w, 21¾" d, 52½" h, c1902–04 .... **4,675.00**

No. 9037, rect top, two half drawers over three long drawers, paneled and arched sides, arched toeboard, stamped numbers, Stickley Bros mark, cleaned, one escutcheon missing, 37¼" w, 21½" d, 46½" h, c1910 .... **1,100.00**

China Closet, No. 746, overhanging top, two doors with six smaller panes over single glass panel, adjustable shelves, arched toeboard, branded L & JG mark, 44" w, 16¼" d, 62" h, c1912 .... **5,250.00**

Day Bed, No. 216, wide crestrail over five vertical slats, cushion, large red Gustav Stickley decal, 79½" l, 31" w, 29¼" h, c1902 .... **2,650.00**

Desk, step down gallery, chamfered drop front, copper strap hinges, two open shelves, chamfered ends with exposed tenons, large Gustav Stickley decal, c1902 .... **6,600.00**

Foot Stool, orig leather seat and tacks, four posts joined by offset lower stretchers, branded mark, 18¾" w, 16" d, 15" h, c1912 .... **715.00**

Frame, 26¾ x 22½", oak, rect, V–shape overhanging crest rail supported by short corbels and vertical stretchers, exposed lower rail tenon, medium brown finish, L & JG mark, c1910 .... **770.00**

Magazine Stand, No. 46, four open shelves, arched rails, three vertical slats, white decal "The Work of L & JG Stickley," 20⅞" w, 11⅞" d, 41⅞" h, c1912, minor stains to shelf ... **1,320.00**

Rocker, No. 2603, arm, concave crestrail, four horizontal back slats, flat cut corner arms, rope seat rails,

box mark, c1902, early refinishing, 35½" h **357.50**

Settle, inlaid flowers, leaves, grasses, naturalistic motifs, 43½" w, 21¾" d, 51¾" h **3,300.00**

Sideboard, No. 734, plate rack, rect top, three drawers flanked by cabinet doors over single long drawer, L & JG decal, later strapwork, 48" w, 20¼" d, 44½" h, c1912 ...... **2,100.00**

Table

No. 575, occasional, round top, four sq legs, cross stretchers, median shelf, branded L & JG mark, minor stain, 24" d, c1910 **880.00**

No. 655, library, oak, thirteen vertical spindles on each side, median shelf, paper label, 36" w, 24¼" d, 29" h, c1905 .... **1,200.00**

No. 722, dining, round top, straight apron cross stretcher, sq legs, three leaves, 48" d, c1912 ..... **1,430.00**

No. 2618, side, oak, rect top, sq tapering legs, double vertical side slats, side, and middle stretchers, metal tag "Quaintfurniture, Stickley Bros, Grand Rapids, MI," 26" h, c1901 .... **385.00**

Tabouret, No. 558, octagonal, oak, white L & JG Stickley decal, c1910, 17" h, 15" d **600.00**

Lamp Base, hammered copper, oviform, brass strapwork, three curved legs, imp mark, wooden base, 9¾" h **550.00**

Lantern, No. 225, wrought iron, heart cut–out design, spade shape mounts, opal cylindrical suspension, c1910, 10" h, pr **2,200.00**

Luggage Rack, orig light finish, large red decal, from Cleveholm Manor, CO, 14 x 35½ x 18" **3,520.00**

Wall Sconce, No. 342, copper, brass accents, separate bobeches for candles, marked "342, Stickley Bros," 15" l **425.00**

Window Seat, No. 178, mortised, raised sides, tacked seat, stretcher mortised with tenon and key, restored dark finish, small decal, c1902–04, 26 x 35½ x 19¼" **1,650.00**

STIEGEL TYPE GLASS

History: Baron Henry Stiegel founded America's first flint glass factory at Manheim, Pennsylvania, in the 1760s. Although clear glass was the most common color made, amethyst, blue (cobalt), and fiery opalescent are found. Products included bottles, creamers, flasks, flips, perfumes, salts, tumblers, and whiskeys. Prosperity was short lived. Stiegel's extravagant living forced the factory to close.

It is very difficult to identify a Stiegel-made item. As a result the term "Stiegel type" is used to identify glass made at that time period in the same shapes and colors.

Enamel decorated ware also is attributed to Stiegel. True Stiegel pieces are rare. An overwhelming majority is of European origin.

Reference: Frederick W. Hunter, *Stiegel Glass*, 1950, available in Dover reprint.

Reproduction Alert: Beware of modern reproductions, especially in enamel wares.

Salt, cobalt blue, twelve heavy vertical ribs, swirled to the right, 2½" h, $275.00.

ENAMELED

Bride's Bottle, clear, enameled dec
   6" h, long neck, rolled mouth, Carpenter's Arms, reverse inscribed "Vivat der Schreiner 1825," red, white, yellow, and blue 200.00
   6⅞" h, large spray of flowers, white, red, yellow, blue, and black, slight haze on bottom 275.00
   7" h, dancing man, playing French horn, urn of flowers, red, blue, yellow, green, and white, orig pewter collar 200.00
Flip, 6½" h, basket of flowers and leaves 375.00
Mug, 3¾" h, blown, red, white, blue, yellow, and green berries, applied handle 100.00
Whiskey, man on prancing horse 265.00

ENGRAVED

Bottle, 7⅞" h, blown clear glass, engraved large tulip on each side, monogram and date 1837, chemical deposit on bottom 150.00
Flip, clear
   6" d, 7¾" h, Phoenix bird between two tulips 150.00

   6⅜" d, 7¼" h, lovebirds in sunburst, frosted 400.00
Mug, cov, floral motif, strap handle ... 400.00
Vase, 9¾" h, clear, hollyhocks and ferns dec, hollow base, hollow stem, pontil 100.00

OTHER

Bowl, amethyst, fifteen expanded diamond pattern, miniature 425.00
Christmas Light, 4" h, yellow–green, expanded diamond, metal fixture 125.00
Creamer, 4⅛" h, cobalt blue, twenty expanded diamonds 300.00
Flask, 4¾" h, amethyst, pattern molded, flattened globular, diamond daisy pattern and fluting 4,620.00
Perfume Bottle, daisy in hexagon pattern, flake on neck 4,000.00
Salt, cobalt blue, expanded diamond . 125.00
Sugar, cov, deep sapphire blue, eleven expanded diamond pattern 2,500.00

STONEWARE

History: Made from dense kaolin clay and commonly salt–glazed, stonewares were hand–thrown and high–fired to produce a simple, bold vitreous pottery. Stoneware crocks, jugs, and jars were produced for storage and utility purposes. This use dictated shape and design—solid, thick–walled forms with heavy rims, necks, and handles with little or no embellishment. When decorated, the designs were simple: brushed cobalt oxide, incised, slip trailed, stamped, or tooled.

Stoneware has been made for centuries. Early American settlers imported stoneware items at first. As English and European potters refined their earthenware, colonists began to produce their own wares. Two major North American traditions emerged based only on the location or type of clay. North Jersey and parts of New York comprise the first area; the second was eastern Pennsylvania spreading westward and into Maryland, Virginia, and West Virginia. These two distinct locations, style of decoration, and shape are discernible factors in classifying and dating early stoneware.

By the late 18th century, stoneware was manufactured in all sections of the country. During the 19th century, this vigorous industry flourished until glass "fruit jars" appeared and the widespread use of refrigeration. By 1910, commercial production of salt–glazed stoneware came to an end.

References: Georgeanna H. Greer, *American Stoneware: The Art and Craft of Utilitarian Potters*, Schiffer Publishing, Ltd., 1981; Don and Carol Raycraft, *Country Stoneware And Pottery*, Collector Books, 1985, 1989 value update; Don and Carol Raycraft, *Collector's Guide To Country Stoneware & Pottery, 2nd Series*, Collector Books, 1990.

Periodical: *Stoneware Collectors' Journal*, 670 Mix Avenue #5L, Hamden, CT 06514.

Bowl, 8¼" d, cobalt blue foliage dec on rim, floral sides, Hickerson, J H, Strasburg, VA, ... **225.00**
Butter Crock
  5¾" d, straight sides, stenciled cobalt blue label, Ratcliff, D L, and Co, Wheeling, WV **120.00**
  6" d, applied handles, brown slip floral motif, imp mark on shoulder, Bell, Samuel and Solomon, Strasburg, VA, c1834–82 .... **250.00**
  10" d, feather motif, matching lid ... **300.00**
Canning Jar
  8" h, narrow mouth, Albany slip, three brushed white flowers, Rouston, Wooster, OH **125.00**
  9¾" h, stenciled label, leaf motif, Weymon and Bros, Pittsburgh, PA **100.00**
Churn, 15½" h, brushed cobalt blue design and "4" **125.00**
Cooler, 23¼" h, ovoid, cobalt blue foliage design, incised label, bung hole with imp design, marked "A B Lake, Hopewell, Ohio" **7,600.00**

Crock, two applied ear handles, marked "L. H. Yeager & Co, Allentown, PA," 8¾" d, 7" h, $225.00.

Crock
  9¼" h, flourish and "2" cobalt blue quill work design **45.00**
  9¾" h, cobalt blue quill work feather design, imp label "J Burger Jr Rochester, NY" and "3" **275.00**
Cuspidor, 11" d, 6¾" h, cobalt blue dec ext., brown Albany slip int., marked "Livingston House" in bold letters .. **70.00**
Flask, 5½" h, flattened ovoid **85.00**
Jar
  7½" h, ovoid, eared handles, imp swags and single flower, cobalt blue wash, Crolius, C, Manhattan–Wells, NY **1,100.00**

8¼" h, ovoid, incised wavy lines, imp "1" **65.00**
8¾" h, ovoid, brushed cobalt blue flower, applied handles **235.00**
8⅝" h, cobalt blue floral dec, open handles **175.00**
9½" h, ovoid, butterfly design in cobalt blue brush work, imp label "S S Perry Troy" **60.00**
11½" h, floral design and stripes with "2," cobalt blue stenciled and free-hand label **125.00**
12¼" h, cobalt blue stenciled label, shields and "2" **85.00**
13¾" h, ovoid, cobalt blue stenciled and freehand label, flowers, marked "Hamilton & Jones, Greensboro, Pa 3" **275.00**
14" h, "3" and flourish cobalt blue quill work **65.00**
14½" h, eared handles, stenciled cobalt label and spread winged eagle, brushed "4" and wavy lines, Reppert, T F, Eagle Pottery, Greensboro, PA **625.00**
15" h, ovoid, imp "6" **65.00**
16¼" h, ovoid, cobalt blue stenciled "5" in wreath **75.00**
16½" h, stenciled and freehand cobalt blue label, "Williams & Reppert, Greensboro, PA 6" **145.00**
Jug
  7½" h, ovoid, gray salt glaze, brown highlights, imp "Charlestown" ... **250.00**
  11" h, semi–ovoid, slip quilled cobalt blue bird perched on scrolling branch, Norton and Co, J E, Bennington, VT **325.00**
  11½" h, cobalt blue quill work, stylized floral design, imp label "Somerset Potters' Works" **200.00**
  12" h, ovoid, cobalt blue slip dash marks, marked "1840" **325.00**
  12½" h, ovoid, brushed brown floral design, imp label "Lyman & Clark, Gardiner" **485.00**
  12¾" h, semi–ovoid, strap handle, brushed cobalt blue leafy floral sprig, imp "Cowden & Wilcox, Harrisburg, Pa, 2," c1870, minor flakes **275.00**
  13" h, cobalt blue slip bird on branch, imp label "Evan B Jones, Pittston, PA" **400.00**
  13¼" h, cobalt blue stenciled griffins, imp label, Webster and Berge ... **135.00**
  13¾" h, cobalt blue slip bird on branch, imp label "White's Utica, 2" **300.00**
  14¼" h, ovoid, strap handle, brushed cobalt blue stylized flower, daub of blue on imp label "H Purdy, Ohio 2," c1840, minor chips and short hairline in base **500.00**

15½" h, cobalt blue quill work flower, imp label "F B Norton Sons, Worcester, Mass" **250.00**

17¼" h, seated polka dot lion, cobalt blue slip, imp label "Troy, NY Pottery 4" **450.00**

18" h, ovoid, "5" and simple dot design in cobalt blue brush work ... **80.00**

19¼" h, semi–ovoid, applied loop handles at rim, fine slip quilled cobalt blue script inscription "Viall Ruckel & Co, Middlebury, O" **2,000.00**

Match Holder, 2¾" h, cone shaped, gray body, imp narrow bands around top and base with cobalt blue wash, serrated striking surface **75.00**

Milk Bowl

10" d, cobalt blue leaf motif Hermann, P, Baltimore, ... **200.00**

12¾" d, pouring spout, applied handles, brushed cobalt blue "2" with foliate detail, brown Albany slip int., imp label "Lyons" **475.00**

Mug, 4¾" h, cylindrical, applied strap handle, slip quilled cobalt blue blossoms, attributed to Daniel P Shenfelder, Marion Township, Berks County, PA, c1869–80 .... **450.00**

Pitcher

8¼" h, gray salt glaze **90.00**

10¼" h, greenish tan glaze **125.00**

Preserving Jar

5½" h, cobalt blue stenciled label, "A P Donaghho, Parkersburg, W VA" **145.00**

6¾" h, cobalt blue stenciled label, "A P Donaghho, Parkersburg, W VA . **145.00**

7¾" h, cobalt blue stenciled label, "Voegtly & Bros, Baresville, Ohio" **175.00**

8" h, cobalt blue stenciled label and pear, "Greensboro" **140.00**

8½" h, cobalt blue stenciled band .. **55.00**

9½" h, cobalt blue stenciled label, "Fine MacCoboy," mismatched lid **125.00**

10" h, cobalt blue stenciled and freehand label "Hamilton & Jones, Greensboro, PA" **205.00**

11½" h, stenciled and freehand cobalt blue label, "E J Miller & Son, Dealers in China and Glassware, Alexandria, VA" **385.00**

12" h, brushed cobalt blue wavy lines and "2" **175.00**

Salt Box, 6¾" w, 6½" h, hanging, emb basketweave design and "SEL," wood lid **55.00**

Spittoon, 8" d, cobalt blue leaf and floral motif **175.00**

Wash Board, 13¾ x 24½", dark brown Albany slip wash board insert in wooden frame, scrubbed finish, insert chipped **50.00**

Water Cooler, 24½" h, domed cov,

ovoid, applied loop handles, incised florals, cobalt blue highlights, Cyrus Fenton **650.00**

STONEWARE, BLUE AND WHITE

History: Blue and white stoneware refers to molded, salt glazed, domestic, utilitarian earthenware with a blue glaze produced in the late 19th and early 20th centuries. Earlier stoneware was usually handthrown and either undecorated, hand decorated in Spencerian script floral and other motifs, or stenciled. The stoneware of the blue and white period is molded with a design impressed, embossed, stenciled, or printed.

Although known as blue and white, the base color is generally grayish in tone. The blue cobalt glaze may coat the entire piece, appear as a series of bands, or accent the decorative elements.

All types of household products were available in blue and white stoneware. Bowls, crocks, jars, pitchers, mugs, and salts are just a few examples. The ware reached its height between 1870 and 1890. The advent of glass jars, tin containers, and chilled transportation brought its end. The last blue and white stoneware was manufactured in the 1920s.

References: Kathryn McNerney, *Blue & White Stoneware*, Collector Books, 1981, 1991 value update; Don and Carol Raycraft, *Collector's Guide To Country Stoneware & Pottery, Second Series*, Collector Books, 1990.

Collectors' Club: Blue & White Pottery Club, 224 12th St., NW, Cedar Rapids, IA 52405.

Reproduction Alert: A vast majority of the blue and white stoneware found in antiques shops and flea markets is unmarked reproductions from Rushville Pottery, Rushville, OH.

Crock, cov, Grape pattern, int. glazed, marked "Robinson Clay, Akron, OH," 7¾" d, $195.00.

Berry Bowl, 4½" d, diffused blues	50.00
Bowl	
5" d, Wedding Ring	50.00
9½" d, currants and diamonds dec .	75.00
10½" d, feather dec	100.00
Butter Crock	
Butterfly	100.00
Panel	80.00
Cake Crock, four blue bands, "cake" stencil, replaced tin lid	325.00
Chamber Pot, Beaded Rose Cluster and Spear Points	100.00
Coffeepot, 11½" h, swirl, blue tipped finial knob, spurs handle, iron base cap	350.00
Cookie Jar, 8" h, grooved blue, orig lid	125.00
Cup, 4½" h, Wildflower, emb ribbon and bow	60.00
Ice Crock, 4½" h, Rope Bands, ice tongs, and ice block dec, late 1800s	125.00
Mug	
Cattails	115.00
Rose, decal	50.00
Pickle Crock, blue band, barrel shape, bail handle	60.00
Pie Plate, 10½" d, blue, brick edge base, imp star shaped mark	100.00
Pitcher	
7¾" h	
Grapes, emb	100.00
Peacock, emb spout	250.00
8" h, Indian Chief, feather headdress medallion on waffle ground	200.00
9" h, Butterfly, large butterfly surrounded by raised rope medallion, diffused blues, small butterflies between raised rope bands top and bottom	150.00
10" h, Old Fashioned Garden Rose .	125.00
Rolling Pin, 13" l, swirl design, orig wood handles	200.00
Salt	
Apricot	140.00
Lovebirds, wooden lid	125.00
Soap Dish	
Cat's Head	125.00
Indian War Bonnet	140.00
Spittoon, emb, sponged blue earthworm pattern	120.00
Toothpick Holder, Swan	55.00

STRETCH GLASS

History: Stretch glass was produced by many glass manufacturers in the United States between the early 1900s and the 1920s. The most prominent makers were Cambridge, Fenton (who probably manufactured more stretch glass than any of the others), Imperial, Northwood, and Steuben. Stretch glass can be identified by its iridescent, onionskin–like effect. Look for mold marks. Imported pieces are blown and show a pontil mark.

Reference: Berry Wiggins, *Stretch Glass*, Antique Publications, 1972 (1987 value update).

Collectors' Club: Stretch Glass Society, P.O. Box 770643, Lakewood, OH 44107.

Dish, scalloped corners, Imperial, 3" h, 6½" w, $135.00

Bobeches, scalloped, vaseline, pr	40.00
Bowl	
8½" d, 4" h, vaseline	15.00
10" d, 4½" h, yellow irid, Imperial . .	85.00
12" d, white, Fenton	40.00
Candlesticks, 10½" h, vaseline, pr . . .	50.00
Candy Dish, topaz, Fenton	60.00
Compote	
7⅝" d, 4½" h, green irid, clear stem, amber base	65.00
12" d, 6" h, gold irid, sgd "LCT Favrile #2776"	1,210.00
Creamer and Sugar, Rings pattern, tangerine	75.00
Hat, 4" h, purple, Imperial	55.00
Nappy, 7" w, vaseline, Fenton	32.00
Pitcher, lemonade, celeste blue, cobalt blue handle	200.00
Plate	
6" d, red, paneled, Imperial	50.00
8¼" d, Aurene, gold	70.00
Rose Bowl, 5" h, 3½" d, pink, melon ribbed	50.00
Sherbet, 4" h, red, melon ribbed	50.00
Vase	
5½" h, baluster, pink, Imperial	75.00
6" h, fan shape, ribbed, green	35.00
10" h, blue, vertical cut	50.00

STRING HOLDERS

History: The string holder developed as a utilitarian tool to assist the merchant or manufacturer who needed tangle-free string or twine to tie packages. The early holders were made of cast iron, some patents dating to the 1860s.

When the string holder moved to the household, lighter and more attractive forms developed, many made of chalkware. The string holder remained a key kitchen element until the early 1950s.

Advertising, "Use Higgins German Laundry Soap. It is the Best," cast iron, black, four wall or counter mounts, 6" h 60.00

Cast-Iron, beehive, 6½" d, 4½" h, $18.00.

Cast Iron
Counter type, openwork beehive, three legs 35.00
Girl ice skating, polychrome paint, 7" h 375.00
Woman, string comes out of mouth, repainted 350.00
Ceramic, bear 10.00
Chalkware
Baby 35.00
Mexican Man 25.00
Scotty Dog 45.00
Spanish Senor and Senorita, pr ... 50.00
Cut Glass, notched prisms, Gorham sterling silver top 185.00
Plaster, cat, cream, red ball 20.00
Porcelain, rooster, Royal Bayreuth ... 220.00
Pottery, figural, dog, Bennington 165.00
Silver Plated, 3⅝" h, 3¾" d, dome shape, repousse wreath around body, Pairpoint 65.00

SUGAR SHAKERS

History: Sugar shakers, sugar castors, or muffineers all served the same purpose: to "sugar" muffins, scones, or toast. They are larger than salt and pepper shakers, were produced in a variety of materials, and were in vogue in the late Victorian era.

CHINA

Nippon, 3⅛ x 4⅞", panels of pink and red roses, cream ground, gold dec handle 65.00

Forget-Me-Not pattern, light pink, Challinor, $110.00.

Schlegelmilch, RS Prussia, 5", scalloped base, pearl finish, roses, red mark 235.00
Wedgwood, classic white dec, blue ground 50.00

GLASS

Milk Glass
Bulbous, three Palmer Cox Brownies dec, pale blue ground 175.00
Challinor's Forget–Me–Not, white, opaque, orig top 100.00
Mt Washington
Egg shape, pansies dec, peach shading to yellow ground 250.00
Lighthouse shape, IVT, bluerina, orig metal top, 5½" 270.00
Melon ribbed, blue and white forget–me–nots, yellow ground 200.00
Opalescent Glass
Reverse Swirl, cranberry, 6" 125.00
Ribbed Lattice, blue 75.00
Pattern Glass
Coin Spot, cranberry, SP top 75.00
Inverted Thumbprint, vaseline, orig top 60.00
Leaf Umbrella, cranberry spatter, white casing 225.00
Medallion Sprig, rubena 165.00
Royal Oak, rubena, frosted 225.00
Wisconsin, orig top 65.00
Satin, MOP, DQ, blue 225.00

SWANSEA

History: This superb pottery and porcelain was made at Swansea (Glamorganshire, Wales) as early as the 1760s with production continuing until 1870.

Marks on Swansea vary. The earliest marks were SWANSEA impressed under glaze and DILLWAN under glaze after 1805. CAMBRIAN POTTERY was stamped in red under glaze from 1803-1805. Many fine examples, including the Botanical series in pearlware, are not marked, but may have the botanical name stamped under glaze.

Fine examples of Swansea often may show imperfections, such as firing cracks. These pieces are considered mint because they left the factory in this condition.

Reference: Susan and Al Bagdade, *Warman's English & Continental Pottery & Porcelain, 2nd Edition,* Wallace–Homestead, 1991.

Reproduction Alert: Swansea porcelain has been copied for many decades in Europe and England. Marks should be studied carefully.

Bowl, 8⅝″ d, blue printed profile of George III and Queen Charlotte, inscribed "A King revered, a Queen beloved," and "Long may they live," chinoiserie scenes **285.00**
Cabinet Cup and Saucer, multicolored bouquets, turquoise border edged with gold foliage, colored sprays, three paw feet **235.00**
Dessert Dish, 11¼″ l, oval, center painted with single sprig, border with four panels of painted roses on white ground, four panels of butterflies reserved on apricot ground, cruciform gilding, c1820 .... **1,500.00**
Figure, 5½″ l, two running pointers, brown markings, molded green and turquoise grass, floral ground, pink gilt lined stepped base, Dillwyn & Co, c1811–17 .... **1,825.00**

Plate, floral, sgd under glaze, c1812, 8½″ d, $120.00.

Plate, 8⅛″ d, spray of three pink roses, two green leaves, dentil rim, scattered floral sprays border, 1814–22 ..... **660.00**
Tea Set, teapot, sugar, and creamer, terra cotta, enameled Etruscan motif band, c1840 .... **1,530.00**
Vase, 12½″ h, ovoid, applied relief pendant biscuit garland flowers, reserved

gilded pink roses and dots, circular foot, sq base, flared neck, baskets of flowers, two scroll handles, ram's head terminals, c1815 .... **3,179.00**

SWORDS

History: The first swords in America came from Europe. The chief cities for sword manufacturing were Solingen in Germany, Klingenthal in France, and Hounslow and Shotley Bridge in England. Among the American importers of these foreign blades was "Horstmann" whose mark is found on many military weapons.

New England and Philadelphia were the early centers for American sword manufacturing. By the Franco-Prussian War, the Ames Manufacturing Company of Chicopee, Massachusetts, was exporting American swords to Europe.

Sword collectors concentrate on a variety of styles: commission vs. non-commission officers' swords, presentation swords, naval weapons, and swords from a specific military branch such as cavalry or infantry. The type of sword helped identify a person's military rank and, depending on how he had it customized, his personality as well.

Following the invention of repeating firearms in the mid-19th century, the sword lost its functional importance as a combat weapon and became a military dress accessory. Condition is a key criterion determining value.

Reference: Harold L. Peterson, *The American Sword 1775–1945,* Ray Riling Arms Books Co, 1965.

Collectors' Club: Japanese Sword Society of the United States, Inc., P.O. Box 4387, Grasso Plaza Branch, St. Louis, MO 63123.

Presentation, presented to General Ulysses S. Grant by his friends in Kentucky when he took control of the Northern Army, 1864, jewel encrusted, $330,000.

AMERICAN

Cavalry, Saber, Model 1840, stamped on obverse ricasso "US JH" and on reverse "N.P. AMES CABOTVILLE

1846," crisp brass hilt, steel scabbard with some polishing marks **800.00**

Confederate, Officer's, 83½" overall, 33¼" unmarked blade with unstopped fuller, brass basket guard with large "CS" in counterguard surrounded by floral patterns, leather grip wound with twisted brass wire, complete with part of orig scabbard, brass throat mount Serial No. 47 and engraved "MADE BY/James Coning/Mobile/ Ala," brass middle mount unmarked, drag missing **5,000.00**

Fraternal, Ames, deluxe, 27" blade, etched against gilt ground for 18½", obverse with profuse scrolls, a standing knight in armor and "Wilson Daniel Rau," reverse with scrolls, a panel showing knights jousting with a castle at the side, a trophy of flags, and "AMES/Sword Co/CHICOPEE/ MASS," fancy cast and silvered hilt with black painted grips, silvered scabbard with fancy openwork mounts with enameled crown and cross, Maltese cross **100.00**

Halberd, Colonial, steel head, 17" overall, 12" leaf shaped blade, 29½" straps for attachment to shaft, deep age patina, small areas of light cleaning, scattered pitting, fitted to restoration 87½" oak shaft **125.00**

Non–commissioned Officer, Model 1840, obverse stamped "US/DFM/ 1860," reverse "EMERSON/&/SILVER/TRENTON, N.J.," orig brass mounted black leather scabbard . . . **300.00**

Polearm, military, 97" overall, 6" iron tip, heavy 4½" point square in cross–section, forged one piece with 17" straps, butt a 2½" iron cone with 8½" straps, again forged as one piece, straps all attached to heavy oak shaft with screws, shaft marked "U.S." and "T.H." **500.00**

EUROPEAN

Continental, Presentation, German silver scabbard with high raised cast brass mounts in oak leaf and acorn pattern, orig script inscription between throat and middle mount, "Presented to/Lt. H. H. Dumont,/By Co. F 189th O.V.I./1865," sword 40" overall, 34" curved "W.CLAUBERG/SOLINGEN" blade, deeply etched for 15½" on each side with trophies of arms, scrolls, etc., hollow silver plate casting grip in dot and leaf pattern **2,100.00**

MIDDLE EAST

Eastern, 30⅝" overall, 25½" blade engraved overall with large figures of various animals, iron hilt with gold damascened dec and ivory scales that are mellowed old replacements, engraved animals with considerable traces of gold dec **125.00**

Persian, Saber, 36" overall, 31" curved blade, damascened panel containing Farsi writing, iron hilt with stylized lion head pommel dec with gold damascening, orig black leather cov wood scabbard with iron drag **375.00**

TEA CADDIES

History: Tea once was a precious commodity. Special boxes or caddies were used as containers to accomodate different teas, including a special cup for blending.

Around 1700 silver caddies appeared in England. Other materials, such as Sheffield plate, tin, wood, china, and pottery, also were used. Some tea caddies became very ornate.

Burl Walnut, string inlay, ivory escutcheon, brass hinges, two compartments, 7½" l, 4⅜" d, 4¾" h, $575.00.

Ivory, rect, carved, scholars, boats, pavilions, and tree scenes, bamboo carved edges, sliding top, Chinese, 19th C **1,250.00**

Lacquer, 8½" l, black, crested, two fitted and chased pewter compartments, ivory handles **350.00**

Porcelain, 5" h, famille rose, arched rect form, blue Nanking border on shoulder, painted shield enclosing monogram front and back, Chinese Export, c1790 . . . . **550.00**

Tortoiseshell
  5¾" h, 6¾" l, rect, stepped top with silverplated panel, canted corners with veneered panels, ivory edge,

silverplated escutcheon, four silver-
plated ball feet, 19th C **3,300.00**
7" h, shaped rect, two lidded contain-
ers, 19th C **3,575.00**
Willow, 7¾" h, blue transfer, labeled
"Rington's Tea Merchants" **125.00**
Wood
5" l, barrel form, walnut, molded
ebonized bands, ivory knob, steel
escutcheon, bouquet of silk flowers
inset on each end, turned circular
ebonized plinth **300.00**
10" l
Regency, sarcophagus form, four
mother–of–pearl inlaid panels,
English **675.00**
Victorian, inlaid walnut, domed lid
with inlaid checkered borders,
two quarter fans, center lozenge
motif on lid, fitted int., 19th C . . **550.00**
12" l, George III, inlaid mahogany,
rect, strung and crossbanded, center oval plate on lid, drop ring han-
dle, fitted int., c1800 . . . . **525.00**
13" h, George III, inlaid and grained
mahogany, strung and crossbanded edge, lion mask drop ring
handle, fitted int., 19th C **300.00**
30½ x 15¾", Victorian, rosewood,
molded case, beaded borders, fitted int., sq tapered shaft, rect plinth,
bun feet, c1840 . . . . **660.00**

TEA LEAF IRONSTONE CHINA

History: Tea Leaf Ironstone china flowed into
America from England in great quantities in the
1860 to 1910 period and graced the tables of working class America. It traveled to California and
Texas in wagons and by boat down the Mississippi
River to Kentucky and Missouri. It was too plain
for the rich homes; its simplicity and strength ap-
pealed to wives forced to watch pennies. Tea Leaf
found its way into the kitchen of Lincoln's Springfield home; sailors ate from it aboard the *Star of
India*, now moored in San Diego and still displaying Tea Leaf.

Tea Leaf was not manufactured exclusively by
English potters in Staffordshire, contrary to popular
opinion. Although there were more than 35 English
potters producing Tea Leaf, at least 26 American
potters helped satisfy the demand. However,
American potters perpetuated the myth by using
backstamps bearing the English coat-of-arms and
the marking "Warrented." The American housewife
favored imported ware to that made by Americans.

Anthony Shaw (1850–1900) first registered the
pattern in 1856 as Luster Band and Sprig. Edward
Walley (1845–56) already was decorating ironstone with luster trefoil leaf, a detached bud, and
trailing green vine. Walley's products are desig-

nated Pre-Tea Leaf and are sought by eclectic
collectors. Other early variants include "Morning
Glory" and "Pepper Leaf" or "Tobacco Leaf" by
Elsmore & Forster (Foster) (1853–57) and "Teaberry" by Clementson Bros. (1832–1916). Clover
leaf, cinquefoil, and pinwheel all may be found in
a collection specializing in early ware.

The most prolific Tea Leaf makers were Anthony
Shaw and Alfred Meakin (1875–). Johnson Bros.
(1883–), Henry Burgess (1864–92) and Arthur J.
Wilkinson (1897–), all of whom shipped much of
their ware to America and followed close behind
Shaw and Meakin.

Although most of the English Tea Leaf is copper
luster, Powell and Bishop (1868–78) and their successors, Bishop and Stonier (1891–1936), worked
exclusively in gold luster. Beautiful examples of
gold luster by H. Burgess still are being found.
Mellor, Taylor & Co. (1880–1904) used gold luster
on their children's tea sets. Other English potters
also used gold lustre. Recently discovered are
gold lustre pieces by W. & E. Corn, Thomas Elsmore, Thomas Hughes.

J. & E. Mayer, Beaver Falls, Pennsylvania, were
English potters who immigrated to America and
produced a large amount of copper luster Tea
Leaf. The majority of the American potters decorated with gold luster, with no brown underglaze
like that found under the copper luster.

East Liverpool, Ohio potters such as Cartwright
Bros. (1864–1924), East End Pottery (1894–
1909), Knowles, Taylor & Knowles (1870–1934),
and others decorated only in gold luster. This is
also true of Trenton, New Jersey potters such as
Glasgow Pottery, American Crockery Co., Fell &
Thropp Co. Since no underglazing was used with
the gold, much of it has been washed away.

By the 1900s Tea Leaf's popularity had waned.
The sturdy ironstone did not disappear. It was
stored in barns and relegated to attics and basements. Much of it was disposed of in dumps, where
one enterprising collector has dug up some beautiful pieces.

A frequent myth about Tea Leaf is that pieces
marked "Wedgwood" are THE Wedgwood, Josiah.
This is not true! Dealers and collectors who per-
petuate this myth should be confronted. Enoch
Wedgwood was the only potter of that name to
produce Tea Leaf. Enoch Wedgwood's product is
beautiful with large showy leaves. He deserves full
credit for his work.

References: Annise Doring Heaivilin, *Grandma's Tea Leaf Ironstone*, Wallace–Homestead,
1981; Jean Wetherbee, *A Look At White Ironstone*,
Wallace–Homestead, 1980; Jean Wetherbee, *A
Second Look At White Ironstone*, Wallace–Homestead, 1985.

Collectors' Club: Tea Leaf Club International,
P.O. Box 2204, Columbus, IN 47202.

Museums: Lincoln Home, Springfield, IL; Sherman Davidson House, Newark OH; Ox Barn Museum, Aurora, OR.

Reproduction Alert: There are reproductions that are collectible, and there are *reproductions*! Avoid the latter. Collectible reproductions were made by Cumbow China Decorating Co. of Abington, Virginia from 1932 to 1980. Wm. Adams & Sons, an old English firm who made Tea Leaf in 1960s, made reproduction Tea Leaf from 1960 to 1972. Red Cliff, who decorated Hall China blanks with Tea Leaf and clearly marked them, worked in the late 1960s and early 1970s.

Ruth Sayer started making Tea Leaf reproductions in 1981. Although her early pieces were not marked, all of it now is marked with a leaf and the initials "RS" on the bottom. In 1968 Blakeney Pottery, a Staffordshire firm, manufactured a poor quality reproduction of Meakin's Bamboo pattern and marked it "Victoria." It was distributed through a Pennsylvania antiques reproduction outlet.

Plate, raised tea leaf border, imp "J & G Meakin," 4¼" d, $35.00.

Apple Bowl, Wilkinson, tall, ftd	450.00
Baker (open vegetable)	
Elsmore, oval	40.00
Johnson Bros, piecrust edge, 8¾" d round	80.00
Meakin, Chelsea shape, 9" sq	52.00
Butter Dish, cov	
Meakin, Bamboo pattern	80.00
Shaw, Hexagon Sunburst pattern, orig liner	225.00
Wedgwood, Chelsea, orig liner	120.00
Butter Pat	
Edwards, sq	15.00
Meakin, Chelsea pattern, pr	35.00
Shaw, octagonal	12.40
Cake Plate	
American, unmarked, copper luster	90.00
Shaw, Daisy pattern	100.00
Chamber Pot	
W & E Corn	150.00
Wedgwood, plain, round	180.00

Children's Dishes	
Cup and Saucer, handleless, Shaw, Lily of the Valley	240.00
Milk Mug	
Tobacco Leaf variant, unmarked, 2½" d, 2½" h	275.00
Unmarked, 2¼" d, 2½" h	250.00
Tea Set, Knowles, Taylor & Knowles, American, teapot, sugar, four cups, saucers, and plates	750.00
Coffeepot	
Davenport, Fig Cousin, slight damage	180.00
Shaw, Cable	190.00
Compote	
Davenport, low, ftd, hairlines in base	200.00
Mellor Taylor, 7⅞" d, 4½" h	235.00
Shaw, Sunburst pattern, 9½" d, 4" h	450.00
Creamer	
Edwards, Peerless (Feather) pattern, 6" h	110.00
Elsmore & Forster, Pepper Leaf variant	105.00
Red Cliff, American	75.00
Unmarked, Pinwheel variant, 5" h, repaired	140.00
Cup and Saucer	
Edge, Malkin, butter yellow	60.00
Furnival, handled cup, six sets	260.00
Red Cliff, handled cup, four sets	90.00
Shaw	
Basketweave, handled cup, pr	160.00
Fuchsia blank, handleless cup	75.00
Egg Cup	
Adams, reproduction, pr	110.00
Meakin, Boston, low, ftd, repaired	190.00
Unmarked	270.00
Gravy Boat	
Mayer, American	55.00
Shaw	
Cable pattern	70.00
Lily of the Valley pattern	180.00
Hot Water Pitcher (chamber set type)	
Johnson Bros, Chelsea	140.00
Wilkinson, Bow Knot pattern	250.00
Mush Bowl, J & E Mayer, American, pr	80.00
Nappy	
Meakin, sq, set of eight	95.00
Powell & Bishop, gold luster, pr	25.00
Wedgwood, set of five	42.00
Oyster Bowl, unmarked	55.00
Pitcher	
Clementson, Teaberry pattern, 9½" h	120.00
Cumbow, American, 6½" h	50.00
East End Pottery, American, copper luster, 7¾" h	125.00
Meakin, Bamboo pattern, 9" h	190.00
Shaw, Chinese pattern	190.00
Wedgwood, 9" h, sq ridged	130.00
Relish Dish	
Mayer, American	80.00
Shaw, Cable pattern	90.00
Wedgwood, Chelsea	55.00

Sauce Ladle, Shaw	200.00
Sauce Tureen, base, cov, ladle, and underplate	
Mellor Taylor, Lions Head, small chip on ladle	250.00
Wilkinson, simple square shape	425.00
Shaving Mug	
Shaw, Lily of the Valley pattern	265.00
Wick, American, gold luster, ribbed	110.00
Wilkinson	110.00
Soap Dish	
Meakin, Bamboo pattern, base, cov, and liner	150.00
Mellor Taylor, open	150.00
Shaw, Cable pattern, base, cov, and liner	200.00
Soup Bowl, Shaw, 11″ d	27.00
Soup Ladle, Meakin	290.00
Soup Tureen, base, cov, ladle, and underplate	
Meakin, Fishhook pattern	725.00
Shaw, Cable pattern	575.00
Spittoon, Shaw, hairline and chip	450.00
Sugar, cov	
Adams, Empress pattern, reproduction	45.00
Edwards, Victory pattern	140.00
Mayer, American, copper luster, emb	60.00
Shaw, Pear shape, early, rare	230.00
Teapot	
Meakin, Bamboo pattern	195.00
Morning Glory, variant, repaired	175.00
Toothbrush Holder	
American, unmarked, hairline	80.00
Meakin	135.00
Unmarked, vase shape	200.00
Wilkinson	105.00
Vegetable, cov	
East End Pottery, American	70.00
Mellor Taylor, underplate	110.00
Shaw, Daisy pattern	100.00
Wilkinson, Daisy pattern, 7″ sq	70.00
Wash Stand Bowl and Pitcher	
Mayer, copper luster	190.00
Meakin, Fishhook pattern	365.00
Mellor Taylor, Lions Head pattern	360.00
Shaw, Lily of the Valley pattern	350.00

TEDDY BEARS

History: Originally thought of as "Teddy's Bears," the name comes from President Theodore Roosevelt. These stuffed toys are believed to have originated in Germany and in the United States during the 1902–03 period.

Most of the earliest Teddy Bears had humps on their backs, elongated muzzles, and jointed limbs. The fabric used was usually mohair; the eyes were either glass with pin backs or black shoe buttons. The stuffing was generally excelsior. Kapok (for softer bears) and wood-wool (for firmer bears) also were used as stuffing materials.

Quality older bears often had elongated limbs, sometimes with curved arms, oversize feet, and felt paws. Noses and mouths were black and embroidered onto fabric.

The earliest Teddy Bears are believed to have been made by the original Ideal Toy Corporation in America and a German company, Margarete Steiff, GmbH. Bears made in the early 1900s by other companies can be difficult to identify because they had a strong similarity in appearance and because most tags or labels were lost through childhood play.

Teddy Bears are rapidly increasing as collectibles and their prices are increasing proportionately. As in other fields, desirability should depend upon appeal, quality, uniqueness, and condition. One modern bear already has been firmly accepted as a valuable collectible among its antique counterparts: the Steiff Teddy put out in 1980 for the company's 100th anniversary. This is a reproduction of that company's first Teddy and has a special box, signed certificate, and numbered ear tag; 11,000 of these were sold worldwide.

References: Peggy and Alan Bialosky, *The Teddy Bear Catalog*, Workman Publishing, 1984, revised edition; Kim Brewer and Carol–Lynn Rössel Waugh, *The Official Price Guide To Antique & Modern Teddy Bears*, House of Collectibles, 1990; Shirley Conway and Jean Wilson, *Steiff Teddy Bears, Dolls, and Toys With Prices*, Wallace–Homestead, 1984, 1991 value update; Margaret Fox Mandel, *Teddy Bears And Steiff Animals*, Collector Books, 1984; Margaret Fox Mandel, *Teddy Bears, Annalee Animals & Steiff Animals, Third Series*, Collector Books, 1990; Linda Mullins, *The Raikes Bear & Doll Story*, Hobby House, 1991; Linda Mullins, *Teddy Bears Past & Present, Vol. II*, Hobby House Press, 1992; Helen Sieverling (comp.) and Albert C. Revi (ed.), *The Teddy Bear And Friends Price Guide*, Hobby House Press, Inc., 1983.

Periodical: *The Teddy Bear And Friends*, Hobby House Press, Inc., 900 Frederick Street, Cumberland, MD 21502.

Collectors' Club: Good Bears Of The World, P.O. Box 13097, Toledo, OH 43613.

Additional Listing: See Steiff.

BEARS

6″, jointed, glass eyes	80.00
7″, gold mohair, squeaker, hump, shoe button eyes, jointed at hips and shoulders, swivel head, long upturned nose, elongated torso, thin limbs, black sewn nose and mouth, straw stuffed	90.00
12″, Teddy Bar, open mouth, glass eyes, Steiff	100.00

Ideal, mohair, brown, felt pads, c1920, 24" h, $325.00.

13"

Knickerbocker, wearing suit, glass eyes, 1940s 55.00
Steiff, shoe button eyes, plain button in ear, 1907 . . . . 530.00
14", yellow haircloth, articulated limbs and head, recovered paw pads, embroidered features, replaced button eyes, repairs 75.00
20", orange yellow, Steiff, 1920s 180.00
21", straw stuffed, gold mohair, pear shape torso, jointed at hips and shoulders, swivel head, felt paws, brown sewn nose and mouth glass stick pin eyes 110.00
24", mohair, glass eyes, missing one ear, worn pads, Ideal, 1910–20 . . . . 210.00
27", articulated, glass eyes, bow around neck 45.00
30", orange–yellow, Knickerbocker, 1920s 180.00
36", worn pads, Knickerbocker, 1940s . 200.00

BEAR RELATED ITEMS

Book
More About The Roosevelt Bears, Seymour Eaton, illus 90.00
Mother Goose's Teddy Bears, Frederick L Cavally, color illus, worn edges 365.00
The Roosevelt Bears Abroad, Seymour Eaton, illus 100.00
The Traveling Bears In New York, Seymour Eaton, illus, page separation at spine 30.00
Dish, 9" d, child's, porcelain, copper backing, holds warm water under plate, teddy bears in various activities, British 155.00
Perfume Bottle, 5" h, mohair, bottle insert, 1920–30 . . . . 415.00

Puppet, hand, Steiff
Polar Bear 80.00
Teddy 60.00
Spoon, 5½" l, figural handle, enameled, silverplated, Soviet Union 50.00
Toy
Loop the Hoop Bear, 8" h, wire, tin, and cloth, key–wind, orig box, Japan 145.00
Roosevelt Bear Balance, 6½" l, litho metal 110.00

TELEPHONES

History: The deregulation of the nation's telephone industry and increasing interest in antique telephones has led to increasing values for old telephones and equipment.

Lovers' telegraphs and other crude sound operated and unpatented telephones existed prior to Alexander Graham Bell's 1876 patent. However, it is generally accepted that Bell invented the telephone powered by electricity.

The most valuable antique telephones come from the pre-1895 period and must be marked, dated, or easily documented. Instruments also must be unaltered and have all major original parts. Telephones marked Charles Williams, Jr., a Boston manufacturer whose factory was the "birthplace" of the infant Bell Telephone Company, are among the most valued.

Post-1895 telephones have value if modified or converted to be compatible with today's modern phone network. Conversions should be done by an expert who will supply additional parts without removing any of the major components to accomplish conversion.

Refinishing also requires expert skills. Do not remove original circuitry. Restoring nickel and black baked enamel finishes is most desirous. Buffing original parts to expose the brass beneath will make it difficult to distinguish those parts from the many dated and old fashioned marked, solid brass fake parts and whole telephones which have been flooding the market for a decade. No mass produced telephone made in the United States prior to 1950 was offered with a shiny brass finish!

References: R.H. Knappen, *History And Identification Of Old Telephones,* 2 volumes, published by author, 1978; R.H. Knappen, *Old Telephones Price Guide And Picture-Index To History Of Old Telephones,* published by author, 1981.

Collectors' Clubs: Antique Telephone Collectors Association, Box 94, Abilene, KS 67410; Telephone Collectors International, Inc., 19 North Cherry Dr., Oswego, IL 60543.

Automatic, Dialing Telephones
Globe Automatic, wall model 950.00
Lorimer Automatic, all models 1,500.00
Monson Automatic, wall model 1,200.00

Candlestick, Western Electric, brass, non dial, patent date "Aug 16, 1904," $55.00.

National Automatic, wall model	1,500.00
Select–O–Phone	200.00
Strowger Patent	
Automatic Electric, candlestick model	1,200.00
Pre–1898 models	2,500.00
Wall Model, large	1,500.00
Double Box Telephones	
48" l, tandem, any manufacturer	550.00
49 to 60" l, tandem two boxes	750.00
60 to 70" l, tandem two boxes	1,200.00
71" and longer	1,500.00
Oak, plain, Stromberg–Carlson type, c1899	350.00
Unusual in any way, any manufacturer	450.00
Fiddleback Telephones	
Gillian, American Bell, Blake or Charles Williams transmitter	1,000.00
Vought Berger, Kellogg, Western Electric, Stromberg Carlson, Dean, Diamond, etc	275.00
Pay Phones	
Common 1950s style	165.00
Gray Pay Station	
Desk Model, wood, slots for coins up to dollar, marked	3,000.00
Wall Phone, 72"	3,000.00
1920s style (Known as Laurel & Hardy style)	400.00
Pay Box, cast iron, small, c1910	150.00
Single Box Wall Telephones, wood	
Picture Frame Front	
Cathedral Top, lightning arrestors at top	300–400.00
1910–15	225.00
Plain Front, 1915–20	200.00
Unusual style	450–600.00
Stands	
Gossip Benches, approx	70.00
Ornate, carvings	600.00

Plain, 1920s style	150.00
Switchboards	
Hotel Annunciators	50–400.00
Mansion Annunciators, depending on size and ornateness	75–450.00
Pre–1894, wall mount, marked American Bell–Blake, Gillian, Edison, National Bell, or Charles Williams	2,000.00
Pre–1910, wall mount	500.00
Pre–1935	
Light Bulbs	250.00
Transmitter broom	400.00
1935 to present	Surplus Value
Telephone Booths	
1890s, leaded glass	2,000–3,500.00
1910 to 1912, single door	2,000.00
1914 to 1940, oak, folding door	1,200.00
Triple Box	
American Electric, Kokomo	1,200.00
Bell Telephone	1,200.00
Chicago	950.00
Elliott	1,200.00
Gilliand	2,000.00
Keystone	900.00
Mianus	900.00
Note: If any of these sets are missing the 7" long exposed terminal receiver, subtract $150.00.	
Upright Desk Stands (Candlestick Phones)	
Hour Glass or Potbelly shape	750.00
Oil Can shape	500.00
Straight Pipe, regular style, dial type	185.00

Notes: Extremely unusual candlestick phones made of wood or in an outrageous style may be worth in excess of $1,000.00. all phones mass produced from WWI to 1950 were made in black. The Western Electric model is now being reproduced in solid shiny brass.

TEPLITZ CHINA

History: Around 1900 twenty-six ceramic manufacturers were located in Teplitz, a town in the Bohemian province of Czechoslovakia. Other potteries were located in the nearby town of Turn. Wares from these factories were molded, cast, and hand decorated. Most are in the Art Nouveau and Art Deco styles. Most pieces do not carry a specific manufacturer's mark. They are simply marked "Teplitz," "Turn-Teplitz," and "Turn."

Reference: Susan and Al Bagdade, *Warman's*

English & Continental Pottery & Porcelain, 2nd Edition, Wallace–Homestead, 1991.

Basket, Arab motif 60.00
Bowl
  3″ d, enameled boy and dog, gray
    ground, marked "Stellmacher" . . . 75.00
  6¾″ d, ecru, enameled flowers, c1912 175.00
Box, cov, turtle shape, children on cov,
  green, gray, and natural colors, satin
  finish, marked "Ernst Wahliss Turn Vienna," c1918 . . . . 375.00
Candlestick, 5¼″ h, figural, woman in
  flowing gown, c1905 . . . . 135.00
Ewer
  6½″ h, hp, pink and gold flowers, light
    green ground, light pink neck, gold
    twig handle 85.00
  9½″ h, cream, red roses, gold trim,
    marked "Royal Teplitz" 60.00
  9¾″ h, earthenware, gold paint, faint
    irid, free form dec of squares and
    flowing lines, red painted berries,
    curving handle, stamped "Turn–
    Teplitz," c1900 . . . . 300.00
Figure
  12½″ h, young girl, peasant clothes,
    basket resting on tree stump 350.00
  15″ h, man and woman, court clothes,
    multicolored, pr 250.00
Jug, 8″ h, classical man, smoking pipe,
  bronze ground, marked "Stellmacher,
  Teplitz" 175.00
Pitcher, 9½″ h, lily pad dec, green and
  pink, c1895 . . . . 185.00
Tobacco Jar, 8″ h, Boxer dog dec 400.00
Vase
  5″ h, bud, relief rooster head in med-
    allion, multicolored geometric dec 90.00

5½″ h, ovoid, intricately painted Art
  Nouveau portrait, imp, red stamp
  mark, blue Turn mark 550.00
7″ h, four handles, pierced rim panels
  of poppies, drip enamel cobalt blue
  and green dec, gold trim 250.00
16″ h, 5″ d base, turned down pierced
  flared lip flows into handle on
  shoulder, hp florals, heavy gold
  panel, cream ground, marked "Te-
  plitz Amphora" 475.00
Window Box, 12″ l, 3″ w, 4″ h, boat
  shape, rose dec, spider web ground,
  orig liner 125.00

TERRA-COTTA WARE

History: Terra-cotta is ware made of a hard, semi-fired ceramic clay. The color of the pottery ranges from a light orange-brown to a deep brownish red. It is usually unglazed, but some pieces can be found partially glazed or decorated with slip designs, incised, or carved. Examples include utilitarian objects as well as statuettes and large architectural pieces. Fine early Chinese terra-cotta pieces recently have brought substantial prices.

Syrup Jug, enamel, center band of Phoenix birds, pewter top, 6½″ h, $110.00.

Bust, 22″ h, young woman, Chas Eu-
  gene Breton, 1916 . . . . 650.00
Figure
  Hercules, 19¾″ h, seated, folding
    fragments of serpents, stepped
    shaped plinth, inscribed "R. J. Au-
    guste F. 1744," remains of paper
    label and wax seal, some restora-
    tion 20,000.00
  Omphale, 29″ h, nude, hands raised
    above her head holding Hercules'
    lion pelt, Hercules crouches on
    ground behind her, dark brown pa-
    tination, oval base inscribed "A
    Carrier–Belleuse" 6,000.00

Vase, soldier holding long rifle, enam-eled, blue–gray ground, double han-dles, gold Stellmacher mark, 8½″ h, $135.00.

Jug, 7½″ h, marked "Cambridge Ale" .	150.00
Pipe Holder, 5 x 9″, Chinese boy, black glaze	80.00
Plaque, 12 x 22″, relief neoclassical figures	35.00
Tobacco Jar, 11″ h, figural, Bismark, sitting in easy chair	250.00
Tray, 9 x 7″, hp, pilgrims resting on gilt, 1920	75.00
Vase, 6″ h, raised daisy dec, green glazed int.	35.00

TEXTILES

History: Textiles are cloth or fabric items, especially anything woven or knitted. Those that survive usually represent the best since these were the objects that were used carefully and stored by the housewife.

Textiles are collected for many reasons—to study fabrics, understand the elegance of an historical period, and for decorative and modern use. The renewed interest in clothing has sparked a revived interest in textiles of all forms.

References: Alda Leake Horner, *The Official Price Guide to Linens, Lace and Other Fabrics*, House of Collectibles, 1991; William C. Ketchum, Jr., *The Knopf Collectors' Guides to American Antiques: Quilts*, Alfred A. Knopf, Inc., 1982; Betty Ring, *Needlework: An Historical Survey*, Main Street Press, 1984, revised edition; Helene Von Rosenstiel, *American Rugs And Carpets: From The Seventeenth Century To Modern Times*, William Morrow And Company, 1978; Carleton L. Safford and Robert Bishop, *America's Quilts And Coverlets*, Bonanza Books, 1985; Jessie A. Turbayne, *Hooked Rugs History and the Continuing Tradition*, Schiffer Publishing, Ltd., 1991.

Collectors' Club: Costume Society of America, P.O. Box 73, Earleville, MD 21919.

Additional Listings: See Clothing, Linens, Quilts, and Samplers.

Blanket
Homespun, wool, natural white and pink, yellow and brown pinstripes, hand sewn hems, 56 x 78″ **155.00**
Wool, chenille embroidery, gray–blue trees and geometric border, ivory ground, one piece weaving, 66 x 90″ **475.00**
Wool, embroidered, attributed to Chester County, PA, panels of linen homespun, central floral circle enclosing small bird, borders with random design of birds, hearts, leaves, pineapples, flowerheads, candlestand with vase of flowers, houses, inscribed "Remember Me, Forget Me Not, S. R., Sarah, 1852," 100 x 84″ **725.00**

Bolster Cover, trapunto, basket of flowers with vintage and floral designs, finely quilted ground, lace trim, worn ball fringe on three sides, stains, wear, and small holes, 23 x 42″ . . .	200.00
Chair Seat Cover, needlepoint, English, 19th C, trapezoidal shape, bright colors, vignettes of shepherds and shepherdesses, travelers, and farmers, petit and gros point, red, rust, gold, lavender, and brown, teal ground, set of nine	3,000.00

Clothes Pin Bag, to be worn around waist, homespun, hand sewn, worn tape tie, 10 x 11½″
Faced with indigo batik printed floral design **90.00**
Faced with ticking like stripe fabric, brown, blue, and natural **90.00**
Comforter, pierced, knotted, blue prints, brown plaid back, minor stains, 78″ sq **115.00**

Coverlet, jacquard blue and white, woven by Samuel Meily, 72 x 85″, $375.00.

Coverlet
Bride's, trapunto, all white, cotton
American, early 19th C, field with luxuriant pendant blossoms and meandering vines, oval reserve of urn with climbing floral vines, heightened with seed stitching, white cotton fringe, 88 x 90″ . . .   **2,450.00**
Baltimore, early 19th C, center area with elegant urn mounted on pedestal, topped with pineapple, feathered tassels pendant from floral chains, borders with undu-

lating grapevines, daisy sprigs, and clover leaves, 100 x 104″ . **1,200.00**

Jacquard

One piece, double weave, Centennial design

Capitol building, floral border with birds, light green, lavender, dark brown, and natural, minor overall and edge wear, bottom fringe loose, 75 x 78″ **175.00**

Memorial Hall, red, green, blue, and linen, wool fringe, 75½ x 82″ **875.00**

One piece, double weave, central floral urn flanked by two pheasants, floral borders, natural white, tomato red, olive, and gray–green, minor wear, 86 x 90″ **250.00**

One piece, single weave, small center floral medallions, border of two rows of stars and meandering foliage vine, two shades of blue, red, and narrow green stripe, corners sgd "Rebecca Funk 1896," some wear and loss to fringe, 76 x 88″ **200.00**

Two piece, double weave, blue and white, eagle corners, dated 1848, 80 x 88″ **700.00**

Two piece, double weave, blue and white snowflake and circle design, sewn on fringe, minor age stains, 78 x 86″ **350.00**

Two piece, double weave, blue, red, and beige snowflake and rose medallions, foliate vine border, inscribed "Daniel Fisher, Southbend, D–Bennett, 1847," wear and staining on one end, 74 x 87″ **550.00**

Two piece, double weave, very dark navy blue and natural blue, floral design, chickens and eagles in borders, inscribed "J. R. Van Houten 1834," 73 x 85″ . . . **2,300.00**

Two piece, single weave, navy blue and natural white, bold floral pattern, some wear, stains, 68 x 87″ **165.00**

Two piece, single weave, navy blue, green, red, and natural white, floral, vintage borders, weaver sgd "W in Mt Vernon, Knox County, Ohio by Jacob and Michael Ardner 1852," some moth damage and stains, 78 x 82″ **500.00**

Two piece, single weave, red, blue, and natural white, floral design, bird border, corners labeled "Charles Melly, Wayne County, Ohio 1835," stains, some fringe wear, rebound, 80 x 84″ **225.00**

Two piece, single weave, compotes of flowers and floral border with corners sgd "Susanna Zech," red, blue, green, and natural, minor age stains, bit of edge wear, 80 x 90″ **375.00**

Two piece, single weave, large center floral medallions, meandering feather borders, abstract tulips in corners, corners sgd "Magdalene Harham 1867," blue and white, 72 x 90″ **300.00**

Two piece, single weave, medallions, birds and floral border, red, olive green, and natural, corners sgd "Jacob Stephen Springvil, Seneca County, Ohio, 1853," 78 x 88″ **500.00**

Overshot, two piece

Blue and white, 61 x 88″ **150.00**

Blue and white plaid, wear, small holes, some repair, 69 x 93″ . . . **50.00**

Blue, red, and natural white, overall and fringe wear, 72 x 88″ **200.00**

Blue, red, olive green, and natural white, optical diamond and star pattern, minor wear, 76 x 84″ . . **225.00**

Dark blue and white, four block and optical plaid design, Shelburne Falls, MA, early 19th C, 71 x 86″ **650.00**

Drapery Panel, 48″ w, 89″ l, handmade crewel, yellow, orange, olive, and tan, 20th C **30.00**

Dresser Scarf, drawn work border of ducks, eight pointed star in corners, 17 x 33″ **40.00**

Handkerchief, homespun cotton, tricorner, muted plaid design, c1830, 24 x 35″ **40.00**

Luncheon Set, 23 pcs, two runners, two rect mats, seven oval mats, and twelve coasters, Point Venise lace . . **465.00**

Mattress Cover

60 x 72″, navy blue and white cotton plaid, white linen backing, hand sewn **150.00**

60 x 104″, blue and white homespun, one seam, white homespun backing, very minor wear and age stains **115.00**

Mourning Picture, needlework, silk, green, blue–green, ivory, tan, and gray, burial monument with classical ftd urn resting on large plinth, drapery swags over medallion, white reserved plaque imprinted with name and 1809 date, willow tree branches, broad meadow, shrubbery and village in background, tinted watercolor on silk with faint trees, hills, and church, blue and rose shaded sky, stretched on wood frame, staining on unworked lower edge, 13½″ h, 17¾″ l **3,000.00**

Napkin, homespun, blue and white, hand sewn hems, 18 x 19½″ **55.00**

Needlepoint Panel, 15½″ h, 14¼″ w, oval, young woman and dog, mostly wool, watercolor on paper face, worn gilt frame **200.00**

Needlework Picture

14½″ h, 10½″ w, wool and silk threads, shades of blue, green, yellow, red, pink, cream, and black, linen ground, worked by Mehitable Goddard, Sutton and Worcester, MA, c1770, inscribed "MM" and "The 24 chapter of Genesis," Rebecca at the well, orig frame, back inscribed, some fiber loss **7,000.00**

21″ h, 24″ w, wool on silk, scene of Moses in the bullrushes, drawn detail of baby and woman's face, orig eglomise glass liner, worn gilt frame **225.00**

Pocketbook, needlework, blue, yellow, green, and brown flamestitch, red satin, pocket int., inscribed Nathaniel Richard of Roxbury and 1769 on front **4,400.00**

Pot Holder, appliqued wool and silk, three brown owls, yellow moon, int. lined with red and white polka dot cotton, American, early 20th C **275.00**

Rug

Fish Scale, wool, bound with cotton tape and embroidery, black center field, embroidered pot of flowers, some fading, wear, and minor damage, 22½ x 40½″ **125.00**

Hooked

11 x 39″, yarn, pictorial, scene of red barn, purple house, green tree, pond in foreground with ducks and chicks, birds in flight in distance, PA, early 20th C . . **275.00**

23¾ x 39½″, rag, spinning wheel, chair, and broom, red, gray walls, olive floor boards, blue, white, and black accents, faded colors **150.00**

24 x 38″, rag, multicolored geometric design, maroon ground, minor wear **70.00**

24 x 46″, yarn, sheared, allover triangular motifs, shades of gray, blue, red, black, and purple, American, late 19th C **285.00**

25¾ x 39½″, coral, green, red, yellow, lavender, and gray, black ground, running buck, stylized flowers, fabric label, printed string tag "Made in Labrador, International Grenfell Association," c1925 . . . . **3,410.00**

26 x 47½″, yarn, eight point stars in green, orange, and blue, green trellis border with orange intersection points, American, c1900 **250.00**

30 x 54″, rag, beige, brown, rose, pink, red, blue, and green, peacock with extravagant spotted tail, large rose blossom at feet, scalloped blue–gray borders . . . **2,475.00**

31 x 86″, yarn, fiery sunburst design, minor edge wear **200.00**

34 x 56″, rag, black dog, beige and gray ground, tan grid and light blue dots **750.00**

34½ x 47″, rag, red, white, blue, black, beige, yellow, orange, and lavender, American flag center, brightly colored double sawtooth borders, late 19th C **5,225.00**

35 x 46″, rag, gray, beige, brown, red, and blue, four masted sailing ship, blue seas, inner chain border, black brown outer border . . **8,250.00**

35 x 48″, shades of beige and gray, polychrome ground, angel trumpeting over three graves, hourglass, verse: "The sands of time are running low soon to my maker I must go—I have no fear tho worried be what I will say to my husbands," some fading and soiling, American, 20th C **2,750.00**

Machine Woven, 19 x 37″, kittens on fence, red poppies **415.00**

Penny, felt, overlapping tan and brown petals, embroidered blue and red edges, center with applied oval brown panel embroidered with vase filled with three red and green floral sprigs, American, early 20th C, 28 x 34½″ **475.00**

Rag

Braided, 52 x 78″, alternating gray and blue squares, border of red and black squares **85.00**

Woven

18½″ x 75″, loom woven, orange and green stripes, bound ends, warp knotted fringe, two strips **120.00**

28 x 114″, loom woven, multicolored wool fabrics **130.00**

65 x 33″, pink, blue, and green squares, American **85.00**

Sewn, 35 x 71″, yarn, red, yellow, green, and brown wool and cotton, low ftd vase, stylized blossoms, corners with dancing five pointed stars, dark blue ground, New England, early 19th C **11,000.00**

Shawl

58 x 112″, stripes with paisley design, frayed ends **330.00**

66 x 70″, wool, woven, paisley **250.00**

68 x 72″, allover paisley pattern, black center **275.00**

Sheet

Homespun, two piece, hand sewn seam and hem, ink sgd in corner
64 x 92", stains, pr ... 110.00
66 x 98", small repairs 25.00
Homespun Cotton, two piece, center seam, hand sewn hems, 77 x 78" 65.00
Linen, two pillow cases, linen, embroidered blue silk, 56" sq 80.00

Show Towel

Homespun, cross stitch and cut work, tied fringe, gray and several shades of brown embroidery floss, 10 x 10" plus fringe, framed, 12¾ x 16¾" 475.00
Homespun, linen and cotton cut work, floral embroidery with "C. L.," minor stains, 13½ x 51" 100.00
Linen, embroidered in pink threads with numerous stars, flowerheads, birds, reindeer, dogs, potted flowering shrubs, zigzag crochet panel with fringe below, sgd "Anna Marie Nies, 1816," 15 x 60" 350.00

Table Cloth

36"
  Oval, organdy, white, stitched floral dec 90.00
  Square, pr, linen, pink, beige lace dec, eight napkins 200.00
39 x 55", homespun linen, gold and white check, unhemmed 125.00
50", sq, linen, beige, geometric dec, eight matching napkins 40.00
54 x 76", homespun, gold and white plaid, two piece, off center seam, one end with hand sewn hem, other with basted selvage, some wear, repaired holes 125.00
58 x 72", homespun
  Cotton, blue and white plaid, hand sewn hem, off center seams, wear, small holes 90.00
  Cotton and Linen, woven diamond design, two piece, center seam 25.00
60 x 74", homespun, woven white on white design, two pieces, hand sewn, embroidered initials and date 1862 .... 25.00
60 x 76", homespun, blue and white plaid, two piece, off center seam, hand sewn hem 165.00
65", round, lace, ivory and ecru ... 300.00
80", round, linen, white, silvery gray floral open work embroidery, twelve napkins 100.00
90 x 56", linen, beige, brown stitched foliate dec, eleven napkins 110.00
105 x 88", organdy, white, embroidered floral and foliate motifs, scalloped edges, eleven napkins 100.00

Table Set, linen

13 pcs, cutwork and filet lace inserts, 76 x 116" tablecloth, twelve matching napkins 310.00
17 pcs, eight placemats, eight napkins, and runner, linen, beige, embroidered foliate dec 140.00

Towel, homespun linen

Natural color, natural and white embroidery, 11½ x 32" 20.00
White on white woven design, tab hangers, ink sgd name, 18 x 56" . 25.00
Woven overshot bands, red embroidered initials "B.M.," 16½ x 51" .. 25.00

Tapestry

20½ x 43½", needlepoint, English, birds among acanthus and rosette motif 425.00
42 x 48", needlepoint, Renaissance style 450.00
4' 3" x 4' 7", machine made, 18th C figures in landscape, floral border 300.00
6' x 6' 4", French, Aubusson, mid 19th C, exotic birds, wooded landscape 2,200.00
6' 6" x 9' 11", Flemish, Baroque Verdure, fortified town in wooded landscape, flowers plants, exotic birds and animals by stream, blue, green, brown, and beige, narrow dark brown and beige border, extensive reweaving to center section, some losses and splitting, borders added 4,950.00
7' 4" x 4' 6", Continental, needlepoint, late 19th C, medieval knight and maiden beneath architectural arch 160.00
7' 11" x 6' 3", French, Gobelins, late 18th C, tree and floral landscape, country house and brook, acanthus leaf border 3,800.00
8' 6" x 7' 4", Flemish, Baroque Verdure, country house, park and trees, blue, green, brown, and ochre, repeating border of palmettes, armorials, and trophies, extensive reweaving, splitting ... 3,850.00
9' 5" x 10' 4", Brussels, late 18th C, exotic birds, wooded setting, floral border 5,950.00
16' 3" x 11' 10", Brussels, second half 17th C, silk, wool, and silver thread, depicting departure of Meleager for the Hunt of the Calydonian Boar, central field filled with equestrians, attendants and hunting dogs, foliate border woven with flower filled urns, fruits, arrow-filled quivers, and masks in rust, burgundy, gold, green, olive, ivory, umber, blue, and pink 21,000.00

THIMBLES

History: Thimbles often are thought of as common household sewing tools. Many are. However, others are miniature works of art, souvenirs of places, people, and events, or gadgets (thimbles with expanded uses such as attached threaders, cutters, or magnets).

There were many thimble manufacturers in the United States prior to 1930. Before we became a "throw–away" society, hand sewing was a never ending chore for the housewife. Garments were mended and altered. When they were beyond repair, pieces were salvaged to make a patchwork quilt. Thimble manufacturers tried to create a new thimble to convince the home sewer that "one was not enough."

By the early 1930s only one manufacturer of gold and silver thimbles remained in business in the United States. The Simons Brothers Company of Philadelphia, which was founded by George Washington Simons in 1839. Simons Brothers thimbles from the 1904 St. Louis World's Fair and the 1893 Columbian Exposition are prized acquisitions for any collector. The Liberty Bell thimble, in the shape of the bell, is one of the most novel.

Today, the company is owned by Nelson Keyser and continues to produce silver and gold thimbles. The Simons Brothers Company designed a special thimble for Nancy Reagan as a gift for diplomats wives who visited the White House. The thimble has a picture of the White House and the initials "N. D. R."

Thimbles have been produced in a variety of materials: gold, silver, steel, aluminum, brass, china, glass, vegetable ivory, ivory, bone, celluloid, plastics, leather, hard rubber, and silk. Common metal thimbles usually are bought by the intended user, who makes sure the size is a comfortable fit. Precious metal thimbles often were received as gifts. Many of these do not show signs of wear from constant use. This may result from ill fit of the thimble or from it simply being too elegant for mundane work.

During the 20th century thimbles were used as advertising promotions. It is not unusual to find a thimble that says "You'll Never Get Stuck Using Our Product" or a political promotion stating "Sew It Up—Vote for John Doe for Senator."

References: Helmut Greif, *Talks About Thimbles,* Fingerhutmuseum, Cregligen, Germany, 1983 (English edition available from Dine–American, Wilmington, DE); Edwin F. Holmes, *A History Of Thimbles,* Cornwall Books, 1985; Mrytle Lundquist, *The Book Of A Thousand Thimbles,* Wallace–Homestead, 1970; Myrtle Lundquist, *Thimble Americana,* Wallace–Homestead, 1981; Myrtle Lundquist, *Thimble Treasury,* Wallace–Homestead, 1975; John Heille, *Thimble Collectors Encyclopedia,* Wallace–Homestead, 1986; Averil Mathis, *Antique and Collectible Thimbles and Accessories,* Collector Books, 1986, 1989 value up-

date; Gay Ann Rogers, *American Silver Thimbles,* Haggerston Press, 1989; Estelle Zalkin, *Zalkin's Handbook Of Thimbles & Sewing Implements, First Edition,* Warman Publishing Co., 1988.

Periodical: *Thimbletter,* 93 Walnut Hill Road, Newton Highlands, MA 02161.

Collectors' Club: Thimble Collectors International, 6411 Montego Bay Dr., Louisville, KY 40228.

Advisor: Estelle Zalkin.

Reproduction Alert: Reproductions can be made by restrikes from an original die or cast from a mold made from an antique thimble. Many reproductions are sold as such and priced accordingly. Among the reproduced thimbles are a pre–revolution Russian enamel thimble and the Salem Witch thimble (the repro has no cap, and the seam is visible).

Souvenir, Statue of Liberty, left: French, $35.00; right: Simons, $15.00.

Advertising	
Brass, advertisement or inscription	5.50
Plastic, old, 1930–1950	
One Color	2.00
Two colors, red top	2.00
Sterling Silver	20.00
Gold, 1900–40	
Plain band	75.00
Scenic band	100.00
Semi precious stones on band	200.00
Ivory	
Modern scrimshaw	20.00
Vegetable ivory	60.00
Metal, common	
Brass	
Fancy band	15.00
Cloisonne design, China	10.00
Cast Pot Metal, "For a Good Girl"	5.00
Silver, 1900–40	
Continental, synthetic stone cap	25.00
Cupid in high relief	100.00
Enameled	60.00
Engraved, two birds on branch	25.00
Flowers in high relief	35.00

Italian, stones on band, modern . .	**35.00**

Raised Design

Bleeding Heart	**25.00**
Wild Rose	**35.00**
Scenic band	**35.00**
Simons, Cupid and Garlands	**90.00**

Souvenir

Liberty Bell, 1976 issue	**75.00**
Palm Beach	**75.00**
Statue of Liberty, France	**35.00**

World's Fairs

1892, Columbian, buildings . . .	**225.00**
1904, St. Louis World's Fair . . .	**200.00**
1933, Chicago World's Fair . . .	**75.00**

Porcelain

Meissen, hp, modern, Germany . . .	**125.00**
Royal Worcester, hp, modern, artist sgd, England	**25.00**
Scrimshaw, antique, whalebone or whale tooth	**90.00**

THREADED GLASS

History: Threaded glass is glass decorated with applied threads of glass. Before the English invention of a glass threading machine in 1876, threads were applied by hand. After this invention, threaded glass was produced in quantity by practically every major glass factory.

Threaded glass was revived by the art glass manufacturers, such as Durand and Steuben, and continues to be made today.

Pitcher, pink and yellow swirls, 6″ h, $185.00.

Bowl, 16″ d, clear, topaz threaded edge, controlled air bubbles, Steuben . . .	**150.00**
Candlestick, 9⅞″ h, clear, cut, flared base, bell nozzle with frosted floral and beaded dec, amethyst rim and threading in stem	**175.00**
Finger Bowl, matching underplate, yellow green opalescent, pr	**80.00**
Ewer, 10¼″ h, 6″ d, rainbow, deep shades of cranberry, blue, vaseline,	

and green swirled stripes, clear applied handle, strips of clear rigaree .	**695.00**
Goblet, pink, threaded bowl, clear base and stem, Steuben	**85.00**
Mayonnaise, matching underplate, cranberry, ground pontil	**75.00**
Perfume Bottle, 5½″ h, clear, pink threading	**175.00**
Stein Set, 14½″ h x 5¼″ d master stein, four matching 7½″ h x 3″ d steins, shaded blue to clear, pewter figured handled lids	**1,195.00**
Rose Bowl, 6″ h, clear, pink threading .	**50.00**

Vase

7″ h, peacock blue, blue threading and white hearts, Quezal	**625.00**
8″ h, stick, MOP, blue, clear applied allover threading	**515.00**

L.C. Tiffany-Favrile

TIFFANY

History: Louis Comfort Tiffany (1849–1934) established a glass house in 1878 primarily to make stained glass windows. There he developed a unique type of colored iridescent glass called Favrile. His Favrile glass differed from other art glass in manufacture as it was a composition of colored glass worked together while hot. The essential characteristic is that ornamentation is found within the glass. Favrile was never further decorated. Different effects were achieved by varying the amount and position of colors which project movement in form and shape.

In 1890, in order to utilize surplus materials at the plant, Tiffany began to design and produce "small glass" such as iridescent glass lamp shades, vases, stemware, and tableware in the Art Nouveau manner.

Commercial production began in 1896. Most Tiffany wares are signed with the name L. C. Tiffany or the initials L.C.T. Some pieces also carry the word "Favrile" as well as a number. A number of other marks can be found, e.g., Tiffany Studios and Louis C. Tiffany Furnaces.

Louis Tiffany and the artists in his studio also are well known for the fine work in other areas—bronzes, pottery, jewelry, silver and enamels.

References: Victor Arwas, *Glass, Art Nouveau and Art Deco*, Rizzoli International Publications, Inc., 1977; Vivienne Couldrey, *Tiffany: The Art of Louis Comfort*, Wellfleet Press, 1989; *The Art Work of Louis C. Tiffany*, Apollo Books, 1987; Robert Koch, *Louis C. Tiffany, Rebel In Glass*, Crown Publishers, Inc., 1966; John A. Shuman III, *The Collector's Encyclopedia of American Art Glass*, Collector Books, 1988.

Note: All glass is of the Favrile type unless otherwise noted.

Vase, conical, white opaque body, white streaks, flat circular pedestal, white opaque base, blue rim, stretched yellow top, marked "1546 L. C. Tiffany Favrile," orig paper label, $1,125.00.

BRONZE

Ashtray, 7" d, circular, cast low relief, graduated band of rect border, three curving cigarette rests, imp "Tiffany Studios/New York/186," c1900 .... **200.00**

Candlesticks, pr, 17¾" h, Queen Anne's Lace pattern, spherical green Favrile glass candle holder, reticulated bronze mount, slender stem, circular base cast with floral sprigs, stamped "Tiffany Studios New York 30055" .. **2,600.00**

Desk Clock, 3¾" w, Adam pattern, gilt bronze, circular gilt dial, black hands and Arabic numerals, hexagonal case, cast low relief, printed on face "Tiffany Studios/New York," imp mark, c1920 .... **250.00**

Desk Set
  Six Pcs, Pine Needle pattern, 10" l paper rack, 7¾" l rect box, sq inkwell, rect perpetual desk calendar, and pen, polished gilt bronze over opaque amber and white marbleized favrile glass, each pc imp "Tiffany Studios/New York" and numbered **1,325.00**
  Ten pcs, Zodiac pattern, 19¼" l blotter ends, utility box, perpetual calendar, pen tray, large paper rack, ink stand, pen brush holder, memoranda pad, paper knife, low relief casting of zodiac signs and interlacing strapwork, green patina, each pc numbered and imp "Tiffany Studios/New York," c1900–28 **1,540.00**

GLASS

Bowl, 8" d, ribbed, scalloped rim, gold irid, stems and leaves etched int., inscribed "L. C. Tiffany Favrile" **1,200.00**

Candlesticks, pr, 4" h, urn form nozzle, downward curving drip pan, spherical standard, quilted circular foot, inscribed "L. C. Tiffany–Favrile 1846," orig paper label **1,800.00**

Candy Dish, 4" h, translucent foot and stem, shallow dish, widely flaring scalloped rim, white linear dec, crackled blue irid, inscribed "L. C. T. Favrile 1924" **950.00**

Center Bowl
  8½" d, 4" h, Favrile, pastel blue, ten lobed bowl, opaque opal–blue stripes, swirled vertical ribbing, sgd "L. C. Tiffany Inc. Favrile 5–7651 N" **2,750.00**
  10½" d, Favrile, deep cobalt blue roundel, five lily pads and swirling vines, strong irid, red and gold highlights, central aperture holds matching looped flower arranger, bowl sgd "L. C. Tiffany Favrile 7193L," holder sgd and numbered **2,200.00**

Compote, 4½" h, slender translucent stem and foot, crackled lemon yellow irid, white petal dec, numbered and inscribed "L. C. T. Favrile" **400.00**

Cordial, conical, etched frieze of grape clusters, vines, and leaves, slender stem, gold irid, inscribed "L. C. T.," set of 7 .... **1,800.00**

Decanter Set, Moravignian pattern, 9" h peacock irid stoppered double gourd decanter, applied lily pads and tendrils dec, eleven matching gold irid globular cordials, each pc inscribed "L. C. T." **2,000.00**

Juice Glass, applied lily pad and trailing stems, inscribed "L. C. T.," set of 11 **2,400.00**

Medallion, 1¾" d, oval, emerald green Favrile, imp "LCT & Co AA Trademark," (Associated Artists), 1872–1882 .... **360.00**

Perfume Bottle, 4¼" h, globular, short cylindrical neck, everted lip, ball shaped stopper, irid green trailing vine and ivy leaves dec, irid amber ground, shaded with pink, numbered, inscribed "L. C. Tiffany, Favrile," c1916 .... **1,000.00**

Salt, master, 2½" d, 1¾" h, Favrile, eighteen ribs, turned over rim, pedestal base, gold, strong blue highlights, sgd "L. C. Tiffany, Favrile, X295" **350.00**

Tile, 6" h, turtle back, rect form, rounded corners, green, molded undulating surface, shaded amber, blue, and violet irid dec **250.00**

Vase

4" h, bud, irregular shaped pinched ribbed body, scalloped rim, blue irid, numbered and inscribed "L. C. Tiffany–Favrile," orig paper label . **1,200.00**

5" h, Favrile, gold, irid **650.00**

6" h, Favrile, Imperial Yellow Gold irid, ten panels, wavy 3" d rim, pulled out snails, sgd "L. C. Tiffany, Favrile–9187H–X144" **950.00**

7⅛" h, flattened oviform, slender neck, eight applied spouts, brilliant gold irid, inscribed "2605D L. C. Tiffany Favrile," c1909 .... **1,800.00**

8" h, ovoid, paperweight, aquamarine body, orange–amber int. wash, red–orange blossoms, green lily pads and stems, std "L. C. T. 9453A," orig paper label **4,125.00**

8¾" h, paperweight, baluster, translucent silver irid body, stems, free form leaves and tiny white millefiore dec, inscribed "L. C. T. R2131," c1902 .... **4,000.00**

9½" h, baluster, ftd, El Amarna, transparent aquamarine–green, ribbed, applied flared gold irid raised cuff, double green and gold–amber Egyptian zigzag necklace, applied tooled golden thread, raised disk foot, sgd "L. C. Tiffany Favrile 3898J," paper foil label **3,300.00**

14¼" h, slender baluster, internally dec with tall shaded green lily leaves, crimson flowerheads with green centers, clear opal ground, sgd "L. C. Tiffany, Inc., Favrile/6401N," c1919 ....**11,000.00**

26" h, flared naturalistic flower stem cylinder, irid gold Favrile with five green pulled leaf elements, sgd "L. C. T.," inserted into bronze holder, raised on four swirl molded legs, stepped disk platform base imp "Tiffany Studios New York 715" .. **2,090.00**

LAMPS

Candle, 18" h, bronze, ten ribbed opal Favrile glass shade, five gold and green pulled feather dec, fitted to bobeche ring, trifid base, green glass blown–out shaft, shade sgd "L. C. T.," base foot imp "22322" **1,760.00**

Chandelier, 19" d, 17" l, half round dome, amber and white striated ripple glass panes, border bands of sq emerald green turtle back tiles, apex dome with gold irid turtleback disk,

overall bronze wire twists, swag beading, ball drops **13,200.00**

Desk, 14½" h, turtle back shade, peacock surface irid, white opaque int., rotating bronze mount cast with petals, circular frieze of irid glass spheres, stamped "Tiffany Studios New York" **7,000.00**

Table

21½" h, 16" d, Crocus, green and gold tiles arranged in four repeating elements of spring blossoms, imp "Tiffany Studios New York," urn form oil lamp base, four ribbed legs, quatraform base, fuel canister imp "Tiffany Studios New York 11416" **8,250.00**

24¼" h, dome shade, wide medial band, meandering lemon yellow and green swirled vine leaves, mottled green ground, wide borders of rect tiles, imp "Tiffany Studios/New York," gilt bronze baluster form base, spreading circular foot, longitudial graining, etched finish, brown patinated bronze finial, imp mark **8,875.00**

SILVER

Asparagus Tongs, Chrysanthemum pattern, cast and pierced design, 7 troy oz **825.00**

Basket, 13" h, flared horizontal stepped and cane cut floral basket, sterling silver floral handle marked "Tiffany & Co Makers Sterling Silver C" **1,980.00**

Bowl, 10" d, circular flat rim, pierced sides, chased flowers and foliage at intervals, 1907–38, 42 troy oz, pr .. **2,970.00**

Box, cov, 9½" l, rect, plain, monogram, wood liner, 1907–38, 24 troy oz ... **880.00**

Crumber, Saratoga pattern **250.00**

Gravy Boat and Underplate, 21 oz, c1873–91 .... **700.00**

Relish Tray, 9 oz, marked "Tiffany & Co" **275.00**

Serving Set, fork and spoon, Richelieu pattern, 7 troy oz **360.00**

Vegetable Dish, cov, 15 oz, marked "Tiffany & Co" **425.00**

TIFFIN GLASS

History: A. J. Beatty & Sons built a glass manufacturing plant in Tiffin, Ohio, in 1888. On January 1, 1892, the firm joined the U. S. Glass Co. and was known as factory "R". Quality and production at this factory were very high and resulted in fine depression era glass.

Beginning in 1916 wares were marked with a paper label. From 1923 to 1936, Tiffin produced a line of black glassware, called Black Satin. The company discontinued operation in 1980.

References: Fred Bickenheuser, *Tiffin Glassmasters, Book I*, Glassmasters Publications, 1979; *Tiffin Glassmasters, Book II*, Glassmasters Publications, 1981; Fred W. Bickenheuser, *Tiffin Glassmasters, Book III*, Glassmasters Publications, 1985.

Collectors' Club: Tiffin Glass Collectors Club, P.O. Box 554, Tiffin, OH 44883.

Ashtray, 6″, Carnegie National Bank, 1902–1928	30.00
Basket, Black Satin	40.00
Cake Plate, Flanders, crystal, 10½″ d, handle	50.00
Champagne	
Cherokee Rose	18.00
Eternally Yours	10.00
Flanders, crystal	14.00
Shawl Dancer, crystal	18.00
Claret	
Canterbury, citron	17.50
Cherokee Rose	32.50
Cocktail	
Cherokee Rose	24.00
Classic, crystal	35.00
Compote, Palais Versailles, gold	100.00
Cordial	
Flanders, crystal	55.00
June Night, crystal	40.00
Killarny, green	20.00
Creamer and Sugar	
Cerice, crystal, matching tray	95.00
June Night, crystal	50.00
Rosalind, yellow	85.00
Cup and Saucer	
Flanders, crystal	35.00
Sylvan, pink	35.00
Decanter, stopper, Cadena, yellow	225.00
Goblet	
Cerice, crystal, pulled stem	20.00
Eternally Yours	15.00
Flanders	
Crystal	17.75
Pink	35.00
Iced Tea	
Canterbury, citron	15.00
Cerice, crystal, ftd	24.00
Cherokee Rose	24.00
Classic, crystal and green	45.00
Flanders, yellow	24.00
Shawl Dancer, crystal, cone shape	20.00
Juice Tumbler	
Cordella, yellow, ftd	15.00
Fontaine, green	30.00
Lamp, Torchere, Santa Maria, orange ground	295.00
Parfait, Flying Nun, green	40.00
Plate	
Byzantine, crystal, 10½″ d	35.00
Cerice, crystal, 12″ d	45.00

Empire Twilight, 8″ d	17.50
Flanders	
Pink, 8″ d	17.50
Yellow, 10½″ d	35.00
Rosalind, yellow, 10½″	35.00
Shawl Dancer, crystal, 7½″ d	15.00
Wistaria, red, 8″ d	16.00
Relish, Rambling Rose, round, three parts	17.50
Sherbet	
Canterbury, citron	12.50
Flying Nun, green	25.00
Sugar	
Cherokee Rose, crystal	22.50
Flying Nun, green	65.00
Sundae, Cerice, crystal	18.00

Vase, bulbous, Poppies pattern, frosted, bright blue, 8″ h, 8″ d, $75.00.

Vase	
Cerice, crystal, bud, 10½″ h	45.00
Princess, crystal, 4″ h	22.50
Whiskey, Flanders, pink, ftd	65.00
Wine	
Cordella, crystal	14.50
Eternally Yours	14.75
Flanders, yellow	30.00
Psyche, green	50.00

TILES

History: The use of decorated tiles peaked during the latter part of the 19th century. Over one hundred companies in England alone were producing tiles by 1880. By 1890 companies had opened in Belgium, France, Australia, Germany, and the United States.

Tiles were not limited to adorning fireplaces. Many were installed into furniture, such as wash stands, hall stands, and folding screens. Since tiles were easily cleaned and, hence, hygienic, they readily were used on the floors and walls of entry halls, hospitals, butcher shops, or any place where sanitation was a concern. Many public buildings and subways also employed tiles to add interest and beauty.

Condition is an important fact in determining price. A cracked, badly scuffed and scratched, or heavily chipped tile has very little value. Slight chipping around the outer edges of a tile is, at times, considered acceptable by collectors, especially if these chips can be covered by a frame.

It is not uncommon for the highly glazed surface of some tiles to have become crazed. Crazing is not considered a deterent as long as it does not detract from the overall appearance of the tile.

References: J. & B. Austwick, *The Decorated Tile,* Pitman House Ltd., 1980; Susan and Al Bagdade, *Warman's English & Continental Pottery & Porcelain, 2nd Edition,* Wallace–Homestead, 1991; Julian Barnard, *Victorian Ceramic Tiles,* N. Y. Graphic Society Ltd., 1972; Terence A. Lockett, *Collecting Victorian Tiles,* Antique Collectors Club, 1979; Hans Van Lemmen, *Tiles: A Collectors' Guide,* Seven Hills Books, 1985.

Periodical: *Flash Point,* P.O. Box 1850, Healdsburg, CA 95448.

Collectors' Club: Tile & Architectural Ceramics Society, Ironbridge Gorge Museum, Ironbridge, Telford, Shropshire, England TF8 7AW.

Wedgwood, Puck, blue transfer, marked "Josiah Wedgwood & Sons, Etruria," 8″ sq, $90.00.

American Encaustic Tiling Co, Zanesville, OH

3″ sq, President McKinley, orig label with biography, slight glaze crazing	50.00
4¼″ sq, white, black design of horseman riding through brush	30.00
6″ sq	
Cherub band, highly emb, brown	160.00
Jack and Jill, polychrome	75.00
6″ sq, set of four tiles in frame, flower in pot design, brown	90.00

California Art

5¾″ sq, landscape, tan and green	50.00
7½ x 11½″, peacock and grapes, multicolored	120.00

Cambridge Art Tile, Covington, KY, 6 x 18″

Goddess and Cherub, amber, pr	200.00
Night and Morning, pr	475.00

J. & J. G. Low, Chelsea, MA

4¼″ sq

Blue, putti carrying grapes, pr	60.00
Teal Blue, swirled foliate	50.00
Yellow–green, floral	25.00
6″ d, circular, yellow, minor edge nicks and glaze wear	30.00

6″ sq

Geometric pattern, pale blue	20.00
Woman wearing hood, brown	85.00
6⅛ x 4½″, rect, blue–green, picture of woman, titled "Autumn"	75.00
7⅜ x 5⅜″, rect, blue–green, portrait of stylish lady, small chip on corner	75.00

Kensington, 6″ sq, classic female head, brown	40.00
KPM, 5¾ x 3⅜″, portrait of monk, titled "Hieronymous of Ferrara sends this image of the prophet to God," small nicks to corners	225.00
Leach Pottery, Bernard, 4″ d, cat against stylized landscape, brown, cream ground, artist initials, framed	200.00
Marblehead, 4⅝″ sq, ships, blue and white, pr	100.00

Minton China Works

6″ sq

Aesops Fables, Fox and Crow, black and white	60.00
Cows crossing stream, brown and cream	75.00
Girl feeding pigeons, blue and white	60.00
6 x 12″, Wild Roses, polychrome slip dec	48.00
8″ sq, Rob Roy, Waverly Tales, brown and cream	85.00

Minton Hollins & Co

6″ sq

Daisies, polychrome	20.00
Urn and floral relief, green ground	30.00
8″ sq, Morning, blue and white	100.00

Mosaic Tile Co, Zanesville, OH

6″ sq

Fortune and the Boy, polychrome	75.00
Leo, Zodiac series, polychrome	25.00
8″ sq, Delft windmill, blue and white, framed	45.00

Pardee, C.

4¼″ sq, chick and griffin, blue–green matte	175.00
4½″ sq, white rabbit, light green ground, sgd	100.00
6″ sq, portrait of Grover Cleveland, gray–lavender	120.00

Paul Revere Pottery

3⅞″ sq, green trees and landscape, circular mark, part of orig label	150.00

4⅜" d, circular
  Paul Revere Trademark, blue, green, black, yellow, and brown on white 200.00
  Swan, yellow, brown, green, and white, slight age crack 125.00
Providential Tile Works, Trenton, NJ
  Round, stove type, hole in center, flowered 10.00
  Square, 6" sq, raspberries 20.00
Rookwood
  4½ x 4¼", blue–green, emblem of Packard Motor Co, 1910 .... 75.00
  5¾" d, circular, seagulls in flight, two colors, 1943 .... 60.00
Sherwin & Cotton
  6" sq, dog head, brown, artist sgd .. 100.00
  6 x 9", Abraham Lincoln, brown ... 135.00
  6 x 12", Quiltmaker and Ledger, orange, pr 250.00
Trenton Tile Co, Trenton, NJ
  6" sq
    Grant, portrait, yellow–green 110.00
    Leaf, emb, green 5.00
U. S. Encaustic Tile Works, Indianapolis, IN
  6" sq
    Boy with umbrella, amber 75.00
    Wreath, flowered, emb, light green 12.00
  6 x 18", panel, Dawn, green, framed 150.00
Wedgwood, England
  6" sq
    Red Riding Hood, black and white 100.00
    November, boy at seashore, peacock blue 85.00
  8" sq
    Shakespeare's Mid–Summer Night's Dream, moth 100.00
    Tally Ho, man riding horse, blue and white 75.00

TINWARE

History: Beginning in the 1700s many utilitarian household objects were made of tin. Tin is non-toxic, rust resistant, and fairly durable, so it can be used for storing food. It often was plated to iron to provide strength. Because it was cheap, tinware and tin plated wares were in the price range of most people.

An early center of tinware manufacture in the United States was Berlin, Connecticut. Almost every small town and hamlet had its own tinsmith, tinner, or whitesmith. Tinsmiths used patterns from which to make items. They cut out the pieces, hammered and shaped them, and soldered the parts. If a piece was to be used with heat, a copper bottom was added because of the low melting point of tin. The Industrial Revolution brought about machine made, mass produced tinware

pieces. The handmade era ended by the late 19th century.

This category is a catchall for tin objects which do not fit into other categories in our book.

Additional Listings: See Advertising, Kitchen Collectibles, Lanterns, Lamps and Lighting, and Tinware: Decorated.

Candle Mold, four candles, handle, 10" h, 3¾" w, $55.00.

Box, 4¼" h, hanging, rounded crest, beaded brass trim, hinged lid 55.00
Candle Mold
  Six tubes, 11" h 40.00
  Ten tubes, makes 8" candles 70.00
  Twelve tubes, makes 10" candles .. 90.00
  Twenty–four tubes, handle with engraved brass label "JEM, 1877" . 220.00
Centerpiece, 12" d, twelve candle sockets 475.00
Chandelier, 24" h, two tiers, fifteen candle arms with crimped pans 400.00
Cheese Strainer, 5¾ x 5⅜ x 3⅝", heart shape, ftd 85.00
Coffeepot
  9" h, brass finial 165.00
  10¼" h, molded detail, cast finial, side spout, turned handle 160.00
Conical Torch, 6" h, spout, handle, and chain hanger, emb label "P Wall, Pittsburgh" 40.00
Dutch Oven, 19" l, wrought iron spit, soldered repair 220.00
Food Mold, 12½" l, curved fish 45.00
Lamp
  Grease, 1⅝" h, colorful glaze 150.00
  Petticoat, 4" h, orig whale oil burner, orig black paint 50.00
  Skater's
    6⅜" h, clear globe 65.00
    6⅝" h, light teal green globe 210.00
    6¾" h, cracked red globe 165.00

7" h, emerald globe marked "Jewel"	55.00
Lamp Stand, 7" h, betty type	125.00

Lantern

7⅝" h, marked "Dietz Sport," globe marked "Dietz Scout"	55.00
9½" h, font with single spout burner, clear pressed paneled globe, ring handle	190.00
Match Box, 2½" h, English post office dec, ivory socket	90.00
Muffin Pan, heart shape wells	35.00
Roaster, 12" w, 9¼" h, used in down hearth	180.00
Sconce, 14" h, pr, candle, crimped circular crests	300.00
Toy, 3½" l, pull, goose, nodding head	385.00

TINWARE: DECORATED

History: Decorating sheet iron, tin, and tin coated sheet iron dates back to the mid-18th century. The Welsh called the practice pontipool, the French To'le Peinte. In America the center for tin decorated ware in the late 1700s was Berlin, Connecticut.

Several styles of decorating techniques were used: painting, japanning, and stenciling. Designs were done by both professionals and itinerants. English and Oriental motifs strongly influenced both form and design.

A special type of decoration was the punch work on unpainted tin practiced by the Pennsylvania tinsmiths. Forms included coffeepots, spice boxes, and grease lamps.

Basket, red, yellow, and green tulips, oval, 12¼" l, $425.00.

Box, 4¼" l, polychrome fruit and foliage, orig dark brown japanning	175.00
Bread Tray, 12¾" l, oblong, painted fruit and leaf motif border, brown ground, 19th C	3,025.00
Canister, 5½" d, 4¾" h, red, green, and yellow floral dec, white band, orig alligatored dark brown japanning	400.00
Chocolate Pot, 10½" h, painted dec, inscribed "Lizzie Lefever 1875"	1,600.00

Coffeepot

8¾" h, polychrome floral dec, orig black paint	1,600.00
11" h, punched potted tulip design above double twisted band, hinged lid with brass finial, Pennsylvania, early 19th C	1,400.00

Deed Box

9" l, stenciled gilt dec, emb lid with orig brass bale, orig brown japanning	120.00
9½" l, dome top, orig black japanning, polychrome bird and floral dec	300.00
9¾" l, red and yellow dec, orig black paint	55.00
Document Box, 4 x 7¾ x 4½", red flowers, green leaves, white band trim, black ground, dome lid	185.00

Foot Warmer, punched diamonds and circles

7¾ x 8½", mortised hardwood case, turned corner posts, old cherry finish	150.00
12½ x 15", mortised cherry frame, turned corner posts	375.00

Lantern, pierced

13" h, candle type	30.00
14" h, fitted candle holder on outside	140.00
Mug, 5⅝" h, red, yellow, green, and white oval stylized floral design, orig brown japanning	625.00
Needle Case, 9" l, red and yellow stylized foliage dec, orig dark brown japanning	105.00
Spice Caddy, 3¾ x 5½", orig brown japanning, yellow stripe, six canisters	90.00
Sugar Bowl, 4" h, floral band, orig dark brown japanning	165.00
Tea Caddy, 4" h, orig dark brown japanning, floral dec, white band, mismatched lid	125.00

Tray

8¾" l, octagonal, dark red crystallized center, white band with foliage and berries, black and brown japanned border with yellow commas, orig paint	275.00
27" l, basket of flowers, black ground, repainted	110.00
Wall Pocket, 7¾" h, punched heart design	250.00

TOBACCO CUTTERS

History: Before pre-packaging, tobacco was delivered to merchants in bulk form. Tobacco cutters were used to cut the tobacco into desired sizes.

Brown's Mule, iron, counter top	55.00
Climax, 17" l	50.00
Cupples Arrow & Superb	50.00

Lorillards Chew Climax Plug, brass, Penn Hardware Co., Reading, PA, 17¼" l, $100.00.

Drummond Tobacco Co	65.00
John Finzer & Brothers, Louisville, KY	45.00
Griswold Tobacco Cutter, Erie, PA ...	55.00
E C Simmons Keen Kutter	225.00
Sprague Warner & Co	75.00
Unmarked, graduated 6¼ to 7¼" w, 10½" l, cast iron cutter, wood base .	45.00

TOBACCO JARS

History: A tobacco jar is a container for storing tobacco. Tobacco humidors were made of various materials and in many shapes, including figurals. The earliest jars date to the early 17th century. However, most examples in today's market were made in the late 19th or early 20th centuries.

Reference: Deborah Gage and Madeleine Marsh, *Tobacco Containers & Accessories*, Gage Bluett & Company, 1988.

Majolica, cottage, blue, green, and tan, yellow ground, 9" h, $300.00.

Brass, 5½" h, tin case int., early 19th C	40.00
Creamware, 9" h, 6" d, plum colored transfers on side, one titled "Success to the British Fleet," striped orange, blue, and yellow molding, domed lid	900.00
Jasperware, raised white Indian chief on cov, Indian regalia on front, green ground	185.00
Majolica, figural	
5" h, American Indian, bust	135.00
6" h, bear smoking pipe	125.00
Milk Glass, hp, hunting dogs, green and maroon ground, metal top, Handel Ware	525.00

Papier Mache, figural, Mandarin	75.00
Porcelain, figural	
Arab Head	100.00
Humpty Dumpty	115.00
Skull, marked "Carlsbad, Austria" ..	150.00
Pottery	
4½ x 5½", Oriental man, black mustache and goatee, hat cov	120.00
8¾" h, pipes, cigarettes, and matches dec, standard glaze, Rookwood, sgd "Jeannette Swing," dated 1903	500.00
Wavecrest, 5" sq	425.00

TOBY JUGS

History: A toby jug is a drinking vessel usually depicting a full–figured, robust, genial drinking man. They originated in England in the late 18th century. The term "Toby" probably related to the character Uncle Toby from *Tristam Shandy* by Laurence Sterne.

References: Susan and Al Bagdade, *Warman's English & Continental Pottery & Porcelain, 2nd Edition*, Wallace–Homestead, 1991; Vic Schuler, *British Toby Jugs*, Kevin Francis Publishing Ltd. (London), 1986.

Additional Listing: Royal Doulton.

Reproduction Alert: Within the last 100 years or more, tobies have been reproduced copiously by many potteries in the United States and England.

Delft, 11¼" h, man seated on barrel, green hat, green and black sponged coat, blue and yellow pants, old cork stopper, c19th C	350.00
Portobello Pottery, 10" h, standing, spatter enamel dec, orig cov, c1840 ...	250.00
Pratt, 10¾" h, Hearty Good Fellow, blue jacket, yellow–green vest, blue and	

Staffordshire, Lord Nelson, multicolored, c1860, 11½" h, $350.00.

yellow striped pants, blue and ochre
sponged base and handle, stopper
missing, slight glaze wear, c1770–80 **1,500.00**
Royal Doulton
6½" h, stoneware, blue coat, double
XX, Harry Simeon **375.00**
7" h, Bacchus, wreath of grapes and
leaves on head, twisted vine han-
dle **80.00**
Staffordshire
9" h, pearl ware, seated figure,
sponged blue jacket, ochre buttons, ochre and lavender speckled
vest and trousers, brown hair and
hat, green glazed base, shallow
flake inside hat rim, attributed to
Ralph Wood, c1770–80 . . . . **1,900.00**
9¼" h, Thin Man, full chair, green,
blue, and brown, holding pipe and
foaming mug, attributed to Ralph
Wood, c1765–75 . . . . **5,000.00**
10½" h, dog, King Charles Spaniel,
enamel dec, restored hat, late 19th
C **225.00**
10¾" h, cat, enamel dec, holding let-
ter, restored hat, late 19th C **200.00**
11" h, dog, spotted enamel dec, restored hat, late 19th C **185.00**
11¾" h, Rodney's Sailor, black hat,
green coat, white trousers with blue
stripes, imp "65" on base, Ralph
Wood, lid missing, c1765–75 . . . . **5,700.00**
Whieldon, 9½" h, pearl ware, seated figure, yellow greatcoat, green vest,
blue trousers, holding brown jug in left
hand, raises foaming glass of ale towards mouth, lid missing, c1770–80 **1,500.00**
Wilkinson, 11¾" h, Winston Churchill,
multicolored, designed by Clarice
Cliff, black printed marks, number,
and facisimile signature, c1940 . . . . **765.00**
Yorkshire Pottery, 7¾" h, underglazed
enamels, red face, tricorn hat, plaid
vest, molded caryatid handle, c1810 **825.00**

TOOLS

History: Before the advent of assembly line and
mass production, practically everything required
for living was handmade at home or by a local
tradesman or craftsmen. The cooper, the blacksmith, the cabinet maker, and the carpenter all had
their special tools.

Early examples of these hand tools are collected
for their workmanship, ingenuity, place of manufacture, or design. Modern day craftsman often
search out old hand tools for use to authentically
recreate the manufacture of an object.

References: Ronald S. Barlow, *The Antique
Tool Collector's Guide to Value*, Windmill Publishing Company, Third Edition, 1991; Kathryn Mc-

Nerney, *Antique Tools, Our American Heritage*,
Collector Books, 1979; R. A. Salaman, *Dictionary
of Tools*, Charles Scribner's Sons, 1974; John Walter, *Antique & Collectible Stanley Tools: A Guide
To Identity and Value*, Tool Merchants, 1990.

Periodical: *Fine Tool Journal*, P.O. Box 4001,
Pittsford, VT 05763.

Collectors' Club: Early American Industries Association, P.O. Box 2128, Empire State Plaza Station, Albany, NY 12220.

Museum: Shelburne Museum, Shelburne, VT.

Plane, walnut, Ohio Tool Co., inscribed
with carpenter's name, 9½" l, $20.00.

Anvil, hand forged, 8" **50.00**
Bench Press, 9½ x 6", Sherman, solid
brass, 12 lbs **60.00**
Clamp, wood, 13½" jaws, pr **110.00**
Chisel, 22½" l, blade stamped "E Con-
nor" **45.00**
Drill, hand, Goodel and Pratt, brass fer-
rules **24.00**
File, 20", half round **10.00**
Hammer, claw type
Iron, wood handle, c1880 . . . . **30.00**
Winchester **55.00**
Hay Rake, wood
62" l **190.00**
67" l, branded "M B Young" **200.00**
Level, wood and brass, patent Dec
1886, marked "Davis & Cook" **40.00**
Mallet, 34" l, burl, hickory handle **200.00**
Mitre Box, laminated maple, birch, and
oak, graduated quadrant, Stanley . . **25.00**
Plane
Keen Kutter, K110 . . . . **20.00**
Stanley, #10½ **100.00**
Pruning Knife, hand forged iron blade,
wood handle, c1800 . . . . **30.00**
Router, Stanley, #71½, patent date
1901 . . . . **35.00**
Rule
K & E, parallel, German silver and
ebony **25.00**
Lumkin #1085, folding, brass **40.00**
Stanley, folding **15.00**
Saw
Band, 76" h, mortised and pinned
wood frame, orig red paint with blue

and white striping, blade and blade guides, laminated cherry and maple top **300.00**
Buck, 30″, wood, worn varnish finial, marked "W T Barnes" **35.00**
Keyhole, 9″, well shaped wood handle **25.00**
Screwdriver, 9″ blade, flat wood handle, round sides **18.00**
Scribe
  7½″ l, hewn wood handle **35.00**
  21″ l, curly maple, adjustable fence and arm **65.00**
Square, cherry, iron, brass bound blade, marked "Set Try" **45.00**
Surveyor's Tape, 50 ft, steel and brass, wind handle **25.00**
Trammel, 29¾″ l, wrought iron, sawtooth **65.00**
Wheel Measure, 14½″ l, wrought iron . **40.00**

TOOTHPICK HOLDERS

History: Toothpick holders, indispensible table accessories of the Victorian era, are small containers used to hold toothpicks.

They were made in a wide range of materials: china (bisque and porcelain), glass (art, blown, cut, opalescent, pattern, etc.), and metals, especially silver plate. Makers include both American and European firms.

Toothpick holders were used as souvenir items by applying decals or transfers. The same blank may contain several different location labels.

References: William Heacock, *Encyclopedia Of Victorian Colored Pattern Glass, Book I, Toothpick Holders From A To Z*, Antique Publications, 1981; William Heacock, *1,000 Toothpick Holders: A Collector's Guide*, Antique Publications, 1977; William Heacock, *Rare & Unlisted Toothpick Holders*, Antique Publications, 1984.

Collectors' Club: National Toothpick Collector's Society, P. O. Box 246, Sawyer, MI 49125.

Additional Listings: See *Warman's Americana & Collectibles* for more examples.

Advisor: Judy Knauer.

China
Bisque, skull, blue anchor shape mark **55.00**
Meissen, clown **55.00**
Royal Bayreuth, elk **100.00**
Royal Doulton, Santa scene, green handles **65.00**
Schlegelmilch, R. S. Germany, mother of pearl luster **35.00**
Unmarked
  Flower form mold **30.00**
  Raised beaded dec, Moriage **35.00**
Glass
Cranberry, coralene beaded flowers **285.00**

Silver, dog, glass eyes, bone in paw, marked "James W Tufts, Boston, 2693," 2½″ h, 3″ w, $175.00.

Cut Glass
Pedestal, chain of hobstars **135.00**
Star, clear, Federal Glass, c1910–14 .... **45.00**
Figural
Anvil, amber **55.00**
Baby Bootie, amber, c1890–95 .. **38.00**
Elephant, amber, c1890 .... **65.00**
Heart, pink, Heacock #142 ..... **135.00**
Pail, amber, metal handle **35.00**
Pig on Railroad Car, amber **225.00**
Milk Glass
Alligator, c1885 .... **50.00**
Parrot and Top Hat, c1895 ..... **28.00**
Rose Urn, dec, two handles, Fostoria Glass Co, c1905 .... **38.00**
Scroll, claw ftd, light pink and blue dec, c1900 .... **40.00**
Opalescent, Reverse Swirl, blue, speckled **85.00**
Pattern glass
Arched Fleur–de–lis, clear **30.00**
California, green with gold **60.00**
Florette, opaque, turquoise **100.00**
Intaglio Sunflower, clear **25.00**
Kansas **45.00**
Michigan, clear, yellow stain **175.00**
Monkey, clear, 3¾″ h **45.00**
Spearpoint Band, ruby stained ... **80.00**
Teardrop and Cracked Ice, c1900–03 .... **75.00**
Texas, gold **27.00**
Wisconsin **40.00**
Ruby Stained Glass
Button Arches, souvenir of Battleview, NJ **30.00**
Truncated Cube **35.00**

TORTOISE SHELL ITEMS

History: For many years amber and mottled colored tortoiseshell has been used in the manufacture of small items such as boxes, combs, dresser sets, and trinkets.

Note: Anyone dealing in the sale of tortoise shell objects should be familiar with the Endangered Species Act and Amendment in its entirety. As of November 1978, antique tortoise shell objects can be legally imported and sold with some restrictions.

Cigarette Case, brass clasps, 3½″ h, 2⅞″ w, $25.00.

Bowl, 8½″ d
Applied amber foot, folded rim 85.00
Enamel butterflies and flower dec,
deep crimped rim 115.00
Box, 4⅞″ h, rect, canted corners, carved
and incised figures seated in pavil-
ions scene, hinged lid, blank car-
touche on sides and top, silver edge
bands and lock, 19th C 660.00
Hair Comb, carved crest, five oval
cameo relief medallions with pierced
borders, 19th C 375.00
Inkwell, sterling silver mounts, marked
"V C Vickerey, 179–81–3 Regent St
W, London," c1900 .... 275.00
Ladle, 10″ l, handle mounted with agate,
coral, and amber, 19th C 200.00
Salt, sterling silver rivets, orig spoon .. 25.00
Tea Caddy, 5½″ h, rect, curved reverse
breakfront frieze, slightly curved
sides, hinged cov with silver monogrammed plaque, ball feet 1,980.00
Vase
3½″ h, dimpled sides, Japanese style
dec, raised gold flowers and highlights, handled 110.00
4″ h, amber drippings 190.00
8½″ h, bulbous, pinched, ruffled rim,
gold bird in flight and bamboo stalk
dec, enamel motifs 250.00

TOYS

History: In America the first cast-iron toys began to appear shortly after the Civil War. Leading
19th century manufacturers included Hubley, Dent,
Kenton, and Schoenhut. In the first decades of the
20th century, Arcade, Buddy L, Marx, and Tootsie
Toy joined these earlier firms. Wooden toys were
made by George Brown and other manufacturers
who did not sign or label their work.

In Europe, Nuremberg, Germany, was the center for the toy industry from the late 18th through
the mid-20th century. Companies such as Lehman
and Marklin produced high quality toys.

Several auction houses, e.g. Lloyd Ralston
Toys, have specialty auctions consisting entirely
of toys.

Every toy is collectible. The key is the condition
and working order if mechanical. Examples listed
are considered to be in good to very good condition to mint condition unless otherwise specified.

References: Linda Baker, *Modern Toys, American Toys, 1930–1980,* Collector Books, 1985,
1991 value update; Robert Carter and Eddy Rub-
instein, *Yesterday's Yesteryears: Lesney "Matchbox" Models,* Haynes Publishing Group (London),
1986; Jurgen and Marianne Cieslik, *Lehmann
Toys,* New Cavendish Books, 1982; Don Cranmer,
Collectors Encyclopedia, Toys–Banks, L–W
Books, 1986; Richard Friz, *The Official Identifica-
tion And Price Guide To Collectible Toys, Fifth
Edition,* House of Collectibles, 1990; Edward
Force, *Corgi Toys,* Schiffer Publishing Ltd., 1984,
1991 value update; Edward Force, *Dinky Toys,*
Schiffer Publishing Ltd., 1988; Edward Force,
Matchbox and Lledo Toys, Schiffer Publishing
Ltd., 1988; Gordon Gardiner and Alistair Morris,
The Illustrated Encyclopedia of Metal Toys, Har-
mony Books, 1984; Lillian Gottschalk, *American
Toy Cars & Trucks,* Abbeville Press, 1985; Dale
Kelley, *Collecting The Tin Toy Car, 1950–1970,*
Schiffer Publishing, Ltd., 1984; Constance King,
Metal Toys & Automata, Chartwell Books, 1989;
Ernest & Ida Long, *Dictionary of Toys Sold in
America,* 2 vols, published by author; Albert W.
McCollough, *The Complete Book of Buddy "L"
Toys,* 2 vol, Greenberg Publishing Co., 1991;
David Longest, *Character Toys and Collectibles,*
Collector Books, 1984; David Longest, *Character
Toys and Collectibles, Second Series,* Collector
Books, 1987; David Longest, *Toys: Antique & Col-
lectible,* Collector Books, 1990, 1992 value up-
date; Brian Moran, *Battery Toys,* Schiffer Publish-
ing, 1984; Richard O'Brien, *Collecting Toys: A
Collectors Identification and Value Guide, 5th Edi-
tion,* Books Americana, 1990; Richard O'Brien,
The Story of American Toys, Abbeville Press,
1990; Maxine A. Pinsky, *Greenberg's Guide To
Marx Toys, Volume I* (1988), *Volume II* (1990),
Greenberg Publishing Co.; David Richter, *Collec-
tor's Guide To Tootsietoys,* Collector Books, 1991;
Harry L. Rinker, *Collector's Guide To Toys,
Games, And Puzzles,* Wallace–Homestead, 1991;
Nancy Schiffer, *Matchbox Toys,* Schiffer Publish-
ing Ltd., 1983; Martyn L. Schorr, *The Guide To
Mechanical Toy Collecting,* Performance Media,
1979; Peter Viemeister, *Micro Cars,* Hamilton's,
1982; Blair Whitton, *Paper Toys of The World,*
Hobby House Press, Inc., 1986; Blair Whitton, *The

Knopf Collector's Guide to American Toys, Alfred A. Knopf, 1984.

Periodicals: *The Antique Toy World*, P.O. Box 34509, Chicago, IL 60634; *Toy Shop*, 700 East State Street, Iola, WI 54990; *Wheel Goods Trader*, P.O. Box 435, Fraser, MI 48026; *YesterDaze Toys*, P.O. Box 57, Otisville, MI 48463.

Collectors' Club: Antique Toy Collectors of America, Two Wall Street, New York, NY 10005.

Museums: American Museum of Automobile Miniatures, Andover, MA; Museum of the City of New York, New York, NY; Smithsonian Institution, Washington, D.C.; Margaret Woodbury Strong Museum, Rochester, NY; Toy Museum of Atlanta, Atlanta, GA.

Additional Listings: Disneyana and Schoenhut. Also see *Warman's Americana & Collectibles* for more examples.

Buffalo Toys, litho tin windup, Silver Dash, silver body, red wheels, two yellow figures, black hats, patent 1925, 12″ l, $250.00.

Arcade, Freeport, IL, 1893–1946
Bus, Greyhound Lines GMC, cast iron, 1933, 10″ l	125.00
Catalog/Storybook, *Arcade Mfg Co, The Wonderful Adventure of Fred and Jane with the Tiny Arcadians*, copyright 1931, 20 pages, two children visit Fairyland, full color illus of Arcade vehicles and toys	60.00
Chester Gump Cart, painted cast iron, 7½″ l	325.00
Coupe, rumble seat, c1920, 5″ l	150.00
Gas Pump, painted cast iron, mechanical, 6¼″ h	115.00
Ice Truck, red, white rubber tires, 6¾″ l	100.00
Yellow Cab Taxi, cast iron, Century of Progress, orig black and orange paint, 7″ l	350.00

Auburn Rubber, Auburn, IN, 1913–1968
Bulldozer and Earthmover, 8″ l bulldozer, 8″ l earthmover, orig 18 x 5″ box	40.00
Early American Frontier Set, 44 pcs of Indians, Frontiersmen, wild animals, cabins, and accessories, orig box, 17 x 12″	115.00
Public Service Set, 17 pcs, soft rubber, seven vehicles, ten figures, c1950, orig box	75.00

Bing, German
Airplane and Tower, painted and litho tin, 7½″ l	250.00
Automobile, litho tin windup, 5″ l	125.00
Combination Railroad Coach, litho and hp tin	100.00
Limousine, litho tin windup, maroon, black, red, and tan striping, black top, printed trademark, 1912–23, 11″ l	4,510.00
Post Card Projector, painted tin, 9″ h, smokestack missing	50.00
Yacht, painted tin, canopy, live steam attachment, 16″	1,750.00

Buddy L, American, 1921–Present, painted pressed steel
Aerial Towers Tramway, orig labels rough, incomplete	7,500.00
Airport, orig plane, spring loaded, 12″ l	325.00
Baggage Line, orig labels	1,500.00
Bus, orig labels	2,000.00
Camper, MIB	85.00
Coach, No. 208, passenger vehicle, 1927, 28¾″ l, repaired	1,210.00
Coal Hopper, doors open, black rubber tires, coal chutes missing	3,600.00
Coal Truck, labels and paint restored	900.00
Dump Truck, Robotoy, mechanical, orig labels, electrical hookup, orig box	1,400.00

Fire Truck
Aerial, 1925–26, fine orig condition, 30″ l	1,430.00
Hook and Ladder, hose reel, orig labels	1,300.00
Steam Pumper, nickel plated, orig labels	850.00
Water Tower, nickel plated hose tower, incomplete	2,300.00
Hanger, two BL12 mono–airplanes, motors missing, orig labels incomplete	650.00
Ice Delivery Truck, orig canvas top	900.00
International Harverster Truck, red, spoked wheels, orig labels	2,500.00
Overhead Crane	1,900.00
Pick–Up Truck, Ford, Model T, Flivver Delivery No. 210, sheet iron, 1924–30, 12¼″ l, repainted black	475.00
Sand Truck, black, red chassis and wheels, 1900s, 25″ l, poor condition decal and paint	440.00
Texaco Tanker, MIB	95.00
Wrecker, orig labels, 1 gear broken, hook missing	2,000.00

Carette, German, limousine, litho metal,

deep read, cream stripes, black top,
c1915, 12¼″ l, not working **5,225.00**
Chein, J., Harrison, NJ, c1930
 Army Truck, tin, cannon, 8½″ l **30.00**
 Clown in Barrel, litho tin windup, 7½″
  h **150.00**
 Clown Noisemaker, litho tin, wooden
  push handle, clicking sounds, four
  different clown faces, c1930, 19″ l **98.00**
 Mickey Mouse Disneyland Ferris
  Wheel, six seats, ringing bell
  sound, orig box, 10 x 17″ **675.00**

Chein & Co, World War I Lorry, $65.00.

Mother Goose Tea Set, tin litho, 7 pcs **35.00**
Organ, Cathedral Player, litho tin
 windup, multicolored, hand crank . **70.00**
Ride–A–Rocket, litho tin windup, 9″ h **135.00**
Roadster, litho tin windup, c1925, 8½″
 l **65.00**
Space Ride, litho tin windup, 9″ l ... **225.00**
Walking Popeye, litho tin windup, 6″
 h **150.00**
Dent
 Bus, Public Service, painted cast iron,
  13½″ l, 2nd series **375.00**
 Coupe, painted cast iron, 9½″ l, 2nd
  series **450.00**
 Zeppelin, painted cast iron, 12½″ l,
  2nd series **275.00**
Einfalt, Gebruder, German, c1928
 Birds with Worm, litho tin windup, 9″
  l, slight rust on spring **385.00**
 Cock Fight, litho tin windup, 10¾″ l,
  some rust on spring **440.00**
Fisher Price, East Aurora, NY, 1930–
Present
 Barky Dog, pull toy **25.00**
 Donald Duck Choo Choo, pull toy, 4
  x 8 x 7″, c1940 .... **80.00**
 Elsie's Dairy Truck, two milk bottles,
  pull toy **150.00**
 Hot Diggety, windup, Black boy, col-
  orful cloth outfit, painted wooden
  head, cardboard body, black metal
  ski–like feet, feet shuffle back and
  forth, c1934, orig box, 6″ h **700.00**

Kriss Kricket, pull toy, #678, paper
 labels, rear jointed leg action, 4 x 9
 x 3″ **60.00**
Peter Bunny Cart, bunny rings bell,
 pull toy **100.00**
Puffy Train, pull toy, paper on wood,
 plastic arms, multicolored, c1950,
 orig box, 6″ l **90.00**
Quacky Family, fourth version, plastic
 beaks, metal connectors, c1949,
 4½ x 13 x 4½″, light wear **85.00**
Squeaky the Clown, pull toy **60.00**
Woodsy–Wee Circus, nine paper litho
 on wood animals, one clown, and
 circus wagon, 1931, orig 16 x 12″
 box, unplayed–with condition **600.00**
Woofy Wagger, pull toy, wooden,
 bright paper labels, c1947, 4 x 8 x
 9½″, light wear **75.00**
Gong Bell Toy
 Black Boy Baiting Alligator, painted
  cast iron, mechanical, 8″ l **1,600.00**
 Centennial Bell Toy, cast iron, four
  wheels, two shields platform sup-
  port bell, flag, late 19th C, 9½″ l . . **825.00**
 Trix, pull toy, litho paper on wood, mechanical, 16¼″ l **150.00**
Greppert & Ketch, German, black man
 and cart, litho tin windup, some rush
 to finish, non functioning mechanism,
 1920s, 6¼″ l **360.00**
Guntherman, Martin, German
 Beetle, litho tin windup, 7″ l **50.00**
 Clown and Acrobatic Dog, litho and
  hp tin windup, clown missing one
  leg **200.00**
 Fiddler, Black man playing fiddle, 8½″
  h, repainted **150.00**
 Musicians, litho and painted tin,
  windup, fabric clothing, paper accordion, 8½″ d base **2,000.00**
 Playing Boy, hp tin windup, vibrating
  movement, side to side body action
  swings celluloid ball in circular mo-
  tion, c1910, 7½″ h **200.00**
Horsman, E. I., Golden ABC Cubes,
 block set, litho paper on wood, c1883,
 orig wood framed 14½ x 9½ x 2″ box,
 40 pcs **340.00**
Hubley, Lancaster, PA, 1894–1965
 Bell Telephone Khaki Mack Truck,
  orig accessories, 10″ l **350.00**
 Circus Chariot, painted cast iron,
  three horses, Kenton clown figure,
  10″ l **300.00**
 Crash Car, motorcycle with rider, 9½″
  l, worn paint **425.00**
 Custom Sports Car, yellow metal Corvette, rubber tires, hood and trunk
  lift, steering wheel turns front
  wheels, orig box marked "Hubley

Kiddie Toy No. 509," 1950s, 12¾"
l **275.00**
Diesel Road Roller, orange metal
body, silvered wheels and roller,
orig box, 9¾" l **250.00**
Life Saver Truck, holds pack in back,
c1930 . . . . **80.00**
Limousine, c1920, 7" l **65.00**
Motorcycle, cast metal, red, two plastic policemen, black rubber tires,
orig box, 8¼" l **330.00**
Royal Circus Bear Cage, 12½" l . . . **125.00**
Sedan, painted cast iron, nickel
plated grill and bumper, white rub-
ber tires, red hubcaps, 7" l **175.00**
Steam Shovel, Panama, red paint,
dual label, 9" l **525.00**
Street Sweeper, cast iron, 8" l **675.00**
Ives, Bridgeport, CT
Cannon, painted cast iron, Hotchkiss,
firecracker, 9½" l **175.00**
Fire Engine, pumper, painted cast
iron, 23" l **2,150.00**
General Butler, mechanical, cloth
clothing, 9½" h **1,500.00**
Magic Snake Toy, japanned and
painted cast iron, 4" h **400.00**
Katz, Red Arrow Airplane, litho tin, copy
of Spirit of St. Louis, framed box lid,
missing tin tab **250.00**

**Kenton, Happy Hooligan, nodder figure
seated in carriage, pulled by horse,
1911, $1,125.00.**

Kenton, Kenton, OH
Buckboard, horse drawn wagon,
painted cast iron, 13" l **125.00**
Cabriolet, painted cast iron, rubber
tires under horse, 2nd series, orig
box, 16" l **275.00**
Carriage, painted cast iron, silver
wheels and shafts, cream body,
black trim, orig lady rider, 17" l . . . **900.00**
Fire Truck, double team, pumper, cast
iron, white horses, gilt finish, red
wheels, fabric hose, c1911, 18⅜" l,
some repainting **220.00**

Log Wagon, painted cast iron, 15" l . **375.00**
Overland Cage Wagon, painted cast
iron and tin, orig white bear and
reins, 14" l **300.00**
Overland Calliope, painted cast iron,
iron wheels under horse, 14" l, 1
wheel and outriders missing **400.00**
Sulky, painted cast iron, 7½" l **100.00**
Keystone, painted pressed steel,
marked "Packard"
American Railway Express, screen
sides, orig labels, rubber tires . . . **2,300.00**
Dump Truck, scissors action, coal
chute, orig labels, all metal wheels **450.00**
Fire Truck
Aerial Ladder, rubber tires, ladders
missing, old repaint **325.00**
Chemical Pump Engine, incom-
plete **800.00**
Water Tower, rubber tires and
hoses **1,200.00**
Koaster Truck, orig labels, rubber
tires **1,000.00**
Moving Van, rubber tires, orig labels
rough **300.00**
Police Patrol, 28" l **575.00**
Steam Roller, orig string for bell, la-
bels, orig box **1,100.00**
Wrecker, rubber tires, orig labels, me-
chanical, 1 brace and hook missing **350.00**
Kilgore, roadster, painted and nickel
plated cast iron, 6" l **400.00**
Kingsbury, Keene, NH, painted pressed
steel, windup
Biplane, white rubber tires, 16" l, 12"
wingspan **375.00**
Bus, Greyhound, white rubber tires,
18" l, restored **125.00**
Fire Truck
Aerial Ladder, airflow design, black
rubber tires, 24" l **60.00**
Ladder, red and yellow, ladder ex-
tends to 37", 18" l **100.00**
Pumper, cast iron and wood details,
10" l, not working **100.00**
Sunbeam Racer, yellow, driver, black
rubber tires, plastic windshield, rub-
ber bumper, c1930 . . . . **340.00**
Lehmann, Nürnberg, Germany, 1881–
Present
Adam, porter with trunk, litho and
painted tin, 1912 . . . . **950.00**
Anxious Bride, litho tin windup, No.
470, not working, dull finish **1,210.00**
Balky Mule, litho tin windup, cloth
dressed **160.00**
Daredevil, litho tin windup **450.00**
Going To The Fair, painted and litho
tin, momentum **600.00**
Mandarin, painted and litho tin
windup, orig braids, 7½" l **1,000.00**
Mars Captive Balloon, 1896 . . . . . . **2,225.00**

Mill and Miller, figure climbs pole, brings down bag of flour on head, c1927, 18" h 550.00

Motor Car, coil spring motor, patent May 12, 1903, 4⅞" l, good finish . 330.00

Na–Nu, litho tin windup, 7" h 500.00

Naughty Boy, 5" l, very fine orig cond, 1904–35 . . . . 935.00

New Century Cycle, 1904, 5½" l, orig working condition 500.00

Oh My Alabama Coon Jigger, litho tin windup, 4½ x 3 x 2" litho tin base, 10" h 375.00

Paddy and the Pig, 1903, 5¾" l, fine working cond 825.00

Performing Sea Lion, litho tin windup, hp features, orig box, 7½" l 460.00

Taku Torpedo Boat, litho tin, floor toy, 1913–35, 9½" l 415.00

Tap Tap, 1903, 6⅜" l, minor chips to finish 385.00

Wild West, bucking bronco and rider 375.00

Linemar

Campus Express, litho tin, multicolored, working crank sound, 4½" l 65.00

Disneyland Roadster, litho tin friction, 1½" celluloid Nephew Duck driver, plastic windshield, c1950, 4½" l . . 160.00

Dockyard Crane, litho tin windup, 8 x 3" base, c1950 . . . . 50.00

Donald Duck In His Convertible, litho tin friction, celluloid Donald at wheel, orig cartoon box, c1950 . . 275.00

Figuro, litho tin friction, multicolored, c1950, 3" l 90.00

Goofy, litho tin windup, multicolored . 250.00

Ham and Sam, litho tin windup, Sam playing piano, Ham dances, c1950, 4 x 5 x 6" 960.00

Jalopy Car, litho tin, graffiti slogans, siren sound, 4½" l 60.00

Jam Licking Bear, mechanical, plush body, tin base, reaches into litho tin strawberry jam can and then licks paw, c1950, orig box 100.00

Mickey Mouse Crazy Car, litho tin windup, orig tin ears and arms, not working 150.00

RC Jalopy, litho graffiti tin car, plastic driver, erratic forward and back driving pattern, orig box, c1950, 7½" l 195.00

Sam The City Gardener, litho tin windup, red, white, and brown plastic figure pushes litho tin cart with seven plastic garden tools, red pressed steel base, c1950, orig box 125.00

Walking Professor Van Drake, litho tin, bright colors, lifts right arm up and down while walking, c1950, Walt Disney Productions and Linemar marks, orig box, 6" l 415.00

Marklin, German

Armored Car, hp tin, clockwork, c1930, 14½" l 975.00

Ocean Liner, painted tin, red, black, and white deck, clockwork, marked on rudder, c1910, 15" l 1,750.00

Marx, American, 1921–Present

Airplane, WWII, US Army, litho tin windup, 8" w 60.00

Charleston Trio, litho tin windup, Black fiddler, dancer, and dog with cane, 1921, 9⅜" h 475.00

Coca–Cola Truck, yellow and red tin litho, cab door marked "Drink Coca–Cola in Bottles," silver plastic air horn, large Coca–Cola decal on back, small soda crates, c1950, 5 x 12½ x 5½" 150.00

Dick Tracy Siren Squad Car, litho tin windup, litho Tracy and friends in windows, orig red and white box, 11" l 288.00

G–Man Pursuit Car, litho tin windup, 14" l, no key 375.00

Hey–Hey the Chicken Snatcher, black man, litho tin windup, c1920 . . . . 650.00

Hopalong Cassidy, rocking horse, litho tin windup 175.00

Joe Penner, litho tin windup, holding basket of ducks in one hand, duck mascot in other, checkered black and white jacket, blue trim, white shirt, red tie, light and dark blue pants, fleshtone face and accents, cigar, tag on basket "Wanna Buy A Duck? Sincerely Joe Penner," c1930, 4 x 4 x 8", three of four wooden wheels replaced, replaced hat 395.00

Lazy Daisy Dairy Truck 50.00

Liberty Bus, litho tin friction, black and red, green metal wheels, c1930, 5" l 100.00

Main Street, litho tin, mechanical, 5" l trucks and buses travel in loop, c1930, orig box, 24" l 850.00

Moon Mullins & Kayo Dynamite Handcar, litho tin windup, not working 300.00

Pinocchio, litho tin windup, blinking eyes, 8½" h, nose glued 200.00

Police Motorcycle with Sidecar, litho tin windup, celluloid pieces, 8½" l . 175.00

Popeye, with parrots, litho tin windup, 8¼" h 200.00

Racer, litho tin windup, red, yellow, and black, black tin tires, c1930, 5" l 100.00

Rocket Racer, litho tin windup, rubber front bumper 225.00

Rolls Royce, litho tin friction, dark maroon, silver accents, orig box, c1960, 2½ x 5 x 2″ 65.00

Running Scotty, litho tin windup, sides marked "Wee Scotty," black rubber ears and tail, orig red and white box, c1950, 2 x 5 x 4″ 90.00

Taxi, windup, bright yellow hard plastic, marked "Sky View," raised coat of arms, c1950, 2 x 5 x 1½″ 35.00

Tin Lizzie, litho tin windup, sedan, black, four doors, slang expressions, orig driver, 1929, 7″ l 220.00

Touring Auto, green and yellow tin, emb side louvers and doors, red tin tires, grill marked "103," red and black litho tin uniformed figure, c1920, 10″ l 275.00

Meier, J. Ph., penny–toy, litho tin

Hay Wagon, double team, 4½″ l, driver missing 125.00

Limousine, chauffer driven, 4⅜″ l, roof rack missing, some rust 135.00

Schieble, c1920, car, Hillclimber Roadster Coupe, pressed steel, friction, black, 17″ l 375.00

Schuco, marked "U.S. Zone Germany," c1940

Car

2002, painted tin body, chrome trim 60.00

3000, cream colored tin, chrome grill and five gears, 4″ l 65.00

Fex 1111, windup, dark orange tin body, chrome grill, tin litho name plate 115.00

Microracer 1043, windup, gray cast body, red int., gray rubber tires, white grill marked "Schuco," orig box, 4″ l 100.00

Old Timer Ford Coupe, 1917 T, tin and plastic, windup, orig box, 6″ l . 50.00

Teddy Bear on Scooter, yellow mohair, steel eyes, felt outfit, friction action, 1930s, 6″ h 1,760.00

Steelcraft

Army Scout Plane, 22″ l 250.00

Fire Truck, painted pressed steel, rubber tires, orig labels

Combination Hook and Ladder and Hose Reel 900.00

Mack Chemical Wagon 2,000.00

Steam Roller, pressed steel 85.00

Strauss, Ferdinand, New York City, 20th C

Leaping Lena Car, litho tin windup, 1920s 275.00

Scissors Grinder, litho tin windup, MIB 175.00

Tank Truck, painted black chassis, open cab, red wheels, gray tank, decal on dashboard, 1920s, 25¼″ l 825.00

Tip Top Porter, litho tin windup, porter pushing blue and yellow cart, c1930, 6″ l 165.00

Tombo The Alabama Coon Jigger, litho tin windup, multicolored, 5 x 3 x 2″ base 400.00

Trikauto The Circus Wonder, litho tin windup, bright yellow and red, orig 7½″ box with circus motif artwork, c1920 . . . . 425.00

Twin Trolleys, litho tin windup, yellow and red, orig box, pole missing 315.00

Unmarked, American, folk art type peddlar's wagon, smoked grain horses, full harness, wagon marked "London Tonic Pills, C. A. Price Co, Richmond, Me," $2,300.00.

Unidentified Maker

American

Tricycle, painted and stenciled wood, cast iron hardware, c1860, 34″ l 1,200.00

Velocipede, painted and stenciled wood, cast iron, c1870, 40″ l . . 1,000.00

German

Dancing Couple, litho tin windup, paint fair to good, not working, 8½″ h 825.00

Balloonist, painted tin, clockwork, straw basket, 15″ h 1,750.00

Ferris Wheel, painted tin, live steam attachment, 15″ h 1,600.00

Fire Truck, penny–toy, litho tin windup, early 20th C, 4½″ l, two men missing 220.00

Minstrel Drummer, painted tin windup, 8½″ h 700.00

Pool Player, penny–toy, litho tin man hits metal cue ball, spring operated pool stick, c1920, 2½ x 4″ 200.00

Unique Art

Bombo The Monkey, litho tin windup, 9½″ h coconut tree, 5″ l Bombo, c1930, 6 x 3½″ base 450.00

Dogpatch Band, litho tin windup . . . 400.00

GI Joe and K9 Pups, litho tin windup, 9½″ h 175.00

Kiddy Cyclist, litho tin windup 100.00

Lincoln Tunnel, litho tin windup, 24″ l 200.00

Police Motorcycle, litho tin windup, multicolored, uniformed officer, 8½″ l 150.00

Rodeo Joe, litho tin windup	**150.00**
Sky Rangers, litho tin windup, orig box	**250.00**

Wilkins

Fire Patrol Wagon, cast iron, triple team, dapple gray horses, red wagon, gong, yellow wheels, driver, four firemen (two missing), c1911	**770.00**
Wagon, cast iron, double team, black horses, gold accents, red whiffletree, yellow wheels, early 1900s, 8¼″ l, minor paint chips	**220.00**

Wolverine

Jet Roller Coaster, litho tin windup .	**85.00**
Luxury Liner, litho tin windup, MIB . .	**80.00**
Merry–Go–Round, litho tin, spring action, horses and airplanes, 12″ h .	**160.00**

Wyandotte

Hoky Poky, litho tin windup, multicolored, 6″ red pressed steel base, two clowns, c1930	**200.00**
Humphrey Mobile, litho tin windup, MIB	**500.00**
Speed King, boy riding scooter, litho tin windup, 1930	**250.00**
Super Mainliner, airplane, painted pressed steel	**75.00**

TRAINS, TOY

History: Railroading has always been an important part of childhood, largely because of the romance associated with the railroad and the emphasis on toy trains.

The first toy trains were cast-iron and tin; windup motors added movement. The Golden Age of toy trains was 1920–1955 when electric powered units were available and names such as Ives, American Flyer, and Lionel were household words. The construction of the rolling stock was of high quality. The advent of plastic in the late 1950s lessened this quality considerably.

Toy trains were designated by a model scale or gauge. The most popular are HO, N, O and standard. Narrow gauge was a response to the modern capacity to miniaturize. Its popularity has lessened in the last few years.

Condition of trains is critical. Items in fair condition (scratched, chipped, dented, rusted or warped) and below generally have little value to a collector. Restoration is accepted, provided it is done accurately. It may enhance the price one or two grades. Prices listed below are for very good to mint condition unless noted.

References: Paul V. Ambrose, *Greenberg's Guide To Lionel Trains, 1945–1969, Volume III*, Greenberg Publishing, 1990; Susan and Al Bagdade, *Collector's Guide To American Toy Trains*, Wallace–Homestead, 1990; John O. Bradshaw, *Greenberg's Guide To Kusan Trains*, Greenberg Publishing Co, 1987; Joe Deger, *Greenberg's Guide To American Flyer S Gauge Volume I, (1991) and Volume II (1991)*, Greenberg Publishing; Richard Friz, *The Official Identification And Price Guide To Toy Trains*, House of Collectibles, 1990; Bruce Greenberg, *Greenberg's Guide to Ives Trains, Volume I, (1991) and Volume II (1991)*, Greenberg Publishing Co; Bruce Greenberg, (edited by Christian F. Rohlfing), *Greenberg's Guide To Lionel Trains: 1901–1942, Volume 1* (1988), *Volume 2* (1988), Greenberg Publishing Co.; Bruce Greenberg (edited by Paul V. Ambrose), *Greenberg's Guide To Lionel Trains: 1945-1969, Volume 1* (1991), *Volume 2* (1991), Greenberg Publishing Co.; John Hubbard, *The Story of Williams Electric Trains*, Greenberg Publishing Co., 1987; Steven H. Kimball, *Greenberg's Guide To American Flyer Prewar O Gauge*, Greenberg Publishing Co., 1987; Roland La Voie, *Greenberg's Guide To Lionel Trains, 1970–1991*, Greenberg Publishing Co., 1991; Lionel Book Committee, *Lionel Trains: Standard Of The World, 1900-1943*, Train Collectors Assocation, 1989; Dallas J. Mallerich, III, *Greenberg's American Toy Trains: From 1900 With Current Values*, Greenberg Publishing Co., 1990; Dallas J. Mallerich, III, *Greenberg's Guide to Athearn Trains*, Greenberg Publishing Co., 1987; Eric J. Matzke, *Greenberg's Guide To Marx Trains, Volume 1*, Greenberg Publishing Co., 1989; Al McDuffie, et al., *Greenberg Guide to Ives Trains, 1901-1932*, Greenberg Publishing Co., 1984; Robert P. Monaghan, *Greenberg's Guide to Markin OO/HO*, Greenberg Publishing Co., 1989; John R. Ottley, *Greenberg's Guide To LGB Trains*, Greenberg Publishing Co., 1989; Vincent Rosa and George J. Horan, *Greenberg Guide To HO Trains*, Greenberg Publishing Co., 1986; Alan R. Schuweiler, *Greenberg's Guide to American Flyer, Wide Gauge*, Greenberg Publishing Co., 1989.

Note: Greenberg Publishing Company (7543 Main Street, Sykesville, MD 21784) is the leading publisher of toy train literature. Anyone interested in the subject should write for their catalog and ask to be put on their mailing list.

Periodical: *Classic Toy Trains*, P.O. Box 1612, Waukesha, WI 53187.

Collectors' Clubs: Lionel Collector's Club, P.O. Box 479, LaSalle, IL 61301; The National Model Railroad Association, 4121 Cromwell Road, Chattanooga, TN 37421; The Toy Train Operating Society, Inc., 25 West Walnut Street, Suite 305, Pasadena, CA 91103; The Train Collector's Association, P.O. Box 248, Strasburg, PA 17579.

Additional Listings: See *Warman's Americana & Collectibles* for more examples.

AMERICAN FLYER

Car

934, caboose, S	**38.00**
3007, gondola, litho, O gauge	**20.00**
4041, American, pullman, light green, S gauge	**75.00**

Locomotive
290, steam, S gauge	**65.00**
360, 361, diesel, S gauge, pr	**125.00**
L2002, Burlington Route, S gauge . .	**185.00**

Set
Locomotive 429, tender, four cars, orig box, O gauge	**450.00**
Locomotive 4670, tender, three Lone Scout coaches, S gauge	**850.00**

IVES

Car
67, Caboose, four wheels	**50.00**
184, Club Car, standard gauge, olive, c1927	**100.00**

Locomotive
1132, steam engine with tender, wide gauge, 1921–26, excellent condition	**750.00**
3243, electric, wide gauge, 1921–28, good condition	**175.00**
3251, electric, O gauge, orange with brown trim	**100.00**
4637, electric, standard gauge, restored, new wheels	**550.00**

Set, American, cast iron, black and red locomotive, tender, 1182 passenger car, 1193 royal blue line passenger cars, finished in blue and red roofs, c1895 . . . . **950.00**

Lionel, No. 10 electric engine, #332 baggage car, #339 pullman car, #341 observation car, standard gauge, late 1920s, $450.00.

LIONEL

Car
58, rotary snowplow, 027 gauge, 1959–61, excellent condition	**400.00**
514, ventilated refrigerator car, white with green, orig box, paint flaking .	**100.00**
602, baggage, dark green body and roof, wood litho doors, O gauge . .	**50.00**
6457, O gauge, caboose, lighted . . .	**45.00**

Locomotive
150, O gauge, maroon, green windows	**160.00**

251E, O gauge, red with cream trim, brass plates	**120.00**
380, electric, standard gauge, 1923–27	**250.00**
1668, steam engine with tender, O gauge, 1937–41	**70.00**
2378, Milwaukee, AB diesel, O gauge	**350.00**

Set, Locomotive 402E, three coaches, standard gauge **1,150.00**

TRAMP ART

History: Tramp art was prevalent in the United States from 1875 to the 1930s. Items were made by itinerant artists who left no record of their identity. They used old cigar boxes and fruit and vegetable crates. The edges of items were chip-carved and layered, creating the "Tramp Art" effect. Finished items usually were given an overall stain. Today they are collected primarily as folk art.

Reference: Helaine Fendelman, *Tramp Art: An Itinerant's Folk Art Guide,* E. P. Dutton & Co., 1975.

Sewing Box, three drawers, pin cushion heart and star cut-out appliqués, 9½" w, 5¾" d, 6¼" h, $250.00.

Box
8¼ x 11", three tiers, geometric designs, brown finish, inlay, carved initials "L D," three drawers in top	**300.00**
8½" l, hinged lid, dark varnish finish	**55.00**
11" l, pedestal base	**45.00**
12" w, 12" h, hanging, bottom crest, old brown paint, black trim	**45.00**

Frame
16" h, 13¾" w, heart design on crest, gold paint traces	**175.00**
19½" h, 17¼" w, holds German diploma, Philadelphia, 1915	**45.00**

Miniatures
Chest, three drawers
6 x 10 x 12", scalloped crest, natural finish, carved green trim edge	**160.00**

12″ l, old varnish finish	**100.00**
Desk, 21 x 15″, pine, multi–layered chip carved stars, compasses, circles, and geometric shapes, slant front hinged lid, compartment int. lined with blue paper, six drawers, c1930	**990.00**
Dresser, 22″ h, 10½″ w, miniature, Gothic arch mirror, triptych–like back, three drawers, old varnish finish	**225.00**
Mirror, 20½″ h, 12¼″ w, pine carved, multi–layered moons, circles, hearts, and geometric designs, c1930	**935.00**

TRANSPORTATION MEMORABILIA

History: The first airlines in the United States depended on subsidies from the government for carrying mail for most of their income. The first non–Post Office Department flight for mail carrying was in 1926 between Detroit and Chicago. By 1930 there were thirty-eight domestic and five international airlines operating in the United States. A typical passenger load was ten. After World War II, four engine planes with a capacity of 100 or more passengers were introduced.

The jet age was launched in the 1950s. In 1955 Capitol Airlines used British made turboprop airliners in domestic service. In 1958 National Airlines began domestic jet passenger service. The giant Boeing 747 went into operation in 1970 as part of the Pan American fleet. The Civil Aeronautics Board, which regulates the airline industry, ended control of routes in 1982 and fares in 1983.

Transoceanic travel falls into two distinct periods—the era of the great clipper ships and the era of the diesel powered ocean liners. The later craft reached their "Golden Age" in the period between 1900 and 1940.

An ocean liner was a city unto itself. Many had their own printing rooms to produce a wealth of daily memorabilia. Companies such as Cunard, Holland–America, and others encouraged passengers to acquire souvenirs with the company logo and ship name.

Certain ships acquired a unique mystic. The *Queen Elizabeth, Queen Mary,* and *United States* became symbols of elegance and style. Today the cruise ship dominates the world of the ocean liner.

References: Aeronautica & Air Label Collectors Club of Aerophilatelic Federation of America, *Air Transport Label Catalog,* published by club; Stan Baumwald, *Junior Crew Member Wings,* published by author; Trev Davis and Fred Chan, *Airline Playing Cards: Illustrated Reference Guide, 2nd Edition,* published by authors, 1987; Richard R. Wallin, *Commercial Aviation Collectibles: An Illustrated Price Guide,* Wallace–Homestead, 1990.

The sales catalogs of Robert L. Loewenthal (10161 Southwest 1st Court, Plantation, FL 33324) and Ken Schultz (Box M753, Hoboken, NJ 07030) are excellent substitutes for the lack of books on the subject of ocean liner collectibles.

Collectors' Clubs: Steamship Historical Society of America, Inc., 3925 Cloverhill Rd, Baltimore, MD 21218; Titanic Historical Society, P. O. Box 51053, Indian Orchard, MA 01151; The World Airline Historical Society, 3381 Apple Tree Lane, Erlanger, KY 41018.

Museum: Owls Head Transportation Museum, Owls Head, ME.

Additional Listings: See Automobilia and Railroad Items in *Warman's Antiques And Their Prices* and Aviation Collectibles, Ocean Liner Collectibles, and Railroad Items in *Warman's Americana & Collectibles.*

AVIATION

Baggage Sticker, Pan American, blue and white, wing over globe emblem, "The System of The Flying Clippers"	**4.00**
Badge, insignia, crew	
TWA, 2 x 2¼″, diecut, emb, bright brassy gold finish, red enamel initials	**20.00**
United Airlines, 2¼ x 3″, black felt and leather over metal, silver and gold finish, red, silver, and blue logo . .	**20.00**
China	
Breakfast Set, American Airlines, butter pat, cup and saucer, 6″ plate, marked "Mayer China"	**35.00**
Cup and Saucer, TWA, white, gold emblem, marked "Rosenthal, Germany"	**25.00**
Plate, Convair Corp, marked "Vernon Kilns"	**25.00**
Soup Bowl, cream, handles, Trans–World Airlines, white, red banner, gold star with RA (Royal Ambassador) in center, marked "Rosenthal China"	**15.00**
Coaster, British Caledonian, cargo adv, tile, orig gift box	**3.00**
Desk Pen Holder, Eastern	**14.00**
Fan, Air India, litho, blue and orange, cream ground, route map, four stylized figures, c1960	**8.00**
Lapel Stud, ½″ d, TWA, brass, red enamel	**18.00**
Monthly Organizer, pocket, Eastern, logo and slogan "Eastern is its People," blue vinyl cov	**2.00**
Pinback Button	
⅞″ d, AMA Pilot, dark blue letters, white ground, bright red rim, c1930	**15.00**
1″ d, Aeronautical Mechanics Lodge 1125/AF of L/IA of M, celluloid,	

bright red plane, dark blue sky, red
rim letters 15.00
1¾" d, Souvenir of Beech–Nut Gum
Autogiro 1931, multicolored scene,
1930s helicopter flying over coun-
tryside, bright red rim 40.00
Post Card
Braniff International, 747 in flight,
oversized 3.00
DC10–30 .... 1.00
707 .... 1.00
Poster, Air France Nordafrika, 25 x 40",
airliner swooping over North African
setting, c1946 .... 250.00
Schedule, Air France, 4 x 9" paper
folder, opens to 9 x 20" sheet, air
route map of Europe, three major
routes, int. black and white photo of
Golden Clipper 10–seater, c1930 .. 20.00
Souvenir Glass, 4¾" h, Eastern Air
Lines, Golden Falcon, gold and blue
inscriptions, "The Newest, Fastest,
Most Luxurious Airliner in the World,"
c1955 .... 10.00
Toy
American Airlines Flagship, orig pro-
pellers, Fisher Price 175.00
Delta Tri–Star Jet, white plastic, give-
away 6.00

**Spoon, Red Star Lines, German silver,
5½" l, $75.00.**

OCEAN LINERS

Ashtray
France III, French Line, cobalt blue,
image and name in gold ....
RMS Queen Elizabeth I, Cunard Line,
wooden ship's wheel, glass insert
over color center photo 30.00
Pacific Far East Steamship, china .. 25.00
Baggage Tag, French Line, France fun-
nel, first class 5.00
Belt Buckle, Queen Elizabeth II, Cunard
Line, chrome plated solid brass, black
outline of ship, name in red 14.00
Booklet
Canadian Pacific, St Lawrence Route
to Europe, 1930, 8 x 11", 16 pgs . 24.00
Independence, American Export
Lines, 1966 Gala Springtime
Cruise, itinerary and deck plan in-
serts 20.00

Compact, Empress of Canada, Cana-
dian Pacific Line, Stratton, line flag
logo, ship's name in enameled front
medallion 40.00
Cigarette Lighter, Queen Elizabeth II,
Cunard Line, Zippo 20.00
Deck Plan
Atlantis, Chandris Line, illus 8.00
SS Hamburg, 1930, fold out 35.00
Dish, Queen Mary, Cunard Line, ce-
ramic, 5" l, oval, color portrait, gold
edge, Staffordshire 35.00
Excursion Announcement, SS Cuba .. 20.00
Menu
Andrea Doria 15.00
Lancastria, Cunard Line, luncheon,
1939, color sailing ship on cov ... 15.00
Queen Elizabeth 20.00
Passenger List, St Louis, American
Line, eastbound trip, Feb 10, 1906 . 35.00
Pennant, SS Princess Anne, 25½" l,
maroon, felt, VFC logo in white, tinted
white, gray, and light green cruise
ship illus, c1930 .... 8.00
Pinback Button,⅞" d
American Line, multicolored, crossed
American and Swedish flags, slo-
gan on upper rim "Utstallingen 1
Stockholm 1897" 20.00
Cunard Line, British, main smokes-
tack, paper back reads "Compli-
ments Of The High Admiral Ciga-
rette," c1898 .... 12.00
Lusitania, black and white, blue smo-
kestacks, blue ocean, yellow–blue
sky 18.00
Playing Cards, Alaska Steamship 15.00
Post Card, Philadelphia, American
Line, color, NY Harbor scene 15.00
Print, Titanic, 15 x 22½", black and
white, text of sinking, published by
Tichnor Bro, Boston 60.00
Souvenir Spoon, Transylvania Anchor
Line, silver plated, twisted handle,
blue enameled ring, flag, and crest . 75.00
Stock Certificate, Cunard Steam Ship
Co, Ltd 7.50
Tin Container, Queen Mary, Cunard
Line, Benson's Candy, McDowell il-
lus, oct, 5 x 8 x 1¾" 24.00
View Book, Royal Mail Cabin Liners, int.
views, 1924 .... 25.00

TRUNKS

History: Trunks are portable containers that
clasp shut for the storage or transportation of personal possessions. Normally "trunk" means the
ribbed flat, or dome top models of the second half
of the 19th century. Unrestored they sell for between $50 and $150. Refinished and relined the

price rises to $200 to $400, with decorators being a principal market.

Early trunks frequently were painted, stenciled, grained, or covered with wallpaper. These are collected for their folk art qualities and as such experience high prices.

Reference: Martin and Maryann Labuda, *Price & Identification Guide to Antique Trunks,* published by authors, 1980.

Dome top, wood rim, wooden slats, 20¼ x 32 x 25″, $95.00.

DOME TOP

11 x 32 x 16″, pine, rect, brass bound, English, early 19th C	50.00
16″ l, leather covered wood, brass stud dec, bail handle	30.00
25″ l, pine, dark green paint, orange striping and yellow dots, orig iron hinges and end handles, replaced lock	65.00
46¾″ l, oak, immigrant type, dovetail, wrought iron strap hinges, banding, end handles, lock, dark finish	270.00

FLAT TOP

14 x 8″, pigskin, red, front and sides with painted Oriental maidens and landscapes within quatrefoils, brass loop handles and lock, Chinese, 19th C	125.00
39⅓ x 19¼″, rect, camphor wood, dovetail, brass bound corners, shaped hasp, escutcheon, carrying handles, fitted int.	550.00
46″ l, campaign, brass bound leather, c1850	400.00

VALENTINES

History: Early cards were handmade, often containing both handwritten verses and hand drawn pictures. Many cards also were hand colored and contained cutwork.

Mass production of machine-made cards featur-

ing chromolithography began after 1840. In 1847 Esther Howland of Worcester, Massachusetts, established a company to make valentines which were hand decorated with paper lace and other materials imported from England. They had a small "H" stamped in red in the top left corner. Howland's company eventually became the New England Valentine Company (N.E.V. Co.).

George C. Whitney and his brother founded a company after the Civil War which dominated the market from the 1870s through the first decades of the twentieth century. They bought out several competitors, one of which was the New England Valentine Company.

Lace paper was invented in 1834. The 1835 to 1860 period is known as the "golden age" of lacy cards.

Embossed paper was used in England after 1800. Embossed lithographs and woodcuts developed between 1825–40, with early examples being hand colored.

References: Roberta B. Etter, *Tokens Of Love,* Abbeville Press Inc., 1990; Ruth Webb Lee, *A History of Valentines*, reprinted by National Valentine Collectors Association; Frank Staff, *The Valentine And Its Origins*, out–of–print.

Collectors' Club: National Valentine Collectors Association, Box 1404, Santa Ana, CA 92702.

Additional Listings: See *Warman's Americana & Collectibles* for more examples.

Advisor: Evalene Pulati.

Diecut, stand–up, German, 6¾″ h, 3¾″ w, $10.00.

Cameo, Berlin and Jones, 5 x 7″, 1860	35.00
Cobweb, Dobbs, 8 x 10″, hand colored, 1860	35.00
Cutwork, Pennsylvania German, 16″, sq, hand colored, 1820	350.00
Easel Back	
6 x 9″, fancy cutwork border, 1900	10.00

8½", girl carrying red honeycomb paper parasol 50.00

Lacy Folder, 3 x 5"
Hand assembled, emb, 1850 ..... 15.00
Howland, signed, 1855 .... 25.00

Layered
3 x 5", lacy, N.E.V. Co., 1875 ..... 18.00
5", hearts and flowers, c1860 ..... 20.00

Mechanical, R. Tuck, large paper doll, 1900 .... 25.00

Pulldown, German
5 x 10", five layers, 1920 .... 20.00
8 x 12", large ship, 1910 .... 75.00

Sailor's, octagonal
Forget Me Not, double, 8½" d, 19th C 1,450.00
Homeward Bound, 10⅜" d, 19th C . 550.00
I'm Yours, Be Mine, 12" d 600.00
To A Lover, double, 9" d 1,150.00

Sheet, emb, Union soldier embracing girl, c1860 .... 50.00

Animal Dish, cov
Dog on rug, amber, sgd 75.00
Hen on nest, aqua opaque, sgd ... 60.00
Rabbit, white, frosted 60.00
Snail, figural strawberry base, milk white, sgd 90.00
Swan, blue milk glass 100.00

Breakfast Set, hen cov dish, six egg cups, basket form master salt, and tray, milk white, 9 pcs 450.00

Butter Dish, cov, turtle, snail finial, milk white 100.00

Candlesticks, Baroque pattern, amber, pr 75.00

Compote, 6¼" d, 6¼" h, sq, blue milk glass 75.00

Dish, cov, figural, lemon, milk white, sgd 65.00

Mustard, cov, swirled ribs, scalloped, matching cov with slot for spoon, milk glass 25.00

Plate, 6" d, Thistle pattern, green 65.00

Salt, cov, hen on nest, white opal 35.00

Sugar, cov, 5" h, Strawberry pattern, salamander finial, milk white, gold trim . 75.00

Tumbler, 4" h, blue 40.00

Vase, 10" h, ribbed body, hp wine blossoms connected by gold branches of thorns, gold accents, ruffled top ... 120.00

VALLERYSTAHL GLASS

History: Vallerystahl (Lorraine), France, has been a glass producing center for centuries. In 1872 two major factories, Vallerystahl glassworks and Portieux glassworks, merged and produced art glass until 1898. Later, pressed glass covered animal dishes were introduced. The factory continues operation today.

Salt, cobalt blue, ram's head dec, three feet, 2½" d, 1½" h, marked, $45.00.

VAL SAINT–LAMBERT

History: Val Saint–Lambert, a twelfth century Cistercian abbey, was located during different historical periods in France, Netherlands, and Belgium (1930 to present). In 1822 Francois Kemlin and Auguste Lelievre, along with a group of financiers, bought the abbey and opened a glassworks. In 1846 Val Saint–Lambert merged with the Société Anonyme des Manufactures de Glaces, Verres à Vitre, Cristaux et Gobeletaries. The company bought many other glassworks.

Val Saint–Lambert developed a reputation for technological progress in the glass industry. In 1879 Val Saint–Lambert became an independent company employing 4,000 workers. Val Saint–Lambert concentrated on the export market making table glass, cut, engraved, etched, and molded pieces, and chandeliers. Some pieces were finished in other countries, e.g., silver mounts added in the United States.

Val Saint–Lambert executed many special commissions for the artists of the Art Nouveau and Art

Deco periods. The tradition continues. The company also made cameo–etched vases, covered boxes, and bowls. The firm celebrated its 150th anniversary in 1975.

Ashtray, 4½" w, hat, frosted clear, paper
  label 25.00
Bowl, cameo
  6" d, blue amethyst, wisteria and
    vines dec, frosted ground 150.00
  6½" d, cov, deep cut purple florals,
    frosted ground, sgd "Val St Lambert" 750.00
Chess Set, crystal, clear crystal half,
  green and clear crystal remaining
  half, each pc labeled and sgd, 6½" h
  tallest pc 300.00

Atomizer, acid etched, raised floral garland, light cranberry flashing, gold washed fittings, bulb missing, 6¾" h, $260.00.

Dresser Jar, cov, 4¾" h, double cut, ruby
  cut to clear, sgd 100.00
Pitcher, clear, paneled, diamond shaped
  cuttings, sgd 85.00
Vase
  6¾" h, cameo, shouldered cylinder,
    clear ruby overlay, cut random blossoms and leaves, blue and white
    enamel, gilt trim, acid stamped .. 1,100.00
  11" h, trumpet, flared, flat base, crystal, ruby overlay, molded rounded
    criss–cross faceted bands, sgd on
    base 385.00
  23¾" h, cameo, slender neck, wide
    sloping foot, clear glass overlaid
    with white, brown, and green,
    c1900 .... 5,000.00
Wine Glass, intaglio cut, ribbons, bows,
  and cranberry cameos, gold trimmed
  stems, set of 12 .... 480.00

VAN BRIGGLE POTTERY

History: Artus Van Briggle, born in 1869, was a talented Ohio artist. He joined Rookwood in 1887 and studied in Paris under Rookwood's sponsorship from 1893 until 1896. In 1899 he moved to Colorado for his health and established his own pottery in Colorado Springs in 1901.

Van Briggle's work was influenced heavily by the Art Nouveau "school" he saw in France. He produced a great variety of matte glazed wares in this style. Colors varied.

The "AA" mark, a date, and "Van Briggle" were incised on all pieces prior to 1907 and sometimes into the 1910s and 1920s. After 1920, "Colorado Springs, Colorado" or an abbreviation was added. Dated pieces are the most desirable.

Artus died in 1904. Anne Van Briggle continued the pottery until 1912.

References: Barbara Arnest (ed.), *Van Briggle Pottery: The Early Years*, The Colorado Springs Fine Art Center, 1975; Scott N. Nelson, Lois Crouch, Euphemia Demmin, and Robert Newton, *Collector's Guide To Van Briggle Pottery,* Halldin Publishing, 1986.

Collectors' Club: American Art Pottery Association, 9825 Upton Circle, Bloomington, MN 55431.

Museum: Pioneer Museum, Colorado Springs, CO.

Reproduction Alert: Van Briggle pottery still is made today. These modern pieces often are confused for older examples. Among the glazes used are Moonglo (off white), Turquoise Ming, Russet, and Midnight (black).

Bowl, Design 268, turquoise, matte, mottled brown glaze around rim, 1906, imp marks, 6¾" d, 3½" h, $550.00.

1901–1920

Bookends, pr, 5½" l, 5" h polar bear,
  Persian rose matte glaze, blue accents 275.00

Bowl
3" d, dragonfly design, deep plum, 1917 . . . . **100.00**
5¾" d, 2" h, buff colored clay body, flowers in panels, shaded light blue glaze, Pattern 322, 1906 . . . . **300.00**
Chamberstick, 5½" h, molded leaf shape, hood over candle socket, green glaze **110.00**
Figure
Elephant, raised trunk, turquoise, AA mark **90.00**
Rabbit, early **45.00**
Plaque
Indian, pr **175.00**
Mermaid, 10" h, AA mark **65.00**
Pot, 3" h, dark teal blue, #688, 1915 mark **150.00**
Urn, 4" h, 4" d, burgundy, blue floral spray band at top, 1919–21 . . . . . . **85.00**
Vase
3¾" h, robin's egg blue wash, buff colored clay, 1908–11 . . . . **120.00**
4¼" h, olive green, rose brushed around bottom, Pattern 549, 1907 **225.00**
4½" h, poppy seed pods, matte moss green curdled to yellow–green, some smooth areas, Shape 452, 1907 . . . . **275.00**
5" h, copper clad, Shape 696, c1907 **1,000.00**
6¼" h, dark green long slender leaves, deep dark blue, matte glaze on leathery texture, Shape 636, 1908–11 . . . . **275.00**
7" h, dark and light blue dragonflies, #792 . . . . **125.00**
7¼" h, brown glaze, Shape 296, 1906 **475.00**
7½" h, medium blue, cream colored clay body, thistle flowers, 1918 . . **225.00**
9½" h, 7" d, burgundy, blue spray, #235, late 1910s **365.00**
Wall Pocket, 7½" l, turquoise matte, relief, AA mark **75.00**

1921–1968

Ashtray, 6½" w, Hopi Indian maiden kneeling, grinding corn, turquoise Ming glaze **75.00**
Boot, 2½" h **35.00**
Bust, 6½" h, child reading book **45.00**
Indian Maiden, 4" w, 6" h, blue–green, bent over rock, ear of corn in hands **50.00**
Lamp, Damsel of Damascus **175.00**
Paperweight, 3" d, maroon, rabbit . . . **60.00**
Pitcher, conical, plain, blue, Pattern 435 **100.00**
Rose Bowl, 5" d, blue–green, spade shaped leaves around top **30.00**
Urn, 3½" h, dark burgundy, Shape 688, late 1920s **75.00**

Vase
3" h, butterfly **45.00**
5" h, rect, blue flower, rose ground . **40.00**

VENETIAN GLASS

History: Venetian glass has been made on the island of Morano, near Venice, since the 13th century. Most of the wares are thin walled. Many types of decoration have been used: embedded gold dust, lace work, and applied fruits or flowers.

Reproduction Alert: Venetian glass continues to be made today.

Paperweight, blue, millefiori, goldstone, crystal base, 13" h, $215.00.

Candlestick, pr, 7" h, swan stems, pink and lace bobeches **220.00**
Compote
5½" h, swirled gold, blue, and white dec **190.00**
6½" h, ruby, gold, and white flashing, coiled snake around stem **150.00**
9" h, latticinio, pink, white lace **140.00**
Cruet
Bulbous, blue and gold ribbons alternating with white filagree, clear handle and stopper, 7" h **200.00**
Latticinio, pink to white lace, hollow stopper **165.00**
Decanter, 12" h, pink to white latticinio design **250.00**
Ewer, 9¼" h, rainbow **145.00**
Figure, 10" h, fish **90.00**
Liquor Set, 7 pcs, 8" h decanter, six stemmed cordials, decanter with clear applied prunts and rigaree, cordials with applied beading over green alternating with gold and white filagree **440.00**
Plate, 7" d, dessert, set of 6, white filagree with gold, ruffled **150.00**

Vase
- 4" h, pr, corset shape, gold and green ribbed with gold and white . . . . . . — 50.00
- 7" h, gold, blue dotted enamel, two handles, ftd . . . . — 80.00
- 8½" h, double gourd, latticinio design — 220.00
- 10" h, boat shape, pink, chartreuse, and white on clear double twist stem with two daffodils . . . . — 90.00
- 10½" h, rubena verde, latticinio stripes, rigaree . . . . — 250.00

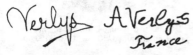

VERLYS GLASS

History: Verlys glass is an art glass originally made in France after 1930. For a period of a few months, Heisey Glass Co., Newark, Ohio, produced the identical glass, having obtained the rights and formula from the French factory.

The French-produced glass can be distinguished from the American product by the signature. The French is mold marked; the American is etched script signed.

Salad Bowl, Poppy, script sgd, 13½" d, $125.00.

Ashtray, 4½" w, frosted doves, floral border, script mark . . . . — 50.00
Bowl
- 6" d, Pinecone, French blue . . . . . . — 100.00
- 8½" d, Thistle, clear, sgd . . . . — 65.00
Box, cov, 6½" w, butterflies, script mark — 100.00
Candy Dish, 7" d, sculptured florals on cov, opal . . . . — 375.00
Candlesticks, 5½" d, leaftip molded nozzle, spreading circular foot with

molded nasturtiums, etched signature on base, minor chips on rim, pr . . . . — 90.00
Centerpiece, 19¼" l, 4⅞" h, oval, high relief molded ext., four exotic fish with long swirling fins and tails, each molded with shaped handle formed by extended fan shaped tails, wavy ground scattered with bubbles, relief molded signature . . . . — 350.00
Charger, 13" d, Waterlily . . . . — 145.00
Console Bowl
- 12" d, Tassels, beige . . . . — 90.00
- 13½" d, Wild Ducks, Directorie Blue — 200.00
Plate, 11¾" d, bird dec . . . . — 165.00
Powder Box, cov, lovebirds, frosted . . — 65.00
Vase, 9¾" h, clear and frosted, high relief molded stalks of wheat, inscribed "Verlys" . . . . — 150.00

VILLEROY & BOCH

History: Pierre Joseph Boch established a pottery near Luxemburg, Germany, in 1767. Jean Francis, his son, introduced the first coal–fired kiln in Europe and perfected a water–power–driven potter's wheel. Pierre's grandson, Eugene Boch, managed a pottery at Mettlach; Nicholas Villeroy also had a pottery nearby.

In 1841 the three potteries were merged into the firm of Villeroy & Boch. Early production included a hard paste earthenware comparable to English ironstone. The factory continues to use this hard paste formula for its modern tablewares.

Reference: Susan and Al Bagdade, *Warman's English & Continental Pottery & Porcelain*, 2nd Edition, Wallace–Homestead, 1991.

Additional Listings: Mettlach.

Bread Board, 5½ x 8½", white . . . . . . — 115.00
Coffeepot, 8", Virginia pattern . . . . . . — 85.00
Creamer, Aragon pattern . . . . — 20.00
Jug, 14¼", brown earthenware, peasants in field, white relief, pewter mounts, 19th C . . . . — 175.00
Mug, elk dec, sgd . . . . — 40.00
Plaque, 10¼", boat scene, blue and white, matte finish . . . . — 85.00
Plate, 10", gaudy stick spatter, polychrome floral design . . . . — 25.00
Punch Bowl, cov, blue, scene of dancing figures, underplate, 3 qt, #2087 . . . — 750.00
Ramekin, blue and white, underplate . — 40.00

Plate, Onion pattern, imp mark, 10″ d, $20.00.

Salt Box, 9½″, blue dec, wood cov . . .	150.00
Stein, ½ L, 6½″ h, five white figures, blue ground, Mercury mark	225.00
Tile, blue and white Dutch scene with windmills	50.00
Vase	
6¼″, Art Deco, green and brown, gold outlining, white ground, pr	185.00
7½″, tan, beige relief figure, silver luster trim	250.00

WARWICK

History: Warwick China Manufacturing Co., Wheeling, West Virginia, was incorporated in 1887 and continued until 1951. The company was one of the first manufacturers of vitreous glazed wares in the United States. Production was extensive and included tableware, garden ornaments, and decorative and utilitarian items.

Pieces were hand painted or decorated by decals. Collectors seek portrait items and fraternal pieces for groups such as the Elks, Eagles, and Knights of Pythias.

Some experimental, eggshell–type porcelain was made before 1887. A few examples are in the market.

Bone Dish, scenic flow blue dec, marked "Warwick China"	48.00
Cuspidor, 6½″ h, floral dec, marked "IOGA"	70.00
Egg Cup, large, Tudor Rose	15.00
Gravy Boat, red currants, green leaves, gold trim	50.00
Marmalade Jar, cov, handles, pale yellow florals, brown ground	100.00
Mug, 4½″ h, singing monk, brown ground	45.00

Vase, two handles, rose dec, brown ground, marked "IOGA," 10″ h, $120.00.

Plate	
9½″ d, monk drinking wine, brown ground	75.00
10″ d	
Herons, green ground	135.00
Portrait, gypsy lady, multicolored, white ground	65.00
Spooner, platinum banded dinnerware	60.00
Tea Set, 3 pcs, teapot, creamer, and cov sugar, gold bands	115.00
Vase	
9¼″ h, charcoal ground, verbena, marked "LG #1"	200.00
10½″ h, urn shape, gypsy girl portrait, blue blouse and hair ribbon, brown shaded ground, twig handles	150.00
11″ h, red hibiscus, brown ground . .	75.00
11½″ h, bouquet shape, portrait, lady with white rose, brown ground . . .	170.00

WATCHES, POCKET

History: Pocket watches can be found from flea markets to the specialized jewelry sales at Butterfield & Butterfield, William Doyle Galleries, and Sothebys. Condition of movement is first priority; design and detailing of case is second.

In pocket watches, listing aids are size (18/0 to 20), number of jewels in movement, open or closed (hunter) face, and whether the case is gold, gold filled, or some other metal. The movement is the critical element since cases often were switched. However, an elaborate case, especially of gold, adds significantly to value.

Pocket watches designed to railroad specifications are desirable. They are 16 to 18 in size, have a minimum of 17 jewels, adjust to at least five positions, and conform to many other specifications. All are open faced.

Study the field thoroughly before buying. The literature is vast, including books and newsletters from clubs and collectors. Abbreviations: S = size; gf = gold filled; yg = yellow gold; j = jewels.

References: August C. Bolino,*The Watchmakers of Massachusetts,* Kensington Historical Press, 1987; Howard Brenner, *Collecting Comic Character Clocks and Watches,* Books Americana, 1987; Roy Ehrhardt & William Meggers, *American Pocket Watches Identification And Price Guide: Beginning To End...1830–1980,* Heart of America Press, 1987; Cedric Jagger, *The Artistry Of The English Watch,* Charles E. Tuttle Co., 1988; Reinhard Meis, *Pocket Watches: From the Pendant Watch To The Tourbillon,* Schiffer Publishing, 1987, orig published in German; Cooksey Shugart and Tom Engle, *The Official Price Guide To Watches, Eleventh Edition,* Cooksey Shugart Publications, 1991.

Collectors' Club: National Association of Watch & Clock Collectors, 514 Poplar Street, Box 33, Columbia, PA 17512. *Bulletin* (bi–monthly) and *Mart* (bi–monthly).

Museums: American Clock & Watch Museum, Bristol, CT; Hoffman Clock Museum, Newark, NY; National Association of Watch and Clock Collectors Museum, Columbia, PA; The Time Museum, Rockford, IL.

Hunter, size 6, Illinois, 14K solid gold case, 15 jewels, $275.00.

Character
Big Bad Wolf, pocket, slogan on reverse, Ingersoll, Disney, c1930	400.00
Buck Rogers, copper lightning bolt hands, one–eyed monster on reverse	300.00
Mickey Mouse, silvered brass, black paint, orig leather strap	75.00

Railroad
Blinn, 24j	650.00
Bunn (Illinois), 16 S, 23j, 10K gf case	325.00
Rockford, 18 S, 21j, open face, Railway King	550.00

Seth Thomas, 18 S, 15j, locomotive engraved on silveroid case	65.00

Regular
American Watch Co, 16 S, 17j, #1899, yg filled hunter case,	165.00
Berlington, 19j, Montgomery dial	180.00
Chicago Watch Co, 18 S, 11j, key wind	450.00
Elgin, 8 S, hunter, 14K, #1141341, lever case, machine turned case	465.00
Eureka, 18 S, 11j	115.00
Hamilton, 16 S, 17j, #987, gold filled open face, Masonic emblems	125.00
Hampden, 18 S, 23j, gold jewel setting, adjusted to heat, cold, isochronism, and five positions, nickel plate case, double roller, two tone	275.00
Howard, open face, 16 S, 17j, gf	135.00
Illinois, 16 S, hunter, 17j, nickel lever movement #1923165, yg filled case #537918	250.00
Ingersoll, 16 S, 17j, white base metal, Reliance	55.00
Movado, 17j, open face, movement #1617359, 14K yg case	500.00
National Watch Co, 18 S, 15j, coin silver, hunter case, key wind	175.00
New York Standard, yellow playing card dial	650.00
Patek Philippe, 18j, open face, circular dial, raised gold bar nos., subsidiary second dial, nickel lever movement, 18K plain case, sgd, #882371	950.00
Rockford, 16 S, 21j, gold jewel setting, open face	650.00
South Bend, 18 S, 21j, gold jewel setting, hunter case, full plate	425.00
Tiffany, 3/0 S, 15j, 18K, open face, swing out	400.00
Waltham, 18 S, 17j, silveroid case, lever set, 1903	90.00
Washington, 18 S, 17j, 25 year, yg filled, open face, single sunk dial, lever set, Senate	175.00

WATCHES, WRIST

History: The definition of a wristwatch is simple: "a small watch that is attached to a bracelet or strap and is worn around the wrist." However, a watch on a bracelet is not necessarily a wristwatch. The key is the ability to read the time. A true wristwatch allows you to read the time at a glance, without making any other motions. Early watches on a bracelet worn on the arm had the axis of their dials, from 6 to 12, perpendicular to the band. Reading them required some extensive arm movement.

The first true wristwatch appeared about 1850. However, the key date is 1880 when the stylish decorative wristwatch appeared and almost universal acceptance occurred. The technology to create the wristwatch existed in the early nineteenth century with Brequet's shock–absorbing "Parachute System" for automatic watches and Ardien Philipe's winding stem.

The wristwatch was a response to the needs of the entreprenuerial age with its emphasis on punctuality and planned free time. By approximately 1930 the sales of wristwatches surpassed that of pocket watches. Swiss and German manufacturers were quickly joined by American makers.

The wristwatch has undergone many technical advances during the twentieth century including self–winding (automatic), shock–resistance, electric operation, etc. It truly is the most significant and dominant clock of the century.

References: Howard S. Brenner, *Identification and Value Guide Collecting Comic Character Clocks and Watches*, Books Americana, 1987; Kahlert Mühe Brunner, *Wristwatches, History Of A Century's Development*, Schiffer Publishing Ltd., 1986; Sherry and Roy Ehrhardt and Joe Demesy, *Vintage American & Europe Wrist Watch Price Guide, Book 5*, Heart of America Press, 1990; Sherry Ehrhardt & Peter Planes, *Vintage American & European Wrist Watch Price Guide 1987 Values*, Heart of America Press, 1987; Helmut Kahlert, Richard Muhee, Gisbert L. Brunner, *Wristwatches: History of a Century's Development*, Schiffer Publishing Ltd., 1991; Cooksey Shugart & Tom Engle, *The Official Price Guide To Watches, Eleventh Edition*, Cooksey Shugart Publications, 1991.

Collectors' Club: National Association of Watch & Clock Collectors, 514 Poplar Street, Box 33, Columbia, PA 17512. *Bulletin* (bi–monthly) and *Mart* (bi–monthly).

Museums: American Clock & Watch Museum, Bristol, CT; Hoffman Clock Museum, Newark, NY; National Association of Watch and Clock Collectors Museum, Columbia, PA; The Time Museum, Rockford, IL.

Gruen, tank, 14K yg fill, 17 j, $45.00.

Character
Babe Ruth	175.00
Cinderella, silver case, green plastic bands with emb pictures, late 1940s	75.00
Davy Crockett, green hard plastic case, orig brown leather strap, c1954	125.00
Donald Duck, rect face, 1940s	100.00
Gene Autry, silvered metal case, full color photo, leather straps, Wilane, c1948	110.00
Howdy Doody, silvered metal case, plaid fabric band, bob Smith copyright, 1948–51	150.00
Roy Rogers and Trigger, chrome metal case, orig tan leather bands, Ingraham Co, c1951	75.00
Snoopy, pilot on doghouse, 1965	50.00

Gentleman's
Baylor, 14K, yg, rect fancy case, small diamond set in white gold on dial	185.00
Corum, 18K, rect, heavy case	600.00
Elgin, 14K, automatic, c1960	250.00
Hamilton, 17j, gf, #987, stem wind, leather band	75.00
Jules Jergensen, quartz, day and date, leather band	150.00
Patek Philippe, 18K, 18j, nickel lever movement, optionally adjusted to heat cold, and isochronism, and five positions, sgd, #794679	850.00

Lady's
Bucherer, 18K, white gold, 12 diamonds with brick work solid band and cov over dial	2,200.00
Bulova, 14K, 23j, yg, surrounded by 24 diamonds	665.00
Girod, 14K	150.00
Le Roy & Fils, London, platinum and diamond, rect, strap set at intervals with six old European cut diamonds, each .65 carat, numerous rose cut diamonds	2,000.00
Longines, 14K	200.00
Nicolet, 17j, flexible band, cabochon crystal, small diamond on each side of ½ sq face	85.00

WATERFORD

History: Waterford crystal is quality flint glass commonly decorated with cuttings. The original factory was established at Waterford, Ireland, in 1729. Glass made before 1830 is darker than the brilliantly clear glass of later production. The factory closed in 1852. After 100 years it reopened and continues in production.

Bowl, 9", leaf cut border over trellis work sides	100.00

Fruit Bowl, turned down rim, standard base, 5¾" h, 6¾" d, $290.00.

Compote, 9½" h, 13½" l, boat shape	**500.00**
Creamer and Sugar, diamond cut	**50.00**
Cruet, 5", waisted body, short fluted neck, fluted rim, strawberry leaves and fan cutting, faceted stopper	**100.00**
Decanter, 10", deep cut Sawtooth Rib pattern, double rope ring neck, orig stopper	**250.00**
Jar, cov, 6", diamond cut body, triple sprig chain bordering thumb cut rim and star cut lid, faceted knob finial	**100.00**
Letter Opener	**45.00**
Salt, 3", cut, star base	**30.00**
Vase, 7", fluted neck, flared rim, hobnail cut, triple sprig chains, star cut centered base	**85.00**
Water Set, 6" pitcher, six tumblers, diamond cut	**600.00**

WAVE CREST WARE

WAVE CREST

History: The C. F. Monroe Company of Meriden, Connecticut, produced the opal glassware known as Wave Crest from 1898 until World War I. The company bought the opaque, blown molded glass blanks for decoration from the Pairpoint Manufacturing Co. of New Bedford, Massachusetts, and other glass makers including European factories. Florals were the most common decorative motif. Trade names used were "Wave Crest Ware," "Kelva," and "Nakara."

References: Wilfred R. Cohen, *Wave Crest: The Glass of C.F. Monroe,* Collector Books, 1987; Elsa H. Grimmer, *Wave Crest Ware,* Wallace-Homestead, 1979.

Bowl, pink flowers, 1½" h, 4½" d, $185.00.

Biscuit Jar, cov, satin glass	
7" h, 6" d, soft yellow and white ground, pink, blue, and yellow pansies dec, emb pattern, resilvered top, rim, and handle	**225.00**
8¼" h, 6" d, soft yellow and white ground, pink, blue, and yellow pansies, emb pattern, resilvered top, rim, and handle	**300.00**
Box	
3" d	
Circular, pink daisies, raised blue tinted double shell design, hinged, shield mark	**200.00**
Square, pink florals, raised light green snowflake design, hinged, shield mark	**250.00**
Yellow twist, white enameled forget–me–not flowers	**165.00**
4" d, circular, blown–out shell, light green, yellow florals, shield mark	**250.00**
5" d, circular, light pink Baroque shell, earthtone lakeside scene framed with mauve enamel scrolls, hinged	**715.00**
5½" l, rect, egg crate, pink roses, hinged, marked "Wavecrest"	**500.00**
7" d, yellow florals encircled with raised gold scrolls and white enamel daisies, Helmschmidt swirl white satin ground, hinged	**1,375.00**
7½" d, blue daisies and pink mum, light pink raised scrolls and webbing ground, shield mark	**715.00**
Cracker Jar	
Robin's egg blue ground, large yellow daisies, green leaves, resilvered collar, cov, and handle	**365.00**
Square, 5" d, pink daisies, raised scrolls, light blue ground	**355.00**
Creamer and Sugar, bulbous, blue floral design, metal rims and bail	**110.00**
Dresser Box, 7" d, sq, egg crate, cov with pink clover and white enamel daisy dec, marked "Wavecrest"	**525.00**
Dresser Set, 5" d cov powder jar, 5" d hair receiver, Kate Greenaway type cherubs, stamped "Nakara CFM Co"	**825.00**
Dresser Tray, 5" d, circular, pink wild roses, white to light green ground, raised floral and scroll design, oval mirror, marked "Wavecrest"	**410.00**

Fernery, 5 x 9", rect, pink wild roses, white to blue ground, raised scrolls, gold metal rim, shield mark 330.00

Jewelry Box, 3½" d, circular, pink wild roses, blue ground, hinged, marked "Nakara" 410.00

Playing Card Holder, 4" l, light pink rose, light green raised scrolls, metal rim, shield mark 275.00

Ring Tree, floral dec, pedestal base, handled ormolu rim 135.00

Salt and Pepper Shakers, pr
  Pillow, pink apple blossoms, dotted centers 200.00
  Pink daisies on olive green and blue daises, pink ground, Nakara 410.00

Urn, ribbed, hp floral dec on white, scroll handles 275.00

Vase
  6" h, cylindrical, pink wild roses, raised scroll base, ftd, shield mark 165.00
  7" h, bud, blue forget-me-nots, ornate metal scroll ftd base, stem, and double handles 220.00

Wall Pocket, 8" h, opal glass, elaborate gilt metal and brass rims and frame, sgd 825.00

WEATHER VANES

History: A weather vane indicates wind direction. The earliest known examples were found on late 17th century structures in the Boston area. The vanes were handcrafted of wood, copper, or tin. By the last half of the 19th century, weather vanes adorned farms and houses throughout the nation. Mass-produced vanes of cast-iron, copper, and sheet metal were sold through mail order catalogs or at country stores.

The champion vane is the rooster. In fact, the name weathercock is synonymous with weather vane. The styles and patterns are endless. Weathering can affect the same vane differently. For this reason, patina is a critical element in collecting vanes.

Whirligigs are a variation of the weather vane. Constructed of wood and metal, often by unskilled craftsmen, whirligigs not only indicate the direction of the wind and its velocity, but their unique movements served as entertainment for children, neighbors, and passersby.

References: Robert Bishop and Patricia Coblentz, *A Gallery of American Weathervanes and Whirligigs*, E. P. Dutton, 1981; Ken Fitzgerald, *Weathervanes and Whirligigs*, Clarkson N. Potter, 1967.

Reproduction Alert: Reproduction of early models exist, are being aged, and sold as originals.

Cow, 32" l, copper, full bodied, standing, molded, cast zinc head, black metal stand, 19th C 4,950.00

Dragon, 78" h, 38" d, copper, scrolled wrought iron direction, wood pedestal, restored, mid 19th C 1,400.00

Eagle, 31" h, 35" w, copper, perched on globe, outstretched wings, American, c1800 . . . . 1,800.00

Horse, 26" h, 36" l, cast iron, left leg raised, molded forelock, incised mane, wavy cut applied sheet iron tail, late 19th C 6,050.00

Horse, MA, flat, cast-iron, 32" l, c1830, $1,200.00.

Horse and Sulky
  24½" h, 49½" l, copper, molded, gilded, running horse pulling sulky with seated driver, mounted on rod, Harris & Co, Boston, MA, 19th C . 15,400.00
  27" h, 40" l, copper and zinc, molded, mounted on rod, black metal base J. W. Fiske & Co, c1880 . . . . 11,000.00

Hunter and Stag, 34" h, 26½" l, sheet iron, hunter wearing tricornered hat and waistcoat taking aim at leaping deer, black and white hunting dog, orig polychrome, mounted on scrolling rod enclosing date 1811 . . . . . . 4,950.00

Indian Chief on Horseback, 21" h, 35" l, sheet iron, silhouette, feathered headdress, holding tomahawk, jagged mane and tail 1,320.00

Locomotive, cast iron, silhouette form, weighted front, American, 19th C . . 3,850.00

Plow, 52 x 23", copper and cast zinc, mounted on rod in black metal base, c1860 . . . . 5,500.00

Ram, 25½" h, 30" l, copper and zinc, molded and gilded, molded fur and curly horns and tail, mounted on rod, black metal base 10,450.00

Rooster, 26½" h, 30" l, copper, comb and painted red wattle, yellow traces on body, white polychrome and gilded base, mounted on black metal stand, mid 19th C **3,850.00**

Sea Captain, 43½" h, copper, black coat and top hat, pointing right forefinger, spyglass under left arm, mid 19th C **22,500.00**

Seaman, 44" l, wood, blowing foghorn, 19th C **2,500.00**

Sloop, 32" h, 46" l, copper, molded, three masts, mounted on black metal base, allover verdigris, 19th C **3,300.00**

WEBB, THOMAS & SONS

History: Thomas Webb & Sons was established in 1837 in Stourbridge, England. The company probably is best known for its very beautiful English cameo glass. However, many other types of colored glass were produced including enameled glass, iridescent glass, pieces with heavy glass ornamentation, cased glass, and other art glass besides cameo.

Additional Listings: Burmese, Cameo, and Peachblow.

Rose Bowl, applied gold flowers and vine dec, 3¼" d, 3" h, $500.00.

Bowl
6" d, satin, raised gold floral branches and butterfly, shaded brown ground, ftd **275.00**
9½" d, 4¼" h, yellow overlay, pink int., ruffled, applied green thorny feet . **195.00**
Bride's Bowl
8¼" d, pink satin to pale yellow, twisted handle **250.00**
12" l, salmon pink, DQ, MOP, raised gold and white enamel bird perched on floral and leafy branches, attached metal dolphin ftd base **850.00**

Cologne Bottle, 6" h, bulbous, cranberry over canary yellow, allover birds of Paradise perched on thistle branches, honeycomb cut neck, matching bulbous teardrop stopper . **1,030.00**

Milk Pitcher, 4½" h, Honeycomb, pink, amber reeded handle **190.00**

Perfume Bottle, 3" h, bulbous, satin, MOP, blue, peacock eye, silver hallmarked top with emb ivy **850.00**

Rose Bowl, 3⅛" d, 3" h, rose overlay, white int., four crimp top, clear wafer foot, heavy gold flowers and branches, enameled "E" and spider web dec on base **275.00**

Salt, master, frosted, Adam and Eve, butterfly signature **75.00**

Scent Bottle, 3½" l, black satin, white floral dec, small label "Lily of the Valley" **90.00**

Sweetmeat, 5" d, sq, satin, MOP, chartreuse, flower and acorn design, silver hallmarked lid **480.00**

Vase
3" h, squatty, cameo, gingo ferns, marked "Webb" **1,210.00**
5¼" h, 3½" d, peachblow, gold branches and leaves, silver flowers, gold band around top, rose shaded to pale pink, cream int. .. **265.00**
6" h, melon ribbed, heavy enamel dec, lavender fleur–de–lis, blue ground **360.00**
6¼" h, ovoid, orange satin, amethyst berries and leaves dec, thorny branches, etched mark **475.00**
6½" h
Cameo, ovoid, simulated ivory, three carved birds perched on leaf and berry laden thorny branch, intricate lattice fence border, stylized floral motif, semi–circular imp "Thomas Webb & Sons" **6,600.00**
Cased, ribbed and swirled, rainbow design, irid luster, acid finish, gold dec on flanged rim, sgd, pr **1,090.00**
7" h, stick, cut velvet, teal blue, zipper design **210.00**
7¼" h, 4½" d, satin, shaded deep apricot, ruffled top, gold prunus blossoms, soft pink int., ormolu stand **525.00**
7½" h, 7⅜" d, flared, polished rock crystal, cut by master engraver William Fritsche, alternating panels of bamboo latticework and scenic Oriental type reserves of fisherman, pagoda, and storks, sgd in script at lower edge **3,025.00**
8" h, bulbous, satin, MOP, chartreuse,

flower and acorn pattern, pinched
sides, tricorn top **600.00**
8¼" h, 4¾" d, opaque cream ground,
gold prunus blossom sprays, gold
bee **295.00**
9" h
  Bulbous, stick, blue, raised gold floral branches, shiny finish **250.00**
  Double gourd shape, red satin . . . **190.00**
10" h, melon, cased, opaque white to
butterscotch, two twisted clear handles, flared top, gold, brown, green
hp florals **295.00**
10¼" h, tapered cylinder, Cluthra,
mottled crystal, shades of amethyst
with yellow, red, blue, and white
striations, gold aventurine inclusions, sgd "W & C England" **330.00**
12" h, bulbous, stick
  Allover floral and leaves dec,
  enamel highlights **180.00**
  Basketweave design, pale blue . . **210.00**
14" h, stick, cased, bright blue to pale
blue, heavy gold thistle and scroll
dec **690.00**

WEDGWOOD

WEDGWOOD

History: In 1754 Josiah Wedgwood entered into a partnership with Thomas Whieldon of Fenton Vivian, Staffordshire, England. Products included marbled, agate, tortoise shell, green glaze, and Egyptian black wares. In 1759 Wedgwood opened his own pottery at the Ivy House works, Burslem. In 1764 he moved to the Brick House (Bell Works) at Burslem. The pottery concentrated on utilitarian pieces.

Between 1766 and 1769 Wedgwood built the famous works at Etruria. Among the most renowned products of this plant were the Empress Catherina of Russia dinner service (1774) and the Portland Vase (1790s). Product lines were cane-ware, unglazed earthenwares (drabwares), pie-crust wares, variegated and marbled wares, black basalt (developed in 1768), Queen's or cream-ware, Jasperware (perfected in 1774), and others.

Bone china was produced under the direction of Josiah Wedgwood II between 1812 and 1822 and revived in 1878. Moonlight luster was made from 1805 to 1815. Fairyland luster began in 1920. All luster production ended in 1932.

A museum was established at the Etruria pottery in 1906. When Wedgwood moved to its modern plant at Barlaston, North Staffordshire, the museum was continued and expanded.

References: Susan and Al Bagdade, *Warman's English & Continental Pottery & Porcelain, 2nd Edition,* Wallace–Homestead, 1991; David Buten and Jane Clancy, *Eighteenth–Century Wedgwood: A Guide For Collectors And Connoisseurs*, Main Street Press, 1980; Robin Reilly, *The Collector's Wedgwood*, Portfolio Press/A Robert Campbell Rowe Book, 1980; Robin Reilly and George Savage, *Dictionary Of Wedgwood*, Antique Collectors Club, 1980; Geoffrey Wills, *Wedgwood*, Chartwell Books, Inc., 1989.

Periodicals: *American Wedgwoodian,* 55 Vandam Street, New York, NY 10013; *ARS Ceramica,* 5 Dogwood Court, Glen Head, NY 11545.

Collectors' Club: The Wedgwood Society, The Roman Villa, Rockbourne, Fordingbridge, Hents, England, SP6 3PG.

Museum: Buten Museum, Merion, PA.

Basalt, box, cov, ribbed body, figural finial, imp mark, 4½" h, $300.00.

BASALT

Bust, 4¼" h, Aristophanes, marked
"Wedgwood" **400.00**
Coffeepot, 9¼" h, basketweave, Widow
Warburton finial **325.00**
Creamer, 2¾" h, black, one side classic
figural scene of old man with serpent
and young man with dish in his hand,
reverse side classical figure of old
woman washing young woman's feet **130.00**
Figure
  3½" h, elephant, standing, trunk lowered, glass eyes, imp mark, c1916 **302.50**
  5½" h, squirrel, holding nut, glass
  eyes, imp mark, c1915, one leg re-
  stored **220.00**
  11" h, Nymph at Well, female figure
  holding shell, seated on shaped
  oval base, inscribed title, imp mark,
  c1840 . . . . **1,045.00**

Pendant, oval, black, lion chasing horse, beaded SS frame and chain . **75.00**

Pitcher, 4¾" h, tankard shape, black, classical women and children scene, grape and vine border, large mark with "8" in circle **155.00**

Urn, cov, 11" h, pedestal, sq base, swags, acanthus leaves at base and cov, c1860 . . . . **1,700.00**

Vase, 7¾" h, urn shape, cov, high relief floral swags suspended from rams heads enclosing flower head motifs, knob finial, scroll handles with foliage motif, sq pedestal, imp mark, c1770 **875.00**

Wine Ewer, 16" h, figural models by John Flaxman on shoulders, swags of vine and water reeds, stiff leaves, bands of overlapping foliage, gadrooned stems, sq bases, imp mark, c1860, pr **900.00**

CANEWARE

Bowl, drabware dec of ferns and stars, c1810 . . . . **425.00**

Dish, 9¾" l, rect, molded with overlapping leaves, imp mark, letter "L", c1790 . . . . **250.00**

Fruit Stand, 12⅜" d, foliate scroll handles, rect flaring foot, imp "Wedgwood," early 19th C **200.00**

Sugar, cov, 6" h, smear glaze, prunus blossoms, c1800 . . . . **300.00**

Teapot, c1820, smear glaze Arabesque scene, dog finial **225.00**

Vase, 8¾" h, sq, pierced domed lid, concave sides, relief brown classical figures, brown foliage caryatid corner supports suspending swags, four brown paw feet, stepped shaped sq base, imp mark, c1800 . . . . **1,200.00**

Waste Bowl, 5½" d, Wicker pattern, imp mark, c1820 . . . . **100.00**

CREAMWARE

Basket, 9" d, round, reticulated, c1790 **200.00**

Compote, 8¼" d, 4¾" h, basketweave, reticulated foliate scroll, rope twist rim handles **175.00**

Dish, 10¼" l, oval, clusters of fruit, green printed rim transfer, scrolling flowering branches, gilt rims, artist sgd "F. H. Cox," imp mark, Pat #G4744, c1880 . . . . **150.00**

Fruit Bowl, oval, wide brown and plum border pattern **550.00**

Sauce Dish, cov, attached underplate, oval, two handles, glazed **250.00**

Serving Dish, 11¾" l, shaped rect, brown edged scalloped rim, low relief int. molded with two fish, small

painted swan below banner, inscribed "Al SIDERA VULTUS," imp "Wedgwood," minor chips **200.00**

Sugar, cov, 8" h, stand, painted iron–red, green, blue, and yellow bands of flowering foliage, disc finial and flower head motif cov, imp mark, iron–red mark "Pat #1173," c1860 . . . . **235.00**

Teapot, 9" h, swelled cylindrical, dome cov, knop finial, brown dec, circular band and floral sprigs, scrolling vines, imp "Wedgwood" **250.00**

Tray, 6¼" w, diamond shape, transfer printed and painted, embracing cupids among clouds, sgd "EL," imp mark, letters "C," "AVO," c1865 . . . **250.00**

Tureen, cov, 17" l, Neo–Classical, painted sepia dec, loop handles, fitted undertray, early 19th C **650.00**

Urn, 6" h, mottled blue and brown, glazed, mounted on basalt plinth, marked "Wedgwood and Bentley," c1768–80 . . . . **475.00**

Water Set, 4 pcs, pitcher, two tumblers, and tray, dog handles, gilt, Victorian **850.00**

DRABWARE

Child's Tea Set, 3½" h teapot, cov sugar bowl, milk jug, waste bowl, basketweave, button knobs, imp mark, early 19th C **275.00**

Cup and Saucer, applied blue bands of flowering foliage **100.00**

Jug, 8" h, classical women emb on panels, loop handle, Wedgwood mark, c1820 . . . . **2,250.00**

Teapot, 8½" h, Gothic dec, bearded man faces on lower section, imp "Wedgwood" **225.00**

Vase, 10" h, blue and white, three sections, figural swan handles **400.00**

Jasper, vase, Portland, white cameos, black ground, imp mark, 9" h, $750.00.

JASPERWARE

Biscuit Jar, 7¾" h, white floral dec, lavender ground, acorn finial, artist sgd "Barnard" **710.00**

Butter Dish, cov, 4" h, 7" d, dark blue, raised white classical figures, SP lid and plate, marked "Wedgwood" ... **165.00**

Candlesticks, 6¼" h, blue, white coat of arms of St. Andrews, inscribed name and motto, scrolling foliage, circular column, flaring feet, imp marks, pr . **325.00**

Chandelier Dish, 10¾" d, light blue, applied white classical panels, chips at mounting hole, imp mark, late 19th C **470.00**

Compote, 7¾" d, 9½" d underplate, yellow, applied grapevine borders, added acanthus leaves, imp marks, c1890, minor int. stain ring .. **825.00**

Cup and Saucer, tricolor, green ground, white relief rams heads suspending floral swags enclosing oval medallions of classical figures on lilac ground, imp marks, 19th C **250.00**

Hair Receiver, cov, heart shape, medium blue, large white angel dec, numbered only **250.00**

Jardiniere, 10¼" d, 8¾" h, bulbous, olive green, white applied classical relief, imp "England," c1920 .... **415.00**

Loving Cup, 4½" h, three handles, olive green, white cameo medallions of Washington, Franklin, and Lafayette, marked "Wedgwood, England" **450.00**

Mantle Lusters, 11½" h, cylindrical, light blue and white jasper base, silver-plated mounts, relief dec of cupids, festoons and rams heads, two center trophies and oval medallions in violet, molded and cut glass bobeche hung with drops, glass floriform nozzle, pr **600.00**

Mug, 5" h, 3¾" d, dark blue, raised white classical figures, rope handle, raised white medallion, SP rim, marked "Wedgwood" **145.00**

Pitcher, 7¾" h, sage green, classical figures, cupid, and cherubs, marked "Wedgwood, England" **85.00**

Plaque, 16" l, 5½" h, light blue, white relief depicting "The Body of Hector Dragged at the Car of Achilles," carved oak frame, imp mark **1,210.00**

Preserve Jar, 6" h, cov, dark blue, matching underplate, four classical Muses in cartouches, marked "Wedgwood, England" **200.00**

Sweetmeat, cov, 3¼" h, cylindrical, dark blue, white horses and figures, knob finial, marked "Wedgwood" **185.00**

Teapot, cov, 5¼" h, 5⅝" d, sage green and white, raised white classical figures, marked "Wedgwood England" **195.00**

Toothpick Holder, 2¼" h, dark blue, white bust of Josiah Wedgwood, marked "Wedgwood, Made In England" **75.00**

Urn, 7½" h, cov, tricolor, white ground, green swags and acanthus leaves, lilac rams masks, two green medallions with white classical figures on lilac ground, floral lilac shoulder band, flared foot, ball finial, scroll handles, imp mark, mid 19th C **900.00**

Vase
 7½" h, tricolor, light green dip to upper and lower body, light blue central panel, white classical relief, stiff leaf borders, scrolled handles, staining, one handle damaged, c1860 .... **440.00**
 10¼" h, dark blue, loop handles, applied white relief of trophies over continuous frieze of classical figures, minor relief loss, imp "Made in England," c1900 .... **495.00**

LUSTERS

Butterfly
 Bowl, 2¾ x 1¾", octagonal, gold outlined multicolored butterflies, gold trim, mottled MOP luster ext., mottled flame int., Portland vase mark **115.00**
 Mug, 2" h, three handles, blue, tan, and pink, gold butterflies, coral int., marked "Wedgwood Lustre" **200.00**

Dragon
 Bowl, octagonal, printed mark, c1925 8¾" w, blue ext., yellow–green int., slight int. wear **465.00**
 9" w, orange ext., purple with mottled blue int. **330.00**
 Garniture Set, 11" h center vase, two 8" h sq vases, flying cranes and dragon breathing flames, 3 pcs .. **900.00**
 Salt, 2¼" h, orange dog's head in bowl, blue ext. **130.00**
 Vase, 8¾" h, shape #2355, mixed blues, MOP int., printed marks, c1925, pr **385.00**

Fairyland
 Bowl, 7¾" w, octagonal, Moorish ext., black ground, Smoke Ribbons int., worn int., c1920 .... **475.00**
 Melba Cup, 4⅞" d, 3½" h, green MOP int. with two elves on branch, midnight luster ext., gold stars, green grass, leapfrogging elves and fairies, Portland vase mark **700.00**
 Plate, 10¾" d, elves on bridge, gold center, lacy gold fairies and florals on gold border, mottled blue back **1,700.00**
 Vase, 8⅜" h, 4¼" d, Candlemas, multicolored, gold details, Portland

vase mark and "Z5157, Wedgwood" 1,275.00

Hummingbird

Bowl, 8" w, octagonal, blue ext., orange int., printed mark, c1925 ... 525.00

Jar, cov, 9" h, gold outlined multicolored hummingbirds, mottled green ext., gold trim, marked "Wedgwood" 725.00

Vase, 5⅛" h, gold outlined multicolored hummingbirds, mottled blue luster ground, mottled flame luster int. 200.00

Moonlight

Goblet, 3¼" h, pink with yellow and green splashes, gilt rim, imp mark, c1810 .... 300.00

Plate, 9¾" d, purple luster splotches, c1810 .... 200.00

Vase, 8⅛" h, Boys on Bridge dec, Portland vase mark 1,150.00

MAJOLICA

Bowl, 9" d, 4⅛" h, white and brown, emb white seashells, rose and gold seaweed, turquoise int., SP rim band, imp mark 125.00

Creamer, 3" h, Strawberry pattern, turquoise int., imp mark 160.00

Game Pie Dish, 11" l, polychrome enamels, chick finial, molded gaming trophies between floral garlands, winged creatures, Queensware liner, imp marks, 1868 .... 3,575.00

Pitcher, 8½" h, jug shape, jeweled design, turquoise int., c1860 .... 350.00

Plate, 6½" d, butterflies, florals, and fans dec 65.00

Sugar, 7" h, Fan pattern, flowering prunus, gray–green, yellow, and pink, turquoise int., two branch handles, imp mark, 1878 .... 165.00

Teapot, cov, 6¼" h, Bamboo pattern, imp mark, 1871 .... 625.00

Water Bottle, 10" h, multicolored florals, horizontal blue stripes, cream ground, 1879 .... 300.00

MISCELLANEOUS

Bulb Pot, 9½" h, figural, hedgehog, light blue, glazed, imp mark 475.00

Calendar Tile, The Mayflower Approaching Land, brown and white, 1910 .... 65.00

Cream Pitcher, 2¾" h, Diceware, tricolor, light green jasper dip, white applied laurel borders, yellow quatrefoils, flake restored to edge of spout, minor staining, c1850 .... 605.00

Honey Pot, cov, 3¾" h, stoneware, bee-

Stoneware, pitcher, ship and grapeleaf border, multicolored, 11⅜" h, $175.00.

hive shape, translucent smear glaze, c1820 .... 225.00

Pepper Pot, 3½" h, bulbous, relief grapes and leaves, white, imp mark 100.00

Tray, 15¾" l, oval, smear glaze, rim relief molded, band of scrolling flowering foliage, imp mark, early 19th C . 280.00

PEARLWARE

Bough Pot, 9", h pierced cov, D–shape, speckled, molded floral swags, still foliage border, gilt, imp mark, c1810, pr 1,200.00

Compote, 10¾" d, Havelock pattern, floral border, imp mark, c1840–68 .... 265.00

Jug, 5¾" h, blue, scenic transfer, gold wreath with initials under spout, gold grim, imp mark, c1820 .... 275.00

Plate, 8½" d, shell shape, ribbon handle, 1882 .... 75.00

Soup Tureen, cov, ladle, blue dahlias, green foliage, black rope edge, imp mark 400.00

Vase, cov, 6⅝" h, tan slip, engine turned gadroons, relief beadwork and swags, imp mark, late 18th C 425.00

QUEEN'S WARE

Box, 4 x 5", powder blue, relief berries, marked "Wedgwood England" 100.00

Crocus Pot, 6" h, rect, bombe shape, classical motifs in oval medallion ... 115.00

Cup and Saucer, relief vintage rim border, #2223 .... 25.00

Tea Set, Edward VIII Coronation, blue, c1937, 3 pcs 400.00

ROSSO ANTICO

Bowl, Egyptian 385.00

Creamer, 6" h, applied center black band of scrolling flowering foliage, imp mark, mid 19th C 225.00

Inkwell, 2⅝" h, Egyptian manner, sq flat base, removable ink pot insert, imp mark, late 18th C **605.00**
Jug, 6" h, pinched spout, applied black formal foliage and bellflowers, c1820 **200.00**
Teapot, cov, squatty, band of hieroglyphs at shoulder, crocodile finial, 1810 . . . . **420.00**

TERRA-COTTA WARE

Ashtray, 4½" d, classical dec, marked "Made in England" **35.00**
Box, heart shaped **85.00**
Pin Dish, 4" l, oval, cupids playing, marked "Made in England" **30.00**
Vase, 5¼" h, Portland shape, black relief lilies and foliage, flaring rim, band of grass, angular handles, applied mask terminals, imp mark, mid 19th C **300.00**

WELLER POTTERY

History: In 1872 Samuel A. Weller opened a small factory in Fultonham, near Zanesville, Ohio, to produce utilitarian stoneware, such as milk pans and sewer tile. In 1882 he moved his facilities to Zanesville. In 1890 Weller built a new plant in the Putnam section of Zanesville along the tracks of the Cincinnati and Miskingum Railway. Additions followed in 1892 and 1894.

In 1894 Weller entered into an agreement with William A. Long to purchase the Lonhuda Faience Company, which had developed an art pottery line under the guidance of Laura A. Fry, formerly of Rookwood. Long left in 1895, but Weller continued to produce Lonhuda under a new name, Louwelsa. Replacing Long as art director was Charles Babcock Upjohn. He, along with Jacques Sicard, Frederick Hurten Rhead, and Gazo Fudji, developed Weller's art pottery lines.

At the end of World War I, many prestige lines were discontinued and Weller concentrated on commercial wares. Rudolph Lorber joined the staff and designed lines such as Roma, Forest, and Knifewood. In 1920 Weller purchased the plant of the Zanesville Art Pottery and claimed to be the largest pottery in the country.

Art pottery enjoyed a revival when the Hudson Line was introduced in the early 1920s. The 1930s saw Coppertone and Graystone Garden ware added. However, the Depression forced the closing of the Putnam plant and one on Marietta Street in Zanesville. After World War II, cheap Japanese imports took over Weller's market. In 1947 Essex Wire Company of Detroit bought the controlling stock. Early in 1948 operations ceased.

References: Sharon and Bob Huxford, *The Collectors Encyclopedia Of Weller Pottery*, Collector Books, 1979, values updated 1992; Ann Gilbert McDonald, *All About Weller: A History And Collectors Guide To Weller Pottery, Zanesville, OH*, Antique Publications, 1989.

Collectors' Club: American Art Pottery Association, P. O. 9825 Upton Circle, Bloomington, MN 55431.

Additional Listings: See *Warman's Americana & Collectibles* for more examples.

Basket, Coppertone, branch handle, relief molded large blossoms **80.00**
Bowl
   Atlas, 4" d, blue glaze **45.00**
   Claywood, 4½" d, etched floral panels **22.00**
Candleholders, pr, Atlas, cream glaze . **16.00**
Clock, 11½" w, 5" d, 10" h, mantel, Dickensware, porcelain dial, Gilbert keywind clock, pottery frame, yellow pansies, standard glazed brown ground, imp oval marks **440.00**
Console Bowl, Silvertone, frog, sgd "DE" **200.00**
Ewer, Cameo, 10" h, ftd, squatty, tapering to tall neck, high spout, blue ground **30.00**
Ginger Jar, cov, Chase, late 1920s . . . **425.00**
Hanging Basket
   Burntwood, 4 x 8" **35.00**
   Souevo, 6½" d **175.00**
Jardiniere
   Blueware, 8½" h, slightly flared, three short feet, dancing ladies, trees, and birds **225.00**
   Silvertone, 10" h **350.00**
Model
   Frog, Coppertone, 15" l **650.00**
   Penguin, 5" h, pr standing on rockwork base **365.00**
Mug
   Dickensware, cavalier portrait, two handles **325.00**
   Jap Birdmal, burnt orange, four slender trees **325.00**
Pitcher
   Aurelian, tankard, slip painted berries, glossy brown glaze, artist sgd **350.00**
   Dickensware, tankard, Indian head portrait, Ghost Bull Dancer, artist sgd **900.00**
Planter, 11¼" d, 9½" h, chrysanthemum dec **125.00**

Tobacco Jar, Louwelsa, brass lid 185.00
Umbrella Stand, 21½" h, cylindrical, relief purple fruited trees, striated brown and green matte glaze ground 465.00

Vase, Warwick, brown, 9¾"h, $150.00.

Vase
  Aurelian
    8" h, sgd "P.A." 395.00
    9½" h, Jonquils, sgd "CJ Dilbouski" 300.00
  Camelot, 7¾" h, funnel shape, white dec, yellow–green ground, c1914 . 315.00
  Coppertone, 8" h, 9" d, handles . . . 145.00
  Dickensware
    10" h, Indian head portrait, "Chief Wolf Robe" 700.00
    17½" h, second line, two ladies strolling in country landscape, blue, green, brown, and yellow, imp marks, c1900 . . . . 2,750.00
  Eocean, 6" h, 5" d, pansies dec . . . 180.00
  Etna, 13" h, daffodils dec, 1906 . . . 150.00
  Hudson Perfecto, 8" h, 5" d, mauve, apple blossoms 285.00
  Kenova, 9" h, cylindrical 80.00
  Lasa, 5¼" h, trees and mountains dec, sgd 195.00
  Malvern, 6" h, brown 45.00
  Sicard
    4" h, triangular, irid blossom glaze, small rim glaze chips 300.00
    4¼" h, angled oval, four flattened ribs ending in extended feet, stylized daisy blossoms and grasses, blue–gold luster, sgd "Sicard Weller" 440.00
Wall Pocket
  Darsie, 1935 . . . . 50.00
  Roma, 10" l 100.00

WHALING

History: Whaling items are a specialized part of nautical collecting. Provenance is of prime impor-

tance since whaling collectors want assurances that their pieces are from a whaling voyage. Since ship's equipment seldom carries the ship's identification, some individuals have falsely attributed a whaling provenance to general nautical items. Know the dealer, auction house, or collector from whom you buy.

Special tools, e.g., knives, harpoons, lances, spades, etc., do not overlap the general nautical line. Makers' marks and condition determine value for these items.

Richard Bourne, Hyannis, Massachusetts, and Chuck DeLuca, York, Maine, regularly hold auctions featuring whaling material.

Reference: Thomas G. Lytle, *Harpoons And Other Whalecraft*, Old Dartmouth Historical Society, 1984.

Periodical: *Whalebone*, P. O. Box 2834, Fairfax, VA 22031.

Museums: Cold Spring Harbor Museum, Long Island, NY; Kendall Whaling Museum, Sharon, MA; Mystic Seaport Museum, Mystic, CT; National Maritime Museum, San Francisco, CA; Old Dartmouth Historical Society, New Bedford, MA; Whaling Museum, Nantucket, MA.

Additional Listings: Nautical Items and Scrimshaw.

Branding Iron, cast and wrought iron, "E. S. Mitchell," Dartmouth, c1850, 32¾" l, $75.00.

Agreement, ship *Rowena,* allows two crew members on whaling voyage, 1845 . . . . 275.00
Bill of Sale
  Whaleship *Meridian,* August 5, 1829 150.00
  Whaleship *William Rotch,* purchase of hull, dated October 29, 1819, New Bedford 125.00
  Whaling Schooner *Rainbow,* August 31, 1865 . . . . 160.00
Blubber Pike
  51½" l, orig handle, early to mid 19th C 55.00
  52" l, curved iron, orig wood handle, 19th C 140.00

Book

Ashley, Clifford W, *The Yankee Whaler*, first edition, Cambridge, MA 220.00

Barron, Captain William, *Old Whaling Days*, London, 1895 .... 75.00

Dow, George Francis, *Whale Ships and Whaling*, first edition, Salem, MA, 1925 .... 250.00

Spears, John R., *The Story of the New England Whalers*, New York, 1908 .... 110.00

Branding Iron, whaleship *Ship R M*, lettering mounted on handwrought iron, 20" l 275.00

Document, gives permission for whaleship *Cadmus* to voyage Pacific Ocean, sgd by President Andrew Jackson, framed, 1831 .... 880.00

Harpoon

Darting, 38¼" l, toggle, orig wood and canvas sheath 440.00

Stocked Bomb, walnut, Grudchos & Eggers, New Bedford, MA 1,100.00

Toggle

29¾" l, marked on side "JDD" ... 600.00

99" l, mounted on yellow painted pole 550.00

Lance, long shaft

55¼" l, unmounted 175.00

119¼" l, mounted on pole 220.00

122" l, iron shaft, mounted on wood pole 330.00

Letter, Abraham Barke discusses whaling industry, New Bedford, 1795 ... 125.00

Log Book

Bark *Milwood*, June 25, 1842 thru June 3, 1844, whale stamps, orig cov 3,750.00

Bark *Otranto*, commences at New Bedford January 17, 1847 thru April 30, 1849, contains whale stamps and ship stamps 3,080.00

Ship *Phoenix*, October 4, 1847 thru October 18, 1847 .... 660.00

Measuring Stick, 72" l, used to measure oil in whale oil barrel 220.00

Paddles, 69" l, whaleboat, marked "SB (Starboard Boat)," pr 440.00

Spade, 36" l, whaleboat, orig wood handle, mid 19th C 40.00

Whale Stamp, wood, fitted with turned whale ivory handle, mid 19th C 575.00

Whalebone Products

Box, 3⅞ x 2⅜ x 1⅜", fitted lid, 19th C 440.00

Cleat, 3⅝" l, early to mid 19th C ... 220.00

Corset Busk, 15" l, engraved ship, monument, and basket of flowers, mid 19th C 440.00

Fid, 10¼" l, 19th C 250.00

Seam Rubber, 4⅞" l, 29th C 385.00

Thimble

Circular, 2⅜", mid 19th C 190.00

Incised, 5⅛", initials "MT," mid 19th C 220.00

Teardrop shape, 2½", mid 19th C 190.00

WHIELDON

WHIELDON

History: The Staffordshire potter, Thomas Whieldon, established his shop in 1740. He is best known for his mottled ware, molded in forms of vegetables, fruits, and leaves. Josiah Spode and Josiah Wedgwood, in different capacities, had connections with Whieldon.

Whieldon ware is a generic term. His wares were never marked and other potters made similar items. Whieldon ware is agate–tortoise shell earthenware, in limited shades of green, brown, blue and yellow. Most pieces are utilitarian items, e.g., dinner ware and plates, but figurines and other decorative pieces are found.

Reference: Susan and Al Bagdade, *Warman's English & Continental Pottery & Porcelain, 2nd Edition,* Wallace–Homestead, 1991.

Plate, octagonal, 8½" d, $500.00.

Coffeepot, 9" h, green, yellow, and brown streaky glaze, repaired 800.00

Cradle, 3¾" l, mottled green, yellow, and brown, c1770 .... 385.00

Dish, 5½" l, leaf shape, gray and brown mottling, splashes of green and yellow on white, three small feet, c1770 400.00

Pitcher, cov, 8¾" h, green, brown, and gray–blue glaze, applied flower and scroll design, three mask and paw feet, matching cov with repaired bird finial, c1755–60 .... 8,000.00

Plate, pr, splashed manganese 8½" d, octagonal, raised rope twist rim, c1755 .... 1,000.00

9½" d, blue, green, and ochre, feather molded edge	**600.00**
Spill Bowl, 5¾" d, mottled brown and white glaze, vertical yellow, green, and blue stripes, c1770	**450.00**
Tea Caddy, 5½" h, rect, canted corners, flat shoulder, splashed brown glaze, c1755	**425.00**

WHIMSIES, GLASS

History: Glass workers occasionally spent time during lunch or after completing their regular work schedule creating unusual glass objects, known as whimsies, e.g. candy striped canes, darners, hats, paperweights, pipes, witch balls, etc. Whimsies were taken home and given as gifts to family and friends.

Because of their uniqueness and infinite variety, whimsies can rarely be attributed to a specific glass house or glass worker. Whimsies occurred wherever glass was made, from New Jersey to Ohio and westward. Some have suggested that style and color can be used to pinpoint region or factory, but no one has yet developed an identification key that is adequate.

One of the most collectible types of whimsies are glass canes. Glass canes range from very short, under one foot, to lengths of ten feet and beyond. They come in both hollow and solid form. Hollow canes can have a bulb type handle or the rarer "C" or "L" shaped handle. Canes are found in many fascinating colors, with the candy striped being a regular favorite with collectors. Many canes are also filled with varied colored powders, gold and white being the most common and silver being harder to find. Sometimes they were even used as candy containers.

References: Joyce E. Blake, *Glasshouse Whimsies*, printed by author, 1984; Joyce E. Blake and Dale Murschell, *Glasshouse Whimsies: An Enhanced Reference*, printed by author, 1989.

Collectors' Club: The Whimsey Club, 4544 Cairo Drive, Whitehall, PA 18052.

Advisors: Joyce E. Blake and Lon Knickerbocker.

Birdfeeder, 5¾" h, bottle green, emb bird and "Don't Forget to Feed Me"	**135.00**
Bracelet	
2" to 3" d, Lutz type, clear, multicolored twists and spirals, gold	**75.00**
3" d, solid glass, varied colored applied stripes	**35.00**
Buttonhook	
5" to 10" l, plain	
Bottle green	**20.00**
Clear glass	**20.00**
7" l, bottle green, elaborately twisted body, amber ends	**75.00**

Witch Ball, decanter vase with wafer type foot, white Nailsea loopings, $665.00.

Cane	
48" l, solid type	
Blue milk glass over white grooved finely twisted handle, attributed to Durand	**250.00**
Cobalt blue, shepherds crook handle	**250.00**
48" to 72" l, blown, baton type, gold, silver, or white powder filled, multicolored stripes on outside	**250.00**
60" l, solid, bottle green, finely twisted, curved handle	**125.00**
60" to 96" l, blown, baton type, multicolored candy stripes, red, blue, and yellow, c1910	**200.00**
Chain	
96" l, bi–colored, alternating white milk glass and amber links	**150.00**
Swag type, fancy twisted links, aqua with color through links, heart or star decoration	**225.00**
Cigarette Holder	
3" l, cobalt blue, yellow stripe	**45.00**
4" l, elaborate, multicolored, yellow with laid on white stripe	**75.00**
Darner	
5" l, bi–colored, amber head, applied clear handle	**200.00**
5" to 8" l, spatter, multicolored, clear or white int. lining	**125.00**
6" l, Aurene, gold, Steuben	**300.00**
7" l, white, blue Nailsea loopings	**150.00**
Egg, hollow, milk glass, various colored splotches	
2" h	**45.00**
4½" h	**85.00**
Hat, free blown	
1½" h, milk glass, c1910	**45.00**
1½" h, 4" d, amber, attributed to Keene, c1860	**150.00**

Horn

8½" l, French horn type, candy stripes	300.00
20" l, trumpet type, red, white, yellow, purple, and green candy stripes . .	150.00

Ladle

10" l, hollow, gold or silver powder filled, colored splotches, curved handle	50.00
12" l, aqua, straight handle	25.00

Pear, hollow

5½" h, amber, stem	65.00

6" h

Peachblow, stem	150.00
White milk glass, colored pink, green, and blue splotches	125.00

Pen

Elaborate, green, finely twisted applied bird finial	75.00
Simple design, amber, clear nib, 7" l	30.00

Pipe

20" l, English style, large bowl	
Nailsea loopings	225.00
Spatter design	225.00
36" l, American style, long twisted stem, small hollow bowl, aqua, c1900	100.00

Potichomanie Ball, blown, aqua, paper cut outs of flowers, etc.

9" d, c1850	250.00
12" d, matching stand, 24" total height, attributed to Lancaster, NY	600.00

Rolling Pin

14" l, black or deep olive glass, white dec, early Keene or Stoddard . . .	140.00
15" l, Nailsea type, various color combinations	150.00

Turtle, 5½" l, doorstop

Amber	140.00
Aqua	60.00

Witch Ball

5" d, clear red, Nailsea loopings . . .	250.00
6" d, milk glass, colored splotches . .	200.00

WHISKEY BOTTLES, EARLY

History: The earliest American whiskey bottles were generic form bottles blown by pioneer glass makers in the 18th century. The Biningers (1820–1880s) were the first bottles specifically designed for whiskey. After the 1860s distillers favored the cylindrical 'fifth' form.

The first embossed brand name bottle was the amber E. G. Booz Old Cabin Whiskey bottle which was issued in 1860. Many stories have been told about this classic bottle. Unfortunately, most are not true. Research has proved that "booze" was a corruption of the words "bouse" and "boosy" from the 16th and 17th centuries. It was only a coincidence that the Philadelphia distributor also was named Booz. This bottle has been reproduced extensively.

Prohibition (1920–1933) brought the legal whiskey industry to a standstill. Whiskey was marked "medicinal purposes only" and distributed by private distillers in unmarked or paper label bottles.

The size and shape of whiskey bottles are standard. Colors are limited to amber, amethyst, clear, green, and cobalt blue (rare). Corks were the common closure in the early period, with the inside screw top being used in the 1880–1910 period.

Bottles made prior to 1880 are the most desirable. In purchasing a bottle with a label, condition is a critical factor. In the 1950s distillers began to issue collectors' special edition bottles to help increase sales.

References: Ralph & Terry Kovel, *The Kovels' Bottle Price List, 8th Edition*, Crown Publishers, 1987; Carlo and Dorothy Sellari, *The Standard Old Bottle Price Guide*, Collector Books, 1989.

Periodical: *Antique Bottle and Glass Collector*, P. O. Box 187, East Greenville, PA 18041.

Additional Listing: See *Warman's Americana & Collectibles* for a listing of Collectors' Special Editions Whiskey Bottles.

Mount Vernon Whiskey, orig box, 1933, $85.00.

Booth & Sedgewicks Cordial Gin, sq, green, iron pontil, 10"	100.00
Brown, Thompson & Co, Louisville, KY, amber, 1860–90	20.00
Casper's, round, cobalt blue, paneled shoulder, 12"	210.00
Chestnut Grove, jug, amber, pontil, applied seal, 8¾"	90.00
Cutter, J. F., olive green, star and shield, whittled	150.00
Davis Rye, pinch bottle, gold paint . . .	55.00
Eagle Liqueur Distilleries, olive	50.00
G. & B. Whiskey, decanter, bulbous, gold letters, backbar	35.00
Hotaling, A. P., light amber, whittled, four pcs	50.00
Imperial, aqua, ½ pint	20.00

Lacey, W. A. Whiskey, two–tone, stenciled, threaded stopper, 4½″	50.00
Macy & Jenkins, NY, amber, handled	18.00
Melchers Finest Canadian, Geneva, dark green	30.00
Moonshine, cylinder, amber, smiling moon face	300.00
Old Club Whiskey, Mach & Jenkins, NY, amber, applied handle	15.00
Peacock, Honolulu, cylinder, light amber, monogram	65.00
Pharazyn, H., figural, Indian warrior, yellow amber, 12¼″	625.00
Turner Brothers, New York, Buffalo, & San Francisco, sq, deep olive green, 9¾″, 1860	70.00

WHITE PATTERNED IRONSTONE

History: White patterned ironstone is a heavy earthenware, first patented in 1813 by Charles Mason, Staffordshire, England, using the name "Patent Ironstone China." Other English potters soon began copying this opaque, feldspathic, white china.

All white ironstone dishes first became available in the American market in the early 1840s. The first patterns had simple Gothic lines similar to the shapes used in transfer wares. Pattern shapes, such as New York, Union, and Atlantic, were designed to appeal to the American housewife. Motifs, such as wheat, corn, oats, and poppies, were embossed on the forms as the American western prairie influenced design. Eventually over 200 shapes and patterns, with variations of finials and handles, were made.

White patterned ironstone is identified by shape names and pattern names. Many potters only named the shape in their catalogs. Pattern names usually refer to the decoration motif.

References: Jean Wetherbee, *A Look At White Ironstone,* Wallace-Homestead, 1980; Jean Wetherbee, *A Second Look At White Ironstone,* Wallace-Homestead, 1985.

Vegetable Tureen, Wheat and Ivy pattern, marked "Stone China, W Taylor Hanley," 11½″ l, $75.00.

Butter, cov, Athens, Podmore Walker, 1857	80.00
Cake Plate, 9″ d, Brocade, Mason, handled	125.00
Chamber Pot, Wheat & Blackberry, Meakin	35.00
Coffeepot, Washington shape, John Meir	125.00
Creamer	
Fig, Davenport	60.00
Wheat in the Meadow, Powell & Bishop, 1870	40.00
Cup and Saucer, handleless	
Ceres, Elsmore & Forster	48.00
Oak Leaf, Pankhurst, 1863	50.00
Ewer, Scalloped Decagon, Wedgwood	140.00
Gravy Boat	
Bordered Fuchsia, Anthony Shaw	40.00
Wheat & Blackberry, Meakin	25.00
Pitcher	
Berlin Swirl, Mayer & Elliot	115.00
Japan pattern, Mason, c1815	275.00
Syndenham, T & R Boote, 7⅞″ h	185.00
Wheat, W E Corn	65.00
Plate	
Ceres, Elsmore & Forster, 8½″ d	12.00
Gothic, Adams, 9½″ d	18.00
Platter	
Columbia, 20 x 15″, octagonal	125.00
Wheat, Meakin, 20¾ x 15⅜″	50.00
Punch Bowl	
Adriatic, scalloped edge	335.00
Berry Cluster, J Furnival	125.00
Relish	
Ceres, Elsmore & Forster, 1860	40.00
Wheat, W E Corn	30.00
Sauce, Vintage, Challinor	15.00
Soup Tureen, cov, Lily of the Valley, Shaw	225.00
Sugar, cov, Hyacinth, Wedgwood	40.00
Teapot	
Hyacinth, Wedgwood	85.00
Ivy, imp "William Adams," 10″ h	75.00
Niagara, Walley	110.00
Trent, T & R Boote	90.00
Toothbrush Holder	
Bell Flower, Burgess	45.00
Cable and Ring, Cockson & Seddon	40.00
Vegetable, cov	
Blackberry	45.00
Cable and Ring, Savoy shape, T & R Boote	50.00
Prairie Flowers, Livesley & Powell	85.00

WILLOW PATTERN CHINA

History: Josiah Spode developed the first "traditional" willow pattern in 1810. The components, all motifs taken from Chinese export china, are: a willow tree, "apple" tree, two pagodas, fence, two birds, and a three figures crossing a bridge. The legend, in its many versions, is an English invention based on the design components.

By 1830, there were over 200 plus makers of willow pattern china in England. The pattern has remained in continuous production. Some of the English firms that still produce willow pattern china are: Burleigh, Johnson Bros. (Wedgwood Group), Royal Doulton's continuation of the Booths pattern, and Wedgwood.

By the end of the 19th century, pattern production spread to France, Germany, Holland, Ireland, Sweden, and the United States. In the United States, Buffalo Pottery made the first willow pattern beginning in 1902. Many other companies followed, developing willow variants using rubber–stamp simplified patterns as well as overglaze decals. The largest American manufacturers of the traditional willow pattern were Royal China and Homer Laughlin, usually preferred because it is dated. Shenango pieces are most desired among restaurant quality ware.

Japan began producing large quantities of willow pattern china in the early 20th century. Noritake began about 1902. Its early pieces used a Nippon "Royal Someteku" mark. Most Japanese pieces are porous earthenware with a dark blue pattern using the traditional willow design, usually with no inner border. Noritake did put the pattern on china bodies. Unusual forms include salt and pepper shakers, one–quarter pound butter dishes, and canisters. "Occupied Japan" may add a small percentage to the value of common table wares. Maruta and Moriyama marked pieces are especially valued. The most sought after Japanese willow is the fine quality NKT Co. ironstone a copy of the old Booths pattern. Recent Japanese willow is a paler shade of blue on a porcelain body.

The most common dinnerware color is blue. However, pieces can also be found in black (with clear glaze or mustard–color glaze by Royal Doulton), brown, green, mulberry, pink (red), and polychrome. Although colors other than blue are hard to find, there is less demand; thus, prices may not necessarily be higher.

The popularity of the willow design has resulted in a large variety of willow–decorated products: candles, fabric, glass, graniteware, linens, needlepoint, plastic, tinware, stationery, watches, and wall coverings. All this material has collectible value.

References: Robert Copeland, *Spode's Willow Pattern and Other Designs After The Chinese,* Studio Vista, 1980, 1990 reprint; Mary Frank Gaston, *Blue Willow: An Identification & Value Guide,* Collector Books, Revised Second Edition, 1990, 1992 value update; Veryl Marie Worth and Louise M. Loehr, *Willow Pattern China: Collector's Guide, 3rd Edition,* H. S. Worth Co, 1986.

Periodicals: *American Willow Report,* P.O. Box 900, Oakridge, OR 97463; *The Willow Word,* P.O. Box 13382, Arlington, TX 76094.

Collector's Club: International Willow Collectors, 145 Maple Drive, Springboro, OH 45066.

Reproduction Alert: The Scio Pottery, Scio, Ohio, currently manufactures a willow pattern set sold in variety stores. The pieces have no marks or back stamps, and the transfer is of poor quality. The plates are flatter in shape than those of other manufacturers.

Additional Listings: Buffalo Pottery. See *Warman's Americana & Collectibles* for more examples.

Bowl, Mason, 9″ d, $48.00.

Bowl	
5″ d, Homer Laughlin	3.00
6″ d, Homer Laughlin	4.00
Cake Plate, handle, Royal	8.00
Cake Stand, Royal Worcester, pedestal base	225.00
Casserole, cov, small	35.00
Chamber Set, wash bowl and pitcher, matching hot water pitcher, Royal Doulton	500.00
Children's Dinner Set, six dinner plates, cups and saucers, 7″ platter, teapot, cov casserole, cov sugar, two serving plates, ftd vase, 29 pcs	325.00
Cup and Saucer	
Booths	25.00
Buffalo Pottery	20.00
Homer Laughlin	8.00
Japanese, design in cup	7.00
Shenango	12.00
Gravy Boat, Buffalo Pottery	75.00
Plate	
6″ d	
Homer Laughlin	2.00
Royal	2.00
9″ d	
England, lighter blue	7.00
Homer Laughlin	6.00
Japan	7.00
10″ d	
Allerton, plain edge	24.00
Japan	10.00

Johnson Bros	15.00
Royal	2.50
Platter	
Allerton, 9" w, 12" l	48.00
Royal	15.00
Salt Shaker, 3½" h	8.00
Snack Plate, 10" d, Johnson Bros	12.00
Soup Plate	
England	10.00
Homer Laughlin	7.00
Royal	5.00
Teapot	
Homer Laughlin	35.00
Johnson Bros	60.00

WOODENWARE

History: Many utilitarian household objects and farm implements were made of wood. Although they were used heavily, these implements were made of the strongest woods and well taken care of by their owners.

This category serves as a catch–all for wood objects which do not fit into other categories.

Additional Listings: See *Warman's Americana & Collectibles* for more examples.

Pantry Box, 7¾" d, 3¾" h, $35.00.

Ballot Box, mahogany	45.00
Bootjack, 19" l, fish shape, relief carving, red stain	30.00
Bowl	
11 x 20½", oblong, refinished	130.00
15½" d, 4½" h, round, maple, refinished	135.00
Box	
8" d, 6¼" h, round, bentwood, reddish finish	200.00
8¾" d, 5½" h, round, bentwood, swivel handle fastened with wood knobs, old patina	195.00
10¾" d, round, bentwood, swivel handle, chipped knobs holds handle	165.00
13" l, poplar, worn grayish green paint	60.00
Bucket, 3⅝" h, stave constructed, wire bale with wood handle, iron bands, red and black repaint	135.00
Bugle Box, 19¼" l, hard and soft wood,	

red striping, gold stenciled designs and initials, polychrome bugle, black repaint over blue, missing handle	300.00
Butter Paddle, 9½" l, curly maple, dark patina	45.00
Candle Dryer, 32" h, turned post, two rows of cross arms, red	475.00
Candlestick, 8" h, silver stick shape, worn silver gilt over gesso	300.00
Canteen	
5" d, 4¼" h, keg shape, red	175.00
6⅝" d, stave constructed, laced bands, branded "O E" and carved initials, old patina	175.00
Chamber Stick, 4⅞" h, pushup	185.00
Checkerboard, 14¼" h, 15" w, pine, black and red paint	195.00
Cheese Box, 15½" d, 11½" h, "Monarch Chicago" label	55.00
Cobbler's Bench, 42" l, pine, nut brown finish, five drawers, worn leather seat, one drawer dated "1806"	450.00
Doll, 8½" h, articulated, paper and paint traces, modern base	65.00
Dough Box	
15½ x 26¾", pine, reddish brown stain, gothic arch feet, lid, refinished	175.00
19 x 34", pine and poplar, splayed base, turned legs, dovetailed, replaced lid, refinished	295.00
Drying Rack	
41" h, pine, gray paint, three mortised and pinned horizontal bars, shoe feet	200.00
48" h unfolded, four arms, single pedestal base, old brown paint	75.00
49" h, pine, three mortised bars, old greenish gray paint, shoe feet	190.00
Footstool, 16" l, pine, old worn green repaint	65.00
Frame, 20½" h, 16½" w, mahogany, beveled, old finish	40.00
Glove Box, ornate	45.00
Grease Bucket, 10" h, Conestoga wagon type, lid, old brown paint	55.00
Jar, 8" h, keg shaped, poplar, turned detail, old finish	200.00
Lantern, barn	
10¼" h, pine, glass sides, hinged door, replaced tin candle socket	325.00
11" h, beech, oak, and pink, glass sides, hinged door, replaced tin candle socket	225.00
Lectern, 32½" h, Country, quarter sawed oak, old finish, late 19th C, early 20th C	25.00
Noggin, 6½" h	60.00
Pipe Box, 18½" h, oak, dark finish, English	170.00
Plate, 7½" d, turned, painted winter landscape scene	145.00

Shelf, 12½" w, pine, carved rayed back,
old brown finish **425.00**
Sleigh, 51" l, 36" h, child's, push type,
old red paint, black striping, wrought
iron fittings, wood runners **625.00**
Spice Box, 10½" w, 14" h, hanging,
pine, shaped crest, divided two part
int., drawer, molded edge, dovetail
corners, old gray paint **300.00**
Spoon Rack, 21" h, 10½" w, oak, chip
carved with baroque spiral posts, fi-
gural finial, old dark finish **110.00**
Sugar Bucket, 9¾" h, stave constructed,
stenciled mark "18XX" on handle . . **85.00**
Swift
25½" h, brown patina, table clamp,
adjustable collar missing thumb
screw **50.00**
30" h, unusual clamping device **55.00**
Towel Rack, 25¾ x 32", folding, poplar,
dark brown finish, peaked finials . . . **400.00**
Toy, pull, 6½" h, cart with wheels, brown
flocked papier mache rabbit, marked
"Germany" **35.00**
Tray
16 x 24½", polychrome stenciled children at play scene, orig black lac-
quer **45.00**
18¾ x 19", pine, scalloped sides with
cut out designs, orig green paint,
red striping **200.00**
Wall Planter, 24¾" h, 15¼" w, hanging,
poplar, scalloped edges, chip carved
cut outs, two compartments lined with
tin, wire nail construction, orig red
paint with yellow striping and detail . **325.00**
Water Bench, 35½ x 12 x 36½", pine,
shaped sides, cut out feet, old mellow
refinishing **575.00**
Whirligig, 29" l, man and kicking mule,
polychrome paint, 20th C **225.00**

WORLD'S FAIRS AND EXPOSITIONS

History: The Great Exhibition of 1851 in London
marked the beginning of the World's Fair and Exposition movement. The fairs generally feature exhibitions from nations around the world displaying
the best of their industrial and scientific achieve-
ments.

Many important technological advances have
been introduced at world's fairs. Examples include
the airplane, telephone, and electric lights. The ice
cream cone, hot dog, and iced tea were products
of vendors at fairs. Art movements often were
closely connected to fairs with the Paris Exhibition
of 1900 generally considered to have assembled
the best of the works of the Art Nouveau artists.

References: *American Art, New York World's
Fair 1939,* Apollo Books, 1987; Carl Abbott, *The*

*Great Extravaganza: Portland and the Lewis and
Clark Exposition,* Oregon Historical Society, 1981;
Stanley Appelbaum, *The New York World's Fair,
1939/1940,* Dover Publications, Inc., 1971; Patricia
F. Carpenter and Paul Totah, *The San Francisco
Fair, Treasure Island, 1939–1940,* Scottwall As-
sociates, 1989; Richard Friz, *World's Fair Memor-
abilia,* House of Collectibles, 1989, out–of–print;
Kurt Krueger, *Meet Me In St. Louis—The Exonu-
mia Of The 1904 World's Fair,* Krause Publica-
tions, 1979; Howard Rossen and John Kaduck,
Columbia World's Fair Collectibles, Wallace-
Homestead, 1976, revised price list 1982.

Periodical: *World's Fair,* P.O. Box 339, Corte
Madera, CA 94925.

Collectors' Club: World's Fair Collectors' Society, Inc., P.O. Box 20806, Sarasota, FL 33583.

**Columbia Exposition, 1895, salt shaker,
egg shaped, orig top, Mount Washington, 3" h, $155.00.**

1876, Philadelphia, Centennial, paperweight, glass, scenes of exposition
buildings **75.00**
1893, Chicago, Columbian Exposition
Badge, 1½ x 2½", brass link, emb,
Columbus on U.S. shore with Indians, 400th Anniversary/Discovery
Of America/Oct. 1892 . . . . **60.00**
Fan, 12¼" h, 23" w opened, full color
illus of fairgrounds, mounted on flat
wood swivel pieces **55.00**
Spoon, 4½" l, silverplate, ornate han-
dle **25.00**
1901, Buffalo, Pan–American Exposi-
tion
Matchsafe, 1½ x 2½", silvered brass,
ladies outstretched arms as crest
of Niagara Falls, Manufacturers &
Liberal Arts Building on back **70.00**
Pin, 2¼" l, pan shape, diecut litho tin,
"C Klinck's Daisy Leaf Lard," red,
white, and blue, full color lard pail
in center **27.50**

Lewis & Clark Centennial, medal, brass, US Government building on reverse, 1⅜" d, $50.00.

1904, St. Louis, Louisiana Purchase Exposition
Ashtray, Cascade Gardens **10.00**
Pin, 1¼" l, composition, raised "Heinz" adv on one side, "St. Louis '04" on other, brass hanging loop . **18.00**
Tray, 3¼ x 5", aluminum, cartoon art panel, red accent border **25.00**
Vase, 5" h, irid blue and purple, double handles, Electricity Bldg picture, numbered **45.00**
1909, Alaska–Yukon Pacific Exposition
Pinback Button, 1¾" d, Hendrick Hud-

Chicago, A Century of Progress Exposition, 1933, Baltimore & Ohio train schedule, 18 pages, folded, 4 x 9", $50.00.

son and Robert Fulton with their ships **110.00**
Plate **55.00**
1915, San Francisco, Panama–Pacific International Exposition
Book, *Red Book of Views of the Panama Intl Exposition in San Francisco* **18.00**
Pin, 1¼" d, brass, enameled, yellow and white stripe accents, olive–green rim, brass lettering **25.00**
1933, Chicago, Century of Progress
Bottle Opener, 5" h, figural, copper–colored metal, mythological Egyptian lady and American Legion logo, Fort Dearborn exhibit and "Chicago 1933" on back **25.00**
Jigsaw Puzzle, 11 x 16", "H. M. Pettit Approved Bird's Eye View Of A Century Of Progress," 8½ x 8½ x 1" box **30.00**
Souvenir Book, 6 x 8¼", 28 pgs, linen–like paper, full color illus, orig marked envelope **30.00**
Ticket, closing day, cardboard, Oct 31, 1934, black inscriptions **15.00**
Watch Box, 2¼ x 2½ x¾", for "Chicago World's Fair Watch #9531," black and white illus of early fort on lid **60.00**
1939, New York, New York World's Fair
Bowl, 10" d, china, creamy white, full color design, geometric floral pattern edge, Paden City Pottery . . . **100.00**
Bracelet, silvered brass, emb buildings around side **40.00**
Candle, orange, inscribed raised gold lettering on each side, orig box . . **75.00**
Cigarette Case, wood, brass plunger knob, dark mahogany center band, Trylon and Perisphere **80.00**
Coin, 1¼" d, brass, emb, raised Trylon and Perisphere, rim inscription "Metropolitan Life Insurance Exhibit" **15.00**
Map, 8 x 11" folded sheet, full color aerial view **15.00**
Pen, 5" l, pearl–like tan, orange and blue Theme Center motif **75.00**
Pennant, 9 x 27", felt, purple, white inscription, green, yellow, and blue design **25.00**
Playing Cards, trick deck, 48 cards, boxed **50.00**
Pocket Knife, 3" l, marbleized plastic, orange and blue design and inscription, Imperial, Providence, RI **75.00**
Pencil, mechanical, 10½" l,¾" d, gold colored wood barrel, cartoon illus of person with camera clinging to Trylon and lady sitting on Peris-

phere, marked "N.Y.W.F. Eagle
Pencil Co.," rubber eraser 30.00
Pin, 1¼″ d, trefoil, clear plastic bakelite, raised Trylon, purple glass Perisphere, inscribed 30.00
Ring, silvered brass, adjustable, Trylon and Perisphere, dated and
copyright symbol 25.00
1939, San Francisco, Golden Gate International Exposition
Guide Book, 5½ x 8″, soft cover, 118
pgs, 16 x 19″ fold out map, diecut
tab index, Junket Dessert adv on
back cov 20.00
Scarf, 27½ x 29″, linen–like, light blue
and brown illus, off–white ground .   40.00
1964, New York, New York World's Fair
Figurine, 3¼″ h, Unisphere, ceramic,
glossy white and dark blue finish .   25.00
Guide Book, *Official Guide New York
World's Fair* 18.00
Plate, 7¼″ d, china, white, full color
illus around border 40.00
Playing Cards, 52 cards, full color ex-
hibit illus 30.00

YELLOW WARE

History: Yellow ware is a heavy earthenware of
differing weight and strength which varies in color
from a rich pumpkin to lighter shades which are
more tan than yellow. Although plates, nappies,
and custard cups are found, kitchen bowls and
other cooking utensils are most prevalent.

The first American yellow ware was produced at
Bennington, Vermont. English yellow ware has additional ingredients which make its body much
harder. Derbyshire and Sharp's were foremost
among the English manufacturers.

References: John Gallo, *Nineteenth and Twentieth Century Yellow Ware,* Heritage Press, 1985;
Joan Leibowitz, *Yellow Ware: The Transitional Ceramic,* Schiffer Publishing, 1985.

**Mixing Bowl, pouring spout, emb dec,
11⅝″ d, 4¾″ h, $75.00.**

Bowl, 9½″ d, brown sponging 130.00
Chamber Pot, 9″ d, mocha, white band,
brown stripes, blue seaweed dec . .   250.00

Creamer, 4½″ h, green and brown
sponging 75.00
Crock, 5½″, brown bands 30.00
Cuspidor, 5 x 7½″, green, blue, and tan
sponge glaze 60.00
Figure, 11⅜″ h, seated cat, oval base,
freestanding front legs, brown and
bluish green running glaze, minor
chips on edge of base 2,000.00
Food Mold, 8″ l, rabbit 105.00
Jar
8¾″ h, brown slip dec 525.00
12¼″ h, brown running glaze, chipped
lid 85.00
Jug, 9″ h, blue Mocha dec 225.00
Lamp, 14½″ h, grease, bluish green running glaze, rayed circle with "W" . . .   55.00
Mixing Bowl, nested set of 3, molded
ridges, brown and green spatter . . .   180.00
Mug
3¼″, brown polka dots 675.00
3⅞″, white band with brown stripes .   115.00
Pitcher
4½″ h, brown and green sponging,
molded ribs, black transfer adv la-
bel 55.00
4¾″ h, brown sponging, molded
Gothic arch design, flaked spout .   40.00
Plate, 9⅛″ d, molded Gothic rim, imp
"Hall & Sons" 60.00
Salt, 3″ d, 2⅛″ h, ftd, white band, blue
seaweed dec, blue stripe 155.00
Sugar Bowl, 4⅝″ h, molded floral de-
sign, classical figures 150.00

ZANE WARE
MADE IN U.S.A.

ZANE POTTERY

History: In 1921 Adam Reed and Harry Mc-
Clelland bought the Peters and Reed Pottery in
Zanesville, Ohio. The firm continued production of
garden wares and introduced several new art
lines: "Sheen," "Powder Blue," "Crystalline," and
"Drip." The factory was sold in 1941 to Lawton
Gonder.

Reference: Jeffery, Sherrie, and Barry Hersone,
*The Peters and Reed and Zane Pottery Experi-
ence,* published by authors, 1990.

Additonal Listings: Gonder and Peters and
Reed.

Bowl
5″ d, brown and blue 45.00
5¼″ d, Wilse Blue, dragonfly dec . . .   50.00
6½″ d, blue, marked "Zanesware" . .   25.00
Figure, 10⅛″ h, cat, black, green eyes   500.00

Jardiniere, green matte glaze, artist sgd "Frank Ferreu," 34" h, $300.00.

Jardiniere
 7⅛" h, 8½" d, waisted cylindrical, blue and green landscape scene, maroon matte glaze, c1907 . . . . **165.00**
 34" h, green matte glaze, artist sgd "Frank Ferreu" **300.00**
Vase
 5" h, green, cobalt blue drip glaze . . **25.00**
 7" h, flowing medium green over dark forest green ground **85.00**

Vase, bulbous, circled collar neck, outward flaring rim, pansy dec, olive to brown left to right glaze, marked "La Moro," 7" h, $125.00.

 marked "Tyces Pottery/Zanesville/ Ohio" **35.00**
Tile, 6" h, 18" l, woman, blowing horn, cream ground **275.00**
Vase, 10¼" h, matte, white–gray portrait of horse, light olive green to blue–green ground, peachblow in back, high glaze brown int., sgd "R. G. Turner" **825.00**

LA MORO

ZANESVILLE POTTERY

History: Zanesville Art Pottery, one of several potteries located in Zanesville, Ohio, began production in 1900. A line of utilitarian products was first produced. Art pottery was introduced shortly thereafter. The major line was La Moro which was hand painted and decorated under glaze. The impressed block print mark La Moro appears on the high glazed and matte glazed decorated ware. The firm was bought by S. A. Weller in 1920 and became known as Weller Plant No. 3.

References: Louise and Evan Purviance and Norris F. Schneider, *Zanesville Art Pottery In Color*, Mid-America Book Company, 1968; Evan and Louise Purviance, *Zanesville Art Tile In Color*, Wallace-Homestead Book Co., 1972.

Bowl, 6½" d, fluted edge, mottled blue **45.00**
Jardiniere
 7⅛" h, 8½" d, waisted cylindrical, blue and green landscape scene, maroon matte glaze, c1907 . . . . **165.00**
 8¼" h, cream to light amber peony blossoms, ruffled rim, shaded brown ground **75.00**
Plate, 4½" d, applied floral dec **25.00**
Teapot, 2¾" h, souvenir, dark green,

ZSOLNAY POTTERY

History: Vilmos Zsolnay (1828–1900) assumed control of his brother's factory in Pécs, Hungary, in the mid-19th century. In 1899 Miklos, Vilmos's son, became manager. The firm still produces ceramic ware.

The early wares are highly ornamental, glazed, and have a cream color ground. "Eosin" glaze, a deep rich play of colors reminiscent of Tiffany's iridescent wares, received a gold medal at the 1900 Paris exhibition. Zsolnay Art Nouveau pieces show great creativity.

Originally no trademark was used. Beginning in 1878 a blue mark depicting the five towers of the cathedral at Pécs was used. The initials "TJM" represent the names of Miklos's three children.

Zsolnay's recent series of iridescent glazed figurines, which initially were inexpensive, now are being sought by collectors and show a steady increase in value.

Reference: Susan and Al Bagdade, *Warman's English & Continental Pottery & Porcelain, 2nd Edition,* Wallace–Homestead, 1991.

Figure, Mountain Goat and Kid, irid blue–green, c1930, "3 Castle Pecs, Hungary" mark, 6" h, $175.00.

Bowl, 10" d, cherubs dec, curved leaf handles	500.00
Centerpiece, 16 x 4 x 5", crescent shape, double walled, reticulated, irid florals, gold trim	285.00
Dish, 8½" w, fan shape, rolled in edge, reticulated, beige, gold, and pink dec, steeple mark	185.00

Ewer, 7½" h, cream, yellow, and beige dec, gold base, gold reticulated neck band, ornate handle	115.00
Figure	
3¾" h, fox, irid green, sgd	50.00
4" h, kitten, irid green	75.00
7½" h, polar bears, irid purple and green	225.00
Jug, 9" h, handles, multicolored enameled flowers, cream ground, lustered	200.00
Mug, 4½" h, irid blue luster	80.00
Pitcher, 9" h, pink cherub design, c1870	100.00
Plate	
8½" d, shell shape, reticulated, red and gold flowers, beige ground, steeple mark	180.00
10¾" d, Persian type design, red, blue, and silver luster	300.00
Puzzle Jug, 6½" h, pierced roundels, irid dec, cream ground, castle mark, imp "Zsolnay"	165.00
Ring Tree, 3½" h, irid gold	75.00
Vase	
5½" h, applied simulated stone with thumbprints, irid red glaze	155.00
6½" h, double walled, reticulated, cobalt blue, beige, and gold dec	350.00
9" h, swirled form, irid blue–green, sgd "Zsolnay Pecs"	250.00
19½" h, globular body, flared base, large foliate pierced handles, polychrome underglaze and overglaze Islamic style dec, marked "Hungary," 20th C, pr	1,650.00

INDEX

Harry and the Rinkettes. Left to right: Jocelyn C. Mousely, Beverly B. Marriner, Ellen T. Schroy, Harry L. Rinker, Terese J. Oswald, Nancy M. Butt, Diane L. Sterner, and Dana N. Morykan.

HARRY L. RINKER is consulting editor for Wallace-Homestead Book Company, editor of *Warman's Antiques and Their Prices* and *Warman's Americana & Collectibles*; author of *Collector's Guide to Toys, Games, and Puzzles, How to Make the Most of Your Investments in Antiques and Collectibles,* and *Rinker on Collectibles*; co-author with Frank Hill of *The Joy of Collecting with Craven Moore*; syndicated columnist of ''Rinker on Collectibles;'' and president of ''Rinker's Antiques and Collectibles Market Report.''

OTHER TOPICS COVERED BY WALLACE-HOMESTEAD

All of the following books can be purchased from your local bookstore, antiques dealer, or can be borrowed from your public library. Books can also be purchased directly from **Chilton Book Company, One Chilton Way, Radnor, PA 19089-0230.** Include code number, title, and price when ordering. Add applicable sales tax and **$2.50** postage and handling for the first book plus 50¢ for each additional book shipped to the same address. VISA/Mastercard orders call **1-800-695-1214** and ask for Customer Service Department (AK, HI, & PA residents call **215-964-4730** and ask for Customer Service Department). Prices and availability are subject to change without notice. Please call for a current Wallace-Homestead catalog.

COLLECTOR'S GUIDE SERIES

Code	Title/Author	Price
W5320	Collector's Guide to American Toy Trains, *Susan & Al Bagdade*	$16.95
W5568	Collector's Guide to Autographs, *George Sanders, Helen Sanders, and Ralph Roberts*	$16.95
W5339	Collector's Guide to Baseball Cards, *Troy Kirk*	$12.95
W5487	Collector's Guide to Comic Books, *John Hegenberger*	$12.95
W5479	Collector's Guide to Early Photographs, *O. Henry Mace*	$16.95
W5347	Collector's Guide to Quilts, *Suzy McLennan Anderson*	$17.95
W572X	Collector's Guide to Toys, Games & Puzzles, *Harry L. Rinker*	$14.95
W5649	Collector's Guide to Treasures from the Silver Screen, *John Hegenberger*	$16.95
W5762	Collector's Guide to Victoriana, *O. Henry Mace*	$17.95

COLLECTIBLES

Code	Title/Author	Price
W5258	American Clocks and Clockmakers, *Robert W. & Harriett Swedberg*	$16.95
W0100	The Button Lover's Book, *Marilyn Green*	$17.95
W4464	Check the Oil: Gas Station Collectibles with Prices, *Scott Anderson*	$18.95

| W4140* | Zalkin's Handbook of Thimbles & Sewing Implements, *Estelle Zalkin* | $24.95 |

COUNTRY

Code	Title/Author	Price
W5428	Baskets, Wallace-Homestead Price Guide to, Second Edition, *Frances Johnson*	$16.95
W3581	Kitchens and Gadgets: 1920 to 1950, *Jane Celehar*	$16.95
W4251	Kitchens and Kitchenware: 1900 to 1950, *Jane Celehar*	$15.95
W443X	Shaker: A Collector's Source, Book II, *Don & Carol Raycraft*	$15.95

FURNITURE

Code	Title/Author	Price
W6203	American Oak Furniture, Book I, 3rd Edition, *Robert W. & Harriett Swedberg*	$16.95
W5878	American Oak Furniture, Book II, 2nd Edition, *Robert W. & Harriett Swedberg*	$16.95
W5886	American Oak Furniture, Book III, 2nd Edition, *Robert W. & Harriett Swedberg*	$16.95
W3883	Country Pine Furniture, Revised Edition, *Robert W. & Harriett Swedberg*	$14.95
W3964	Victorian Furniture, Book III, *Robert W. & Harriett Swedberg*	$16.95

GENERAL

Code	Title/Author	Price
W4189	Antique Radios: Restoration and Price Guide, *Betty & David Johnson*	$14.95
W5274	Antiquing in England: A Guide to Antique Centres, *Robert W. & Harriett Swedberg*	$16.95
W5614*	Bessie Pease Gutmann: Her Life and Works, *Victor J. W. Christie*	$29.95
W5304	Buy Art Smart, *Alan S. Bamberger*	$12.95
W6181	Collector's Information Bureau Collectibles Market Guide & Price Index, 9th Edition, *Diane Carnevale, ed.*	$19.95
W5592	Flea Market Handbook: How to Make Money Selling in Flea Markets, Co-ops, and Antiques Malls, Second Edition, *Robert G. Miner*	$12.95

W636X	Flea Market Treasures, Price Guide to, *Harry L. Rinker, Jr.*	$14.95
W4618	The Joy of Collecting with Craven Moore, *Harry Rinker & Frank Hill*	$ 6.95
W6106	1992 Collector's Information Clearinghouse Antiques and Collectibles Resource Directory, *David Maloney*	$19.95
W4855	Oriental Antiques & Art: An Identification and Value Guide, *Sandra Andacht*	$19.95

GENERAL PRICE GUIDES

Code	Title/Author	Price
W5843	American Country Antiques, Wallace-Homestead Price Guide to, 11th Edition, *Don & Carol Raycraft*	$14.95
W6157	Warman's Americana & Collectibles, 5th Edition, *Edited by Harry L. Rinker*	$14.95
W6238	Warman's Antiques and Their Prices, 26th Edition, *Edited by Harry L. Rinker*	$14.95

GLASS

Code	Title/Author	Price
W4308*	American Cut and Engraved Glass of the Brilliant Period, *Martha Louise Swan*	$35.00
W5452*	Early American Pattern Glass—1850 to 1910: Major Collectible Table Settings with Prices, *Bill Jenks & Jerry Luna*	$29.95
W4626	Glass Signatures, Trademarks, and Trade Names, *Anne Geffken Pullin*	$16.95
W4421	Pattern Glass, Wallace-Homestead Price Guide to, Eleventh Edition, *Robert W. Miller & Dori Miles*	$15.95
W5444*	Perfume and Scent Bottle Collecting with Prices, Second Edition, *Jean Sloan*	$35.00
W5754	Tomart's Price Guide to Character & Promotional Glasses, *Carol and Gene Markowski*	$21.95

JEWELRY/METALS

Code	Title/Author	Price
W6289	Antique Jewelry with Prices, Updated Edition, *Doris J. Snell*	$15.95
W5746	Collectible Costume Jewelry, Revised Edition, *S. Sylvia Henzel*	$16.95
W4121	Jewelers' Circular-Keystone Sterling Flatware Pattern Index, Second Edition, *Binder*	$69.95

PAPER EPHEMERA

Code	Title/Author	Price
W4987	Currier & Ives: An Illustrated Value Guide, *Craig McClain*	$16.95
W5363	Hancer's Price Guide to Paperback Books, Third Edition, *Kevin Hancer*	$16.95
W5193*	Postcard Companion: The Collector's Reference, *Jack H. Smith*	$39.95
W5673	The Price Guide to Autographs, Second Edition, *George Sanders, Helen Sanders, & Ralph Roberts*	$21.95
W6033	Tomart's Price Guide to Golden Book Collectibles, *Rebecca Greason*	$21.95

POTTERY & PORCELAIN

Code	Title/Author	Price
7982X	A History of World Pottery, Revised and Updated Edition, *Emmanuel Cooper*	$27.95
W5770	Warman's English & Continental Pottery & Porcelain, 2nd Edition, *Susan & Al Bagdade*	$19.95

* Denotes hardcover, all others are paperback.